Lecture Notes in Computer Science 14369

Founding Editors

Gerhard Goos

Juris Hartmanis

Editorial Board Members

The series Lecture Notes in Computer Science (LNCS), including its subseries Lecture Notes in Artificial Intelligence (LNAI) and Lecture Notes in Bioinformatics (LNBI), has established itself as a medium for the publication of new developments in computer science and information technology research, teaching, and education.

LNCS enjoys close cooperation with the computer science R & D community, the series counts many renowned academics among its volume editors and paper authors, and collaborates with prestigious societies. Its mission is to serve this international community by providing an invaluable service, mainly focused on the publication of conference and workshop proceedings and postproceedings. LNCS commenced publication in 1973.

Guy Rothblum · Hoeteck Wee
Editors

Theory
of Cryptography

21st International Conference, TCC 2023
Taipei, Taiwan, November 29 – December 2, 2023
Proceedings, Part I

 Springer

Editors
Guy Rothblum 🆔
Apple
Cupertino, CA, USA

Hoeteck Wee
NTT Research
Sunnyvale, CA, USA

ISSN 0302-9743   ISSN 1611-3349 (electronic)
Lecture Notes in Computer Science
ISBN 978-3-031-48614-2   ISBN 978-3-031-48615-9 (eBook)
https://doi.org/10.1007/978-3-031-48615-9

This Springer imprint is published by the registered company Springer Nature Switzerland AG
The registered company address is: Gewerbestrasse 11, 6330 Cham, Switzerland

Paper in this product is recyclable.

Preface

The 21st Theory of Cryptography Conference (TCC 2023) was held during November 29 – December 2, 2023, at Academia Sinica in Taipei, Taiwan. It was sponsored by the International Association for Cryptologic Research (IACR). The general chairs of the conference were Kai-Min Chung and Bo-Yin Yang.

The conference received 168 submissions, of which the Program Committee (PC) selected 68 for presentation giving an acceptance rate of 40%. Each submission was reviewed by at least three PC members in a single-blind process. The 39 PC members (including PC chairs), all top researchers in our field, were helped by 195 external reviewers, who were consulted when appropriate. These proceedings consist of the revised versions of the 68 accepted papers. The revisions were not reviewed, and the authors bear full responsibility for the content of their papers.

We are extremely grateful to Kevin McCurley for providing fast and reliable technical support for the HotCRP review software. We also thank Kay McKelly for her help with the conference website.

This was the ninth year that TCC presented the Test of Time Award to an outstanding paper that was published at TCC at least eight years ago, making a significant contribution to the theory of cryptography, preferably with influence also in other areas of cryptography, theory, and beyond. This year, the Test of Time Award Committee selected the following paper, published at TCC 2007: "Multi-authority Attribute Based Encryption" by Melissa Chase. The award committee recognized this paper for "the first attribute-based encryption scheme in which no small subset of authorities can compromise user privacy, inspiring further work in decentralized functional encryption." The author was invited to deliver a talk at TCC 2023.

This year, TCC awarded a Best Young Researcher Award for the best paper authored solely by young researchers. The award was given to the paper "Memory Checking for Parallel RAMs" by Surya Mathialagan.

We are greatly indebted to the many people who were involved in making TCC 2023 a success. First of all, a big thanks to the most important contributors: all the authors who submitted fantastic papers to the conference. Next, we would like to thank the PC members for their hard work, dedication, and diligence in reviewing and selecting the papers. We are also thankful to the external reviewers for their volunteered hard work and investment in reviewing papers and answering questions. For running the conference itself, we are very grateful to the general chairs, Kai-Min Chung and Bo-Yin Yang, as well as the staff at Academia Sinica (Institute of Information Science and Research Center of Information Technology Innovation). For help with these proceedings, we thank the team at Springer. We appreciate the sponsorship from IACR, Hackers in Taiwan, Quantum Safe Migration Center (QSMC), NTT Research and BTQ. Finally, we are thankful to

Tal Malkin and the TCC Steering Committee as well as the entire thriving and vibrant TCC community.

October 2023   Guy Rothblum
                                                                                                            Hoeteck Wee

Organization

General Chairs

Kai-Min Chung   Academia Sinica, Taiwan
Bo-Yin Yang   Academia Sinica, Taiwan

Program Committee Chairs

Guy N. Rothblum   Apple, USA and Weizmann Institute, Israel
Hoeteck Wee   NTT Research, USA and ENS, France

Steering Committee

Jesper Buus Nielsen   Aarhus University, Denmark
Krzysztof Pietrzak   Institute of Science and Technology, Austria
Huijia (Rachel) Lin   University of Washington, USA
Yuval Ishai   Technion, Israel
Tal Malkin   Columbia University, USA
Manoj M. Prabhakaran   IIT Bombay, India
Salil Vadhan   Harvard University, USA

Program Committee

Prabhanjan Ananth   UCSB, USA
Christian Badertscher   Input Output, Switzerland
Chris Brzuska   Aalto University, Finland
Ran Canetti   Boston University, USA
Nico Döttling   CISPA, Germany
Rosario Gennaro   CUNY and Protocol Labs, USA
Aarushi Goel   NTT Research, USA
Siyao Guo   NYU Shanghai, China
Shai Halevi   AWS, USA
Pavel Hubáček   Czech Academy of Sciences and Charles
                                     University, Czech Republic
Yuval Ishai   Technion, Israel

Aayush Jain	CMU, USA
Zhengzhong Jin	MIT, USA
Yael Kalai	Microsoft Research and MIT, USA
Chethan Kamath	Tel Aviv University, Israel
Bhavana Kanukurthi	IISc, India
Jiahui Liu	MIT, USA
Mohammad Mahmoody	University of Virginia, USA
Giulio Malavolta	Bocconi University, Italy and Max Planck Institute for Security and Privacy, Germany
Peihan Miao	Brown University, USA
Eran Omri	Ariel University, Israel
Claudio Orlandi	Aarhus, Denmark
João Ribeiro	NOVA LINCS and NOVA University Lisbon, Portugal
Doreen Riepel	UC San Diego, USA
Carla Ràfols	Universitat Pompeu Fabra, Spain
Luisa Siniscalchi	Technical University of Denmark, Denmark
Naomi Sirkin	Drexel University, USA
Nicholas Spooner	University of Warwick, USA
Akshayaram Srinivasan	University of Toronto, Canada
Stefano Tessaro	University of Washington, USA
Eliad Tsfadia	Georgetown University, USA
Mingyuan Wang	UC Berkeley, USA
Shota Yamada	AIST, Japan
Takashi Yamakawa	NTT Social Informatics Laboratories, Japan
Kevin Yeo	Google and Columbia University, USA
Eylon Yogev	Bar-Ilan University, Israel
Mark Zhandry	NTT Research, USA

Additional Reviewers

Damiano Abram	Benedikt Auerbach
Hamza Abusalah	Renas Bacho
Abtin Afshar	Saikrishna Badrinarayanan
Siddharth Agarwal	Chen Bai
Divesh Aggarwal	Laasya Bangalore
Shweta Agrawal	Khashayar Barooti
Martin Albrecht	James Bartusek
Nicolas Alhaddad	Balthazar Bauer
Bar Alon	Shany Ben-David
Benny Applebaum	Fabrice Benhamouda
Gal Arnon	Jean-François Biasse

Alexander Bienstock
Olivier Blazy
Jeremiah Blocki
Andrej Bogdanov
Madalina Bolboceanu
Jonathan Bootle
Pedro Branco
Jesper Buus Nielsen
Alper Çakan
Matteo Campanelli
Shujiao Cao
Jeffrey Champion
Megan Chen
Arka Rai Choudhuri
Valerio Cini
Henry Corrigan-Gibbs
Geoffroy Couteau
Elizabeth Crites
Hongrui Cui
Marcel Dall'Agnol
Quang Dao
Pratish Datta
Koen de Boer
Leo Decastro
Giovanni Deligios
Lalita Devadas
Jack Doerner
Jelle Don
Leo Ducas
Jesko Dujmovic
Julien Duman
Antonio Faonio
Oriol Farràs
Danilo Francati
Cody Freitag
Phillip Gajland
Chaya Ganesh
Rachit Garg
Gayathri Garimella
Romain Gay
Peter Gaži
Ashrujit Ghoshal
Emanuele Giunta
Rishab Goyal
Yanqi Gu

Ziyi Guan
Jiaxin Guan
Aditya Gulati
Iftach Haitner
Mohammad Hajiabadi
Mathias Hall-Andersen
Shuai Han
Dominik Hartmann
Aditya Hegde
Alexandra Henzinger
Shuichi Hirahara
Taiga Hiroka
Charlotte Hoffmann
Alex Hoover
Yao-Ching Hsieh
Zihan Hu
James Hulett
Joseph Jaeger
Fatih Kaleoglu
Ari Karchmer
Shuichi Katsumata
Jonathan Katz
Fuyuki Kitagawa
Ohad Klein
Karen Klein
Michael Klooß
Dimitris Kolonelos
Ilan Komargodski
Yashvanth Kondi
Venkata Koppula
Alexis Korb
Sabrina Kunzweiler
Thijs Laarhoven
Jonas Lehmann
Baiyu Li
Xiao Liang
Yao-Ting Lin
Wei-Kai Lin
Yanyi Liu
Qipeng Liu
Tianren Liu
Zeyu Liu
Chen-Da Liu Zhang
Julian Loss
Paul Lou

Steve Lu

Ji Luo

Fermi Ma

Nir Magrafta

Monosij Maitra

Christian Majenz

Alexander May

Noam Mazor

Bart Mennink

Hart Montgomery

Tamer Mour

Alice Murphy

Anne Müller

Mikito Nanashima

Varun Narayanan

Hai Nguyen

Olga Nissenbaum

Sai Lakshmi Bhavana Obbattu

Maciej Obremski

Kazuma Ohara

Aurel Page

Mahak Pancholi

Guillermo Pascual Perez

Anat Paskin-Cherniavsky

Shravani Patil

Sikhar Patranabis

Chris Peikert

Zach Pepin

Krzysztof Pietrzak

Guru Vamsi Policharla

Alexander Poremba

Alex Poremba

Ludo Pulles

Wei Qi

Luowen Qian

Willy Quach

Divya Ravi

Nicolas Resch

Leah Namisa Rosenbloom

Lior Rotem

Ron Rothblum

Lance Roy

Yusuke Sakai

Pratik Sarkar

Sruthi Sekar

Joon Young Seo

Akash Shah

Devika Sharma

Laura Shea

Sina Shiehian

Kazumasa Shinagawa

Omri Shmueli

Jad Silbak

Pratik Soni

Sriram Sridhar

Akira Takahashi

Ben Terner

Junichi Tomida

Max Tromanhauser

Rotem Tsabary

Yiannis Tselekounis

Nikhil Vanjani

Prashant Vasudevan

Marloes Venema

Muthuramakrishnan Venkitasubramaniam

Hendrik Waldner

Michael Walter

Zhedong Wang

Gaven Watson

Weiqiang Wen

Daniel Wichs

David Wu

Ke Wu

Zhiye Xie

Tiancheng Xie

Anshu Yadav

Michelle Yeo

Runzhi Zeng

Jiaheng Zhang

Rachel Zhang

Cong Zhang

Chenzhi Zhu

Jincheng Zhuang

Vassilis Zikas

Contents – Part I

Multi-party Computation I

Proofs and Outsourcing

Beyond MPC-in-the-Head: Black-Box Constructions of Short Zero-Knowledge Proofs

Carmit Hazay[1,2], Muthuramakrishnan Venkitasubramaniam[2], and Mor Weiss[1(✉)]

[1] Bar-Ilan University, Ramat Gan, Israel
{carmit.hazay,mor.weiss}@biu.ac.il
[2] Georgetown University and Ligero Inc., Washington, USA
mv783@georgetown.edu

Abstract. In their seminal work, Ishai, Kushilevitz, Ostrovsky, and Sahai (STOC'07) presented the MPC-in-the-Head paradigm, which shows how to design Zero-Knowledge Proofs (ZKPs) from secure Multi-Party Computation (MPC) protocols. This paradigm has since then revolutionized and modularized the design of efficient ZKP systems, with far-reaching applications beyond ZKPs. However, to the best of our knowledge, all previous instantiations relied on *fully-secure* MPC protocols and have not been able to leverage the fact that the paradigm only imposes relatively weak privacy and correctness requirements on the underlying MPC.

In this work, we extend the MPC-in-the-Head paradigm to *game-based* cryptographic primitives supporting homomorphic computations (e.g., fully-homomorphic encryption, functional encryption, randomized encodings, homomorphic secret sharing, and more). Specifically, we present a simple yet generic compiler from these primitives to ZKPs which use the underlying primitive as a black box. We also generalize our paradigm to capture commit-and-prove protocols, and use it to devise tight black-box compilers from Interactive (Oracle) Proofs to ZKPs, assuming One-Way Functions (OWFs).

We use our paradigm to obtain several new ZKP constructions:

1. The first ZKPs for NP relations $\mathcal{R}$ computable in (polynomial-time uniform) NC^1, whose round complexity is bounded by a *fixed* constant (independent of the depth of $\mathcal{R}$'s verification circuit), with communication approaching witness length (specifically, $n \cdot \mathsf{poly}(\kappa)$, where n is the witness length, and κ is a security parameter), assuming DCR. Alternatively, if we allow the round complexity to scale with the depth of the verification circuit, our ZKPs can make black-box use of OWFs.

2. Constant-round ZKPs for NP relations computable in bounded polynomial space, with $O(n) + o(m) \cdot \mathsf{poly}(\kappa)$ communication assuming OWFs, where m is the instance length. This gives a black-box alternative to a recent non-black-box construction of Nassar and Ron (CRYPTO'22).

3. ZKPs for NP relations computable by a logspace-uniform family of depth-$d(m)$ circuits, with $n \cdot \mathsf{poly}(\kappa, d(m))$ communication assuming OWFs. This gives a black-box alternative to a result of Goldwasser, Kalai and Rothblum (JACM).

© International Association for Cryptologic Research 2023
G. Rothblum and H. Wee (Eds.): TCC 2023, LNCS 14369, pp. 3–33, 2023.
https://doi.org/10.1007/978-3-031-48615-9_1

1   Introduction

Zero-Knowledge Proofs (ZKPs) [GMR85,GMR89] enable a prover $\mathcal{P}$ to prove to an efficient verifier $\mathcal{V}$ that $x \in \mathcal{L}$ for some NP-language $\mathcal{L}$, while revealing nothing except the validity of the statement. ZKPs have numerous applications, and are a fundamental building block in the design of many secure Multi-Party Computation (MPC) protocols.

In their seminal work that introduced the "MPC-in-the-Head" paradigm, Ishai, Kushilevitz, Ostrovsky, and Sahai [IKOS07] established a surprising connection between MPC protocols and ZKPs. Specifically, they gave a construction in the reverse direction, showing how to construct ZKPs from MPC protocols. The high-level idea is to associate an NP-relation $\mathcal{R} = \mathcal{R}(x, w)$ for $\mathcal{L}$ with a function f whose input is x and additive shares of w, and generate the proof using an MPC protocol Π for f. More specifically, $\mathcal{P}$ secret shares w, emulates "in her head" the execution of Π on x and the witness shares, and commits to the views of all parties in this execution. The verifier then chooses a subset of parties whose views are opened and checked for consistency. Importantly, this ZKP makes *black-box* use of the underlying primitives (e.g., the one-way function used to instantiate the commitment scheme) as well as the algorithms of Π's participants. Moreover, Π is only required to satisfy relatively weak security guarantees, specifically correctness and privacy against *semi-honest* corruptions.

The "MPC-in-the-Head" paradigm draws its power from its generality: it can be instantiated with *any* secure MPC protocol Π for f (with essentially any number of parties), utilizing the efficiency properties of Π to obtain different tradeoffs between the parameters of the resultant ZKP (e.g., communication complexity, supported class of languages, etc.). The versatility of the paradigm was demonstrated in [IKOS07], who – by instantiating the construction with "appropriate" MPC protocols – designed two types of constant-round communication-efficient ZKPs. Specifically, using a protocol of [BI05], they construct ZKPs for AC^0 (i.e., constant-depth circuits over $\land, \lor, \oplus, \neg$ gates of unbounded fan-in) whose communication complexity approaches the witness length, namely it is $n \cdot \mathsf{poly}(\kappa, \log s)$ bits (here, n is the witness length, κ is the security parameter, and s is the size of the verification circuit for $\mathcal{R}$). And, using a protocol of [DI06], they construct "constant rate" ZKPs for all NP, namely ZKPs whose communication complexity is $O(s) + \mathsf{poly}(\kappa, \log s)$, where s is the size of the verification circuit using gates of *bounded* fan in. Both constructions use the underlying commitment scheme (which can be based on one-way functions) as a black box.

Following its introduction, the "MPC-in-the-Head" paradigm has been extensively used to obtain black-box constructions [IPS08,HIKN08,IPS09,IW14, GOSV14,IKP+16,GIW16,HVW20], and communication-efficient protocols by using highly-efficient MPC protocols [GIW16,IPS08,IKO+11,GMO16,AHIV17, HIMV19,HVW20,BFH+20,HVW22]. In many of these works, the paradigm was used to compile protocols from semi-honest to malicious security. In the context of designing sublinear ZK arguments (and ZK-SNARKs), recent works [AHIV17,BFH+20] have leveraged the MPC-in-the-Head paradigm to obtain highly-efficient succinct proofs [AHIV22].

However, Ishai et al. [IKOS07] and, to the best of our knowledge, all follow-up works, relied on *fully-secure* MPC protocols (in the simulation-based paradigm). In particular, the constructions presented in the 15 years since [IKOS07] have not utilized the fact that the MPC protocol is only required to be correct (when all parties are honest), and private against semi-honest corruptions. Since such protocols could potentially be made more efficient than fully-secure protocols, "MPC-in-the-Head" might not have yet realized its full potential.

1.1   Our Contribution

We extend the "MPC-in-the-Head" paradigm to use *game-based* primitives that only guarantee *correctness and privacy* against semi-honest adversaries. Thus, we can exploit – for the first time – the observation of [IKOS07] that full security is not needed, and rely on the weaker requirements essential for the "MPC-in-the-Head" paradigm. We then use our paradigm to obtain new (also, black-box) constructions of succinct ZKPs.

ZKPs from Game-Based Primitives: A General Paradigm. We present a paradigm for constructing ZKPs that can be applied to a wide range of primitives, including Fully Homomorphic Encryption (FHE), Functional Encryption (FE), Homomorphic Secret Sharing (HSS), Function Secret Sharing (FSS), Randomized Encodings (REs), and Laconic Function Evalaution (LFE). Roughly speaking, the underlying primitive should contain a method of encoding secret information, a procedure for generating keys associated with computations, and a method of performing homomorphic computations on the encoded messages using the keys. For example, in an FE scheme, encoding the secret is simply encrypting it, function keys can be generated for different functions, and the computation can be executed homomorphically over ciphertexts by decrypting the ciphertext using an appropriate function key. Importantly, our paradigm preserves the efficiency of the underlying primitive in the following sense: the communication complexity of the resultant ZKP is proportional to the sum of (1) the size of the keys; (2) the size of encodings, and (3) the randomness complexity of the primitive (namely; the amount of randomness needed to generate encodings and keys).[1] In particular, the communication complexity does *not* depend directly on the *size of the computation*.

More specifically, we obtain the following result, where the soundness error is the probability that the verifier accepts a false claim (see Sect. 4 and the theorems therein for formal statements of the transformation from different primitives):

**Theorem 1 (ZKPs from Game-Based Non-Interactive Primitives –
Informal).** *Let $\mathcal{R} = \mathcal{R}(x, w)$ be an NP-relation with verification circuit C, and let κ be a security parameter. Let $\mathsf{P} = (\mathsf{Gen}, \mathsf{Enc}, \mathsf{Eval}, \mathsf{Dec})$ be a game-based*

---

[1] This dependence on the randomness can be removed by generating the randomness using a PRG whose output is indistinguishable from random, against non-uniform distinguishers. This causes only a negligible increase in the soundness error.

non-interactive primitive $\mathsf{P} \in \{\mathsf{FHE}, \mathsf{FE}, \mathsf{FSS}, \mathsf{HSS}, \mathsf{LFE}, \mathsf{RE}\}$ *for a circuit class containing* C. *Assuming ideal commitments, there exists a constant-round ZKP with constant soundness error, which uses* P *as a black-box.*

Moreover, assume that:

- *Keys generated by* Gen *have length* $\ell_k(\kappa)$,
- *Encodings generated by* Enc *have length* $\ell_c(\kappa, l)$ *(l denotes the length of the encrypted message)*,
- *And the executions of* $\mathsf{Gen}, \mathsf{Enc}$ *and* Eval *each consume* $\ell_r(\kappa)$ *random bits,*

Then the communication complexity of the proof is $O\big(n + \ell_r(\kappa) + \ell_k(\kappa) + \ell_c(\kappa, n)\big)$ *bits, where* n *denotes the witness length.*

Our paradigm is quite versatile: it can be applied to primitives in which the homomorphic computation is performed by a single party (as in FE and FHE), or distributed between multiple parties (as in HSS and FSS); it can handle primitives with a correctness error, in which decryption might not always yield the correct output of the computation; and it can rely on secret- or public-key primitives. See Sect. 4 for the various constructions.

Generalization to Interactive Protocols. We generalize our paradigm to use *interactive protocols* as the underlying building block, showing that our paradigm can be used to design protocols for *commit-and-prove* style functionalities. In particular, this generalized paradigm can be applied to Interactive Proofs (IPs) and Interactive Oracle Proofs (IOPs). As described below, this is useful for designing black-box variants of (succinct) ZKPs.

(Succinct) Black-Box ZKP Constructions. Similar to [IKOS07], the generality of our paradigm means it can be instantiated with various underlying primitives. We can additionally *exploit the relatively weak security properties* required from the underlying primitives to obtain efficiency gains in the communication complexity of the resultant ZKP. Specifically, by instantiating our paradigm with appropriate primitives, we construct ZKPs with new tradeoffs between the communication complexity, the supported class of languages, and the underlying assumptions. Moreover, we reprove several known results by casting known construction as special cases of our paradigm. Another attractive feature of our paradigm is that any future constructions of the underlying primitives can be plugged-into the compiler of Theorem 1 to obtain a new ZKP system. This is particularly important given the recent rapid improvement in the design of some of the underlying primitives (e.g., the relatively new notion of HSS).

We now give more details on these ZKP constructions.

Constant-Round ZKPs Approaching Witness Length. Instantiating Theorem 1 with an appropriate HSS scheme, we obtain constant-round ZKPs approaching witness length for (polynomial-time uniform) NC^1,[2] assuming the

---

[2] By polynomial-time uniform NC^1 we mean that there exist a polynomial $p(n)$ and a Turing machine that on input 1^n runs in time $p(n)$ and outputs the circuit (in NC^1) for input length n.

DCR assumption. (In fact, our ZKPs make a black-box use of HSS, which can be instantiated with the appropriate parameters assuming DCR.) The round complexity of our ZKPs is bounded by a *universal* constant, independent of the depth of the relation's verification circuit. This should be contrasted with [IKOS07], who obtain similar ZKPs for AC^0 assuming One-Way Functions (OWFs). See Sect. 4.1 for the construction and proof.

Corollary 1 (Constant-Rnd. ZKPs of Quasi-Linear Length from DCR). *Assume that the DCR hardness assumption (Definition 1) holds. Then there exists a universal constant c such that any NP-relation in (polynomial-time uniform) NC^1 has a c-round ZKP with 1/8 soundness error and $n \cdot \text{poly}(\kappa)$ communication complexity, where n denotes the witness length, and κ is the security parameter.*

Next, we show that if the round complexity of the ZKP is allowed to scale with the depth of the relation's verification circuit, then our ZKPs can make black-box use of *OWFs* (instead of the DCR assumption). This should be contrasted with Goldwasser et al. [GKR15], who obtain ZKPs approaching witness length for NC (with log-many rounds), and $O(1)$-round ZKPs for (polynomial-time uniform) NC^1 relations which follows from [GR20]. Both results are based on OWFs and use it in a *non-black-box* way; see Sect. 1.3 for a more detailed comparison.

Corollary 2 (Constant-Rnd. ZKPs of Quasi-Linear Length from OWFs). *Assume that OWFs exist. Then any NP-relation in (polynomial-time uniform) NC^1 has a constant-round ZKP with 1/2 soundness error and $n \cdot \text{poly}(\kappa)$ communication complexity, where n denotes the witness length, and κ is the security parameter. Moreover, the ZKP uses the OWF as a black box.*

As a second application, instantiating Theorem 1 with an FHE scheme, we obtain constant-round ZKPs for all NP, whose communication is proportional to the witness length. Moreover, our construction is black-box in the underlying FHE scheme. This gives a black-box alternative to a non-interactive ZKP construction of Gentry et al. [GGI+15] with similar parameters. More formally, we have the following corollary.

Corollary 3 (Constant-Rnd. ZKPs for all NP from FHE). *Assume the existence of an FHE scheme for all polynomial sized circuits. Then every NP language has a constant-round ZKP with 3/4 soundness error and $O(n)$ communication complexity, where n denotes the witness length. Moreover, the construction uses the underlying FHE scheme as a black-box.*

We note that similar to [GGI+15], to instantiate our construction of Corollary 3 we need an FHE scheme that can evaluate any polynomial-size circuit, and such constructions are known assuming LWE and circular-security of a particular encryption, or indistinguishability obfuscation.

Constant-Round ZKPs from OWFs. Instantiating Theorem 1 with an appropriate Randomized Encoding (RE) [IK00, AIK04] scheme (specifically, an appropriate garbling scheme), we reprove the following theorem from [HV16], who explored 2PC-in-the-Head as an intermediate step toward building black-box adaptively-secure ZKPs from OWFs.

Corollary 4. *Assume that OWFs exist. Then any polynomial-size Boolean circuit C has a constant-round ZKP with $2/3$ soundness error and $O(\kappa|C|)$ communication complexity, where κ is the security parameter. Moreover, the ZKP uses the OWF as a black-box.*

Everything Provable is Provable in Black-Box ZK. Ben-Or et al. [BGG+88] compiled a public-coin IP[3] for any language $\mathcal{L}$ to a ZKP for $\mathcal{L}$, by making non-black-box use of a OWF. Instantiating our generic C&P abstraction with randomized encodings as the underlying primitive, we obtain a similar transformation from IPs to ZKPs, which makes only *black-box* use of the underlying OWF. Specifically, we show the following:

Corollary 5 (Everything Provable is Provable in Black-Box ZK). *Assume OWFs exist. Then any $\mathcal{L} \in$ IP has a zero-knowledge proof which uses the underlying OWF as a black-box.*

Succinct Black-Box ZKPs for Bounded-Space/Bounded-Depth NP. We use our C&P abstraction to provide an IP-to-ZKP compiler which makes *black-box* use of a OWF. Applying this compiler to the "doubly-efficient" IPs of [GKR15] yields ZKPs for bounded-depth NP, as specified in Corollary 6 (see the full version for the formal statement). Prior to our work, succinct black-box ZKPs from OWFs were only known for AC^0 [IKOS07].

Corollary 6 (Succinct ZKPs for Bounded-Depth NP – Informal). *Assume OWFs exist, and let $\kappa(m) \geq \log(m)$ be a security parameter. Let $\mathcal{R}$ be an NP-relation computable by a logspace-uniform family of Boolean circuits of size $\mathsf{poly}(m)$ and depth $d(m)$, where m is the instance length. Then there exists a ZKP for $\mathcal{R}$ in which the prover runs in time $\mathsf{poly}(m)$ (given a witness), the verifier runs in time $\mathsf{poly}(m, \kappa)$, and the communication complexity is $n \cdot \mathsf{poly}(\kappa, d(m))$, where n denotes the witness length. Moreover, the protocol uses the underlying OWF as a black-box.*

We extend our black-box IP-to-ZKP compiler to apply to IOPs. Combined with ideas from [NR22], the compiler can be made to incur only a *constant* overhead (as low as roughly 2) in the communication complexity. This gives a *black-box* alternative to the recent IOP-to-ZKP compiler of [NR22], with slightly higher overhead (the compiler of [NR22] has essentially no overhead). Applying our compiler to the succinct IOPs of [RR20] gives the following result (see the full version for the formal statement):

Corollary 7 (Succinct ZKPs for Bounded-Space NP – Informal). *Assume OWFs exist, and let κ be a security parameter. Let $\mathcal{R}$ be an NP relation computable in polynomial time and bounded polynomial space (n^δ-space for some*

---

[3] In a *public-coin* IP, the verifier's messages are simply random bits.

fixed $\delta \in (0,1)$)). Then for any constant $\beta \in (0,1)$, there exists a public-coin, constant-round, ZKP for $\mathcal{R}$ with constant soundness error, and communication complexity $O(n) + m^\beta \cdot \text{poly}(\kappa)$, where m, n denote the instance and witness lengths, respectively. Moreover, the ZKP uses the underlying OWF as a black box.

1.2 Technical Overview

Our construction is conceptually simple. It relies in a black-box manner on a non-interactive game-based primitive, that allows for homomorphic computation of a function f while hiding both *the function* and *the input to it*. We first describe the properties needed from such primitives, then explain how they are used in our ZKP constructions.

The Building Block: Game-Based Non-interactive Primitive with Homomorphic Computations. Let $\mathcal{R} = \mathcal{R}(x, w)$ be an NP relation, and let $\mathcal{L}$ be the corresponding NP language. Let P be a cryptographic primitive consisting of the following four algorithms:

- Gen is a key generation algorithm used to generate keys, and all setup parameters needed to execute the primitive.
- Enc is an encoding procedure used to encode secrets.
- Eval is an evaluation procedure used to homomrphically compute over encoded secrets.
- Dec is a decoding procedure used to decode the outcome of homomorphic computations.

These algorithms are required to satisfy the following properties:

- **Correctness:** homomorphic computations yield the correct outcome; namely, they emulate the computation over unencoded messages. For simplicity, we assume *perfect* correctness in this section; however, our paradigm (described in Sect. 4) extends to primitives with a correctness error. (See, e.g., Sect. 4.1.)
- **Input Privacy:** encodings generated by Enc computationally hide the encoded secrets. (In particular, this implies that the output of a homomorphic computation over an encoding c hides the secret encoded by c.)
- **Function Privacy:** outputs of homomorphic computations generated by Eval reveal only the outcome of the computation, hiding all other information regarding the evaluated function.

One example of such a primitive is circuit-private Fully Homomorphic Encryption (FHE). Nevertheless, our abstraction captures a rich class of cryptographic objects, including function-private Functional Encryption (FE) and homomorphic forms of secret sharing, such as Homomorphic Secret Sharing (HSS) and Function Secret Sharing (FSS). The latter two examples (HSS and FSS) differ significantly from the former two (FHE and FE) because, in HSS/FSS, evaluation is *distributed* between k parties. We call such primitives *k-party primitives*, where a 1-party primitive is a primitive in which evaluation is not distributed (this is the case in, e.g., FHE and FE). For simplicity, we present our ZKP blueprint below for 1-party primitives, and it might be helpful for the reader to keep the FHE example in mind as an instantiation of the blueprint. We then describe how to generalize our abstraction to k-party primitives (see also the full abstraction in Fig. 3, Sect. 3). This allows us to obtain Theorem 1 by instantiating our paradigm with recent HSS constructions.

Blueprint of Our ZKP Construction. Similar to the MPC-in-the-head paradi-gm of [IKOS07], the prover $\mathcal{P}$ emulates the primitive's algorithms "in her head" and commits to (the transcripts of) these executions. The verifier $\mathcal{V}$ then checks that the primitive was honestly executed. If this is the case, the computation's output would be 1 if and only if $x \in \mathcal{L}$. Our constructions assume an ideal commitment oracle $\mathcal{F}_{\mathsf{Com}}$, which can be instantiated with computationally-hiding commitments (see Sect. 2.1). We now describe the construction in more detail. Let $C(\cdot, \cdot)$ be the verification circuit of $\mathcal{R}$. The ZKP between $\mathcal{P}$ with input $x \in \mathcal{L}$ and witness w, and $\mathcal{V}$ with input x, is executed as follows (see also Fig. 1).

In the first – and most crucial – step of the ZKP, $\mathcal{P}$ additively shares the witness $w = w_1 \oplus w_2$, and lets $\widetilde{C}(u) := C(x, w_1 \oplus u)$. Intuitively, this sharing divides w into two parts: one is tied to the homomorphic computation, and the other is the secret over which the computation is executed. This division is essential because we rely on *weak* primitives which *only guarantee correctness* (i.e., in an honest execution), with no correctness guarantees against *malicious* corruptions. Indeed, in this case $\mathcal{V}$ must check *all* parts of the execution – including encoding and homomorphic computation – so none of these steps can depend directly on the witness w. By separating w into two parts, we can remove the direct dependence on w from both the encoding and the homomorphic evaluation steps.[4] The prover's goal now reduces to proving that w_2 satisfies $\widetilde{C}$.

For this, $\mathcal{P}$ performs the following "in her head". $\mathcal{P}$ first generates the keys for homomorphic computation (by running Gen), then encodes w_2 (using Enc) to an encoding c, and homomorphically evaluates $\widetilde{C}$ over c (using Eval) to obtain an encoded outcome c'. $\mathcal{P}$ then commits to all values generated during these executions, namely: the randomness needed for the executions of $\mathsf{Gen}, \mathsf{Enc}$ and Eval, the encoding c of w_2, and the encoded output c'. Notice that to homomorphically evaluate $\widetilde{C}$ on w_2, one must perform the following four steps: (1) generate keys for the homomorphic computation; (2) encode w_2; (3) homomorphically evaluate $\widetilde{C}$ over w_2; (4) decode the outcome of the homomorphic computation. As noted above, if all these steps were honestly executed, the outcome is 1 if and only if $x \in \mathcal{L}$ (because of perfect correctness). Therefore, the verifier's goal is to check

---

[4] This is reminiscent of the [IKOS07] construction from passively-secure MPC protocols, in which the witness is secret-shared between the parties participating in the execution "in-the-head". We note, however, that our use of secret sharing is conceptually different: in our case, there is no underlying *two-* or *multi-party* computation. Instead, one of the shares is hard-wired into the computed function, making its identity secret, whereas [IKOS07] compute a *public* function by emulating *multiple parties* "in-the-head".

that the steps were honestly executed. For this, he randomly chooses one of the steps and checks that it was honestly executed, where $\mathcal{P}$ decommits the inputs, outputs, and randomness used in the step. The construction is described more explicitly in Fig. 1.

ZKPs from Game-Based Primitives

Let $\mathcal{R} = \mathcal{R}(x, w)$ be an NP-relation with verification circuit $C(\cdot, \cdot)$. The ZKP uses a non-interactive, game-based primitive $\mathsf{P} = (\mathsf{Gen}, \mathsf{Enc}, \mathsf{Eval}, \mathsf{Dec})$ as a building block, and is executed between a prover $\mathcal{P}$ with input $(x, w) \in \mathcal{R}$ and a verifier $\mathcal{V}$ with input x.

1. **Witness Secret Sharing:** $\mathcal{P}$ additively shares w by picking w_1, w_2 uniformly at random subject to $w = w_1 \oplus w_2$, and commits to w_1, w_2. Let $\widetilde{C}(u) := C(x, w_1 \oplus u)$.

2. **Setup:** $\mathcal{P}$ executes Gen to generate keys, and any public parameters needed for the execution of P, and commits to the randomness used by Gen, and its output. (This step might depend on $\widetilde{C}$, and consequently also on w_1, but not on w_2.)

3. **Witness Encoding:** $\mathcal{P}$ generates an encoding c of w_2 using Enc, and commits to c and any randomness used for encoding. (This step depends on w_2, but not on w_1.)

4. **Evaluation:** $\mathcal{P}$ homomorphically evaluates $\widetilde{C}$ on w_2, by executing Eval on c, to obtain an encoded outcome c', and commits to c' and any randomness used for evaluation. (This step depends on $\widetilde{C}$, and consequently also on w_1, but depends only on a *computationally-hiding encoding* of w_2.)

5. **Verification:** $\mathcal{V}$ randomly chooses one of the four steps of homomorphic evaluation and checks that it was executed correctly, as follows:

   (a) **Checking Setup:** $\mathcal{P}$ decommits w_1, the randomness used to execute Gen, as well as all keys and public parameters, and $\mathcal{V}$ check that Gen was executed correctly.

   (b) **Checking Witness Encoding:** $\mathcal{P}$ decommits w_2, c, the randomness used for encoding, as well as the keys needed for encoding (as generated in Step 2), and $\mathcal{V}$ checks that Enc was executed correctly.

   (c) **Checking Evaluation:** $\mathcal{P}$ decommits c, c', w_1, and the randomness used for evaluation, and $\mathcal{V}$ checks that Eval was executed correctly.

   (d) **Checking Output:** $\mathcal{P}$ decommits c', and any keys needed for decoding (as generated in Step 2), and $\mathcal{V}$ checks that c' decodes to 1.

Fig. 1. ZKP Abstraction (Informal, see Fig. 3 and Sect. 4)

Example: ZKPs from FHE. To demonstrate how to use our paradigm, we briefly describe an instantiation based on FHE (see the full version for the detailed construction and proof).[5] Let $\mathsf{FHE} = (\mathsf{Gen}, \mathsf{Enc}, \mathsf{Eval}, \mathsf{Dec})$ be an FHE

---

[5] We note that a similar construction could be obtained from the paradigm of [IKOS07] by instantiating an appropriate 2-party protocol from FHE.

scheme. The Setup step (Step 2) consists of executing Gen to generate a public encryption key pk and secret decryption key sk. pk can be sent to $\mathcal{V}$ in the clear, whereas $\mathcal{P}$ commits to sk and the randomness r_G used by Gen. The witness encoding step (Step 3) consists of $\mathcal{P}$ executing Enc with sk to encrypt w_2, and committing to w_2, the ciphertext c, and the randomness r_E used to generate it. Evaluation (Step 4) consists of $\mathcal{P}$ executing Eval to homomorphically evaluate $\widetilde{C}$ on c, to obtain a ciphertext c'. $\mathcal{P}$ commits to c' and the randomness r_C used for evaluation. During verification, $\mathcal{V}$ performs one of the following. (1) Checking setup (Step 5a), by reading r_G, pk, sk and checking the execution of Gen. (2) Checking encryption (Step 5b), by reading r_E, w_2, pk, c and checking the execution of Enc. (3) Checking evaluation (Step 5c), by reading r_C, w_1, pk, c, c' and checking the execution of Eval. (4) Checking decryption (Step 5d), by reading sk, c' and checking that c' decrypts to 1.

Analysis. We give a high-level intuition for the security of our paradigm; full proofs (relying on the specific properties of the underlying primitives) appear in Sect. 4. *Completeness*, when $\mathcal{P}, \mathcal{V}$ are honest, follows directly from the (perfect) correctness of the underlying primitive.[6] As for *soundness*, any $x \notin \mathcal{L}$ is rejected with constant probability. Indeed, the witness sharing step (Step 1) binds $\mathcal{P}$ to some "witness" $w^* = w_1^* \oplus w_2^*$, for which $C(x, w^*) = 0$ (because $x \notin \mathcal{L}$), and in particular $\widetilde{C}^*(w_2^*) = 0$ where $\widetilde{C}^*(u) := C(x, w_1^* \oplus u)$. Therefore, if $\mathcal{P}$ executed Steps 2–4 correctly (for $\tilde{C}^*$), then the output will decode to 0, in which case $\mathcal{V}$ rejects if he performs Step 5d, which happens with probability 1/4. Otherwise, $\mathcal{P}$ cheated in one of Steps 2–4, which will be detected if $\mathcal{V}$ checks the corresponding computation in Step 5 (which happens with probability 1/4).

Finally, *zero-Knowledge* follows from the input and function privacy of the underlying primitive. The high-level (though somewhat inaccurate) idea is to describe a simulator Sim which guesses in advance which of the substeps of Step 5 will be carried out by (the possibly malicious) $\mathcal{V}^*$, committing to "correct" values for that step, and dummy values for the other steps. If Sim had guessed correctly, it can continue the simulation; otherwise, it rewinds $\mathcal{V}^*$. Since the verifier has only four possible choices, in expectation, Sim succeeds in completing the simulation with overwhelming probability.

We now explain how Sim generates the committed values. The setup and witness encoding checks (Steps 5a–5b) depend only on w_1 and w_2 (respectively). Therefore, these steps can be simulated separately by picking w_1 or w_2 uniformly at random (which is identical to their distribution in the real execution because each witness share in isolation is independent of w). Once w_1 (respectively, w_2) have been fixed, the keys (respectively, witness encoding) can then be honestly generated from this witness share. Moreover, the input privacy of the underlying primitive guarantees that Sim can simulate the evaluation check in Step 5c. Indeed, this step depends only on an encoding c of w_2, which is computationally indistinguishable from the encoding of any other value. Thus, to simulate this

---

[6] See Sect. 4 for a generalization to imperfect correctness; e.g., in the HSS-based construction of Theorem 2.

step, the simulator can choose a random w_1, and indistinguishability between the real and simulated views reduces to indistinguishability between the encodings of two different messages. Finally, by function privacy, the output check (Step 5d) can be simulated by generating an encoding of 1.

The (simplified) ZK analysis provided here gives a flavor of how the splitting of w into two witness shares is used in the proof. The actual proofs are more intricate and depend on the specific notion of input and function privacy guaranteed by the underlying primitive. We refer the interested reader to Sect. 4 for the complete proofs.

Extension to k-Party Primitives. The ZKP construction of Fig. 1 is based on a 1-party primitive, namely a primitive in which a single party performs the evaluation, as is the case in FHE and FE. However, our paradigm generalizes to k-distributed primitives in which evaluation is *distributed* between multiple parties, each generating an *output share*, where the output can later be recovered from all shares. (See Fig. 3 in Sect. 3 for the full description.) This flexibility of our paradigm allows us to use a wider range of underlying primitives, and, in particular, enables us to obtain the succinct ZKPs of Corollary 1, which are based on 2-party HSS schemes. While we can rely on a k-distributed primitive for any $k \geq 1$, using $k > 2$ does not seem to be useful for constructing succinct ZKPs. Therefore, in the following, we focus on the case that $k = 2$. (The case of $k = 1$ was already discussed above.)

In a 2-distributed primitive, Gen generates a public state pk, as well as secret keys sk_1, sk_2 for the parties, and the evaluation is distributed between two parties, each using its secret key sk_i to homomorphically compute an output share y_i from the encoded inputs. Output decoding is possible given both output shares y_1, y_2. Therefore, using a 2-distributed primitive requires the following changes to the ZKP described in Fig. 1. First, the setup step (Step 2) generates the public state pk and both secret keys sk_1, sk_2. Second, the evaluation step (Step 4) is performed twice (once with each key sk_i) to generate a pair of output shares y_1, y_2. $\mathcal{P}$ then commits to all these values. Moreover, to check the evaluation (Step 5c), $\mathcal{V}$ picks $i \leftarrow \{1, 2\}$ and checks the execution of Eval with sk_i. Finally, to check the output value (Step 5d) $\mathcal{P}$ decommits y_1, y_2. (See Fig. 3 for a more detailed description.)

Variants and Extensions. We described our abstraction for public-key 1- and 2-distributed primitives with perfect correctness, but our paradigm is flexible and can be instantiated using a wide range of primitives. As discussed above, we can use k-distributed primitives also for $k > 2$. We can further support secret-key primitives (see, e.g., the FE-based construction in the full version), as well as primitives with a correctness error (see, e.g., the HSS-based construction of Sect. 4.1). This latter case is handled by having $\mathcal{P}, \mathcal{V}$ engage in a coin-tossing protocol before Step 2, which results in $\mathcal{P}$ holding a random string r and $\mathcal{V}$ holding a commitment to it. This protocol can be trivially realized in the $\mathcal{F}_{\mathsf{Com}}$-hybrid model with nearly no overhead in communication. Some of our constructions do not require the function-privacy property of the underlying primitive. In particular, this is the case for our RE-based construction.

Black-Box Commit-and-Prove. We extend our ZKP paradigm to Commit-and-Prove (C&P) functionalities that support an iterative commit phase. More specifically, a C&P protocol for a relation $\mathcal{R}$ is executed between $\mathcal{P}, \mathcal{V}$ with common input x, and consists of an iterative Commit phase, followed by a Prove phase. In the ith round of the commit phase, $\mathcal{V}$ sends a message z^i, following which $\mathcal{P}$ commits to a message y^i. In the Prove phase following l commit rounds, $\mathcal{P}$ proves that $((x, z_1, \ldots, z_l), (y_1, \ldots, y_l)) \in \mathcal{R}$. Roughly, the C&P construction is obtained by having $\mathcal{P}$ repeat the witness sharing phase of Step 1 (Fig. 1) for every message y^i, committing to shares y_1^i, y_2^i. Then, the Prove phase is executed by repeating Steps 2–5 of Fig. 1 for the circuit

$$\widetilde{C}'(u_1, \ldots, u_l) := C\left(\left(x, z^1, \ldots, z^l\right), \left(y_1^1 \oplus u_1, \ldots, y_1^l \oplus u_l\right)\right)$$

where C denotes the verification circuit of $\mathcal{R}$. Instantiating the generic C&P construction with randomized encodings as the underlying primitive yields a C&P protocol which makes a black box use of OWFs. See the full version for further details.

Succinct ZKP Constructions. An important advantage of the C&P construction is that the iterative nature of the Commit phase allows us to apply it to *interactive* protocols. In particular, we obtain a generic compiler from any public-coin IP for a language $\mathcal{L}$ to a ZKP for $\mathcal{L}$, as follows. In the Commit phase, $\mathcal{P}$ and $\mathcal{V}$ emulate the original IP protocol, except that $\mathcal{P}$ commits to her messages (instead of sending them directly to $\mathcal{V}$). The Prove phase is then executed for the relation consisting of all accepting transcripts. That is, C is taken to be the circuit which the IP verifier applies to the transcript to determine his output. Importantly, the communication complexity of the ZKP scales with the sum of the communication complexity of the IP, and the communication complexity of the Prove phase (which depends only on the size of the verification circuit of the IP verifier). By applying this compiler to the IPs of Ben-Or et al. [BGG+88] and Goldwasser et al. [GKR15] we obtain the new black-box ZKPs from OWFs of Corollaries 5 and 6, respectively. Furthermore, we show that our C&P can also be used to compile IOPs into ZKPs. Applying this compiler to the succinct IOPs of [RR20] gives our succinct ZKPs of Corollary 7, that make a black box use of OWFs. This improves a recent result of [NR22], who achieve a (tighter) non-black-box compilation in the OWF. We note that obtaining the ZKPs of Corollaries 1–4 reduces to instantiating the generic construction of Theorem 1 with a primitive with appropriate efficiency guarantees. In particular, the communication complexity of the ZKP scales with the sum of the key length, encoding length, and the randomness complexity of the underlying primitive.

1.3   Related Works

Interactive (Oracle) Proofs and Short Zero-Knowledge Proofs. Ben-Or et al. [BGG+88] showed a general compiler transforming any interactive proof system to one that is also zero-knowledge, assuming only the existence of one-way functions. In particular, as a corollary, they showed that every language in PSPACE has a zero-knowledge proof. Kalai and Raz [KR08], and independently

Ishai, Kushilevitz, Ostrovsky, and Sahai [IKOS07], gave the first doubly-efficient (zero-knowledge) interactive proof for NP relations computable by AC^0 circuits. While the work of [IKOS07] achieved communication complexity $n \cdot \text{poly}(\kappa)$ where n is the length of the witness, [KR08] achieved a communication of $\text{poly}(n, \kappa)$. In an influential work, Goldwasser Kalai and Rothblum gave the first (doubly-efficient) interactive proof for all bounded-depth computations computable by a logspace-uniform circuit [GKR15] with communication complexity $d \cdot \text{poly} \log S$ where d is the depth of the circuit and S is its size. An important feature of their construction was succinct verification, where the verifier's runtime was $m \cdot \text{poly}(d, \log(m))$, where m is the instance length. Applying the Ben-Or et al. compilation [BGG+88] technique to their protocol, they obtained as a corollary a ZKP for NP languages whose corresponding relation is computable by logspace-uniform circuits with communication complexity $n \cdot \text{poly}(\kappa, d)$. Implicit in their construction is a protocol for (polynomial-time) uniform circuits with the same communication complexity where the verifier's runtime is quasi-linear in circuit size.[7] While such a construction is not a useful interactive proof for a language in P when compiled using [BGG+88], it yields a non-trivial short zero-knowledge proof for NP-languages whose relations can be computed by polynomial-time uniform bounded-depth circuits.

Reingold, Rothblum, and Rothblum gave a constant-round IP for bounded-space computations [RRR16] with communication complexity $m^\delta \cdot \text{poly}(S)$ and verification time $m^\delta \cdot \text{poly}(S) + \tilde{O}(m)$ for any constant $\delta \in (0, 1)$ and language computable in space S. Similar to [GKR15], they compiled their IP to obtain a ZKP for NP languages with corresponding relations that can be computed via a space-bounded Turing machine. Goldreich and Rothblum [GR20] tightened the results of [RRR16] for $AC^0[2]$ and NC^1 by providing a constant-round IP with communication $m^{\delta+o(1)}$ and verification time $m^{1+o(1)}$. Ron-Zewi and Rothblum [RR20] gave a succinct IOP for NP languages whose relation can be computed in m^ζ-space for some fixed constant $\zeta \in (0, 1)$ where the communication complexity is $(1 + \epsilon)n$ for a constant $\epsilon \in (0, 1)$ (assuming the witness is larger than the instance), with constant query complexity. Nassar and Rothblum [NR22] showed how to compile this protocol into a zero-knowledge proof, with essentially no overhead in the communication complexity. The result of [GR20] yields constant-round ZKPs for (polynomial-time uniform) NC^1 with communication complexity $n \cdot \text{poly}(\kappa)$, making non-black box use of OWFs.[8] We note that Xie et al. [XZZ+19] design ZK-IOPs that work for GKR-style protocols (i.e., where the verifier needs to evaluate a low-degree extension of the wiring predicate), that are black-box in the underlying OWF, but whose length is polynomial

---

[7] The reason the protocol requires logspace-uniformity is to provide an efficient way for the verifier to evaluate a point on the low-degree extension of the circuit wiring predicate. If the circuit class was just polynomial-time uniform, the verifier would need time that is quasi-linear in the size of the predicate.

[8] [GR20] provide a constant-round protocol for sufficiently uniform (i.e., adjacency predicate) circuits in NC^1. However, following the observation made on the protocol of [GKR15], the protocol of [GR20] also yields a constant-round protocol for polynomial-time uniform NC^1 with short communication.

in the witness length $|n|$. On the other hand, our compiler uses the underlying IP/IOP as a black-box, and can therefore be applied to any IP/IOP.

The round complexity in all these works, except [IKOS07], scales with the size/depth of the verification circuit for the relation, whereas the round complexity in our ZKPs from DCR (Corollary 1) is bounded by a universal constant, independent of the circuit depth.

Going beyond one-way functions, the work of [GGI+15] shows how to design a ZKP for all NP approaching witness length based on fully-homomorphic encryption schemes.

Other Black-Box Transformations. The work of Hazay and Venkitasubramaniam [HV16] used MPC-in-the-Head to compile 2PC protocols into zero-knowledge proofs. While their constructions do not yield succinct proofs, they achieve other features such as input-delayed proofs and adaptive zero-knowledge. Their work provided a general framework for designing zero-knowledge proofs from randomized-encodings. Their 2PC-in-the-head paradigm was later used by Brakerski and Yuen [BY22] to obtain a quantum-secure zero-knowledge proof by first designing a quantum-secure randomized encoding (actually, a garbled circuit) and then applying the compiler. Ishai et al. [IKP+16] provide a different compiler for 2PC protocols by designing a framework of black-box compilers.

Restricting to black-box constructions from one-way functions and succinct proofs, only the work of [IKOS07] provides a construction for NP-languages whose relation can be computed by an AC^0 circuit. Several works design zero-knowledge variants of IOPs, referred to as ZK-IOPs, for circuit SAT (or its generalization to R1CS) [BCGV16, BCG+17a, BCF+17, BBHR19, BCR+19, BCL22] or based on the GKR protocol [WTS+18, BBHR19, XZZ+19, ZLW+21], but none yield succinct proofs. The GKR-based ZK-IOPs of Xie et al. [XZZ+19] can be compiled into ZKP with communication complexity $\mathsf{poly}(n, \kappa)$ and logarithmic rounds for NC^1 circuits, and it is conceivable that a similar technique could be used to compile the protocols of [RRR16, GR20], perhaps with communication complexity $\mathsf{poly}(n, \kappa)$ and constant rounds. It is plausible that this communication can be brought down further to $n \cdot \mathsf{poly}(\kappa)$ by using the ZK variant of the code-switching technique of [RR20] from [BCL22], thus providing an alternative path to obtain Corllary 2. However, this approach will only apply to GKR-style protocols, whereas our approach is more general and works for any IOP while preserving the efficiency parameters.

Black-Box Commit and Prove. The (single) commit-and-prove functionality dates back to the work of Goldreich et al. [GMW87] and was formalized in [CLOS02]. Implicit in [IKOS07] was the first black-box commit-and-prove protocol based on collision-resistant hash functions. Follow-up works have optimized the round complexity and achieved other features such as adaptive security. [GLOV12, GOSV14, OSV15, HV16, KOS18, HV18] improved the concrete round complexity and also constructed zero-knowledge argument systems from one-way functions.

Homomorphic Secret Sharing (HSS). HSS were introduced by [BGI16], who constructed a 2-party HSS scheme for polynomial-length deterministic branching programs with an inverse-polynomial correctness error, assuming the DDH assumption. Using this result in our HSS-based ZKPs (Fig. 4, Sect. 4.1) would result in a ZKP with inverse polynomial *simulation* error. Instead, we rely on the HSS scheme of [RS21] for polynomial-length branching programs (with negligible correctness error) which are based on the DCR assumption. A similar HSS construction was provided in [OSY21].

Functional Encryption (FE). Functional encryption, introduced in [BSW11, O'N10], is a generalization of (public-key) encryption in which function keys can be used to compute a function of the plaintext directly from the ciphertext (without knowledge of the decryption key). We instantiate our construction with the state-of-the-art FE for circuits from [GWZ22] that gives rate-1 ciphertext size based on indistinguishability obfuscation.

Randomized Encoding (RE). Formalized in the works of [IK00, IK02, AIK06], randomized encoding explores to what extent the task of securely computing a function can be simplified by settling for computing an "encoding" of the output. Loosely speaking, a function $\hat{f}(x, r)$ is said to be a randomized encoding of a function f if the output distribution depends only on $f(x)$. One of the earliest constructions of a randomized encoding for Boolean circuits is that of "garbled circuits" and originates in the work of Yao [Yao86]. Additional variants have been considered in the literature in the early works of [Kil88, FKN94]. Instantiating our paradigm with RE implies a theorem proven in [HV16].

Fully Homomorphic Encryption (FHE). First constructed by Gentry [Gen09], fully homomorphic encryption is a public-key encryption scheme allowing arbitrary computations to be performed on ciphertexts. That is, given a function f and a ciphertext ct encrypting a message m, it is possible to compute a ciphertext ct' that encrypts $f(m)$, without knowing the secret decryption key. FHE can be constructed based on LWE where the approximation factor in the underlying lattice problem can be polynomial [BV14]. Instantiating our construction with a rate-1 FHE scheme (e.g., using hybrid encryption) that can evaluate all polynomial-sized circuits, gives constant-round ZKPs for all NP languages with total communication complexity $O(n)$.

1.4   Paper Organization

In Sect. 2, we introduce basic preliminaries and security definitions. In Sect. 3 we introduce our abstraction. In Sect. 4 we instantiate our abstraction with HSS. Due to space limitations, we defer instantiations of our abstraction with other primitives, its generalization to commit-and-prove, our black-box compilers from IPs and IOPs to ZKPs, and most proofs, to the full version.

2   Preliminaries

Notation. Let κ denote the security parameter, and $\mathbb{G}$ denote a finite abealian group. We use PPT to denote probabilsitic polynomial time computation. For a distribution $\mathcal{D}$, sampling according to $\mathcal{D}$ is denote by $X \leftarrow \mathcal{D}$, or $X \in_R \mathcal{D}$. For a pair $\mathcal{D}, \mathcal{D}'$ of distributions, we use $\mathcal{D} \approx \mathcal{D}'$ to denote that they are computationally indistinguishable. We assume familiarity with standard notions of Turing machines, probabilistic polynomial-time and bounded-space computations.[9] When we refer to Turing Machines running in time $t(n)$ and/or space $s(n)$, we assume $t(\cdot)$ and $s(\cdot)$ are time-constructible and space-constructible (respectively).

Complexity Classes. A language $\mathcal{L}$ is in NP if there is a polynomial-time computable relation $\mathcal{R}_\mathcal{L}$ that consists of pairs (x, w), such that $x \in \mathcal{L}$ if and only if there exists a w such that $(x, w) \in \mathcal{R}_\mathcal{L}$. We denote the instance size $|x|$ by m, and the witness size $|w|$ by n.

A circuit ensemble $\{C_m\}_{m=1}^\infty$ is a family of circuits indexed by an integer m, where C_m is a circuit that accepts inputs of length m. AC^0 consists of ensembles of Boolean circuits with polynomial size, constant depth, and unbounded fan-in. For $i \in \mathbb{N}$, NC^i contains the ensembles of constant fan-in Boolean circuits where the mth circuit is of depth $\log^i(m)$, and $\mathsf{NC} = \cup_{i \in \mathbb{N}}\mathsf{NC}^i$. The notion of circuit uniformity describes the complexity of generating the description of the mth circuit on input 1^m. For example, a popular uniformity notion is *log-space* uniformity, where there should exist a log-space Turing machine that, on input 1^m, outputs a description of C_m. Similarly, polynomial-time uniform means there exist a polynomial $p(m)$ and a Turing machine that on input 1^m runs in time $p(m)$ and outputs a description of the circuit C_m. In this work we focus on NP languages whose relations can be expressed via circuits in a particular complexity class (e.g., AC^0 or NC^1).

Assumptions. Our HSS-based construction relies on the DCR hardness assumption [Pai99] that holds in the presence of non-uniform adversaries and a properly generated RSA number (namely, a product of two random safe primes[10] of the same length).

Definition 1 (Non-uniform DCR [Pai99]). *The Decisional Composite Residuosity (DCR) assumption states that the uniform distribution over $\mathbb{Z}_{N^2}^*$ is indistinguishable from the uniform distribution on the subgroup of perfect powers of N in $\mathbb{Z}_{N^2}^*$[11] in the presence of non-uniform adversaries, for a properly generated RSA number N.*

---

[9] We will assume the multi-tape formulation to capture sub-linear space computations.

[10] A safe prime is a prime number of the form $2p + 1$, where p is also a prime.

[11] We say that $t \in \mathbb{Z}_{N^2}^*$ is a perfect power of N if there exists $r \in \mathbb{Z}_N^*$ such that $t = r^N \mod \mathbb{Z}_{N^2}^*$.

2.1 Commitment Schemes

Our constructions are proven in the $\mathcal{F}_{\text{COM}}$-hybrid model depicted in Fig. 2, where our communication complexity analysis only counts the lengths of committed/decommitted messages.

Functionality $\mathcal{F}_{\text{COM}}$

Functionality $\mathcal{F}_{\text{COM}}$ communicates with sender sender and receiver receiver, and adversary Sim.

1. Upon receiving input (commit, sid, m) from sender where $m \in \{0, 1\}^t$, internally record (sid, m) and send message $(sid, \text{sender}, \text{receiver})$ to the adversary. Upon receiving approve from the adversary send sid, to receiver. Ignore subsequent (commit, ., ., .) messages.
2. Upon receiving (reveal, sid) from sender, where a tuple (sid, m) is recorded, send message m to adversary Sim and receiver. Otherwise, ignore.

Fig. 2. The string commitment functionality.

Remark 1 (Commitment Schemes). We use the commitment-hybrid model to emphasize that our constructions rely on the underlying commitment instantiation in a black-box manner. However, analogously to [IKOS07], the ideal commitment primitive in all our protocols can be instantiated with any statistically-binding commitment protocol. We recall that rate-1 non-interactive perfectly-binding commitment schemes can be constructed based on one-way permutations (or injective one-way functions), whereas two-round statistically binding commitment schemes can be constructed based on one-way functions [Nao91].

2.2 Zero-Knowledge Proofs (ZKPs)

A zero-knowledge proof system for an NP language $\mathcal{L}$ is a protocol between a prover $\mathcal{P}$ and a computationally bounded verifier $\mathcal{V}$ where $\mathcal{P}$ wishes to convince $\mathcal{V}$ of the validity of some public statement x. Namely, $\mathcal{P}$ wishes to prove that there exists a witness w such that $(x, w) \in \mathcal{R}$, where $\mathcal{R}$ is an NP relation for verifying membership in $\mathcal{L}$. More formally, We denote by $\langle A(w), B(z) \rangle(x)$ the random variable representing the (local) output of machine B when interacting with machine A on common input x, when the random-input to each machine is uniformly and independently chosen, and A has an auxiliary input w.

Definition 2 (Interactive Proof (IP)). *A pair of interactive PPT machines $(\mathcal{P}, \mathcal{V})$ is called a $(1 - \delta)$-complete, $(1 - \varepsilon)$-sound Interactive Proof (IP) system for a language $\mathcal{L}$ if the following two conditions hold:*

– $(1-\delta)$-*completeness: For every* $x \in \mathcal{L}$,

$$\Pr[\langle \mathcal{P}, \mathcal{V} \rangle(x) = 1] \geq 1 - \delta.$$

where $\langle \mathcal{P}, \mathcal{V} \rangle(x)$ *denotes the output of* $\mathcal{V}$ *after he interacts with* $\mathcal{P}$ *on common input* x.

– $(1-\varepsilon)$-*soundness: For every* $x \notin \mathcal{L}$ *and every interactive machine* $\mathcal{P}^*$,

$$\Pr[\langle \mathcal{P}^*, \mathcal{V} \rangle(x) = 1] \leq \varepsilon.$$

Definition 3 (μ-Zero-Knowledge). *Let* $(\mathcal{P}, \mathcal{V})$ *be an interactive proof system for some language* $\mathcal{L}$. *We say that* $(\mathcal{P}, \mathcal{V})$ *is* computational zero-knowledge *with* μ-*simulation error if for every PPT interactive machine* $\mathcal{V}^*$ *there exists a PPT algorithm* Sim *such that for every PPT distinguisher* $\mathcal{D}$,

$$\left| \Pr[\mathcal{D}(\langle \mathcal{P}, \mathcal{V}^* \rangle(x)) = 1] - \Pr \mathcal{D}(\langle \mathsf{Sim} \rangle(x)) = 1] \right| \leq \mu(n)$$

where $\langle \mathsf{Sim} \rangle(x)$ *denotes the output of* Sim *on* x *and* n *is the witness length.*

Notation 1. *We say that a proof system is a* $(1-\varepsilon)$-*sound ZKP if it is a* $(1-\delta)$-*complete,* $(1-\varepsilon)$-*sound ZKP with* μ *simulation error, for* $\delta, \mu = \mathsf{negl}\,(n)$, *where* n *is the witness length.*

2.3 Interactive Oracle Proofs (IOP)

Interactive Oracle Proofs (IOPs) [BCS16, RRR16] are proof systems that combine aspects of Interactive Proofs (IPs) [Bab85, GMR85] and Probabilistically Checkable Proofs (PCPs) [BFLS91, AS98, ALM+98]. They also generalize Interactive PCPs (IPCPs) [KR08]. In this model, similar to the PCP model, the verifier does not need to read the whole proof, and instead can query the proof at some locations, while similar to the IP model, there are several interaction rounds between the prover and verifier. More specifically, a public-coin k-round IOP has k rounds of interaction, where in the ith round the verifier sends a uniformly random message m_i to the prover, and the prover responds with a proof oracle π_i. Once the interaction ends, the verifier makes some queries to the proofs $\pi_1, \ldots, \pi_k$ (via oracle access), and either accepts or rejects. More formally,

Definition 4. (Interactive Oracle Proofs). *A* k-*round* q-*query public-coin IOP system for a language* $\mathcal{L}$ *is a pair of PPT algorithms* $(\mathcal{P}, \mathcal{V})$ *satisfying the following properties:*

– **Syntax:** *On common input* x *and prover input* w, $\mathcal{P}$ *and* $\mathcal{V}$ *run an interactive protocol of* k *rounds. In each round* i, $\mathcal{V}$ *sends a uniformly random message* m_i *and* $\mathcal{P}$ *generates a proof oracle* π_i, *to which* $\mathcal{V}$ *has oracle access. Let* $\pi := (\pi_1, \pi_2, \ldots, \pi_k)$. *Following the* k^{th} *round,* $\mathcal{V}$ *makes* q *queries to* π, *and either accepts or rejects.*

- $(1-\delta)$-**completeness:** *For every* $x \in \mathcal{L}$,

$$\Pr[\langle \mathcal{P}, \mathcal{V}^\pi \rangle (x) = 1] \geq 1 - \delta.$$

where $\langle \mathcal{P}, \mathcal{V}^\pi \rangle(x)$ *denotes the output of* $\mathcal{V}$ *after he interacts with* $\mathcal{P}$ *on common input* x, *and* $\mathcal{V}^\pi$ *denotes that* $\mathcal{V}$ *has oracle access to* π.
- $(1-\varepsilon)$-**soundness:** *For every* $x \notin \mathcal{L}$, *every interactive machine* $\mathcal{P}^*$, *and every proof* $\tilde{\pi}$

$$\Pr[\langle \mathcal{P}^*, \mathcal{V}^{\tilde{\pi}} \rangle (x) = 1] \leq \varepsilon.$$

2.4 Homomorphic Secret Sharing (HSS)

Homomorphic secret sharing is an alternative approach to FHE, allowing for homomorphic evaluation to be distributed among two parties who do not interact with each other. We follow the definition from [BCG+17b].

Definition 5. (Homomorphic Secret Sharing with δ Error). *A (2-party, public-key) Homomorphic Secret Sharing (HSS) scheme for a class of circuits $\mathcal{C}$ with output group $\mathbb{G}$ consists of algorithms* (Gen, Enc, Eval) *with the following syntax:*

- Gen(1^κ) *is a key generation algorithm, which on input a security parameter* 1^κ *outputs a public key* pk *and a pair of evaluation keys* (ek_0, ek_1).
- Enc(pk, x) *is an encryption algorithm which given public key* pk *and secret input value* $x \in \{0,1\}^n$, *outputs a ciphertext* ct. *We assume the input length n is included in* ct.
- Eval$(b, ek_b, (ct_1, \ldots, ct_m), C)$ *is an evaluation algorithm, which on input party index* $b \in \{0,1\}$, *evaluation key* ck_b, *ciphertext* ct_i, *and a circuit* $C \in \mathcal{C}$ *with m inputs and n' output bits, the homomorphic evaluation algorithm outputs* $y_b \in \mathbb{G}$, *constituting party $b's$ share of an output $y \in \mathbb{G}$ where $\mathbb{G}$ is an abelian group.*

The scheme is required to satisfy the following semantic properties:

- **Correctness:** *For all security parameters κ, all circuits $C \in \mathcal{C}$, and all inputs $x_1, \ldots, x_m$, we have:*

$$\Pr\left[y_1 \oplus y_2 = C(x_1, \ldots, x_m) : \begin{array}{c} (pk, ek_1, ek_2) \leftarrow \text{HSS.Gen}(1^\kappa) \\ \forall 1 \leq j \leq m, \left(c_1^j, c_2^j\right) \leftarrow \text{HSS.Enc}(pk, x_j) \\ \forall i \in \{1,2\}, y_i \leftarrow \text{HSS.Eval}(i, ek_i, c_i^1, \ldots, c_i^m, C) \end{array} \right] \geq 1 - \delta(\kappa)$$

where the probability is over the randomness of Gen, Enc *and* Eval.
- **Security:** *For every $x, x' \in \{0,1\}^n$ the distribution ensembles $C_b(\kappa, x)$ and $C_b(\kappa, x')$ are computationally indistinguishable in the presence of non-uniform distinguishers, where $C_b(\kappa, x)$ is obtained by sampling $(pk, (ek_0, ek_1)) \leftarrow$ Gen(1^κ), sampling $ct_x \leftarrow$ Enc(pk, x), and outputting (pk, ek_b, ct_x). $C_b(\kappa, x')$ is generated similarly.*

Remark 2. (Single ciphertext.). Our ZK construction (Sect. 4.1) requires a simpler definition where Eval is invoked on a single ciphertext.

3   ZKPs from Game-Based Primitives

In this section we describe our abstraction, which uses non-interactive game-based primitives to design ZKPs. In Sect. 4 we instantiate this abstraction with various primitives. The abstraction is given in Fig. 3.

At a high level, the building block is a k-distributed, game-based, non-interactive primitive. More specifically, the primitive should support homomorphic evaluation which is distributed between k parties. The primitive consists of the following algorithms:

1. A key generation algorithm Gen that generates a public state pk and secret keys $sk_1, \ldots, sk_k$ for the k parties.
2. An Encoding algorithm Enc which, given a message w, the public key pk, and a secret key sk_i, generates an encoding c_i of w with respect to sk_i.
3. An evaluation procedure Eval which, given the public state pk (and possibly also sk_i), an encoding c_i of w, and a circuit C, generates an output share y_i of $C(w)$.
4. An output decoder Dec which, given the k output shares $y_1, \ldots, y_k$, can decode the output. (We note that decoding might require knowledge of the secret keys $sk_1, \ldots, sk_k$.)

Roughly, the primitive is required to satisfy the following semantic properties:

1. **Correctness:** evaluation over encoded inputs yields the correct output. That is, if the input is encoded using Enc, and the output shares are computed from the input encodings using Eval, then Dec decodes the correct output.
2. **Input privacy:** the encodings semantically hide the secret input.
3. **Function privacy:** the output of Eval hides all information about the computed function, except for the output of the computation.

4   Zero-Knowledge Proof Constructions

In this section, we instantiate our paradigm with an HSS scheme and obtain constant-round, black-box ZKPs for NC^1 assuming the DCR assumption, proving Corollary 1. In the full version, we instantiate our paradigm with other game-based primitives such as FSS, FHE, FE, REs and LFEs. Our constructions are described in the $\mathcal{F}_{Com}$-hybrid model, and use the underlying cryptographic primitive (as well as any instantiation of the commitment oracle) as a black box.

Remark 3 (On using k-distributed primitives for k > 2). Some of our constructions (e.g. the HSS- and FSS-based constructions) are based on k-distributed primitives for $k \geq 2$. For simplicity, we chose to describe these constructions for the special case that $k = 2$, but they naturally extend to any $k \geq 2$. We note that choosing $k = 2$ also results in lower communication complexity in the resultant ZKP. This is not only because the communication complexity scales with k, but also because the most efficient HSS and FSS schemes to date are in the 2-party setting.

ZKP Abstraction

Let $P = (\mathsf{Gen}, \mathsf{Enc}, \mathsf{Eval}, \mathsf{Dec})$ be a k-party primitive as described above. The ZKP for an NP-relation $\mathcal{R} = \mathcal{R}(x, w)$ with verification circuit $C(\cdot, \cdot)$ is executed between a prover $\mathcal{P}$ that has input $(x, w) \in \mathcal{R}$ and a verifier $\mathcal{V}$ that has input x. The parties have access to an ideal commitment functionality $\mathcal{F}_{\mathsf{Com}}$.

1. **Witness secret sharing:** $\mathcal{P}$ additively shares w by picking w_1, w_2 uniformly at random subject to $w = w_1 \oplus w_2$, and uses $\mathcal{F}_{\mathsf{Com}}$ to commit to w_1, w_2. Additionally, $\mathcal{P}$ defines $\widetilde{C}(u) := C(x, w_1 \oplus u)$.

2. **Randomness generation:** $\mathcal{P}$ and $\mathcal{V}$ run a coin tossing protocol to generate randomness r for $\mathsf{Gen}, \mathsf{Enc}$ and Eval. At the end of this phase, $\mathcal{P}$ knows r, and $\mathcal{V}$ holds a commitment to r. (This can be easily done using $\mathcal{F}_{\mathsf{Com}}$.) The bits of r are used by $\mathcal{P}$ in the following steps when executing a randomized algorithm of P.[a]

3. **Setup:** $\mathcal{P}$ executes Gen to generate a public state pk (which might be empty), and k secret states $\mathsf{sk}_1, \ldots, \mathsf{sk}_k$. This step might depend on $\widetilde{C}$ (and consequently also on w_1). $\mathcal{P}$ sends pk to $\mathcal{V}$ (in the clear), and uses $\mathcal{F}_{\mathsf{Com}}$ to commit to $\mathsf{sk}_1, \ldots, \mathsf{sk}_k$.

4. **Witness encoding:** $\mathcal{P}$ uses $\mathsf{pk}, \mathsf{sk}_1, \ldots, \mathsf{sk}_k$ to generate encoding $c_1, \ldots, c_k$ of w_2, and uses $\mathcal{F}_{\mathsf{Com}}$ to commit to these encodings.

5. **Evaluation:** For each $i \in [k]$, $\mathcal{P}$ executes Eval using $c_i, \widetilde{C}, \mathsf{pk}$ and sk_i (as appropriate) to generate an output share y_i of $\widetilde{C}(w_2)$, and uses $\mathcal{F}_{\mathsf{Com}}$ to commit to these output shares.

6. **Verification:** $\mathcal{V}$ checks that one of the three steps (Steps 3.-5.) was executed correctly, or that the output is 1 (each check is performed with probability $1/4$). Specifically, this is done as follows:

   (a) **Checking setup:** $\mathcal{P}$ decommits the randomness used to execute Gen, as well as $\mathsf{sk}_1, \ldots, \mathsf{sk}_k, w_1$, and $\mathcal{V}$ checks that Gen was executed correctly.

   (b) **Checking witness encoding:** $\mathcal{P}$ decommits the randomness used for encoding, as well as $w_2, c_1, \ldots, c_k$ and all the keys in $\{\mathsf{sk}_1, \ldots, sk_k\}$ which are used by Enc, and $\mathcal{V}$ checks that Enc was executed correctly on these values.

   (c) **Checking evaluation:** $\mathcal{V}$ picks $i \leftarrow [k]$, and $\mathcal{P}$ decommits the randomness used for the ith execution of Eval, as well as to sk_i, c_i and y_i, and *one* of w_1, w_2 (if it is needed for evaluation), and $\mathcal{V}$ checks that the ith execution of Eval was done correctly on these values.

   (d) **Checking output decoding:** $\mathcal{P}$ decommits $y_1, \ldots, y_k$, and all the keys in $\{\mathsf{sk}_1, \ldots, sk_k\}$ which are used by Dec, and $\mathcal{V}$ uses Dec to decode the output y from $y_1, \ldots, y_k$, and checks that $y = 1$.

---

[a] This step is needed only when P has imperfect correctness, otherwise $\mathcal{P}$ can choose the random bits on her own.

Fig. 3. ZKP Construction from Game-Based Secure Primitives

Recall from Sect. 3 that in our protocols, we secret share the NP witness w into two additive secret shares $w = w_1 \oplus w_2$, hard-wire w_1 into the verification circuit C, and then (homomorphically) evaluate this circuit $C_{x,w_1}(u) = C(x, w_1 \oplus u)$ on the second witness share w_2. Therefore, we will need the underlying primitive to support homomorphic computations over circuits of the form C_{x,w_1}, for any possible witness share w_1. More specifically, we will use the following circuit class which, intuitively, contains all the circuits of the form C_{x,w_1}, where w_1 has the same length as a witness w for x.

Notation 2 *Let $\mathcal{R} = \mathcal{R}(x, w)$ be an NP relation, with verification circuit C, and let $\mathcal{L}$ denote the corresponding NP language. For $x \in \mathcal{L}$, we define the following class of circuits:*

$$\tilde{\mathcal{C}}(C) = \{C_{x,w_1}(u) = C(x, w_1 \oplus u) :$$
$$\exists w, w_1 \in \{0,1\}^* \ s.t. \ (x, w) \in \mathcal{R} \land |w| = |w_1|\}.$$

4.1 Zero-Knowledge Proofs from Homomorphic Secret Sharing (HSS)

The construction uses a 2-party Homomorphic Secret Sharing (HSS) scheme HSS = (HSS.Setup, HSS.Enc, HSS.Eval). Since this is a 2-distributed primitive, the Setup phase (Step 3 in Fig. 4) generates a public key pk and a pair of evaluation keys $\mathsf{ek}_1, \mathsf{ek}_2$. Moreover, the witness encoding step generates a pair of witness ciphertexts c_1, c_2, and the evaluation algorithm is executed with each pair of evaluation key and ciphertext, generating an output share y_i. The output is decoded by computing $y = y_1 \oplus y_2$, so the prover need not perform this step ($\mathcal{V}$ can check the output directly by reading y_1, y_2, see Step 6d in Fig. 4).

Theorem 2 (ZKPs from HSS). *Let $\mathcal{R} = \mathcal{R}(x, w)$ be an NP-relation with verification circuit C, and let κ be a security parameter. Let $\mathsf{HSS} = (\mathsf{HSS.Gen}, \mathsf{HSS.Enc}, \mathsf{HSS.Eval})$ be an HSS scheme with δ error for the class $\tilde{\mathcal{C}}(C)$ of circuits (see Notation 2) with output group $\mathbb{G}$. The ZKP of Fig. 4, when instantiated with HSS, is a $(1 - \delta/4)$-complete, $(1 - \varepsilon)$-sound ZKP, with $\delta + \mathsf{negl}(\kappa)$ simulation error, in the $\mathcal{F}_{\mathsf{Com}}$-hybrid model, where $\varepsilon = \max\{3/4 + \delta/4, 7/8\}$. Furthermore, the ZKP uses HSS as a black-box.*

Moreover, assume that:

- *Evaluation and public keys generated by HSS.Gen have length $\ell_k(\kappa)$,*
- *Ciphertexts generated by HSS.Enc have length $\ell_c(\kappa, m)$ (m denotes the length of the encrypted message),*
- *And the executions of HSS.Gen, HSS.Enc and (the two executions of) HSS.Eval each consume $\ell_r(\kappa)$ random bits,*

Then $\mathcal{P}, \mathcal{V}$ exchange at most $4\ell_r(\kappa) + \ell_k(\kappa) + 3$ bits, at most $2n + 4\ell_r(\kappa) + 2 \cdot \ell_k(\kappa) + 2 \cdot \ell_c(\kappa, n) + 2\log|\mathbb{G}|$ bits are committed, and at most $n + \ell_r(\kappa) + 2 \cdot \ell_c(\kappa, n) + 2 \cdot \ell_k(\kappa) + 2\log|\mathbb{G}|$ bits are decommitted, where n denotes the witness length.

Proof Given an ideal commitment functionality, Step 2 can be executed with perfect security. Therefore, we assume that r_G, r_1, r_2 are uniformly random in the following.

$(1 - \delta/4)$-*Completeness.* When both parties are honest, verification can fail only due to a correctness error of the HSS (see Definition 5), which causes $y_1 \oplus y_2 \neq 1$. (Indeed, all other steps in the proof are deterministic given the randomness generated in Step 2.) Since the HSS is executed with uniformly random bits, the correctness of the HSS scheme guarantees that $y_1 \oplus y_2 \neq 1$ only with probability δ. Since $\mathcal{V}$ checks that $y_1 \oplus y_2 = 1$ if and only if he chooses to perform Step 6d, $\mathcal{V}$ rejects only with probability $\delta/4$.

$(1 - \varepsilon)$-*Soundness.* Assume that $x \notin \mathcal{L}$. Let w_1^*, w_2^* denote the witness shares which $\mathcal{P}$ committed to in Step 1, and let $w^* := w_1^* \oplus w_2^*$, then $C(x, w^*) = 0$. We consider two possible cases. First, if $\mathcal{P}$ executed Steps 3-5 honestly, then $y_1 \oplus y_2 = 1$ only with probability δ. This follows from the correctness of the HSS scheme since it is executed with uniformly random bits. Therefore, if $\mathcal{V}$ chooses to check Step 6d, he rejects with probability at least $1 - \delta$. Since Step 6d is performed with probability $1/4$, in this case $\mathcal{V}$ accepts with probability at most $1 - (1 - \delta)/4 = 3/4 + \delta/4$.

Second, assume that $\mathcal{P}$ cheated in one of the Steps 3-5. Since the execution of each of these steps is deterministic (given the appropriate randomness from $\{r_G, r_1, r_2\}$), then if $\mathcal{V}$ checks that step, he will reject. More specifically, if $\mathcal{P}$ cheated in Step 3 or Step 4, then $\mathcal{V}$ will accept with probability at most $3/4$. If $\mathcal{P}$ cheated in Step 5 then $\mathcal{P}$ cheated in the execution of HSS.Eval for $i = 1$ or $i = 2$, and this will be detected by $\mathcal{V}$ if he chooses to execute Step 6c with i, so, in this case, $\mathcal{V}$ accepts with probability at most $7/8$. Overall, $\mathcal{V}$ accepts with probability $\max \{3/4 + \delta/4, 7/8\}$.

Zero-Knowledge. Let $\mathcal{V}^*$ be a (possibly malicious) PPT verifier. We describe a simulator Sim for $\mathcal{V}^*$. Sim, on input $1^\kappa, x$, operates as follows.

1. Picks $i \leftarrow \{1, 2\}$. (Intuitively, Sim guesses that if $\mathcal{V}^*$ will choose to perform Step 6c, it will be with index i.)
2. Executes Steps 1-4 honestly with $\mathcal{V}^*$, using an arbitrary string w^* as the witness.
3. Executes Step 5 honestly for i, and sets $y_{3-i} := 1 \oplus y_i$ (in particular, $y_1 \oplus y_2 = 1$). Sim then commits to y_1, y_2 as the honest prover does.
4. When $\mathcal{V}^*$ makes his choice in Step 6:
   (a) If $\mathcal{V}^*$ chose Step 6c with $3 - i$ then Sim rewinds $\mathcal{V}^*$ back to Step 1 of the simulation, unless rewinding has already occurred κ times, in which case Sim halts with no output.
   (b) Otherwise, Sim honestly completes the proof by decommitting the appropriate values.

ZKP from Homomorphic Secret Sharing

Let $\mathsf{HSS} = (\mathsf{HSS.Gen}, \mathsf{HSS.Enc}, \mathsf{HSS.Eval})$ be a homomorphic secret sharing scheme. The ZKP for an NP-relation $\mathcal{R} = \mathcal{R}(x, w)$ with verification circuit $C(\cdot, \cdot)$ is executed between a prover $\mathcal{P}$ that has input $(x, w) \in \mathcal{R}$ and a verifier $\mathcal{V}$ that has input x. The scheme is parameterized by a security parameter κ, and both parties have access to an ideal commitment functionality $\mathcal{F}_{\mathsf{Com}}$.

1. **Witness secret sharing:** $\mathcal{P}$ additively shares w by picking w_1, w_2 uniformly at random subject to $w = w_1 \oplus w_2$, and uses $\mathcal{F}_{\mathsf{Com}}$ to commit to w_1, w_2. Additionally, $\mathcal{P}$ defines $\widetilde{C}(u) := C(x, w_1 \oplus u)$.

2. **Randomness generation:** $\mathcal{P}$ and $\mathcal{V}$ run a coin tossing protocol to generate randomness r_G, r_E, r_1, r_2 for $\mathsf{HSS.Gen}, \mathsf{HSS.Enc}$ and the two executions of $\mathsf{HSS.Eval}$, at the end of which the randomness is known to $\mathcal{P}$, and $\mathcal{V}$ holds commitments to it.

3. **Setup:** $\mathcal{P}$ executes $(\mathsf{pk}, \mathsf{ek}_1, \mathsf{ek}_2) = \mathsf{HSS.Gen}(1^\kappa; r_G)$ to generate a public encryption key pk, and evaluation keys $\mathsf{ek}_1, \mathsf{ek}_2$, and uses $\mathcal{F}_{\mathsf{Com}}$ to commit to $\mathsf{ek}_1, \mathsf{ek}_2$. $\mathcal{P}$ sends pk to $\mathcal{V}$ in the clear.

4. **Witness encryption:** $\mathcal{P}$ computes a pair of ciphertexts $(c_1, c_2) = \mathsf{HSS.Enc}(\mathsf{pk}, w_2; r_E)$ of w_2, and uses $\mathcal{F}_{\mathsf{Com}}$ to commit to c_1, c_2.

5. **Evaluation:** For $i = 1, 2$, $\mathcal{P}$ computes the ith output share $y_i = \mathsf{HSS.Eval}\left(i, \mathsf{ek}_i, c_i, \widetilde{C}; r_i\right)$ of $\widetilde{C}(w_2)$, and uses $\mathcal{F}_{\mathsf{Com}}$ to commit to y_i.

6. $\mathcal{V}$ performs one of the following verification steps (each with probability $1/4$):

   (a) **Checking setup:** $\mathcal{P}$ decommits $r_G, \mathsf{ek}_1, \mathsf{ek}_2$, and $\mathcal{V}$ checks that $\mathsf{HSS.Gen}$ was executed correctly.

   (b) **Checking witness encryption:** $\mathcal{P}$ decommits r_E, w_2, c_1, c_2, and $\mathcal{V}$ checks that $\mathsf{HSS.Enc}$ was executed correctly on these values.

   (c) **Checking evaluation:** $\mathcal{V}$ chooses $i \leftarrow \{1, 2\}$, $\mathcal{P}$ decommits $r_i, \mathsf{ek}_i, c_i, y_i$ and w_1, and $\mathcal{V}$ checks that $\mathsf{HSS.Eval}$ was executed correctly on these values.

   (d) **Checking decoding:** $\mathcal{P}$ decommits y_1, y_2, and $\mathcal{V}$ checks that $y_1 \oplus y_2 = 1$.

Fig. 4. A ZKP from HSS

We claim that the real and simulated views – denoted **Real** and **Ideal** respectively – are computationally indistinguishable. To prove this, we show that both are computationally close to the following hybrid distribution $\mathcal{H}$. $\mathcal{H}$ is generated by having Sim secret share the actual witness w when executing Step 1 of the proof. The rest of the simulation is carried out as described above.

Bounding the Computational Distance Between Real and $\mathcal{H}$. The two differences between **Real** and $\mathcal{H}$ are: (1) in $\mathcal{H}$, the simulator may abort the simulation in Step 4a; and (2) in **Real**, y_{3-i} was generated as the output of $\mathsf{HSS.Eval}$, whereas in $\mathcal{H}$ it is generated as $y_{3-i} := 1 \oplus y_i$. We claim first that (1) happens only with probability $2^{-\kappa}$. Indeed, the choice that $\mathcal{V}^*$ makes in Step 4 of the simulation is independent of i (because the commitments are ideal). Therefore, the fact that i is random guarantees that rewinding occurs in Step 4a of the simulation only with probability $1/2$ (only if $\mathcal{V}^*$ chooses $3 - i$, which happens with probability at most $1/2$ because i is random). Therefore, the probability of κ rewinds is $2^{-\kappa}$.

Therefore, bounding the computational distance conditioned on the event that Sim did not abort in $\mathcal{H}$ suffices. We can further condition on the witness shares w_1, w_2, which are identically distributed in both cases. In this case, y_i is also identically distributed in both cases (since it was generated from w_1, w_2 given the committed randomness) so we can further condition on y_i. Consequently, the only difference is in the distribution of y_{3-i}, which is included in the view if $\mathcal{V}^*$ chooses to execute Step 6d. Notice that if the output shares satisfy $y_1 \oplus y_2 = 1$, conditioning on y_i determines y_{3-i}. This is always the case in $\mathcal{H}$, and is also the case in **Real**, unless a correctness error occurred in the execution of HSS. That is, unless a correctness error occurred, $y_{3-1} = 1 \oplus y_i$ also in **Real**, namely $\mathcal{H}$ and **Real** would be identically distributed. By the correctness of HSS, a correctness error occurs only with probability δ. We conclude that the computational distance between **Real, Ideal** is $2^{-\kappa} + \delta$.

Bounding the Computational Distance Between **Ideal** and $\mathcal{H}$. The only difference between the distributions is the witness shares w_1, w_2 (and any values computed from them), which in $\mathcal{H}$ are random secret shares of the actual witness w, and in **Ideal** are secret shares of some arbitrary w^*. Since the commitments are ideal, these are identically distributed in both views. We consider the following possible cases, based on which check $\mathcal{V}^*$ chooses to perform in Step 6 of the proof.

Case (1): checking Step (a). This step is independent of the witness shares, and therefore, in this case, $\mathcal{H}$ and **Ideal** are identically distributed.

Case (2): checking Step (b). This step is independent of w_1. Notice that w_2 is uniformly random in both distributions when considered separately from w_1. Therefore, $\mathcal{H}$ and **Ideal** are identically distributed in this case.

Case (3): checking Step 6c. Notice that by the definition of Sim, in this case $\mathcal{V}^*$ chose to check i (i.e., not $3-i$, otherwise Sim would have rewinded or aborted, and in this case $\mathcal{H}$, **Ideal** would be identically distributed). Since w_1 is identically distributed in both distributions, we will analyze this case conditioned on w_1 and show that computational indistinguishability of $\mathcal{H}$, **Ideal** follows from the security of HSS. More specifically, we show that conditioned on $\mathcal{V}^*$ checking Step 6c (with index i), a distinguisher $\mathcal{D}$ between $\mathcal{H}$, **Ideal** will enable distinguishing between encryptions of the witness share w_2 in **Ideal**, and the witness share w_2' in $\mathcal{H}$, and this contradicts the security of HSS (Definition 5). We describe a distinguisher $\mathcal{D}'$ between such encryptions, with w_1 hard-wired into it. $\mathcal{D}'$ on input the public key pk, evaluation key ek_i, and a ciphertext c (generated either as $c \leftarrow \mathsf{HSS.Enc}\,(\mathsf{pk}, w_2)$ or $c \leftarrow \mathsf{HSS.Enc}\,(\mathsf{pk}, w_2')$) picks randomness r for $\mathsf{HSS.Eval}$, computes $y_i = \mathsf{HSS.Eval}\left(i, \mathsf{ek}_i, c, \widetilde{C}; r\right)$ ($\mathcal{D}'$ can compute $\widetilde{C}$ because it knows w_1), runs $\mathcal{D}$ on $(\mathsf{pk}, \mathsf{ek}_i, c, w_1, y_i, r)$ and outputs whatever $\mathcal{D}$ outputs.[12] Notice that if c encrypts w_2 then $\mathcal{D}$ is executed with a sample from **Ideal**, otherwise $\mathcal{D}$ is executed with a sample from $\mathcal{H}$, and so $\mathcal{D}'$ obtains the same distinguishing advantage as $\mathcal{D}$. The security of HSS guarantees that this advantage is $\mathsf{negl}(\kappa)$.

Case (4): checking Step 6d. We show that the views, in this case, are deterministically computable from the views in case (3), and therefore computational indistinguishability follows from the analysis of case (3). In case (4), y_{3-i} is generated in the same way in both $\mathcal{H}$, **Ideal**: $y_{3-i} := 1 \oplus y_i$. Therefore, it is computable deterministically from the view of case (3) (in which y_1 was generated from an encryption of w_2 in **Ideal** and from an encryption of w_2' in $\mathcal{H}$).

In summary, by the triangle inequality, the computational distance between **Real** and **Ideal** is $\delta + \mathsf{negl}(\kappa)$.

Communication Complexity. The communication between the parties consists of both direct messages and committed/decommitted messages. In the analysis, we use the fact that in the $\mathcal{F}_{\mathsf{Com}}$-hybrid model, tossing r coins in Step 2 can be implemented with r bits of direct communication, and r committed and decommitted bits. Therefore, the direct communication consists of $4\ell_r(\kappa) + \ell_k(\kappa) + 3$ bits. The committed messages consist of a total of $2n + 4\ell_r(\kappa) + 2 \cdot \ell_k(\kappa) + 2 \cdot \ell_c(\kappa, n) + 2\log|\mathbb{G}|$ bits. Finally, $\mathcal{P}$ decommits at most $n + \ell_r(\kappa) + 2 \cdot \ell_c(\kappa, n) + 2 \cdot \ell_k(\kappa) + 2\log|\mathbb{G}|$ bits.

4.2 Constant-Round ZKPs Approaching Witness Length

We use our HSS-based ZKP construction (Fig. 4 and Theorem 2) to design constant-round ZKPs for NC^1 whose total communication complexity (in the plain model) is quasi-linear in the witness length. The construction is based on the DCR assumption (Definition 1). This can be thought of as a scaling-up of a similar result by [IKOS07] who obtain such ZKPs for AC^0 based on OWFs, and a scaling-down of a result by [GKR15] who obtain ZKPs for NC based on OWFs with the same communication complexity, but whose round complexity scales with the depth of the circuit. See Sect. 1.3 for further discussion.

Instantiating the ZKPs of Theorem 2 with the following HSS scheme yields Corollary 1 (see the full version for the proof).

Theorem 3 [RS21]. *Assuming the DCR hardness assumption (Definition 1), there exists an HSS scheme for the class of polynomial size Boolean branching programs with output group $\mathbb{G}$ of size $|\mathbb{G}| = 2^{O(\kappa)}$, with $O(\kappa)$ output shares, $O(\kappa)$ key sizes, $\mathsf{poly}(\kappa)$ randomness and a negligible correctness error, where κ is the security parameter.*

---

[12] We note that $\mathcal{D}'$ does not need to generate the commitments - these do not contribute to distinguishability because the commitments are ideal.

Acknowledgments. We thank Shweta Agarwal, Elette Boyle, Yuval Ishai, Justin Thaler, and Daniel Wichs for several discussions on the various cryptographic primitives. We also thank Guy Rothblum and Ron Rothblum for substantial discussions on the state-of-the-art for succinct proofs. We thank the anonymous TCC reviewers for their insightful comments and suggestions. Distribution Statement "A" (Approved for Public Release, Distribution Unlimited). The first and second authors are supported by DARPA under Contract No. HR001120C0087. Any opinions, findings and conclusions or recommendations expressed in this material are those of the author(s) and do not necessarily reflect the views of the United States Government or DARPA.

References

AHIV17. Ames, S., Hazay, C., Ishai, Y., Venkitasubramaniam, M.: Ligero: lightweight sublinear arguments without a trusted setup. In: CCS, pp. 2087–2104 (2017)

AHIV22. Ames, S., Hazay, C., Ishai, Y., Venkitasubramaniam, M.: Ligero: lightweight sublinear arguments without a trusted setup. IACR Cryptol. ePrint Arch. **2022**(1608) (2022). https://eprint.iacr.org/2022/1608

AIK04. Applebaum, B., Ishai, Y., Kushilevitz, E.: Cryptography in NC^0. In: FOCS, pp. 166–175 (2004)

AIK06. Applebaum, B., Ishai, Y., Kushilevitz, E.: Cryptography in NC^0. SIAM J. Comput. **36**(4), 845–888 (2006)

ALM+98. Arora, S., Lund, C., Motwani, R., Sudan, M., Szegedy, M.: Proof verification and the hardness of approximation problems. J. ACM **45**(3), 501–555 (1998)

AS98. Arora, S., Safra, S.: Probabilistic checking of proofs: a new characterization of NP. J. ACM **45**(1), 70–122 (1998)

Bab85. Babai, L.: Trading group theory for randomness. In: STOC, pp. 421–429 (1985)

BBHR19. Ben-Sasson, E. Bentov, I., Horesh, Y., Riabzev, M.: Scalable zero knowledge with no trusted setup. In: Boldyreva, A., Micciancio, D. (eds.) CRYPTO 2019. LNCS, vol. 11694, pp. 701–732. Springer, Cham (2019). https://doi.org/10.1007/978-3-030-26954-8_23

BCF+17. Ben-Sasson, E., Chiesa, A., Forbes, M.A., Gabizon, A., Riabzev, M., Spooner, N.: Zero knowledge protocols from succinct constraint detection. In: Kalai, Y., Reyzin, L. (eds.) TCC 2017. LNCS, vol. 10678, pp. 172–206. Springer, Cham (2017). https://doi.org/10.1007/978-3-319-70503-3_6

BCG+17a. Bootle, J., Cerulli, A., Ghadafi, E., Groth, J., Hajiabadi, M., Jakobsen, S.K.: Linear-time zero-knowledge proofs for arithmetic circuit satisfiability. In: Takagi, T., Peyrin, T. (eds.) ASIACRYPT 2017. LNCS, vol. 10626, pp. 336–365. Springer, Cham (2017). https://doi.org/10.1007/978-3-319-70700-6_12

BCG+17b. Boyle, E., Couteau, G., Gilboa, N., Ishai, Y., Orrù, M.: Homomorphic secret sharing: optimizations and applications. In: CCS, pp. 2105–2122 (2017)

BCGV16. Ben-Sasson, E., Chiesa, A., Gabizon, A., Virza, M.: Quasi-linear size zero knowledge from linear-algebraic PCPs. In: Kushilevitz, E., Malkin, T. (eds.) TCC 2016. LNCS, vol. 9563, pp. 33–64. Springer, Heidelberg (2016). https://doi.org/10.1007/978-3-662-49099-0_2

BCL22. Bootle, J., Chiesa, A., Liu, S.: Zero-knowledge IOPs with linear-time prover and polylogarithmic-time verifier. In: Dunkelman, O., Dziembowski, S. (eds.) Advances in Cryptology—EUROCRYPT 2022, LNCS, vol. 13276, pp. 275–304. Springer, Cham (2022). https://doi.org/10.1007/978-3-031-07085-3_10

BCR+19. Ben-Sasson, E., Chiesa, A., Riabzev, M., Spooner, N., Virza, M., Ward, N.P.: Aurora: transparent succinct arguments for R1CS. In: Ishai, Y., Rijmen, V. (eds.) EUROCRYPT 2019. LNCS, vol. 11476, pp. 103–128. Springer, Cham (2019). https://doi.org/10.1007/978-3-030-17653-2_4

BCS16. Ben-Sasson, E., Chiesa, A., Spooner, N.: Interactive oracle proofs. In: Hirt, M., Smith, A. (eds.) TCC 2016. LNCS, vol. 9986, pp. 31–60. Springer, Heidelberg (2016). https://doi.org/10.1007/978-3-662-53644-5_2

BFH+20. Bhadauria, R., et al.: Ligero++: a new optimized sublinear IOP. In: CCS, pp. 2025–2038 (2020)

BFLS91. Babai, L., Fortnow, L., Levin, L.A., Szegedy, M.: Checking computations in polylogarithmic time. In: STOC, pp. 21–31 (1991)

BGG+88. Ben-Or, M., et al.: Everything provable is provable in zero-knowledge. In: Goldwasser, S. (ed.) CRYPTO 1988. LNCS, vol. 403, pp. 37–56. Springer, New York (1990). https://doi.org/10.1007/0-387-34799-2_4

BGI16. Boyle, E., Gilboa, N., Ishai, Y.: Breaking the circuit size barrier for secure computation under DDH. In: Robshaw, M., Katz, J. (eds.) CRYPTO 2016. LNCS, vol. 9814, pp. 509–539. Springer, Heidelberg (2016). https://doi.org/10.1007/978-3-662-53018-4_19

BI05. Barkol, O., Ishai, Y.: Secure computation of constant-depth circuits with applications to database search problems. In: Shoup, V. (ed.) CRYPTO 2005. LNCS, vol. 3621, pp. 395–411. Springer, Heidelberg (2005). https://doi.org/10.1007/11535218_24

BSW11. Boneh, D., Sahai, A., Waters, B.: Functional encryption: definitions and challenges. In: Ishai, Y. (ed.) TCC 2011. LNCS, vol. 6597, pp. 253–273. Springer, Heidelberg (2011). https://doi.org/10.1007/978-3-642-19571-6_16

BV14. Brakerski, Z., Vaikuntanathan, V.: Lattice-based FHE as secure as PKE. In: ITCS, pp. 1–12. ACM (2014)

BY22. Brakerski, Z., Yuen, H.: Quantum garbled circuits. In: STOC, pp. 804–817. ACM (2022)

CLOS02. Canetti, R., Lindell, Y., Ostrovsky, R., Sahai, A.: Universally composable two-party and multi-party secure computation. In: STOC, pp. 494–503. ACM (2002)

DI06. Damgård, I., Ishai, Y.: Scalable secure multiparty computation. In: Dwork, C. (ed.) CRYPTO 2006. LNCS, vol. 4117, pp. 501–520. Springer, Heidelberg (2006). https://doi.org/10.1007/11818175_30

FKN94. Feige, U., Kilian, J., Naor, M.: A minimal model for secure computation (extended abstract). In: STOC, pp. 554–563 (1994)

Gen09. Gentry, C.: Fully homomorphic encryption using ideal lattices. In: STOC, pp. 169–178 (2009)

GGI+15. Gentry, C., Groth, J., Ishai, Y., Peikert, C., Sahai, A., Smith, A.D.: Using fully homomorphic hybrid encryption to minimize non-interactive zero-knowledge proofs. J. Cryptol. 28(4), 820–843 (2015)

GIW16. Genkin, D., Ishai, Y., Weiss, M.: Binary AMD circuits from secure multiparty computation. In: Hirt, M., Smith, A. (eds.) TCC 2016. LNCS, vol.

9985, pp. 336–366. Springer, Heidelberg (2016). https://doi.org/10.1007/978-3-662-53641-4_14

GKR15. Goldwasser, S., Tauman Kalai, Y., Rothblum, G.N.: Delegating computation: interactive proofs for muggles. J. ACM **62**(4), 27:1–27:64 (2015)

GLOV12. Goyal, V., Lee, C.-K., Ostrovsky, R., Visconti, I.: Constructing non-malleable commitments: a black-box approach. In: FOCS, pp. 51–60. IEEE Computer Society (2012)

GMO16. Giacomelli, I., Madsen, J., Orlandi, C.: ZKBoo: faster zero-knowledge for boolean circuits. In: USENIX, pp. 1069–1083 (2016)

GMR85. Goldwasser, S., Micali, S., Rackoff, C.: The knowledge complexity of interactive proof-systems (extended abstract). In: STOC, pp. 291–304 (1985)

GMR89. Goldwasser, S., Micali, S., Rackoff, C.: The knowledge complexity of interactive proof systems. SIAM J. Comput. **18**(1), 186–208 (1989)

GMW87. Goldreich, O., Micali, S., Wigderson, A.: How to play any mental game or a completeness theorem for protocols with honest majority. In: STOC, pp. 218–229 (1987)

GOSV14. Goyal, V., Ostrovsky, R., Scafuro, A., Visconti, I.: Black-box non-black-box zero knowledge. In: STOC, pp. 515–524 (2014)

GR20. Goldreich, O., Rothblum, G.N.: Constant-round interactive proof systems for $AC^0[2]$ and NC^1. In: Goldreich, O. (ed.) Computational Complexity and Property Testing. LNCS, vol. 12050, pp. 326–351. Springer, Cham (2020). https://doi.org/10.1007/978-3-030-43662-9_18

GWZ22. Guan, J., Wichs, D., Zhandry, M.: Incompressible cryptography. In: Dunkelman, O., Dziembowski, S. (eds.) Advances in Cryptology – EUROCRYPT 2022, Part I, pp. 700–730. Springer, Cham (2022). https://doi.org/10.1007/978-3-031-06944-4_24

HIKN08. Harnik, D., Ishai, Y., Kushilevitz, E., Nielsen, J.B.: OT-combiners via secure computation In: Canetti, R. (ed.) TCC 2008. LNCS, vol. 4948, pp. 393–411. Springer, Heidelberg (2008). https://doi.org/10.1007/978-3-540-78524-8_22

HIMV19. Hazay, C., Ishai, Y., Marcedone, A., Venkitasubramaniam, M.: Leviosa: Lightweight secure arithmetic computation. In: CCS, pp. 327–344 (2019)

HV16. Hazay, C., Venkitasubramaniam, M.: On the Power of Secure Two-Party Computation. In: Robshaw, M., Katz, J. (eds.) CRYPTO 2016. LNCS, vol. 9815, pp. 397–429. Springer, Heidelberg (2016). https://doi.org/10.1007/978-3-662-53008-5_14

HV18. Hazay, C., Venkitasubramaniam, M.: Round-optimal fully black-box zero-knowledge arguments from one-way permutations. In: Beimel, A., Dziembowski, S. (eds.) TCC 2018. LNCS, vol. 11239, pp. 263–285. Springer, Cham (2018). https://doi.org/10.1007/978-3-030-03807-6_10

HVW20. Hazay, C., Venkitasubramaniam, M., Weiss, M.: The price of active security in cryptographic protocols. In: Canteaut, A., Ishai, Y. (eds.) EUROCRYPT 2020. LNCS, vol. 12106, pp. 184–215. Springer, Cham (2020). https://doi.org/10.1007/978-3-030-45724-2_7

HVW22. Hazay, C., Venkitasubramaniam, M., Weiss, M.: Your reputation's safe with me: framing-free distributed zero-knowledge proofs. IACR Cryptol. ePrint Arch. **2022**(1523) (2022). https://eprint.iacr.org/2022/1523 (to appear at TCC 2023)

IK00. Ishai, Y., Kushilevitz, E.: Randomizing polynomials: a new representation with applications to round-efficient secure computation. In: FOCS, pp. 294–304 (2000)

IK02. Ishai, Y., Kushilevitz, E.: Perfect constant-round secure computation via perfect randomizing polynomials. In: Widmayer, P., Eidenbenz, S., Triguero, F., Morales, R., Conejo, R., Hennessy, M. (eds.) ICALP 2002. LNCS, vol. 2380, pp. 244–256. Springer, Heidelberg (2002). https://doi.org/10.1007/3-540-45465-9_22

IKO+11. Ishai, Y., Kushilevitz, E., Ostrovsky, R., Prabhakaran, M., Sahai, A.: Efficient non-interactive secure computation. In: Paterson, K.G. (ed.) EURO-CRYPT 2011. LNCS, vol. 6632, pp. 406–425. Springer, Heidelberg (2011). https://doi.org/10.1007/978-3-642-20465-4_23

IKOS07. Ishai, Y., Kushilevitz, E., Ostrovsky, R., Sahai, A.: Zero-knowledge from secure multiparty computation. In: STOC, pp. 21–30 (2007)

IKP+16. Ishai, Y., Kushilevitz, E., Prabhakaran, M., Sahai, A., Yu, C.-H.: Secure protocol transformations. In: Robshaw, M., Katz, J. (eds.) CRYPTO 2016. LNCS, vol. 9815, pp. 430–458. Springer, Heidelberg (2016). https://doi.org/10.1007/978-3-662-53008-5_15

IPS08. Ishai, Y., Prabhakaran, M., Sahai, A.: Founding cryptography on oblivious transfer – efficiently. In: Wagner, D. (ed.) CRYPTO 2008. LNCS, vol. 5157, pp. 572–591. Springer, Heidelberg (2008). https://doi.org/10.1007/978-3-540-85174-5_32

IPS09. Ishai, Y., Prabhakaran, M., Sahai, A.: Secure arithmetic computation with no honest majority. In: Reingold, O. (ed.) TCC 2009. LNCS, vol. 5444, pp. 294–314. Springer, Heidelberg (2009). https://doi.org/10.1007/978-3-642-00457-5_18

IW14. Ishai, Y., Weiss, M.: Probabilistically checkable proofs of proximity with zero-knowledge. In: Lindell, Y. (ed.) TCC 2014. LNCS, vol. 8349, pp. 121–145. Springer, Heidelberg (2014). https://doi.org/10.1007/978-3-642-54242-8_6

Kil88. Kilian, J.: Founding cryptography on oblivious transfer. In: STOC, pp. 20–31 (1988)

KOS18. Khurana, D., Ostrovsky, R., Srinivasan, A.: Round optimal black-box "Commit-and-Prove". In: Beimel, A., Dziembowski, S. (eds.) TCC 2018. LNCS, vol. 11239, pp. 286–313. Springer, Cham (2018). https://doi.org/10.1007/978-3-030-03807-6_11

KR08. Kalai, Y.T., Raz, R.: Interactive PCP. In: ICALP, pp. 536–547 (2008)

Nao91. Naor, M.: Bit commitment using pseudorandomness. J. Cryptology 4(2), 151–158 (1991)

NR22. Nassar, S., Rothblum, R.D.: Succinct interactive oracle proofs: applications and limitations. In: Dodis, Y., Shrimpton, T. (eds.) Advances in Cryptology – CRYPTO 2022, Part I, pp. 504–532. Springer, Cham (2022). https://doi.org/10.1007/978-3-031-15802-5_18

O'N10. O'Neill, A.: Definitional issues in functional encryption. IACR Cryptol. ePrint Arch. 2010(556) (2010). https://eprint.iacr.org/2010/556

OSV15. Ostrovsky, R., Scafuro, A., Venkitasubramanian, M.: Resettably sound zero-knowledge arguments from OWFs - the (semi) black-box way. In: Dodis, Y., Nielsen, J.B. (eds.) TCC 2015. LNCS, vol. 9014, pp. 345–374. Springer, Heidelberg (2015). https://doi.org/10.1007/978-3-662-46494-6_15

OSY21. Orlandi, C., Scholl, P., Yakoubov, S.: The rise of Paillier: homomorphic secret sharing and public-key silent OT. In: Canteaut, A., Standaert, F.-X. (eds.) EUROCRYPT 2021. LNCS, vol. 12696, pp. 678–708. Springer, Cham (2021). https://doi.org/10.1007/978-3-030-77870-5_24

Pai99. Paillier, P.: Public-key cryptosystems based on composite degree residuosity classes. In: Stern, J. (ed.) EUROCRYPT 1999. LNCS, vol. 1592, pp. 223–238. Springer, Heidelberg (1999). https://doi.org/10.1007/3-540-48910-X_16

RR20. Ron-Zewi, N., Rothblum, R.D.: Local proofs approaching the witness length (extended abstract). In: FOCS, pp. 846–857. IEEE (2020)

RRR16. Reingold, O., Rothblum, G.N., Rothblum, R.D.: Constant-round interactive proofs for delegating computation. In: STOC, pp. 49–62. ACM (2016)

RS21. Roy, L., Singh, J.: Large message homomorphic secret sharing from DCR and applications. In: Malkin, T., Peikert, C. (eds.) CRYPTO 2021. LNCS, vol. 12827, pp. 687–717. Springer, Cham (2021). https://doi.org/10.1007/978-3-030-84252-9_23

WTS+18. Wahby, R.S., Tzialla, I., Shelat, A., Thaler, J., Walfish, M.: Doubly-efficient zkSNARKs without trusted setup. In: S&P, pp. 926–943 (2018)

XZZ+19. Xie, T., Zhang, J., Zhang, Y., Papamanthou, C., Song, D.: Libra: succinct zero-knowledge proofs with optimal prover computation. In: Boldyreva, A., Micciancio, D. (eds.) CRYPTO 2019. LNCS, vol. 11694, pp. 733–764. Springer, Cham (2019). https://doi.org/10.1007/978-3-030-26954-8_24

Yao86. Yao, A.C.-C.: How to generate and exchange secrets (extended abstract). In: FOCS, pp. 162–167 (1986)

ZLW+21. Zhang, J., et al.: Doubly efficient interactive proofs for general arithmetic circuits with linear prover time. In: CCS, pp. 159–177 (2021)

Your Reputation's Safe with Me: Framing-Free Distributed Zero-Knowledge Proofs

Carmit Hazay[1], Muthuramakrishnan Venkitasubramaniam[2], and Mor Weiss[1(✉)]

[1] Bar-Ilan University, Ramat Gan, Israel
{Carmit.Hazay,Mor.Weiss}@biu.ac.il
[2] Georgetown University and Ligero Inc., Washington, USA
mv783@georgetown.edu

Abstract. *Distributed Zero-Knowledge (dZK) proofs*, recently introduced by Boneh et al. (CRYPTO'19), allow a prover $\mathcal{P}$ to prove NP statements on an input x which is *distributed* between k verifiers $\mathcal{V}_1, \ldots, \mathcal{V}_k$, where each $\mathcal{V}_i$ holds only a piece of x. As in standard ZK proofs, dZK proofs guarantee *Completeness* when all parties are honest; *Soundness* against a malicious prover colluding with t verifiers; and *Zero Knowledge* against a subset of t malicious verifiers, in the sense that they learn nothing about the NP witness and the input pieces of the honest verifiers.

Unfortunately, dZK proofs provide no correctness guarantee for an honest prover against a subset of maliciously corrupted verifiers. In particular, such verifiers might be able to "frame" the prover, causing honest verifiers to reject a true claim. This is a significant limitation, since such scenarios arise naturally in dZK applications, e.g., for proving honest behavior, and such attacks are indeed possible in existing dZKs (Boneh et al., CRYPTO'19).

We put forth and study the notion of *strong completeness* for dZKs, guaranteeing that true claims are accepted even when t verifiers are maliciously corrupted. We then design strongly-complete dZK proofs using the "MPC-in-the-head" paradigm of Ishai et al. (STOC'07), providing a novel analysis that exploits the unique properties of the distributed setting.

To demonstrate the usefulness of strong completeness, we present several applications in which it is instrumental in obtaining security. First, we construct a certifiable version of Verifiable Secret Sharing (VSS), which is a VSS in which the dealer additionally proves that the shared secret satisfies a given NP relation. Our construction withstands a constant fraction of corruptions, whereas a previous construction of Ishai et al. (TCC'14) required $k = \mathsf{poly}(t)$. We also design a *reusable* version of certifiable VSS that we introduce, in which the dealer can prove an *unlimited* number of predicates on the *same* shared secret.

Finally, we extend a compiler of Boneh et al. (CRYPTO'19), who used dZKs to transform a class of "natural" semi-honest protocols in the honest-majority setting into maliciously secure ones with abort. Our compiler uses *strongly-complete* dZKs to obtain *identifiable* abort.

G. Rothblum and H. Wee (Eds.): TCC 2023, LNCS 14369, pp. 34–64, 2023.
https://doi.org/10.1007/978-3-031-48615-9_2

1 Introduction

Zero-Knowledge (ZK) Proofs, namely proofs that yield nothing but their validity, are an essential component of many cryptographic systems. Recently, [BBC+19b] introduced a *distributed* model for ZK proofs which captures the types of proof systems that appear in many existing application scenarios such as anonymous messaging [CBM15], verifiable function secret sharing [BGI16], and systems for privately computing aggregate statistics [CB17]. This distributed model proved particularly suited for proving honest behaviour in Multi-Party Computation (MPC) protocols [BBC+19b, BGIN19, BGIN20, BGIN21].

ZK Proofs. A standard ZK proof [GMR85] is a 2-party protocol between a prover $\mathcal{P}$ and a verifier $\mathcal{V}$. Both parties are Probabilistic Polynomial Time (PPT), and have a joint input x. The prover's goal is to convince $\mathcal{V}$ that $x \in \mathcal{L}$ for some language $\mathcal{L}$ (i.e., a subset of strings). When $\mathcal{L}$ is an NP language, $\mathcal{P}$ is additionally given a witness for the membership of x in $\mathcal{L}$. A ZK proof guarantees the following properties. (1) *Correctness*, meaning if $x \in \mathcal{L}$ and both parties honestly follow the protocol, then $\mathcal{V}$ outputs accept (with high probability). (2) *Soundness*, namely if $x \notin \mathcal{L}$ then any (possibly malicious and computationally unbounded) $\mathcal{P}^*$ can only cause $\mathcal{V}$ to accept x with small probability. (3) *Zero Knowledge (ZK)*, guaranteeing that even a (possibly malicious and computationally unbounded) $\mathcal{V}^*$ learns nothing from the execution, except that $x \in \mathcal{L}$. In particular, $\mathcal{V}$ learns nothing about the corresponding witness. This is formalized by requiring the existence of a PPT simulator $\mathsf{Sim}_{\mathcal{V}^*}$ who on input x can simulate the entire view of $\mathcal{V}^*$ – consisting of x, the random coin tosses of $\mathcal{V}^*$, and the messages it received from the honest $\mathcal{P}$.

Distributed ZK (dZK) Proofs. [BBC+19b] generalize standard ZK proofs to a distributed setting with multiple verifiers $\mathcal{V}_1, \ldots, \mathcal{V}_k$, where the input statement x is distributed among them but no verifier knows x in full. (For example, x could be a secret sharing of some secret, and each $\mathcal{V}_i$ holds a share).[1] Parties are connected via secure point-to-point channels as well as a broadcast channel. In fact, our protocols have the additional feature that following the first round in which the prover send a single message to each verifier, all communication is over the broadcast channel and private point-to-point channels are not needed (except in the first round).

The standard properties of completeness and soundness naturally extend to the distributed setting, where completeness should hold when all parties are honest, and soundness should hold against a cheating prover $\mathcal{P}^*$ that colludes with a subset of at most t verifiers. As for zero knowledge, in the distributed setting one would generally wish to hide not only the witness w, but also the parts of the input statement held by the honest parties. More specifically, assume

---

[1] Various works have considered other models, e.g., when security is only computational, or when the input statement is known in full to all verifiers. These models are discussed in Sect. 1.5, but similar to [BBC+19b] our focus is on information-theoretic security when the input statement is distributed between the verifiers.

the input statement x is distributed between the verifiers, where each verifier $\mathcal{V}_i$ holds an *input piece* $x^{(i)}$. Then we require that a subset $T \subseteq [k], |T| \leq t$ of possibly malicious verifiers learn nothing except $\left(x^{(i)}\right)_{i \in T}$ and the fact that $x \in \mathcal{L}$, in the sense that there exists a PPT simulator Sim that can simulate their entire view in the protocol given only $\left(x^{(i)}\right)_{i \in T}$.

Boneh et al. [BBC+19b] constructed such dZK proofs for NP whose communication is linear in the size of the verification circuit, and additionally presented sublinear dZK proofs for structured languages. (See Sect. 1.5 for further details.) A main feature of the dZKs of [BBC+19b] — which is crucial to their applications for designing efficient MPC protocols — is having sublinear communication between the verifiers. Notice that while generic MPC protocols could be used to achieve dZK, they would not generally have this feature (see Sect. 1.1 for further details).

Several recent works [BBC+19b, BGIN19, BGIN20, BGIN21] have demonstrated the usefulness of dZK proofs towards constructing *maliciously-secure* MPC protocols, i.e., ones which guarantee correctness of the outputs and privacy of the inputs of the honest parties, even when some parties deviate from the protocol specification. This is done by transforming an MPC protocol Π with semi-honest security – namely whose security only holds when all parties follow the protocol, though corrupted parties might still try to learn information about the inputs of honest parties – into a *maliciously secure* protocol $\widetilde{\Pi}$. The high-level idea is to execute Π except for its final round (in which the outputs are revealed), and use dZK proofs to prove honest behavior in this execution.[2] In this context, "honest behaviour" of a party $\mathcal{P}_i$ roughly means that there exist an input x_i and random coins r_i for which the messages that $\mathcal{P}_i$ sent to the other parties are consistent with x_i, r_i, the messages $\mathcal{P}_i$ received from the other parties, and Π. This is an NP statement (with witness x_i, r_i) which is distributed between the parties $\mathcal{P}_j, j \neq i$ because $\mathcal{P}_j$ knows (only) the messages exchanged between $\mathcal{P}_i, \mathcal{P}_j$, and is known in full to $\mathcal{P}_i$.

"Framing-Free" dZK Proofs. In the 2-party setting, the properties of standard ZK proofs capture all possible corruption models, namely no corruptions (completeness), corrupt prover (soundness), or corrupt verifier (ZK). However, the corresponding properties of dZK proofs do *not* capture all possible corruption models in the *distributed* setting. Indeed, there is no guarantee for an honest $\mathcal{P}$ when the dZK is executed in the presence of maliciously corrupted verifiers, and in particular, such corrupted verifiers could potentially *frame* the prover, i.e., cause the proof of a correct claim to fail. This corruption model was not explored in previous works on dZK proofs [BBC+19b], and in fact maliciously corrupted verifiers *can* frame the prover in their constructions. We note that the dZKs of [BBC+19b] do implicitly provide a partial guarantee in this case, since

---

[2] More specifically, this paradigm applies to a class of *natural* protocols which guarantee, among other things, that privacy is preserved up to the final round even in the presence of *malicious corruptions*; see the full version for further details.

$\mathcal{P}$ is able to identify cheating verifiers.[3] However, the best one can do in this case is to identify a pair of parties – namely $\mathcal{P}$ and one of the verifiers $\mathcal{V}_i$ – such that at least one of them is corrupted, but it is impossible to determine which one. In particular, one cannot deduce that $x \in \mathcal{L}$, otherwise this would lead to a successful soundness-violating cheating strategy for $\mathcal{P}$ colluding with a verifier $\mathcal{V}_i$: "sacrifice" $\mathcal{V}_i$ by causing an inconsistency between $\mathcal{P}$ and $\mathcal{V}_i$, which will lead the other verifiers to (falsely) conclude that $x \in \mathcal{L}$.

A "framing-free" guarantee is desirable since such situations naturally arise in applications of dZK, e.g., when using dZK proofs to prove honest behavior in MPC protocols as discussed above, and more generally in distributed systems over shared data. Indeed, when an MPC protocol Π is executed with a subset T of corrupted parties, the dZK proof of an honest $\mathcal{P}_i, i \notin T$ *will be* executed in the presence of corrupted verifiers (namely, the parties in T). In previous works applying dZK to prove honest behavior [BGIN20, BGIN21], the "solution" is to have the prover identify a cheating verifier whenever the proof fails, and then disqualify both parties from the next protocol execution. This "player elimination" techniques is standard in protocol design (and can even be used to obtain guaranteed output delivery), but it gives no indication as to which of the eliminated parties is corrupted. For an honest party who was eliminated from the execution in this manner, the fact that the computation can be successfully completed without it might provide little consolation.

In particular, a protocol in which framing is possible encourages attacks where the adversary targets honest parties and disqualifies them, thus excluding their inputs from the computation and consequently biasing the outcome. This is of particular importance in settings – such as voting, auctions, and secure aggregation – in which elimination harms the reputation of the eliminated party, or when a biased outcome has severe consequences. Moreover, player elimination is only useful when there are repeated executions (or multiple phases) of the protocol, which is not the case in some of the application scenarios in which framing arises (see the full version [HVW22] for a more detailed discussion).

Thus, "framing-free" dZK proofs are motivated not only by the goal of guaranteeing security against all possible corruption patterns, but also because such attacks naturally arise in many application scenarios of dZK.

1.1 Our Contribution

We put forth a strong completeness notion for dZK proofs which guarantees that honest provers cannot be framed. More specifically, we define *t-strong completeness* which guarantees that when the prover is honest and the verifiers hold pieces of an $x \in \mathcal{L}$ then all honest verifiers accept the proof, even in the presence of a subset of t maliciously-corrupted and computationally-unbounded verifiers. In terms of communication, we distinguish between the *proof generation phase*

---

[3] Roughly, this holds in their protocols because the verifiers do not have any private coins, and $\mathcal{P}$ knows the entire input statement x.

in which the prover distributes the proof among the verifiers (with no communication between the verifiers), and the *verification phase* in which the proof is verified. Our goal is for the total communication complexity during verification to be independent of the computation size (ideally, polynomial in the number of verifiers, the security parameter, and $\log|x|$). We call such protocols *verification efficient*. This feature is especially important when verifiers are lightweight devices and stable communication between a large number of verifiers in not available. A related attractive feature that our protocols provide (in certain settings) is that verifiers require small space to process and verify the proofs. Our protocols will have the added feature that all communication during verification is only through broadcasts.

Strongly-Complete dZK Proofs. We construct strongly-complete dZK proofs by employing the so-called "MPC-in-the-head" paradigm [IKOS07]. Specifically, we construct strongly-complete dZK proofs from an MPC protocol Π with t-privacy – namely, in which secrecy of the honest parties' inputs holds in the presence of t semi-honest corruptions – and t-robustness (which, roughly, guarantees correctness of the honest parties' outputs in the presence of t malicious corruptions, see Definition 8).

Our construction is informally summarized in the following theorem, where an unconditionally secure t-dZK is a dZK proof system with completeness, strong completeness, soundness, and zero-knowledge (as informally defined above) in the information-theoretic setting in the presence of t corruptions; $\widehat{\mathcal{L}}$ for an NP-language $\mathcal{L}$ consists of all robust encodings of $x \in \mathcal{L}$ (e.g., encoding x using an error correcting code with good distance);[4] and a dZK proof system is verification efficient if the total communication complexity during verification if $\mathrm{poly}(k, \kappa, \log|x|)$ where k denotes the number of verifiers and κ is a security parameter. (See Theorem 5 for the formal statement.)

Theorem 1 (dZK from MPC-in-the-Head – Informal). *Let $t, k \in \mathbb{N}$ such that $k > 6t + 2$. Let $\mathcal{L}$ be an NP-language, and let Π be a perfectly correct, t-private and perfectly t-robust k-party protocol verifying membership in $\widehat{\mathcal{L}}$. Then assuming ideal coin-tossing, there exists a 2-round unconditionally-secure verification-efficient t-dZK for $\widehat{\mathcal{L}}$.*

Moreover, the total proof length in our dZK proof system is qusilinear in the size of the circuit verifying membership in $\mathcal{L}$, and can be reduced to linear by increasing the round complexity to 3. Furthermore, we define the ideal dZK functionality and show that our constructions realize it (see the full version [HVW22] for details).

---

[4] Notice that the dZK proof is for input statements that are distributed between the verifiers *using a robust encoding*. [BBC+19b] make the same assumption. The reason to focus on such languages is because they show [BBC+19a, Sec. 6.3.2] limitations on the existence of dZK proofs for languages that are not robustly encoded.

We note that while strong completeness can be obtained fairly easily in the *computational* setting using standard tools such as commitments and signatures, obtaining it in the *information theoretic* setting seems significantly harder. Specifically, in the computational model the prover can commit to its messages to the verifiers, and parties can then prove consistency with respect to these commitments. (This is exactly the method used to obtain strong completenss in the GMW compiler [GMW87].) Achieving strong completeness information theoretically is much harder since the prover is not committed to its messages to the verifiers.

Theorem 1 gives an alternative approach towards designing dZK proofs (even *without* strong completeness) compared to previous works [BBC+19b], who relied on fully-linear probabilistically-checkable proofs and fully-linear interactive oracle proofs. One advantage of our approach is that the general construction of Theorem 1 can be instantiated with various MPC protocols to obtain dZK proofs with different tradeoffs between the parameters. This is particularly appealing since one could potentially leverage the major research effort devoted towards optimizing MPC protocols, and employ it to obtain dZK proofs whose parameters are optimized for specific applications. We demonstrate this versatility of our approach by instantiating our general transformation with two different MPC protocols, obtaining dZK proofs with different parameters.

The proof of Theorem 1 uses a novel analysis for MPC-in-the-head, exploiting the distributed setting, as well as a novel protocol for *batched* verifiable secret sharing. Both of these might be of independent interest. See Sects. 1.2, 3, and 4 for further details.

dZK Proof Systems Without Strong Completeness. As noted above, our construction gives an alternative approach towards designing dZK proof systems. To demonstrate this, we describe in the full version [HVW22] a scaled-down variant of our construction *without* strong completeness (i.e., in the same security model as that considered in [BBC+19b], and relying on the same assumption of ideal coin tossing) with an improved corruption threshold. This gives an alternative approach towards designing dZK proofs *without* strong completeness.

Theorem 2 (dZK Without Strong Completeness – Informal). *Let* $t, k \in \mathbb{N}$ *such that* $k > 2t + 2$. *Let* $\mathcal{L}$ *be an NP-language, and let* Π *be a perfectly correct, t-private and perfectly t-robust k-party protocol verifying membership in* $\widehat{\mathcal{L}}$. *Then assuming ideal coin-tossing, there exists a 2-round unconditionally-secure verification-efficient t-dZK for* $\mathcal{L}$ *without strong completeness.*

dZK from Generic MPC Protocols. An alternative route towards designing dZK protocols is to view dZK as an ideal functionality (see the full version [HVW22] for further discussion of this functionality), and then use *generic fully-secure* MPC protocols to instantiate it. In slightly more details, such a functionality would take as input each verifier's input piece, as well as all input pieces and the witness from the prover. Then, it will check that: (1) for at least $k - t$ of the verifiers, the input pieces they provided are consistent with the input pieces the prover provided; and (2) the input pieces define an instance in the relation. While this gives a generic mechanism for constructing strongly-complete dZK proofs, unfortunately, it does not yield *verification efficient* dZKs. Indeed, even when the most communication-efficient protocols (e.g., [DI06]) are used to instantiate the ideal dZK functionaility, the total communication between the verifiers will be proportional to the size of the circuit verifying the relation. In contrast, in our protocol, following the initial proof generation phase, the communication between the verifiers is *independent* of the circuit size. (See Sect. 1.5 for further details and comparison with generic MPC protocols.)

Applications. We demonstrate the usefulness of strong completeness by showing several applications of dZK proofs in which strong completeness is crucial.

Verifiable Secret Sharing (VSS) and Extensions. A (robust) t-private secret sharing scheme allows an honest dealer $\mathcal{D}$ to distribute a secret x between a k parties $\mathcal{P}_1, \ldots, \mathcal{P}_k$, such that any t parties learn nothing about x, but when all parties come together they can reconstruct x even in the presence of t maliciously corrupted parties. a *Verifiable Secret Sharing (VSS)* scheme additionally guarantees soundness against a corrupted dealer colluding with t parties. Specifically, it guarantees that the secret shares define *some* secret x^* which the honest parties will reconstruct regardless of the shares that the corrupted parties provide during reconstruction. Ishai and Weiss [IW14] put forth the notion of *Certifiable VSS (cVSS)* which additionally guarantees that x is in some NP language $\mathcal{L}$ (and, when the dealer is corrupted, that $x^* \in \mathcal{L}$). They construct such schemes based on zero-knowledge probabilistically checkable proofs of proximity, in which $t = k^\varepsilon$ for a small $\varepsilon < 1$.

We use strongly-complete dZK proofs to construct cVSS schemes, in which the corruption threshold is "inherited" from the underlying dZK. Specifically, using the dZKs of Theorem 1, we obtain $t < (k-2)/6$. Very roughly, the high-level idea is for the dealer to share x using a standard secret sharing scheme, and then have all parties engage in a dZK proving that the input pieces held by the parties share an $x \in \mathcal{L}$. We note that strong completeness is essential for obtaining correctness, which in VSS and cVSS is required to hold for an honest dealer even if t parties are maliciously corrupted. Indeed, if the underlying dZK does not have strong completeness then corrupted parties who actively cheat during the dZK proof can cause it to fail, thus violating correctness.

We also introduce a *reusable* variant of cVSS, in which the dealer can prove that $x \in \mathcal{L}_i$ for a sequence of NP-languages $\mathcal{L}_i$. In particular, there is no bound on the *number* of languages $\mathcal{L}_i$, which are determined (i.e., provided to the dealer and all other parties) in an online fashion, and all membership claims are proven with relation to *the same* secret x. We construct reusable cVSS schemes from strongly-complete dZK proofs. See the full version [HVW22] for further details.

MPC with Identifiable Abort (IA-MPC). Aborts pose a major obstacle in the malicious corruption setting, or even when parties are honest but have poor network connections. Indeed, a deviating/crashed party could potentially cause the entire computation to fail. The natural mitigation against such "denial-of-completion" attacks is to support *Identifiable Abort (IA)*, i.e., when the executions fails to complete, the parties can (publicly) identify at least one malicious/crashed party.

We use strongly-complete dZK proofs to transform a class of "natural" protocols that are secure in the *semi-honest* setting (in which even corrupted parties follow the protocol) to protocols that guarantee security with identifiable abort in the presence of *malicious* corruptions. This class of "natural" protocols was introduced by [BBC+19b], who used dZK proofs *without strong completeness* to transform such protocols into maliciously-secure protocols with (*non*-identifiable) abort. Thus, our compiler shows that *strong completeness* can be used to obtain *identifiable* abort. This result is summarized in the following theorem (see the full version [HVW22] for the formal statement):

Theorem 3 (IA-MPC from Natural Protocols – Informal). *Let $t, k \in \mathbb{N}$ such that $k > 6t + 3$, and let Π_{nat} be a natural k-party protocol computing a function f in the presence of t semi-honest corruptions. Then assuming ideal coin tossing, there exists a protocol Π which securely computes f with identifiable abort in the presence of t malicious corruptions.*

Our compiler is very similar to the compiler of [BBC+19b]. Their main observation is that dZK proofs can be used to replace the standard ZK proofs used in GMW-style compilers [GMW87], and in fact seem to be a more natural tool in this context. Indeed, the ZK proofs are used to prove honest behavior in an execution of a semi-honest protocol, and this task exactly requires running a zero-knowledge proof on a distributed input.

More specifically, the high-level idea of our compiler is to execute all rounds of Π_{nat} except the final round, then run dZK proofs attesting to the honest behavior of all parties during this execution, before executing the final round of Π_{nat} to reveal the output. One notable property of our compiler is that the compiler itself *does not use any broadcasts*. In particular, all broadcasted messages in Π are either broadcasts of Π_{nat} or of the underlying dZK proofs. When instantiated with our dZK proofs of Theorem 1, the number of broadcast bits introduced by the dZK proofs could be as low as k^2polylog$(\mathsf{CC}(\Pi_{nat}))$, where $\mathsf{CC}(\Pi_{nat})$ denotes the communication complexity of Π_{nat}. We note that the use of broadcasts is inherent to obtaining identifiable abort [CL14]. Previous works obtaining identifiable abort either built on specific maliciously-secure protocols that a broadcast channel for every multiplication gate, or increased the number of broadcasts to equal the number of multiplication gates. This includes the generic compiler from [IOZ14] discussed next.

Our compiler gives an alternative, conceptually simple, approach towards transforming protocols with semi-honest security into maliciously-secure protocols with identifiable abort in the information-theoretic setting, compared to an existing compiler of Ishai, Ostrovsky and Zikas [IOZ14]. These approaches result in incomparable compilers. Specifically, the compiler of [IOZ14] works in the correlated randomness setting, transforming *any* semi-honest secure protocol into a maliciously-secure protocol with identifiable abort, by broadcasting *every* message of the semi-honest protocol (and proving honest behavior with relation to the broadcasted messages). Our compiler works only for "natural" protocols, but uses much fewer broadcasts. See Sect. 1.5 and the full version [HVW22] for further discussion and comparison of these compilers.

"Framing-Free" Proofs on Committed or Secret-Shared Data. [BBC+19b] use dZK proofs to construct proofs on secret shared data. Special cases of such proofs have been considered in several recent works, e.g., [BGI16, CB17]. Roughly, they allow a client to secret share a (potentially large) input x among multiple servers, and then prove to the servers that x satisfies various NP statements. The construction from dZK is conceptually simple: the client plays the role of the dZK prover, and the servers play the role of the verifiers. The client first shares x using a robust secret sharing scheme, and distributes the shares between the servers. The client and servers can then engage in multiple dZK executions to prove various NP statements on x. Instantiating this construction with our *strongly complete* dZK proofs yields "framing-free" proofs on secret shared data, namely in which a subset of corrupted servers cannot cause the proof of a true statement to fail. This strengthens the proofs obtained in [BBC+19b] (based on dZKs *without* strong completeness), which do not provide this guarantee.

1.2   Highlights of Our Techniques

In this section we highlight the main techniques used to obtain our results.

dZK Proofs from MPC-in-the-Head. Our dZK proofs are based on the MPC-in-the-head paradigm, introduced by [IKOS07] in the context of constructing (standard) ZK proofs. The high-level idea of the paradigm is that an MPC protocol Π computing a predicate "$x \in \mathcal{L}$" for some NP language $\mathcal{L}$ and some public x (where the corresponding NP witness w is secret-shared between the parties executing Π), can be used to design a ZK proof for the membership of $x \in \mathcal{L}$. Indeed, an *honest* execution of Π on x will result in output 1 if and only if $x \in \mathcal{L}$. Moreover, a main observation made in [IKOS07] is that verifying that Π was honestly emulated – i.e., that the views of all parties participating in Π are globally consistent – can be done by checking *pairwise consistency* of the views. (The view of a party consists of its input, random coins tosses, and the messages it received from other parties in the execution.) That is, if the set of all parties' views does not correspond to an honest execution of Π on x, then there is a pair of parties whose views are inconsistent with each other.

This observation immediately gives rise to the following proof system: the prover $\mathcal{P}$ emulates "in its head" the entire execution of Π on x (and the shares of w), and commits to the views of all parties in this execution. The verifier $\mathcal{V}$ then picks a pair of parties whose views $\mathcal{P}$ opens, and $\mathcal{V}$ accepts if these views are pairwise consistent, and these parties output 1 in the execution. Thus, soundness follows from the (perfect) correctness of Π, whereas if Π is private against semi-honest corruptions then the proof is also ZK, because the verifier learns only a pair of views in Π, and these reveal only two secret shares of the witness w which, in turn, reveal no information about w.

The resultant proof system has a large soundness error, i.e., the probability that $\mathcal{V}$ accepts false claims is large. [IKOS07] then show how to reduce the soundness error by relying on a stronger correctness guarantee – known as *robustness* – which holds even in the presence of *malicious* corruptions. Roughly, robustness means that if $x \notin \mathcal{L}$ then even maliciously-corrupted parties cannot cause honest parties to output 1 in Π. In particular, while $\mathcal{V}$ might not open a pair of inconsistent views during verification (since $\mathcal{V}$ opens only a small subset of views), still robustness guarantees that cheating that occurred in the un-opened views cannot "propogate" and cause honest parties to accept a false claim in the execution. Consequently, if $x \notin \mathcal{L}$ then the output reported in the honest parties' views which $\mathcal{V}$ opened will be 0, and so $\mathcal{V}$ will reject. This should be contrasted with the basic construction described above – using Π that is only secure against semi-honest corruptions – in which $\mathcal{V}$ rejects only if it opened a pair of inconsistent views, namely the view of a corrupted party.

Novel Verification for MPC-in-the-Head in Distributed Settings. Our dZK proofs employ the MPC-in-the-Head paradigm, using a novel verification procedure that exploits the properties of the distributed setting.[5] Specifically, the proof is executed between a prover $\mathcal{P}$ that knows x and a corresponding NP witness w, and k verifiers $\mathcal{V}_1, \ldots, \mathcal{V}_k$, where each $\mathcal{V}_i$ holds a *piece* $x^{(i)}$ of the input x (and $\mathcal{P}$ knows all input pieces). To simplify the presentation, we describe here a simplified dZK proof in the *correlated randomness* model, in which an honest party samples ahead of time a random string $R = (R_1, \ldots, R_k)$ from a pre-defined distribution $\mathcal{D}$, and gives R_i to $\mathcal{V}_i$. We explain below how to remove this assumption. We stress that the final dZK proof (Fig. 2 in Sect. 4) is *in the plain model* and does *not* use correlated randomness.

The dZK proof proceeds as follows. The correlated randomness consists of (long) random masks r_{ij} for every pair of verifiers $\mathcal{V}_i, \mathcal{V}_j$, where $R_i = (r_{ij})_{j \neq i, j \in [k]}$. The prover emulates "in its head" a k-party protocol Π computing the predicate $(x^{(1)}, \ldots, x^{(k)}) \in \mathcal{L}$ as in the 2-party ZK proof described above. However, instead of committing to the views, $\mathcal{P}$ sends the i'th view to $\mathcal{V}_i$. The parties then jointly execute the following verification procedure:

1. Each $\mathcal{V}_i$ checks *local* consistency of its view, namely that the input reported in the view is $x^{(i)}$, and that the output of the ith party given this view is 1. If the view is not locally consistent then $\mathcal{V}_i$ broadcasts a complaint against the prover. Let C_1 denote the set of verifiers that complained against the prover.
2. Each pair $\mathcal{V}_i, \mathcal{V}_j$ check *pairwise* consistency of their views by comparing the messages exchanged between parties i, j in Π.[6] This pairwise consistency

---

[5] See Sect. 1.5 for a comparison between our construction and other constructions using this technique in the two-party and in other distributed settings.

[6] The messages sent from party i to party j appear explicitly in the view of party j, and the messages it sent to party i can be computed from its view.

check is done *publicly*, by having $\mathcal{V}_i, \mathcal{V}_j$ broadcast the values to be compared, masked using r_{ij}.
3. The prover broadcasts complaints against verifiers who broadcasted incorrect messages in Step 2. Let C_2 denote the set of verifiers against whome the prover complained.
4. Finally, each verifier $\mathcal{V}_i$ determines its output as follows. If $|C_1 \cup C_2| > t$, or there exist $i, j \notin C_1 \cup C_2$ who broadcasted inconsistent messages in Step 2, then reject. Otherwise, accept.

We note that while this describes the main steps in the dZK proof, the actual construction is more involved, in several respects. First, to reduce the communication complexity, instead of sending in Step 2 all the messages exchanged in Π, the verifiers send information-theoretic MACs of these values. More specifically, the messages exchanged between i, j are interpreted as the of coefficients of a univariate polynomial, and the MAC is the evaluation of this polynomial at a random point (see Step 3 in Fig. 2). This requires the verifiers to jointly sample a random element of a sufficiently large field. The resultant protocol therefore uses an ideal coin-tossing functionality as in [BBC+19b] (and makes *minimal* use of it). Second, by using MACs we can eliminate the correlated randomness and have *the prover* provide random masks as part of the proof, and moreover each mask will consist of a *single* field element. Since the random masks are chosen *before* the MAC key is sampled, inconsistent views will, with overwhelming probability, result in inconsistent MACs, even when the prover chooses the masks.

Finally, the input pieces held by the verifiers should constitute an encoding of the underlying input x in some robust code, and the parties need to verify that their input pieces are indeed "close" to a valid encoding. This is done using a standard technique for batch-testing of code membeship. Specifically, the verifiers broadcast a random linear combination of the codeword symbols they hold, which they also mask with a random codeword (masking is needed to guarantee ZK). Soundness of this test has been studied in several previous works [AHIV17, BBHR18, BCI+20] (and plays an important role in improving the concrete efficiency of succinct ZK arguments). However, relying on the analysis directly in our distributed setting will not guarantee strong completeness (only identifiable abort). We refine this soundness analysis to apply in the distributed verification setting while guaranteeing strong completeness. See Sect. 4 for further details and the full construction.

We note that the dZK proofs of [BBC+19b] also require the input pieces to form a robust encoding, and they show [BBC+19a, Sec. 6.3.2] some limitations on the existence of dZK proofs when the input statement is *not* robustly encoded, at least when security should hold against collusions of the prover and verifiers, as we consider in this work.

The Security Analysis. Proving security of our dZK proof is more complex than in standard (in particular, 2-party) settings of MPC-in-the-Head, and requires a novel analysis which combines techniques from the VSS literature. Intuitively, this is because while in the analysis of ZK proofs such as those of [IKOS07] the verifier can safely reject if an inconsistency is detected, we cannot immediately reject because inconsistencies might be due to corrupted verifiers trying to "frame" an honest prover (and so rejecting in this case would violate strong completeness). Thus, the strong completeness guarantee leads to a much more intricate soundness analysis.

Proving strong completeness is fairly simple, and it follows from the fact that all complaints arise from the corrupted parties. That is, either a corrupted party falsely complaining that its view is not locally consistent, or a corrupted verifier broadcasting an incorrect MAC in Step 2, causing the prover to complain against it. Thus, we will have $|C_1 \cup C_2| \leq t$ in Step 4, and all other parties' views will be pairwise consistent, so all honest verifiers will accept.

The soundness analysis, however, is much more involved. At a high level, it proceeds by showing that if $\left(x^{(1)}, \ldots, x^{(k)}\right) \notin \mathcal{L}$ then there exists a subset H of parties which constitutes an honest majority in the execution of Π with input pieces $\left(x^{(1)}, \ldots, x^{(k)}\right)$, and therefore their outputs in Π would be 0. Thus, the checks performed in Step 4 would fail and all honest verifiers would reject. More specifically, in the analysis we gradually eliminate verifiers (alternatively, parties in Π, since there is a correspondence between the dZK verifiers and the parties in Π) until we are left with the set H. We stress that unlike MPC applications employing the "player elimination" technique, we *do not actually eliminate* any verifier from the computation, but rather this "elimination" is only done *in the analysis*. Moreover, an "eliminated" verifier is not necessarily corrupted – for example, it might be an honest verifier who received an incorrect view from the prover – but rather these are verifiers whose views in Π might not correspond to honest strategies, and therefore cannot be relied on for verification.

More specifically, the set H is obtained as follows. First, since the verifiers check that their input pieces are close to a valid codeword, if the test passes then we are guaranteed that the input pieces of the honest verifiers are at most t-far from the code, in the following sense. There exists a subset $T, |T| \leq t$ of honest verifiers, and a valid codeword, such that the input pieces of all honest verifiers $i \notin T$ are identical to the corresponding pieces of the codeword. (Intuitively, the parties in T hold "incorrect" input pieces.) We then eliminate the verifiers in T.

Next, in the remaining set of $\geq k - t$ verifiers, there are at most t corrupted verifiers (i.e., corrupted in the dZK), and we eliminate them as well. These verifiers need to be eliminated because they cannot be relied on to honestly check their views. In particular, they might not complain against the prover, even if their output in Π is 0, or they might cheat in Step 2, sending messages which are not actually consistent with their views. We note that the existence of such corrupted verifiers *in the dZK execution* is also the reason that we need to rely on *robust* MPC protocols even though we seemingly check *all* views in Π (indeed, the views held by the corrupted verifiers are never checked). Finally, we eliminate the (at most t) verifiers in $C_1 \cup C_2$.

We thus remain with $\geq k - 3t$ *honest* verifiers, whose views are both locally and pairwise consistent. Their views therefore correspond to an execution of Π on $\left(x^{(1)}, \ldots, x^{(k)}\right)$ with an honest majority (when $k > 6t + 2$), and so the robustness of Π guarantees that the outputs of these parties must be correct. (This description is a gross over simplification of the actual analysis, see Sect. 4 for further details, and for a clarification why we need $k > 6t + 2$ instead of $k > 6t$.)

Finally, our verification procedure provides a strong ZK guarantee – verifiers learn nothing beyond the view of the corresponding party in Π (whereas in [IKOS07] the verifier learns multiple views).

Certifiable VSS (cVSS) and Reusable cVSS. Certifiable VSS (cVSS) schemes follow naturally from strongly-complete dZK proofs, using a standard robust secret sharing scheme. Specifically, in a t-robust secret sharing scheme, reconstruction succeeds even if t parties provide incorrect shares. We note that many standard VSS schemes employ robust secret sharing as a building block. Moreover, as discussed in Sect. 1.2, robustly encoding the input seems necessary in dZKs with security against coalitions of the prover and a subset of verifiers.

Our cVSS Scheme for an NP-language $\mathcal{L}$ consists of a dealer $\mathcal{D}$ and k parties $\mathcal{P}_1, \ldots, \mathcal{P}_k$. The dealer shares its secret x using the robust secret sharing scheme, and distributes the shares among the parties. The parties then run a "code membership" test to check that their shares are "close" to a valid secret sharing of some secret. Then, the parties execute a dZK, in which $\mathcal{P}_i$'s input piece is its share, attesting to the fact that the shared secret is in $\mathcal{L}$. If the dZK fails then the parties revert to some fixed sharing of an arbitrary $x^* \in \mathcal{L}$. Reconstruction is performed by simply running the reconstruction procedure of the underlying secret sharing scheme (and correcting errors if necessary). The strong completeness of the dZK guarantees that when the dealer is honest, corrupted parties cannot "frame" the dealer during the dZK test. Since the code membership test has a similar strong completeness guarantee, the cVSS is correct (in the presence of t active corruptions).

Our cVSS scheme is incomparable to the cVSS of [IW14]. Specifically, the communication during the verification part of their sharing phase (i.e., the part corresponding to executing the code test and the dZK in our cVSS) is polylogarithmic in the total number of parties, and the total communication during sharing is linear. In contrast, when instantiated with the dZK proofs of Theorem 1, the communication of our cVSS scheme during sharing would be at least quadratic. However, to contend with t corruptions, the number of parties in the cVSS of [IW14] must be a (large) polynomial in t, whereas our cVSS has $k = O(t)$. Therefore, in many settings, our cVSS might have lower overall communication complexity due to the smaller number of parties it employs. Moreover, our cVSS can be generalized to the *reusable* setting, as we now discuss.

Reusable cVSS. We generalize the notion of cVSS to allow the dealer to prove *multiple* NP statements – which are determined in an online fashion – on the *same* shared secret, using the same secret shares. In particular, the scheme now includes a *Prove* phase that can be executed following the Sharing phase an unlimited number of times. In each Prove phase the parties are given an NP language $\mathcal{L}$, and $\mathcal{D}$ is additionally given a corresponding witness, and the dealer proves to the parties that the secret their shares encode is in $\mathcal{L}$.

We note that several subtleties arise when defining reusability, and in particular, reusabe cVSS is not a strict strengthening of cVSS. The main reason for this is that since during the Sharing phase the parties still do not know all the NP languages which will be used during the Prove phases, we cannot generally guarantee that the secret x which the shares will reconstruct to will be in all NP languages (and in fact, it might be the case that there exists no such x). Instead, binding only guarantees that when the Sharing phase terminates, even a malicious dealer $\mathcal{D}^*$ is committed to *some* secret x, but there is no further guarantee on x. Binding additionally guarantees that $\mathcal{D}^*$ cannot prove false claims about x, namely if $x \notin \mathcal{L}$ then an execution of the Prove phase with language $\mathcal{L}$ will fail. This should be contrasted with standard cVSS which isn't reusable, i.e., it can be executed only for a single NP language $\mathcal{L}$, but whose binding property guarantees that the secret x which will be reconstructed, satisfies $x \in \mathcal{L}$. Further subtleties are discussed in the full version [HVW22].

Our reusable cVSS scheme operates similarly to the cVSS scheme described above. Specifically, to share x the dealer secret shares it using a robust secret sharing scheme, and the parties then run a code membership test on the shares. Each Prove phase with NP language $\mathcal{L}$ consists of running a dZK for the claim that the shares reconstruct to a secret in $\mathcal{L}$, and reconstruction is by running the reconstructor of the underlying secret sharing scheme.

1.3   Open Problems and Future Directions

Our work gives rise to many interesting questions in the context of dZK and MPC-in-the-Head. First, we did not explore the possibility of obtaining more efficient constructions for simple NP languages, e.g., with low degree. In particular, using an appropriate MPC instantiation, it might be possible to design special-purpose dZKs for simpler languages, with sublinear communication complexity and improved computational complexity. Round complexity is another important complexity measure. Our construction achieves a 2-round dZK assuming ideal coin-tossing, and leaves open the question of proving this is optimal, or further improving the round complexity as in the computational setting for related proof systems [AKP22]. Finally, it would be interesting to find further applications of dZK proofs, and in particular of strongly-complete ones.

1.4   Paper Organization

In Sect. 2 we introduce basic preliminaries. In Sect. 3 we present our batch code membership test, and in Sect. 4 we present our dZK proof construction. Due to space limitations, we defer all proofs, as well as the description of our dZK applications and the ideal dZK functionality, and an extensive comparison between dZK and VRS, to the full version [HVW22].

1.5   Related Works

Zero-Knowledge Proofs in Distributed Settings. The notion of ZK in distributed settings has been extensively explored in a recent sequence of works [CBM15, CB17, BBC+19b, BGIN20, BGIN21]. The motivation for such models is that they present a useful abstraction that captures many scenarios naturally arising in distributed computation. The first two works discussed how to embed distributed ZK into real-world applications such as anonymous broadcast messaging practical at a large scale [CBM15], and a federated learning system, denoted by Prio, with input certification to securely compute aggregate statistics [CB17]. The latter system has been deployed in various real world scenarios. For instance, Mozilla uses a modified version of Prio to privately collect web usage statistics, and Apple and Google use Prio for their exposure notifications express (ENX) system. Nevertheless, the model considered for both [CBM15, CB17] is limited because they assume that the verifiers are semi-honest, and moreover they only consider a specific functionality. On the other hand, their dZKs achieve information-theoretic security.

Different settings have been considered in this context, depending on whether the input statement is known in full to all verifiers (starting with the work of [BD91], and more recently in, e.g., [GO07, YW22, BJO+22, AKP22]), or distributed between them (as in the distributed ZK proofs discussed below); and whether the resultant scheme is information-theoretically, or only computationally, secure while optimizing different parameters of the proof system.

Another related model is that of Verifiable Relation Sharing (VRS) [GIKR02], which is similar to the model of dZK proofs considered in this work, in the sense that the input statement is distributed between the verifiers, but differs from it because the prover chooses the statement and the verifiers' shares (whereas in dZK proofs the prover has no control over the input statement). Works on VRS [GIKR02, AKP20, AKP22] consider both the information theoretic [GIKR02] and the computational setting [AKP20, AKP22], with progressively improving corruption thresholds. Specifically, the VRS of [GIKR02] is for $k \geq 6t$, which the latter pair of works improved by moving to the computational setting. More specifically, [GIKR02] obtain a 2-round perfectly-secure VRS protocol whose communication complexity (and in particular, the communication between the verifiers) scales with the circuit size. This protocol can be made to be verification efficient (i.e., where the communication between the verifiers is independent of the circuit size) using the MAC-based verification techniques used in our dZK proofs. This requires coin tossing, and also relaxing security to statistical. [AKP22] obtain a 2-round VRS with computational security against $t < (k-1)(1/2 - \varepsilon)$ for an arbitrarily small $\varepsilon > 0$, assuming non-interactive commitments (their protocol is not verification-efficient).[7] Their result extends

---

[7]   [AKP22] also obtain a fully information-theoretically secure VRS assuming ideal non-interactive commitments, as well as a computationally sound and statistically ZK (statistically sound and computationally ZK, respectively) VRS based on computationally binding and statistically hiding (statistically binding and computationally hiding, respectively) non-interactive commitments [App22].

to any *single input functionality*, resolving the round complexity of such functionalities. (As noted in Sect. 1.3, the round complexity of dZK – which is not a single input functionality – is not yet resolved for optimal thresholds.)

It is instructive to note that this difference in who chooses the input statement makes VRS and dZK incomparable. Indeed, dZK can be used to prove correctness "after the fact" (namely, after the parties already have their inputs fixed), while in VRS the prover chooses the inputs. Therefore, when used in settings when parties already hold their inputs, VRS necessitates some external mechanism for verifying consistency of the parties' inputs, and the inputs provided by the prover.[8] On the other hand, both primitives can be useful in constructing similar applications, such as the certified VSS primitive discussed above. We note that while VRS can also be used to obtain IA-MPC, the construction from dZK is conceptually simpler and more efficient (only additively increases the round and communication complexities). Using VRS complicates the protocol (as it requires sending the protocol messages as part of the VRS), and also increases the round and communication complexities by a multiplicative factor that grows with the respective complexities of the underlying VRS. See the full version [HVW22] for further discussion of the connection between the two primitives.

Distributed Zero-Knowledge Proofs. Out of the multitude of distributed models for ZK, the focus of this work is on the "distributed zero-knowledge" (dZK) proofs presented in [BBC+19b]. In dZK, the input statement is distributed between the verifiers (where no verifier knows it in full), and security is unconditional. [BBC+19b] consider two possible corruption models in the context of soundness: a malicious prover interacting with honest verifiers ("setting I"), and a malicious prover colluding with a subset of verifiers ("setting II"). (In this work we consider only the latter corruption model.) They design dZK systems based on fully-linear probabilistically checkable proofs or fully-linear interactive oracle proofs. Specifically, assuming ideal coin tossing, they construct dZKs for *"low-degree languages"* in which the communication and round complexities are logarithmic in the size of the statement.

Assuming ideal coin-tossing, they also provide a 2-round construction for arbitrary circuits in which the communication complexity is proportional to the circuit size, and ZK (soundness, respectively) holds against t corrupted verifiers ($t - 1$ corrupted verifiers colluding with the prover, respectively), where $k > 2t$. We note that their constructions do not achieve strong completeness. In the full version we adapt our techniques to obtain a 2-round dZK scheme (assuming ideal coin tossing) without strong completeness with ZK (soundness, respectively) against t corrupted verifiers (t corrupted verifiers colluding with the prover, respectively) for $k > 2(t + 1)$, where the communication complexity is quasi-linear in the circuit size, and can be reduced to linear with one additional round.

---

[8] In the computational setting one can use standard tools such as commitments to help resolve disputes between parties, but in the information theoretic setting this seems to require a more sophisticated dispute-resolution sub-protocol.

See the full version [HVW22] for further details and comparison with the results of [BBC+19b].

Following the formalization of [BBC+19b], several follow-up works [BGIN19, BGIN20, BGIN21] explored the applicability of dZKs in the context of MPC, starting with [BGIN19] that focused on the three-party setting with an honest majority. This simpler case excludes the corruption model of a prover colluding with a verifier, and therefore only requires a simpler dZK. Building on [BGIN19], the protocol introduced in [BGIN20] works in the honest majority setting for a constant number of parties by applying the sublinear dZK from [BBC+19b]. [BGIN21] extends the techniques from [BGIN20] to the dishonest majority setting with preprocessing.

dZK as an Ideal Functionality. As mentioned before, our notion of dZK can be specified as an ideal functionality, and such a functionality can be realized generically using a fully secure MPC protocol against active adversaries. However, all these works will result in communication that is proportional to the circuit size between the verifiers, so they are not verification efficient.

MPC-in-the-head is a powerful technique, originally introduced in [IKOS07] as a novel approach towards designing zero-knowledge proofs, based on MPC protocols. Following this seminal work, this approach has been improved and optimized [GMO16, AHIV17, CDG+17, KKW18, BFH+20, GSV21].

COMPARISON WITH OUR MPC-IN-THE-HEAD CONSTRUCTION. Our novel verification technique for the distributed setting has several advantages over MPC-in-the-head techniques used in the 2-party setting. First, it does not require commitments, and in particular gives information-theoretic security. Commitments are not needed because sending the views in Π to the verifiers effectively commits the prover to these views (at least, to the ones given to honest verifiers). Moreover, usually (e.g., this is the case in [IKOS07]) the soundness error depends on the number of parties. Indeed, the soundness error depends on the size of the challenge space, namely the number of possible subsets of views which the verifier opens, where obtaining negl (s) soundness error requires opening $\Omega(s)$ views. Since a single verifier receives all the opened views, the privacy parameter of the system, and consequently the total number of parties, increases proportionally to s, and the communication complexity of Π (i.e., the view size) increases accordingly. In contrast, in our verification procedure *all* views are simultaneously checked, but each verifier sees a single view. Thus, the privacy parameter, and the total number of parties in Π, is *independent* of the security parameter. Instead, the soundness error is roughly proportional to the ratio between the communication complexity of Π and the size of the field used to generate the MACs. Obtaining negl (s) soundness error thus requires the field size to be superpolynomial in s and the communication complexity $CC(\Pi)$ of Π. Therefore, the overall communication in Step 2 (Sect. 1.2) would be only *polylogarithmic in s*.

COMPARISON WITH OTHER MPC-IN-THE-HEAD CONSTRUCTIONS IN A DISTRIBUTED SETTING. [AKP22] employ the MPC-in-the-head paradigm in the *distributed* computational setting. Similar to [IKOS07], the prover in their construction commits to the views in the MPC. However, instead of opening a subset of views (and checking their consistency), [AKP22] exploit the distributed setting to simultaneously check consistency of *all* views. Nonetheless, their method of doing so differs significantly from ours. Specifically, they check *local* consistency of each view (roughly, verifying that the party honestly generated its messages given its input and randomness), by running an appropriate MPC with a "committee" (i.e., a subset) of the parties. In contrast, we check pairwise consistency between views by revealing a view in full to a single party and have the parties compare their messages in the clear (i.e., without any MPC computation). We are thus able to avoid using commitments and get information-theoretic security.

Identifiable Abort MPC (IA-MPC). Secure computation in the dishonest majority setting has a significant limitation: it *inherently* cannot prevent even a single deviating party from causing the protocol to fail [Cle86]. While guaranteed output delivery is possible when there is an *honest* majority, aborts still create substantial obstacles. In particular, obtaining guaranteed output delivery often incurs a large overhead in rounds and communication complexity due to the player elimination technique. A natural solution to the problem of parties repeatedly failing the protocol is to support *identifiable abort*. That is, if the protocol fails to complete, it must provide a method to (publicly) identify at least one malicious/crashed party. Identifying cheaters is highly non-trivial for concretely efficient protocols [IOZ14,SF16,BOS16,CFY17,BOSS20,BMMM20, Bra21,SSY22] since the parties must reach consensus on the cheater's identity. This property is very useful for deterring malicious behavior; in particular, when *penalties* are used against malicious parties, as is the case with smart contracts that run on distributed ledgers and realize a bulletin board.

Amongst these works, only [IOZ14] introduces a *generic* compiler from any semi-honestly secure MPC protocol which uses correlated randomness into a similar protocol which is secure with identifiable abort against malicious adversaries. This compiler works by broadcasting each semi-honest message, together with a zero-knowledge proof of consistency with that party's committed input and correlated randomness obtained from the setup phase. It therefore increases the broadcast complexity of the semi-honest protocol proportionally to the size of the computation. More recent works (e.g., [BOS16,SF16,BOSS20]) on identifiable abort have refined this approach but the overall communication complexity of these approaches is $\Omega(\kappa \cdot |C|)$ to generate correlated randomness in the offline phase, and $\Omega(|C|)$ in the online phase, where κ the (computational) security parameter and $|C|$ is the circuit size. While the more recent works achieve identifiable abort property for specific protocols (e.g., SPDZ-type protocols), the work of [IOZ14] presents a generic compiler for any semi-honest protocol in the correlated-randomness model. In this work, we use dZKs to provide a compiler in similar vein to achieve identifiable abort, but for a class of protocols in the honest-majority setting.

2   Preliminaries

Notation. $\mathbb{F}$ denotes a finite field. A *language* $\mathcal{L}$ *over* $\mathbb{F}$ is a subset $\mathcal{L} \subseteq \mathbb{F}^*$. For a pair of vectors $v, u \in \mathbb{F}^k$, we denote their Hamming distance by $d(u,v) = |\{i \ : \ u_i \neq v_i\}|$. We associate with a code $\mathcal{C} \subseteq \mathbb{F}^k$ an *encoding procedure* Enc and a *decoding procedure* Dec such that for every x, $\mathsf{Dec}(\mathsf{Enc}(x)) = x$. We will also allow for encoding to be randomized (this would be useful for our applications of dZK). We use PPT to denote probabilsitic polynomial time computation. For a distribution $\mathcal{D}$, sampling according to $\mathcal{D}$ is denote by $X \leftarrow \mathcal{D}$, or $X \in_R \mathcal{D}$. For a pair of random variables X, Y, we use $X \equiv Y$ to denote that X, Y are identically distributed. For random variables X and Y over a finite domain Ω, the *statistical distance* between them is defined as

$$\mathsf{SD}(X,Y) = \frac{1}{2} \sum_{w \in \Omega} \big| \Pr[X = w] - \Pr[Y = w] \big|.$$

X and Y are *ε-statistically close* if their statistical distance is at most ε. Ensembles $\{X_s\}_s, \{Y_s\}_s$ are *statistically close*, denoted $X_s \approx Y_s$, if there exist an $\epsilon(s) = \mathsf{negl}(s)$ such that X_s, Y_s are $\epsilon(s)$-close for every s.

The Ideal Coin-Tossing Functionality. For modularity, our construction will employ an ideal implementation of coin-tossing, a standard primitive that generates unpredictable, public randomness.

Coding Notation. For a code $\mathcal{C} \subseteq \mathbb{F}^k$ and vector $v \in \mathbb{F}^k$, denote by $d(v,\mathcal{C})$ the minimal distance of v from $\mathcal{C}$, namely $d(v,\mathcal{C}) = \min_{u \in \mathcal{C}} d(v,u)$, and denote by $\Delta(v,\mathcal{C})$ the set of positions in which v differs from such a closest codeword (in case of ties, take the lexicographically first closest codeword). We further denote, for a vector set $V \subseteq \mathbb{F}^k$ and a code $\mathcal{C}$, $\Delta(V,\mathcal{C}) = \bigcup_{v \in V}\{\Delta(v,\mathcal{C})\}$, and denote by $d(V,C)$ the minimal distance between a V and the code $\mathcal{C}$, namely $d(V,\mathcal{C}) = \min_{v \in V}\{d(v,\mathcal{C})\}$. Our constructions will employ robust codes which, intuitively, are error correcting.

Definition 1 (Robust Code). *A code $\mathcal{C} \in \mathbb{F}^k$ is (ε,t)-robust if for every $u \in \mathcal{C}$ and for every $v \in \mathbb{F}^k$ such that $d(u,v) \leq t$, $\Pr[\mathsf{Dec}(u) = \mathsf{Dec}(v)] \geq 1 - \varepsilon$. $\mathcal{C}$ is perfectly t-robust if it is $(0,t)$-robust.*

Distributed Inputs, Distributed Relations, and Distributed Languages. Let $n \in \mathbb{N}$ be a length parameter, $\mathbb{F}$ be a finite field, and $\mathcal{C} \subseteq \mathbb{F}^k$ be a robust code with encoding procedure Enc and decoding procedure Dec. The following notions are defined for a fixed n, but naturally extends to a family of length parameters by using families of codes. For an input $x \in \mathbb{F}^n$, a corresponding *k-distributed input* $X \in \mathbb{F}^{k \times n}$ is a matrix such that for every $i \in [n]$, the i'th column $X[i]$ of X satisfies $x_i = \mathsf{Dec}(X[i])$ (intuitively, the i'th column of X encodes the i'th symbol x_i of x, possibly with some errors).[9] We will write $X = (x^{(1)}, \ldots, x^{(k)})$,

---

[9] Notice that if Enc is randomized then x might have several corresponding k-distributed inputs X.

where for every $i \in [k]$, the *input piece* $x^{(i)}$ is the i'th row of X (i.e., it is the list of i'th symbols in the codewords encoding $x_1, \ldots, x_n$).

Definition 2 (Distributed Languages and Relations). *For a language $\mathcal{L} \subseteq \mathbb{F}^n$ over $\mathbb{F}$, the corresponding k-distributed language $\widehat{\mathcal{L}}_{\mathcal{C}}$ over $\mathbb{F}$ with relation to $\mathcal{C}$ is defined as*

$$\widehat{\mathcal{L}}_{\mathcal{C}} = \left\{ X = \left(x^{(1)}, \ldots, x^{(k)} \right) \ : \ (x_1, \ldots, x_n) \in \mathcal{L}, \right.$$
$$\left. \text{where } x_i = \mathsf{Dec}\left(X[i] \right) \text{ for all } 1 \le i \le n \right\}.$$

For an NP-relation $\mathcal{R} = \mathcal{R}(x, w) \in \mathbb{F}^n \times \mathbb{F}^*$ over $\mathbb{F}$, the corresponding k-distributed relation $\widehat{\mathcal{R}}$ with relation to $\mathcal{C}$ is defined as

$$\widehat{\mathcal{R}}_{\mathcal{C}} = \left\{ \left(\left(x^{(1)}, \ldots, x^{(k)} \right), w \right) \ : \ ((x_1, \ldots, x_n), w) \in \mathcal{R}, \right.$$
$$\left. \text{where } x_i = \mathsf{Dec}\left(X[i] \right) \text{ for all } 1 \le i \le n \right\}.$$

We call $\widehat{\mathcal{L}}_{\mathcal{C}}, \widehat{\mathcal{R}}_{\mathcal{C}}$ the k-distributed language and the k-distributed relation that *correspond* to $\mathcal{L}, \mathcal{R}$, respectively. When $\mathcal{C}$ is clear from the context, we omit it and simply write $\widehat{\mathcal{L}}, \widehat{\mathcal{R}}$. For a (distributed) NP-relation $\mathcal{R}$, we denote $\mathcal{L}(\mathcal{R}) = \{x \ : \ \exists w \text{ s.t. } (x, w) \in \mathcal{R}\}$.

2.1 Distributed Zero-Knowledge (dZK) Proofs

Following Boneh et al. [BBC+19b], we consider a distributed setting in which a single prover $\mathcal{P}$ interacts with k verifiers $\mathcal{V}_1, \ldots, \mathcal{V}_k$. Each verifier $\mathcal{V}_i$ holds a *piece* $x^{(i)} \in \mathbb{F}^*$ of a distributed input $\left(x^{(1)}, \ldots, x^{(k)} \right)$ encoding some input $x \in \mathbb{F}^*$, and the prover's goal is to convince the verifiers that $\left(x^{(1)}, \ldots, x^{(k)} \right) \in \widehat{\mathcal{L}}$ for some language $\mathcal{L}$. We assume that $\left(x^{(1)}, \ldots, x^{(k)} \right)$ is known to the prover. When $\mathcal{L}$ is an NP language, the prover additionally knows a witness w for the fact that $x \in \mathcal{L}$. The parties can communicate over point-to-point channels, as well as a broadcast channel.

Similar to standard (i.e., 2-party) ZK proofs, the system should satisfy completeness (when all parties are honest), zero knowledge (against a subset of corrupted verifiers), and soundness. The two latter properties have several possible interpretations in the distributed setting, as we now explain.

In terms of ZK, following [BBC+19b] we require that a subset of corrupted verifiers learn nothing on the NP witness, *as well as on the input pieces of the honest verifiers*. This is formalized by requiring, as in the standard setting, the existence of an efficient simulator that can simulate the corrupted verifiers' views given only their input pieces. This provides a strong ZK property which is meaningful also for languages and relations in P. There are also two possible interpretations of the soundness property. We choose to consider the stronger requirement of soundness against a corrupted prover colluding with a subset of verifiers, namely for $\left(x^{(1)}, \ldots, x^{(k)} \right) \notin \widehat{\mathcal{L}}$, the honest verifiers should reject with high probability. ([BBC+19b] consider also a weaker notion in which soundness is only required to hold when all verifiers are honest.)

Another concern naturally arises in this distributed setting: that of corrupted verifiers trying to "frame" an honest prover, namely trying to cause the honest verifiers to reject a true claim $(x^{(1)}, \ldots, x^{(k)}) \in \widehat{\mathcal{L}}$. We require that they succeed only with small probability. This property, which we call *strong completeness*, was not required in the distributed model of [BBC+19b] (and their dZK proofs do not obtain it), but will be needed for the applications. This discussion is summarized in the following definition:

Definition 3 (Distributed Zero-Knowledge Proofs). *Let* $\widehat{\mathcal{R}} = \widehat{\mathcal{R}}((x^{(1)}, \ldots, x^{(k)}), w)$ *be a* k-*distributed relation over a finite field* $\mathbb{F}$. *A* k-*verifier* $(\varepsilon_p, \varepsilon_r, t_p, t_r)$ *distributed Zero-Knowledge proof* $((\varepsilon_p, \varepsilon_r, t_p, t_r)$-*dZK)* Π_{dist} *for* $\mathcal{R}_k$ *consists of a prover* $\mathcal{P}$ *and verifiers* $\mathcal{V}_1, \ldots, \mathcal{V}_k$ *satisfying the following:*

– **Syntax.** *The input of each* $\mathcal{V}_i$ *is an input piece* $x^{(i)}$, *and the input of* $\mathcal{P}$ *is* $(x^{(1)}, \ldots, x^{(k)})$ *and a witness* w *such that* $((x^{(1)}, \ldots, x^{(k)}), w) \in \widehat{\mathcal{R}}$.[10] *The parties interact in rounds over point-to-point channels and a broadcast channel, where the messages sent by a party in round* i *are determined given a next-message function, and depend on its input, randomness, and messages it received in previous rounds. The protocol terminates after a fixed number of rounds, and each verifier outputs either* accept *or* reject, *based on its view (which consists of its input and the messages it received throughout the execution).*

– **Completeness.** *For every* $(x^{(1)}, \ldots, x^{(k)}, w) \in \widehat{\mathcal{R}}$, *when all parties are honest then all verifiers accept in the execution of* Π *on* $((x^{(1)}, \ldots, x^{(k)}), w)$ *with probability* 1.

– (ε_r, t_r)-**Strong Completeness.** *For every* $(x^{(1)}, \ldots, x^{(k)}, w) \in \widehat{\mathcal{R}}$, *in an execution of* Π *on* $((x^{(1)}, \ldots, x^{(k)}), w)$ *with an honest prover, except with probability at most* ε_r *all honest verifiers accept, even if* t_r *verifiers are corrupted, computationally unbounded, and may arbitrarily deviate from the protocol.*

– (ε_r, t_r)-**Soundness.** *For every (possibly malicious and unbounded) prover* $\mathcal{P}^*$, *and any* $(x^{(1)}, \ldots, x^{(k)}) \notin \widehat{\mathcal{L}}(\widehat{\mathcal{R}})$, *even if a subset* C *of at most* t_r *verifiers are maliciously corrupted, computationally unbounded and colluding with* $\mathcal{P}$, *then except with probability* ε_r *all honest verifiers reject in the execution of* Π_{dist} *on input* $(x^{(1)}, \ldots, x^{(k)})$ *with prover* $\mathcal{P}^*$ *colluding with the verifiers in* C.

– (ε_p, t_p)-**Distributed Zero Knowledge (dZK).** *For every adversary* $\mathcal{A}$ *corrupting a subset* T *of at most* t_p *verifiers, there exists a PPT simulator* Sim *such that for every* $((x^{(1)}, \ldots, x^{(k)}), w) \in \widehat{\mathcal{R}}$, *it holds that*

$$SD\left(Sim\left(\left(x^{(j)}\right)_{j \in T} \right), \mathsf{View}_{\Pi, \mathcal{A}}\left(\left(x^{(1)}, \ldots, x^{(k)}\right), w \right) \right) \leq \varepsilon_p$$

---

[10] We note that w may also be the empty string, e.g., if $\widehat{\mathcal{R}}$ corresponds to a language in P.

where $\mathsf{View}_{\Pi,\mathcal{A}}\left(x^{(1)}, \ldots, x^{(k)}, w\right)$ *denotes the view of the adversary* $\mathcal{A}$ *in an execution of* Π *with an honest prover on inputs* $\left(x^{(1)}, \ldots, x^{(k)}, w\right)$.

The following notation will be useful.

Notation 1 (t-dZK). *We say that a protocol between a prover* $\mathcal{P}$ *and* k *verifiers is a* t-dZK *proof, if it is a* $(\mathsf{negl}\,(s), \mathsf{negl}\,(s), t, t)$-dZK *proof, where* s *is a statistical security parameter.*

Next, we describe a special structure of dZK proofs, which the systems constructed in this work satisfy. Specifically, the execution is divided into a proof generation phase in which the prover sends a proof share to each verifier, and a verification phase in which the proof shares are verified. We are particularly interested in dZK proofs in which the communicated during the verification phase is independent of the size of the verification circuit.

Definition 4. *We say that a dZK proof is* verification efficient *if it is a dZK between the prover and* k *verifiers, whose execution can be divided into a proof generation phase in which the prover sends a message to each verifier, and a verification phase in which all parties interact, and moreover, the communication complexity during the verification phase is* poly $(k, s, \log n)$, *where* s *is a statistical security parameter, and* n *is the input length. In particular, the communication complexity during verification is* independent *of the size of the computation.*

Remark 1 (Round Complexity of dZK Proofs). Our dZK proofs are designed in the coin-tossing hybrid model, in which parties can obtain truly random coins by calling an ideal coin-tossing oracle. Calls to this oracle are done separately from communication rounds, namely parties do not exchange any messages in rounds during which the oracle is called. When counting the round complexity of a dZK proof, the rounds in which the oracle is called are not counted towards the round complexity of the system. Thus, if the coin-tossing oracle is replaced with a secure MPC implementation of coin-tossing, the round complexity of the resultant system will be the sum of the round complexity of the dZK and of the secure coin-tossing.

2.2   Secure Multi-Party Computation (MPC) Protocols

In this section we set some notation and terminology relating to MPC protocols, which will be used in subsequent sections.

Let Π be an MPC protocol between parties $P_1, \ldots, P_k$. The *view* View_i *of party* P_i consists of its input, random coin tosses, and all the messages it received throughout the protocol execution.

Definition 5 (Pairwise Consistent Views). *a pair of views* $\mathsf{View}_i, \mathsf{View}_j$ *of parties* P_i, P_j *in an MPC protocol* Π *is* pairwise consistent *if the outgoing messages from* P_i *to* P_j *implicit in* View_i *are identical to the incomming messages from* P_i *to* P_j *reported in* View_j, *and vice versa.*

Definition 6 (ε-Correctness). *We say that a k-party protocol Π realizes a deterministic k-party functionality $f\left(x^{(1)}, \ldots, x^{(k)}\right)$ with ε-correctness if for every $x^{(1)}, \ldots, x^{(k)}$,*

$$\Pr\left[\exists i \in [k] \; : \; y_i \neq f\left(x^{(1)}, \ldots, x^{(k)}\right)\right] \leq \varepsilon$$

where y_i denotes the output of P_i in Π.
We say that Π is perfectly correct if it is ε-correct for $\varepsilon = 0$.

Definition 7 ((ε, t)-Privacy). *Let $1 \leq t < k$. We say that a protocol Π realizing a k-party functionality f is (ε, t)-private if for every subset $\mathsf{C} \subset [k]$ of size $|\mathsf{C}| \leq t$ there exists a PPT simulator Sim_C such that for every $x^{(1)}, \ldots, x^{(k)}$,*

$$SD\left(\mathsf{View}_\mathsf{C}\left(x^{(1)}, \ldots, x^{(k)}\right), \mathsf{Sim}_\mathsf{C}\left(\left\{x^{(i)}\right\}_{i \in \mathsf{C}}, f\left(x^{(1)}, \ldots, x^{(k)}\right)\right)\right) \leq \varepsilon$$

where $\mathsf{View}_\mathsf{C}\left(x^{(1)}, \ldots, x^{(k)}\right)$ denotes the joint view of the parties in C (including their inputs, random coin tosses, and the messages they received) in a semi-honest execution of Π in which the parties have inputs $x^{(1)}, \ldots, x^{(k)}$.
We say that Π is perfectly t private if it is $(0, t)$-private.

Definition 8 ((ε, t)-Robustness). *Let f be a k-party functionality whose outputs are in $\{0, 1\}$, and let $1 \leq t < k$. We say that a protocol Π realizing f is (ε, t)-robust if for every subset $\mathsf{C} \subset [k]$ of size $|\mathsf{C}| \leq t$ and for every $x^{(1)}, \ldots, x^{(k)}$, the following holds. If there exists no $x^{(1\prime)}, \ldots, x^{(k\prime)}$ such that: (1) $x^{(i)} = x^{(i\prime)}$ for every $i \notin \mathsf{C}$, and (2) $f\left(x^{(1\prime)}, \ldots, x^{(k\prime)}\right) = 1$, then except with probability ε, all parties $i \notin \mathsf{C}$ output 0 in an execution of Π in which the honest parties have inputs $\left\{x^{(i)}\right\}_{i \notin \mathsf{C}}$, even if the parties in C are maliciously corrupted, colluding, and computationally unbounded.*
We say that Π is perfectly t robust if it is $(0, t)$-robust.

3   Checking Membership in a Robust Code

In this section, we describe and analyze a batch code membership test. As we show in the full version [HVW22], this test yields a *batched* Verifiable Secret Sharing (VSS) scheme – which allows the dealer to share multiple secrets simultaneously – in which the complexity of verifying the shares is *independent* of the batch size. First, we establish some notations.

Our test pertains to Reed-Solomon (RS) codes, defined next. We recall that a $[k, \delta, d]$ code refers to a linear code over some underlying field $\mathbb{F}$ where k is block length, δ is the message length (dimension) and d is the minimal distance.

Definition 9 (Reed-Solomon Code). *For positive integers k, δ, finite field $\mathbb{F}$, and a vector $\eta = (\eta_1, \ldots, \eta_k) \in \mathbb{F}^k$ of distinct field elements, the code $\mathsf{RS}_{\mathbb{F}, k, \delta, \eta}$ is the $[k, \delta, k - \delta + 1]$ linear code over $\mathbb{F}$ that consists of all k-tuples $(p(\eta_1), \ldots, p(\eta_k))$ where p is a polynomial of degree $< \delta$ over $\mathbb{F}$.*

It will be convenient to view m-tuples of codewords in a linear code L as codewords in an interleaved code L^m, formally:

Definition 10 (Interleaved Code). *Let $L \subset \mathbb{F}^k$ be a $[k, \delta, d]$ linear code over $\mathbb{F}$. We let L^m denote the $[mk, m\delta, d]$ (interleaved) code over $\mathbb{F}$ whose codewords are all $k \times m$ matrices U such that every column $U[i]$ of U satisfies $U[i] \in L$. For $U \in L^m$ and $j \in [k]$, we denote by U_j the jth symbol (row) of U.*

Definition 11 (Encoded Message). *Let $L = \mathsf{RS}_{\mathbb{F}, k, \delta, \eta}$ and $\zeta = (\zeta_1, \ldots, \zeta_\ell)$ be a sequence of distinct elements of $\mathbb{F}$ for $\ell \leq \delta$. For $u \in L$ we define the message $\mathsf{Dec}_\zeta(u)$ to be $(p_u(\zeta_1), \ldots, p_u(\zeta_\ell))$, where p_u is the polynomial (of degree $< \delta$) corresponding to u (i.e., $p_u(x) = \sum_{i=0}^{\delta-1} u_i x^i$). For $U \in L^m$ with columns $U[1], \ldots, U[m] \in L$, we let $\mathsf{Dec}_\zeta(U)$ be the length-$m\ell$ vector $x = (x_{11}, \ldots, x_{1\ell}, \ldots, x_{m1}, \ldots, x_{m\ell})$ such that $(x_{i1}, \ldots, x_{i\ell}) = \mathsf{Dec}_\zeta(U[i])$ for $i \in [m]$. Finally, when ζ is clear from the context, we say that U encodes x if $x = \mathsf{Dec}_\zeta(U)$.*

Private (Interleaved) RS Codes. We will in fact use a *private* variant of the (interleaved) RS code. Intuitively, in a t-private code encoding is randomized, and any subset of t codeword symbols reveals no information about the encoded message (when the codeword was randomly generated). In particular, privacy requires a randomized encoding procedure Enc. We will sometime explicitly state the randomness r used for encoding, denoted by $\mathsf{Enc}(\cdot; r)$. Formally,

Definition 12 (Private Code). *Let $t, k \in \mathbb{N}$, and $\varepsilon \in [0, 1]$. A code $\mathcal{C} \subseteq \mathbb{F}^k$ with a randomized encoding procedure Enc is (ε, t)-private if for every x, x', and every subset $\mathcal{I} \subset [k]$ of size $|\mathcal{I}| \leq t$, it holds that $\mathsf{SD}(\mathsf{Enc}(x)|_\mathcal{I}, \mathsf{Enc}(x')|_\mathcal{I}) \leq \varepsilon$, where $\mathsf{Enc}(x)|_\mathcal{I}$ denotes the restriction of $\mathsf{Enc}(x)$ to the coordinates in $\mathcal{I}$, and the distance is over the randomness used to encode x, x'. We say that $\mathcal{C}$ is perfectly t-private if it is $(0, t)$-private.*

Intuitively, to guarantee that the RS codeword reveals no information about the underlying secret, we rely on a *randomized* version of the code which concatenates the message with randomness before encoding it. Specifically, we use the following private version of RS codes (for our purposes, $\ell = 1$ suffices; but the notion easily extends to larger ℓ).

Definition 13 (Randomized Reed-Solomon (RRS) Code). *For positive integers k, δ, finite field $\mathbb{F}$, and a vector $\eta = (\eta_1, \ldots, \eta_k) \in \mathbb{F}^k$ of distinct field elements, the code $\mathsf{RRS}_{\mathbb{F}, k, \delta, \eta}$ is defined by the following encoding and decoding procedures.*

- *Enc is a PPT procedure that on input $x \in \mathbb{F}$ samples $r \leftarrow \mathbb{F}^{\delta-1}$ and applies the encoding procedure of the RS code $\mathsf{RS}_{\mathbb{F}, k, \delta, \eta}$ (Definition 9) to (x, r). That is, it computes $(p(\eta_1), \ldots, p(\eta_k))$ where $p(y) = x + \sum_{i=1}^{\delta-1} r_i y^i$.*
- *Dec is a deterministic procedure that on input a purported codeword $c \in \mathbb{F}^k$ applies the decoding procedure of the RS code $\mathsf{RS}_{\mathbb{F}, k, \delta, \eta}$ and (if decoding succeeds) outputs the first symbol of the decoded message.*

We will need the following simple fact regarding the RRS code, which follows from the properties of Shamir's secret sharing.

Fact 31 (RRS is Robust and Private). *For every positive integers k, δ such that $k > 3(\delta - 1)$, any finite field $\mathbb{F}$, and any vector $\eta = (\eta_1, \ldots, \eta_k) \in \mathbb{F}^k$ of distinct field elements, the code $\mathsf{RRS}_{\mathbb{F}, k, \delta, \eta}$ is $(0, \delta - 1)$-private and $(0, \delta - 1)$-robust.*

Moreover, the code is $(0, \delta - 1)$-private for any $k \geq \delta$.

Batch Verification of RS Codewords. We describe a simple procedure for batch verification of membership in the (randomized) RS code, namely membership in the *Interleaved RS (IRS)* code $\mathsf{RS}^m_{\mathbb{F}, k, \delta, \eta}$. First, we recall a Lemma from [BCI+20] regarding IRS codes.

Lemma 32 *[BCI+20, Theorem 1.2] Let $L = \mathsf{RS}_{\mathbb{F}, k', \delta, \eta}$ be a Reed-Solomon code with minimal distance $d = k' - \delta + 1$ and e a positive integer such that $e < d/2$. Suppose $d(U', L^m) > e$. Then, for a random w^* in the column-span of U', we have $\Pr[d(w^*, L') \leq e] \leq k'/|\mathbb{F}|$.*

The IRS Test

Let $L = \mathsf{RS}_{\mathbb{F}, k, \delta, \eta}$ and $\delta = t + \ell - 1$. The IRS test is executed between a prover $\mathcal{P}$ and k verifiers $\mathcal{V}_1, \ldots, \mathcal{V}_k$. Let $x \in \mathbb{F}^{\ell \times m}$ (we think of x as a batch of m length-ℓ secrets), and let $U \in L^m$ such that $\mathsf{Dec}_\zeta(U) = x$. In the protocol, $\mathcal{P}$ has input U, and each verifier $\mathcal{V}_i$ has as input the ith row U_i of U. The protocol proceeds as follows.

1. $\mathcal{P}$ samples a random vector $r_b \in \mathbb{F}^\ell$ and a random codeword $U^* \in L$ such that $\mathsf{Dec}_\zeta(U^*) = r_b$. It sends U_i^* to $\mathcal{V}_i$.
2. The verifiers call $\mathcal{F}_{\mathsf{coin}}$ to obtain a random $r \in_R \mathbb{F}^m$.
3. Each verifier $\mathcal{V}_i$ computes $w_i = \sum_{j=1}^m r_j \cdot U_{i,j} + U_i^*$ and broadcasts w_i.
4. Denote $w = (w_1, \ldots, w_k)$. The verifiers accepts iff $d(w, L) \leq t$.

Fig. 1. Verifying Membership in the IRS Code with t Corruptions

Our batched code-membership test, which we call the *IRS test*, is described in Fig. 1. Its properties are summarized in the following theorem.

Theorem 4 (IRS Test, Figure 1). *Let $k > 4\delta$ where $\delta = t + \ell$. Then, the protocol described in Fig. 1 satisfies the following properties, even if t verifiers are maliciously corrupted.*

- **Correctness.** *If $U \in L^m$ (i.e. the shares held by the parties form a valid codeword), and the prover is honest, then all honest verifiers accept with probability 1.*

- **Soundness/Commitment.** If $U \notin L^m$, then except with probability $k/|\mathbb{F}|$ one of the following hold even if the prover and t verifiers are maliciously corrupted and colluding.
  - All honest verifiers reject.
  - Let H denote the set of honest parties, and let L' and L'^m denote the restrictions of the codes L and L^m (respectively) to the coordinates corresponding to the parties in H. Let U' denote the restriction of U to the coordinates held by the parties in H. Then $d(U', L'^m) \leq t$, and there exists a unique codeword $\widetilde{U} \in L'^m$ that agrees with U' on $H - \Delta(U', L'^m)$.
- **Secrecy.** For every x, x', and any subset $T \subseteq [k], |T| \leq t$, we have $\mathsf{View}_T(x) \equiv \mathsf{View}_T(x')$, where $\mathsf{View}_T(x)$ denotes the view of the parties in T in an execution of the protocol on a random encoding U of x (i.e., U is random subject to $\mathsf{Dec}_\zeta(U) = x$), in which the prover and the verifeirs $\mathcal{V}_i, i \notin T$ are honest.

4 dZK Proofs from Secure MPC Protocols

In this section we describe our dZK proofs and prove Theorem 1. Instantiations and extentions can be found in the full version [HVW22].

Overview of the dZK Proof System. Let $\mathcal{R} = \mathcal{R}(x, w)$ be a relation over $\mathbb{F}$. Our dZK proves membership in the corresponding k-distributed relation $\widehat{\mathcal{R}}_{\mathsf{RRS}}$ (see Definition 2 in Sect. 2, and Definition 13 in Sect. 3). Roughly, we employ the MPC-in-the-head paradigm in the following way. The prover generates the proof by emulating "in its head" an MPC protocol Π which checks membership in $\widehat{\mathcal{R}}_{\mathsf{RRS}}$. More specifically, Π is a $(k+1)$-party protocol between $\mathcal{P}_0, \ldots, \mathcal{P}_k$, in which every $\mathcal{P}_i, i > 0$ has input $x^{(i)}$ and $\mathcal{P}_0$ holds a corresponding witness w, and the protocols checks whether $((x^{(1)}, \ldots, x^{(k)}), w) \in \widehat{\mathcal{R}}_{\mathsf{RRS}}$. The emulation of Π results in views $\mathsf{View}_0, \ldots, \mathsf{View}_k$ of the parties, and the prover sends $\mathsf{View}_i, i \in [k]$ to $\mathcal{V}_i$ (notice that View_0 is not given to any verifier). The verifiers then verify the proof by performing the following. First, they run the IRS test (Fig. 1) to verify that their input pieces are close to an RRS codeword. If so, the verifiers call $\mathcal{F}_{\mathsf{coin}}$ to sample a public random value r which will be used when checking pairwise consistency of the views. More specifically, every pair of verifiers exchange short authentication tags which are computed from their views using r. The proof is accepted if these checks pass, allowing for a small (at most t) number of "errors". This "error tolerance" is essential to guaranteeing strong completeness, namely that corrupted verifiers cannot "frame" an honest prover. We note that this "error tolerance" significantly complicates the soundness analysis. Indeed, even if an inconsistency was revealed, the verifiers cannot immediately reject because that might violate strong completeness. The soundness analysis thus needs to show that a malicious prover cannot exploit the error tolerance to convince verifiers of false claims.

Theorem 5 (dZK from MPC-in-the-Head). Let $t_p, t_r, k \in \mathbb{N}$ such that $k > 6t_r + 2$. Let $\widehat{\mathcal{R}}_{\mathsf{RRS}}$ be a k-distributed relation over a field $\mathbb{F}$, and let Π be a perfectly

---

dZK from Secure MPC Protocols

For an NP relation $\mathcal{R}$ over $\mathbb{F}$, let $\widehat{\mathcal{R}}_{\mathsf{RRS}}$ be the corresponding k-distributed relation (see Definition 2, and Definition 13), and let $\widehat{\mathcal{L}} := \widehat{\mathcal{L}}\left(\widehat{\mathcal{R}}_{\mathsf{RRS}}\right).^{a}$ The dZK proof system is executed between a prover $\mathcal{P}$ and k verifiers $\mathcal{V}_1, \ldots, \mathcal{V}_k$. It employs a $(k+1)$-party MPC protocol Π for $\widehat{\mathcal{R}}_{\mathsf{RRS}}$, and is parameterized by a bound $t < (k-2)/6$ on the number of corrupt verifiers.

Proof Generation. The prover $\mathcal{P}$ on input $\left(\left(x^{(1)}, \ldots, x^{(k)}\right), w\right) \in \widehat{\mathcal{R}}_{\mathsf{RRS}}$ operates as follows:

1. Runs Π "in its head" with parties $P_0, P_1, \ldots, P_k$ holding inputs $w, x^{(1)}, \ldots, x^{(k)}$ (respectively).^{b} That is, it honestly emulates the operations of all parties in Π. Let $\mathsf{View}_1, \ldots, \mathsf{View}_k$ denotes the views of $P_1, \ldots, P_k$ in this execution, *excluding their inputs*. That is, P_i's view consists of its coin tosses, and all the messages it received throughout the execution.
2. For every pair $i < j$ of verifiers, picks $r_{ij} \leftarrow \mathbb{F}$.
3. Emulates the prover in Step 1. of the IRS test of Figure 1 (with $\ell = 1$) to generate the messages $\mathsf{m}_1, \ldots, \mathsf{m}_k$ which the prover sends to $\mathcal{V}_1, \ldots, \mathcal{V}_k$.
4. For every $i \in [k]$, sends $\mathsf{View}_i, \{r_{ij}\}_{i<j}, \{r_{ji}\}_{j<i}, \mathsf{m}_i$ to $\mathcal{V}_i$.

Verification.

1. The verifiers execute the IRS test of Figure 1 (with $\ell = 1$) on their input pieces $x^{(1)}, \ldots, x^{(k)}$, using $\mathsf{m}_1, \ldots, \mathsf{m}_k$ as the messages from $\mathcal{P}$. For each $\mathcal{V}_i$, if the i'th verifier rejects in the IRS test then $\mathcal{V}_i$ outputs reject.
2. The verifiers call $\mathcal{F}_{\mathsf{coin}}$ to obtain a random $r \in_R \mathbb{F}$.
3. Every $\mathcal{V}_i$ performs the following, for every $j \neq i$. Let $z_1^j, \ldots, z_l^j$ denote the field elements exchanged between P_i, P_j in the execution of Π, as they appear in View_i. (The messages from P_j to P_i appear in View_i. The messages from P_i to P_j can be computed from View_i.) Let $r'_{ij} := r_{ij}$ if $i < j$, otherwise $r'_{ij} := r_{ji}$. Then $\mathcal{V}_i$ broadcasts $m_{ij} := p_{ij}(r)$ where $p_{ij}(x) := \sum_{f=1}^{l} z_f^j \cdot x^f + r'_{ij}$.
4. Every $\mathcal{V}_i$ checks local consistency of View_i, by checking that the output of P_i given input $x^{(i)}$ and the messages reported in View_i is 1. If View_i is not locally consistent then $\mathcal{V}_i$ broadcasts a complaint against $\mathcal{P}$ and rejects. Let C_1 denote the set of verifiers who broadcasted a complaint against $\mathcal{P}.^{c}$
5. $\mathcal{P}$ broadcasts a set C_2 of parties which it claims are corrupted (i.e., broadcasted false m_{ij} values). Let $\mathsf{C} := \mathsf{C}_1 \cup \mathsf{C}_2$.
6. Every verifier $\mathcal{V}_i$ checks that:
   (a) $|\mathsf{C}| \leq t$.
   (b) for every $j, l \notin \mathsf{C}$, $m_{jl} = m_{lj}$.
   If $i \in \mathsf{C}_1$ or one of the tests failed, then $\mathcal{V}_i$ outputs reject. Otherwise, it outputs accept.

---

^{a} We note that $\widehat{\mathcal{L}}$ is a subset of the code obtained by instantiating Definition 10 with the RRS code; this is because in $\widehat{\mathcal{L}}$, not only is every column a RRS codeword, but the underlying encoded message is also in $\mathcal{L}$.
^{b} We note that if $\mathcal{R}$ is a relation in P then Π can be a protocol for k parties $P_1, \ldots, P_k$.
^{c} We note that Steps 3. and 4. can be implemented in a single round.

Fig. 2. A t-dZK Protocol for $k > 6t + 2$

*correct, (ε_p, t_p)-private and perfectly $(3t_r + 1)$-robust k-party protocol for $\widehat{\mathcal{R}}_{\mathsf{RRS}}$.
Then the proof system Π_{dist} of Fig. 2 is an $(\varepsilon_p, \varepsilon_r, t_p, t_r)$-dZK for $\widehat{\mathcal{L}}\left(\widehat{\mathcal{R}}_{\mathsf{RRS}}\right)$, for*

$$\varepsilon_r = \max\left\{\varepsilon', \binom{k}{2}\frac{N}{|\mathbb{F}|}\right\}$$

*where ε' denotes the error of the IRS test (specified in Theorem 4), and N bounds
the total number of field elements exchanged between a pair of parties in Π.*

Due to space limitations, we defer several remarks, extensions and instantiations, as well as a dZK with improved threshold (but without strong completeness), to the full version [HVW22].

Acknowledgment. We thank Benny Applebaum for helpful discussions and for pointing out to us the reduction from VRS to dZK. The first and third authors are supported by the BIU Center for Research in Applied Crypytography and Cyber Security in conjunction with the Israel National Cyber Bureau in the Prime Minister's Office. The first author is supported by ISF grant No. 1316/18. The first and second authors are supported by DARPA under Contract No. HR001120C0087. Any opinions, findings and conclusions or recommendations expressed in this material are those of the author(s) and do not necessarily reflect the views of the United States Government or DARPA. The first author is supported by the Algorand Centres of Excellence programme managed by Algorand Foundation. Any opinions, findings, and conclusions or recommendations expressed in this material are those of the author(s) and do not necessarily reflect the views of Algorand Foundation.

References

[AHIV17] Ames, S., Hazay, C., Ishai, Y., Venkitasubramaniam, M.: Ligero: lightweight sublinear arguments without a trusted setup. In: CCS, pp. 2087–2104 (2017)

[AKP20] Applebaum, B., Kachlon, E., Patra, A.: The resiliency of MPC with low interaction: the benefit of making errors (extended abstract). In: Pass, R., Pietrzak, K. (eds.) TCC 2020. LNCS, vol. 12551, pp. 562–594. Springer, Cham (2020). https://doi.org/10.1007/978-3-030-64378-2_20

[AKP22] Applebaum, B., Kachlon, E., Patra, A.: Verifiable relation sharing and multi-verifier zero-knowledge in two rounds: trading NIZKs with honest majority: (extended abstract). In: Dodis, Y., Shrimpton, T. (eds.) Advances in Cryptology – CRYPTO 2022, Part IV, pp. 33–56. Springer, Cham (2022). https://doi.org/10.1007/978-3-031-15985-5_2

[App22] Benny Applebaum. Private communication (2022)

[BBC+19a] Boneh, D., Boyle, E., Corrigan-Gibbs, H., Gilboa, N., Ishai, Y.: How to prove a secret: zero-knowledge proofs on distributed data via fully linear PCPs. IACR Cryptol. ePrint Arch. 188 (2019)

[BBC+19b] Boneh, D., Boyle, E., Corrigan-Gibbs, H., Gilboa, N., Ishai, Y.: Zero-knowledge proofs on secret-shared data via fully linear PCPs. In: Boldyreva, A., Micciancio, D. (eds.) CRYPTO 2019. LNCS, vol. 11694, pp. 67–97. Springer, Cham (2019). https://doi.org/10.1007/978-3-030-26954-8_3

[BBHR18] Ben-Sasson, E., Bentov, I., Horesh, Y., Riabzev, M.: Fast Reed-Solomon interactive oracle proofs of proximity. In: ICALP, pp. 14:1–14:17 (2018)

[BCI+20] Ben-Sasson, E., Carmon, D., Ishai, Y., Kopparty, S., Saraf, S.: Proximity gaps for Reed-Solomon codes. In: FOCS, pp. 900–909 (2020)

[BD91] Burmester, M., Desmedt, Y.: Broadcast interactive proofs. In: Davies, D.W. (ed.) EUROCRYPT 1991. LNCS, vol. 547, pp. 81–95. Springer, Heidelberg (1991). https://doi.org/10.1007/3-540-46416-6_7

[BFH+20] Bhadauria, R., Fang, Z., Hazay, C., Venkitasubramaniam, M., Xie, T., Zhang, Y.: Ligero++: a new optimized sublinear IOP. In: CCS, pp. 2025–2038 (2020)

[BGI16] Boyle, E., Gilboa, N., Ishai, Y.: Function secret sharing: improvements and extensions. In: CCS, pp. 1292–1303. ACM (2016)

[BGIN19] Boyle, E., Gilboa, N., Ishai, Y., Nof, A.: Practical fully secure three-party computation via sublinear distributed zero-knowledge proofs. In: CCS, pp. 869–886. ACM (2019)

[BGIN20] Boyle, E., Gilboa, N., Ishai, Y., Nof, A.: Efficient fully secure computation via distributed zero-knowledge proofs. In: Moriai, S., Wang, H. (eds.) ASIACRYPT 2020. LNCS, vol. 12493, pp. 244–276. Springer, Cham (2020). https://doi.org/10.1007/978-3-030-64840-4_9

[BGIN21] Boyle, E., Gilboa, N., Ishai, Y., Nof, A.: Sublinear GMW-style compiler for MPC with preprocessing. In: Malkin, T., Peikert, C. (eds.) CRYPTO 2021. LNCS, vol. 12826, pp. 457–485. Springer, Cham (2021). https://doi.org/10.1007/978-3-030-84245-1_16

[BJO+22] Baum, C., Jadoul, R., Orsini, E., Scholl, P., Smart, N.P.: Feta: efficient threshold designated-verifier zero-knowledge proofs. In: CCS, pp. 293–306. ACM (2022)

[BMMM20] Brandt, N.-P., Maier, S., Müller, T., Müller-Quade, J.: Constructing secure multi-party computation with identifiable abort. IACR Cryptol. ePrint Arch. 153 (2020)

[BOS16] Baum, C., Orsini, E., Scholl, P.: Efficient secure multiparty computation with identifiable abort. In: Hirt, M., Smith, A. (eds.) TCC 2016. LNCS, vol. 9985, pp. 461–490. Springer, Heidelberg (2016). https://doi.org/10.1007/978-3-662-53641-4_18

[BOSS20] Baum, C., Orsini, E., Scholl, P., Soria-Vazquez, E.: Efficient constant-round MPC with identifiable abort and public verifiability. In: Micciancio, D., Ristenpart, T. (eds.) CRYPTO 2020. LNCS, vol. 12171, pp. 562–592. Springer, Cham (2020). https://doi.org/10.1007/978-3-030-56880-1_20

[Bra21] Brandt, N.: Tight setup bounds for identifiable abort. IACR Cryptol. ePrint Arch. 684 (2021)

[CB17] Corrigan-Gibbs, H., Boneh, D.: Prio: private, robust, and scalable computation of aggregate statistics. In: USENIX, pp. 259–282 (2017)

[CBM15] Corrigan-Gibbs, H., Boneh, D., Mazières, D.: Riposte: an anonymous messaging system handling millions of users. In: SP, pp. 321–338 (2015)

[CDG+17] Chase, M., et al.: Post-quantum zero-knowledge and signatures from symmetric-key primitives. In: CCS, pp. 1825–1842 (2017)

[CFY17] Cunningham, R.K., Fuller, B., Yakoubov, S.: Catching MPC cheaters: identification and openability. In: ICITS, pp. 110–134 (2017)

[CL14] Cohen, R., Lindell, Y.: Fairness versus guaranteed output delivery in secure multiparty computation. In: Sarkar, P., Iwata, T. (eds.) ASIACRYPT 2014. LNCS, vol. 8874, pp. 466–485. Springer, Heidelberg (2014). https://doi.org/10.1007/978-3-662-45608-8_25

[Cle86] Cleve, R.: Limits on the security of coin flips when half the processors are faulty (extended abstract). In: STOC (1986)

[DI06] Damgård, I., Ishai, Y.: Scalable secure multiparty computation. In: Dwork, C. (ed.) CRYPTO 2006. LNCS, vol. 4117, pp. 501–520. Springer, Heidelberg (2006). https://doi.org/10.1007/11818175_30

[GIKR02] Gennaro, R., Ishai, Y., Kushilevitz, E., Rabin, T.: On 2-round secure multiparty computation. In: Yung, M. (ed.) CRYPTO 2002. LNCS, vol. 2442, pp. 178–193. Springer, Heidelberg (2002). https://doi.org/10.1007/3-540-45708-9_12

[GMO16] Giacomelli, I., Madsen, J., Orlandi, C.: ZKBoo: faster zero-knowledge for boolean circuits. In: USENIX, pp. 1069–1083 (2016)

[GMR85] Goldwasser, S., Micali, S., Rackoff, C.: The knowledge complexity of interactive proof-systems (extended abstract). In: STOC, pp. 291–304. ACM (1985)

[GMW87] Goldreich, O., Micali, S., Wigderson, A.: How to play any mental game or a completeness theorem for protocols with honest majority. In: STOC, pp. 218–229. ACM (1987)

[GO07] Groth, J., Ostrovsky, R.: Cryptography in the multi-string model. In: Menezes, A. (ed.) CRYPTO 2007. LNCS, vol. 4622, pp. 323–341. Springer, Heidelberg (2007). https://doi.org/10.1007/978-3-540-74143-5_18

[GSV21] Gvili, Y., Scheffler, S., Varia, M.: BooLigero: improved sublinear zero knowledge proofs for boolean circuits. In: Borisov, N., Diaz, C. (eds.) FC 2021. LNCS, vol. 12674, pp. 476–496. Springer, Heidelberg (2021). https://doi.org/10.1007/978-3-662-64322-8_23

[HVW22] Hazay, C., Venkitasubramaniam, M., Weiss, M.: Your reputation's safe with me: framing-free distributed zero-knowledge proofs. IACR Cryptol. ePrint Arch. 2022(1523) (2022). https://eprint.iacr.org/2022/1523

[IKOS07] Ishai, Y., Kushilevitz, E., Ostrovsky, R., Sahai, A.: Zero-knowledge from secure multiparty computation, pp. 21–30. In: STOC (2007)

[IOZ14] Ishai, Y., Ostrovsky, R., Zikas, V.: Secure multi-party computation with identifiable abort. In: Garay, J.A., Gennaro, R. (eds.) CRYPTO 2014. LNCS, vol. 8617, pp. 369–386. Springer, Heidelberg (2014). https://doi.org/10.1007/978-3-662-44381-1_21

[IW14] Ishai, Y., Weiss, M.: Probabilistically checkable proofs of proximity with zero-knowledge. In: Lindell, Y. (ed.) TCC 2014. LNCS, vol. 8349, pp. 121–145. Springer, Heidelberg (2014). https://doi.org/10.1007/978-3-642-54242-8_6

[KKW18] Katz, J., Kolesnikov, V., Wang, X.: Improved non-interactive zero knowledge with applications to post-quantum signatures. In: CCS, pp. 525–537 (2018)

[SF16] Spini, G., Fehr, S.: Cheater detection in SPDZ multiparty computation. In: Nascimento, A.C.A., Barreto, P. (eds.) ICITS 2016. LNCS, vol. 10015, pp. 151–176. Springer, Cham (2016). https://doi.org/10.1007/978-3-319-49175-2_8

[SSY22] Simkin, M., Siniscalchi, L., Yakoubov, S.: On sufficient oracles for secure computation with identifiable abort. In: Galdi, C., Jarecki, S. (eds.) Security and Cryptography for Networks: 13th International Conference, SCN 2022, Proceedings, pp. 494–515. Springer, Cham (2022). https://doi.org/10.1007/978-3-031-14791-3_22

[YW22] Yang, K., Wang, X.: Non-interactive zero-knowledge proofs to multiple verifiers. In: Agrawal, S., Lin, D. (eds.) Advances in Cryptology – ASIACRYPT 2022. LNCS, vol. 13793, pp. 517–546. Springer, Cham (2022). https://doi.org/10.1007/978-3-031-22969-5_18

Locally Verifiable Distributed SNARGs

Eden Aldema Tshuva[1]([✉]), Elette Boyle[2,3], Ran Cohen[2], Tal Moran[2],
and Rotem Oshman[1]

[1] Tel-Aviv University, Tel Aviv, Israel
{aldematshuva,roshman}@tau.ac.il
[2] Reichman University, Herzliya, Israel
{elette.boyle,cohenran,talm}@runi.ac.il
[3] NTT Research, Sunnyvale, USA

Abstract. The field of *distributed certification* is concerned with certifying properties of distributed networks, where the communication topology of the network is represented as an arbitrary graph; each node of the graph is a separate processor, with its own internal state. To certify that the network satisfies a given property, a prover assigns each node of the network a certificate, and the nodes then communicate with one another and decide whether to accept or reject. We require *soundness* and *completeness*: the property holds if and only if there exists an assignment of certificates to the nodes that causes all nodes to accept. Our goal is to minimize the length of the certificates, as well as the communication between the nodes of the network. Distributed certification has been extensively studied in the distributed computing community, but it has so far only been studied in the information-theoretic setting, where the prover and the network nodes are computationally unbounded.

In this work we introduce and study computationally bounded distributed certification: we define *locally verifiable distributed* SNARGs (LVD-SNARGs), which are an analog of SNARGs for distributed networks, and are able to circumvent known hardness results for information-theoretic distributed certification by requiring both the prover and the verifier to be computationally efficient (namely, PPT algorithms).

We give two LVD-SNARG constructions: the first allows us to succinctly certify any network property in P, using a global prover that can see the entire network; the second construction gives an efficient distributed prover, which succinctly certifies the execution of any efficient distributed algorithm. Our constructions rely on non-interactive batch arguments for NP (BARGs) and on RAM SNARGs, which have recently been shown to be constructible from standard cryptographic assumptions.

R. Oshman's research is supported by ISF grant no. 2801/20. E. Boyle's research is supported in part by AFOSR Award FA9550-21-1-0046 and ERC Project HSS (852952). R. Cohen's research is supported in part by NSF grant no. 2055568 and by the Algorand Centres of Excellence programme managed by Algorand Foundation. Any opinions, findings, and conclusions or recommendations expressed in this material are those of the authors and do not necessarily reflect the views of Algorand Foundation. T. Moran's research is supported by ISF grant no. 2337/22.

G. Rothblum and H. Wee (Eds.): TCC 2023, LNCS 14369, pp. 65–90, 2023.
https://doi.org/10.1007/978-3-031-48615-9_3

1   Introduction

Distributed algorithms are algorithms that execute on multiple processors, with each processor carrying out part of the computation and often seeing only part of the input. This class of algorithms encompasses a large variety of scenarios and computation models, ranging from a single computer cluster to large-scale distributed networks such as the internet. Distributed algorithms are notoriously difficult to design: in addition to the inherent unpredictability that results from having multiple processors that are usually not tightly coordinated, distributed algorithms are required to be robust and fault-tolerant, coping with an environment that can change over time. Moreover, distributed computation introduces bottlenecks that are not present in centralized computation, including *communication* and *synchronization* costs, which can sometimes outweigh the cost of local computation at each processor. All of these reasons make distributed algorithms hard to design and to reason about.

In this work we study *distributed certification*, a mechanism that is useful for ensuring correctness and fault-tolerance in distributed algorithms: the goal is to efficiently check, on demand, whether the system is in a legal state or not (here, "legal" varies depending on the particular algorithm and its purpose). To that end, we compute in advance auxiliary information in the form of *certificates* stored at the processors, and we design an efficient *verification procedure* that allows the processors to interact with one another and use their certificates to verify that the system is in a legal state. The certificates are computed once, and therefore we are traditionally less interested in how hard they are to compute; however, the verification procedure may be executed many times to check whether the system state is legal, and therefore it must be highly efficient. Since we do not trust that the system is in a legal state, we think of the certificates as given by a *prover*, whose goal is to convince us that the system is in a legal state even when it is not. One can therefore view distributed certification as a distributed analog of NP.

Distributed certification has recently received extensive attention in the context of *distributed network algorithms*, which execute in a network comprising many nodes (processors) that communicate over point-to-point communication links. The communication topology of the network is modeled as an arbitrary undirected network graph, where each node is a vertex; the edges of the graph represent bidirectional communication links. The goal of a network algorithm is to solve some global problem related to the network topology, and so the network graph is in some sense both the input to the computation and also the medium over which the computation is carried out. Typical tasks in this setting include setting up network infrastructure such as low-weight spanning trees or subgraphs, scheduling and routing, and various forms of resource allocation; see the textbook [Pel00] for many examples. We usually assume that the network nodes initially know only their own unique identifier (UID), their immediate neighbors, and possibly a small amount of global information about the network, such as its size or its diameter. An efficient network algorithm will typically have each node learn as little as possible about the network as a whole, as this requires both communication and time. This is sometimes referred to as *locality* [Pel00].

Distributed certification arises naturally in the context of fault tolerance and correctness in network algorithms (even in early work, e.g., [APV91]), but it was first formalized as an object of independent interest in [KKP05]. A certification scheme for a network property $\mathcal{P}$ (for example, "the local states of the network nodes encode a valid spanning tree of the network") consists of a *prover*, which is usually thought of as unbounded, and a *verification procedure*, which is an efficient distributed algorithm that uses the certificates. Here, "efficiency" can take many forms (see the textbook [Pel00] for some), but it is traditionally measured only in *communication* and in *number of synchronized communication rounds*, not in local computation at the nodes. (A *synchronized communication round*, or *round* for short, is a single interaction round during which each network node sends a possibly-different message on each of its edges, receives the messages sent by its neighbors, and performs some local computation.) At the end of the verification procedure, each network node outputs an acceptance bit, and the network as a whole is considered to accept if and only if all nodes accept; it suffices for one node to "raise the alarm" and reject in order to indicate that there is a problem. Our goal is to minimize the length of the certificates while providing soundness and completeness, that is — there should exist a certificate assignment that convinces all nodes to accept if and only if the network satisfies the property $\mathcal{P}$.

To our knowledge, all prior work on distributed certification is in the information-theoretic setting: the prover and the network nodes are computationally unbounded, and we are concerned only with space (the length of the certificates) and communication (at verification time). As might be expected, some strong lower bounds are known: while any property of a communication topology on n nodes can be proven using $O(n^2)$-bit certificates by giving every node the entire network graph, it is shown in [GS16] that some properties do in fact require $\Omega(n^2)$-bit certificates in the deterministic setting, and similar results can be shown when the verification procedure can be randomized [FMO+19].

Our goal in this work is to circumvent the hardness of distributed certification in the information-theoretic setting by moving to the *computational setting*: we introduce and study *computationally sound distributed proofs*, which we refer to as *locally verifiable distributed* SNARGs (LVD-SNARGs), extending the centralized notion of a succinct non-interactive argument (SNARG).

Distributed SNARGs. In recent years, the fruitful line of work on delegation of computation has culminated in the construction of succinct, non-interactive arguments (SNARGs) for all properties in P [CJJ21b, WW22, KLVW23, CGJ+22]. A SNARG is a computationally sound proof system under which a PPT prover certifies a statement of the form "$x \in \mathcal{L}$", where x is an input and $\mathcal{L}$ is a language, by providing a PPT verifier with a short proof π. The verifier then examines the input x and the proof π, and decides (in polynomial time) whether to accept or reject. It is guaranteed that an honest prover can convince the verifier to accept any true statement with probability 1 (*perfect completeness*), and at the same time, no PPT cheating prover can convince the verifier to accept with non-negligible probability (*computational soundness*).

In this work, we first ask:

Can we construct locally verifiable distributed SNARGs *(LVD-SNARGs), a distributed analog of* SNARGs *which can be verified by an efficient (i.e., local) distributed algorithm?*

In contrast to prior work on distributed verification, here when we say "efficient" we mean in communication and in rounds, but also in computation, combining both distributed and centralized notions of efficiency. (We defer the precise definition of our model to Sect. 2.

We consider two types of provers: first, as a warm-up, we consider a *centralized prover*, which is a PPT algorithm that sees the entire network and computes succinct certificates for the nodes. We show that in this settings, there is an LVD-SNARG for any property in P, using RAM SNARGs [KP16, KLVW23] as our main building block.

The centralized prover can be applied in the distributed context by first collecting information about the entire network at one node, and having that node act as the prover and compute certificates for all the other nodes. However, this is very inefficient: for example, in terms of total communication, it is easy to see that collecting the entire network topology in one location may require $\Omega(n^2)$ bits of communication to flow on some edge. In contrast, "efficient" network algorithms use sublinear and even poly-logarithmic communication.[1] This motivates us to consider another type of prover – a *distributed* prover—and ask:

If a property can be decided by an efficient distributed algorithm, can it be succinctly certified by an efficient distributed prover?

Of course, we still require that the verifier be an efficient distributed algorithm, as in the case of the centralized prover above. We give a positive answer to this question as well: given a distributed algorithm $\mathcal{D}$, we construct a distributed prover that runs alongside $\mathcal{D}$ with low overhead (in communication and rounds), and produces succinct certificates at the network nodes.

We give more formal statements of our results in Sect. 1.3 below, but before doing so, we provide more context and background on distributed certification and on delegation of computation.

1.1   Background on Distributed Certification

The classical model for distributed certification was formally introduced by Korman, Kutten and Peleg in [KKP05] under the name *proof labeling schemes (PLS)*, but was already present implicitly in prior work on self-stabilization, such as [APV91]. To certify a property $\mathcal{P}$ of a network graph $G = (V, E)$,[2] we first run a *marker algorithm* (i.e., a prover), a computationally-unbounded algorithm that sees the entire network, to compute a proof in the form of a labeling $\ell : V \rightarrow \{0, 1\}^*$. We refer to these labels as *certificates*; each node $v \in V$ is given only its own certificate, $\ell(v)$. We refer to this as the *proving stage*.

---

[1] As just one example of many, in [KP98] it is shown that one can construct a k-dominating set of the network graph in $\tilde{O}(k)$ communication per edge, and this is used to construct a minimum-weight spanning tree in $\tilde{O}(\sqrt{n})$ communication per edge.

[2] In general, the nodes of the network may have *inputs*, on which the property may depend, but for simplicity we ignore inputs for the time being and discuss only properties of the graph topology itself.

Next, whenever we wish to verify that the property $\mathcal{P}$ holds, we carry out the *verification stage*: each node $v \in V$ sends its certificate $\ell(v)$ to its immediate neighbors in the graph. Then, each node examines its direct neighborhood, its certificates, and the certificate it received from its neighbors, and deterministically outputs an acceptance bit.

The proof is considered to be accepted if and only if all nodes accept it. During the verification stage, the nodes are honest; however, the prover may not be honest during the proving stage, and in general it can assign arbitrary certificates to any and all nodes in the network. We require *soundness* and *completeness*: the property $\mathcal{P}$ holds if and only if there exists an assignment of certificates to the nodes that causes all nodes to accept.

The focus in the area of distributed certification is on schemes that use short certificates. Even short certificates can be extremely helpful: to illustrate, and to familiarize the reader with the model, we describe a scheme from [KKP05] for certifying the correctness of a spanning tree: each node $v \in V$ is given a parent pointer $p_v \in V \cup \{\bot\}$, and our goal is to certify that the subgraph induced by these pointers, $\{(v, p_v) : v \in V \text{ and } p_v \neq \bot\}$, is a spanning tree of the network graph G. In the scheme from [KKP05], each node $v \in V$ is given a certificate $\ell(v) = (r_v, d_v)$, containing the following information:

- The purported name r_v of the root of the tree, and
- The distance d_v of v from the root r_v.

(Note that even though the tree has a single root, the prover can try to cheat by claiming different roots at different nodes, and hence we use the notation r_v for the root given to node v.) To verify, the nodes send their certificates to their neighbors, and check that:

- Their root r_v is the same as the root r_u given to each neighbor u, and
- If $p_v \neq \bot$, then $d_{p_v} = d_v - 1$, and if $p_v = \bot$, then $d_v = 0$.

This guarantees the correctness of the spanning tree,[3] and requires only $O(\log n)$-bit certificates, where n is the number of nodes in the network; the verification stage incurs communication $O(\log n)$ on every edge, and requires only one round (each node sends one message to each neighbor). In contrast, *generating* a spanning tree from scratch requires $\Omega(D)$ communication rounds, where D is the diameter of the network; *verifying without certificates* that a given (claimed) spanning tree is correct requires $\tilde{\Omega}(\sqrt{n}/B)$ communication rounds, if each node is allowed to send B bits on every edge in every round [SHK+12].

The original model of [KKP05] is highly restricted: it does not allow randomization, and it allows only one round of communication, during which each node sends its certificate to all of its neighbors (this is the only type of message allowed). Subsequent work studied many variations on this basic model, featuring different generalizations and communication constraints during the verification stage (e.g., [GS16, OPR17, PP17, FFH+21, BFO22]), different restrictions on how certificates may depend

---

[3] Assuming the underlying network is connected, which is a standard assumption in the area; otherwise additional information, such as the size of the network, is required.

on the nodes' identifiers (e.g., [FHK12, FGKS13, BDFO18]), restricted classes of properties and network graphs (e.g., [FBP22, FMRT22]), allowing randomization [FPP19, FMO+19] or interaction with the prover (e.g., [KOS18, NPY20, BKO22]), and in the case of [BKO22], also preserving the privacy of the nodes using a distributed notion of zero knowledge. We refer to the survey [Feu21] for an overview of much of the work in this area.

To our knowledge, all work on distributed certification so far has been in the *information-theoretic* setting, which requires soundness against a computationally unbounded prover, and does not take the local computation time of either the prover or the verifier into consideration as a complexity measure (with one exception, [AO22], where the running time of the nodes is considered, but perfect soundness is still required). Information-theoretic certification is bound to run up against barriers arising from communication complexity: it is easy to construct synthetic properties that essentially encode lower bounds from nondeterministic or Merlin-Arthur communication complexity into a graph problem. More interestingly, it is possible to use reductions from communication complexity to prove lower bounds on some natural problems: for example, in [GS16] it was shown that $\Omega(n^2)$-bit certificates are required to prove the existence of a non-trivial automorphism, or non-3-colorability. In addition to this major drawback, in the information-theoretic setting there is no clear connection between whether a property is efficiently checkable in the traditional sense (P, or even NP) and whether it admits a short distributed proof: even computationally easy properties, such as "the network has diameter at most k" (for some constant k), or "the identifiers of the nodes in the network are unique," are known to require $\tilde{\Omega}(n)$-bit certificates [FMO+19]. (These lower bounds are, again, proven by reduction from 2-party communication complexity.) In this work we show that introducing computational assumptions allows us to efficiently certify any property in P, overcoming the limitations of the information-theoretic model.

1.2 Background on Delegation of Computation

Computationally sound proof systems were introduced in the seminal work of Micali [Mic00], who gave a construction for such proofs in an idealized model, the random-oracle model (ROM). Following Micali's work, extensive effort went into obtaining non-interactive arguments (SNARGs) in models that are closer to the plain model, such as the *Common Reference String* (CRS) model. Earlier work in this line of research, such as [ABOR00, DLN+04, DL08, Gro10, BCCT12], relied on *knowledge assumptions*, which are non-falsifiable; for languages in NP, Gentry and Wichs [GW11] proved that relying on non-falsifiable assumptions is unavoidable. This led the research community to focus some attention on delegating efficient deterministic computation, that is, computation in P.

Initial progress on delegating computation in P assumed the weaker model of a *designated verifier*, where the verifier holds some secret that is related to the CRS [KRR13, KRR14, KP16, BKK+18, HR18]. However, a recent line of work has led to the construction of publicly-verifiable SNARGs for deterministic computation, first for space-bounded computation [KPY19, JKKZ21] and then for general polynomial-time computation [CJJ21a, WW22, KLVW23]. These latter constructions exploit a connection to *non-interactive batch arguments for* NP (BARGs), which can be constructed from various standard cryptographic assumptions [BHK17, CJJ21a, WW22, KLVW23, CGJ+22]. We use BARGs as the basis for the distributed prover that we construct in Sect. 4.

1.3 Our Results

We are now ready to give a more formal overview of our results, although the full formal definitions are deferred to the Sect. 2. For simplicity, in this overview we restrict attention to network properties that concern only the topology of the network—in other words, in the current section, a property $\mathcal{P}$ is a family of undirected graphs. (In the more general case, a property can also involve the internal states of the network nodes, as in the spanning tree example from Sect. 1.1. This will be discussed in the Technical Overview.)

Defining LVD-SNARGs. Like centralized SNARGs, LVD-SNARGs are defined in the common reference string (CRS) model, where the prover and the verifier both have access to a shared unbiased source of randomness.

An LVD-SNARG for a property $\mathcal{P}$ consists of

- A *prover algorithm*: given a network graph $G = (V, E)$ of size $|V| = n$ and the common reference string (CRS), the prover algorithm outputs an assignment of $O(\text{poly}(\lambda, \log n))$-bit certificates to the nodes of the network. The prover may be either a PPT centralized algorithm, or a distributed algorithm that executes in G in a polynomial number of rounds, sends messages of polynomial length on every edge, and involves only PPT computations at each network node. [4]
- A *verifier algorithm*: the verifier algorithm is a one-round distributed algorithm, where each node of the network simultaneously sends a (possibly different) message of length $O(\text{poly}(\lambda, \log n))$ on each of its edges, receives the messages sent by its neighbors, carries out some local computation, and then outputs an acceptance bit.
  Each message sent by a node is produced by a PPT algorithm that takes as input the CRS, the certificate stored at the node, and the input and neighborhood of the node; the acceptance bit is produced by a PPT algorithm that takes the CRS, the certificate of the node, the messages received from its neighbors, the input and the neighborhood.

We require that certificates produced by an honest execution of the prover in the network be accepted by all verifiers with overwhelming probability, whereas for any graph failing to satisfy the property $\mathcal{P}$, certificates produced by any poly-time cheating prover (allowing stronger, centralized provers in both cases) will be rejected by at least one node with overwhelming probability, as a function of the security parameter λ.[5] We refer the reader to Sect. 2.1 for the formal definition.

---

[4] In fact, as we mentioned in Sect. 1, a centralized prover can also be implemented by a distributed algorithm where one node learns the entire network graph and then generates the certificates. This is easy to do in polynomial rounds and message length.

[5] The schemes we construct actually satisfy *adaptive* soundness: there is no PPT algorithm that can, with non-negligible probability, output a network graph and certificates for all the nodes, such that the property does not hold for the network graph but all of the nodes accept.

LVD-SNARGs *with a global prover.* We begin by considering a global (i.e., centralized) prover, which sees the entire network graph G. In this setting, we give a very simple construction that makes black-box use of the recently developed RAM SNARGs for P [KP16, CJJ21b, KLVW23, CGJ+22] to obtain the following:

Theorem 1. *Assuming the existence of* RAM SNARGs *for* P *and collision-resistant hash families, for any property* $\mathcal{P} \in$ P*, there is an* LVD-SNARG *with a global prover.*

LVD-SNARG *s with a distributed prover.* As explained in Sect. 1, one of the main motivations for distributed certification is to be able to quickly check that the network is in a legal state. One natural special case is to check whether the results of a previously executed distributed algorithm are still correct, or whether they have been rendered incorrect by changes or faults in the network. To this end, we ask whether we can augment any given computationally efficient distributed algorithm $\mathcal{D}$ with a *distributed prover*, which runs alongside $\mathcal{D}$ and produces an LVD-SNARG certifying the execution of $\mathcal{D}$ in the specific network. The distributed prover may add some additional overhead in communication and in rounds, but we would like the overhead to be small.

We show that indeed this is possible:

Theorem 2. *Let* $\mathcal{D}$ *be a distributed algorithm that runs in* $\mathrm{poly}(n)$ *rounds in networks of size* n*, where in each round, every node sends a* $\mathrm{poly}(\log n)$*-bit message on every edge, receives the messages sent by its neighbors in the current round, and then carries out* $\mathrm{poly}(n)$ *local computation steps.*

Assuming the existence of BARGs *for* NP *and collision-resistant hash families, there exists an augmented distributed algorithm* $\mathcal{D}'$*, which carries out the same computation as* $\mathcal{D}$*, but also produces an* LVD-SNARG *certificate attesting that* $\mathcal{D}$*'s output is correct.*

- *The overhead of* $\mathcal{D}'$ *compared to* $\mathcal{D}$ *is an additional* $O(\mathrm{diam}(G))$ *rounds, during which each node sends only* $\mathrm{poly}(\lambda, \log n)$*-bit messages, for security parameter* λ*.*
- *The certificates produced are of size* $\mathrm{poly}(\lambda, \log n)$*.*

Using known constructions of RAM SNARGs for P and of SNARGs for batch-NP [CJJ21b, CJJ21a, WW22, KLVW23, CGJ+22], we obtain both types of LVD-SNARGs (global or distributed prover) for P from either LWE, DLIN, or subexponential DDH.

Distributed Merkle trees (DMTs). To construct our distributed prover, we develop a data structure that we call a *distributed Merkle tree* (DMT), which is essentially a global Merkle tree of a distributed collection of $2|E|$ values, with each node u initially holding a value $x_{u \to v}$ for each neighbor v. (At the "other end of the edge", node v also holds a value $x_{v \to u}$ for node v. There is no relation between the value $x_{u \to v}$ and the value $x_{v \to u}$.)

The unique property of the DMT is that it can be constructed by an efficient distributed algorithm, at the end of which each node u holds both the root of the global Merkle tree and a succinct opening to each value $x_{(u,v)}$ that it held initially.

The DMT is used in the construction of the LVD-SNARG of Theorem 2 to allow nodes to "refer" to messages sent by their neighbors. We cannot afford to have node v store these messages, or even a hash of the messages v received on each of its edges, as we do not want the certificates to grow linearly with the degree. Instead, we construct a DMT that allows nodes to "access" the messages sent by their neighbors: we let each value $x_{v \to u}$ be a hash of the messages sent by node v to node u, and construct a DMT over these hashes. When node u needs to "access" a message sent by v to construct its proof, node v produces the appropriate opening path from the root of the DMT, and sends it to node u. All of this happens implicitly, inside a BARG proof asserting that u's local computation is correct.

The remainder of the paper gives a technical overview of our results.

2 Model and Definitions

In this section, we give a more formal overview of our network model; this model is standard in the area of distributed network algorithms (see, e.g., the textbook [Pel00]). We then formally define LVD-SNARGs, the object we aim to construct.

Modeling Distributed Networks. A distributed network is modeled as an undirected, connected[6] graph $G = (V, E)$, where the nodes V of the network are the processors participating in the computation, and the edges E represent bidirectional communication links between them.

For a node $v \in V$, we denote by $N_G(v)$ (or by $N(v)$, if G is clear from context) the neighborhood of v in the graph G. The communication links (i.e., edges) of node v are indexed by *port numbers*, with $I_{u \to v} \in [n]$ denoting the port number of the channel from v to its neighbor u. The port numbers of a given node need not be contiguous, nor do they need to be symmetric (that is, it might be that $I_{v \to u} \neq I_{u \to v}$). We assume that the neighborhood $N(v)$ and the port numbering at node v are known to node v during the verification stage; the node does not necessarily need to have them stored in memory at the beginning of the verification stage, but it should be able to generate them at verification time (e.g., by probing its neighborhood, opening communication sessions with its neighbors one after the other; or, in the case of a wireless network, by running a neighbor-discovery protocol).

In addition to knowing their neighborhood, we assume that each node $v \in V$ has a unique identifier; for convenience we conflate the unique identifier of a node v with the vertex v representing v in the network graph. We assume that the UID is represented by a logarithmic number of bits in the size of the graph. No other information is available; in particular, we do not assume that the nodes know the size of the network, its diameter, or any other global properties.

A *(synchronous) distributed network algorithm* proceeds in synchronized rounds, where in each round, each node $v \in V$ sends a (possibly different) message on each edge $\{v, u\} \in E$. The nodes then receive the messages sent to them, perform some internal computation, and then the next round begins. Eventually, each node halts and produces some output.

---

[6] We consider only connected networks, since in disconnected networks one can never hope to carry out any computation involving more than one connected component. Also, it is fairly standard to assume an undirected graph topology, i.e., bidirectional communication links, although directed networks are also considered sometimes (for instance, in [BFO22]).

Distributed Decision Tasks. In the literature on distributed decision and certification, network properties are referred to as *distributed languages*. A distributed language is a family of *configurations* (G, x), where G is a network graph and $x : V \to \{0, 1\}^*$ assigns a string $x(v)$ to each node $v \in V$. The assignment x may represent, for example, the input to a distributed computation, or the internal states of the network nodes. We assume that $|x(v)|$ is polynomial of the size of the graph. We usually refer to x as an *input assignment*, since for our purposes it represents an input to the decision task.

A distributed decision algorithm is a distributed algorithm at the end of which each node of the network outputs an acceptance bit. The standard notion of *acceptance* in distributed decision [FKP13] is that the network accepts if and only if all nodes accept; if any node rejects, then the network is considered to have rejected.

Notation. When describing the syntax (interface) of a distributed algorithm, we describe the input to the algorithm as a triplet $(\alpha; G; \beta)$, where

- α is a value that is given to all the nodes in the network. Typically this will be the common reference string.
- $G = (V, E)$ is the network topology on which the algorithm runs.
- $\beta : V \to \{0, 1\}^*$ is a mapping assigning a local input to every network node. Each node $v \in V$ receives only $\beta(v)$ at the beginning of the algorithm, and does not initially know the local values $\beta(u)$ of other nodes $u \neq v$.

We frequently abuse notation by writing a sequence of values or mappings instead of a single one for α or β (respectively); e.g., when we write that the input to a distributed algorithm is $(a, b; G; x, y)$, we mean that every node $v \in V(G)$ is initially given $a, b, x(v), y(v)$, and the algorithm executes in the network described by the graph G.

The *output* of a distributed algorithm in a network $G = (V, E)$ is described by a mapping $o : V \to \{0, 1\}^*$ which specifies the output $o(v)$ of each node $v \in V$. In the case of *decision algorithms*, the output is a mapping $o : V \to \{0, 1\}$, and we say that the algorithm *accepts* if and only if all nodes output 1 (i.e., $\bigwedge_{v \in V} o(v) = 1$). We denote this event by "$\mathcal{D}(\alpha; G; \beta) = 1$", where $\mathcal{D}$ is the distributed algorithm, and $(\alpha; G; \beta)$ is its input (as explained above).

In general, when describing objects that depend on a specific graph G, we include G as a subscript: e.g., the neighborhood of node v in G is denoted $N_G(v)$. However, when G is clear from the context, we omit the subscript and write, e.g., $N(v)$.

2.1 Locally Verifiable Distributed SNARGs

In this section we give the formal definition of locally-verifiable distributed SNARGs (LVD-SNARGs). This definition allows for provers that are either global (centralized) or distributed.

Syntax. A locally verifiable distributed SNARG consists of the following algorithms.

$\mathsf{Gen}(1^\lambda, n) \to \mathsf{crs}$. A randomized algorithm that takes as input a security parameter 1^λ and a graph size n, and outputs a common reference string crs.

$\mathcal{P}(\text{crs}; G; x) \rightarrow \pi$. A deterministic algorithm (centralized or distributed)[7] that takes a crs obtained from $\text{Gen}(1^\lambda, n)$ and a configuration (G, x), and outputs an assignment of certificates to the nodes $\pi : V(G) \rightarrow \{0, 1\}^*$.

$\mathcal{V}(\text{crs}; G; x, \pi) \rightarrow b$. A *distributed decision algorithm* that takes a common reference string crs obtained from $\text{Gen}(1^\lambda, n)$, an input assignment $x : V \rightarrow \{0, 1\}^*$, and a proof $\pi : V \rightarrow \{0, 1\}^*$, and outputs acceptance bits $b : V \rightarrow \{0, 1\}^*$. In the distributed algorithm, each node v is initially given the crs, its own local input $x(v)$ (which is assumed to include its unique identifier), and its own proof $\pi(v)$. During the algorithm nodes communicate with their neighbors over synchronized rounds, and eventually each node produces its own acceptance bit $b(v)$.

Definition 1. *Let $\mathcal{L}$ be a distributed language. An* LVD-SNARG *$(\text{Gen}, \mathcal{P}, \mathcal{V})$ for $\mathcal{L}$ must satisfy the following properties:*

Completeness. For any $(G, x) \in \mathcal{L}$,

$$\Pr\left[\mathcal{V}(\text{crs}; G; x, \pi) = 1 \,\middle|\, \begin{array}{l} \text{crs} \leftarrow \text{Gen}(1^\lambda, n) \\ \pi \leftarrow \mathcal{P}(\text{crs}; G; x) \end{array} \right] = 1.$$

Soundness. For any PPT algorithm $\mathcal{P}^*$, there exists a negligible function $\text{negl}(\cdot)$ such that

$$\Pr\left[\begin{array}{l} (G, x) \notin \mathcal{L} \\ \wedge\, \mathcal{V}(\text{crs}; G; x, \pi) = 1 \end{array} \,\middle|\, \begin{array}{l} \text{crs} \leftarrow \text{Gen}(1^\lambda, n) \\ (G, x, \pi) \leftarrow \mathcal{P}^*(\text{crs}) \end{array} \right] \leq \text{negl}(\lambda).$$

Succinctness. The crs and the proof $\pi(v)$ at each node v are of length at most $\text{poly}(\lambda, \log n)$.

Verifier Efficiency. $\mathcal{V}$ runs in a single synchronized communication round, during which each node sends a (possibly different) message of length $\text{poly}(\lambda, \log n)$ to each neighbor. At each node v, the local computation executed by $\mathcal{V}$ runs in time $\text{poly}(\lambda, |\pi(v)|) = \text{poly}(\lambda, \log n)$.

Prover Efficiency. If the prover $\mathcal{P}$ is centralized, then it runs in time $\text{poly}(\lambda, n)$. If the prover $\mathcal{P}$ is distributed, then it runs in $\text{poly}(\lambda, n)$ rounds, sends messages of $\text{poly}(\lambda, \log n)$ bits, and uses $\text{poly}(\lambda, n)$ local computation time at every network node.

---

[7] For the centralized case, we denote $\mathcal{P}(\text{crs}, G, x)$ instead of $(\text{crs}; G; x)$ as we have one entity that receives the entire input.

3   LVD-SNARGs with a Global Prover

We begin by describing a simple construction for LVD-SNARGs with a global prover for any property in P. (When we refer to P here, we mean from the centralized point of view: a distributed language $\mathcal{L}$ is in P iff there is a deterministic poly-time Turing machine that takes as input a configuration (G, x) and accepts iff $(G, x) \in \mathcal{L}$.)

Throughout this overview, we assume for simplicity that the nodes of the network are named $V = \{1, \ldots, n\}$, with each node knowing its own name (but not necessarily the size n of the network).

Commit-and-Prove. Fix a language $\mathcal{L} \in$ P and an instance $(G, x) \in \mathcal{L}$. A global prover that sees the entire instance G can use a (centralized) SNARG for the language $\mathcal{L}$ in a black-box manner, to obtain a succinct proof for the statement "$(G, x) \in \mathcal{L}$." However, regular SNARGs (as opposed to RAM SNARGs) assume that the verifier *holds the entire input* whose membership in $\mathcal{L}$ it would like to verify; in our case, no single node knows the entire instance G, so we cannot use the verification procedure of the SNARG as-is.

Our simple work-around to the nodes' limited view of the network is to ask the prover to give the nodes a *commitment with local openings* C to the entire network graph (for instance, a Merkle tree [Mer89]), and to each node, a proof π_{SNARG} that the graph under the commitment is in the language $\mathcal{L}$.

Note that the language for which π_{SNARG} is a SNARG proof is a set of commitments, not of network configurations—it is the language of all commitments to configurations in $\mathcal{L}$. However, this leaves us with the burden of relating the commitment C to the true instance (G, x) in which the verifier executes, to ensure that the prover did not choose some arbitrary C that is unrelated to the instance at hand. To that end, we ask the prover to provide each node v with the following:

- The commitment C and proof π_{SNARG}. The nodes verify that they all received the same values by comparing with their neighbors, and they verify the SNARG proof π_{SNARG}.
- A succinct opening to v's neighborhood. Node v verifies that indeed, C opens to its true neighborhood $N(v)$.

Intuitively, by verifying that the commitment is consistent with the view of all the nodes, and by verifying the SNARG that the graph "under the commitment" is in the language $\mathcal{L}$, we verify that the true instance (G, x) is in fact in $\mathcal{L}$.

Although the language $\mathcal{L}$ is in P, if we proceed carelessly, we might find ourselves asking the prover to prove an NP-statement, such as "there exists a graph configuration (G, x) whose commitment is C, such that $(G, x) \in \mathcal{L}$." Moreover, to prove the soundness of such a scheme, we would need to *extract* the configuration (G, x) from the proof π_{SNARG}, in order to argue that a cheating adversary that produces a convincing proof of a false statement can be used to break either the SNARG or the commitment scheme. Essentially, we would require a SNARK, a succinct non-interactive argument *of knowledge* for NP, but significant barriers are known [GW11] on constructing SNARKs from standard assumptions. To avoid this, we use RAM SNARGs rather than plain SNARGs.

RAM SNARGs *for* P. A RAM SNARG ([KP16,BHK17]) is a SNARG that proves that a given RAM machine M^8 performs some computation correctly; however, instead of holding the input x to the computation, the verifier is given only a *digest* of x—a hash value, typically obtained from a hash family with local openings (for instance, the root of a Merkle tree of x). In our case, we ask the prover to use a polynomial-time machine $M_{\mathcal{L}}$ that decides $\mathcal{L}$ as the RAM machine for the SNARG, and the commitment C as the digest; the prover computes a RAM SNARG proof for the statement "$M_{\mathcal{L}}(G,x) = 1$."

Defining the soundness of RAM SNARGs is delicate: because the verifier is not given the full instance but only a digest of it, there is no well-defined notion of a "false statement"—a given digest d could be the digest of multiple instances, some of which satisfy the claim and some of which do not. However, the digest is collision resistant, so intuitively, it is hard for the adversary to *find* two instances that have the same digest. We adopt the original RAM SNARG soundness definition from [KP16,BHK17,KLVW23], which requires that it be computationally hard for an adversary to prove "contradictory statements"; given the common reference string, it must be hard for an adversary to find:

- A digest d, and
- Two different proofs π_0 and π_1, *which are both accepted with input digest d*, such that π_0 proves that the output of the computation is 0, and π_1 proves that the output of the computation is 1.

In our construction, the prover is asked to provide the nodes with a digest C, which is a commitment to the configuration (G, x), and a RAM SNARG proof π_{SNARG} for the statement "$(G, x) \in \mathcal{L}$," which the prover constructs using a RAM machine $M_{\mathcal{L}}$ that decides membership in $\mathcal{L}$ in polynomial time.

Tying the Digest to the Real Network Graph. By themselves, the digest C and the RAM SNARG proof π_{SNARG} do not say much about the actual instance (G, x) that we have at hand. As we explained above, we can relate the digest to the real network by having every node verify that it opens correctly to its local view (neighborhood). However, this is not quite enough: the prover can commit to (i.e., provide a digest of) a graph $G' \in \mathcal{L}$ that is *larger* than the true network graph G, such that G' agrees with G on the neighborhoods of all the "real nodes" (the nodes of G).[9] We prevent the prover from doing this by:

- Asking the prover to provide the nodes with the size n of the network, and a certificate proving that the size is indeed n. There is a simple and elegant scheme for doing this [KKP05], based on building and certifying a rooted spanning tree of the network; it has perfect soundness and completeness, and requires $O(\log n)$-bit certificates.

---

[8] A RAM machine M is given query access to an input x and an unbounded random-access memory array, and returns some output y. Each query to the input x or the memory is considered a unit-cost operation.

[9] This requires that G' not be connected, but that is not necessarily a problem for the prover, depending on the property $\mathcal{L}$.

- The Turing machine $M_{\mathcal{L}}$ that verifies membership in $\mathcal{L}$ is assumed to take its input in the form of an adjacency list $L_{G,x} = ((v_1, x(v_1), N(v_1)), \ldots, (v_n, x(v_n), N(v_n)), \bot)$, where $\bot$ is a special symbol marking the end of the list, and each triplet $(v_i, x(v_i), N(v_i))$ specifies a node v_i, its input $x(v_i)$, and its neighborhood $N(v_i)$. Since $\bot$ marks the end of the list, the machine $M_{\mathcal{L}}$ is assumed (without loss of generality) to ignore anything following the symbol $\bot$ in its input.
- Recall that we assumed for simplicity that $V = \{1, \ldots, n\}$. The prover computes a digest C of $L_{G,x}$, and gives each node i the opening to the ith entry. Each node verifies that its entry opens correctly to its local view (name, input, and neighborhood).
- The last node, node n, is also given the opening to the $(n + 1)^{th}$ entry, and verifies that it opens to $\bot$. Node n knows that it is the last node, because the prover gave all nodes the size n of the network (and certified it).

To prove the soundness of the resulting scheme, we show that if all nodes accept, then C is a commitment to some adjacency list L' which has $L_{G,x}$ as a prefix—in the format outlined above, including the end-of-list symbol $\bot$. Since the machine $M_{\mathcal{L}}$ interprets $\bot$ as the end of its input, it ignores anything past this point, and thus, the prover's SNARG proof is essentially a proof for the statement "$M_{\mathcal{L}}$ accepts (G, x)." If we assume for the sake of contradiction that $(G, x) \notin \mathcal{L}$ then we can generate an honest SNARG proof π_0 for the statement "$M_{\mathcal{L}}$ rejects (G, x)," using the same digest C, [10] and this breaks the soundness of the SNARG.

4   LVD-SNARGs with a Distributed Prover

One of the main motivations for distributed certification is to help build fault-tolerant distributed algorithms. In this setting, there is no omniscient global prover that can provide certificates to all the nodes. Instead, the labels must themselves be produced by a distributed algorithm, and comprise a proof that a previous execution phase completed successfully and that its outputs are still valid (in particular, they are still relevant given the current state of the communication graph and the network nodes). Formally, given a distributed algorithm $\mathcal{D}$, we want to construct a distributed prover $\mathcal{D}'$ that certifies the language

$$\mathcal{L}_{\mathcal{D}} = \left\{ (G, x, y) : \begin{array}{c} \text{when } \mathcal{D} \text{ executes in the network } G \\ \text{with inputs } x : V \to \{0, 1\}^*, \\ \text{it produces the outputs } y : V \to \{0, 1\}^* \end{array} \right\}.$$

Furthermore, $\mathcal{D}'$ should not have much overhead compared to $\mathcal{D}$ in terms of communication and rounds.

Certifying the execution of the distributed algorithm $\mathcal{D}$ essentially amounts to proving a collection of "local" statements, each asserting that at a specific node $v \in V(G)$, the algorithm $\mathcal{D}$ indeed produces the claimed output $y(v)$ when it executes in G. The

---

[10] This step is a little delicate, and relies on the fact that in recent RAM SNARG constructions (e.g., [CJJ21b, KLVW23]), completeness holds for any digest d that opens to the input instance at every location the RAM machine reads from.

prover at node v can record the local computation at node v as $\mathcal{D}$ executes, including the messages that node v sends and receives. As a first step towards certifying that $\mathcal{D}$ executes correctly, we could store at each node v a (centralized) SNARG proving that in every round, v produced the correct messages according to $\mathcal{D}$, handled incoming messages correctly, and performed its local computation correctly, eventually outputting $y(v)$. However, this does not suffice to guarantee that the *global* computation is correct, because we must verify consistency across the nodes: how can we be sure that incoming messages recorded at node v were indeed sent by v's neighbors when $\mathcal{D}$ ran, and vice-versa?

A naïve solution would be for node v to record, for each neighbor $u \in N(v)$, a hash $H_{(v,u)}$ of all the messages that v sends and receives on the edge $\{v, u\}$; at the other end of the edge, node u would do the same, producing a hash $H_{(u,v)}$. At verification time, nodes u and v could compare their hashes, and reject if $H_{(v,u)} \neq H_{(u,v)}$. Unfortunately, this solution would require too much space, as node v can have up to $n - 1$ neighbors; we cannot afford to store a separate hash for each edge as part of the certificate. Our solution is instead to hash all the messages sent in the entire network together, but in a way that allows each node to "access" the messages sent by itself and its neighbors. To do this we use an object we call a *distributed Merkle tree* (DMT), which we introduce next.

Distributed Merkle Trees. A DMT is a single Merkle tree that represents a commitment to an unordered collection of values $\{x_{u \to v}\}_{\{u,v\} \in E}$, one value for every directed edge $u \to v$ such that $\{u, v\} \in E$. (The total number of values is $2|E|$.) It is constructed by a distributed algorithm called DistMake, at the end of which each node v obtains the following information:

- val: the global root of the DMT.
- rt_v: the "local root" of node v, which is the root of a Merkle tree over the local values $\{x_{v \to u}\}_{u \in N(v)}$.
- I_v and ρ_v: the index of rt_v inside the global DMT, and the corresponding opening path ρ_v for rt_v from the global root val.
- $\beta_v = \{(I_{v \to u}, \rho_{v \to u})\}_{u \in N(v)}$: for each neighbor $u \in N(v)$, the index $I_{v \to u}$ is a relative index for the position of $x_{v \to u}$ under the local root rt_v, and the opening path $\rho_{v \to u}$ is the corresponding relative opening path from rt_v. For every pair of neighbors v and u, the index $I_{v \to u}$ also equals the number of the port of u in v's neighborhood.

The DMT is built such that for any value $x_{v \to u}$, the index of the value in the DMT is given by $I_v \parallel I_{v \to u}$, and the corresponding opening path is $\rho_v \parallel \rho_{v \to u}$. Thus, node v holds enough information to produce an opening and to verify any value that it holds.[11]

---

[11] For simplicity we assume that nodes can query the communication infrastructure for a consistent order of their neighbors (e.g., by "port number"); thus the relative ordering $I_{v \to u}$ does not count against v's storage. This is a standard assumption in the area. In the general case, the port numbers themselves, which may stand for MAC addresses or similar, do not necessarily need to be consecutive numbers from $1, \ldots, \deg(v)$, but we can order v's neighbors in order of increasing port number.

(Here and throughout, $\|$ denotes concatenation; we treat indices as binary strings representing paths from the root down (with "0" representing a left turn, and "1" a right.)

The novelty of the DMT is that it can be constructed by an efficient distributed algorithm, which runs in $O(D)$ synchronized rounds (where D is the diameter of the graph), and sends $\text{poly}(\lambda, \log n)$-bit messages on every each in each round. We remark that it would be trivial to construct a DMT in a *centralized* manner, but the key to the efficiency of our distributed prover is to provide an efficient *distributed* construction; in particular, we cannot afford to, e.g., collect all the values $\{x_{u \to v}\}_{\{u,v\} \in E}$ in one place, as this would require far too much communication. We avoid this by giving a distributed construction where each node does some of the work of constructing the DMT, and eventually obtains only the information it needs.

We give an overview of the construction of the DMT in Sect. 5, but first we explain how we use it in the distributed prover.

Using the **DMT.** We assume for simplicity that in each round r, instead of sending and receiving messages on all its edges, each node v either sends or reads a message from one specific edge, determined by its current state. We further assume that each message sent is a single bit. (Both assumptions are without loss of generality, up to a polynomial blowup in the number of rounds.)

While running the original distributed algorithm $\mathcal{D}$, the distributed prover stores the internal computation steps, the messages sent and the messages received at every node.[12] For each node v and neighbor u, node v computes two hashes:

– A hash $h_{v \to u}$ of the messages v sent to u, and
– a hash $h_{u \to v}$ of the messages v received from u.

A message sent in round r is hashed at index r. Note that both endpoints of the edge $\{u, v\}$ compute the same hashes $h_{u \to v}$ and $h_{v \to u}$, but they "interpret" them differently: node v views $h_{u \to v}$ as a hash of the messages it received from u, while node u views it as a hash of the messages it sent to v, and vice-versa for $h_{v \to u}$.

The messages hashes are used to construct the proof, but they are discarded at the end of the proving stage, so as not to exceed our storage requirements. We use a hash family with local openings, so that node v is able to produce a succinct opening from $h_{v \to u}$ or $h_{u \to v}$ to any specific message that was sent or received in a given round.

Next we construct a DMT over the values $\{h_{u \to v}\}_{\{u,v\} \in E}$. Let val^{msg} be the root of the DMT. For each neighbor $u \in N(v)$, node v obtains from the DMT the index and opening for the message hash $h_{v \to u}$, and it sends them to the corresponding neighbor u.

For a given node v and a neighbor of it, u, let $I^{\text{msg}}_{v,u,r}$ be the index in the DMT of the message sent by node v to node u in round r, which is given by $I_v \| I_{v \to u} \| r$ (recall that r is the index of the r-round message inside $h_{v \to u}$). Node v is able to compute both $I^{\text{msg}}_{v,u,r}$ and $I^{\text{msg}}_{u,v,r}$ and the corresponding opening paths, since it holds both hashes $h_{v \to u}$ and $h_{u \to v}$, learns I_v and $\beta_v = \{I_{v \to u}\}_{u \in N(v)}$ during the construction of the DMT, and receives $I_u \| I_{u \to v}$ from node v.

---

[12] We believe that this additional temporary storage requirement can be avoided using incrementally verifiable computation, but we have not gone through the details.

With these values in hand, the nodes can jointly use val^{msg} as a hash of all the messages sent or received during the execution of $\mathcal{D}$. Each node v holds indices and openings for all the messages that it sent or received during the execution. Note that this is the *only* information that v obtains; although val^{msg} is a hash of *all* the messages sent in the network, each node can only access the messages that it "handled" (sent or received) during its own execution. This is all that is required to certify the execution of $\mathcal{D}$, because a message that was neither sent nor received by a node does not influence its immediate execution.

Modeling the Distributed Algorithm in Detail. Before proceeding with the construction we must give a formal model for the internal computation at each network node, as our goal will be to certify that each step of this computation was carried out correctly. It is convenient to think of each round of a distributed algorithm as comprising three phases:

1. A *compute* phase, where each node computes the messages it will send in the current round and writes them on a special output tape. In this phase nodes may also change their internal state.
2. A *send* phase, where nodes send the messages that they produced in the compute phase. The internal states of the nodes do not change.
3. A *receive* phase, where nodes receive the messages sent by their neighbors and write them on a special tape. The internal states of the nodes do not change.

The compute phase at each node is modeled by a RAM machine $M_\mathcal{D}$ that uses the following memory sections:

- Env: a read-only memory section describing the node's environment—its neighbors and port numbers, and any additional prior information it might have about the network before the computation begins.
- In: a read-only memory section that contains the input to the node.
- Read: a read-only input memory section that contains the messages that the node received in the previous round.
- Mem: a read-write working memory section, which contains the node's internal state.
- Write: a write-only memory section where the machine writes the messages that the node sends to its neighbors in the current round. In the final round of the distributed algorithm, this memory section contains the final output of the node.

The state of the RAM machine, which we denote by st, includes the following information:

- Whether the machine will read or write in the current step,
- The memory location that will be accessed,
- If the next step is a write, the value to be written and the next state to which the RAM machine will transition after writing,
- If the next step is a read, the states to which the RAM machine will transition upon reading 0 or 1 (respectively).

(We assume for simplicity that the memory is Boolean, that is, each cell contains a single bit.)

The send and receive phases can be thought of as follows:

- The send phase is a sequence of $2|E|$ *send steps*, each indexed by a directed edge $v \rightarrow u$, ordered lexicographically, first by sender v and then by receiver u. In send step $v \rightarrow u$ the message created by v for u in the current round is sent on the edge between them.
- The receive phase is similarly a sequence of $2|E|$ *receive steps*, indexed by the directed edges of the graph, and ordered lexicographically, again first by the sending node and then the receiving node. In receive step $v \rightarrow u$ the message created by v for u in the current round is received at node u.

Intuitively, using the same ordering for both the send and the receive phase means that messages are received in the exact same order in which they are sent.

Certifying the Computation of One Node. After constructing the DMT, each node has access to hashes of the messages it received during the execution of the algorithm. It would be tempting think of these hashes as input digests, since in some sense incoming messages do serve as inputs, and to use a RAM SNARG in a black-box manner to certify that the node carried out its computation correctly. The problem with this approach is the notion of soundness we require, which is similar to that of a plain SNARG, but differs from the soundness of a RAM SNARG: in our model, the nodes have access to their neighborhoods and their individual inputs at verification time, so in some sense they jointly have the entire input to the computation. We require that the prover should not be able to *prove a false statement*, that is, find a configuration (G, x) and a convincing proof that $\mathcal{D}(G, x)$ outputs a value y which is not the true output of $\mathcal{D}$ on (G, x). In contrast, the RAM SNARG verifier has only a digest of the input—although it may also have a short explicit input, the bulk of the input is implicit and is "specified" only by the digest, i.e., it is not uniquely specified. The soundness of RAM SNARGs, in turn, is weaker: they only require that the prover not be able to find a single digest and two convincing proofs for contradictory statements about the same digest. Because of this difference, we cannot use RAM SNARGs as a black box, and instead we directly build the LVD-SNARG from the same primary building block used in recent RAM SNARG constructions [CJJ21b, KLVW23]: a *non-interactive batch argument for* NP (BARG).

A (non-interactive) BARG is an argument that proves a set (a batch) of NP statements $x_1, \ldots, x_k \in \mathcal{L}$, for an NP language $\mathcal{L}$, such that the size of the proof increases very slowly (typically, polylogarithmically) with the number of statements k. (This is not a SNARG for NP, since the proof size does grow polynomially with the length of *one* witness.) Several recent works [CJJ21a, KLVW23] have constructed from standard assumptions BARGs with proof size $\text{poly}(\lambda, s, \log k)$, where s is the size of the circuit that verifies the NP-language. These BARGs were then used in [CJJ21b, KLVW23] to construct RAM SNARGs for P. Following their approach, we use BARGs to construct our desired LVD-SNARG. Roughly, our method is as follows.

At each node v, we use a hash family with local openings to commit to the sequence of RAM machine configurations that v goes through: for example, if the history of the memory section Read at node v is given by $\text{Read}_v^0, \text{Read}_v^1, \ldots$ (with Read_v^0 being the initial contents of the memory section, Read_v^1 being the contents following the first step of the algorithm, and so on), then we first compute individual hashes of $\mathsf{Read}_v^0, \mathsf{Read}_v^1, \ldots$, and then hash together all these hashes to obtain a hash $\mathsf{val}_v^{\mathsf{Read}}$ representing the sequence of contents on this memory section at node v. Similarly, let $\mathsf{val}_v^{\mathsf{Mem}}, \mathsf{val}_v^{\mathsf{Write}}$ be commitments to the memory section contents of Mem and Write at v, and let $\mathsf{val}_v^{\mathsf{st}}$ be a hash of the sequence of internal RAM machine states that node v went through during the execution of $\mathcal{D}$ (in all rounds).

We now construct a BARG to prove the following statement (roughly speaking): for each round r and each internal step i of the compute phase of that round, there exist openings of $\mathsf{val}_v^{\mathsf{Read}}, \mathsf{val}_v^{\mathsf{Mem}}, \mathsf{val}_v^{\mathsf{Write}}$ and $\mathsf{val}_v^{\mathsf{st}}$ in indices (r, i) and $(r, i + 1)$ to values $\mathsf{st}_{r,i}, \mathsf{st}_{r,i}, \mathsf{hRead}_{r,i}, \mathsf{hRead}_{r,i+1}, \mathsf{hMem}_{r,i}, \mathsf{hMem}_{r,i+1}, \mathsf{hWrite}_{r,i}, \mathsf{hWrite}_{r,i+1}$, such that the following holds:

- If i is a step of the compute phase, and $\mathsf{st}_{r,i}$ indicates that the machine reads from location ℓ in memory section $\mathsf{TP} \in \{\mathsf{Read}, \mathsf{Mem}, \mathsf{Write}\}$, then there exists an opening of $\mathsf{hTP}_{r,i}$ in location ℓ to a bit b such that upon reading b, $M_{\mathcal{D}}$ transitions to $\mathsf{st}_{r,i+1}$. Moreover, the hash values of the memory sections $\mathsf{hRead}, \mathsf{hMem}, \mathsf{hWrite}$ do not change in step (r, i): we have $\mathsf{hRead}_{r,i} = \mathsf{hRead}_{r,i+1}$, $\mathsf{hMem}_{r,i} = \mathsf{hMem}_{r,i+1}$, and $\mathsf{hWrite}_{r,i} = \mathsf{hWrite}_{r,i+1}$.
- If i is a step of the compute phase, and $\mathsf{st}_{r,i}$ indicates that the machine writes the value b to location ℓ in memory section $\mathsf{TP} \in \{\mathsf{Mem}, \mathsf{Write}\}$, then there exists an opening of $\mathsf{hTP}_{r,i+1}$ in location ℓ to the bit b. Moreover, the hash values of the other memory sections $\{\mathsf{hRead}, \mathsf{hMem}, \mathsf{hWrite}\} \setminus \mathsf{TP}$ do not change in step (r, i).
- If i is a step of the send phase indexed by $v \to u$ (i.e., a step where v sends a message to u), then there exists a message m such that $\mathsf{val}^{\mathsf{msg}}$ opens to m in index $I_{v,u,r}^{\mathsf{msg}}$ and hWrite opens to m in index d.
- If i is a step of the receive phase indexed by $u \to v$ (i.e., a step where v receives a message from u), and u is the dth neighbor of v, then there exists a message m such that $\mathsf{val}^{\mathsf{msg}}$ opens to m in index $I_{u,v,r}^{\mathsf{msg}}$ and hRead opens to m in index d.

In addition to the requirements above, we ust ensure that whenever the contents of a memory section change, they change only in the location to which the machine writes, and the hash value for the memory section changes accordingly; for example, if in step i of the compute phase of round r the machine writes value b to location ℓ of memory section TP, then we must ensure not only that $\mathsf{TP}_{r,i+1}$ opens to b in location ℓ, but also that $\mathsf{hTP}_{r,i}$ and $\mathsf{hTP}_{r,i+1}$ are hash values of arrays that differ *only* in location ℓ. To do so, we use a hash family that also supports write operations (in addition to local openings), as in the definition of a *hash tree* in [KPY19]. For example, a Merkle tree [Mer89] satisfies all of the requirements for a hash tree.

We use the hash write operations to include the following additional requirements as part of our BARG statement:

- For each step i of the compute phase of each round r, if $\mathsf{st}_{r,i}$ indicates that the machine writes value b to location ℓ in memory section $\mathsf{TP} \in \{\mathsf{Mem}, \mathsf{Write}\}$, then there exists an opening showing that $\mathsf{hTP}_{r,i}$ and $\mathsf{hTP}_{r,i+1}$ differ only in location ℓ.
- For each step of the receive phase of each round r, if the message received in this step is written to location ℓ of Read, then there exists an opening showing that $\mathsf{hRead}_{r,i}, \mathsf{hRead}_{r,i+1}$ differ only location ℓ.

There is one main obstacle remaining: in all known BARG constructions, the BARG is only as succinct as the circuit that verifies the statements it claims. In our case, the statements involve the indices $I_{v,u,r}^{\mathsf{msg}}$, as well as port numbers of the various neighbors of v, and the corresponding opening paths. These must be "hard-wired" into the circuit, because they are obtained from the DMT, i.e., they are external to the BARG itself. Each node v may need to use up to $n-1$ indices and openings, one for every neighbor, so we cannot afford to use a circuit that explicitly encodes them.

Indirect Indexing. To avoid hard-wiring the indices and openings into the BARG, each node v computes a commitment to the indices, in the form of a locally openable hash of the following arrays:

- $\mathsf{Ind}^{in}(v)$, an array containing at each index $I_{v \to u}$ the value $I_v \parallel I_{v \to u}$.
- $\mathsf{Ind}^{out}(v)$, an array containing at each index $I_{v \to u}$ the value $I_u \parallel I_{u \to v}$.
- $\mathsf{Port}(v)$, an array containing at each index k the value $\bot$ if $v_k \notin N(v)$, or the value d if v_k is the dth neighbor of v.

Denote these hash values by $\mathsf{val}^{in}(v)$, $\mathsf{val}^{out}(v)$, and $\mathsf{val}^{\mathsf{Port}}(v)$, respectively.

Now we can augment the BARG, and have it prove the following: at every round r and step i of the send phase, there exists a port number d, an index I, a message m, and appropriate openings to the hash values $\mathsf{val}^{\mathsf{Port}}$, val^{out}, $\mathsf{hWrite}_{r,i}$, $\mathsf{val}^{\mathsf{msg}}$ such that

- $\mathsf{val}^{\mathsf{Port}}$ opens to d in location ℓ such that v_ℓ is the node that v sends a message to in step i of every send phase,
- val^{out} opens to I in location d,
- $\mathsf{hWrite}_{r,i}$ opens to m in location d, and
- $\mathsf{val}^{\mathsf{msg}}$ opens to m in location $I \parallel r$.

Similarly, at every round r and step i of the receive phase, there exist a port number d, an index I, a message m, and appropriate openings to the hash values $\mathsf{val}^{\mathsf{Port}}$, $\mathsf{val}^{\in}$, $\mathsf{hRead}_{r,i+1}$, $\mathsf{val}^{\mathsf{msg}}$ such that

- $\mathsf{val}^{\mathsf{Port}}$ opens to d in location k such that v_k is the node that v receives a message to in step i of every send phase,
- val^{in} opens to I in location d,
- $\mathsf{hRead}_{r,i+1}$ opens to m in location d,[13] and
- $\mathsf{val}^{\mathsf{msg}}$ opens to m in location $I \parallel r$.

The circuit verifying this BARG's statement requires only the following values to be hard-wired: $\mathsf{val}^{\mathsf{st}}$, $\mathsf{val}^{\mathsf{msg}}$, val^{in}, val^{out}, $\mathsf{val}^{\mathsf{Port}}$, $\mathsf{val}^{\mathsf{Read}}$, $\mathsf{val}^{\mathsf{Mem}}$, $\mathsf{val}^{\mathsf{Write}}$. During verification, however, node v must verify that indeed, the hashes $\mathsf{val}^{in}(v)$, $\mathsf{val}^{out}(v)$, $\mathsf{val}^{\mathsf{Port}}(v)$ are correct: node v can do this by re-computing the hashes, using the index I_v which is stored as part of its certificate, the port numbers $\{I_{v \to u}\}_{u \in N(v)}$ that it accesses during verification, and also indices $\{I_u\}_{u \in N(v)}$ and port numbers $\{I_{u \to v}\}_{u \in N(v)}$ that v's neighbors can provide in verification time.

---

[13] As explained above, we actually require that this opening show that $\mathsf{hRead}_{r,i}$ and $\mathsf{hRead}_{r,i+1}$ only differ in the location d and $\mathsf{hRead}_{r,i+1}$ opens to m in that location.

The Soundness of our Construction. Following [KLVW23], instead of using regular BARGs, we use *somewhere extractable* BARGs (seBARGs): an seBARG is a BARG with the following somewhere argument of knowledge property: for some index i, using the appropriate trapdoor, the seBARG proof completely reveals an NP-witness for the ith statement. Importantly, the trapdoor is generated alongside the crs and the crs *hides* the binding index i: the (computationally bounded) prover cannot tell from the crs alone the binding index i. Conveniently, BARGs can be easily transformed into seBARGs [CJJ21b, KLVW23], without adding more assumptions.

The overall idea of our soundness proof is similar to the one in [CJJ21b, KLVW23], although there are some complications (e.g., the need to switch between different nodes of the network as we argue correctness). Assume for the sake of contradiction that a cheating prover is able to convince the network to accept a false statement with non-negligible probability. We proceed by induction over the rounds and internal steps (inside each compute, send and receive phase) of the distributed algorithm: in the induction we track the true state of the distributed algorithm, and compare witnesses extracted from the seBARG to this state. Informally speaking, we prove that from a proof that is accepted, using the appropriate trapdoor and crs, we can extract at each step a witness that must be compatible with the true execution of the distributed algorithm, otherwise we break the seBARG. In the last round, this means that the output encoded in the witness is the correct output of the distributed algorithm. But this contradicts our assumption that the adversary convinces the network of a *false* statement.

5   Distributed Merkle Trees

Finally, we briefly sketch the construction of the distributed Merkle tree used in the previous section.

The Structure of the DMT. Recall that our goal with the distributed Merkle tree (DMT) is to hash together all the messages sent during the execution of the distributed algorithm, in such a way that a node can produce openings for its own sent messages. Accordingly, we construct the DMT in several layers (see Fig. 1):

- At the lowest level, for each node v and neighbor $u \in N(v)$, node v hashes together the messages $(m_1^{v \to u}, m_2^{v \to u}, \dots)$ that it sent to node u, obtaining a hash $\mathsf{rt}_{v \to u}$.
- At the second level, each node v hashes together the hashes of its different edges, $\{\mathsf{rt}_{v \to u}\}_{u \in N(v)}$, ordered by the port numbers $I_{v \to u}$, obtaining a hash rt_v which we refer to as v's *local root*.
- Finally, the nodes collaborate to hash their local roots $\{\mathsf{rt}_v\}_{v \in V}$ together to obtain a global root val. The nodes are initially not ordered, but during the creation of the DMT, the local roots $\{\mathsf{rt}_v\}_{v \in V}$ are ordered; and each node v obtains an index I_v for its local root, and the corresponding opening path from val to rt_v.

Constructing the DMT. After each node computes the hash values $\mathsf{rt}_{v \to u}$ for each of its neighbors $u \in N(v)$, we continue by having the network nodes compute a spanning tree ST of the network, with each node v learning its parent $p_v \in N(v) \cup \{\bot\}$, and its

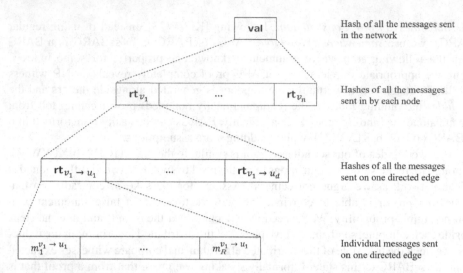

Fig. 1: The structure of the DMT constructed over the messages

children $C_v \subseteq N(v)$. The root v_0 of the spanning tree is the only node that has a null parent, i.e., $p_{v_0} = \bot$.

We note that using standard techniques, a rooted spanning tree can be constructed in $O(D)$ rounds in networks of diameter D, using $O(\log n)$-bit messages in every round; this can be done even if the nodes do not initially know the diameter D or the size n of the network, and it does not require the root to be chosen or known in advance [Lyn96].

After constructing the spanning tree, we compute the DMT in three stages: in the first stage nodes compute a Merkle tree of their own values, in the second we go "up the spanning tree" to compute the global Merkle tree, and the third stage goes "down the tree" to obtain the indices and the openings.

Stage 1: Local Hash Trees. Let x_v be a vector containing the values $\{rt_{v \to u}\}_{u \in N(v)}$ held by node v, ordered by the port number of the neighbor $u \in N(v)$ at node v (padded up to a power of 2, if necessary). For each node v and neighbor $u \in N(v)$, let $I_{v \to u}$ be a binary representation of the port number of u at v (again, possibly padded).

Each node v computes its local root rt_v by building a Merkle tree over the vector x_v, as well as an opening $\rho_{v \to u}$ for the index $I_{v \to u}$, for each neighbor $u \in N(v)$. We let $\beta_v = \{(I_{v \to u}, \rho_{v \to u})\}_{u \in N(v)}$.

Stage 2: Spanning Tree Computation. The nodes jointly compute a spanning tree ST of the network, storing at every node v the parent $p_v \in N(v)$ of v and the children $C_v \subseteq N(v)$ of v. In the sequel, we denote by v_0 the root of the spanning tree.

Stage 3: Convergecast of hash-tree forests. In this stage, we compute the global hash tree up the spanning tree ST, with each node v merging some or all of the hash-trees received from its children and sending the result upwards in the form of a set of HT-roots annotated with height information.

Each node v receives from each child $c \in C_v$ a set S_c of pairs (rt, h), where rt is a Merkle-tree root, and $h \in \mathbb{N}$ is the cumulative height of the Merkle tree. Node v now creates a forest F_v, as follows:

1. Initially, F_v contains the roots sent up by v's children, and a new leaf representing v's local hash tree: $F_v = \{(\mathsf{rt}_v, 0)\} \cup \bigcup_{c \in C_v} S_c$.
2. While there remain two trees in F_v whose roots rt_0 and rt_1 have the same cumulative height h (note—we do not care about the actual height of the trees in the forest F_v, but rather about their cumulative height, represented by the value h in the node (rt, h)): node v chooses two such trees and merges them, creating a new root rt of cumulative height $h+1$ and placing (rt_0, h) and (rt_1, h) as the left and right children of $(\mathsf{rt}, h + 1)$, respectively.
3. When there no longer remain two trees in F_v whose roots have the same cumulative height:
   – If $v \neq v_0$ (that is, v is not the root of the spanning tree), node v sends its parent, p_v, the set S_v of tree-roots in F_v. The size of this set is at most $O(\log n)$, since it contains at most one root of any given cumulative height (if there were two roots of the same cumulative height, node v would merge them).
   – At the root v_0, we do not want to halt until F_v is a single tree. If F_v is not yet a single tree, node v_0 must pad the forest by adding "dummy trees" so that it can continue to merge. To do so, node v_0 finds the tree-root (rt, h) that has the smallest cumulative height h in F_v. It then creates a "dummy" Merkle-tree of height h, with root $(\perp, h)$, and adds it to F_{v_0}. Following this addition, there exist two tree-roots of cumulative-height h (the original tree-root (rt, h) and the "dummy" tree-root $(\perp, h)$), which v_0 now merges. It continues on with this process, at each step choosing a tree with the smallest remaining height, and either merging it with another same-height tree if there is one, or creating a dummy tree and merging the shortest tree with it.

When the last stage completes, the forest F_{v_0} computed by node v_0 (the root of the spanning tree) is in fact a single tree, whose root is the root of the global Merkle tree. Let val be this root.

Stage 4: Computing Hash-Tree Indices and Openings. In this stage we proceed down the spanning tree, forwarding the global root val downwards. In addition, as we move down the tree, each node v annotates its forest F_v with indices and opening paths: first, it receives from its parent p_v an index and opening for every tree-root $(\mathsf{rt}, h) \in F_v$ that it sent upwards to p_v. Then, it extends this information "downwards" inside F_v, annotating each inner node and leaf in F_v with their index and opening path from the global root val: for example, if (rt_0, h) and (rt_1, h) are the left and right children of $(\mathsf{rt}, h + 1)$ in F_v, and the index and opening path for $(\mathsf{rt}, h + 1)$ are already known to be I and ρ (resp.), then the index and opening path for (rt_0, h) are $I \parallel 0$ and $\rho \parallel \mathsf{rt}_1$ (resp.).

Outputs. The final output at node v is $(\mathsf{val}, \mathsf{rt}_v, I_v, \rho_v, \beta_v)$. (For the LVD-SNARG, at the end of the proving stage, β_v is discarded, as it is too long to store. However, $\mathsf{val}, \mathsf{rt}_v, I_v$ and ρ_v are part of node v's certificate.)

We remark that for our purposes, it is not necessary for the nodes to *certify* that they computed the DMT correctly: after obtaining the global root and the relevant openings, the nodes simply use the DMT as they would use a centralized hash with local openings. The completeness proof of our LVD-SNARG relies on the fact that a correctly-computed DMT will open to the correct information everywhere, but the soundness proof does not rely the details of the construction, only on the fact that the value obtained by opening various locations of the DMT matches the true execution of the algorithm.

Acknowledgments. We would like to thank Omer Paneth for fruitful and illuminating iscussions.

References

[ABOR00] Aiello, W., Bhatt, S.N., Ostrovsky, R., Rajagopalan, S.: Fast verification of any remote procedure call: short witness-indistinguishable one-round proofs for np. In: Proceedings of the 27th International Colloquium on Automata, Languages and Programming, pp. 463–474 (2000)

[AO22] Aldema Tshuva, E., Oshman, R.: Brief announcement: on polynomial-time local decision. In: Proceedings of the 2022 ACM Symposium on Principles of Distributed Computing, pp. 48–50 (2022)

[APV91] Awerbuch, B., Patt-Shamir, B., Varghese, G.: Self-stabilization by local checking and correction. In: Proceedings 32nd Annual Symposium of Foundations of Computer Science, pp. 268–277 (1991)

[BCCT12] Bitansky, N., Canetti, R., Chiesa, A., Tromer, E.: From extractable collision resistance to succinct non-interactive arguments of knowledge, and back again. In: Proceedings of the 3rd Innovations in Theoretical Computer Science Conference, pp. 326–349 (2012)

[BDFO18] Balliu, A., D'Angelo, G., Fraigniaud, P., Olivetti, D.: What can be verified locally? J. Comput. Syst. Sci. **97**, 106–120 (2018)

[BFO22] Ben Shimon, Y., Fischer, O., Oshman, R.: Proof labeling schemes for reachability-related problems in directed graphs. In: Parter, M. (ed.) SIROCCO 2022. LNCS, vol. 13298, pp. 21–41. Springer, Heidelberg (2022). https://doi.org/10.1007/978-3-031-09993-9_2

[BHK17] Brakerski, Z., Holmgren, J., Kalai, Y.T.: Non-interactive delegation and batch np verification from standard computational assumptions. In: Proceedings of the 49th Annual ACM SIGACT Symposium on Theory of Computing, pp. 474–482 (2017)

[BKK+18] Badrinarayanan, S., Kalai, Y.T., Khurana, D., Sahai, A., Wichs, D.: Succinct delegation for low-space non-deterministic computation. In: Proceedings of the 50th Annual ACM SIGACT Symposium on Theory of Computing, pp. 709–721 (2018)

[BKO22] Bick, A., Kol, G., Oshman, R.: Distributed zero-knowledge proofs over networks. In: SODA, pp. 2426–2458. SIAM (2022)

[CGJ+22] Choudhuri, A.R., Garg, S., Jain, A., Jin, Z., Zhang, J.: Correlation intractability and SNARGs from sub-exponential DDH. Cryptology ePrint Archive (2022)

[CJJ21a] Choudhuri, A.R., Jain, A., Jin, Z.: Non-interactive batch arguments for NP from standard assumptions. In: Malkin, T., Peikert, C. (eds.) CRYPTO 2021. LNCS, vol. 12828, pp. 394–423. Springer, Cham (2021). https://doi.org/10.1007/978-3-030-84259-8_14

[CJJ21b] Choudhuri, A.R., Jain, A., Jin, Z.: SNARGs for P from LWE. In: 62nd IEEE Annual Symposium on Foundations of Computer Science (FOCS), pp. 68–79 (2021)

[DL08]   Di Crescenzo, G., Lipmaa, H.: Succinct NP proofs from an extractability assumption. In: Beckmann, A., Dimitracopoulos, C., Löwe, B. (eds.) CiE 2008. LNCS, vol. 5028, pp. 175–185. Springer, Heidelberg (2008). https://doi.org/10.1007/978-3-540-69407-6_21

[DLN+04] Dwork, C., Langberg, M., Naor, M., Nissim, K., Reingold, O.: Succinct proofs for np and spooky interactions (2004). http://www.cs.bgu.ac.il/kobbi/papers/spooky_sub_crypto.pdf

[FBP22] Feuilloley, L., Bousquet, N., Pierron, T.: What can be certified compactly? compact local certification of MSO properties in tree-like graphs. In: PODC, pp. 131–140. ACM (2022)

[Feu21] Feuilloley, l.: Introduction to local certification. Disc. Math. Theor. Comput. Sci. 23(3) (2021)

[FFH+21] Feuilloley, L., Fraigniaud, P., Hirvonen, J., Paz, A., Perry, M.: Redundancy in distributed proofs. Distrib. Comput. 34(2), 113–132 (2021)

[FGKS13] Fraigniaud, P., Göös, M., Korman, A., Suomela, J.: What can be decided locally without identifiers? In: Proceedings of the 2013 ACM Symposium on Principles of Distributed Computing, pp. 157–165. ACM, New York (2013)

[FHK12] Fraigniaud, P., Halldórsson, M.M., Korman, A.: On the impact of identifiers on local decision. In: Baldoni, R., Flocchini, P., Binoy, R. (eds.) OPODIS 2012. LNCS, vol. 7702, pp. 224–238. Springer, Heidelberg (2012). https://doi.org/10.1007/978-3-642-35476-2_16

[FKP13] Fraigniaud, P., Korman, A., Peleg, D.: Towards a complexity theory for local distributed computing. J. ACM (JACM) 60(5), 1–26 (2013)

[FMO+19] Fraigniaud, P., Montealegre, P., Oshman, R., Rapaport, I., Todinca, I.: On distributed merlin-arthur decision protocols. In: Censor-Hillel, K., Flammini, M. (eds.) SIROCCO 2019. LNCS, vol. 11639, pp. 230–245. Springer, Cham (2019). https://doi.org/10.1007/978_3_030_24922-9_16

[FMRT22] Fraigniaud, P., Montealegre, P., Rapaport, I., Todinca, I.: A meta-theorem for distributed certification. In: Parter, M. (ed.) SIROCCO 2022. LNCS, vol. 13298, pp. 116–134. Springer, Heidelberg (2022). https://doi.org/10.1007/s00453-023-01185-1

[FPP19] Fraigniaud, P., Patt-Shamir, B., Perry, M.: Randomized proof-labeling schemes. Distrib. Comput. 32, 217–234 (2019)

[Gro10] Groth, J.: Short pairing-based non-interactive zero-knowledge arguments. In: Abe, M. (ed.) ASIACRYPT 2010. LNCS, vol. 6477, pp. 321–340. Springer, Heidelberg (2010). https://doi.org/10.1007/978-3-642-17373-8_19

[GS16]   Göös, M., Suomela, J.: Locally checkable proofs in distributed computing. Theory Comput. 12(1), 1–33 (2016)

[GW11]   Gentry, C., Wichs, D.: Separating succinct non-interactive arguments from all falsifiable assumptions. In: Proceedings of the Forty-Third Annual ACM Symposium on Theory of Computing, pp. 99–108 (2011)

[HR18]   Holmgren, J., Rothblum, R.: Delegating computations with (almost) minimal time and space overhead. In: 2018 IEEE 59th Annual Symposium on Foundations of Computer Science (FOCS), pp. 124–135. IEEE (2018)

[JKKZ21] Jawale, R., Kalai, Y.T., Khurana, D., Zhang, R.: SNARGs for bounded depth computations and PPAD hardness from sub-exponential LWE. In: Proceedings of the 53rd Annual ACM SIGACT Symposium on Theory of Computing, pp. 708–721 (2021)

[KKP05] Korman, A., Kutten, S., Peleg, D.: Proof labeling schemes. In: Proceedings of the Twenty-Fourth Annual ACM Symposium on Principles of Distributed Computing, pp. 9–18 (2005)

[KLVW23] Kalai, Y., Lombardi, A., Vaikuntanathan, V., Wichs, D.: Boosting batch arguments and RAM delegation. In: Proceedings of the 55th Annual ACM Symposium on Theory of Computing (STOC), pp. 1545–1552 (2023)

[KOS18] Kol, G., Oshman, R., Saxena, R.R.: Interactive distributed proofs. In: Symposium on Principles of Distributed Computing (PODC), pp. 255–264 (2018)

[KP98]   Kutten, S., Peleg, D.: Fast distributed construction of small k-dominating sets and applications. J. Algor. **28**, 27 (1998)

[KP16]   Kalai, Y., Paneth, O.: Delegating RAM computations. In: Hirt, M., Smith, A. (eds.) TCC 2016. LNCS, vol. 9986, pp. 91–118. Springer, Heidelberg (2016). https://doi.org/10.1007/978-3-662-53644-5_4

[KPY19] Kalai, Y.T., Paneth, O., Yang, L.: How to delegate computations publicly. In: Proceedings of the 51st Annual ACM SIGACT Symposium on Theory of Computing, pp. 1115–1124 (2019)

[KRR13] Kalai, Y.T., Raz, R., Rothblum, R.D.: Delegation for bounded space. In Proceedings of the Forty-Fifth Annual ACM Symposium on Theory of Computing, pp. 565–574 (2013)

[KRR14] Kalai, Y.T., Raz, R., Rothblum, R.D.: How to delegate computations: the power of no-signaling proofs. In: Proceedings of the Forty-Sixth Annual ACM Symposium on Theory of Computing, pp. 485–494 (2014)

[Lyn96] Lynch, N.A.: Distributed Algorithms. Morgan Kaufmann, Burlington (1996)

[Mer89] Merkle, R.C.: A certified digital signature. In: Brassard, G. (ed.) CRYPTO 1989. LNCS, vol. 435, pp. 218–238. Springer, New York (1990). https://doi.org/10.1007/0-387-34805-0_21

[Mic00] Micali, S.: Computationally sound proofs. SIAM J. Comput. **30**(4), 1253–1298 (2000)

[NPY20] Naor, M., Parter, M., Yogev, E.: The power of distributed verifiers in interactive proofs. In: Chawla, S. (ed.) Symposium on Discrete Algorithms (SODA), pp. 1096–115 (2020)

[OPR17] Ostrovsky, R., Perry, M., Rosenbaum, W.: Space-time tradeoffs for distributed verification. In: Das, S., Tixeuil, S. (eds.) SIROCCO 2017. LNCS, vol. 10641, pp. 53–70. Springer, Cham (2017). https://doi.org/10.1007/978-3-319-72050-0_4

[Pel00] Peleg, D.: Distributed Computing: A Locality-Sensitive Approach. Society for Industrial and Applied Mathematics, Philadelphia (2000)

[PP17]   Patt-Shamir, B., Perry, M.: Proof-labeling schemes: broadcast, unicast and in between. In: Spirakis, P., Tsigas, P. (eds.) SSS 2017. LNCS, vol. 10616, pp. 1–17. Springer, Cham (2017). https://doi.org/10.1007/978-3-319-69084-1_1

[SHK+12] Sarma, A.D., et al. Distributed verification and hardness of distributed approximation. SIAM J. Comput. (special issue of STOC 2011) (2012)

[WW22]   Waters, B., Wu, D.J.: Batch arguments for and more from standard bilinear group assumptions. In: Dodis, Y., Shrimpton, T. (eds.) CRYPTO 2022. LNCS, vol. 13508, pp. 433–463. Springer, Heidelberg (2022). https://doi.org/10.1007/978-3-031-15979-4_15

Distributed-Prover Interactive Proofs

Sourav Das[1]($\boxtimes$), Rex Fernando[2], Ilan Komargodski[3,4], Elaine Shi[2], and Pratik Soni[5]

[1] UIUC, Champaign, IL, USA
souravd2@illinois.edu
[2] Carnegie Mellon University, Pittsburgh, PA, USA
[3] Hebrew University of Jerusalem, Jerusalem, Israel
ilank@cs.huji.ac.il
[4] NTT Research, Sunnyvale, CA, USA
[5] University of Utah, Salt Lake City, UT, USA
psoni@cs.utah.edu

Abstract. Interactive proof systems enable a verifier with limited resources to decide an intractable language (or compute a hard function) by communicating with a powerful but untrusted prover. Such systems guarantee soundness: the prover can only convince the verifier of true statements. This is a central notion in computer science with far-reaching implications. One key drawback of the classical model is that the data on which the prover operates must be held by a single machine.

In this work, we initiate the study of distributed-prover interactive proofs (dpIPs): an untrusted cluster of machines, acting as a distributed prover, interacts with a single verifier. The machines in the cluster jointly store and operate on a massive data-set that no single machine can store. The goal is for the machines in the cluster to convince the verifier of the validity of some statement about its data-set. We formalize the communication and space constraints via the massively parallel computation (MPC) model, a widely accepted analytical framework capturing the computational power of massive data-centers.

Our main result is a compiler that generically augments any verification algorithm in the MPC model with a (computational) soundness guarantee. Concretely, for any language L for which there is an MPC algorithm verifying whether $x \in L$, we design a new MPC protocol capable of convincing a verifier of the validity of $x \in L$ and where if $x \notin L$, the verifier rejects with overwhelming probability. The new protocol requires only slightly more rounds, i.e., a $\mathsf{poly}(\log N)$ blowup, and a slightly bigger memory per machine, i.e., $\mathsf{poly}(\lambda)$ blowup, where N is the total size of the dataset and λ is a security parameter independent of N.

En route, we introduce distributed-prover interactive oracle proofs (dpIOPs), a natural adaptation of the (by now classical) IOP model to the distributed prover setting. We design a dpIOP for verification algorithms in the MPC model and then translate them to "plain model" dpIPs via an adaptation of existing polynomial commitment schemes into the distributed prover setting.

P. Soni—Work was done partially when the author was visiting Carnegie Mellon University.

G. Rothblum and H. Wee (Eds.): TCC 2023, LNCS 14369, pp. 91–120, 2023.
https://doi.org/10.1007/978-3-031-48615-9_4

1   Introduction

Interactive proofs are a natural extension of non-determinism and have become a fundamental concept in complexity theory and cryptography. The study of interactive proofs has led to many of the exciting notions that are at the heart of several areas of theoretical computer science, including zero-knowledge proofs [40,41] and probabilistically checkable proofs (PCPs) [4,10,11].

An interactive proof is a protocol between a randomized verifier and a powerful but untrusted prover. The goal of the prover is to convince the verifier regarding the validity of some statement. If the statement is indeed correct, we require that the verifier should accept an honestly generated proof with high probability. Otherwise, if the statement is false, the verifier should reject with high probability any maliciously crafted proof. A particularly interesting and practical case is when the verifier is significantly weaker than the prover in some aspect. Typically, verifiers that are weaker in terms of computational abilities are studied, but other sorts of limitations are relevant.

The standard model of interactive proofs, as described above, has a key limitation: *The data must be held by a prover modeled as a single machine.* A scenario where the data is distributed among multiple parties is not natively supported. Indeed, large organizations nowadays store vast amounts of data, often reaching petabytes or even exabytes in size. To store and efficiently manage such enormous volumes of data, these organizations utilize massive data-centers. With existing succinct arguments, if such an organization takes up the role of the prover, the only way to use existing interactive proofs technology is by essentially aggregating the data at a single machine. However, the latter is physically impossible as there is no one machine that can store so much data.

Motivated by the above scenario, in this work, we study *interactive proofs for distributed provers.* We first define a concrete model that captures the constraints of such a distributed setting, and then design new interactive proofs in our model.

The Distributed Computation Model. We imagine an enormous data-set, the size of which is denoted N. The data is stored in a cluster split among M machines; i.e., every machine stores roughly a size N/M portion of the data-set. As an example, imagine that $N = 10^{17}$ bytes (100 petabytes) and that each machine has a hard-disc capable of storing 10^{13} bytes (10 terabytes). Then, a cluster consisting of $10^4 = 10,000$ machines is needed. (Clearly, there is no single machine capable of storing 100 petabytes).

The distributed prover is the above cluster, consists of M server machines. The verifier is another machine, as powerful as a single machine in the cluster, i.e., it can store N/M bits of information. The goal of the distributed prover is to convince the verifier of the validity of some statement about its data-set. The distributed prover can perform arbitrary communication (server-to-server or server-to-client) and local computation, as long as it respects the space constraint of each machine. If we care about computational complexity of the (honest or malicious) prover, we shall also require that the local computation of the (honest or malicious) provers is polynomial time. Each server machine and the client have their own private source of randomness.

The above logic coincides with the rationale behind the *Massively Parallel Computation* (MPC) model. This model was invented to capture popular modern parallel computation programming paradigms such as MapReduce, Hadoop, and Spark, designed to utilize parallel computation power to manipulate and analyze huge amounts of data. In this model, first introduced by Karloff, Suri, and Vassilvitskii [42], the size N data-set is stored in a distributed manner among M machines. The machines are connected via pairwise communication channels and each machine can only store $S = N^\epsilon$ bits of information locally for some $\epsilon \in (0, 1)$. Naturally, we assume that $M \geq N^{1-\epsilon}$ so that all machines can jointly at least store the entire data-set.

The primary metric for the complexity of algorithms in this model is their *round complexity*. Reasonable polynomial-time computations that are performed within a machine are considered "for free" since the communication is often the bottleneck. We typically want algorithms in the MPC framework to have a small number of rounds, say, poly-logarithmically or even sub-logarithmically many rounds (in the total data size N). With the goal of designing efficient algorithms in the MPC model, there is an immensely rich algorithmic literature suggesting various non-trivial efficient algorithms for tasks of interest, including graph problems [1–3,6–9,12,15,16,26,28,31], clustering [13,14,33,39] and submodular function optimization [32,34,46].

Succinct Arguments in the MPC Model. In this work, we study the question of constructing interactive argument systems in the MPC model, where the "prover" is a cluster of machines, each with N^ϵ maximum storage, where N is the size of the witness, and the client is also a machine with the same storage restriction. Note that it is unrealistic to achieve an argument system for all polynomial-time computable functions in this model, because there are various results showing that not all such functions can be computed in the MPC model [30,54]. Thus, we aim for the best-possible goal: to prove a statement whose verification algorithm is itself an MPC algorithm.

We design an argument system that supports clusters acting as provers and where the protocol respects the requirements of the MPC model. Specifically, we prove the following theorem.

Theorem 1 (Main result; Informal). *Let $R = \{(x, w)\}$ be any relation which has a massively-parallel verification algorithm Π among $M = N^{1-\epsilon}$ parties each with space N^ϵ, where $N = |w|$, and $|x| \leq N^\epsilon$.*

Then there exists an argument system Π' for R in the MPC model, which has M space-bounded provers $P_1, \ldots, P_M$, and convinces a space-bounded verifier V that $x \in L_R$. The protocol Π' has space overhead multiplicative in $\mathsf{poly}(\lambda)$ relative to Π, where λ is a security parameter, and has round overhead multiplicative in $\mathsf{polylog}(N)$.

Under standard falsifiable cryptographic assumptions, the argument Π' is sound in the CRS model against malicious provers with arbitrary $\mathsf{poly}(N, \lambda)$ running time and space.

Our protocol's soundness relies on the existence of groups of hidden order, which can be instantiated based on the RSA assumption [53] or on class groups [27,57].

To put the above result in better context, we mention a recent work of Fernando et al. [35] (building on [36]) who built a secure computation compiler for arbitrary MPC protocols. That is, they compile any MPC protocol into secure counterparts, which still respect the constraints of the model. In particular, their protocol can be used as an argument system in the cluster-verifier model we introduce above. Unfortunately, their compiler relies on (publicly verifiable) succinct non-interactive proofs of knowledge (SNARKs), which are well-known not to be constructible based on falsifiable assumptions [38,49]. Our main contribution, and the main technical challenge we overcome, is achieving such an argument system relying only on falsifiable assumptions. As a bonus, we mention that if we instantiate the hidden order group using class groups, our protocol requires only a common *random* string, whereas the SNARK based solution requires a structured common *reference* string.

1.1 Techniques: Distributed IOPs and Distributed Streaming Polynomial Commitments

To achieve our main result, we use recent work on interactive oracle proofs (IOPs). Recall that the IOP model is a proof system model that combines features of interactive proofs (IPs) and probabilistically checkable proofs (PCPs). In this model, the verifier is not required to read the prover's messages in their entirety; rather, the verifier has oracle access to some of the prover's messages (viewed as strings), and may probabilistically query these messages during its interaction with the prover. IOPs strictly generalize PCPs, and serve as a convenient intermediate model for getting succinct "plain model" protocols. Many recent succinct arguments have been constructed by first giving a protocol in the IOP model, and then using a vector commitment or polynomial commitment to instantiate the IOP oracle [18,21,22,27,29,37].

We extend the IOP model to a setting where the prover is distributed — here on referred to as the distributed IOP. We imagine a prover that is made up of a collection of servers that can communicate between themselves via peer-to-peer channels, as in the classical distributed cluster-verifier MPC model. But, communication between any server and the verifier occurs as in the IOP model: the verifier has oracle access to a large string committed to by the server, in addition to being able to communicate directly with any of the parties comprising the server.

We build a distributed IOP in the MPC model analogous to the "plain model" protocol we stated above. Specifically, given a distributed, massively-parallel protocol Π for verifying a relation R, we construct a distributed argument system Π' which works in this new IOP model, and where a distributed group of provers convince a verifier V that some $x \in L_R$. Our argument uses a *polynomial commitment oracle,* where each prover first streams evaluations of some multilinear polynomial W over some subset of the Boolean hypercube, and where at the end the provers have collectively defined W by their evaluations. The verifier then interacts with the prover and queries this polynomial IOP oracle in order to verify the statement x.

Our IOP is inspired by the work of Blumberg et al. [23], who give an IOP for RAM programs, where the prover's running time and space are approximately preserved in relation to the running time and space of the verification algorithm. At a very high level, the [23] IOP has the prover commit to a polynomial $\hat{W}$, which encodes the RAM computation, and then has the prover and verifier run a sumcheck argument in relation to a polynomial h that is based on $\hat{W}$. The polynomial h has the property that it can be evaluated at any point via a constant number of evaluations of $\hat{W}$. At the end of the sumcheck, the verifier can thus query the IOP oracle in order to do the final random evaluation of h.

We would like to use a similar strategy to [23], having the provers encode a polynomial $\hat{W}$ which encodes the MPC computation, and then using a sumcheck argument to verify the truthfulness of $\hat{W}$. However, since $\hat{W}$ now encodes an *interactive protocol between RAM programs* Π_L, instead of just a RAM computation, it is unclear how the provers would be able to generate sumcheck messages without rerunning the MPC protocol many times, thus blowing up the communication complexity.

To solve this, we use several ideas. First, for each round of the MPC protocol, the provers commit to a concatenation π_r of their states after the round is finished, using a Merkle tree-based succinct commitment. This defines a statement (r, π_{r-1}, π_r), where a witness for this statement is a set of decommitments for π_{r-1} and π_r which show honest behavior during this round. If we can build a knowledge-sound argument for this statement which works in the MPC model and is round-efficient, this is sufficient to build an argument for honest execution of the whole protocol Π_L. We then design an IOP similar to [23] for proving the statement (r, π_{r-1}, π_r). Note that even though we have reduced to proving honesty of one round, we still have the problem that knowledge of $\hat{W}$ is spread across all the provers, and no single prover knows the whole description of $\hat{W}$. Thus it is still unclear how the provers will generate the sumcheck provers' messages in a round-efficient way. The main technical part of our paper deals with how to do this.

Polynomial Commitments. Once we have an IOP for L, we still need to instantiate it using a polynomial commitment scheme. Informally, a polynomial commitment scheme allows a prover to commit to some low degree polynomial f, and provide evaluations $f(x)$ to a verifier along with a (interactive) proof that the provided evaluation is consistent with the commitment. Polynomial commitments were introduced by [43] and have recently drawn significant attention due to their use in compiling oracle proof systems (e.g., PCPs and IOPs) into real world proof systems (e.g., arguments). A sequence of works [5, 17, 19, 24, 25, 27, 44, 47, 52, 55, 56, 59] have studied several different aspects of efficiency including getting constant-sized proofs/commitments, sublinear (even polylogarithmic) time verification, as well as linear prover time. However, these works consider a monolithic prover that stores the entire polynomial locally. This is in stark contrast with our setting where there are multiple provers $P_1, \ldots, P_M$, each of which only have *streaming* access to a *small piece* of the description of the polynomial. Looking ahead, the polynomial in our context is the description of the transcript of the RAM computation, which can be generated as a stream.

The works that come closest to our requirements are that of Block et al. [21,22] who introduced the *streaming model* of access where a monolithic prover has streaming access to the description of the polynomial. They build a logarithmic round polynomial commitment scheme in the streaming model where the prover's memory usage is logarithmic, the prover time is quasilinear, and requires only a logarithmic number of passes over the stream. Using such a polynomial commitment scheme they build a succinct argument for RAM computation where the prover is both time- and space- optimal. The key structural property of their construction that allows for this small-space implementation in the streaming model is: they show that *for each of the logarithmic rounds*, prover's messages in the interactive proof of consistency can be expressed as a *linear combination of the elements in the description stream*. Therefore, it is sufficient for the monolithic prover to take a single pass over its stream to compute its message in every round. Although, their work still considers a monolithic prover, this structural property is the starting point of our work. In particular, we observe that the natural adaptation of Block et al. [22] commitment scheme to our setting suffices for our purposes. In fact, when the cluster of provers $P_1, \ldots, P_M$ is viewed as a monolithic prover, then the two schemes are identical. This allows us to base our security on that of Block et al. [22], which in turn, is based on groups of hidden order (e.g., RSA and class groups). Due to the above structural property, in each of the rounds, each of the provers in the cluster can (a) first compute their contributions to this round's message in small space, while making a single pass over their stream, and (b) then all provers can combine their contributions in logarithmic (in M) rounds via a tree-based protocol to compute the full round message.

We present our construction in the MPC model in Sect. 6.2. Along the way, we introduce the definition of polynomial commitments in the MPC model tailored to the case of multilinear polynomials in Sect. 4.

1.2   Related Work

The terminology of distributed interactive proofs appeared in several prior works, all of which differ significantly from our notion. The works [20,45,50] all study a variant of interactive proofs where the verifier is distributed but the prover is a single machine. The work of [51,58] allow multiple (potentially mutually-distrusting) provers to efficiently derive a single SNARK for a large statement/witness pair. While their goal on the surface is similar to ours, both works inherently require non-falsifiable assumptions since they rely on SNARKs. In contrast, the main contribution of our work is in building a succinct argument system that *does not* require non-falsifiable assumptions.

1.3   Organization

The rest of the paper is organized as follows. Section 2 contains preliminaries. In Sect. 3, we define the MPC model and security properties required for argument systems in this model. In Sect. 4, we define polynomial commitments that work with distributed committers. Section 5 contains the main construction of succinct arguments in the MPC model. Section 6 contains our adaptation of the [22] polynomial commitment.

2   Preliminaries

Let S be some finite, non-empty set. By $x \leftarrow S$ we denote the process of sampling a random element x from S. For any $k \in \mathbb{N}$, by S^k we denote the set of all sequences/vectors of length k containing elements of S where $S^0 = \{\epsilon\}$ for empty string ϵ. We let $\mathbb{F} = \mathbb{F}_p$ denote a finite field of prime cardinality p. We assume that $\vec{b} = (b_n, \ldots, b_1)$, where b_n is the most significant bit and b_1 is the least significant bit. For bitstrings $\vec{b} \in \{0,1\}^n$, we naturally associate $\vec{b}$ with integers in the set $\{0, \ldots, 2^n - 1\}$, i.e., $\vec{b} = \sum_{i=1}^n b_i \cdot 2^{i-1}$. For any two equal sized vectors $\vec{u}, \vec{v}$, by $\vec{u} \odot \vec{v}$ we denote the coordinate-wise multiplication of $\vec{u}$ and $\vec{v}$. We use uppercase letters to denote matrices, e.g., $A \in \mathbb{Z}^{m \times n}$. For $m \times n$ dimensional matrix A, $A(i, *)$ and $A(j, *)$ denote the i-th row and j-th column of A, respectively.

Notation for Matrix-Vector "Exponents". For some group $\mathbb{G}$, $A \in \mathbb{Z}^{m \times n}$. $\vec{u} = (u_1, \ldots, u_m) \in \mathbb{G}^{1 \times m}$, and $\vec{v} = (v_1, \ldots, v_m)^\top \in \mathbb{G}^{n \times 1}$, we let $\vec{u} \star A$ and $A \star \vec{v}$ denote a matrix-vector exponent, defined for every $j \in [n]$, $i' \in [m]$ as

$$(\vec{u} \star A)_j = \prod_{i=1}^m u_i^{A(i,j)} \ ; \ (A \star \vec{v})_{i'} = \prod_{j'=1}^n v_{j'}^{A(i',j')} ,$$

For any vector $\vec{x} \in \mathbb{Z}^n$ and group element $g \in \mathbb{G}$, we define $g^{\vec{x}} = (g^{x_1}, \ldots, g^{x_n})$. Finally, for $k \in \mathbb{Z}$ and a vector $\vec{u} \in \mathbb{G}^n$, we let $\vec{u}^k$ denote the vector $(u_1^k, \ldots, u_n^k)$.

2.1   Multilinear Polynomials

An n-variate polynomial $f : \mathbb{F}^n \to \mathbb{F}$ is *multilinear* if the individual degree of each variable in f is at most 1.

Fact 1. *A multilinear polynomial $f : \mathbb{F}^n \to \mathbb{F}$ (over a finite field $\mathbb{F}$) is uniquely defined by its evaluations over the Boolean hypercube. Moreover, for every $\vec{\zeta} \in \mathbb{F}^n$,*

$$f(\vec{\zeta}) = \sum_{\vec{b} \in \{0,1\}^n} f(\vec{b}) \cdot \prod_{i=1}^n \chi(b_i, \zeta_i) ,$$

where $\chi(b, \zeta) = b \cdot \zeta + (1 - b) \cdot (1 - \zeta)$.

As a shorthand, we will often denote $\prod_{i=1}^{n} \chi(b_i, \zeta_i)$ by $\overline{\chi}(\vec{b}, \vec{\zeta})$ for $n = |\vec{b}| = |\vec{\zeta}|$.

Notation for Multilinear Polynomials. Throughout, we denote a multilinear polynomial f by the 2^n sized sequence $\mathcal{Y}$ containing its evaluations over the Boolean hypercube. That is, $\mathcal{Y} = (f(\vec{b}) : \vec{b} \in \{0,1\}^n)$, and denote the evaluation of the multilinear polynomial defined by $\mathcal{Y}$ on the point $\vec{\zeta}$ as $\mathsf{ML}(\mathcal{Y}, \vec{\zeta}) = \sum_{\vec{b} \in \{0,1\}^n} \mathcal{Y}_{\vec{b}} \cdot \overline{\chi}(\vec{b}, \vec{\zeta})$.

3   Model Definition

In the massively-parallel computation (MPC) model, there are M parties (also called machines) and each party has a local space of S bits. The input is assumed to be distributed across the parties. Let N denote the total input size in bits; it is standard to assume $M \geq N^{1-\varepsilon}$ and $S = N^{\varepsilon}$ for some small constant $\varepsilon \in (0,1)$. Note that the total space is $M \cdot S$ which is large enough to store the input (since $M \cdot S \geq N$), but at the same time it is not desirable to waste space and so it is commonly further assumed that $M \cdot S \in \tilde{O}(N)$ or $M \cdot S = N^{1+\theta}$ for some small constant $\theta \in (0,1)$. Further, assume that $S = \Omega(\log M)$.

At the beginning of a protocol, each party receives an input, and the protocol proceeds in rounds. During each round, each party performs some local computation given its current state (modeled as a RAM program with maximum space S), and afterwards may send messages to some other parties through private authenticated pairwise channels. An MPC protocol must respect the space restriction throughout its execution, even during the communication phase—to send a message at the end of a round, a party must write that message in some designated place in memory, and in order to receive a message at the end of a round, a party must reserve some space in memory equal to the size of the message. This in turn implies that each party can send or receive at most S bits in each round. An MPC algorithm may be randomized, in which case every machine has a sequential-access random tape and can read random coins from the random tape. The size of this random tape is not charged to the machine's space consumption.

3.1   Succinct Arguments in the MPC Model

We are interested in building a succinct argument in this model for some NP language L, where the witness $w = (w_1, \ldots, w_M)$ for $x \in L$ has size much larger than S. The prover role is carried out by a group of S-space-bounded parties $P_1, \ldots, P_M$, each of which has the statement x and one piece w_i of the witness. They work together to convince a verifier V, which is also S-space-bounded. Since any prover must at least be powerful enough to verify that $(x, w) \in R_L$, and the MPC model is not known to capture P when the rounds are bounded, we only consider languages L where the verification algorithm $R_L \colon ((x, w_1), \ldots, (x, w_M)) \to \{0,1\}$ is implementable by a MPC protocol Π_L where each party is S-space-bounded. Given such a protocol, our goal is to build a new MPC protocol Π'_L between $M + 1$ parties $P_1, \ldots, P_M, V$, where P_i has input (x, w_i) and V has input x, which satisfies the properties discussed below.

Communication Model and Setup. We assume a synchronous setting, with pairwise channels between parties. We also allow for a CRS Setup$(1^\lambda) \rightarrow (\alpha_1, \ldots, \alpha_M)$, where party i receives α_i at the beginning of the protocol. Since each party must store some α_i, it is clear that $|\alpha_i| \leq S$ for all i. Looking ahead, in our protocol, all parties get the same CRS string α which is a description of a group of size 2^λ, that is, $\alpha_i = \alpha$ for all $i \in [M]$.

Efficiency Requirements. We want to build a protocol Π'_L which has efficiency properties as close as possible to the original verification protocol Π_L. Specifically, if in Π_L each party uses space bounded by S, in Π'_L each party's space should be bounded by $S \cdot p(\lambda)$, for some fixed polynomial p. Moreover, if Π_L takes r rounds, Π'_L should take a small multiplicative factor $r \cdot \beta$ rounds. In this paper, we set $\beta = \mathsf{polylog}(N)$.

Security Requirements. Let α be the output of the setup algorithm, and denote with

$$\Pi'_L \langle [P_1, \ldots, P_M], V \rangle \left(1^\lambda, \alpha, x, w = (w_1, \ldots, w_M)\right)$$

the output of the protocol Π'_L with interactive RAM programs $P_1, \ldots, P_M$ playing the roles of the M provers, and with the interactive RAM program V playing the role of the verifier, where each P_i is initialized with input $(1^\lambda, \alpha, x, w_i)$, and V is initialized with input $(1^\lambda, \alpha, x)$. Similarly, denote with

$$\Pi'_L \langle \mathcal{A}, V \rangle \left(1^\lambda, \alpha, x, w = (w_1, \ldots, w_M)\right)$$

the output of the protocol Π'_L with an interactive *monolithic* RAM program $\mathcal{A}$ playing the role of all provers $P_1, \ldots, P_M$, and with the interactive RAM program V playing the role of the verifier, where $\mathcal{A}$ is initialized with the inputs of all P_i as defined above, and V is initialized in the same way as above.

We require Π'_L satisfies completeness and soundness, defined as follows.

Definition 1 (Completeness). *Let L be a language with a corresponding MPC protocol Π_L which implements the verification functionality for R_L. For all $(x, w) \in R_L$ and for all λ, letting $m = m(|x|)$,*

$$\Pr\left[\Pi'_L \langle [P_1, \ldots, P_M], V \rangle \left(1^\lambda, \mathsf{Setup}(1^\lambda), x, w\right) = 1\right] = 1,$$

where $P_1, \ldots, P_M$ (resp., V) are the honest provers (resp., verifier), and the probability is taken over random coins of the parties and of the setup algorithm.

Definition 2 (Soundness). *Let L be a language with a corresponding MPC protocol Π_L which implements the verification functionality R_L. Fix a PPT adversary $\mathcal{A} = (\mathcal{A}_1, \mathcal{A}_2)$, where $\mathcal{A}_1$ takes as input the security parameter and the output of Setup, and chooses an input x, and where $\mathcal{A}_2$ plays the roles of* the provers $P_1, \ldots, P_M$. Then Π_L is said to satisfy soundness if there exists a negligible function negl such that for all λ,

$$\Pr\left[\begin{array}{c} x \notin L \wedge \\ \Pi'_L \langle \mathcal{A}_2, V\rangle \left(1^\lambda, \alpha, x, \perp\right) = 1 \end{array} : \begin{array}{c} (\alpha_1, \ldots, \alpha_M) \leftarrow \mathsf{Setup}(1^\lambda) \\ x \leftarrow \mathcal{A}_1(\lambda, \alpha_1, \ldots, \alpha_M) \end{array}\right] < \mathsf{negl}(\lambda).$$

To prove soundness of our protocol, we show the stronger property of witness-extended emulation as formalized by Lindell [48]. Intuitively, witness-extended emulation requires the existence of an efficient extractor that can simulate an adversarial prover's view while extracting the underlying witness. Below we formally extend the standard definition to the MPC setting in the natural way.

Definition 3 (Witness-Extended Emulation). *Let L be a language with a corresponding MPC protocol Π_L which implements the verification functionality R_L. Fix a PPT adversary $\mathcal{A} = (\mathcal{A}_1, \mathcal{A}_2)$, where $\mathcal{A}_1$ takes as input the security parameter and the output of Setup and chooses an input x along with a private state σ, and where $\mathcal{A}_2$ takes this σ as input and plays the roles of the provers $P_1, \ldots, P_M$. Then Π_L is said to satisfy witness-extended emulation with respect to L (and R_L) if there exists an (expected) PPT machine $\mathcal{E}$ (called the "extractor") and a negligible function negl such that the following holds. Define two distributions $\mathcal{D}_1^\lambda$ and $\mathcal{D}_2^\lambda$ based on $\mathcal{A}$ and $\mathcal{E}$, as follows:*

- $\mathcal{D}_1^\lambda$: *Compute the setup $\alpha \leftarrow \mathsf{Setup}(1^\lambda)$ and then compute $(x, \sigma) \leftarrow \mathcal{A}_1(1^\lambda, \alpha)$, then output $(\alpha, r_\mathcal{A}, r_V, x, \tau)$, where τ is the transcript of messages obtained by the execution $\Pi'_L \langle \mathcal{A}_2(\sigma), V\rangle \left(1^\lambda, \alpha, x, \perp\right)$, $r_\mathcal{A}$ is the random tape of $\mathcal{A}_1$ and $\mathcal{A}_2$, and r_V is the random tape of V.*
- $\mathcal{D}_2^\lambda$: *Compute the setup $\alpha \leftarrow \mathsf{Setup}(1^\lambda)$ and then compute $(x, \sigma) \leftarrow \mathcal{A}_1(1^\lambda, \alpha)$, then output $(\alpha, r_\mathcal{A}, r_V, x, \tau, w) \leftarrow \mathcal{E}^\mathcal{O}(1^\lambda, \alpha, x)$, where $\mathcal{O}$ is an oracle which provides an execution of $\Pi'_L \langle \mathcal{A}_2(\sigma), V\rangle \left(1^\lambda, \alpha, x, \perp\right)$, and allows for rewinding of the protocol and choosing the randomness of $\mathcal{A}_2$ during each round.*

With respect to these distributions, for all λ, the following holds:

1. *The distributions $\mathcal{D}_1^\lambda$ and $\mathcal{D}_2^\lambda\big|_{\alpha, r, x, \tau}$ are identical, where $\mathcal{D}_2^\lambda\big|_{\alpha, r, x, \tau}$ is the restriction of $\mathcal{D}_2$ to the first four components of the tuple (α, r, x, τ, w).*
2. *It holds that $\Pr\left[V \text{ accepts and } (x, w) \notin R_L : (\alpha, r, x, \tau, w) \leftarrow \mathcal{D}_2^\lambda\right] < \mathsf{negl}(\lambda)$.*

4   Defining Multilinear Polynomial Commitments in the MPC Model

In this section, we discuss how to define a polynomial commitment scheme which works in the MPC model starting with a discussion on how the polynomial is distributed across all of the M many S-space-bounded parties. Let M be a power of 2 and let $\mathcal{Y} \in \mathbb{F}^N$ define an n variate multilinear polynomial where $N = 2^n$. We assume that $\mathcal{Y}$ is distributed across all parties in the following way: Let $\{I_1, \ldots, I_M\}$ be the canonical partition of $\{0,1\}^n$, that is, $I_i = \{(i - 1) \cdot N/M, \ldots, i \cdot N/M - 1\}$. We associate each party P_i with the subset I_i, and assume that P_i holds only the partial vector $\mathcal{Y}_i$ containing elements from $\mathcal{Y}$ restricted to the indices in I_i. That is,

$$\mathcal{Y}_i = (\mathcal{Y}_{\vec{b}})_{\vec{b} \in I_i} .$$

Furthermore, for the canonical partition, if i-th party holds the partial vector $\mathcal{Y}_i$, then they collectively define the multilinear polynomial $\mathcal{Y}$ where $\mathcal{Y} = \mathcal{Y}_1 \parallel \mathcal{Y}_2 \parallel \cdots \parallel \mathcal{Y}_M$, where $\parallel$ refers to the concatenation of two vectors.

Definition 4 (Multilinear Polynomial Commitment Syntax). *A multilinear polynomial commitment has the following syntax.*

- PC.Setup$(1^\lambda, p, 1^n, M) \to pp$: *On input the security parameter 1^λ (in unary), a field size p less than 2^λ, the number of variables 1^n (also in unary), and the number of parties M, the setup algorithm PC.Setup is a randomized PPT algorithm that outputs a CRS pp whose size is at most $\mathsf{poly}(\lambda, n, \log(M))$.*
- PC.PartialCom$(pp, \mathcal{Y}_i) \to (\mathsf{com}_i; \mathcal{Z}_i)$: *On input a CRS pp, and a vector $\mathcal{Y}_i \in \mathbb{F}$ which is the description of a multilinear polynomial restricted to the set $I_i \subset \{0,1\}^n$, PC.PartialCom outputs a "partial commitment" com_i as well as the corresponding decommitment $\mathcal{Z}_i \in \mathbb{Z}$.*
- PC.CombineCom$(pp, \{\mathsf{com}_i\}_{i \in [M]}) \to \mathsf{com}$: *This is an interactive PPT protocol in the MPC model computing the following functionality: each party P_i holds the string (pp, com_i), they jointly compute the full commitment com such that P_1 learns com, and outputs it.*
  PC.PartialEval$(pp, \mathcal{Y}_i, \vec{\zeta}) \to y_i$: *On input a CRS pp, a partial description vector $\mathcal{Y}_i$, and an evaluation point $\vec{\zeta} \in \mathbb{F}^n$, PC.PartialEval is a PPT algorithm that outputs the partial evaluation y_i.*
- PC.CombineEval$(pp, \{y_i\}_{i \in [M]}, \zeta) \to y$: *This is an interactive PPT protocol in the MPC model computing the following functionality: each party P_i holds the string (pp, y_i), they jointly compute the full evaluation y such that P_1 learns y, and outputs it.*
- PC.IsValid$(pp, \mathsf{com}, \mathcal{Y}, \mathcal{Z}) \to 0$ or 1: *On input the CRS pp, a commitment com, a multilinear polynomial $\mathcal{Y}$ and a decommitment $\mathcal{Z}$, PC.IsValid is a PPT algorithm that returns a decision bit.*
- PC.Open: *Is a public-coin succinct interactive argument system $\langle [P_1, \ldots, P_M], V \rangle$ in the MPC model, where the statement $(pp, \mathsf{com}, \vec{\zeta}, y)$ and witness $(\mathcal{Y} = \{\mathcal{Y}_i\}_{i \in [M]}, \mathcal{Z} = \{\mathcal{Z}_i\}_{i \in [M]})$, with respect to the relation*

$$R = \left\{ \left((pp, \mathsf{com}, \vec{\zeta}, y), (\mathcal{Y}, \mathcal{Z}) \right) : \begin{array}{l} \mathsf{IsValid}(pp, \mathsf{com}, \mathcal{Y}, \mathcal{Z}) = 1, \text{ and} \\ \mathsf{ML}(\mathcal{Y}, \vec{\zeta}) = y \end{array} \right\},$$

where each prover P_i has input $(pp, \mathsf{com}, \vec{\zeta}, y, \mathcal{Y}_i, \mathcal{Z}_i)$ and V has input $(pp, \mathsf{com}, \vec{\zeta}, y)$.

In the following sections, we assume that PC.PartialCom works even if we are given streaming access to $\mathcal{Y}_i$.

We now specify the security properties which are required of PC.

Definition 5 (Multilinear Polynomial Commitment Security). *We require the following three properties from a polynomial commitment scheme:*

- **Correctness:** *For every prime p, number of variables n, and all $\mathcal{Y}$ and $\vec{\zeta}$,*

$$
\Pr \left[1 = \mathsf{PC.Open}(pp, \mathsf{com}, \vec{\zeta}, y; \mathcal{Y}, \mathcal{Z}) : \begin{array}{c} pp \leftarrow \mathsf{PC.Setup}(1^\lambda, p, 1^n) \\ \{\mathsf{com}_i, \mathcal{Z}_i \leftarrow \mathsf{PC.PartialCom}(pp, \mathcal{Y}_i)\}_{i \in [M]} \\ \mathsf{com}, \mathcal{Z} \leftarrow \mathsf{PC.CombineCom}(pp, \{\mathsf{com}_i\}_{i \in [M]}) \end{array} \right] = 1.
$$

- **Computational Binding:** *For every prime q, number of variables n, number of parties M, and nonuniform polynomial machine $\mathcal{A}$, there exists a negligible function $\mathsf{negl} : \mathbb{N} \to [0,1]$ such that for every $\lambda \in \mathbb{N}$ and every $z \in \{0,1\}^*$, following holds:*

$$
\Pr \left[\begin{array}{c} b_0 = 1 \\ b_1 = 1 \\ \mathcal{Y}_0 \neq \mathcal{Y}_1 \end{array} : \begin{array}{c} pp \leftarrow \mathsf{PC.Setup}(1^\lambda, q, 1^n, M) \\ (\mathsf{com}, \mathcal{Y}_0, \mathcal{Y}_1, \mathcal{Z}_0, \mathcal{Z}_1) \leftarrow \mathcal{A}(1^\lambda, pp, z) \\ b_0 \leftarrow \mathsf{PC.IsValid}(pp, \mathsf{com}, \mathcal{Y}_0, \mathcal{Z}_0) \\ b_1 \leftarrow \mathsf{PC.IsValid}(pp, \mathsf{com}, \mathcal{Y}_1, \mathcal{Z}_1) \end{array} \right] < \mathsf{negl}(\lambda).
$$

- **Properties of PC.Open:** *The argument PC.Open satisfies the efficiency, completeness and witness-extended emulation properties defined in Sect. 3.*

Looking ahead, in Sect. 6, we will prove the following theorem, showing the existence of a scheme PC which satisfies the properties above.

Theorem 2. *Assume $\mathcal{G}$ is a group sampler where the Hidden Order Assumption holds. Let n be the number of variables, $M \leq 2^n$ be the number of parties. Then, the scheme defined in Sect. 6.2 is a polynomial commitment scheme (as in Sect. 4) for n variate multilinear polynomials over finite field of prime-order p in the MPC model with M parties with the following efficiency guarantees:*

1. *PC.PartialCom outputs a partial commitment of size $\mathsf{poly}(\lambda)$ bits, runs in time $2^n \cdot \mathsf{poly}(\lambda, n, \log(p))$, and uses a single pass over the stream.*
2. *PC.PartialEval outputs a partial evaluation of size $\lceil \log(p) \rceil$, runs in time $(2^n/M) \cdot \mathsf{poly}(n, \log(p))$, and uses a single pass over the stream.*
3. *PC.CombineCom and PC.CombineEval have $O(\log(M))$ rounds, and each party in it requires $\mathsf{poly}(\lambda)$ bits of space.*
4. *PC.Open takes $O(n \cdot \log(M))$ rounds with $\mathsf{poly}(n, \lambda, \log(p), \log(M))$ communication.*
5. *The verifier in PC.Open runs in time $\mathsf{poly}(\lambda, n, \log(p))$.*
6. *Each party P_i in PC.Open runs in time $2^n \cdot \mathsf{poly}(n, \lambda, \log(p))$, requires space $n \cdot \mathsf{poly}(\lambda, \log(p), \log(M))$, and uses $O(n)$ passes over its stream.*

5   Constructing Succinct Arguments in the MPC Model

Our construction uses the subprotocols Distribute, Combine, and CalcMerkleTree introduced in [35]. These protocols take $O(\log_\nu M)$ rounds and the communication is $O(S \cdot \nu)$ per round for each machine, for small integral branching factor $\nu \geq 2$.

5.1 Tools from Prior Work

We import two major tools from previous work. The first is the following lemma, which says that any RAM program can be transformed into a circuit C, where the wire assignments of C can be streamed in time and space both proportional to the time and space of the RAM program, respectively. In addition, the circuit logic can be represented succinctly by low-degree polynomials which have properties amenable to sumcheck arguments.

Lemma 1 (From Blumberg et al. [23]). *Let M be an arbitrary (non-deterministic) RAM program that on inputs of length n runs in time $T(n)$ and space $S(n)$. M can be transformed into an equivalent (non-deterministic) arithmetic circuit C over a field $\mathbb{F}$ of size $\mathsf{polylog}(T(n))$. Moreover, there exist cubic extensions $\widehat{\mathsf{add}}$ and $\widehat{\mathsf{mult}}$ of the wiring predicates add and mult of C that satisfy:*

1. *C has size $O(T(n) \cdot \mathsf{polylog}(T(n)))$.*
2. *The cubic extensions $\widehat{\mathsf{add}}$ and $\widehat{\mathsf{mult}}$ of C can be evaluated in time $O(\mathsf{polylog}(T(n)))$.*
3. *an (input,witness) pair (x, w) that makes M accept can be mapped to a correct transcript W for C in time $O(T(n) \cdot \mathsf{polylog}(T(n)))$ and space $O(S(n)) \cdot \mathsf{polylog}(T(n))$. Furthermore, w is a substring of the transcript W, and any correct transcript W' for C possesses a witness w' for (M, x) as a substring.*
4. *C can be evaluated "gate-by-gate" in time $O(T(n) \cdot \mathsf{polylog}(T(n)))$ and space $O(S(n) \cdot \mathsf{polylog}(T(n)))$.*
5. *The prover's sumcheck messages can be computed in space $O(S(n) \cdot \mathsf{polylog}(T(n)))$.*

5.2 Notation

We make the following notational assumptions about the MPC algorithm Π_L which verifies membership in L.

Let R be the number of rounds that Π_L takes. In each round $r \in [R]$ of an execution of Π_L, the behavior of party $i \in [M]$ is described as a succinct RAM program $\mathsf{NextSt}(i, r, \cdot)$. Thus the program NextSt is a succinct representation of the entire protocol Π_L. We assume NextSt has size much less than S. For convenience, we write $\mathsf{NextSt}_{i,r}(\cdot) = \mathsf{NextSt}(i, r, \cdot)$. We assume that $\mathsf{NextSt}_{i,r}$ takes a string $\mathsf{st}_{i,r-1} \| \mathsf{msg}_{i,r-1}^{\mathsf{in}}$ as an input and outputs string $\mathsf{st}_{i,r} \| \mathsf{msg}_{i,r}^{\mathsf{out}}$, where $\mathsf{st}_{i,r}$ is the internal, private state of party i in round r and $\mathsf{msg}_{i,r-1}^{\mathsf{in}}$ is the list of messages which party i received in round $r - 1$, and $\mathsf{msg}_{i,r}^{\mathsf{out}}$ are the outgoing messages of party i in round r. Note that the space of each party is limited to S bits, so in particular $|\mathsf{st}_{i,r}\| \mathsf{msg}_{i,r}^{\mathsf{in}}\| \mathsf{msg}_{i,r}^{\mathsf{out}}| \leq S$ for each $i \in [M]$ and $r \in [R]$. We assume that the first-round private state $\mathsf{st}_{i,0}$ of each party i is equal to its private input (x, w_i) (or x if $i = M + 1$). In addition, we assume that $\mathsf{msg}_{i,r}^{\mathsf{out}} = \{(j, \ell_j, m_j)\}_j$, where each triple (j, ℓ_j, m_j) means that party i should send message m_j to party j, and that party j should store this message at position ℓ_j in $\mathsf{msg}_{j,r-1}^{\mathsf{in}}$. Finally, we assume that if r is the final round then P_1 writes 1 to the first position of $\mathsf{st}_{1,r}$ iff $x \in L$.

5.3   The Construction

The main construction of a succinct argument in the MPC model works as follows. First, we construct a succinct argument for the following scenario. Fix a round r and corresponding starting states $\mathsf{st}_{i,r-1}\|\mathsf{msg}^{\mathsf{in}}_{i,r-1}$ for each party $i \in [M]$, and let π_{r-1} be a Merkle commitment to the concatenation of all these starting states. Let $\mathsf{st}_{i,r}\|\mathsf{msg}^{\mathsf{out}}_{i,r}\|\mathsf{msg}^{\mathsf{in}}_{i,r}$ be the state of party i after an honest execution of round r, and let π_r be a Merkle commitment to the concatenation of all these end states. Assuming V has x, π_{r-1}, and π_r, the goal is to convince V that π_r is a commitment to states which have been obtained by an honest round-r interaction, starting with the states committed to by π_{r-1}. If we construct an argument for this language, and this argument satisfies witness-extended emulation, this is sufficient for achieving an argument system which verifies an honest execution of the full protocol Π_L with respect to a witness for L.

In the following, we construct such a "round verification protocol," which is our main technical contribution. In Sect. 5.4, we show how to use this round verification protocol to build an argument system for L.

To start, we define a new machine, which we call NextSt'. As before, we write $\mathsf{NextSt}'_{i,r}(\cdot) = \mathsf{NextSt}'(i,r,\cdot)$. Let

$$\mathsf{NextSt}'_{i,r}(\pi_{r-1}, \pi_r, \mathsf{st}_{i,r-1}, \mathsf{msg}^{\mathsf{in}}_{i,r-1}, \rho_{i,r-1}, \rho_{i,r}, \{\rho_{i \to j,r}\}_j) = 1$$

if the all following holds:

- $\rho_{i,r-1}$ is an opening of π_{r-1} to $(\mathsf{st}_{i,r-1}, \mathsf{msg}^{\mathsf{in}}_{i,r-1})$ at position i,
- $\rho_{i,r}$ is an opening of π_r to $\mathsf{st}_{i,r}\|\mathsf{msg}^{\mathsf{out}}_{i,r}\|\mathsf{msg}^{\mathsf{in}}_{i,r}$ at position i, where

$$\mathsf{NextSt}_{i,r}(\mathsf{st}_{i,r-1}, \mathsf{msg}^{\mathsf{in}}_{i,r-1}) = \mathsf{st}_{i,r}\|\mathsf{msg}^{\mathsf{out}}_{i,r}\|\mathsf{msg}^{\mathsf{in}}_{i,r},$$

- Writing $\mathsf{msg}^{\mathsf{out}}_{i,r}$ as $\{(j, \ell_j, m_j)\}_j$, for each j, $\rho_{i \to j,r}$ is an opening to m_j at position ℓ_j in $\mathsf{msg}^{\mathsf{in}}_{j,r}$.

Otherwise, let

$$\mathsf{NextSt}'_{i,r}(\pi_{r-1}, \pi_r, \mathsf{st}_{i,r-1}, \mathsf{msg}^{\mathsf{in}}_{i,r-1}, \rho_{i,r-1}, \rho_{i,r}, \{\rho_{i \to j,r}\}_j) = 0.$$

Note that since $\mathsf{NextSt}_{i,r}$ is succinct, $\mathsf{NextSt}'_{i,r}$ is also succinct. Let $C_{i,r}$ be the circuit corresponding to $\mathsf{NextSt}'_{i,r}$ via Lemma 1. Also from Lemma 1, party i can stream the gate assignments $W_{i,r}$ of $C_{i,r}$ in space proportional to the space taken by an execution of $\mathsf{NextSt}'_{i,r}$.

We take an approach inspired by that of [22,23] in constructing a sumcheck polynomial that encodes the computation, and using a polynomial commitment to allow for a succinct verifier. Let $s = \lceil \log T' \rceil$, where T' is the number of wires in $C_{i,r}$ (which is constant across i and r). We can index every wire in $C_{i,r}$ with some string $\vec{x} \in \{0,1\}^s$. Define the polynomial $\hat{W}_{i,r}(X_1, \ldots, X_s)$ to be the multilinear extension of $W_{i,r}$, i.e., for all $\vec{x} \in \{0,1\}^s$, $W_{i,r}(\vec{x})$ is the value that $W_{i,r}$ assigns to wire $\vec{x}$. Now, letting $m = \lceil \log M \rceil$, we can index each party by a string $\vec{z} \in \{0,1\}^m$. Define $\hat{W}_r(X_1, \ldots, X_s, Z_1, \ldots, Z_m)$ to be the multilinear polynomial such that $\hat{W}_r(\vec{x}, \vec{z}) = \hat{W}_{i,r}(\vec{x})$, where i is the index which corresponds to $\vec{z}$. Let $\widehat{\mathsf{add}}(X_1, \ldots, X_{3s})$ be the succinct, low-degree polynomial from Lemma 1 where $\widehat{\mathsf{add}}(\vec{x}_1, \vec{x}_2, \vec{x}_3) = 1$ if in $C_{i,r}$ the unique gate which has input wires $\vec{x}_1$ and $\vec{x}_2$ and output wire $\vec{x}_3$ is an addition gate. Note that $\widehat{\mathsf{add}}$ does not depend on i (or r for that matter) since, except for some hardcoded input wires, $C_{i,r} = C_{i',r'}$ for all i, i', r, r'. Similarly, define $\widehat{\mathsf{mult}}(X_1, \ldots, X_{3s})$. Finally, define $\widehat{\mathsf{inout}}(X_1, \ldots, X_{3s})$ so that $\widehat{\mathsf{inout}}(\vec{x}_1, \vec{x}_2, \vec{x}_3) = 1$ if either $\vec{x}_3$ is an input wire which is known by V, or $\vec{x}_3$ is an output wire which is known by V and $\vec{x}_1$ and $\vec{x}_2$ are the input wires for the gate whose output wire is $\vec{x}_3$. Define $\hat{I}(X_1, \ldots, X_m)$ to be the multilinear polynomial such that $\hat{I}(\vec{x})$ is the corresponding bit of π_{r-1} (or π_r) if $\vec{x}$ is an input wire which takes the value of a bit of π_{r-1} (or π_r, respectively), and is the corresponding bit of the statement to the argument system if $r = 0$ $\vec{x}$ is an input wire which takes the value of the statement, and is 1 if $\vec{x}$ is an output wire which V knows should be 1.

Given above, we can define the polynomial g as follows:

$$
\begin{aligned}
g(\vec{X}_1, \vec{X}_2, \vec{X}_3, \vec{Z}) = {}& \widehat{\mathsf{add}}(\vec{X}_1, \vec{X}_2, \vec{X}_3)(\hat{W}_r(\vec{X}_3, \vec{Z}) - (\hat{W}_r(\vec{X}_1, \vec{Z}) + \hat{W}_r(\vec{X}_2, \vec{Z}))) \\
{}+{}& \widehat{\mathsf{mult}}(\vec{X}_1, \vec{X}_2, \vec{X}_3)(\hat{W}_r(\vec{X}_3, \vec{Z}) - (\hat{W}_r(\vec{X}_1, \vec{Z}) \cdot \hat{W}_r(\vec{X}_2, \vec{Z}))) \\
{}+{}& \widehat{\mathsf{inout}}(\vec{X}_1, \vec{X}_2, \vec{X}_3)(\hat{W}_r(\vec{X}_3, \vec{Z}) - \hat{I}(\vec{X}_3)).
\end{aligned}
$$

With this definition, g vanishes on all boolean inputs if and only if $\hat{W}_r$ encodes transcripts of the correct computations of each party i with respect to starting states committed to in π_{r-1} and ending states committed to in π_r, and if all messages sent by i have been stored in the respective $\mathsf{msg}^{in}_{j,r}$. For $q \in \mathbb{Z}_p$, let $h_q(\vec{X}) = g(\vec{X}) \cdot \prod_{\beta \in [m+3\,s]} (1 - (1 - q^{2^{\beta-1}})X_i)$. Then, $h_q(\vec{x}) = g(\vec{x}) \cdot q^{\mathsf{bin}^{-1}(\vec{x})}$ for all $\vec{x} \in \{0,1\}^{m+3\,s}$, where $\mathsf{bin}^{-1}(\vec{X})$ is the integer represented by the binary representation $\vec{X}$. We now have defined the polynomials required for the protocol below. If $P_1, \ldots P_M$ can collectively construct the prover's sumcheck messages for the polynomial h_q for a randomly chosen q, then this is sufficient to build an argument that convinces V that g vanishes on the boolean hypercube. We now describe the protocol, assuming the provers have an efficient subprotocol CalcSumcheckProverMsg (defined below) for constructing their responses. This protocol is heavily inspired by the IOP in [22]. However, that protocol was significantly simpler, since in their setting, there is only one prover who can stream the whole polynomial $\hat{W}_r$. In contrast, we have the task of showing that it is possible to construct the prover's sumcheck responses in a round-efficient way, even given that $\hat{W}_r$ is spread across many different machines.

VerifyRound: **Protocol to verify correctness of one round of Π_L.**

Parameters: Tree fan-in $\nu = s/\log N$.

Inputs: P_i has input $(r, \pi_{r-1}, \pi_r, \mathsf{st}_{i,r-1}, \mathsf{msg}^{\mathsf{in}}_{i,r-1}, \rho_{i,r-1}, \rho_{i,r}, \{\rho_{i \to j,r}\}_j)$. V has input (x, r, π_{r-1}, π_r). In addition, all parties have the setup α for a polynomial commitment scheme.

Execution:

1. Independently in parallel, each prover computes $\phi_i = \mathsf{PC.PartialCom}(\alpha, \hat{W})$, where for each $\vec{x} \in \{0,1\}^s$, $\hat{W}(\vec{x})$ is the wire assignment for wire $\vec{x}$ in $C_{i,r}$. By Lemma 1, the wire assignments can be computed in a streaming fashion, and $\mathsf{PC.PartialCom}$ works given streaming access to $\hat{W}$.
2. $\mathsf{com} \leftarrow \mathsf{PC.CombineCom}(\alpha, \{\phi_i\}_{i \in [M]})$, so that each party obtains com, the commitment of the polynomial $\hat{W}_r$ defined above.
3. P_1 sends this commitment com to V.
4. V chooses $q \xleftarrow{\$} \mathbb{F}$ and sends q to P_1.
5. The provers run $\mathsf{Distribute}_\nu(q)$ so that every prover obtains q.
6. The parties now run the sumcheck protocol with respect to h_q defined above. Set $y_1 \leftarrow 0$. For each $\gamma \in [m + 3s]$:
   (a) Provers run the subprotocol $\mathsf{CalcSumcheckProverMsg}$ to generate sumcheck prover's message f_γ. P_1 sends f_γ to V.
   (b) V checks that $\deg f_\gamma = \deg_\gamma h_q$, and halts and outputs 0 if the degrees are different.
   (c) V checks that $f_\gamma(0) + f_\gamma(1) = y_\gamma$, and halts and outputs 0 if the equality does not hold.
   (d) V then chooses $\zeta_\gamma \xleftarrow{\$} \mathbb{F}$, sets $y_{\gamma+1} \leftarrow f_\gamma(\zeta_\gamma)$, and sends ζ_γ to P_1.
7. Write $\vec{\zeta} = (\vec{\zeta_1}, \vec{\zeta_2}, \vec{\zeta_3}, \vec{\zeta_4})$. The provers and verifier run $\mathsf{PC.Open}$ with respect to statements $(\alpha, \mathsf{com}, (\vec{\zeta_1}, \vec{\zeta_4}), \hat{W}_r(\vec{\zeta_1}, \vec{\zeta_4})), (\alpha, \mathsf{com}, (\vec{\zeta_2}, \vec{\zeta_4}), \hat{W}_r(\vec{\zeta_2}, \vec{\zeta_4}))$, and $(\alpha, \mathsf{com}, (\vec{\zeta_3}, \vec{\zeta_4}), \hat{W}_r(\vec{\zeta_3}, \vec{\zeta_4}))$. V halts and outputs 0 if any of these protocols fail to verify.
8. V uses the openings to compute $h_q(\vec{\zeta})$. It checks whether $h_q(\vec{\zeta}) = y_{m+3s}$; if the equality does not hold, V outputs 0; otherwise, it outputs 1.

The $\mathsf{CalcSumcheckProverMsg}$ subprotocol

We now show how the parties $P_1, \ldots, P_M$ can generate the sumcheck prover's polynomials f_γ in a round- and space-efficient manner. For each round γ, the honest $f_\gamma(X)$ is defined to be the following univariate polynomial:

$$f_\gamma(X) = \sum_{\vec{x} \in \{0,1\}^{m+3\,s-\gamma}} h_q(\vec{\zeta}, X, \vec{x}),$$

for the random vector $\vec{\zeta}$ chosen by the verifier in previous rounds. (In round one, $\vec{\zeta}$ is the empty vector of length 0.) Recall that $h_q(\vec{X}) = g(\vec{X}) \cdot \prod_{i \in [m+3\,s]}(1 - (1 - q^{2^i} X_i))$, for g as defined below (setting $\vec{X} = (\vec{X}_1, \vec{X}_2, \vec{X}_3, \vec{Z})$):

$$g(\vec{X}_1, \vec{X}_2, \vec{X}_3, \vec{Z}) = \widehat{\mathsf{add}}(\vec{X}_1, \vec{X}_2, \vec{X}_3)(\hat{W}_r(\vec{X}_3, \vec{Z}) - (\hat{W}_r(\vec{X}_1, \vec{Z}) + \hat{W}_r(\vec{X}_2, \vec{Z})))$$
$$+ \widehat{\mathsf{mult}}(\vec{X}_1, \vec{X}_2, \vec{X}_3)(\hat{W}_r(\vec{X}_3, \vec{Z}) - (\hat{W}_r(\vec{X}_1, \vec{Z}) \cdot \hat{W}_r(\vec{X}_2, \vec{Z})))$$
$$+ \widehat{\mathsf{inout}}(\vec{x}_1, \vec{x}_2, \vec{x}_3)(\hat{W}_r(\vec{X}_3, \vec{Z}) - \hat{I}(\vec{X}_3)).$$

Observe that $h_q(\vec{X})$ can be written as

$$h_q(\vec{X}_1, \vec{X}_2, \vec{X}_3, \vec{Z}) = \sum_{i=j}^{5} p_j(\vec{X}_1, \vec{X}_2, \vec{X}_3, \vec{Z}),$$

where $p_5(\vec{X}_1, \vec{X}_2, \vec{X}_3, \vec{Z}) = \widehat{\mathsf{inout}}(\vec{x}_1, \vec{x}_2, \vec{x}_3) \cdot \hat{I}(\vec{X}_3)$ and can be computed locally by each party,

$$p_4(\vec{X}_1, \vec{X}_2, \vec{X}_3, \vec{Z}) = p_4'(\vec{X}_1, \vec{X}_2, \vec{X}_3, \vec{Z})\hat{W}_r(\vec{X}_1, \vec{Z})\hat{W}_r(\vec{X}_2, \vec{Z}),$$

and for all $j \in \{1, 2, 3\}$

$$p_j(\vec{X}_1, \vec{X}_2, \vec{X}_3, \vec{Z}) = p_j'(\vec{X}_1, \vec{X}_2, \vec{X}_3, \vec{Z})\hat{W}_r(\vec{X}_j, \vec{Z}) .$$

Here each p_j' is a succinct low-degree polynomial known by V. Thus, to compute the polynomial $f_\gamma(X)$ in small rounds and space, it is sufficient to compute

$$\sum_{\vec{x} \in \{0,1\}^{m+3\,s-\gamma}} p_j(\vec{\zeta}, X, \vec{x}) \tag{1}$$

in small rounds and space for each $j \in [4]$ (and p_5 locally) and sum the results.

We now show how to do this, focusing first on the case of $i \in \{1, 2, 3\}$. Note that in every round except the first, computing the sum in Eq. (1) involves computing $O(2^{|\vec{x}|})$ interpolations of $\hat{W}_r$. Since the evaluations of $\hat{W}_r$ are distributed among the M parties $P_1, \ldots, P_M$, doing these interpolations requires communication among these parties. If we interpolated $p_j(\vec{\zeta}, X, \vec{x})$ for each $\vec{x}$ and then summed the result, then even if the communication per interpolation is a constant number of rounds, this would mean that computing Eq. (1) would involve a number of rounds linear in the total computation time. So we need something slightly more clever than the naive strategy.

Before we go on, we note that for Eq. (1), it suffices to compute

$$\sum_{\vec{x} \in \{0,1\}^{m+3\,s-\gamma}} p_j(\vec{\zeta}, \zeta', \vec{x}),$$

for each $\zeta' \in \{0, \ldots, \delta\}$, where δ is the degree of p_j. Once we have these $\delta+1$ field elements, we can interpolate Eq. (1) in constant space. So we focus on computing this; i.e., we focus on computing the following for an arbitrary $\vec{\zeta} \in \mathbb{F}^\gamma$

$$\sum_{\vec{x}\in\{0,1\}^{m+3\,s-\gamma}} p_j(\vec{\zeta},\vec{x}). \tag{2}$$

Note that each term in the sum above is of the form $p'_j(\vec{\zeta},\vec{x})\hat{W}_r(\vec{\zeta}',\vec{x}')$, where $\vec{\zeta}'$ is obtained from $\vec{\zeta}$ by deleting some (possibly zero) indices, and $\vec{x}'$ is obtained from $\vec{x}$ in the same manner. The key insight which allows us to compute Eq. (2) in low rounds is as follows. Imagine that $\vec{\zeta}' = (\zeta_1)$ is a single element. Then, by the multilinearity of $\hat{W}_r$, it follows that $\hat{W}_r(\zeta_1,\vec{x}') = \zeta_1 \cdot \hat{W}_r(1,\vec{x}') + (1-\zeta_1) \cdot \hat{W}_r(0,\vec{x}')$. In the same way, if $\vec{\zeta}' = (\zeta_1,\zeta_2)$, then

$$\hat{W}_r(\zeta_1,\zeta_2,\vec{x}') = \zeta_1 \cdot \hat{W}_r(1,\zeta_2,\vec{x}') + (1-\zeta_1) \cdot \hat{W}_r(0,\zeta_2,\vec{x}')$$
$$= \zeta_1 \cdot \Big(\zeta_2 \cdot \hat{W}_r(1,1,\vec{x}') + (1-\zeta_2) \cdot \hat{W}_r(1,0,\vec{x}')\Big)$$
$$+ (1-\zeta_1) \cdot \Big(\zeta_2 \cdot \hat{W}_r(0,1,\vec{x}') + (1-\zeta_2) \cdot \hat{W}_r(0,0,\vec{x}')\Big).$$

By a simple use of induction, we can write $\hat{W}_r(\vec{\zeta}',\vec{x}')$, for arbitrary $\vec{\zeta}'$, as

$$\hat{W}_r(\vec{\zeta}',\vec{x}') = \sum_{\vec{y}\in\{0,1\}^{|\vec{\zeta}'|}} c_{\vec{\zeta}',\vec{y}} \cdot \hat{W}_r(\vec{y},\vec{x}') \tag{3}$$

where

$$c_{\vec{\zeta}',\vec{y}} = \prod_{j=1}^{|\vec{\zeta}'|} (\zeta_j \cdot y_j + (1-\zeta_j)(1-y_j)) = \prod_{j=1}^{|\vec{\zeta}'|} \{\zeta_j \text{ if } y_j = 1, \text{ otherwise } (1-\zeta_j)\}.$$

It follows that we can rewrite Eq. (2) as

$$\sum_{\vec{x}\in\{0,1\}^{m+3\,s-\gamma}} p_j(\vec{\zeta},\vec{x}) = \sum_{\vec{x}\in\{0,1\}^{m+3\,s-\gamma}} p'_j(\vec{\zeta},\vec{x}) \left(\sum_{\vec{y}\in\{0,1\}^{|\vec{\zeta}'|}} c_{\vec{\zeta}',\vec{y}} \cdot \hat{W}_r(\vec{y},\vec{x}')\right) \tag{4}$$
$$= \sum_{\vec{x}\in\{0,1\}^{m+3\,s-\gamma}} \sum_{\vec{y}\in\{0,1\}^{|\vec{\zeta}'|}} c'_{\vec{x},\vec{\zeta}',\vec{y}} \cdot \hat{W}_r(\vec{y},\vec{x}'), \tag{5}$$

where $c'_{\vec{x},\vec{\zeta}',\vec{y}}$ is computable in space proportional to the space required to compute $c_{\vec{\zeta}',\vec{y}}$ and $p'_j(\vec{\zeta},\vec{x})$.

Since Eq. (2) can be written as a weighted sum of evaluations of $\hat{W}_r$ on points in the boolean hypercube, and since all such evaluations are partitioned across the provers, each prover can compute a component of the sum by streaming the computation in space $O(S)$, and then the provers can all sum their components together using a large-arity tree in constant rounds.

The case where $j = 4$ is more involved. Recall that the goal is to compute

$$\sum_{\vec{x}\in\{0,1\}^{m+3\,s-\gamma}} p_4(\vec{\zeta},\vec{x}), \tag{6}$$

for some given $\vec{\zeta} \in \mathbb{F}^\gamma$. We first handle the case where $\gamma \leq 3s$. In this case,

$$\sum_{\vec{x} \in \{0,1\}^{m+3\,s-\gamma}} p_4(\vec{\zeta}, \vec{x}) = \sum_{\vec{z} \in \{0,1\}^m} \sum_{\vec{x}' \in \{0,1\}^{3\,s-\gamma}} p_4'(\vec{\zeta}, \vec{x}', \vec{z}) \hat{W}_r(\vec{\zeta}_1, \vec{z}) \hat{W}_r(\vec{\zeta}_2, \vec{z}), \quad (7)$$

where $\vec{\zeta}_1$ and $\vec{\zeta}_2$ are both a combination of $\vec{\zeta}$ and $\vec{x}$. Observe that from the discussion above, for each $\vec{z} \in \{0,1\}^m$, the values $\{\hat{W}_r(\vec{\zeta}_j)\}_{\vec{\zeta}_j}$ can be streamed by a single party P_i, where $\vec{z}$ is the binary representation of i, by streaming the values of $\hat{W}_r$ in the boolean hypercube and then using Eq. (3). Thus, for each $\vec{z}$, the inner sum $\sum_{\vec{x}' \in \{0,1\}^{3\,s-\gamma}} p_4'(\vec{\zeta}, \vec{x}', \vec{z}) \hat{W}_r(\vec{\zeta}_1, \vec{z}) \hat{W}_r(\vec{\zeta}_2, \vec{z})$ can be computed by a single party in $O(S)$ space. The parties can then sum these terms in a large-arity tree, thus computing Eq. (6) in $O(1)$ rounds and $O(S)$ space.

We now consider the case where $\gamma > 3s$. Write $\gamma = 3\,s + m'$, for some $m' > 1$, and write $\vec{\zeta} = (\vec{\zeta}_1, \vec{\zeta}_2, \vec{\zeta}_3, \vec{\zeta}_4)$. In this case,

$$\sum_{\vec{x} \in \{0,1\}^{m+3\,s-\gamma}} p_4(\vec{\zeta}, \vec{x}) = \sum_{\vec{z}' \in \{0,1\}^{m-m'}} p_4'(\vec{\zeta}, \vec{z}') \hat{W}_r(\vec{\zeta}_1, \vec{\zeta}_4, \vec{z}') \hat{W}_r(\vec{\zeta}_2, \vec{\zeta}_4, \vec{z}'),$$

and then again by Eq. (3), this is equal to

$$\sum_{\vec{z}' \in \{0,1\}^{m-m'}} \text{term}_{\vec{z}'} \quad (8)$$

where $\text{term}_{\vec{z}'}$ is the following:

$$p_4'(\vec{\zeta}, \vec{z}') \left(\sum_{\vec{y}_4^{(1)} \in \{0,1\}^{m'}} c_{\vec{\zeta}_4, \vec{y}_4^{(1)}} \cdot \hat{W}_r(\vec{\zeta}_1, \vec{y}_4^{(1)}, \vec{z}') \right) \left(\sum_{\vec{y}_4^{(2)} \in \{0,1\}^{m'}} c_{\vec{\zeta}_4, \vec{y}_4^{(2)}} \cdot \hat{W}_r(\vec{\zeta}_2, \vec{y}_4^{(2)}, \vec{z}') \right).$$
$$(9)$$

Note that for any $\hat{W}_r(\vec{\zeta}_j, \vec{y}_4^{(2)}, \vec{z}')$, there is a party (indexed by $(\vec{y}_4^{(2)}, \vec{z}')$ who can compute this value locally, so WLOG, we assume each party has precomputed this corresponding value. Observe that $\vec{z}'$ defines a *subset* of parties, indexed by the set $S_{\vec{z}'} = \{\vec{y}_4, \vec{z}' : y_4 \in \{0,1\}^{m'}\}$, and distinct from $S_{\vec{z}''}$ for all $\vec{z}'' \neq \vec{z}'$. Observe also that for each $\vec{z}'$, to compute $\text{term}_{\vec{z}'}$, only the parties in $S_{\vec{z}'}$ must interact, and they can compute the sum in Eq. (9) in constant rounds and $O(S)$ space by first computing the two inner sums via large-arity trees as in all the previous cases, and then multiplying these two summed values together and weighting them according to $p_4'(\vec{\zeta}, \vec{z}')$. Thus, to compute the outer sum, for each $\vec{z}'$, the parties in $S_{\vec{z}'}$ can interact in the manner described above, simultaneously with all other $S_{\vec{z}''}$. Then, once each set has their term of the sum, representative parties for each of the sets can again use a large-arity tree to obtain the final result in constant rounds and $O(S)$ space.

We now give the description of CalcSumcheckProverMsg.

The protocol CalcSumcheckProverMsg.

Parameters: Tree fan-in $\nu = s/\log N$.

Inputs: P_i has input $(r, \pi_{r-1}, \pi_r, \mathsf{st}_{i,r-1}, \mathsf{msg}^{\mathsf{in}}_{i,r-1}, \rho_{i,r-1}, \rho_{i,r}, \{\rho_{i\to j,r}\}_j)$. In addition, all parties have the setup α for a polynomial commitment scheme, a field element $q \in \mathbb{F}$, the round γ of the sumcheck, and the verifier queries $\vec{\zeta}$, where $|\vec{\zeta}| = \gamma - 1$.

Execution:

1. Write $h_q(\vec{X}_1, \vec{X}_2, \vec{X}_3, \vec{Z}) = \sum_{i=j}^{5} p_j(\vec{X}_1, \vec{X}_2, \vec{X}_3, \vec{Z})$. Party P_1 locally computes $\mathsf{summand}_5 = \sum_{\vec{x}\in\{0,1\}^{m+3s-\gamma}} p_5(\vec{\zeta}, X, \vec{x})$, where

$$p_5(\vec{X}_1, \vec{X}_2, \vec{X}_3, \vec{Z}) = \widehat{\mathsf{inout}}(\vec{x}_1, \vec{x}_2, \vec{x}_3) \cdot \hat{I}(\vec{X}_3),$$

   and stores the result.

2. For $j \in \{1,\ldots,3\}$, the parties compute $\sum_{\vec{x}\in\{0,1\}^{m+3s-\gamma}} p_j(\vec{\zeta}, X, \vec{x})$ as:
   (a) For $\zeta' \in \{0,\ldots,\deg(p_j)\}$, compute $\sum_{\vec{x}\in\{0,1\}^{m+3s-\gamma}} p_j(\vec{\zeta}, \zeta', \vec{x})$ as:
      i. Each party P_i streams the computation of $C_{i,r}$ in order to compute the component $\mathsf{component}_i$ of the sum in eq. (5) which it has access to.
      ii. The parties run the protocol $\mathsf{Combine}_\nu(+, \{\mathsf{component}_i\}_{i\in[M]})$ so that P_1 learns $\sum_{\vec{x}\in\{0,1\}^{m+3s-\gamma}} p_j(\vec{\zeta}, \zeta', \vec{x})$.
   (b) Once P_1 has these $\deg(p_j) + 1$ values, it interpolates $\mathsf{summand}_j = \sum_{\vec{x}\in\{0,1\}^{m+3s-\gamma}} p_j(\vec{\zeta}, X, \vec{x})$.
3. The parties now compute $\mathsf{summand}_4 = \sum_{\vec{x}\in\{0,1\}^{m+3s-\gamma}} p_4(\vec{\zeta}, X, \vec{x})$. If $\gamma \le 3s$, then for each $\zeta' \in \{0,\ldots,\deg(p_4)\}$:
   (a) Each party P_i computes the inner sum

$$\mathsf{component}_i = \sum_{\vec{x}'\in\{0,1\}^{3s-\gamma}} p'_4(\vec{\zeta}, \vec{x}', \vec{z})\hat{W}_r(\vec{\zeta}_1, \vec{z})\hat{W}_r(\vec{\zeta}_2, \vec{z})$$

   from eq. (7), where $\vec{z}$ is the index of i in binary form.
   (b) The parties run the protocol $\mathsf{Combine}_\nu(+, \{\mathsf{component}_i\}_{i\in[M]})$ so that P_1 learns $\sum_{\vec{x}\in\{0,1\}^{m+3s-\gamma}} p_4(\vec{\zeta}, \zeta', \vec{x})$.
4. On the other hand, if $\gamma > 3s$ then for each $\zeta' \in \{0,\ldots,\deg(p_4)\}$:
   (a) For each $\vec{z}'' \in \{0,1\}^{m-m'}$, the parties in the set $S_{\vec{z}''}$ do the following to compute $\mathsf{term}_{\vec{z}''}$:
      i. Each party P_i in $S_{\vec{z}''}$ computes the component $\mathsf{component}_i$ of $\left(\sum_{\vec{y}_4^{(1)}\in\{0,1\}^{m'}} c_{\vec{\zeta}_4, \vec{y}_4^{(1)}} \cdot \hat{W}_r(\vec{\zeta}_1, \vec{y}_4^{(1)}, \vec{z}'')\right)$ which it has access to.
      ii. The parties in $S_{\vec{z}''}$ run $\mathsf{Combine}_\nu(+, \{\mathsf{component}_i\}_{i\in S_{\vec{z}''}})$ so that the lexicographically first party in $S_{\vec{z}''}$ learns factor_1.

    iii. Each party P_i in $S_{\vec{z}'}$ computes the component component$_i$ of
$$\left(\sum_{\vec{y}_4^{(2)} \in \{0,1\}^{m'}} c_{\vec{\zeta}_4, \vec{y}_4^{(2)}} \cdot \hat{W}_r(\vec{\zeta}_2, \vec{y}_4^{(2)}, \vec{z}')\right) \text{ which it has access to.}$$
    iv. The parties in $S_{\vec{z}'}$ run $\mathsf{Combine}_\nu(+, \{\text{component}_i\}_{i \in S_{\vec{z}'}})$ so that
the lexicographically first party in $S_{\vec{z}'}$ learns factor$_2$.
    v. The lexicographically first party in $S_{\vec{z}'}$ now computes term$_{\vec{z}'}$ =
$p_4'(\vec{\zeta}, \vec{z}') \cdot$ factor$_1$ · factor$_2$ locally, by eq. (9).
  (b) Let $P_{i_{\vec{z}'}}$ be the lexicographically first party in $S_{\vec{z}'}$. The parties
$\{P_{i_{\vec{z}'}} : \vec{z}' \in \{0,1\}^{m-m'}\}$ runs $\mathsf{Combine}_\nu(+, \{\text{term}_{\vec{z}'}\}_{\vec{z}' \in \{0,1\}^{m-m'}})$ so
that P_1 learns $\sum_{\vec{x} \in \{0,1\}^{m+3s-\gamma}} p_4(\vec{\zeta}, \zeta', \vec{x})$, as in eq. (8).
5. Once P_1 has these $\deg(p_j) + 1$ values, it interpolates them to compute
summand$_4 = \sum_{\vec{x} \in \{0,1\}^{m+3s-\gamma}} p_4(\vec{\zeta}, X, \vec{x})$.
6. P_1 outputs $\sum_{j=1}^5$ summand$_j$.

Efficiency

We now discuss the efficiency of the VerifyRound protocol.

Round complexity. The protocol VerifyRound can be separated into two steps: first, the provers commit to the polynomial $\hat{W}_r$ and receive a random q from V, and then second, the parties carry out a sumcheck protocol. The first step is dominated by the subprotocols PC.CombineCom($\alpha, \{\phi_i\}_{i \in [M]}$) and Distribute$_\nu(q)$. Note that since $\nu = \lambda$, and each of these two protocols take $O(\log_\nu(M))$ rounds, the first step takes a constant number of rounds. The second step takes $(m + 3s) \cdot (R_{\mathsf{CalcSumcheckProverMsg}} + C_1) + C_2 \cdot R_{\mathsf{PC.Open}}$ rounds, where $m + 3s$ is polylog(N), $R_{\mathsf{CalcSumcheckProverMsg}}$ and $R_{\mathsf{PC.Open}}$ are the number of rounds required for the CalcSumcheckProverMsg and PC.Open subprotocols respectively, and C_1 and C_2 are constants. As explained in Sect. 6, $R_{\mathsf{PC.Open}} = \text{polylog}(|\hat{W}_r|)$, which is polylog($N$). As explained in Sect. 5.3, $R_{\mathsf{CalcSumcheckProverMsg}}$ is constant. Thus, $(m + 3s) \cdot (R_{\mathsf{CalcSumcheckProverMsg}} + C_1) + C_2 \cdot R_{\mathsf{PC.Open}}$ is polylog(N). It follows that the entire protocol VerifyRound takes polylog(N) rounds.

Space complexity per party. By the properties of the polynomial commitment and the sumcheck protocol, the verifier takes space polylog(N) · poly(λ). The provers each take space $S \cdot \text{poly}(\lambda)$; this follows from the following:

– Each party's polynomial $\hat{W}$ which encodes the wire assignments of $C_{i,r}$ can be streamed in space $O(S)$ by Lemma 1, and PC.PartialCom works assuming streaming access to $\hat{W}$.
– PC.CombineCom and PC.Open are MPC protocols where the provers require at most $S \cdot \text{poly}(\lambda)$ space, as per the properties of PC.
– CalcSumcheckProverMsg is an MPC protocol where the provers require at most $S \cdot \text{poly}(\lambda)$ space, as discussed in the previous section.

5.4 From Round Verification to a Full Argument

In this section, we use the VerifyRound protocol from Sect. 5 and the polynomial commitment PC from Sect. 6.2 to achieve a succinct argument for a language L, assuming L has a MPC verification algorithm Π_L as described in Sect. 5.2.

The formal description of the argument system is as follows. Assume the original protocol Π_L runs for R rounds.

The argument system for L.

Parameters: Tree fan-in $\nu = s/\log N$.

Inputs: P_i has input (x, w_i). V has input x. In addition, all parties have the CRS α for a polynomial commitment scheme.

Execution:

1. V samples a hash key h and sends it to P_1. The provers run Distribute$_\nu(h)$.
2. Each P_i sets $\mathsf{st}_{i,0} = (x, w_i)$, and sets $\mathsf{msg}_{i,0}^{\mathsf{in}}$ to be the empty string.
3. The provers run the subprotocol CalcMerkleTree$_h(\{\mathsf{st}_{i,0}\}_{i \in [M]})$ so that each P_i learns a Merkle root π_0 along with an opening $\rho_{i,0}$ for $\mathsf{st}_{i,r}$.
4. P_1 sends π_0 to V.
5. For each round $r \in [R]$, the parties do the following:
   (a) Each P_i runs NextSt$_{i,r}(\mathsf{st}_{i,r-1}, \mathsf{msg}_{i,r-1}^{\mathsf{in}})$ to obtain $\mathsf{st}_{i,r}$ and $\mathsf{msg}_{i,r}^{\mathsf{out}}$.
   (b) For prover P_i, for each triple $(j, \ell_j, m_j) \in \mathsf{msg}_{i,r}^{\mathsf{out}}$, P_i sends (ℓ_j, m_j) to prover P_j, who stores m_j at position ℓ_j in $\mathsf{msg}_{j,r}^{\mathsf{in}}$.
   (c) The provers run the subprotocol CalcMerkleTree$_h$ on inputs $(\{(\mathsf{st}_{i,r}, \mathsf{msg}_{i,r}^{\mathsf{out}}, \mathsf{msg}_{i,r}^{\mathsf{in}})\}_{i \in [M]})$ so that each P_i learns a Merkle root π_r along with an opening $\rho_{i,r}$ for $(\mathsf{st}_{i,r}, \mathsf{msg}_{i,r}^{\mathsf{out}}, \mathsf{msg}_{i,r}^{\mathsf{in}})$.
   (d) P_1 sends π_r to V.
   (e) For prover P_i, for each message in $\mathsf{msg}_{i,r}^{\mathsf{in}}$, P_i sends an opening $\rho_{i \to j,r}$ of that position in $\mathsf{msg}_{i,r}^{\mathsf{in}}$ to the sender P_j of that message.
   (f) The parties run the subprotocol VerifyRound, where each prover P_i has input $(r, \pi_{r-1}, \pi_r, \mathsf{st}_{i,r-1}, \mathsf{msg}_{i,r-1}^{\mathsf{in}}, \rho_{i,r-1}, \rho_{i,r}, \{\rho_{i \to j,r}\}_j)$, and the verifier V has input (x, r, π_{r-1}, π_r).
   (g) If VerifyRound aborts, then V aborts and rejects.
6. P_1 sends an opening ρ of the first position of $\mathsf{st}_{i,R}$ w.r.t. π_R to V.
7. V accepts if the opening bit is 1, and rejects otherwise.

Efficiency. The round complexity of the above argument is $R \cdot \mathsf{polylog}(N)$, where R is the number of rounds taken by Π_L. The space complexity is $S \cdot \mathsf{poly}(\lambda)$ per party. The round and space complexity of the argument follows from those of VerifyRound discussed above.

Security. We have the following theorem and defer its proof to the full version.

Theorem 3. *Assume the polynomial commitment scheme* PC *satisfies the security properties in Definition 5. Then the argument system above satisfies witness-extended emulation with respect to the language* L.

6   Constructing Polynomial Commitments in the MPC Model

Our construction extensively uses the polynomial commitment scheme of Block et al. [22], which we describe in detail in the full version. To describe our construction, we first introduce the *distributed streaming model* in Sect. 6.1, then describe the construction in Sect. 6.2 with its proof in Sect. 6.3.

6.1   Distributed Streaming Model

Looking ahead to our goal of designing succinct arguments in the MPC model, we consider an enhancement of the streaming model [22] to the MPC setting. We refer to the model as the *distributed streaming model*: Let $\mathcal{Y} \in \mathbb{F}^N$ be some multilinear polynomial and let $\{\mathcal{Y}_i \in \mathbb{F}^{N/M}\}_{i \in [M]}$ be the set of partial descriptions vectors such that $\mathcal{Y} = \mathcal{Y}_1 \| \mathcal{Y}_2 \| \dots \| \mathcal{Y}_M$. In the distributed streaming model, we assume that each of the S-space bounded parties P_i have streaming access only to the elements of their partial description vector $\mathcal{Y}_i$, where $S \ll N/M$.

While adapting Block et al. [22] to the distributed streaming model, we need to ensure two properties: (a) *low-space provers* and (b) a *low-round protocol*. A naive low space implementation is achieved by blowing up the number of rounds of interaction. Similarly, a naive polylogarithmic round protocol is achieved by simply having each party communicate their whole input (in a single round) to a single party, but this incurs high space for the prover. Achieving the two properties together is the main technical challenge. We build a low-space and a low-round protocol by heavily exploiting the algebraic structure of [22].

6.2   Our New Construction

To support n variate polynomials, recall that each party P_i holds a partial vector $\mathcal{Y}_i$ over $\mathbb{F}$ of size N/M and the corresponding index set $I_i = \{(i-1) \cdot N/M, \dots, iN/M - 1\}$. The PC.Setup algorithm is identical to [22], and the PC.PartialCom and PC.CombineCom collectively implement the commitment algorithm of [22], and PC.Open implements their open algorithm.

PC.Setup$(1^\lambda, p, 1^n, M)$: The public parameters pp output by PC.Setup contains the tuple $(g, p, \mathbb{G})$ where g is a random element of the hidden order group $\mathbb{G}$ and q is a sufficiently large integer odd integer (i.e., $q > p \cdot 2^{n \cdot \mathsf{poly}(\lambda)}$).

PC.PartialCom$(pp, \mathcal{Y}_i)$: Each of the parties locally run this algorithm to compute their partial commitment to the polynomial. In particular, on inputs $pp = (q, g, \mathbb{G})$ and the partial sequence $\mathcal{Y}_i \in \mathbb{F}^{N/M}$, the algorithm PartialCom outputs a commitment com_i to $\mathcal{Y}_i$ by encoding its elements as an integer in base q. Specifically, $\mathsf{com}_i = g^{z_i}$ where

$$z_i = q^{(i-1)N/M} \left(\sum_{\vec{b} \in \{0,1\}^{n-m}} q^{\vec{b}} \cdot \mathcal{Y}_{i\vec{b}} \right), \tag{10}$$

and private partial decommitment is the sequence $\mathcal{Z}_i = \mathsf{lift}(\mathcal{Y}_i)$. We give the formal description of this algorithm in the streaming model below.

Protocol 1 PC.PartialCom$_\nu(pp, \mathcal{Y}_i)$

Require: Party P holds a string $pp = (q, g, \mathbb{G})$ where $|pp| \leq S$ and has
   streaming access to the elements in the sequence $\mathcal{Y}_i$ in lexicographic order.
Ensure: P party holds com where com $= g^{z_i}$ is as defined in Equation (10).
1: Let com $= 1 \in \mathbb{G}$, temp $= g$.
2: **for** $\vec{b} \in \{0,1\}^{n-m}$ **do**
3:    com $=$ com $\cdot$ temp$^{(\mathcal{Y}_i)_{\vec{b}}}$
4:    temp $=$ temp^q
5: com $=$ com$^{q^{(i-1)N/M}}$.
6: output com

PC.CombineCom$(pp, \{\mathsf{com}_i\})$: Parties each holding their partial commitments com$_i$ want to jointly compute a full commitment com $= \prod_{i \in [M]} \mathsf{com}_i$. For this, parties run the Combine subprotocol on their inputs with op as the group multiplication and P_1 as the receiver. Then, P_1 outputs com as the commitment.

PC.PartialEval$(pp, \mathcal{Y}_i, \vec{\zeta})$: Each of the parties locally run this algorithm to compute their contributions to the evaluation. In particular, on input the CRS pp, a partial vector $\mathcal{Y}_i \in \mathbb{F}^{N/M}$ and a evaluation point $\vec{\zeta} \in \mathbb{F}^n$, the partial evaluation algorithm outputs $y_i \in \mathbb{F}$ such that

$$y_i = \sum_{\vec{b} \in \{0,1\}^{n-m}} \mathcal{Y}_{i\vec{b}} \cdot \overline{\chi}(\vec{\zeta}, \vec{b} + (i-1) \cdot M) . \tag{11}$$

We give the formal description of this algorithm in the streaming model below.

Protocol 2 PC.PartialEval$_\nu(pp, \mathcal{Y}_i, \vec{\zeta})$

Require: Party P holds a string $pp = (q, g, \mathbb{G})$ and $\vec{\zeta}$ where $|pp|, |\vec{\zeta}| \leq S$, and
   has streaming access to the elements in $\mathcal{Y}_i$ in lexicographic order.
Ensure: P party holds y_i as defined in Equation (11).
1: Let $y_i = 0 \in \mathbb{F}$.
2: **for** $\vec{b} \in \{0,1\}^{n-m}$ **do**
3:    $y_i = y_i + (\mathcal{Y}_i)_{\vec{b}} \cdot \overline{\chi}(\vec{\zeta}, \vec{b} + (i-1) \cdot M)$
4: output y_i

PC.CombineEval$(pp, y_i, \vec{\zeta})$: Parties each holding their partial evaluations y_i want to jointly compute the full evaluation $y = \sum_{i \in [M]} y_i$. For this, parties run the Combine subprotocol on their inputs with the field addition as the associate operator op and P_1 as the receiver. Then, P_1 outputs y as the evaluation.

PC.Open The PC.Open algorithm is the natural adaptation of the Open algorithm in [22] to the distributed streaming model. Specifically, all parties (including V) hold the public parameters $pp = (q, p, \mathbb{G})$, the claimed evaluation $y \in \mathbb{F}$, the evaluation point $\vec{\zeta} \in \mathbb{F}^n$ and the commitment com. Further, each party P_i has streaming access to the entries in its partial decommitment vector $\mathcal{Z}_i$.

The protocol PC.Open.

Inputs: Each party P_i holds a string $pp = (q, g, \mathbb{G})$, $\vec{\zeta}$, y and com where $|pp|, |\vec{\zeta}|, |\text{com}|, |y| \leq S$, and has streaming access to the elements in the sequence $\mathcal{Y}_i$ in lexicographic order. The verifier V holds $pp, \vec{\zeta}, \text{com}, y$.

Execution:

1. All parties and the verifier compute the λ-fold repetitions $\vec{\text{com}}^{(0)}$ and $\vec{y}^{(0)}$ of com and y respectively as done in the Open algorithm of [22]. P_i views $\mathcal{Y}_i$ as a vector $\mathcal{Z}_i = \text{lift}(\mathcal{Y}_i)$ over the integers. Further, let $\mathcal{Z} = \mathcal{Z}_1 || \mathcal{Z}_2 || \dots \mathcal{Z}_M$, and let $Z^{(0)}$ be the λ-fold repetition of $\mathcal{Z}$ as done in the Open algorithm of [22]. By $Z_i^{(0)}$ we denote the part of $Z^{(0)}$ corresponding to $\mathcal{Z}_i$.

2. For $k \in [0, \dots, n - 1]$, do the following:
   (a) Each party P_i, having streaming access to columns in $Z_i^{(0)}$, computes their contribution to $\vec{y}_L^{(k)}$, $\vec{y}_R^{(k)}$, $\vec{\text{com}}_L^{(k)}$ and $\vec{\text{com}}_R^{(k)}$.
   (b) Then, each party run the Combine protocol on their respective contributions such that P_1 learns $\vec{y}_L^{(k)}$, $\vec{y}_R^{(k)}$, $\vec{\text{com}}_L^{(k)}$ and $\vec{\text{com}}_R^{(k)}$. P_1 then forwards these values to the verifier V.
   (c) V checks that $\vec{y}^{(k)} = \vec{y}_L^{(k)} \cdot (1 - \zeta_{k+1}) + \vec{y}_R^{(k)} \cdot \zeta_{k+1}$.
   (d) P_1 and V run a PoE protocol on inputs $(\vec{\text{com}}_R^{(k)}, \vec{\text{com}}^{(k)} / \vec{\text{com}}_L^{(k)}, q, n - k - 1, \lambda)$ as in line 9 of MultiEval procedure of [22].
   (e) V samples $U^{(k)} = [U_L^{(k)} || U_R^{(k)}] \leftarrow \{0, 1\}^{\lambda \times 2\lambda}$ and sends $U^{(k)}$ to P_1 where $U_L^{(k)}, U_R^{(k)} \in \{0, 1\}^{\lambda \times \lambda}$.
   (f) P_1 runs the Distribute subprotocol with input $U^{(k)}$ with other P_i's.
   (g) All parties P_i and V locally compute the following:

   $$\vec{y}^{(k+1)} = U_L^{(k)} \cdot \vec{y}_L^{(k)} + U_R^{(k)} \cdot \vec{y}_R^{(k)}$$
   $$\vec{\text{com}}^{(k+1)} = (U_L^{(k)} \star \vec{\text{com}}_L^{(k)}) \odot (U_R^{(k)} \star \vec{\text{com}}_R^{(k)}) .$$

3. Each party P_i computes $Z_i^{(n)}$ where $Z_i^{(n)}$ is obtained by restricting the summation in the expression for $Z^{(n)}$ to I_i.

4. Parties run the Combine protocol on $Z_i^{(n)}$ with the integer addition operation to compute $Z^{(n)}$, and forward to V.

5. V accepts iff $||Z^{(n)}||_\infty \leq p(2\lambda)^n$, $\vec{y}^{(n)} = Z^{(n)} \mod p$, and $\vec{\text{com}}^{(n)} = g^{Z^{(n)}}$.

6.3   Proof of Theroem 2

We now prove Theorem 2 – our main theorem statement for multilinear polynomial commitments in the MPC model. The correctness, binding and witness-extended emulation properties follow readily from that of [22]: this is because, for these properties, it suffices to view the cluster of provers as monolithic. In such a setting, the above described polynomial commitment scheme is then identical to that of [22]. Finally, we argue about the efficiency of each of the algorithms next.

Efficiency of PC.PartialCom. In PC.PartialCom (Sect. 6.2), each party P_i runs through the stream of $\mathcal{Y}_i$ once, and for each of the $2^n/M$ elements performs the following computation: In line 3, it does a single group exponentiation where the exponent is an $\mathbb{F}$ value, and performs a single group multiplicaton. In line 4, it performs a group exponentiation where the exponent is q. Thus, lines 3–4 results in total runtime of $(2^n/M) \cdot \mathsf{poly}(\lambda, \log(p), \log(q))$. On line 5, it performs a single group exponentiation where the exponent is $q^{(i-1)N/M}$ followed by a single group multiplication. The former requires $(i-1)(N/M)\mathsf{poly}(\lambda, \log(q))$ time whereas latter requires $\mathsf{poly}(\lambda)$ run time. Plugging the value of q, results in an overall time of $2^n \cdot \mathsf{poly}(\lambda, n, \log(p))$. The output is a single group elements which require $\mathsf{poly}(\lambda)$ bits, and only one pass over the stream $\mathcal{Y}_i$ is required.

Efficiency of PC.CombineCom. Recall from Sect. 6.2, that in PC.CombineCom, all parties run the Combine subprotocol on local inputs of $\mathsf{poly}(\lambda)$ bits. This requires $O(\log M)$ rounds and each party only requires $\mathsf{poly}(\lambda)$ bits of space.

Efficiency of PC.PartialEval. Recall from Sect. 6.2, each party P_i runs through the stream of $\mathcal{Y}_i$ once, and for each of the $2^n/M$ elements performs the following operations in line 3: (a) computes the polynomial $\overline{\chi}$ on inputs of size n, and (b) performs a single field multiplication and addition. Thus PC.PartialEval's running time is bounded by $(2^n/M) \cdot \mathsf{poly}(\lambda, n, \log(p))$, the output is a single field element of $\lceil \log(p) \rceil$ bits, and only one pass over $\mathcal{Y}_i$ is required.

Efficiency of PC.CombineEval. Recall from Sect. 6.2, that in PC.CombineEval, all parties run the Combine subprotocol on local inputs of $\mathsf{poly}(\lambda)$ bits. This requires $O(\log M)$ rounds and each party only requires $\mathsf{poly}(\lambda)$ bits of space.

Communication/Round Complexity of PC.Open. The round complexity of PC.Open as described in Sect. 6.2 is dominated by line 2. In particular, line 2 is executed for $O(n)$ times where in each iteration k: parties perform local computations in all lines except 2-(b), 2-(d) and 2-(f). In particular, in 2-(b) (resp., 2-(f)), an instantiation of the Combine (resp., Distribute)subprotocol is run which requires $O(\log(M))$ rounds. Additionally, in 2-(d), party P_1 and the verifier engage in a POE protocol which requires $O(n-k)$ rounds. Therefore, overall, the round complexity of PC.Open is $O(n \cdot \log(M))$ rounds. In terms of communication complexity, in each round of the protocol at most $\mathsf{poly}(\lambda, n, \log(p), \log(M))$ bits are transmitted, therefore overall its bounded by $\mathsf{poly}(\lambda, n, \log(p), \log(M))$.

The Efficiency of PC.Open. The verifier efficiency is dominated by its computation in the PoE execution in line 2 of each of the n rounds, which is bounded by $\mathsf{poly}(\lambda, n, \log(p), \log(q))$. Now onto the prover efficiency. The efficiency of each party P_i is dominated by the n iterative executions of line 2 of the PC.Open(Sect. 6.2). In each iteration: in line 2-(a), P_i runs through the stream of $\mathcal{Y}_i$ once, and for each of the $2^n/M$ elements performs some $\mathsf{poly}(\lambda, n)$ computation for computing the matrices $M_{\tilde{c}}$ as well as an $O(n)$ size-product of evaluations of the χ function. Further, the prover computation in lines 2-(d) through 2-(g), doesn't depend on the stream. In particular, its running time is dominated by its computation in lines 2-(d) where P_1 acts as a prover in the PoE protocol where the exponent is of the form $q^{2^{n-k-1}}$. This results in overall running time of $2^n \cdot \mathsf{poly}(\lambda, n, \log(p))$. Further, the prover's space in each of the n iterations is $\mathsf{poly}(\lambda, \log(p), \log(M))$. Finally, in each run of line 2, a single pass over the entire stream is sufficient, resulting in $O(n)$ passes over the stream for each party P_i.

Acknowledgements. Rex Fernando, Elaine Shi, and Pratik Soni were sponsored by the Algorand Centres of Excellence (ACE) Programme, the Defense Advanced Research Projects Agency under award number HR001120C0086, the Office of Naval Research under award number N000142212064, and the National Science Foundation under award numbers 2128519 and 2044679. The views and conclusions contained in this document are those of the author and should not be interpreted as representing the official policies, either expressed or implied, of any sponsoring institution, the U.S. government or any other entity. Ilan Komargodski is the incumbent of the Harry & Abe Sherman Senior Lectureship at the School of Computer Science and Engineering at the Hebrew University, supported in part by an Alon Young Faculty Fellowship, by a grant from the Israel Science Foundation (ISF Grant No. 1774/20), and by a grant from the US-Israel Binational Science Foundation and the US National Science Foundation (BSF-NSF Grant No. 2020643).

References

1. Kook Jin Ahn and Sudipto Guha: Access to data and number of iterations: dual primal algorithms for maximum matching under resource constraints. ACM Trans. Parallel Comput. (TOPC) 4(4), 17 (2018)
2. Andoni, A., Nikolov, A., Onak, K., Yaroslavtsev, G.: Parallel algorithms for geometric graph problems. In: STOC 2014 (2014)
3. Andoni, A., Stein, C., Zhong, P.: Log diameter rounds algorithms for 2-vertex and 2-edge connectivity. arXiv preprint arXiv:1905.00850 (2019)
4. Arora, S., Lund, C., Motwani, R., Sudan, M., Szegedy, M.: Proof verification and hardness of approximation problems. In: 33rd Annual Symposium on Foundations of Computer Science, FOCS, pp. 14–23 (1992)
5. Arun, A., Ganesh, C., Lokam, S.V., Mopuri, T., Sridhar, S.: Dew: a transparent constant-sized polynomial commitment scheme. In: Public Key Cryptography, pp. 542–571 (2023)
6. Assadi, S.: Simple round compression for parallel vertex cover. CoRR, abs/1709.04599 (2017)
7. Assadi, S., Bateni, M.H., Bernstein, A., Mirrokni, V., Stein, C.: Coresets meet EDCS: algorithms for matching and vertex cover on massive graphs. arXiv preprint arXiv:1711.03076 (2017)

8. Assadi, S., Khanna, S.: Randomized composable coresets for matching and vertex cover. In: Proceedings of the 29th ACM Symposium on Parallelism in Algorithms and Architectures, pp. 3–12. ACM (2017)
9. Assadi, S., Sun, X., Weinstein, O.: Massively parallel algorithms for finding well-connected components in sparse graphs. CoRR, abs/1805.02974 (2018)
10. Babai, L., Fortnow, L., Levin, L.A., Szegedy, M.: Checking computations in poly-logarithmic time. In: Proceedings of the 23rd Annual ACM Symposium on Theory of Computing, STOC, pp. 21–31 (1991)
11. Babai, L., Fortnow, L., Lund, C.: Non-deterministic exponential time has two-prover interactive protocols. Comput. Complex. **1**, 3–40 (1991)
12. Bahmani, B., Kumar, R., Vassilvitskii, S.: Densest subgraph in streaming and MapReduce. Proc. VLDB Endow. **5**(5), 454–465 (2012)
13. Bahmani, B., Moseley, B., Vattani, A., Kumar, R., Vassilvitskii, S.: Scalable k-means++. Proc. VLDB Endow. **5**(7), 622–633 (2012)
14. Bateni, M.H., Bhaskara, A., Lattanzi, S., Mirrokni, V.: Distributed balanced clustering via mapping coresets. In: Advances in Neural Information Processing Systems, pp. 2591–2599 (2014)
15. Behnezhad, S., Derakhshan, M., Hajiaghayi, M.T., Karp, R.M.: Massively parallel symmetry breaking on sparse graphs: MIS and maximal matching. CoRR, abs/1807.06701 (2018)
16. Behnezhad, S., Hajiaghayi, M.T., Harris, D.G.: Exponentially faster massively parallel maximal matching. arXiv preprint arXiv:1901.03744 (2019)
17. Ben-Sasson, E., Bentov, I., Horesh, Y., Riabzev, M.: Fast reed-Solomon interactive oracle proofs of proximity. In: 45th International Colloquium on Automata, Languages, and Programming (ICALP), pp. 14:1–14:17. Schloss Dagstuhl-Leibniz-Zentrum fuer Informatik, Dagstuhl, Germany (2018)
18. Ben-Sasson, E., Chiesa, A., Riabzev, M., Spooner, N., Virza, M., Ward, N.P.: Aurora: transparent succinct arguments for R1CS. In: Ishai, Y., Rijmen, V. (eds.) EUROCRYPT 2019. LNCS, vol. 11476, pp. 103–128. Springer, Cham (2019). https://doi.org/10.1007/978-3-030-17653-2_4
19. Ben-Sasson, E., Goldberg, L., Kopparty, S., Saraf, S.: DEEP-FRI: sampling outside the box improves soundness, pp. 5:1–5:32 (2020)
20. Bick, A., Kol, G., Oshman, R.: Distributed zero-knowledge proofs over networks. In: SODA, pp. 2426–2458 (2022)
21. Block, A.R., Holmgren, J., Rosen, A., Rothblum, R.D., Soni, P.: Public-coin zero-knowledge arguments with (almost) minimal time and space overheads. In: Theory of Cryptography, pp. 168–197 (2020)
22. Ben-Sasson, E., Chiesa, A., Riabzev, M., Spooner, N., Virza, M., Ward, N.P.: Aurora: transparent succinct arguments for R1CS. In: Ishai, Y., Rijmen, V. (eds.) EUROCRYPT 2019. LNCS, vol. 11476, pp. 103–128. Springer, Cham (2019). https://doi.org/10.1007/978-3-030-17653-2_4
23. Blumberg, A.J., Thaler, J., Vu, V., Walfish, M.: Verifiable computation using multiple provers. IACR Cryptol. ePrint Arch., p. 846 (2014)
24. Bootle, J., Cerulli, A., Chaidos, P., Groth, J., Petit, C.: Efficient zero-knowledge arguments for arithmetic circuits in the discrete log setting. In: Fischlin, M., Coron, J.-S. (eds.) EUROCRYPT 2016. LNCS, vol. 9666, pp. 327–357. Springer, Heidelberg (2016). https://doi.org/10.1007/978-3-662-49896-5_12
25. Bootle, J., Chiesa, A., Hu, Y., Orrú, M.: Gemini: elastic snarks for diverse environments. In: Dunkelman, O., Dziembowski, S. (eds.) Advances in Cryptology–EUROCRYPT 2022. LNCS, vol. 13276, pp. 427–457. Springer, Cham (2022). https://doi.org/10.1007/978-3-031-07085-3_15

26. Brandt, S., Fischer, M., Uitto, J.: Matching and MIS for uniformly sparse graphs in the low-memory MPC model. CoRR, abs/1807.05374 (2018)
27. Bünz, B., Fisch, B., Szepieniec, A.: Transparent SNARKs from DARK compilers. In: Canteaut, A., Ishai, Y. (eds.) EUROCRYPT 2020. LNCS, vol. 12105, pp. 677–706. Springer, Cham (2020). https://doi.org/10.1007/978-3-030-45721-1_24
28. Chang, Y.-J., Fischer, M., Ghaffari, M., Uitto, J., Zheng, Y.: The complexity of $(\varDelta+1)$ coloring incongested clique, massively parallel computation, and centralized local computation. arXiv preprint arXiv:1808.08419 (2018)
29. Chiesa, A., Hu, Y., Maller, M., Mishra, P., Vesely, N., Ward, N.: Marlin: preprocessing zkSNARKs with universal and updatable SRS. In: Canteaut, A., Ishai, Y. (eds.) EUROCRYPT 2020. LNCS, vol. 12105, pp. 738–768. Springer, Cham (2020). https://doi.org/10.1007/978-3-030-45721-1_26
30. Chung, K.-M., Ho, K.-Y., Sun, X.: On the hardness of massively parallel computation. In: 32nd ACM Symposium on Parallelism in Algorithms and Architectures, SPAA, pp. 153–162 (2020)
31. Czumaj, A., Łącki, J., Mądry, A., Mitrović, S., Onak, K., Sankowski, P.: Round compression for parallel matching algorithms. In: STOC (2018)
32. da Ponte Barbosa, R., Ene, A., Nguyen, H.L., Ward, J.: A new framework for distributed submodular maximization. In: FOCS, pp. 645–654 (2016)
33. Ene, A., Im, S., Moseley, B.: Fast clustering using MapReduce. In: Proceedings of the 17th ACM SIGKDD International Conference on Knowledge Discovery and Data Mining, pp. 681–689. ACM (2011)
34. Ene, A., Nguyen, H.: Random coordinate descent methods for minimizing decomposable submodular functions. In: International Conference on Machine Learning, pp. 787–795 (2015)
35. Fernando, R., Gelles, Y., Komargodski, I., Shi, E.: Maliciously secure massively parallel computation for all-but-one corruptions. In: Dodis, Y., Shrimpton, T. (eds.) Advances in Cryptology. CRYPTO 2022. LNCS, vol. 13507, pp. 688–718. Springer, Cham (2022). https://doi.org/10.1007/978-3-031-15802-5_24
36. Fernando, R., Komargodski, I., Liu, Y., Shi, E.: Secure massively parallel computation for dishonest majority. In: Theory of Cryptography - 18th International Conference, TCC, pp. 379–409 (2020)
37. Gabizon, A., Williamson, Z.J., Ciobotaru, O.: Plonk: permutations over Lagrange-bases for oecumenical noninteractive arguments of knowledge. Cryptology ePrint Archive (2019)
38. Gentry, C., Wichs, D.: Separating succinct non-interactive arguments from all falsifiable assumptions. In: Proceedings of the 43rd ACM Symposium on Theory of Computing, STOC, pp. 99–108 (2011)
39. Ghaffari, M., Lattanzi, S., Mitrović, S.: Improved parallel algorithms for density-based network clustering. In: International Conference on Machine Learning, pp. 2201–2210 (2019)
40. Goldreich, O., Micali, S., Wigderson, A.: Proofs that yield nothing but their validity for all languages in NP have zero-knowledge proof systems. J. ACM 38(3), 691–729 (1991)
41. Goldwasser, S., Micali, S., Rackoff, C.: The knowledge complexity of interactive proof systems. SIAM J. Comput. 18(1), 186–208 (1989)
42. Karloff, H.J., Suri, S., Vassilvitskii, S.: A model of computation for MapReduce. In: Proceedings of the Twenty-First Annual ACM-SIAM Symposium on Discrete Algorithms, SODA, pp. 938–948 (2010)

43. Kate, A., Zaverucha, G.M., Goldberg, I.: Constant-size commitments to polynomials and their applications. In: Abe, M. (ed.) Constant-size commitments to polynomials and their applications. LNCS, vol. 6477, pp. 177–194. Springer, Heidelberg (2010). https://doi.org/10.1007/978-3-642-17373-8_11
44. Kattis, A.A., Panarin, K., Vlasov, A.: Redshift: transparent snarks from list polynomial commitments. In: CCS, pp. 1725–1737 (2022)
45. Kol, G., Oshman, R., Saxena, R.R.: Interactive distributed proofs. In: PODC, pp. 255–264 (2018)
46. Kumar, R., Moseley, B., Vassilvitskii, S., Vattani, A.: Fast greedy algorithms in MapReduce and streaming. TOPC. **2**(3), 1–22 (2015)
47. Lee, J.: Dory: efficient, transparent arguments for generalised inner products and polynomial commitments. In: Theory of Cryptography, pp. 1–34 (2021)
48. Lindell: Parallel coin-tossing and constant-round secure two-party computation. J. Cryptol. **16**, 143–184 (2003)
49. Naor, M.: On cryptographic assumptions and challenges. In: Boneh, D. (ed.) CRYPTO 2003. LNCS, vol. 2729, pp. 96–109. Springer, Heidelberg (2003). https://doi.org/10.1007/978-3-540-45146-4_6
50. Naor, M., Parter, M., Yogev, E.: The power of distributed verifiers in interactive proofs. In: SODA, pp. 1096–115 (2020)
51. Ozdemir, A., Boneh, D.: Experimenting with collaborative ZK-snarks: zero-knowledge proofs for distributed secrets. In: USENIX, pp. 4291–4308 (2022)
52. Papamanthou, C., Shi, E., Tamassia, R.: Signatures of correct computation. In: Theory of Cryptography, pp. 222–242 (2013)
53. Rivest, R.L., Shamir, A., Adleman, L.: A method for obtaining digital signatures and public-key cryptosystems. Commun. ACM. **21**(2), 120–126 (1978)
54. Roughgarden, T., Vassilvitskii, S., Wang, J.R.: Shuffles and circuits (on lower bounds for modern parallel computation). J. ACM **65**(6), 1–24 (2018)
55. Setty, S., Lee, J.: Quarks: quadruple-efficient transparent Zksnarks. Cryptology ePrint Archive, Paper 2020/1275 (2020)
56. Wahby, R.S., Tzialla, I., Shelat, A., Thaler, J., Walfish, M.: Doubly-efficient Zksnarks without trusted setup. In: S&P, pp. 926–943 (2018)
57. Wesolowski, B.: Efficient verifiable delay functions. J. Cryptol. **33**(4), 2113–2147 (2020)
58. Wu, H., Zheng, W., Chiesa, A., Popa, R.A., Stoica, I.: DIZK: a distributed zero knowledge proof system. In: USENIX, pp. 675–692 (2018)
59. Zhang, J., Xie, T., Zhang, Y., Song, D.: Transparent polynomial delegation and its applications to zero knowledge proof. In: S&P, pp. 859–876 (2020)

Rogue-Instance Security for Batch Knowledge Proofs

Gil Segev[1]([✉])(iD), Amit Sharabi[2], and Eylon Yogev[2](iD)

[1] School of Computer Science and Engineering, Hebrew University of Jerusalem,
91904 Jerusalem, Israel
segev@cs.huji.ac.il
[2] Department of Computer Science, Bar-Ilan University, Ramat Gan, Israel
amit.sharabi1@live.biu.ac.il, eylon.yogev@biu.ac.il

Abstract. We propose a new notion of knowledge soundness, denoted *rogue-instance security*, for interactive and non-interactive *batch* knowledge proofs. Our notion, inspired by the standard notion of rogue-key security for multi-signature schemes, considers a setting in which a malicious prover is provided with an honestly-generated instance x_1, and may then be able to maliciously generate related "rogue" instances $x_2, \ldots, x_k$ for convincing a verifier in a batch knowledge proof of corresponding witnesses $w_1, \ldots, w_k$ for all k instances – without actually having knowledge of the witness w_1 corresponding to the honestly-generated instance. This setting provides a powerful security guarantee for batch versions of a wide variety of practically-relevant protocols, such as Schnorr's protocol and similar ones.

We present a highly-efficient generic construction of a batch proof-of-knowledge applicable to any *algebraic* Sigma protocols. The algebraic property refers to a homomorphic structure of the underlying group and includes Schnorr's protocol and others. We provide an almost tight security analysis for our generic batch protocol, which significantly improves upon the previously known security bounds even for the specific case of batch Schnorr protocol. We extend our results beyond algebraic Sigma protocols. We analyze the rogue-instance security of a general batch protocol with plus-one special soundness (a generalization of standard special soundness) and achieve improved security bounds in the generic case.

Our results use a particular type of *high-moment* assumptions introduced by Rotem and Segev (CRYPTO 2021). These assumptions consider the hardness of a relation against algorithms with bounded *expected*

Gil Segev is supported by the Israel Science Foundation (Grant No. 1336/22) and by the European Union (ERC, FTRC, 101043243). Views and opinions expressed are however those of the author(s) only and do not necessarily reflect those of the European Union or the European Research Council. Neither the European Union nor the granting authority can be held responsible for them.
Amit Sharabi is sponsored by the Israel Science Foundation (Grant No. 2439/20).
Eylon Yogev is supported by an Alon Young Faculty Fellowship, by the Israel Science Foundation (Grant No. 2302/22), and by the BIU Center for Research in Applied Cryptography and Cyber Security in conjunction with the Israel National Cyber Bureau in the Prime Minister's Office.

G. Rothblum and H. Wee (Eds.): TCC 2023, LNCS 14369, pp. 121–157, 2023.
https://doi.org/10.1007/978-3-031-48615-9_5

running time. Although Rotem and Segev introduced these assumptions, they did not provide evidence to support their hardness. To substantiate and validate the high-moment assumptions, we present a new framework for assessing the concrete hardness of cryptographic problems against oracle algorithms with bounded expected runtime. Our framework covers generic models, including the generic group model, random oracle model, and more. Utilizing our framework, we achieve the first hardness result for these high-moment assumptions. In particular, we establish the second-moment hardness of the discrete-logarithm problem against expected-time algorithms in the generic group model.

1   Introduction

A zero-knowledge proof-of-knowledge protocol is a powerful cryptographic tool with diverse applications. It enables a prover to convincingly demonstrate to a verifier, who holds an instance x, that it possesses knowledge of a valid witness w for x. The fundamental power of such protocols lies in the ability to *extract* a witness from a given prover, a property that varies in its precise formulation across different protocols. Proofs of knowledge play a pivotal role in cryptographic protocols, both from a theoretical standpoint and in practical implementations.

One notable example is Schnorr's protocol [31,32], which serves as a zero-knowledge proof-of-knowledge for the knowledge of the discrete-logarithm of a group element. In its interactive form, this protocol offers an efficient identification scheme, while in its non-interactive form, it translates into a signature scheme via the Fiat-Shamir transformation. The widespread influence of the Schnorr identification and signature schemes stems from their conceptual simplicity and practical efficiency. Another compelling example is a proof-of-knowledge for a Pedersen commitment or hash function, which is the product of two Schnorr instances. In this scenario, the prover demonstrates the ability to "open" the commitment without actually revealing its contents, thus maintaining the privacy of the committer [27]. The wide-ranging applicability of these protocols within the field of cryptography has garnered substantial attention and interest in a tight analysis of their security bounds.

Extraction from Special Soundness. Both of the examples presented above exemplify Sigma protocols, which are three-move protocols that exhibit the unique soundness notion called "special soundness". This property plays a vital role in the construction of an extractor. Specifically, the property states that it is possible to extract a witness when provided with two accepting transcripts that share the same first message but differ in the second message. Consequently, to establish the protocol's security based on the hardness of the underlying relation, the extractor must successfully extract two such valid transcripts from a potentially malicious prover.

To achieve this goal, existing approaches employ a strategy of executing the protocol multiple times. The analysis of these approaches draws upon the classic "forking lemma" introduced by Pointcheval and Stern [28] (see also [1, 7,10,21]). These different approaches showcase a trade-off between the success probability and the running time of the extractor. To provide a concrete example, let us examine the Schnorr identification scheme and signature scheme, which derive their security from the hardness of the discrete-logarithm problem. For the Schnorr identification scheme, suppose we have a malicious prover who runs in time t and succeeds in impersonating with probability ϵ. We can transform this malicious prover into a discrete-logarithm algorithm that runs in time $2t$ and succeeds with probability ϵ^2. Similarly, for the Schnorr signature scheme, suppose the attacker additionally performs at most q queries to the random oracle. We can transform this attacker into a discrete-logarithm algorithm that runs in time $2t$ and succeeds with probability ϵ^2/q. For any group of order p, where generic hardness of discrete-log is believed to hold [33], this leads to the bound $\epsilon \leq (t^2/p)^{1/2}$ for the Schnorr identification scheme, and a bound of $\epsilon \leq (q \cdot t^2/p)^{1/2}$ for the Schnorr signature scheme. Other trade-offs that were established lead to the same bound [5,19]. In idealized models, such as the generic group model [22,33] and the algebraic group model [2,4,14,15,25,29], it is possible to achieve an optimal bound of $\epsilon \leq t^2/p$ (see [15,33]).

High-Moment Forking Lemma. The extractor runs the given adversary for the second time, only if the first time succeeded. Thus, it is convenient to analyze the *expected* running-time of the extractor, rather than its strict running-time [20]. In this case, the result is an algorithm for solving discrete-logarithm with a bound on its expected running time. Recently, Segev and Rotem [30] have leveraged this type of analysis to derive tighter bounds for Schnorr's protocols (and similar Sigma protocols). Towards this end, they established a hardness of discrete-logarithm for excepted time algorithms.

In simple terms, their *second-moment assumption* states that the success probability ϵ of any algorithm A solving discrete-logarithm for a group of order p satisfies $\epsilon \leq \mathbb{E}\left[T_A^2\right]/p$, where T_A denotes the random variable corresponding to A's running time.[1] Under this assumption, Segev and Rotem were able to derive the bound of $\epsilon \leq (t^2/p)^{2/3}$, which is the best-known bound for Schnorr in the standard model. Achieving the optimal bound in the standard model remains an open problem that continues to drive ongoing research and exploration.

Batch Protocols. The Schnorr protocol and the Pedersen protocol both admit efficient *batch* versions [16]. A batch protocol is given k instances, $x_1, \ldots, x_k$, and allows to prove the knowledge of *all* corresponding k witnesses with a communication complexity that is approximately the same as that of a single proof of knowledge. The efficiency gain provided by batch protocols is a highly desirable property in many domains. In the context of blockchain, batching is a widely adopted practice aimed at reducing costs and optimizing resource utilization, the instances are usually public-keys and the witnesses are private-keys. By grouping

---

[1] They originally stated their assumption for a general d-moment but, in this paper, we focus on the second-moment.

multiple transactions or operations into a single batch, the associated overhead, such as communication and computation costs (which affect the transaction fees), can be significantly reduced.

However, the security analysis of batch protocols raises several concerns. The security bounds vary depending on how the instances are chosen in the security game (a modeling issue that does not appear with a single instance). For example, in a permissionless blockchain network, the attacker can choose the instances (its public-keys) adaptively as a function of existing instances sampled by honest parties. In such a case, the security reduction cannot assume hardness of the instances chosen by the adversary. These types of security games are known in the context of multi-signatures and are called rogue-key attacks (see [6,7,9,23,26] and the many references therein).

The special soundness property extends to the multiple instance case. In this setting, the extractor must extract $k+1$ valid transcripts from which it can compute all k corresponding witnesses (actually, it needs all $k+1$ transcripts even if it aims to compute a single witness). This is a generalization of the standard special soundness property, which we call *plus-one* special soundness. However, deriving tight security bounds for the batch setting is even more challenging than the single case. A straightforward extension of the single extractor to the batch version would run the malicious prover $k+1$ times and would yield an extractor that runs in approximately $(k+1) \cdot t$ time, but with a success probability of ϵ^{k+1}, i.e., an exponential decay in the number of instances. This is indeed the case in the batch Schnorr protocol given in [16]. Furthermore, the tighter bound of Segev and Rotem [30] does not seem to extend to the multiple instance case (regardless of the precise security game definition). This raises the question of how to derive tight security bounds for batch protocols.

1.1 Our Contributions

We give several contributions towards a better understanding of batch proof-of-knowledge protocols.

Rogue-Instance Soundness. Our first contribution is a strong security notion for batch protocols, denoted *rogue-instance security*, for interactive and non-interactive *batch* knowledge proofs. Our notion is inspired by the standard notion of rogue-key security for multi-signature schemes. We consider a setting in which a malicious prover is provided with an honestly-generated instance x_1 (according to some distribution), and is then allowed to maliciously generate related "rogue" instances $x_2, \ldots, x_k$ for convincing a verifier in a batch knowledge proof of corresponding witnesses $w_1, \ldots, w_k$ for all k instances. This is done without the malicious prover having knowledge of the witness w_1 corresponding to the honestly-generated instance. This setting provides a powerful security guarantee for batch versions of numerous practical and relevant protocols, such as Schnorr's protocol and similar ones. See Sect. 4 for the precise definition.

Batching Algebraic Sigma Protocols We construct batch protocols for a large family of Sigma protocols and provide a relatively tight analysis. Our construction works for *algebraic* Sigma protocols, which captures the proof-of-knowledge protocol for discrete-logarithm (Schnorr) [31,32], Pedersen commitment [27], Guillou-Quisquater identification scheme [17] and more. The algebraic property refers to a homomorphic structure of the underlying group. Algebraic Sigma protocols consist of an algebraic one-way function f such that the prover aims to prove knowledge of a preimage under f. The notion of algebraic one-way function introduced by Catalano et al. [11] which relates to the notion of group-homomorphic one-way generators introduced by Cramer and Damgård [13]. We analyze the security of our construction in the rogue-instance game and achieve the bound $\epsilon \leq (t^2/p)^{2/3}$ (for groups of order p) which matches the state-of-the-art bound of Segev and Rotem [30] for a single instance. In particular, our bound does not depend on the number of rogue instances. In more general form, our theorem is as follows.

Theorem 1 (Informal). *Let Π be an algebraic Sigma protocol for a relation $\mathcal{R} \subseteq \mathcal{X} \times \mathcal{W}$. If $\mathcal{R}$ is second-moment hard with respect to a distribution $\mathcal{D}$, then $\mathcal{R}$ has a batch protocol with rogue soundness error $\epsilon(t) \leq (t^2/|\mathcal{W}|)^{2/3}$.*

In particular, our theorem gives us tighter security bounds for the batch version of Schnorr and Pederson protocols. Specifically, the batch version of Schnorr's protocols immediately implies the same bounds for the corresponding batch identification scheme.

Corollary 1. *Assuming that the discrete-logarithm problem is second-moment hard, any adversary that runs in time t wins in the rogue soundness game for the batch Schnorr and Okamoto identification schemes with probability at most $(t^2/p)^{2/3}$, where p is the order of the underlying group.*

We extend our results for general batch Sigma protocols. We analyze the rogue-instance security of a general batch protocol with plus-one special soundness and achieve the bound of $\epsilon \leq (k^2 \cdot t^2/p)^{1/2}$, which is inferior to our bound for the specific case of algebraic protocols, but superior to previously known bounds.

Theorem 2 (Informal). *Let Π be k-batch Sigma protocol for a relation $\mathcal{R} \subseteq \mathcal{X} \times \mathcal{W}$ with plus-one special soundness. If $\mathcal{R}$ is second-moment hard with respect to a distribution $\mathcal{D}$, then Π has rogue soundness error $\epsilon(t) \leq (k^2 \cdot t^2/|\mathcal{W}|)^{1/2}$.*

In Table 1 we exemplify the concrete improvements we get in Theorem 1 and Theorem 2 for various parameter settings.

Non-interactive Proof-of-Knowledge. We construct non-interactive batch arguments from algebraic Sigma protocols by applying the Fiat-Shamir paradigm to the batch Sigma protocols. Given Theorem 1, the generic analysis of the Fiat-Shamir yields a bound on the rogue-instance game of $\epsilon \leq q \cdot (t^2/p)^{2/3}$ when considering malicious prover who runs in time t and performs at most q queries

Table 1. A comparison of the security guarantees for the batch Schnorr scheme provided by [16] compared to our bounds given in Theorem 2 and in Theorem 1.

Attacker's running time t	Security parameter λ	Batch parameter k	Bound of [16] $(t^2/p)^{1/(k+1)}$	Generic bound Theorem 2 $(k^2 \cdot t^2/p)^{1/2}$	Algebraic bound Theorem 1 $(t^2/p)^{2/3}$
2^{64}	256	2	$2^{-42.67}$	2^{-63}	$2^{-85.33}$
2^{64}	256	4	$2^{-25.6}$	2^{-62}	$2^{-85.33}$
2^{80}	256	6	$2^{-13.71}$	$2^{-45.42}$	2^{-64}
2^{80}	512	8	$2^{-39.11}$	2^{-173}	$2^{-234.66}$
2^{100}	512	16	$2^{-18.35}$	2^{-152}	2^{-208}
2^{100}	512	24	$2^{-12.48}$	$2^{-151.42}$	2^{-208}
2^{128}	512	24	$2^{-10.24}$	$2^{-123.42}$	$2^{-170.66}$
2^{128}	512	32	$2^{-7.76}$	2^{-123}	$2^{-170.66}$

to the random oracle. However, direct analysis of the rogue-instance game yields a bound of $\epsilon \leq (kq \cdot t^2/p)^{2/3}$ which is again matches the bound of Rotem and Segev [30], for a single instance. Informally, we show the following.

Theorem 3 (Informal). *Let Π be an algebraic Sigma protocol for a relation $\mathcal{R} \subseteq \mathcal{X} \times \mathcal{W}$. If $\mathcal{R}$ is second-moment hard with respect to a distribution $\mathcal{D}$, then $\mathcal{R}$ has a non-interactive batch argument with rogue soundness error $\epsilon(t) \leq (kq \cdot t^2/|\mathcal{W}|)^{2/3}$.*

Establishing Hardness for High-Moment Assumptions. Theorem 1 and Theorem 3 rely on the second-moment-hardness of a relation, an assumption introduced in [30]. While the use of these assumptions is beneficial, there is no evidence to support their hardness. To remedy the situation, we present a new framework that allows to establish bounds for oracle-algorithms with expected running time. Utilizing our framework, we achieve the first hardness result for these high-moment assumptions, relative to a oracle. The general statement of our framework is somewhat technical and is given in Theorem 2. Thus, we present two main implications of our framework, which are easier to state.

First, we establish the second-moment hardness of the discrete-logarithm problem against expected-time algorithms in the generic group model. Shoup [33] analyzed the generic hardness of the discrete-logarithm problem with respect to strict time algorithms. He showed that any generic t-time algorithm that solves the discrete-logarithm problem has success probability at most $\epsilon \leq t^2/p$. Applying our framework yields a bound of $\epsilon \leq \mathbb{E}\left[T_A^2\right]/p$ when considering *unbounded* algorithms where T_A denotes the random variable indicating the algorithm's running time.

Theorem 4 (second-moment hardness in generic group model; Informal). *For any query algorithm A, let $T_A = T_A(\lambda)$ be a random variable indicating the number of queries performed by A until he stops. For every algorithm*

A that solves the discrete-logarithm problem in a generic group of prime order p and succeeds with probability ϵ_A it holds that

$$\epsilon_A \leq \frac{\mathbb{E}\left[T_A^2\right]}{p} \ .$$

Our framework is inspired by [19] which showed a generic framework to prove bounds with respect to expected-time algorithms when considering only the first-moment of the expected running time. Their result proves the first-moment assumption (Definition 1), but cannot be used to derive second-moment hardness. Moreover, our framework achieves tighter bounds than theirs and is arguably easier to use (see Corollary 3).

Second, we derive expected-time bounds for SNARKs in the random oracle model (ROM). We focus on the construction of Micali [24], which compiles a PCP to a SNARK in the ROM. It is known that if the underlying PCP has soundness error ϵ_{PCP}, then every malicious prover that makes at most t-queries to the random oracle can convince the verifier of a false statement with probability at most $\epsilon \leq t \cdot \epsilon_{PCP} + \frac{3}{2} \cdot \frac{t^2}{2^\lambda}$ (see analysis in [8]). Using our framework, we derive the following bound.

Theorem 5 (second-moment hardness of SNARKs; Informal) *Suppose the Micali construction is instantiated for a relation $\mathcal{R}$ with a PCP with error ϵ_{PCP}, and random oracle with output length λ. Then, for every $x \notin \mathcal{L}(\mathcal{R})$ and every malicious argument prover $\tilde{P}$ that performs $T_{\tilde{P}}$ oracle queries (as a random variable) and outputs a proof $\tilde{\pi}$ it holds that*

$$\Pr\left[\mathcal{V}^f(x, \tilde{\pi}) = 1\right] \leq \mathbb{E}\left[T_{\tilde{P}}\right] \cdot \epsilon_{PCP} + 4 \cdot \frac{\mathbb{E}\left[T_{\tilde{P}}^2\right]}{2^\lambda} \ .$$

In Sect. 2.6, we further discuss the type of cryptographic problems relative to an oracle captured by our framework. A formal treatment of the framework, including definitions, statements, and further examples, is given in Sect. 6.1.

2   Our Techniques

We summarize the main ideas behind our results.

- In Sect. 2.1 we discuss the computational assumptions we consider in this work.
- In Sect. 2.2 we define batch Sigma protocols and extend the notion of rogue-key security for multi-signature, to rogue-instance security of batch proof-of-knowledge.
- In Sect. 2.3 we first show a general compiler from a large family of Σ-protocols to a batch Σ-protocol. Then, we show the high-level proof of the rogue-security of batch Σ-protocols constructed via the general compiler.
- In Sect. 2.4 we start by showing how to construct non-interactive batch arguments using the general compiler, then, we bound their rogue-security.

- In Sect. 2.5 we show how to apply our techniques on a general batch Σ-protocol and derive a concrete bound on their rogue-soundness error.
- In Sect. 2.6 we describe our framework for establishing high-moment hardness assumptions.

2.1 High-Moment Hardness

We begin by describing the computational assumptions that underlie our work. Let $\mathcal{R} \subseteq \mathcal{X} \times \mathcal{W}$ be a relation, where $\mathcal{X}$ is the set of instances and $\mathcal{W}$ is the set of witnesses. We note that the relation (and in fact all algorithms that will be described later on) are with respect to a setup algorithm that produces public parameters. For the simplicity of this high-level overview, we omit the public parameters (where formal definitions take them into account).

We consider distribution $\mathcal{D}$ over instance-witness pairs such that $(x, w) \in \mathcal{R}$. For example, the distribution can sample a discrete-logarithm challenge. Typically, the hardness of the distribution is stated with respect to strict-time algorithms, that is, algorithms that run in some fixed time t. Here, we consider hardness with respect to an algorithm where the running time, t, is a random variable. We denote by $T_{A,\mathcal{D}}$ the random variable indicating the running time of A on input x where $(x, w) \leftarrow \mathcal{D}$. Informally, we say that $\mathcal{R}$ is *first-moment hard* with respect to the distribution $\mathcal{D}$ if for every algorithm A, it holds that

$$\textbf{first-moment hardness:} \quad \Pr\left[(x, A(x)) \in \mathcal{R}\right] \leq \frac{\mathbb{E}\left[T_{A,\mathcal{D}}\right]}{|\mathcal{W}|^{0.5}}, \tag{1}$$

where the probability is taken over $(x, w) \leftarrow \mathcal{D}$ and over A. The first-moment assumption is justified by the work of Jaeger and Tessaro [19]. They developed a framework for proving tight bounds on the advantage of an adversary with expected-time guarantees in generic models (a.k.a. "bad flag analysis"). In particular, they prove the first-moment hardness of the discrete-logarithm problem in the generic group model. That is, they show that every algorithm A with an expected running time $\mathbb{E}[T_A]$ computes the discrete-logarithm problem in the generic group model with probability at most $\mathbb{E}[T_A]/p^{1/2}$ (where p is the group size).

Recently, Rotem and Segev [30] have generalized this assumption for higher moments, where most important for our work is the second-moment assumption. We say that a relation is *second-moment hard* with respect to a distribution $\mathcal{D}$ if for every algorithm A it holds that

$$\textbf{second-moment hardness:} \quad \Pr\left[(x, A(x)) \in \mathcal{R}\right] \leq \frac{\mathbb{E}\left[T_{A,\mathcal{D}}^2\right]}{|\mathcal{W}|}, \tag{2}$$

where the probability is taken over $(x, w) \leftarrow \mathcal{D}$ and the algorithm A. The hardness of the second-moment assumption does not follow from the framework of [19], and has no justification even in generic models. In order to validate this assumption, we develop a framework (see Sect. 2.6), in the spirit of [19] which *does* allow us to establish bounds for second-moments. In particular, it allows us to prove the second-moment hardness of the discrete-logarithm problem in the generic group model. That is, we show that every algorithm A with an expected running time $\mathbb{E}[T_A]$ computes the discrete-logarithm problem in the generic group model with probability at most $\mathbb{E}[T_A^2]/p$.

2.2 Rogue-Instance Security for Batch Protocols

We move on to describe our notion of rogue-instance soundness for batch protocols. In a batch Σ-protocol, we are given k instance-witness pairs $(x_1, w_1), \ldots, (x_k, w_k)$. The prover consists of two algorithms $\mathbf{P} = (\mathbf{P}_1, \mathbf{P}_2)$, where $\mathbf{P}_1$ sends a message α, the verifier $\mathbf{V}$ sends a random challenge $\beta \in \mathcal{C}$, $\mathbf{P}_2$ responds with a message γ, and the verifier $\mathbf{V}$ decides whether to accept.

The standard adaptive soundness requirement considers the case where a malicious prover wishes to convince the verifier on k instances of its choice. However, we consider batch Σ-protocols with rogue-instance security, where one instance x_1 is sampled according to a given hard distribution, and the rest of the instances $x_2, \ldots, x_k$ are chosen adaptively as a function of x_1.

Specifically, a batch Σ-protocol Π has ϵ rogue-soundness error if for every malicious prover $\tilde{\mathbf{P}} = (\tilde{\mathbf{P}}_1, \tilde{\mathbf{P}}_2)$ that runs in time t it holds that

$$\Pr\left[\mathsf{RogueExp}_\Pi(\tilde{\mathbf{P}}, \lambda) = 1\right] \leq \epsilon(t),$$

where the experiment $\mathsf{RogueExp}_\Pi(\tilde{\mathbf{P}}, \lambda)$ defined as follows:

1. $(x_1, w_1) \leftarrow \mathcal{D}_\lambda$
2. $((\tilde{x}_2, \ldots, \tilde{x}_k), \alpha, \mathsf{st}) \leftarrow \tilde{\mathbf{P}}_1(x_1)$
3. $\beta \leftarrow \mathcal{C}$
4. $\gamma \leftarrow \tilde{\mathbf{P}}_2(\mathsf{st}, \beta)$
5. Output $\mathbf{V}(x_1, \tilde{x}_2, \ldots, \tilde{x}_k, \alpha, \beta, \gamma)$.

Recall that the definition above omits the setup phase, see Sect. 4 for the precise definition.

2.3 Batching Algebraic Sigma Protocols

We first describe our general compiler for batching algebraic Σ-protocols. This compiler takes an algebraic protocol (which we define next) and outputs a batch version of it (for the same relation). Then, we show the high-level proof of our (almost tight) rogue-security for the batch protocol.

Algebraic Sigma Protocols. Algebraic Σ-protocols are defined with respect to an algebraic one-way function F. The protocol is a proof-of-knowledge of a preimage of $\mathsf{F}(r)$, for randomly sampled r. It is a generalization of the *preimage protocol* presented by Cramer and Damgård [13]. Algebraic one-way functions were introduced by [11], a closely related notion to group-homomorphic one-way functions introduced by [13].

Informally, we say that a one-way function $\mathsf{F}\colon \mathcal{A}^m \to \mathcal{B}$ is algebraic if $\mathcal{A}$ and $\mathcal{B}$ are abelian cyclic groups and for every $x, x' \in \mathcal{A}^m$ it holds that $\mathsf{F}(x + x') = \mathsf{F}(x) \cdot \mathsf{F}(x')$. We say that a Σ-protocol $\Pi = (\mathbf{P}_1, \mathbf{P}_2, \mathbf{V})$ is algebraic if the protocol has the following general recipe:

1. The prover $\mathbf{P}_1$ produces a message $\alpha = \mathsf{F}(r)$ for $r \in \mathcal{A}$.
2. A challenge β is sampled from $\mathbb{Z}_p$ where p is the order of $\mathcal{A}$.
3. The prover $\mathbf{P}_2$ produces a message $\gamma = r + \beta \cdot \mathrm{w}$.
4. The verifier checks correctness by checking whether $\mathsf{F}(\gamma) \overset{?}{=} \alpha \cdot \mathrm{x}^\beta$.

General Compiler to Batch Sigma Protocols. We construct a batch Σ protocol $\Pi^* = (\mathbf{P}_1^*, \mathbf{P}_2^*, \mathbf{V}^*)$ from algebraic Σ-protocol by invoking the Σ-protocol k times. Specifically, given k instances, $\mathbf{P}_1^*$ invokes $\mathbf{P}_1(\mathrm{x}_i)$ and produces the message α which is the multiplication of all α_i's. Then, given k challenges, $\mathbf{P}_2^*$ invokes $\mathbf{P}_2$ for each challenge and produces the compressed message γ by summing the messages γ_i. More formally, given an algebraic Σ-protocol $\Pi = (\mathbf{P}_1, \mathbf{P}_2, \mathbf{V})$, we construct a batch Σ-protocol $\Pi^* = (\mathbf{P}_1^*, \mathbf{P}_2^*, \mathbf{V}^*)$ as follows:

1. The prover $\mathbf{P}_1^*$ invokes $\alpha_i \leftarrow \mathbf{P}_1(\mathrm{x}_i)$ and produces the message $\alpha = \Pi_{i=1}^k \alpha_i$.
2. k challenges β_i are sampled from $\mathbb{Z}_p$ where p is the order of $\mathcal{A}$.
3. The prover $\mathbf{P}_2^*$ invokes $\gamma_i \leftarrow \mathbf{P}_2(\beta_i)$ for each challenge β_i and produces the compressed message $\gamma = \sum_{i=1}^k \gamma_i$.
4. The verifier checks correctness by checking whether $\mathsf{F}(\gamma) \overset{?}{=} \alpha \cdot \Pi_{i=1}^k \mathrm{x}_i^{\beta_i}$.

One can observe that the completeness of Π^* follows from the homomorphic property of F. The prover-to-verifier communication is two group elements. The verifier sends k elements, but since they are all uniformly random strings, they can be easily compressed to a single group element using any pseudo-random generator (e.g., using a random oracle).

Our objective is now to bound the rogue-soundness error of Π^*. To achieve this, we consider a malicious prover $\tilde{\mathbf{P}}$ that given as input an instance x_1 which is sampled from a distribution $\mathcal{D}$, and chooses the rest of the instances $\mathrm{x}_2, \ldots, \mathrm{x}_k$ as a function of x_1. Its goal is to convince the verifier on $\mathrm{x}_1, \ldots, \mathrm{x}_k$. We construct an algorithm that given as input an instance x, invokes $\tilde{\mathbf{P}}$ on x in order to obtain a witness for x. Combined with the second-moment assumption, it allows us to bound $\tilde{\mathbf{P}}$'s success probability (which is the rogue-soundness error).

In order to construct A, we make use of the special soundness property of Σ-protocols. Note that if a Σ-protocol has special soundness, then our construction yields a batch protocol which has *plus-one* special soundness (i.e., given $k + 1$ accepting transcripts on k instances with a common first message and pairwise distinct challenges, one can extract all k witnesses). Obtaining $k + 1$ valid transcripts from the adversary is very costly. However, in our case, we are only interested in extracting a single witness. Thus, we define a relaxed notion called *local special soundness* that allows to extract a single witness from two specifically designed transcripts.

Local Special Soundness. Informally, a batch Σ-protocol has *local special soundness* if there exists an extractor E such that given k instances $x_1, \ldots, x_k$ and a pair of accepting transcripts with a common first message and only one different challenge $\beta_i \neq \beta'_i$, outputs a valid witness for x_i. We now show that every batch Σ-protocol constructed from algebraic Σ-protocol as above, has local special soundness.

Claim 1 (Informal). *The batch Σ-protocol Π^* constructed above from algebraic Σ-protocol has local special soundness.*

Proof (Proof sketch). Consider the algorithm E which takes as input a pair of accepting transcripts $(\alpha, \beta_1, \ldots, \beta_k, \gamma)$, $(\alpha, \beta'_1, \ldots, \beta'_k, \gamma')$ such that there exists only one index j on which $\beta_j \neq \beta'_j$, defined as follows:

1. Let i^* be the index on which $\beta_{i^*} \neq \beta'_{i^*}$.
2. Output $(\gamma - \gamma')/(\beta_{i^*} - \beta'_{i^*})$ on the group $\mathbb{Z}_p$ where p is the order of $\mathcal{A}_{pp}$.

The proof follows from the homomorphic property of F (see Sect. 5.1 for a complete proof).

Due to the local special soundness property, it is sufficient to construct an algorithm A that invokes $\tilde{\mathsf{P}}$ on x and outputs two accepting transcripts $(\alpha, \beta_1, \ldots, \beta_k, \gamma), (\alpha, \beta'_1, \ldots, \beta'_k, \gamma')$ such that $\beta_1 \neq \beta'_1$.

We reduce the problem of finding two such transcripts to the "collision game" first introduced in [12]. In more detail, we show that given an algorithm that succeeds in the collision game, we can construct an algorithm that outputs two such transcripts, which conclude extracting a witness.

The Collision Game. We consider the collision game first introduced in [12] and used in [3,18] which consists of a binary matrix $H \in \{0,1\}^{R \times N}$. The output of the game is 1 if and only if two 1-entries in the same row have been found.

Informally, the R rows correspond to the prover's randomness and the N columns correspond to the verifier's randomness. An entry of H equals 1 if and only if the corresponding transcript is accepting. Then, finding two 1-entries in the same row corresponds to finding two accepting transcripts with a common first message and distinct challenges. Therefore, an algorithm for the collision game can be transformed into an algorithm that finds two accepting transcripts, which by the local special soundness, allows extracting a witness (see Sect. 5.3 for a complete proof).

We now focus on constructing an algorithm for the collision game. In contrast to the collision game algorithm of [12] which runs in strict polynomial time, our algorithm runs in expected polynomial time. A similar approach can be found in [3,18], however, their algorithm minimizes only the first-moment of the expected running time. The collision game algorithm of [3,18] samples an entry of H, if this entry equals 1, the algorithm continues to sample the entire row till it finds another 1-entry. One can observe that the second-moment of the expected running time of this algorithm is too high to get improved bounds.

Our goal is to construct an algorithm that maximizes the trade-off between the success probability and the second-moment of the expected running time, in order to use the second-moment assumption.

Lemma 1 (Informal). *Let $H \in \{0,1\}^{R \times N}$ be a binary matrix and let ϵ be the fraction of 1-entries in H. Then, there exists an algorithm A with oracle access to H such that the following holds:*

1. *The expected number of queries performed by A to H is at most 2.*
2. *The second-moment of the expected number of queries performed by A to H is at most 4.*
3. *The probability that A succeeds in the collision game is at least $\epsilon^{1.5}$.*

Proof (Proof sketch). Let $B = \frac{1}{\sqrt{\epsilon}}$ and consider the following algorithm A:

A^H

1. Sample an entry (ρ, β) in H. If $H[\rho, \beta] = 0$, abort. Let $F = \emptyset$.
2. For every $i \in [B]$: sample without replacement entries in the same row ρ. If $H[\rho, \beta_i] = 1$, set $F \leftarrow F \cup \{\beta_i\}$.
3. If $F = \emptyset$, abort. Otherwise, choose uniformly at random an index $\beta' \in F$ and output ρ, β, β'.

Let $\mathcal{Q}_A$ be a random variable indicating the number of queries performed by A to H. For this section only, we omit the bound on the expected number of queries and refer to the second-moment only. A complete proof of the formal lemma can be found in Sect. 5.2.

By the description of A it performs 1 query to H with probability $(1 - \epsilon)$ and $(1 + B)$ queries with probability ϵ. Therefore,

$$\mathbb{E}\left[\mathcal{Q}_A^2\right] = (1 - \epsilon) \cdot 1^2 + \epsilon \cdot (1 + B)^2 \leq 1 + 2\sqrt{\epsilon} + 1 \leq 4 \ .$$

For now, we give a high-level overview of the proof of A's success probability. A complete proof can be found in Sect. 5.2. Assuming the first query to H was 1-entry, the algorithm continues to sample entries in the same row. Thus, if it hit a row with only one 1-entry, it succeeds in the game with probability zero. Therefore, we divide the rows by the number of 1-entries in it and look at the probability to sample such a row. Formally, for every $0 \leq d \leq N$, we let δ_d be the fraction of rows with exactly d 1-entries. Assuming the first query was 1-entry, A succeeds in the game if it finds at least one more 1-entry with B draws. Let X_d be a random variable indicating the number of 1-entries found in B draws in a row with exactly d 1-entries. Overall,

$$\Pr\left[\mathsf{CollGame}(A, H) = 1\right] \geq \sum_{d=2}^{N} \delta_d \cdot \frac{d}{N} \cdot \Pr\left[X_d \geq 1\right] \ .$$

In Sect. 5.2, we show that the above term is bounded by $\approx \epsilon^{1.5}$.

2.4 Non-interactive Batch Arguments

In the previous subsection we showed a general compiler for batching algebraic Σ-protocols and bound their rogue-soundness error. Similarly, in this subsection we refer to the non-interactive analog. We first construct non-interactive batch arguments from algebraic Σ-protocols and then bound their rogue-instance security.

Non-interactive Batch Arguments from Sigma Protocols. We show how to construct non-interactive batch arguments from algebraic Σ-protocols.

The construction is given by applying the Fiat-Shamir paradigm on the batch Σ-protocol constructed in Sect. 2.3 except for one minor change. Recall that in the construction of batch Σ-protocols, the prover is given as input k different challenges for each input. We wish to keep this property in the non-interactive analog. Specifically, we construct a non-interactive batch argument NARG $= (\mathcal{P}, \mathcal{V})$ from algebraic Σ-protocol by invoking the Σ-protocol k times and obtaining the challenges from a random oracle function $f \in \mathcal{U}(\lambda)$. In more detail, given k instances, the prover $\mathcal{P}$ invokes $\alpha_i \leftarrow \mathbf{P}_1(\mathbbm{x}_i)$ and computes α as the multiplication of α_i's. Then, it obtains each challenge β_i by querying $f(\mathbbm{x}_1, \ldots, \mathbbm{x}_k, \alpha, i)$. Finally, it invokes $\mathbf{P}_2$ for each challenge and computes γ by summing the messages γ_i. The prover $\mathcal{P}$ outputs the proof string (α, γ). The verifier $\mathcal{V}$ computes β_i by querying the random oracle f and checking whether $\mathsf{F}(\gamma) \overset{?}{=} \alpha \cdot \Pi_{i=1}^{k} \mathbbm{x}_i^{\beta_i}$. One can observe that the completeness of NARG follows from the homomorphic property of F and that the proof size is two group elements.

Our objective now is to bound the rogue-soundness error of NARG. Similarly to the interactive case, the NARG constructed above has local special soundness. Therefore, in order to extract a witness, it suffices to construct an algorithm that outputs a pair of transcripts with a common first message and only one different challenge $\beta_i \neq \beta_i'$.

Collision Game for the Non-interactive Analog. Similar to the interactive case, our goal is to reduce the task of finding two such transcripts to the collision game. However, this transformation presents certain challenges. First, in the interactive case, we have two elements of randomness - the prover's randomness and the verifier's randomness which can be straightforwardly represented as a matrix. In contrast, in the non-interactive settings, the verifier's randomness is replaced by random oracle queries. A malicious prover performs at most q queries to the random oracle in order to obtain the challenges. Each answer from the random oracle may affect the prover's algorithm.

Secondly, in the interactive case, a prover $\mathbf{P}$ can be represented by two algorithms $\mathbf{P}_1, \mathbf{P}_2$. The algorithm $\mathbf{P}_1$ outputs the first message α and a state st, and $\mathbf{P}_2$ given as input the challenges β_i and the state st. Consequently, in order to obtain a pair of transcripts with a common first message, we can invoke $\mathbf{P}_1$ and $\mathbf{P}_2$, followed by invoking $\mathbf{P}_2$ again, on the same state and different challenges. In the non-interactive analog, a prover $\mathcal{P}$ outputs the instances $\mathbbm{x}_2, \ldots, \mathbbm{x}_k$ along with (α, γ). We assume without loss of generality that $\mathcal{P}$ always outputs α that it queried the random oracle f with $(x_1, \tilde{x}_2, \ldots, \tilde{x}_k, \alpha)$. Then, in order to obtain two transcripts with a common first message, we need to "guess" which random oracle query the prover is going to output. We invoke the prover once to obtain $(\tilde{x}_2, \ldots, \tilde{x}_k, \alpha, \gamma)$ and let i^* be the random oracle on which the prover queried $(x_1, \tilde{x}_2, \ldots, \tilde{x}_k, \alpha)$. Then, we invoke the prover, replicating the same random oracle responses up to the i^*-th query. With probability $\approx 1/q$ the prover outputs the same instances and first message α.

Therefore, we reduce the problem of finding two such transcripts into the "tree game". In this game, we consider a fixed randomness for the prover and consider a tree of depth q and degree 2^λ. The depth corresponds to the number of queries performed by the prover and the degree corresponds to the possible answers from the random oracle f. Consequently, the execution of the prover corresponds to a random walk on the tree and a leaf corresponds to the output of the prover. We let the value of a leaf be the random oracle query on which the prover queried f with this output. More precisely, each leaf corresponds to an output $(x_2, \ldots, x_k, \alpha, \gamma)$, we consider the value of a leaf to be the random oracle query in which the prover queried f with $(x_2, \ldots, x_k, \alpha)$. Then, finding two transcripts with a common first message and distinct challenges corresponds to finding two leaves with the same value i such that their lowest common ancestor is an internal node v of height i. A formal proof of the reduction appears in the full version.

The Tree Game. We introduce a tree game where an algorithm is given oracle access to a tree T where the value of each leaf is a number. Consider a complete tree T of depth l and degree r. Let $\mathsf{Leaves}(T)$ be the leaves of T and for every $u \in \mathsf{Leaves}(T)$ let $\mathsf{val}(u)$ be the value "stored" in u. Note that not all leaves hold a number value, we consider the value of such a leaf as $\bot$. During the execution of the game, the algorithm A is given as input a number k and oracle access to the tree T and aims to find $k+1$ leaves $u_1, \ldots, u_{k+1}$ with the same value i that have the same lowest common ancestor v such that $\mathsf{height}(v) = i$.

Due to the local special soundness property, it is sufficient to construct an algorithm that outputs two accepting transcripts, then in this section, we consider the specific case where $k = 1$.

Lemma 2 (Informal). *Let T be a complete tree of depth l and degree r and let ϵ be the fraction of non-bot leaves in T. Then, there exists an algorithm A with oracle access to T such that on input $k = 1$ the following holds:*

1. *The expected number of queries performed by A to H is at most 2.*
2. *The second-moment of the expected number of queries performed by A to H is at most 4.*
3. *The probability that A succeeds in the collision game is at least $\epsilon^{1.5}/l$.*

Proof (Proof sketch). Let $B = \frac{1}{\sqrt{\epsilon}}$ and consider the following algorithm A:

A^T

1. Sample a leaf $u \in \mathsf{Leaves}(T)$. If $\mathsf{val}(u) = \bot$, abort.
2. Let v be the parent of u of height $\mathsf{val}(u)$ and let w be the parent of u of height $(\mathsf{val}(u) - 1)$. Let $F = \emptyset$.
3. For every $i \in [B]$: sample without replacement leaves from $T_v \setminus T_w$. If $\mathsf{val}(u_i) = \mathsf{val}(u)$, set $F \leftarrow F \cup \{u_i\}$.
4. If $F = \emptyset$, abort. Otherwise, choose uniformly at random a leaf $u' \in F$ and output u, u'.

Let $\mathcal{Q}_A$ be a random variable indicating the number of queries performed by A to T. For this section only, we omit the bound on the expected number of queries and refer to the second-moment only. A complete proof of the formal lemma appears in the full version.

By the description of A it performs 1 query to T with probability $(1 - \epsilon)$ and $(1 + B)$ queries with probability ϵ. Therefore,

$$\mathbb{E}\left[\mathcal{Q}_A^2\right] = (1 - \epsilon) \cdot 1^2 + \epsilon \cdot (1 + B)^2 \leq 1 + 2\sqrt{\epsilon} + 1 \leq 4 .$$

For now, we give an informal high-level overview of the proof of A's success probability. A complete proof appears in the full version. Assume A samples a leaf u with the value h, then, A continues to sample leaves from the same sub-tree in order to find another leaf with the value h. Let v be the parent of u of height h. Note that for every h and v, the number of leaves with the value h in T_v may be different, which affects its success probability. Therefore, for every value h, we "divide" the internal nodes to "buckets" by the probability to sample a leaf with the value h in its sub-tree, and then we look at the probability to "reach" each bucket.

Formally, for every $0 \leq d \leq l \log r$ and $0 \leq h \leq l - 1$, we let

$$\delta_{d,h} = \Pr_{v:\mathsf{height}(v)=h}\left[\frac{|\{u \in \mathsf{Leaves}(T_v) : \mathsf{val}(u) = h\}|}{|\mathsf{Leaves}(T_v)|} \in \left[2^{-d}, 2^{-d+1}\right]\right] .$$

Note that a node v is in the d-th "bucket" if the probability to sample a leaf with the value h in the sub-tree T_v is in $\left[2^{-d}, 2^{-d+1}\right]$. Assuming the first query to the tree is a leaf u with the value h, the remainder of the game can be modeled by a hypergeometric distribution. Informally, B elements from a population of size $|T_v \setminus T_w|$ containing $\approx 2^{-d}$ successes are drawn without replacement. Let $X_{\delta_{d,h}}$ be a random variable indicating the number of leaves with the value h found in B draws in a sub-tree T_v such that v is in the d-th "bucket". Thus,

$$\Pr\left[\mathsf{TreeCollGame}(A, T) = 1\right] \geq \sum_{h=0}^{l-1} \sum_{d=2}^{N} \delta_{d,h} \cdot 2^{-d} \cdot \Pr\left[X_{\delta_{d,h}} \geq 1\right] .$$

In the full version, we show that the above term is bounded by $\approx \epsilon^{1.5}/l$.

2.5   General Batch Sigma Protocols

Batch Sigma protocols. In the general case, we consider batch Σ-protocols where given k instance-witness pairs $(\mathrm{x}_i, \mathrm{w}_i)$, the prover $\mathbf{P}_1$ sends a message α, the verifier $\mathbf{V}$ samples a challenge β and sends it, the prover $\mathbf{P}_2$ responds with a message γ, and the verifier $\mathbf{V}$ decides whether to accept or reject by applying a predicate to $(\mathrm{x}_1, \ldots, \mathrm{x}_k, \alpha, \beta, \gamma)$. In order to bound the rogue-soundness error of batch Σ-protocols, we make use of the special soundness property. In particular, we consider the *plus-one special soundness* which guarantees the existence of an extractor E. When it is given as input $k + 1$ transcripts of an execution of a batch Sigma protocol on k instances, the extractor outputs k corresponding witnesses. More precisely, the extractor is given as input $k + 1$ transcripts with a common first message and distinct pairwise challenges.

We construct an algorithm A that given as input an instance x invokes a malicious prover on input x to obtain $k + 1$ transcripts, which by the plus-one special soundness allows extracting k witnesses, specifically, to output a witness for x. Note that the algorithm needs to invoke the prover multiple times in order to achieve approximately the same probability as in the specific case of batch protocols constructed from algebraic Σ-protocols. Unfortunately, it appears that finding a good trade-off between the second-moment of the expected running time and the success probability of the algorithm is challenging in this context. As a result, in the general case, we rely on the first-moment assumption.

Similarly, we reduce the problem of finding $k + 1$ accepting transcripts to a generalized version of the collision game first introduced in [12]. In more detail, we construct an algorithm for the collision game and then use it in order to obtain $k + 1$ accepting transcripts (with a common first message and pairwise distinct challenges), which conclude extracting a witness.

General Collision Game. We provide a general version of the collision game first introduced in [12] and used in [3,18], which consists of a binary matrix $H \in \{0,1\}^{R \times N}$. We generalize the collision game by an additional input, a number $k \in \mathbb{N}$. The output of the game is 1 if and only if $k + 1$ entries with the value 1 in the same row have been found. An algorithm for the collision game is given as input a number $k \in \mathbb{N}$ and an oracle access to the matrix H.

Informally, the R rows correspond to the prover's randomness and the N columns correspond to the verifier's randomness. An entry of H equals 1 if and only if the corresponding transcript is accepting. Then, finding $k + 1$ entries with the value 1 in the same row corresponds to finding $k + 1$ accepting transcripts with a common first message and pairwise distinct challenges. Therefore, an algorithm for the collision game can be transformed into an algorithm that finds $k + 1$ accepting transcripts, which as discussed above, allows extracting a witness (see the full version for a complete proof).

Lemma 3 (Informal). *Let $H \in \{0,1\}^{R \times N}$ be a binary matrix and let ϵ be the fraction of 1-entries in H. Then, there exists an algorithm A with oracle access to H such that on input k the following holds:*

1. *The expected number of queries performed by A to H is at most $k + 1$.*
2. *The probability that A succeeds in the game is at least ϵ.*

Proof (Proof sketch). We consider the following algorithm:

$A^H(k)$

1. Sample an entry (ρ, β) in H. If $H[\rho, \beta] = 0$, abort.
2. Sample without replacement entries in the same row ρ, until $k + 1$ entries with the value 1 are found or the row has been exhausted.

Let $\mathcal{Q}_A$ be a random variable indicating the number of queries performed by A to H. Note that the number of 1-entries in each row affects the expected number of queries performed by A. Thus, we let ϵ_ρ be the fraction of 1-entries in row ρ. Assuming the first query to H lies in row ρ and equals 1, the remainder of the algorithm can be modeled by a negative hypergeometric distribution. Elements from a population of size $N - 1$ containing $\epsilon_\rho N - 1$ successes are drawn without replacement till k successes are counted. Thus, assuming that the first query lies in a row ρ and equals 1, the expected number of queries performed by A is $\frac{k(N-1+1)}{\epsilon_\rho N-1+1} = \frac{k}{\epsilon_\rho}$. Overall,

$$\mathbb{E}[\mathcal{Q}_A] = 1 + \frac{1}{R} \sum_{1}^{R} \epsilon_\rho \cdot \frac{k}{\epsilon_\rho} = k + 1 \ .$$

As discussed in Sect. 2.3, in order to bound the success probability we divide the rows by the number of 1-entries in it. Formally, for every $0 \le d \le N$, we let δ_d be the fraction of rows with exactly d 1-entries. Note that if A's first query to H lies in a row with at least $k + 1$ entries with the value 1, it succeeds in the game with probability 1. Thus,

$$\Pr[\mathsf{CollGame}_k(A, H) = 1] \ge \sum_{d=k+1}^{R} \delta_d \cdot \frac{d}{N} \ .$$

In the full version, we show that the above term is bounded by $\approx \epsilon$.

2.6 Expected Time Hardness Framework

In this subsection, we present our framework for analyzing the expected-time hardness of cryptographic problems in generic models. Our framework allows bounding the success probability of query-algorithms in experiments that involve access to an oracle (e.g., solving discrete-logarithm in the generic group model). Here, we consider the number of queries performed by the algorithm and ignore its actual runtime.

Our overall goal is to prove statements of the form: if any algorithm that performs t queries (as a strict parameter) has success probability $\epsilon(t)$ in a particular experiment, then any algorithm A has success probability $\mathbb{E}[\epsilon(T_A)]$, where T_A is a *random variable* for the number of queries performed by A. Such a statement would allow us to derive the desired first-moment and second-moment hardness that we need for discrete-logarithm and other problems.

Perhaps surprisingly, such a general statement is *incorrect*, which we demonstrate via the multiple discrete-logarithm problem. Yun [34] showed that any generic t-time algorithm given k instances of the discrete-logarithm problem solves all of them with probability at most $\epsilon(t) \le (k \cdot t^2/p)^k$ (which is tight). However, this bound does not translate to $\mathbb{E}[\epsilon(T_A)] = k^k \cdot \mathbb{E}[T_A^{2k}]/p^k$. To illustrate this, consider the following generic algorithm A for the case where $k = 2$:

1. Perform $p^{1/4}$ distinct queries to the group generation oracle and store the query-answer list μ.
2. If there does not exist $(x,y), (x',y') \in \mu$, such that $x \ne x'$ and $y = y'$, abort.
3. Otherwise, perform another $p^{1/2}$ queries to the group generation oracle.

A careful analysis shows that the success probability of this algorithm is $\approx 1/\sqrt{p}$ and the 4-moment of the expected number of queries is $\approx p$, which does not satisfy the bound of $\epsilon \le 4 \cdot \mathbb{E}[T_A^4]/p^2$.

This raises the question of when can we derive bounds for expected algorithms. What distinguishes the multiple discrete-logarithm (for which we have no non-trivial bounds for expected algorithms) compared to the single discrete-logarithm (for which we derive tight bounds for expected algorithms)? We define a (relatively natural) property of the experiment, called *history oblivious*, that can precisely distinguish the two cases and allows us to derive our bounds. Roughly speaking, history oblivious experiment is defined via the existence of a predicate on the sequence of query/answer pairs (the trace). When the predicate of the trace is true, then the algorithm is able to solve its task with no additional queries. When the predicate is false, the trace has a limited effect on its success probability (only the size of the trace affects the probability and not its contents).

For example, in the discrete-logarithm problem, the trace to the generic group would be true if it contains a collision. When the predicate is true, one can easily deduce a solution. Otherwise, the trace gives almost no helpful information to the algorithm except for specific elements which are not the discrete-logarithm. That is, in this case, the advantage only depends on the size of the trace. Any two traces of the same size for which the predicate is false yield equal success probability for the algorithm. Observe that this is not the case for multiple discrete-logarithm. Here, we have three types of interesting traces (rather than two). A trace can contain no collisions, or a single collision (from which one can deduce one discrete-logarithm but not the other), or two collisions (from which one can derive both discrete-logarithms). The predicate in this case would identify a trace with two collisions. Thus, two traces of the same size, one from the first type and one from the second type would have drastic different effect on the success probability, as in the latter it needs to solve only a single discrete-logarithm.

In summary, for any history oblivious experiment we show that:

$$\Pr[\textbf{strict algorithms succeeds}] \le \epsilon(t) \implies \Pr[\textbf{expected-time algorithms succeeds}] \le \mathbb{E}[\epsilon(t)] \ .$$

We formalize the above statement in Theorem 2. This allows us to prove first and second-moment hardness of discrete-logarithm Eqs. 1 and 2, which are the basis for our results. It also allows us to derive our bounds for the Micali SNARK construction given in Theorem 5. Our framework is inspired by the work of Jaeger and Tessaro [19], however, their tools do not allow us to prove the second-moment hardness assumptions in generic models. Furthermore, our approach is arguably simpler to use and provides tighter security bounds even for first-moment assumptions. We show that our framework recovers the bounds of [19] in Corollary 3.

3 Preliminaries

For any $n \in \mathbb{N}$, we denote the set of all positive integers up to n as $[n] := \{1, \ldots, n\}$. For any finite set S, $x \leftarrow S$ denotes a uniformly random element x from the set S. Similarly, for any distribution $\mathcal{D}$, $x \leftarrow \mathcal{D}$ denotes an element x drawn from distribution $\mathcal{D}$.

3.1 High-Moment Hardness

A relation $\mathcal{R}$ is a set $\mathcal{R} = \{\mathcal{R}_\lambda\}_{\lambda \in \mathbb{N}}$, where $\mathcal{R}_\lambda \subseteq \mathcal{P}_\lambda \times \mathcal{X}_\lambda \times \mathcal{W}_\lambda$ for any $\lambda \in \mathbb{N}$, for sets $\mathcal{X} = \{\mathcal{X}_\lambda\}_{\lambda \in \mathbb{N}}$, $\mathcal{W} = \{\mathcal{W}_\lambda\}_{\lambda \in \mathbb{N}}$ and $\mathcal{P} = \{\mathcal{P}_\lambda\}_{\lambda \in \mathbb{N}}$. The corresponding language $\mathcal{L}(\mathcal{R}_\lambda)$ is the set of public parameters pp and instances x for which there exists a witness w such that $(\text{pp}, \text{x}, \text{w}) \in \mathcal{R}_\lambda$.

We consider distributions $\mathcal{D} = \{\mathcal{D}_\lambda\}_{\lambda \in \mathbb{N}}$ over the relation where each $\mathcal{D}_\lambda$ produces $(\text{pp}, \text{x}, \text{w}) \in \mathcal{R}_\lambda$. We note by $\mathcal{D}_\lambda(\text{pp})$ the distribution that produces (x, w) such that $(\text{pp}, \text{x}, \text{w}) \in \mathcal{R}_\lambda$.

For any such distribution $\mathcal{D}_\lambda(\text{pp})$ and an algorithm A, we denote by $T_{A, \mathcal{D}_\lambda}$ the random variable indicating the running time of A on input x where $(\text{x}, \text{w}) \leftarrow \mathcal{D}_\lambda(\text{pp})$.

Definition 1 (First-moment hard relation). *Let $\Delta = \Delta(\lambda), \omega = \omega(\lambda)$ be functions of the security parameter, and let $\mathcal{R} = \{\mathcal{R}_\lambda\}_{\lambda \in \mathbb{N}}$ be a relation where $\mathcal{R}_\lambda \subseteq \mathcal{P}_\lambda \times \mathcal{X}_\lambda \times \mathcal{W}_\lambda$. Let Setup be a setup algorithm that on input 1^λ, outputs $\text{pp} \in \mathcal{P}_\lambda$. We say that $\mathcal{R}$ is first-moment hard (with respect to a distribution $\mathcal{D} = \{\mathcal{D}_\lambda\}_{\lambda \in \mathbb{N}}$ and a setup algorithm Setup) if for every algorithm A and for every $\lambda \in \mathbb{N}$ it holds that*

$$\Pr \left[(\text{pp}, \text{x}, \tilde{\text{w}}) \in \mathcal{R}_\lambda \ \middle| \ \begin{array}{l} \text{pp} \leftarrow \text{Setup}(1^\lambda) \\ (\text{x}, \text{w}) \leftarrow \mathcal{D}_\lambda(\text{pp}) \\ \tilde{\text{w}} \leftarrow A(\text{pp}, \text{x}) \end{array} \right] \leq \frac{\Delta \cdot \mathbb{E}\left[T_{A, \mathcal{D}_\lambda}\right]}{|\mathcal{W}_\lambda|^\omega}.$$

Definition 2 (Second-moment hard relation). *Let $\Delta = \Delta(\lambda), \omega = \omega(\lambda)$ be functions of the security parameter, and let $\mathcal{R} = \{\mathcal{R}_\lambda\}_{\lambda \in \mathbb{N}}$ be a relation where $\mathcal{R}_\lambda \subseteq \mathcal{P}_\lambda \times \mathcal{X}_\lambda \times \mathcal{W}_\lambda$. Let Setup be a setup algorithm that on input 1^λ, outputs $\text{pp} \in \mathcal{P}_\lambda$. We say that $\mathcal{R}$ is second-moment hard (with respect to a distribution*

$\mathcal{D} = \{\mathcal{D}_\lambda\}_{\lambda \in \mathbb{N}}$ and a setup algorithm Setup) if for every algorithm A and for every $\lambda \in \mathbb{N}$ it holds that

$$
\Pr \left[(\mathrm{pp}, \mathrm{x}, \tilde{\mathrm{w}}) \in \mathcal{R}_\lambda \;\middle|\; \begin{array}{l} \mathrm{pp} \leftarrow \mathsf{Setup}(1^\lambda) \\ (\mathrm{x}, \mathrm{w}) \leftarrow \mathcal{D}_\lambda(\mathrm{pp}) \\ \tilde{\mathrm{w}} \leftarrow A(\mathrm{pp}, \mathrm{x}) \end{array} \right] \leq \frac{\Delta \cdot \mathbb{E}\left[T^2_{A,\mathcal{D}_\lambda}\right]}{|\mathcal{W}_\lambda|^\omega} .
$$

3.2   Sigma Protocols

Definition 3 (Σ-Protocol). Let $\mathcal{R} = \{\mathcal{R}_\lambda\}_{\lambda \in \mathbb{N}}$ be a relation, where $\mathcal{R}_\lambda \subseteq \mathcal{P}_\lambda \times \mathcal{X}_\lambda \times \mathcal{W}_\lambda$ for any $\lambda \in \mathbb{N}$. A Σ-protocol Π for relation $\mathcal{R}$ is a 5-tuple $(\mathsf{Setup}, \boldsymbol{P}_1, \boldsymbol{P}_2, \boldsymbol{V}, \mathcal{C})$ where Setup and $\boldsymbol{P}_1$ are probabilistic polynomial-time algorithms, $\boldsymbol{P}_2$ and $\boldsymbol{V}$ are deterministic polynomial-time algorithms, and $\mathcal{C} = \{\mathcal{C}_{\mathrm{pp}}\}_{\mathrm{pp} \in \mathcal{P}}$ is an ensemble of efficiently sampleable sets. The protocol Π is defined as follows:

1. The algorithm $\mathsf{Setup}(1^\lambda)$ produces public parameters pp.
2. The algorithm $\boldsymbol{P}_1(\mathrm{pp}, \mathrm{x}, \mathrm{w})$ produces a message α and a state st.
3. A challenge β is sampled uniformly at random from the challenge set $\mathcal{C}_{\mathrm{pp}}$.
4. The algorithm $\boldsymbol{P}_2(\mathsf{st}, \beta)$ produces a message γ.
5. The algorithm $\boldsymbol{V}(\mathrm{pp}, \mathrm{x}, \alpha, \beta, \gamma)$ determines the output of the protocol by outputting 0 or 1.

We require that for every $\lambda \in \mathbb{N}$ and $(\mathrm{x}, \mathrm{w}) \in \mathcal{R}_\lambda$ it holds that

$$
\Pr \left[\boldsymbol{V}(\mathrm{pp}, \mathrm{x}, \alpha, \beta, \gamma) = 1 \;\middle|\; \begin{array}{l} \mathrm{pp} \leftarrow \mathsf{Setup}(1^\lambda) \\ (\alpha, \mathsf{st}) \leftarrow \boldsymbol{P}_1(\mathrm{pp}, \mathrm{x}, \mathrm{w}) \\ \beta \leftarrow \mathcal{C}_{\mathrm{pp}} \\ \gamma \leftarrow \boldsymbol{P}_2(\mathsf{st}, \beta) \end{array} \right] = 1 .
$$

Definition 4 (Special soundness). Let $\Pi = (\mathsf{Setup}, \boldsymbol{P}_1, \boldsymbol{P}_2, \boldsymbol{V}, \mathcal{C})$ be a Σ-protocol for a relation $\mathcal{R}$, and let $t = t(\lambda)$ be a function of the security parameter $\lambda \in \mathbb{N}$. Then, Π has t-time special soundness if there exists a deterministic t-time algorithm E that on any public parameters $\mathrm{pp} \in \mathcal{P}$, any input statement $\mathrm{x} \in \mathcal{X}_\lambda$ and any two accepting transcripts with a common first message and distinct challenges, outputs a witness w such that $(\mathrm{pp}, \mathrm{x}, \mathrm{w}) \in \mathcal{R}$.

Definition 5 (Zero knowledge Σ-protocol). Let $\Pi = (\mathsf{Setup}, \boldsymbol{P}_1, \boldsymbol{P}_2, \boldsymbol{V}, \mathcal{C})$ be a Σ-protocol for a relation $\mathcal{R}$, and let $t = t(\lambda)$ be a function of the security parameter $\lambda \in \mathbb{N}$. Then, Π is t-time zero-knowledge if there exists a probabilistic t-time algorithm Sim such that for every $\lambda \in \mathbb{N}$ and public parameters-instance-witness tuple $(\mathrm{pp}, \mathrm{x}, \mathrm{w}) \in \mathcal{R}_\lambda$ the distributions

$$
\left\{ (\mathrm{pp}, \mathrm{x}, \alpha, \beta, \gamma) \;\middle|\; \begin{array}{l} (\alpha, \mathsf{st}) \leftarrow \boldsymbol{P}_1(\mathrm{pp}, \mathrm{x}, \mathrm{w}) \\ \beta \leftarrow \mathcal{C}_{\mathrm{pp}} \\ \gamma \leftarrow \boldsymbol{P}_2(\mathsf{st}, \beta) \end{array} \right\} \qquad and \qquad \{\mathsf{Sim}(\mathrm{pp}, \mathrm{x})\}
$$

are identical.

3.3 Batch Sigma Protocols

Definition 6 (Batch Σ-protocol). *Let $\mathcal{R} = \{\mathcal{R}_\lambda\}_{\lambda \in \mathbb{N}}$ be a relation, where $\mathcal{R}_\lambda \subseteq \mathcal{P}_\lambda \times \mathcal{X}_\lambda \times \mathcal{W}_\lambda$ for any $\lambda \in \mathbb{N}$ and let $\boldsymbol{K} \in \mathbb{N}$ be a bound on the number of instances. A batch Σ-protocol Π for relation $\mathcal{R}$ is a 5-tuple $(\mathsf{Setup}, \boldsymbol{P}_1, \boldsymbol{P}_2, \boldsymbol{V}, \mathcal{C})$ where Setup and $\boldsymbol{P}_1$ are probabilistic polynomial-time algorithms, $\boldsymbol{P}_2$ and $\boldsymbol{V}$ are deterministic polynomial-time algorithms, and $\mathcal{C} = \{\mathcal{C}_{\mathsf{pp}}\}_{\mathsf{pp} \in \mathcal{P}}$ is an ensemble of efficiently sampleable sets. For any $k \leq \boldsymbol{K}$, the protocol Π is defined as follows:*

1. *The algorithm $\boldsymbol{P}_1(\mathsf{pp}, (\mathbb{x}_1, \mathbb{w}_1), \ldots, (\mathbb{x}_k, \mathbb{w}_k))$ produces a message α and a state st.*
2. *A challenge β is sampled uniformly at random from the challenge set $\mathcal{C}_{\mathsf{pp}}$.*
3. *The algorithm $\boldsymbol{P}_2(\mathsf{st}, \beta)$ produces a message γ.*
4. *The algorithm $\boldsymbol{V}(\mathsf{pp}, \mathbb{x}_1, \ldots, \mathbb{x}_k, \alpha, \beta, \gamma)$ determines the output of the protocol by outputting 0 or 1.*

We require that for every $\lambda, k \in \mathbb{N}$ such that $k \leq \boldsymbol{K}$, for any $(\mathbb{x}_1, \mathbb{w}_1), \ldots, (\mathbb{x}_k, \mathbb{w}_k) \in \mathcal{R}_\lambda$ it holds that

$$
\Pr\left[\boldsymbol{V}(\mathsf{pp}, \mathbb{x}_1, \ldots, \mathbb{x}_k, \alpha, \beta, \gamma) = 1 \,\middle|\, \begin{array}{l} \mathsf{pp} \leftarrow \mathsf{Setup}(1^\lambda, \boldsymbol{K}) \\ (\alpha, \mathsf{st}) \leftarrow \boldsymbol{P}_1(\mathsf{pp}, (\mathbb{x}_1, \mathbb{w}_1), \ldots, (\mathbb{x}_k, \mathbb{w}_k)) \\ \beta \leftarrow \mathcal{C}_{\mathsf{pp}} \\ \gamma \leftarrow \boldsymbol{P}_2(\mathsf{st}, \beta) \end{array} \right] = 1 .
$$

Definition 7 (Plus-one special soundness). *Let $\Pi = (\mathsf{Setup}, \boldsymbol{P}_1, \boldsymbol{P}_2, \boldsymbol{V}, \mathcal{C})$ be a batch Σ-protocol for a relation $\mathcal{R}$ with a bound $\boldsymbol{K}$ on the number of instances, and let $t = t(\lambda, \boldsymbol{K})$ be a function of $\boldsymbol{K}$ and the security parameter $\lambda \in \mathbb{N}$. Then, Π has t-time plus-one special soundness if there exists a deterministic t-time algorithm E that for every $\lambda \in \mathbb{N}$ and $k \leq \boldsymbol{K}$, on any public parameters pp, any k inputs statements $\mathbb{x}_1, \ldots, \mathbb{x}_k \in \mathcal{X}_\lambda$ and any $k + 1$ accepting transcripts with a common first message and pairwise distinct challenges, outputs k witnesses $\mathbb{w}_1, \ldots, \mathbb{w}_k$ such that for every $i \in [k]$ it holds that $(\mathsf{pp}, \mathbb{x}_i, \mathbb{w}_i) \in \mathcal{R}_\lambda$.*

Definition 8 (Zero knowledge batch Σ-protocol). *Let $\Pi = (\mathsf{Setup}, \boldsymbol{P}_1, \boldsymbol{P}_2, \boldsymbol{V}, \mathcal{C})$ be a batch Σ-protocol for a relation $\mathcal{R}$ with a bound $\boldsymbol{K}$ on the number of instances, and let $t = t(\lambda, \boldsymbol{K})$ be a function of $\boldsymbol{K}$ and the security parameter $\lambda \in \mathbb{N}$. Then, Π is t-time zero-knowledge if there exists a probabilistic t-time algorithm Sim such that for any $k \leq \boldsymbol{K}$, for every $\lambda \in \mathbb{N}$ and $(\mathsf{pp}, \mathbb{x}_1, \mathbb{w}_1), \ldots, (\mathsf{pp}, \mathbb{x}_k, \mathbb{w}_k) \in \mathcal{R}_\lambda$ the distributions*

$$
\left\{ (\mathsf{pp}, \mathbb{x}_1, \ldots, \mathbb{x}_k, \alpha, \beta, \gamma) \,\middle|\, \begin{array}{l} (\alpha, \mathsf{st}) \leftarrow \boldsymbol{P}_1(\mathsf{pp}, (\mathbb{x}_1, \mathbb{w}_1), \ldots, (\mathbb{x}_k, \mathbb{w}_k)) \\ \beta \leftarrow \mathcal{C}_{k, \lambda} \\ \gamma \leftarrow \boldsymbol{P}_2(\mathsf{st}, \beta) \end{array} \right\} \quad and \quad \{\mathsf{Sim}(\mathsf{pp}, \mathbb{x}_1, \ldots, \mathbb{x}_k)\}
$$

are identical.

4   Rogue-Instance Security

In this section, we give our definition of rogue-instance security notion for batch protocols and non-interactive batch arguments, which is inspired by the rogue-key security notion for multi-signatures.

4.1   Batch Sigma Protocols

In a batch Σ-protocol, we are given k instance-witness pairs $(x_1, w_1), \ldots,$ (x_k, w_k). The standard adaptive soundness requirement considers the case where a malicious prover wishes to convince the verifier on k instances of its choice. However, we consider batch Σ-protocols with rogue-instance security, where one instance x_1 is sampled according to a given hard distribution, and the rest of the instances $x_2, \ldots, x_k$ are chosen adaptively as a function of x_1. Formally,

Definition 9 (Rogue soundness). *Let* $\Pi = (\mathsf{Setup}, P_1, P_2, V, \mathcal{C})$ *be a batch* Σ-*protocol for a relation* $\mathcal{R}$ *with a bound* $\boldsymbol{K}$ *on the number of instances. Then,* Π *has* $(t, \epsilon_{\mathcal{D}})$-*rogue soundness (with respect to a distribution* $\mathcal{D} = \{\mathcal{D}_\lambda\}_{\lambda \in \mathbb{N}}$ *and the setup algorithm* Setup) *if for every* $\lambda, k \in \mathbb{N}$ *such that* $k \leq \boldsymbol{K}$ *and for any* t-*time malicious prover* $\tilde{\boldsymbol{P}} = (\tilde{\boldsymbol{P}}_1, \tilde{\boldsymbol{P}}_2)$:

$$\Pr\left[V(\mathsf{pp}, x_1, \tilde{x}_2, \ldots, \tilde{x}_k, \alpha, \beta, \gamma) = 1 \left| \begin{array}{l} \mathsf{pp} \leftarrow \mathsf{Setup}(1^\lambda, \boldsymbol{K}) \\ (x_1, w_1) \leftarrow \mathcal{D}_\lambda(\mathsf{pp}) \\ ((\tilde{x}_2, \ldots, \tilde{x}_k), \alpha, \mathsf{st}) \leftarrow \tilde{P}_1(\mathsf{pp}, x_1) \\ \beta \leftarrow \mathcal{C}_{\mathsf{pp}} \\ \gamma \leftarrow \tilde{P}_2(\mathsf{st}, \beta) \end{array} \right. \right] \leq \epsilon_{\mathcal{D}}(\lambda, t, \boldsymbol{K}) \ .$$

In the full version of the paper, we provide an analogous non-interactive definition.

5   Batching Algebraic Sigma Protocols

In this section, we define algebraic Σ-protocols and construct their batch version. Then, we bound the rogue-soundness error of such batch Σ-protocols using the second-moment assumption (Definition 2).

In Sect. 5.1 we define algebraic one-way functions and construct batch Σ-protocols from algebraic Σ-protocols. Then, in Sect. 5.2 we generalize the "collision game" presented in [3,12,18] for multiple instances while referring to the second-moment of the expected running time. Finally, in Sect. 5.3 we prove the rogue-instance security of batch Σ-protocols constructed from algebraic Σ-protocols.

5.1   Algebraic Sigma Protocols

In this section, we refer to Σ-protocols that have a specific structure we call *algebraic* Σ-*protocols* and then, we define their batch analog.

Our definition of algebraic Σ-protocols relies on algebraic one-way function, presented in [11,13].

Definition 10 (Algebraic one-way function). *A family of m-variate one-way functions consists of two algorithms* $(\mathsf{Setup}, \mathsf{F})$ *that work as follows. On input* 1^λ, *the algorithm* $\mathsf{Setup}(1^\lambda)$ *produces public parameters. Any such public parameters* pp, *determines the function* $\mathsf{F}_{\mathsf{pp}} \colon \mathcal{A}_{\mathsf{pp}}^m \to \mathcal{B}_{\mathsf{pp}}$ *such that for every* $x \in \mathcal{A}_{\mathsf{pp}}^m$, *it is efficient to compute* $\mathsf{F}_{\mathsf{pp}}(x)$. *A family of one-way functions is algebraic if for every* $\lambda \in \mathbb{N}$ *and* $\mathsf{pp} \leftarrow \mathsf{Setup}(1^\lambda)$ *the following holds:*

- **Algebraic:** The sets $\mathcal{A}_{pp}, \mathcal{B}_{pp}$ are abelian cyclic groups with operators $(+)$, and $(\cdot)$, respectively.
- **Homomorphic:** For any input $x, x' \in \mathcal{A}_{pp}^m$ it holds that $\mathsf{F}(x + x') = \mathsf{F}(x) \cdot \mathsf{F}(x')$.

We now define the notion of algebraic Σ-protocols, which is a generalization of the *preimage protocol* presented in [13].

Definition 11 (Algebraic Σ-protocol). *Let $\mathcal{R} = \{\mathcal{R}_\lambda\}_{\lambda \in \mathbb{N}}$ be a relation, where $\mathcal{R}_\lambda \subseteq \mathcal{P}_\lambda \times \mathcal{X}_\lambda \times \mathcal{W}_\lambda$ for any $\lambda \in \mathbb{N}$. A Σ-protocol $\Pi = (\mathsf{Setup}, \boldsymbol{P}_1, \boldsymbol{P}_2, \boldsymbol{V}, \mathcal{C})$ for relation $\mathcal{R}$ is algebraic if there exists m-variate algebraic one-way function $(\mathsf{Setup}, \mathsf{F})$ such that for every pp produced by $\mathsf{Setup}(1^\lambda)$ the following holds:*

- *For every x, w it holds that $(pp, \mathrm{x}, \mathrm{w}) \in \mathcal{R}_\lambda$ if and only if $\mathsf{F}_{pp}(\mathrm{w}) = \mathrm{x}$.*
- *The challenge space $\mathcal{C}_{pp} \subseteq \mathbb{Z}_p$ where p is the order of $\mathcal{A}_{pp}$.*
- *The protocol Π is defined as follows:*
  1. *The algorithm $\boldsymbol{P}_1(\mathrm{x}, \mathrm{w})$ produces a message $\alpha = \mathsf{F}(r)$ for some $r \in \mathcal{A}_{pp}$ and a state st.*
  2. *A challenge β is sampled uniformly at random from the challenge set $\mathcal{C}_{pp}$.*
  3. *The algorithm $\boldsymbol{P}_2(\mathsf{st}, \beta)$ produces a message $\gamma = r + \beta \cdot \mathrm{w}$.*
  4. *The algorithm $\boldsymbol{V}(\mathrm{x}, \alpha, \beta, \gamma)$ determines the output of the protocol by checking whether $\mathsf{F}(\gamma) \overset{?}{=} \alpha \cdot \mathrm{x}^\beta$.*

Note that the setup algorithm of the function is the setup algorithm of the protocol. In fact, the prover holds a public parameters-instance-witness tuple such that $\mathrm{x} = \mathsf{F}_{pp}(\mathrm{w})$. Thus, the prover convinces the verifier that it knows the preimage of x. Note that the verifier's computation can be performed using exponentiation by squaring, however there may exist more efficient algorithms.

Next, we construct a batch version of any algebraic Σ-protocol as follows.

Construction 1 (Batch Σ-protocol). *Let $\mathcal{R} = \{\mathcal{R}_\lambda\}_{\lambda \in \mathbb{N}}$ be a relation, where $\mathcal{R}_\lambda \subseteq \mathcal{P}_\lambda \times \mathcal{X}_\lambda \times \mathcal{W}_\lambda$ for any $\lambda \in \mathbb{N}$ and let $\boldsymbol{K} \in \mathbb{N}$ be a bound on the number of instances. Let $\Pi = (\mathsf{Setup}, \boldsymbol{P}_1, \boldsymbol{P}_2, \boldsymbol{V}, \mathcal{C})$ be an algebraic Σ-protocol with an algebaric one-way function $(\mathsf{Setup}, \mathsf{F})$. We define $\Pi^* = (\mathsf{Setup}^*, \boldsymbol{P}_1^*, \boldsymbol{P}_2^*, \boldsymbol{V}^*, \mathcal{C})$ to be a batch Σ-protocol for relation $\mathcal{R}$ as follows. The algorithms Setup^* and $\boldsymbol{P}_1^*$ are probabilistic polynomial-time algorithms, $\boldsymbol{P}_2^*$ and $\boldsymbol{V}^*$ are deterministic polynomial-time algorithms, and $\mathcal{C} = \{\mathcal{C}_{pp}\}_{pp \in \mathcal{P}}$ is an ensemble of efficiently sampleable sets. For every $k \leq \boldsymbol{K}$ the protocol is defined as follows:*

1. *The algorithm $\mathsf{Setup}^*(1^\lambda, \boldsymbol{K})$ is the same algorithm as $\mathsf{Setup}(1^\lambda)$.*
2. *The algorithm $\boldsymbol{P}_1^*(pp, (\mathrm{x}_1, \mathrm{w}_1), \ldots, (\mathrm{x}_k, \mathrm{w}_k))$ invokes $(R_i, \mathsf{st}_i) \leftarrow \boldsymbol{P}_1(pp, \mathrm{x}_i, \mathrm{w}_i)$ for every $i \in [k]$ and produces a message $\alpha = \Pi_{i=1}^k R_i$ and a state $\mathsf{st} = (\mathsf{st}_1 \| \ldots \| \mathsf{st}_k)$.*
3. *k different challenges $\beta_1, \ldots, \beta_k$ are sampled uniformly at random from the challenge set $\mathcal{C}_{pp}$.*
4. *The algorithm $\boldsymbol{P}_2^*(\mathsf{st}, \beta_1, \ldots, \beta_k)$ parses $\mathsf{st} = (\mathsf{st}_1 \| \ldots \| \mathsf{st}_k)$, invokes $\gamma_i \leftarrow \boldsymbol{P}_2(\mathsf{st}_i, \beta_i)$ and produces a message $\gamma = \sum_{i=1}^k \gamma_i$.*

5. *The algorithm $V(\mathsf{pp}, \mathsf{x}_1, \ldots, \mathsf{x}_k, \alpha, \beta, \gamma)$ determines the output of the protocol checking whether $\mathsf{F}(\gamma) \overset{?}{=} \alpha \cdot \Pi_{i=1}^{k} \mathsf{x}_i^{\beta_i}$.*

Note that the completeness of the protocol above follows from the homomorphic property of F and that the prover-to-verifier communication is two-group elements. The verifier sends k elements, but since they are all uniformly random strings, they can be easily compressed to a single group element using any pseudo-random generator (e.g., using a random oracle).

Definition 12 (Local special soundness). *Let $\Pi = (\mathsf{Setup}, P_1, P_2, V, C)$ be an algebraic Σ-protocol for a relation $\mathcal{R}$ and let Π^* be the batch Σ-protocol defined in Lemma 1 with a bound K on the number of instances. Then, Π^* has local special soundness if there exists a deterministic polynomial time algorithm E that for every $\lambda \in \mathbb{N}$ and $k \le K$, given public parameters pp, any k inputs statements $\mathsf{x}_1, \ldots, \mathsf{x}_k \in \mathcal{X}_\lambda$ and any pair of accepting transcripts $(\alpha, \beta_1, \ldots, \beta_k, \gamma), (\alpha, \beta'_1, \ldots, \beta'_k, \gamma')$ such that there exists only one index j on which $\beta_j \ne \beta'_j$, outputs a witness w_j such that $(\mathsf{x}_j, \mathsf{w}_j) \in \mathcal{R}_\lambda$.*

We now show that every batch Σ-protocol defined in Lemma 1 has local special soundness.

Claim 2. *Let $\Pi = (\mathsf{Setup}, P_1, P_2, V, C)$ be an algebraic Σ-protocol for a relation $\mathcal{R}$ and let Π^* be the batch Σ-protocol constructed from Π as defined in Lemma 1 with a bound K on the number of instances. Then, Π^* has local special soundness.*

Proof. Consider the algorithm E which takes as input public parameters pp, instances $\mathsf{x}_1, \ldots, \mathsf{x}_k$ and a pair of accepting transcripts $(\alpha, \beta_1, \ldots, \beta_k, \gamma)$, $(\alpha, \beta'_1, \ldots, \beta'_k, \gamma')$ such that there exists only one index j on which $\beta_j \ne \beta'_j$, defined as follows:

1. Let i^* be the index on which $\beta_{i^*} \ne \beta'_{i^*}$.
2. Output $(\gamma - \gamma')/(\beta_{i^*} - \beta'_{i^*})$ on the group $\mathbb{Z}_p$ where p is the order of $\mathcal{A}_{\mathsf{pp}}$.

Observe that since the two transcripts are accepting it holds that

$$\mathsf{F}_{\mathsf{pp}}(\gamma) = \alpha \cdot \Pi_{i=1}^{k} \mathsf{x}_i^{\beta_i} \qquad \text{and} \qquad \mathsf{F}_{\mathsf{pp}}(\gamma') = \alpha \cdot \Pi_{i=1}^{k} \mathsf{x}_i^{\beta'_i} .$$

Since $\beta_i = \beta'_i$ for every $i \ne i^*$, it holds that

$$\mathsf{x}_{i^*}^{\beta_{i^*}} \cdot \mathsf{F}_{\mathsf{pp}}(\gamma') = \mathsf{x}_{i^*}^{\beta'_{i^*}} \cdot \mathsf{F}_{\mathsf{pp}}(\gamma) .$$

Note that $\mathsf{x}_{i^*} = \mathsf{F}_{\mathsf{pp}}(\mathsf{w}_{i^*})$, therefore, by the homomorphic property, it holds that

$$\mathsf{F}_{\mathsf{pp}}((\beta_{i^*} - \beta'_{i^*})\mathsf{w}_{i^*}) = \mathsf{F}_{\mathsf{pp}}(\gamma - \gamma') .$$

Thus, $(\gamma - \gamma')/(\beta_{i^*} - \beta'_{i^*})$ is a preimage of x_{i^*}, i.e., a valid witness for x_{i^*}. The extractor E performs only three group operations, therefore, Π^* has local special soundness.

In Sect. 5.3, we show a concrete bound on the rogue soundness error of batch Σ-protocols defined in Lemma 1. Formally, we prove the following.

Theorem 1. *Let* $\Delta = \Delta(\lambda), \omega = \omega(\lambda), t_{\tilde{P}} = t_{\tilde{P}}(\lambda, \boldsymbol{K}), t_V = t_V(\lambda, \boldsymbol{K}), t_W = t_W(\lambda, \boldsymbol{K})$ *be functions of the security parameter* $\lambda \in \mathbb{N}$ *and the bound on the number of instances* $\boldsymbol{K} \in \mathbb{N}$. *Let* Π *be an algebraic* Σ-protocol for a relation $\mathcal{R}$ *and let* $\Pi^* = (\mathsf{Setup}, \boldsymbol{P}_1, \boldsymbol{P}_2, \boldsymbol{V}, \mathcal{C})$ *be the batch* Σ-protocol constructed from Π *as defined in Lemma 1. If* $\mathcal{R}$ *is second-moment hard with respect to a distribution* $\mathcal{D}$ *and the setup algorithm* Setup, *then* Π^* *has* $(t_{\tilde{P}}, \epsilon)$-rogue soundness error such that

$$\epsilon_{\mathcal{D}}(\lambda, t_{\tilde{P}}, t_V, t_W, \boldsymbol{K}) \leq \left(\frac{\Delta \cdot 32 \cdot (t_{\tilde{P}} + t_V + t_W)^2}{|\mathcal{W}_\lambda|^\omega} \right)^{2/3} + \frac{4}{|\mathcal{C}_{\mathsf{pp}}|} ,$$

where t_V *denotes the running time of the verifier* $\boldsymbol{V}$ *and* t_W *denotes the running time of the witness extractor.*

5.2 The Collision Game

Similar to the collision game presented in [3,12,18], we consider a binary matrix $H \in \{0, 1\}^{R \times N}$. However, instead of looking for two 1-entries in the same row, the generalized algorithm A is given as input a number $k \in \mathbb{N}$ and oracle access to the matrix and its goal is to find $k + 1$ entries with the value 1 in the same row in H. Formally, the game is constructed as follows:

$\mathsf{CollGame}_k(A, H)$

1. The algorithm $A(k)$ is given oracle access to H and outputs ρ and $\beta_1, \ldots, \beta_{k+1}$.
2. The output of the game is 1 if and only if $H[\rho, \beta_1] = \ldots = H[\rho, \beta_{k+1}] = 1$ and $\beta_1, \ldots, \beta_{k+1}$ are distinct.

In particular, in this section, we refer to the collision game when $k = 1$. We construct an algorithm that finds two 1-entries in the same row in H with probability at least $\approx \epsilon^{3/2}$ and performs ≈ 2 queries to H where ϵ is the fraction of 1-entries in H. Formally, we prove the following.

Lemma 3. *Let* $H \in \{0, 1\}^{R \times N}$ *be a binary matrix and let* ϵ *be the fraction of 1-entries in* H. *Let* $\mathcal{Q}_A$ *be a random variable indicating the number of queries performed by* A *to* H. *Then, there exists an algorithm* A *with oracle access to* H *such that on input* $k = 1$ *the following holds:*

1. $\mathbb{E}[\mathcal{Q}_A] \leq 2$.
2. $\mathbb{E}[\mathcal{Q}_A^2] \leq 4$.
3. *Either* $\epsilon < \frac{4}{N}$ *or* $\Pr[\mathsf{CollGame}(A, H) = 1] \geq \frac{\epsilon^{1.5}}{8}$.

Proof. Let $B = \left\lceil \frac{1}{\sqrt{\epsilon}} - 1 \right\rceil$ and consider the following algorithm A:

$A^H(1)$

1. Sample $\rho \leftarrow R$ and $\beta \leftarrow N$. If $H[\rho, \beta] = 0$ abort.
2. Let $S = \emptyset$. For every $i \in [B]$, sample $\beta_i \leftarrow N \setminus S$ and set $S = S \cup \{\beta_i\}$.
   If for every $i \in [B]$ it holds that $H[\rho, \beta_i] = 0$, abort.
3. Choose uniformly at random an index i for which $H[\rho, \beta_i] = 1$.
4. Return ρ, β and β_i.

We now prove each claim separately.

Claim 4. *It holds that* $\mathbb{E}[\mathcal{Q}_A] \leq 2$.

Proof. By the description of A, it performs a single query to H, and then only with probability ϵ it performs B queries. Thus, we can bound the expectation by

$$\mathbb{E}[\mathcal{Q}_A] = 1 + \epsilon \cdot B \leq 1 + \frac{1}{\sqrt{\epsilon}} \cdot \epsilon \leq 2 \ .$$

Claim 5. *It holds that* $\mathbb{E}\left[\mathcal{Q}_A^2\right] \leq 4$.

Proof. By the description of A, with probability $1 - \epsilon$, it performs a single query, and with probability ϵ it performs $(1 + B)$ queries. Thus, we can bound the expectation squared by

$$\mathbb{E}\left[\mathcal{Q}_A^2\right] = (1 - \epsilon) \cdot 1^2 + \epsilon \cdot (1 + B)^2 = 1 - \epsilon + \epsilon(1 + 2B + B^2)$$
$$= 1 + 2\epsilon B + \epsilon B^2 \leq 1 + 2\sqrt{\epsilon} + 1 \leq 4 \ .$$

Claim 6 (Success probability). *Either* $\epsilon < \frac{4}{N}$ *or* $\Pr[\mathsf{CollGame}(A, H) = 1] \geq \frac{\epsilon^{1.5}}{8}$.

In order to bound A's success probability, we first show a lower bound on the probability that A does not abort in Item 2.

Claim 7. *Let* X_d *be a random variable indicating the number of 1-entries found in B draws in a row with exactly d 1-entries. For every $d > 1$, it holds that* $\Pr[X_d \geq 1] \geq \min\{0.5, \frac{d \cdot B}{2N}\}$.

The proof of Claim 7 appears in the full version.

Proof (Proof of Claim 6). Assuming the first query to the matrix was 1-entry, A continues to sample entries from the same row. Note that for each row, the number of 1-entries may be different which affects the success probability of the algorithm. Therefore, we "divide" the rows into "buckets" by the number of 1-entries in it. Formally, for every $0 \leq d \leq N$, we define δ_d be the fraction of rows with exactly d 1-entries.

When $d \leq 1$, we know that the success probability is 0. Thus, we consider only δ_d for $d \geq 2$. This lets us derive the following:

$$\Pr[\mathsf{CollGame}(A, H) = 1] \geq \sum_{d=2}^{N} \delta_d \frac{d}{N} \cdot \Pr[X_d \geq 1] \geq \sum_{d=2}^{N} \delta_d \frac{d}{N} \cdot \left(\min \left\{ \frac{1}{2}, \frac{(d-1) \cdot B}{2(N-1)} \right\} \right)$$

Let $n := \lfloor 1 + \frac{N-1}{B} \rfloor$, then,

$$\Pr[\mathsf{CollGame}(A, H) = 1] \geq \sum_{d=2}^{n} \delta_d \frac{d}{N} \cdot \frac{(d-1) \cdot B}{2(N-1)} + \sum_{d=n+1}^{N} \delta_d \frac{d}{N} \cdot \frac{1}{2}$$

$$= \frac{B}{2} \sum_{d=2}^{n} \delta_d \frac{d(d-1)}{N(N-1)} + \frac{1}{2} \cdot \sum_{d=n+1}^{N} \delta_d \frac{d}{N}$$

$$= \frac{B}{2N(N-1)} \sum_{d=0}^{n} \delta_d \cdot d(d-1) + \frac{1}{2} \cdot \sum_{d=n+1}^{N} \delta_d \frac{d}{N}$$

Let $\epsilon_1 := \sum_{d=0}^{n} \delta_d \frac{d}{N}$ and $\epsilon_2 := \sum_{d=n+1}^{N} \delta_d \frac{d}{N}$. By Jensen's inequality we get that

$$\frac{1}{N(N-1)} \sum_{d=0}^{n} \delta_d \cdot d(d-1) \geq \frac{1}{N(N-1)} \cdot \epsilon_1 N (\epsilon_1 N - 1) \geq \frac{\epsilon_1^2 \cdot N - \epsilon_1}{N} = \epsilon_1^2 - \frac{\epsilon_1}{N} .$$

Therefore we get, $\Pr[\mathsf{CollGame}(A, H) = 1] \geq \frac{B}{2} \left(\epsilon_1^2 - \frac{\epsilon_1}{N} \right) + \frac{1}{2} \epsilon_2$. Since $\epsilon_1 + \epsilon_1 = \epsilon$, the minimum of the above expression is where $\epsilon_1 = \epsilon$. Thus, we can write

$$\Pr[\mathsf{CollGame}(A, H) = 1] \geq \frac{B}{2} \left(\epsilon^2 - \frac{\epsilon}{N} \right) \geq \frac{1}{2 \cdot 2\sqrt{\epsilon}} \cdot \epsilon^2 - \frac{\epsilon}{2 \cdot \sqrt{\epsilon} N} = \frac{\epsilon^{1.5}}{4} - \frac{\sqrt{\epsilon}}{2N} .$$

Since $\epsilon \geq \frac{4}{N}$, it holds that,

$$\frac{\sqrt{\epsilon}}{2N} \leq \frac{\sqrt{\epsilon}}{2 \left(\frac{4}{\epsilon} \right)} = \frac{\epsilon^{1.5}}{8} .$$

This leads to,

$$\Pr[\mathsf{CollGame}(A, H) = 1] \geq \frac{\epsilon^{1.5}}{8} ,$$

which completes the proof.

5.3   Rogue Soundness Error Bound from the Collision Game

We now use the algorithm for the collision game in order to construct an algorithm that extracts a witness w for an instance x. Then, combined with the second-moment assumption we prove Theorem 1.

First, we prove the following lemma (which is interesting on its own):

Lemma 8. *Let $t_{\tilde{P}} = t_{\tilde{P}}(\lambda, K), t_V = t_V(\lambda, K), t_W = t_W(\lambda, K)$ be functions of the security parameter $\lambda \in \mathbb{N}$ and the bound on the number of instances $K \in \mathbb{N}$. Let Π be an algebraic batch Σ-protocol for a relation $\mathcal{R}$ and let $\Pi^* = (\mathsf{Setup}, P_1, P_2, V, \mathcal{C})$ be the batch Σ-protocol constructed from Π as defined in Lemma 1. Let t_V denote the running time of the verifier V and let t_W denote the running time of the witness extractor. Let $\mathcal{D} = \{\mathcal{D}_\lambda\}_{\lambda \in \mathbb{N}}$ be a distribution over the relation where each $\mathcal{D}_\lambda$ produces $(\mathsf{pp}, \mathbb{x}, \mathbb{w}) \in \mathcal{R}_\lambda$. For every prover $\tilde{P} = (\tilde{P}_1, \tilde{P}_2)$ that runs in time $t_{\tilde{P}}$, there exists an algorithm A^* such that:*

1. $\mathbb{E}\left[T_{A^*, \mathcal{D}_\lambda}\right] \leq 2 \cdot (t_{\tilde{P}} + t_V + t_W)$.
2. $\mathbb{E}\left[T_{A^*, \mathcal{D}_\lambda}^2\right] \leq 4 \cdot (t_{\tilde{P}} + t_V + t_W)^2$.
3. *Either $\epsilon < \frac{4}{|\mathcal{C}_{\mathsf{pp}}|}$ or $\Pr\left[(\mathsf{pp}, \mathbb{x}_1, \tilde{\mathbb{w}}_1) \in \mathcal{R} \,\middle|\, \begin{array}{l} \mathsf{pp} \leftarrow \mathsf{Setup}(1^\lambda, K) \\ (\mathbb{x}_1, \mathbb{w}_1) \leftarrow \mathcal{D}_\lambda(\mathsf{pp}) \\ \tilde{\mathbb{w}}_1 \leftarrow A^*(\mathsf{pp}, \mathbb{x}_1) \end{array}\right] \geq \frac{\epsilon^{1.5}}{8}$ where ϵ is the rogue-soundness error of Π^* with respect to a distribution $\mathcal{D}$ and the setup algorithm Setup.*

Proof. We denote by aux the variable for tuples of $(\mathsf{pp}, \mathbb{x}, \boldsymbol{\beta})$ where $\boldsymbol{\beta} = (\beta_2, \ldots, \beta_k)$ and $\beta_i \in \{0, 1\}^r$. We consider binary matrices $H = \{H_{\mathsf{aux}}\}_{\mathsf{pp}, \mathbb{x}\boldsymbol{\beta}} \in \{0, 1\}^{R \times N}$, where the R rows correspond to $\tilde{P}$'s randomness and the N columns correspond to V's randomness for one instance. Note that although $\tilde{P}$'s and V's randomness depends on the number of instances that the prover outputs, we can always bound it by the randomness size when $\tilde{P}$ outputs K instances.

An entry of H_{aux} equals 1 if and only if the corresponding transcript (between $\tilde{P}$ and V) is accepting. Recall that every algorithm A for the collision game aims to find $k + 1$ entries with the value 1 in the same row. As $\tilde{P}$'s randomness is fixed along one row, finding two 1-entries in the same row correspond to finding two accepting transcripts $(\alpha, \beta_1, \boldsymbol{\beta}, \gamma), (\alpha, \beta_1', \boldsymbol{\beta}, \gamma')$. Given Claim 2, Π^* has local special soundness, i.e., there exists an algorithm E that runs in time t_W which given two accepting transcripts as considered above, extracts a witness for the instance $\mathbb{x}_1$.

Let A be the algorithm for the collision game constructed in Lemma 3, we construct the algorithm A^* as follows:

$A^*(\mathsf{pp}, \mathbb{x}_1)$

1. Initialize an empty mapping M between the randomness used by $\tilde{\mathbf{P}}$ and $\mathbf{V}$ and the transcript between them.
2. Let r be $\mathbf{V}$'s randomness size for each instance. For $2 \leq i \leq \mathbf{K}$, sample $\beta_i \leftarrow \{0,1\}^r$.
3. Invoke $A(1)$. When A performs a query on (ρ, β) answer as follows:
   (a) Invoke $((\tilde{\mathbb{x}}_2, \ldots, \tilde{\mathbb{x}}_k), \alpha, \mathsf{st}) \leftarrow \tilde{\mathbf{P}}_1(\mathsf{pp}, \mathbb{x}_1; \rho)$.
   (b) Invoke $\gamma \leftarrow \tilde{\mathbf{P}}_2(\beta, \beta_2, \ldots, \beta_k, \mathsf{st})$.
   (c) Set $M[(\rho, \beta)] \leftarrow (\tilde{\mathbb{x}}_2, \ldots, \tilde{\mathbb{x}}_k, \alpha, \beta, \beta_2, \ldots, \beta_k, \gamma)$.
   (d) Return $\mathbf{V}(\mathsf{pp}, \mathbb{x}_1, \tilde{\mathbb{x}}_2, \ldots, \tilde{\mathbb{x}}_k, \alpha, \beta, \beta_2, \ldots, \beta_k, \gamma)$ as the answer to the query.
4. When A outputs ρ, β_1, β_2: set $(\tilde{\mathbb{x}}_2, \ldots, \tilde{\mathbb{x}}_k, \alpha_1^*, \beta_1^*, \beta_{1,2}^* \ldots, \beta_{1,k}^*, \gamma_1^*) \leftarrow M[\rho, \beta_1]$ and $(\tilde{\mathbb{x}}_2, \ldots, \tilde{\mathbb{x}}_k, \alpha_2^*, \beta_2^*, \beta_{2,2}^* \ldots, \beta_{2,k}^*, \gamma_2^*) \leftarrow M[\rho, \beta_2]$.
5. Run $\tilde{\mathbb{w}}_1 \leftarrow E(\tilde{\mathbb{x}}_2, \ldots, \tilde{\mathbb{x}}_k, \alpha_1^*, \beta_{1,2}^*, \ldots, \beta_{1,k}^*, (\beta_{1,1}^*, \gamma_{1,1}^*), (\beta_{2,1}^*, \gamma_{2,1}^*))$.
6. Output $\tilde{\mathbb{w}}_1$.

We prove each claim separately.

Claim 9 (Expected running time). *It holds that* $\mathbb{E}\left[T_{A^*, \mathcal{D}_\lambda}\right] \leq 2 \cdot (t_{\tilde{P}} + V + t_W)$.

Proof. Observe that whenever A query H, the algorithm A^* invokes $\tilde{\mathbf{P}}$ and $\mathbf{V}$. Thus, the expected number of invocations that A^* performs to $\tilde{\mathbf{P}}$ and $\mathbf{V}$ is the expected number of queries performed by A. Thus, $\mathbb{E}\left[T_{A^*, \mathcal{D}_\lambda}\right] \leq \mathbb{E}\left[\mathcal{Q}_A\right] \cdot (t_{\tilde{P}} + V) + t_W \leq 2 \cdot (t_{\tilde{P}} + t_V + t_W)$.

Claim 10 (Second-moment of expected running time). *It holds that* $\mathbb{E}\left[T_{A^*, \mathcal{D}_\lambda}^2\right] \leq 4 \cdot (t_{\tilde{P}} + t_V + t_W)^2$.

Proof. Following the same observation as in Claim 9 we obtain that

$$\mathbb{E}\left[T_{A^*, \mathcal{D}_\lambda}^2\right] \leq \left(\mathbb{E}[\mathcal{Q}_A] \cdot (t_{\tilde{P}} + t_V)\right)^2 + t_W^2 \leq \left(\mathbb{E}[\mathcal{Q}_A] \cdot (t_{\tilde{P}} + t_V + t_W)\right)^2 = \mathbb{E}[\mathcal{Q}_A]^2 \cdot (t_{\tilde{P}} + t_V + t_W)^2 .$$

Jensen's inequality leads to $\mathbb{E}\left[T_{A^*, \mathcal{D}_\lambda}^2\right] \leq \mathbb{E}\left[\mathcal{Q}_A^2\right] \cdot (t_{\tilde{P}} + t_V + t_W)^2 \leq 4(t_{\tilde{P}} + t_V + t_W)^2$.

Claim 11 (Success probability). *Either* $\epsilon < \frac{4}{|\mathcal{C}_{\mathsf{pp}}|}$ *or*

$$\Pr\left[(\mathsf{pp}, \mathbb{x}_1, \tilde{\mathbb{w}}_1) \in \mathcal{R} \; \middle| \; \begin{array}{l} \mathsf{pp} \leftarrow \mathsf{Setup}(1^\lambda, K) \\ (\mathbb{x}_1, \mathbb{w}_1) \leftarrow \mathcal{D}_\lambda(\mathsf{pp}) \\ \tilde{\mathbb{w}}_1 \leftarrow A^*(\mathsf{pp}, \mathbb{x}_1) \end{array}\right] \geq \frac{\epsilon^{1.5}}{8}$$ *where* ϵ *is the rogue-soundness error of* Π^* *with respect to a distribution* $\mathcal{D}$ *and the setup algorithm* Setup.

Proof. Whenever A succeeds in the collision game with H_{aux}, the algorithm A^* outputs a witness for $\mathbb{x}_1$. Thus,

$$\Pr\left[(\mathsf{pp}, \mathbb{x}_1, \tilde{\mathbb{w}}_1) \in \mathcal{R} \,\middle|\, \begin{array}{l} \mathsf{pp} \leftarrow \mathsf{Setup}(1^\lambda, \mathbf{K}) \\ (\mathbb{x}_1, \mathbb{w}_1) \leftarrow \mathcal{D}_\lambda(\mathsf{pp}) \\ \tilde{\mathbb{w}}_1 \leftarrow A^*(\mathsf{pp}, \mathbb{x}_1) \end{array}\right] = \sum_{\mathsf{aux}} \Pr[\mathsf{aux}] \cdot \Pr\left[\mathsf{CollGame}(A, H_{\mathsf{aux}}) = 1\right] \ .$$

For every $\mathsf{aux} = (\mathsf{pp}, \mathbb{x}, \boldsymbol{\beta})$, we let

$$\epsilon_{\mathsf{aux}} = \Pr\left[\begin{array}{l} \mathbf{V}(\mathsf{pp}, \mathbb{x}, \tilde{\mathbb{x}}_2, \ldots, \tilde{\mathbb{x}}_k, \alpha, \beta, \beta_2, \ldots, \beta_k, \gamma) = 1 \\ \text{conditioned on } \mathsf{pp} \leftarrow \mathsf{Setup}(1^\lambda, \mathbf{K}) \\ \wedge (\mathbb{x}_1, \mathbb{w}_1) \leftarrow \mathcal{D}_\lambda(\mathsf{pp}) \\ \wedge \beta_2, \ldots, \beta_k \leftarrow \mathcal{C}_{\mathsf{pp}} \end{array} \,\middle|\, \begin{array}{l} ((\tilde{\mathbb{x}}_2, \ldots, \tilde{\mathbb{x}}_k), \alpha, \mathsf{st}) \leftarrow \tilde{\mathbf{P}}_1(1^\lambda, \mathsf{pp}, \mathbb{x}) \\ \beta_2, \ldots, \beta_k \leftarrow \mathcal{C}_{\mathsf{pp}} \\ \gamma \leftarrow \tilde{\mathbf{P}}_2(\mathsf{st}, \beta_2, \ldots, \beta_k) \end{array}\right] .$$

The collision game matrix H_{aux} has ϵ_{aux} fraction of 1-entries. Thus, conditioned on aux, the probability that A succeeds in the collision game is $\frac{\epsilon_{\mathsf{aux}}^{1.5}}{8}$. Therefore,

$$\Pr\left[(\mathsf{pp}, \mathbb{x}_1, \tilde{\mathbb{w}}_1) \in \mathcal{R} \,\middle|\, \begin{array}{l} \mathsf{pp} \leftarrow \mathsf{Setup}(1^\lambda, \mathbf{K}) \\ (\mathbb{x}_1, \mathbb{w}_1) \leftarrow \mathcal{D}_\lambda(\mathsf{pp}) \\ \tilde{\mathbb{w}}_1 \leftarrow A^*(\mathsf{pp}, \mathbb{x}_1) \end{array}\right] = \sum_{\mathsf{aux}} \Pr[\mathsf{aux}] \cdot \frac{\epsilon_{\mathsf{aux}}^{1.5}}{8} = \mathop{\mathbb{E}}_{\mathsf{aux}}\left[\frac{\epsilon_{\mathsf{aux}}^{1.5}}{8}\right]$$

$$\geq \frac{\mathop{\mathbb{E}}_{\mathsf{aux}}[\epsilon_{\mathsf{aux}}]^{1.5}}{8} \geq \frac{\epsilon^{1.5}}{8} \ ,$$

where first inequality follows from Jensen's inequality and the last inequality follows from the fact that $\mathop{\mathbb{E}}_{\mathsf{aux}}[\epsilon_{\mathsf{aux}}] = \epsilon$.

We are now ready to show a bound on the rogue soundness error of batch Σ-protocol defined in Lemma 1.

Proof (Proof of Theorem 1). Let $\tilde{\mathbf{P}}$ be a cheating prover and let $\epsilon_\mathcal{D}$ be the rogue soundness error with respect to $\mathcal{D}$ and Setup. Given Lemma 8 and the assumption that $\mathcal{R}$ is second-moment hard with respect to the distribution $\mathcal{D}$ and the setup algorithm Setup, it holds that either $\epsilon_\mathcal{D} < \frac{4}{|\mathcal{C}_{\mathsf{pp}}|}$ or,

$$\frac{\epsilon_\mathcal{D}^{1.5}}{8} \leq \Pr\left[(\mathsf{pp}, \mathbb{x}_1, \tilde{\mathbb{w}}_1) \in \mathcal{R} \,\middle|\, \begin{array}{l} \mathsf{pp} \leftarrow \mathsf{Setup}(1^\lambda, \mathbf{K}) \\ (\mathbb{x}_1, \mathbb{w}_1) \leftarrow \mathcal{D}_\lambda(\mathsf{pp}) \\ \tilde{\mathbb{w}}_1 \leftarrow A^*(\mathsf{pp}, \mathbb{x}_1) \end{array}\right] \leq \frac{\Delta \cdot \mathbb{E}\left[T_{A^*, \mathcal{D}}^2\right]}{|\mathcal{W}_\lambda|^\omega} \leq \frac{\Delta \cdot 4 \cdot (t_{\tilde{\mathbf{P}}} + t_{\mathbf{V}} + t_W)^2}{|\mathcal{W}_\lambda|^\omega} \ .$$

This leads to

$$\epsilon_\mathcal{D} \leq \left(\frac{\Delta \cdot 32 \cdot (t_{\tilde{\mathbf{P}}} + t_{\mathbf{V}} + t_W)}{|\mathcal{W}_\lambda|^\omega}\right)^{2/3} \ .$$

Overall we derive the following bound

$$\epsilon_\mathcal{D} \leq \max\left\{\left(\frac{\Delta \cdot 32 \cdot (t_{\tilde{\mathbf{P}}} + t_{\mathbf{V}} + t_W)}{|\mathcal{W}_\lambda|^\omega}\right)^{2/3}, \frac{4}{|\mathcal{C}_{\mathsf{pp}}|}\right\} \leq \left(\frac{\Delta \cdot 32 \cdot (t_{\tilde{\mathbf{P}}} + t_{\mathbf{V}} + t_W)}{|\mathcal{W}_\lambda|^\omega}\right)^{2/3} + \frac{4}{|\mathcal{C}_{\mathsf{pp}}|} .$$

5.4 Algebraic Batch Identification Schemes

An identification scheme consists of a Σ-protocol for relation $\mathcal{R}$ and an algorithm Gen that produces a distribution over $(\mathbb{x}, \mathbb{w}) \in \mathcal{R}$ where the public key is the instance $\mathbb{x}$ and the secret key is the witness $\mathbb{w}$. Similarly, we construct a batch identification scheme that consists of batch Σ-protocol defined in Lemma 1 and an algorithm Gen that given public parameters pp, produces a distribution over $(x, w) \in \mathcal{R}(pp)$.

Note that the execution of ID is as the execution of the batch Σ-protocol where each public key pk corresponds to an instance, and a secret key sk corresponds to a witness.

We consider the rogue-security notion of batch identification scheme, asking a cheating prover $\tilde{P}$ given as input an instance x produced by Gen, to convince the verifier V on $(x, \tilde{x}_2, \ldots, \tilde{x}_k)$ where $\tilde{x}_2, \ldots, \tilde{x}_k$ are adaptively chosen by $\tilde{P}$ while given access to an honest transcript-generator for the instance x and another $(k - 1)$ instances by its choice. Formally, we let $\text{Trans}_{pk_1, sk_1}(\cdot)$ denote an oracle that when queried with input $(pk_2, sk_2), \ldots (pk_k, sk_k)$, runs an honest execution of the protocol on input $(pk_1, sk_1), \ldots (pk_k, sk_k)$ and returns the resulting transcripts (α, β, γ). We define the rogue-security of a batch identification scheme as follows:

Definition 13 (Rogue soundness). *Let* ID $= (\text{Setup}, \text{Gen}, P_1, P_2, V, C)$ *be a batch identification scheme for a relation $\mathcal{R}$. Then,* ID *is (t, ϵ)-rogue soundness (with respect to* Gen *and* Setup*) if for every $\lambda, k \in \mathbb{N}$ such that $k \leq K$ and for any t-time malicious prover $\tilde{P} = (\tilde{P}_1, \tilde{P}_2)$ that performs q queries to the transcript-generation oracle it holds that:*

$$\Pr\left[\text{StrongIdent}_{ID}(\tilde{P}, \lambda)\right] \leq \epsilon(\lambda, t, q, K) \ ,$$

where the experiment $\text{StrongIdent}_{ID}(\tilde{P}, \lambda)$ *defined as follows:*

$\text{StrongIdent}_{ID}(\tilde{P}, \lambda)$:

1. $pp \leftarrow \text{Setup}(1^\lambda, K)$.
2. $(pk_1, sk_1) \leftarrow \text{Gen}(pp)$.
3. $((\tilde{pk}_2, \ldots, \tilde{pk}_k), \alpha, st) \leftarrow \tilde{P}_1^{\text{Trans}_{pk_1, sk_1}(\cdot)}(pp, pk_1)$.
4. $\beta \leftarrow C_{pp}$.
5. $\gamma \leftarrow \tilde{P}_2(st, \beta)$.
6. Output $V(pp, pk_1, \tilde{pk}_2, \ldots, \tilde{pk}_k, \alpha, \beta, \gamma) = 1$.

Recall that batch identification scheme ID consists of a batch Σ-protocol Π^* defined in Lemma 1 such that the execution of ID is as the execution of Π^* where each public key pk corresponds to an instance and a secret key sk corresponds to a witness. Thus, if Π^* is zero-knowledge, we can assume that every malicious prover does not query the transcript-generation oracle, as such queries can be internally simulated given the public keys. Formally, if Π^* is t-time zero-knowledge (Definition 8), for every malicious prover that performs q queries to the transcript-generation oracle $\text{Trans}_{pk_1, sk_1}(\cdot)$, we can construct a malicious prover that does not query the transcript-generation oracle and instead runs the simulator q times to generate transcripts. Specifically, if Π^* has t_{Sim}-time zero-knowledge, any malicious prover that runs in time $t_{\tilde{P}}$ and performs q queries to $\mathsf{Trans}_{\mathsf{pk}_1,\mathsf{sk}_1}(\cdot)$, can be simulated by a malicious prover that runs in time $t_{\tilde{P}} + \mathsf{q} \cdot t_{\mathsf{Sim}}$.

Recall that every batch Σ-protocol Π^* defined in Lemma 1 is constructed from an algebraic Σ-protocol Π. We now show that if Π is t_{Sim}-time zero-knowledge, then Π^* is $(k \cdot t_{\mathsf{Sim}})$-zero-knowledge. Formally, we prove the following.

Claim 12. *Let $\Pi = (\mathsf{Setup}, P_1, P_2, V, \mathcal{C})$ be an algebraic Σ-protocol for a relation $\mathcal{R}$ and let Π^* be the batch Σ-protocol constructed from Π as defined in Lemma 1 with a bound K on the number of instances. If Π is t_{Sim}-time zero-knowledge, then Π^* is $(K \cdot t_{\mathsf{Sim}})$-time zero-knowledge.*

The proof of Claim 12 appears in the full version. Combined with Theorem 1, we derive the following corollary:

Corollary 2. *Let $\Delta = \Delta(\lambda), \omega = \omega(\lambda), t_{\tilde{P}} = t_{\tilde{P}}(\lambda), t_V = t_V(\lambda, K), t_W = t_W(\lambda, K), t_{\mathsf{Sim}} = t_{\mathsf{Sim}}(\lambda, K), \mathsf{q} = \mathsf{q}(\lambda)$ be functions of the security parameter $\lambda \in \mathbb{N}$ and the bound on the number of instances $K \in \mathbb{N}$. Let Π be an algebraic Σ-protocol for relation $\mathcal{R}$ with t_{Sim}-time zero-knowledge and let $\Pi^* = (\mathsf{Setup}, P_1, P_2, V, \mathcal{C})$ be the batch Σ-protocol constructed from Π as defined in Lemma 1. Let $\mathsf{ID} = (\mathsf{Setup}, \mathsf{Gen}, P_1, P_2, V, \mathcal{C})$ be the batch identification scheme consists with Π^*. If $\mathcal{R}$ is second-moment hard with respect to Gen, then for any malicious prover $\tilde{P}$ that runs in time $t_{\tilde{P}}$ and issues q transcript-generation queries it holds that*

$$\Pr\left[\mathsf{StrongIdent}_{\mathsf{ID}}(\tilde{P}, \lambda)\right] \leq \left(\frac{\Delta \cdot 32 \cdot (t_{\tilde{P}} + \mathsf{q} \cdot K \cdot t_{\mathsf{Sim}} + t_V + t_W)^2}{|\mathcal{W}_\lambda|^\omega}\right)^{2/3} + \frac{4}{|\mathcal{C}_{\mathsf{pp}}|},$$

where t_V is the running time of the verifier V and t_W is the running time of the witness extractor.

6 Proving Expected-Time Hardness in Generic Models

In this section, we present a generic framework for analyzing expected-time hardness of cryptographic problems. In fact, applying our framework proves the second-moment assumption (Definition 2) for the discrete-logarithm problem in the generic group model. Shoup [33] analyzed generic hardness of the discrete-logarithm problem with respect to strict time algorithms. He showed that any generic t-time algorithm that solves the discrete-logarithm problem has success probability at most $\epsilon \leq t^2/p$. Applying our framework yields a bound of $\epsilon \leq \mathbb{E}\left[T_A^2\right]/p$ when considering *unbounded* algorithms where T_A denotes the random variable indicating the algorithm's running time.

Our framework is inspired by [19] which showed a generic framework to prove bounds with respect to expected-time algorithms when considering only the first-moment of the expected running time. Their result proves the first-moment assumption (Definition 1) but cannot be used to derive the second-moment assumption.

In Sect. 6.1 we introduce our framework for proving expected-time hardness.

6.1   Our Framework

Definition 14 (Monotonic predicate). *A predicate P is* monotonic *if for every* tr *such that $P(\text{tr}) = 1$, it holds that $P(\text{tr}\|\text{tr}') = 1$ for every* tr'.

We consider distributions $\mathcal{D}(\lambda)$ which produces an oracle $\mathcal{O}$ and define the hardness of a predicate as follows:

Definition 15 (Hard predicate). *A predicate P is* ϵ-hard *if for every strict time algorithm $\mathcal{A}_t$ it holds that*

$$\Pr\left[P(\text{tr}) = 1 \;\middle|\; \begin{array}{l} \mathcal{O} \leftarrow \mathcal{D}(\lambda) \\ \text{out} \xleftarrow{\text{tr}} \mathcal{A}_t{}^{\mathcal{O}}(\text{in}) \end{array}\right] \le \epsilon(t) \ .$$

In addition, we define history-oblivious predicates. Intuitively, this family of predicates includes predicates on which each query is oblivious to the history of the query-answer list (see Sect. 2.6 for further discussion). We define history-oblivious by considering the hardness to set the predicate to output 1 on input $\text{tr}\|(x, y)$ where (x, y) is a fresh query-answer pair and tr is a query-answer list on which the predicate outputs 0.

For any list of query-answer pairs μ we denote by $\mathcal{D}(\lambda, \mu)$ the distribution $\mathcal{D}(\lambda)$ of all oracles such that for every $(x_i, y_i) \in \mu$ it holds that $y_i = \mathcal{O}(x_i)$. We let X, Y be the query and answer spaces.

Definition 16 (History-oblivious predicate). *Let P be an ϵ-hard predicate. We say that P is* history-oblivious *with respect to $\mathcal{O}$ if there is a function $\kappa(\cdot)$, such that for every $t \in \mathbb{N}$ the following holds:*

1. *For every $0 \le i \le t$, every trace* tr *of length i with $P(\text{tr}) = 0$, and any query $x \in X$:*

$$\Pr\left[P(\text{tr}\|(x, y)) = 1 \;\middle|\; \begin{array}{l} \mathcal{O} \leftarrow \mathcal{D}(\lambda, \text{tr}) \\ y = \mathcal{O}(x) \end{array}\right] \le \kappa(i) \ .$$

2. $\sum_{j=0}^{t} \kappa(j) \le \epsilon(t)$.

(Above, the length of a trace is the number of query/answer pairs it contains.) We consider experiments relative to an oracle, for which their security relies on the trace between the adversary and the oracle. We capture this using a monotonic predicate on the trace. Formally, we define the following:

Definition 17 (δ-bounded experiment). *Let $\mathsf{Exp}^{\mathcal{O}}$ be an experiment with oracle access $\mathcal{O}$, and let $\delta = \delta(\lambda)$ be a function of the security parameter $\lambda \in \mathbb{N}$. We say that $\mathsf{Exp}^{\mathcal{O}}$ is δ-bounded with respect to a monotonic predicate P if for every (bounded and unbounded) algorithm $\mathcal{A}$ it holds that,*

$$\Pr\left[\mathsf{Exp}^{\mathcal{O}}(\text{in}, \text{out}) = 1 \;\middle|\; \begin{array}{l} \mathcal{O} \leftarrow \mathcal{D}(\lambda) \\ \text{out} \xleftarrow{\text{tr}} \mathcal{A}^{\mathcal{O}}(\text{in}) \end{array}\right] \le \Pr\left[P(\text{tr}) = 1 \;\middle|\; \begin{array}{l} \mathcal{O} \leftarrow \mathcal{D}(\lambda) \\ \text{out} \xleftarrow{\text{tr}} \mathcal{A}^{\mathcal{O}}(\text{in}) \end{array}\right] + \delta \ .$$

Given the definitions above, we prove the following theorem.

Theorem 2. *Let* $\mathsf{Exp}^{\mathcal{O}}$ *be a δ-bounded experiment with respect to a predicate P which is ϵ-hard. If P is history-oblivious, then, for every* unbounded *algorithm $\mathcal{A}$ it holds that,*

$$\Pr\left[\mathsf{Exp}^{\mathcal{O}}(\mathsf{in},\mathsf{out}) = 1 \;\middle|\; \begin{array}{c}\mathcal{O} \leftarrow \mathcal{D}(\lambda) \\ \mathsf{out} \xleftarrow{\mathsf{tr}} \mathcal{A}^{\mathcal{O}}(\mathsf{in})\end{array}\right] \leq \mathbb{E}\left[\epsilon(t)\right] + \delta \;.$$

In particular, Theorem 2 allows us to recover the same bounds given in [19], which is captured in the following corollary.

Corollary 3. *Let* $\mathsf{Exp}^{\mathcal{O}}$ *be a δ-bounded experiment with respect to a predicate P which is ϵ-hard where $\epsilon(t) = \frac{\Delta t^d}{N}$ for $\Delta, d, N \geq 1$. If P is history-oblivious, then, for every* unbounded *algorithm $\mathcal{A}$ it holds that,*

$$\Pr\left[\mathsf{Exp}^{\mathcal{O}}(\mathsf{in},\mathsf{out}) = 1 \;\middle|\; \begin{array}{c}\mathcal{O} \leftarrow \mathcal{D}(\lambda) \\ \mathsf{out} \xleftarrow{\mathsf{tr}} \mathcal{A}^{\mathcal{O}}(\mathsf{in})\end{array}\right] \leq \sqrt[d]{\epsilon(\mathbb{E}\left[T_{\mathcal{A}}\right])} + \delta = \sqrt[d]{\frac{\Delta}{N}} \cdot \mathbb{E}\left[T_{\mathcal{A}}\right] + \delta \;,$$

where $T_{\mathcal{A}}$ is a random variable indicating the number of queries performed by $\mathcal{A}$ until he stops, when given access to an oracle $\mathcal{O}$.

The proof of Corollary 3 appears in the full version, we now prove Theorem 2.

Proof (Proof of Theorem 2). Let tr_i be the first i pairs in the query-answer list between the algorithm and the oracle $\mathcal{O}$. Let Y_i be an indicator random variable for the event that (i) $|\mathsf{tr}| \geq i$; (ii) $P(\mathsf{tr}_i) = 1$; and (iii) $P(\mathsf{tr}_{i-1}) = 0$. Note that, the events $Y_i = 1$ are mutually exclusive, thus:

$$\Pr\left[P(\mathsf{tr}) = 1 \;\middle|\; \begin{array}{c}\mathcal{O} \leftarrow \mathcal{D}(\lambda) \\ \mathsf{out} \xleftarrow{\mathsf{tr}} \mathcal{A}^{\mathcal{O}}(\mathsf{in})\end{array}\right] = \sum_{i=1}^{\infty} \Pr\left[Y_i = 1 \;\middle|\; \begin{array}{c}\mathcal{O} \leftarrow \mathcal{D}(\lambda) \\ \mathsf{out} \xleftarrow{\mathsf{tr}} \mathcal{A}^{\mathcal{O}}(\mathsf{in})\end{array}\right] \;,$$

To simplify the notation throughout the proof, we omit the explicit reference to the probability taken over the sampling of the oracle $\mathcal{O} \leftarrow \mathcal{D}(\lambda)$ and the execution of the algorithm.

Let $T_{\mathcal{A}} = T_{\mathcal{A}}(\lambda)$ be a random variable indicating the number of queries performed by $\mathcal{A}$ until he stops, when given access to an oracle $\mathcal{O}$. Note that for every $i \in \mathbb{N}$ it holds that $Y_i = 1$ only if the number of queries performed by the algorithm is at least i. Thus,

$$\Pr\left[P(\mathsf{tr}) = 1 \;\middle|\; \begin{array}{c}\mathcal{O} \leftarrow \mathcal{D}(\lambda) \\ \mathsf{out} \xleftarrow{\mathsf{tr}} \mathcal{A}^{\mathcal{O}}(\mathsf{in})\end{array}\right] = \sum_{i=1}^{\infty} \Pr\left[Y_i = 1 \mid T_{\mathcal{A}} \geq i\right] \cdot \Pr[T_{\mathcal{A}} \geq i]$$

$$\leq \sum_{i=1}^{\infty} \Pr\left[Y_i = 1 \mid T_{\mathcal{A}} \geq i\right] \cdot \sum_{t=i}^{\infty} \Pr[T_{\mathcal{A}} = t]$$

The following claim shows an upper bound on the above term $\Pr\left[Y_i = 1 \mid T_{\mathcal{A}} \geq i\right]$. The proof of the claim appears in the full version.

Claim 13. *If P is ϵ-hard and history-oblivious, then for every $i \in \mathbb{N}$, it holds that $\Pr\left[Y_i = 1 \mid T_{\mathcal{A}} \geq i\right] \leq \kappa(i)$.*

Given Claim 13 it holds that,

$$
\Pr\left[P\left(\mathsf{tr}\right) = 1 \,\middle|\, \begin{array}{c} \mathcal{O} \leftarrow \mathcal{D}(\lambda) \\ \mathsf{out} \xleftarrow{\mathsf{tr}} \mathcal{A}^{\mathcal{O}}\left(\mathsf{in}\right) \end{array}\right] \leq \sum_{i=1}^{\infty} \kappa(i) \cdot \sum_{t=i}^{\infty} \Pr\left[T_{\mathcal{A}} = t\right]
$$

$$
= \sum_{t=1}^{\infty} \Pr\left[T_{\mathcal{A}} = t\right] \cdot \sum_{i=1}^{t} \kappa(i) \leq \sum_{t=1}^{\infty} \Pr\left[T_{\mathcal{A}} = t\right] \cdot \epsilon(t) = \mathbb{E}\left[\epsilon(t)\right] \ ,
$$

where the first equality follows from rearranging the summation, and the last inequality follows from the fact that P is ϵ-hard and history-oblivious. Overall, we conclude that,

$$
\Pr\left[\mathsf{Exp}^{\mathcal{O}}(\mathsf{out}) = 1 \,\middle|\, \begin{array}{c} \mathcal{O} \leftarrow \mathcal{D}(\lambda) \\ \mathsf{out} \xleftarrow{\mathsf{tr}} \mathcal{A}^{\mathcal{O}}\left(\mathsf{in}\right) \end{array}\right] \leq \mathbb{E}\left[\epsilon(t)\right] + \delta \ .
$$

References

1. Abdalla, M., An, J.H., Bellare, M., Namprempre, C.: From identification to signatures via the fiat-shamir transform: minimizing assumptions for security and forward-security. In: Knudsen, L.R. (ed.) EUROCRYPT 2002. LNCS, vol. 2332, pp. 418–433. Springer, Heidelberg (2002). https://doi.org/10.1007/3-540-46035-7_28

2. Agrikola, T., Hofheinz, D., Kastner, J.: On instantiating the algebraic group model from falsifiable assumptions. In: Canteaut, A., Ishai, Y. (eds.) EUROCRYPT 2020. LNCS, vol. 12106, pp. 96–126. Springer, Cham (2020). https://doi.org/10.1007/978-3-030-45724-2_4

3. Attema, T., Cramer, R., Kohl, L.: A compressed Σ-protocol theory for lattices. In: Malkin, T., Peikert, C. (eds.) CRYPTO 2021. LNCS, vol. 12826, pp. 549–579. Springer, Cham (2021). https://doi.org/10.1007/978-3-030-84245-1_19

4. Bauer, B., Fuchsbauer, G., Loss, J.: A classification of computational assumptions in the algebraic group model. In: Micciancio, D., Ristenpart, T. (eds.) CRYPTO 2020. LNCS, vol. 12171, pp. 121–151. Springer, Cham (2020). https://doi.org/10.1007/978-3-030-56880-1_5

5. Bellare, M., Dai, W.: The multi-base discrete logarithm problem: tight reductions and non-rewinding proofs for Schnorr identification and signatures. In: Bhargavan, K., Oswald, E., Prabhakaran, M. (eds.) INDOCRYPT 2020. LNCS, vol. 12578, pp. 529–552. Springer, Cham (2020). https://doi.org/10.1007/978-3-030-65277-7_24

6. Bellare, M., Dai, W.: Chain reductions for multi-signatures and the HBMS scheme. In: Tibouchi, M., Wang, H. (eds.) ASIACRYPT 2021. LNCS, vol. 13093, pp. 650–678. Springer, Cham (2021). https://doi.org/10.1007/978-3-030-92068-5_22

7. Bellare, M., Neven, G.: Multi-signatures in the plain public-key model and a general forking lemma. In: Proceedings of the ACM Conference on Computer and Communications Security, pp. 390–399 (2006)

8. Ben-Sasson, E., Chiesa, A., Spooner, N.: Interactive oracle proofs. In: Hirt, M., Smith, A. (eds.) TCC 2016. LNCS, vol. 9986, pp. 31–60. Springer, Heidelberg (2016). https://doi.org/10.1007/978-3-662-53644-5_2

9. Boneh, D., Drijvers, M., Neven, G.: Compact multi-signatures for smaller blockchains. In: Peyrin, T., Galbraith, S. (eds.) ASIACRYPT 2018. LNCS, vol. 11273, pp. 435–464. Springer, Cham (2018). https://doi.org/10.1007/978-3-030-03329-3_15

10. Bootle, J., Cerulli, A., Chaidos, P., Groth, J., Petit, C.: Efficient zero-knowledge arguments for arithmetic circuits in the discrete log setting. In: Fischlin, M., Coron, J.-S. (eds.) EUROCRYPT 2016. LNCS, vol. 9666, pp. 327–357. Springer, Heidelberg (2016). https://doi.org/10.1007/978-3-662-49896-5_12

11. Catalano, D., Fiore, D., Gennaro, R., Vamvourellis, K.: Algebraic (trapdoor) one-way functions: constructions and applications. Theoret. Comput. Sci. **592**, 143–165 (2015)

12. Cramer, R.: Modular design of secure yet practical cryptographic protocols. Ph.D. thesis, CWI and University of Amsterdam (1996)

13. Cramer, R., Damgård, I.: Zero-knowledge proofs for finite field arithmetic, or: can zero-knowledge be for free? In: Krawczyk, H. (ed.) CRYPTO 1998. LNCS, vol. 1462, pp. 424–441. Springer, Heidelberg (1998). https://doi.org/10.1007/BFb0055745

14. Fuchsbauer, G., Kiltz, E., Loss, J.: The algebraic group model and its applications. In: Shacham, H., Boldyreva, A. (eds.) CRYPTO 2018. LNCS, vol. 10992, pp. 33–62. Springer, Cham (2018). https://doi.org/10.1007/978-3-319-96881-0_2

15. Fuchsbauer, G., Plouviez, A., Seurin, Y.: Blind Schnorr signatures and signed ElGamal encryption in the algebraic group model. In: Canteaut, A., Ishai, Y. (eds.) EUROCRYPT 2020. LNCS, vol. 12106, pp. 63–95. Springer, Cham (2020). https://doi.org/10.1007/978-3-030-45724-2_3

16. Gennaro, R., Leigh, D., Sundaram, R., Yerazunis, W.: Batching Schnorr identification scheme with applications to privacy-preserving authorization and low-bandwidth communication devices. In: Lee, P.J. (ed.) ASIACRYPT 2004. LNCS, vol. 3329, pp. 276–292. Springer, Heidelberg (2004). https://doi.org/10.1007/978-3-540-30539-2_20

17. Guillou, L.C., Quisquater, J.-J.: A "paradoxical" indentity-based signature scheme resulting from zero-knowledge. In: Goldwasser, S. (ed.) CRYPTO 1988. LNCS, vol. 403, pp. 216–231. Springer, New York (1990). https://doi.org/10.1007/0-387-34799-2_16

18. Hazay, C., Lindell, Y.: Efficient Secure Two-Party Protocols - Techniques and Constructions. Information Security and Cryptography, Springer, Heidelberg (2010). https://doi.org/10.1007/978-3-642-14303-8

19. Jaeger, J., Tessaro, S.: Expected-time cryptography: generic techniques and applications to concrete soundness. In: Pass, R., Pietrzak, K. (eds.) TCC 2020. LNCS, vol. 12552, pp. 414–443. Springer, Cham (2020). https://doi.org/10.1007/978-3-030-64381-2_15

20. Katz, J., Lindell, Y.: Handling expected polynomial-time strategies in simulation-based security proofs. J. Cryptol. **21**(3), 303–349 (2008)

21. Kiltz, E., Masny, D., Pan, J.: Optimal security proofs for signatures from identification schemes. In: Robshaw, M., Katz, J. (eds.) CRYPTO 2016. LNCS, vol. 9815, pp. 33–61. Springer, Heidelberg (2016). https://doi.org/10.1007/978-3-662-53008-5_2

22. Maurer, U.: Abstract models of computation in cryptography. In: Smart, N.P. (ed.) Cryptography and Coding 2005. LNCS, vol. 3796, pp. 1–12. Springer, Heidelberg (2005). https://doi.org/10.1007/11586821_1

23. Maxwell, G., Poelstra, A., Seurin, Y., Wuille, P.: Simple Schnorr multi-signatures with applications to Bitcoin. Des. Codes Crypt. **87**(9), 2139–2164 (2019). https://doi.org/10.1007/s10623-019-00608-x

24. Micali, S.: Computationally sound proofs. SIAM J. Comput. **30**(4), 1253–1298 (2000)

25. Mizuide, T., Takayasu, A., Takagi, T.: Tight reductions for Diffie-Hellman variants in the algebraic group model. In: Matsui, M. (ed.) CT-RSA 2019. LNCS, vol. 11405, pp. 169–188. Springer, Cham (2019). https://doi.org/10.1007/978-3-030-12612-4_9

26. Nick, J., Ruffing, T., Seurin, Y.: MuSig2: simple two-round Schnorr multi-signatures. In: Malkin, T., Peikert, C. (eds.) CRYPTO 2021. LNCS, vol. 12825, pp. 189–221. Springer, Cham (2021). https://doi.org/10.1007/978-3-030-84242-0_8

27. Okamoto, T.: Provably secure and practical identification schemes and corresponding signature schemes. In: Brickell, E.F. (ed.) CRYPTO 1992. LNCS, vol. 740, pp. 31–53. Springer, Heidelberg (1993). https://doi.org/10.1007/3-540-48071-4_3

28. Pointcheval, D., Stern, J.: Security arguments for digital signatures and blind signatures. J. Cryptol. **13**, 361–396 (2000)

29. Rotem, L., Segev, G.: Algebraic distinguishers: from discrete logarithms to decisional uber assumptions. In: Pass, R., Pietrzak, K. (eds.) TCC 2020. LNCS, vol. 12552, pp. 366–389. Springer, Cham (2020). https://doi.org/10.1007/978-3-030-64381-2_13

30. Rotem, L., Segev, G.: Tighter security for Schnorr identification and signatures: a high-moment forking lemma for Σ-protocols. In: Malkin, T., Peikert, C. (eds.) CRYPTO 2021. LNCS, vol. 12825, pp. 222–250. Springer, Cham (2021). https://doi.org/10.1007/978-3-030-84242-0_9

31. Schnorr, C.P.: Efficient identification and signatures for smart cards. In: Brassard, G. (ed.) CRYPTO 1989. LNCS, vol. 435, pp. 239–252. Springer, New York (1990). https://doi.org/10.1007/0-387-34805-0_22

32. Schnorr, C.P.: Efficient signature generation by smart cards. J. Cryptol. **4**(3), 161–174 (1991). https://doi.org/10.1007/BF00196725

33. Shoup, V.: Lower bounds for discrete logarithms and related problems. In: Fumy, W. (ed.) EUROCRYPT 1997. LNCS, vol. 1233, pp. 256–266. Springer, Heidelberg (1997). https://doi.org/10.1007/3-540-69053-0_18

34. Yun, A.: Generic hardness of the multiple discrete logarithm problem. In: Oswald, E., Fischlin, M. (eds.) EUROCRYPT 2015. LNCS, vol. 9057, pp. 817–836. Springer, Heidelberg (2015). https://doi.org/10.1007/978-3-662-46803-6_27

On Black-Box Verifiable Outsourcing

Amit Agarwal[1]([✉])[iD], Navid Alamati[2][iD], Dakshita Khurana[1][iD],
Srinivasan Raghuraman[3][iD], and Peter Rindal[2][iD]

[1] University of Illinois Urbana-Champaign, Champaign, USA
{amita2,dakshita}@illinois.edu
[2] Visa Research, Palo Alto, USA
{nalamati,perindal}@visa.com
[3] Visa Research and MIT, Cambridge, USA

Abstract. We study verifiable outsourcing of computation in a model where the verifier has black-box access to the function being computed. We introduce the problem of oracle-aided batch verification of computation (OBVC) for a function class $\mathcal{F}$. This allows a verifier to efficiently verify the correctness of any $f \in \mathcal{F}$ evaluated on a batch of n instances $x_1, \ldots, x_n$, while only making λ calls to an oracle for f (along with $O(n\lambda)$ calls to low-complexity helper oracles), for security parameter λ. We obtain the following positive and negative results:

- We build OBVC protocols for the class of all functions that admit *random-self-reductions*. Some of our protocols rely on homomorphic encryption schemes.
- We show that there cannot exist OBVC schemes for the class of all functions mapping λ-bit inputs to λ-bit outputs, for any $n = \mathsf{poly}(\lambda)$.[1]([1] The authors grant IACR a non-exclusive and irrevocable license to distribute the article under the https://creativecommons.org/licenses/by-nc/3.0/.)

1 Introduction

We study the problem of *verifiably outsourcing computation* in a model where the verifier has *black-box access* to the function being computed as well as to certain *low-complexity* helper functions.

A large body of work in the study of delegation, starting with [24,26], consider the setting where a computationally bounded prover generates efficiently checkable proofs π attesting to the correctness of relatively inefficient computation. A major downside of existing works is that they require the prover and verifier to agree on and use a *specific* circuit C_f for computing the function f. In other words, the verification scheme is inherently tied to a fixed (arbitrary) implementation of f which is publicly known to both the prover (server) and the verifier (client).

On the other hand, consider a scenario where a cloud-based service provider offers a service computing f (for example, f can be matrix multiplication) on arbitrary client data. The client would like to ensure correctness of returned

© International Association for Cryptologic Research 2023
G. Rothblum and H. Wee (Eds.): TCC 2023, LNCS 14369, pp. 158–187, 2023.
https://doi.org/10.1007/978-3-031-48615-9_6

outcomes. There are a few reasons why the "circuit-dependent verification" approach above poses a barrier to verifiable computation in this scenario. First of all, the service provider may be using a proprietary code/implementation C_f to compute f (e.g. some proprietary matrix multiplication algorithm) which it is unwilling to disclose to its clients. As such, running a verifiable outsourcing protocol where the client/verifier depends on the code C_f is simply not feasible. Second, even if the company is willing to disclose its code/implementation, the client would have to audit it (for e.g. using formal verification) to make sure that C_f is indeed a sound implementation of f, which can be quite complex. Third, the company may make frequent updates to C_f (for e.g. to add performance optimizations) which would require the client to keep checking this code continually. Finally, making verification independent of the code of f may also lead to efficiency improvements for the verifier in certain settings. Motivated by these questions, we study the following problem:

What classes of functions admit oracle-aided verifiable computation schemes?

The notion of oracle-aided computation captures "circuit-independence" in the context of verifiable computation, as we discuss next. We consider a batch verification scenario: suppose a verifier is given access to an oracle O_f for function $f \in \mathcal{F}$. Is it possible for the verifier, using only $\lambda = \log^2 n$ queries to O_f, to verify the correctness of a large batch of computations $y_1 = f(x_1), \ldots, y_n = f(x_n)$? Oracle access to O_f ensures that the verification scheme is oblivious to any specific implementation C_f that the server may use to perform the computation. Indeed, the client can instantiate such an oracle using any arbitrary implementation C'_f which need not depend on the server's implementation C_f. The restriction of λ oracle queries ensures that even if the oracle O_f is instantiated with a naive/inefficient implementation C'_f on the client side, the total work performed by the client over the entire batch will be relatively small (as long as the security parameter λ is smaller than the batch size).

1.1 Our Results

Motivated by the above considerations, we formalize the notion of oracle aided verifiable computation (OBVC) in the batched setting. At a high level, an OBVC protocol for function class $\mathcal{F}$, defined on ℓ bit inputs, consists of a weak client who wishes to outsource the computation of some function $f \in \mathcal{F}$ on a batch of n instances, let's say $x_1, \ldots, x_n$, to a powerful server. The client is assisted by a function oracle $\mathcal{O}_f$ along with some helper oracles $\mathcal{O}_{g_1}, \ldots, \mathcal{O}_{g_m}$ which are computationally "weaker" than $\mathcal{O}_f$. This is formalized by requiring that the combined time complexity of helper oracles be smaller than the time complexity of the function f i.e. $\sum_{i=1}^{m} T_{g_i}(\ell) = o(T_f(\ell))$. The server can use an arbitrary implementation C_f of the function f. The completeness guarantee of OBVC ensures that the client, when interacting with an honest server (i.e. a server holding a correct circuit C_f for f and following the protocol steps), always outputs the correct evaluation i.e. $f(x_1), \ldots, f(x_n)$. On the other hand, the soundness guarantee of OBVC ensures that a malicious server (i.e. a server who deviates from the protocol or uses an incorrect circuit C'_f) cannot make the client accept incorrect evaluations on any input in the batch, except with some negligible probability.

We require the scheme to have the following efficiency properties: i) the number of oracle queries made by V to the function oracle $\mathcal{O}_f$ is $O(\lambda)$, ii) the number of queries made to each helper oracle $\mathcal{O}_{g_i}$ is $O(n\lambda)$, iii) there is a constant c such that the running time of the verifier (as an oracle machine) is $\lambda^c \cdot o(n \cdot T_f(\ell))$, where $T_f(\ell)$ is the time complexity of computing f on ℓ bit inputs. Note that the efficiency condition ensures that the OBVC protocol is non-trivial in that the verifier efficiency is better than computing the function on all n inputs in time $n \cdot O(T_f(\ell))$ or, by making $O(n)$ oracle queries to $\mathcal{O}_f$.

Random Self Reducible Functions. In this work, we build an OBVC scheme for the class of all Random Self-Reducible (RSR) functions. We now briefly describe this property. If a function f admits K RSR, then computing f on any chosen input x can be reduced to computing f on a set of uniformly random (not necessarily independent) inputs $r^1, \ldots, r^K$, where K is some fixed constant dependent on f. More formally, there exists a randomized algorithm called RSR.Encode which takes as input x and outputs a set of random instances $r^1, \ldots, r^K$. We will sometimes call these random instances as "shares" of the original input x (borrowing the terminology from secret-sharing literature). Given the evaluation of f on these random instances, $f(r^1), \ldots, f(r^K)$, there exists a deterministic algorithm called RSR.Decode which outputs $f(x)$. Moreover, RSR.Encode and RSR.Decode are much "simpler" to compute than f and this is formalized by requiring that the combined time complexity of RSR.Encode and RSR.Decode is much less than that of f. (Note that these only depend on the functionality f and not on its circuit/implementation.) Many useful functions such as integer multiplication, matrix multiplication, polynomial multiplication, integer division, exponentiation, and trigonometric functions such as sine and cos admit RSR. In our positive result, we assume that the RSR.Encode and RSR.Decode functions are available to the verifier as helper oracles.

Theorem 1. *(Informal) Let $\mathcal{F}_\ell$ be the class of all Random Self-Reducible functions on $\ell = \ell(\lambda)$ bit inputs. Assuming homomorphic encryption scheme (HE) for $\mathcal{F}_\ell$, there exists an OBVC scheme for $\mathcal{F}_\ell$.*

In this work, we are also interested in studying the limitations of OBVC schemes. In other words, we would like to understand whether all large classes of functions can admit OBVC schemes. To that end, we have the following result:

Theorem 2. *(Informal) Let $\mathcal{F}_\lambda$ be the class of all functions mapping λ bit inputs to λ bit outputs. Then, $\mathcal{F}_\lambda$ does not admit an OBVC scheme.*

We will elaborate upon these two results in the next section.

1.2   Our Techniques

Positive result. Let us start by describing a simplified version of our idea (which doesn't directly work). Consider the following protocol: The client sends all n instances, $x_1, \ldots, x_n$, to the server and the server is supposed to respond with $y_1 = f(x_1), \ldots, y_n = f(x_n)$. On receiving $y_1, \ldots, y_n$ from the server, the client performs a cut-and-chose style check on some small subset T, where $|T| = \lambda$ (λ being the security parameter), in the following way: It randomly selects $T \subset [n]$ and checks whether $y_i = \mathcal{O}_f(x_i)$ for all $i \in T$, where $\mathcal{O}_f$ is an oracle that returns the evaluation of f. If the check fails, the client aborts. Otherwise, the client outputs $y_1, \ldots, y_n$. On an intuitive level, if the server is cheating on some instance x_{i_0} where $i_0 \in [n]$, then it runs the risk of being caught in the cut-and-chose check. However, this strategy fails since even if $|T| = n - 1$, the prover can get away with a probability atleast $\frac{1}{n}$, which is non-negligible. Hence this basic scheme does not work.

The major downside of the above scheme is that a malicious server can corrupt the computation on a single instance and go undetected with non-negligible probability. One may attempt to resolve this issue is that of error correction. In more detail, we could force a malicious server to corrupt the computation on many parts of a codeword in order to successfully corrupt the computation on a single instance. This would hopefully reduce the probability of a malicious server going undetected. However, this alone does not suffice. The real issue that the above example highlights is that a malicious server can, *with probability* 1, *selectively* corrupt the computation on a single instance x_i in the batch where $i \in [n]$, error-corrected or otherwise. Unless the verifier is invoking the oracle $\mathcal{O}_f$ on all n instances, it runs the risk of accepting a bad set of $y_1, \ldots, y_n$. This is true even if one employs error correction techniques on each instance as the adversary may be able to identify the error-corrected instances corresponding to each instance. Our idea to tackle this is to leverage the property of Random Self-Reduction (RSR). In the following description, we will assume that we are dealing with the class of functions admitting RSR, and that the RSR.Encode and RSR.Decode functions are available to the verifier as helper oracles.

Suppose our function f of interest admits K RSR with $K = 1$. As a first step, we will show that RSR helps us to reduce the probability of *selective* corruptions from 1 to $\frac{1}{n}$. Looking ahead, our next step will be to show that assuming this lower probability of *selective* corruptions, error-correction tools, i.e., repetition and majority decoding, can be used to achieve negligible soundness error. For our first step, we modify our previous basic protocol in the following way: Instead of sending $x_1, \ldots, x_n$ to the server, we will first map each instance x_i to a uniformly random instance r_i using RSR.Encode, shuffle the set $\{r_1, \ldots, r_n\}$, and send this shuffled set to the server. After receiving the answers from the server, the client will perform a cut-and-chose check as described earlier. If the cut-and-chose check passes, it reverse shuffles the server's responses and applies RSR.Decode to each of them to get the actual outputs. We claim that this protocol reduces the probability of *selective* corruptions to $\frac{1}{n}$, i.e., the prover cannot *selectively* corrupt the computation on a particular instance x_{i_0} with probability better than $\frac{1}{n}$. This follows because a 1 RSR is a random mapping, and have shuffled the random mappings of the instance as well.

Having achieved this lower probability of *selective* corruptions, we move on to our next and final step for the case of $K = 1$. We claim that we can now boost the soundness of this protocol by performing repetitions and majority decoding in the following way: For each instance x_i in the batch, we apply RSR.Encode independently λ times, where λ is a security parameter, to get $\{r_{i,j}\}_{i\in[n],j\in[\lambda]}$. We then proceed as described earlier i.e. the client randomly shuffles $\{r_{i,j}\}_{i\in[n],j\in[\lambda]}$, sends this shuffled set to the server and performs cut-and-chose check on the server's responses. If the cut-and-chose check passes, it reverse shuffles the server's responses and applies RSR.Decode to each of them. Additionally, it performs a majority decoding on the results of RSR.Decode to get the final outputs. If the cut-and-chose check passes, it ensures that any random subset of size λ of the server's responses will have less than $\frac{\lambda}{2}$ corruptions (except with negligible probability) due to Hoeffding's bound. Note that this holds regardless of having achieved a low probability of *selective* corruptions. But crucially, the low probability of *selective* corruptions allows to translate the guarantee on random subsets of size λ to subsets that precisely correspond to the repetitions of each instance. This, in turn, ensures that the majority decoding for each instance will always result in the correct output. To further illustrate this, note that if we skip the shuffling step (that was partially responsible for a low probability of *selective* corruptions) and only perform random mapping (using RSR.Encode) along with repetitions, it won't get us negligible soundness error. This is because a cheating server can again selectively corrupt only $\{r_{i_0,j}\}_{j\in[\lambda]}$ i.e., all the random instances in every repetition corresponding to a particular input x_{i_0} and avoid detection with non-negligible probability.

We now turn towards the case of functions which admit K RSR where $K > 1$. Compared to $K = 1$ case, this case is much more tricky to handle for the following reason. Suppose we invoke RSR.Encode on each instance x_i (without any repetitions) to form a set of random instances $\{r_i^1, \ldots, r_i^K\}$. As with the $K = 1$ case, a natural extension of the previous approach in order to thwart *selective* corruptions would be to gather all the $n \cdot K$ random instances $\{r_i^k\}_{i\in[n],k\in[K]}$, shuffle them, and send them to the server. In the $K = 1$ setting, we argued that the prover cannot *selectively* corrupt the computation on a particular instance x_{i_0} with probability better than $\frac{1}{n}$ due to the random mapping and shuffling step. However, this is no longer true for the $K > 1$ case. The reason is that although each individual share in the set $\{r_{i_0}^1, \ldots, r_{i_0}^K\}$, corresponding to a particular instance x_{i_0}, is uniformly random, the joint distribution is not necessarily uniform. For example, it may happen that any two shares in the set $\{r_{i_0}^1, \ldots, r_{i_0}^K\}$ completely reveal the instance x_{i_0}. Therefore, an unbounded server can potentially try a brute force approach to find out which shares correspond to a particular instance x_{i_0} and then selectively corrupt the computation on those shares.

To handle this, we make the following observation. Suppose we are dealing with a restricted kind of "non-communicating" prover $\mathsf{P}_{\mathsf{no\text{-}com}}$. Such a prover is defined as a tuple of K non-communicating provers $\mathsf{P}_{\mathsf{no\text{-}com}} =$

$(\mathsf{P}^1_{\text{no-com}}, \ldots, \mathsf{P}^K_{\text{no-com}})$. While each prover in the tuple can be an arbitrary unbounded machine, the restriction is that they are not allowed to communicate with each other during the protocol execution. The idea then is to modify the protocol in the following manner: Instead of sending all K shares corresponding of each instance x_i to a single prover, we will only send the kth shares of each instance to the kth non-communicating prover $\mathsf{P}^k_{\text{no-com}}$. On receiving the responses from each $\mathsf{P}^k_{\text{no-com}}$, the verifier applies an independent cut-and-chose check on the responses sent by each $\mathsf{P}^k_{\text{no-com}}$. Since each individual prover is now receiving only a single share (for each instance x_i), we can re-apply the soundness logic discussed for the $K = 1$ RSR case after doing λ independent repetitions. This means that for each individual non-communicating prover $\mathsf{P}^k_{\text{no-com}}$, if the cut-and-chose check passes, then any random subset of size λ of the $\mathsf{P}^k_{\text{no-com}}$ responses will have less than $\frac{\lambda}{2K}$[1] corruptions (except with negligible probability) due to Hoeffding's bound. It turns out that ensuring fewer than $\frac{\lambda}{2K}$ corruptions with respect to each instance $i \in [n]$ and prover $\mathsf{P}^k_{\text{no-com}}$ suffices for the majority decoding argument (as mentioned in the $K = 1$ RSR case) to go through.

Note that eventually we would like to construct a protocol which is sound against a single prover P. To this end, we introduce an intermediate notion of a "no-signaling prover" where we ease the non-communicating restriction in $\mathsf{P}_{\text{no-com}}$. Formally, a "no-signaling prover" is defined as a tuple of K provers $\mathsf{P}_{\text{no-com}} = (\mathsf{P}^1_{\text{no-sig}}, \ldots, \mathsf{P}^K_{\text{no-sig}})$. While each prover in the tuple can be an arbitrary unbounded machine, the restriction is that for all $k \in [K]$, the distribution of the responses of the kth prover $\mathsf{P}^k_{\text{no-sig}}$ should be independent of the shares received by the other provers $\{\mathsf{P}^i_{\text{no-sig}}\}_{i \in [K], i \neq k}$. We then show that our modified protocol for handling arbitrary non-communicating provers is also sound against arbitrary no-signaling provers. Intuitively, the reason why this works is because the cut-and-chose check that we apply on each individual $\mathsf{P}^k_{\text{no-sig}}$ responses is *local*. In more detail, suppose Pred^k is a binary predicate capturing the following event: there exists $i_0 \in [n]$ such that the server $\mathsf{P}^k_{\text{no-sig}}$ responds incorrectly to more than $\frac{\lambda}{2K}$ fraction of RSR instances $\{r_{i_0,j}\}_{j \in [\lambda]}$ and the cut-and-chose check on its responses passes. Since this predicate is local, i.e., the predicate output depends only on the responses of $\mathsf{P}^k_{\text{no-sig}}$, it can be shown that any $\mathsf{P}^k_{\text{no-sig}}$ which makes Pred^k true with non-negligible probability (over the randomness of the verifier) directly implies a non-communicating prover $\mathsf{P}^k_{\text{no-com}}$ which makes Pred^k true with non-negligible probability (thus contradicting our soundness analysis for arbitrary non-communicating provers).

Finally, we show that the restriction to a no-signaling set of provers can be removed by a slight modification to the protocol where the verifier simply encrypts each RSR instance $\{r^k_{i,j}\}_{i \in [n], j \in [\lambda], k \in [K]}$ under an independent public-key $\mathsf{pk}_{i,j,k}$ before sending it to a single server P. If the public-key encryption scheme is homomorphic, then the server can compute the answers to verifier messages "under the hood" of the HE scheme (using $\mathsf{HE.Eval}$) and send the

---

[1] We use $\frac{\lambda}{2K}$ as opposed to $\frac{\lambda}{2}$ as this is what we need in the setting of K provers to make the rest of the analysis work out.

encrypted responses back to the verifier. The verifier then simply decrypts all the responses and runs the no-signaling verifier (which is identical to the non-communicating verifier) to derive the final output. With this transformation, it can be shown that the soundness of the previous protocol (i.e., without applying encryption) against arbitrary unbounded no-signaling provers $P_{no\text{-}sig}$ directly implies soundness of the transformed protocol (i.e., after applying encryption) against arbitrary *computationally bounded* provers P. Formally, the analysis uses a reduction to the semantic security of the encryption scheme.

Negative result. Towards a negative result, an ideal goal would be to tightly characterize functions that do not admit an OBVC scheme. However, getting such a strong negative result seems difficult as there might be arbitrary properties of functions (other than RSR) that one could potentially leverage in order to construct an OBVC scheme. Therefore, we settle for a weaker goal where we show that it is impossible to construct an OBVC scheme for a "large enough" function class $\mathcal{F}$. Specifically, we consider the function class $\mathcal{F}_\lambda = \{\{0,1\}^\lambda \to \{0,1\}^\lambda\}$, the class consisting of all functions mapping λ bit inputs to λ bit outputs.

We now adopt the following approach: Suppose there exists a OBVC scheme Π for $\mathcal{F}_\lambda$ and let f_λ be a function sampled randomly from $\mathcal{F}_\lambda$. Then we show that there exists a malicious prover P^* that breaks the soundness of Π with non-negligible probability. Allowing f_λ to be sampled randomly from $\mathcal{F}_\lambda$ enables us to model this game in the well-known Random Oracle Model (ROM) [6]. In this terminology, the oracle $\mathcal{O}_f$ will be identical to a Random Oracle (RO). Let n be the number of instances in the batch and t be the number of queries that V is allowed to make to $\mathcal{O}_f$. For the OBVC scheme to be meaningful, we know that t should be strictly less than n. However, note that in our OBVC definition, we also allow the verifier to have access to $poly(\lambda)$ function-dependent helper oracles, each of which be invoked $O(n\lambda)$ times. To model these helper oracles faithfully in ROM, we will assume that these are encoded as an s-bit auxiliary input aux and handed over to the verifier as a preprocessing advice. Note that this aux can depend arbitrarily on the entire RO function table, for example, it can contain global information about the entire RO function f.

Our idea to construct a malicious prover P^* that breaks the soundness of any potential OBVC scheme Π in this ROM setting is as follows. Let $\mathcal{Q}$ denote the set of queries that the V makes to $\mathcal{O}_f$ during the protocol. Since $t < n$, it holds that a randomly sampled instance x_ϕ from the batch $\{x_1, \ldots, x_n\}$ will be outside $\mathcal{Q}$ with probability atleast $1 - t/n$. Therefore, we can switch into a hybrid where the prover locally reprograms the value of $f(x_\phi)$ to a random value Δ in the image of f. Intuitively, one could invoke a lazy-sampling argument for ROM to argue that this change will go unnoticed to the verifier if it does not query $\mathcal{O}_f$ at x_ϕ. Indeed, if this were true, then it would have been sufficient to break soundness with non-negligible probability. However, there is a subtle flaw in directly applying such a lazy-sampling argument. Recall that we are in a setting where the verifier is allowed to compute auxiliary information aux about $\mathcal{O}_f$ before the protocol begins. This hinders a direct application of lazy-sampling argument as aux might potentially contain information (for e.g. a small digest) about the *entire* $\mathcal{O}_f$. Hence, it is no longer true that points outside $\mathcal{Q}$ are independent from the verifier's view.

To resolve this, we apply some of the techniques that were developed in earlier works [16,17,28] which studied security of cryptographic protocols where adversary can contain auxiliary information about the Random Oracle, also known as the Auxiliary Input Random Oracle (AI-RO) model. We specifically use the results in [16] where authors define a new relaxed model called Bit-Fixing Random Oracle (BF-RO) model. At a high level, in the BF-RO model, the aux is constrained so that it only contains information about p points (p is a tunable parameter) in $\mathcal{O}_f$ which can be chosen arbitrarily. Based on this modeling, the authors show that security theorems proved in BF-RO model can be carried over to the AI-RO model with a loss in advantage proportional to st/p (recall that s is the length of advice string in AI-RO model and t is the number of queries to $\mathcal{O}_f$). By setting s, t, p appropriately, one can get negligible loss in advantage.

Returning to our setting, recall that it was not possible to apply lazy sampling in the AI-RO model we were dealing with. Therefore, as a first step, we will restrict ourselves to the BF-RO model where aux is constrained so that it only contains information about/fixes some p points of the random oracle. Let us denote these set of p points by $\mathcal{P}$. Fortunately, in this model, we can apply the lazy-sampling technique for the points outside $\mathcal{P}$. Therefore, as long as we can ensure that x_ϕ is outside both $\mathcal{P}$ and $\mathcal{Q}$ (recall that $\mathcal{Q}$ is the set of queries that the verifier makes during the protocol), then the malicious prover P* which we described earlier will work. We show formally that this is indeed the case for all $\alpha' \in (0,1], p \in 2^{(1-\alpha')\lambda}$, thus giving us an impossibility result for OBVC in the BF-RO model. Finally, we are also able to apply a lemma from [16] to lift our impossibility result from the BF-RO model to the AI-RO model with appropriate setting of parameters.

1.3 Related Work

Our idea of verifiable computation of functions in a "circuit-independent" fashion is inspired from the early works on Self-Testing/Self-Correcting programs [7,25]. In these works, it was shown that if a program P correctly computes a random self-reducible (RSR) function f on "most" inputs, then it can be used to correctly compute f on "all" inputs using only oracle access to P. However, a major limitation of these works is that the adversarial program is limited to a stateless machine. In other words, the response provided by P on a particular query is not allowed to depend on the previous queries. In our work, we consider the setting of arbitrary stateful prover which is strictly general than a stateless program.

Later works [8] extended this idea to deal with adaptive programs (i.e. programs whose response in a particular query can depend on the previous queries arbitrarily) but protocols in this setting required two or more independent copies of the program which, analogously, can be thought of as non-communicating provers. This work requires an additional property of "downward self-reducibility" (which roughly means that computing f on input x of size ℓ can be reduced to computing f on random "smaller" instances of size $\ell - 1$).

Thus, our result, which only relies on random-self-reducibility to instances of the same size, is more general.

Rubinfeld [27] extended the work on program checking to a batched setting where the verifier is trying to verify the computation of P on batch of n inputs. Again, this work was limited to stateless program as opposed to stateful prover which we consider. Bellare et. al. [5] proposed a different approach to batch verification for the specific case of modular exponentiation function by allowing the verifier to compute the function on some small number of inputs on its own.

As discussed earlier in the introduction, succinct non-interactive arguments (SNARGs) for P (where proof size and verification time are polylogarithmic in the security parameter) and batch arguments (BARGs) for NP, where a batch of statements can be verified in time that is sublinear in the number of statements [10,12,13,21,22,29] are closely related primitives. A related line of work [2,14,19] similarly considers the possibility of using FHE and a preprocessing stage to perform verifiable computation. Unfortunately, all of these works require the verifier to have non-black-box access to the circuit C_f for the function f, and are therefore not applicable to the setting of black-box verification.

2   Preliminaries

Throughout the paper, we use bold-letters to indicate vectors (which can sometimes be equivalently represented as strings). For a vector $\mathbf{v}$ of length n, we use the notation v_i to indicate the ith co-ordinate of $\mathbf{v}$ where $i \in [n]$. For a subset $S \subseteq [n]$, we use $\mathbf{v}_S := (v_i)_{i \in S}$ to denote the subvector of $\mathbf{v}$ restricted to the positions $i \in S$. For a bit string $\mathbf{b} = (b_1, \ldots, b_n) \in \{0,1\}^n$ of arbitrary length $n \geq 0$, we use $\mathsf{RW}(\mathbf{b})$ and $\mathsf{HW}(\mathbf{b})$ to indicate the relative and absolute hamming weight of $\mathbf{b}$ respectively. Throughout the paper, we use λ to indicate the security parameter. By $\mathsf{poly}(\lambda)$ and $\mathsf{negl}(\lambda)$, we mean the class $\lambda^{O(1)}$ and $\frac{1}{\lambda^{\omega(1)}}$. We sometimes abuse notation and use $\mathsf{poly}(\lambda)$ and $\mathsf{negl}(\lambda)$ to refer to a member from the class $\mathsf{poly}(\lambda)$ and $\mathsf{negl}(\lambda)$ respectively. Given a security parameter λ, we use PPT to denote probabilitic $\mathsf{poly}(\lambda)$-time Turing Machines and non-uniform PPT to denote PPT machines with $\mathsf{poly}(\lambda)$-sized advice. We say that two distribution ensembles $X = \{X_\lambda\}_{\lambda \in \mathbb{N}}$ and $Y = \{Y_\lambda\}$ are computationally indistinguishable, denoted by $X \approx_c Y$, if for every non-uniform PPT algorithm $\mathcal{D}$, there exists a negligible function $\mathsf{negl}(\lambda)$ such that for all $\lambda \in \mathbb{N}$, we have $|\Pr[\mathcal{D}(X_\lambda) = 1] - \Pr[\mathcal{D}(Y_\lambda) = 1]| \leq \mathsf{negl}(\lambda)$.

2.1   Mathematical Preliminaries and Definitions

Theorem 3 (Hoeffding's inequality [20]). *Let $\mathbf{b} \in \{0,1\}^{nm}$ be a bitstring with relative hamming weight $\mu = \mathsf{RW}(\mathbf{b})$. Let the random variables $X_1, \ldots, X_k$ be obtained by sampling k entries from $\mathbf{b}$ with replacement, i.e. the X_i's are independent and $\Pr[X_i = 1] = \mu$. Furthermore, let the random variables $Y_1, \ldots, Y_k$ be obtained by sampling k entries from $\mathbf{b}$ without replacement. Then, for any $\delta > 0$, the random variables $\bar{X} = \frac{1}{k} \sum_i X_i$ and $\bar{Y} = \frac{1}{k} \sum_i Y_i$ satisfy:*

$$\Pr[|\bar{Y} - \mu| \geq \delta] \leq \Pr[|\bar{X} - \mu| \geq \delta] \leq 2 \cdot e^{-2\delta^2 k}$$

Definition 1. *An (N, M) source is a random variable X with range $[M]^N$. A source is called p-bit-fixing if it is fixed on at most p coordinates and uniform on the rest.*

Theorem 4 ([16]). *Let X be distributed uniformly over $[M]^N$ and $Z := f(X)$, where $f : [M]^N \to \{0,1\}^s$ is an arbitrary function. For any $\gamma > 0$ and $p \in \mathbb{N}$, there exists a family $\{Y_z\}_{z \in \{0,1\}^s}$ of convex combinations Y_z of p-bit-fixing (N, M)-sources such that for any distinguisher D taking an s-bit input and querying at most $t < p$ coordinates of its oracle,*

$$|\Pr[D^X(f(X) = 1)] - \Pr[D^{Y_{f(X)}}(f(X)) = 1]| \leq \frac{(s + \log 1/\gamma) \cdot t}{p} + \gamma$$

2.2 Bit Fixing Random Oracle Model

In this section, we will define the Auxiliary Input Random Oracle (AI-RO) and Bit fixing Random Oracle (BF-RO) model as described in Coretti et. al. [16]. An oracle $\mathcal{O}$ consists of two interfaces $\mathcal{O}.\text{pre}$ and $\mathcal{O}.\text{main}$. We will define two types of entities (modeled as turing machines) and their access to $\mathcal{O}$.

- Two-stage entity : Such an entity $\mathcal{E}$ is split up into two parts $\mathcal{E} = (\mathcal{E}_1, \mathcal{E}_2)$. The first part $\mathcal{E}_1$ can access $\mathcal{O}.\text{pre}$ and the second part $\mathcal{E}_2$ can access $\mathcal{O}.\text{main}$. Furthermore, $\mathcal{E}_1$ can pass on some auxiliary information to the second part.
- Single stage entity: Such an entity $\mathcal{E}$ only accesses $\mathcal{O}.\text{main}$.

Let $\mathcal{F}_{M,N}$ be the set of all possible functions $f : [M] \to [N]$. Now we will define different types of oracles that we will use:

- Auxiliary Input Random Oracle AI-RO(M, N): Samples a random function table $F \leftarrow \mathcal{F}_{M,N}$; outputs F at $\mathcal{O}.\text{pre}$; answers queries $x \in [M]$ at $\mathcal{O}.\text{main}$ by the corresponding value $F(x) \in [N]$.
- Bit fixing Random Oracle BF-RO(p, M, N): Samples a random function table $F \leftarrow \mathcal{F}_{M,N}$; outputs F at $\mathcal{O}.\text{pre}$; takes a list at $\mathcal{O}.\text{pre}$ of at most p query/answer pairs (called "bit-fixing" pairs), $\{(x_i, y_i)\}_{i \in [p]}$, that override F in the corresponding position i.e. $\forall i \in [p]$, we set $F(x_i) = y_i$. Then it answers queries $x \in [M]$ at $\mathcal{O}.\text{main}$ by the corresponding value $F(x) \in [N]$.

2.3 Homomorphic Encryption

A homomorphic (public-key) encryption scheme $\text{HE} = (\text{HE.Keygen}, \text{HE.Enc}, \text{HE.Dec}, \text{HE.Eval})$ is a quadruple of PPT algorithms as follows.

- Key Generation: The algorithm $(\text{pk}, \text{sk}) \leftarrow \text{HE.Keygen}(1^\lambda)$ takes a unary representation of the security parameter λ and outputs a public encryption key pk, and a secret decryption key sk.

- Encryption: The algorithm $c \leftarrow \mathsf{HE.Enc_{pk}}(\mu)$ takes the public key pk and a single bit message $\mu \in \{0,1\}$ and outputs a ciphertext c. For encrypting ℓ bit messages, we can simply invoke HE.Enc bit-by-bit.
- Decryption: The algorithm $\mu^* \leftarrow \mathsf{HE.Dec_{sk}}(c)$ takes the secret key sk and a ciphertext c and outputs a message $\mu^* \in \{0,1\}$.
- Homomorphic Evaluation: The algorithm $c_f \leftarrow \mathsf{HE.Eval_{pk}}(f, c_1, \ldots, c_\ell)$ takes the public key pk, a function $f : \{0,1\}^\ell \rightarrow \{0,1\}$ and a set of ciphertexts $c_1, \ldots, c_\ell$ and outputs a ciphertext $c_f{}^2$.

As mentioned in [11], the representation of function f can vary between schemes, and it is best to leave this issue outside of the syntactic definition for our purposes.

The above algorithms must satisfy the following properties:

- CPA-security: A scheme HE is IND-CPA secure if the following holds:

$$\{c \leftarrow \mathsf{HE.Enc_{pk}}(0) : (\mathsf{pk}, \mathsf{sk}) \leftarrow \mathsf{HE.Keygen}(1^\lambda)\}_\lambda$$

$$\approx_c$$

$$\{c \leftarrow \mathsf{HE.Enc_{pk}}(1) : (\mathsf{pk}, \mathsf{sk}) \leftarrow \mathsf{HE.Keygen}(1^\lambda)\}_\lambda$$

where $\lambda \in \mathbb{N}$.
- $\mathcal{F}$-homomorphism: Let $\mathcal{F}_\ell \subseteq \{\{0,1\}^\ell \rightarrow \{0,1\}\}$ be a set of functions where $\ell = \ell(\lambda)$. A scheme HE is $\mathcal{F}$-homomorphic (or, homomorphic for the class $\mathcal{F}$) if for any sequence of functions $f_\ell \in \mathcal{F}_\ell$ and respective inputs $\mu_1, \ldots, \mu_\ell \in \{0,1\}$, it holds that:

$$\Pr\left[\mathsf{HE.Dec_{sk}}(\mathsf{HE.Eval_{pk}}(f, c_1, \ldots, c_\ell)) \neq f(\mu_1, \ldots, \mu_\ell) : \begin{array}{l} \mathsf{pk}, \mathsf{sk} \leftarrow \mathsf{HE.Keygen}(1^\lambda) \\ \forall i \in [\ell], c_i \leftarrow \mathsf{HE.Enc_{pk}}(\mu_i) \end{array}\right] = \mathsf{negl}(\lambda)$$

- Compactness: A scheme HE is compact if there exists a polynomial $s = s(\lambda)$ such that the output length of HE.Eval is at most s bits long (regardless of f or the number of inputs).

2.4   Random Self Reducibility

Intuitively, a function f has Random Self Reducibility (RSR) property if computing f on a given input x can be "easily" reduced to computing f on uniformly random inputs. We now provide a formal definition inspired by [4, 7].

Definition 2 (Random Self Reduction (RSR)). *A function $f : \mathsf{D} \rightarrow \mathsf{R}$ is K random self reducible (henceforth denoted by K-RSR) if there exists a pair of algorithms* (RSR.Encode, RSR.Decode) *where,*

---

[2] For syntactic simplicity, we only consider functions with a single bit output. The generalization to functions with arbitrary output length can be done by splitting a multi-bit output function into multiple functions with single bit output.

– RSR.Encode(x) : *This is a randomized algorithm which takes an ℓ bit input $x \in \{0,1\}^{\ell} \cap D$ and outputs K values $r_1, \ldots r_K$, where each $r_i \in \{0,1\}^{\ell} \cap D$. It also outputs a state* st.
– RSR.Decode($\{y_1, \ldots, y_K\}$, st): *This is a deterministic algorithm which takes as input K values $\{y_i\}_{i \in [K]}$ from* R, *along with a state* st, *and outputs a value $y \in$* R.

The above algorithms must satisfy the following properties.

– *Correctness: For all $\ell \in \mathbb{N}$ and $x \in \{0,1\}^{\ell} \cap D$, we have:*

$$\Pr\left[\text{RSR.Decode}(\{y_1, \ldots, y_K\}, \text{st}) = f(x) : \begin{matrix} \{r_1, \ldots, r_K\}, \text{st} \leftarrow \text{RSR.Encode}(x) \\ \forall i \in [K] : y_i := f(r_i) \end{matrix}\right] = 1$$

– *Uniformity: For all $\ell \in \mathbb{N}$, $x \in \{0,1\}^{\ell} \cap D, i \in [K]$,*

$$\{r_i : r_1, \ldots, r_K \leftarrow \text{RSR.Encode}(x)\} \equiv \mathcal{U}_{\ell}$$

where $\mathcal{U}_{\ell}$ is the uniform distribution on ℓ bit strings.
– *Efficiency: Let $T_{\text{RSR.Encode}}(\ell)$ and $T_{\text{RSR.Decode}}(\ell)$ be the time complexity of* RSR.Encode *and* RSR.Decode *respectively on inputs of size ℓ. Let $T_f(\ell)$ be the (worst-case, over all inputs of size ℓ) time complexity of computing f[3]. Then, the efficiency condition requires that for all constants $c > 0$:*

$$T_{\text{RSR.Encode}}(\ell) + T_{\text{RSR.Decode}}(\ell) = o(T_f(\ell))$$

Blum et. al. [7] showed that many interesting and useful functions, such as modular multiplication, modular exponentiation, integer division, matrix multiplication, polynomial multiplication (over a ring) admit efficient random self reductions. Later works also extended RSR to trigonometric functions such as sine and cosine [3,15], and real-valued functions such as floating-point exponentiation and floating point logarithm [18].

2.5   No-Signaling Prover

We define the notion of no-signaling prover in a manner similar to prior works [9,23]. Intuitively, for a no-signaling set of provers $P_{\text{no-sig}} = (P_1, \ldots, P_K)$, the response of each prover P_i is allowed to depend on the queries to all provers as a function but the distribution of each prover's response (modeled as a random variable) should be (computationally) independent of the queries sent to the other provers.

---

[3] In cases where $T_f(\ell)$ is not known, due to circuit lower bound barriers, we can fix $T_f(\ell)$ to be the best known time complexity for computing f on (worst-case) inputs of size ℓ. For example, if f is the matrix multiplication function of two $\ell \times \ell$ bit matrices, then we can set $T_f(\ell) = \ell^{2.3728596}$ for inputs of length $2\ell^2$ (encoding two $\ell \times \ell$ sized bit-matrix as a bit-string) based on the fastest known matrix multiplication algorithm [1].

Definition 3 (No-signaling prover). *Let $\mathcal{Q}$ denote the alphabet of the queries. A prover system $\mathsf{P}_{\text{no-sig}} = (\mathsf{P}_1, \ldots, \mathsf{P}_K)$ is called a no-signaling multi-prover system if the following holds:*

$$\left\{ \mathsf{Game}_k^0(x, \{y_0^i\}_{i \in [K], i \neq k}, \{y_1^i\}_{i \in [K], i \neq k}) \right\}_{k \in [K], x \in \mathcal{Q}, y_0^i \in \mathcal{Q}, y_1^i \in \mathcal{Q}}$$

$$\approx_c \left\{ \mathsf{Game}_k^1(x, \{y_0^i\}_{i \in [K], i \neq k}, \{y_1^i\}_{i \in [K], i \neq k}) \right\}_{k \in [K], x \in \mathcal{Q}, y_0^i \in \mathcal{Q}, y_1^i \in \mathcal{Q}}$$

where the games are formally defined below:

$\mathsf{Game}_k^0(x, \{y_0^i\}_{i \in [K], i \neq k}, \{y_1^i\}_{i \in [K], i \neq k})$	$\mathsf{Game}_k^1(x, \{y_0^i\}_{i \in [K], i \neq k}, \{y_1^i\}_{i \in [K], i \neq k})$
1 : *Send x to P_k.*	1 : *Send x to P_k.*
2 : *$\forall i \in [K], i \neq k$: send y_0^i to P_i.*	2 : *$\forall i \in [K], i \neq k$: send y_1^i to P_i.*
3 : *Receive z from P_k.*	3 : *Receive z from P_k.*
4 : *Output z.*	4 : *Output z.*

3   Defining Oracle-Aided Batch Verifiable Computation

We provide two definitions for Oracle-aided Batch Verifiable Computation - one in the single server setting (OBVC) and the other in multi-server setting (MOBVC).

Definition 4 (Oracle-aided Batch Verifiable Computation). *Let $\ell \in \mathbb{N}$ parameterize input length, $m = \mathsf{poly}(\ell)$ for some polynomial $\mathsf{poly}(\cdot)$, n denote a number of instances, and λ denote a security parameter. Let f_ℓ be an arbitrary function in a class $\mathcal{F}_\ell \subseteq \{\{0,1\}^\ell \to \{0,1\}^*\}$, and let $\mathcal{X} = \{0,1\}^\ell$ denote the domain of f_ℓ.*

An oracle-aided batch verifiable computation OBVC for the function class $\mathcal{F}_\ell$ is an interactive protocol between a randomized client/verifier V and a deterministic server/prover P, with the following syntax.

- *The client V obtains input a batch of n inputs, $\mathbf{x} = x_1, \ldots, x_n$, where each $x_i \in \mathcal{X}$.*
- *The server P obtains a circuit C_f for computing f.*
- *The client V interacts with the server P, and can additionally make oracle calls to a function oracle $\mathcal{O}_f$ as well as to m helper oracles $\mathcal{O}_{g_1}, \ldots, \mathcal{O}_{g_m}$. Finally, V outputs OUT where OUT is either $y_1, \ldots, y_n$ where $y_i \in \mathsf{Range}(f)$ or OUT $= \perp$.*

The protocol satisfies the following properties.

- *Non-triviality: The combined time complexity of helper oracles is smaller than the time complexity of the function f i.e. $\sum_{i=1}^m T_{g_i}(\ell) = o(T_f(\ell))$.*

- *Completeness: Let* $\mathsf{OUT}(\langle \mathsf{P}(C_f), \mathsf{V}^{\mathcal{O}_f, \{\mathcal{O}_{g_i}\}_{i\in[m]}} \rangle)$ *denote the output of* V *at the end of protocol. For all* $l \in \mathbb{N}, f_l \in \mathcal{F}_l, n \in \mathbb{N}, \mathbf{x} \in \mathcal{X}^n, \lambda \in \mathbb{N}$,

$$\Pr_{\mathsf{V}}[\mathsf{OUT} = f_l(x_1), \ldots, f_l(x_n)] = 1$$

  where the probability is taken over the internal coin tosses of V.
- *Soundness: There exists a negligible function* $\mathsf{negl}(\cdot)$ *s.t. for all adversarial* P^*, *for all* $l \in \mathbb{N}, f_l \in \mathcal{F}_l, n = \mathsf{poly}(\lambda), \mathbf{x} \in \mathcal{X}^n, \lambda \in \mathbb{N}$,

$$\Pr_{\mathsf{V}}[\mathsf{OUT} = f(x_1), \ldots, f(x_n) \vee \mathsf{OUT} = \bot] \geq 1 - \mathsf{negl}(\lambda)$$

  where the probability is taken over the internal coin tosses of V.
  When referring to computational soundness, we quantify over all non-uniform PPT provers P^*.
- *Privacy: For all adversarial* P^*, *there exists a simulator* $\mathsf{Sim_P}$ *s.t. there exists a negligible function* $\mathsf{negl}(\cdot)$ *s.t. for all* $\lambda \in \mathbb{N}, f_\lambda \in \mathcal{F}_\lambda, n \in \mathbb{N}, \mathbf{x} \in \mathcal{X}^n$,

$$\mathsf{VIEW}(\mathsf{P}^*) \approx_c \mathsf{Sim}(1^\lambda, 1^n, \mathcal{X})$$

- *Efficiency: For every* $\ell \in \mathbb{N}, f_\ell \in \mathcal{F}_\ell, n \in \mathbb{N}, x \in \mathcal{X}^n$ *and* $\lambda \in \mathbb{N}$, *the number of oracle queries made by* V *to the function oracle* $\mathcal{O}_f$ *is* $O(\lambda)$ *and the number of queries made to each helper oracle* $\mathcal{O}_{g_i}$ *is* $O(n\lambda)$. *Furthermore, there is a constant* c *such that the running time of the verifier (as an oracle machine) is* $\lambda^c \cdot o(n \cdot T_f(\ell))$.

Note that the efficiency condition ensures that the OBVC protocol is non-trivial in the sense that the V is doing something better than the trivial strategies where it computes the function on all n inputs on its own using an internal algorithm in time $n \cdot O(T_f(\ell))$ or, alternatively, does the same task by making $O(n)$ oracle queries to $\mathcal{O}_f$.

We now define K-Multi-server Oracle-aided Batch Verifiable Computation (K-MOBVC) which is a straightforward generalization of the single server definition to a multi-server/multi-prover system $\mathsf{P} = (\mathsf{P}_1, \ldots, \mathsf{P}_K)$ with K provers. Also, in this definition, we do not require the privacy condition.

Definition 5 (Multi-server Oracle-aided Batch Verifiable Computation).
  Refer to the full version of this paper.

4   Protocol for Functions Admitting 1-RSR

In the following section, we provide a construction of OBVC scheme for functions admitting 1-RSR. The idea behind our protocol is simple: First the verifier maps each of its instance x_i to a uniformly random instance s_i using the RSR.Encode function. Then it sends all the randomized instances $\{s_i\}_{i\in[n]}$ to the prover in a shuffled order, and the prover is supposed to respond back with $\{f(s_i)\}_{i\in[n]}$. Intuitively, this shuffling, coupled with the fact that RSR.Encode outputs a uniformly random sample, prevents a malicious prover from selectively providing incorrect responses on some instances (for e.g. the seventh instance x_7). However, note that a malicious prover might still provide incorrect responses on some indices not knowing which instances they correspond to. To tackle this, the verifier uses a cut-and-choose based checking mechanism. Specifically, it selects a small random subset of the indices, gets the correct answer for those indices from the oracle $\mathcal{O}_f$, and then checks whether the prover's responses match. This check ensures that if the prover is misbehaving on "too many" indices, then he will be caught with "overwhelming" probability. Formally, once the check passes, it is ensured that the prover is not lying on more than some (fixed) constant fraction of indices except with some negligible probability. However, note that, our soundness condition requires the output of the verifier be correct on *all* instances (and not just *most* of the instances). To achieve this, we perform a parallel repetition of each instance for some security parameter λ many times and then select the majority of responses as the correct answer. Intuitively, we can select our parameters in a way so that if the cut-and-chose check passes, then it is ensured that the majority, among λ repetitions, encodes the correct answer for that instance.

Theorem 5. *There exists a* OBVC *scheme, specifically Protocol 4, for the class* $\mathcal{F}_\ell^{1\text{-}RSR}$ *consisting of all ℓ bit functions that admit* 1-RSR *with soundness against arbitrary unbounded provers.*

Corollary 6. *For all* $0 < \delta < 1$, $n \in O(2^{\lambda^\delta})$, *Protocol 4 is an* OBVC *scheme for* $\mathcal{F}_\ell^{1\text{-}RSR}$ *with soundness error* $\mathsf{negl}(\lambda)$. *Alternatively, one could set* $\lambda = \omega(\log n)$ *and get a soundness error of* $\mathsf{negl}(n)$.

In the rest of this section, we will prove Theorem 5. We note that the completeness of our protocol follows directly from the correctness property of RSR. We now proceed to discuss non-triviality, privacy, efficiency and prove soundness.

Non-triviality, Privacy and Efficiency Analysis. In our protocol, the verifier uses two helper oracles namely $\mathcal{O}_{\mathsf{RSR.Encode}_f}$ and $\mathcal{O}_{\mathsf{RSR.Decode}_f}$. By Definition 2, we know that $T_{\mathsf{RSR.Encode}}(\ell) + T_{\mathsf{RSR.Decode}}(\ell) = o(T_f(\ell))$. Hence, our protocol satisifes the non-triviality condition.

The privacy of our scheme follows directly from the uniformity condition of RSR. More formally, the simulator $\mathsf{Sim}(1^\lambda, 1^n, \mathcal{X})$ simply samples $n\lambda$ uniformly random instances from $\mathcal{X}$ and outputs it. Since each share $s_{i,j}$ in Protocol 4 is a uniformly random and independent (from everything else) element from $\mathcal{X}$, the simulation is perfect.

For efficiency, we note that each helper oracle is invoked exactly $n\lambda$ times, the function oracle $\mathcal{O}_f$ is invoked exactly λ times and the running time of V is exactly $O(n\lambda)$ as shuffling, majority and cut-and-chose check can be computed in linear time.

Protocol 4

Common input: 1^λ, 1^n
V's additional input: Inputs $x_1, \ldots, x_n$, oracle $\mathcal{O}_f$, helper oracles $\mathcal{O}_{\mathsf{RSR.Encode}_f}$, $\mathcal{O}_{\mathsf{RSR.Decode}_f}$
P's additional input: Circuit C_f for computing f.

1. $\forall i \in [n]$, V generates λ independent RSR instances, $s_{i,1}, \ldots, s_{i,\lambda}$, where $s_{i,j}, \mathsf{st}_{i,j} \leftarrow \mathcal{O}_{\mathsf{RSR.Encode}_f}(x_i)$. It sets $\mathbf{s} := s_{1,1}, \ldots, s_{1,\lambda}, \ldots, s_{n,1}, \ldots, s_{n,\lambda}$.
2. V samples a random permutation π on $[n\lambda]$ and sets $\mathbf{s}' := \pi(\mathbf{s})$. It sends $\mathbf{s}'$ to P.
3. $\forall i \in [n], j \in [\lambda]$, P computes $z'_{i,j} = C_f(s'_{i,j})$.
4. P sets $\mathbf{z}' := z_{1,1}, \ldots, z_{1,\lambda}, \ldots, z_{n,1}, \ldots, z_{n,\lambda}$ and sends $\mathbf{z}'$ to V.
5. V samples a random subset $T \subset [n] \times [\lambda]$ of size λ and checks whether the following holds:
$$\forall (i,j) \in T : z'_{i,j} = f(s'_{i,j})$$
6. If the check fails, then V outputs $\bot$. Otherwise it proceeds.
7. V computes $\mathbf{z} = \pi^{-1}(\mathbf{z}')$.
8. $\forall i \in [n], j \in [\lambda]$, V computes $u_{i,j} \leftarrow \mathcal{O}_{\mathsf{RSR.Decode}_f}(z_{i,j}, \mathsf{st}_{i,j})$.
9. $\forall i \in [n]$, V computes $u_i^{\mathsf{final}} = \mathsf{Majority}(u_{i,1}, \ldots, u_{i,\lambda})$.
10. V outputs $u_1^{\mathsf{final}}, \ldots, u_n^{\mathsf{final}}$.

Soundness Analysis. The high level intuition behind the soundness is the following: If the checking phase in Protocol step 5, 6 passes, then with high probability the verifier will output correct values i.e. with high probability, all u_i^{final} will equal $f(x_i)$. To prove this, we will have to show that, for each $i \in [n]$, the majority of $\{u_{i,j}\}_{j \in [\lambda]}$ will be equal to $f(x_i)$ (with high probability) if the testing phase passes. To do so, we first consider the following experiment which basically captures the execution of Protocol 4 with an arbitrary fixed prover P* and defines random variables $\mathbf{b}$ and its inverse $\mathbf{b}^{\mathsf{inv}}$.

Experiment $\mathsf{Exp}^{\mathsf{1\text{-}RSR}}(\mathsf{P}^*, \mathbf{x})$

1: $\forall i \in [n], j \in [\lambda], s_{i,j} \leftarrow \mathsf{RSR.Encode}(x_i)$

2: $\mathbf{s} := s_{1,1}, \ldots, s_{1,\lambda}, \ldots, s_{n,1}, \ldots, s_{n,\lambda}$

3: $\pi \leftarrow$ random permutation on $[n\lambda]$

4: $\mathbf{s}' := \pi(\mathbf{s})$

5: $\mathbf{z}' \leftarrow \mathsf{P}^*(\mathbf{s}')$

6: $T \leftarrow$ random λ sized subset of $[n] \times [\lambda]$

7: $\forall i \in [n], j \in [\lambda], b_{i,j} = \begin{cases} 0 & ; z'_{i,j} = f(s'_{i,j}) \\ 1 & ; \text{otherwise} \end{cases}$

8: $\mathbf{b} := b_{1,1}, \ldots, b_{1,\lambda}, \ldots, b_{n,1}, \ldots, b_{n,\lambda}$

9: $\mathbf{b}^{\mathsf{inv}} := \pi^{-1}(\mathbf{b})$

Now, based on the above experiment, we define the advantage of an adversarial prover P^* for an arbitrary instance $\mathbf{x}$:

$$\mathsf{Adv}_{\delta,\Delta}^{\text{1-RSR}}(P^*, \mathbf{x}) = \Pr \left[\begin{array}{c} \exists i \in [n], \mathsf{RW}(b_{i,1}^{\text{inv}} || \ldots || b_{i,\lambda}^{\text{inv}}) > \delta + \Delta \\ \\ \wedge \\ \\ \mathsf{RW}(\mathbf{b}_T) = 0 \end{array} \quad : \ \mathsf{Exp}^{\text{1-RSR}}(P^*, \mathbf{x}) \right]$$

In a protocol execution with malicious prover P^*, $\mathbf{b}$ will be an arbitrary bitstring. We will now prove some properties about any arbitrary bitstring $\mathbf{b}$ which will enable us to finally establish the soundness claim.

Lemma 1. *Suppose* $\mathbf{b} \in \{0,1\}^{n\lambda}$ *is an arbitrary bitstring of length* $n\lambda$. *We sample a uniformly random subset* $T \subset [n\lambda]$ *and use* $\mathbf{b}_T$ *to denote the corresponding* $|T|$ *sized substring of* b. *Let* $B_T^\delta = \{\mathbf{b}' \in \{0,1\}^{n\lambda} : |\mathsf{RW}(\mathbf{b}') - \mathsf{RW}(\mathbf{b}_T)| < \delta\}$ *be the set of all* $n\lambda$-*length strings which are"* δ-*close" to the substring* b_T *in terms of relative Hamming weight. Then, for all* $\mathbf{b} \in \{0,1\}^{n\lambda}$ *and real-valued* $\delta \in (0,1)$:

$$\Pr_T[\mathbf{b} \notin B_T^\delta] \leq 2 \cdot e^{-2\delta^2 |T|}$$

where the probability is over the sampling of subset T.

Proof. The proof for the above lemma follows directly from Hoeffding's bound (Theorem 3).

Lemma 2. *Suppose* $\mathbf{b} \in \{0,1\}^{n\lambda}$ *is an arbitrary bitstring of length* $n\lambda$. *Let* $P_1, \ldots, P_n$ *be a random partitioning of the bits of* $\mathbf{b}$ *where each partition contains exactly* λ *bits. Then, for all* $\mathbf{b} \in \{0,1\}^{n\lambda}$, $\forall i \in [n]$, $\forall \Delta \in (0,1)$:

$$\Pr[|\mathsf{RW}(\mathbf{b}) - \mathsf{RW}(\mathbf{b}_{P_i})| \geq \Delta] \leq 2 \cdot e^{-2\Delta^2 \lambda}$$

where the probability is over the sampling of random partition.

Proof. The proof follows directly from Hoeffding's bound (Theorem 3).

Corollary 7. *Let* F *denote a indicator random variable denoting the following failure event:*

$$F = \begin{cases} 1 & \exists i \in [n], s.t. \ |\mathsf{RW}(\mathbf{b}) - \mathsf{RW}(\mathbf{b}_{P_i})| \geq \Delta \\ 0 & otherwise \end{cases}$$

Then, we have that:

$$\Pr[F = 1] \leq n \cdot 2 \cdot e^{-2\Delta^2 \lambda}$$

Proof. The proof follows directly by applying Lemma 2 and union bounding across all n partitions.

Lemma 3. *Suppose* $\mathbf{b}$ *is an arbitrary bitstring from* $\{0,1\}^{n\lambda}$. *We probe a random substring* $\mathbf{b}_T$, *of size* $|T|$, *from* $\mathbf{b}$. *Also, let* $P_1, \ldots, P_n$ *be a random partitioning of the bits of* $\mathbf{b}$ *where each partition contains exactly* λ *bits. Then, for all* $n \in \mathbb{N}, \lambda \in \mathbb{N}, \mathbf{b} \in \{0,1\}^{n\lambda}$, *real valued* $\delta, \Delta \in (0,1)$, *it holds that:*

$$\Pr \begin{bmatrix} \exists i \in [n], \mathsf{RW}(P_i) \geq \delta + \Delta \\ \wedge \\ \mathsf{RW}(\mathbf{b}_T) = 0 \end{bmatrix} \leq 2 \cdot e^{-2\delta^2 |T|} + n \cdot 2 \cdot e^{-2\Delta^2 \lambda}$$

Proof. Consider the following indicator random variables.

$$E_1^\delta = \begin{cases} 1 & \mathbf{b} \in \{\mathbf{b}' \in \{0,1\}^{n\lambda} : |\mathsf{RW}(\mathbf{b}') - \mathsf{RW}(\mathbf{b}_T)| \geq \delta\} \\ 0 & \text{otherwise} \end{cases}$$

$$E_2^\Delta = \begin{cases} 1 & \exists i \in [n], \text{s.t. } |\mathsf{RW}(\mathbf{b}) - \mathsf{RW}(\mathbf{b}_{P_i})| \geq \Delta \\ 0 & \text{otherwise} \end{cases}$$

$$E_3 = \begin{cases} 1 & \mathsf{RW}(\mathbf{b}_T) \neq 0 \\ 0 & \text{otherwise} \end{cases}$$

From the probability bounds from Lemma 1 and Lemma 2, we get the following bound. For all $\mathbf{b} \in \{0,1\}^{n\lambda}$, for all real-valued $\delta, \Delta \in (0,1)$:

$$\Pr[E_1^\delta = 1 \wedge E_2^\Delta = 1] \leq 2 \cdot e^{-2\delta^2 |T|} + n \cdot 2 \cdot e^{-2\Delta^2 \lambda} \tag{1}$$

This implies that:

$$\Pr[(E_1^\delta = 1 \wedge E_2^\Delta = 1) \bigwedge E_3 = 0] \leq 2 \cdot e^{-2\delta^2 |T|} + n \cdot 2 \cdot e^{-2\Delta^2 \lambda}$$

$$\implies \Pr \begin{bmatrix} \exists i \in [n], \mathsf{RW}(P_i) \geq \delta + \Delta \\ \wedge \\ \mathsf{RW}(\mathbf{b}_T) = 0 \end{bmatrix} \leq 2 \cdot e^{-2\delta^2 |T|} + n \cdot 2 \cdot e^{-2\Delta^2 \lambda}$$

Claim 1. *For all* $n \in \mathbb{N}, x \in \mathcal{X}^n$ *and for all arbitrary unbounded provers* P^*:

$$\mathsf{Adv}_{\delta,\Delta}^{\text{1-RSR}}(\mathsf{P}^*, \mathbf{x}) \leq 2 \cdot e^{-2\delta^2 |T|} + n \cdot 2 \cdot e^{-2\Delta^2 \lambda}$$

Proof. This follows directly from Lemma 3 and the definition of $\mathsf{Adv}_{\delta,\Delta}^{\text{1-RSR}}$.

Claim 2. *Fix* $|T| = \lambda$. *Then for all* $0 < \delta < 1$, *for* $n = 2^{\lambda^\delta}$, *for all* $\mathbf{x} \in \mathcal{X}^n$ *and for all arbitrary unbounded provers* P^*,

$$\mathsf{Adv}_{\delta=0.25,\Delta=0.25}^{\text{1-RSR}}(\mathsf{P}^*, \mathbf{x}) = \mathsf{negl}(\lambda)$$

Proof. By setting $\delta = 0.25$, $\Delta = 0.25$ in Claim 1, we get:

$$\mathsf{Adv}_{\delta=0.25,\Delta=0.25}^{\text{1-RSR}}(\mathsf{P}^*, \mathbf{x}) \leq \frac{2}{2^{0.18|T|}} + \frac{2n}{2^{0.18\lambda}}$$

For $n \leq 2^{0.17\lambda}$ and $|T| = \lambda$, we get,

$$\mathsf{Adv}_{\delta=0.25, \Delta=0.25}^{\text{1-RSR}}(\mathsf{P}^*, \mathbf{x}) \leq \frac{2}{2^{0.18\lambda}} + \frac{2n}{2^{0.18\lambda}}$$
$$= \mathsf{negl}(\lambda)$$

which proves the claim.

Remark 1. Claim 2 shows that one of the following two events will happen (except with some negligible probability): 1) the relative hamming weight in each random partition P_i of $\mathbf{b}$ is less than 0.5 or 2) the relative hamming weight of the random substring $\mathbf{b}_T$ is non-zero. In Case 1, this implies that for all $i \in [n]$, more than 50% of the $z_{i,j}$ are correct. This ensures that for all $i \in [n]$, more than 50% of $\{u_{i,j}\}_{j \in [\lambda]}$ will equal to $f(x_i)$. If this happens, for all $i \in [n]$, u_i^{final} will be equal to $f(x_i)$ due to the majority rule. In Case 2, the verifier will simply detect and abort as prescribed in Step 5 and 6 of the protocol. This concludes our soundness analysis.

5 Protocol for Functions Admitting K-RSR

In this section, we will extend the basic protocol from Sect. 4 to the more general case of functions which admit K-RSR for any constant $K > 1$. As an intermediate step, we will construct a protocol which is sound against a restricted class of provers. Specifically, we will consider a setting where the prover is a tuple of K no-signaling provers as defined in Definition 3. Finally, we will show how this "no-signaling" constraint can be computationally enforced using homomorphic encryption. Our final protocol will be sound against an arbitrary non-uniform PPT prover P.

5.1 OBVC with Multiple Provers

Protocol 5.1 describes our OBVC construction for functions that admit K-RSR. At a high level, the protocol is a simple extension of Protocol 4 in the following way: In K-RSR, each invocation of RSR.Encode(x_i) will yield K shares, each being uniformly random (although jointly they may be not). The verifier simply executes K instances of the protocol for 1-RSR setting where the kth prover P_k receives all the kth shares. In the end, the verifier simply aggregates the result from all the K provers and computes the output.

Theorem 8. *There exists a K-MOBVC scheme, specifically Protocol 5.1, for the class $\mathcal{F}_\ell^{K\text{-}RSR}$ consisting of all ℓ bit functions that admit K-RSR for any $K \geq 1$ with soundness against arbitrary unbounded no-signaling provers $\mathsf{P}_{\mathsf{no\text{-}sig}} = (\mathsf{P}_{\mathsf{no\text{-}sig}_1}, \ldots, \mathsf{P}_{\mathsf{no\text{-}sig}_K})$.*

Corollary 9. *For all $0 < \delta < 1$, $n \in O(2^{\lambda^\delta})$, Protocol 5.1 is an MOBVC scheme for $\mathcal{F}_\ell^{K\text{-}RSR}$ with soundness error $\mathsf{negl}(\lambda)$. Alternatively, one could set $\lambda = \omega(\log n)$ and get a soundness error of $\mathsf{negl}(n)$.*

In the rest of this section, we will prove Theorem 8. We note that the completeness of Protocol 5.1 follows directly from the correctness property of RSR. We now proceed to discuss non-triviality, efficiency and prove soundness.

Protocol 5.1

Common input: 1^λ, 1^n, f
V's additional input: Inputs $x_1, \ldots, x_n$, oracle $\mathcal{O}_f$, helper oracles $\mathcal{O}_{\mathsf{RSR.Encode}_f}$, $\mathcal{O}_{\mathsf{RSR.Decode}_f}$.
P's additional input: Circuit C_f for computing f.

1. For each x_i, V generates λ independent RSR instances. Formally, $\forall i \in [n], j \in [\lambda]$: $\{s_{i,j,k}\}_{k \in [K]}, \mathsf{st}_{i,j} \leftarrow \mathcal{O}_{\mathsf{RSR.Encode}_f}(x_i)$.
2. $\forall k \in [K]$, the following steps are performed:
   (a) V sets $\mathbf{s}^k := s_{1,1,k}, \ldots, s_{1,\lambda,k}, \ldots, s_{n,1,k}, \ldots, s_{n,\lambda,k}$.
   (b) V samples a random permutation π^k on $[n\lambda]$ and sets $\mathbf{s}'^k := \pi^k(\mathbf{s}^k)$. It sends $\mathbf{s}'^k$ to P_k.
   (c) $\forall i \in [n], j \in [\lambda], \mathsf{P}_k$ computes $z'_{i,j,k} := C_f(s'^k_{i,j})$
   (d) P_k sets $\mathbf{z}'^k := z'_{1,1,k}, \ldots, z'_{1,\lambda,k}, \ldots, z'_{n,1,k}, \ldots, z'_{n,\lambda,k}$. It sends $\mathbf{z}'^k$ to V.
   (e) V samples a random subset $T^k \subset [n] \times [\lambda]$ of size λ and checks whether the following holds:

$$\forall (i,j) \in T^k : z'^k_{i,j} = \mathcal{O}_f(s'^k_{i,j})$$

   (f) If the check fails, then V outputs $\bot$. Otherwise it proceeds.
   (g) V computes $\mathbf{z}^k := (\pi^k)^{-1}(\mathbf{z}'^k)$.
3. $\forall i \in [n], j \in [\lambda]$, V computes $u_{i,j} \leftarrow \mathcal{O}_{\mathsf{RSR.Decode}_f}(\{z^k_{i,j}\}_{k \in [K]}, \mathsf{st}_{i,j})$.
4. $\forall i \in [n]$, V sets $u_i^{\mathsf{final}} = \mathsf{Majority}(u_{i,1}, \ldots, u_{i,\lambda})$
5. V outputs $u_1^{\mathsf{final}}, \ldots, u_n^{\mathsf{final}}$

Non-triviality. In our protocol, the verifier uses two helper oracles namely $\mathcal{O}_{\mathsf{RSR.Encode}_f}$ and $\mathcal{O}_{\mathsf{RSR.Decode}_f}$. By Definition 2, we know that $T_{\mathsf{RSR}}.\mathsf{Encode}(\ell) + T_{\mathsf{RSR}}.\mathsf{Decode}(\ell) = o(T_f(\ell))$. Hence, our protocol satisifes the non-triviality condition.

Efficiency. For efficiency, we note that each helper oracle is invoked exactly $n\lambda$ times, the function oracle $\mathcal{O}_f$ is invoked exactly $K\lambda$ times and the running time of V is exactly $O(nK\lambda)$ as shuffling, majority and cut-and-chose check can be computed in linear time. Here K is a constant which depends on the function f (but independent of n, λ and ℓ).

Before proving soundness against no-signaling provers, we consider a relaxed case of "non-communicating" provers as an intermediate step. Such a prover is a tuple of K "non-communicating" local algorithms i.e. $\mathsf{P}_{\mathsf{no\text{-}com}} = (\mathsf{P}_1, \ldots, \mathsf{P}_K)$ where the next-message function of each P_i only depends on the messages it exchanges with V, and not on the interaction of V with other provers $\{P_j\}_{j \in [K], j \neq i}$.

Soundness analysis for non-communicating provers. We consider the following experiment capturing the execution of Protocol 5.1 with an arbitrary non-communicating prover $P^*_{\text{no-com}}$ and defines random variables $\mathbf{b}^k$ and its inverse $\mathbf{b}^{\text{inv}^k}$.

Experiment $\text{Exp}^{K\text{-RSR}}(P^*_{\text{no-com}}, \mathbf{x})$

1 : $\forall i \in [n], j \in [\lambda], \{s_{i,j,k}\}_{k \in [K]} \leftarrow \text{RSR.Encode}^j(x_i)$

2 : $\forall k \in [K]$:

3 : $\mathbf{s}^k := s_{1,1,k}, \ldots, s_{1,\lambda,k}, \ldots, s_{n,1,k}, \ldots, s_{n,\lambda,k}$

4 : $\pi^k \leftarrow$ random permutation on $[n\lambda]$

5 : $\mathbf{s}'^k := \pi^k(\mathbf{s}^k)$

6 : $\mathbf{z}'^k \leftarrow P^*_{\text{no-com} k}(\mathbf{s}'^k)$

7 : $T^k \leftarrow$ random λ sized subset of $[n] \times [\lambda]$

8 : $\forall i \in [n], j \in [\lambda], b^k_{i,j} = \begin{cases} 0 & ; z'^k_{i,j} = f(s'^k_{i,j}) \\ 1 & ; \text{otherwise} \end{cases}$

9 : $\mathbf{b}^k := b^k_{1,1}, \ldots, b^k_{1,\lambda}, \ldots, b^k_{n,1}, \ldots, b^k_{n,\lambda}$

10 : $\mathbf{b}^{\text{inv}^k} := (\pi^k)^{-1}(\mathbf{b}^k)$

11 :   Parse $\mathbf{b}^{\text{inv}^k}$ as $b^{\text{inv}^k}_{1,1}, \ldots, b^{\text{inv}^k}_{1,\lambda}, \ldots, b^{\text{inv}^k}_{n,1}, \ldots, b^{\text{inv}^k}_{n,\lambda}$

Based on the above experiment, we now define the advantage of the kth prover $P^*_{\text{no-com} k}$, for any arbitrary $k \in [K]$, on an arbitrary instance $\mathbf{x}$ in the following way.

$$\text{Adv}^{K\text{-RSR}}_{\delta, \Delta}(P^*_{\text{no-com} k}, \mathbf{x}) = \Pr \left[\begin{array}{c} \exists i \in [n], \text{RW}(b^{\text{inv}^k}_{i,1} || \ldots || b^{\text{inv}^k}_{i,\lambda}) > \delta + \Delta \\ \wedge \\ \text{RW}(\{b^k_{i,j}\}_{(i,j) \in T^k}) = 0 \end{array} : \text{Exp}^{K\text{-RSR}}(P^*_{\text{no-com}}, \mathbf{x}) \right] \quad (2)$$

Lemma 4. *For all $n \in \mathbb{N}$, $\lambda \in \mathbb{N}$, $\mathbf{x} \in \mathcal{X}^n$ and for all arbitrary unbounded non-communicating provers $P^*_{\text{no-com}} = (P^*_{\text{no-com} 1}, \ldots, P^*_{\text{no-com} K})$, $k \in [K]$ and real valued $\delta, \Delta \in (0, 1)$,*

$$\text{Adv}^{K\text{-RSR}}_{\delta, \Delta}(P^*_{\text{no-com} k}, \mathbf{x}) \leq 2 \cdot e^{-2\delta^2 T^k|} + n \cdot 2 \cdot e^{-2\Delta^2 \lambda}$$

Proof. This follows from Claim 1 and the fact that each individual share in K-RSR is uniformly random (and hence the view of $P^*_{\text{no-com} k}$ in Protocol 5.1 is identical to the view of P^* in Protocol 4).

Soundness analysis for no-signaling provers. In this section, we will extend the soundness analysis of Protocol 5.1 from non-communicating multi-provers to multi-provers who can communicate arbitrarily but follow a special "no-signaling" requirement which we formalize in Definition 3. To do so, we consider an experiment $\mathsf{Exp}^{K\text{-RSR}}(\mathsf{P}^*_{\text{no-sig}}, \mathbf{x})$ which captures the execution of Protocol 5.1 with an arbitrary fixed no-signaling prover $\mathsf{P}^*_{\text{no-sig}} = (\mathsf{P}_{\text{no-sig}_1}, \ldots, \mathsf{P}_{\text{no-sig}_K})$ and defines random variables $\mathbf{b}^k$ and its inverse $\mathbf{b}^{\text{inv}^k}$. This experiment is identical to $\mathsf{Exp}^{K\text{-RSR}}(\mathsf{P}^*_{\text{no-com}}, \mathbf{x})$ defined earlier except that we have switched from $\mathsf{P}^*_{\text{no-com}}$ to $\mathsf{P}^*_{\text{no-sig}}$.

Based on the experiment $\mathsf{Exp}^{K\text{-RSR}}(\mathsf{P}^*_{\text{no-sig}}, \mathbf{x})$, we now define the advantage of the kth prover $\mathsf{P}_{\text{no-sig}_k}$ in Eq. 3 and denote it by $\mathsf{Adv}^{K\text{-RSR}}(\mathsf{P}^*_{\text{no-sig}_k}, \mathbf{x})$.

$$\mathsf{Adv}^{K\text{-RSR}}_{\delta,\Delta}(\mathsf{P}^*_{\text{no-sig}_k}, \mathbf{x}) = \Pr \left[\begin{array}{c} \exists i \in [n], \mathsf{RW}(b^{\text{inv}^k}_{i,1} || \ldots || b^{\text{inv}^k}_{i,\lambda}) > \delta + \Delta \\ \wedge \\ \mathsf{RW}(\mathbf{b}^k_{T^k}) = 0 \end{array} : \mathsf{Exp}^{K\text{-RSR}}(\mathsf{P}^*_{\text{no-sig}}, \mathbf{x}) \right] \quad (3)$$

Lemma 5. *Assume there exists a function $\epsilon(\cdot, \cdot, \cdot, \cdot, \cdot)$ such that for any arbitrary non-communicating multi-prover $\mathsf{P}^*_{\text{no-com}} = (\mathsf{P}^*_1, \ldots, \mathsf{P}^*_K)$, for all $\delta \in [0,1], \Delta \in [0,1], k \in K, n \in \mathsf{poly}(\lambda), x \in \mathcal{X}^n, \lambda \in \mathbb{N}$, it holds that $\mathsf{Adv}^{K\text{-RSR}}_{\delta,\Delta}(\mathsf{P}^*_{\text{no-com}_k}, \mathbf{x}) \leq \epsilon(\lambda, n, \delta, \Delta, K)$. Then it follows that for any arbitrary no-signaling multi-prover $\mathsf{P}^*_{\text{no-sig}} = (\mathsf{P}^*_1, \ldots, \mathsf{P}^*_K)$, there exists a negligible function $\mathsf{negl}(\cdot)$ such that for all $\delta \in [0,1], \Delta \in [0,1], k \in K, n = \mathsf{poly}(\lambda), x \in \mathcal{X}^n, \lambda \in \mathbb{N}$, it holds that:*

$$\mathsf{Adv}^{K\text{-RSR}}_{\delta,\Delta}(\mathsf{P}^*_{\text{no-sig}_k}, \mathbf{x}) \leq \epsilon(\lambda, n, \delta, \Delta, K) + \mathsf{negl}(\lambda)$$

Proof. Suppose the lemma is false i.e. there exists a no-signaling multi-prover $\mathsf{P}^*_{\text{no-sig}} = (\mathsf{P}^*_{\text{no-sig}_1}, \ldots, \mathsf{P}^*_{\text{no-sig}_K})$ and a fixed polynomial $p(\cdot)$ such that for infinitely many $\lambda \in \mathbb{N}$, there exists $\delta^* \in [0,1], \Delta^* \in [0,1], k^* \in K, n^* \in \mathsf{poly}(\lambda), x^* \in \mathcal{X}^n$ such that

$$\mathsf{Adv}^{K\text{-RSR}}_{\delta,\Delta}(\mathsf{P}^*_{\text{no-sig}_{k^*}}, \mathbf{x}^*) \geq \epsilon(\lambda, n^*, \delta^*, \Delta^*, K) + \frac{1}{\mathsf{poly}(\lambda)}$$

Given this, we can construct a new prover $\mathsf{P}^*_{\text{no-com}} = (\mathsf{P}^*_{\text{no-com}_1}, \ldots, \mathsf{P}^*_{\text{no-com}_K})$ which will contradict the ϵ upper bound for the advantage of $\mathsf{P}^*_{\text{no-com}_k}$.

$$P^*_{\text{no-com}_{k=k^*}}$$

1 : Receive $\mathbf{s}'^{k=k^*}$.

2 : For all $k \in [K], k \neq k^*$, set $\mathbf{s}'^k := \mathbf{0}^{n\lambda}$, where $\mathbf{0}$ is a default element.

3 :

4 : For all $k \in [K]$, send $\mathbf{s}'^k$ to $P^*_{\text{no-sig}_k}$.

5 : For all $k \in [K]$, receive $\mathbf{z}'^k$ from $P^*_{\text{no-sig}_k}$.

6 : Output $\mathbf{z}'^{k^*}$.

$$P^*_{\text{no-com}_{k \neq k^*}}$$

1 : Receive $\mathbf{s}'^k$.

2 : Output $\perp$.

From the above construction, it follows that:

$$\text{Adv}^{K\text{-RSR}}_{\delta,\Delta}(P^*_{\text{no-com}\,k^*}, \mathbf{x}^*) = \Pr \left[\begin{array}{c} \exists i \in [n], \text{RW}(b^{\text{inv}^{k^*}}_{i,1} || \ldots || b^{\text{inv}^{k^*}}_{i,\lambda}) > \delta + \Delta \\ \wedge \\ \text{RW}(\mathbf{b}^{k^*}_T) = 0 \end{array} : \text{Exp}'^{K\text{-RSR}}(P^*_{\text{no-sig}}, \mathbf{x}) \right],$$

$$(4)$$

where the experiment $\text{Exp}'^{K\text{-RSR}}(P^*_{\text{no-sig}}, \mathbf{x})$ is defined as follows (the difference from $\text{Exp}^{K\text{-RSR}}(P^*_{\text{no-sig}}, \mathbf{x})$ have been highlighted in blue):

Experiment $\text{Exp}'^{K\text{-RSR}}(P^*_{\text{no-sig}}, \mathbf{x})$
1 : $\forall i \in [n], j \in [\lambda], \{s_{i,j,k}\}_{k \in [K]} \leftarrow \text{RSR.Encode}^j(x_i)$
2 : $\forall k \in [K]$:
3 : $\mathbf{s}^k := \begin{cases} s_{1,1,k}, \ldots, s_{1,\lambda,k}, \ldots, s_{n,1,k}, \ldots, s_{n,\lambda,k} & ; k = k^* \\ \mathbf{0}^{n\lambda} & ; \text{otherwise} \end{cases}$
4 : $\pi^k \leftarrow$ random permutation on $[n\lambda]$
5 : $\mathbf{s}'^k := \pi^k(\mathbf{s}^k)$
6 : $\mathbf{z}'^k \leftarrow P^*_{\text{no-sig}_k}(\mathbf{s}'^k)$
7 : $T^k \leftarrow$ random λ sized subset of $[n] \times [\lambda]$
8 : $\forall i \in [n], j \in [\lambda], b^k_{i,j} = \begin{cases} 0 & ; z'^k_{i,j} = f(s'^k_{i,j}) \\ 1 & ; \text{otherwise} \end{cases}$
9 : $\mathbf{b}^k := b^k_{1,1}, \ldots, b^k_{1,\lambda}, \ldots, b^k_{n,1}, \ldots, b^k_{n,\lambda}$
10 : $\mathbf{b}^{\text{inv}^k} := (\pi^k)^{-1}(\mathbf{b}^k)$
11 : Parse $\mathbf{b}^{\text{inv}^k}$ as $b^{\text{inv}^k}_{1,1}, \ldots, b^{\text{inv}^k}_{1,\lambda}, \ldots, b^{\text{inv}^k}_{n,1}, \ldots, b^{\text{inv}^k}_{n,\lambda}$

Let p indicate the R.H.S probability value in Eq. 4. By the no-signaling property established in Definition 3, there exists $\mathsf{negl}(\cdot)$ such that:

$$p \geq \mathsf{Adv}_{\delta,\Delta}^{K\text{-RSR}}(\mathsf{P}^*_{\text{no-sig}\,k=k^*}, \mathbf{x}^*) - \mathsf{negl}(\lambda)$$

Since we have assumed (towards contradiction) that $\mathsf{Adv}_{\delta,\Delta}^{K\text{-RSR}}(\mathsf{P}^*_{\text{no-sig}\,k=k^*}, \mathbf{x}^*) \geq \epsilon(\lambda, n^*, \delta^*, \Delta^*, K) + \frac{1}{\mathsf{poly}(\lambda)}$, it follows that:

$$\mathsf{Adv}_{\delta,\Delta}^{K\text{-RSR}}(\mathsf{P}^*_{\text{no-com}\,k^*}, \mathbf{x}^*) = p \geq \epsilon(\lambda, n^*, \delta^*, \Delta^*, K) + \frac{1}{\mathsf{poly}(\lambda)} - \mathsf{negl}(\lambda)$$

This directly contradicts the fact that for any arbitrary non-communicating multi-prover $\mathsf{P}^*_{\text{no-com}} = (\mathsf{P}^*_1, \ldots, \mathsf{P}^*_K)$, for all $\delta \in [0,1], \Delta \in [0,1], k \in K, n = \mathsf{poly}(\lambda), x \in \mathcal{X}^n, \lambda \in \mathbb{N}$, it holds that $\mathsf{Adv}_{\delta,\Delta}^{K\text{-RSR}}(\mathsf{P}^*_{\text{no-com}\,k}, \mathbf{x}) \leq \epsilon(\lambda, n, \delta, \Delta, K)$.

We will now define the advantage of the overall prover system $\mathsf{P}^*_{\text{no-sig}} = (\mathsf{P}^*_{\text{no-sig}\,1}, \ldots, \mathsf{P}^*_{\text{no-sig}\,K})$ as follows:

$$\mathsf{Adv}_{\delta,\Delta}^{K\text{-RSR}}(\mathsf{P}^*_{\text{no-sig}}, \mathbf{x}) = \Pr \left[\begin{array}{c} \exists i \in [n], \mathsf{RW}\big(\big\|_{j\in[\lambda],k\in[K]}\, b_{i,j}^{\mathsf{inv}\,k}\big) > (\delta + \Delta) \\ \wedge \\ \mathsf{RW}(b_{T^1}^1 || \ldots || b_{T^K}^1) = 0 \end{array} \;\middle|\; \mathsf{Exp}^{K\text{-RSR}}(\mathsf{P}^*_{\text{no-sig}}, \mathbf{x}) \right] \quad (5)$$

Claim 3. *Fix $|T^1| = \ldots = |T^K| = \lambda$ and let K be some fixed constant. Then, for all $0 < \delta < 1$, for $n \in O(2^{\lambda^\delta})$, for all $\mathbf{x} \in \mathcal{X}^n$ and for all arbitrary unbounded no-signaling provers $\mathsf{P}^*_{\text{no-sig}}$,*

$$\mathsf{Adv}_{\delta=0.25/K,\Delta=0.25/K}^{K\text{-RSR}}(\mathsf{P}^*_{\text{no-sig}}, \mathbf{x}) = \mathsf{negl}(\lambda)$$

Proof. From Lemma 4 and Lemma 5, we know that:

$$\mathsf{Adv}_{\delta,\Delta}^{K\text{-RSR}}(\mathsf{P}^*_{\text{no-sig}\,k}, \mathbf{x}) \leq \epsilon(\lambda, n, \delta, \Delta, K) + \mathsf{negl}(\lambda)$$

where $\epsilon(\lambda, n, \delta, \Delta, K) = 2 \cdot e^{-2\delta^2|T^k|} + n \cdot 2 \cdot e^{-2\Delta^2\lambda}$.

By union bound, we note that $\mathsf{Adv}_{\delta,\Delta}^{K\text{-RSR}}(\mathsf{P}^*_{\text{no-sig}}, \mathbf{x}) \leq \Sigma_{k\in K}\mathsf{Adv}_{\delta,\Delta}^{(1,K)\text{-RSR}}(\mathsf{P}^*_{\text{no-sig}\,k}, \mathbf{x})$.

Assuming $|T^1| = \ldots = |T^K| = |T|$, we get that:

$$\mathsf{Adv}_{\delta,\Delta}^{K\text{-RSR}}(\mathsf{P}^*_{\text{no-sig}}, \mathbf{x}) \leq 2K \cdot e^{-2\delta^2 T|} + n \cdot 2K \cdot e^{-2\Delta^2\lambda} + K \cdot \mathsf{negl}(\lambda)$$

By setting $\delta = 0.25/K, \Delta = 0.25/K$, we get:

$$\mathsf{Adv}_{\delta=0.25/K,\Delta=0.25/K}^{K\text{-RSR}}(\mathsf{P}^*_{\text{no-sig}}, \mathbf{x}) \leq \frac{2K}{2^{0.18\,T|/K^2}} + \frac{2nK}{2^{0.18\lambda/K^2}} + K \cdot \mathsf{negl}(\lambda)$$

For constant K, $n \leq 2^{\frac{0.17\lambda}{K^2}}$ and $|T| = \lambda$, we get,

$$\mathsf{Adv}^{K\text{-RSR}}_{\delta=0.25/K, \Delta=0.25/K}(\mathsf{P}^*_{\text{no-sig}}, \mathbf{x}) \leq \frac{2K}{2^{\frac{0.18}{K^2}\lambda}} + \frac{2nK}{2^{\frac{0.18}{K^2}\lambda}} + K \cdot \mathsf{negl}(\lambda)$$
$$= \mathsf{negl}(\lambda)$$

Remark 2. Claim 3 shows that one of the following two events will happen (except with some negligible probability): 1) For all $i \in [n]$, the relative hamming weight of the string $\big\|_{j \in [\lambda], k \in [K]} b^{\mathsf{inv}^k}_{i,j}$ is less than $0.5/K$ or 2) the relative hamming weight of the substring $\mathbf{b}^1_{T^1} \| \ldots \| \mathbf{b}^1_{T^K}$ is non-zero. In Case 1, this implies that for all $i \in [n]$, for more than 50% of the j values, all $\{z^k_{i,j}\}_{k \in [K]}$ are correct. This ensures that for all $i \in [n]$, more than 50% of $\{u_{i,j}\}_{j \in [\lambda]}$ will equal to $f(x_i)$. If this happens, for all $i \in [n]$, u^{final}_i will be equal to $f(x_i)$ due to the majority rule. In Case 2, the verifier will simply detect and abort as prescribed in the protocol. This concludes our soundness proof.

5.2   OBVC with a Single Prover

We will now provide a OBVC protocol for all the class of all K-RSR functions which is sound against a single non-uniform PPT prover. The protocol construction is almost identical to the Protocol 5.1 except for the following modification: The verifier samples a fresh HE key pair for each RSR instance and encrypts it before sending it to the prover. The prover is supposed to respond with HE encrypted values obtained by performing a homomorphic evaluation of the circuit C_f on the ciphertexts sent by the verifier. We describe the protocol formally in Fig. 5.2.

Theorem 10. *Let $\mathcal{F}^{K\text{-RSR}}_\ell$ denote the class of all ℓ bit functions that admit K-RSR for any $K \geq 1$. Assuming a homomorphic encryption scheme for $\mathcal{F}^{K\text{-RSR}}_\ell$, there exists a OBVC scheme, specifically Protocol 5.2, for $\mathcal{F}^{K\text{-RSR}}_\ell$ with soundness against arbitrary non-uniform PPT provers.*

Corollary 11. *For all $\lambda = \omega(\log n)$, Protocol 5.2 is an OBVC scheme for $\mathcal{F}^{K\text{-RSR}}_\ell$ with soundness error $\mathsf{negl}(n)$ against non-uniform PPT provers.*

In the rest of this section, we will prove Theorem 10. We note that the completeness of Protocol 5.2 follows directly from the correctness property of RSR and $\mathcal{F}$-homomorphism property of the HE scheme. We now proceed to discuss non-triviality, privacy, efficiency and prove soundness.

Non-triviality, Privacy and Efficiency Analysis. In our protocol, the verifier uses two helper oracles namely $\mathcal{O}_{\mathsf{RSR.Encode}_f}$ and $\mathcal{O}_{\mathsf{RSR.Decode}_f}$. By Definition 2, we know that $T_{\mathsf{RSR}}.\mathsf{Encode}(\ell) + T_{\mathsf{RSR}}.\mathsf{Decode}(\ell) = o(T_f(\ell))$. Hence, our protocol satisfies the non-triviality condition.

The privacy of our protocol follows directly from the CPA-security of the underlying HE scheme. More formally, the simulator $\mathsf{Sim}(1^\lambda, 1^n, \mathcal{X})$ simply runs the verifier V on inputs $x_1 = \ldots = x_n = \mathbf{0}$ where $\mathbf{0}$ is a default element in the domain of f. By the CPA-security of HE scheme and a standard hybrid argument, the view of the server in the real protocol will be computationally indistinguishable from the simulated view.

For efficiency, note that each helper oracle is invoked exactly $n\lambda$ times and the $\mathcal{O}_f$ is invoked exactly $K\lambda$ times. For security parameter λ, let $T_{\mathsf{HE.Keygen}}(\lambda)$, $T_{\mathsf{HE.Enc}}(\lambda)$ and $T_{\mathsf{HE.Dec}}(\lambda)$ denote the time-complexity of HE.Keygen, HE.Enc and HE.Dec respectively. Then the running time of V is exactly $O(nK\lambda(T_{\mathsf{HE.Keygen}}(\lambda) + \ell \cdot T_{\mathsf{HE.Enc}}(\lambda) + \ell \cdot T_{\mathsf{HE.Dec}}(\lambda)))$ as the bottleneck cost comes from generating HE keys for each of the $nK\lambda$ shares i.e. $\{s_{i,j,k}\}_{i\in[n],j\in[\lambda],k\in[K]}$ and then encrypting and decrypting them. The other steps like shuffling, majority and cut-and-chose check can be computed in linear time. Here K is a constant which depends on the function f (but independent of n, λ and ℓ).

Protocol 5.2

Common input: 1^λ, 1^n, f
V's additional input: Inputs $x_1, \ldots, x_n$, oracle $\mathcal{O}_f$, helper oracles $\mathcal{O}_{\mathsf{RSR.Encode}_f}$, $\mathcal{O}_{\mathsf{RSR.Decode}_f}$.
P's additional input: Circuit C_f for computing f.

1. For each x_i, V generates λ independent RSR instances Formally, $\forall i \in [n], j \in [\lambda]$: $\{s_{i,j,k}\}_{k\in[K]}, \mathsf{st}_{i,j} \leftarrow \mathcal{O}_{\mathsf{RSR.Encode}_f}(x_i)$.
2. $\forall i \in [n], j \in [\lambda], k \in [K]$, V generates $\mathsf{pk}_{i,j,k}, \mathsf{sk}_{i,j,k} \leftarrow \mathsf{HE.Keygen}(1^\lambda)$.
3. $\forall i \in [n], j \in [\lambda], k \in [K]$, V computes $\mathsf{ct}_{i,j,k} \leftarrow \mathsf{HE.Enc}_{\mathsf{pk}_{i,j,k}}(1^\lambda, s_{i,j,k})$.
4. For all $k \in [K]$, it sets $\mathbf{s}^k := (\mathsf{ct}_{1,1,k}, \mathsf{pk}_{1,1,k}), \ldots, (\mathsf{ct}_{1,\lambda,k}, \mathsf{pk}_{1,\lambda,k}), \ldots, (\mathsf{ct}_{n,1,k}, \mathsf{pk}_{n,1,k}), \ldots, (\mathsf{ct}_{n,\lambda,k}, \mathsf{pk}_{n,\lambda,k})$.
5. $\forall k \in [K]$, V samples a random permutation π_k on $[n\lambda]$ and sets $\mathbf{s}'^k := \pi_k(\mathbf{s}^k)$.
6. V sends $\mathbf{s}'^1, \ldots, \mathbf{s}'^K$ to P.
7. $\forall k \in [K]$, P parses $s'^k_{i,j}$ as $(\mathsf{ct}_*, \mathsf{pk}_*)$ and computes $\mathsf{ct}'_{i,j,k} := \mathsf{HE.Eval}_{\mathsf{pk}_*}(C_f, \mathsf{ct}_*)$.
8. $\forall k \in [K]$, P sets $\mathbf{z}'^k := \mathsf{ct}'_{1,1,k}, \ldots, \mathsf{ct}'_{1,\lambda,k}, \ldots, \mathsf{ct}'_{n,1,k}, \ldots, \mathsf{ct}'_{n,\lambda,k}$.
9. P sends $\mathbf{z}'^1, \ldots, \mathbf{z}'^K$ to V.
10. $\forall k \in [K]$, V samples a random subset $T^k \subset [n] \times [\lambda]$ of size λ and checks whether the following holds:

$$\forall (i,j) \in T^k : \mathsf{HE.Dec}_{\mathsf{sk}_{i',j',k}}(\mathbf{z}'^k_{i,j}) = f(s^k_{i',j'})$$

where $(i', j') := \pi_k^{-1}(i,j)$.
11. If the check fails, then V outputs $\bot$. Otherwise it proceeds.
12. $\forall k \in [K]$, V computes $\mathbf{z}^k := \pi_k^{-1}(\mathbf{z}'^k)$.
13. $\forall i \in [n], j \in [\lambda]$, V computes $u_{i,j} \leftarrow \mathcal{O}_{\mathsf{RSR.Decode}_f}(\{w_{i,j,k}\}_{k\in[K]}, \mathsf{st}_{i,j})$, where $w_{i,j,k} = \mathsf{Dec}_{sk_{i,j,k}}(z^k_{i,j})$
14. $\forall i \in [n]$, V sets $u_i^{\mathsf{final}} = \mathsf{Majority}(u_{i,1}, \ldots, u_{i,\lambda})$
15. V outputs $u_1^{\mathsf{final}}, \ldots, u_n^{\mathsf{final}}$

Soundness Analysis. Now we will show how the security of Protocol 5.1 against arbitrary no-signaling multi-prover $P_{no\text{-}sig}$ can be carried over to the security of Protocol 5.2 against arbitrary non-uniform PPT prover P. As mentioned earlier, the main ingredient used in Protocol 5.2 is an HE scheme. The main idea behind the security proof amounts to showing that any malicious PPT prover in Protocol 5.2 will conform to the notion of no-signaling prover as defined in Definition 3. The formal proof follows via reduction to the CPA-security of the HE scheme. We refer the readers to the full version.

6 Impossibility of Oracle-Aided Batch Verifiable Computation

Definition 6. *A $(s(\lambda), t(\lambda), q(\lambda), n(\lambda))$ OBVC scheme $\Pi = (P, V)$ in the $\mathcal{O}$ model is defined as follows.*

- *The verifier V which is a two-staged entity i.e. $V = (V_1, V_2)$. V_1 is computationally unbounded; it interacts with $\mathcal{O}$.pre and outputs an s-bit "advice" string. V_2 is computationally bounded and also query bounded. It takes an s-bit auxiliary input and makes at most t queries to $\mathcal{O}$.main.*
- *The prover P which is a single staged entity and makes at most q queries to $\mathcal{O}$.main. There is no computational bound on the prover.*

We will use the notation $\langle P^{\mathcal{O}}, V^{\mathcal{O}} \rangle_\Pi$ to denote the following protocol interaction:

- *V_1 interacts with $\mathcal{O}$.pre and outputs an s-bit "advice" string.*
- *V_1 passes a s-bit auxiliary input aux to V_2.*
- *Sample a batch of instances $I \subseteq [M]$ where $|I| = n$. Send I to V_2.*
- *P and V_2 interact with each other while having access to $\mathcal{O}$.main.*
- *V_2 returns OUT in the end.*

The scheme Π satisfies the following properties.

- *Completeness: For all $\lambda \in \mathbb{N}$,*

$$\Pr[\text{OUT} = \mathcal{O}(x_1^I), \ldots, \mathcal{O}(x_n^I)] = 1$$

- *Soundness: For all adversarial P^*, there exists a negligible function $\mathsf{negl}(\cdot)$ s.t. for all $\lambda \in \mathbb{N}$:*

$$\Pr[\text{OUT} = \mathcal{O}(x_1^I), \ldots, \mathcal{O}(x_n^I) \vee \text{OUT} = \bot] = 1 - \mathsf{negl}(\lambda)$$

- *Efficiency: We say that an OBVC scheme is efficient if the $s(\lambda) \in \mathsf{poly}(\lambda)$ and $t(\lambda) \in o(n(\lambda))$.*

Theorem 12. *For all $n \in \mathsf{poly}(\lambda)$, $\alpha' \in (0, 1]$, $t \in o(n)$, $q = q(\lambda)$, $s \in \mathsf{poly}(\lambda)$, for every (s, t, q, n) OBVC scheme $\Pi = (P, V)$ in the $\mathcal{O} := \mathsf{BF\text{-}RO}(M = 2^\lambda, N = 2^\lambda, p = 2^{(1-\alpha')\lambda})$ model, there exists a malicious prover P_{mal} and noticeable function $\epsilon'(\lambda)$ s.t. for all $\lambda \in \mathbb{N}$:*

$$\Pr\left[\text{OUT} \neq \mathcal{O}(x_1^I), \ldots, \mathcal{O}(x_n^I) \wedge \text{OUT} \neq \bot : \text{OUT} \leftarrow \langle P_{mal}^{\mathcal{O}}, V^{\mathcal{O}} \rangle_\Pi \right] \geq \epsilon'(\lambda)$$

Proof. Refer to the full version.

We will now lift the above theorem from the Bit-fixing RO model to Auxiliary-input RO model.

Theorem 13. *For all $n \in \mathsf{poly}(\lambda)$, $\alpha \in (0, 1]$, $q = 2^{(1-\alpha)\lambda}$, $t \in o(n)$, $s \in \mathsf{poly}(\lambda)$, for every (s, t, q, n) OBVC scheme $\Pi = (\mathsf{P}, \mathsf{V})$ in the $\mathcal{O} := \mathsf{AI\text{-}RO}(M = 2^\lambda, N = 2^\lambda)$, there exists a malicious prover P_{mal} and noticeable function $\epsilon(\lambda)$ s.t. for all $\lambda \in \mathbb{N}$:*

$$\Pr\left[\,\mathsf{OUT} \neq \mathcal{O}(x_1^I), \ldots, \mathcal{O}(x_n^I) \wedge \mathsf{OUT} \neq \perp : \mathsf{OUT} \leftarrow \langle \mathsf{P}_{mal}^{\mathcal{O}}, \mathsf{V}^{\mathcal{O}} \rangle_\Pi\,\right] \geq \epsilon(\lambda)$$

Proof. The formal proof leverages Theorem 4. We refer the readers to the full version.

Disclaimer

Acknowledgments. A. Agarwal and D. Khurana were supported in part by NSF CAREER CNS-2238718, DARPA SIEVE and an award from Visa Research. This material is based upon work supported by the Defense Advanced Research Projects Agency through Award HR00112020024.

References

1. Alman, J., Williams, V.V.: A refined laser method and faster matrix multiplication. In: Proceedings of the 2021 ACM-SIAM Symposium on Discrete Algorithms (SODA), pp. 522–539. SIAM (2021)

2. Applebaum, B., Ishai, Y., Kushilevitz, E.: From secrecy to soundness: efficient verification via secure computation. In: Abramsky, S., Gavoille, C., Kirchner, C., Meyer auf der Heide, F., Spirakis, P.G. (eds.) ICALP 2010. LNCS, vol. 6198, pp. 152–163. Springer, Heidelberg (2010). https://doi.org/10.1007/978-3-642-14165-2_14

3. Ar, S., Blum, M., Codenotti, B., Gemmell, P.: Checking approximate computations over the reals. In: Proceedings of the Twenty-Fifth Annual ACM Symposium on Theory of Computing, pp. 786–795 (1993)

4. Beaver, D., Feigenbaum, J., Kilian, J., Rogaway, P.: Locally random reductions: improvements and applications. J. Cryptol. **10**(1), 17–36 (1997)

5. Bellare, M., Garay, J.A., Rabin, T.: Batch verification with applications to cryptography and checking. In: Lucchesi, C.L., Moura, A.V. (eds.) LATIN 1998. LNCS, vol. 1380, pp. 170–191. Springer, Heidelberg (1998). https://doi.org/10.1007/BFb0054320

6. Bellare, M., Rogaway, P.: Random oracles are practical: a paradigm for designing efficient protocols. In: Proceedings of the 1st ACM Conference on Computer and Communications Security, pp. 62–73 (1993)

7. Blum, M., Luby, M., Rubinfeld, R.: Self-testing/correcting with applications to numerical problems. In: Proceedings of the Twenty-Second Annual ACM Symposium on Theory of Computing, pp. 73–83 (1990)

8. Blum, M., Luby, M., Rubinfeld, R.: Program result checking against adaptive programs. In: Distributed Computing and Cryptography: Proceedings of a DIMACS Workshop, October 4–6, 1989, vol. 2, p. 107. American Mathematical Soc. (1991)

9. Brakerski, Z., Holmgren, J., Kalai, Y.: Non-interactive ram and batch NP delegation from any PIR. Cryptology ePrint Archive (2016)

10. Brakerski, Z., Holmgren, J., Kalai, Y.: Non-interactive delegation and batch NP verification from standard computational assumptions. In: Proceedings of the 49th Annual ACM SIGACT Symposium on Theory of Computing, pp. 474–482 (2017)

11. Brakerski, Z., Vaikuntanathan, V.: Efficient fully homomorphic encryption from (standard) LWE. SIAM J. Comput. **43**(2), 831–871 (2014)

12. Choudhuri, A.R., Jain, A., Jin, Z.: Non-interactive batch arguments for NP from standard assumptions. In: Malkin, T., Peikert, C. (eds.) CRYPTO 2021. LNCS, vol. 12828, pp. 394–423. Springer, Cham (2021). https://doi.org/10.1007/978-3-030-84259-8_14

13. Choudhuri, A.R., Jain, A., Jin, Z.: Snargs for $\mathcal{P}$ from LWE. In: 62nd IEEE Annual Symposium on Foundations of Computer Science, FOCS 2021, Denver, CO, USA, February 7–10, 2022. pp. 68–79. IEEE (2021). https://doi.org/10.1109/FOCS52979.2021.00016

14. Chung, K.-M., Kalai, Y., Vadhan, S.: Improved delegation of computation using fully homomorphic encryption. In: Rabin, T. (ed.) CRYPTO 2010. LNCS, vol. 6223, pp. 483–501. Springer, Heidelberg (2010). https://doi.org/10.1007/978-3-642-14623-7_26

15. Cleve, R., Luby, M.: A note on self-testing/correcting methods for trigonometric functions. International Computer Science Inst. (1990)

16. Coretti, S., Dodis, Y., Guo, S., Steinberger, J.: Random oracles and non-uniformity. In: Nielsen, J.B., Rijmen, V. (eds.) EUROCRYPT 2018. LNCS, vol. 10820, pp. 227–258. Springer, Cham (2018). https://doi.org/10.1007/978-3-319-78381-9_9

17. Dodis, Y., Guo, S., Katz, J.: Fixing cracks in the concrete: random oracles with auxiliary input, revisited. In: Coron, J.-S., Nielsen, J.B. (eds.) EUROCRYPT 2017. LNCS, vol. 10211, pp. 473–495. Springer, Cham (2017). https://doi.org/10.1007/978-3-319-56614-6_16

18. Gemmell, P., Lipton, R., Rubinfeld, R., Sudan, M., Wigderson, A.: Self-testing/Correcting for polynomials and for approximate functions. In: STOC, vol. 91, pp. 32–42. Citeseer (1991)
19. Gennaro, R., Gentry, C., Parno, B.: Non-interactive verifiable computing: outsourcing computation to untrusted workers. In: Rabin, T. (ed.) CRYPTO 2010. LNCS, vol. 6223, pp. 465–482. Springer, Heidelberg (2010). https://doi.org/10.1007/978-3-642-14623-7_25
20. Hoeffding, W.: Probability inequalities for sums of bounded random variables. The Collected Works of Wassily Hoeffding, pp. 409–426 (1994)
21. Hulett, J., Jawale, R., Khurana, D., Srinivasan, A.: SNARGs for P from sub-exponential DDH and QR. In: Dunkelman, O., Dziembowski, S. (eds.) Advances in Cryptology - EUROCRYPT 2022, Part II. Lecture Notes in Computer Science, vol. 13276, pp. 520–549. Springer, Heidelberg, Germany, Trondheim, Norway (May 30 - Jun 3, 2022). https://doi.org/10.1007/978-3-031-07085-3_18
22. Jawale, R., Kalai, Y.T., Khurana, D., Zhang, R.Y.: SNARGs for bounded depth computations and PPAD hardness from sub-exponential LWE. In: Khuller, S., Williams, V.V. (eds.) STOC '21: 53rd Annual ACM SIGACT Symposium on Theory of Computing, Virtual Event, Italy, June 21–25, 2021, pp. 708–721. ACM (2021). https://doi.org/10.1145/3406325.3451055
23. Kalai, Y.T., Raz, R., Rothblum, R.D.: How to delegate computations: the power of no-signaling proofs. In: Proceedings of the Forty-Sixth Annual ACM Symposium on Theory of Computing, pp. 485–494 (2014)
24. Kilian, J.: A note on efficient zero-knowledge proofs and arguments. In: Proceedings of the Twenty-Fourth Annual ACM Symposium on Theory of Computing, pp. 723–732 (1992)
25. Lipton, R.: New directions in testing. Distrib. Comput. Crypt. 2, 191–202 (1991)
26. Micali, S.: Computationally sound proofs. SIAM J. Comput. 30(4), 1253–1298 (2000)
27. Rubinfeld, R.: Batch checking with applications to linear functions. Inf. Process. Lett. 42(2), 77–80 (1992)
28. Unruh, D.: Random oracles and auxiliary input. In: Menezes, A. (ed.) CRYPTO 2007. LNCS, vol. 4622, pp. 205–223. Springer, Heidelberg (2007). https://doi.org/10.1007/978-3-540-74143-5_12
29. Waters, B., Wu, D.J.: Batch arguments for np and more from standard bilinear group assumptions. In: Annual International Cryptology Conference, pp. 433–463. Springer, Cham (2022). https://doi.org/10.1007/978-3-031-15979-4_15

Theoretical Foundations

Counting Unpredictable Bits: A Simple PRG from One-Way Functions

Noam Mazor[1](✉) and Rafael Pass[1,2]

[1] Cornell Tech, New York, USA
noammaz@gmail.com, rafaelp@tau.ac.il
[2] Tel-Aviv University, Tel Aviv, Israel

Abstract. A central result in the theory of Cryptography, by Håstad, Imagliazzo, Luby and Levin [SICOMP'99], demonstrates that the existence one-way functions (OWF) implies the existence of pseudo-random generators (PRGs). Despite the fundamental importance of this result, and several elegant improvements/simplifications, analyses of constructions of PRGs from OWFs remain complex (both conceptually and technically).

Our goal is to provide a construction of a PRG from OWFs with a *simple proof of security*; we thus focus on the setting of *non-uniform* security (i.e., we start off with a OWF secure against non-uniform PPT, and we aim to get a PRG secure against non-uniform PPT).

Our main result is a construction of a PRG from OWFs with a self-contained, simple, proof of security, relying only on the Goldreich-Levin Theorem (and the Chernoff bound). Although our main goal is simplicity, the construction, and a variant there-of, also improves the efficiency— in terms of invocations and seed lengths—of the state-of-the-art constructions due to [Haitner-Reingold-Vadhan, STOC'10] and [Vadhan-Zheng, STOC'12], by a factor $O(\log^2 n)$.

The key novelty in our analysis is a generalization of the Blum-Micali [FOCS'82] notion of unpredictabilty—rather than requiring that every bit in the output of a function is unpredictable, we count how many unpredictable bits a function has, and we show that any OWF on n input bits (after hashing the input and the output) has $n + O(\log n)$ unpredictable output bits. Such unpredictable bits can next be "extracted" into a pseudorandom string using standard techniques.

N. Mazor—Part of this work was done while at Tel Aviv University and while visiting the Simons Institute. Research partly supported by Israel Science Foundation grant 666/19, NSF CNS-2149305 and NSF CNS-2128519.

R. Pass—Part of this work was done while visiting the Simons Institute. Supported in part by NSF Award CNS 2149305, NSF Award SATC-1704788, NSF Award RI-1703846, AFOSR Award FA9550-18-1-0267, and a JP Morgan Faculty Award. This material is based upon work supported by DARPA under Agreement No. HR00110C0086. Any opinions, findings and conclusions or recommendations expressed in this material are those of the author(s) and do not necessarily reflect the views of the United States Government or DARPA.

© International Association for Cryptologic Research 2023
G. Rothblum and H. Wee (Eds.): TCC 2023, LNCS 14369, pp. 191–218, 2023.
https://doi.org/10.1007/978-3-031-48615-9_7

1   Introduction

Pseudorandom generators (PRGs) are one of the most fundamental crypto-graphic building blocks [BM82]. Roughly speaking, a PRG is a function taking a seed of length n and expanding it into a longer string, of say, length $2n$, such that the output string is indistinguishable from random. While the existence of PRGs almost immediately implies the existence of one-way functions (OWF), it is significantly harder to show that OWFs imply the existence of PRGs. Indeed, the first construction of PRGs from OWFs was obtained in the seminal work by Håstad, Impagliazzo, Luby and Levin (HILL) [HILL99]. This beautiful work introduced a host of new notions and techniques and is a technical *tour-de-force*. To understand the importance of this result, let us remark that still today, known constructions of e.g., secure private-key encryption [GM84], commitment schemes [Nao91], zero-knowledge [GMW87], pseudorandom functions [GGM84] from the minimal assumption of OWFs, all pass through the notion of a PRG and the result of [HILL99].

Consequently, it would be desirable to come up with simpler construc-tions/proofs of the existence of PRGs from OWFs. Additionally, the PRGs con-struction of HILL, while asymptotically efficient, has a large polynomial running time. In particular, the PRG requires invoking the underlying OWFs $O(n^{11})$ times, where n is the security parameter. Since then, several simplifications and improvements (in terms of the efficiency of the construction) were obtained by Holenstein [Hol06a], Haitner, Harnik and Reingold [HHR06], Haitner, Reingold and Vadhan [HRV13], Vadhan and Zheng [VZ12], leading up to constructions of PRGs from OWFs using only $\omega(n^3)^1$ *non-adaptive* invocations of the underlying OWF, and using a seed of length $\omega(n^4)$; additionally, Vadhan and Zheng [VZ12] show how to improve the seed length to $\omega(n^3 \log n)$, but at the price of using an adaptive construction. Finally, Haitner and Vadhan [HV17] obtained a construc-tion with a simpler security proof (focusing only on the setting on non-uniform security), but which required $\omega(n^6 \log n)$ invocations of the OWF. But despite these beautiful works—and the intriguing new notions that they introduce—the security proofs involved remain quite complicated (even the simplest one with looser parameters in [HV17]).

Our Results. The goal of this paper is to provide a simple, self-contained, proof of the existence of PRGs from any OWFs. Our proof relies only on standard results such as the Goldreich-Levin (GL) Theorem [GL89] and the Chernoff bound (and in case we want to optimize the seed-length using an adaptive construction, also the Leftover-hash Lemma (LHL) [HILL99]). The hope is that our proof will enable teaching the construction of a PRG from any OWF in graduate course in Cryptography.

---

[1] More formally, for any function $q(n) = \omega(n^3)$, there exists a construction of a PRG from OWFs that uses q calls. HRV [HRV13] state their result with additional $\log n$ factor in both the seed length and the number of calls. However, the improved parameters can be easily deduced from their main theorem.

Following Haitner and Vadhan [HV17], as our (main) goal is to present a security proof that is as easy as possible, we focus on the setting of *non-uniform* security (i.e., we start off with a OWF that is secure against non-uniform poly-time algorithms, and obtain a PRG secure against non-uniform polytime algorithms). (As we note in the full version of this paper, our proof of security also readily adapts to the uniform setting if we rely on Holenstein's Uniform Hard-core Lemma [Hol06b].)

Perhaps surprisingly, along the way, we manage to also improve the concrete efficiency of the PRG, obtaining a construction that only requires invoking the underlying OWF $\omega(n^3/\log^2 n)$ number of times, shaving a factor $\log^2 n$ from the best constructions [HRV13, VZ12], both in terms of number of invocations and seed length. (On a very high level, this improvement comes from the fact that we are relying on a simpler notion of "pseudo-entropy" and can next rely on a simpler 0–1 Chernoff bound instead of a "multi-valued" Chernoff bound as in [HRV13], which results in a tighter bound.)

Our main result is a non-adaptive construction of a PRG from any OWFs, with a simple proof of security.

Theorem 1.1 (Non-adaptive Construction of a PRG from OWFs).
Assume the existence of a one-way function secure against non-uniform polynomial-time algorithms. Then there exists a PRG secure against non-uniform polynomial-time algorithms that non-adaptively invokes the underlying OWF $\omega(n^3/\log^2 n)$ times, and that has a seed of length $\omega(n^4/\log^2 n)$.

As mentioned above, Vadhan and Zheng [VZ12] showed how to use adaptive calls to the underlying OWF to improve the seed length in the construction of [HRV13]; we note that the same method applies also to our construction enabling us again to shave $\log^2 n$ in the number of invocations of f and the seed length.

Theorem 1.2 (Adaptive PRG Construction from OWF with improved seed length). *Assume the existence of a one-way function secure against non-uniform polynomial-time algorithms. Then there exist a PRG secure against non-uniform polynomial-time algorithms that adaptively invokes the underlying OWF $\omega(n^3/\log^2 n)$ times, and that has a seed of length $\omega(n^3/\log n)$.*

On Concrete Efficiency (Exponentially-Hard OWFs). While shaving a $\log^2 n$ factor may not seem significant (when the running time is $O(n^3)$, this does make a significant difference in the regime of exponential security, or in the regime of concrete security. In particular, if we start off with an exponentially-secure OWF (i.e., a OWF secure against circuits of size $2^{\Omega(n)}$), then we can get a PRG that only invokes the OWF $\omega(\log n)$ times. This matches the bound of the best PRG from exponentially-secure OWFs from Haitner, Harnik and Reingold [HHR06], but only uses *non-adaptive* calls to the underlying OWF, whereas [HHR06] required adaptive calls, and may make the construction more feasible in practice. On the downside, our construction uses a seed of length $O(n^2)$, while [HHR06] uses seed of length $\omega(n \log n)$. We believe we can get a similar seed length using a better hash function, but we defer the details to a future version.

Theorem 1.3. *Assume the existence of a one-way function secure against circuits of size $2^{\Omega(n)}$. Then there exists a PRG secure against non-uniform polynomial-time algorithms that non-adaptively invokes the underlying OWF $\omega(\log n)$ times.*

We remark that the final PRG is also secure against exponential-size attackers, but only achieves negligible indisitinguishability gap.

The Key Insight: Counting Unpredictable Bits. Starting with the work of HILL, the key method for constructing a PRG from OWFs is to start with a OWF and turning it into a generator of some "weak" form of pseudorandomness. Later these weak forms of pseudorandomness can be gradually amplified to achieve full pseudorandomness. Towards this, HILL introduced the notion of *pseudo-entropy*—roughly speaking, which requires a distribution to be indistinguishable from a distribution with some entropy. Haitner, Reingold and Vadhan [HRV13](HRV) improved and simplified the HILL construction by introducing and working with a relaxed notion of *next-block pseudo-entropy*, where following earlier notions of pseudorandomness by Shamir [Sha83] and Blum-Micali [BM82], we focus on the ability of a distinguisher to learn something about the next "block" in a sequence—and in more detail, this next block is required to have "high pseudo-entropy in expectation over random blocks (see [HRV13] for the formal definition).

In this work, we consider a strengthening of the HRV notion (which is incomparable to HILL notion): We start by going back to the "plain" notion of *unpredictability* from Blum-Micali [BM82]: Recall that we say that a function satisfies *unpredictability for the i-th bit*, if no non-uniform PPT attacker can guess the i-th bit of the output of the function on a random input given the first $i-1$ bits. We are interesting in *counting* how many unpredictable bits a function has. The simplest way to do this would be to say that a function has k unpredictable bits if there exists a set S of indexes, with $|S| \geq k$, such that for each $i \in S$, the i-th bit is unpredictable for f.

Such a notion will be a bit too strong for our needs—we want to allow the indexes of the unpredictable bits to depend on the inputs. We do this by allowing the set $S(x)$ of "unpredictable bits" to be a function of the input x, and we require that for each bit i in the union of the support of $S(U_n)$, we have that unpredictability of the i-th bit holds *conditioned* on sampling an input x such that $i \in S(x)$ (That is, unpredictability of bit i holds whenever i is in the set of "unpredictable bits"). To measure the number of such unpredictable bits, we simply consider the expected size of $S(U_n)$: Roughly speaking, we say that a function has $k(\cdot)$ unpredictable bits if for every inverse polynomial ϵ, there exists function S such that (1) the expected size of $S(U_n)$ is at least $k(n)$, and (2) the bits specified by S are ϵ-unpredictable. More formally,

Definition 1.4. *We say that a function $g : \{0,1\}^{m(n)} \rightarrow \{0,1\}^{\ell(n)}$ has $k(\cdot)$-unpredictable bits if for every inverse polynomial $\epsilon(\cdot)$, there exists some S such that (1) for all $n \in \mathbb{N}$, $\mathrm{E}\left[\left|S(U_{m(n)})\right|\right] \geq k(n)$, and (2) for all nonuniform PPT*

A, *every sufficiently large* n, *every* $i \in \bigcup_{x \in \{0,1\}^{m(n)}} \text{Supp}(\mathcal{S}(x))$, A *distinguishes between*

- $\{x \leftarrow \{0,1\}^{m(n)} | i \in \mathcal{S}(x) \ : \ g(x)_{<i}, g(x)_i\}$
- $\{x \leftarrow \{0,1\}^{m(n)} | i \in \mathcal{S}(x) \ : \ g(x)_{<i}, U\}$

with probability at most $\epsilon(n)$.

For our purposes, we will need to generalize this definition to also apply to *families* of functions $\{g_h\}_{h \in \{0,1\}^*}$, where the above conditions hold for g_h for a randomly sampled "key" h (looking forward, for us, this key will just be the description of a hash function based on inner-products mod 2).

2   Proof Overview

We present here our whole construction and provide a detailed proof overview—in essence, the below description provides *the whole proof* except that it omits standard hybrid arguments/reductions. (The formal proof in Sects. 4 to 7 of course provides those details). We note that our construction closely follows the construction paradigm of HRV but due to the use of our notion of unpredictability, as opposed to next-bit pseudoentropy, we are able to simplify the analysis in the non-uniform setting (and improve its parameters).

Let M be an $n \times n$ binary matrix, and we define the hash function $M(x) = Mx$ mod 2, where x is interpreted as a binary vector. A simple form of the Leftover-hash Leamm (LHL) [HILL99] states that $\{M, M(X)_k)\}$ is $1/\text{poly}(n)$-close to $\{M, U_k\}$, if X has min-entropy $k + c \log n$ for a sufficiently large c, and when M is sampled at random from the set of $n \times n$ binary matrices.[2]

- **Step 1: Unpredictability Generators from Regular OWF.** We start by showing how to turn any *regular* OWF—recall that for a $r(\cdot)$-regular OWF, each element in the support of the function on inputs of length n has between $2^{r(n)-1}$ and $2^{r(n)}$ pre-images—into a function family that has $n + O(\log n)$ unpredictable bits; we refer to such function as an "unpredictability generator".

  For inputs of length n, the construction is defined as:

$$g_M(x) = M(f(x)) \| M(x),$$

  where the "hash function" M is described by an $n \times n$ binary matrix. In other words, we are applying n GL-predicates to $f(x)$, and then the same n GL

---

[2]   As an additional didactic contribution, we show that this simple form of the LHL follows as a direct corollary of the GL-theorem; while this observation may already be folklore, as far as we know, it has not been explicitly stated anywhere (more than for the case of extracting 1, or $O(\log n)$ bits).

predicates to x.[3]

First, note that the since $f(\cdot)$ is $r(\cdot)$-regular, $f(U_n)$ has min-entropy $n-r(n)-1$ and thus by the (simple) LHL the first $n - r(n) - O(\log n)$ bits of $M(f(x))$ are $1/\mathrm{poly}(n)$-close to uniform, and thus unpredictable. Next, we want to argue that bits $n + 1, \ldots, n + r(n) + c \log n$, for any c, also are unpredictable. Assume not; that is, there exists some efficient algorithm P and some index i such that

$$P(f(x), M, M(x)_{<i}) = M(x)_i$$

with inverse polynomial advantage. By the GL theorem, this means that there exists some PPT algorithm E such that $E(f(x), M, M(x)_{<i}) = x$ with inverse polynomial probability, which in turn means that there exists some E' that computes x with probability $2^{-i}/\mathrm{poly}(n) \geq 2^{-r(n)-O(\log n)}$ given just $f(x)$ (by guessing $M(x)_{<i}$). But since $f(x)$ has at least $2^{r(n)-1}$ pre-images, and all of which are equally likely, we have that the probability that $\Pr\left[E'(f(x)) = x\right] = \Pr\left[E'(f(x)) \in f^{-1}(f(x))\right]/2^{r(n)-1}$, and thus E' inverts f with inverse polynomial probability, which is a contradiction.

Thus, we conclude that for every inverse polynomial ϵ, there exists a set S of ϵ-unpredictable indexes of size $[n - r(n) - O(\log n)] + [r(n) + c \log n] = n + (c - O(1)) \log n$ (and which contains indexes $1, \ldots n - r(n) - O(\log n)$, as well as $n + 1, \ldots n + r(n) + c \log n$).

(Note that the set S depends on the unpredictability advantage ϵ, but so far does not depend on the input x.)

- **Step 2: Unpredictability Generators from Any OWF.** We next show that the same construction actually works also for *any* (not necessarily regular) OWF. This directly follows from the observation that any OWF can be essentially split into regular OWFs on a partition of the input domain. In more detail, we can partition the input domain of the OWF into domains $D_1, D_2, \ldots$, such that (1) for each r, f is r-regular when restricted to D_r— refer to this function as f^r, and (2) for each r such that D_r has inverse polynomial density in $\{0, 1\}^n$,[4] we have that f is one-way also on D_j. The set D_j is simply the inputs $x \in \{0, 1\}^n$ such that $f(x)$ has between 2^{j-1} and 2^j pre-images, and note that condition 2 follows directly from the assumption that f is one-way.

---

[3] We note that this step differs from the next-bit pseudo-entropy generator of HRV where H is only applied to x and not $f(x)$; this is the crucial difference that allows us to get unpredictability as opposed to next-bit pseudo-entropy. Additionally, we note that HRV has to work with a specially constructed hash function H (based on concatenation of a Reed-Solomon Code and the Hadamard code); Haitner and Vadhan [HV17] showed how to just use the standard GL predicate, but this gave a final PRG construction with significantly worse parameters. Finally, Vadhan and Zheng [VZ12] show how to analyze also the construction without any hash function (achieving the same parameters as HRV), but this requires a much more complicated proof.

[4] Formally, $r = r(n)$ is a function of the input length n, and we here require the density condition to hold for all $n \in N$.

Now, consider the set of "common" r's such that D_r has inverse polynomial density (and thus f^r is one-way). By Step 1, we have shown that there exists some (appropriately large) set S_r of unpredictable indexes for every f^r such that r is "common", and for every such $x \in D_r$ we define $S(x) = S_r$. For the remaining x's (that correspond to rare regularities), let $S(x)$ simply be the empty set. By a union bound over the n possible regularities, it follows that $S(x)$ is set to the empty set only for a small fraction of inputs, and thus the expected size of $S(U_n)$ is still $n + O(\log n)$.

To show that unpredictability holds, assume for contradiction that there exists some i in the (union) of the support of $S(U_n)$ such that bit i can be predicted with inverse polynomial probability conditioned on $i \in S(x)$ for infinitely many input lengths n. Then, note that $i \in S(x)$ implies that $x \in D_r$ for some "common" regularity r, so we can always find some common r (for each input length n) such that prediction also succeeds conditioned on $x \in D_r$ (for infinitely many input lengths), but this contradicts the unpredictability of bit i for the function f^r.

- **Step 3: From Unpredictability to Random-Index Unpredictability.** In the next step, we consider a slightly stronger notion of unpredictability. Rather than bounding the expected size of the unpredictable set, the notion of $k(\cdot)$-**random bits unpredictability** requires that for each index i, we have that $\Pr[i \in S(U_n)] \geq k(n)/\ell(n)$, where $\ell(\cdot)$ denotes the output length of the function. Note that by the linearity of expectation, this directly implies "plain" k-bits unpredictability (so this notion is a strengthening of "plain" unpredictability).

To turn an unpredictability generator into a random bit unpredictability generator, we rely on the same transformation as Haitner et al. [HRV13] used in their "entropy equalization step" (and which was first used by [HRVW09]). Given a function $g : \{0,1\}^n \to \{0,1\}^{\ell(n)}$ that has k-bit unpredictability, consider the "shifted" direct-product function g':

$$g'(i, x^1, \ldots, x^r) = g(x^1)_{\geq i} || g(x^2) || \ldots || g(x^{r-1}) || g(x^r)_{<i}$$

where $i \in [\ell(n)], x^j \in \{0,1\}^n$ (see Fig. 1). That is, we apply the function g on r random inputs, output the concatenation (i.e., the direct product) and then simply truncate the $i-1$ bits from the beginning and the $\ell - (i-1)$ bits from the end, for a random i (specified by the inputs).

Note that each bit of g' is part of the unpredictable set for f with probability $k(n)/\ell(n)$. To see this, note that clearly a random index into g is part of the unpredictable set for g with probability $k(n)/\ell(n)$; but each bit of g' has exactly the same distribution as a random bit of g. Thus, g' has $(r-1)k(n)$ random unpredictable bits (while using a seed of length $n \cdot r + \log \ell(n)$).

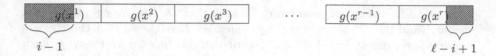

$i - 1$ $\ell - i + 1$

Fig. 1. The construction of a function with random-bits-unpredictability from a function $g: \{0,1\}^n \to \{0,1\}^{\ell(n)}$ with bits-unpredictability. We take r copies of g, and truncate the $i - 1$ first bits and $\ell - i + 1$ last bits, such that the output, marked in white, is of length $(r - 1)\ell$.

Finally, recall that the function obtained in Step 2 has a seed of length n, outputs $2n$ bits and has $(n + c \log n)$-bit unpredictability, for any c. If we plug in this function into g, we get a function with seed length $nr + O(\log n)$, output length $2(r-1)n$ and satisfying $(r-1)(n + c \log n)$-random bit unpredictability. To get "expansion" (i.e., more unpredictable bits than the seed length), we set $r = n/\log n$, which results in a function $g : \{0,1\}^{n^2/\log n + O(\log n)} \to \{0,1\}^{2n^2/\log n - 2n}$ that has $n^2/\log n + c \cdot n)$ random unpredictable bits, for any c.

- **Step 4: Pseudorandomness from Random-Bit Unpredictability.** In the final step, we show how to turn any generator of random-bit unpredictability into a standard PRG. The transformation is simple and goes back to HILL; it was also used by HRV to turn next-bit pseudo-entropy into pseudorandomness, but for us, it will be even simpler (and due to this reason we can also improve the parameters from HRV).

  The transformation consists of doing a t-wise direct product of a function $g : \{0,1\}^{m(n)} \to \{0,1\}^{\ell(n)}$ that has $k(n)$ random unpredictable bits, and then applying any (seeded) extractor *coordinate-wise* to the outputs of g. In more details, the ith block of the output will be $H(g(x^1)_i, g(x^2)_i, \ldots g(x^t)_i)$, where H is an appropriate hash function, selected as part of the seed (and which also can be included in the output). (See Fig. 2).

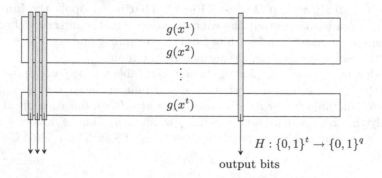

Fig. 2. Extracting pseudoentropy from a function g with random-bits unpredictability. We take t copies of g and apply a hash function (random matrix) on every column.

To analyze this construction, first note that by a standard hybrid argument, we simply need to show that each such output block i is indistinguishable from uniform given the prefix up to block i. Next—and this is the key step— note that we can furthermore move to a hybrid where for each $j \in [t]$, we replace $g(x^j)_i$ with a random bit whenever i is in the unpredictable set for x^j. Indistinguishability of the real experiment and this hybrid follows from the definition of unpredictability through an essentially standard hybrid argument, but there is an important subtlety: The set $S(x)$ is not efficiently computable, so in the hybrid argument it is not clear how to efficiently emulate the hybrids (and in particular, in Hybrid j, how to simulate all other "rows" $j' \neq j$). Since we are in the non-uniform setting, this issue, however, is easy to deal with: we can simply non-uniformly pick the best choices for those values.Finally, by the Chernoff bound, we have that except with negligible probability, the number of "rows" j such bit i is unpredictable for g is at least $t \cdot k(n)/\ell(n) - \sqrt{tw(\log n)}$, and thus all those bits will be uniform in the above hybrid. It follows that the min-entropy of the string on which we apply the extractor is $t \cdot k(n)/\ell(n) - \sqrt{tw(\log n)}$ and thus roughly this many bits may be extracted from each block; thus in total, we get $t \cdot k(n) - \ell\sqrt{tw(\log n)}$ pseudorandom bits.

The input is of length $t \cdot m(n)$, so we need to choose t such that $t \cdot k(n) - \ell\sqrt{tw(\log n)} > t \cdot m(n)$, which yields $t \geq \omega(\log n)\ell^2/(k - m)^2$. Plugging in the construction from Step 3, we have that $k(n) = m(n) + O(n)$, $\ell(n) = O(n^2/\log n)$ which yields $t \geq \omega(\log n\ell^2/n^2) = \omega(n^2/\log n)$.

Note that the total seed length becomes $t \cdot m(n) + |H| = \omega(n^4/\log^2 n) + |H|$. If we rely on a random matrix as a hash function (and the above simplified LHL), its description length will be $t(n)^2 = n^4/\log^2 n$ (see Fig. 3 for the complete construction).[5]

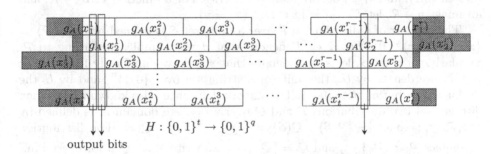

$$H : \{0,1\}^t \to \{0,1\}^q$$

output bits

Fig. 3. The non-adaptive PRG construction. There are $t \approx n^2/\log n$ rows, each row has $r \approx n/\log n$ i.i.d copies of $g_A(x) = (A(f(x)), A(x))$, shifted by a random offset. Every fully populated column, marked in white, is hashed by H.

---

[5] In this step we save $\log^2 n$ factor over HRV. The reason is that we apply the Chernoff bound on a random variable that can only take zero-one values, while HRV consider the *sample entropy* of the next bit, which can take larger values.

Further Improving the Seed Length: Vadhan and Zheng [VZ12] presented an elegant approach for shaving a factor $n/\log n$ in terms of the seed length in the construction of HRV. Their idea is to note that to compute "coordinate" j, we do not actually need to know the "seed" $x^{j'}$ to earlier coordinates $j' < j$, and thus we can take the input to coordinate $j - 1$ from coordinate j (while additionally outputting $O(\log n)$ bits). The same method can be applied to our construction and can be analyzed in a modular way. (We note that we do not claim any original contributions w.r.t. this step on top of [VZ12]; the only "novelty" here is the modular analysis of their construction.) Doing this yields an (adaptive) construction with seed length $\omega(n^3/\log n) + |H|$. So, to take advantage of this saving, we also need to have a hash function with a better description length. This is easily obtain by using a standard constructions of pair-wise independent hash functions (e.g., $h_{a,b}(x) = ax + b$ where the operations are over $\mathbb{F}_{2^n}$) and appealing to the standard LHL [HILL99] (instead of the above simplified form), which yields a description length of $O(t(n)) = O(n^2/\log^2 n)$, and thus a total seed length of $\omega(n^3/\log n)$.

3 Preliminaries

3.1 Notations

All logarithms are taken in base 2. We use calligraphic letters to denote sets and distributions, uppercase for random variables, and lowercase for values and functions. Let poly stand for the set of all polynomials. Let PPT stand for probabilistic poly-time, and n.u.-poly-time stand for non-uniform poly-time. An n.u.-poly-time algorithm A is equipped with a (fixed) poly-size advice string set $\{z_n\}_{n \in \mathbb{N}}$ (that we typically omit from the notation). Let neg stand for a negligible function. For $n \in \mathbb{N}$, let $[n] := \{1, \ldots, n\}$. Given a vector $s \in \{0,1\}^n$, let s_i denote its i-th entry, and $s_{1,\ldots,i}$ denote its first i entries. For a function $f : \mathcal{D} \to \mathcal{R}$, and an image $y \in \mathcal{R}$, let $f^{-1}(y) = \{x \in \mathcal{D} : f(x) = y\}$.

The support of a distribution $\mathcal{P}$ over a finite set $\mathcal{S}$ is defined by $\mathrm{Supp}(\mathcal{P}) := \{x \in \mathcal{S} : \mathcal{P}(x) > 0\}$. Let $d \leftarrow \mathcal{P}$ denote that d was sampled according to $\mathcal{P}$. Similarly, for a set $\mathcal{S}$, let $s \leftarrow \mathcal{S}$ denote that s is drawn uniformly from $\mathcal{S}$. For $n \in \mathbb{N}$, we denote by U_n the uniform distribution over $\{0,1\}^n$, and by U the uniform distribution over $\{0,1\}$. The statistical distance (also known as, variation distance) of two distributions $\mathcal{P}$ and $\mathcal{Q}$ over a discrete domain $\mathcal{X}$ is defined by $\mathrm{SD}(\mathcal{P}, \mathcal{Q}) := \max_{\mathcal{S} \subseteq \mathcal{X}} |\mathcal{P}(\mathcal{S}) - \mathcal{Q}(\mathcal{S})| = \frac{1}{2} \sum_{x \in \mathcal{S}} |\mathcal{P}(x) - \mathcal{Q}(x)|$. For distribution ensembles $\mathcal{P} = \{\mathcal{P}_n\}_{n \in \mathbb{N}}$ and $\mathcal{Q} = \{\mathcal{Q}_n\}_{n \in \mathbb{N}}$ we write $\mathcal{P} \overset{c}{\approx}_\epsilon \mathcal{Q}$ if for every n.u.-poly-time A, for all but finitely many n's, $|\Pr[A(\mathcal{P}_n) = 1] - \Pr[A(\mathcal{Q}_n) = 1]| \leq \epsilon(n)$. We write $\mathcal{P} \overset{c}{\approx} \mathcal{Q}$ if $|\Pr[A(\mathcal{P}_n) = 1] - \Pr[A(\mathcal{Q}_n) = 1]| = \mathrm{neg}(n)$ for every such A.

Lastly, we identify a matrix $M \in \{0,1\}^{n \times m}$ with a function $M : \{0,1\}^n \to \{0,1\}^m$ by $M(x) := x \cdot M \bmod 2$, thinking of $x \in \{0,1\}^n$ as a vector with dimension n.

3.2   One-Way Functions and Pseudorandom Generators

We now formally define basic cryptographic primitives. We start with the definition of one-way function.

Definition 3.1 (One-way function). *A polynomial-time computable function* $f : \{0,1\}^* \to \{0,1\}^*$ *is called a* n.u-one-way *function if for every n.u.-poly-time algorithm A, there is a negligible function $\nu : \mathbb{N} \to [0,1]$ such that for every $n \in \mathbb{N}$*

$$\Pr_{x \leftarrow \{0,1\}^n} \left[A(f(x)) \in f^{-1}(f(x)) \right] \leq \nu(n)$$

For simplicity, we assume that the one-way function f is length-preserving. That is, $|f(x)| = |x|$ for every $x \in \{0,1\}^*$. This can be assumed without loss of generality, and is not crucial for our constructions.

In Sect. 4 we use one-way functions to construct PRGs. The latter is formally defined below.

Definition 3.2 (Pseudorandom generator). *Let n be a security parameter. A polynomial-time computable function $G : \{0,1\}^n \to \{0,1\}^{m(n)}$ is called a* n.u-pseudorandom generator *if for every $n > 0$ it holds that $m(n) > n$ and, for every n.u.-poly-time algorithm D, there is a negligible function $\nu : \mathbb{N} \to [0,1]$ such that for every $n > 0$,*

$$\left| \Pr_{x \leftarrow \{0,1\}^n} [D(G(x)) = 1] - \Pr_{x \leftarrow \{0,1\}^{m(n)}} [D(x) = 1] \right| \leq \nu(n).$$

As in this paper we are focusing on the non-uniform setting, we will refer to n.u-one-way functions and n.u-PRGs simply by one-way functions and PRGs.

A key ingredient in the construction of PRG from one way function is the Goldreich-Levin hardcore predicate. We will use the following version, which is a combination between Goldreich-Levin and Yao's distinguishing to prediction lemma [Yao82].

Lemma 3.3 (Goldreich-Levin [GL89, Yao82]). *There exists an oracle-aided PPT A such that the following holds. Let $n \in N$ be a number, and $\mathcal{Q}$ a distribution over $\{0,1\}^n \times \{0,1\}^*$, and let D be an algorithm such that*

$$\Pr_{(x,z) \leftarrow \mathcal{Q}, r \leftarrow \{0,1\}^n} [D(z, r, \mathrm{GL}(x,r)) = 1]$$

$$- \Pr_{(x,z) \leftarrow \mathcal{Q}, r \leftarrow \{0,1\}^n} [D(z, r, U) = 1] \geq \alpha$$

for some α, where $\mathrm{GL}(x,r) := \langle x, r \rangle$ is the Goldreich-Levin predicate. Then

$$\Pr_{(x,z) \leftarrow \mathcal{Q}} \left[A^D(1^n, 1^{\lceil 1/\alpha \rceil}, z) = x \right] \geq \alpha^3/8n.$$

3.3   Min-Entropy and Extraction

The min-entropy of a distribution $\mathcal{Q}$, denoted by $\mathrm{H}_\infty(\mathcal{Q})$ is defined by

$$\mathrm{H}_\infty(\mathcal{Q}) := -\log(\max_{q \in \mathrm{Supp}(\mathcal{Q})} \{\Pr[\mathcal{Q} = q]\}).$$

We will use the following simplified version of the leftover hash lemma, which shows that a random matrix is a strong extractor.

Lemma 3.4 (Leftover hash lemma, simplified version). *Let $n \in \mathbb{N}$, $\varepsilon \in [0,1]$, and let X be a random variable over $\{0,1\}^n$. Let $M \leftarrow \{0,1\}^{n \times \ell}$ be a random matrix for $\ell \leq H_\infty(X) - 3\log 1/\varepsilon - 4\log n - 4$. Then,*

$$SD((M, M(X)), (M, U_\ell)) \leq \varepsilon$$

for U_ℓ being the uniform distribution over $\{0,1\}^\ell$.

The above (simplified) version of the leftover hash lemma can be proven using GL. (The proof may be folklore, but we have not previously seen it in the literature.)

Proof. Let $\ell \leq H_\infty(X) - 3\log(1/\epsilon) - 4\log n - 4 < n$, and let $M \leftarrow \{0,1\}^{n \times \ell}$ be a random matrix. Assume there exists an (inefficient) algorithm that distinguishes $M, M(X)$ from M, U_ℓ with advantage ϵ. By a simple hybrid argument, there exists an (inefficient) distinguisher D and an index $i \in [\ell]$, such that

$$\Pr\left[D(M, M(X)_{<i}, M(X)_i) = 1\right] - \Pr\left[D(M, M(X)_{<i}, U) = 1\right] \geq \epsilon/\ell \geq \epsilon/n.$$

Observe that $M(X)_i = \langle M_i, X \rangle$ is the GL hard-core predicate, and thus we get that there exists algorithm A such that $\Pr[A(M, M(X)_{<i}) = X] \geq \epsilon^3/8n^4$. Consider the algorithm A' that given M, guess $M(X)_{<i}$ and runs A. Clearly,

$$\Pr[A'(M) = X] \geq 2^{-i} \cdot \epsilon^3/8n^4 \geq 2^{-\ell} \cdot \epsilon^3/8n^4 > 2^{-H_\infty(X)},$$

which is a contradiction, since M is independent from X.   □

We will also use the well-known Chernoff bound in our proof.

Fact 3.5 (Chernoff bound). *Let $A_1, ..., A_n$ be independent random variables s.t. $A_i \in \{0,1\}$. Let $\widehat{A} = \Sigma_{i=1}^n A_i$ and $\mu = E\left[\widehat{A}\right]$. For every $\epsilon \in [0,1]$ It holds that:*

$$\Pr\left[\left|\widehat{A} - \mu\right| \geq \epsilon \cdot \mu\right] \leq 2 \cdot e^{-\epsilon^2 \cdot \mu/3}.$$

4   Unpredictable Bits

In this section we define bits-unpredictability, which is the main building block in the construction. We will consider such a notion of unpredictability for families of functions.

Definition 4.1 (Unpredictable bits). *Let $m = m(n)$, $\ell = \ell(n)$, $\lambda = \lambda(n)$ and $k = k(n)$ be integer functions, and let $\epsilon = \epsilon(n) \in [0,1]$. We say that a function family $g = \left\{g_a \colon \{0,1\}^{m(n)} \to \{0,1\}^{\ell(n)}\right\}_{a \in \{0,1\}^{\lambda(n)}}$ has (k, ϵ)-bits-unpredictability if for every $n \in \mathbb{N}$ and $x \in \{0,1\}^{m(n)}$, there exists a set $\mathcal{S}(x) \subseteq [\ell(n)]$, such that, for $X_n \leftarrow \{0,1\}^{m(n)}$ and $A \leftarrow \{0,1\}^{\lambda(n)}$:*

1. *For every n, $\mathrm{E}\left[|S(X_n)|\right] \geq k(n)$, and,*
2. *for every sequence $\{i_n\}_{n \in \mathbb{N}}$ such that $i_n \in \bigcup_{x \in \{0,1\}^{m(n)}} S(x)$,*

$$\left\{\left(A, g_A(X_n)_{<i_n}, g_A(X_n)_{i_n}\right)|_{i_n \in S(X_n)}\right\}_{n \in \mathbb{N}}$$

$$\overset{c}{\approx}_\epsilon \left\{\left(A, g_A(X_n)_{<i_n}, U\right)|_{i_n \in S(X_n)}\right\}_{n \in \mathbb{N}}.$$

We say that g has k-bits-unpredictability if it has (k, n^{-c})-bits-unpredictability for every $c \in \mathbb{N}$.

We will also consider a stronger notion of unpredictability—called k-*random-bit unpredictability*, that requires each individual bit to be unpredictable with probability k/ℓ where ℓ is the output length.

Definition 4.2 (Random bits unpredictability). *Let $m = m(n)$, $\ell = \ell(n)$ and $k = k(n)$ be integer functions, and let $\epsilon = \epsilon(n) \in [0,1]$. We say that a function family $g = \left\{g_a \colon \{0,1\}^{m(n)} \to \{0,1\}^{\ell(n)}\right\}_{a \in \{0,1\}^{\lambda(n)}}$ has (k, ϵ)-random-bits-unpredictability if it satisfies Definition 4.1 except that condition (1) is replaced by:*

1. *For every $i \in [\ell(n)]$, $\Pr\left[i \in S(X_n)\right] \geq k(n)/\ell(n)$.*

We say that g has k-random-bits-unpredictability if it has (k, n^{-c})-bits- unpredictability for every $c \in \mathbb{N}$.

5   OWFs $\Rightarrow$ Unpredictable Bits

In this section, we prove the next theorem, which shows how to construct a function family with non-trivial bits-unpredictability from one-way functions.

Theorem 5.1 (OWFs imply unpredictability). *Let $f \colon \{0,1\}^n \to \{0,1\}^n$ be a one-way function and let $\mathcal{M}_n = \{0,1\}^{n \times n}$ be the family of all $n \times n$ matrices. Let $g = \left\{g_M \colon \{0,1\}^n \to \{0,1\}^{2n}\right\}_{M \in \mathcal{M}_n}$ defined by*

$$g_M(x) = M(f(x)), M(x).$$

Then g has $(n + \log n)$-bits-unpredictability.

We start with proving Theorem 5.1 for the case that f is a regular one-way function on a partial domain. We later show how Theorem 5.1 follows from this case.

Definition 5.2 (Regular one-way function, partial domain). *For every $n \in \mathbb{N}$, let $\Omega_n \subseteq \{0,1\}^n$ be a set. An efficiently computable function $f \colon \Omega_n \to \{0,1\}^n$ is a one-way function if for every n.u.-poly-time algorithm E,*

$$\Pr\left[E(f(W_n)) \in f^{-1}(f(W_n))\right] = neg(n)$$

for $W_n \leftarrow \Omega_n$. Such a function is $r = r(n)$ regular if for every n and $x \in \Omega_n$,

$$2^r > \left|f^{-1}(f(x))\right| \geq 2^{r-1}.$$

Lemma 5.3. *Let* $\epsilon = \epsilon(n) \in [0,1]$ *and* $r = r(n) \in \mathbb{N}$ *be functions. Let* $\Omega_n \subseteq \{0,1\}^n$ *be a set such that* $|\Omega_n| = \epsilon(n) \cdot 2^n$, *and let* $f\colon \Omega_n \to \{0,1\}^n$ *be a* r-*regular one-way function. Let* $M_n \leftarrow \mathcal{M}_n$ *be a random matrix, and* $Y_n = (M_n(f(W_n)), M_n(W_n))$ *for* $W_n \leftarrow \Omega_n$. *Then the following holds for every* $c \in \mathbb{N}$:

For every $n \in \mathbb{N}$ *there exists a set* $\mathcal{S}_n \subseteq [2n]$ *such that* $|\mathcal{S}_n| = n + 4c\log n - \log(1/\epsilon)$, *and for every sequence* $\{i_n\}_{n \in \mathbb{N}}$ *with* $i_n \in \mathcal{S}_n$ *it holds that*

$$\{(M_n, (Y_n)_{\leq i_n})\}_{n \in \mathbb{N}} \overset{c}{\approx}_{n^{-c}} \{(M_n, (Y_n)_{< i_n}, U)\}_{n \in \mathbb{N}}.$$

In the following, fix $c \in \mathbb{N}$, and let $r, \epsilon, \Omega_n, M_n, W_n$ and Y_n be as defined in Lemma 5.3. For every $n \in \mathbb{N}$, let

$$\mathcal{S}_n = [n - r(n) - 8c\log n - \log(1/\epsilon(n))] \cup \{n < i \leq n + r(n) + 12c\log n\}. \quad (1)$$

Clearly, the size of $\mathcal{S}$ is $n + 4c\log n - \log(1/\epsilon)$, as stated in Lemma 5.3. To prove the lemma, we use the following two claims.

Claim 5.4. *For every* $n \in \mathbb{N}$ *and every* $i \in [n - r(n) - 8c\log n - \log(1/\epsilon(n))]$ *it holds that*

$$SD((M_n, M_n(f(W_n))_{\leq i}), (M_n, M_n(f(W_n))_{< i}, U)) \leq n^{-c},$$

for $M \leftarrow \mathcal{M}_n$.

Proof. To prove the claim we will show that $\mathrm{H}_\infty(f(W_n)) \geq n - r(n) - \log(1/\epsilon(n))$. The proof is then immediate from the leftover hash lemma (Lemma 3.4) and a simple hybrid argument, as by Lemma 3.4, $M_n(f(W_n))_{\leq i}$ is statistically close to i uniform bits. To show the bound on the min-entropy of f, compute,

$$\mathrm{H}_\infty(f(X)) = -\log(\max_y \Pr[f(X) = y])$$
$$\geq -\log(\max_y \frac{|f^{-1}(y)|}{|\Omega_n|}) > -\log(\frac{2^r}{\epsilon 2^n}) = n - r - \log(1/\epsilon)$$

as stated.   □

Claim 5.5. *For every sequence* $\{i_n\}_{n \in \mathbb{N}}$, *with* $i_n \in [r(n) + 12c\log n]$ *it holds that*

$$\{(M_n, f(W_n), M_n(W_n)_{\leq i_n})\}_{n \in \mathbb{N}} \overset{c}{\approx} \{(M_n, f(W_n), M_n(W_n)_{< i_n}, U)\}_{n \in \mathbb{N}}.$$

Proof. Assume towards a contradiction that the claim does not hold. That is, there exists some algorithm E and a sequence $\{i_n\}_{n \in \mathbb{N}}$, such that

$$|\Pr[E(M_n, f(W_n), M_n(W_n)_{\leq i_n}) = 1]$$
$$- \Pr[E(M_n, f(W_n), M_n(W_n)_{< i_n}, U) = 1]| \geq n^{-d}$$

for some constant $d \in \mathbb{N}$ and for infinitely many n's. Fix such $n \in \mathbb{N}$, and omit it from the notation. Let $i^* = i_n$, assume without loss of generality that

$$\Pr\left[E(M, f(W), M(W)_{\leq i^*}) = 1\right] - \Pr\left[E(M, f(W), M(W)_{< i^*}, U) = 1\right] \geq n^{-d}.$$

By Lemma 3.3 (Goldreich-Levin), the existence of E implies that there exists an algorithm E' such that

$$\Pr\left[E'(1^{n^c}, M, f(W), M(W)_{< i^*}) = W\right] \geq n^{-2d}.$$

Let $\widehat{E}$ be the algorithm that on input $f(W)$, sample $M \leftarrow \{0,1\}^{n \times n}$, and guess $r \leftarrow \{0,1\}^{i^*-1}$. It then outputs $E'(1^{n^c}, M, f(W), r)$. Since $\Pr\left[M(W)_{< i^*} = r\right] = 2^{-i^*+1}$, it holds that

$$\Pr\left[\widehat{E}(f(W)) = W\right] \geq n^{-2d} \cdot 2^{-i^*+1}. \tag{2}$$

Since f has at least $2^{r-1} \geq 2^{i^*-12c\log n}$ pre-images, it holds that

$$\Pr\left[\widehat{E}(f(W)) \in f^{-1}(f(W))\right] \geq 2^{r-1} \cdot \Pr\left[\widehat{E}(f(W)) = W\right]$$
$$\geq 2^{i^*-12c\log n-1} \cdot \Pr\left[\widehat{E}(f(W)) = W\right]. \tag{3}$$

Combining Eqs. (2) and (3), we get that

$$\Pr\left[\widehat{E}(f(W)) = W\right] \geq n^{-2d-12c-1}$$

which is a contradiction since f is a one-way function. $\square$

5.1   Proving Lemma 5.3.

We are now ready to prove Lemma 5.3.

Proof (Proof of Lemma 5.3). Assume towards a contradiction that the lemma does not hold. That is, there exists a constant c, a n.u.-poly-time algorithm E and a sequence $\{i_n\}_{n \in \mathbb{N}}$ with $i_n \in \mathcal{S}_n$ such that,

$$\left|\Pr\left[E(M_n, (Y_n)_{\leq i_n}) = 1\right] - \Pr\left[E(M_n, (Y_n)_{< i_n}, U) = 1\right]\right| > n^{-c}$$

for infinitely many n's, where $\mathcal{S}_n$ is the set defined in Eq. (1) with respect to the constant c. We conclude the proof by the observation that, either for infinitely many such n's it holds that $i_n \leq n$, or for infinitely many such n's $i_n > n$. In the first case, E contradicts Claim 5.4. In the second, E contradicts Claim 5.5 by a simple data-processing argument. $\square$

5.2   Proving Theorem 5.1

Proof (Proof of Theorem 5.1). Fix $c \in \mathbb{N}$. The proof follows by the observation that every one-way function is a combination of regular one-way functions. Let $f \colon \{0,1\}^n \to \{0,1\}^n$ be a one-way function, and for every $x \in \{0,1\}^n$, let $D_f(x) = \lfloor \log |f^{-1}(f(x))| \rfloor$. For every $n \in N$ and $r \in [n]$, let $\Omega_n^r = \{x \in \{0,1\}^n \colon D_f(x) = r\}$. Let $\epsilon^r(n) = |\Omega_n^r|/2^n$ and let $\mathcal{S}_n^r$ be the set $\mathcal{S}_n$ promised by Lemma 5.3 with respect to r. Observe that for every function $r = r(n)$, $f^r \colon \Omega_n^r \to \{0,1\}^n$ is r-regular function. Moreover, for every such r with $\epsilon^r(n) \geq n^{-2c}$ for every $n \in \mathbb{N}$, it holds that the function f^r is one-way. Indeed, an algorithm E that inverts f^r with probability $\alpha(n)$ inverts f with probability at least $\alpha(n) \cdot \Pr[D_f(X_n) = r(n)] \geq \alpha(n) \cdot n^{-2c}$.

For $x \in \{0,1\}^n$, let $\mathcal{S}(x) = \mathcal{S}_n^{D_f(x)}$ if $\epsilon^{D_f(x)}(n) \geq n^{-2c}$ or $\emptyset$ otherwise. In the following we show that

$$\Pr[|\mathcal{S}(X_n)| < n + 2c \log n] \leq n^{-c}. \tag{4}$$

It then follows that

$$E[|\mathcal{S}(X_n)|] \geq (n + 2c \log n)(1 - n^{-c}) \geq n + c \log n$$

as stated. To see Eq. (4), let $\mathcal{G}_n = \{r \in [n] \colon \epsilon^r(n) \geq n^{-2c}\}$. By definition of $\mathcal{S}$ and $\mathcal{G}_n$ we get that for every $r \in \mathcal{G}_n$ and x with $D_f(x) = r$

$$|\mathcal{S}(x)| \geq (n + 4c \log n - \log(1/n^{-2c}))$$
$$= n + 2c \log n.$$

Thus, $\Pr[|\mathcal{S}(X_n)| < n + 2c \log n] \leq \Pr[D_f(X_n) \notin \mathcal{G}_n]$, and it is enough to bound $\Pr[D_f(X_n) \notin \mathcal{G}_n]$. By union bound, as $D_f(x)$ can get at most n values, and for every $r \notin \mathcal{G}_n$ it holds that $\Pr[D_f(X_n) = r] \leq n^{-2c}$, we get that $\Pr[D_f(X_n) \notin \mathcal{G}_n] \leq n^{-2c} \cdot n \leq n^{-c}$, as we wanted to show.

Next, assume toward a contradiction that g has no $(n + \log n, n^{-c})$-bits-unpredictability with respect to the above sets $\mathcal{S}(x)$. Namely, there exists an algorithm E such that

$$|\Pr[E(M_n, g_{M_n}(X_n)_{\leq i_n}) = 1 \mid i_n \in \mathcal{S}(X_n)]$$
$$- \Pr[E(M_n, g_{M_n}(X_n)_{<i_n}, U) = 1 \mid i_n \in \mathcal{S}(X_n)]| > n^{-c}$$

for some sequence $\{i_n\}_{n \in \mathbb{N}}$ and for infinite many n's. Below we show how to construct a regular one-way function on partial domain f^{r^*}, such that E contradicts Lemma 5.3 with respect to f^{r^*}. To do so, fix such n and observe that, by an averaging argument, there exists some $r^* \in [n]$ such that $i_n \in \mathcal{S}_n^{r^*}$, and,

$$|\Pr[E(M_n, g_{M_n}(X_n)_{\leq i_n}) = 1 \mid i_n \in \mathcal{S}(X_n), D_f(X_n) = r^*]$$
$$- \Pr[E(M_n, g_{M_n}(X_n)_{<i_n}, U) = 1 \mid i_n \in \mathcal{S}(X_n), D_f(X_n) = r^*]| > n^{-c}.$$

Since $\mathcal{S}(X_n)$ is determined by $D_f(X_n)$, we get that,

$$\left| \Pr\left[E(M_n, g_{M_n}(X_n)_{\leq i_n}) = 1 \mid D_f(X_n) = r^*\right] \right.$$
$$\left. - \Pr\left[E(M_n, g_{M_n}(X_n)_{<i_n}, U) = 1 \mid D_f(X_n) = r^*\right] \right| > n^{-c}.$$

Lastly, observe that the event $D_f(X_n) = r$ does not depend on M_n, and only depend on $f(X_n)$. Thus, we can write the above as

$$\left| \Pr_{x \leftarrow \Omega_n^{r^*}}\left[E(M_n, g_{M_n}(x)_{\leq i_n}) = 1\right] - \Pr_{x \leftarrow \Omega_n^{r^*}}\left[E(M_n, g_{M_n}(x)_{<i_n}, U) = 1\right] \right| \geq n^{-c}.$$

Moreover, since $i_n \in \mathcal{S}_n^{r^*}$, it holds that $\epsilon^{r^*}(n) \geq n^{-2c}$. For every n let $r^*(n)$ be as described above (or, if no such r^* exists, let $r^*(n)$ be arbitrary r with $\epsilon^r(n) \geq n^{-2c}$).[6] The above is a contradiction to Lemma 5.3, as by construction $f^{r^*} \colon \Omega_n^{r^*} \to \{0,1\}^n$ is a regular one-way function (note that, while r^* may not be an efficiently computable function, f^{r^*} is).   □

6   Bits Unpredictability $\Rightarrow$ Random Bits Unpredictability

The next theorem, proven below, shows how to convert bits unpredictability to random bits unpredictability.

Theorem 6.1 (Bits unpredictability to random bits unpredictability).
Let $m = m(n)$, $\ell = \ell(n)$, $\lambda = \lambda(n)$ *and* $k = k(n)$ *be integer functions and let* $g = \left\{ g_a \colon \{0,1\}^{m(n)} \to \{0,1\}^{\ell(n)} \right\}_{a \in \{0,1\}^{\lambda(n)}}$ *be a function family with* k-*bits-unpredictability. Then, for every polynomial* $r = r(n)$, *the function family* $g^r = \left\{ g_a^r \colon [\ell(n)] \times (\{0,1\}^{m(n)})^{r(n)} \to \{0,1\}^{(r(n)-1)\ell(n)} \right\}_{a \in \{0,1\}^{\lambda(n)}}$ *defined by*

$$g_a^r(i, x^1, \ldots, x^r) = g_a(x^1)_{\geq i}, g_a(x^2), \ldots, g_a(x^{r-1}), g_a(x^r)_{<i}$$

has $(r(n) - 1)k(n)$-*random-bits unpredictability.*

We get the following corollary, on construction of random-bits unpredictability from a one-way function.

Corollary 6.2 (OWF to random-bits unpredictability). *Let* $f \colon \{0,1\}^n \to \{0,1\}^n$ *be a one-way. Then there exists an efficiently computable function family* $g' = \left\{ g_a' \colon \{0,1\}^{m'(n)} \to \{0,1\}^{\ell'(n)} \right\}_{a \in \{0,1\}^{\lambda(n)}}$ *with* k'-*random-bits unpredictability, for* $m'(n) = O(n^2/\log n)$, $\ell'(n) = O(n^2/\log n)$, $\lambda(n) = n^2$ *and* $k'(n) \geq m'(n) + n$.
Moreover, the construction uses $r(n)$ *non-adaptive calls to* f.

---

[6] That is, for every n for which E distinguishes $g_{M_n}(X_n)_{\leq i_n}$ from $(g_{M_n}(X_n)_{<i_n}, U)$ given $i_n \in \mathcal{S}(X^n)$, we define $r^*(n)$ as described, and for all other n's we define $r^*(n)$ arbitrarily such that $\Pr[D_f(X_n) = r^*(n)]$ is noticeable.

Proof. Let g be the function family defined in Theorem 5.1. Let $r(n) = \lceil 2n/\log n \rceil + 3$, and let $g' = g^r$, as defined in Theorem 6.1. It holds that $m'(n) = \lceil \log n \rceil + n \cdot r(n) = O(n^2/\log n)$, and $\ell'(n) = 2n \cdot (r(n) - 1) = O(n^2/\log n)$. Moreover, by Theorem 6.1,

$$k'(n) = (r(n)-1)(n+\log n) = \log n + n \cdot r(n) + \log n \cdot (r(n)-2) - n \geq m'(n) + 2n - n.$$

$\square$

6.1 Proving Theorem 6.1

Proof (Proof of Theorem 6.1). Let ℓ, m, λ, k and g be as in Theorem 6.1, and fix a polynomial $r = r(n)$ and a constant c. In the following we prove that g^r has $((r-1)k, n^{-c})$-random bits unpredictability. For every $n \in \mathbb{N}$ and $x \in \{0,1\}^{m(n)}$, let $\mathcal{S}^g(x)$ be the set promised by Definition 4.1 with respect to the (k, n^{-c})-bits-unpredictability of g.

For $i \in [\ell(n)]$ and $x^1, \ldots, x^r \in (\{0,1\}^{m(n)})^{r(n)}$, define the set

$$S(i, x^1, \ldots, x^r) = \left(\bigcup_{j \in [r]} \{z + (j-1)n - (i-1) : z \in \mathcal{S}^g(x^j)\} \right) \bigcap [\ell(n) \cdot (r(n)-1)].$$

let $X_n^1, \ldots, X_n^r \leftarrow \{0,1\}^{m(n)}$ and $I_n \leftarrow [\ell(n)]$. Clearly, for every $i \in [\ell(n) \cdot (r(n) - 1)]$, it holds that

$$\Pr\left[i \in S(I_n, X_n^1, \ldots, X_n^r)\right] = \Pr\left[(i + I_n \bmod \ell(n)) \in \mathcal{S}^g(X_n)\right]$$
$$= \frac{\mathrm{E}\left[|\mathcal{S}^g(X_n)|\right]}{\ell(n)} \geq \frac{k(n)}{\ell(n)} = \frac{(r(n)-1)k(n)}{(r(n)-1)\ell(n)}.$$

Let $S_n = S(I_n, X_n^1, \ldots, X_n^r)$. Assume toward a contradiction that g^r does not have $(r-1)k$-random-bits unpredictability with respect to the above set S. That is, there exists an algorithm E and an index $z = z(n) \in [\ell \cdot (r-1)]$, such that, for $A_n \leftarrow \{0,1\}^{\lambda(n)}$,

$$\left|\Pr\left[E(A_n, g_{A_n}^r(I_n, X_n^1, \ldots, X_n^r)_{\leq z}) = 1 \mid z \in S_n\right]\right.$$
$$\left. - \Pr\left[E(A_n, g_{A_n}^r(I_n, X_n^1, \ldots, X_n^r)_{<z}, U) = 1\right] \mid z \in S_n\right| \geq n^{-c}.$$

For infinitely many n's. Fix such n and omit n from the notation. By an averaging argument, there exists an index $i^* \in [\ell(n)]$ such that

$$\left|\Pr\left[E(A, g_A^r(i^*, X^1, \ldots, X^r)_{\leq z}) = 1 \mid z \in S\right]\right.$$
$$\left. - \Pr\left[E(A, g_A^r(i^*, X^1, \ldots, X^r)_{<z}, U) = 1\right] \mid z \in S\right| \geq n^{-c}.$$

Recall that g_A^r is produced by r blocks of the form $g_A(X^j)$ (with a random shift). Let $s = \lceil \frac{z+(i^*-1)}{\ell} \rceil$ be the index of the block in which the index z belongs to, and i be the index of z inside the block. That is, s and i are such that

$g_A^r(i^*, X^1, \ldots, X^r)_{\leq z} = g_A(X^1)_{\geq i^*}, g_A(X^2), \ldots, g_A(X^s)_{\leq i}$. Consider the algorithm E' that, given $a, g_a(x)_{\leq i}$ and a bit b, sample $X^1, \ldots, X^{s-1}$ uniformly at random and executes $E(a, g_a(X^1)_{>i^*}, g_a(X^2), \ldots, g_a(x)_{<i}, b)$.

Observe that,

$$\begin{aligned}
&|\Pr[E'(A, g_A(X)_{<i}, g_A(X)_i) = 1 \mid i \in \mathcal{S}^g(X)] \\
&\quad - \Pr[E'(A, g_A(X)_{<i}, U) = 1 \mid i \in \mathcal{S}^g(X)]| \\
&= |\Pr[E(A, g_A(i^*, X^1, \ldots, X^r)_{\leq z}) = 1 \mid z \in \mathcal{S}] \\
&\quad - \Pr[E(A, g_A(i^*, X^1, \ldots, X^r)_{<z}, U) = 1 \mid z \in \mathcal{S}]| \\
&\geq n^{-c}.
\end{aligned}$$

The above is a contradiction to the (k, n^{-c})-bits unpredictability of g, since by assumption, it holds for infinitely many n's □

7   Extracting Pseudorandomness and the Main Theorem

In this section we prove Theorem 7.1, which is the last step in our main construction. Theorem 7.1 shows how to extract pseudorandomness from random bits unpredictability.

Theorem 7.1 (Extracting from random bits unpredictability). *Let* $s = \omega(1)$, $m = m(n)$, $\ell = \ell(n)$, $\lambda = \lambda(n)$ *and* $k = k(n)$ *be integer functions, and let* $g = \left\{ g_a \colon \{0,1\}^{m(n)} \to \{0,1\}^{\ell(n)} \right\}_{u \in \{0,1\}^{\lambda(n)}}$ *be a function family with* $k(n)$-*random-hits-unpredictability. Then the following holds for every polynomial* $t = t(n)$. *Let* $\alpha(n) = k(n)/\ell(n)$, *and let* $H_n \leftarrow \{0,1\}^{t(n) \times q(n)}$ *be a random matrix, for* $q = \lfloor \alpha t - \sqrt{\alpha t \cdot s \log n} - s \log n \rfloor$. *Then for* $X_n^1 \ldots, X_n^{t(n)} \leftarrow (\{0,1\}^{m(n)})^{t(n)}$ *and* $A_n \leftarrow \{0,1\}^{\lambda(n)}$, *the distribution ensemble*

$$\left\{ H_n, A_n, H_n(g_{A_n}(X_n^1)_1, \ldots, g_{A_n}(X_n^{t(n)})_1), \ldots, H_n(g_{A_n}(X_n^1)_{\ell(n)}, \ldots, g_{A_n}(X_n^{t(n)})_{\ell(n)}) \right\}_{n \in \mathbb{N}}$$

is pseudorandom.

We prove Theorem 7.1 below, but first let us deduce our main theorem.

Theorem 7.2 (PRG construction).
For any function $s(n) = \omega(1)$, *there exists a construction of a PRG from a one-way function, that uses* $O(s(n) \cdot n^3 / \log^2 n)$ *non-adaptive calls to the one-way function and a seed of length* $O(s^2(n) \cdot n^4 / \log^2 n))$.

Proof (Proof of Theorem 7.2). Let $f \colon \{0,1\}^n \to \{0,1\}^n$ be a one-way function, $g' = \left\{ g_a' \colon \{0,1\}^{m'(n)} \to \{0,1\}^{\ell'(n)} \right\}_{a \in \{0,1\}^{\lambda(n)}}$ be the function family promised by Corollary 6.2, and let $\alpha = k'/\ell' \leq 1$.

Let s be as in Theorem 7.2 (assume without loss of generality that $s(n) \leq \log n$), $t = 4 \lceil \frac{\ell'^2 s \log n}{(k'-m')^2} \rceil = O(s \cdot n^2 / \log n)$, $m = t \cdot m'$ and $\ell = (\lfloor \alpha t - \sqrt{\alpha t s \log n} -$

$s \log n \rfloor)\ell'$. Let $\mathcal{H} = \{0,1\}^{t \times (\lfloor \alpha t - \sqrt{\alpha t s \log n} - s \log n \rfloor)}$ be the set of all matrices of size $t \times (\lfloor \alpha t - \sqrt{\alpha t s \log n} - s \log n \rfloor)$, and let $G : \mathcal{H} \times \{0,1\}^\lambda \times \{0,1\}^m \to \mathcal{H} \times \{0,1\}^\lambda \times \{0,1\}^\ell$ be the function defined by

$$G(H, A, W_1, \dots, W_t) :=$$
$$H, A, H(g_A^r(W_1)_1, \dots g_A^r(W_t)_1), \dots, H(g_A^r(W_1)_{\ell'}, \dots, g_A^r(W_t)_{\ell'}).$$

By Theorem 7.1, the output of G is pseudorandom when $H \leftarrow \mathcal{H}$, and $W_1, \dots, W_t \leftarrow (\{0,1\}^{m_2})^t$. We need to show that G is expanding. To do so, it is enough to verify that $m < \ell$.

Indeed,

$$
\begin{aligned}
\ell - m &= (\lfloor \alpha t - \sqrt{\alpha t s \log n} - s \log n \rfloor)\ell' - tm' \\
&> \alpha t \ell' - 2\ell' \sqrt{t s \log n} - tm' \\
&= tk' - 2\ell' \sqrt{t s \log n} - tm' \\
&= t(k' - m') - 2\ell' \sqrt{t s \log n} \\
&\geq 0,
\end{aligned}
$$

where the last inequality holds since $m = m't$ and since $t(k' - m') \geq 2\ell' \sqrt{t s \log n}$ by our choice of t.

Moreover, G uses $tr = O(s \cdot n^3 / \log n)$ calls to f and has seed length $\log |\mathcal{H}| + \lambda + t \cdot m_2 = \log |\mathcal{H}| + O(t^2 + n^2 + s \cdot n^4 / \log^2 n) = O(s^2 \cdot n^4 / \log^2 n)$. $\square$

7.1   Exponentially-Hard OWFs

Before proving Theorem 7.1, we state and prove our results for exponentially-hard one-way functions. We start with a formal definition of the latter.

Definition 7.3 (Exponentially hard one-way function). *A polynomial-time computable function $f : \{0,1\}^* \to \{0,1\}^*$ is called a $T = T(n)$-hard one-way function if for every n.u. algorithm A of size at most $T(n)$, for all but finitely many $n \in \mathbb{N}$,*

$$\Pr_{x \leftarrow \{0,1\}^n} \left[A(f(x)) \in f^{-1}(f(x)) \right] \leq 1/T(N).$$

f is n.u exponentially-hard one-way function if it is 2^{cn}-hard one-way function for some constant $c > 0$.

We get the following theorem:

Theorem 7.4 (PRG construction from exponentially-hard OWFs). *For any function $s(n) = \omega(1)$, there exists a construction of a poly-time secure PRG from an exponentially-hard one-way function, that uses $O(s(n) \cdot \log n)$ non-adaptive calls to the one-way function.*

Proof. Let f be an 2^{cn}-hard one-way function. We use the well-known fact that we can extract δn GL hard-core bits from the input of f, for some constant $c > \delta > 0$. Thus, by the construction in Theorem 5.1, we get a function family g with $(n + \epsilon n)$-bits-unpredictability, for some constant $\epsilon > 0$ (and g only makes one call to f).

Next, by Theorem 6.1, and taking $r = \lceil 3/\epsilon \rceil + 1 = O(1)$, we get that the function family $g' = g^r$ has $k'(n) = (\lceil 3/\epsilon \rceil (1+\epsilon)n)$-random-bits-unpredictability. Moreover, g^r has input length $m'(n) = O(\log n) + n(\lceil 3/\epsilon \rceil + 1)$, output length $\ell'(n) = 2n(\lceil 3/\epsilon \rceil)$. We get that $k'(n) - m'(n) = \Omega(n) = \Omega(\ell'(n))$.

Let $\alpha = k'(n)/\ell'(n)$. Let s be as in Theorem 7.4, $t = 4\lceil \frac{\ell'^2 s \log n}{(k'-m')^2} \rceil = O(s \log n)$, $m = t \cdot m'$ and $\ell = (\lfloor \alpha t - \sqrt{\alpha t s \log n} - s \log n \rfloor)\ell'$. Let $\mathcal{H}$ be the set of all matrices of size $t \times (\lfloor \alpha t - \sqrt{\alpha t s \log n} - s \log n \rfloor)$, and let $G \colon \mathcal{H} \times \{0,1\}^\lambda \times \{0,1\}^m \to \mathcal{H} \times \{0,1\}^\lambda \times \{0,1\}^\ell$ be the function defined by

$$G(H, A, W_1, \ldots, W_t) :=$$
$$H, A, H(g^r_A(W_1)_1, \ldots g^r_A(W_t)_1), \ldots, H(g^r_A(W_1)_{\ell'}, \ldots, g^r_A(W_t)_{\ell'}).$$

By Theorem 7.1, the output of G is pseudorandom when $H \leftarrow \mathcal{H}$, and $W_1, \ldots, W_t \leftarrow (\{0,1\}^{m_2})^t$. By the same calculation as in the proof of Theorem 7.2, G is expanding. Moreover, G uses $tr = O(s \log n)$ calls to f.

7.2 Proving Theorem 7.1

By a simple hybrid argument, it is enough to prove the following claim.

Claim 7.5. *Let g, t, H_n, A_n and $X^1_n, \ldots, X^t_n$ be as in Theorem 7.1. Then for every sequence $\{i_n\}_{n \in \mathbb{N}}$, and for every n.u.-poly-time algorithm E,*

$$|\Pr\left[E(H_n, A_n, g_{A_n}(X^1_n)_{<i_n}, \ldots, g_{A_n}(X^t_n)_{<i_n}, H_n(g_{A_n}(X^1_n)_{i_n}, \ldots, g_{A_n}(X^t_n)_{i_n})) = 1\right]$$
$$- \Pr\left[E(H_n, A_n, g_{A_n}(X^1_n)_{<i_n}, \ldots, g_{A_n}(X^t_n)_{<i_n}, U_{q(n)}) = 1\right]| = neg(n).$$

Proof. (Proof of Theorem 7.1). Theorem 7.1 follows from Claim 7.5 by a simple hybrid argument. $\qquad\square$

In the following we prove Claim 7.5. Fix $c \in \mathbb{N}$, a n.u.-poly-time E and a constant d such that $t(n) \le n^d$ for large enough n. We want to show that

$$|\Pr\left[E(H_n, A_n, g_{A_n}(X^1_n)_{<i_n}, \ldots, g_{A_n}(X^t_n)_{<i_n}, H_n(g_{A_n}(X^1_n)_{i_n}, \ldots, g_{A_n}(X^t_n)_{i_n})) = 1\right]$$
$$- \Pr\left[E(H_n, A_n, g_{A_n}(X^1_n)_{<i_n}, \ldots, g_{A_n}(X^t_n)_{<i_n}, U_{q(n)}) = 1\right]| < n^{-c}. \quad (5)$$

for all but finitely many n's. Let $c' = c + d + 2$. For every $n \in \mathbb{N}$ and $j \in [t(n)]$, let $\mathcal{S}^j_n = \mathcal{S}^g(X^j_n)$ be the set promised by the assumed $(k, n^{-c'})$-random-bits-unpredictability property of g. We define the random variables $Q^1, \ldots, Q^t$ as follows. For every $j \in t$, let $Q^j = g_A(X^j_n)_{i_n}$ if $i_n \notin \mathcal{S}^j_n$, or a uniform bit otherwise.

By the definition of bits-unpredictability, it holds that for every n.u.-poly-time algorithm E',

$$\left| \Pr\left[E'(g_A(X_n^j)_{<i_n}, g_A(X_n^j)_{i_n}) = 1 \right] - \Pr\left[E'(g_A(X_n^j)_{<i_n}, Q^j) = 1 \right] \right| \le n^{-c'}.$$
(6)

The proof of Claim 7.5 follows from the following two claims.

Claim 7.6. *For all but infinitely many n's,*

$$\left| \Pr\left[E(H_n, A_n, g_{A_n}(X_n^1)_{<i_n}, \ldots, g_{A_n}(X_n^t)_{<i_n}, H_n(Q^1, \ldots, Q^t)) = 1 \right] \right.$$
$$\left. - \Pr\left[E(H_n, A_n, g_{A_n}(X_n^1)_{<i_n}, \ldots, g_{A_n}(X_n^t)_{<i_n}, U_{q(n)}) = 1 \right] \right| < n^{-c}/2$$

Claim 7.7. *For all but infinitely many n's,*

$$\left| \Pr\left[E(H_n, A_n, g_{A_n}(X_n^1)_{<i_n}, \ldots, g_{A_n}(X_n^t)_{<i_n}, H_n(g_{A_n}(X_n^1)_{i_n}, \ldots, g_{A_n}(X_n^t)_{i_n})) = 1 \right] \right.$$
$$\left. - \Pr\left[E(H_n, A_n, g_{A_n}(X_n^1)_{<i_n}, \ldots, g_{A_n}(X_n^t)_{<i_n}, H_n(Q^1, \ldots, Q^t)) = 1 \right] \right| < n^{-c}/2$$

We will prove Claim 7.6 and Claim 7.7 below, but first let us prove Claim 7.5.

Proof. (Proof of Claim 7.5). Equation (5) holds by Claim 7.6 and Claim 7.7 and the triangle inequality. The claim follows since Eq. (5) holds for every $c \in \mathbb{N}$. $\square$

7.3 Proving Claim 7.6

Proof. (Proof of Claim 7.6).

We will show that given $g_{A_n}(X_n^1)_{<i_n}, \ldots, g_{A_n}(X_n^t)_{<i_n}$, the distribution of $(Q^1, \ldots, Q^t)$ is $n^{-c}/3$-close to a distribution with min-entropy at least $q(n) + \omega(\log n)$. The proof then follows by the leftover hash lemma.

To do so, we start by showing that with probability $1 - n^{-c}/3$, there are at least $q(n) + \omega(\log n)$ indexes j such that $i_n \in \mathcal{S}^j$. To see the above, fix n and omit it from the notation. Let $q' = q + s \log n$, and for every $j \in [t]$, let δ_j be an indicator for the event that $i \in \mathcal{S}_j$. By construction, $\delta_1, \ldots, \delta_t$ are independent random variables, and by the definition of k-random-bits-unpredictability, for each $j \in [t]$, it holds that $\Pr[\delta_j = 1] \ge k/\ell = \alpha$. Thus, by Chernoff inequality, for large enough n it holds that

$$\Pr\left[\sum_{j=1}^t \delta_j < q' \right] = \Pr\left[\sum_{j=1}^t \delta_j < \alpha t - \sqrt{\alpha t s \log n} \right] \le 2^{-s \log n/3} < n^{-c}/3,$$

as we wanted to show. Next, let $\mathcal{J} = \{j : i_n \in \mathcal{S}^j\}$ be the set of j's for which Q^j is uniform independent bit. By the above $\Pr[|\mathcal{J}| < q'] < n^{-c}/3$, and thus the distribution $(Q^1, \ldots, Q^t)$ is $n^{-c}/3$ close to the distribution $(Q^1, \ldots, Q^t)|_{|\mathcal{J}| \ge q'}$. To bound the min-entropy of the latter, we want to show that for every $q^1, \ldots, q^t$, it holds that $\Pr\left[Q^1,\ldots,Q^t = q^1,\ldots,q^t \mid |\mathcal{J}| \geq q'\right] \leq 2^{-q'}$, which concludes the proof. It holds that,

$$
\begin{aligned}
&\Pr\left[Q^1,\ldots,Q^t = q^1,\ldots,q^t \mid |\mathcal{J}| \geq q'\right] \\
&= \mathbb{E}_{J\leftarrow \mathcal{J}_{||\mathcal{J}|>q'}}\left[\Pr\left[Q^1,\ldots,Q^t = q^1,\ldots,q^t \mid J = J\right]\right] \\
&\leq \mathbb{E}_{J\leftarrow \mathcal{J}_{||\mathcal{J}|>q'}}\left[2^{-|J|}\right] \\
&\leq 2^{-q'},
\end{aligned}
$$

where the first inequality holds since for every $j \in J$, Q^j is a uniform and independent random bit. $\qquad\square$

7.4 Proving Claim 7.7

Proof. (Proof of Claim 7.7). Assume towards a contradiction that the claim does not hold. That is,

$$
\begin{aligned}
&\left|\Pr\left[E\big(H_n, A_n, g_{A_n}(X_n^1)_{<i_n},\ldots,g_{A_n}(X_n^t)_{<i_n}, H_n(g_{A_n}(X_n^1)_{i_n},\ldots,g_{A_n}(X_n^t)_{i_n})\big) = 1\right]\right. \\
&\left.- \Pr\left[E\big(H_n, A_n, g_{A_n}(X_n^1)_{<i_n},\ldots,g_{A_n}(X_n^t)_{<i_n}, H_n(Q^1,\ldots,Q^t)\big) = 1\right]\right| \geq n^{-c}/2
\end{aligned}
$$

for some algorithm E and for infinitely many n's. By data-processing inequality, it holds that for some n.u.-poly-time $\widehat{E}$ and for infinitely many n's,

$$
\begin{aligned}
&\left|\Pr\left[\widehat{E}\big(A_n, g_{A_n}(X_n^1)_{<i_n},\ldots,g_{A_n}(X_n^t)_{<i_n}, g_{A_n}(X_n^1)_{i_n},\ldots,g_{A_n}(X_n^t)_{i_n}\big) = 1\right]\right. \\
&\left.- \Pr\left[\widehat{E}\big(A_n, g_{A_n}(X_n^1)_{<i_n},\ldots,g_{A_n}(X_n^t)_{<i_n}, Q^1,\ldots,Q^t\big) = 1\right]\right| \geq n^{-c}/2.
\end{aligned}
$$

Fix such n. By a simple hybrid argument, we get that there exists some $j^* \in [t]$, such that,

$$
\begin{aligned}
&\left|\Pr\left[\widehat{E}\big(A_n, g_{A_n}(X_n^1)_{<i_n},\ldots,g_{A_n}(X_n^t)_{<i_n}, g_{A_n}(X_n^1)_{i_n},\ldots,g_{A_n}(X_n^{j^*})_{i_n}, Q^{j^*+1},\ldots,Q^t\big) = 1\right]\right. \\
&\left.- \Pr\left[\widehat{E}\big(A_n, g_{A_n}(X_n^1)_{<i_n},\ldots,g_{A_n}(X_n^t)_{<i_n}, g_{A_n}(X_n^1)_{i_n},\ldots,g_{A_n}(X_n^{j^*-1})_{i_n}, Q^{j^*},\ldots,Q^t\big) = 1\right]\right| \\
&\geq n^{-c'}/2.
\end{aligned}
$$

By a simple averaging argument, there is a fixing $x^1,\ldots,x^{j^*-1}, x^{j+1},\ldots,x^t$ for $X_n^1,\ldots,X_n^{j^*-1}, X_n^{j+1},\ldots,X_n^t$, and b^j for every Q^j with $i_n \in \mathcal{S}^g(x^j)$, such that the following holds. Let $q^j(a) = g_a(x^j)$ if $i_n \notin \mathcal{S}^g(x^j)$, or b^j otherwise. Then it holds that

$$
\begin{aligned}
&\left|\Pr[\widehat{E}\big(A_n, g_{A_n}(x^1)_{<i_n},\ldots,g_{A_n}(X_n^{j^*}),\ldots,g_{A_n}(x^t)_{<i_n},\right. \\
&\qquad\qquad g_{A_n}(x^1)_{i_n},\ldots,g_{A_n}(X_n^{j^*})_{i_n}, q^{j^*+1}(A_n),\ldots,q^t(A_n)\big) = 1] \\
&- \Pr[\widehat{E}\big(A_n, g_{A_n}(x^1)_{<i_n},\ldots,g_{A_n}(X_n^{j^*}),\ldots,g_{A_n}(x^t)_{<i_n}, \\
&\left.\qquad\qquad g_{A_n}(x^1)_{i_n},\ldots,Q^{j^*}, q^{j^*+1}(A_n),\ldots,q^t(A_n)\big) = 1]\right| \\
&\geq n^{-c'}/2.
\end{aligned}
$$

The above is a contradiction to the bit-unpredictability property of g. Indeed, Let

$$E'(a, g_a(x)_{<i}, b)$$
$$= \widehat{E}(A_n, g_{A_n}(x^1)_{<i_n}, \ldots, g_a(x)_{<i}, \ldots, g_{A_n}(x^t)_{<i_n},$$
$$g_{A_n}(x^1)_{i_n}, \ldots, g_{A_n}(x^{j^*-1})_{i_n}, b, q^{j^*+1}(A_n), \ldots, q^t(A_n)).$$

We get that

$$|\Pr[E'(A_n, g_{A_n}(X_n)_{<i_n}, g_{A_n}(X_n)_{i_n}) = 1]$$
$$- \Pr[E'(A_n, g_{A_n}(X_n)_{<i_n}, Q) = 1]| \geq n^{-c'}/2.$$

where Q is equal to $g_{A_n}(X_n)_{i_n}$ if $i_n \notin \mathcal{S}^g(X_n)$, or uniform bit otherwise. This is a contradiction to Eq. (6).   □

8 Saving Seed Length

In this section we show how to use the transformation from [VZ12] to get the following theorem.

Theorem 8.1. (PRG construction). *For any function $s = \omega(1)$, there exists a construction of a PRG from a one-way function, that uses $O(s(n) \cdot n^3 / \log^2 n)$ calls to the one-way function and a seed of length $O(s(n) \cdot n^3 / \log n)$.*

To get an improvement in the seed length, we will also need to use a hash function with a shorter description in the extraction step, described in Sect. 7. For this, we need to define 2-universal families.

Definition 8.2. (2-universal family). *A family of function $\mathcal{F} = \{f : \{0,1\}^n \to \{0,1\}^\ell\}$ is 2-universal if for every $x \neq x' \in \{0,1\}^n$ it holds that $\Pr_{f \leftarrow \mathcal{F}}[f(x) = f(x')] = 2^{-\ell}$.*

A universal a family is explicit *if given a description of a function $f \in \mathcal{F}$ and $x \in \{0,1\}^n$, $f(x)$ can be computed in polynomial time (in n, ℓ).*

The family of all matrices of size $n \times m$ is an explicit 2-universal family, but it is well known that there are explicit 2-universal families with description size $O(n+m)$. An important property of 2-universal families is that they can be used to construct a strong extractor. This is stated in the leftover hash lemma:

Lemma 8.3. (Leftover hash lemma, standard version, [ILL89]).
Let $n \in \mathbb{N}$, $\varepsilon \in [0,1]$, and let X be a random variable over $\{0,1\}^n$. Let $\mathcal{H} = \{h : \{0,1\}^n \to \{0,1\}^\ell\}$ be a 2-universal hash family with $\ell \leq H_\infty(X) - 2\log 1/\varepsilon$. Then,

$$SD((H, H(X)), (H, U_\ell)) \leq \varepsilon$$

for U_ℓ being the uniform distribution over $\{0,1\}^\ell$ and H being the uniform distribution over $\mathcal{H}$.

We are now ready to prove the main result of this section.

Proof. Observe that the significant parts of the seed of the PRG G defined in the proof of Theorem 7.2 are the description of $\mathcal{H}$, and t inputs to the function g^r.

More Efficient Hash Function. We start with reducing the description length of $\mathcal{H}$ by using more efficient 2-universal family. Indeed, the proof of Claim 7.5 holds also when H_n is a random function from a 2-universal family instead of a random matrix. We change the proof of Theorem 7.2, such that

$$\mathcal{H} = \left\{ h \colon \{0,1\}^{t(n)} \to \{0,1\}^{\alpha t - \sqrt{\alpha t s \log n} - s \log n} \right\}$$

is a 2-universal family of description size $\log |\mathcal{H}| = O(t)$.

Using the transformation of [VZ12]. Next, we use the transformation of [VZ12] to avoid the need to get t independent inputs for g^r as input to the PRG. Let us first recall the construction given in Sects. 5 to 7. The construction starts with a function family g which has non-trivial bits-unpredictability. Then, for every $j \in [t]$ we compute

$$Y^j = g_A^r(I^j, X_j^1, \dots, X_j^r) = g_A(X^{j,1})_{\geq I^j}, g_A(X^{j,2}), \dots, g_A(X^{j,r})_{< I^j}.$$

Finally, we extract pseudorandom bits by applying an extractor on $Y_i^1, \dots Y_i^t$ for every $i \in [(r-1)\ell]$. We prove that $H(Y_i^1, \dots Y_i^t)$ is indistinguishable from uniform, given $A, Y_{i<}^1, \dots Y_{<i}^t$. Moreover, by inspecting the reductions in the proofs of Theorems 6.1 and 7.1, it is not hard to see that $H(Y_i^1, \dots Y_i^t)$ is indistinguishable from uniform, even given $I^1, \dots, I^t$ (in addition to $A, Y_{i<}^1, \dots Y_{<i}^t$).

Vadhan and Zheng [VZ12] observed that for computing Y_i^j, we only need to know the value of A, I^j and exactly one (specific) of the values of $X^{j,1}, \dots, X^{j,r}$. In particular, we don't need to know the value of $X^{j,1}, \dots, X^{j,\alpha-1}$, where α is such that $i = \alpha \cdot \ell + \beta$ for $\beta \in [\ell]$, to compute Y_i^j. Thus, we can sample each input to g only when it is used. This gives rise to an algorithm G' that computes the output of the PRG in the following way: First, G' samples A, and for each $j \in [t]$, the G' samples I^j, and $X^{j,r}, X^{j,r-1}$ uniformly at random. Then, for each i from $(r-1)\ell$ to $(r-2)\ell+1$, the algorithm computes $H(Y_i^1, \dots Y_i^t)$ (notice that the relevant bits have already been fixed by $A, I^j, X^{j,r}$ and $X^{j,r-1}$) and outputs the hashed value. The total length of the output of G' so far is $q = \ell \cdot t(m/\ell + \Omega(\log n/\ell)) = tm + \Omega(t \cdot \log n)$. After finishing, the algorithm samples $X^{j,r-2}$ uniformly at random for every j, and continues this process for another ℓ indexes (i from $(r-2)\ell$ to $(r-3)\ell+1$), and so on. This process of sampling and hashing continues until it gets to $i = 1$, where in the k-th iteration, G' samples $X^{j,r-k}$ for each j, and the hashes $H(Y_i^1, \dots Y_i^t)$ for each i between $(r-k)\ell$ to $(r-k-1)\ell+1$. This results with $tm + \Omega(t \cdot \log n)$ pseudorandom bits in every iteration.

Clearly, the output of the described G' is equal to the output of the PRG. Moreover, the output in the k-th iteration is indistinguishable from uniform, even given the parts of $Y^j_{<(r-k-1)\ell}$ that have already been sampled up to the k-th iteration (that is, A, I^j and

$$Y^j[k] := Y^j_{(r-k-1)\ell-(I^j-1)}, \ldots, Y^j_{(r-k-1)\ell-1} = g_A(X^{j,r-k})_{<I^j}).$$

More formally, for every $k \in [r-1]$, let Z^k be the output of G' in the k-th iteration. It follows from the proof of Theorem 7.1 that for every such k,

$$(A, I^1, \ldots, I^t, Y^1[k], \ldots, Y^t[k], Z^k) \overset{c}{\approx} (A, I^1, \ldots, I^t, Y^1[k], \ldots, Y^t[k], U_q). \quad (7)$$

Using an hybrid argument we can also see that

$$(A, I^1, \ldots, I^t, Y^1[k], \ldots, Y^t[k], Z^1, \ldots, Z^k) \quad (8)$$
$$\overset{c}{\approx} (A, I^1, \ldots, I^t, Y^1[k], \ldots, Y^t[k], U_{k\cdot q}).$$

The idea in [VZ12] is to output only $\Omega(t \cdot \log n)$ bits of the above algorithm in each iteration k, and to use the other tm pseudorandom bits to sample the inputs $X^{1,r-k-1}, \ldots X^{t,r-k-1}$ of g for the next iteration. Since the output of G' in each iteration is indistinguishable from uniform, the output of this process is pseudorandom by a simple hybrid argument.

Indeed, fix a distinguisher E, a constant $c \in \mathbb{N}$ and a large enough $n \in N$, and for each $\tau \in [r-1]$ let $G'(\tau)$ be the algorithm that samples $X^{1,r-k-1}, \ldots X^{t,r-k-1}$ uniformly at random in the beginning of each iteration $k \leq \tau$, and uses the first tm bits of the output of each iteration $k > \tau$ as $X^{1,r-k-1}, \ldots X^{t,r-k-1}$. That is, $G'(r-1)$ is simply the algorithm G' described above, while $G'(1)$ is the algorithm considered by [VZ12], that only uses randomness to sample $X^{1,r-1}, X^{1,r}, \ldots, X^{t,r-1}, X^{t,r}$. Let $Z^1(\tau), \ldots, Z^{r-1}(\tau)$ be the output of $G'(\tau)$ in each iteration respectively, and let $Z^k(\tau)_{>tm}$ be the last $w - tm$ bits of $Z^k(\tau)$. Since the output of G' is pseudorandom, we get that,

$$|\Pr\left[E(Z^1(r-1)_{>tm}, \ldots, Z^{r-1}(r-1)_{>tm}) = 1\right]$$
$$- \Pr\left[E(U_{(r-1)\cdot(q-tm)}) = 1\right]| < n^{-c}.$$

We want to show that it also holds that

$$|\Pr\left[E(Z^1(1)_{>tm}, \ldots, Z^{r-1}(1)_{>tm}) = 1\right] - \Pr\left[E(U_{(r-1)\cdot(q-tm)}) = 1\right]| < 2n^{-c},$$

and thus it is enough to show that

$$|\Pr\left[E(Z^1(r-1)_{>tm}, \ldots, Z^{r-1}(r-1)_{>tm}) = 1\right]$$
$$- \Pr\left[E(Z^1(1)_{>tm}, \ldots, Z^{r-1}(1)_{>tm}) = 1\right]| < n^{-c}.$$

Assume towards a contradiction that the above does not hold. By an hybrid argument, there exists some $\tau \in [r-1]$ such that E distinguish between $(Z^1(\tau)_{>tm}, \ldots, Z^{r-1}(\tau)_{>tm})$ and $(Z^1(\tau+1)_{>tm}, \ldots, Z^{r-1}(\tau+1)_{>tm})$ with advantage n^{-c}/r.

Observing that $(Z^{\tau+1}(\tau)_{>tm}, \dots, Z^{r-1}(\tau)_{>tm})$ can be computed from $Z^{\tau}(\tau)$ and $A, I^1, \dots, I^t, Y^1[\tau], \dots, Y^t[\tau]$, while $(Z^{\tau+1}(\tau+1)_{>tm}, \dots, Z^{r-1}(\tau+1)_{>tm})$ can be computed by the same function from U_q and $A, I^1, \dots, I^t, Y^1[\tau], \dots, Y^t[\tau]$, we get the following by data processing. E distinguishes between

$$A, I^1, \dots, I^t, Y^1[\tau], \dots, Y^t[\tau], Z^1(\tau)_{>tm}, \dots, Z^{\tau}(\tau)_{>tm}, Z^{\tau}(\tau)_{\le tm}$$

and

$$A, I^1, \dots, I^t, Y^1[\tau], \dots, Y^t[\tau], Z^1(\tau+1)_{>tm}, \dots, Z^{\tau}(\tau+1)_{>tm}, U_{tm}$$

with the same advantage, n^{-c}/r. Since by definition $(Z^1(\tau), \dots, Z^{\tau}(\tau)) \equiv (Z^1(\tau+1), \dots, Z^{\tau}(\tau+1)) \equiv (Z^1, \dots, Z^{\tau})$, we get a contradiction to Eq. (8).

To see that $G'(1)$ outputs more pseudorandom bits than the randomness used, observe that $G'(1)$ uses $2tm$ random bits to sample

$$X^{1,r-1}, X^{1,r}, \dots, X^{t,r-1}, X^{t,r},$$

and outputs $\Omega(t \cdot \log n)$ pseudorandom bits in each iteration. Thus, for $r = \Omega(m/\log n)$, $G'(1)$ an expanding function. $\qquad \square$

References

[BM82] Blum, M., Micali, S.: How to generate cryptographically strong sequences of pseudo random bits. In: Annual Symposium on Foundations of Computer Science (FOCS), pp. 112–117 (1982). (cit. on pp. 2, 4)

[GGM84] Goldreich, O., Goldwasser, S., Micali, S.: On the cryptographic applications of random functions (extended abstract). In: Blakley, G.R., Chaum, D. (eds.) CRYPTO 1984. LNCS, vol. 196, pp. 276–288. Springer, Heidelberg (1985). https://doi.org/10.1007/3-540-39568-7_22

[GL89] Goldreich, O., Levin, L.A.: A hard-core predicate for all one-way functions. In: Proceedings of the 21st Annual ACM Symposium on Theory of Computing (STOC), pp. 25–32 (1989). (cit. on pp. 2, 11)

[GM84] Goldwasser, S., Micali, S.: Probabilistic encryption. J. Comput. Syst. Sci. 270–299 (1984). (cit. on p. 2)

[GMW87] Goldreich, O., Micali, S., Wigderson, A.: How to play any mental game or a completeness theorem for protocols with honest majority. In: Stoc 19, pp. 218–229 (1987). (cit. on p. 2)

[HHR06] Haitner, I., Harnik, D., Reingold, O.: On the power of the randomized iterate. In: Dwork, C. (ed.) CRYPTO 2006. LNCS, vol. 4117, pp. 22–40. Springer, Heidelberg (2006). https://doi.org/10.1007/11818175_2

[HILL99] Hastad, J., Impagliazzo, R., Levin, L.A., Luby, M.: A pseudorandom generator from any one-way function. SIAM J. Comput. 1364–1396 (1999). (cit. on pp. 2, 5, 10)

[Hol06a] Holenstein, T.: Pseudorandom generators from one-way functions: a simple construction for any hardness. In: Halevi, S., Rabin, T. (eds.) TCC 2006. LNCS, vol. 3876, pp. 443–461. Springer, Heidelberg (2006). https://doi.org/10.1007/11681878_23

[Hol06b] Holenstein, T.: Strengthening key agreement using hard-core sets. Ph.D. thesis. ETH Zurich (2006). (cit. on pp. 3, 9)

[HRV13] Haitner, I., Reingold, O., Vadhan, S.: Efficiency improvements in constructing pseudorandom generators from one-way functions. SIAM J. Comput. **42**(3), 1405–1430 (2013). (cit. on pp. 2–4, 7)

[HRVW09] Haitner, I., Reingold, O., Vadhan, S., Wee, H.: Inaccessible entropy. In: Proceedings of the 41st Annual ACM Symposium on Theory of Computing (STOC), pp. 611–620 (2009). (cit. on p. 7)

[HV17] Haitner, I., Vadhan, S.: The many entropies in one-way functions. In: Tutorials on the Foundations of Cryptography. ISC, pp. 159–217. Springer, Cham (2017). https://doi.org/10.1007/978-3-319-57048-8_4

[ILL89] Impagliazzo, R., Levin, L.A., Luby, M.: Pseudorandom generation from one-way functions. In: Annual ACM Symposium on Theory of Computing (STOC), pp. 12–24 (1989). (cit. on p. 24)

[Nao91] Naor, M.: Bit commitment using pseudorandomness. J. Cryptol. 151–158 (1991). (cit. on p. 2)

[Sha83] Shamir, A.: On the generation of cryptographically strong pseudorandom sequences. ACM Trans. Comput. Syst. (TOCS) **1**(1), 38–44 (1983). (cit. on p. 4)

[VZ12] Vadhan, S., Zheng, C.J.: Characterizing pseudoentropy and simplifying pseudorandom generator constructions. In: Annual ACM Symposium on Theory of Computing (STOC), pp. 817–836 (2012). (cit. on pp. 2, 3, 6, 9, 10, 23–26)

[Yao82] Yao, A.C.: Theory and applications of trapdoor functions. In: Annual Symposium on Foundations of Computer Science (FOCS), pp. 80–91 (1982). (cit. on p. 11)

On One-Way Functions and Sparse Languages

Yanyi Liu[1][(✉)] and Rafael Pass[2]

[1] Cornell Tech, New York, USA
ttyl2866@cornell.edu
[2] Tel-Aviv University & Cornell Tech, Tel Aviv-Yafo, Israel
ttrafaelp@tau.ac.il

Abstract. We show equivalence between the existence of one-way functions and the existence of a *sparse* language that is hard-on-average w.r.t. some efficiently samplable "high-entropy" distribution. In more detail, the following are equivalent:
- The existence of a $S(\cdot)$-sparse language L that is hard-on-average with respect to some samplable distribution with Shannon entropy $h(\cdot)$ such that $h(n) - \log(S(n)) \geq 4 \log n$;
- The existence of a $S(\cdot)$-sparse language $L \in \mathsf{NP}$, that is hard-on-average with respect to some samplable distribution with Shannon entropy $h(\cdot)$ such that $h(n) - \log(S(n)) \geq n/3$;
- The existence of one-way functions.

where a language L is said to be $S(\cdot)$-sparse if $|L \cap \{0,1\}^n| \leq S(n)$ for all $n \in \mathbb{N}$. Our results are inspired by, and generalize, results from the elegant recent paper by Ilango, Ren and Santhanam (IRS, STOC'22), which presents similar connections for *specific* sparse languages

1 Introduction

A *one-way function* [4] (OWF) is a function f that can be efficiently computed (in polynomial time), yet no probabilistic polynomial-time (PPT) algorithm can invert f with inverse polynomial probability for infinitely many input lengths n. Whether one-way functions exist is unequivocally the most important open problem in Cryptography (and arguably the most important open problem in the theory of computation, see e.g., [18]): OWFs are both necessary [15] and sufficient for many of the most central cryptographic primitives and protocols (e.g., pseudorandom generators [2,10], pseudorandom functions [6], private-key encryption [7], digital signatures [22], commitment schemes [20], identification

---
Supported by a JP Morgan fellowship.
Supported in part by NSF Award CNS 2149305, NSF Award CNS-2128519, NSF Award RI-1703846, AFOSR Award FA9550-18-1-0267, FA9550-23-1-0312, a JP Morgan Faculty Award, the Algorand Centres of Excellence programme managed by Algorand Foundation, and DARPA under Agreement No. HR00110C0086. Any opinions, findings and conclusions or recommendations expressed in this material are those of the author(s) and do not necessarily reflect the views of the United States Government, DARPA or the Algorand Foundation.

G. Rothblum and H. Wee (Eds.): TCC 2023, LNCS 14369, pp. 219–237, 2023.
https://doi.org/10.1007/978-3-031-48615-9_8

protocols [5], coin-flipping protocols [1], and more). These primitives and protocols are often referred to as *private-key primitives*, or "Minicrypt" primitives [13] as they exclude the notable task of public-key encryption [4,21]. Additionally, as observed by Impagliazzo [8,13], the existence of a OWF is equivalent to the existence of polynomial-time method for sampling hard *solved* instances for an NP language (i.e., hard instances together with their witnesses).

A central open question at the intersection of Cryptography and Complexity-theory, however, is whether the existence of just an average-case hard problem in NP suffices to get the existence of OWFs:

> *Does the existence of a language in* NP *that is hard-on-average imply the existence of OWFs?*

(In Impagliazzo's language, can we rule out "Pessiland"—a world where NP is hard on average but OWFs do not exist.) There has been some recent progress towards this question. Most notably, Liu and Pass [19] recently showed that (mild) average-case hardness, w.r.t. the uniform distribution of instances, of a particular natural problem in NP—the time-bounded Kolmogorov Complexity problem [9,16,17,23,24]—characterizes the existence of OWFs. This problem, however is not average-case complete for NP so it does not resolve the above question.

In this work, our goal is to identify properties of languages such that their average-case hardness implies OWFs:

> *Can we identify simple/natural properties of a distribution-language pair* $(\mathcal{D}, L)$ *such that average-case hardness of* L *with respect to distribution* $\mathcal{D}$ *implies the existence of OWFs?*

Our starting point towards answering this problem is an elegant recent work by Ilango, Ren and Santhanam [11,12] (IRS). IRS first show that the existence of OWFs is equivalent to average-case hardness of a Gap version of the Kolmogorov complexity problem w.r.t. *any* efficiently computable distribution. In a second step, they next show that average-case hardness of some specific sparse languages implies average-case hardness of this Gap problem.

In more detail, their first step shows that OWFs exist iff there exists some samplable distribution $\mathcal{D}$ and efficiently computable thresholds t_0, t_1, $t_1(n) - t_0(n) > \omega(\log n)$, so that it is hard to decide whether $K(x) > t_1(|x|)$ or $K(x) < t_0(|x|)$. Let us highlight that this characterization differs from the one in [19] in three aspects: (1) it considers unbounded, as opposed to time-bounded Kolmogorov complexity, (2) hardness holds w.r.t. to a gap problem, as opposed to a decisional problem, and (3) it considers hardness w.r.t. *any* efficient distribution, as opposed to the uniform distribution considered in [19]. (In particular, this result does not provide a candidate distribution for which the Gap problem may be hard—and it is provably *easy* with respect to the uniform distribution.) In the second step, they present some concrete languages (k-SAT and t-Clique) such that average-case hardness of these languages with respect to high-entropy distributions implies (but does not characterize) the existence of OWFs.

In this work, we show how to generalize the results obtained in the second step and to demonstrate that the existence of OWFs is equivalent to the existence of a *sparse* language that is hard-on-average w.r.t. some efficiently samplable "high-entropy" distribution. In more details, the Shannon entropy of the sampler needs to be just slightly bigger than the logarithm of the density of the language.

As a result of independent interest, we additionally show how to generalize the results of IRS in their Step 1 with respect to K-complexity (but note that the results with respect to sparse languages no longer pass through this result).[1]

1.1 Our Results

To formalize the statements of our results, let us briefly state some preliminaries.

Preliminaries We say that a language $L \subset \{0,1\}^*$ is $S(\cdot)$-*sparse* if for all $n \in \mathbb{N}$, $|L_n| \leq S(n)$, where $L_n = |L \cap \{0,1\}^n|$. Given a language L, we abuse the notation and let $L(x) = 1$ iff $x \in L$. For a random variable X, let $H(X) = \mathsf{E}[\log \frac{1}{\Pr[X=x]}]$ denote the Shannon entropy of X. A function μ is said to be *negligible* if for every polynomial $p(\cdot)$ there exists some n_0 such that for all $n > n_0$, $\mu(n) \leq \frac{1}{p(n)}$.

We say that $\mathcal{D} = \{D_n\}_{n \in \mathbb{N}}$ is an *ensemble* if for all $n \in \mathbb{N}$, D_n is a probability distribution over $\{0,1\}^n$. We say that an ensemble $\mathcal{D} = \{D_n\}_{n \in \mathbb{N}}$ is *samplable* if there exists a probabilistic polynomial-time Turing machine S such that $S(1^n)$ samples D_n; we use the notation $S(1^n; r)$ to denote the algorithm S with randomness fixed to r. We say that an ensemble $\mathcal{D}$ has entropy $h(\cdot)$ if for all sufficiently large $n \in \mathbb{N}$, $H(D_n) \geq h(n)$.

We say that a language $L \subset \{0,1\}^*$ is $\alpha(\cdot)$ *hard-on-average* (α-*HoA*) on an ensemble $\mathcal{D} = \{D_n\}_{n \in \mathbb{N}}$ if for all probabilistic polynomial-time heuristics $\mathcal{H}$, for all sufficiently large $n \in \mathbb{N}$,

$$\Pr[x \leftarrow D_n : \mathcal{H}(x) = L(x)] < 1 - \alpha(n).$$

We simply say that L is *hard-on-average (HoA)* on $\mathcal{D}$ if for every c, $\alpha(n) = \frac{1}{2} - \frac{1}{n^c}$, L is α-HoA.

Let $f : \{0,1\}^* \to \{0,1\}^*$ be a polynomial-time computable function. f is said to be a *one-way function (OWF)* if for every PPT algorithm $\mathcal{A}$, there exists a negligible function μ such that for all $n \in \mathbb{N}$,

$$\Pr[x \leftarrow \{0,1\}^n; y = f(x) : A(1^n, y) \in f^{-1}(f(x))] \leq \mu(n)$$

Main Theorem We are now ready to state our main theorem.

Theorem 11 *The following are equivalent:*

1. *The existence of a $S(\cdot)$-sparse language L that is $(\frac{1}{2} - \frac{1}{4n})$-HoA with respect to some samplable distribution with Shannon entropy $h(\cdot)$ such that $h(n) - \log(S(n)) \geq 4 \log n$;*

---

[1] It appears that a similar generalization was concurrently and independently obtained by IRS in the proceedings version [12]; see Sect. 5 for more details.

2. *The existence of a $S(\cdot)$-sparse language $L \in$ NP, that is HoA with respect to some samplable distribution with Shannon entropy $h(\cdot)$ such that $h(n) - \log(S(n)) \geq n/3$;*
3. *The existence of one-way functions.*

Theorem 11 is proven by, in Sect. 2 showing that (1) implies (3), and in Sect. 3 showing that (3) implies (2); the fact that (2) implies (1) is trivial. We present some corollaries of Theorem 11 in Sect. 4. In Sect. 5, we finally present some result of independent interest that generalize the result in [11] with respect to the particular K-complexity problem—in particular, we strengthen the result from [11] to show that that it suffices to assume hardness of approximating K-complexity (as opposed to assuming hardness of deciding a threshold version of a Gap-K problem).

1.2 Proof Overview

To explain the proof of our results, and to put it in context, let us start by reviewing the results of Ilango, Ren and Santhanam (IRS) [11].

IRS Part 1: OWFs from Hardness of Gap-K. As mentioned, IRS first show that OWFs exist iff there exists some samplable distribution $\mathcal{D}$ and efficiently computable thresholds t_0, t_1 where $t_1(n) - t_0(n) > \omega(\log n)$ so that it is hard to decide whether $K(x) > t_1(|x|)$ or $K(x) < t_0(|x|)$ when sampling x from $\mathcal{D}$. We here focus only on the "if" direction which will be most relevant to us.[2] On a high level, the IRS result is obtained by showing that any sampler that makes this Gap problem hard must itself be a OWF. In more detail, they first appeal to the result of [14, 15] showing that if OWFs do not exist, then approximate counting is possible on average. They next show how to use an approximate counter to solve the Gap-K problem: Given an instance x, approximately count the number of random strings r that lead the sampler $\mathcal{D}$ (given randomness r) to generate x. If the number is "small"—we refer to such strings x as rare, where "small" is appropriately defined as a function of $t_1(|x|)$ (which, recall, is required to be efficiently computable), then output NO (i.e., that the K-complexity is large), and otherwise (i.e., if x is common) output YES.

It remains to analyze that this deciding algorithm works (on average). The key observation is that common instances x must be YES-instances: their K-complexity must be small simply by enumerating all common strings (since there can only be a small number of them!). Thus (whenever the approximate counter is correct), the decider always gives the right answer on NO-instances. On the other hand, since YES-instances are sparse, it directly follows by a Union bound, that the probability that we sample a YES-instance that is rare must be small. Consequently, the decider will also give the right answer on YES-instances with high probability. This concludes the existence of OWFs assuming the hardness of the Gap-K problem.

---

[2] The only-if direction is a direct consequence of [10].

IRS Part 2: OWF from Specific Sparse Languages. In the second part of their paper, IRS next present some concrete languages—k-SAT and t-Clique—and show that average-case hardness with respect to *high-entropy* distributions of these concrete languages imply hardness of Gap-K (which in turn by the first result implies OWFs). This argument relies on the following three steps:

- **Step 1** (Language-specific): Proving—*using language specific structures*—that YES instances have small K-complexity.
- **Step 2** (Generic): Rely on a generic counting argument (following a similar statement in [19]) to show that elements sampled from any high-entropy distribution need to have high K-complexity with reasonable (roughly $1/n$) probability.
- **Step 3** (Language-specific): Finally, to argue that average-case hardness of these languages w.r.t. any high-entropy distribution implies average-case hardness of Gap-K, we additionally need to argue that the thresholds t_0, t_1 for the K-complexity problem are efficiently computable. Another language specific argument is used to show that the number of YES-instances in these languages can be efficiently estimated and this can be used to give the thresholds.

Towards Sparse Languages: A Warm-Up We start by observing that Step 1, in fact, holds for *any* sparse language that is *decideable*, or even *recursively enumerable*: If the language is sparse and recursively enumerable, then we can simply compress an instance by writing down its index, so YES-instances need to have small K-complexity. We additionally note that if the sparsity threshold, $S(\cdot)$, is efficiently computable, the thresholds t_0, t_1 for the Gap-K problem also become efficiently computable and we can also carry out Step 3 (and Step 2 is obviously generic). Thus, relying on these observations, we can directly obtain a *weaker* version of Theorem 11 by appealing to the results of [11]. Let us highlight, however, that this version is weaker in two important ways:

1. We require the sparse language to be recursively enumerable (to deal with Step 1).
2. We require the sparsity threshold to be efficiently computable (to deal with Step 3).

Proving the Full Result To remove the above two restrictions, our key observation is that passing through K-complexity may not be the right approach. Rather, we can directly redo Part 1 of IRS (i.e., decide the language using an approximate counter) for any sparse language w.r.t. to a high-entropy distribution. Our decider proceeds as follows given an instance x:

- Just as IRS, use the approximate counter to check if the string x is rare (i.e., that there is a small number of random coins r for $\mathcal{D}$ that generate x).
- If x is deemed rare, then output NO, and otherwise output a *random guess* (as opposed to outputting YES as in IRS).

In the above approach, we still need to define the threshold for what counts as rare. To do this, we note that we can use approximate counting to estimate the Shannon entropy of any efficiently sampleable distribution (see Lemma 25), and we can use the (estimated) Shannon entropy as the threshold for determining when to deem a string rare. More precisely, we call a string x rare if it is sampled by $\mathcal{D}$ with probability $\leq 2^{-h+3}$, where h is the Shannon entropy of $\mathcal{D}$.

To argue that this approach works, we proceed as follows:

- We first note that any distribution $\mathcal{D}$ needs to output strings that are rare (where recall, rare is defined w.r.t. the Shannon-entropy of $\mathcal{D}$) with probability $1/n$ (See Lemma 22). (This statement is a stronger version of a result shown in [19], and relies on essentially the same proof as used in [11] to argue that high-entropy distributions output strings with high K-complexity with reasonable probability.)
- We next argue that conditioned on $\mathcal{D}$ sampling a rare instance, our decider succeeds with high probability. First, note that the decider always outputs NO on rare instances (unless the approximate counter fails, which happens with small probability so we can ignore this event). Next, by the sparsity of the language and the Union bound, we have that the probability that $\mathcal{D}$ samples a YES-instance that is rare is tiny (technically, $\leq 1/n^2$) (see Lemma 23). But since the probability that $\mathcal{D}$ samples a rare instance is a lot larger, we have that our decider succeeds with high probability conditioned on rare instances.
- On common instances, our decider succeeds with probability $1/2$ (again, as long as the approximate counter does not fail, which happens with tiny probability). So, we conclude that the decider succeeds with probability roughy $1/2 + 1/(2n)$.

This concludes that (1) implies (3) in Theorem 11. To show that (3) implies (2) we simply note that one-way functions imply pseudo-random generators (PRG) by [10], and by considering the language of images of the PRG (which is extremely sparse) and the distribution that with probability $1/2$ samples a random string and with probability $1/2$ samples an image of the PRG (which has Shannon-entropy entropy $1/2n$); this language is hard-on-average on this distribution by the security of the PRG.

Concluding Corollaries for Concrete Languages We finally observe—using standard arguments—that the languages considered in [11] (k-SAT and t-Clique) are sparse, and so is the language of strings with small K-complexity. See Sect. 4 for more details.

In our view, these results show that for many of the corollaries of [11], K-complexity was perhaps a mirage, and in our eyes, sparsity is the central feature. We note that a similar phenomena actually happened also with respect to the vein of work on "hardness magnification", as shown in the elegant work by Chen, Jin, Williams [3].

Musings on the Relevance of our Results The reader may wonder why it matters to deal with non-recursively enumerable languages and with non-efficiently computable sparsity. After all, the natural sparse languages we consider in Sect. 4 are both recursively enumerable and have efficiently computable sparsity. In our opinion, the difference is significant. In particular, removing these restriction opens up for the possibility of using a probabilistic argument to define a candidate language that is hard-on-average. Probabilistic arguments are typically used for proving lower-bounds and our hope is that our result opens up the avenue for using such techniques.

Back to K-complexity Motivated by the above results, one may wonder whether the efficient computability condition in the results of [11] w.r.t. K-complexity is inherent (i.e., whether the efficient computability of the thresholds t_0, t_1 in the Gap-K problem is inherent). As a result of independent interest, we show how to strengthen the result of IRS to show that it suffices to assume average-case hardness of *approximately computing K-complexity* within an additive term of $\omega(\log n)$ to deduce the existence of one-way function (i.e., that hardness of the search version suffices, and thus we no longer need to consider any thresholds).[3]

Theorem 12 *The following are equivalent:*

- *One-way functions exist;*
- *There exists some efficiently samplable distribution $\mathcal{D}$ such that K-complexity is mildly hard to approximate within an additive term of $\omega(\log n)$.*
- *There exists some efficiently samplable distribution $\mathcal{D}$ such that K-complexity is hard to approximate within an additive term of $n - n^{o(1)}$.*

Let us first compare this result to IRS; the result is strictly stronger as our hardness of approximating K-complexity assumption is trivially implied the decisional Gap-K hardness condition considered in IRS. In fact, as a corollary of this result (of independent interest), we get a decision-to-search reduction for K-complexity (for efficiently computable thresholds); See Theorem 51 for more details.

It is also worthwhile to compare it to the results of [19]; here the results is incomparable. [19] shows that mild average-case hardness of *time-bounded* Kolmogorov complexity (even to approximate) with respect to the *uniform distribution* characterizes OWF. We note that K-complexity (and also time-bounded K-complexity) is *easy* to approximate within an additive factor of $\omega(\log n)$ with overwhelming probability with respect to the uniform distribution so it was crucial for [19] that an approximate factor of $O(\log n)$ was employed. Theorem 12 thus cannot hold w.r.t. the uniform distribution, and just as the result in IRS, it gives no indication of what the hard distribution may be—in fact, as mentioned before, the distribution $\mathcal{D}$ gives the OWF.

---

[3] As mentionned above, it appears that a similar generalization was concurrently and independently obtained by IRS in the proceedings version [12]; see Sect. 5 for more details.

2   OWFs from Avg-Case Hardness of Sparse Languages

Theorem 21 *Let $S(\cdot)$ be a function, let $h(n) \geq \log S(n) + 4 \log n$, and let L be a $S(\cdot)$-sparse language. Assume there exists some samplable ensemble $\mathcal{D}$ with entropy $h(\cdot)$ such that L is $(\frac{1}{2} - \frac{1}{4n})$-HoA on $\mathcal{D}$. Then, one-way functions exist.*

Before proving the theorem, we will state some useful lemmas.

Lemma 22 (Implicit in [11,19]) *Let D_n be a distribution over $\{0,1\}^n$ with entropy at least h. Then, with probability at least $\frac{1}{n}$ over $x \leftarrow D_n$, it holds that*

$$\Pr[D_n = x] \leq 2^{-h+3}$$

Proof. Assume for contradiction that with probability less than $\frac{1}{n}$ over $x \leftarrow D_n$, $\Pr[D_n = x] \leq 2^{-h+3}$. Let Freq denote the set of strings $x \subseteq \{0,1\}^n$ such that $\Pr[D_n = x] > 2^{-h+3}$, and let Rare denote the set of strings $\subseteq \{0,1\}^n$ such that $\Pr[D_n = x] \leq 2^{-h+3}$. Let flag be a binary random variable such that flag $= 0$ if $D_n \in$ Freq and 1 otherwise (i.e. if $D_n \in$ Rare). Let p_{Freq} be the probability that $D_n \in$ Freq and p_{Rare} be the probability that $D_n \in$ Rare. By the chain rule for entropy, it holds that

$$H(D_n) \leq H(D_n, \mathsf{flag})$$
$$= H(\mathsf{flag}) + p_{\mathsf{Freq}} H(D_n \mid D_n \in \mathsf{Freq}) + p_{\mathsf{Rare}} H(D_n \mid D_n \in \mathsf{Rare})$$

In the RHS, the first term is at most 1 (since flag is a binary variable). The second term is at most $h-3$ since $|\mathsf{Freq}| \leq 2^{h-3}$. Recall that by assumption, we have that $p_{\mathsf{Rare}} < \frac{1}{n}$; furthermore, $H(D_n \mid D_n \in \mathsf{Rare}) \leq n$ (since $|\mathsf{Rare}| \leq 2^n$) and thus the last term of the RHS is at most 1. Therefore, $H(D_n) \leq 1 + (h-3) + 1 < h$, which is a contradiction.

Lemma 23 *Let $L_n \subset \{0,1\}^n$ be a set of strings such that $|L_n| \leq S(n)$. Let D_n be a distribution over $\{0,1\}^n$. Let ε be any number satisfying $\varepsilon \leq \frac{1}{S(n)n^2}$. Then, the following holds:*

$$\Pr_{x \leftarrow D_n}[L_n(x) = 1 \wedge \Pr[D_n = x] \leq \varepsilon] \leq \frac{1}{n^2}$$

Proof. By taking a union bound over the at most $S(n)$ instances in L_n, it follows that $\Pr_{x \leftarrow D_n}[L_n(x) = 1 \wedge \Pr[D_n = x] \leq \varepsilon]$ is bounded by $S(n) \times \frac{1}{S(n)n^2} = \frac{1}{n^2}$.

We will rely on the following important lemma showing that approximate counting can be efficiently done infinitely often if one-way functions do not exist.

Lemma 24 ([11,14,15]) *Assume that one-way functions do not exist. Then, for any samplable ensemble $\mathcal{D} = \{D_n\}_{n \in \mathbb{N}}$ and any constant $q \geq 1$, there exist a PPT algorithm $\mathcal{A}$ and a constant $\delta > 0$ such that for infinitely many n,*

$$\Pr_{x \leftarrow D_n}[\delta \cdot p_x \leq \mathcal{A}(x) \leq p_x] \geq 1 - \frac{1}{n^q}$$

where $p_x = \Pr[D_n = x]$.

In addition, we observe that if approximate counting can be done, the Shannon entropy of any samplable distribution $\mathcal{D}$ can be estimated efficiently.

Lemma 25 *Let $\mathcal{D} = \{D_n\}_{n \in \mathbb{N}}$ be a samplable ensemble, let Samp be the corresponding sampler, and let $m(\cdot)$ be a polynomial such that $m(n)$ is greater than the number of random coins used by $\mathsf{Samp}(1^n)$. Assume that there exist a PPT algorithm $\mathcal{A}$, a constant δ, and an infinite set $I \subseteq \mathbb{N}$ such that for all $n \in I$,*

$$\Pr_{x \leftarrow D_n} [\delta \cdot p_x \leq \mathcal{A}(x) \leq p_x] \geq 1 - \frac{1}{m(n)}$$

where $p_x = \Pr[D_n = x]$. Then, there exist a PPT algorithm est and a constant δ' such that for all $n \in I$, with probability at least $1 - \frac{1}{n^2}$,

$$|\mathsf{est}(1^n) - H(D_n)| \leq \delta'$$

Proof. Let $n \in I$ be a sufficiently large input length on which $\mathcal{A}$ succeeds, and let $m = m(n)$. Let p_x denote $\Pr[D_n = x]$. Let $\mathcal{A}'$ be the algorithm defined as $\mathcal{A}'(x) = \max(2^{-m}, \min(1, \mathcal{A}(x)))$. $\mathcal{A}'$ will have the same property that $\mathcal{A}$ has in the assumption since for all x in the support of D_n, it holds that $2^{-m} \leq p_x \leq 1$. We first claim that

$$|\mathbb{E}_{x \leftarrow D_n}[-\log \mathcal{A}'(x)] - H(D_n)| \leq -\log \delta + 1 \qquad (1)$$

If this holds, note that $\mathcal{D}$ is samplable and $\mathcal{A}'$ runs in PPT, it follows that we can empirically estimate $\mathbb{E}_{x \leftarrow D_n}[-\log \mathcal{A}'(x)]$ in polynomial time by collecting at least polynomially many samples and taking the average. By Hoeffding's inequality, the difference between this estimation and the real expectation value is at most 1 with very high probability $(\geq 1 - \frac{1}{n^2})$.

Thus, it remains to show that inequality 1 holds. Notice that

$$|\mathbb{E}_{x \leftarrow D_n}[-\log \mathcal{A}'(x)] - H(D_n)|$$
$$= |\mathbb{E}_{x \leftarrow D_n}[-\log \mathcal{A}'(x)] - \mathbb{E}_{x \leftarrow D_n}[-\log p_x]|$$
$$\leq \mathbb{E}_{x \leftarrow D_n}[|-\log \mathcal{A}'(x) - (-\log p_x)|]$$
$$= \Pr_{x \leftarrow D_n}[\mathcal{A}' \text{ succeeds}] \cdot \mathbb{E}_{x \leftarrow D_n}[|-\log \mathcal{A}'(x) - (-\log p_x)| \mid \mathcal{A}' \text{ succeeds}]$$
$$+ \Pr_{x \leftarrow D_n}[\mathcal{A}' \text{ fails}] \cdot \mathbb{E}_{x \leftarrow D_n}[|\log \mathcal{A}'(x) - (-\log p_x)| \mid \mathcal{A}' \text{ fails}]$$
$$\leq \mathbb{E}_{x \leftarrow D_n}[|\log \frac{p_x}{\mathcal{A}'(x)}| \mid \mathcal{A}' \text{ succeeds}] + \frac{1}{m} \cdot m$$
$$\leq \mathbb{E}_{x \leftarrow D_n}[-\log \delta \mid \mathcal{A}' \text{ succeeds}] + 1$$
$$\leq -\log \delta + 1$$

Now we are ready to prove Theorem 21.

Proof (Proof of Theorem 21). Assume for contradiction that one-way functions do not exist. Then, by Lemma 24, there exist a PPT algorithm $\mathcal{A}$ and a constant δ such that for infinitely many n,

$$\Pr_{x \leftarrow D_n} [\delta \cdot p_x \leq \mathcal{A}(x) \leq p_x] \geq 1 - \frac{1}{n^2}$$

where $p_x = \Pr[D_n = x]$. By Lemma 25, there exist a PPT algorithm est and a constant δ' such that for all n on which $\mathcal{A}$ succeeds, with probability at least $1 - \frac{1}{n^2}$,

$$|\mathsf{est}(1^n) - H(D_n)| \leq \delta' \tag{2}$$

Consider some sufficiently large input length n on which $\mathcal{A}$ succeeds. Let the random variable

$$\varepsilon = 2^{-\mathsf{est}(1^n) + \log n}$$

We are now ready to describe our heuristic $\mathcal{H}$ for L. On input $x \leftarrow D_n$, $\mathcal{H}$ computes ε and outputs 0 if $\mathcal{A}(x) \leq \varepsilon$; otherwise, $\mathcal{H}$ outputs a random guess $b \in \{0,1\}$. We will show that $\mathcal{H}$ solves L with probability $\frac{1}{2} + \frac{1}{4n}$ on the input length n (whenever n is sufficiently large).

Towards this, let us first assume we have access to a "perfect" approximate-counter algorithm $\mathcal{O}$ such that $\delta \cdot p_x \leq \mathcal{O}(x) \leq p_x$ with probability 1 when x sampled from D_n; let us also assume we have access to a "perfect" entropy-estimator algorithm est^* such that $|\mathsf{est}^*(1^n) - H(D_n)| \leq \delta'$ with probability 1; consider the heuristic $\mathcal{H}'$ that behaves just as $\mathcal{H}$ except that $\mathcal{H}'$ uses $\mathcal{O}$ and est^* instead of $\mathcal{A}$ and est.

We first show that $\mathcal{H}'$ solves L with high probability on D_n. Note that

$$\Pr_{x \leftarrow D_n}[\mathcal{H}'(x) = L(x)]$$

$$= \Pr_{x \leftarrow D_n}[\mathcal{H}'(x) = L(x) \mid \mathcal{O}(x) > \varepsilon] \Pr[\mathcal{O}(x) > \varepsilon]$$

$$\quad + \Pr_{x \leftarrow D_n}[\mathcal{H}'(x) = L(x) \mid \mathcal{O}(x) \leq \varepsilon] \Pr[\mathcal{O}(x) \leq \varepsilon]$$

$$= \frac{1}{2}(1 - \Pr[\mathcal{O}(x) \leq \varepsilon]) + \left(1 - \Pr_{x \leftarrow D_n}[\mathcal{H}'(x) \neq L(x) \mid \mathcal{O}(x) \leq \varepsilon]\right) \Pr[\mathcal{O}(x) \leq \varepsilon]$$

$$= \frac{1}{2}(1 - \Pr[\mathcal{O}(x) \leq \varepsilon]) + \left(1 - \Pr_{x \leftarrow D_n}[L(x) = 1 \mid \mathcal{O}(x) \leq \varepsilon]\right) \Pr[\mathcal{O}(x) \leq \varepsilon]$$

$$= \frac{1}{2} + \frac{1}{2}\Pr[\mathcal{O}(x) \leq \varepsilon] - \Pr_{x \leftarrow D_n}[L(x) = 1 \mid \mathcal{O}(x) \leq \varepsilon] \Pr[\mathcal{O}(x) \leq \varepsilon]$$

$$= \frac{1}{2} + \frac{1}{2}\Pr[\mathcal{O}(x) \leq \varepsilon] - \Pr_{x \leftarrow D_n}[L(x) = 1 \wedge \mathcal{O}(x) \leq \varepsilon]$$

Note that $p_x \leq \varepsilon$ implies $\mathcal{O}(x) \leq \varepsilon$ (since $\mathcal{O}$ is a prefect approximate-counter). In addition, for sufficiently large n, $p_x \leq 2^{-H(D_n)+3}$ implies $p_x \leq \varepsilon$ since

$$2^{-H(D_n)+3} \leq 2^{-\mathsf{est}^*(1^n)+\delta'+3} \leq 2^{-\mathsf{est}^*(1^n)+\log n} = \varepsilon.$$

Thus,

$$\Pr[\mathcal{O}(x) \leq \varepsilon] \geq \Pr_{x \leftarrow D_n}[p_x \leq \varepsilon] \geq \Pr_{x \leftarrow D_n}[p_x \leq 2^{-H(D_n)+3}] \geq \frac{1}{n}$$

where the last inequality follows from by Lemma 22.

Next, observe that $\varepsilon/\delta \leq \frac{1}{S(n)n^2}$ (for sufficiently large n). This follows since if n is sufficiently large, we have:

$$\varepsilon = 2^{-\text{est}^*(1^n)+\log n} \leq 2^{-H(D_n)+\delta'+\log n} = 2^{-H(D_n)+\log n} \cdot 2^{\delta'}$$

$$\leq 2^{-H(D_n)+\log n} \cdot \delta n = 2^{-H(D_n)+2\log n}\delta$$

$$\leq 2^{-h(n)+2\log n}\delta \leq 2^{-\log S(n)-4\log n+2\log n}\delta$$

$$= \frac{\delta}{S(n)n^2}$$

Finally, since $p_x \leq \mathcal{O}(x)/\delta$ holds with probability 1, it follows that

$$\Pr_{x \leftarrow D_n}[L(x) = 1 \wedge \mathcal{O}(x) \leq \varepsilon] \leq \Pr_{x \leftarrow D_n}[L(x) = 1 \wedge p_x \leq \varepsilon/\delta] \leq \frac{1}{n^2}$$

where the last inequality follows from Lemma 23 and the fact that $\varepsilon/\delta \leq \frac{1}{S(n)n^2}$. Thus, we conclude that

$$\Pr_{x \leftarrow D_n}[\mathcal{H}'(x) = L(x)] \geq \frac{1}{2} + \frac{1}{2} \cdot \frac{1}{n} - \frac{1}{n^2}$$

We now turn to analyzing $\mathcal{H}$ as opposed to $\mathcal{H}'$ and note that $\mathcal{H}$ and $\mathcal{H}'$ work identically the same except when either $\mathcal{A}$ or est "fail". Observe that the probability that $\mathcal{A}(x) \neq \mathcal{O}(x)$ on x sampled from D_n is at most $\frac{1}{n^2}$. Additionally, the probability that $|\text{est}(1^n) - H(D_n)| > \delta'$ is at most $\frac{1}{n^2}$. Thus, by a union bound, we have that

$$\Pr_{x \leftarrow D_n}[\mathcal{H}(x) = L(x)] \geq \frac{1}{2} + \frac{1}{2n} - \frac{3}{n^2} \geq \frac{1}{2} + \frac{1}{4n}$$

on infinitely many $n \in \mathbb{N}$, which is a contradiction.

3   Avg-Case Hardness of Sparse Languages from OWFs

Theorem 31 *Assume the existence of one-way functions. Let $S(n) = 2^{n/10}$ and $h(n) = n/2$. Then there exists a $S(\cdot)$-sparse language $L \in$ NP and a samplable ensemble $\mathcal{D}$ with entropy $h(\cdot)$ such that L is HoA on $\mathcal{D}$.*

Proof. Assume the existence of OWFs. By [10], there exists some pseudorandom generator $g : \{0,1\}^{n/10} \rightarrow \{0,1\}^n$. Consider the NP-language $L = \{g(s) \mid s \in \{0,1\}^*\}$. Note that L is $S(\cdot)$-sparse for $S(n) = 2^{n/10}$. Let $\mathcal{D} = \{D_n\}_{n\in\mathbb{N}}$ be an ensemble such that D_n samples from $g(\mathcal{U}_{n/10})$ with probability $1/2$ and from $\mathcal{U}_n$ with probability $1/2$. Note that $\mathcal{D}$ has entropy at least $h(n) = n/2$ (since with probability $1/2$, we sample from $\mathcal{U}_n$). Finally, it follows from the pseudorandomness property of g (using a standard argument) that L is HoA over $\mathcal{D}$.

4 Corollaries

In this section, we present some direct corollaries that follow by applying our main theorem to known sparse languages. For convenience of the reader, we recall the (standard) proofs that these languages are sparse.

4.1 Kolmogorov Complexity

The Kolmogorov complexity (K-complexity) of a string $x \in \{0,1\}^*$ is defined to be the length of the shortest program Π that outputs the string x. More formally, let U be a fixed Universal Turing machine, for any string $x \in \{0,1\}^*$, we define $K(x) = \min_{\Pi \in \{0,1\}^*}\{|\Pi| : U(\Pi) = x\}$. Let MINK$[s]$ denote the language of strings x having the property that $K(x) \leq s(|x|)$. We observes that MINK$[s]$ is a sparse language when $s(n)$ is slightly below n.

Lemma 41 *For all $n \in \mathbb{N}$, $|\text{MINK}[s] \cap \{0,1\}^n| \leq 2^{s(n)+1}$.*

Proof. The lemma directly follows from the fact that the number of strings with length $\leq s(n)$ is at most $2^{s(n)+1}$.

Combining Lemma 41, we get:

Corollary 42 *Let $s(n) \leq n - 4\log n - 1$ be a function. Assume that there exists some samplable ensemble $\mathcal{D}$ with entropy $h(n) \geq s(n) + 4\log n + 1$ such that MINK$[s]$ is $(\frac{1}{2} - \frac{1}{4n})$-HoA on $\mathcal{D}$. Then, one-way functions exist.*

Proof. By Lemma 41, the number of n-bit YES instances is at most $S(n) = 2^{s(n)+1}$. Since $\mathcal{D}_n$ has entropy $h(n) \geq s(n) + 1 + 4\log n$, the corollary follows directly from Theorem 11.

4.2 k-SAT

Let k, c be two positive integers. The language k-SAT(m, cm) is defined to consist of all satisfiable k-CNF formulas on m variables with cm clauses. We recall the well-known fact that k-SAT(m, cm) is a sparse language when $c \geq 2^{k+1}$.

Lemma 43 *The number of satisfiable k-CNF formulas on m variables with cm clauses is at most $2^m \left((2^k - 1)\binom{m}{k}\right)^{cm}$, and the number of all such k-CNF formulas is $\left((2^k)\binom{m}{k}\right)^{cm}$.*

Proof. We first show that there are $\left((2^k)\binom{m}{k}\right)^{cm}$ k-CNF formulas on m variables with cm clauses. Note that are $2^k \binom{m}{k}$ choices for a single k-clause; therefore, the number of cm k-clauses is $\left((2^k)\binom{m}{k}\right)^{cm}$.

We then show that there are at most $2^m((2^k - 1)\binom{m}{k})^{cm}$ satisfiable k-CNF formulas on m variables with cm clauses. Consider any possible assignment x; the number of k-clauses that is satisfied by x is at most $(2^k - 1)\binom{m}{k}$ since given the choice of k variables, there are at most $2^k - 1$ possible choices of the polarities. Finally, since there are cm such k-clauses with m variables, we have that the total number of satisfiable formulas is at most $2^m((2^k - 1)\binom{m}{k})^{cm}$

To consider average-case hardness of this problem, we need to have a way to encode formulas as strings. We use the following standard encoding scheme for k-SAT from [11]: a m-variable cm-clause k-CNF is represented by using $n(m, k, c) = cm(k\lceil \log m \rceil + k)$ bits to describe a sequence of cm clauses (and here n denotes the length of the input bit string encoding the instance). In each clause, we specify k literals one-by-one, and each of them takes $\lceil \log m \rceil$ bits to specify the index of a variable and 1 bit to fix the polarity. When n is not of the form $n(m, k, c)$, for an input of length n, we ignore as few bits as possible in the end of the input such that the prefix of the input is of length $n(m, k, c)$ for some m. Following [11], let the *entropy deficiency* of a distribution D_n over n bits denote the difference between n and $H(D_n)$. The following corollary implies [11, Theorem 4, Term 1].

Corollary 44 *Let k, c be two integers such that $c \geq 2^{k+2}$. Let $m = m(n)$ be a polynomial. Assume that there exists some samplable ensemble $\mathcal{D} = \{D_n\}_{n \in \mathbb{N}}$ with entropy deficiency at most $cm(n)/2^{k+1}$ distributed over k-CNF formulas on $m(n)$ variables and $cm(n)$ clauses such that k-SAT is $(\frac{1}{2} - \frac{1}{4n})$-HoA on $\mathcal{D}$. Then, one-way functions exist.*

Proof. Recall that k-CNF formulas are represented by binary strings using the standard encoding scheme. Let $n' = n(m(n), k, c)$ (be the length of the input without padding); by the encoding scheme, it follows that every $m(n)$-variable $cm(n)$-clause k-CNF formula will be encoded by $2^{n-n'}$ n-bit strings. By Lemma 43, it follows that n' is at least

$$\log \left(\left((2^k) \binom{m}{k} \right)^{cm} \right) - cm \log 2^k + cm \log \binom{m}{k}$$

Since D_n has entropy deficiency at most $cm/2^{k+1}$, it follows that D_n has entropy lower bounded by:

$$n' + (n - n') - cm/2^{k+1} \geq cm \left(\log 2^k - \frac{1}{2^{k+1}} + \log \binom{m}{k} \right) + (n - n')$$

By Lemma 43, the number of n-bit YES instances is at most

$$S(n) = 2^m \left((2^k - 1) \binom{m}{k} \right)^{cm} \times 2^{n-n'}$$

It follows that

$$
\begin{aligned}
H(D_n) - \log S(n) \geq & cm\left(\log 2^k - \frac{1}{2^{k+1}} + \log\binom{m}{k}\right) + (n - n') \\
& - \log\left(2^m\left((2^k - 1)\binom{m}{k}\right)^{cm} \times 2^{n-n'}\right) \\
= & m(c\log 2^k - c\log(2^k - 1) - \frac{c}{2^{k+1}} - 1) \\
\geq & m(\frac{c}{2^k} - \frac{c}{2^{k+1}} - 1) \\
\geq & m \\
\geq & 4\log n.
\end{aligned}
$$

where the second inequality follows from the standard inequality that $\log x - \log(x-1) \geq \frac{1}{x}$ for all $x \geq 2$, the third one from the fact that, by assumption, $c \geq 2^{k+2}$, and the fourth one inequality follows from the fact that due to the encoding scheme, $m \geq \Omega(\sqrt{n})$.

4.3 t-Clique

Let $t : \mathbb{N} \to \mathbb{N}$ be a function and let t-Clique(m) be the set of graphs on m vertices having a clique of size at least $t(m)$. We recall the well-known fact that t-Clique(m) is sparse when $t(\cdot)$ is large enough.

Lemma 45 *The number of m-vertex graphs with at least a t-size clique is at most $\binom{m}{t}2^{\binom{m}{2}-\binom{t}{2}}$. However, the number of m-vertex graphs is $2^{\binom{m}{2}}$.*

Proof. There are $\binom{m}{2}$ edges in a m-vertex graph, and thus the number of possible graphs is $2^{\binom{m}{2}}$. There are $\binom{m}{t}$ choices of cliques in a graph, and after fixing a clique, there are $\binom{m}{2} - \binom{t}{2}$ edges in the rest of the graph and therefore the number of graphs with at least 1 clique is at most $\binom{m}{t}2^{\binom{m}{2}-\binom{t}{2}}$.

We use the standard encoding scheme for t-Clique from [11]. A m-vertex graph is encoded by a $(n = n(m) = \binom{m}{2})$-bit string where the i-th bit is 1 iff the i-th edge appears in the graph. For input lengths n that are not of the form $n(m)$, we ignore as few bits as possible at the end of the input such that the prefix of the input is of length $n(m)$ for some m.

Corollary 46 *Let $m(n), t(n) \in \omega(\log m)$ be two polynomials. Assume that there exists some samplable ensemble $\mathcal{D} = \{D_n\}_{n\in\mathbb{N}}$ with entropy deficiency at most $0.99\binom{t(n)}{2}$ distributed over $m(n)$-vertex graphs such that t-Clique(m) is $(\frac{1}{2} - \frac{1}{4n})$-HoA on $\mathcal{D}$. Then, one-way functions exist.*

Proof. Recall that graphs are represented by binary strings using the standard encoding scheme. Let $n' = n(m(n))$ (be the length of the input without padding);

by the encoding scheme, it follows that every $m(n)$-vertex graph will be encoded by at least $2^{n-n'}$ n-bit strings. By Lemma 45, it follows that n' is at least

$$\log 2^{\binom{m}{2}} = \binom{m}{2}$$

Since D_n has entropy deficiency $0.99\binom{t}{2}$, it follows that D_n has entropy lower bounded by:

$$n' + (n - n') - 0.99\binom{t}{2} \geq \binom{m}{2} - 0.99\binom{t}{2} + (n - n')$$

By Lemma 45, the number of n-bit YES instances is at most

$$S(n) = \binom{m}{t} 2^{\binom{m}{2} - \binom{t}{2}} \times 2^{n-n'}$$

It follows that

$$H(D_n) - \log S(n) \geq \binom{m}{2} - 0.99\binom{t}{2} + (n - n')$$
$$- \log\left(\binom{m}{t} 2^{\binom{m}{2} - \binom{t}{2}} \times 2^{n-n'}\right)$$
$$\geq \binom{m}{2} - 0.99\binom{t}{2} - \log\binom{m}{t} - \left(\binom{m}{2} - \binom{t}{2}\right)$$
$$\geq \binom{t}{2} - 0.99\binom{t}{2} - t\log m$$
$$\geq 4\log n$$

since $t(n) = \omega(\log m)$.

5   OWF from Hardness of Approximating K-Complexity

We turn to showing how to (slightly) generalize the result in [11] with respect to K-complexity, and show that the hardness of approximating K-complexity (even with respect to unknown thresholds) is equivalent to the existence of OWFs. We refer the reader to Sect. 4.1 for a formal definition of the notion of K-complexity.

It appears that a similar generalization was concurrently and independently obtained by IRS in the proceedings version [12] for a general class of complexity measures satisfying a so-called "coding theorem"—see Theorem 2.2 in [12]—but their full version has not appeared yet as far as we can tell. The corollary of this Theorem 2.2 to K-complexity is still stated w.r.t. a gap problem with a computable threshold.

We start by recalling what it means for a function to be hard on average to approximate. We say that a function $f : \{0,1\}^* \to \mathbb{N}$ is $\alpha(\cdot)$ *hard-on-average (α-HoA) to $\beta(\cdot)$-approximate on an ensemble* $\mathcal{D} = \{D_n\}_{n \in \mathbb{N}}$ if for all probabilistic polynomial-time heuristics $\mathcal{H}$, for all sufficiently large $n \in \mathbb{N}$,

$$\Pr[x \leftarrow D_n : |\mathcal{H}(x) - f(x)| \leq \beta(n)] < 1 - \alpha(n).$$

We simply say that f is *mildly hard-on-average (mildly HoA) to approximate* on $\mathcal{D}$ if there exists a polynomial $p(\cdot)$ such that f is $\frac{1}{p}$-HoA to approximate; We say that f is *hard-on-average (HoA) to approximate* on $\mathcal{D}$ if for every c, $\alpha(n) = \frac{1}{2} - \frac{1}{n^c}$, L is α-HoA to approximate.

The hardness notion above is defined with respect to the search version of approximating the function f and when considering K-complexity, it asserts that approximating the value of the K-complexity is hard. We can also consider its decisional version, parametrized by two efficiently computable thresholds $t_0(\cdot), t_1(\cdot)$, where we aim at deciding whether the input string x is of K-complexity below $t_0(|x|)$ or above $t_1(|x|)$. Let $\mathsf{GapK}[t_0, t_1]$ be a promise problem where YES-instances are strings $x \in \Pi_{\mathsf{YES}}$ such that $K(x) \leq t_0(|x|)$, and NO-instances are strings $x \in \Pi_{\mathsf{NO}}$ such that $K(x) \geq t_1(|x|)$. We say that $\mathsf{GapK}[t_0, t_1]$ is *mildly hard on average (mildly HoA)* on an ensemble $\mathcal{D} = \{D_n\}_{n \in \mathbb{N}}$ if there exists a polynomial $p(\cdot)$ such that for all probabilistic polynomial-time heuristics $\mathcal{H}$, for all sufficiently large $n \in \mathbb{N}$,

$$\Pr[x \leftarrow D_n : (x \in \Pi_{\mathsf{YES}} \wedge \mathcal{H}(x) = 0) \vee (x \in \Pi_{\mathsf{NO}} \wedge \mathcal{H}(x) = 1)] \geq 1/p(n).$$

The result in [11] showed that the existence of a samplable distribution $\mathcal{D}$ and efficiently computable $t_0, t_1, t_1(n) - t_0(n) \in \omega(\log n)$ such that $\mathsf{GapK}[t_0, t_1]$ is mildly HoA on $\mathcal{D}$ is equivalent to the existence of OWFs. We show in the following Theorem that it suffices to assume hardness with respect to the search version (with an additive factor $\omega(\log n)$) to obtain OWFs, therefore giving a search to decision reduction for this problem by going through the notion of OWFs.

We are not aware of any "direct" way of showing such a decision-to-search reduction. While one direction is trivial (hardness of decision—with respect to *efficiently computable* thresholds—to hardness of search), it is not clear how to show the converse direction.[4]

Theorem 51 (Theorem 12, restated) *The following are equivalent:*

1. *One-way functions exist;*
2. *There exists some efficiently samplable distribution such that K-complexity is mildly hard to approximate within an additive term of $\omega(\log n)$.*
3. *There exists some efficiently samplable distribution such that K-complexity is hard to approximate within an additive term of $n - n^{o(1)}$.*
4. *There exist some efficiently samplable distribution and efficiently computable thresholds $t_0, t_1, t_1(n) - t_0(n) = \omega(\log n)$ such that $\mathsf{GapK}[t_0, t_1]$ is mildly HoA.*

---

[4] The naive approach to try to prove such a result would be to simply try running the decision heuristic on different thresholds. There are several problems with this approach. First, for every threshold $t = (t_0, t_1)$, there may exist a *different* heuristic H_t that solves the decision problem for that threshold, so it's not clear how to get a uniform search heuristic. Next, its not even clear how to define efficient threshold functions as we require n/Gap thresholds to approximate within an additive term of Gap. Finally, it is not a-prior clear how to use a Gap-K heuristic to approximate K given that the Gap-K heuristic only works on *average*.

Proof (of Theorem 12). (2) $\Rightarrow$ (1) follows from Theorem 52 (stated and proved below). The implications (1) $\Rightarrow$ (3) and (1) $\Rightarrow$ (4) essentially follow from the argument proving Theorem 31 (and see also [11]). (3) $\Rightarrow$ (2) trivially holds. (4) $\Rightarrow$ (2) follows from the following argument. Assume that there exists a heuristic $\mathcal{H}$ for approximating K-complexity within $(t_1 - t_0)/2$. To solve $\mathsf{GapK}[t_0, t_1]$ on input x, we simply output 1 if $\mathcal{H}(x) \leq t_0(|x|) + (t_1(|x|) - t_0(|x|))/2$. Note that if $\mathcal{H}$ succeeds on x (with some probability), our algorithm also succeeds in solving $\mathsf{GapK}[t_0, t_1]$ on x (with the same probability). This concludes our proof.

Theorem 52 *For any constant $\gamma \geq 3$, there exists a polynomial p such that if there exists a samplable ensemble $\mathcal{D}$ on which K-complexity is $\frac{1}{p}$-HoA to $(\gamma \log n)$-approximate, then OWFs exist.*

Proof. Consider some fixed constant $\gamma \geq 3$ and let $p(n) = n^{\gamma-2}$. We assume for contradiction that OWFs do not exist. Then, by Lemma 24, there exist a constant δ and an approximate counter $\mathcal{A}$ for $\mathcal{D} = \{D_n\}$ with an (multiplicative) approximate factor δ and an error probability $\leq \frac{1}{2p(n)}$. We will use $\mathcal{A}$ to compute the K-complexity of strings sampled by $\mathcal{D}$.

On input $x \leftarrow D_n$, our heuristic $\mathcal{H}$ simply outputs $-\lfloor \log \mathcal{A}(x) \rfloor$ as (our estimate of) $K(x)$. $\mathcal{H}$ runs in polynomial time since $\mathcal{A}$ is a PPT machine. We next show that $\mathcal{H}(x)$ approximates $K(x)$ with probability at least $1 - \frac{1}{p(n)}$ (over $x \sim D_n$). Fix some input length n on which $\mathcal{A}$ succeeds (and there are infinitely many such input lengths). Let us first assume that $\mathcal{A}$ is a "perfect" approximate counter and $\delta \cdot p_x \leq \mathcal{A}(x) \leq p_x$ with probability 1 (where p_x is defined to be $\Pr[D_n = \tau]$) The following two claims will show that $\mathcal{H}$ approximate K with high probability.

Claim 1 $K(x) \leq \mathcal{H}(x) + \gamma \log n$ holds with probability 1.

Proof. We will show that $K(x) \leq -\lfloor \log p_x \rfloor + 2\log(n) + O(1)$ with probability 1. Note that $\mathcal{H}(x) = -\lfloor \log \mathcal{A}(x) \rfloor \geq -\lfloor \log p_x \rfloor$ (due to the correctness of $\mathcal{A}$) and $\gamma \geq 3$, the claim follows. For any string $x \in \{0,1\}^n$, let $S = \{y \in \{0,1\}^n : -\lfloor \log p_y \rfloor = -\lfloor \log p_x \rfloor\}$. Note that for each $y \in S$, it holds that $\Pr[D_n = y] = p_y \geq 2^{\lfloor \log p_x \rfloor}$. So S is of size at most $2^{-\lfloor \log p_x \rfloor}$. Membership of S can be checked by using an exponential time algorithm computing p_y (enumerating all randomness used in D_n) with the values $-\lfloor \log p_x \rfloor$ and n. Therefore, we can compress each element in S (including x) into $-\lfloor \log p_x \rfloor + 2\log(n) + O(1)$ bits by hardwiring its index and running an exhaustive search with the membership checker, which shows that $K(x) \leq -\lfloor \log p_x \rfloor + 2\log(n) + O(1)$.

Claim 2 $K(x) \geq \mathcal{H}(x) - \gamma \log n$ holds with probability at least $1 - \frac{1}{2p(n)}$

Proof. Towards this, we show that $\mathcal{H}(x) > K(x) + \gamma \log n$ with probability at most $\frac{1}{2p(n)}$. This follows from a union bound.

$$
\Pr_{x \leftarrow D_n} [\mathcal{H}(x) > K(x) + \gamma \log n]
$$

$$
= \sum_{w=1}^{n+O(1)} \Pr_{x \leftarrow D_n} [K(x) = w \wedge \mathcal{H}(x) > w + \gamma \log n]
$$

$$
\leq \sum_{w=1}^{n+O(1)} \Pr_{x \leftarrow D_n} [K(x) = w \wedge \Pr[D_n = x] < \frac{1}{\delta} \cdot 2^{-w-\gamma \log n}]
$$

$$
\leq \sum_{w=1}^{n+O(1)} 2^w \cdot \frac{1}{\delta} \cdot 2^{-w-\gamma \log n}
$$

$$
\leq \frac{1}{2p(n)}.
$$

where the second to last line follows from a union bound.

Finally, we note that $\mathcal{A}$ is not necessarily a perfect approximate counter and $\mathcal{A}$ fails with probability $\frac{1}{2p(n)}$. By a union bound, it follows that

$$
\Pr_{x \leftarrow D_n} [|\mathcal{H}(x) - K(x)| \leq \gamma \log n] \geq 1 - \frac{1}{2p(n)} - \frac{1}{2p(n)} \geq 1 - \frac{1}{p(n)}
$$

on infinitely many n.

References

1. Blum, M.: Coin flipping by telephone - a protocol for solving impossible problems. In: COMPCON'82, Digest of Papers, Twenty-Fourth IEEE Computer Society International Conference, San Francisco, California, USA, February 22–25, 1982, pp. 133–137. IEEE Computer Society (1982)
2. Blum, M., Micali, S.: How to generate cryptographically strong sequences of pseudo-random bits. SIAM J. Comput. **13**(4), 850–864 (1984)
3. Chen, L., Jin, C., Williams, R.R.: Hardness magnification for all sparse np languages. In: 2019 IEEE 60th Annual Symposium on Foundations of Computer Science (FOCS), pp. 1240–1255. IEEE (2019)
4. Diffie, W., Hellman, M.: New directions in cryptography. IEEE Trans. Inf. Theory **22**(6), 644–654 (1976)
5. Feige, U., Shamir, A.: Witness indistinguishable and witness hiding protocols. In: STOC '90, pp. 416–426 (1990). http://doi.acm.org/10.1145/100216.100272
6. Goldreich, O., Goldwasser, S., Micali, S.: On the cryptographic applications of random functions. In: CRYPTO, pp. 276–288 (1984)
7. Goldwasser, S., Micali, S.: Probabilistic encryption. J. Comput. Syst. Sci. **28**(2), 270–299 (1984)
8. Gurevich, Y.: The challenger-solver game: variations on the theme of p=np. In: Logic in Computer Science Column, The Bulletin of EATCS (1989)

9. Hartmanis, J.: Generalized kolmogorov complexity and the structure of feasible computations. In: 24th Annual Symposium on Foundations of Computer Science (sfcs 1983), pp. 439–445 (1983). https://doi.org/10.1109/SFCS.1983.21
10. Håstad, J., Impagliazzo, R., Levin, L.A., Luby, M.: A pseudorandom generator from any one-way function. SIAM J. Comput. **28**(4), 1364–1396 (1999)
11. Ilango, R., Ren, H., Santhanam, R.: Hardness on any samplable distribution suffices: New characterizations of one-way functions by meta-complexity. Electron. Colloquium Comput. Complex. **28**, 82 (2021)
12. Ilango, R., Ren, H., Santhanam, R.: Robustness of average-case meta-complexity via pseudorandomness. In: Proceedings of the 54th Annual ACM SIGACT Symposium on Theory of Computing, pp. 1575–1583 (2022)
13. Impagliazzo, R.: A personal view of average-case complexity. In: Structure in Complexity Theory '95, pp. 134–147 (1995)
14. Impagliazzo, R., Levin, L.A.: No better ways to generate hard NP instances than picking uniformly at random. In: 31st Annual Symposium on Foundations of Computer Science, St. Louis, Missouri, USA, October 22–24, 1990, Volume II, pp. 812–821 (1990)
15. Impagliazzo, R., Luby, M.: One-way functions are essential for complexity based cryptography (extended abstract). In: 30th Annual Symposium on Foundations of Computer Science, Research Triangle Park, North Carolina, USA, 30 October - 1 November 1989, pp. 230–235 (1989)
16. Ko, K.: On the notion of infinite pseudorandom sequences. Theor. Comput. Sci. **48**(3), 9–33 (1986). https://doi.org/10.1016/0304-3975(86)90081-2
17. Kolmogorov, A.N.: Three approaches to the quantitative definition of information. Int. J. Comput. Math. **2**(1–4), 157–168 (1968)
18. Levin, L.A.: The tale of one-way functions. Problems of Information Transmission **39**(1), 92–103 (2003). https://doi.org/10.1023/A:1023634616102
19. Liu, Y., Pass, R.: On one-way functions and Kolmogorov complexity. In: 61st IEEE Annual Symposium on Foundations of Computer Science, FOCS 2020, Durham, NC, USA, November 16–19, 2020, pp. 1243–1254. IEEE (2020)
20. Naor, M.: Bit commitment using pseudorandomness. J. Cryptol. **4**(2), 151–158 (1991). https://doi.org/10.1007/BF00196774
21. Rivest, R.L., Shamir, A., Adleman, L.M.: A method for obtaining digital signatures and public-key cryptosystems (reprint). Commun. ACM **26**(1), 96–99 (1983). https://doi.org/10.1145/357980.358017
22. Rompel, J.: One-way functions are necessary and sufficient for secure signatures. In: STOC, pp. 387–394 (1990)
23. Sipser, M.: A complexity theoretic approach to randomness. In: Proceedings of the 15th Annual ACM Symposium on Theory of Computing, 25–27 April, 1983, Boston, Massachusetts, USA, pp. 330–335. ACM (1983)
24. Trakhtenbrot, B.A.: A survey of Russian approaches to perebor (brute-force searches) algorithms. Ann. Hist. Comput. **6**(4), 384–400 (1984)

Security Proofs for Key-Alternating Ciphers with Non-Independent Round Permutations

Liqing Yu[1,3], Yusai Wu[3(✉)], Yu Yu[2,3], Zhenfu Cao[1], and Xiaolei Dong[1]

[1] East China Normal University, Shanghai, China
lqyups@126.com, {zfcao,dong-xl}@sei.ecnu.edu.cn
[2] Shanghai Jiao Tong University, Shanghai, China
yuyu@yuyu.hk
[3] Shanghai Qi Zhi Institute, Shanghai, China
yusaiwu@126.com

Abstract. This work studies the key-alternating ciphers (KACs) whose round permutations are not necessarily independent. We revisit existing security proofs for key-alternating ciphers with a single permutation (KACSPs), and extend their method to an arbitrary number of rounds. In particular, we propose new techniques that can significantly simplify the proofs, and also remove two unnatural restrictions in the known security bound of 3-round KACSP (Wu et al., Asiacrypt 2020). With these techniques, we prove the first tight security bound for t-round KACSP, which was an open problem. We stress that our techniques apply to all variants of KACs with non-independent round permutations, as well as to the standard KACs.

1 Introduction

The key-alternating ciphers (see Eq. (1)) generalize the Even-Mansour construction [EM97] over multiple rounds. They can be viewed as abstract constructions of many substitution-permutation network (SPN) block ciphers (e.g. AES [DR02]). In addition, there are various variants of the key-alternating ciphers.

This work only considers the case of independent round keys, and reducing their independence is a relatively parallel topic. That is, we are concerned with different variants of KACs on round permutations, while the round keys are always independent and random. For convenience, we simply use KAC to represent the standard KAC with independent permutations, and refer to all the other variants as *KAC-type constructions*. In particular, KACSP is a KAC-type construction in which all the round permutations are identical.

In a t-round KAC or KAC-type construction, the number of different round permutations, denoted t', is an important parameter. Clearly, we have $t' = t$ in the case of KAC and $t' = 1$ in the case of KACSP. When $t' < t$, it means that there are different rounds using the same permutation. For a given construction, we name the round permutations as follows. In particular, the name P_k will be

© International Association for Cryptologic Research 2023
G. Rothblum and H. Wee (Eds.): TCC 2023, LNCS 14369, pp. 238–267, 2023.
https://doi.org/10.1007/978-3-031-48615-9_9

assigned to each round permutation in order from round 1 to round t, where $k \in \{1, \ldots, t'\}$. For round i, we check if there exists $j < i$ such that round j uses the same permutation as round i. If so, we use the same name as the permutation in round j; otherwise, we use the name P_k, where $k \in \{1, \ldots, t'\}$ is the smallest integer not used in previous rounds. For simplicity, we sometimes only use the permutation names to denote a construction, such as $P_1 P_2 P_3$-construction (i.e. 3-round KAC), $P_1 P_1 P_1$-construction (i.e. 3-round KACSP), $P_1 P_1 P_2$-construction, etc.

We now give a more formal definition of KAC and KACSP constructions. Let $x \in \{0,1\}^n$ denote the plaintext, $\kappa_0, \kappa_1, \ldots, \kappa_t \in \{0,1\}^{n \times (t+1)}$ denote the $t+1$ round keys, and $P_1, \ldots, P_t$ denote the permutations over $\{0,1\}^n$, then the outputs of t-round KAC and t-round KACSP are computed as follows.

$$\mathsf{KAC}^{P_1,\ldots,P_t;\ \kappa_0,\kappa_1,\ldots,\kappa_t}(x) \stackrel{\text{def}}{=} \kappa_t \oplus P_t(\kappa_{t-1} \oplus P_{t-1}(\cdots P_2(\kappa_1 \oplus P_1(\kappa_0 \oplus x)) \cdots)), \tag{1}$$

$$\mathsf{KACSP}^{P_1;\ \kappa_0,\kappa_1,\ldots,\kappa_t}(x) \stackrel{\text{def}}{=} \kappa_t \oplus P_1(\kappa_{t-1} \oplus P_1(\cdots P_1(\kappa_1 \oplus P_1(\kappa_0 \oplus x)) \cdots)). \tag{2}$$

Related Works. Bogdanov et al. [Bog+12] were the first to study the provable security of t-round KAC (for $t \geq 2$), and showed that it is secure up to $\mathcal{O}(2^{\frac{2}{3}n})$ queries. On the other hand, they presented a simple distinguishing attack using $\mathcal{O}(2^{\frac{t}{t+1}n})$ queries, and conjectured that this attack cannot be improved intrinsically. Thus, their result is optimal for 2-round KAC. After a series of papers [Ste12, LPS12, CS14, HT16], the above conjecture was proved. Roughly, it says that unless $\Omega(2^{\frac{t}{t+1}n})$ queries are used, one cannot distinguish t-round KAC from a truly random permutation with non-negligible advantage, where the round permutations are public and random.

Another line of research focuses on the variants of KAC constructions, where round permutations and keys may not be independent of each other. [DKS12] was the first to study the minimalism of Even-Mansour cipher, and showed that several of its single-key variants could achieve the same level of security as it. Later, Chen et al. [Che+18] proved that a variant of 2-round KAC still enjoys security close to $\mathcal{O}(2^{\frac{2}{3}n})$ when only n-bit key and a single permutation are used. Next, [WYCD20] generalized Chen et al.'s technique and proved a tight security bound (with two unnatural restrictions) for 3-round KACSP. Recently, Tessaro and Zhang [TZ21] showed that $(t-2)$-wise independent round keys are sufficient for t-round KAC to achieve the tight security bound, where $t \geq 8$.

Our Contributions. This work focuses on the provable security of KAC or KAC-type constructions in random permutation model. Our main contribution is to prove the tight security bound $\mathcal{O}(2^{\frac{t}{t+1}n})$ for t-round KACSP.

We revisit the security proofs in [Che+18, WYCD20]. The idea of their proofs is not hard to understand, but the analysis is quite laborious. In particular, the security bound of [WYCD20] (see Theorem 1) has two unnatural restrictions, making the result far from elegant. The first is the existence of an error function

$\zeta(\cdot)$, and the second is that it requires $28q_e^2/2^n \leq q_p \leq q_e/5$, where q_p and q_e denote the number of two types of queries made by the distinguisher respectively.

We propose new techniques that can significantly simplify proofs, thus making the security proofs of KAC-type constructions easier to understand and read. One of the key techniques is a general transformation, which reduces our task to bounding only one probability in the form of (9) (even for t-round constructions). Note that [WYCD20] needs to bound at least 3 such probabilities. We stress that the transformation is general and may also be used to simplify other security proofs. To increase the number of constructive methods, we introduce a new notion of *recycled-edge* which is different from the *shared-edge* used in [Che+18, WYCD20]. Roughly speaking, recycled-edge is to reuse existing permutation queries made by distinguisher to save resources, while shared-edge is to reuse the permutation queries generated on-the-fly. We point out that recycled-edge has the following features compared to shared-edge. First, the analysis of recycled-edge is easier, which is another important reason why our proof is simpler. Second, the recycled-edge has wider applicability and is less sensitive to constructions.

Moreover, we provide new ideas to remove the two unnatural restrictions in the security bound of [WYCD20]. For the first restriction, our approach is to consider the security proof in two disjoint cases, and provide separate proofs for each case. It should be pointed out here that these two proofs will be almost identical, except for slightly different calculations. For the second restriction, our approach is to increase the number of variables[1] so that we can better exploit the power of multivariate hypergeometric distribution used in the calculation. Our main finding here is that the improvements in security bound are largely influenced by computational rather than conceptual factors. This is a key to addressing the security bound of t-round KACSP. More details about our new techniques can be found in Sect. 3.

With the above new techniques, we first obtain a neat security bound for the 3-round KACSP (see Theorem 2), and discuss its proof in detail in Sect. 4. We then generalize the proof to the general t-round KACSP (see Theorem 3), using almost the same techniques. It should be emphasized that our proof techniques apply to KAC and all kinds of KAC-type constructions. For example, we also apply the proof techniques to other variants of 3-round KAC (see Thms. 17 and 18 in the full version [Yu+23] of this paper).

2 Preliminaries

2.1 Notation

Let $N = 2^n$ and $\mathcal{P}_n$ be the set of all permutations over $\{0, 1\}^n$. For a permutation $P \in \mathcal{P}_n$, we let P^{-1} denote its inverse permutation. If A is a finite set, then $|A|$ and $\overline{A}$ represent the cardinality and complement of A, respectively. Given a set

---

[1] Each variable represents the number of new edges that can be saved by some constructive method, usually denoted by h_i in the proofs.

of n-bit strings A and a fixed $k \in \{0,1\}^n$, we will use $A \oplus k$ to denote the set $\{a \oplus k : a \in A\}$. For a finite set S, let $x \leftarrow_\$ S$ denote the act of sampling uniformly from S and then assigning the value to x. The falling factorial is usually written by $(a)_b = a(a-1)\ldots(a-b+1)$, where $1 \le b \le a$ are two integers. For a set of pairs $\mathcal{Q} = \{(x_1, y_1), \ldots, (x_q, y_q)\}$, where x_i's (resp. y_i's) are distinct n-bit strings, and a permutation $P \in \mathcal{P}_n$, we say that P extends the set $\mathcal{Q}$, denoted as $P \downarrow \mathcal{Q}$, if $P(x_i) = y_i$ for $i = 1, 2, \ldots, q$. In particular, we write $\mathsf{Dom}(\mathcal{Q}) := \{x_1, \ldots, x_q\}$ (resp. $\mathsf{Ran}(\mathcal{Q}) := \{y_1, \ldots, y_q\}$) as the domain (resp. range) of $\mathcal{Q}$.

2.2   Random Permutation Model, Transcripts and Graph View

Random Permutation Model. This work studies the security of KAC or KAC-type constructions under the *random permutation model*. The model can be viewed as an enhanced version of black-box indistinguishability with additional access to the underlying permutations, making security analysis more operable.

Given a t-round KAC or KAC-type construction, the task of distinguisher $\mathcal{D}$ is to tell apart two worlds, the *real world* and the *ideal world*. In the real world, the distinguisher can interact with $t'+1$ oracles $(E_K, P_1, \ldots, P_{t'})$, where E_K is the t-round target cipher (denoted as E) computed based on t' independent random permutations $P_1, \ldots, P_{t'}$ and a key K. In the ideal world, there are also $t'+1$ oracles but the first oracle E_K is replaced by an independent random permutation P_0. That is, what interact with the distinguisher $\mathcal{D}$ are $t'+1$ independent random permutations $(P_0, P_1, \ldots, P_{t'})$. Furthermore, we allow the distinguisher to be adaptive and query each permutation oracle in both directions. We can then define the *super-pseudorandom permutation* (SPRP) advantage of distinguisher $\mathcal{D}$ on t-round E_K (with t' different permutations) as follows.

$$\mathbf{Adv}_{E,t}^{\mathsf{SPRP}}(\mathcal{D}) = \Big| \Pr_{\substack{K \leftarrow_\$ \{0,1\}^{(t+1)n}; \\ P_1, \ldots, P_{t'} \leftarrow_\$ \mathcal{P}_n}} [\mathcal{D}^{E_K, P_1, \ldots, P_{t'}} = 1]$$

$$- \Pr_{P_0, P_1, \ldots, P_{t'} \leftarrow_\$ \mathcal{P}_n} [\mathcal{D}^{P_0, P_1, \ldots, P_{t'}} = 1] \Big|, \tag{3}$$

where all oracles can be queried bidirectionally. In particular, we refer to the queries on the first oracle (i.e. E_K or P_0) as *construction queries* and to the set formed by them and their answers as $\mathcal{Q}_0$. Similarly, the queries on the other t' oracles are called *permutation queries* and the resulting sets are denoted as Q_i, where $i = 1, \ldots, t'$.

Transcripts. Formally, the interaction between $\mathcal{D}$ and $t'+1$ oracles can be represented by an ordered list of queries, which is often called *transcript*. Each query in the transcript is in the form of (i, b, u, v), where $i \in \{0, 1, \ldots, t'\}$ represents the oracle being queried, b indicates whether it is a forward query or backward query, u is the query value and v is the corresponding answer. We can assume *wlog* that the adversary $\mathcal{D}$ is deterministic and does not make redundant queries, since it is computationally unbounded. That means the output of $\mathcal{D}$ is entirely determined by its transcript, which can also be encoded (requiring a description of $\mathcal{D}$) into $t'+1$ unordered lists of queries.

In addition, we are more generous to the distinguisher $\mathcal{D}$ in the analysis, so that it will receive the actual key used in the real world (after all queries are done but before a decision is made). To maintain consistency, $\mathcal{D}$ would also receive a dummy key in the ideal world (even the key is not used). This modification is justified since it only increases the advantage of $\mathcal{D}$. From the perspective of $\mathcal{D}$, a transcript $\tau \in \mathcal{T}$ has the form of $\tau = (\mathcal{Q}_0, \mathcal{Q}_1, \ldots, \mathcal{Q}_{t'}, K)$, and can be rewritten as the following unordered lists.

$$
\tau = \left\{
\begin{array}{l}
\mathcal{Q}_0 = \{(x_1, y_1), \ldots, (x_{q_e}, y_{q_e})\}, \\
\mathcal{Q}_1 = \{(u_{1,1}, v_{1,1}), \ldots, (u_{1,q_1}, v_{1,q_1})\}, \\
\cdots, \\
\mathcal{Q}_{t'} = \{(u_{t',1}, v_{t',1}), \ldots, (u_{t',q_{t'}}, v_{t',q_{t'}})\}, \\
K = (\kappa_0, \ldots, \kappa_t)
\end{array}
\right\},
\tag{4}
$$

where $y_j = E_K(x_j)$ or $y_j = P_0(x_j)$ (depending on which world) for all $j \in \{1, \ldots, q_e\}$ and $v_{i,j} = P_i(u_{i,j})$ for all $i \in \{1, \ldots, t'\}$ and $j \in \{1, \ldots, q_i\}$, and where $K \in \{0,1\}^{(t+1)n}$ is a $(t+1)n$-bit key.

Statistical Distance of Transcript Distributions. We already know that the output of $\mathcal{D}$ is a deterministic function on transcript. For any fixed distinguisher $\mathcal{D}$, its advantage is obviously bounded by the statistical distance of transcript distributions in two worlds. That is, it is usually to determine the upper bound of the value (3) as follows,

$$
(3) \leq \|\mathcal{T}_{\text{real}} - \mathcal{T}_{\text{ideal}}\| \overset{\text{def}}{=} \frac{1}{2} \sum_\tau |\Pr[\mathcal{T}_{\text{ideal}} = \tau] - \Pr[\mathcal{T}_{\text{real}} = \tau]|
$$
$$
= \sum_\tau \max\{0, \Pr[\mathcal{T}_{\text{ideal}} = \tau] - \Pr[\mathcal{T}_{\text{real}} = \tau]\},
\tag{5}
$$

where $\| \cdot \|$ represents the statistical distance, and $\mathcal{T}_{\text{real}}$ (resp. $\mathcal{T}_{\text{ideal}}$) denotes the transcript random variable generated by the interaction of $\mathcal{D}$ with the real (resp. ideal) world. We let $\mathcal{T}$ denote the set of *attainable* transcripts τ such that $\Pr[\mathcal{T}_{\text{ideal}} = \tau] > 0$. It is worth noting that although the set $\mathcal{T}$ depends on $\mathcal{D}$, the probabilities $\Pr[\mathcal{T}_{\text{ideal}} = \tau]$ and $\Pr[\mathcal{T}_{\text{real}} = \tau]$ (for any $\tau \in \mathcal{T}$) are independent of $\mathcal{D}$, since they are inherent properties of the two worlds. The task of bounding (5) is to figure out two (partial) distributions, of which the one for ideal world is simple and easy to deal with. Thus, the main effort in various proofs is essentially to study the random value $\mathcal{T}_{\text{real}}$.

Crucial Probability in the Real World. The basis of studying $\mathcal{T}_{\text{real}}$ is the probability $\Pr[\mathcal{T}_{\text{real}} = \tau]$, which can be reduced to a conditional probability with intuitive meaning (see Eq. (7)). For any fixed transcript $\tau = (\mathcal{Q}_0, \mathcal{Q}_1, \ldots, \mathcal{Q}_{t'}, K) \in \mathcal{T}$, it has

$$\Pr[\mathcal{T}_{\text{real}} = \tau] = \Pr_{\substack{\kappa \leftarrow_\$ \{0,1\}^{(t+1)n} \\ P_1,\dots,P_{t'} \leftarrow_\$ \mathcal{P}_n}}[E_\kappa \downarrow \mathcal{Q}_0 \wedge P_1 \downarrow \mathcal{Q}_1 \wedge \cdots \wedge P_{t'} \downarrow \mathcal{Q}_{t'} \wedge \kappa = K]$$

$$= \Pr_{\substack{\kappa \leftarrow_\$ \{0,1\}^{(t+1)n} \\ P_1,\dots,P_{t'} \leftarrow_\$ \mathcal{P}_n}}[P_1 \downarrow \mathcal{Q}_1 \wedge \cdots \wedge P_{t'} \downarrow \mathcal{Q}_{t'} \wedge \kappa = K] \tag{6}$$

$$\times \Pr_{P_1,\dots,P_{t'} \leftarrow_\$ \mathcal{P}_n}[E_K \downarrow \mathcal{Q}_0 \mid P_1 \downarrow \mathcal{Q}_1 \wedge \cdots \wedge P_{t'} \downarrow \mathcal{Q}_{t'}] \tag{7}$$

The central task of calculating $\Pr[\mathcal{T}_{\text{real}} = \tau]$ is to evaluate Eq. (7)[2], since the value of Eq. (6) can be solved trivially for any KAC or KAC-type construction. In this work, we will use a *graph view* (basically taken from [CS14] and to be defined in next part), then Eq. (7) can be interpreted as the probability that all the paths between x_j and y_j (where $(x_j, y_j) \in \mathcal{Q}_0$) are completed, when each random permutation P_i extending the corresponding set $\mathcal{Q}_i$.

Graph View. It is often more convenient to work with constructions and transcripts in graph view. Here we take only the t-round KAC or KAC-type construction as an example, and other constructions are similar. For a given construction, all the information of transcript $\tau = (\mathcal{Q}_0, \mathcal{Q}_1, \dots, \mathcal{Q}_{t'}, K) \in \mathcal{T}$ can be encoded into a *round graph* $G(\tau)$. First, one can view each set $\mathcal{Q}_i$ as a bipartite graph with shores $\{0,1\}^n$ and containing q_i (resp. q_e, in the case of $\mathcal{Q}_0$) disjoint edges. To have maximum generality, we here keep the value of $K = (\kappa_0, \dots, \kappa_t)$ in graph $G(\tau)$[3], where each mapping of XORing round key κ_i is viewed as a full bipartite graph (i.e. it contains 2^n disjoint edges).

More specifically, graph $G(\tau)$ contains $2(t+1)$ shores, each of which is identified with a copy of $\{0,1\}^n$. The $2(t+1)$ shores are indexed as $0, 1, 2, \dots, 2t+1$. We use the ordered pair $\langle i, u \rangle$ to represent the string u in shore i, where $i \in \{0, 1, \dots, 2t+1\}$ and $u \in \{0,1\}^n$. For convenience, we simply use u to denote a string if it is clear from the context which shore the u is in. In particular, the vertices in shore 0 and shore $2t+1$ are often called *plaintexts* and *ciphertexts*, respectively. More care should be taken when $t' < t$, as this means that the target construction uses the same permutation in different rounds. For any $i \neq j \in \{1, \dots, t\}$ that round i and round j use the same permutation, the shores $2i - 1$ and $2j - 1$ are actually the same, and the shores $2i$ and $2j$ are also the same. That is, $\langle 2i - 1, u \rangle = \langle 2j - 1, u \rangle$ and $\langle 2i, v \rangle = \langle 2j, v \rangle$ for all $u, v \in \{0,1\}^n$.

We define the even-odd edges between shore $2i$ and shore $2i+1$ as $E_{(2i,2i+1)} := \{(v, v \oplus \kappa_i) : v \in \{0,1\}^n\}$ and call them *key-edges*, where $i \in \{0, \dots, t\}$. The key-edges $E_{(2i,2i+1)}$ correspond to the step of XORing round key κ_i in the KAC or KAC-type construction, and form a perfect matching of bipartite graph.

For $i \in \{1, \dots, t\}$, we use the odd-even edges between shore $2i - 1$ and shore $2i$ to represent the queries made to the permutation in round i, and call them

---

[2] For t-round KAC, the technical lemma of [CS14] (see Lemma 1) solves exactly this probability when $|\mathcal{Q}_0| = 1$.

[3] Although this leads to a somewhat redundant notation, it is still relatively easy to understand. For a concrete example, you can refer to Fig. 1 in the full version [Yu+23, Appendix C].

permutation-edges. Naturally, the term P_k-permutation-edge is used to indicate the round permutation associated with it, where $k \in \{1, \ldots, t'\}$. Based on the definition of strings above, more care should also be taken when $t' < t$. For any $i \neq j \in \{1, \ldots, t\}$ that round i and round j use the same permutation, the bipartite graph between the shore $2i - 1$ and $2i$, and the bipartite graph between the shore $2j - 1$ and $2j$ are the same one. More specifically, we define the permutation-edges between shore $2i - 1$ and $2i$ as $E_{(2i-1,2i)} := \{\langle u, P_k, v\rangle :$ $(u, v) \in \mathcal{Q}_k\}^4$ for $i = 1, \ldots, t$, where P_k $(1 \leq k \leq t')$ is the name of round permutation between shore $2i-1$ and $2i$ (see the naming in Sect. 1). That is, we distinguish strings and permutation-edges by the round permutation associated with them, rather than by shores.

In addition, we should keep in mind that there are implicit permutation-edges (i.e., $\{\langle x_i, \mathcal{Q}_0, y_i\rangle : (x_i, y_i) \in \mathcal{Q}_0\}$, although not drawn) directly from shore 0 to shore $2t + 1$ according to the construction queries in $\mathcal{Q}_0$, i.e. these edges are from the plaintexts x_i's to the corresponding ciphertexts y_i's. Throughout this work, we use symbols related to x (e.g., x_i and x_i') and y (e.g., y_i and y_i') to denote plaintexts (i.e., strings in shore 0) and ciphertexts (i.e., strings in shore $2t + 1$), respectively.

Basic Definitions about Graph. We say shore i is to the left of shore j if $i < j$, and view paths as oriented from left to right. For convenience, the index of the shore containing vertex u is written as $\mathsf{Sh}(u)$. A vertex u in a shore i is called *right-free*, if no edge connects u to any vertex in shore $i + 1$. A vertex v in a shore j is called *left-free*, if no edge connects v to any vertex in shore $j - 1$. Notice that right-free vertices and left-free vertices must be located on the odd and even shores, respectively.

We write $\mathsf{R}(u)$ for the rightmost vertex in the path of $G(\tau)$ starting at u, and $\mathsf{L}(v)$ for the leftmost vertex in the path of $G(\tau)$ ending at v. For any odd $i \in \{0, \ldots, 2t + 1\}$ and $i < j \in \{0, \ldots, 2t + 1\}$, we let U_{ij} denote the set of paths that starts at a left-free vertex in shore i and reaches a vertex in shore j. Similarly, for any $i < j \in \{0, \ldots, 2t + 1\}$, we use Z_{ij} to denote the set of paths that starts at a vertex in shore i and reaches a vertex in shore j. That is, the only difference between Z_{ij} and U_{ij} is that the starting vertices on shore i in the former need not be left-free.

Path-Growing Procedure. In this work, we usually imagine the crucial probability (7) as connecting all x_j with y_j through a (probabilistic) *path-growing procedure*, where $(x_j, y_j) \in \mathcal{Q}_0$. Note that all the key-edges already exist, so we only need to generate edges from odd shores to the next shore. Given $G(\tau)$ and a vertex u, we define the following procedure to generate a path $(u, w_1, \ldots, w_r)$ from u.

Let $w_0 = u$. For i from 1 to r, if w_{i-1} is not right-free and adjacent to some vertex z in shore i, then let $w_i = z$; otherwise, sample u_i uniformly at random from all left-free vertices in shore i, and let $w_i = u_i$.

---

^{4} Due to the uniqueness, we will interchangeably use the permutation-edge $\langle u, P_k, v\rangle$ and the input-output pair (u, v) under P_k.

For convenience, we let $u \to v$ denote the event that u is connected to v through the above path-growing procedure and write $\Pr_G[u \to v] = \Pr_G[w_r = v]$, where v is a vertex in shore $\mathsf{Sh}(u) + r$. We are now ready to give the key lemma of [CS14] (adapted slightly to fit here) as follows.

Lemma 1 (Lemma 1 of [CS14]). *Given any $G(\tau)$ as described above, let u be any right-free vertex in shore 1 and v be any left-free vertex in shore $2t$, then it has*

$$\Pr_{G(\tau)}[u \to v] = \frac{1}{N} - \frac{1}{N} \sum_{\sigma} (-1)^{|\sigma|} \prod_{j=1}^{|\sigma|} \frac{|U_{i_{j-1}i_j}|}{N - |\mathcal{Q}_{(i_j-1)/2}|}. \tag{8}$$

where the sum is taken over all sequences $\sigma = (i_0, \ldots, i_s)$ with $1 = i_0 < \cdots < i_s = 2t + 1$ (where $i_0, i_1, \ldots, i_s$ are required to be odd integers), and $|\sigma| = s$.

2.3 Two Useful Lemmas

The H-coefficient technique [CS14] is a very popular tool for bounding the statistical distance between two distributions (e.g. Eq. (5)). Its core idea is to properly partition the set of attainable transcripts $\mathcal{T}$ into two disjoint sets, the good transcripts set $\mathcal{T}_1$ and the bad transcripts set $\mathcal{T}_2$. If for any $\tau \in \mathcal{T}_1$, we are able to obtain a lower bound (e.g. $1 - \varepsilon_1$) on the ratio $\Pr[\mathcal{T}_{\mathsf{real}} = \tau]/\Pr[\mathcal{T}_{\mathsf{ideal}} = \tau]$. And we can also obtain an upper bound (e.g. ε_2) on the value of $\Pr[\mathcal{T}_{\mathsf{ideal}} \in \mathcal{T}_2]$. The statistical distance is then bounded by $\varepsilon_1 + \varepsilon_2$. All of the above are formalized in the following lemma.

Lemma 2 (H-Coefficient Technique, [CS14]). *Let E denote the target t-round KAC or KAC-type construction, and $\mathcal{T} = \mathcal{T}_1 \cup \mathcal{T}_2$ be the set of attainable transcripts. Assume that there exists a value $\varepsilon_1 > 0$ such that*

$$\frac{Pr[\mathcal{T}_{\mathsf{real}} = \tau]}{Pr[\mathcal{T}_{\mathsf{ideal}} = \tau]} \geq 1 - \varepsilon_1$$

holds for any $\tau \in \mathcal{T}_1$, and there exists a value $\varepsilon_2 > 0$ such that $Pr[\mathcal{T}_{\mathsf{ideal}} \in \mathcal{T}_2] \leq \varepsilon_2$. Then for any information-theoretic distinguisher $\mathcal{D}$, it has $\mathbf{Adv}_{E,t}^{\mathsf{SPRP}}(\mathcal{D}) \leq \varepsilon_1 + \varepsilon_2$.

To apply Lemma 2, the main task is usually to determine the value of ε_1. As we have argued in the previous section, it is essentially to calculate the crucial probability (7). The following lemma re-emphasizes this fact.

Lemma 3 (Lemma 2 of [Che+18]). *Let E denote the target t-round KAC or KAC-type construction, and $\tau = (\mathcal{Q}_0, \mathcal{Q}_1, \ldots, \mathcal{Q}_{t'}, K) \in \mathcal{T}$ be an attainable transcript, where K is the $(t+1)n$-bit key. We denote $p(\tau) = \Pr_{P_1, \ldots, P_{t'} \leftarrow_{\$} \mathcal{P}_n}[(E_K \downarrow \mathcal{Q}_0) \mid (P_1 \downarrow \mathcal{Q}_1) \wedge \cdots \wedge (P_{t'} \downarrow \mathcal{Q}_{t'})]$, then*

$$\frac{Pr[\mathcal{T}_{\mathsf{real}} = \tau]}{Pr[\mathcal{T}_{\mathsf{ideal}} = \tau]} = (N)_{q_e} \cdot p(\tau).$$

3   Technical Overview

This section outlines the techniques used in security proofs of this work. We first review the known proof method, then propose a general transformation to simplify it, and finally give new proof strategies to further simplify security proofs and remove unnatural restrictions in the known result.

3.1   Proof Method of [Che+18]

The proof method for KAC-type constructions was originally proposed by Chen et al. [Che+18] in their analysis of the minimization of 2-round KAC. We note that [WYCD20] also follows this method and further refines it into an easy-to-use framework. Our approach is more closely inspired by that of [WYCD20] than by [Che+18].

At a high level, the proof method uses the H-coefficient technique (see Theorem 2), so the values of ε_1 and ε_2 need to be determined for good and bad transcripts, respectively. We focus here only on the main challenge, the value of ε_1, which is equivalent to the crucial probability (7) (see Lemma 3).

For a given construction and transcript (represented equivalently in graph view), we call a set of pairs of strings $A^{\equiv} = \{(\langle 0, a_1 \rangle, \langle 2t + 1, b_1 \rangle), \ldots, (\langle 0, a_m \rangle, \langle 2t+1, b_m \rangle)\}$ a *uniform-structure-group*, if $\mathsf{Sh}(\mathsf{R}(a_1)) = \cdots = \mathsf{Sh}(\mathsf{R}(a_m)) < \mathsf{Sh}(\mathsf{L}(b_1)) = \cdots = \mathsf{Sh}(\mathsf{L}(b_m))$. Clearly, all pairs in $A^{\equiv}$ have a uniform structure in graph view, i.e., the numbers and locations of missing permutation-edges are the same for each pair of strings $(\langle 0, a_i \rangle, \langle 2t + 1, b_i \rangle)$. We now give the general problem abstracted in [WYCD20], but slightly different to fit better here.

Definition 1 (Completing A Uniform-Structure-Group, [WYCD20]). *Consider a t-round KAC or KAC-type construction E, and fix arbitrarily an attainable transcript* $\tau = (Q_0, Q_1, \ldots, Q_{t'}, K)$. *Let* $Q_0^{\equiv} = \{(x_{i_1}, y_{i_1}), (x_{i_2}, y_{i_2}), \ldots, (x_{i_s}, y_{i_s})\} \subseteq Q_0$ *be a uniform-structure-group of plaintext-ciphertext pairs[5], then the problem is to evaluate the probability that $Q_0^{\equiv}$ is completed (i.e. all plaintext-ciphertext pairs in $Q_0^{\equiv}$ are connected), written as*

$$p_\tau(Q_0^{\equiv}) = \mathrm{Pr}_{P_1, \ldots, P_{t'} \leftarrow_\$ \mathcal{P}_n}[(E_K \downarrow Q_0^{\equiv}) \mid (P_1 \downarrow Q_1) \wedge \cdots \wedge (P_{t'} \downarrow Q_{t'})]. \quad (9)$$

For 3-round KACSP, [WYCD20] showed that the set Q_0 can be divided into six disjoint uniform-structure-groups $Q_{0,1}^{\equiv}, Q_{0,2}^{\equiv}, Q_{0,3}^{\equiv}, Q_{0,4}^{\equiv}, Q_{0,5}^{\equiv}, Q_{0,6}^{\equiv}$, and the crucial probability (7) can be decomposed into six probabilities (in the form of (9)) associated with them. Then, all that remains is to find a good lower bound on the probability (9).

It is shown in [WYCD20] that there exists a general framework for the task. To state it, we should first look at a useful concept called Core.

---

[5] Recall that x_i's and y_i's are by default in shore 0 and shore $2t + 1$ respectively, so we use the simplified notation here.

Definition 2 (Core, [WYCD20]). *For a complete path from x_j to y_j, we refer to the set of permutation-edges that make up the path as the* Core *of (x_j, y_j), and denote it as* Core(x_j, y_j). *That is,*

$$\text{Core}(x_j, y_j) := \{\langle u, P_k, v \rangle : \langle u, P_k, v \rangle \text{ is in the path from } x_j \text{ to } y_j\}.$$

Similarly, when a uniform-structure-group $\mathcal{Q}_0^{\overline{\equiv}}$ is completed, we can also define its Core *, i.e. the set of permutation-edges used to connect all plaintext-ciphertext pairs in $\mathcal{Q}_0^{\overline{\equiv}}$, denoted as* Core$(\mathcal{Q}_0^{\overline{\equiv}})$. *That is,*

$$\text{Core}(\mathcal{Q}_0^{\overline{\equiv}}) := \bigcup_{(x_j, y_j) \in \mathcal{Q}_0^{\overline{\equiv}}} \text{Core}(x_j, y_j).$$

In order to illustrate the definition of Core more clearly, we also provide several concrete examples in the full version [Yu+23, Appendix B].

Note that the probability (9) is equivalent to counting all possible permutations $P_1, \ldots, P_{t'}$ that complete $\mathcal{Q}_0^{\overline{\equiv}}$ and also satisfy the known queries $\mathcal{Q}_1, \cdots, \mathcal{Q}_{t'}$. The idea of the general framework is to classify all such possible permutations $P_1, \ldots, P_{t'}$, according to the number of new edges added to each round permutation (relative to the known $\mathcal{Q}_1, \cdots, \mathcal{Q}_{t'}$) in Core$(\mathcal{Q}_0^{\overline{\equiv}})$. Since the goal is to obtain a sufficiently large lower bound, a constructive approach can be used. In particular, for each sequence of the numbers of newly added edges in round permutations, we should construct as many permutations $P_1, \ldots, P_{t'}$ as possible that complete $\mathcal{Q}_0^{\overline{\equiv}}$ and satisfy these parameters. Summing up a sufficient number of sequences will give a desired lower bound.

More precisely, we let $\mathcal{P}_C = \{(P_1, \ldots, P_{t'}) \in \mathcal{P}_n^{t'} : (E_K \downarrow \mathcal{Q}_0^{\overline{\equiv}}) \wedge (P_1 \downarrow \mathcal{Q}_1) \wedge \cdots \wedge (P_{t'} \downarrow \mathcal{Q}_{t'})\}$ denote the set of all permutations that complete $\mathcal{Q}_0^{\overline{\equiv}}$ and extend respectively $\mathcal{Q}_1, \ldots, \mathcal{Q}_{t'}$, and let $\mathcal{C} = \{\text{Core}(\mathcal{Q}_0^{\overline{\equiv}}) : \mathcal{Q}_0^{\overline{\equiv}}$ is completed by a sequence of round permutations$(P_1, \ldots, P_{t'}) \in \mathcal{P}_C\}$ denote the set of all possible Cores. For each $\widetilde{C} \in \mathcal{C}$, we can determine a tuple of numbers $(|\widetilde{C}_1|, |\widetilde{C}_2|, \ldots, |\widetilde{C}_{t'}|)$, where $|\widetilde{C}_j|$ represents the number of *edges newly added* to $\mathcal{Q}_j$ in the $\widetilde{C}$. Then, we can give a more general form than the framework in [WYCD20] (i.e., setting $t' = 1$) as follows,

$$(9) = \Pr_{P_1, \ldots, P_{t'} \leftarrow_{\$} \mathcal{P}_n}[(E_K \downarrow \mathcal{Q}_0^{\overline{\equiv}}) \mid (P_1 \downarrow \mathcal{Q}_1) \wedge \cdots \wedge (P_{t'} \downarrow \mathcal{Q}_{t'})]$$

$$= \frac{|\mathcal{P}_C|}{(N - |\mathcal{Q}_1|)! \times \cdots \times (N - |\mathcal{Q}_{t'}|)!}$$

$$= \frac{\sum_{\widetilde{C} \in \mathcal{C}} |(P_1, \ldots, P_{t'}) \in \mathcal{P}_C : \text{Core}(\mathcal{Q}_0^{\overline{\equiv}}) = \widetilde{C}|}{(N - |\mathcal{Q}_1|)! \times \cdots \times (N - |\mathcal{Q}_{t'}|)!}$$

$$= \frac{\sum_{\widetilde{C} \in \mathcal{C}} \prod_{j=1}^{t'} (N - |\mathcal{Q}_j| - |\widetilde{C}_j|)!}{(N - |\mathcal{Q}_1|)! \times \cdots \times (N - |\mathcal{Q}_{t'}|)!}$$

$$= \frac{\sum_{(m_1, m_2, \ldots, m_{t'})} |\{\widetilde{C} \in \mathcal{C} : |\widetilde{C}_1| = m_1, \ldots, |\widetilde{C}_{t'}| = m_{t'}\}| \times \prod_{j=1}^{t'} (N - |\mathcal{Q}_j| - m_j)!}{(N - |\mathcal{Q}_1|)! \times \cdots \times (N - |\mathcal{Q}_{t'}|)!}$$

$$= \sum_{m_1} \cdots \sum_{m_{t'}} \frac{|\{\widetilde{C} \in \mathcal{C} : |\widetilde{C}_1| = m_1, \ldots, |\widetilde{C}_{t'}| = m_{t'}\}|}{(N - |\mathcal{Q}_1|)_{m_1} \times \cdots \times (N - |\mathcal{Q}_{t'}|)_{m_{t'}}}. \tag{10}$$

As mentioned earlier, Eq. (10) essentially turns the task into constructing as many Cores as possible for different tuples $(m_1, \ldots, m_{t'})$, and then summing their results. In general, the framework can be carried out in three steps. The first step is to design a method that, for each given tuple $(m_1, \ldots, m_{t'})$, ensures to generate Cores $\widetilde{C}$ satisfying $|\widetilde{C}_1| = m_1, \ldots, |\widetilde{C}_{t'}| = m_{t'}$. The second step is then to count the possibilities that can be generated by the first step. And the third step is to perform a summation calculation, where a trick[6] of hypergeometric distribution (pioneered by [Che+18]) will be used.

Note. It should be pointed out here that all proofs in this work are conducted under the guidance of this framework (i.e., Eq. (10)). In particular, we showed that the key task of H-coefficient technique (i.e., Lemma 2) is to bound the probability (7) in the real world, which can then be reduced to bound the probabilities of the form (9). Therefore, the framework provides a *high-level intuition* that we can always accomplish the above task in three steps (for any KAC or KAC-type construction[7]): constructing Cores with specific cardinalities, counting the number of Cores and performing a summation calculation. When analyzing different constructions, such as the KACs (setting $t' = t$) and KACSPs (setting $t' = 1$), the subtle difference mainly lies in step 1, where the available constructive methods will be slightly different. In contrast, the detailed analysis and calculations in steps 2 and 3 are similar.

3.2 A General Transformation

We propose a general transformation to simplify the above proof method of [Che+18], such that only one probability (9) needs to be bounded. As we shall see, it does cut out a lot of tedious work and significantly simplify the proof. We apply this transformation to the security proofs of various constructions in this work.

For each pair (x_j, y_j), there are $r_j := \left(\mathsf{Sh}(\mathsf{L}(y_j)) - \mathsf{Sh}(\mathsf{R}(x_j)) + 1\right)/2$ undefined edges between x_j and y_j, where $r_j \in \{1, \ldots, t\}$ for a good transcript[8]. We call r_j the *actual distance* between x_j and y_j. We say that (x_i, y_i) is *farther* than (x_j, y_j) if $r_i > r_j$; or *closer* if $r_i < r_j$; or *equidistant*, otherwise. Clearly, all pairs in a uniform-structure-group are equidistant.

The idea of our general transformation is quite natural. First note that the set $\mathcal{Q}_0$ usually contains pairs with various actual distances, leading to the existence of multiple uniform-structure-groups. Just by intuition, the farther pair (x_i, y_i) feels more "hard" (conditionally, in fact) to connect than the closer pair (x_j, y_j), given the same available resources. After all, the former tends to consume more

---

[6] The terms arising from a (multivariate) hypergeometric distribution are introduced to help calculate a lower bound on the target probability, see the full version [Yu+23, Eq. (30)] for an example.

[7] In fact, the idea of this framework is quite general and it can be easily generalized to other constructions.

[8] The definition of good transcripts usually excludes the case where $r_j = 0$. Please note that we keep all key-edges in the graph view here for maximum generality.

resources (e.g. new edges), so fewer edges can be freely defined. Assuming this argument holds, we can define a set $\widehat{\mathcal{Q}_0}$ satisfying $|\widehat{\mathcal{Q}_0}| = |\mathcal{Q}_0|$ and in which all pairs have the maximal actual distance t. That is, all the easier pairs in $\mathcal{Q}_0$ are replaced with the hardest ones, thus making $\widehat{\mathcal{Q}_0}$ itself a uniform-structure-group. Then, for the same known queries $\mathcal{Q}_1, \ldots, \mathcal{Q}_{t'}$, it should have

$$\text{Eq. (7)} = \Pr_{P_1,\ldots,P_{t'} \leftarrow_\$ \mathcal{P}_n}[(E_K \downarrow \mathcal{Q}_0) \mid (P_1 \downarrow \mathcal{Q}_1) \wedge \cdots \wedge (P_{t'} \downarrow \mathcal{Q}_{t'})]$$
$$\geq \Pr_{P_1,\ldots,P_{t'} \leftarrow_\$ \mathcal{P}_n}[(E_K \downarrow \widehat{\mathcal{Q}_0}) \mid (P_1 \downarrow \mathcal{Q}_1) \wedge \cdots \wedge (P_{t'} \downarrow \mathcal{Q}_{t'})] \stackrel{\text{def}}{=} p_\tau(\widehat{\mathcal{Q}_0}).$$
$$(11)$$

Clearly, if we can obtain a good lower bound for $p_\tau(\widehat{\mathcal{Q}_0})$, it holds for the target crucial probability as well. The advantage of this treatment is that we only need to bound a single probability (9), namely $p_\tau(\widehat{\mathcal{Q}_0})$. Of course it comes at a price, so we need to keep the probability loss within an acceptable range. In short, this transformation can be seen as sacrificing a small amount of accuracy for great computational convenience.

All that remains is to find a method to transform closer pairs into farther ones, and make sure that they are less likely to be connected. We first point out that *the direct transformation* does not necessarily hold, although it is intuitively sound. Taking KAC as an example, we can know from the well-known Lemma 1 that the direct transformation does hold in the average case. However, it does not hold in the worst case, since counterexamples are not difficult to construct.

We next show that the direct transformation can be proved to hold, if a simple constraint is added on the replaced farther pairs. First of all, we say that a vertex u is connected to a vertex v *in the most wasteful way*[9], if all growing permutation-edges in the path are new (i.e. not defined before then) and each of them is used exactly once. Similarly, we can also connect a group of pairs of nodes in the most wasteful way, where all growing permutation-edges in these paths are new and each of them is used exactly once. The following is a *useful property*: for a given group of pairs, the number of new edges added to each round permutation P_j is fixed (denoted as m_j), among all possible paths generated in the most wasteful way. These numbers $m_1, \ldots, m_{t'}$ must be the maximum values (i.e. the number of missing edges between the group of pairs), determined by the construction and the number of pairs.

---

[9] Intuitively, this kind of paths require the most new-edges and do not share any edges with other paths. In the words of [WYCD20], the most wasteful way actually means *sampling an exclusive element for each inner-node*. It had also been shown in [WYCD20] that such samples are easy to analyze. More concrete examples and analysis can be found in the security proofs, such as the Fig. 1 and Appendix C.3 in the full version [Yu+23].

More formally, we give below the definition of the most wasteful way (in the contex of plaintext-ciphertext pairs for ease of notation; other cases can be defined similarly).[10]

Definition 3 (The Most Wasteful Way). *Consider a t-round KAC or KAC-type construction E, and fix arbitrarily the set of construction queries $\mathcal{Q}_0$ and the key K. Let $\mathcal{Q}'_k$ denote the set of all P_k-permutation-edges fixed so far, where $k = \{1,\ldots,t'\}$. Let $\tilde{\mathcal{Q}}_0 = \{(x_{i_1}, y_{i_1}), (x_{i_2}, y_{i_2}), \ldots, (x_{i_s}, y_{i_s})\} \subseteq \mathcal{Q}_0$ be a set of plaintext-ciphertext pairs to be connected, where $\mathsf{Sh}(\mathsf{R}(x_{i_j})) < \mathsf{Sh}(\mathsf{L}(y_{i_j}))$ for all $j \in \{1,\ldots,s\}$. We denote by m_k the total number of P_k-permutation-edges missing in the paths between all pairs in $\tilde{\mathcal{Q}}_0$ (given $\mathcal{Q}'_1, \ldots, \mathcal{Q}'_{t'}$), where $k = \{1,\ldots,t'\}$.*

Then, $\tilde{\mathcal{Q}}_0$ is said to be connected in the most wasteful way (with respect to $\mathcal{Q}'_1, \ldots, \mathcal{Q}'_{t'}$), if the Core of the completed $\tilde{\mathcal{Q}}_0$ contains exactly m_k new P_k-permutation-edges compared to $\mathcal{Q}'_k$ for all $k \in \{1,\ldots,t'\}$.

At this point, we are ready to describe our transformation from $\mathcal{Q}_0$ to $\widehat{\mathcal{Q}}_0$: all pairs in $\mathcal{Q}_0$ whose actual distance is less than t are replaced with new pairs whose actual distance is equal to t, and it is required that these replaced new pairs must be connected in the most wasteful way. The correctness of this transformation can be verified by repeatedly using the general Lemma 4, the proof of which is given in the full version [Yu+23, Appendix E.1].

Lemma 4 (The Closer The Easier) *Consider a t-round ($t \geq 2$) KAC or KAC-type construction E, and fix arbitrarily the sets of known queries $\mathcal{Q}_1, \ldots, \mathcal{Q}_{t'}$ and the key K.*

Let $A^{\equiv} = \{(x_1, y_1), \ldots, (x_s, y_s)\}$ be a uniform-structure-group of s plaintext-ciphertext pairs, where $\mathsf{Sh}(\mathsf{R}(x_1)) = \cdots = \mathsf{Sh}(\mathsf{R}(x_s)) = 3$ and $\mathsf{Sh}(\mathsf{L}(y_1)) = \cdots = \mathsf{Sh}(\mathsf{L}(y_s)) = 2t$. That is, the actual distance of each pair in $A^{\equiv}$ is $t - 1$.

Let $B^{\equiv} = \{(x'_1, y'_1), \ldots, (x'_s, y'_s)\}$ be a uniform-structure-group of s plaintext-ciphertext pairs, where $\mathsf{Sh}(\mathsf{R}(x'_1)) = \cdots = \mathsf{Sh}(\mathsf{R}(x'_s)) = 1$ and $\mathsf{Sh}(\mathsf{L}(y'_1)) = \cdots = \mathsf{Sh}(\mathsf{L}(y'_s)) = 2t$. That is, the actual distance of each pair in $B^{\equiv}$ is t.

Assume that $s \cdot t \leq |\mathcal{Q}_{i_2}|/2$ and $|U_{04}| \leq |\mathcal{Q}_{i_2}|/2$, where $\mathcal{Q}_{i_2}$ denotes the set of known queries to the second round permutation P_{i_2} (where $i_2 \in \{1,\ldots,t'\}$). If we both connect $A^{\equiv}$ and $B^{\equiv}$ in the most wasteful way, then the closer $A^{\equiv}$ is relatively easier. That is, for sufficiently large n, we have

$$\Pr_{P_1,\ldots,P_{t'} \leftarrow_{\$} \mathcal{P}_n}[(E_K \downarrow_w A^{\equiv}) \mid (P_1 \downarrow \mathcal{Q}_1) \wedge \cdots \wedge (P_{t'} \downarrow \mathcal{Q}_{t'})]$$
$$\geq \Pr_{P_1,\ldots,P_{t'} \leftarrow_{\$} \mathcal{P}_n}[(E_K \downarrow_w B^{\equiv}) \mid (P_1 \downarrow \mathcal{Q}_1) \wedge \cdots \wedge (P_{t'} \downarrow \mathcal{Q}_{t'})],$$

where $E_K \downarrow_w A^{\equiv}$ (resp. $E_K \downarrow_w B^{\equiv}$) denotes the event that $A^{\equiv}$ (resp. $B^{\equiv}$) is completed in the most wasteful way.

---

[10] It can be verified that the Examples 2 and 4 in full version [Yu+23, Appendix B] are both connected in the most wasteful way (we purposely assume $\mathcal{Q}_1 = \mathcal{Q}_2 = \emptyset$ over there to ensure that each permutation-edge fixed in the path(s) is new compared to $\mathcal{Q}_1$ and $\mathcal{Q}_2$).

The Lemma 4 tells us that the closer pairs are easier to connect than the farther pairs, even if they are both in the wasteful way. Also note that the ordinary probability of connecting given pairs must be greater than when only the most wasteful way is allowed, since there may be other ways of connecting (e.g. reusing edges). Thus, our general transformation replaces the closer uniform-structure-group (whose connections are unrestricted) by a farther one that can only be connected in the most wasteful way, the connecting probability of course becoming smaller (i.e. Eq. (11) holds). We should also stress that the assumptions $s \cdot t \leq |\mathcal{Q}_{i_2}|/2$ and $|U_{04}| \leq |\mathcal{Q}_{i_2}|/2$ are quite loose, and their only effect on the security proof is to add a few conditions to the definition of good transcripts. For convenience, we can simply ignore the assumptions, except that there is a negligible deviation in the value of ε_2. To see this more clearly, we first point out that the number of pairs that need to be replaced s is often much smaller than $|\mathcal{Q}_i|$ and the number of rounds t is a constant. In particular, the largest s encountered in the security proof for a t-round construction is $s = \mathcal{O}(|\mathcal{Q}_i|/N^{1/(t+1)})$. Second, since the expectation of $|U_{04}|$ is $|\mathcal{Q}_1| \cdot |\mathcal{Q}_{i_2}|/N$, the well-known Markov's inequality is sufficient to give a good upper bound on the probability $\Pr[|U_{04}| > |\mathcal{Q}_{i_2}|/2]$.

Finally, we illustrate how the general transformation can be applied in practical security proofs. The process is quite simple. Given a good transcript $\tau = (\mathcal{Q}_0, \mathcal{Q}_1, \ldots, \mathcal{Q}_{t'}, K)$, we first partition the set $\mathcal{Q}_0$ into disjoint uniform-structure-groups, such as $\mathcal{Q}_{\overline{0},1}^{\equiv}, \ldots, \mathcal{Q}_{\overline{0},k}^{\equiv}$. Typically, there is only one uniform-structure-group, say $\mathcal{Q}_{\overline{0},k}^{\equiv}$, whose actual distance is t and $|\mathcal{Q}_{\overline{0},k}^{\equiv}| = |\mathcal{Q}_0| \cdot (1 - \mathcal{O}(\frac{1}{N^{t+1}}))$. That is, only about $s = \mathcal{O}(\frac{1}{N^{t+1}}) \cdot |\mathcal{Q}_0|$ plaintext-ciphertext pairs need to be replaced by the general transformation. We write $wlog$ that $\mathcal{Q}_0 = \{(x_1, y_1), \ldots, (x_q, y_q)\}$ and $\mathcal{Q}_{\overline{0},k}^{\equiv} = \{(x_{s+1}, y_{s+1}), \ldots, (x_q, y_q)\}$. We first arbitrarily choose s right-free vertices $u_1, \ldots, u_s$ in the shore 1, and s left-free vertices $v_1, \ldots, v_s$ in the shore $2t$ (this always works since both s and $|\mathcal{Q}_i|$ are much smaller than N). Then, we define $(x_{q+i}, y_{q+i}) := (u_i \oplus \kappa_0, v_i \oplus \kappa_t)$ for $i = 1, \ldots, s$, and denote the set they form as $\mathcal{Q}_0^*$. Next, we set $\widehat{\mathcal{Q}_0} = \mathcal{Q}_{\overline{0},k}^{\equiv} \cup \mathcal{Q}_0^*$, i.e. $\widehat{\mathcal{Q}_0} = \{(x_{s+1}, y_{s+1}), \ldots, (x_q, y_q), (x_{q+1}, y_{q+1}), \ldots, (x_{q+s}, y_{q+s})\}$. It is easy to see that $\widehat{\mathcal{Q}_0}$ is indeed a uniform-structure-group with actual distance t. Please note that all the known queries $\mathcal{Q}_1, \ldots, \mathcal{Q}_{t'}$ remain unchanged throughout. Also, don't forget that the last s pairs (i.e. $\mathcal{Q}_0^*$) must be connected in the most wasteful way. Lastly, the property of general transformation (see Eq. (11)) allows us to focus only on the lower bound of the new probability

$$\begin{aligned} \Pr_{P_1, \ldots, P_{t'} \leftarrow_\$ \mathcal{P}_n}[E_K \downarrow \widehat{\mathcal{Q}_0} \mid (P_1 \downarrow \mathcal{Q}_1) \wedge \cdots \wedge (P_{t'} \downarrow \mathcal{Q}_{t'})] \\ = \Pr_{P_1, \ldots, P_{t'} \leftarrow_\$ \mathcal{P}_n}[E_K \downarrow \mathcal{Q}_{\overline{0},k}^{\equiv} \wedge E_K \downarrow_w \mathcal{Q}_0^* \mid (P_1 \downarrow \mathcal{Q}_1) \wedge \cdots \wedge (P_{t'} \downarrow \mathcal{Q}_{t'})], \end{aligned} \quad (12)$$

where $E_K \downarrow_w \mathcal{Q}_0^*$ denotes the event that the plaintext-ciphertext pairs in $\mathcal{Q}_0^*$ are connected in the most wasteful way.

3.3   New Proof Strategies

Although we are guided by the proof method of [Che+18], the low-level proof strategies are quite different.

We introduce a new notion of *recycled-edge*, while [WYCD20] only uses the *shared-edge*. Intuitively, our use of a recycled-edge means that an edge is recycled from the known queries (i.e. from $Q_1, \ldots, Q_{t'}$) to build the path, so that one less new edge is added. Thus, recycled-edges serve the same purpose as shared-edges, i.e. to reduce the use of new edges when growing paths (relative to the most wasteful way). The difference between them is that the former reuses known edges, while the later reuses the newly added edges. We point out that recycled-edge has the following features compared to shared-edge. First, the analysis of recycled-edges is easier because each of recycled-edge involves only one path, whereas each shared-edge involves multiple paths. Second, the recycled-edge is less sensitive to the construction, and its analysis is relatively uniform in different constructions. In particular, it exists in the KAC construction where edges cannot be shared as in [WYCD20].

We provide new ideas to remove the two unnatural restrictions in the security bound of [WYCD20] (i.e., Theorem 1). The first restriction is the existence of an error term $\zeta(q_e)$, making it impossible to obtain a uniform bound for all q_e's. To get a good bound, [WYCD20] needs to choose an appropriate c for different values of q_e. In particular, it is unnatural that their bound does not converge to 0 as the number of queries q_e decreases to 0. Our observation is that this problem may be due to the nature of the hypergeometric distribution, whose variance is not a monotonic function. This leads to the fact that the tail bound obtained by Chebyshev's inequality (see Lemma 16 in the full version [Yu+23]) is also not monotonic, and thus only works well for part of the q_e's, e.g. $q_e = \omega(N^{1/2})$. A natural solution is to give a different proof for the range of $q_e = \mathcal{O}(N^{1/2})$. But one thing to note here is that we need to get a beyond-birthday-bound (i.e. $\mathcal{O}(N^{1/2+\epsilon})$-bound for $\epsilon > 0$), so that the bound is negligible for all $q_e = \mathcal{O}(N^{1/2})$. We found that the proof for $q_e = \omega(N^{1/2})$ can be adapted to the case of $q_e = \mathcal{O}(N^{1/2})$ just by modifying several constants defined in the proof (e.g., the values of M and M_0 in Sect. 4). Therefore, the security proofs in this work usually consider two cases, one is large $q_e = \omega(N^{1/2})$ and the other is small $q_e = \mathcal{O}(N^{1/2})$. Their proofs are almost identical except for slightly different calculations.

The second restriction is that it requires $q_p \leq q_e/5$, where q_p and q_e are the number of permutation queries and construction queries respectively. This is an unnatural limitation on the access ability of distinguisher. After a lot of effort and calculation, we found that under the proof method of [Che+18], the main factor affecting the final security bound is the number of *variables*. Each variable is used to represent the number of new edges reduced in a Core (relative to the most wasteful way), and is denoted by h_i in our proofs. That is, more variables usually means a more accurate bound. It is important to note here that each variable actually corresponds to a constructive method of reducing new edges, and the results generated by these different methods are required to be disjoint. On the other hand, there seems to be an upper bound on the number of constructive methods of reducing new edges. Therefore, a big challenge is to perform a fine-grained analysis that allows us to find an appropriate number of variables to meet both requirements (i.e., accuracy and feasibility).

4 Improved Security Bound of $P_1P_1P_1$-Construction

4.1 Comparison of the Results

Known Result. Wu et al. [WYCD20] were the first to prove a tight security bound for the $P_1P_1P_1$-construction, and their proof was quite laborious.

Theorem 1 ($P_1P_1P_1$-Construction, Theorem 1 of [WYCD20]). *Consider the $P_1P_1P_1$-construction. Assume that $n \geq 32$ is sufficiently large, $\frac{28(q_e)^2}{N} \leq q_p \leq \frac{q_e}{5}$ and $2q_p + 5q_e \leq \frac{N}{2}$, then for any $6 \leq c \leq \frac{N^{1/2}}{8}$, the following upper bound holds:*

$$\mathbf{Adv}^{\mathrm{SPRP}}_{P_1P_1P_1}(\mathcal{D}) \leq 98c \cdot \left(\frac{q_e}{N^{3/4}}\right) + 10c^2 \cdot \left(\frac{q_e}{N}\right) + \zeta(q_e), \tag{13}$$

where $\zeta(q_e) = \begin{cases} \frac{32}{c^2}, & \text{for } q_e \leq \frac{c}{6}N^{1/2} \\ \frac{9N}{q_e^2}, & \text{for } q_e \geq \frac{7c}{6}N^{1/2} \end{cases}$ and $\mathcal{D}$ can be any distinguisher making q_e construction queries and q_p permutation queries.

It can be seen that the above security bound has two unnatural restrictions. The first is the error term $\zeta(q_e)$, where the entire range of q_e cannot be covered by a single value c. In particular, this term is non-negligible for small values of q_e, such as $q_e = \mathcal{O}(N^{1/2})$, making the security bound quite counter-intuitive. The second is the requirement on q_e and q_p, that is, $28(q_e)^2/N \leq q_p \leq q_e/5$, which is not a reasonable limit on the ability of distinguisher.

Our Result. Using the general transformation and new proof strategies outlined in Sect. 3, we obtain a neat security bound for the $P_1P_1P_1$-construction and the proof is much simpler.

Theorem 2 ($P_1P_1P_1$-Construction, Improved Bound). *Consider the $P_1P_1P_1$-construction. For any distinguisher $\mathcal{D}$ making q_e construction queries and q_p permutation queries, the following upper bound holds:*

$$\mathbf{Adv}^{\mathrm{SPRP}}_{P_1P_1P_1}(\mathcal{D}) \leq \begin{cases} \dfrac{69q}{N^{3/4}} + \dfrac{125q^2}{N^{3/2}} + \dfrac{8q^4}{N^3} + \dfrac{6q^6}{N^5} + \dfrac{78q}{N} + \dfrac{32N}{q^2}, & \text{for } q = \omega(N^{1/2}) \\[2ex] \dfrac{12q}{N^{7/10}} + \dfrac{125q^2}{N^{7/5}} + \dfrac{135q}{N^{3/4}} + \dfrac{8q^4}{N^3} + \dfrac{6q^6}{N^5} + \dfrac{32}{N^{1/10}}, & \text{for } q = \mathcal{O}(N^{1/2}) \end{cases}$$

where $q := \max\{q_e, q_p\}$.

In contrast to Theorem 1, our bound does give a negligible bound for all $q = \mathcal{O}(N^{1/2})$ (which is better than $\mathcal{O}(N^{2/3})$-bound but slightly worse than $\mathcal{O}(N^{3/4})$-bound), and has no restriction on the values of q_e and q_p. In fact, the bound for $q = \mathcal{O}(N^{1/2})$ can be easily improved to $\mathcal{O}(N^{3/4-\epsilon})$-bound for any $\epsilon > 0$, by modifying M to $q/N^{1/2-\epsilon}$ and M_0 to $q/N^{1/4+\epsilon}$, where M and M_0 are two constants to be defined in the proof. Even if we focus only on the large $q = \omega(N^{1/2})$, our bound is better than Eq. (13) (for which the optimal $c = 6$ is set). Most importantly, the proof of Theorem 2 is simpler and can be found in Sect. 4.2.

Remarks. It should be pointed out that the tightness of our bound is with respect to attacks achieving constant probability, i.e., an adversary needs $q = \Omega(N^{3/4})$ queries to distinguish $P_1 P_1 P_1$-construction from random with a high advantage. The curve of our bound (i.e., roughly $(q^4/N^3)^{\frac{1}{4}}$) is not as sharp as the tigher bound (i.e., roughly q^4/N^3) achieved in the study of KACs (e.g., [HT16]).

We here show that the exact threshold of the two bounds in Theorem 2 can be determined. In fact, there are values of q that satisfy both bounds (for these q's, we can choose the better one at the time of use). More specifically, the first bound holds for all $q >= N^{1/2+\epsilon}$ for any $\epsilon > 0$, and the second bound holds for all $q \leq N^{11/20}/2$. Thus, any value in the interval $[N^{1/2+\epsilon}, N^{11/20}/2]$ (e.g., $N^{0.53}$) can be safely chosen as the threshold.

The main reason that leads us to discuss two cases is the Eq. (35) in the full version [Yu+23], where the magnitudes of MN and q^2 need to be compared. For more details, please refer to the calculation below Eq. (34) in the full version [Yu+23], which shows the analysis for all $q \geq N^{1/2+\epsilon}$. If we set $M = \frac{q}{N^{9/20}}$ there, then it can be verified that the second bound holds for $q \leq N^{11/20}/2$.

4.2 Proof of Theorem 2

As discussed in Sect. 3, we will consider two disjoint cases separately to remove the first restriction, namely the case $q = \omega(N^{1/2})$ and the case $q = \mathcal{O}(N^{1/2})$. For each case, the proof is guided by the proof method of [Che+18], thus using the H-coefficient technique (see Lemma 2) at a high level. Following the technique, we define the sets of good and bad transcripts, and then determine the values of ε_1 and ε_2, respectively. When calculating the value of ε_1, we apply the general transformation (see Eq. (11)) so that only a single probability need to be considered. Finally, we address this single probability using the general framework (see Eq. (10)) combined with our new proof strategies.

Preparatory Work. First, we point out the simple fact that for every distinguisher $\mathcal{D}$ that makes q_e construction queries and q_p permutation queries, there exists a $\mathcal{D}'$ making q construction queries and q permutation queries with at least the same distinguishing advantage, where $q = \max\{q_e, q_p\}$. We can just let $\mathcal{D}'$ simulate the queries of $\mathcal{D}$, and then perform additional $q - q_e$ construction queries and $q - q_p$ permutation queries, which obviously increases its advantage. For computational convenience, we consider the distinguisher $\mathcal{D}'$ that makes q

construction queries and q permutation queries in the analysis. That is, for each attainable transcript $\tau = (\mathcal{Q}_0, \mathcal{Q}_1, K) \in \mathcal{T}$, it has $|\mathcal{Q}_0| = |\mathcal{Q}_1| = q$.

To illustrate the key probability (7) of a good transcript, we can assume that there is no path of length 7 starting from $x_i \in \mathsf{Dom}(\mathcal{Q}_0)$ in shore 0 or ending at $y_i \in \mathsf{Ran}(\mathcal{Q}_0)$ in shore 7 (otherwise, it would be a bad transcript). Then, as in [WYCD20], the set $\mathcal{Q}_0$ can be partitioned into the following 6 uniform-structure-groups.

- Denote WLOG that $\mathcal{Q}_{0,1}^{\equiv} = \{(x_1, y_1), \ldots, (x_{\alpha_2}, y_{\alpha_2})\} \subset \mathcal{Q}_0$, where $\mathsf{Sh}(\mathsf{R}(x_i)) = 5$ and $\mathsf{Sh}(\mathsf{L}(y_i)) = 6$ for $i = 1, \ldots, \alpha_2$. That is, the actual distance of $\mathcal{Q}_{0,1}^{\equiv}$ is 1 and $|\mathcal{Q}_{0,1}^{\equiv}| = \alpha_2$. We also denote by $\mathsf{R}(\mathcal{Q}_{0,1}^{\equiv}) = \{\mathsf{R}(x_i) : i = 1, \ldots, \alpha_2\}, \mathsf{L}(\mathcal{Q}_{0,1}^{\equiv}) = \{\mathsf{L}(y_i) : i = 1, \ldots, \alpha_2\}$.
- Denote WLOG that $\mathcal{Q}_{0,2}^{\equiv} = \{(x_{\alpha_2+1}, y_{\alpha_2+1}), \ldots, (x_{\alpha_2+\beta_2}, y_{\alpha_2+\beta_2})\} \subset \mathcal{Q}_0$, where $\mathsf{Sh}(\mathsf{R}(x_i)) = 1$ and $\mathsf{Sh}(\mathsf{L}(y_i)) = 2$ for $i = \alpha_2 + 1, \ldots, \alpha_2 + \beta_2$. That is, the actual distance of $\mathcal{Q}_{0,2}^{\equiv}$ is 1 and $|\mathcal{Q}_{0,2}^{\equiv}| = \beta_2$. We also denote by $\mathsf{R}(\mathcal{Q}_{0,2}^{\equiv}) = \{\mathsf{R}(x_i) : i = \alpha_2 + 1, \ldots, \alpha_2 + \beta_2\}, \mathsf{L}(\mathcal{Q}_{0,2}^{\equiv}) = \{\mathsf{L}(y_i) : i = \alpha_2 + 1, \ldots, \alpha_2 + \beta_2\}$.
- Denote WLOG that $\mathcal{Q}_{0,3}^{\equiv} = \{(x_{\alpha_2+\beta_2+1}, y_{\alpha_2+\beta_2+1}), \ldots, (x_{\delta_2}, y_{\delta_2})\} \subset \mathcal{Q}_0$, where $\mathsf{Sh}(\mathsf{R}(x_i)) = 3$ and $\mathsf{Sh}(\mathsf{L}(y_i)) = 4$ for $i = \alpha_2 + \beta_2 + 1, \ldots, \delta_2$. That is, the actual distance of $\mathcal{Q}_{0,3}^{\equiv}$ is 1 and $|\mathcal{Q}_{0,3}^{\equiv}| := \gamma_2 = \delta_2 - \alpha_2 - \beta_2$. We also denote by $\mathsf{R}(\mathcal{Q}_{0,3}^{\equiv}) = \{\mathsf{R}(x_i) : i = \alpha_2 + \beta_2 + 1, \ldots, \delta_2\}, \mathsf{L}(\mathcal{Q}_{0,3}^{\equiv}) = \{\mathsf{L}(y_i) : i = \alpha_2 + \beta_2 + 1, \ldots, \delta_2\}$.
- Denote WLOG that $\mathcal{Q}_{0,4}^{\equiv} = \{(x_{\delta_2+1}, y_{\delta_2+1}), \ldots, (x_{\delta_2+\alpha_1}, y_{\delta_2+\alpha_1})\} \subset \mathcal{Q}_0$, where $\mathsf{Sh}(\mathsf{R}(x_i)) = 3$ and $\mathsf{Sh}(\mathsf{L}(y_i)) = 6$ for $i = \delta_2 + 1, \ldots, \delta_2 + \alpha_1$. That is, the actual distance of $\mathcal{Q}_{0,4}^{\equiv}$ is 2 and $|\mathcal{Q}_{0,4}^{\equiv}| = \alpha_1$. We also denote by $\mathsf{R}(\mathcal{Q}_{0,4}^{\equiv}) = \{\mathsf{R}(x_i) : i = \delta_2 + 1, \ldots, \delta_2 + \alpha_1\}, \mathsf{L}(\mathcal{Q}_{0,4}^{\equiv}) = \{\mathsf{L}(y_i) : i = \delta_2 + 1, \ldots, \delta_2 + \alpha_1\}$.
- Denote WLOG that $\mathcal{Q}_{0,5}^{\equiv} = \{(x_{\delta_2+\alpha_1+1}, y_{\delta_2+\alpha_1+1}), \ldots, (x_{\delta_2+\delta_1}, y_{\delta_2+\delta_1})\} \subset \mathcal{Q}_0$, where $\mathsf{Sh}(\mathsf{R}(x_i)) = 1$ and $\mathsf{Sh}(\mathsf{L}(y_i)) = 4$ for $i = \delta_2 + \alpha_1 + 1, \ldots, \delta_2 + \delta_1$. That is, the actual distance of $\mathcal{Q}_{0,5}^{\equiv}$ is 2 and $|\mathcal{Q}_{0,5}^{\equiv}| := \beta_1 = \delta_1 - \alpha_1$. We also denote by $\mathsf{R}(\mathcal{Q}_{0,5}^{\equiv}) = \{\mathsf{R}(x_i) : i = \delta_2 + \alpha_1 + 1, \ldots, \delta_2 + \delta_1\}, \mathsf{L}(\mathcal{Q}_{0,5}^{\equiv}) = \{\mathsf{L}(y_i) : i = \delta_2 + \alpha_1 + 1, \ldots, \delta_2 + \delta_1\}$.
- Denote WLOG that $\mathcal{Q}_{0,6}^{\equiv} = \{(x_{\delta_2+\delta_1+1}, y_{\delta_2+\delta_1+1}), \ldots, (x_q, y_q)\} \subset \mathcal{Q}_0$, where $\mathsf{Sh}(\mathsf{R}(x_i)) = 1$ and $\mathsf{Sh}(\mathsf{L}(y_i)) = 6$ for $i = \delta_2 + \delta_1 + 1, \ldots, q$. That is, the actual distance of $\mathcal{Q}_{0,6}^{\equiv}$ is 3 and $|\mathcal{Q}_{0,6}^{\equiv}| = \delta_0 = q - \delta_1 - \delta_2$. We also denote by $\mathsf{R}(\mathcal{Q}_{0,6}^{\equiv}) = \{\mathsf{R}(x_i) : i = \delta_2 + \delta_1 + 1, \ldots, q\}, \mathsf{L}(\mathcal{Q}_{0,6}^{\equiv}) = \{\mathsf{L}(y_i) : i = \delta_2 + \delta_1 + 1, \ldots, q\}$.

It is easy to see that the crucial probability

$$(7) = \Pr_{P_1 \leftarrow_\$ \mathcal{P}_n}[E_K \downarrow \mathcal{Q}_0 \mid P_1 \downarrow \mathcal{Q}_1] = \Pr_{P_1 \leftarrow_\$ \mathcal{P}_n}[\bigwedge_{j=1}^{6} E_K \downarrow \mathcal{Q}_{0,j}^{\equiv} \mid P_1 \downarrow \mathcal{Q}_1].$$

$$(14)$$

In [WYCD20], the probability (14) was decomposed into several conditional probabilities, which were quite cumbersome to analyze.

Applying General Transformation. We use the general transformation (see Eq. (11)) here to reduce the task to bounding only one probability. The basic idea is to replace the uniform-structure-groups whose actual distance is less than 3 (i.e. $\mathcal{Q}_{0,1}^{\equiv}, \mathcal{Q}_{0,2}^{\equiv}, \mathcal{Q}_{0,3}^{\equiv}, \mathcal{Q}_{0,4}^{\equiv}, \mathcal{Q}_{0,5}^{\equiv}$) with a new uniform-structure-group whose actual distance is 3, and make the connecting probability smaller.

First note that when $q = \mathcal{O}(N^{3/4})$, the expectation of $\alpha_2, \beta_2, \gamma_2$ is $q^3/N^2 = \mathcal{O}(q/N^{1/2})$, and the expectation of α_1, β_1 is $q^2/N = \mathcal{O}(q/N^{1/4})$. Then, we denote $s = \delta_1 + \delta_2 = \alpha_1 + \beta_1 + \alpha_2 + \beta_2 + \gamma_2 = \mathcal{O}(q/N^{1/4})$ as the number of pairs to be replaced. As discussed in Sect. 3, we take arbitrarily s vertices in shore 0 from the set $\{0,1\}^n \setminus \mathrm{Dom}(\mathcal{Q}_0) \setminus \mathrm{Dom}(\mathcal{Q}_1) \oplus \kappa_0$ and denote them as $x_{q+1}, \ldots, x_{q+s}$. We also take arbitrarily s vertices in shore $2t+1$ from the set $\{0,1\}^n \setminus \mathrm{Ran}(\mathcal{Q}_0) \setminus \mathrm{Ran}(\mathcal{Q}_1) \oplus \kappa_3$ and denote them as $y_{q+1}, \ldots, y_{q+s}$. Then, we define the new uniform-structure-group $\mathcal{Q}_0^* := \{(x_i, y_i) : i = q+1, \ldots, q+s\}$ and set $\widehat{\mathcal{Q}_0} := \mathcal{Q}_{0,6}^{\equiv} \cup \mathcal{Q}_0^*$, where the pairs in $\mathcal{Q}_0^*$ must be connected in the most wasteful way. Using Lemma 4 several times, we can know that

$$
(14) = \Pr_{P_1 \leftarrow_\$ \mathcal{P}_n}\left[\bigwedge_{j=1}^{6} E_K \downarrow \mathcal{Q}_{0,j}^{\equiv} \mid P_1 \downarrow \mathcal{Q}_1\right]
$$

$$
\geq \Pr_{P_1 \leftarrow_\$ \mathcal{P}_n}[E_K \downarrow \widehat{\mathcal{Q}_0} \mid P_1 \downarrow \mathcal{Q}_1]
$$

$$
= \Pr_{P_1 \leftarrow_\$ \mathcal{P}_n}[E_K \downarrow \mathcal{Q}_{0,6}^{\equiv} \wedge E_K \downarrow_w \mathcal{Q}_0^* \mid P_1 \downarrow \mathcal{Q}_1]. \tag{15}
$$

4.2.1   Case 1: $q = \omega(N^{1/2})$ We mainly focus on the large values of $q = \omega(N^{1/2})$, and the other case of $q = \mathcal{O}(N^{1/2})$ is similar. Let $M = \frac{q}{N^{1/2}}$ and $M_0 = \frac{q}{N^{1/4}}$. We first give the definition of good and bad transcripts.

Definition 4 (Bad and Good Transcripts, $P_1P_1P_1$-Construction). *For an attainable transcript $\tau = (\mathcal{Q}_0, \mathcal{Q}_1, K) \in \mathcal{T}$, we say that τ is bad if $K \in \bigcup_{i=1}^{5} \mathsf{BadK}_i$; otherwise τ is good. The definitions of BadK_i are shown below:*

$K \in \mathsf{BadK}_1 \Leftrightarrow$ *there exists a path of length 7 starting from a vertex $x_i \in \mathrm{Dom}(\mathcal{Q}_0)$*
   in shore 0 or ending at a vertex $y_i \in \mathrm{Ran}(\mathcal{Q}_0)$ in shore 7

$K \in \mathsf{BadK}_2 \Leftrightarrow$ $\alpha_2 > M \vee \beta_2 > M \vee \gamma_2 > M \vee \alpha_1 > M_0 \vee \beta_1 > M_0$

$K \in \mathsf{BadK}_3 \Leftrightarrow$ $\mathrm{Dom}(\mathcal{Q}_1), \mathrm{R}(\mathcal{Q}_{0,1}^{\equiv}), \mathrm{R}(\mathcal{Q}_{0,2}^{\equiv}), \mathrm{R}(\mathcal{Q}_{0,3}^{\equiv})$ *are not pairwise disjoint*
   $\vee\ \mathrm{Ran}(\mathcal{Q}_1), \mathrm{L}(\mathcal{Q}_{0,1}^{\equiv}), \mathrm{L}(\mathcal{Q}_{0,2}^{\equiv}), \mathrm{L}(\mathcal{Q}_{0,3}^{\equiv})$ *are not pairwise disjoint*

$K \in \mathsf{BadK}_4 \Leftrightarrow$
$$
\begin{cases}
|\{x \in \mathrm{Dom}(\mathcal{Q}_0) : x \oplus \kappa_0 \oplus \kappa_1 \text{ is not left-free}\}| > M_0 \\
\vee\ |(\mathrm{Dom}(\mathcal{Q}_0) \oplus \kappa_0 \oplus \kappa_1) \cap (\mathrm{Ran}(\mathcal{Q}_0) \oplus \kappa_3)| > M_0 \\
\vee\ |\{y \in \mathrm{Ran}(\mathcal{Q}_0) : y \oplus \kappa_3 \oplus \kappa_2 \text{ is not right-free}\}| > M_0 \\
\vee\ |(\mathrm{Ran}(\mathcal{Q}_0) \oplus \kappa_3 \oplus \kappa_2) \cap (\mathrm{Dom}(\mathcal{Q}_0) \oplus \kappa_0)| > M_0 \\
\vee\ |\{x \in \mathrm{Dom}(\mathcal{Q}_0) : x \oplus \kappa_0 \oplus \kappa_2 \text{ is not left-free}\}| > M_0 \\
\vee\ |(\mathrm{Dom}(\mathcal{Q}_0) \oplus \kappa_0 \oplus \kappa_2) \cap (\mathrm{Ran}(\mathcal{Q}_0) \oplus \kappa_3)| > M_0 \\
\vee\ |\{y \in \mathrm{Ran}(\mathcal{Q}_0) : y \oplus \kappa_3 \oplus \kappa_1 \text{ is not right-free}\}| > M_0 \\
\vee\ |(\mathrm{Ran}(\mathcal{Q}_0) \oplus \kappa_3 \oplus \kappa_1) \cap (\mathrm{Dom}(\mathcal{Q}_0) \oplus \kappa_0)| > M_0
\end{cases}
$$

$K \in \mathsf{BadK}_5 \Leftrightarrow |U_{05}| > M_0 \vee |U_{27}| > M_0.$

We can determine the value of $\varepsilon_2 = \frac{12q}{N^{3/4}} + \frac{3q^2}{N^{3/2}} + \frac{8q^4}{N^3} + \frac{6q^6}{N^5}$ from the following lemma, the proof of which can be found in the full version [Yu+23, Appendix E.2].

Lemma 5 (Bad Transcripts, $q = \omega(N^{1/2})$). *For any given $\mathcal{Q}_0, \mathcal{Q}_1$ such that $|\mathcal{Q}_0| = |\mathcal{Q}_1| = q$, we have*

$$\mathrm{Pr}_{K \leftarrow_\$ \{0,1\}^{4n}}[\tau = (\mathcal{Q}_0, \mathcal{Q}_1, K) \text{ is bad}] \leq \frac{12q}{N^{3/4}} + \frac{3q^2}{N^{3/2}} + \frac{8q^4}{N^3} + \frac{6q^6}{N^5}.$$

The following lemma gives a lower bound on Eq. (15) for any good transcript.

Lemma 6 (Good Transcripts, $q = \omega(N^{1/2})$). *Fix arbitrarily a good transcript $\tau = (\mathcal{Q}_0, \mathcal{Q}_1, K) \in \mathcal{T}$ as defined in Definition 4. Let $\mathcal{Q}_{0,6}^{\equiv}$ and $\mathcal{Q}_0^*$ be as described in Eq. (15), then we have*

$$\mathrm{Pr}_{P_1 \leftarrow_\$ \mathcal{P}_n}[E_K \downarrow \mathcal{Q}_{0,6}^{\equiv} \wedge E_K \downarrow_w \mathcal{Q}_0^* \mid P_1 \downarrow \mathcal{Q}_1] \tag{16}$$
$$\geq \frac{1}{(N)_q} \times \left(1 - \frac{57q}{N^{3/4}} - \frac{122q^2}{N^{3/2}} - \frac{78q}{N} - \frac{32\,N}{q^2}\right).$$

Before giving the proof of Lemma 6, we first show how to obtain the final security bound from the above two lemmas. First note that (16) is also a lower bound on the crucial probability (7), i.e. $p(\tau)$ in Lemma 3 when $t = 3, t' = 1$. Then it is not difficult to determine the value of $\varepsilon_1 = \frac{57q}{N^{3/4}} + \frac{122q^2}{N^{3/2}} + \frac{78q}{N} + \frac{32\,N}{q^2}$. According to the H-coefficient technique (see Lemma 2), we can obtain

$$\mathbf{Adv}_{\Gamma_1 P_1 P_1}^{\mathsf{SPRP}}(\mathcal{D}) \leq \varepsilon_1 + \varepsilon_2$$
$$= \frac{12q}{N^{3/4}} + \frac{3q^2}{N^{3/2}} + \frac{8q^4}{N^3} + \frac{6q^6}{N^5} + \frac{57q}{N^{3/4}} + \frac{122q^2}{N^{3/2}} + \frac{78q}{N} + \frac{32\,N}{q^2}$$
$$= \frac{69q}{N^{3/4}} + \frac{125q^2}{N^{3/2}} + \frac{8q^4}{N^3} + \frac{6q^6}{N^5} + \frac{78q}{N} + \frac{32\,N}{q^2},$$

which is the result of large $q = \omega(N^{1/2})$ in Theorem 2.

Proof (Proof of Lemma 6). Let $\mathcal{Q}_0^{\equiv} = \widehat{\mathcal{Q}_0} := \mathcal{Q}_{0,6}^{\equiv} \cup \mathcal{Q}_0^*$ and $t = 3, t' = 1$, then the target probability is exactly an instantiation of the general problem (9). We apply the general framework (10) to bound it, so roughly in three steps.

The first step is to generate Cores with specific numbers of new edges. We will use four variables (denoted as h_1, h_2, h_3, h_4) to obtain a sufficiently accurate security bound, so four constructive methods of reducing new edges are needed.

The first method we use is called *recycled-edge-based method*, which exploits recycled-edges to reduce a specified number of new edges when building paths. Intuitively, when we construct a path connecting plaintext-ciphertext pair (x_i, y_i) with an actual distance of 3, the choice of the permutation-edge between shore 3 and 4 is quite free and can be "recycled" from the known edges in $\mathcal{Q}_1$ for use.

Thus, we can construct the path with one less new edge. Furthermore, most of the known edges in $\mathcal{Q}_1$ (about the proportion of $1 - \mathcal{O}(1/N^{1/4})$) can be used as recycled-edges. More details about the recycled-edge-based method can be found in the full version [Yu+23, Appendix C.1].

The other three methods we use are *shared-edge-based methods*, each of which exploits a different type of shared-edges to reduce a specified number of new edges when building paths. Intuitively, we consider two plaintext-ciphertext pairs together and let them share exactly 1 permutation edge. The two paths can then be connected with one less new edge than the most wasteful way. In particular, this work only considers shared-edges of this type, each of which saves 1 new edge for 2 paths. To distinguish, we refer to a shared-edge as (i,j)-*shared-edge*, where i and j represent the rounds that the shared-edge lies in two paths respectively. Note that the positions of the two paths are interchangeable, so (i,j)-shared-edges and (j,i)-shared-edges are essentially the same type. More details about the shared-edge-based methods can be found in the full version [Yu+23, Appendix C.2].

Recalling the Eq. (15), our task is to connect the q pairs of $\widehat{\mathcal{Q}_0} = \mathcal{Q}_{\overline{0},6}^{\equiv} \cup \mathcal{Q}_0^*$ using a specified number of new edges, where $\mathcal{Q}_0^*$ is connected in the most wasteful way. Let h_1, h_2, h_3, h_4 be four integer variables in the interval $[0, M]$, where $M = \frac{q}{N^{1/2}}$ is a constant determined by q. We combine the recycled-edge-based method, the shared-edge-based methods and the most wasteful way to accomplish the task in five steps.

1. Select h_1 distinct pairs from $\mathcal{Q}_{\overline{0},6}^{\equiv}$, and connect each of these pairs using the recycled-edge-based method.
2. Apart from the h_1 pairs selected in Step 1, select $2h_2$ appropriate pairs from $\mathcal{Q}_{\overline{0},6}^{\equiv}$, and connect these pairs using the $(1,2)$-shared-edge-based method.
3. Apart from the $h_1 + 2h_2$ pairs selected in Steps 1 and 2, select $2h_3$ appropriate pairs from $\mathcal{Q}_{\overline{0},6}^{\equiv}$, and connect these pairs using the $(1,3)$-shared-edge-based method.
4. Apart from the $h_1 + 2h_2 + 2h_3$ pairs selected in Steps 1–3, select $2h_4$ appropriate pairs from $\mathcal{Q}_{\overline{0},6}^{\equiv}$, and connect these pairs using the $(2,3)$-shared-edge-based method.
5. Connect the remaining $\delta_0 - h_1 - \sum_{i=2}^{4} 2h_i$ pairs in $\mathcal{Q}_{\overline{0},6}^{\equiv}$ and the s pairs in $\mathcal{Q}_0^*$ in the most wasteful way.

Clearly, the above procedure must generate a $\mathsf{Core}(\widehat{\mathcal{Q}_0})$ containing exactly $3q - \sum_{i=1}^{4} h_i$ new edges, and all the pairs of $\mathcal{Q}_0^*$ are connected in the most wasteful way.

As mentioned in Sect. 3, the main factor affecting the final security bound is the number of variables. A simple explanation is that more variables make the multivariate hypergeometric distribution used in the calculations more tunable. That is why we define four variables h_1, h_2, h_3, h_4 here (i.e., to improve the accuracy), and it can be verified that these four methods necessarily produce different types of paths (i.e., to ensure the plausibility). Note that even considering only the shared-edge-based methods, our strategy is simpler than [WYCD20].

In particular, a single selection operation of theirs may generate three different types of shared-edges, whereas each of our selection operations will only generate shared-edges of the same type.

The second step is to evaluate the number of Cores that can be generated in the first step. According to the above procedure of connecting q plaintext-ciphertext pairs of $\widehat{\mathcal{Q}_0}$, we determine the number of possibilities for each step as follows. In the following, $RC_i(j)$ denotes the *Range (set) of all possible Candidate values* for the to-be-assigned nodes in shore j (according to the constructive method used in Step i).

1. Since $|\mathcal{Q}_{\overline{0},6}^{\equiv}| = \delta_0$, it has $\binom{\delta_0}{h_1}$ possibilities to select h_1 distinct pairs from $\mathcal{Q}_{\overline{0},6}^{\equiv}$. After the h_1 pairs are chosen, we use the recycled-edge-based method to connect them by first determining a set $RC_1(3)$ (the analysis of which is referred to the $RC(3)$ in full version [Yu+23, Appendix C.1]) and choosing h_1 different u's from it, and then assigning one u to each pair. In total, the possibilities of Step 1 is at least $\binom{\delta_0}{h_1} \cdot (|RC_1(3)|)_{h_1}$.

2. For simplicity, we can define a set of plaintext-ciphertext pairs $Z \subset \mathcal{Q}_{\overline{0},6}^{\equiv}$ (see Eq. (17) for the definition of Z), so that the $2(h_2 + h_3 + h_4)$ distinct pairs in Step 2–4 can all be selected from Z. Then in Step 2, we have $\binom{|Z|}{h_2} \cdot \binom{|Z|-h_2}{h_2}$ possibilities to sequentially select h_2 distinct pairs from Z twice, where the first (resp. second) selected h_2 pairs will be constructed as the upper-paths (resp. lower-paths)[11] in the $(1, 2)$-shared-edge-based method. We then use the $(1, 2)$-shared-edge-based method to connect these $2h_2$ pairs. According to the discussion in the full version [Yu+23, Appendix C.2], the core task of $(1, 2)$-shared-edge-based method is to determine two sets denoted by $RC_2(2)$ and $RC_2(4)$. By simple counting, the possibilities of Step 2 is at least $\frac{(|Z|)_{2h_2}}{h_2!} \cdot (|RC_2(2)|)_{h_2} \cdot (|RC_2(4)|)_{h_2}$, where $\frac{(|Z|)_{2h_2}}{h_2!} = \binom{|Z|}{h_2} \cdot \binom{|Z|-h_2}{h_2} \cdot h_2!$.

3. For Step 3, we can select $2h_3$ distinct pairs from Z after removing the $2h_2$ pairs chosen in Step 2. Then, we have $\binom{|Z|-2h_2}{h_3} \cdot \binom{|Z|-2h_2-h_3}{h_3}$ possibilities to sequentially select h_3 distinct pairs from the rest of Z twice (similar to Step 2, the first and second selected h_3 pairs will play different roles). After the $2h_3$ pairs are chosen, we use the $(1, 3)$-shared-edge-based method to connect them. According to an analysis similar to that in the full version [Yu+23, Appendix C.2], the core task of $(1, 3)$-shared-edge-based method is also to determine two sets denoted by $RC_3(4)$ and $RC_3(2)$. By simple counting, the possibilities of Step 3 is at least $\frac{(|Z|-2h_2)_{2h_3}}{h_3!} \cdot (|RC_3(2)|)_{h_3} \cdot (|RC_3(4)|)_{h_3}$.

4. For Step 4, we can select $2h_4$ distinct pairs from Z after removing the $2(h_2 + h_3)$ pairs chosen in Step 2 and Step 3. Then, we have $\binom{|Z|-2h_2-2h_3}{h_4} \cdot \binom{|Z|-2h_2-2h_3-h_4}{h_4}$ possibilities to sequentially select h_4 distinct pairs from the rest of Z twice (similar to Step 2, the first and second selected h_4 pairs will play different roles). After the $2h_4$ pairs are chosen, we use the $(2, 3)$-shared-edge-based method to connect them. According to an analysis similar to that in the full version [Yu+23, Appendix C.2], the core

---

[11] In Fig. 1 of the full version [Yu+23, Appendix C], the paths between (x_2, y_2) and (x'_2, y'_2) are called the *upper-path* and *lower-path*, respectively.

task of $(2, 3)$-shared-edge-based method is to determine two sets denoted by $RC_4(4)$ and $RC_4(2)$. By simple counting, the possibilities of Step 4 is at least $\frac{(|Z|-2h_2-2h_3)_{2h_4}}{h_4!} \cdot (|RC_4(2)|)_{h_4} \cdot (|RC_4(4)|)_{h_4}$.

5. Step 5 is to connect the remaining $(\delta_0 - h_1 - \sum_{i=2}^{4} 2h_i)$ pairs in $\mathcal{Q}_{0,6}^{\equiv}$ and the s pairs in $\mathcal{Q}_0^*$ in the most wasteful way. According to the analysis in the full version [Yu+23, Appendix C.3], we can determine a set $RC_5(2)$ and choose $(\delta_0 - h_1 - \sum_{i=2}^{4} 2h_i) + s = q - h_1 - \sum_{i=2}^{4} 2h_i$ different $w_{3,2}$'s from it, and assign one $w_{3,2}$ to each pair; then determine a set $RC_5(4)$ and choose $q - h_1 - \sum_{i=2}^{4} 2h_i$ different $w_{3,4}$'s from it, and then assign one $w_{3,4}$ to each pair. In total, the possibilities of Step 5 is at least $(|RC_5(2)|)_{q-h_1-\sum_{i=2}^{4} 2h_i} \cdot (|RC_5(4)|)_{q-h_1-\sum_{i=2}^{4} 2h_i}$.

All that's left is to give a lower bound on the cardinality for Z and each $RC_j(i)$ mentioned above. Let Λ_1 denote the set of h_1 pairs selected from $\mathcal{Q}_{0,6}^{\equiv}$ in Step 1. We first give the definition of set Z below[12], and denote by $|Z| = q_0$.

$$
\begin{aligned}
Z := \{(x_i, y_i) \in \mathcal{Q}_{0,6}^{\equiv} \setminus \Lambda_1 : \\
x_i \notin \mathsf{Ran}(\mathcal{Q}_0) \oplus \kappa_0 \oplus \kappa_1 \oplus \kappa_3 \wedge x_i \notin \mathsf{Ran}(\mathcal{Q}_0) \oplus \kappa_0 \oplus \kappa_2 \oplus \kappa_3 \\
\wedge y_i \notin \mathsf{Dom}(\mathcal{Q}_0) \oplus \kappa_0 \oplus \kappa_1 \oplus \kappa_3 \wedge y_i \notin \mathsf{Dom}(\mathcal{Q}_0) \oplus \kappa_0 \oplus \kappa_2 \oplus \kappa_3 \quad (17) \\
\wedge x_i \oplus \kappa_0 \oplus \kappa_1 \text{ is left-free} \wedge x_i \oplus \kappa_0 \oplus \kappa_2 \text{ is left-free} \\
\wedge y_i \oplus \kappa_1 \oplus \kappa_3 \text{ is right-free} \wedge y_i \oplus \kappa_2 \oplus \kappa_3 \text{ is right-free} \}
\end{aligned}
$$

From the BadK_4 in Defn. 4, we can know that

$$
q_0 = |Z| \geq \delta_0 - h_1 - 8M_0. \tag{18}
$$

Based on the analysis in the full version [Yu+23, Appendix C.1–C.3], we proceed to lower-bound the cardinality of each $RC_j(i)$ as follows.

$$
\begin{aligned}
|RC_1(3)| &\geq |\mathsf{Dom}(\mathcal{Q}_1) \setminus S_1 \setminus S_2| \tag{19} \\
&\geq q - 2M_0,
\end{aligned}
$$

since $|S_1| = |U_{05}| \leq M_0, |S_2| = |U_{27}| \leq M_0$ hold in any good transcript (see BadK_5 in Defn. 4).

$$
\begin{aligned}
|RC_2(2)| &\geq |\{0,1\}^n \setminus \mathsf{Ran}(\mathcal{Q}_0) \oplus \kappa_3 \setminus V \setminus \mathsf{Dom}(\mathcal{Q}_0) \oplus \kappa_0 \oplus \kappa_1 \setminus U \oplus \kappa_1 \\
&\quad \setminus \mathsf{Dom}(\mathcal{Q}_0) \oplus \kappa_0 \oplus \kappa_2 \setminus U \oplus \kappa_2| \tag{20} \\
&\geq |\{0,1\}^n \setminus \mathsf{Ran}(\mathcal{Q}_0) \oplus \kappa_3 \setminus \mathsf{Ran}(\mathcal{Q}_1) \setminus \mathsf{Dom}(\mathcal{Q}_0) \oplus \kappa_0 \oplus \kappa_1 \\
&\quad \setminus \mathsf{Dom}(\mathcal{Q}_1) \oplus \kappa_1 \setminus \mathsf{Dom}(\mathcal{Q}_0) \oplus \kappa_0 \oplus \kappa_2 \setminus \mathsf{Dom}(\mathcal{Q}_1) \oplus \kappa_2| \\
&\quad - 3 \cdot (2h_1) \\
&\geq N - 6q - 6h_1,
\end{aligned}
$$

---

[12] See Appendix D of the full version [Yu+23] for an analysis of the constraints on Z, which are the sum of constraints from the three shared-edge-based methods.

where U (resp. V) denotes the domain (resp. range) of all P_1-input-output-pairs fixed so far (i.e., after Step 1) and $3 \cdot (2h_1) = 6h_1$ is the maximum number[13] of new values generated by Step 1 that fall within the constraints of $RC_2(2)$. This is exactly the consequence of updating U, V discussed in the full version [Yu+23, Appendix C.2]. Due to the similarity, we directly give the remaining lower bounds without explanation.

$$|RC_2(4)| \geq N - 4q - 4h_1 - 10h_2, \tag{21}$$

$$|RC_3(4)| \geq N - 4q - 4h_1 - 10h_2, \tag{22}$$

$$|RC_3(2)| \geq N - 4q - 4h_1 - 10h_2 - 10h_3, \tag{23}$$

$$|RC_4(4)| \geq N - 6q - 6h_1 - 15h_2 - 15h_3, \tag{24}$$

$$|RC_4(2)| \geq N - 4q - 4h_1 - 10h_2 - 10h_3 - 10h_4, \tag{25}$$

$$|RC_5(2)| \geq N - 4q - 4h_1 - 10h_2 - 10h_3 - 10h_4, \tag{26}$$

$$|RC_5(4)| \geq N - 5q - 3h_1 - 8h_2 - 8h_3 - 8h_4. \tag{27}$$

Let $\#\mathsf{Cores}_i$ denote the number of $\mathsf{Cores}(\widehat{\mathcal{Q}_0})$ containing exactly i new edges (relative to $\mathcal{Q}_1$). Combining all the above, we finally obtain that

$$
\begin{aligned}
&\#\mathsf{Cores}_{3q - \sum_{i=1}^{4} h_i} \\
&\geq \binom{\delta_0}{h_1} \cdot (|RC_1(3)|)_{h_1} \cdot \frac{(|Z|)_{2h_2 + 2h_3 + 2h_4}}{h_2! \cdot h_3! \cdot h_4!} \cdot (|RC_2(2)|)_{h_2} \cdot (|RC_2(4)|)_{h_2} \\
&\quad \times (|RC_3(4)|)_{h_3} \cdot (|RC_3(2)|)_{h_3} (|RC_4(4)|)_{h_4} \cdot (|RC_4(2)|)_{h_4} \\
&\quad \times (|RC_5(2)|)_{q - h_1 - 2h_2 - 2h_3 - 2h_4} \cdot (|RC_5(4)|)_{q - h_1 - 2h_2 - 2h_3 - 2h_4} \\
&\geq \frac{(\delta_0)_{h_1} (q - 2M_0)_{h_1}}{h_1!} \cdot \frac{(q_0)_{2h_2 + 2h_3 + 2h_4}}{h_2! \cdot h_3! \cdot h_4!} \\
&\quad \cdot (N - 6q - 6h_1)_{h_2} \cdot (N - 4q - 4h_1 - 10h_2)_{h_2} \\
&\quad \cdot (N - 4q - 4h_1 - 10h_2)_{h_3} \cdot (N - 4q - 4h_1 - 10h_2 - 10h_3)_{h_3} \\
&\quad \cdot (N - 6q - 6h_1 - 15h_2 - 15h_3)_{h_4} \\
&\quad \cdot (N - 4q - 4h_1 - 10h_2 - 10h_3 - 10h_4)_{h_4} \\
&\quad \cdot (N - 4q - 4h_1 - 10h_2 - 10h_3 - 10h_4)_{q - h_1 - 2h_2 - 2h_3 - 2h_4} \\
&\quad \cdot (N - 5q - 3h_1 - 8h_2 - 8h_3 - 8h_4)_{q - h_1 - 2h_2 - 2h_3 - 2h_4}.
\end{aligned}
\tag{28}
$$

---

[13] Note that Step 1 will generate $2h_1$ new permutation-edges, so there will be $2h_1$ new elements added to U and V respectively (compared to $\mathsf{Dom}(\mathcal{Q}_1)$ and $\mathsf{Ran}(\mathcal{Q}_1)$). It can be seen that there are only three constraints related to U and V in Eq. (20), $6h_1$ is obviously the maximum number of changes. We need to point out that this is actually an overestimation. For example, newly added permutation-edges in Step 1 of the form $\langle x_i \oplus \kappa_0, P_1, * \rangle$ cause the set $U \oplus \kappa_1$ to add new elements (i.e., $x_i \oplus \kappa_0 \oplus \kappa_1$) which are already included in $\mathsf{Dom}(\mathcal{Q}_0) \oplus \kappa_0 \oplus \kappa_1$. A finer analysis could provide more accurate results, but this simplified treatment is sufficient here since we are not seeking to optimize the constant coefficients in security bounds. Also, we use this easily verifiable overestimation in the evaluation of Eqs. (21)–(26) below.

The third step is to perform the summation calculation. Since the lower bound on $\#\mathsf{Cores}_{3q-\sum_{i=1}^4 h_i}$ is known, we are now ready to calculate the final result. From the Eqs. (10) and (28), we have

$$(15) = \Pr_{P_1 \leftarrow_\$ \mathcal{P}_n}[E_K \downarrow \mathcal{Q}^{\equiv}_{0,6} \wedge E_K \downarrow_w \mathcal{Q}^*_0 \mid P_1 \downarrow \mathcal{Q}_1]$$

$$\geq \sum_{0 \leq h_1,\ldots,h_4 \leq M} \frac{\#\mathsf{Cores}_{3q-\sum_{i=1}^4 h_i}}{(N-q)_{3q-\sum_{i=1}^4 h_i}} \geq \sum_{0 \leq h_1,\ldots,h_4 \leq M} \frac{\text{Eq. (28)}}{(N-q)_{3q-\sum_{i=1}^4 h_i}} \qquad (29)$$

By lower-bounding[14] the Eq. (29), we end up with

$$(15) = \Pr_{P_1 \leftarrow_\$ \mathcal{P}_n}[E_K \downarrow \mathcal{Q}^{\equiv}_{0,6} \wedge E_K \downarrow_w \mathcal{Q}^*_0 \mid P_1 \downarrow \mathcal{Q}_1]$$

$$\geq \frac{1}{(N)_q} \times \left(1 - \frac{57q}{N^{3/4}} - \frac{122q^2}{N^{3/2}} - \frac{78q}{N} - \frac{32\,N}{q^2}\right),$$

which completes the proof. $\qquad\qquad\square$

4.2.2 Case 2: $q = \mathcal{O}(N^{1/2})$

The entire proof is almost the same as in the case $q = \omega(N^{1/2})$, except for a slight modification to the calculations related to M and M_0. As mentioned before, for any positive $\epsilon > 0$, if we set $M = q/N^{1/2-\epsilon}$ and $M_0 = q/N^{1/4+\epsilon}$, then we can get a $\mathcal{O}(N^{3/4-\epsilon})$-bound.

For simplicity, we here set $M = \frac{q}{N^{9/20}}$ and $M_0 = \frac{q}{N^{3/10}}$, i.e. $\epsilon = \frac{1}{20}$. We omit the details of proof and only list the following two technical lemmas.

Lemma 7 (Bad Transcripts, $q = \mathcal{O}(N^{1/2})$). *For any given $\mathcal{Q}_0, \mathcal{Q}_1$ such that $|\mathcal{Q}_0| = |\mathcal{Q}_1| = q$, we have*

$$\Pr_{K \leftarrow_\$ \{0,1\}^{4n}}[\tau = (\mathcal{Q}_0, \mathcal{Q}_1, K) \text{ is bad}] \leq \frac{12q}{N^{7/10}} + \frac{3q^2}{N^{7/5}} + \frac{8q^4}{N^3} + \frac{6q^6}{N^5}.$$

Lemma 8 (Good Transcripts, $q = \mathcal{O}(N^{1/2})$). *Fix arbitrarily a good transcript $\tau = (\mathcal{Q}_0, \mathcal{Q}_1, K) \in \mathcal{T}$ as defined in Definition 4. Let $\mathcal{Q}^{\equiv}_{0,6}$ and $\mathcal{Q}^*_0$ be as described in Eq. (15), then we have*

$$\Pr_{P_1 \leftarrow_\$ \mathcal{P}_n}[E_K \downarrow \mathcal{Q}^{\equiv}_{0,6} \wedge E_K \downarrow_w \mathcal{Q}^*_0 \mid P_1 \downarrow \mathcal{Q}_1]$$

$$\geq \frac{1}{(N)_q} \times \left(1 - \frac{122q^2}{N^{7/5}} - \frac{135q}{N^{3/4}} - \frac{32}{N^{1/10}}\right).$$

According to the H-coefficient technique (see Lemma 2), we can obtain

$$\mathbf{Adv}^{\mathsf{SPRP}}_{P_1 P_1 P_1}(\mathcal{D}) \leq \varepsilon_1 + \varepsilon_2$$

$$= \frac{12q}{N^{7/10}} + \frac{3q^2}{N^{7/5}} + \frac{8q^4}{N^3} + \frac{6q^6}{N^5} + \frac{122q^2}{N^{7/5}} + \frac{135q}{N^{3/4}} + \frac{32}{N^{1/10}}$$

$$= \frac{12q}{N^{7/10}} + \frac{125q^2}{N^{7/5}} + \frac{135q}{N^{3/4}} + \frac{8q^4}{N^3} + \frac{6q^6}{N^5} + \frac{32}{N^{1/10}},$$

which is the result of small $q = \mathcal{O}(N^{1/2})$ in Theorem 2.

---

[14] Although the calculation involves a large number of terms, it is actually simple and regular; the details can be found in the full version [Yu+23].

5   Tight Security Bound of t-Round KACSP

In this section, we generalize the proof of 3-round KACSP to the general t-round KACSP. The proof idea is basically the same, except the notation is heavier.

Theorem 3 (t-Round KACSP). *Consider the t-round KACSP (where $t \geq 4$), denoted as $P_1^{(t)}$-construction. For any distinguisher $\mathcal{D}$ making q_e construction queries and q_p permutation queries, the following upper bound holds:*

$$\mathbf{Adv}_{P_1^{(t)}}^{\mathsf{SPRP}}(\mathcal{D})$$

$$\leq \begin{cases} \dfrac{27t^4 q}{N^{t/(t+1)}} + \dfrac{15t^5 q^2}{N^{2t/(t+1)}} + \dfrac{2t^2 q^{t+1}}{N^t} + \dfrac{4t^2 N}{q^2}, & \text{for } q = \omega(N^{1/2}) \\[3mm] \dfrac{4tq}{N^{7/10}} + \dfrac{15t^5 q^2}{N^{7/5}} + \dfrac{q^{t-1}}{N^{7(t-1)/10}} + \dfrac{22t^4 q}{N^{3/4}} + \dfrac{tq}{N^{t/(t+1)}} + \dfrac{2t^2 q^{t+1}}{N^t} + \dfrac{4t^2}{N^{1/10}}, & \text{for } q = \mathcal{O}(N^{1/2}) \end{cases}$$

where $q := \max\{q_e, q_p\}$.

Note that the value of $t = \mathcal{O}(1)$ is a constant. Therefore, the above bound does show that unless $\mathcal{D}$ makes $q = \Omega(N^{t/(t+1)})$ queries, its advantage of distinguishing $P_1^{(t)}$ from a truly random permutation is negligible (for sufficiently large n). In other words, t-round KACSP has the same security level as the t-round KAC.

Proof (Proof of Theorem 3). As discussed in Sect. 4.2, we also consider that the distinguisher makes q construction queries and q permutation queries in the analysis. That is, for each attainable transcript $\tau = (\mathcal{Q}_0, \mathcal{Q}_1, K) \in \mathcal{T}$, it has $|\mathcal{Q}_0| = |\mathcal{Q}_1| = q$. Furthermore, we let $\mathsf{AD}_{t-i} \subset \mathcal{Q}_0$ denote the set of pairs $(x_i, y_i) \in \mathcal{Q}_0$ whose actual distance is i, where $i = 1, \ldots, t$. We also let $\delta_i := |\mathsf{AD}_i|$. For convenience, we simply use $\mathcal{Q}_{0,t}^{\equiv}$ to denote AD_0 since it is a uniform-structure-group.

Applying General Transformation. First of all, we also use the general transformation (see Eq. (11)) here to reduce the task to bounding only one probability. The basic idea is to replace the uniform-structure-groups whose actual distance is less than t with a new uniform-structure-group whose actual distance is t, and make the connecting probability smaller.

Note that the expectation of δ_i is $\mathcal{O}(q/N^{i/(t+1)})$ and we can *wlog* assume that $q = \mathcal{O}(N^{t/(t+1)})$ (otherwise the security bound is invalid). Then, we denote $s = \sum_{i=1}^{t-1} \delta_i = \mathcal{O}(q/N^{1/(t+1)})$ as the number of pairs to be replaced. As discussed in Sect. 3, it is easy to construct a new uniform-structure-group $\mathcal{Q}_0^* := \{(x_i, y_i) : i = q+1, \ldots, q+s\}$ and set $\widehat{\mathcal{Q}}_0 := \mathcal{Q}_{0,t}^{\equiv} \cup \mathcal{Q}_0^*$, where the pairs in $\mathcal{Q}_0^*$ must be connected in the most wasteful way. Using Lemma 4 several times, we can know that the crucial probability

$$(7) \geq \mathrm{Pr}_{P_1 \leftarrow_\$ \mathcal{P}_n}[E_K \downarrow \widehat{\mathcal{Q}}_0 \mid P_1 \downarrow \mathcal{Q}_1]$$
$$= \mathrm{Pr}_{P_1 \leftarrow_\$ \mathcal{P}_n}[E_K \downarrow \mathcal{Q}_{0,t}^{\equiv} \wedge E_K \downarrow_w \mathcal{Q}_0^* \mid P_1 \downarrow \mathcal{Q}_1]. \tag{30}$$

Thus, Eq. (30) becomes the target probability for which we need a lower bound.

5.1   Case 1: $q = \omega(N^{1/2})$

As in Sect. 4.2, we mainly focus on the large values of $q = \omega(N^{1/2})$, and the other case of $q = \mathcal{O}(N^{1/2})$ is similar. We also first give the definition of good and bad transcripts.

Let $\mathsf{R}_{t-1} = \{\mathsf{R}(x_i) : (x_i, y_i) \in \mathsf{AD}_{t-1}\}$ and $\mathsf{L}_{t-1} = \{\mathsf{L}(y_i) : (x_i, y_i) \in \mathsf{AD}_{t-1}\}$ denote the set of all rightmost and leftmost vertices of the pairs whose actual distance is 1, respectively. Next, we define $t - 1$ constants $M_j = \frac{q}{N^{j/(t+1)}}$ related to the value of q, where $j = 1, 2, \ldots, t - 1$.

Definition 5 (Bad and Good Transcripts, $P_1^{(t)}$-Construction). *For an attainable transcript* $\tau = (\mathcal{Q}_0, \mathcal{Q}_1, K) \in \mathcal{T}$, *we say that* τ *is bad if* $K \in \bigcup_{i=1}^{5} \mathsf{BadK}_i$; *otherwise* τ *is good. The definitions of* BadK_i *are shown below:*

$K \in \mathsf{BadK}_1 \iff$ *there exists a path of length* $2t + 1$ *starting from a vertex*
$\qquad\qquad\qquad\qquad x_i \in \mathsf{Dom}(\mathcal{Q}_0)$ *in shore 0 or ending at a vertex* $y_i \in \mathsf{Ran}(\mathcal{Q}_0)$
$\qquad\qquad\qquad\qquad$ *in shore* $2t + 1$

$K \in \mathsf{BadK}_2 \iff \delta_i > M_i$ *where* $i = 1, 2, \ldots, t - 1$

$K \in \mathsf{BadK}_3 \iff |\mathsf{R}_{t-1} \cup \mathsf{Dom}(\mathcal{Q}_1)| < \delta_{t-1} + q \lor |\mathsf{L}_{t-1} \cup \mathsf{Ran}(\mathcal{Q}_1)| < \delta_{t-1} + q$

$$K \in \mathsf{BadK}_4 \iff \begin{cases} \bigvee_{i=1}^{t-1} |\{x \in \mathsf{Dom}(\mathcal{Q}_0) : x \oplus \kappa_0 \oplus \kappa_i \text{ is not left-free}\}| > M_1 \\[2ex] \bigvee_{i=1}^{t-1} |(\mathsf{Dom}(\mathcal{Q}_0) \oplus \kappa_0 \oplus \kappa_i) \cap (\mathsf{Ran}(\mathcal{Q}_0) \oplus \kappa_t)| > M_1 \\[2ex] \bigvee_{i=1}^{t-1} |\{y \in \mathsf{Ran}(\mathcal{Q}_0) : y \oplus \kappa_3 \oplus \kappa_i \text{ is not right-free}\}| > M_1 \\[2ex] \bigvee_{i=1}^{t-1} |(\mathsf{Ran}(\mathcal{Q}_0) \oplus \kappa_3 \oplus \kappa_i) \cap (\mathsf{Dom}(\mathcal{Q}_0) \oplus \kappa_0)| > M_1 \end{cases}$$

$K \in \mathsf{BadK}_5 \iff |U_{05}| > M_1 \lor |U_{27}| > M_1.$

We can determine the value of $\varepsilon_2 = \frac{5tq}{N^{t/(t+1)}} + \frac{2t^2 q^{t+1}}{N^t}$ from the following lemma, the proof of which can be found in the full version [Yu+23, Appendix E.3].

Lemma 9 (Bad Transcripts, $q = \omega(N^{1/2})$). *For any given* $\mathcal{Q}_0, \mathcal{Q}_1$ *such that* $|\mathcal{Q}_0| = |\mathcal{Q}_1| = q$, *we have*

$$\Pr_{K \leftarrow_\$ \{0,1\}^{(t+1)n}} [\tau = (\mathcal{Q}_0, \mathcal{Q}_1, K) \text{ is bad}] \leq \frac{5tq}{N^{t/(t+1)}} + \frac{2t^2 q^{t+1}}{N^t}.$$

The following lemma gives a lower bound on Eq. (30) for any good transcript.

Lemma 10 (Good Transcripts, $q = \omega(N^{1/2})$). *Fix arbitrarily a good transcript $\tau = (\mathcal{Q}_0, \mathcal{Q}_1, K) \in \mathcal{T}$ as defined in Definition 5. Let $\mathcal{Q}_{0,t}^{\equiv}$ and $\mathcal{Q}_0^*$ be as described in Eq. (30), then we have*

$$
\Pr_{P_1 \leftarrow_\$ \mathcal{P}_n}[E_K \downarrow \mathcal{Q}_{0,t}^{\equiv} \wedge E_K \downarrow_w \mathcal{Q}_0^* \mid P_1 \downarrow \mathcal{Q}_1]
$$
$$
\geq \frac{1}{(N)_q} \times \left(1 - \frac{22t^4 q}{N^{t/(t+1)}} - \frac{15t^5 q^2}{N^{2t/(t+1)}} - \frac{4t^2 N}{q^2}\right). \tag{31}
$$

The proof of Lemma 10 is given in the full version [Yu+23, Appendix E.4]. We next show how to obtain the final security bound from the above two lemmas. First note that (31) is also a lower bound on the crucial probability (7), i.e. $p(\tau)$ in Lemma 3 when $t' = 1$. Then it is not difficult to determine the value of ε_1. According to the H-coefficient technique (see Lemma 2), we can obtain

$$
\mathbf{Adv}_{(P_1)^t}^{\mathsf{SPRP}}(\mathcal{D}) \leq \varepsilon_1 + \varepsilon_2
$$
$$
= \frac{5tq}{N^{t/(t+1)}} + \frac{2t^2 q^{t+1}}{N^t} + \frac{22t^4 q}{N^{t/(t+1)}} + \frac{15t^5 q^2}{N^{2t/(t+1)}} + \frac{4t^2 N}{q^2} \tag{32}
$$
$$
\leq \frac{27t^4 q}{N^{t/(t+1)}} + \frac{15t^5 q^2}{N^{2t/(t+1)}} + \frac{2t^2 q^{t+1}}{N^t} + \frac{4t^2 N}{q^2},
$$

which is the result of large $q = \omega(N^{1/2})$ in Theorem 3.

5.2 Case 2: $q = \mathcal{O}(N^{1/2})$

The entire proof is almost the same as in the case $q = \omega(N^{1/2})$, except for a slight modification to the calculations related to M_1 and M_{t-1} and we here set $M_1 = \frac{q}{N^{3/10}}$ and $M_{t-1} = \frac{q}{N^{9/20}}$. We omit the details of proof and only list the following two technical lemmas.

Lemma 11 (Bad Transcripts, $q = \mathcal{O}(N^{1/2})$). *For any given $\mathcal{Q}_0, \mathcal{Q}_1$ such that $|\mathcal{Q}_0| = |\mathcal{Q}_1| = q$, we have*

$$
\Pr_{K \leftarrow_\$ \{0,1\}^{(t+1)n}}[\tau = (\mathcal{Q}_0, \mathcal{Q}_1, K) \text{ is bad}] \leq \frac{4tq}{N^{7/10}} + \frac{q^{t-1}}{N^{7(t-1)/10}} + \frac{tq}{N^{t/(t+1)}} + \frac{2t^2 q^{t+1}}{N^t}.
$$

Lemma 12 (Good Transcripts, $q = \mathcal{O}(N^{1/2})$). *Fix arbitrarily a good transcript $\tau = (\mathcal{Q}_0, \mathcal{Q}_1, K) \in \mathcal{T}$ as defined in Definition 5. Let $\mathcal{Q}_{0,t}^{\equiv}$ and $\mathcal{Q}_0^*$ be as described in Eq. (30), then we have*

$$
\Pr_{P_1 \leftarrow_\$ \mathcal{P}_n}[E_K \downarrow \mathcal{Q}_{0,t}^{\equiv} \wedge E_K \downarrow_w \mathcal{Q}_0^* \mid P_1 \downarrow \mathcal{Q}_1] \geq \frac{1}{(N)_q} \times \left(1 - \frac{15t^5 q^2}{N^{7/5}} - \frac{22t^4 q}{N^{3/4}} - \frac{4t^2}{N^{1/10}}\right).
$$

According to the H-coefficient technique (see Lemma 2), we can obtain

$$
\mathbf{Adv}_{P_1 P_1 P_1}^{\mathsf{SPRP}}(\mathcal{D}) \leq \varepsilon_1 + \varepsilon_2
$$
$$
= \frac{4tq}{N^{7/10}} + \frac{q^{t-1}}{N^{7(t-1)/10}} + \frac{tq}{N^{t/(t+1)}} + \frac{2t^2 q^{t+1}}{N^t} + \frac{15t^5 q^2}{N^{7/5}} + \frac{22t^4 q}{N^{3/4}} + \frac{4t^2}{N^{1/10}}
$$
$$
= \frac{4tq}{N^{7/10}} + \frac{15t^5 q^2}{N^{7/5}} + \frac{q^{t-1}}{N^{7(t-1)/10}} + \frac{22t^4 q}{N^{3/4}} + \frac{tq}{N^{t/(t+1)}} + \frac{2t^2 q^{t+1}}{N^t} + \frac{4t^2}{N^{1/10}},
$$

which is the result of small $q = \mathcal{O}(N^{1/2})$ in Theorem 2.

6   Remarks on Other Variants of KACS

Our proof technology in this work applies to various KAC-type constructions as well as the standard KAC construction. Our general transformation also works and the proof idea is similar. The core task is to find enough constructive methods of reducing new edges, so that the final security bound is sufficiently accurate.

We also find that the more rounds means more methods, so it seems easier to find enough methods in constructions with more rounds. This is somewhat counter-intuitive. It might be interesting to figure out whether this phenomenon is an artifact of the proof technology, or because larger constructions inherently have more security redundancy.

Acknowledgements. We would like to thank the anonymous reviewers of TCC 2023 for their valuable comments. Yu Yu is supported by the National Natural Science Foundation of China (Grant Nos. 62125204 and 92270201), the National Key Research and Development Program of China (Grant No. 2018YFA0704701), and the Major Program of Guangdong Basic and Applied Research (Grant No. 2019B030302008). Yu Yu also acknowledges the support from the XPLORER PRIZE. This work is supported in part by the National Key Research and Development Program of China (Grant No. 2022YFB2701400) and in part by the National Natural Science Foundation of China (Grant No. 62132005, 62172162).

References

[Bog+12] Bogdanov, A., Knudsen, L.R., Leander, G., Standaert, F.-X., Steinberger, J., Tischhauser, E.: Key-alternating ciphers in a provable setting: encryption using a small number of public permutations. In: Pointcheval, D., Johansson, T. (eds.) EUROCRYPT 2012. LNCS, vol. 7237, pp. 45–62. Springer, Heidelberg (2012). https://doi.org/10.1007/978-3-642-29011-4_5 (cited on p. 2)

[Che+18] Chen, S., Lampe, R., Lee, J., Seurin, Y., Steinberger, J.P.: Minimizing the two-round even-Mansour cipher. J. Cryptol. 4, 1064–1119 (2018). https://doi.org/10.1007/s00145-018-9295-y (cited on pp. 2, 3, 8, 9, 11, 15, 17)

[CS14] Chen, S., Steinberger, J.: Tight security bounds for key-alternating ciphers. In: Nguyen, P.Q., Oswald, E. (eds.) EUROCRYPT 2014. LNCS, vol. 8441, pp. 327–350. Springer, Heidelberg (2014). https://doi.org/10.1007/978-3-642-55220-5_19 (cited on pp. 2, 6, 8)

[DKS12] Dunkelman, O., Keller, N., Shamir, A.: Minimalism in cryptography: the even-Mansour scheme revisited. In: Pointcheval, D., Johansson, T. (eds.) EUROCRYPT 2012. LNCS, vol. 7237, pp. 336–354. Springer, Heidelberg (2012). https://doi.org/10.1007/978-3-642-29011-4_21 (cited on p. 2)

[DR02] Daemen, J., Rijmen, V.: The advanced encryption standard process. In: The Design of Rijndael. Information Security and Cryptography. Springer, Berlin, Heidelberg (2002).https://doi.org/10.1007/978-3-662-04722-4 (cited on p. 1)

[EM97] Even, S., Mansour, Y.: A construction of a cipher from a single pseudorandom permutation. J. Cryptol. 3, 151–162 (1997). https://doi.org/10.1007/s001459900025 (cited on p. 1)

[HT16] Hoang, V.T., Tessaro, S.: Key-alternating ciphers and key-length extension: exact bounds and multi-user security. In: Robshaw, M., Katz, J. (eds.) CRYPTO 2016. LNCS, vol. 9814, pp. 3–32. Springer, Heidelberg (2016). https://doi.org/10.1007/978-3-662-53018-4_1 (cited on pp. 2, 17)

[LPS12] Lampe, R., Patarin, J., Seurin, Y.: An asymptotically tight security analysis of the iterated even-Mansour cipher. In: Wang, X., Sako, K. (eds.) ASIACRYPT 2012. LNCS, vol. 7658, pp. 278–295. Springer, Heidelberg (2012). https://doi.org/10.1007/978-3-642-34961-4_18 (cited on p. 2)

[Ste12] Steinberger, J.P.: Improved security bounds for key-alternating ciphers via Hellinger distance. In: IACR Cryptology ePrint Archive, p. 481 (2012). http://eprint.iacr.org/2012/481 (cited on p. 2)

[TZ21] Tessaro, S., Zhang, X.: Tight security for key-alternating ciphers with correlated sub-keys. In: Tibouchi, M., Wang, H. (eds.) ASIACRYPT 2021. LNCS, vol. 13092, pp. 435–464. Springer, Cham (2021). https://doi.org/10.1007/978-3-030-92078-4_15 (cited on p. 2)

[WYCD20] Wu, Y., Yu, L., Cao, Z., Dong, X.: Tight security analysis of 3-round key-alternating cipher with a single permutation. In: Moriai, S., Wang, H. (eds.) ASIACRYPT 2020. LNCS, vol. 12491, pp. 662–693. Springer, Cham (2020). https://doi.org/10.1007/978-3-030-64837-4_22 (cited on pp. 2, 3, 9, 10, 12, 15, 16, 18, 21)

[Yu+23] Yu, L., Wu, Y., Yu, Y., Cao, Z., Dong, X.: security proofs for key-alternating ciphers with non-independent round permutations. In: IACR Cryptology ePrint Archive, Paper 2023/1355 (2023). https://eprint.iacr.org/2023/1355 (cited on pp. 3, 6, 10, 11, 12, 13, 15, 17, 19, 21, 22, 23, 24, 25, 27, 28)

Public-Key Encryption, Local Pseudorandom Generators, and the Low-Degree Method

Andrej Bogdanov[1(✉)], Pravesh K. Kothari[2], and Alon Rosen[3,4]

[1] University of Ottawa, Ottawa, Canada
abogdano@uottawa.ca
[2] Carnegie Mellon University, Pittsburgh, USA
praveshk@cs.cmu.edu
[3] Bocconi University, Milan, Italy
alon.rosen@unibocconi.it
[4] Reichman University, Herzliya, Israel

Abstract. The low-degree method postulates that no efficient algorithm outperforms low-degree polynomials in certain hypothesis-testing tasks. It has been used to understand computational indistinguishability in high-dimensional statistics.

We explore the use of the low-degree method in the context of cryptography. To this end, we apply it in the design and analysis of a new public-key encryption scheme whose security is based on Goldreich's pseudorandom generator. The scheme is a combination of two proposals of Applebaum, Barak, and Wigderson, and inherits desirable features from both.

Keywords: Public-key encryption · local cryptography · hypothesis testing

1 Introduction

Hypothesis testing is concerned with the computational task of detecting a noisy signal. The question is cast as a distinguishing problem between a pure noise distribution Q and an alternative distribution P that contains a planted signal. The goal is to understand tradeoffs between the "amplitude" θ and the "frequency" m.

Several works [BR13, HWX15, BB20] uncover that such problems exhibit statistical-to-computational gaps: depending on θ, there is a range of frequencies $m \in [m_{\mathrm{stat}}, m_{\mathrm{comp}}]$ for which hypothesis testing is possible, but no efficient algorithm is known.

The *low-degree method* is a heuristic for generating remarkably accurate estimates of the *computational threshold* m_{comp} at which the hypothesis testing problem becomes feasible [HKP+17]. It relies on the observation that for several natural average-case hypothesis testing problems, the optimal polynomial time distinguisher amounts to computing a low-degree polynomial in input samples.

The method was first employed [BHK+19] in constructing lower bound witnesses for the sum-of-squares semidefinite programming hierarchy for the *planted*

© International Association for Cryptologic Research 2023
G. Rothblum and H. Wee (Eds.): TCC 2023, LNCS 14369, pp. 268–285, 2023.
https://doi.org/10.1007/978-3-031-48615-9_10

clique problem. It was later [HKP+17] shown to be powerful enough to capture natural spectral algorithms and in fact used to design new algorithms for certain Bayesian estimation problems [HS17]. Indeed, no efficient algorithm appears to outperform what can be inferred by observing "local statistics".

In [HKP+17], the authors make the *pseudocalibration conjecture* positing that hardness in the low-degree model implies sum-of-squares lower bounds for average-case refutation problems under certain mild niceness conditions. Later works [HS17, Hop18, KWB19] have proposed a stronger variant of the pseudocalibration conjecture positing that thresholds computed in the low-degree method are in fact m_{comp} i.e., a threshold for all polynomial time computable distinguishers. In the past few years, a sequence of works have used the low-degree method to find evidence of gap between computational and statistical thresholds for a number of average-case algorithmic problems.

In this work we will be interested in exploring the applicability of the low-degree method to cryptography, and in particular to the design and analysis of a new public-key cryptosystem. While we do not claim that the method's predictions always coincide with the computational infeasibility threshold m_{comp}, we do believe that it can serve a guideline for sound design, in addition to being a sanity-check for assessing security.

1.1 Goldreich's Pseudorandom Generator

The main object underlying our new public-key encryption scheme is *Goldreich's candidate one-way function* [Gol11]. We will instantiate it in a way that may allow us to conjecture it to be a pseudorandom generator given known attacks.

The function, denoted F_H, maps n bits to m bits. It is described in terms of two main objects:

- A d-hypergraph H on on n vertices and m (ordered) hyperedges, each of size d. See Fig. 2 where the vertices are represented by circles ($\circ$) and the hyperedges are represented by squares ($\blacksquare$).
- A d-ary predicate that is applied to the projection of an n-bit input x on each one of the m hyperedges of H (Fig. 1).

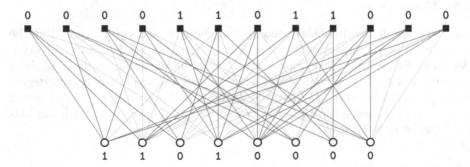

Fig. 1. An instance of Goldreich's function with predicate $x_1 \oplus x_2 \oplus x_3 \oplus x_4x_5$. The non-linear part x_4x_5 is shaded light grey. (Color figure online)

For concreteness, we set H to be a 5-hypergraph on n vertices and m hyperedges, let $d = k + 3$, and $k = 2$. In Sect. 6 we give a more general description parametrized by k. We set the predicate to be $x_1 \oplus x_2 \oplus x_3 \oplus x_4 x_5$ [MST06].

1.2   A New Public-Key Encryption Scheme

Recall that a public-key encryption scheme involves three algorithms: Key generation, Encryption, and Decryption (see Sect. 2). Our scheme has binary message space and we allow both imperfect correctness and security.

Encryption. In our scheme, encryptions of 0 are outputs $y = F_H(x)$ of Goldreich's function applied to a random input x. Encryptions of 1 are random m-bit strings y. Indistinguishability of encryptions of 0 from encryptions of 1 follows from pseudorandomness of F_H given H.

Decryption. Decryption is made possible thanks to logarithmic size hypergraphs (called "hyperloops") that are planted in H in the key generation process. These hyperloops make it effectively possible to distinguish between $y = F_H(x)$ and a random m-bit string y (see Sect. 1.3).

Key-generation. A *hyperloop* is a 3-hypergraph in which every vertex has degree two. Let L_0 be a fixed hyperloop with $\ell_0 = O(\log n)$ hyperedges. The public key of our scheme consists of a 5-hypergraph H sampled as follows. Let:

- L be the union of $t = 2^{\Theta(\ell_0)}$ vertex-disjoint copies of L_0,
- Q be a random 3-hypergraph with n vertices and hyperedge probability $O(n^{-3/2-\delta})$,
- $P = Q \cup L$ where L is planted on a random subset of vertices of Q,
- H be obtained by randomly adding 2 vertices to each hyperedge in P.

The public key is the 5-hypergraph H and the secret key is $S_1, \ldots, S_t$, where $S_i \subseteq \{1, \ldots, m\}$ are the hyperedges corresponding to the ith planted copy of L_0.

1.3   Correctness

The hypergraph H is published, enabling anybody to encrypt by evaluating the function F_H on a random input. Knowledge of $S_1, \ldots, S_t$ enables correct decryption, since each planted hyperloop S gives noticeable advantage in distinguishing the output of F_H from a random string: all vertices in a hyperloop S have degree two, and so whenever $y = F_H(x)$, the linear part $\oplus_{j \in S}(x_{j_1} \oplus x_{j_2} \oplus x_{j_3})$ in the bit $z = \oplus_{j \in S} y_j$ cancels out to 0. It follows that $z = \oplus_{j \in S} x_{j_4} x_{j_5}$, which has bias $2^{-|S|}$ (when H is "typical").

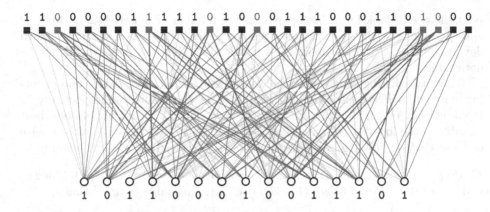

Fig. 2. A public key and ciphertext with a single planted hyperloop L_0 (from Fig. 4). The secret key and the ciphertext section used in decryption are marked in red.

The decryption function is then a majority of parities over hyperloops $S \subseteq \{1, \ldots, m\}$. Specifically, testing whether more than $(1+2^{-|S|})t/2$ of $z_1, \ldots, z_t$ are zero enables it to distinguish $y = F_H(x)$ from random with advantage $1 - o(1)$ (see Claim 6) .

1.4 Security

For the scheme to be secure it is necessary that the output of the function F_H is pseudorandom and that the public key H hides the planted hyperloops $S_1, \ldots, S_t$. This will in particular be true if:

1. A planted hypergraph $P = Q \cup L$ is indistinguishable from a random one Q.
2. The output of F_H is pseudorandom when H is a random hypergraph Q.

While these two properties may be strictly stronger than required, we will analyze their individual plausibility. Our examination is conducted both in light of the best known asymptotic attacks, and within the low-degree framework.

A distinguisher of non-negligible advantage exists as there is already noticeable probability that F_H contains a constant-sized subset of output bits that always XOR to zero. Our security argument applies to distinguishers of any *constant* advantage. Ruling those out is sufficient to obtain a gap between decryption advantage and distinguishing advantage, which can then be amplified (at some cost in efficiency). On the other hand, the secret key can be inverted by exhaustive search in time $\binom{m}{\ell_0} = n^{O(\log n)}$ so we will restrict the analysis to distinguishers that run in time $n^{o(\log n)}$.

Indistinguishability of P and Q. The distributions P and Q are statistically distinguishable since the planted hyperloops L of size ℓ_0 in P are unlikely to appear in Q. There are two natural distinguishers to try in this context. Exhaustive search for a hyperloop of size ℓ_0 has complexity at least $n^{-O(1)}\binom{m}{\ell_0}$. Another possibility is to look for a discrepancy in the number of hyperedges between P and Q. As long as the $2^{\Theta(\ell_0)}$ hyperedges present are within $o(1)$ of the standard deviation $n^{0.75-\delta/2}$ in the number of edges of Q this discrepancy will not be noticeable.

These two distinguishers are based on counting size-ℓ_0 hyperloops and counting hyperedges. The counts are polynomials of degree ℓ_0 and one, respectively, in the adjacency tensor of H. In Proposition 1 we show that they are close to best possible in the low-degree framework: For every ϵ there exists an δ and a choice of L_0 so that no polynomial of degree at most $(1-\epsilon)\ell_0$ has constant advantage.

Conjecture 1. For a sufficiently small constant δ, $m = n^{1.5-\delta}$, $\ell_0 = 0.36 \log n$, and $t = n^{0.75-\delta}$, P and Q are $(1 - \Omega(1))$-indistinguishable in $n^{O(1)}$-time.

Pseudorandomness of F_Q. For a random Q, the output $y = F_Q(x)$ has been conjectured to be computationally indistinguishable from a random $y \in \{0,1\}^m$ given Q. When the hyperedge probability is $O(n^{-3/2-\delta})$ the graph has $m = \Theta(n^{1.5-\delta})$ edges with high probability. The best known distinguisher has complexity $m^{\Theta(n^{2\delta})}$ and is based on a landmark result of Feige, Kim, and Ofek [FKO06]. They prove that H is likely to contain $2^{\Theta(\ell_1)}$ hyperloops each of size $\ell_1 \approx n^{2\delta}$. The distinguisher effectively inverts the secret key and runs our decryption algorithm assuming the "public key" is sampled from the model distribution Q.

In Proposition 2 we show that the advantage of any statistic that depends arbitrarily in Q but has most degree d in y in distinguishing $y = F_Q$ from random is upper bounded by the expected number of hyperloops of size at most d in Q. This expectation is $o(1)$ when $d = o(n^{-2\delta})$, that is for any statistic of degree just too low to "see" the hyperloops in Q. This complements results on the small-bias of F_Q [MST06, ABR16, OW14, AL18].

Conjecture 2. For every δ, $m = n^{1.5-\delta}$, random $x \in \{0,1\}^n$, $y \in \{0,1\}^m$, $(Q, F_Q(x))$ and (Q, y) are $o(1)$-indistinguishable in $n^{O(1)}$-time.

1.5   The Low-Degree Method

The low-degree method is a formal framework for arguing *computational* hardness of hypothesis testing. Although the method is, in full generality, neither complete or sound, it correctly predicts the computational threshold m_{comp} for a variety of problems. The method is effective in settings where the computational advantage is non-negligible but vanishing (e.g., $n^{-\Omega(1)}$), and where the model distribution is a high-dimensional product distribution. It is in particular applicable for analyzing the two security claims from Sect. 1.4 and for detecting vulnerabilities in alternative design choices.

We are in particular interested in the following question: For which planted structures L are the distributions Q and $P = Q \cup L$ computationally indistinguishable? Perhaps the simplest attack is to try and detect a discrepancy in the number of edges. Should the edge numbers be close, could the attacker rely on discrepancies on other fixed-size substructures such as 5-cycles? It turns out that this won't help as long as the planted substructure L is sufficiently small-set expanding (see Proposition 1).

Consider for example an alternative construction $P' = Q \cup L'$ in which L' now consists of a union of $2^{\Theta(\ell_0)}$ *independent* random size-ℓ_0 hyperloops. P' and Q are now distinguishable as L' will induce a significant discrepancy in the number of 4-cliques. These additional structures completely break security of encryption.

The low-degree method is in general incomplete as it does not model algebraic attacks. For example it predicts that random n-bit strings of parities 0 and 1 are degree-$(n-1)$ indistinguishable. Nevertheless we believe that it can be a useful guide in "noisy linear algebra" type constructions with noticeable security error.

One technical difficulty in low-degree analysis is the lack of a triangle inequality. In our case we show that $P = Q \cup L$ is low-degree indistinguishable from Q and that (Q, F_Q) is low-degree indistinguishable from (Q, random). However we cannot compose the two claims to conclude that (P, F_P) is low-degree indistinguishable from (Q, random). Nevertheless, we prove a weaker security claim with an additional assumption on the "distinguisher" in Theorem 7.

1.6   Relation to the ABW Schemes

Applebaum, Barak, and Wigderson [ABW10] proposed two closely related public-key encryption schemes that differ from ours in the choice of planted structure L and predicate used in the underlying pseudorandom generator.

In their first scheme (ABW1) L is a single hyperloop of size $\ell = \Theta(n^{2\delta})$ and the predicate is the randomized function $x_1 \oplus x_2 \oplus x_3 \oplus e$, where e is a noise bit of probability $n^{-2\delta}$. Alternatively, e can be replaced by an AND of $k = \log \ell + O(1)$ input bits. This encryption is not local (although in any reasonable parameter setting a small value of k may suffice.) Their security analysis relies on *statistical* indistinguishability of Q and $P = Q \cup L$ thus obviating the need for additional computational assumptions.

The main difference is that, unlike ABW1, our proposal has constant locality. Another difference is that our construction doesn't use extrinsic noise bits e. The role of the noise is played by the nonlinear part $x_4 x_5$ of our predicate.

In their second scheme (ABW2) L is a single subgraph of size $\ell = \ell_0 = \Theta(\log n)$, with fewer vertices than hyperedges. The predicate in this construction can be arbitrary. To decrypt one checks whether the ℓ-bit part of the ciphertext restricted to L has a preimage. (With a small modification this scheme supports errorless decryption.)

Unlike in ABW2, our secret key consists of *multiple* planted known linear dependencies between the output bits. This endows our scheme with natural leakage-resilience: Even if a small subset of these dependencies becomes public encryption remains secure. Another difference is that our decryption may be of lower complexity in some models as it is a majority of parities, while ABW2 rely on a hardcoded lookup table.

Moreover, we believe that our scheme may be marginally more secure than theirs. A brute-force search for the secret key would have complexities $\binom{m}{\ell_0}$ and $\binom{n}{\ell_0}$ in our and their variant, respectively. The gap is most prominent when $m = n^{3/2-\delta}$ is large, i.e., when δ is small. In the regime where δ approaches $1/2$ lower-degree attacks (based on detecting some substructure present in L) become possible. A more precise low-degree analysis is needed for a fair comparison.

As for security guarantees, Applebaum, Barak, and Widgerson identify a discrepancy in the number of small cycles as a potential vulnerability of their schemes and account for it in parameter setting. The low-degree method systematically rules out all attacks of this type and more. While the low-degree method readily applies to ABW1 and ABW2, its relevance in security analysis is better highlighted in our scheme as it informs choices in the construction (hyperloop sampling in key generation) and parameters (size and density of hyperloops) (Fig. 3).

Scheme	Locality	Security	Planted analysis
ABW1 ($\ell = \Theta(n^{2\delta})$)	$\log n + O(1)$	$\exp(cn^{2\delta})$	all polynomials (statistical)
ABW2 ($\ell_0 = \Theta(\log n)$)	$O(1)$	$n^{c\log n}$	short cycle count
This work ($\ell_0 = \Theta(\log n)$)	$O(1)$	$m^{c\log n}$	all deg $(1-\varepsilon)\ell_0$ polynomials

Fig. 3. Comparison with ABW1 and ABW2

1.7 Open Questions

One weakness of our security analysis is that it relies on *computational* indistinguishability of the model hypergraph distribution Q and the planted distribution P that contains $2^{\Theta(\ell_0)}$ copies of the planted hyperloop L_0 with $\ell_0 = \Theta(\log n)$ edges. Might it be possible to argue that the proximity is statistical?

Feige, Kim, and Ofek prove that a random 3-hypegraph with n vertices and hyperedge probability $p = O(n^{-3/2}/\ell_0^{1/2})$ is likely to contain K^{ℓ_0} hyperloops of size ℓ_0 (for any desired constant K). We believe, however, that the number of *disjoint* hyperloops of size ℓ_0 is at most polynomial by the following heuristic argument. In expectation a large fraction of the hyperloop pairs intersect. If we model the intersection graph as a random graph its maximum independent set would have expected size logarithmic in the number of hyperloops 2^{ℓ_0}, namely polynomial in the hyperloop size ℓ_0. Thus it appears that the planted instance P is statistically far apart from the model instance Q.

Is it is possible to efficiently sample the public-key L of K^{ℓ_0} intersecting size-ℓ_0 hyperloops jointly with the *random* hypergraph Q? If so security would follow directly from the pseudorandomness of F_Q. Our current proof of correctness (Claim 6) would no longer apply owing to intersections between the hyperloops which result in statistical dependencies in decryption. Nevertheless, decryption remains correct as most of the intersections between the K^{ℓ_0} hyperloops are small on average. Although the information bits $z_1, \ldots, z_t$ arising from the different hyperloops in the decryption process would be dependent, their correlations are sufficiently small to enable reliable decryption.

Concerning empirical security, it is unclear if the noise Q is needed at all in the construction. Could the scheme be secure even if P consists of nothing but $n^{1.1}$ randomly planted copies of L_0?

2   Public Key Encryption

Our encryption scheme has binary message space, decrypts incorrectly with bounded probability δ, and has noticeable (but still bounded) computational distance ε between the distribution of encryptions of zero and those of one. Assuming both errors are sufficiently small constants they can be amplified to be negligible at a loss of parameters [DNR04].

Definition 1 (Syntax). *A public key encryption scheme consists of three algorithms* (Gen, Enc, Dec) *such that for $n \in \mathbb{N}$,* Gen(1^n) *outputs a pair of keys* (sk, pk); Enc(pk, b) *encrypts a message b with the public key pk and outputs a ciphertext c;* Dec(sk, c) *decrypts a ciphertext c using the secret key sk and outputs a message b.*

Both key-generation, Gen, and encryption, Enc, are randomized. As mentioned above, we allow the decryption algorithm, Dec, to make errors.

Definition 2 (δ correctness).
A public key encryption scheme (Gen, Enc, Dec) *is correct with probability δ if*

$$\Pr\left[\mathrm{Dec}(sk, \mathrm{Enc}(pk, b)) = b\right] \geq \delta,$$

where probability is taken over the randomness of Gen and Enc. We call $1 - \delta$ the decryption error.

Security is defined through indistingushability of encryptions [GM84]. To this end, we rely on the notion computational indistinguishability.

Definition 3 (ε-indistinguishability). *Two distributions X, Y are ε-indistinguishable if for any probabilistic polynomial time algorithm A:*

$$|\Pr[A(X) = 1] - \Pr[A(Y) = 1]| \leq \varepsilon.$$

Definition 4 (ε-security). *A public key encryption scheme* (Gen, Enc, Dec) *is said to have security error $\varepsilon \in [0, 1]$ if the distributions $(pk, \mathrm{Enc}(pk, 0))$ and $(pk, \mathrm{Enc}(pk, 1))$ are ε-indistinguishable, where probabilities are over the randomness of Gen and Enc.*

3   The Low-Degree Method

Suppose we want to distinguish distribution P from model distribution Q. One way is to sort the outcomes x in order of decreasing likelihood ratio $L(x) = P(x)/Q(x)$, say "p" if it is large and "q" if it is small. The Neyman-Pearson Lemma says that this test minimizes the false positive error among all tests with a given false negative error.

The likelihood ratio can also be used to argue indistinguishability. For any test T,

$$|P(T)-Q(T)| = |\mathbb{E}_Q[(L-1)\cdot 1_T]| \le \sqrt{\mathbb{E}_Q[(L-1)^2] \cdot \mathbb{E}_Q[1_T^2]} = \sqrt{\mathrm{Var}_Q[L] \cdot Q(T)}.$$

Therefore the statistical distance is at most the standard deviation of L under Q. Even if the variance is greater than one but bounded, this bound rules out the possibility that $P(T) \to 1$ and $Q(T) \to 0$ so the statistical distance between P and Q must be bounded away from one.

Example. Let Q and P consist of n i.i.d. ± 1 bits that are unbiased and ϵ-biased, respectively. The likelihood ratio is $L(x) = \prod(1 + \epsilon x_i)$, its variance is $\mathrm{Var}[L] = \prod \mathbb{E}[(1 + \epsilon x_i)^2] - 1 = (1 + \epsilon^2)^n - 1$. The variance is $o(1)$ as long as $\epsilon \ll 1/\sqrt{n}$, which matches the regime in which we cannot distinguish reliably. If we expand $L(x)$ as a polynomial we get $L(x) = 1 + \epsilon \sum x_i + \epsilon^2 \sum_{i \neq j} x_i x_j + \cdots$. The degree-$d$ part contributes $\binom{n}{d}\epsilon^{2d}$ to the variance so the main contribution comes from the degree-1 part $L^1(x) = 1 + \epsilon \sum x_i$. In fact we can use the value of L^1 to distinguish P and Q when $\mathrm{Var}_Q[L^1]$ is large.

This example suggests using the low-degree projection L^1 or more generally L^d to distinguish P from Q assuming Q is a product distribution over bits. (The theory generalizes to product distributions over other domains.) The advantage of L^d is that it can be computed in size $\binom{n}{d}$. In contrast, L may not be efficiently computable in general. For a number of statistical hypothesis testing problems, the best efficient distinguishers are based on the value of some low-degree polynomial. Among those distinguishers, L^d is optimal in the following sense:

Claim 1. *Among all degree-d polynomials f, L^d maximizes the advantage*

$$a_d = \max_f \frac{\mathbb{E}_P[f] - \mathbb{E}_Q[f]}{\sqrt{\mathrm{Var}_Q[f]}}.$$

Moreover, $a_d = \|L^d - 1\|_Q$.

A degree-d polynomial can capture any "d-local" statistic. For example, if P and Q are graphs (represented by their adjacency matrices) then f can compute the number of copies of any given induced subgraph with d edges. A natural distinguisher in this context is a test of the form $f(x) > t$ for a suitable threshold t. If it happens that $\mathrm{Var}_P[f] = O(\mathrm{Var}_Q[f])$ then f will be concentrated around its means under both P and Q so a large value of a_d means that $f(P)$ will typically be large while $f(Q)$ will typically be small. If on the other hand $\mathrm{Var}_P[f] \gg \mathrm{Var}_Q[f]$ then it may be reasonable to try $g(x) = (f(x) - \mathbb{E}_Q[f])^2$ as a distinguisher of degree $2d$. Thus small advantage is evidence of failure for all distinguishers of this type.

Proof (Proof of Claim 1). The maximum advantage can be rewritten as $\max \mathbb{E}_P[f]$ where f is constrained to have degree d, mean $\mathbb{E}_Q[f] = 0$ and variance $\mathbb{E}_Q[f^2] = 1$. Since f has degree at most d,

$$\mathbb{E}_P[f] = \mathbb{E}_Q[f \cdot L] = \mathbb{E}_Q[f \cdot (L^d - \mathbb{E}_Q[L^d])] = \mathbb{E}_Q[f \cdot (L^d - 1)],$$

This expression is maximized when $f = (L^d - 1)/\|L^d - 1\|$. (As the maximum is invariant under scaling and shifting we can also take $f = L^d$.) The advantage is

$$\frac{\mathbb{E}_P[L^d - 1]}{\|L^d - 1\|_Q} = \frac{\mathbb{E}_Q[L^d(L^d - 1)]}{\|L^d - 1\|_Q} = \|L^d - 1\|_Q.$$

If Q is the p-biased product distribution over $\{\pm 1\}^n$ so that $\Pr(X_i = -1) = p$, $\Pr(X_i = 1) = q = 1 - p$. The Fourier basis is given by $\phi_S(x) = \prod_{i \in S} \phi(x_i)$, where $\phi(-1) = -\sqrt{q/p}$ and $\phi(1) = \sqrt{p/q}$. The squared degree-d advantage a_d^2 is

$$a_d^2 = \|L^d - 1\|_Q^2 = \sum_{1 \le |S| \le d} \mathbb{E}_P[\phi_S]^2. \qquad (1)$$

4   Planting Hyperloops

A *hyperloop* is a 3-hypergraph in which every vertex has degree two. Let Q be a random 3-hypergraph on n vertices with edge probability p and $P = Q \cup L$ where L is a hyperloop on ℓ edges.

Proposition 1. *Assume that for every $1 \le s \le d$, every set of s hyperedges in L touches at least $(3/2 - \delta)(s + 1) - 2\delta$ vertices. If $p \ge C\sqrt{d}n^{-3/2-\delta}$ and $\ell \le \eta\sqrt{pn^3/Cd^{3/2}}$ for some constant C and sufficiently large n then the degree-d advantage $a_d(P, Q)$ is $\le \eta$.*

The proposition guarantees degree-d indistinguishability as long as L is small-set expanding and the number of planted hyperedges is within $o(\eta/d^{3/4})$ standard deviations of the expected number of hyperedges pn^3 in the host hypergraph Q. Thus in this regime, no low-degree distinguisher can significantly improve over counting hyperedges.

In our intended application L will consist of ℓ/ℓ_0 vertex-disjoint copies of a single hyperloop L_0 with $\ell_0 = O(\log n)$ hyperedges. By Claim 5 a random choice of L_0 will have the desired expansion with constant probability.

Proof. We expand a_d in the Fourier basis as:

$$a_d^2 = \sum_{1 \le |S| \le d} \mathbb{E}_P[\phi_S]^2 = \sum_{1 \le |S| \le d} \left(\frac{1-p}{p}\right)^{|S|} \Pr[S \subseteq L]^2.$$

A copy of S in L is a map from the vertices of S to the vertices of L that maps edges into edges. Let $C(S,L)$ be the number of such copies. By a union bound $\Pr[S \subseteq L] \leq C(S,L)/n(n-1)\cdots(n-v(S)+1)$ where $v(S)$ is the number of vertices in S. Assuming that $v(S) \leq 3d = O(\sqrt{n})$ the denominator dominates $n^{v(S)}$ so $\Pr[S \subseteq L] \lesssim C(S,L)n^{-v(S)}$. Therefore $a_d^2 \leq \sum_{1 \leq |S| \leq d} f(S)$ where $f(S) = ((1-p)/p)^{|S|}C(S,L)^2 n^{-2v(S)}$.

If the vertex sets of S and S' are disjoint then $f(S \cup S') \leq f(S)f(S')$. Therefore $f(S') \leq \prod_C f(S)$ where the product ranges over the connected components S of S':

$$a_d^2 \leq \sum_{1 \leq |S'| \leq d} \prod_{\text{c.c. } S \text{ of } S'} f(S) \leq \left(1 + \sum_{\substack{1 \leq |S| \leq d \\ S \text{ connected}}} f(S)\right)^d - 1.$$

To obtain $a_d \leq \eta$ it is therefore sufficient to show that the summation over connected S is at most $\eta^2/2d$.

Claim 2. *If S is connected then $C(S,L) \leq 3|L| \cdot 2^{|S|}$.*

Proof. Let $s = |S|$ and let $e_1, \ldots, e_s$ be an ordering of the edges so that e_i is connected to $e_1, \ldots, e_{i-1}$ for all i. The first edge $e_1 = \{v_1, v_2, v_3\}$ of S can map into L into at most ℓ ways, and there are $3! = 6$ ways to assign v_1, v_2, v_3 that are consistent with this edge map. Since L has degree two and e_2 intersects e_1, the image of e_2 is fixed by this assignment. There are then at most two ways to assign the vertices of $e_2 \setminus e_1$. By the same argument there are at most two ways to assign the vertices of $e_i \setminus (e_1 \cup \cdots \cup e_{i-1})$. Therefore $C(S,L) \leq 3|L| \cdot 2^{s-1} = 3|L| \cdot 2^s$.

Applying this bound and disregarding the $(1-p)^{|S|}$ factor (which will be small) we obtain

$$\sum_{\substack{1 \leq |S| \leq d \\ S \text{ connected}}} f(S) \leq 9\ell^2 b_d \quad \text{where} \quad b_d = \sum_{1 \leq |S| \leq d} \frac{1}{(p/2)^{|S|} n^{2v(S)}}.$$

Let $N(s,v)$ be the number of connected 3-hypergraphs with s edges that span a fixed set of v vertices and appear at least once in L. Then

$$b_d \leq \sum_{s=1}^{d} \sum_v \binom{n}{v} N(s,v)(p/2)^{-s} n^{-2v} \leq \sum_{s=1}^{d} \sum_v \frac{N(s,v)}{v!} \cdot (p/2)^{-s} n^{-v}. \tag{2}$$

The leading term $s = 1$, for which v must equal 3, contributes $O(1/pn^3)$. The objective is to show that it dominates the summation assuming that L is sufficiently expanding. If this is the case then the advantage will be bounded as long as $1/pn^3 = O(\eta^{-2}/d\ell^2)$, or $\ell = O(\eta\sqrt{pn^3/d})$. Owing to some slackness in the calculation we will only show that the dominating term is at most $O(\sqrt{d}/pn^3)$, thereby accounting for the additional $\sqrt{d}$ factor in the statement.

Claim 3. $N(s,v)/v! = O(c^s s^{s/2})$ *for some constant c.*

Proof. Let u be the number of degree-1 vertices. Since all vertices have degree 1 or 2 we must have $v = (3s + u)/2$. There are $\binom{v}{u}$ ways to choose the degree-1 vertices. Once these are fixed we argue that the hypergraph can be chosen in $\Theta(h(s, u))$ ways, where

$$h(s, u) = \frac{(3\,s)!}{s! \cdot 6^s \cdot 2^{(3\,s-u)/2}}.$$

Using Stirling's formula we obtain $N(s, v) = O(c'^s s^{2s}/u!(v-u)!)$ for some constant c'. The denominator is minimized when $u = \lfloor v/2 \rfloor$ which gives, again applying Stirling's formula, $N(s, v) = O(c^s s^{2s}/v^v)$. As the maximum degree is 2, v must be at least $3s/2$ and the claim follows.

Let C be the set of $3s$ "clones" consisting two copies of each degree-2 vertex and all the degree-1 vertices. The clones can be partitioned into s hyperedges in $(3s)!/(s! \cdot 6^s)$ ways. Each (s, u)-hypercycle arises from $2^{(3s-u)/2}$ partitions of clones in which no pair of clones is covered by the same hyperedge.

Thus the number of (s, u)-hypercycles is between $qh(s, u)$ and $h(s, u)$, where q is the probability that no pair of clones is covered by the same hyperedge when the partition is chosen at random.

It remains to lower bound q by a constant. The random partition can be sampled by randomly arranging the $3s$ clones and assigning clones $3j$, $3j + 1$, and $3j + 2$ to the j-th hyperedge. After arranging the u degree-one vertices and the first clone of the remaining $(3s - u)/2$ vertices, no pair is covered by the same hyperedge as long as each of the second clones is separated by the corresponding first clone by at least two other clones when its position in the arrangement is chosen. For any given second clone, this happens with probability at least $1 - 4/((3s + u)/2)$ (as there are at most four forbidden positions). Thus q is at least $(1 - 4/((3s + u)/2))^{(3s-u)/2} \geq (1 - 4/(3s/2))^{3s/2} \geq e^{-4}$.

Plugging into (2) we obtain

$$b_d \lesssim \sum_{s=1}^{d} \sum_{v} (p/2c\sqrt{s})^{-s} n^{-v} \lesssim \sum_{s=1}^{d} (p/2c\sqrt{d})^{-s} n^{-v(s)},$$

where $v(s) = \min_{S \subseteq L, S \text{ connected}, |S|=s} v(S)$.

Assume $p/2c\sqrt{d} \geq n^{-3/2-\delta}$ for some constant $\delta > 0$. Then the summation is dominated by the term $s = 1$ as long as $(3/2 + \delta)s - v(s) < -3/2 + \delta$, or

$$v(s) \geq (3/2 + \delta)(s + 1) - 2\delta \quad \text{for every } s \leq d. \tag{3}$$

4.1 Expansion of 3-Regular Graphs

Assume L consists of ℓ/ℓ_0 vertex-disjoint copies of a single hyperloop L_0 with ℓ_0 edges. If L_0 satisfies (3) so will L. It will be more convenient to analyze the dual object L_0^* of L_0 obtained by transposing the incidence matrix of L_0. Then L_0^* is a simple 3-regular graph with ℓ_0 vertices and $3\ell_0/2$ edges. Equation (3) then any set of $s \leq d$ vertices in L_0^* must touch at least $(3/2 + \delta)(s + 1) - 2\delta$ edges.

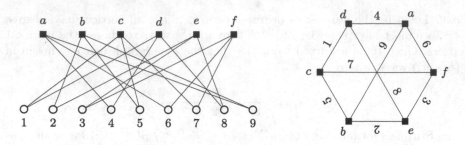

Fig. 4. (a) A hyperloop L and (b) its dual representation L^*

Claim 4. *If a set S of size s touches e edges then the cut $(S, \overline{S})$ has size at least $2e - 3s$.*

Proof. We can write $e = in + out$ where in and out is the number of edges inside S and leaving S, respectively. Since every vertex (in S) has degree 3, $2in + out = 3s$. Therefore $out = 2e - 3s$.

It is therefore sufficient that the cut $(S, \overline{S})$ has size at least $2\delta(s - 1) + 3$ for every set S of s vertices in L_0^*. If L_0^* has sufficiently high girth and high spectral expansion this would hold for sets up to size linear in ℓ_0. However this type of analysis would likely give poor concrete parameters: Even if L_0^* is Ramanujan its spectral expansion would be at most $1 - 2\sqrt{2}/3 \approx 0.06$, which merely guarantees that $|(S, \overline{S})| \geq 0.17s$. To obtain the desired expansion for small sets the girth would need to be at least 18 resulting in a prohibitively large L_0^*.

In terms of concrete parameters there exists a hyperloop L_0 on 14 vertices that satisfies (3) with $d = 9$ and $\delta = 1/8$ (see Fig. 5). A random construction also works well asymptotically:

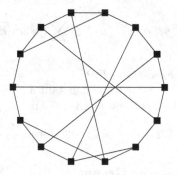

Fig. 5. A size 14 hyperloop L_0^* with $\delta = 1/8$ for $d = 9$.

Claim 5. *For every $\epsilon > 0$ there exists a $\delta > 0$ so that for sufficiently large ℓ_0 and for a random L_0 (3) is satisfied with constant probability up to $d = (1 - \epsilon)\ell_0$.*

Proof. We sample L_0 from the configuration model in which vertices are cloned thrice and then the clones are randomly matched. We consider three parameter ranges.

If $\epsilon\ell_0 < s \leq (1-\epsilon)\ell_0$, with probability approaching one as $\ell_0 \to \infty$, L_0 is a edge-expander [HLW06] so $|(S,\overline{S})| \geq \alpha\min\{|S|,|\overline{S}|\}$ for every S for some absolute expansion constant α. This is at least $2\delta(|S|-1)+3$ for all $|S| = s$ in the desired range as long as $\delta \leq \alpha\epsilon/2 - 3/2(\ell_0 - 1)$.

If $4 \leq s \leq \epsilon\ell_0$, the probability that there exists a set of s vertices that touches at most $v = \alpha s$ edges is at most

$$\binom{\ell_0}{s}\binom{3\ell_0/2}{v} \cdot \frac{2v}{3\ell_0} \cdot \frac{2v-1}{3\ell_0-1} \cdot \frac{2v-3s+1}{3\ell_0-3s+1} \leq \left(\frac{e\ell_0}{s}\right)^s \left(\frac{3e\ell}{2v}\right)^v \left(\frac{2v}{3\ell_0}\right)^{3s}$$

$$= \left(c(\alpha)\left(\frac{s}{\ell_0}\right)^{2-\alpha}\right)^s,$$

where $c(\alpha) = (8e\alpha^3/27)(3e/2\alpha)^\alpha$. Setting $\alpha = 1/8 - 3\delta/4$ we obtain that (3) can be satisfied for all $4 \leq d \leq \ell_0$ with probability that approaches one as ϵ approaches zero.

If $1 \leq s \leq 3$ we will argue that $v(1) = 3$, $v(2) = 5$, and $v(3) = 7$, namely the graph has no parallel edges, no self-loops, and has girth at least five, with probability $\Omega(1)$. Consider the following procedure for sampling the graph. Start with the integer sequence $s = (1, 2, \ldots, 3\ell_0/2)$. Now insert another copy of each integer at a random position in the sequence. In the resulting sequence of length $3\ell_0$ identify the integers with edges and the "clones" at positions $3j, 3j+1, 3j+2$ with vertex j. We describe a sequence of events $G_1, \ldots, G_{3\ell/2}$ where G_i is measurable in the filtration obtained by exposing the j-th insertion, each G_i has probability at least $1-O(1/\ell_0)$ conditioned on $G_1, \ldots, G_{i-1}$, and the conjunction $G_1 \cap \ldots \cap G_{3\ell/2}$ implies the desired properties.

The property $v(1) = 3$ (no parallel edges or self-loops) will be satisfied as long as the two copies of every integer are spaces at least three items apart. It is clearly sufficient that this holds at the time of insertion as subsequent insertions can only increase the distance. The corresponding event G_j has clearly the desired properties as at the time of each insertion there are only four forbidden positions out of at least $3\ell_0/2$.

Similarly, $v(2) = 5$ and $v(3) = 7$ (the girth is at least five) is satisfied as long at when i is inserted it does not land two slots within any number that is within "two hops" to the copy of i that is already present, where a hop between i and i' is allowed if they appear within two positions of each other. This specifies at most 160 forbidden positions so the corresponding event G_j still has probability $1 - O(1/\ell_0)$.

5   Low-Degree Security of Goldreich's Function

We show that Goldreich's function on a random hypergraph is secure with respect to low-degree tests. We consider tests f that receive as input a hypergraph H and a string y that is either an output F_H of Goldreich's function or a random string R. The test f may depend arbitrarily on H but must have degree at most d in y.

Proposition 2. *The squared low-degree advantage of f is at most the expected number of projections of F_H on nonempty subsets of size at most d that have nonzero bias.*

In particular, if the predicate is of the form $X_1 + X_2 + X_3 + g(Y)$ then all nonzero bias subsets must come from hyperloops induced by the X-variables. Therefore a_d^2 is at most the expected number of hyperloops of size at most d in a random 3-hypergraph. Any hyperloop that spans a specific set of v vertices must have at least $2v/3$ hyperedges, so in the $H(n, p)$ model the expected number of hyperloops that span some set of v vertices is at most

$$\binom{n}{v}\binom{\binom{v}{3}}{2v/3}p^{2v/3} \leq \left(\frac{en}{v}\right)^v \left(\frac{ev^2p}{4}\right)^{2v/3}.$$

Assuming $d \leq 0.4p^{-2}n^{-3} = \tilde{\Omega}(n^{2\delta})$, the expectation is dominated by the first term $v = 6$ for which it has value $\tilde{O}(n^{-4\delta})$.

Proof (Proof of Proposition 2). As in the proof of Claim 1, the advantage is $\max_f \mathbb{E}[f(H, F_H)]$ where f is constrained to have zero mean and unit variance under the model distribution (H, R). We can write $\mathbb{E}_{H, F_H}[f] = \mathbb{E}_{H, R}[f \cdot L]$ where L is the joint likelihood ratio

$$L(h, r) = \frac{\Pr(H = h, F_H = r)}{\Pr(H = h, r = R)} = \frac{\Pr(F_H = r | H = h)}{\Pr(r = R)}.$$

Namely, $L(h, r)$ equals the conditional likelihood ratio $L(r|h)$. Thus the optimal choice of f is the conditional degree-d projection $L^d(r|h)$ and the squared advantage is $\mathrm{Var}[L^d]$. By the total variance formula, $\mathrm{Var}[L^d] = \mathbb{E}\,\mathrm{Var}[L^d|H] + \mathrm{Var}\,\mathbb{E}[L^d|H]$. For fixed h, L^d has the Fourier expansion

$$L^d(\cdot \,|h) = \sum_{|S| \leq d} \mathbb{E}[L(R|h)\chi_S(R)]\chi_S = \sum_{|S| \leq d} \mathbb{E}[\chi_S(F_H)]\chi_S,$$

In particular, $\mathbb{E}[L^d(\cdot|h)] = 1$ for every h and $\mathrm{Var}\,\mathbb{E}[L^d|H] = 0$. It follows that the advantage is

$$\mathrm{Var}[L^d] = \mathbb{E}\,\mathrm{Var}[L^d|H] = \mathbb{E}\sum_{1 \leq |S| \leq d} \mathbb{E}[\chi_S(F_H)|H]^2.$$

As $\chi_S(F_H)$ is nonzero only when F_H is nonuniform and it is at most one otherwise, the right hand side is at most the expected number of biased subsets of F_H.

6   The Encryption Scheme

We present a general construction that exhibits a tradeoff between the parameter k that governs the locality of encryption and the size of the hyperloop ℓ_0.

We will assume that the vertices in a hyperedge are ordered. Let

- Q be a random 3-hypergraph with n vertices and hyperedge probability $C\sqrt{d}n^{-3/2-\delta}$,
- L_0 be a fixed 3-hypergraph on $\ell_0 = 0.09 \cdot 2^k \log n$ vertices satisfying Claim 5,
- L consists of $t = O(1/\beta^2 \log 1/\delta)$ vertex-disjoint copies of L_0, $\beta = (1 - 2^{-k+1})^{\ell_0}$,
- P be the m-edge hypergraph union of Q and a copy of L planted on a random subset of $3\ell/2$ vertices of Q,
- H be $(k+3)$-hypergraph obtained by extending each hyperedge of P with k random vertices,
- $F\colon \{0,1\}^n \to \{0,1\}^m$ be the function obtained by evaluating the $(k+3)$-ary predicate $x_1 \oplus x_2 \oplus x_3 \oplus (w_1 \wedge \cdots \wedge w_k)$ on all sequences of input bits indexed by hyperedges in H.

The key generation procedure outputs H as the public key and disjoint ℓ_0-subsets $S_1, \ldots, S_t$ of $\{1, \ldots, m\}$ indexing the copies of L_0 in P as the secret key.

To encrypt a 0, output $y = F(x)$ for a random x. To encrypt a 1, output a random string of length m.

To decrypt y, calculate the parities $z_i = \oplus_{j \in S_i} y_j$ for all $1 \leq j \leq t$. If more than $(1 + \beta)t/2$ of them are zero output 0, otherwise output 1.

Call the public key good if all extensions of the hyperedges in L are pairwise disjoint. By a union bound the public key is good except with probability $O(\ell^2 k^2/n) = n^{-\Omega(1)}$.

Claim 6. *Assuming H is good, decryption is correct except with probability δ.*

Proof. For an encryption of 1, the bits $z_1, \ldots, z_t$ are independent random so the probability that more than $(1 + \beta)t/2$ of them are zero is at most δ by Chernoff bounds.

For an encryption of 0, each bit z_i evaluates to an ℓ_0-XOR of disjoint k-ANDs so it has bias β. As $z_1, \ldots, z_\ell$ are independent the probability that fewer than $(1 + \beta)t/2$ are zero is at most δ again.

Theorem 7. *If f has degree less than $(1 - \epsilon)\ell_0$ and bounded 4-norm, the distinguishing advantage $\mathbb{E}[f(P, F_P)] - \mathbb{E}[f(Q, R)]$ is $n^{-\Omega(1)}$.*

We do not know if a bounded variance assumption on f would suffice.

Proof. We may assume $\mathbb{E}[f(Q, R)] = 0$. By Proposition 1, for every g of degree at most $d = (1 - \epsilon)\ell_0$, $\mathbb{E}[g(P)] - \mathbb{E}[g(Q)] \leq n^{-\Omega(1)}\sqrt{\mathrm{Var}[g(Q)]}$. Given f of degree d let $g(G) = \mathbb{E}[f(G, F_G)|G]$. Then g has the same degree as f and

$$\mathbb{E}[f(P, F_P)] - \mathbb{E}[f(Q, F_Q)] \leq n^{-\Omega(1)}\sqrt{\mathrm{Var}[f(Q, F_Q)]}.$$

By Proposition 2 applied to f^2,

$$|\mathbb{E}[f(Q, F_Q)^2] - \mathbb{E}[f(Q, R)^2]| \le n^{-\Omega(1)} \sqrt{\mathrm{Var}[f(Q, R)^2]}.$$

By the boundedness of the 4-norm of f,

$$\mathrm{Var}[f(Q, F_Q)^2] \le \mathrm{Var}[f(Q, R)^2] + n^{-\Omega(1)}$$

so $\mathbb{E}[f(P, F_P)] - \mathbb{E}[f(Q, F_Q)] = n^{-\Omega(1)}$. By Proposition 2 applied to f this time,

$$\mathbb{E}[f(Q, F_Q)] - \mathbb{E}[f(Q, R)] = n^{-\Omega(1)} \sqrt{\mathrm{Var}[f(Q, R)]} = O(n^{-\Omega(1)}).$$

The claim follows by the triangle inequality.

Acknowledgments. We thank Caicai Chen, Yuval Ishai, and Chris Jones for their advice and feedback. Part of this work done when the first and second authors visited Bocconi University. Andrej Bogdanov is supported by an NSERC Discovery Grant and Hong Kong RGC GRF CUHK14209920. Pravesh Kothari is supported by NSF CAREER Award #2047933, Alfred P. Sloan Fellowship and a Google Research Scholar Award. Alon Rosen is supported by the European Research Council (ERC) under the European Union's Horizon 2020 research and innovation programme (Grant agreement No. 101019547) and Cariplo CRYPTONOMEX grant.

References

[ABR16] Applebaum, B., Bogdanov, A., Rosen, A.: A dichotomy for local small-bias generators. J. Cryptol. **29**(3), 577–596 (2016)

[ABW10] Applebaum, B., Barak, B., Wigderson, A.: Public-key cryptography from different assumptions. In: Proceedings of the Forty-Second ACM Symposium on Theory of Computing, STOC 2010, pp. 171–180. Association for Computing Machinery, New York (2010)

[AL18] Applebaum, B., Lovett, S.: Algebraic attacks against random local functions and their countermeasures. SIAM J. Comput. **47**(1), 52–79 (2018)

[BB20] Brennan, M.S., Bresler, G.: Reducibility and statistical-computational gaps from secret leakage. In: Abernethy, J.D., Agarwal, S. (eds.) Conference on Learning Theory, COLT 2020, Graz, Austria, 9–12 July 2020, Virtual Event, vol. 125 of Proceedings of Machine Learning Research, pp. 648–847. PMLR (2020)

[BHK+19] Barak, B., Hopkins, S.B., Kelner, J.A., Kothari, P.K., Moitra, A., Potechin, A.: A nearly tight sum-of-squares lower bound for the planted clique problem. SIAM J. Comput. **48**(2), 687–735 (2019)

[BR13] Berthet, Q., Rigollet, P.: Complexity theoretic lower bounds for sparse principal component detection. In: Shalev-Shwartz, S., Steinwart, I. (eds.) Proceedings of the 26th Annual Conference on Learning Theory, vol. 30 of Proceedings of Machine Learning Research, Princeton, NJ, USA, 12–14 June 2013, pp. 1046–1066. PMLR (2013)

[DNR04] Dwork, C., Naor, M., Reingold, O.: Immunizing encryption schemes from decryption errors. In: Cachin, C., Camenisch, J.L. (eds.) EUROCRYPT 2004. LNCS, vol. 3027, pp. 342–360. Springer, Heidelberg (2004). https://doi.org/10.1007/978-3-540-24676-3_21

[FKO06] Feige, U., Kim, J.H., Ofek, E.: Witnesses for non-satisfiability of dense random 3cnf formulas. In: 2006 47th Annual IEEE Symposium on Foundations of Computer Science (FOCS 2006), pp. 497–508 (2006)

[GM84] Goldwasser, S., Micali, S.: Probabilistic encryption. J. Comput. Syst. Sci. **28**(2), 270–299 (1984)

[Gol11] Goldreich, O.: Candidate one-way functions based on expander graphs. In: Goldreich, O. (ed.) Studies in Complexity and Cryptography. Miscellanea on the Interplay between Randomness and Computation. LNCS, vol. 6650, pp. 76–87. Springer, Heidelberg (2011). https://doi.org/10.1007/978-3-642-22670-0_10

[HKP+17] Hopkins, S.B., Kothari, P.K., Potechin, A., Raghavendra, P., Schramm, T., Steurer, D.: The power of sum-of-squares for detecting hidden structures. In: Umans, C. (ed.) 58th IEEE Annual Symposium on Foundations of Computer Science, FOCS 2017, Berkeley, CA, USA, 15–17 October 2017, pp. 720–731. IEEE Computer Society (2017)

[HLW06] Hoory, S., Linial, N., Wigderson, A.: Expander graphs and their applications. Bull. Am. Math. Soc. **43**(04), 439–562 (2006)

[Hop18] Hopkins, S.: Statistical Inference and the Sum of Squares Method. PhD thesis, Cornell University (2018)

[HS17] Hopkins, S.B., Steurer, D.: Efficient bayesian estimation from few samples: community detection and related problems. In: Umans, C. (ed.) 58th IEEE Annual Symposium on Foundations of Computer Science, FOCS 2017, Berkeley, CA, USA, 15–17 October 2017, pp. 379–390. IEEE Computer Society (2017)

[HWX15] Hajek, B., Wu, Y., Xu, J.: Computational lower bounds for community detection on random graphs. In: Proceedings of The 28th Conference on Learning Theory, vol. 40 of Proceedings of Machine Learning Research, Paris, France, 03–06 July 2015, pp. 899–928. PMLR (2015)

[KWB19] Kunisky, D., Wein, A.S., Bandeira, A.S.: Notes on computational hardness of hypothesis testing: predictions using the low-degree likelihood ratio. In: Cerejeiras, P., Reissig, M. (eds.) ISAAC 2019, vol. 385, pp. 1–50. Springer, Cham (2022). https://doi.org/10.1007/978-3-030-97127-4_1

[MST06] Mossel, E., Shpilka, A., Trevisan, L.: On epsilon-biased generators in nc^0. Random Struct. Algor. **29**(1), 56–81 (2006)

[OW14] O'Donnell, R., Witmer, D.: Goldreich's PRG: evidence for near-optimal polynomial stretch. In: 2014 IEEE 29th Conference on Computational Complexity (CCC), pp. 1–12 (2014)

Cryptography from Planted Graphs:
Security with Logarithmic-Size Messages

Damiano Abram[1], Amos Beimel[2], Yuval Ishai[3](✉), Eyal Kushilevitz[3],
and Varun Narayanan[4]

[1] Aarhus University, Aarhus, Denmark
[2] Ben-Gurion University, Beersheba, Israel
[3] Technion, Haifa, Israel
yuval.ishai@gmail.com
[4] University of California, Los Angeles, USA

Abstract. We study the following broad question about cryptographic primitives: is it possible to achieve security against arbitrary $\mathsf{poly}(n)$-time adversary with $O(\log n)$-size messages? It is common knowledge that the answer is "no" unless information-theoretic security is possible. In this work, we revisit this question by considering the setting of cryptography with *public information* and computational security.

We obtain the following main results, assuming variants of well-studied intractability assumptions:
- A *private simultaneous messages* (PSM) protocol for every $f : [n] \times [n] \to \{0, 1\}$ with $(1 + \epsilon) \log n$-bit messages, beating the known lower bound on information-theoretic PSM protocols. We apply this towards *non-interactive* secure 3-party computation with similar message size in the preprocessing model, improving over previous 2-round protocols.
- A *secret-sharing scheme* for any "forbidden-graph" access structure on n nodes with $O(\log n)$ share size.
- On the negative side, we show that computational *threshold* secret-sharing schemes with public information require share size $\Omega(\log \log n)$. For arbitrary access structures, we show that computational security does not help with 1-bit shares.

The above positive results guarantee that any adversary of size $n^{o(\log n)}$ achieves an $n^{-\Omega(1)}$ distinguishing advantage. We show how to make the advantage negligible by slightly increasing the asymptotic message size, still improving over all known constructions.

The security of our constructions is based on the conjectured hardness of variants of the planted clique problem, which was extensively studied in the algorithms, statistical inference, and complexity theory communities. Our work provides the first applications of such assumptions to improving the efficiency of mainstream cryptographic primitives, gives evidence for the *necessity* of such assumptions, and suggests new questions in this domain that may be of independent interest.

© International Association for Cryptologic Research 2023
G. Rothblum and H. Wee (Eds.): TCC 2023, LNCS 14369, pp. 286–315, 2023.
https://doi.org/10.1007/978-3-031-48615-9_11

1   Introduction

We consider the following broad question about cryptographic primitives:

> Is it possible to achieve security against arbitrary $\mathsf{poly}(n)$-time adversaries
> with messages of size $O(\log n)$?

It is not hard to see that the answer is "no" unless information-theoretic security is possible. Indeed, a non-uniform adversary can simply apply a brute-force distinguisher implemented by a circuit of size $2^{O(\log n)} = \mathsf{poly}(n)$. A similar argument works for efficient uniform adversaries. In this work, we revisit this question by considering the setting of cryptography with *public information*. Public information may be viewed as a cheap resource: it can often be preprocessed (i.e., generated in an offline phase), it does not require secure storage, and (under strong cryptographic assumptions) can even be generically compressed [HJK+16].

As a concrete example, consider the problem of 2-out-of-n secret sharing. It is known that in any such information-theoretic scheme, even when sharing a 1-bit secret, the bit-length of at least one share must be at least $\log n$ [KN90, CCX13].[1] We ask whether the share size can be reduced, in the computational setting, if the dealer is allowed to publish public information that is generated jointly with the shares. As argued above, this relaxation is *necessary* for breaking the $\log n$ lower bound even in the computational security setting. Moreover, by a simple conditioning argument, public information is not helpful at all in the information-theoretic setting.

We start with a seemingly unrelated observation that if such a 2-out-of-n scheme exists, then (a variant of) the planted clique problem is computationally hard. Specifically, for a fixed public information I, we generate a polynomial-size, n-partite graphs G whose nodes are all pairs (i, s_i), where $i \in [n]$ and s_i is a possible share for the i-th party (any string of the appropriate length). We put an edge in G between (i, s_i) and (j, s_j) (where $i \neq j$) if the parties i, j on shares s_i, s_j respectively, and with public information I, reconstruct the secret 1. Note that a legal sharing of the secret 1 forms a size-n clique in G between $(1, s_1), \ldots, (n, s_n)$. A legal sharing of the secret 0 forms instead a size-n independent set in G. The 1-security of the secret-sharing scheme implies that if we pick a random secret b and apply the sharing algorithm to get $(I, s_1, \ldots, s_n)$ then, given a node (i, s_i) (corresponding to the view of the i-th party in the secret-sharing), it is hard to decide whether it belongs to a size-n clique or a size-n independent set of G (defined by the selected I).

The above observation suggests that the hardness of finding planted cliques is necessary for improved 2-out-of-n secret sharing in the public information setting. It is natural to ask whether it is also sufficient. Next, we outline an idea in this direction. This construction does not improve the share size, but it demonstrates in a simple way a high-level idea that we will apply to improve the efficiency of other primitives. First, sample an n-partite random graph, where each part is of size L, and each potential edge between two parts appears with

---

[1] Here and elsewhere, $\log n$ stands for $\log_2 n$.

probability 0.5. Then, if the secret is 1, plant in this graph a random n-partite clique (i.e., select one random node from each of the n parts and add to the graph all the edges between them, if they do not already exist); similarly, if the secret is 0, plant in the graph a random n-partite anti-clique. The resulting graph will be the public information. The share of party i will be the i-th node of the planted clique/anti-clique. The reconstruction is simple: given two shares (i, s_i) and (j, s_j) the share is determined by whether there is an edge between them in the public graph. For the security of the scheme, we assume that an adversary that sees the graph and gets the share of a party, i.e., a node in a clique or anti-clique, cannot distinguish between these two cases. Unfortunately, with the above simple planting procedure, the problem can be conjectured to be hard only if $L \geq n$ (see Sect. 2.1); hence the share size, which is $\log L$, is at least logarithmic.

Generalizing the above example, in this work we systematically explore the possibility of obtaining computational security with logarithmic-size messages using public information. We show that plausible intractability conjectures about different variants the planted clique problem, collectively referred to as "planted graph" problems, can be used to construct secret-sharing schemes and secure computation protocols that beat the best known, and typically the best possible, information-theoretic protocols.

We apply our approach to several different problems. These include private simultaneous messages (PSM) protocols and secure 3-party computation, as well as secret sharing for "forbidden-graph" access structures. For all these primitives, we show how relaxing the standard model by allowing public information can improve over the communication complexity of the best known solutions, assuming plausible hardness conjectures about planted graph problems. Similar results are not known under any other cryptographic assumptions, or even by using ideal forms of obfuscation. In fact, as in the above examples, assuming the hardness of planted graph problems can be shown to be necessary. Finally, we also study the extent to which one can go below logarithmic-size messages. For the case of secret sharing, we get both positive and negative results about the access structures that can be realized using computational secret sharing schemes with public information and very short shares.

Different variants of the *planted clique* problem, introduced in [Jer92, Kuč95], were studied within the algorithms, statistical inference, and complexity-theory communities. While such problems have already found some crypto-graphic applications, these are either in the context of diversifying assumptions [JP00, ABW10] or specialized tasks [GKVZ22]. Our work gives the first applications of planted graph problems to improving the efficiency of mainstream cryptographic tasks, and suggests new questions about such problems that may be of independent interest outside the cryptography community.

1.1   Our Results

We now give a more detailed account of our results. For each result, we describe the task that we study, the previously known results, and our new results obtained by using hardness assumptions about planted graphs. For a more detailed and technical overview, see Sect. 2.

3-Party 2-Input Offline-Online MPC. In this setting, we have 3 semi-honest parties, Alice and Bob who have inputs x and y, respectively, and Carol who has no input and should receive the output $f(x, y)$. We allow an offline stage (that does not depend on the inputs x, y) and generates correlated randomness to Alice and Bob and some public information. The goal is for the online stage to be non-interactive and highly efficient. That is, each of Alice and Bob sends a single short message to Carol. Based on these messages and the public information, Carol computes the output. As far as we know, the construction in the literature that achieves the most lightweight online phase in this setting is the one-time truth table protocol of Ishai *et al.* [IKM+13]. This solution, however, uses at least two rounds of communication. Our new construction, in contrast, uses only one round and, as [IKM+13], for every function $f : [n] \times [n] \to \{0,1\}$ has message size of $O(\log n)$ bits. It relies on a planted graph assumption, and is achieved via a PSM protocol, as described next.

PSM Protocols with Public Information. The private simultaneous messages (PSM) model, introduced in [FKN94], is similar to the above MPC model: after being given common randomness, Alice and Bob simultaneously send a single message encoding their inputs x and y; each message only depends on the input of the party and the common randomness. Carol should be able to compute $f(x, y)$ from these messages and is required to learn no additional information. Most of the study of PSM protocols [IK97, BIKK14, LVW17, AHMS18] focused on the information-theoretic setting, where the best known protocols for arbitrary functions $f : [n] \times [n] \to \{0,1\}$ has communication complexity $O(n^{0.5})$ [BIKK14].

The [BIKK14] protocol can be transformed into a computational PSM protocol with public information and short messages, as follows. Sample shared randomness r for Alice and Bob, and let the public information include the encryptions of the [BIKK14] protocol message of Alice on (x, r) under some secret key K_x, for every $x \in [n]$, in a randomly permuted order and, similarly, encryptions of the message of Bob on (y, r), for every $y \in [n]$. Then, given the actual inputs x, y, Alice sends to Carol the key K_x and the location of the corresponding encryption (according to the permutation) and, similarly, Bob sends the key K_y and the location of the corresponding encryption. Carol then decrypts the two messages and compute the output, as in the [BIKK14] protocol. The public information length is $O(n^{1.5})$ and the communication complexity is $O(\log n + \lambda)$, where λ denotes a security parameter.

In this paper, we show how to use a planted graph assumption, to construct a PSM protocol with messages of size $O(\log n)$. For the PSM protocol, we plant the bipartite graph representing the function f, denoted H_n, in a larger random graph to obtain a graph G. The public information consists of G and the shared randomness (only known by Alice and Bob) is the mapping of all nodes in H_n to the corresponding nodes in G. On input x, y, Alice and Bob send to Carol the corresponding nodes in G according to this mapping. Carol outputs 1 if and only if there is an edge between the two nodes in G she received.

The security of the protocol relies on the assumption that the graph H_n is hidden within the graph G. This assumption seems to be at least as plausible as the planted Clique assumption that was studied more extensively. More concretely, the planted graph assumption that we use assumes that an adversary that receives two nodes x, y from the bipartite graph, cannot distinguish, in time $n^{o(\log n)}$ and advantage $1/n^c$, for some constant c, between the case that the function graph H_n was planted in a random graph, as above, and the case of a random graph where only the edge (x, y) was set according to $f(x, y)$ (see Sect. 2.1 for a detailed discussion of the planted graph assumption and its variants). The security of the above MPC and PSM protocols inherits the property that the adversary cannot achieve $1/n^c$ advantage for some constant c (but we do not obtain negligible advantage, and this is inherent for the planted clique assumption). Moreover, they achieve security only against quasi-polynomial-time adversaries. This is weaker than the typical sub-exponential security achieved under standard cryptographic assumptions but stronger than fine-grained security [Mer78, BRSV18], where security holds against fixed poly-time adversaries. Note that a similar notion of quasi-polynomial security is achieved by other constructions (e.g., [ABW10, BLVW19]).

Forbidden Graph Secret-Sharing Schemes. For a fixed graph G with n nodes, a dealer is required to distribute a secret bit b to the n nodes (parties) so that any 2 nodes can reconstruct the secret if and only if they are connected by an edge (there is no additional requirements on sets of size different than 2). Forbidden Graph Secret-Sharing schemes (FGSS) were introduced in [SS97] and studied in [BIKK14]. The best known information theoretic FGSS scheme has share size $2^{\tilde{O}(\sqrt{\log n})}$ [LVW17]. The best known computational FGSS scheme has share size poly($\log n$) (assuming the existence of one-way functions) [ABI+23b]. We show a computational FGSS scheme with public information and share size $O(\log n)$ based on the hardness of deciding whether a random graph H appears in a large random graph G (both graphs are included in the public information of the FGSS scheme).

We also accompany the above positive results by some negative results. In the full version of the paper [ABI+23a, Section 8], we show that computational threshold secret-sharing schemes even with public information require share size $\Omega(\log \log n)$. Furthermore, in the full version of the paper [ABI+23a, Section 9], we show that, when considering secret-sharing schemes with *one-bit shares*, all access structures that can be realized with computational security with public information can also be realized information-theoretically. A summary of our main results is presented in Table 1 below.

2   Overview of Techniques

This paper studies the relation between cryptographic primitives, such as PSM protocols and secret-sharing schemes, and *planted subgraph problems*.

Table 1. Bounds on the complexity of 2-party PSM protocols, n-party forbidden graph secret-sharing schemes, and 2-out-of-n secret-sharing schemes for the information-theoretic case and the computational case with public information. The values refer to constructions with privacy error $\epsilon = n^{-1/2}$ and perfect correctness. The complexity is defined as the maximum message-size (resp. share-size) for a single party. The PSH and PRSH assumptions are informally described in Sect. 2.1.

	Information Theoretic		Computational with Public Information		
	Bound	*Reference*	*Bound*	*Assumption*	*Reference*
PSM	$\leq \sqrt{n}$	[BIKK14]	$\leq 1.01 \cdot \log n^a$	PSH	[ABI+23a]
	$\geq 1.25 \cdot \log n^a$	[AHMS18]	$\geq \log n$		
Forbidden Graph	$\leq 2^{O(\sqrt{\log n})}$	[LVW17]	$\leq 1.01 \cdot \log n$	PRSH	[ABI+23a]
Secret Sharing	$\geq \log n$	[CCX13]	$\geq \frac{1}{5} \log \log n$		[ABI+23a]
2-out-of-n	$\leq \log n$	[Sha79]	$\leq \log n$		[Sha79]
Secret Sharing	$\geq \log n - O_n(1)$	[ABI+23a]	$\geq \frac{1}{5} \log \log n$		[ABI+23a]

^{a} The bound holds for a $1 - o_n(1)$ fraction of functions $f : [n] \times [n] \to \{0, 1\}$.

2.1 Planted Subgraph Assumptions

Suppose that G and H are graphs with N and n nodes respectively, where $N > n$. The operation of planting H into G consists in selecting a random subset S of n vertices in G and modifying the edges so that the subgraph induced by S is isomorphic to H. In other words, we are hiding a copy of H inside G. We are particularly interested in the case in which G is an Erdős-Rényi random graph, i.e. each edge is independently drawn with probability $1/2$. We denote its distribution by $\mathcal{G}(N, 1/2)$.

We analyse three main subfamilies of assumptions: planted clique (PC), planted subgraph (PS), and planted subgraph with hints (PSH). The first one has a long history: it was introduced in the '90 s [Jer92, Kuč95] and has been studied since then [AKS98, FK03, Ros08, Ros10, FGR+13, BHK+16, ABdR+18, MRS21]. The other two assumptions are introduced for the first time in this work. We describe them below.

The Planted Clique (PC) Assumption. The PC assumption states that a random graph with a large planted clique looks random. Formally, for an appropriate choice of parameters N, T, and ϵ, it claims that, for every $T(n)$-time adversary $\mathcal{A}$,

$$\left| \Pr[\mathcal{A}(G) = 1 | G \xleftarrow{\$} \mathcal{G}(N, 1/2, n)] - \Pr[\mathcal{A}(G) = 1 | G \xleftarrow{\$} \mathcal{G}(N, 1/2)] \right| \leq \epsilon(n).$$

Above, $\mathcal{G}(N, 1/2, n)$ denotes the distribution that plants an n-node clique in a random N-node graph.

The assumption was independently introduced by Jerrum [Jer92] and Kučera [Kuč95] and has been studied since then. The hardness of the problem is supported by the NP-hardness of finding, or even approximating, the largest clique in a graph [Kar72, Hås96a].

Trivial attacks, such as counting the number of edges in G, break the assumption for any $\epsilon = \mathsf{negl}(n)$. However, the assumption is believed to hold against PPT adversaries when $\epsilon = n^{-c}$ for a constant $c > 0$, and N is sufficiently large. Indeed, all the known attacks fail when $N = \omega(n^2)$ [Kuč95, AKS98, DM15a, CX16]. In this parameter setting, the assumption is also supported by many results proving hardness against particular classes of adversaries [FK03, Ros08, FGR+13, GS14, BHK+16, ABdR+18, FGN+20]. Finally, concerning the computational power of the attacker, it is known that $n^{O(\log n)}$-time algorithms can detect the planted clique with $\Theta(1)$ advantage [HK11]. This leads to the following conjecture.

Conjecture 1 (PC – Informal). *For any constant $\delta > 0$, the PC assumption holds with $N = n^{2+\delta}$ and $\epsilon = n^{-c}$ against all $n^{o(\log n)}$-time adversaries.*

We refer to Sect. 4.1 for a more rigorous discussion about this assumption.

The Planted Subgraph (PS) Assumption. The PS assumption generalizes what we described above: instead of hiding a clique in a random graph, we hide an n-node subgraph H coming from some distribution $\mathcal{D}$. The assumption claims the resulting graph looks random even when H is revealed. The concept is formalized similarly to the PC problem: for every T-time adversary $\mathcal{A}$,

$$\left| \Pr\left[\mathcal{A}(G, H) = 1 \,\middle|\, \begin{matrix} H \xleftarrow{\$} \mathcal{D} \\ G \xleftarrow{\$} \mathcal{G}(N, 1/2, H) \end{matrix} \right] - \Pr\left[\mathcal{A}(G, H) = 1 \,\middle|\, \begin{matrix} H \xleftarrow{\$} \mathcal{D} \\ G \xleftarrow{\$} \mathcal{G}(N, 1/2) \end{matrix} \right] \right| \leq \epsilon.$$

Above, $\mathcal{G}(N, 1/2, H)$ denotes the distribution that plants H in a random N-node graph.

We are particularly interested in two variants of the PS assumption: the case in which $\mathcal{D}$ is deterministic and the case in which the $\mathcal{D}$ outputs a random n-node graph. We refer to the latter as the *planted random subgraph* (PRS) assumption.

It is generally believed that breaking the PS assumption is easiest when $\mathcal{D}$ deterministically outputs an n-node clique. For instance, the successful attacks against the PC problem leverage the particular structure of cliques. If we plant a generic subgraph, these algorithms do not perform as well. It is therefore conjectured that, for an overwhelming fraction of subgraphs H, the PS assumption holds for $\mathcal{D} \equiv H^2$ with parameters $T = n^{o(\log n)}$ and $\epsilon = n^{-c}$ even when $N = n^{1+\delta}$ (planted cliques needed $N = n^{2+\delta}$). This implies that the PRS assumption holds with similar parameters. We refer to Sect. 4.2 for more details.

The Planted Subgraph with Hints (PSH) Assumption. The PSH assumption is a variant of the PS assumption in which the adversary is provided with hints: we reveal where we hid a subset S of nodes of the planted graph. The size of S is bounded by a parameter t. Usually, t is small, e.g., $t = 2$. Clearly, after revealing the hints, the graph does not look random anymore: the adversary notices that G hides the subgraph induced by S. The PSH assumption claims, however, that

---

[2] We use $\mathcal{D} \equiv H$ to denote the distribution that always outputs the subgraph H.

the adversary cannot tell if G hides the whole graph H or just the subgraph induced by S. Formally, for any subset S with fewer than t vertices and every T-time adversary $\mathcal{A}$,

$$\left| \Pr\left[\mathcal{A}\big(G_b, H, (u_i^b)_{i\in S}\big) = b \; \middle| \; \begin{array}{l} b \xleftarrow{\$} \{0,1\} \\ H \xleftarrow{\$} \mathcal{D}, \; H' \leftarrow \mathsf{Subgraph}(H,S) \\ (G_1, (u_i^1)_{i\in S}) \xleftarrow{\$} \mathcal{G}(N,1/2,H,S) \\ (G_0, (u_i^0)_{i\in S}) \xleftarrow{\$} \mathcal{G}(N,1/2,H',S) \end{array} \right] - \frac{1}{2} \right| \le \epsilon.$$

Above, $\mathcal{G}(N,1/2,H,S)$ denotes the distribution that plants H in a random N-node graph and reveals where the nodes in S are hidden. The algorithm $\mathsf{Subgraph}(H,S)$ outputs instead the subgraph of H induced by S. When $\mathcal{D}$ outputs random n-node graph, we refer to the assumption as *PRSH* (planted random subgraph with hints).

It is believed that revealing $t = O(1)$ nodes on the planted graph does not affect the security of the assumption. This leads to the following conjectures.

Conjecture 2 (Weak-PSH, PSH, PRSH – Informal)

- *(Weak-PSH)*. Let $(H_n)_{n\in\mathbb{N}}$ be a family of n-node graphs. For any constants $\delta > 0$ and $t \in \mathbb{N}$, the PSH assumption holds for $\mathcal{D} \equiv H_n$ with $N = n^{2+\delta}$, t leaked nodes, and $\epsilon = n^{-c}$ against all $n^{o(\log n)}$-time adversaries.
- *(PSH)*. For any constants $\delta > 0$ and $t \in \mathbb{N}$, the PSH assumption holds for most $\mathcal{D} \equiv H_n$ with $N = n^{1+\delta}$, t leaked nodes, and $\epsilon = n^{-c}$ against all $n^{o(\log n)}$-time adversaries.
- *(PRSH)*. For any constants $\delta > 0$ and $t \in \mathbb{N}$, the PRSH assumption holds with $N = n^{1+\delta}$, t leaked nodes, and $\epsilon = n^{-c}$ against all $n^{o(\log n)}$-time adversaries.

We highlight that all the variations of planted problems we considered above are statistically hard only when $n = O(\log N)$ (e.g., the largest clique in a random N-node graph has $O(\log N)$ size [BE76]). In this parameter regime, our constructions would be outperformed by known information-theoretic upper bounds [BIKK14, LVW17].

We provide evidence supporting our conjectures: we show that the Weak-PSH assumption holds against any adversary that can be represented as a degree-D multivariate polynomial, where $D = (\log n)^{2-\epsilon}$ and $\epsilon > 0$ (a *low-degree polynomial*). We also show that, independently of N and the number of hints, cliques are the planted subgraph that are most easily detected by low-degree polynomials. In the domain of planted problems, low-degree polynomials are a powerful class of adversaries. For instance, all known attacks against the planted clique problem belong to this class. For this reason, it was even conjectured that, for planted problems, security against degree-D polynomials implies security against generic 2^D-time adversaries [Hop18, Conjecture 2.2.4]. We refer to Sect. 4.3 for further details.

Future Work. All variants of planted problems we described above can easily be solved by quasi-polynomial-time adversaries (the advantage is $\Omega(1)$). Furthermore, there exist explicit PPT adversaries that solve the problems with inverse-polynomial advantage. These facts contrast with the security level usually desired in cryptographic assumptions: we would like that, for every subexponential-time adversary, the advantage is negligible. One could therefore wonder whether there exist more clever ways of planting subgraphs (e.g., choosing the graph G from a more sophisticated distribution than $\mathcal{G}(N, 1/2)$) so that we either achieve

- negligible advantage against all PPT adversaries, or
- inverse-polynomial advantage against all subexponential-time adversaries, or (even better)
- negligible advantage against all subexponential-time adversaries.

All these questions remain open. We leave them for future work.

2.2 PSM Protocols with Logarithmic Message-Size

We use the (Weak-)PSH conjecture to build a computational PSM protocol with $O(\log n)$ message-size.

Private Simultaneous Messages Protocols with Public Information. PSM protocols are a cryptographic primitive that specifies how two parties can simultaneously encode their inputs (each encoding only depends on the input of the party and a common random string) and non-interactively evaluate from the encodings a function f on the parties' inputs. An external observer that only sees the encoding of the inputs is guaranteed to learn no information beyond the output of the function.

We consider a computational version of the primitive in which a setup is used to generate common randomness for the parties (which is kept secret) along with some public information I. The latter is necessary for the reconstruction of the output, however, it does not help in learning additional information about the inputs.

We highlight that PSM protocol always needs an algorithms that sets up the randomness of the parties, no matter what[3]. The main novelty in this work is that we allow some information to be public. Since we are considering security in a computational setting, the public information can help in decreasing the size of the message of the parties: I can hide all the information about the function f and its outputs. By revealing the encodings of their inputs x, y, the parties can make the extraction of $f(x, y)$ from I easy, while all other information remains secret. This is exactly the blueprint used by our constructions. In the paper, we focus our attention to functions of the form $f : [n] \times [n] \to \{0, 1\}$.

---

[3] If the parties use independent randomness, an adversary can run a *residual function attack*. Check the full version of the paper [ABI+23a, Section 5.1] for more details.

A Trivial Construction from OWFs. Before using techniques based on planted subgraphs, we linger for a moment on the notion of PSM protocols with public information and we check what can be achieved using more standard cryptographic primitives.

We can obtain a trivial construction using OWFs. Represent the function f as an $n \times n$ truth table T in which each row is associated with an input of the first party and each column is associated with an input of the second party. We permute all the rows and all the columns of T independently using permutations ϕ_0 and ϕ_1. Let T' be the result. For every i, we encrypt all the elements in the i-th row of T' using a key k_i^0. We then perform a similar operation on the already encrypted matrix switching to columns: for every j, we encrypt all the elements in the j-th column using the key k_j^1. The public information I will consist of the resulting doubly-encrypted matrix.

In order for the parties to evaluate f on input x and y, they just need to send $(x', k_{x'}^0)$ and $(y', k_{y'}^1)$, where $x' = \phi_0(x)$ and $y' = \phi_1(y)$. The output is obtained by decrypting the element in position (x', y') in I using the keys sent by the parties. Observe that even if we assume exponentially secure OWFs and we opt for security against $n^{o(\log n)}$-time adversaries, this construction requires $\Omega(\log^2 n)$ message-size.

PSM Protocols with Public Information from PSH. Using planted subgraphs, we obtain a PSM protocol with public information where the message-size is nearly optimal: under the PSH conjecture, for most functions $f : [n] \times [n] \to \{0,1\}$, the parties just need to communicate $(1 + \delta) \cdot \log n$ bits where δ is an arbitrarily small positive constant. Under the Weak-PSH conjecture, we achieve instead $(2 + \delta) \cdot \log n$ message-size for all functions. Observe that there is an information-theoretical lower bound that requires at least $\log n$ bits of communication. Importantly, our construction achieves security against $n^{o(\log n)}$-time adversaries with *inverse-polynomial privacy error*.

The construction is rather simple: we represent the function f as a bipartite graph H with n nodes per part. Each node on the left will be associated with a different input for the first party. Similarly, each node on the right will be associated with a different input for the second party. We connect two nodes with an edge if the evaluation of f on the corresponding values gives 1. The public information will consist of a large random graph G in which we plant a copy of H. The setup will provide the parties with the position of the hidden subgraph. In order to evaluate the function, all the parties need to do is to reveal where the node associated to their input is hidden. The output of the function is 1 if and only if there is a edge connecting the broadcast nodes.

Under the PSH assumption with $t = 2$, the view of an external observer is as if it was given a random graph with a planted edge (if the output is 1) or a planted "non-edge" (if the output is 0). So, no information about the inputs is revealed beyond the result of the evaluation.

Theorem 3 (Informal). *Under the PSH conjecture for $t = 2$, for most functions $f : [n] \times [n] \to \{0,1\}$, the construction described above is a PSM proto-*

col with public information that is secure against $n^{o(\log n)}$-time adversaries with $\epsilon = n^{-c}$ privacy error. The message size is $(1 + \delta) \cdot \log n$ for a small positive constant δ.

Under the Weak-PSH conjecture for $t = 2$, the construction is secure against the same class of adversaries for every function $f : [n] \times [n] \to \{0, 1\}$ and achieves $(2 + \delta) \cdot \log n$ message-size.

Privacy Amplification. The disadvantage of the construction we just described is the inverse-polynomial privacy error ϵ. We therefore tried to amplify it to $\epsilon = \mathsf{negl}(n)$. Unfortunately, techniques such as Yao's XOR lemma, do not seem to help. Another possible approach would have been the technique used in [BGIK22]. This solution, however, would have increased the message size to $\Omega(\log^2 n)$. We recall that the trivial solution from OWF achieves exactly this complexity.

In the end, we came up with a candidate construction that we believe to achieve negligible privacy error against $n^{o(\log n)}$-time adversaries with $\omega(1) \cdot \log n$ message-size. The idea is rather simple: we additively secret share the function f among $r = \omega(1)$ virtual parties. As we did for f in the previous paragraph, we can represent each share g_j as a $2n$-node graph H_j. The public information will consist of a vector $I = (G_1, \ldots, G_r)$ where G_j is a random N-node graph in which we planted H_j.

In order to evaluate the function, the parties encode their inputs as in the original construction with respect to each graph G_j. In particular, the parties reveal where the node associated with their input is hidden in G_j. For every $j \in [r]$, the parties obtain a different output bit z_j (z_j will be equal to 1, if the broadcast nodes in G_j are adjacent). By XORing all these values, they reconstruct the output of the evaluation.

To support our claim of security, observe that an adversary cannot learn where H_j is hidden by solely looking at G_j: it has to work on the joint distribution $(G_1, \ldots, G_r)$. Indeed, each H_j is secret and uniformly distributed, so G_j is just a random graph. The natural attack would require the adversary to find a permutation of the graphs $G_1, \ldots, G_r$, so that their "XOR" hides a copy of f^4. However, only a negligible fraction of all permutations satisfies the desired property. In the full version of the paper [ABI+23a, Section 5.3], we consider more sophisticated attacks.

Offline-Online 2-Input Non-Interactive 3-PC with Logarithmic Communication. Our PSM protocols give rise to very lightweight 2-input 3-party protocols with an offline phase. Our setting is the following: suppose that Alice and Bob have some input $x, y \in [n]$. After receiving some correlated randomness from a trusted dealer, in the so called *offline phase*, they want to reveal the evaluation of a function $f : [n] \times [n] \to \{0, 1\}$ on their inputs to their friend, Carol. Carol should be the only one that learns such output. In our setting, Alice and Bob are,

---

^{4} We "XOR" two graphs by XORing their adjacency matrices.

however, lazy: they want to send a single immediate message that is as short as possible.

PSM protocols with public information are the solution to this problem: the trusted dealer provides the common randomness to Alice and Bob and the public information to Carol. At that point, Alice and Bob independently encode their inputs using the PSM protocol and send their messages to Carol. The public information allows Carol to retrieve the output.

The construction withstands a semi-honest adversary that corrupts at most one party. Observe that the online phase requires a single round of interaction. Furthermore, our PSM protocols allow us to achieve $\omega(1) \cdot \log n$ communication. To our knowledge, the only solution that achieves lower communication complexity is the one-time truth table protocol of [IKM+13]. Such solution would, however, require more than one round of interaction.

Compressing the Public Information. In this work, we decreased the message-size of PSM protocols by introducing public information. A natural question is how big the public information needs to be and whether this can be reused (e.g., the construction based on graph cannot be used more than once).

A partial answer is given by *universal samplers* [HJK+16]. This primitive can be thought as a small public obfuscated program that, on input the description of a distribution $\mathcal{D}$, it outputs a sample from $\mathcal{D}$ without revealing any additional information about it. For instance, if $\mathcal{D}$ produces large random RSA moduli, nobody will learn the factorisation of the output of the universal sampler.

Now, suppose that a trusted dealer provides the parties of the PSM protocol with a key pair (pk, sk) and a universal sampler U. Everybody can evaluate U on input the distribution that generates the PSM public information I and encrypts the common randomness under pk. Everybody is able to retrieve I, but only the PSM participants can recover the common randomness using sk [ASY22].

The universal samplers presented in [HJK+16] set an upper-bound L on the size of the distributions that can be evaluated. In particular, the size of the sampler is $\text{poly}(\lambda, L)$ where λ is a security parameter. In these constructions, the size of U would therefore be greater than the one of I. Using a sampler has nevertheless an advantage: if we rely on a programmable random oracle, U can be reused without limits. In other words, universal samplers allow us to compile a single-use PSM protocol into a reusable one.

The good news is that the issue with sizes can be fixed: Abram, Obremski and Scholl [AOS23] built an *unbounded universal sampler* (again, using a programmable random oracle). This is a universal sampler that sets no bound the size of the distributions that can be given as input. The size of U is simply $\text{poly}(\lambda)$. Notice that if we aim for security against $n^{o(\log n)}$-time adversaries, the size of the sampler is $\text{polylog}\, n$.

We formalize our results about PSM protocols in the full version of this paper [ABI+23a, Section 5].

2.3   Forbidden Graph Secret-Sharing Schemes with Logarithmic Share-Size

We use the PRSH assumption to build forbidden graph secret-sharing schemes with $O(\log n)$ share-size.

Forbidden Graph Secret-Sharing Schemes. Secret-sharing schemes are a primitive that allows to share a secret among n parties. In order to reconstruct the secret, the participants need to collaborate. Whether the reconstruction succeeds or not depends on the set of players that collaborate: some subsets are guaranteed to succeed, some of them are guaranteed to learn no information about the secret, some of them have no guarantee (they may get the whole secret, just some leakage or nothing at all). This reconstruction policies are described by the so called *access structure*.

We are interested in a particular version of primitive called *forbidden graph secret-sharing schemes* [SS97]: the access structure is described by an n-node graph Q. Each party is associated with a different node. A pair of players is guaranteed to reconstruct the secret if and only if there is an edge connecting their nodes. If such edge does not exist, they learn no information about the secret. Finally, if a subset of more than 2 parties collaborates, the construction gives no guarantee on whether the secret can be recovered.

Secret-Sharing Schemes with Public Information. Similarly to what we did for PSM protocols, we consider security against computational adversaries and we augment the primitive with public information: in order to secret-share a value x, a player will broadcast large public information I along with small shares $s_1, \ldots, s_n$, one for each party. The public information will be necessary to reconstruct the secret, however, it will not help in learning x. Since we are in a computational setting, the public information can help in decreasing the size of the shares.

This version of the primitive is motivated by the fact that, in many settings, the cost of storing private information is higher than the one for public information. Moreover, in this kind of schemes, the reconstruction of the secret requires minimal communication. This is even more interesting whenever the public information is reusable.

A Trivial Construction from OWFs. Before presenting our solution based on graphs, we linger for a moment on the definition and we try to check what can be achieved using already known primitives. We can consider a forbidden graph secret-sharing scheme in which the share of each party P_i consists just of a λ-bit key k_i for a symmetric encryption scheme. The public information consists instead of a list of n ciphertexts, the i-th one of which is an encryption under k_i of the i-th share of information-theoretical forbidden-graph secret-sharing (e.g. [BIKK14]) of our secret.

It is trivial to see that this scheme is secure. If we opted for security against $n^{o(\log n)}$-time adversaries, the share size would be $\log^2 n$.

Forbidden Graph Secret-Sharing Schemes with Public Information from PRSH.
Using planted subgraphs, we obtain a forbidden graph secret-sharing scheme
with public information in which the share-size is $O(\log n)$ and the secret is a
bit. Under the PRSH conjecture, we obtain $(1 + \delta) \cdot \log n$ share-size where δ
is a small positive constant. Under the Weak-PSH conjecture, the complexity
becomes instead $(2 + \delta) \cdot \log n$. Importantly, our construction achieves security
against $n^{o(\log n)}$-time adversaries with inverse-polynomial privacy error.

The construction works as follows: we sample a random n-node graph H
and we plant it in a larger random graph G. Each node in H is associated to a
different party. Next, we modify H: we compare it to the graph access structure
Q. For any edge that does not appear in Q, we remove the corresponding edge
in H (if such edge exists). Let H' be the graph obtained in this way. In order to
secret-share $b = 1$, we publish the pair (H', G) and we provide each party with
the position of its node in G. In order to secret-share $b = 0$, we perform the same
operations except that we publish $(H', \overline{G})$ where $\overline{G}$ is the complementary graph
of G (i.e., $\overline{G}$ will have all the edges that do not appear in G).

If a pair of parties is allowed to reconstruct, they can recover b by just
comparing the edge that connects their nodes in H' with the edge that connects
their shares in G. If both edges exist or both do not, the secret is 1. Otherwise,
it is 0.

Observe that under the PRSH assumption with $t = 2$, all the information
the parties see in G is the edge (or non-edge) that connects their shares. All the
rest looks random. If the pair is not allowed to reconstruct the secret, their edge
in G will be independent of the graph H' (their edge was removed from H).

Theorem 4 (Informal). *Under the PRSH conjecture for $t = 2$, the construction described above is a forbidden graph bit secret-sharing scheme with public
information that is secure against $n^{o(\log n)}$-time adversaries with $\epsilon = n^{-c}$ privacy
error. The share size is $(1 + \delta) \cdot \log n$ for a small positive constant δ.*

In the context of secret sharing, amplifying privacy to a negligible error is
easy. We just need to apply Yao's XOR lemma with $r = \omega(1)$ repetitions. The
share-size becomes therefore $\omega(1) \cdot \log n$ (we recall that the trivial VBB solution
requires $\log^2 n$ share-size).

Theorem 5 (Informal). *Under the Weak-PSH conjecture, for every graph
access structure, there exists a forbidden graph secret-sharing scheme with public
information, a one-bit secret, and $\omega(1) \cdot \log n$ share-size. The scheme is secure
against $n^{o(\log n)}$-time adversaries with $\epsilon = \mathsf{negl}(n)$ privacy error.*

Compressing the Public Information. Similarly to PSM protocols, we can use
universal samplers to compress the public information and make it reusable. The
technique requires the use of a programmable random oracle.

Suppose that a trusted setup provides the parties with an unbounded universal sampler U. Suppose also that each party P_i is associated with a key pair
$(\mathsf{pk}_i, \mathsf{sk}_i)$. In order for P_1 to share a bit b, the players can run U on input the
distribution that generates the secret-sharing of a random bit c and outputs the

public information, the encryption of the share s_i under pk_i for every i and the encryption of c under pk_1. Each party can retrieve its share, P_1 also learns the random secret c. At that point, P_1 can simply broadcast $b \oplus c$. Observe that b can be recovered if and only the parties are able to reconstruct c.

This solution decreases the size of the public information and makes it reusable. A minor disadvantage is that the size of the private information stored by each party increases as the size of sk_i is at least λ bits where λ is a security parameter. The cost of such storage is however amortized over many executions of the secret-sharing scheme. Notice that the communication complexity of the reconstruction is as before: the parties just need to communicate $\omega(1) \cdot \log n$ bits.

We formalize our results about forbidden-graph secret-sharing schemes in the full version of this paper [ABI+23a, Section 6].

2.4 On Breaking the $\log n$ Barrier for 2-out-of-n Secret-Sharing Schemes

Unlike PSM protocols, in the context of secret-sharing schemes with public information, the lower bound on the share size is unclear. In particular, is it possible to design schemes with $\delta \cdot \log n$ share size for any $\delta < 1$? We studied this question in the simplest setting: 2-out-n secret-sharing schemes. Unfortunately, we could not find an answer, however, we came up with necessary and sufficient conditions for this to happen.

An Equivalent Condition. We show that 2-out-of-n secret-sharing schemes with public information and share-size ℓ is equivalent to a multipartite version of the planted clique problem: given the public information I, we can derive an n-partite graph with 2^ℓ nodes per part. Each of the nodes in the i-th partition corresponds to a different share for party P_i. We connect all the pairs of nodes that correspond to shares that reconstruct to 1.

By the correctness of the secret-sharing scheme, if the public information hides the secret $b = 1$, the graph we derived hides an n-node clique (the nodes containing the shares of the n parties with the secret 1 and a random string of the dealer generating the public information I). If instead the secret is $b = 0$, the graph hides an n-node independent set. Independently of the secret, each of the nodes in the hidden subgraph lies on a different part. The security of the 2-out-of-n secret-sharing scheme guarantees that the two distributions on graphs are indistinguishable even if we leak one of the nodes in the hidden subgraphs.

The above argument can be reversed to show that distributions over graphs with the described properties imply a 2-out-of-n secret-sharing scheme with public information. Finding them is however not simple when $\ell < \log n$. Indeed, we would need to hide an n-node clique in a graph that has less than n^2 nodes. In this parameter setting, the attacks of [Kuč95, AKS98] succeed in recovering the clique for all the graph distributions we tried. The multipartite nature of the graph makes our goal even harder.

Necessary Conditions and Sufficient Conditions. We consider a somewhat similar problem. We look for a distribution $\mathcal{D}$ over N-node graphs that contain both a t-node clique and a t-node independent set, where t is large. We would like that, for such distribution, it is infeasible to distinguish between a random node in the clique and a random node in the independent set.

We prove that this problem is strictly related to 2-out-of-n secret sharing: if the distribution $\mathcal{D}$ is possible for $t = \omega(N^{3/4})$, then 2-out-of-n secret-sharing schemes with $\delta \cdot \log n$ share-size exists for some $\delta < 1$. If instead, $\mathcal{D}$ does not exist for any $t = \omega(N^{1/2})$, then 2-out-of-n secret-sharing schemes with $\delta \cdot \log n$ share-size are impossible for all $\delta < 1$.

Theorem 6 (Necessary condition – Informal). *Suppose that 2-out-of-n secret-sharing schemes with public information and $\delta \cdot \log n$ share-size exist for some $\delta < 1$. Then, there exists a distribution $\mathcal{D}$ that outputs an N-node graph with an $\omega(N^{1/2})$-node clique and an $\omega(N^{1/2})$-node independent set, such that it is hard to distinguish a random node on the clique from a random node on the independent set.*

Theorem 7 (Sufficient condition – Informal). *Suppose there exists a distribution $\mathcal{D}$ that outputs an N-node graph with an $\omega(N^{3/4})$-node clique and an $\omega(N^{3/4})$-node independent set, such that it is hard to distinguish between a random node on the clique and a random node on the independent set. Then, for some $\delta < 1$ there exist 2-out-of-n secret-sharing schemes with public information and $\delta \cdot \log n$ share-size.*

We formalize these results in the full version [ABI+23a, Section 7].

A Lower-Bound on the Share-Size. We prove a lower-bound for 2-out-of-n secret-sharing schemes with public information: the share-size needs to be at least $\frac{1}{5} \log \log n$.

The idea is rather simple: a 2-out-of-n secret-sharing scheme induces a 2-out-of-n' scheme for any $n' \leq n$. The security of the construction does not depend on n' but only on n. On the other hand, the size of the public information I decreases with n'. Indeed, as we discussed above, I can be represented as an n-partite graph. If we restrict the scheme to n' parties, we just need to consider n' of the parts.

Now, if the share-size ℓ is smaller than $\frac{1}{5} \log \log n$, there exists an $n' > 2^\ell$ for which the size of the public information becomes $O(\log n)$. Such public information is too small to help against $\mathsf{poly}(n)$-time adversaries. Therefore, it must be that the induced scheme is statistically secure. Lower bounds for the information-theoretical case require that $\ell \geq \log n'$. That contradicts the choice of our n'.

We formalize the lower bound in the full version of this paper [ABI+23a, Section 8].

On the Relation between our Primitives and Planted Subgraph Problems. The discussion about breaking the $\log n$ barrier for 2-out-of-n secret-sharing schmes highlighted something important: planted subgraph assumptions are not only sufficient to obtain PSM protocols and forbidden graph secret-sharing schemes with $O(\log n)$ share size, they are also necessary.

For instance, consider a function $f : [n] \times [n] \to \{0, 1\}$ and let H be the corresponding graph representation. We can reframe the security of any PSM protocol for f with $O(\log n)$ message-size as a planted subgraph problem: we create a bipartite graph. Each node on the left side corresponds to a different message the first party can send. Similarly, each node on the right side corresponds to a different message for the second party. We connect any pair of nodes with an edge if the corresponding PSM messages give output 1. It is easy to see that the graph hides at least one copy of H. Breaking the security of the protocol corresponds to recognising which nodes of H were broadcast by the parties.

We can use an analogous argument to show that also forbidden graph secret-sharing schmees with $O(\log n)$ share-size can be reframed as a planted subgraph problem.

Secret-Sharing Schemes with 1-bit Shares. We study the following scenario: employing public information, when can we construct secret-sharing schemes with one-bit shares?

If an n-party gap access structure has at least $\omega(\log n)$-gap between the size of every qualified set and the size of every forbidden set, using virtual black box obfuscation (VBB), we can construct a secret-sharing scheme with one-bit shares as follows: The dealer with secret s distributes an independently and uniformly chosen bit r_i to each party P_i and publishes a VBB obfuscation of the function that, when queried with $Q, (r_i)_{i \in Q}$ for any qualified set Q, outputs s and outputs $\perp$ otherwise. Then, a computationally bounded adversary with shares $(r_i)_{i \in F}$ needs to correctly guess $\omega(\log n)$ random bits to recover the share, hence succeeds with negligible probability.

However, for a perfect access structure, where every set is either qualified or forbidden, we show that a secret-sharing scheme with one-bit shares even with public information achieves less than 1/6-indistinguishability advantage and perfect correctness only if it admits a perfectly secure secret-sharing scheme. In other words, access structures that are not binary ideal do not admit a secret-sharing scheme with one-bit shares even with public information.

To prove this impossibility, we develop an alternative characterization for binary ideal access structures: an access structure is binary ideal if and only if the set difference between any minimal qualified set and a maximal forbidden set has odd sized. We then prove using a combinatorial argument that whenever this condition is not satisfied, there exists a minimal qualified set Q and a maximal forbidden set F such that $|Q \setminus F| = 2$. We show that an adversary who randomly corrupts one amongst the forbidden sets $F, Q \setminus \{i\}$ or $Q \setminus \{j\}$, where $\{i, j\} = Q \setminus F$ can recover the secret with 2/3 advantage. We formalize these results in the full version of the paper [ABI+23a, Section 8].

3   Preliminaries

Notation. For any integer $n \in \mathbb{N}$, we use $[n]$ to denote the set $\{1, \ldots, n\}$. For every $n, N \in \mathbb{N}$ such that $n \leq N$, we use $[n; N]$ to denote the set $\{n, n+1, \ldots, N\}$. Notice that $[0, 1]$ denotes the interval of real values $x \in \mathbb{R}$ such that $0 \leq x \leq 1$. For any $n, N \in \mathbb{N}$ such that $n \leq N$, $\mathsf{Inj}(n, N)$ represents the set of injective functions $[n] \rightarrow [N]$. We use $\mathsf{Sym}(n)$ to denote the set of permutations of $[n]$.

We use $\mathsf{negl} : \mathbb{N} \rightarrow \mathbb{R}$ to denote a generic negligible function, i.e., $\mathsf{negl}(n) = o(n^{-c})$ for every constant $c \in \mathbb{N}$. We use $\mathsf{poly}(n)$ to denote a generic function that is $O(n^c)$ for some constant $c > 0$. Given a distribution μ over the space Ω and a function $f : \Omega \rightarrow \mathbb{R}$, we use $\mathbb{E}_\mu[f]$ to denote the expectation of $f(x)$ for $x \xleftarrow{\$} \mu$. In a similar way, we use $\mathsf{Var}_\mu[f]$ to denote the variance of $f(x)$ for $x \xleftarrow{\$} \mu$.

Give two vectors $x, y \in \{0, 1\}^n$, we use $\langle x, y \rangle$ to denote their inner-product. We use $w(x)$ to denote the Hamming weight of x, i.e., the number of non-zero entries of x.

4   The Planted Subgraph Problem

In this section, we study the hardness of planted subgraph problems. Before presenting our assumptions, we introduce some notation. All the graphs in the paper are finite, undirected and simple. Furthermore, we assume that the set of nodes is $[n]$ for some $n \in \mathbb{N}$. Given a graph G, we denote its complementary by $\overline{G}$: this is the graph in which, for every $i \neq j$, the edge (i, j) appears if and only if (i, j) does not appear in G. We use $\mathcal{G}(n, 1/2)$ to denote a Erdős-Rényi random graph, i.e., the uniform distribution over n-node graphs. Observe that each edge appears independently of the others with probability $1/2$. We denote the clique with n-nodes by K_n. For any n-node graph H and $S \subseteq [n]$, $\mathsf{Subgraph}(H, S)$ denotes the subgraph of H induced by the nodes in S. Notice that this graph has only $|S|$ nodes and its edges are in one-to-one correspondence with the edges of H having both endpoints in S. We will make extensive use of the following *planting* experiment, where we sample a random graph R and then hide inside it a *public* random graph H.

Definition 1 (Planting). *Let $\mathcal{D}_R(\mathbb{1}^n)$ and $\mathcal{D}_H(\mathbb{1}^n)$ be distributions over graphs.*

We define the distribution $\mathcal{G}(\mathcal{D}_R, \mathcal{D}_H)$ as follows:

1. $R \xleftarrow{\$} \mathcal{D}_R(\mathbb{1}^n)$
2. $H \xleftarrow{\$} \mathcal{D}_H(\mathbb{1}^n)$
3. *Let N and ℓ be the number of nodes of R and H respectively.*
4. *If $\ell > N$, output $\perp$.*
5. $\phi \xleftarrow{\$} \mathsf{Inj}(\ell, N)$
6. $G \leftarrow R$
7. *For all $i, j \in [\ell]$, if (i, j) appears in H, add $(\phi(i), \phi(j))$ to G.*
8. *For all $i, j \in [\ell]$, if (i, j) does not appear in H, remove $(\phi(i), \phi(j))$ from G.*
9. *Output (G, H, ϕ).*

We often refer to the graph generated by $\mathcal{D}_R$ as the *ambient graph*. We call the output of $\mathcal{D}_H$ the *hidden graph*. Observe that $\mathcal{G}(\mathcal{D}_R, \mathcal{D}_H)$ hides a copy of H in the ambient graph. More specifically, the copy is the subgraph induced by $\phi([\ell])$. In other words, the edge (i, j) will appear in H if and only if $(\phi(i), \phi(j))$ appears in G.

In the paper, we will rarely use the general notation $\mathcal{G}(\mathcal{D}_R, \mathcal{D}_H)$. Instead, we will typically refer to the following special cases:

- When $\mathcal{D}_R = \mathcal{G}(N, 1/2)$, we write $\mathcal{G}(N, 1/2, \mathcal{D}_H)$.
- When $\mathcal{D}_R = \mathcal{G}(N, 1/2)$ and $\mathcal{D}_H(\mathbb{1}^n) \equiv K_n$, we write $\mathcal{G}(N, 1/2, n)$.
- When $\mathcal{D}_R = \mathcal{G}(N, 1/2)$ and $\mathcal{D}_H(\mathbb{1}^n) \equiv H_n$ where H_n is a fixed graph, we write $\mathcal{G}(N, 1/2, H_n)$.
- When $\mathcal{D}_R = \mathcal{G}(N, 1/2)$ and $\mathcal{D}_H(\mathbb{1}^n) = \mathcal{G}(n, 1/2)$, we write $\mathcal{G}(N, 1/2, n, 1/2)$.

4.1   The Planted Clique Assumption

We now present the assumptions we will use in this paper. We start by recalling the planted clique assumption, a problem that has been extensively studied by the computational complexity community over the last decades [Jer92, Kuč95, AKS98, FK03, BHK+16, MRS21]. The assumption states that it is hard to distinguish a random graph with a large planted clique from a random graph. The problem is related to the NP-hardness of finding or even approximating the largest clique contained in a graph [Kar72, ALM+92, AS92, BGLR93, BS94, BGS95, FGL+95, Hås96a, Hås96b].

Definition 2 (The planted clique assumption [Jer92, Kuč95]). *Let $N : \mathbb{N} \to \mathbb{N}$ be a function such that $N(n) \geq n$ for every $n \in \mathbb{N}$. Let $T : \mathbb{N} \to \mathbb{N}$ be a time bound and let $\epsilon : \mathbb{N} \to [0, 1]$ be an indistinguishability bound. We say that the (N, T, ϵ)-planted clique (PC) assumption holds if the following distributions are $\epsilon(n)$-computationally indistinguishable for any $(T(n) \cdot \mathrm{poly}(n))$-time probabilistic adversary.*

$$\left\{ G \middle| (G, R, \phi) \xleftarrow{\$} \mathcal{G}(N, 1/2, n) \right\} \quad and \quad \left\{ G \middle| G \xleftarrow{\$} \mathcal{G}(N, 1/2) \right\}$$

It is easy to see that the (N, T, ϵ)-PC assumption implies the (N', T', ϵ')-PC assumption for any functions $N' \geq N$, $T' \leq T$ and $\epsilon' \geq \epsilon$.

Attacks Against the PC Assumption. A result by Bollobás and Erdős [BE76] proves that the largest clique in an N-node random graph has almost always $\Theta(\log N)$ size. Therefore, the PC assumption cannot hold against computationally unbounded adversaries when $N = \mathrm{poly}(n)$.

The most natural attack against the PC assumption is *edge-counting*: if the graph G hides a clique, it will be denser on average. When $N = \mathrm{poly}(n)$, this leads to a polynomial-time attack with n^{-c} advantage (c is a positive constant).

Another almost as straightforward attack is the *degree attack*: the planted nodes have on average higher degree. In a random N-node graph, the degree of the nodes is described by a binomial probability distribution with average $(N-1)/2$ and standard deviation $\Theta(\sqrt{N})$. After planting the clique, the distribution of the degree of the planted nodes is shifted by n. As noticed by Kučera in [Kuč95], this not only gives a probabilistic polynomial time attack with inverse-polynomial advantage: when $n = \Omega(\sqrt{N \cdot \log N})$, it is possible to recover the planted clique with constant probability by simply picking the nodes with highest degree.

This approach can be generalized to a *common-neighbour attack*: for any constant $d > 0$, we consider all subsets of d pair-wise adjacent nodes and we count the number of common neighbours. In a random graph, the average number of common neighbours is $\Theta(N/2^d)$ and its standard deviation is still $\Theta(\sqrt{N})$. On the other hand, when the d nodes lie on the planted clique, the distribution of common neighbours is shifted by $n - d$.

In [HK11], it was also noticed that the PC assumption can be broken in time $n^{O(\log n)}$: the adversary can iterate through all subsets of $d = 3 \log n$ nodes. If the graph is random, with high probability, none of these subsets will form a clique.

The last common family of attacks relies on *spectral analysis*. For instance, in [AKS98], Alon *et al.* showed that the planted clique can be found with constant probability whenever $N < n^2/100$. Other attacks were studied in [FK00, McS01, FR10, AV11, DGGP14, DM15a, CX16]. To this day, none of the approaches discussed above succeeds in describing an $n^{o(\log n)}$-time attack with $o_n(1)$-advantage when $N = \omega(n^2)$.

Conjectured Hardness. Motivated by the failed attacks described above, it is conjectured that, for $N = n^{2+\delta}$, the advantage of any $n^{o(\log n)}$ time adversary against the PC problem is dominated by n^{-c} for some constant $c > 0$ [MRS21]. As discussed in [BBB19], the assumption is also supported by its hardness against several classes of attacks: greedy algorithms [McD74, GM75, Kar76, Pit82, Jer92], local algorithms [GS14, COE15, RV17], query models [FGN+20], bounded-depth circuits [Ros08], monotone circuits [Ros10], statistical query algorithms [FGR+13] and resolution [ABdR+18]. Hardness was also proven in the Lovász-Shrijver [FK03] and Sum-of-Squares convex programming hierarchies [MPW15, BHK+16, DM15b, HKP+18].

Conjecture 8 (The PC assumption). *For any constant $\delta > 0$, there exists a constant $c > 0$ such that the $(n^{2+\delta}, T, n^{-c})$-PC assumption holds for every $T = n^{o(\log n)}$.*

The PC assumption has been previously used in cryptography. Juels and Peinado [JP00] used a planted clique hardness assumption to build one-way functions, zero-knowledge proofs, and hierarchical key generation. More recently, in the context of machine learning, Goldwasser *et al.* [GKVZ22] used planted cliques to show how a malicious learner can hide a backdoor in a classifier. The assumption was also used to prove hardness of k-wise dependence testing [AAK+07], approximating Nash equilibria [HK11], sparse principal component detection [BR13, BBH18, BB19], restricted isometry sensing [KZ14, WBP16], community detection [HWX15], adaptive estimators [SBW19], matrix completion [Che15], and submatrix detection [MW15, CLR17, BBH19, MRS21]. In [ERSY22], the PC assumption was used to prove that the NP-Complete Clique problem admits a non-adaptive pseudorandom self-reduction.

4.2   The Planted Subgraph Assumption

We now generalize the PC assumption: instead of planting an n-sized clique in a random graph, we plant a generic n-node graph coming from a distribution $\mathcal{D}(\mathbb{1}^n)$. We say that the planted subgraph assumption holds for $\mathcal{D}$ if the resulting graph looks random even if we reveal the output of $\mathcal{D}$.

The idea of generalizing the PC problem to a different distribution of hidden subgraphs is not new. For instance, the planted dense subgraph assumption, which hides a dense subgraph in a large and sparser ambient graph, has been used in learning theory [HWX15, BBH19]. The DUE assumption, introduced by Applebaum et al. [ABW10] to build PKE, is also somewhat related: it conjectures the hardness of detecting a subset of nodes with a small number of neighbours hidden in a random regular bipartite graph.

Definition 3 (The planted subgraph assumption). Let $\mathcal{D}(\mathbb{1}^n)$ be an efficient distribution outputting an n-node graph. Let $N : \mathbb{N} \to \mathbb{N}$ be a function such that $N(n) \geq n$ for every $n \in \mathbb{N}$. Let $T : \mathbb{N} \to \mathbb{N}$ be a time bound and let $\epsilon : \mathbb{N} \to [0,1]$ be an indistinguishability bound. We say that the $(\mathcal{D}, N, T, \epsilon)$-planted subgraph (PS) assumption holds if the distributions

$$\left\{ (G, H) \Big| (G, H, \phi) \xleftarrow{\$} \mathcal{G}(N, 1/2, \mathcal{D}) \right\} \quad and \quad \left\{ (G, H) \Big| G \xleftarrow{\$} \mathcal{G}(N, 1/2), H \xleftarrow{\$} \mathcal{D}(\mathbb{1}^n) \right\}$$

are $\epsilon(n)$-computationally indistinguishable for any $\big(T(n) \cdot \mathrm{poly}(n)\big)$-time probabilistic adversary We say that the (N, T, ϵ)-planted random subgraph (PRS) assumption holds if the $(\mathcal{D}, N, T, \epsilon)$-PS assumption holds for $\mathcal{D} = \mathcal{G}(n, 1/2)$.

Observe that if $\mathcal{D}(\mathbb{1}^n) \equiv K_n$, we obtain exactly the PC assumption. Once again, it is easy to see that, for any distribution $\mathcal{D}$, the $(\mathcal{D}, N, T, \epsilon)$-PS assumption implies the $(\mathcal{D}, N', T', \epsilon')$-PS whenever $N' \geq N$, $T' \leq T$ and $\epsilon' \geq \epsilon$.

Planting Fixed Families of Graphs. We are particularly interested in a variation of the PS assumption: the case in which $\mathcal{D}(\mathbb{1}^n) \equiv H_n$ where $(H_n)_{n \in \mathbb{N}}$ is a fixed family of n-node graphs. It is believed that hiding any subgraph H_n is at least as easy as hiding a clique, i.e., detecting H_n is harder. Indeed, cliques have easily recognisable characteristics that do not occur on most graphs: they are extremely dense, their nodes have large degree, and any subset of their vertices has a lot of common neighbours. The common approaches to solve the PC problem try to leverage these traits.

On the other hand, the vast majority of n-node graphs do not satisfy any of these properties. It is conjectured that, for all $\delta > 0$, the PS assumption holds for every family $(H_n)_{n \in \mathbb{N}}$ with parameters $N = n^{2+\delta}$, $\epsilon = n^{-c}$ and $T = n^{o(\log n)}$. In Sect. 4.3, we provide some evidence to support this claim: we show that the assumption holds against any adversary that can be represented as a degree-$(\log n)^{2-\epsilon}$ polynomial where $\epsilon > 0$. In the domain of planted problems, this kind of adversaries have always turned out to lead to the best known attacks. For this reason, it was even conjectured that if no degree-D polynomial can distinguish, then the planted assumption holds against any adversary running in time $2^{O(D)}$ [Hop18, Conjecture 2.2.4].

We additionally conjecture that, except for an inverse-polynomial fraction of n-node graphs H_n, the PS assumption holds, for every $\delta > 0$, with parameters $N = n^{1+\delta}$, $\epsilon = n^{-c}$ and $T = n^{o(\log n)}$. In other words, the size of the graph is $n^{1+\delta}$ (compared to $n^{2+\delta}$ for hiding cliques). In some sense, these conjectures give information about the worst-case hardness and the average-case hardness of detecting a subgraph planted in a random graph.

Planting Random Graphs. Another interesting version of the PS problem is the case in which $\mathcal{D}(\mathbb{1}^n) = \mathcal{G}(n, 1/2)$. We refer to this variation as the *PRS assumption*. Even in this case, the assumption is believed to hold with parameters $N = n^{1+\delta}$, $\epsilon = n^{-c}$ and $T = n^{o(\log n)}$. This fact is actually implied by the conjectured average-case hardness of detecting planted subgraphs. The PRS assumption is however strictly weaker: if we plant a fixed graph H_n, the adversary receives an H_n-dependent non-uniform advice. The same would not happen when H_n is sampled at random.

4.3   The Planted Subgraph Assumption with Hints

We finally present a variation of the PS assumption in which we provide the adversary with hints: we leak the position of t nodes in the hidden subgraph. Formally, the assumption states that even if we reveal where a subset S of t nodes is hidden, then we cannot distinguish between a graph in which we plant $H \xleftarrow{\$} \mathcal{D}(\mathbb{1}^n)$ and a random graph in which we hide the subgraph of H induced by S. We will consider small t, e.g., $t = 2$.

The PC assumption is considered robust against leakage. For instance, Brennan and Bresler [BB20] studied several variations of the PC problem in which the adversary is provided with leakage about the position of the planted clique. The authors consider e.g. the case in which the clique is planted in a multipartite graph (the clique will have a single node in each part of the graph).

Definition 4 (The planted subgraph assumption with hints). *Let $\mathcal{D}(\mathbb{1}^n)$ be an efficient distribution outputting an n-node graph. Let $N, t : \mathbb{N} \to \mathbb{N}$ be functions such that $N(n) \geq n \geq t$ for every $n \in \mathbb{N}$. Let $T : \mathbb{N} \to \mathbb{N}$ be a time bound and let $\epsilon : \mathbb{N} \to [0, 1]$ be an indistinguishability bound. We say that the $(\mathcal{D}, N, t, T, \epsilon)$-planted subgraph with hints (PSH) assumption holds if, for every subset $S \subseteq [n]$ such that $|S| \leq t$, the following distributions are $\epsilon(n)$-computationally indistin-*

guishable for any $(T(n) \cdot \text{poly}(n))$-time probabilistic adversary

$$\left\{ G, H \;\middle|\; \begin{aligned} &(G, H, \phi) \xleftarrow{\$} \mathcal{G}(N, 1/2, \mathcal{D}) \\ &(u_i)_{i \in S} \mid \forall i \in S: \; u_i \leftarrow \phi(i) \end{aligned} \right\} \quad and \quad \left\{ G, H \;\middle|\; \begin{aligned} &H \xleftarrow{\$} \mathcal{D}(\mathbb{1}^n) \\ &H' \leftarrow \text{Subgraph}(H, S) \\ &(u_i)_{i \in S} \mid (G, H', \phi) \xleftarrow{\$} \mathcal{G}(N, 1/2, H') \\ &\forall i \in S: \; u_i \leftarrow \phi(i) \end{aligned} \right\}$$

We say that the (N, t, T, ϵ)-planted random subgraph with hints (PRSH) assumption holds if the $(\mathcal{D}, N, t, T, \epsilon)$-PSH assumption holds for $\mathcal{D} = \mathcal{G}(n, 1/2)$.

Observe that if $t = 0$, we obtain exactly the PS assumption.

Conjectured Hardness. Revealing $t = O_n(1)$ nodes on the planted graph is believed to not affect the overall security of the planted subgraph assumptions.

When t is super-constant, the hardness of the problem becomes, however, less clear. For instance, revealing $t = \log n$ nodes on a planted clique would allow distinguishing the graph from a random one with constant advantage by simply counting the number of common neighbours of the t nodes. This leads to the following conjectures.

Conjecture 9 (wPSH, PSH, and PRSH). *Let $(H_n)_{n \in \mathbb{N}}$ be a family of n-node graphs.*

- WEAK-PSH CONJECTURE (WEAK PLANTED SUBGRAPH WITH HINTS). *For every constants $\delta > 0$ and $t \in \mathbb{N}$, there exists a constant $c > 0$ such that the $(\mathcal{D}_H, n^{2+\delta}, t, T, n^{-c})$-PSH assumption holds for $\mathcal{D}_H(\mathbb{1}^n) \equiv H_n$, for all $T = n^{o(\log n)}$.*
- PSH CONJECTURE (PLANTED SUBGRAPH WITH HINTS). *For every $n \in \mathbb{N}$, there exits a subset of n-node graphs $\mathcal{R}_n$ with the following characteristics:*
  1. *$|\mathcal{R}_n| \geq (1 - \text{negl}(n)) \cdot 2^m$ where $m = n(n-1)/2$.*
  2. *For every constants $\delta > 0$ and $t \in \mathbb{N}$, there exists a constant $c > 0$ such that, for all $T = n^{o(\log n)}$, the $(\mathcal{D}_H, n^{1+\delta}, t, T, n^{-c})$-PSH assumption holds for $\mathcal{D}_H \equiv H_n \in \mathcal{R}_n$.*
- PRSH CONJECTURE (PLANTED RANDOM SUBGRAPH WITH HINTS). *For every constants $\delta > 0$ and $t \in \mathbb{N}$, there exists a constant $c > 0$ such that the $(n^{1+\delta}, t, T, n^{-c})$-PRSH assumption holds for all $T = n^{o(\log n)}$.*

Security Against Low-Degree Polynomials. We now provide some evidence to support our conjectures: we show that the weak PSH assumption holds for any graph H_n against all adversaries that can be represented as degree-$(\log n)^{1+\epsilon}$ polynomials where $\epsilon < 1$. In the domain of planted problems, interestingly, all known successful attacks belong to this class [Hop18]. Low-degree polynomials can be incredibly useful in detecting structures planted in large objects. To give an example, given a graph H with D edges, we can use a degree-D polynomial p to tell how many copies of H are hidden in another larger graph. Moreover, if the polynomial p is M-variate, we can always evaluate it in time $D \cdot \binom{M}{D}$. For these reasons, Hopkins conjectured that if there exists no degree-D distinguisher, then the planted assumption holds against generic $2^{O(D)}$-time adversaries [Hop18, Conjecture 2.2.4]. We highlight that such conjecture was introduced in the context of the study of algorithms, where a different notion of indistinguishability is in use: two distributions are "algorithmically indistinguishable" if the advantage of any efficient adversary is $1 - \Omega(1)$ (i.e., it is impossible to efficiently distinguish with vanishing error probability). It is, however, reasonable to assume that the conjecture scales to other notions of indistinguishability, e.g., the standard one in cryptography, where we require the advantage to be negligible, or the main notion we adopt here, where the advantage is required to be $n^{-\Omega(1)}$.

Theorem 10. *Let $(H_n)_{n \in \mathbb{N}}$ be a sequence of graphs where H_n has n nodes and let $t \in \mathbb{N}$ be a constant. Let $(S_n)_{n \in \mathbb{N}}$ be a sequence of sets where $S_n = \{u_{n,1}, \ldots, u_{n,\ell_n}\} \subseteq [n]$ and $\ell_n \leq t$. Let $N(n) := n^{2+\delta}$ where $\delta > 0$ is a constant. Let μ_n be the distribution that samples $(G, H'_n, \phi) \overset{\$}{\leftarrow} \mathcal{G}(N(n), 1/2, H'_n)$, where $H'_n \leftarrow \mathsf{Subgraph}(H_n, S_n)$, then reorders the nodes in G so that $\phi(u_i)$ ends up in the i-th position and, finally, outputs a bit string encoding the edges of the graph except those that have both endpoints in $\phi(S_n)$. Let ν_n be the analogous distribution where, instead, we sample G from $\mathcal{G}(N(n), 1/2, H_n)$. Let $M(n)$ be the length of the strings generated by μ_n and ν_n.*

For any constant $0 < \epsilon \leq 2$ and sequence of polynomials $(p_n)_{n \in \mathbb{N}}$, where $p_n \in \mathbb{R}[X_1, \ldots, X_M]$ has degree at most $D(n) := (\log n)^{2-\epsilon}$, we have

$$\mathsf{Adv}(p_n) := \frac{|\mathbb{E}_{\nu_n}[p_n] - \mathbb{E}_{\mu_n}[p_n]|}{\sqrt{\mathsf{Var}_{\mu_n}[p_n]}} \leq n^{-\Omega(1)}. \tag{1}$$

More in detail, $\max_{p_n} \mathsf{Adv}(p_n)$ is

$$\frac{(N-n)! \cdot \sqrt{(n-\ell_n)!}}{(N-\ell_n)!} \sqrt{\sum_{w(\alpha) \leq D(n)} \binom{N - V(\alpha) - \ell_n}{n - V(\alpha) - \ell_n}^2 \cdot \sum_{\pi \in \mathsf{Sym}(n-\ell_n)} (-1)^{\langle \pi \circ h + h, \alpha' \rangle}} \tag{2}$$

where α denotes a subset of at most D edges in an n-node graph. We encode α as a vector of bits (the i-th bit indicates whether the i-th edge is in the subset or not). We use a similar representation for H (therefore, the inner-product is well-defined). We use $\pi \circ H$ to denote the graph obtained by permuting the nodes (n.b. not the edges) of H according to π (once again we represent this graph as a vector). Finally, $V(\alpha)$ denotes the total number of nodes touched by the edges in α.

The notion of advantage used for low-degree polynomials may first look a bit odd. We explain why it is a meaningful definition. Suppose that $\mathsf{Var}_{\mu_n}[p_n] \sim \mathsf{Var}_{\nu_n}[p_n]$. When (1) does not hold, then, it is usually easy to distinguish between μ_n and ν_n just based on the result of the evaluation of p_n: since the distributions $p_n(\mu_n)$ and $p_n(\nu_n)$ are concentrated around their mean, one can effectively distinguish between the distributions by determining whether the sample is "large" or "small." Conversely, if (1) holds, an attacker has a hard time distinguishing between μ_n and ν_n just based on the evaluation of p_n: if the result is close to $\mathbb{E}_{\nu_n}[p_n]$, it could be that we actually received a sample from ν_n, or it could be that, due to its variance, $p_n(\mu_n)$ produced a sample that is relatively far away from its expectation. Since $\text{Var}_{\mu_n}[p_n] \sim \text{Var}_{\nu_n}[p_n]$, the adversary faces a similar dilemma even if we obtain a value that is close to $\mathbb{E}_{\mu_n}[p_n]$ or far from both $\mathbb{E}_{\mu_n}[p_n]$ and $\mathbb{E}_{\nu_n}[p_n]$. If instead $\text{Var}_{\mu_n}[p_n]$ and $\text{Var}_{\nu_n}[p_n]$ are far apart, the polynomials $q_n := \left(p_n(X) - \mathbb{E}_{\mu_n}[p_n]\right)^2$ and $q_n' := \left(p_n(X) - \mathbb{E}_{\nu_n}[p_n]\right)^2$ most likely do not satisfy (1). We prove Theorem 10 in the full version of this work [ABI+23a].

Interpretation. Theorem 10 highlights some important facts. First of all, it confirms the intuition that cliques are the easiest subgraph we can detect (independently of N, t and D). Indeed, equation (2) reaches its maximum when $\pi \circ h = h$ for every $\pi \in \text{Sym}(n)$. We observe that the vectors $(\pi \circ H + H)_{\pi \in \text{Sym}(n)}$ give a good description of how "structured" H is (e.g., if H is a clique or an independent set, all these vectors are 0). We conjecture that, for most graphs H, the sum $\sum_{\pi \in \text{Sym}(n)} (-1)^{\langle \pi \circ H + H, \alpha \rangle}$ should be small for all choices of α, as $\langle \pi \circ H + H, \alpha \rangle$ should assume the values 0 and 1 almost equally often. We leave the rigorous study of this problem to future work.

The PRSH Conjecture. The PSH conjecture tells us information about the average-case hardness of detecting planted subgraphs: if $N = n^{1+\delta}$, the assumption holds for an overwhelming fraction of n-node graphs. The conjecture is therefore related to the hardness of the PRSH problem: in the following theorem, we prove that the former implies the latter.

Theorem 11. *The PSH conjecture implies the PRSH conjecture.*

Proof. Suppose this is not the case: there exists a $\bar{\delta} > 0$ and $\bar{t} \in \mathbb{N}$ such that, for every $c > 0$, there exists an adversary $\mathcal{A}$ that breaks the PRSH assumption for $N = n^{1+\bar{\delta}}$ with advantage asymptotically greater than n^{-c}. In the context of this proof, we say that an n-node graph H_n is good if $H_n \in \mathcal{R}_n$. Now, consider the PSH conjecture and let $\bar{c} > 0$ be the constant associated with $\bar{\delta}$ and $\bar{t}$. Consider the adversary $\mathcal{A}$ that breaks the PRSH assumption for parameters $\bar{\delta}$, $\bar{t}$ and $\bar{c}/2$. For any $n \in \mathbb{N}$, we consider the good graph H_n for which the advantage of the adversary $\mathcal{A}$ in the PRSH game conditioned on the hidden subgraph being H_n is greatest (the maximum exists as there are only a finite number of n-node graphs for a fixed n). Since a random graph is good with probability $1 - \text{negl}(n)$ and since $\mathcal{A}$ has advantage asymptotically greater than $n^{-\bar{c}/2}$ against the PRSH game, the advantage of the adversary $\mathcal{A}$ in the PRSH game conditioned on the hidden subgraph being H_n must be asymptotically greater than $n^{-\bar{c}/2} - \text{negl}(n) > n^{-\bar{c}}$. Such adversary would therefore contradict the PSH conjecture for the graph family $(H_n)_{n \in \mathbb{N}}$. $\square$

Acknowledgements. We thank Uriel Feige, Prasad Raghavendra, and Daniel Reichman for helpful discussions and literature pointers. Damiano Abram was supported by a GSNS travel grant from Aarhus University and by the Aarhus University Research Foundation (AUFF). Amos Beimel was supported by ERC Project NTSC (742754) and ISF grant 391/21. Yuval Ishai and Varun Narayanan were supported by ERC Project NTSC (742754), BSF grant 2018393, and ISF grant 2774/20. Work of Varun

Narayanan was done while working at Technion, Israel Institute of Technology. Eyal Kushilevitz was supported by BSF grant 2018393 and ISF grant 2774/20.

References

[AAK+07] Alon, N., Andoni, A., Kaufman, T., Matulef, K., Rubinfeld, R., Xie, N. Testing k-wise and almost k-wise independence. In: Johnson, D.S., Feige, U. (eds.), 39th ACM STOC, pp. 496–505. ACM Press, June 2007

[ABdR+18] Atserias, A., et al. Clique is hard on average for regular resolution. In: Diakonikolas, I., Kempe, D., Henzinger, M. (eds.), 50th ACM STOC, pp. 866–877. ACM Press, June 2018

[ABI+23a] Abram, D., Beimel, A., Ishai, Y., Kushilevitz, E., Narayanan, V.: Cryptography from planted graphs: security with logarithmic-size messages. Cryptology ePrint Archive, 2023 (2023)

[ABI+23b] Applebaum, B., Beimel, A., Ishai, Y., Kushilevitz, E., Liu, T., Vaikuntanathan, V.: Succinct computational secret sharing. In: Proceedings of the 55th Annual ACM Symposium on Theory of Computing, STOC 2023 (2023)

[ABW10] Applebaum, B., Barak, B., Wigderson, A.: Public-key cryptography from different assumptions. In: Schulman, L.J. (ed.), 42nd ACM STOC, pp. 171–180. ACM Press, June 2010

[AHMS18] Applebaum, B., Holenstein, T., Mishra, M., Shayevitz, O.: The communication complexity of private simultaneous messages, revisited. In: Nielsen, J.B., Rijmen, V. (eds.) EUROCRYPT 2018. LNCS, vol. 10821, pp. 261–286. Springer, Cham (2018). https://doi.org/10.1007/978-3-319-78375-8_9

[AKS98] Alon, N., Krivelevich, M., Sudakov, B.: Finding a large hidden clique in a random graph. Random Struct. Algorithms 13(3-4), 457–466 (1998)

[ALM+92] Arora, S., Lund, C., Motwani, R., Sudan, M., Szegedy, M.: Proof verifiaction and hardness of approximation problems. In: Proceedings of the 33rd IEEE Annual Symposium on Foundations of Computer Science, FOCS 1992 (1992)

[AOS23] Abram, D., Obremski, M., Scholl, P.: On the (Im)possibility of distributed samplers: lower bounds and party-dynamic constructions. Cryptology ePrint Archive, 2023 (2023)

[AS92] Arora, S., Safra, S.: Approximating clique is NP complete. In: Proceedings of the 33rd IEEE Annual Symposium on Foundations of Computer Science, FOCS 1992 (1992)

[ASY22] Abram, D., Scholl, P., Yakoubov, S.: Distributed (Correlation) samplers: how to remove a trusted dealer in one round. In: Dunkelman, O., Dziembowski, S. (eds.) Advances in Cryptology - EUROCRYPT 2022. EUROCRYPT 2022. LNCS, vol. 13275, pp. 790–820. Springer, Cham (2022). https://doi.org/10.1007/978-3-031-06944-4_27

[AV11] Ames, B., Vavasis, S.: Nuclear norm minimization for the planted clique and biclique problems. In: Mathematical Programming (2011)

[BB19] Brennan, M., Bresler, G.: Optimal average-case reductions to sparse PCA: from weak assumptions to strong hardness. In: Proceedings of 32nd Conference on Learning Theory (2019)

[BB20] Brennan, M., Bresler, G.: Reducibility and statistical-computational gaps from secret leakage. In: Proceedings of 33rd Conference on Learning Theory (2020)

[BBB19] Boix-Adserà, E., Brennan, M., Bresler, G.: The average-case complexity of counting cliques in Erdős-Rényi hypergraphs. In: Zuckerman, D. (ed.), 60th FOCS, pp. 1256–1280. IEEE Computer Society Press, November 2019

[BBH18] Brennan, M., Bresler, G., Huleihel, W.: Reducibility and computational lower bounds for problems with planted sparse structure. In: Proceedings of 31st Conference on Learning Theory (2018)

[BBH19] Brennan, M., Bresler, G., Huleihel, W.: Universality of computational lower bounds for submatrix detection. In: Proceedings of 32nd Conference on Learning Theory (2019)

[BE76] Bollobás, B., Erdős, P.: Cliques in random graph. In: Mathematical Proceedings of the Cambridge Philosophical Society (1976)

[BGIK22] Boyle, E., Gilboa, N., Ishai, Y., Kolobov, V.I.: Programmable distributed point functions. In: Dodis, Y., Shrimpton, T. (eds.) CRYPTO 2022. Part IV, vol. 13510 of LNCS, pp. 121–151. Springer, Heidelberg, August 2022. https://doi.org/10.1007/978-3-031-15985-5_5

[BGLR93] Bellare, M., Goldwasser, S., Lund, C., Russell, A.: Efficient probabilistic checkable proofs and application to approximation. In: Proceedings of the 25th Annual ACM Symposium on Theory of Computing, STOC 1993 (1993)

[BGS95] Bellare, M., Goldreich, O., Sudan, M.: Free bits, PCPs and non-approximability: towards tight results. In: Proceedings of the 36th IEEE Annual Symposium on Foundations of Computer Science, FOCS 1995 (1995)

[BHK+16] Barak, B., Hopkins, S., Kelner, J., Kothari, P.K., Moitra, A., Potechin, A.: A nearly tight sum-of-squares lower bound for the planted clique problem. In: Dinur, I. (ed.), 57th FOCS, pp. 428–437. IEEE Computer Society Press, October 2016

[BIKK14] Beimel, A., Ishai, Y., Kumaresan, R., Kushilevitz, E.: On the cryptographic complexity of the worst functions. In: Lindell, Y. (ed.) TCC 2014. LNCS, vol. 8349, pp. 317–342. Springer, Heidelberg (2014). https://doi.org/10.1007/978-3-642-54242-8_14

[BLVW19] Brakerski, Z., Lyubashevsky, V., Vaikuntanathan, V., Wichs, D.: Worst-case hardness for LPN and cryptographic hashing via code smoothing. In: Ishai, Y., Rijmen, V. (eds.) EUROCRYPT 2019. LNCS, vol. 11478, pp. 619–635. Springer, Cham (2019). https://doi.org/10.1007/978-3-030-17659-4_21

[BR13] Berthet, Q., Rigollet, P.: Complexity theoretic lower bounds for sparse principal component detection. In: The 26th Annual Conference on Learning Theory, COLT 2013 (2013)

[BRSV18] Ball, M., Rosen, A., Sabin, M., Vasudevan, P.N.: Proofs of work from worst-case assumptions. In: Shacham, H., Boldyreva, A. (eds.) CRYPTO 2018. LNCS, vol. 10991, pp. 789–819. Springer, Cham (2018). https://doi.org/10.1007/978-3-319-96884-1_26

[BS94] Bellare, M., Sudan, M.: Improved non-approximability results. In: Proceedings of the 26th Annual ACM Symposium on Theory of Computing, STOC 1994 (1994)

[CCX13] Cascudo, I., Cramer, R., Xing, C.: Bounds on the threshold gap in secret sharing and its applications. In: IEEE Transactions on Information Theory (2013)

[Che15] Chen, Y.: Incoherence-optimal matrix completion. In: IEEE Transactions on Information Theory (2015)

[CLR17] Cai, T.T., Liang, T., Rakhlin, A.: Computational and statistical boundaries for submatrix localization in a large noisy matrix. In: The Annals of Statistics (2017)

[COE15] Coja-Oghlan, A., Efthymiou, C.: On independent sets in random graphs. In: Random Structures and Algorithms (2015)

[CX16] Chen, Y., Xu, J.: Statistical-computational tradeoffs in planted problems and submatrix localization with a growing number of clusters and submatrices. J. Mach. Learn. Res. 17(1), 882–938 (2016)

[DGGP14] Dekel, Y., Gurel-Gurevich, O., Peres, Y.: Finding hidden cliques in linear time with high probability. In: Combinatorics, Probability and Computing (2014)

[DM15a] Deshpande, Y. and Montanari, A.: Finding hidden cliques of size $\sqrt{N/e}$ in nearly linear time. In: Foundations of Computational Mathematics (2015)

[DM15b] Deshpande, Y., Montanari, A.: Improved sum-of-squares lower bounds for hidden clique and hidden submatrix problems. In: Proceedings of 28th Conference on Learning Theory (2015)

[ERSY22] Elrazik, R.A., Robere, R., Schuster, A., Yehuda, G.: Pseudorandom self-reductions for NP-complete problems. In: ITCS 2022 (2022)

[FGL+95] Feige, U., Goldwasser, S., Lovász, L., Safra, S., Szegedy, M.: Interactive proofs and the hardness of approximating cliques. J. ACM **43**(2), 268–292 (1995)

[FGN+20] Feige, U., Gamarnik, D., Neeman, J., Rácz, M.Z., Tetali, P.: Finding cliques using few probes. Random Struct. Algorithms **56**(1), 142–153 (2020)

[FGR+13] Feldman, V., Grigorescu, E., Reyzin, L., Vempala, S.S., Xiao, Y.: Statistical algorithms and a lower bound for detecting planted cliques. In: Boneh, D., Roughgarden, T., Feigenbaum, J. (eds.), 45th ACM STOC, pp. 655–664. ACM Press, June 2013

[FK00] Feige, U., Krauthgamer, R.: Finding and certifying a large hidden clique in a semirandom graph. In: Random Structures Algorithms (2000)

[FK03] Feige, U., Krauthgamer, R.: The probable value of the lovász-schrijver relaxations for maximum independent set. In: SIAM Journal of Computing (2003)

[FKN94] Feige, U., Kilian, J., Naor, M.: A minimal model for secure computation (extended abstract). In: Proceedings of the Twenty-Sixth Annual ACM Symposium on Theory of Computing, STOC, vol. 1994, pp. 554–563 (1994)

[FR10] Feige, U., Ron, D.: Finding hidden cliques in linear time. In: 21st International Meeting on Probabilistic, Combinatorial, and Asymptotic Methods in the Analysis of Algorithms (2010)

[GKVZ22] Goldwasser, S., Kim, M.P., Vaikuntanathan, V., Zamir, O.: Planting undetectable backdoors in machine learning models. In: Proceedings of the 63rd IEEE Annual Symposium on Foundations of Computer Science, FOCS 2022 (2022)

[GM75] Grimmett, G.R., McDiarmid, C.J.: On colouring random graphs. In: Mathematical Proceedings of the Cambridge Philosophical Society (1975)

[GS14] Gamarnik, D., Sudan, M.: Limits of local algorithms over sparse random graphs. In: Naor, M. (ed.), ITCS 2014, pp. 369–376. ACM, January 2014

[Hås96a] Håstad, J.: Clique is hard to approximate within $n^{1-\epsilon}$. In: 37th FOCS, pp. 627–636. IEEE Computer Society Press, October 1996

[Hås96b] Håstad, J.: Testing of the long code and hardness for clique. In: 28th ACM STOC, pp. 11–19. ACM Press, May 1996

[HJK+16] Hofheinz, D., Jager, T., Khurana, D., Sahai, A., Waters, B., Zhandry, M.: How to generate and use universal samplers. In: Cheon, J.H., Takagi, T. (eds.) ASIACRYPT 2016, Part II. LNCS, vol. 10032, pp. 715–744. Springer, Heidelberg (2016). https://doi.org/10.1007/978-3-662-53890-6_24

[HK11] Hazan, E., Krauthgamer, R.: How hard is it to approximate the best nash equilibrium? SIAM J. Comput. **40**(1), 79–91 (2011)

[HKP+18] Hopkins, S.B., Kothari, P., Potechin, A.H., Raghavendra, P., Schramm, T.: On the integrality gap of degree-4 sum of squares for planted clique. In: ACM Transactions on Algorithm, vol. 14, no. 3, Article No.: 28, pp. 1–31 (2018)

[Hop18] Hopkins, S.: Statistical inference and the sum of squares method. Phd thesis, Cornell University (2018)

[HWX15] Hajek, B., Wu, Y. and Xu, J.: Computational lower bounds for community detection on random graphs. In: The 28th Annual Conference on Learning Theory, COLT 2015 (2015)

[IK97] shai, Y., Kushilevitz, E.: Private simultaneous messages protocols with applications. In: Proceedings of Fifth Israel Symposium on Theory of Computing and Systems, ISTCS 1997, Ramat-Gan, Israel, 17–19 June 1997, pp. 174–184 (1997)

[IKM+13] Ishai, Y., Kushilevitz, E., Meldgaard, S., Orlandi, C., Paskin-Cherniavsky, A.: On the power of correlated randomness in secure computation. In: Sahai, A. (ed.) TCC 2013. LNCS, vol. 7785, pp. 600–620. Springer, Heidelberg (2013). https://doi.org/10.1007/978-3-642-36594-2_34

[Jer92] Jerrum, M.: Large cliques elude the metropolis process. In: Random Structures and Algorithms (1992)

[JP00] Juels, A.: Peinado, M.: Hiding cliques for cryptographic security. Des. Codes Cryptography **20**, 269–280 (2000)

[Kar72] Karp, R.: Reducibility among combinatorial problems. In: The Complexity of Computer Computations, Plenum Press (1972)

[Kar76] Karp, R.: Probabilistic analysis of some combinatorial search problems. New directions and recent results. In: Algorithms and Complexity (1976)

[KN90] Kilian, J., Nisan, N.: Private communication (1990)

[Kuč95] Kučera, L.: Expected complexity of graph partitioning problems. In: Discrete Applied Mathematics, vol. 57 (1995)

[KZ14] Koiran, P., Zouzias, A.: Hidden cliques and the certification of the restricted isometry property. In: IEEE Transactions on Information Theory (2014)

[LVW17] Liu, T., Vaikuntanathan, V., Wee, H.: Conditional disclosure of secrets via non-linear reconstruction. In: Katz, J., Shacham, H. (eds.) CRYPTO 2017, Part I. LNCS, vol. 10401, pp. 758–790. Springer, Cham (2017). https://doi.org/10.1007/978-3-319-63688-7_25

[McD74] McDiarmid, C.: Colouring random graphs. In: Annals of Operations Research, vol. 1, no. 3 (1974)

[McS01] McSherry, F.: Spectral partitioning of random graphs. In: 42nd FOCS, pp. 529–537. IEEE Computer Society Press, October 2001

[Mer78] Merkle, R.: Secure communications over insecure channels. In: Communications of the ACM (1978)

[MPW15] Meka, R., Potechin, A., Wigderson, A.: Sum-of-squares lower bounds for planted clique. In: Servedio, R.A., Rubinfeld, R. (eds.), 47th ACM STOC, pp. 87–96. ACM Press, June 2015

[MRS21] Manurangsi, P., Rubinstein, A., Schramm, T.: The strongish planted clique hypothesis and its consequences. In: Lee, J.R. (ed.), ITCS 2021, vol. 185, pp. 10:1–10:21. LIPIcs, January 2021

[MW15] Ma, Z., Wu, Y.: Computational barriers in minimax submatrix detection. In: The Annals of Statistics (2015)

[Pit82] Pittel, B.: On the probable behaviour of some algorithms for finding the stability number of a graph. In: Mathematical Proceedings of the Cambridge Philosophical Society (1982)

[Ros08] Rossman, B.: On the constant-depth complexity of k-clique. In: Ladner, R.E., Dwork, C. (eds.), 40th ACM STOC, pp. 721–730. ACM Press, May 2008

[Ros10] Rossman, B.: The monotone complexity of k-clique on random graphs. In: 51st FOCS, pp. 193–201. IEEE Computer Society Press, October 2010

[RV17] Rahman, M., Virag, B.: Local algorithms for independent sets are half-optimal. In: The Annals of Probability (2017)

[SBW19] Shah, N., Balakrishnan, S., Wainwright, M.: Feeling the bern: adaptive estimators for bernoulli probabilities of pairwise comparisons. In: IEEE Transactions
on Information Theory (2019)

[Sha79] Shamir, A.: How to share a secret. Commun. Assoc. Comput. Mach. **22**(11),
612–613 (1979)

[SS97] Sun, H.M., Shieh, S.P.: Secret sharing in graph-based prohibited structures. In:
INFOCOM 1997 (1997)

[WBP16] Wang, T., Berthet, Q., Plan, Y.: Average-case hardness of rip certification.
In: Advances in Neural Information Processing Systems (2016)

Multi-party Computation I

Randomized Functions with High Round Complexity

Saugata Basu[1]([⊠]), Hamidreza Amini Khorasgani[1], Hemanta K. Maji[1], and Hai H. Nguyen[2]

[1] Department of Computer Science, Purdue University, West Lafayette, USA
{sbasu,haminikh,hmaji}@purdue.edu
[2] Department of Computer Science, ETH Zurich, Zürich, Switzerland
haihoang.nguyen@inf.ethz.ch

Abstract. Consider two-party secure function evaluation against an honest-but-curious adversary in the information-theoretic plain model. We study the round complexity of securely realizing a given secure function evaluation functionality.

Chor-Kushilevitz-Beaver (1989) proved that the round complexity of securely evaluating a deterministic function depends solely on the cardinality of its domain and range. A natural conjecture asserts that this phenomenon extends to functions with randomized output.

Our work falsifies this conjecture – revealing intricate subtleties even for this elementary security notion. For every r, we construct a function f_r with binary inputs and five output alphabets that has round complexity r. Previously, such a construction was known using $(r + 1)$ output symbols. Our counter-example is optimal – we prove that any securely realizable function with binary inputs and four output alphabets has round complexity at most four.

We work in the geometric framework Basu-Khorasgani-Maji-Nguyen (FOCS–2022) introduced to investigate randomized functions' round complexity. Our work establishes a connection between secure computation and the lamination hull (geometric object originally motivated by applications in hydrodynamics). Our counterexample constructions are related to the "tartan square" construction in the lamination hull literature.

Keywords: Two-party secure computation · Information-theoretic security · Semi-honest adversary · Round complexity · Geometry of secure computation · Generalized convex hull · Lamination hull · Hydrodynamics

H. H. Nguyen—This work was done while the author was at Purdue.
Basu was partially supported by NSF grants CCF-1910441 and CCF-2128702. Khorasgani, Maji, and Nguyen are supported in part by an NSF CRII Award CNS–1566499, NSF SMALL Awards CNS–1618822 and CNS–2055605, the IARPA HECTOR project, MITRE Innovation Program Academic Cybersecurity Research Awards (2019–2020, 2020–2021), a Ross-Lynn Research Scholars Grant, a Purdue Research Foundation (PRF) Award, and The Center for Science of Information, an NSF Science and Technology Center, Cooperative Agreement CCF–0939370.

G. Rothblum and H. Wee (Eds.): TCC 2023, LNCS 14369, pp. 319–348, 2023.
https://doi.org/10.1007/978-3-031-48615-9_12

1   Introduction

Secure multi-party computation (MPC) [13,18] allows mutually distrusting parties to compute securely over their private data. In general, MPC requires an honest majority or oblivious transfer to compute tasks securely. Even if honest parties are not in the majority, several tasks are securely computable in the information-theoretic plain model without oblivious transfer or other hardness of computation assumptions. For example, the Dutch auction mechanism [6] securely performs auctions. These information-theoretic protocols, if they exist, are highly desirable – they are perfectly secure, fast, and require no setup or preprocessing. With rapid increases in the computational power of parties, the round complexity of these protocols becomes the primary bottleneck, significantly impacting their adoption.

This work studies the round complexity of MPC in the two-party information-theoretic plain model against honest-but-curious adversaries. Alice and Bob have private inputs $x \in X$ and $y \in Y$, respectively, and their objective is to securely sample an output z from the distribution $f(x, y)$ over the sample space Z. The distribution $f(x, y)$ is publicly known, and both parties must receive the identical output z. Parties have unbounded computational power and honestly follow the protocol; however, they are curious to obtain additional information about the other party's private input. An ideal communication channel connects the parties, and they send messages in alternating rounds.[1] The *round complexity* of securely computing f is the (worst-case) minimum number of rounds required to perform this sampling task securely.

We aim to investigate factors causing high round complexity for these secure sampling tasks. Increasing the size of the input or output sets would certainly lead to higher round complexity. However, even after fixing the input and output sets, the complexity of representing the probability distributions could influence the round complexity. There is a natural conjecture in this context.

It is conjectured that only the sizes of the input and output sets determine the round complexity. The complexity of representing the probability distributions $f(x, y)$ is absorbed within the private computation that parties perform, and it does not impact the round complexity.

This (extremely strong) conjecture is known to hold for (a) classical communication complexity where correctness (not security) is considered, (b) the secure computation tasks with deterministic output, and (c) randomized output tasks with a small output set. In the sequel, Sect. 1.1, Sect. 1.2, and Sect. 1.4 present evidence supporting the credibility of this conjecture. Our work refutes this conjecture. Section 2 presents our contributions and Sect. 3 highlights the underlying technical approach.

1.1   Discussion: Interaction in a World Without Security

Consider the *classical communication complexity* objective of correctly (possibly insecurely) evaluating a randomized output function with minimum interaction.

---

[1] Both parties know which party speaks in which round.

In this context, the following canonical interactive protocol is natural. Alice sends her input x to Bob. Bob samples $z \sim f(x, y)$ and sends the output z to Alice.[2] The round complexity of this (insecure) protocol is two. More generally, its communication complexity is $\log \text{card}(X) + \log \text{card}(Z)$, where $\text{card}(S)$ represents the cardinality of the set S. These upper bounds on the interaction complexity hold irrespective of the complexity of representing the individual probabilities $f(x, y)_z$, the probability to output $z \in Z$ conditioned on the input $(x, y) \in X \times Y$. The computational complexity of sampling their output did not overflow into the interaction complexity because its impact was contained within the respective parties' private computation.

1.2 Round Complexity of Deterministic Functions

A particular class of functions widely studied in communication complexity and cryptography is the class of deterministic functions. The function f is deterministic if the support of the distribution $f(x, y)$ is a singleton set for every $(x, y) \in X \times Y$ – the output z is determined entirely by the parties' private inputs (x, y). For example, in an auction, the price is determined by all the bids.

Chor-Kushilevitz-Beaver [4,8,17] characterized all deterministic functions that are securely computable in the two-party information-theoretic plain model against honest-but-curious adversaries. The secure protocols for such functions follow a general template – parties rule out specific outputs in each round. Excluding outputs, in turn, rules out private input pairs (because each input pair produces one output). For example, the Dutch auction mechanism rules out the price that receives no bids. Such functions are called *decomposable functions* because these secure protocols incrementally decompose the feasible input-output space during their evolution. Decomposable functions are securely computable with *perfect security*.

Let us reason about the round complexity of a deterministic function $f \colon X \times Y \to Z$, represented by $\text{round}(f)$. One has to exclude $\text{card}(Z) - 1$ outputs so that only the output $z = f(x, y)$ remains feasible. So, if f has a secure protocol in this model, then

$$\text{round}(f) \leqslant \text{card}(Z) - 1.$$

Furthermore, the Markov property for interactive protocols holds in the information-theoretic plain model. The joint distribution of inputs conditioned on the protocol's evolution is always a product distribution. Excluding output also excludes private inputs of the parties. For example, if Alice sends a message in a round, she rules out some of her private inputs. This observation leads to the bound

$$\text{round}(f) \leqslant 2 \cdot \text{card}(X) - 1.$$

---

[2] We assume that parties have access to randomness with arbitrary bias; more concretely, consider the Blum-Schub-Smale model of computation [5]. For example, parties can have a random bit that is 1 with probability $1/\pi$.

Likewise, we also have

$$\text{round}\,(f) \leqslant 2 \cdot \text{card}\,(Y) - 1.$$

Combining these observations, Chor-Kushilevitz-Beaver [4,8,17] concluded that

$$\text{round}\,(f) \leqslant \min\,\{\text{card}\,(Z), 2 \cdot \text{card}\,(X), 2 \cdot \text{card}\,(Y)\} - 1. \tag{1}$$

The cardinalities of the private input and output sets determine the upper bound on the round complexity of f if it has a secure protocol. This phenomenon from the classical communication complexity extends to the cryptographic context for deterministic functions.

1.3 Round Complexity of Randomized Functions with Small Output Set

For functions with randomized output, the first conjecture already holds for small values of $\text{card}\,(Z)$. For example, $\text{card}\,(Z) \leqslant 3$ implies that $\text{round}\,(f) \leqslant 2$ [11]. In fact, this paper will prove that $\text{card}\,(Z) \leqslant 4$ implies $\text{round}\,(f) \leqslant 4$. It is fascinating that the complexity of sampling from the distributions $f(x, y)$ does not impact the round complexity; its role is localized to the parties' private computation.

1.4 Round Complexity of Randomized Functions (General Case)

For three decades, there was essentially no progress in determining the round complexity of securely computing general randomized functions – barring a few highly specialized cases [11]. Last year, Basu, Khorasgani, Maji, and Nguyen (FOCS 2022) [1] showed that determining "whether a randomized f has an r-round protocol or not" is decidable. They reduced this question to a geometric analog: "does a query point Q belong to a recursively-generated set $\mathcal{S}^{(r)}$." They start with an initial set of points $\mathcal{S}^{(0)}$, and recursively build $\mathcal{S}^{(i+1)}$ from the set $\mathcal{S}^{(i)}$ using a geometric action, for $i \in \{0, 1, \dots\}$. The function f has an (at most) r-round protocol if (and only if) a specific query point Q belongs to the set $\mathcal{S}^{(r)}$.

These set of points $\{\mathcal{S}^{(i)}\}_{i \geqslant 0}$ lie in the ambient space

$$\mathbb{R}^{\text{card}(X)-1} \times \mathbb{R}^{\text{card}(Y)-1} \times \mathbb{R}^{\text{card}(Z)}.$$

Again, the dimension of the ambient space (of their embedding) is determined entirely by the cardinalities of the inputs and output sets. This feature of their embedding added additional support to the conjecture.

Consider an analogy from geometry. Consider n initial points in $\mathbb{R}^d$, where $n \gg d$. At the outset, any point inside the convex hull can be expressed as a convex linear combination of the initial points that lie on the convex hull; their number can be $\gg d$. However, Carathéodory's theorem [7] states that every point in its interior is expressible as a convex linear combination of (at most) $(d+1)$

initial points on the convex hull. At an abstract level: *canonical representations may have significantly lower complexity*. It is similar to the Pumping lemma for regular languages and (more generally) the Ogden lemma for context-free languages.

Likewise, a fascinating possibility opens up in the context of Basu et al.'s geometric problem. The canonical protocol for f could have round complexity determined solely by the dimension of their ambient space, which (in turn) is determined by the cardinality of the input and output sets. In fact, an optimistic conjecture of $\mathcal{O}\left(\operatorname{card}(Z)^2\right)$ upper bound on the round complexity appears in the full version of their paper [2, Section 7, Conjecture 1].

We Refute This Conjecture. The analogies break exactly at $|Z| = 5$. Represent a randomized function with input set $X \times Y$ and output set Z as $f \colon X \times Y \to \mathbb{R}^Z$. For every $r \in \{1, 2, \dots\}$, we construct a function $f_r \colon \{0,1\} \times \{0,1\} \to \mathbb{R}^{\{1,2,3,4,5\}}$ with round complexity r. Previously, Basu et al. constructed functions $g_r \colon \{0,1\} \times \{0,1\} \to \mathbb{R}^{\{1,2,\dots,r+1\}}$ with round complexity r, i.e., their example had $\operatorname{card}(Z) = (r+1)$. In our example, $\operatorname{card}(Z) = 5$, a constant. Moreover, we prove the optimality of the counterexamples: Any $f \colon \{0,1\} \times \{0,1\} \to \mathbb{R}^{\{1,2,3,4\}}$ has round complexity $\leqslant 4$.

Looking Ahead. Our results indicate that any upper bound on the round complexity of f must involve the complexity of representing (the probabilities appearing in) the function f. For example, consider a randomized function whose probabilities are integral multiples of $1/B$. Then, the round complexity of f should be upper bounded by some function of $\operatorname{card}(X)$, $\operatorname{card}(Y)$, $\operatorname{card}(Z)$, and B. The B-term represents (intuitively) "the condition number of the function f." If this dependence on B can, in fact, be a $\operatorname{poly}(\log(B))$ dependence, then it will lead to efficient secure algorithms, ones with round complexity of $\operatorname{poly}(\log B)$.

Our work considers the round complexity of perfectly secure protocols. The case of statistically secure protocols remains an interesting open problem. In fact, the decidability of the question: "Is there an r-round ε-secure protocol for f?" remains unknown, which is a more fundamental problem. Basu et al. [1] only considered the perfect security case. The technical machinery to handle statistical security for general randomized output functions *does not exist. This work does not contribute to these two research directions.*

1.5   Overview of the Paper

We discuss our contributions in Sect. 2. In Sect. 3, we provide a technical overview of our paper. In Sect. 4, we discuss the relation of our work with lamination hull. Section 5 presents the BKMN geometric framework. Section 6 introduces notations and preliminaries. Section 7 contains all results pertaining to constructing high-round complexity randomized functions. Section 8 shows that our counterexamples are optimal.

2   Our Contributions

Theorem 1 (Functions with arbitrarily high round complexity). *For any $r \in \{1, 2, \ldots, \}$, there is a function $f_r \colon \{0,1\} \times \{0,1\} \to \mathbb{R}^{\{1,2,3,4,5\}}$ such that* round $(f_r) = r$.

The function f_r has an r-round perfectly secure protocol (and r bits of communication) but no $(r-1)$-round perfectly secure protocol. This result proves that there are functions with arbitrary large round complexity with a constant input and output set size. Previously, Basu et al. [1] constructed functions with high round complexity with $(r+1)$ output alphabets. This result is a counterexample to the folklore conjecture. Section 7 presents the definition of the functions and the proof.

Our counterexample is also optimal, which is a consequence of our following result.

Theorem 2 (Bounded Round Complexity for card $(Z) \leqslant 4$**).** *Any function $f \colon \{0,1\} \times \{0,1\} \to \mathbb{R}^Z$ with* card $(Z) \leqslant 4$ *has* round $(f) \leqslant 4$.

Section 8 proves this theorem.

3   Technical Overview of Our Results

The presentation in this work is entirely geometric. *No background in security is necessary.* We use the geometric embedding of BKMN [1] to translate round complexity problems into geometric problems. Security is already folded inside their geometric embedding.

3.1   High-Level Summary of the BKMN Geometric Framework

Section 5 presents a detailed version of this section. Consider a randomized output function $f \colon \{0,1\} \times \{0,1\} \to \mathbb{R}^Z$. BKMN approach considers the ambient space $\mathbb{R}^d$, where $d = \text{card}(Z) + 2$. They present the following maps

1. Function encoding. $f \mapsto (A, B, V)$, where the matrix $A \in \mathcal{M}_{2 \times \text{card}(Z)}(\mathbb{R})^3$, the matrix $B \in \mathcal{M}_{2 \times \text{card}(Z)}(\mathbb{R})$, and the vector $V \in \mathbb{R}^{\text{card}(Z)}$
2. Query point. $f \mapsto Q(f) \in \mathbb{R}^{\text{card}(Z)}$
3. Initial set. $(A, B) \mapsto \mathcal{S}^{(0)} \subseteq \mathbb{R}^d$ satisfying card $(\mathcal{S}^{(0)}) = \text{card}(Z)$.

They present the following recursive definition of $\mathcal{S}^{(i+1)} \subseteq \mathbb{R}^d$ from $\mathcal{S}^{(i)} \subseteq \mathbb{R}^d$, for all $i \in \{0, 1, \ldots\}$.

$$
\mathcal{S}^{(i+1)} = \left\{ \sum_{k=1}^{t} \lambda^{(k)} \cdot Q^{(k)} : \begin{array}{l} t \in \{1, 2, \ldots\}, \\ \lambda^{(1)}, \lambda^{(2)}, \ldots, \lambda^{(t)} \geqslant 0, \\ \lambda^{(1)} + \lambda^{(2)} + \cdots + \lambda^{(t)} = 1, \\ Q^{(1)}, Q^{(2)}, \ldots, Q^{(t)} \in \mathcal{S}^{(i)}, \text{ and} \\ \left(Q_1^{(1)} = Q_1^{(2)} = \cdots = Q_1^{(t)} \text{ or} \right. \\ \left. Q_2^{(1)} = Q_2^{(2)} = \cdots = Q_2^{(t)} \right) \end{array} \right\}.
$$

---

[3] $\mathcal{M}_{m \times n}(\mathbb{R})$ denotes the set of all m-by-n matrices with elements in $\mathbb{R}$.

Intuitively, this recursive definition ensures the following. Pick any t points $Q^{(1)}, Q^{(2)}, \ldots, Q^{(t)} \in \mathcal{S}^{(i)}$, where $t \in \{1, 2, \ldots\}$. If the first coordinates of all these t points are identical, or the second coordinates of all these t points are identical, then add all possible convex linear combinations (i.e., the convex hull) of $\{Q^{(1)}, Q^{(2)}, \ldots, Q^{(t)}\}$ to the set $\mathcal{S}^{(i+1)}$.

Remark 1 (Communication complexity). Restricting the recursive definition to $t = 2$ corresponds to investigating the communication complexity of f. This version of the recursion is closely connected to the lamination hull defined in Sect. 4.

Observe that, in the recursive definition, the points need not be distinct. Therefore, choosing $Q^{(1)} = Q^{(2)} = \cdots = Q^{(t)}$ ensures that $\mathcal{S}^{(i)} \subseteq \mathcal{S}^{(i+1)}$. Using this recursive definition, we have the following sequence of sets in $\mathbb{R}^d$:

$$\mathcal{S}^{(0)} \subseteq \mathcal{S}^{(1)} \subseteq \mathcal{S}^{(2)} \subseteq \cdots$$

Connection to Round Complexity of Secure Computation. BKMN [1] proved that, for all $r \in \{0, 1, \ldots\}$, round $(f) \leqslant r$ if and only if $Q(f) \in \mathcal{S}^{(r)}$. Therefore, to prove round $(f) = r$, it suffices to prove that $Q(f) \in \mathcal{S}^{(r)} \setminus \mathcal{S}^{(r-1)}$.

3.2 The "Tartan Square" Meets Secure Computation

Our objective is to prove that there is a function $f_r \colon \{0, 1\} \times \{0, 1\} \to \mathbb{R}^Z$, where $Z = \{1, 2, \ldots, 5\}$, such that $f_r \in \mathcal{S}^{(r)} \setminus \mathcal{S}^{(r-1)}$, for every $r \in \{1, 2, \ldots\}$. Recall that $\mathcal{S}^{(0)}$ is determined by f_r and card $(\mathcal{S}^{(0)}) = \text{card}(Z) = 5$. Furthermore, all the sets $\mathcal{S}^{(i)}$ are in ambient space $\mathbb{R}^7$, for $i \in \{0, 1, \ldots\}$.

A preliminary step towards designing such functions is to determine an initial set of points $\mathcal{S}^{(0)}$ such that we have

$$\mathcal{S}^{(0)} \subsetneq \mathcal{S}^{(1)} \subsetneq \mathcal{S}^{(2)} \subsetneq \cdots$$

Otherwise, suppose $\mathcal{S}^{(i)} = \mathcal{S}^{(i+1)}$, for some $i \in \{0, 1, \ldots\}$. Then, $\mathcal{S}^{(j)} = \mathcal{S}^{(i)}$, for all $j \geqslant i$, and the round complexity cannot surpass i. So, our objective is to construct an *initial set $\mathcal{S}^{(0)}$ of constant size in an ambient space of constant dimension* such that the evolution of the sequence $\mathcal{S}^{(0)} \to \mathcal{S}^{(1)} \to \mathcal{S}^{(2)} \to \cdots$ does not stabilize. It is unclear whether such an initial set $\mathcal{S}^{(0)}$ even exists.

Illustrative Example. We present an initial set $\mathcal{S}^{(0)} \subseteq \mathbb{R}^3$ such that the evolution of the recursively defined sets does not stabilize. We emphasize that this illustrative example is for intuition purposes only. The actual constructions are presented in Sect. 7, where the ambient space is $\mathbb{R}^7$.

We work in the ambient space $\mathbb{R}^3$ for the illustrative example. Consider an initial set of points

$$\mathbb{R}^3 \supseteq \mathcal{S}^{(0)} := \Big\{ (2, 0, 0),\ (0, 1, 0),\ (1, 3, 0),\ (3, 2, 0),\ (2, 1, 1) \Big\}$$

1. For example, consider the points $(0, 1, 0)$ and $(2, 1, 1)$ in the set $\mathcal{S}^{(0)}$. The recursive definition allows the addition of the line segment $\overline{PQ}$ to the set $\mathcal{S}^{(1)}$. In particular, this line segment's midpoint $(1, 1, 1/2)$ is in the set $\mathcal{S}^{(1)}$.
2. Similarly, considering the points $(1, 3, 0)$ and $(1, 1, 1/2)$ in the set $\mathcal{S}^{(1)}$, we conclude that their midpoint $(1, 2, 1/4)$ is in the set $\mathcal{S}^{(2)}$.
3. Now, consider the points $(3, 2, 0)$ and $(1, 2, 1/4)$ in the set $\mathcal{S}^{(2)}$. Their midpoint $(2, 2, 1/8)$ is in the set $\mathcal{S}^{(3)}$.
4. Finally, the midpoint of the points $(2, 0, 0)$ and $(2, 2, 1/8)$ in the set $\mathcal{S}^{(3)}$ is $(2, 1, 1/16)$, which is in the set $\mathcal{S}^{(4)}$.

Let us summarize what we have achieved thus far. Beginning with the point $(2, 1, 1) \in \mathcal{S}^{(0)}$, we identified the point $(2, 1, 1/16) \in \mathcal{S}^{(4)}$. One can prove that this point $(2, 1, 1/16) \notin \mathcal{S}^{(3)}$. Therefore, we conclude that the point $(2, 1, 1/16) \in \mathcal{S}^{(4)} \setminus \mathcal{S}^{(3)}$.

Using analogous steps as above, starting instead with the point $(2, 1, 1/16) \in \mathcal{S}^{(4)} \setminus \mathcal{S}^{(3)}$ will lead to the point $\left(2, 1, 1/(16)^2\right) \in \mathcal{S}^{(8)} \setminus \mathcal{S}^{(7)}$ In general, using this construction, we will have

$$\left(2, 1, \frac{1}{16^k}\right) \in \mathcal{S}^{(4k)} \setminus \mathcal{S}^{(4k-1)}.$$

This sequence of points, for $k \in \{0, 1, 2, \dots\}$, demonstrate that the sequence $\mathcal{S}^{(0)} \to \mathcal{S}^{(1)} \to \mathcal{S}^{(2)} \to \cdots$ does not stabilize. This example is the "tartan square" from the lamination hull literature; refer to Remark 2 in Sect. 4.

This illustrative example leads to the following conclusion. In an ambient space of constant dimension and starting with a suitable initial set $\mathcal{S}^{(0)}$ of constant size, the sequence $\mathcal{S}^{(0)} \to \mathcal{S}^{(1)} \to \mathcal{S}^{(2)} \to \cdots$ may not stabilize.

3.3 Overview: Proof of Theorem 1

For $r \in \{1, 2, \dots\}$, we will appropriately choose the probabilities of the function $f_r \colon \{0, 1\} \times \{0, 1\} \to \mathbb{R}^Z$, such that $\operatorname{card}(Z) = 5$. Using the BKMN geometric framework (see Sect. 3.1), we will generate:

1. Function encoding (A, B, V_r). We emphasize that all our functions f_r are designed so that they map to the same (A, B); only V_r is different.
2. Query point $Q(f_r) \in \mathbb{R}^7$.
3. Initial point set $\mathcal{S}^{(0)} \subseteq \mathbb{R}^7$, which is identical for all f_r because (a) all functions map to identical (A, B), and (b) (A, B) alone determine $\mathcal{S}^{(0)}$.

Sect. 5.1 presents the definition of the function f_r.

Next, the choice of the $\mathcal{S}^{(0)}$ ensures that the evolution of the sets $\mathcal{S}^{(0)} \to \mathcal{S}^{(1)} \to \mathcal{S}^{(2)} \to \cdots$ does not stabilize. It essentially mimics the tartan square construction of Sect. 3.2. However, we emphasize that in this section, the ambient space is $\mathbb{R}^7$ (the ambient space for the tartan square example was $\mathbb{R}^3$). Furthermore, we design our function f_r such that the corresponding query point $Q(f_r) \in \mathcal{S}^{(r)} \setminus \mathcal{S}^{(r-1)}$. Consequently, we have $\operatorname{round}(f_r) = r$.

3.4   Overview: Proof of Theorem 2

We aim to prove that $\text{round}(f) \leqslant 4$, for any function $f\colon \{0,1\} \times \{0,1\} \to \mathbb{R}^Z$ such that $\text{card}(Z) \leqslant 4$. Toward this objective, we begin with the following observations.

1. Recall that in the BKMN framework $\text{card}(\mathcal{S}^{(0)}) = \text{card}(Z)$.
2. Furthermore, if $\mathcal{S}^{(4)} = \mathcal{S}^{(5)}$, then $\mathcal{S}^{(j)} = \mathcal{S}^{(4)}$, for all $j \geqslant 4$. In this case, $\text{round}(f) \leqslant 4$, because $\mathcal{S}^{(r)} \setminus \mathcal{S}^{(r-1)} = \emptyset$, for all $r \in \{5, 6, \dots\}$.

To prove our theorem, it will suffice to prove that the evolution of the sets $\mathcal{S}^{(0)} \to \mathcal{S}^{(1)} \to \mathcal{S}^{(2)} \to \cdots$ stabilizes by $i = 4$ when $\text{card}(\mathcal{S}^{(0)}) \leqslant 4$.[4] We prove this result using an exhaustive case analysis (see Sect. 8).

4   Lamination Hull

Consider an ambient space $\mathbb{R}^d$. The *lamination hull* is parameterized by a set of points $\Lambda \subseteq \mathbb{R}^d$. Given a set of initial point $\mathcal{S}^{(0,\Lambda)} \subseteq \mathbb{R}^d$, recursively define $\mathcal{S}^{(i+1,\Lambda)}$ from $\mathcal{S}^{(i)}$ as follows

$$\mathcal{S}^{(i+1,\Lambda)} := \left\{ \lambda \cdot Q^{(1)} + (1-\lambda) \cdot Q^{(2)} : \begin{array}{l} Q^{(1)}, Q^{(2)} \in \mathcal{S}^{(i,\Lambda)}, \\ \lambda \in [0,1], \text{ and} \\ Q^{(1)} - Q^{(2)} \in \Lambda \end{array} \right\}.$$

Intuitively, one can add the line segment $\overline{Q^{(1)}Q^{(2)}}$ to the set $\mathcal{S}^{(i+1,\Lambda)}$ for any $Q^{(1)}, Q^{(2)} \in \mathcal{S}^{(i,\Lambda)}$ if $Q^{(1)} - Q^{(2)} \in \Lambda$. The lamination hull is the limit of the sequence $\mathcal{S}^{(0,\Lambda)} \to \mathcal{S}^{(1,\Lambda)} \to \mathcal{S}^{(2,\Lambda)} \to \cdots$. This hull is tied to computing the stationary solutions to the following differential equations underlying incompressible porous media [9,10,12,14].

Incompressible Porous Media (IPM) Equations

Conservation of Mass, Incompressibility, and Darcy's Law

$$\partial_t \rho + \nabla \cdot (\rho \boldsymbol{v}) = 0, \qquad \nabla \cdot \boldsymbol{v} = 0, \qquad \frac{\mu}{\kappa} \boldsymbol{v} = -\nabla p - \rho \boldsymbol{g}, \qquad (2)$$

where ρ is the fluid density, $\boldsymbol{v}$ is the fluid velocity, and $\boldsymbol{g}$ is the gravity.

When $\Lambda = (0, \mathbb{R}, \dots, \mathbb{R}) \cup (\mathbb{R}, 0, \mathbb{R}, \dots, \mathbb{R}) \subseteq \mathbb{R}^d$, the sequence $\mathcal{S}^{(0,\Lambda)} \to \mathcal{S}^{(1,\Lambda)} \to \mathcal{S}^{(2,\Lambda)} \to \cdots$ is identical to the sequence defined by Basu et al. [1] for the communication complexity case (see Remark 1). Basu et al. [1] proved that the points in the recursively defined sets are related to secure computation protocols. As a consequence of this connection, secure computation protocols manifest in physical processes in nature. This connection is mentioned in [3, Page 20].

---

[4] We highlight a subtlety. We only need to prove that $\mathcal{S}^{(4)} = \mathcal{S}^{(5)}$. It is inconsequential if they have stabilized even earlier. For example, it may be the case that $\mathcal{S}^{(j)} = \mathcal{S}^{(j+1)}$ for some $j \in \{0,1,2,3\}$.

Remark 2 (Independent discovery of the "tartan square" construction). Our work independently discovered the "tartan square" construction in the lamination hull literature [16, Figure 2, Page 3]. Consider ambient dimension $\mathbb{R}^3$ and $\Lambda = (0, \mathbb{R}, \mathbb{R}) \cup (\mathbb{R}, 0, \mathbb{R}) \subseteq \mathbb{R}^d$. The "tartan square" is a set of 5 points in $\mathbb{R}^3$ such that the sequence $\mathcal{S}^{(0,\Lambda)} \to \mathcal{S}^{(1,\Lambda)} \to \mathcal{S}^{(2,\Lambda)} \to \cdots$ does not stabilize. Section 3 uses this example to provide the intuition underlying our counterexample constructions.

5   BKMN Geometric Framework: A Formal Introduction

Basu-Khorasgani-Maji-Nguyen [1] presents a new approach for studying the round complexity of any (symmetric) functionality $f \colon X \times Y \to \mathbb{R}^Z$. In the following discussion, we shall recall this approach for the particular case where the input domain satisfies $X = Y = \{0, 1\}$.

From the given functionality f, BKMN22 defines the following maps.

1. Function encoding: $f \mapsto (A, B, V)$
2. Query point: $f \mapsto Q(f)$
3. Initial set: $(A, B) \mapsto \mathcal{S}^{(0)}$
4. Recursive construction: $\mathcal{S}^{(i)} \mapsto \mathcal{S}^{(i+1)}$ for any $i \in \{0, 1, 2, \dots\}$.

Function Encoding

There are matrices $A \in \mathcal{M}_{2 \times \mathrm{card}(Z)}(\mathbb{R})$, $B \in \mathcal{M}_{2 \times \mathrm{card}(Z)}(\mathbb{R})$, and vector $V \in \mathbb{R}^{\mathrm{card}(Z)}$ such that

$$f(x, y)_z = A_{x,z} \cdot B_{y,z} \cdot V_z \text{ for all } x \in X, y \in Y, z \in Z, \text{ and}$$

$$\sum_{x \in X} A_{x,z} = 1, \qquad \sum_{y \in Y} B_{y,z} = 1 \text{ for all } z \in Z.^a$$

---

^{a} If such an encoding does not exist, there is no secure protocol for f [15].

The query point $Q(f)$ is constructed as follows.

Query Point Construction

$$Q(f) := \left(1/2,\ 1/2,\ \frac{1}{4} \cdot V \right) \in \mathbb{R} \times \mathbb{R} \times \mathbb{R}^{\mathrm{card}(Z)}$$

The initial set $\mathcal{S}^{(0)}$ is constructed from (A, B) as follows.

Constructing the initial set $\mathcal{S}^{(0)}$ from (A, B)

$$\mathcal{S}^{(0)} := \{(A_{0,z}, B_{0,z}, e(z)) \colon z \in Z\} \subseteq \mathbb{R}^d,$$

where $d := \operatorname{card}(Z) + 2$, and $e(z)$ is the standard unit vector whose coordinates are all zeros except that the z-th coordinate is one.

They consider the sequence $\mathcal{S}^{(0)}, \mathcal{S}^{(1)}, \ldots, \mathcal{S}^{(i)}, \ldots$ where for any $i \in \{0, 1, \ldots\}$, the geometric action that recursively generates $\mathcal{S}^{(i+1)}$ from $\mathcal{S}^{(i)}$ is defined as follows:

Geometric Action: Constructing $\mathcal{S}^{(i+1)}$ from $\mathcal{S}^{(i)}$

For any $t \in \{1, 2, \ldots\}$ and points $Q^{(1)}, Q^{(2)}, \ldots, Q^{(t)} \in \mathcal{S}^{(i)}$, add all convex linear combinations of the points $\{Q^{(1)}, Q^{(2)}, \ldots, Q^{(t)}\}$ to the set $\mathcal{S}^{(i+1)}$ if (and only if)

1. $Q_1^{(1)} = Q_1^{(2)} = \cdots = Q_1^{(t)}$, or
2. $Q_2^{(1)} = Q_2^{(2)} = \cdots = Q_2^{(t)}$.

For a point $Q \in \mathbb{R}^d$, Q_1 represents the first coordinate of Q, and Q_2 represents the second coordinate of Q.

Some Clarifications.

1. A convex linear combination of the points $Q^{(1)}, \ldots, Q^{(t)}$, is a point of the form $\lambda^{(1)} \cdot Q^{(1)} + \cdots + \lambda^{(t)} \cdot Q^{(t)}$, where $\lambda^{(1)}, \ldots, \lambda^{(t)} \geqslant 0$ and $\sum_{i=1}^{t} \lambda^{(i)} = 1$. All possible convex linear combinations consider all possible such $\lambda^{(1)}, \ldots \lambda^{(t)}$ values.
2. The points $Q^{(1)}, \ldots, Q^{(t)}$ in the definition need not be distinct
3. Considering $t = 1$ in the definition above ensures that $\mathcal{S}^{(i)} \subseteq \mathcal{S}^{(i+1)}$.
4. Since efficiency is not a consideration in the current context, we consider $t \in \{1, 2, \ldots\}$. Otherwise, by Carathéodory's theorem [7], it suffices to consider only $t = (d + 1)$.

BKMN's Reduction. Given the initial set $\mathcal{S}^{(0)}$, one constructs the sequence $\mathcal{S}^{(0)} \to \mathcal{S}^{(1)} \to \mathcal{S}^{(2)} \to \ldots$ recursively based on the geometric action. Basu et al. reduce the problem of the round complexity of secure computation of randomized functions to the problem of testing whether a point belongs to a set in a high dimensional space.

5.1 An Example

In this section, we consider an example and find the corresponding encoding, query point, and sets $S^{(0)}, S^{(1)}, \dots$ based on BKMN's approach. For any $r = 4k + 1$ where $k \in \{0, 1, \dots\}$, we construct a functionality $f_r \colon \{0, 1\} \times \{0, 1\} \to \mathbb{R}^{\{1,2,3,4,5\}}$ and then show in Sect. 7 that round $(f_r) = r$. We emphasize that it is also possible to construct such functionality for the cases that $r = 4k$ or $r = 4k + 2$ or $r = 4k + 3$ where $k \in \{0, 1, 2, \dots\}$.

Consider the following functionality

$$f_{4k+1}(0,0) = \left(\frac{3}{16} \cdot \sigma_k, \ \frac{1}{4} \cdot \sigma_{k+1}, \ \frac{1}{8} \cdot \sigma_k, \ \frac{3}{8} \cdot \sigma_k, \ \frac{3}{2^{4k+2}} \right),$$

$$f_{4k+1}(0,1) = \left(\frac{9}{16} \cdot \sigma_k, \ \frac{1}{4} \cdot \sigma_{k+1}, \ 0 \cdot \sigma_k, \ \frac{1}{8} \cdot \sigma_k, \ \frac{3}{2^{4k+2}} \right),$$

$$f_{4k+1}(1,0) = \left(\frac{1}{16} \cdot \sigma_k, \ \frac{3}{4} \cdot \sigma_{k+1}, \ \frac{1}{8} \cdot \sigma_k, \ 0 \cdot \sigma_k, \ \frac{1}{2^{4k+2}} \right),$$

$$f_{4k+1}(1,1) = \left(\frac{3}{16} \cdot \sigma_k, \ \frac{3}{4} \cdot \sigma_{k+1}, \ 0 \cdot \sigma_k, \ 0 \cdot \sigma_k, \ \frac{1}{2^{4k+2}} \right),$$

where $\sigma_k := \frac{1-(1/16)^k}{1-1/16}$ for $k \in \{0, 1, 2, \dots\}$. Following BKMN's approach (refer to Sect. 5), the encoding of f_{4k+1} is the triplet (A, B, V_{4k+1}), where

$$A = \begin{pmatrix} 3/4, & 1/4, & 1/2, & 1, & 3/4 \\ 1/4, & 3/4, & 1/2, & 0, & 1/4 \end{pmatrix} \in \mathcal{M}_{2\times 5}(\mathbb{R}),$$

$$B = \begin{pmatrix} 1/4, & 1/2, & 1, & 3/4, & 1/2 \\ 3/4, & 1/2, & 0, & 1/4, & 1/2 \end{pmatrix} \in \mathcal{M}_{2\times 5}(\mathbb{R}),$$

$$V_{4k+1} = \left(\sigma_k, 2\sigma_{k+1}, \frac{\sigma_k}{4}, \frac{\sigma_k}{2}, \frac{1}{2^{4k-1}} \right) \in \mathbb{R}^5.$$

Note that the first row of matrix A corresponds to input $X = 0$, and its second row corresponds to $X = 1$. Similarly, the first row of B corresponds to input $Y = 0$, and the other row corresponds to $Y = 1$. The initial set $S^{(0)}$ is derived from (A, B, V_{4k+1}) as follows.

$$S^{(0)} = \{P^{(z)} \colon z \in \{1, 2, 3, 4, 5\}\}, \text{ where}$$
$$P^{(1)} = (3/4, \ 1/4, \ 1, 0, 0, 0, 0),$$

$$P^{(2)} = (1/4, \ 1/2, \ 0, 1, 0, 0, 0),$$
$$P^{(3)} = (1/2, \ \ 1 \ \ , \ 0, 0, 1, 0, 0),$$
$$P^{(4)} = (\ \ 1 \ \ , \ 3/4, \ 0, 0, 0, 1, 0),$$
$$P^{(5)} = (3/4, \ 1/2, \ 0, 0, 0, 0, 1).$$

Note that $\mathcal{S}^{(i)} \subseteq \mathbb{R}^7$ for all $i \in \{0, 1, \dots\}$. The query point is defined as

$$Q(f_{4k+1}) = \left(\frac{1}{2}, \ \frac{1}{2}, \ \frac{1}{4} \cdot \frac{\sigma_k}{4}, \ \frac{\sigma_{k+1}}{2}, \ \frac{\sigma_k}{16}, \ \frac{\sigma_k}{8}, \ \frac{1}{2^{4k+1}} \right) \in \mathbb{R}^7.$$

To prove that $round(f_{4k+1}) = 4k + 1$, it suffices to prove the following result.

Lemma 1. *It holds that* $Q(f_{4k+1}) \in \mathcal{S}^{(4k+1)} \setminus \mathcal{S}^{(4k)}$.

We provide a proof for Lemma 1 in Sect. 7 (refer to the proof of Theorem 3).

6 Preliminaries

This section introduces some notations and definitions to facilitate our presentation.

6.1 Notations

We will use the following notations for a point $p \in \mathbb{R}^d$, a scalar $c \in \mathbb{R}$, and a set $\mathcal{S} \subseteq \mathbb{R}^d$.

$$p + \mathcal{S} := \{p + q \colon q \in \mathcal{S}\}, \quad c \cdot \mathcal{S} := \{c \cdot q \colon q \in \mathcal{S}\}.$$

We use the standard notations $\setminus, \cup, \cap$ to denote the minus, union, and intersection operators on sets, respectively.

6.2 Convex Geometry

For any two points $x, y \in \mathbb{R}^d$, the *line segment* between x and y, denoted as $\overline{xy}$, is the set of all points $t \cdot x + (1 - t) \cdot y$ for $t \in [0, 1]$. A subset of $\mathbb{R}^d$ is a *convex set* if, given any two points in the subset, the subset contains the whole line segment joining them. A *convex combination* is a linear combination of points in which all coefficients are non-negative and sum up to 1. An *extreme point* of a convex set $S \subseteq \mathbb{R}^d$ is a point that does not lie on any open line segment joining two distinct points of S.

Definition 1 (Convex Hull). *For any set* $S \subseteq \mathbb{R}^d$, *the convex hull of* S, *denoted as* $\mathsf{conv}(S)$, *is the set of all convex combinations of points in* S.

For example, every line segment is the convex hull of the two endpoints. The following facts follow directly from the definition of the convex hull.

Fact 1. *For any subset* $S \subseteq \mathbb{R}^d$, *it holds that* $\mathsf{conv}(\mathsf{conv}(S)) = \mathsf{conv}(S)$.

Fact 2. *For any* $S \subseteq T \subseteq \mathbb{R}^d$, *it holds that* $\mathsf{conv}(S) \subseteq \mathsf{conv}(T)$.

7   Functions with High Round Complexity

This section provides a formal proof for Theorem 1 restated as follows.

Theorem 3. *For every $r \in \mathbb{N}$, there exists a function $f_r \colon \{0,1\} \times \{0,1\} \to \mathbb{R}^Z$ such that $\mathrm{card}\,(Z) = 5$ and f_r has r-round perfectly secure protocol but no $(r-1)$-round secure protocol.*

We begin with introducing some notations. Let $P = (P_1, P_2, P_3, P_4, P_5, P_6, P_7)$ denote a point in $\mathbb{R}^2 \times \mathbb{R}^5$. We define the following projections

$$
\begin{aligned}
\pi &\colon \mathbb{R}^2 \times \mathbb{R}^5 \to \mathbb{R}^2, & \pi(P) &:= (P_1, P_2) \\
\pi_1 &\colon \mathbb{R}^2 \times \mathbb{R}^5 \to \mathbb{R}, & \pi_1(P) &:= P_1 \\
\pi_2 &\colon \mathbb{R}^2 \times \mathbb{R}^5 \to \mathbb{R}, & \pi_2(P) &:= P_2 \\
\rho &\colon \mathbb{R}^2 \times \mathbb{R}^5 \to \mathbb{R}^5, & \rho(P) &:= (P_3, P_4, P_5, P_6, P_7)
\end{aligned}
$$

We use $e_i \in \mathbb{R}^5$, where $i \in \{1, \ldots, 5\}$, to represent the ith vector of the standard basis for $\mathbb{R}^5$. All coordinates of e_i are 0 except the ith coordinate, which is equal to 1. For example, if $P = (1/4, 1/2, 0, 1, 0, 0, 0)$, then

$$\pi(P) = (1/4, 1/2), \quad \pi_1(P) = 1/4, \pi_2(P) = 1/2, \quad \rho(P) = (0, 1, 0, 0, 0) = e_2.$$

Our Initial Set of Points. We define the following five points in $\mathbb{R}^2$

$$a_1 = (3/4, 1/4), \ a_2 = (1/4, 1/2), \ a_3 = (1/2, 1), \ a_4 = (1, 3/4), \ a_5 = (3/4, 1/2).$$

The initial set $\mathcal{S}^{(0)}$ is defined as

$$\mathcal{S}^{(0)} := \{P \in \mathbb{R}^2 \times \mathbb{R}^5 \colon \exists\, i \in \{1, 2, 3, 4, 5\}, \ \pi(P) = a_i \text{ and } \rho(P) = e_i\}.$$

Recursive construction of $\mathcal{S}^{(i)}$. For $i \in \{1, 2, \ldots\}$, let $\mathcal{S}^{(i)} \subseteq \mathbb{R}^2 \times \mathbb{R}^5$ be the set defined recursively from $\mathcal{S}^{(i-1)}$ according to Fig. 1.

For $t \in \{1, 2, \ldots\}$ and any points $Q^{(1)}, Q^{(2)}, \ldots, Q^{(t)} \in \mathcal{S}^{(i-1)}$ satisfying

$$\pi_1(Q^{(1)}) = \pi_1(Q^{(2)}) = \cdots = \pi_1(Q^{(t)}), \text{ or}$$
$$\pi_2(Q^{(1)}) = \pi_2(Q^{(2)}) = \cdots = \pi_2(Q^{(t)})$$

add all possible convex linear combinations of $Q^{(1)}, Q^{(2)}, \ldots, Q^{(t)}$ to the set $\mathcal{S}^{(i)}$.

Fig. 1. Recursive procedure to construct $\mathcal{S}^{(i)}$ from $\mathcal{S}^{(i-1)}$ for $i \in \{1, 2, \ldots\}$.

In addition to Theorem 3, we shall also prove the following result.

Theorem 4 (Does not Stabilize). *For all $i \in \{1, 2, \ldots\}$, $\mathcal{S}^{(i-1)} \subsetneq \mathcal{S}^{(i)}$.*

Intuitively, the choice of the $\mathcal{S}^{(0)}$ ensures that the evolution of the sets $\mathcal{S}^{(0)} \to \mathcal{S}^{(1)} \to \mathcal{S}^{(2)} \to \cdots$ does not stabilize.

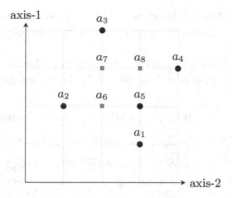

Fig. 2. An example showing that the sequence $\{\mathcal{S}^{(i)}\}_{i=0}^{\infty}$ does not stabilize.

Additional points and notations. We define the following additional points for our analysis (refer to Fig. 2).

$$a_6 = (1/2, 1/2), \ a_7 = (1/2, 3/4), \ a_8 = (3/4, 3/4)$$

Let $\overline{a_1 a_8}$ denote the set of points on the line segment that connects the point a_1 to the point a_8. The segments $\overline{a_2 a_5}, \overline{a_3 a_6}, a_4 a_7$ are defined similarly. For any set $\Omega \subseteq \mathbb{R}^2$, we define the set $\mathcal{S}_{\Omega}^{(i)}$ as follows.

$$\mathcal{S}_{\Omega}^{(i)} := \{Q \in \mathcal{S}^{(i)} : \pi(Q) \in \Omega\}$$

Whenever Ω is a singleton set, we omit the brackets. For example,

$$\mathcal{S}_{a_1}^{(0)} = \{(3/4, 1/4, 1, 0, 0, 0, 0)\}, \quad \mathcal{S}_{a_2}^{(0)} = \{(1/4, 1/2, 0, 1, 0, 0, 0)\},$$
$$\mathcal{S}_{a_3}^{(0)} = \{(1/2, \quad 1, 0, 0, 1, 0, 0)\}, \quad \mathcal{S}_{a_4}^{(0)} = \{(1, 3/4, 0, 0, 0, 1, 0)\},$$
$$\mathcal{S}_{a_5}^{(0)} = \{(3/4, 1/2, 0, 0, 0, 0, 1)\}, \quad \mathcal{S}_{a_6}^{(0)} = \mathcal{S}_{a_7}^{(0)} = \mathcal{S}_{a_8}^{(0)} = \emptyset.$$

Moreover, for any set $\Omega \subseteq \mathbb{R}^2 \times \mathbb{R}^5$, we define $\rho(\Omega) := \{\rho(P) : P \in \Omega\}$. For example, $\rho(\mathcal{S}_{a_4}^{(0)}) = \{(0, 0, 0, 1, 0)\} = \{e_4\}$.

For $i \in \{0, 1, 2, \dots\}$, we define

$$\sigma_i := \sum_{k=0}^{i-1} \frac{1}{16^k} = \frac{1 - (1/16)^i}{1 - 1/16},$$

$$\alpha_i := \sigma_i \cdot \frac{e_1}{2} + \sigma_i \cdot \frac{e_4}{4} + \sigma_i \cdot \frac{e_3}{8} + \sigma_i \cdot \frac{e_2}{16} + \frac{e_5}{16^i},$$

$$\beta_i := \sigma_{i+1} \cdot \frac{e_2}{2} + \sigma_i \cdot \frac{e_1}{4} + \sigma_i \cdot \frac{e_4}{8} + \sigma_i \cdot \frac{e_3}{16} + \frac{e_5}{2^{4i+1}},$$

$$\gamma_i := \sigma_{i+1} \cdot \frac{e_3}{2} + \sigma_{i+1} \cdot \frac{e_2}{4} + \sigma_i \cdot \frac{e_1}{8} + \sigma_i \cdot \frac{e_4}{16} + \frac{e_5}{2^{4i+2}},$$

$$\delta_i := \sigma_{i+1} \cdot \frac{e_4}{2} + \sigma_{i+1} \cdot \frac{e_3}{4} + \sigma_{i+1} \cdot \frac{e_2}{8} + \sigma_i \cdot \frac{e_1}{16} + \frac{e_5}{2^{4i+3}}.$$

Moreover, $\alpha^*, \beta^*, \gamma^*, \delta^*$ are defined as the limit of sequences $\alpha_i, \beta_i, \gamma_i, \delta_i$ respectively (refer to Proposition 4). We prove some algebraic properties of $\alpha_i, \beta_i, \gamma_i, \delta_i$ in Sect. 7.4.

Now, we state all claims needed for the proof of Theorem 3. Assuming these claims, we first prove Theorem 3 in Sect. 7.1. Then, we prove these claims in Sect. 7.2

Lemma 2. *For every* $i \in \{0, 1, 2, \dots\}$, *the following identities hold.*

$$\rho(S_{a_5}^{(4i)}) = \rho(S_{a_5}^{(4i+1)}) = \rho(S_{a_5}^{(4i+2)}) = \rho(S_{a_5}^{(4i+3)}),$$
$$\rho(S_{a_6}^{(4i+1)}) = \rho(S_{a_6}^{(4i+2)}) = \rho(S_{a_6}^{(4i+3)}) = \rho(S_{a_6}^{(4i+4)}),$$
$$\rho(S_{a_7}^{(4i+2)}) = \rho(S_{a_7}^{(4i+3)}) = \rho(S_{a_7}^{(4i+4)}) = \rho(S_{a_5}^{(4i+5)}),$$
$$\rho(S_{a_8}^{(4i+3)}) = \rho(S_{a_8}^{(4i+4)}) = \rho(S_{a_8}^{(4i+5)}) = \rho(S_{a_8}^{(4i+6)}).$$

Lemma 3. *For all* $i \in \{0, 1, \dots\}$,

$$\rho(S_{a_5}^{(4i)}) = \mathrm{conv}(\{\alpha_0, \alpha_i\}), \quad \rho(S_{a_6}^{(4i+1)}) = \mathrm{conv}(\{\beta_0, \beta_i\}),$$
$$\rho(S_{a_7}^{(4i+2)}) = \mathrm{conv}(\{\gamma_0, \gamma_i\}), \quad \rho(S_{a_8}^{(4i+3)}) = \mathrm{conv}(\{\delta_0, \delta_i\}).$$

Lemma 4. *For any* $i \in \{0, 1, 2, \dots\}$, *it holds that*

$$\alpha_{i+1} \notin \rho(S_{a_5}^{(4i)}), \quad \beta_{i+1} \notin \rho(S_{a_6}^{(4i+1)}), \quad \gamma_{i+1} \notin \rho(S_{a_7}^{(4i+2)}), \quad \delta_{i+1} \notin \rho(S_{a_8}^{(4i+3)}).$$

7.1 Proofs of Theorem 3 and Theorem 4

Proof (of Theorem 3). Suppose $r = 4k + 1$, where $k \in \{0, 1, 2, \dots\}$. Recall the functionality f_{4k+1} defined in Sect. 5.1

$$f_{4k+1}(0, 0) = \left(\frac{3}{16} \cdot \sigma_k, \frac{1}{4} \cdot \sigma_{k+1}, \frac{1}{8} \cdot \sigma_k, \frac{3}{8} \cdot \sigma_k, \frac{3}{2^{4k+2}} \right)$$

$$f_{4k+1}(0, 1) = \left(\frac{9}{16} \cdot \sigma_k, \frac{1}{4} \cdot \sigma_{k+1}, 0 \cdot \sigma_k, \frac{1}{8} \cdot \sigma_k, \frac{3}{2^{4k+2}} \right)$$

$$f_{4k+1}(1, 0) = \left(\frac{1}{16} \cdot \sigma_k, \frac{3}{4} \cdot \sigma_{k+1}, \frac{1}{8} \cdot \sigma_k, 0 \cdot \sigma_k, \frac{1}{2^{4k+2}} \right)$$

$$f_{4k+1}(1, 1) = \left(\frac{3}{16} \cdot \sigma_k, \frac{3}{4} \cdot \sigma_{k+1}, 0 \cdot \sigma_k, 0 \cdot \sigma_k, \frac{1}{2^{4k+2}} \right)$$

where $\sigma_k := \frac{1-(1/16)^k}{1-1/16}$ for $k \in \{0, 1, 2, \dots\}$. As we discussed in Sect. 5.1, the encoding of f_{4k+1} is the triplet (A, B, V_{4k+1}), where

$$A = \begin{pmatrix} 3/4, & 1/4, & 1/2, & 1, & 3/4 \\ 1/4, & 3/4, & 1/2, & 0, & 1/4 \end{pmatrix} \in \mathcal{M}_{2\times5}(\mathbb{R}),$$

$$B = \begin{pmatrix} 1/4, & 1/2, & 1, & 3/4, & 1/2 \\ 3/4, & 1/2, & 0, & 1/4, & 1/2 \end{pmatrix} \in \mathcal{M}_{2\times5}(\mathbb{R}),$$

$$V_{4k+1} = \left(\sigma_k, 2\sigma_{k+1}, \frac{\sigma_k}{4}, \frac{\sigma_k}{2}, \frac{1}{2^{4k-1}} \right) \in \mathbb{R}^5.$$

and the query point is the following:

$$Q(f_{4k+1}) = \left(\frac{1}{2}, \frac{1}{2}, \frac{1}{4} \cdot \frac{\sigma_k}{4}, \frac{\sigma_{k+1}}{2}, \frac{\sigma_k}{16}, \frac{\sigma_k}{8}, \frac{1}{2^{4k+1}}\right) \in \mathbb{R}^7.$$

Now, recall that

$$\beta_k = \sigma_{k+1} \cdot \frac{e_2}{2} + \sigma_k \cdot \frac{e_1}{4} + \sigma_k \cdot \frac{e_4}{8} + \sigma_k \cdot \frac{e_3}{16} + \frac{e_5}{2^{4k+1}}$$

This implies $\rho(Q(f_{4k+1})) = \beta_k$. Thus, it follows from Lemma 3 and Lemma 4 that $\rho(Q(f_{4k+1})) \in S_{a_6}^{(4k+1)}$ but $\rho(Q(f_{4k+1})) \notin S_{a_6}^{(4(k-1)+1)}$. Moreover, Lemma 2 implies that $S_{a_6}^{(4(k-1)+1)} = S_{a_6}^{(4k)}$. Thus, we conclude that

$$Q(f_{4k+1}) \in S^{(4k+1)} \setminus S^{(4k)}$$

which is what we promised to prove in Lemma 1. This implies that f_r has r round secure protocol but no $(r-1)$ secure protocol.

We can extend the proof to the case that $r \neq 4k+1$ for any k. The idea is similar. We can find 3 different family of functions corresponding to $r = 4k, r = 4k+2, r = 4k+3$. We only need to choose a different query point in Fig. 2, a_5, a_7, or a_8 and scale that figure and transfer it appropriately such that query points $(1/2, 1/2)$ is on a_5, a_7, or a_8 depending on the remainder of division of r by 4. Then, we can find appropriate functionalities. This completes the proof of the theorem.

Proof (of Theorem 4). Theorem 4 follows directly from Lemma 3 and Lemma 2.

7.2   Proofs of Claims Needed for Theorem 3

This section proves all the claims needed for Theorem 3 assuming other results that will be proved in Sect. 7.3.

Proof (of Lemma 2). We prove by induction on i.

Base Case. From the recursion in Lemma 6, one can verify that

$$\rho(S_{a_5}^{(0)}) = \rho(S_{a_5}^{(1)}) = \rho(S_{a_5}^{(2)}) = \rho(S_{a_5}^{(3)}) = \{e_5\},$$

$$\rho(S_{a_6}^{(1)}) = \rho(S_{a_6}^{(2)}) = \rho(S_{a_6}^{(3)}) = \rho(S_{a_6}^{(4)}) = \frac{e_2 + e_5}{2},$$

$$\rho(S_{a_7}^{(2)}) = \rho(S_{a_7}^{(3)}) = \rho(S_{a_7}^{(4)}) = \rho(S_{a_7}^{(5)}) = \frac{e_3}{2} + \frac{e_2 + e_5}{4},$$

$$\rho(S_{a_8}^{(3)}) = \rho(S_{a_8}^{(4)}) = \rho(S_{a_8}^{(5)}) = \rho(S_{a_8}^{(6)}) = \frac{e_4}{2} + \frac{e_3}{4} + \frac{e_2 + e_5}{8}.$$

Induction Step. Suppose the induction hypothesis holds for $(i-1)$. It follows from Lemma 6 that

$$\rho(S_{a_5}^{(4i+3)}) = \text{conv}\left(\rho(S_{a_5}^{(4i+2)}) \cup \frac{1}{2} \cdot \left(e_1 + \rho(S_{a_8}^{(4i+2)})\right)\right)$$

$$= \text{conv}\left(\text{conv}\left(\rho(\mathcal{S}_{a5}^{(4i+1)}) \cup \frac{1}{2} \cdot \left(e_1 + \rho(\mathcal{S}_{a8}^{(4i+1)})\right)\right) \cup \frac{1}{2} \cdot \left(e_1 + \rho(\mathcal{S}_{a8}^{(4i+2)})\right)\right)$$

By the induction hypothesis, $\rho(\mathcal{S}_{a8}^{(4i+2)}) = \rho(\mathcal{S}_{a8}^{(4i+1)})$. Therefore, we have

$$\frac{1}{2} \cdot \left(e_1 + \rho(\mathcal{S}_{a8}^{(4i+1)})\right) = \frac{1}{2} \cdot \left(e_1 + \rho(\mathcal{S}_{a8}^{(4i+2)})\right)$$

This, together with Fact 1 and Lemma 6, implies that

$$\rho(\mathcal{S}_{a5}^{(4i+3)}) = \text{conv}\left(\rho(\mathcal{S}_{a5}^{(4i+1)}) \cup \frac{1}{2} \cdot \left(e_1 + \rho(\mathcal{S}_{a8}^{(4i+1)})\right)\right) = \rho(\mathcal{S}_{a5}^{(4i+2)}).$$

Likewise, one can show that $\rho(\mathcal{S}_{a5}^{(4i+2)}) = \rho(\mathcal{S}_{a5}^{(4i+1)})$ and $\rho(\mathcal{S}_{a5}^{(4i+1)}) = \rho(\mathcal{S}_{a5}^{(4i)})$. These imply that

$$\rho(\mathcal{S}_{a5}^{(4i)}) = \rho(\mathcal{S}_{a5}^{(4i+1)}) = \rho(\mathcal{S}_{a5}^{(4i+2)}) = \rho(\mathcal{S}_{a5}^{(4i+3)}).$$

The proof of other equalities is similar.

Proof (of Lemma 3). We prove by induction on i (refer to Fig. 3).

Base Case. For $i = 0$,

$$\rho(\mathcal{S}_{a5}^{(0)}) = \{\alpha_0\} = \{e_5\},$$

$$\rho(\mathcal{S}_{a6}^{(1)}) = \{\beta_0\} = \left\{\frac{e_2 + e_5}{2}\right\},$$

$$\rho(\mathcal{S}_{a7}^{(2)}) = \{\gamma_0\} = \left\{\frac{e_3}{2} + \frac{e_2 + e_5}{4}\right\},$$

$$\rho(\mathcal{S}_{a8}^{(3)}) = \{\delta_0\} = \left\{\frac{e_4}{2} + \frac{e_3}{4} + \frac{e_2 + e_5}{8}\right\}.$$

Induction Step. Suppose the lemma is true for i. We shall show that it is true for $i + 1$.

$$\rho(\mathcal{S}_{a5}^{(4i+4)}) = \text{conv}\left(\rho(\mathcal{S}_{a5}^{(4i+3)}) \cup \frac{1}{2}\left(e_1 + \rho(\mathcal{S}_{a8}^{(4i+3)})\right)\right) \qquad \text{(Lemma 6)}$$

$$= \text{conv}\left(\rho(\mathcal{S}_{a5}^{(4i)}) \cup \frac{1}{2}\left(e_1 + \rho(\mathcal{S}_{a8}^{(4i+3)})\right)\right) \qquad \text{(Lemma 2)}$$

$$= \text{conv}\left(\text{conv}(\{\alpha_0, \alpha_i\}) \cup \frac{1}{2}\left(e_1 + \text{conv}(\{\delta_0, \delta_i\})\right)\right) \qquad \text{(Induction hypothesis)}$$

$$= \text{conv}\left(\{\alpha_0, \alpha_i\} \cup \left\{\frac{e_1 + \delta_0}{2}, \frac{e_1 + \delta_i}{2}\right\}\right) \qquad \text{(Fact 1)}$$

$$= \text{conv}\left(\{\alpha_0, \alpha_i\} \cup \{\alpha_1, \alpha_{i+1}\}\right) \qquad \text{Proposition 2}$$

$$= \text{conv}(\{\alpha_0, \alpha_{i+1}\}) \qquad \text{(Proposition 5 and Fact 2)}$$

Similarly, it holds that

$$\rho(\mathcal{S}_{a6}^{(4i+5)}) = \text{conv}(\{\beta_0, \beta_{i+1}\}),$$

$$\rho(\mathcal{S}_{a7}^{(4i+6)}) = \text{conv}(\{\gamma_0, \gamma_{i+1}\}),$$

$$\rho(\mathcal{S}_{a8}^{(4i+7)}) = \text{conv}(\{\delta_0, \delta_{i+1}\}),$$

which completes the proof.

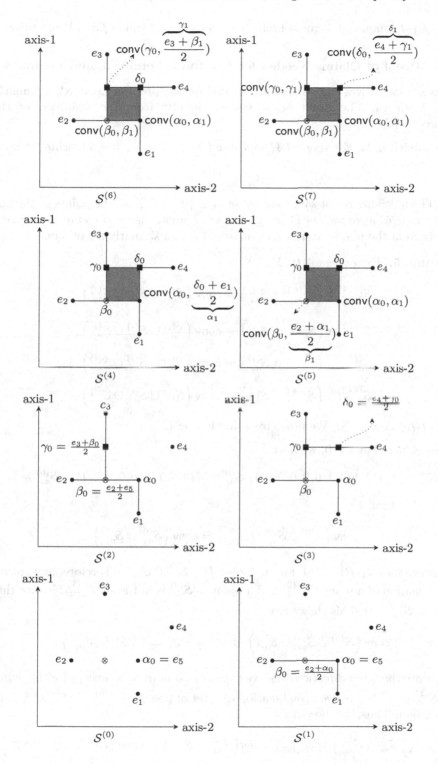

Fig. 3. The evolution of $\rho(\mathcal{S}_{a_5}^{(i)})$, $\rho(\mathcal{S}_{a_6}^{(i)})$, $\rho(\mathcal{S}_{a_7}^{(i)})$, $\rho(\mathcal{S}_{a_8}^{(i)})$ up to step eight.

Proof (of Lemma 4). Lemma 4 follows directly from Lemma 3 and Proposition 5.

7.3   Proof of Claims Needed for Lemma 2, Lemma 3, and Lemma 4

This section proves results that are needed for the proof of Lemma 2, Lemma 3, and Lemma 4. The result below follows directly from the definition of the sequence $\{S_i\}_{i=0}^{\infty}$.

Proposition 1. *For any set Ω and any $i \in \{0, 1, \dots\}$, the following property holds.*

$$S_{\Omega}^{(i)} \subseteq S_{\Omega}^{(i+1)}.$$

The following result says that for any $i \in \{0, 1, \dots\}$, all the points in the line segment $\overline{a_1 a_8}$ at round $(i+1)$ except the new ones at the point a_8 are constructed solely from the points at a_1, a_8, a_5 at round i, and similarly for others.

Lemma 5. *For every $i \in \{0, 1, \dots\}$,*

$$S_{\overline{a_1 a_8}}^{(i+1)} \setminus \left(S_{a_8}^{(i+1)} \setminus S_{a_8}^{(i)} \right) = \mathsf{conv} \left(S_{a_1}^{(i)} \cup S_{a_8}^{(i)} \cup S_{a_5}^{(i)} \right),$$

$$S_{\overline{a_2 a_5}}^{(i+1)} \setminus \left(S_{a_5}^{(i+1)} \setminus S_{a_5}^{(i)} \right) = \mathsf{conv} \left(S_{a_2}^{(i)} \cup S_{a_5}^{(i)} \cup S_{a_6}^{(i)} \right),$$

$$S_{\overline{a_3 a_6}}^{(i+1)} \setminus \left(S_{a_6}^{(i+1)} \setminus S_{a_6}^{(i)} \right) = \mathsf{conv} \left(S_{a_3}^{(i)} \cup S_{a_6}^{(i)} \cup S_{a_7}^{(i)} \right),$$

$$S_{\overline{a_4 a_7}}^{(i+1)} \setminus \left(S_{a_7}^{(i+1)} \setminus S_{a_7}^{(i)} \right) = \mathsf{conv} \left(S_{a_4}^{(i)} \cup S_{a_7}^{(i)} \cup S_{a_8}^{(i)} \right).$$

Proof (of Lemma 5). We prove by induction on i.

Base Case. For $i = 0$, we have

$$S_{a_1}^{(0)} = \{(3/4, 1/4, 1, 0, 0, 0, 0, 0)\}, \quad S_{a_5}^{(0)} = \{(3/4, 1/2, 0, 0, 0, 0, 0, 1)\}, \quad S_{a_8}^{(0)} = \emptyset.$$

It implies that

$$\mathsf{conv} \left(S_{a_1}^{(0)} \cup S_{a_8}^{(0)} \cup S_{a_5}^{(0)} \right) = \mathsf{conv} \left(S_{a_1}^{(0)} \cup S_{a_5}^{(0)} \right).$$

Observe that $\pi_1(P) = 3/4$, for any point $P \in S_{a_1}^{(0)} \cup S_{a_5}^{(0)}$. Therefore, any convex combination of a point in $S_{a_1}^{(0)}$ and a point in $S_{a_5}^{(0)}$ is in the set $S_{\overline{a_1 a_8}}^{(1)}$. Notice that $S_{a_8}^{(0)} = S_{a_8}^{(1)} = \emptyset$. This shows that

$$\mathsf{conv} \left(S_{a_1}^{(0)} \cup S_{a_8}^{(0)} \cup S_{a_5}^{(0)} \right) \subseteq S_{\overline{a_1 a_8}}^{(1)} = S_{\overline{a_1 a_8}}^{(1)} \setminus \left(S_{a_8}^{(1)} \setminus S_{a_8}^{(0)} \right).$$

To prove the other direction, observe that any point in $S_{\overline{a_1 a_8}}^{(1)}$ except for the points in $S_{a_8}^{(1)} \setminus S_{a_8}^{(0)}$ is a convex combination of a set of points in $S_{\overline{a_1 a_8}}^{(0)} = S_{a_1}^{(0)} \cup S_{a_5}^{(0)}$ by definition. Thus, it follows that

$$S_{\overline{a_1 a_8}}^{(1)} \setminus \left(S_{a_8}^{(1)} \setminus S_{a_8}^{(0)} \right) = S_{\overline{a_1 a_8}}^{(1)} \subseteq \mathsf{conv} \left(S_{a_1}^{(0)} \cup S_{a_5}^{(0)} \right) = \mathsf{conv} \left(S_{a_1}^{(0)} \cup S_{a_8}^{(0)} \cup S_{a_5}^{(0)} \right).$$

Induction Hypothesis. We assume that

$$\mathcal{S}^{(i)}_{\overline{a_1 a_8}} \setminus \left(\mathcal{S}^{(i)}_{a_8} \setminus \mathcal{S}^{(i-1)}_{a_8} \right) = \mathrm{conv}\left(\mathcal{S}^{(i-1)}_{a_1} \cup \mathcal{S}^{(i-1)}_{a_8} \cup \mathcal{S}^{(i-1)}_{a_5} \right),$$

and similarly for other equations.

Induction Step. Note that for any point P in the set $\mathcal{S}^{(i)}_{a_1} \cup \mathcal{S}^{(i)}_{a_8} \cup \mathcal{S}^{(i)}_{a_5}$, we have $\pi_1(P) = 3/4$. Therefore,

$$\mathrm{conv}\left(\mathcal{S}^{(i)}_{a_1} \cup \mathcal{S}^{(i)}_{a_8} \cup \mathcal{S}^{(i)}_{a_5} \right) \subseteq \mathcal{S}^{(i+1)}_{\overline{a_1 a_8}}$$

Since $\overline{a_4 a_7}$ is the only line segment that contains a_8 such that a_8 is not an end point of it, we have:

$$\left(\mathcal{S}^{(i+1)}_{a_8} \setminus \mathcal{S}^{(i)}_{a_8} \right) \cap \mathrm{conv}\left(\mathcal{S}^{(i)}_{a_1} \cup \mathcal{S}^{(i)}_{a_8} \cup \mathcal{S}^{(i)}_{a_5} \right) = \left(\mathcal{S}^{(i+1)}_{a_8} \setminus \mathcal{S}^{(i)}_{a_8} \right) \cap \mathrm{conv}\left(\mathcal{S}^{(i)}_{a_8} \right) = \emptyset.$$

Therefore, we conclude that

$$\mathrm{conv}\left(\mathcal{S}^{(i)}_{a_1} \cup \mathcal{S}^{(i)}_{a_8} \cup \mathcal{S}^{(i)}_{a_5} \right) \subseteq \mathcal{S}^{(i+1)}_{\overline{a_1 a_8}} \setminus \left(\mathcal{S}^{(i+1)}_{a_8} \setminus \mathcal{S}^{(i)}_{a_8} \right).$$

To prove the other direction, note that any point in $\mathcal{S}^{(i+1)}_{\overline{a_1 a_8}} \setminus \mathcal{S}^{(i+1)}_{a_8}$ is constructed from a convex combination of the points in $\mathcal{S}^{(i)}_{\overline{a_1 a_8}} \setminus \mathcal{S}^{(i)}_{a_8}$. Thus, we have

$$
\begin{aligned}
\mathcal{S}^{(i+1)}_{\overline{a_1 a_8}} \setminus \mathcal{S}^{(i+1)}_{a_8} &\subseteq \mathrm{conv}\left(\mathcal{S}^{(i)}_{\overline{a_1 a_8}} \setminus \mathcal{S}^{(i)}_{a_8} \right) \\
&\subseteq \mathrm{conv}\left(\mathcal{S}^{(i)}_{\overline{a_1 a_8}} \setminus \left(\mathcal{S}^{(i)}_{a_8} \setminus \mathcal{S}^{(i-1)}_{a_8} \right) \right) && (Fact\ 2) \\
&= \mathrm{conv}\left(\mathrm{conv}\left(\mathcal{S}^{(i-1)}_{a_1} \cup \mathcal{S}^{(i-1)}_{a_8} \cup \mathcal{S}^{(i-1)}_{a_5} \right) \right) && (\text{Induction hypothesis}) \\
&= \mathrm{conv}\left(\mathcal{S}^{(i-1)}_{a_1} \cup \mathcal{S}^{(i-1)}_{a_8} \cup \mathcal{S}^{(i-1)}_{a_5} \right) && (Fact\ 1) \\
&\subseteq \mathrm{conv}\left(\mathcal{S}^{(i)}_{a_1} \cup \mathcal{S}^{(i)}_{a_8} \cup \mathcal{S}^{(i)}_{a_5} \right), && (Proposition\ 1\ \text{and}\ Fact\ 2)
\end{aligned}
$$

Since $\mathcal{S}^{(i)}_{a_8} \subseteq \mathrm{conv}\left(\mathcal{S}^{(i)}_{a_1} \cup \mathcal{S}^{(i)}_{a_8} \cup \mathcal{S}^{(i)}_{a_5} \right)$, it follows that

$$\mathcal{S}^{(i+1)}_{\overline{a_1 a_8}} \setminus \left(\mathcal{S}^{(i+1)}_{a_8} \setminus \mathcal{S}^{(i)}_{a_8} \right) = \left(\mathcal{S}^{(i+1)}_{\overline{a_1 a_8}} \setminus \mathcal{S}^{(i+1)}_{a_8} \right) \cup \mathcal{S}^{(i)}_{a_8} \subseteq \mathrm{conv}\left(\mathcal{S}^{(i)}_{a_1} \cup \mathcal{S}^{(i)}_{a_8} \cup \mathcal{S}^{(i)}_{a_5} \right).$$

We have shown that

$$\mathcal{S}^{(i+1)}_{\overline{a_1 a_8}} \setminus \left(\mathcal{S}^{(i+1)}_{a_8} \setminus \mathcal{S}^{(i)}_{a_8} \right) = \mathrm{conv}\left(\mathcal{S}^{(i)}_{a_1} \cup \mathcal{S}^{(i)}_{a_8} \cup \mathcal{S}^{(i)}_{a_5} \right).$$

We prove other equations in a similar manner, which completes the proof.

Next, using Lemma 5, we prove a recursive construction of the projection ρ at the points a_i for $1 \leqslant i \leqslant 8$.

Lemma 6. *For all $i \in \{0, 1, \dots\}$,*

$$\rho(\mathcal{S}_{a_1}^{(i)}) = \{e_1\}, \ \rho(\mathcal{S}_{a_2}^{(i)}) = \{e_2\}, \ \rho(\mathcal{S}_{a_3}^{(i)}) = \{e_3\}, \ \rho(\mathcal{S}_{a_4}^{(i)}) = \{e_4\}.$$

Furthermore, for all $i \in \{1, 2, \dots, \}$,

$$\rho(\mathcal{S}_{a_5}^{(0)}) = \{e_5\}, \ \rho(\mathcal{S}_{a_5}^{(i+1)}) = \mathrm{conv}\left(\rho(\mathcal{S}_{a_5}^{(i)}) \cup \frac{1}{2} \cdot \left(e_1 + \rho(\mathcal{S}_{a_8}^{(i)})\right)\right),$$

$$\rho(\mathcal{S}_{a_6}^{(0)}) = \emptyset, \ \rho(\mathcal{S}_{a_6}^{(i+1)}) = \mathrm{conv}\left(\rho(\mathcal{S}_{a_6}^{(i)}) \cup \frac{1}{2} \cdot \left(e_2 + \rho(\mathcal{S}_{a_5}^{(i)})\right)\right),$$

$$\rho(\mathcal{S}_{a_7}^{(0)}) = \emptyset, \ \rho(\mathcal{S}_{a_7}^{(i+1)}) = \mathrm{conv}\left(\rho(\mathcal{S}_{a_7}^{(i)}) \cup \frac{1}{2} \cdot \left(e_3 + \rho(\mathcal{S}_{a_6}^{(i)})\right)\right),$$

$$\rho(\mathcal{S}_{a_8}^{(0)}) = \emptyset, \ \rho(\mathcal{S}_{a_8}^{(i+1)}) = \mathrm{conv}\left(\rho(\mathcal{S}_{a_8}^{(i)}) \cup \frac{1}{2} \cdot \left(e_4 + \rho(\mathcal{S}_{a_7}^{(i)})\right)\right).$$

Proof (of Lemma 6). Initially, $\rho(\mathcal{S}_{a_1}^{(0)}) = \{e_1\}$. At any round $i \in \{1, 2 \dots\}$, there is no new point constructed at a_1, since a_1 is an extreme point of $\mathrm{conv}(a_1, a_2, a_3, a_4, a_5)$. Therefore, $\rho(\mathcal{S}_{a_1}^{(i)}) = \{e_1\}$. Similarly, we have

$$\rho(\mathcal{S}_{a_2}^{(i)}) = \{e_2\}, \ \rho(\mathcal{S}_{a_3}^{(i)}) = \{e_3\}, \ \rho(\mathcal{S}_{a_4}^{(i)}) = \{e_4\}, \text{ for every } i \in \{0, 1, \dots\}.$$

Let $P \in \mathcal{S}_{a_5}^{(i+1)}$. It follows from Lemma 5 that there are points $P_{a_1} \in \mathcal{S}_{a_1}^{(i)}$, $P_{a_8} \in \mathcal{S}_{a_8}^{(i)}$, $P_{a_5} \in \mathcal{S}_{a_5}^{(i)}$, and $\lambda_1, \lambda_8, \lambda_5 \geq 0$ such that

$$P = \lambda_1 \cdot P_{a_1} + \lambda_8 \cdot P_{a_8} + \lambda_5 \cdot P_{a_5}, \text{ and } \lambda_1 + \lambda_8 + \lambda_5 = 1.$$

Projecting these points into the second coordinate, we have

$$\pi_2(P) = \lambda_1 \cdot \pi_2(P_{a_1}) + \lambda_8 \cdot \pi_2(P_{a_8}) + \lambda_5 \cdot \pi_2(P_{a_5}).$$

This together with $\pi_2(P) = \pi_2(P_{a_5}) = \frac{1}{2}(\pi_2(P_{a_1}) + \pi_2(P_{a_8}))$ implies that $\lambda_1 = \lambda_8$. Thus, the point P is in the set $\mathrm{conv}\left(\mathcal{S}_{a_5}^{(i)} \cup \frac{1}{2} \cdot \left(\mathcal{S}_{a_1}^{(i)} + \mathcal{S}_{a_8}^{(i)}\right)\right)$. This implies that

$$\mathcal{S}_{a_5}^{(i+1)} \subseteq \mathrm{conv}\left(\mathcal{S}_{a_5}^{(i)} \cup \frac{1}{2} \cdot \left(\mathcal{S}_{a_1}^{(i)} + \mathcal{S}_{a_8}^{(i)}\right)\right).$$

Projecting this fact into coordinates $\{3, 4, 5, 6, 7\}$ yields

$$\rho(\mathcal{S}_{a_5}^{(i+1)}) \subseteq \mathrm{conv}\left(\rho(\mathcal{S}_{a_5}^{(i)}) \cup \frac{1}{2} \cdot \left(\rho(\mathcal{S}_{a_1}^{(i)}) \cup \rho(\mathcal{S}_{a_8}^{(i)})\right)\right)$$

$$= \mathrm{conv}\left(\rho(\mathcal{S}_{a_5}^{(i)}) \cup \frac{1}{2} \cdot \left(e_1 + \rho(\mathcal{S}_{a_8}^{(i)})\right)\right) \qquad \text{(since } \rho(\mathcal{S}_{a_1}^{(i)}) = \{e_1\}).$$

Conversely, it suffices to show that

$$\mathrm{conv}\left(\mathcal{S}_{a_5}^{(i)} \cup \frac{1}{2} \cdot \left(\mathcal{S}_{a_1}^{(i)} + \mathcal{S}_{a_8}^{(i)}\right)\right) \subseteq \mathcal{S}_{a_5}^{(i+1)}.$$

This follows directly from the fact that a_5 is the midpoint of the segment $\overline{a_1 a_8}$. We have proved that

$$\rho(\mathcal{S}_{a_5}^{(i+1)}) = \text{conv}\left(\rho(\mathcal{S}_{a_5}^{(i)}) \cup \frac{1}{2} \cdot \left(e_1 + \rho(\mathcal{S}_{a_8}^{(i)})\right)\right).$$

Similarly, the other three equations for a_6, a_7, a_8 also hold.

7.4 Properties of the Four Sequences

We first recall the definition of the four sequences $\alpha_i, \beta_i, \gamma_i, \sigma_i$ as follows. For $i \in \{0, 1, 2, \dots\}$,

$$\sigma_i := \sum_{k=0}^{i-1} \frac{1}{16^k} = \frac{1 - (1/16)^i}{1 - 1/16},$$

$$\alpha_i := \quad \sigma_i \cdot \frac{e_1}{2} + \quad \sigma_i \cdot \frac{e_4}{4} + \quad \sigma_i \cdot \frac{e_3}{8} + \sigma_i \cdot \frac{e_2}{16} + \frac{e_5}{16^i},$$

$$\beta_i := \sigma_{i+1} \cdot \frac{e_2}{2} + \quad \sigma_i \cdot \frac{e_1}{4} + \quad \sigma_i \cdot \frac{e_4}{8} + \sigma_i \cdot \frac{e_3}{16} + \frac{e_5}{2^{4i+1}},$$

$$\gamma_i := \sigma_{i+1} \cdot \frac{e_3}{2} + \sigma_{i+1} \cdot \frac{e_2}{4} + \quad \sigma_i \cdot \frac{e_1}{8} + \sigma_i \cdot \frac{e_4}{16} + \frac{e_5}{2^{4i+2}},$$

$$\delta_i := \sigma_{i+1} \cdot \frac{e_4}{2} + \sigma_{i+1} \cdot \frac{e_3}{4} + \sigma_{i+1} \cdot \frac{e_2}{8} + \sigma_i \cdot \frac{e_1}{16} + \frac{e_5}{2^{4i+3}}.$$

Proposition 2. *For all* $i \in \{0, 1, \dots\}$,

$$\alpha_{i+1} = \frac{e_1 + \delta_i}{2}, \quad \beta_i = \frac{e_2 + \alpha_i}{2}, \quad \gamma_i = \frac{e_3 + \beta_i}{2}, \quad \delta_i = \frac{e_4 + \gamma_i}{2}.$$

Proof. By definition,

$$\frac{e_2 + \alpha_i}{2} = \frac{e_2}{2} + \frac{\sigma_i}{2} \cdot \left(\frac{e_1}{2} + \frac{e_4}{4} + \frac{e_3}{8} + \frac{e_2}{16}\right) + \frac{e_5}{2 \cdot 16^i}$$

$$= \frac{e_2}{2} + \frac{\sigma_i}{2} \cdot \left(\frac{e_1}{2} + \frac{e_4}{4} + \frac{e_3}{8} + \frac{e_2}{16}\right) + \frac{e_5}{2 \cdot 16^i}$$

$$= \left(1 + \frac{\sigma_i}{16}\right) \cdot \frac{e_2}{2} + \sigma_i \cdot \left(\frac{e_1}{4} + \frac{e_4}{8} + \frac{e_3}{16}\right) + \frac{e_5}{2 \cdot 16^i}$$

$$= \sigma_{i+1} \cdot \frac{e_2}{2} + \sigma_i \cdot \left(\frac{e_1}{4} + \frac{e_4}{8} + \frac{e_3}{16}\right) + \frac{e_5}{2 \cdot 16^i} \qquad (\textit{Proposition 3})$$

$$= \beta_i$$

The proofs of the other equations are similar.

The following proposition follows from the definition of σ_i.

Proposition 3. *For all* $i \in \{1, 2, \dots\}$,

$$\sigma_i = 1 + \frac{1}{16}\sigma_{i-1}.$$

Proposition 4. *The following statements hold.*

$$\lim_{i\to\infty} \alpha_i = \frac{8}{15}e_1 + \frac{4}{15}e_4 + \frac{2}{15}e_3 + \frac{1}{15}e_2 =: \alpha^*,$$

$$\lim_{i\to\infty} \beta_i = \frac{8}{15}e_2 + \frac{4}{15}e_1 + \frac{2}{15}e_4 + \frac{1}{15}e_3 =: \beta^*,$$

$$\lim_{i\to\infty} \gamma_i = \frac{8}{15}e_3 + \frac{4}{15}e_2 + \frac{2}{15}e_1 + \frac{1}{15}e_4 =: \gamma^*,$$

$$\lim_{i\to\infty} \delta_i = \frac{8}{15}e_4 + \frac{4}{15}e_3 + \frac{2}{15}e_2 + \frac{1}{15}e_1 =: \delta^*.$$

Proof. First, note that

$$\lim_{i\to\infty} \sigma_{i-1} = \lim_{i\to\infty} \sigma_i = \lim_{i\to\infty} \frac{1-(1/16)^i}{1-1/16} = 16/15.$$

Now, we have

$$\lim_{i\to\infty} \alpha_i = \lim_{i\to\infty} \sigma_i \cdot \left(\frac{e_1}{2} + \frac{e_4}{4} + \frac{e_3}{8} + \frac{e_2}{16}\right) + \frac{e_5}{16^i}$$

$$= \frac{16}{15} \cdot \left(\frac{e_1}{2} + \frac{e_4}{4} + \frac{e_3}{8} + \frac{e_2}{16}\right)$$

$$= \frac{8}{15}e_1 + \frac{4}{15}e_4 + \frac{2}{15}e_3 + \frac{1}{15}e_2 = \alpha^*.$$

Similarly, we can find the $\lim_{i\to\infty} \beta_i = \beta^*$, $\lim_{i\to\infty} \gamma_i = \gamma^*$, and $\lim_{i\to\infty} \delta_i = \delta^*$ (Fig. 4).

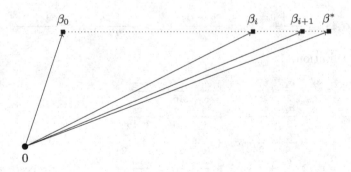

Fig. 4. Visualization of sequence $\{\beta_i\}_{i=1}^{\infty}$ (refer to Proposition 5)

Proposition 5. *For all $i \in \{0, 1, \dots\}$,*

$$\alpha_{i+1} = \frac{15}{16} \cdot \alpha^* + \frac{1}{16} \cdot \alpha_i, \quad \beta_{i+1} = \frac{15}{16} \cdot \beta^* + \frac{1}{16} \cdot \beta_i,$$

$$\gamma_{i+1} = \frac{15}{16} \cdot \gamma^* + \frac{1}{16} \cdot \gamma_i, \quad \delta_{i+1} = \frac{15}{16} \cdot \delta^* + \frac{1}{16} \cdot \delta_i.$$

Consequently, α_i is on the line segment between $\alpha_0 = e_5$ and α_{i+1}; and α_{i+1} is on the line segment between α_i and α^*. More formally,

$$\alpha_i \in \mathsf{conv}(\alpha_0, \alpha_{i+1}), \quad \alpha_{i+1} \in \mathsf{conv}(\alpha_i, \alpha^*),$$
$$\beta_i \in \mathsf{conv}(\beta_0, \beta_{i+1}), \quad \beta_{i+1} \in \mathsf{conv}(\beta_i, \beta^*),$$
$$\gamma_i \in \mathsf{conv}(\gamma_0, \gamma_{i+1}), \quad \gamma_{i+1} \in \mathsf{conv}(\gamma_i, \gamma^*),$$
$$\delta_i \in \mathsf{conv}(\delta_0, \delta_{i+1}), \quad \delta_{i+1} \in \mathsf{conv}(\delta_i, \delta^*).$$

Proof. By definition,

$$\alpha_i = \sigma_i \cdot \left(\frac{e_1}{2} + \frac{e_4}{4} + \frac{e_3}{8} + \frac{e_2}{16} \right) + \frac{e_5}{16^i}.$$

So, we have

$$
\begin{aligned}
\alpha_{i+1} &= \sigma_{i+1} \cdot \left(\frac{e_1}{2} + \frac{e_4}{4} + \frac{e_3}{8} + \frac{e_2}{16} \right) + \frac{e_5}{16^{i+1}} \\
&= \left(1 + \frac{\sigma_i}{16} \right) \cdot \left(\frac{e_1}{2} + \frac{e_4}{4} + \frac{e_3}{8} + \frac{e_2}{16} \right) + \frac{e_5}{16^{i+1}} \quad \text{(\textit{Proposition} 3)} \\
&= \left(\frac{e_1}{2} + \frac{e_4}{4} + \frac{e_3}{8} + \frac{e_2}{16} \right) + \frac{1}{16} \cdot \left(\sigma_i \cdot \left(\frac{e_1}{2} + \frac{e_4}{4} + \frac{e_3}{8} + \frac{e_2}{16} \right) + \frac{e_5}{16^i} \right) \\
&= \frac{15}{16} \cdot \alpha^* + \frac{1}{16} \cdot \alpha_i
\end{aligned}
$$

The proofs of the three other equations are similar.

8 On the Optimality of Our Constructions

This section proves Theorem 2 mentioned in Sect. 2. It suffices to prove the following Theorem 5.

Theorem 5. *Let $\mathcal{S}^{(0)}$ be a subset of $\mathbb{R}^6$ of size 4. Then, there exists an $i^* \in \{0, 1, 2, 3, 4\}$ such that $\mathcal{S}^{(i^*)} = \mathcal{S}^{(i^*+1)}$.*

According to the above theorem, if the initial set $\mathcal{S}^{(0)}$ is a subset of $\mathbb{R}^6$ of size 4, the sequence $\mathcal{S}^{(0)} \to \mathcal{S}^{(1)} \to \mathcal{S}^{(2)} \to \dots$ stabilizes after at most 4 rounds. The following result is a consequence of the above theorem and [1,11].

Corollary 1. *Let $f \colon \{0,1\} \times \{0,1\} \to \mathbb{R}^Z$ such that $\mathrm{card}\,(Z) \leqslant 4$. If f has a perfectly secure protocol, then there is a perfectly secure protocol for f with at most 4 rounds.*

8.1 Proof of Theorem 5

To prove Theorem 5, We will enumerate over all possible cases for $\mathcal{S}^{(0)}$ and show that in each case the sequence $\mathcal{S}^{(0)}, \mathcal{S}^{(1)}, \dots$ stabilizes in at most four rounds i.e. $\mathcal{S}^{(4)} = \mathcal{S}^{(5)}$. It was already shown in [11] that there is an at most two-round secure protocol for a secure function with $\mathrm{card}\,(Z) \leqslant 3$. Therefore, without loss of generality, we only need to enumerate over the cases that the final result in $\mathcal{S}^{(\infty)}$ is connected. Moreover, we only need to consider one case among a set of cases that are similar. For example, in case 1, we consider 4 horizontally aligned points. The case that 4 points are aligned vertically is similar to case 1 and we do not need to consider it. We complete the proof by stating and proving the following lemma (Lemma 7).

Lemma 7. *The following table states the values of i^* (defined in Theorem 5) for each enumerated case (Table 1).*

Table 1. The number of rounds needed to stabilize the sequence $\mathcal{S}^{(0)}, \mathcal{S}^{(1)}, \ldots$ for each enumerated case.

Case Number	1	2	3	4	5	6	7	8	9	10	11	12	13	14	15	16	17
i^*		1	1	2	1	2	2	1	2	2	1	2	2	4	2	3	3	2

Proof. In all cases except case 6, one can easily verify that $\mathcal{S}^{(i^*)} = \mathcal{S}^{(i^*+1)}$ for the i^* mentioned in the table. The reason is that in all those cases, when the final shape in the projected space (projection under π) stabilizes, then the whole shape stabilizes. More formally, in all cases except case 6, one can verify that $\pi(\mathcal{S}^{(i^*)}) = \pi(\mathcal{S}^{(i^*+1)})$ implies that $\mathcal{S}^{(i^*)} = \mathcal{S}^{(i^*+1)}$. For all cases except case 6, we show in the following that $\pi(\mathcal{S}^{(i^*)}) = \pi(\mathcal{S}^{(i^*+1)})$.

Now, we discuss case 6 in the following figure. At time 0, there are four points. Suppose $\rho(\mathcal{S}_{a_i}^{(0)}) = e_i$ where $e_i \in \mathbb{R}^4$ represents the i-th standard basis vector in $\mathbb{R}^4$. The points a_1 and a_2 are axis aligned, so $\rho(\mathcal{S}_{a_1 a_2}^{(1)}) = \mathsf{conv}(e_1, e_2)$. Similarly, $\rho(\mathcal{S}_{a_3 a_4}^{(1)}) = \mathsf{conv}(e_3, e_4)$. Now, notice that at the end of time 1, there are two objects at point p. One of them is $(p, \frac{e_1 + e_2}{2})$ and the other one is $(p, \frac{e_3 + e_4}{2})$. They are both axis aligned. So, we have $\rho(\mathcal{S}_p^{(2)}) = \mathsf{conv}(\frac{e_1 + e_2}{2}, \frac{e_3 + e_4}{2})$ and the shape stabilizes at step 2.

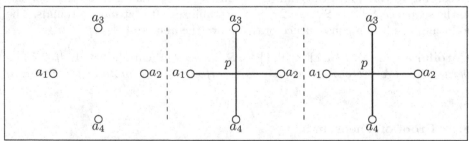

In the following, we enumerate over all possible cases and study the evolution of the sequence $\mathcal{S}^{(0)}, \mathcal{S}^{(1)}, \ldots$.

If There are 3 Collinear Points. There will be 4 cases as follows.

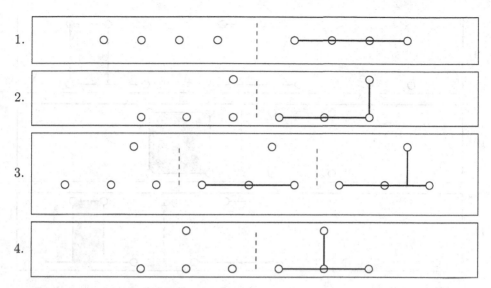

There are No 3 Collinear Points

Subcase 1: Two points are horizontally collinear and the other two points are vertically collinear. There are 2 cases as follows.

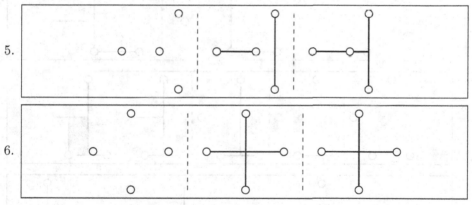

Subcase 2: Two points are horizontally collinear and the other two are also horizontally collinear.

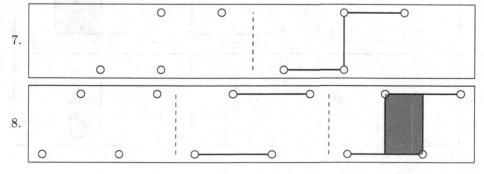

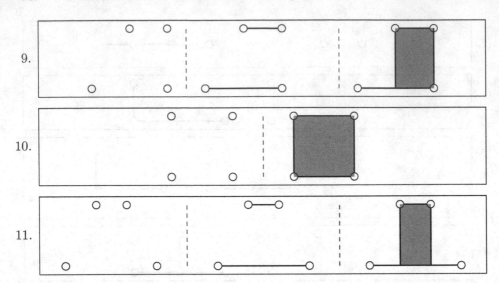

Subcase 3: Two points are horizontally collinear, and the other two points are not collinear.

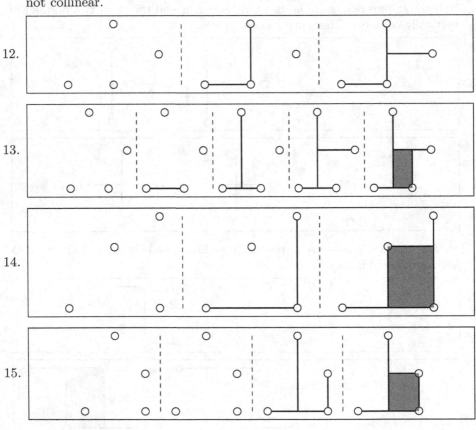

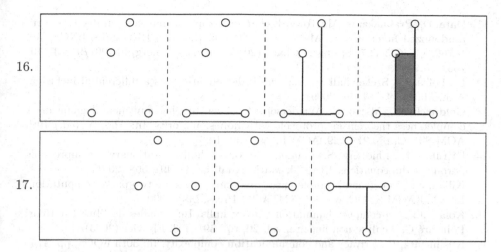

16.

17.

We have exhaustively enumerated all possible cases and proved that the sequence $S^{(0)}, S^{(1)}, \ldots$ stabilizes after at most four rounds, which completes the proof.

References

1. Basu, S., Khorasgani, H.A., Maji, H.K., Nguyen, H.H.: Geometry of secure two-party computation. In: 63rd FOCS, pp. 1035–1044. IEEE Computer Society Press, October/November 2022
2. Basu, S., Khorashgani, H.A., Maji, H.K., Nguyen, H.H.: Geometry of secure two-party computation (2022). https://www.cs.purdue.edu/homes/hmaji/papers/BKMN22.pdf. Accessed 15 Feb 2023
3. Basu, S., Kummer, M., Netzer, T., Vinzan, C.: New directions in real algebraic geometry. https://publications.mfo.de/bitstream/handle/mfo/4031/OWR_2023_15.pdf?sequence=-1&isAllowed=y
4. Beaver, D.: Perfect privacy for two-party protocols. In: Proceedings of DIMACS Workshop on Distributed Computing and Cryptography, vol. 2, pp. 65–77 (1991)
5. Blum, L., Shub, M., Smale, S.: On a theory of computation and complexity over the real numbers: Np-completeness, recursive functions and universal machines (1989)
6. Bogetoft, P., et al.: Secure multiparty computation goes live. In: Dingledine, R., Golle, P. (eds.) FC 2009. LNCS, vol. 5628, pp. 325–343. Springer, Heidelberg (2009). https://doi.org/10.1007/978-3-642-03549-4_20
7. Carathéodory, C.: Über den variabilitätsbereich der fourier'schen konstanten von positiven harmonischen funktionen. Rendiconti Del Circolo Matematico di Palermo (1884–1940), **32**(1), 193–217 (1911)
8. Chor, B., Kushilevitz, E.: A zero-one law for Boolean privacy (extended abstract). In: 21st ACM STOC, pp. 62–72. ACM Press, May 1989
9. Cordoba, D., Faraco, D., Gancedo, F.: Lack of uniqueness for weak solutions of the incompressible porous media equation. Arch. Ration. Mech. Anal. **200**, 725–746 (2011)
10. Córdoba, D., Gancedo, F.: Contour dynamics of incompressible 3-d fluids in a porous medium with different densities. Commun. Math. Phys. **273**, 445–471 (2007)

11. Data, D., Prabhakaran, M.: Towards characterizing securely computable two-party randomized functions. In: Abdalla, M., Dahab, R. (eds.) PKC 2018. LNCS, vol. 10769, pp. 675–697. Springer, Cham (2018). https://doi.org/10.1007/978-3-319-76578-5_23

12. De Lellis, C., Székelyhidi Jr., L.: The Euler equations as a differential inclusion. Ann. Math. 1417–1436 (2009)

13. Goldreich, O., Micali, S., Wigderson, A.: How to play any mental game or A completeness theorem for protocols with honest majority. In: Aho, A. (ed.) 19th ACM STOC, pp. 218–229. ACM Press, May 1987

14. Hitruhin, L., Lindberg, S.: Lamination convex hull of stationary incompressible porous media equations. SIAM J. Math. Anal. **53**(1), 491–508 (2021)

15. Kilian, J.: More general completeness theorems for secure two-party computation. In: 32nd ACM STOC, pp. 316–324. ACM Press, May 2000

16. Kolář, J.: Non-compact lamination convex hulls. In: Annales de l'Institut Henri Poincaré C, Analyse non linéaire, vol. 20, pp. 391–403. Elsevier (2003)

17. Kushilevitz, E.: Privacy and communication complexity. In: 30th FOCS, pp. 416–421. IEEE Computer Society Press, October/November 1989

18. Yao, A.C.-C.: How to generate and exchange secrets (extended abstract). In: 27th FOCS, pp. 162–167. IEEE Computer Society Press, October 1986

Towards Topology-Hiding Computation from Oblivious Transfer

Marshall Ball[1], Alexander Bienstock[1], Lisa Kohl[2], and Pierre Meyer[3(✉)]

[1] New York University, New York, USA
marshall.ball@cs.nyu.edu, abienstock@cs.nyu.edu
[2] CWI, Cryptology Group, Amsterdam, The Netherlands
lisa.kohl@cwi.nl
[3] IDC Herzliya, ISRAEL and IRIF, Université Paris Cité, CNRS, Paris, France
pierre.meyer@irif.fr

Abstract. *Topology-Hiding Computation (THC)* enables parties to securely compute a function on an incomplete network without revealing the network topology. It is known that secure computation on a *complete* network can be based on oblivious transfer (OT), even if a majority of the participating parties are corrupt. In contrast, THC in the dishonest majority setting is only known from assumptions that imply (additively) homomorphic encryption, such as Quadratic Residuosity, Decisional Diffie-Hellman, or Learning With Errors.

In this work we move towards closing the gap between MPC and THC by presenting a protocol for THC on general graphs secure against all-but-one semi-honest corruptions from *constant-round constant-overhead secure two-party computation*. Our protocol is therefore the first to achieve THC on arbitrary networks without relying on assumptions with rich algebraic structure. As a technical tool, we introduce the notion of *locally simulatable MPC*, which we believe to be of independent interest.

1 Introduction

A secure multi-party computation (MPC) protocol enables a set of mutually distrusting parties with private inputs to jointly perform a computation over their inputs such that no adversarial coalition can learn anything beyond the output of the computation. Results in the 1980 s showed that, under widely-believed assumptions, any function that can be feasibly computed can be computed securely [Yao82, GMW87, BGW88, CCD88].

However, these early protocols and most of the subsequent work (as well as their corresponding security definitions), assume that the communication graph is a complete network: any two parties can communication directly. In many situations communication networks are incomplete and, additionally, the structure of the communication network itself may be sensitive information which the participants desire to keep private (e.g. network topology may reveal information about users' locations, or relationships between users).

The full version [BBKM23] is available as entry 2023/849 in the IACR eprint archive.

© International Association for Cryptologic Research 2023
G. Rothblum and H. Wee (Eds.): TCC 2023, LNCS 14369, pp. 349–379, 2023.
https://doi.org/10.1007/978-3-031-48615-9_13

Topology Hiding Computation. Moran et al. [MOR15] noticed that there are situations where the communication network should additionally be kept private: secure computation over a social network, securely computing a function using individual location data, low locality MPC [BBC+19]. Motivated as such, Moran et al. [MOR15] then formalized the notion of *topology-hiding computation (THC)*, where parties can securely compute a function without revealing anything about the communication network (graph), beyond the immediate neighbors they are communicating with and what can be derived from the output of the function computed (which might be either topology independent, such as a message broadcast, or topology dependent, such as a routing table). In general, we say that a protocol is topology-hiding with respect to a class of graphs, if nothing is revealed beyond membership in that parties only see their immediate neighborhood and wish to jointly compute a function without revealing anything about the graph topology beyond what can be derived from the output (which might be topology independent, e.g., a message broadcast, or topology dependent, e.g., a routing table).

It turns out that even simply *broadcasting* a message to all parties in topology-hiding manner (with no privacy guarantees on the information sent) is challenging, even in the semi-honest setting where adversarial parties are assumed to follow the protocol execution.[1] But exactly how difficult it is to construct THC protocols remains poorly understood. In this vein, a line of work has sought to investigate the following question:

> *Is semi-honest MPC equivalent to semi-honest THC? Are additional assumptions required to make a secure computation topology-hiding?*

The feasibility of semi-honest MPC (for arbitrary functions) obeys a dichotomy based on the number of corruptions and following this we can collect the work on semi-honest THC into two categories.

– **Honest majority ($< n/2$ corruptions):** In this regime, we know that semi-honest MPC (on fully connected networks) can be achieved information-theoretically [BGW88, CCD88, RB89].

  For THC (on arbitrary, connected communication graphs) it has been shown that key agreement is necessary with even just *one* corruption [BBC+20]. On the other hand, information-theoretic THC with a single corruption is possible if (and only if) one is promised that the communication graph is two-connected [BBC+20] (albeit at high cost).

  For *single corruption*, key agreement is not just necessary but sufficient to achieve THC (on arbitrary connected graphs) [BBC+20]. For a *constant* number of corruptions, THC is possible (on arbitrary connected graphs) assuming constant round MPC with constant computational overhead [MOR15, BBMM18].

---

[1] In contrast, this is trivial to achieve (in the semi-honest setting) if hiding network topology is not a concern: simply forward the message through the network.

– **Dishonest majority ($\geq n/2$ corruptions):** In the dishonest majority setting, no separation between MPC and THC is known. On the other hand,
  constructions of dishonest majority THC from general *MPC* (with a dishonest majority) are only known for very restricted graph classes [MOR15,
  BBMM18]: graphs of *constant diameter.*

Assuming *constant round MPC with constant computational overhead,*[2] THC
is possible for graphs of *constant* degree and *logarithmic* diameter [MOR15,
BBMM18].[3]

THC for *arbitrary (connected) graphs* is only known from *structured hardness
assumptions* (such as quadratic residuosity (QR), decisional Diffie-Hellman
(DDH) and Learning with Errors (LWE)) [AM17, ALM17, LZM+18], or idealized obfuscation [BBMM18].

So while there is a clear separation between MPC and THC (with respect to
general graphs) in the honest majority setting, no such separation is known in
the dishonest majority setting. While OT is necessary and sufficient for MPC, it
is unclear if it suffices to construct THC.[4] The motivation of this work is, thus,
the following question:

Are THC and MPC equivalent in the dishonest majority setting?

1.1 Our Result

In this work, we make a step towards answering this question in the affirmative,
by proving the following theorem:

Theorem 1 (Topology-Hiding Computation on All Graphs, Informal).
*If there exists a two-party MPC protocol with constant rounds and constant com-
putational overhead, then there exists a protocol securely realizing topology-hiding
computation on every network topology in the presence of a semi-honest adversary corrupting any number of parties.*

---

[2] MPC with constant computational overhead means that a circuit of size $s(n)$ can
  be securely evaluated in time $O(s(n)) + \text{poly}(\lambda)$, where the latter term is a fixed
  polynomial of the security parameter.
[3] [HMTZ16] gave an early construction of a more efficient protocol for such graphs
  from the decisional Diffie-Hellman assumption.
[4] On the other hand, it is known that oblivious transfer is necessary to simply *communicate* in a topology-hiding manner in the presence of a dishonest majority. In
  particular, OT is implied by topology-hiding *broadcast* with a dishonest majority
  for graphs with just 4 nodes [BBMM18]. Again, because the broadcast functionality does not hide its inputs it is trivial to realize without hiding the topology.
  [BBC+20] showed that OT is necessary for topology-hiding *anonymous broadcast*
  on even simpler graphs.

The main feature of this construction is that it is the first construction of semi-honest topology-hiding computation tolerating any number of corruptions *on all graphs* from unstructured assumptions. As mentioned above, prior to this work it was only known how to construct THC against a semi-honest majority from constant round, constant computational overhead MPC for graphs with at most logarithmic diameter [MOR15, BBMM18], or from structured hardness assumptions [AM17, ALM17, LZM+18]. For the case of topology-hiding for general graphs, it was only known how to construct THC from constant round, constant computational MPC if the adversary was restricted to a *constant* number of corruptions [MOR15, BBMM18].

As an aside, our protocol is secure in the "pseudonymous neighbors" model (i.e. "knowledge-till-radius-zero" KT_0 [AGPV88]), where parties only know pseudonomyms of their neighbors (in this model, two colluding parties cannot determine if they share an honest neighbor). In contrast, Moran et al.'s protocol [MOR15] is only secure in the KT_1 model ("knowledge-till-radius-one" [AGPV88]) where parties know globally consistent names for their neighbors (in this model, colluding parties can identify exactly which neighbors they have in common).

On instantiating constant-round constant-overhead secure computation. By [IKOS08], constant-round and constant-overhead two-party secure computation is implied by any constant-round OT protocol (which can be based, e.g., on the learning parity with noise (LPN) assumption [DDN14, YZ16, DGH+20], or on the computational Diffie-Hellman (CDH) assumption [BM90, DGH+20]) together with a constant-locality PRG with polynomial stretch (which can be based on a variant of an assumption by Goldreich [Gol00, MST03, OW14]).

In contrast, all previous constructions of THC for all graphs rely on structured hardness assumptions such as key-homomorphic encryption ("privately-key commutative and re-randomizable encryption, PKCR" [AM17, ALM17, LZM+18]), which does not seem to be implied by LPN/CDH and constant-locality PRGs (in fact, such a result would be rather surprising). We would like to point out though that the main focus of this work is not to build THC from different concrete assumptions, but to move away from structured assumptions, which are not necessary for secure computation without topology hiding, and—as we show in this work—are also not necessary for achieving topology-hiding computation on general graphs.

2 Technical Overview

We first present a high-level overview of our techniques in Sect. 2.1, then present a more technical description of our core protocol in Sect. 2.2.

First, note that the difficulty in constructing protocols for THC can be reduced to the ability to perform topology-hiding broadcast (THB) of a single-bit message. Indeed, once parties can broadcast messages to the network in a topology-hiding way, one can use generic techniques that allow to establish secure computation given any OT protocol (leaking only the total number of nodes in the network). In the following overview, we therefore restrict ourselves to explaining how to achieve THB. With this simplification, we can capture our main result in the following theorem:

Theorem 2 (Topology-Hiding Computation on All Graphs, Informal). *If there exists a two-party MPC protocol with constant rounds and constant computational overhead, then there exists a topology-hiding protocol securely realizing broadcast on the class of all graphs in the presence of a semi-honest adversary corrupting any number of parties.*

For simplicity, we do not explicitly address the subtleties of the neighborhood models (KT_0, where neighbors are pseudonymized, or KT_1, where neighbor are identified "in the clear") in this exposition, but the following high-level overview applies to both models.

2.1 A High-Level Overview

Our contribution is three-fold. First, we observe that many topology-hiding computation protocols implicitly follow the following informal paradigm: the parties run in parallel many instances of some (non topology-hiding on its own) subroutine, each one computing the desired function. Topology-hiding properties of the overall protocol emerge from the fact that the parties participate in each instance *obliviously*, meaning that each party is able to perform their role in each subroutine without being able to identify which execution is which (even while colluding with other parties). Of particular interest is the protocol of Akavia et al. [ALM17, ALM20], which can be abstracted out as having the parties locally setup a mesh of *correlated random walks* along the topology, then perform some special-purpose MPC subprotocol along each path. In [ALM17, ALM20], these subroutines are instantiated by heavily leaning on assumptions with a rich algebraic structure. The first step in removing the need for these assumptions is to identify the properties we need from these MPC subroutines (or at least some sufficient properties we can instantiate from a form of oblivious transfer).

We then put forward the notion of *local simulation* as a sufficient security property to impose on these subroutines in order to allow for oblivious participant evaluation. A secure computation protocol over an incomplete network is *locally simulatable* if the view of each connected component in the adversary's subgraph can be generated independently. As an example, in the network ①-②-③-④-⑤-⑥-⑦-⑧ (where parties ②, ③, ⑥, and ⑦ are corrupt), the views of parties {②, ③} and {⑥, ⑦} should be simulated independently. Intuitively, this means that the adversary cannot tell if {②, ③} and {⑥, ⑦} are participating in the same protocol or, *e.g.* in two different executions ①-②-③-④-Ⓐ-Ⓑ-Ⓒ-Ⓓ and Ⓔ-Ⓕ-Ⓖ-Ⓗ-⑤-⑥-⑦-⑧. Ultimately, if using *correlated random walks*, that means that each party can participate in the MPC along each path without the adversary learning which chunk of walk corresponds to which other.

Finally, we provide a protocol for locally simulatable MPC on a path, assuming (semi-honest, static) secure two-party computation with *constant rounds* and *constant overhead.* By plugging this into the correlated random walks (*i.e.* the parties are obliviously participating in a locally simulatable secure computation along each random walk), we obtain (dishonest majority, semi-honest, static) topology-hiding computation on all graphs. Previously, topology-hiding computation under this assumption was limited to the class of logarithmic-diameter graphs or to a constant number of corruptions on all graphs [MOR15].

We now expand (still at a high level) on each of these three points, without assuming familiarity with topology-hiding computation.

A Modular Approach to Topology-Hiding Computation. Topology-hiding computation allows parties communicating through an incomplete network of point-to-point channels, where each party initially only knows their local neighborhood (possibly pseudonymized), to perform some secure computation without revealing any information about the network (beyond what they already know, *e.g.* each party's respective neighborhood).

Our starting point is the observation that many topology-hiding protocols can be described informally in a very modular fashion, and yet their formal description (and the corresponding security proof) are inaccessibly monolithic. We start by a gentle introduction to this concept, with a modular presentation of the "simplest THC protocol", realizing an information-theoretic topology-hiding sum in the presence of a single semi-honest corruption on cycles (more precisely, we fix a party/vertex set and consider all cycles on this set)[5]. Every party already knows they are on a cycle, but the secret part of the topology is the *order* in which they are arranged. We then provide a modular description of Akavia et al.'s [ALM17, ALM20] protocol, realizing (computational, semi-honest, dishonest majority) topology-hiding computation on the class of all graphs. The latter introduces the notion of *correlated random walks*, which form the basis for essentially all topology-hiding computation protocols *on all graphs*, tolerating any number of corruptions [ALM17, ALM20, LZM+18, Li22] (and now, also ours).

An Introductory Example to Modular THC. Assume n parties are arranged in a cycle, each party only having access to a secure point-to-point channel with its neighbors in the cycle. Consider the following protocol (illustrated in Fig. 1a), which is arguably the simplest (non topology-hiding) MPC protocol for securely computing a sum in the presence of a single semi-honest corruption. In the first round, an agreed upon party, which we will refer to as the *initiator*, samples a random value and uses it as a one-time pad to mask its input, then sends the resulting ciphertext to one of its neighbors (chosen arbitrarily). In each subsequent round, if a party received a message from one of its neighbors, it

---

[5] In fact, the protocol we describe can be seen as a conceptually simpler alternative to Ball et al.'s [BBC+19, Theorem 4.1] 1-secure, semi-honest, information-theoretic topology-hiding anonymous broadcast on the class of all cycles with a given vertex set.

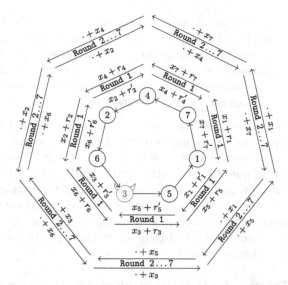

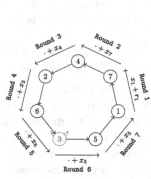

(a) The "simplest MPC protocol ever", securely computing a sum in the presence of a single semi-honest corruption. The "initiator", who can retrieve the output, is ①. The view of the corrupt party, ③, is a single message, obtained in round 5, masked by r_1.

(b) The "simplest THC protocol ever", securely computing a sum in the presence of a single semi-honest corruption. In each round, the corrupt party ③'s view is comprised of two messages, masked by fresh one-time pads: r_6 and r_5', then r_2 and r_1', then r_4 and r_7', then r_7 and r_4', then r_1 and r_2', and finally r_5 and r_6'.

Fig 1. The topology-hiding protocol of Fig. 1b can be seen as running to $2n$ parallel instances of the (non topology-hiding protocol) of Fig. 1a.

sums this message with its own input and passes on the result to its other neighbor. After n rounds, the initiator receives the sum of all inputs masked by the one-time pad they themselves sampled, and they can therefore recover the desired output. Keeping in mind the parties are semi-honest and non-colluding, correctness and security are straightforward to verify (in essence, a single message is being passed around the cycle, containing the partial sum of previously visited parties' inputs and masked by the initiators' one-time pad). This only allows the initiator to get the output, however this can be addressed by running this "single-initiator" protocol n times sequentially with a fresh initiator for each instance.

As described, the protocol is not topology-hiding as, by noting in which round they receive a message, every party can learn their distance to the initiator, which leaks information about the graph. This can be addressed by considering the following augmented protocol (illustrated in Fig. 1b):

– In the first round, each party samples two random masks, uses them as one-time pads for their input, and sends one of the resulting ciphertexts to each of its neighbors;

- In each subsequent round, every party receives two messages, one from each neighbor. Each party can add their input to these two messages, before forwarding them along the cycle (the message received from one neighbor is sent to the other neighbor, after the input is added).
- After n rounds, each party can receive the sum of all inputs by removing the appropriate mask from either of the messages received in the last round.

The above protocol could be described as running $2n$ parallel instances of the "single-initiator" protocol. Each party's instructions in the augmented protocol can be seen as participating in each of these protocols: in two of them with the role of initiator, in another two with the role of the party one hop away from the initiator, and so on for each of the n possible roles. Crucially, both for correctness and security, each party is able to participate in each subroutine *obliviously*, meaning that they are able to fulfill their role without being able to distinguish these executions and thus, most importantly, recognize which one corresponds to which initiator.

Takeway for Our Protocol: Skipping ahead, our main protocol will follow this abstract template: the parties will be participating in a slew of subroutines, where each party knows exactly their role in the process, but non-neighboring colluding parties cannot determine if they both participate in any given subroutine or not.

Correlated random walks [ALM17, ALM20]. In retrospect, the above protocol remains relatively simple to analyze, even without breaking it down into these subroutines. We now turn our attention to Akavia et al.'s [ALM17, ALM20] construction, for which taking a modular approach is significantly more interesting. In order to isolate Akavia et al.'s [ALM17, ALM20] key contribution of *correlated random walks*, we propose the following abstraction. Say there are n parties in some incomplete communication network wishing to securely compute an OR of their inputs. As a starting model, assume one party possesses an idealized hardware "black box". This box is unclonable and has the following properties: any party may enter an input into the box, and after T inputs have been registered, the box returns their OR, where T is some parameter to be defined. The first party can place their input in the box, then pass on the latter to a randomly chosen neighbor. In subsequent rounds, the party who just received the box adds its input then passes the box to a randomly chosen neighbor. From a global point of view, the box is performing a random walk and therefore, by known results on the *cover time* of a *simple random walk* in a connected graph, after $T = \lambda \cdot n^3$ steps the box will have, with all but negligible probability, visited every party at least once each. This means that the last party will receive the correct OR from the box, and because we assumed the box was unclonable, the protocol securely computes OR[6]. This allows a randomly chosen[7] party to

---

[6] If the box was clonable, a party could make a local copy then learn the partial OR of the inputs of all parties who previously handled the box by simply plugging 0s until they receive an output.

[7] The stationary distribution is not uniform, but nevertheless each party has non-negligible probability of being the last party.

learn the output, and we could for instance sequentially repeat the process until every party obtains the OR. This protocol is not topology-hiding however, since colluding parties could learn an upper bound on their distance in the graph by counting the number of steps between when they handled the box[8].

Akavia et al.'s [ALM17, ALM20] elegant solution is to have each party initially send a box to each of their neighbors. In every subsequent round, each party takes all the boxes it just received (one per neighbor), plugs in their input, then shuffles all boxes and sends one to each neighbor. After T rounds, each party opens any of the boxes it holds to recover the result. Observe that each box, taken individually, performs a random walk through the graph. While the walks of each box are not independent, but *correlated*, [ALM20, Lemma 3.14] establishes that setting $T = \Theta(\lambda \cdot n^3)$ guarantees that with all but negligible probability all boxes will have individually covered the graph.

For completeness, we mention that in reality, Akavia et al. [ALM17, ALM20] do not rely on this idealized hardware to perform the secure OR on the fly, but use *linearly homomorphic Privately Key-Commutative and Rerandomizable encryption* (lhPKCR) [AM17], which can be instantiated from DDH [AM17], LWE [LZM+18], or QR [Li22]. In a nutshell, the parties pass around ciphertexts containing the homomorphically computed partial OR of the inputs of all visited nodes. In order to not have these ciphertexts be opened prematurely (*c.f.* the unclonability assumption on the black boxes), the secret key is re-randomized (and therefore secret-shared) along the walk: whenever a party receives a ciphertext they also "add a layer of randomization" to the key, which is possible for PKCR encryption. After $\Theta(\lambda \cdot n^3)$ steps, when the random walk of every message is guaranteed to have visited every node with all but negligible probability, the parties return the ciphertexts to their source, along the reverse walks, and peeling off layers of encryption as they go.

Takeaway for Our Protocol: Abstracting out, Akavia et al.'s [ALM17, ALM20] protocol can be seen as first having each party sample T permutations on their neighborhood (as illustrated in Fig. 2, this globally define a mesh of random walks, where each party knows only their position), and then having the parties run a special-purpose MPC along each walk. These instances of MPC along each path are indistinguishable to the parties by using structural properties of lhPKCR encryption.

Information-Local Simulation. Correlated random walks can be used to reduce the task of *topology-hiding computation on all graphs* to that of designing an MPC the parties can run along each walk without being able to tell when they are participating in the same execution (i.e. in the same walk) or not. To

---

[8] While this is beyond the scope of this exposition, we could quantify the leakage in terms of the *electric conductance* of the graph. What this means additionally is that the protocol is even insecure against a single corruption as a party can learn information from just counting the number of rounds between two consecutive visits of the box.

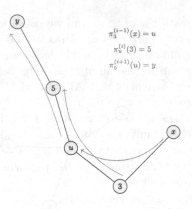

$$\pi_3^{(i-1)}(x) = u$$
$$\pi_u^{(i)}(3) = 5$$
$$\pi_5^{(i+1)}(u) = y$$

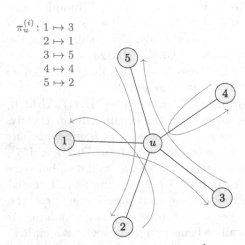

$\pi_u^{(i)}:$ $1 \mapsto 3$
$\phantom{\pi_u^{(i)}:}$ $2 \mapsto 1$
$\phantom{\pi_u^{(i)}:}$ $3 \mapsto 5$
$\phantom{\pi_u^{(i)}:}$ $4 \mapsto 4$
$\phantom{\pi_u^{(i)}:}$ $5 \mapsto 2$

(b) The family $(\pi_v^{(j)})_{v \in V, j \in [T]}$ defines a family of correlated[a] random walks. Each party knows their position in the walk (e.g. party ⓤ knows they are the ith party in the highlighted walk, but they have no way of identifying if this walk is the same as another one in which ⓤ also knows its position).

(a) Visual representation of the ith permutation on ⓤ's neighborhood ($\pi_u^{(i)}$), defining ⓤ's neighborhood in five distinct walks.

[a]The walks are *correlated* in the sense that no two walks borrow the same edge at the same time.

Fig. 2. Local and global views of correlated random walks, obtained by having each party sampled uniformly at random T permutations on their neighborhood.

instantiate the latter, we put forward the notion of *locally simulatable computation*.

Introducing Locally Simulatable Computation. Locally simulatable computation is an MPC over an incomplete network G where the view of disconnected corrupt parties can be simulated *independently*. More formally consider the connected components $\mathcal{Z}_1, \mathcal{Z}_2, \ldots$ of the subgraph $G[\mathcal{Z}]$ induced by the set of corrupted parties $\mathcal{Z}$. The views of the parties in each component $\mathcal{Z}_i$ should be simulated given only their inputs, outputs, and local views of the graph, independently of the views of the parties in $\mathcal{Z} \setminus \mathcal{Z}_i$. Note that this requirement is orthogonal to the notion of being topology-hiding[9]:

---

[9] However our final protocol will turn out to be both topology-hiding and locally simulatable.

- *THC is not necessarily locally simulatable:* Without loss of generality, a topology-hiding computation protocol can be made to be *not* locally simulatable, by first broadcasting a long random string (in a topology-hidding manner). The views of disconnected adversaries cannot be simulated independently, as they expect to receive the same string (which is not passed as input to the simulators, since it is neither an input nor an output).
- *Locally simulatable MPC is not necessarily topology-hiding:* In locally simulatable MPC, each party is assumed to know their position in the graph (or in other words, the graph class is a singleton). There is no guarantee the parties can correctly run a locally simulatable MPC protocol if they are in an unknown graph setting (and having the parties learn information about the graph to be able to run the protocol would not be topology-hiding).

From Local Simulation to Execution-Obliviousness. Because the views of two adversarial components $\mathcal{Z}_1$ and $\mathcal{Z}_2$ are generated independently, the adversary corrupting the parties cannot tell if $\mathcal{Z}_1$ and $\mathcal{Z}_2$ are in fact participating in the same protocol or in different protocols (provided of course they have the same inputs, outputs, and neighborhoods in all these instances).

We are now ready to sketch our topology-hiding broadcast on all graphs, assuming the existence of locally simulatable computation on paths of length $T = \lambda \cdot n^3$ (which we will instantiate next). Each party P_u samples T random permutations on their neighborhood (recall this defines $2|E| = \sum_{v \in V} \deg_v$ paths, each one visiting each node at least once *w.h.p.*), from which they derive $2T \cdot \deg_u$ different "path neighborhoods" with the corresponding positions (more precisely, $2 \deg_u$ of these neighborhoods are as the ith node on the path, for each $i \in [T]$). Each party fulfills in parallel their $2T \cdot \deg_u$ roles in the $2T \cdot |E|$ parallel executions of locally simulatable OR (the broadcaster always uses the broadcast bit as input and the other parties use 0, in all their roles), one along each path. Their output in each of the protocols is then the broadcast bit.

Locally Simulatable MPC on a Path from OT. By what precedes, topology-hiding broadcast on the class of all graphs can be reduced to a locally simulatable OR on a path. At a high-level, our OR protocol on the path proceeds by recursively emulating a two-party computation (2PC) of an OR. Each party in this top-level 2PC is itself emulated by a 2PC whose two parties are further emulated by a lower-level 2PC, and so on, until we get to 2PCs between two real parties on the path. For a 2PC at any given recursion level, each virtual party is recursively emulated by half of the real parties on the current subset of the path being considered. That is, at the highest level, the first (resp. second) half of the real parties emulates the first (resp. second) virtual party. Then, every $(1/4)$-th of the real parties emulate a separate virtual parties at recursion depth 1, and so on, until we reach 2PCs between every pair of neighboring real parties. In a nutshell, local simulatability stems from the fact that each party only sees 2PC messages that come from its direct neighbors. For a more detailed overview of this protocol, we refer the reader to the next subsection.

2.2   Technical Overview of the Core Protocol: Locally Simulatable MPC on a Path

We now focus on presenting our main technical contribution of building locally simulatable OR on a path. We first describe our construction (see Fig. 3) and then explain the primary ways in which the protocol enables proper topology-hiding emulation and local simulatability. In the full version of this paper [BBKM23], we note some differences between our protocol and the protocol of [MOR15].

Building Locally-Simulatable OR on a Path. The core step in building our full THB protocol is building a *locally-simulatable* OR protocol on a directed path of length $\ell = 2^l$, for some $l \geq 1$ (each such path will be a random walk, so we can specify its length to be a power of 2). In this setting, each party knows their position on the path (for $i \in [0, \ell - 1]$), and we refer to the party at position i as $\widetilde{P}_i$. Given each party $\widetilde{P}_i$'s input bit b_i, the protocol outputs $\bigvee_{i=0}^{\ell-1} b_i$ to every party. When used in the full THB protocol, if $\widetilde{P}_i$ is the broadcaster, then $b_i = b$, the broadcast bit; otherwise, $b_i = 0$.

In order to compute the OR of their input bits b_i, the parties emulate recursive (constant-overhead) 2PC computations. At a high-level, the first and second $\ell/2$ real parties will emulate the first and second virtual parties, $P_{0,0}$ and $P_{0,1}$, respectively, of a 2PC computation. The virtual parties input $(b_0||b_1||\ldots||b_{\ell/2-1})$ and $(b_{\ell/2}||b_{\ell/2+1}||\ldots||b_{\ell-1})$, respectively, and the 2PC computation outputs to both virtual parties $\bigvee_{i=0}^{\ell-1} b_i$. Now, in each round of this 2PC, virtual party $P_{0,0}$ is emulated recursively via another 2PC between virtual parties $P_{1,0}$ and $P_{1,1}$, which are in turn emulated by, respectively, the first and second $\ell/4$ real parties recursively (and similarly for virtual party $P_{0,1}$). Virtual party $P_{0,0}$ is emulated by virtual parties $P_{1,0}$ and $P_{1,1}$ as follows: $P_{1,0}$ and $P_{1,1}$ combine their inputs $(b_0||b_1||\ldots||b_{\ell/4-1})$ and $(b_{\ell/4}||b_{\ell/4+1}||\ldots||b_{\ell/2-1})$ (via the 2PC) so that $P_{0,0}$'s input is emulated by $x_{0,0} = (b_0||b_1||\ldots||b_{\ell/2-1})$. Similarly, $P_{1,0}$ and $P_{1,1}$ each take as input random strings $\widetilde{r}'_{1,0}$ and $\widetilde{r}'_{1,1}$ and combine them (via the 2PC) so that $P_{0,0}$'s random tape is emulated by $\widetilde{r}_{0,0} = \widetilde{r}'_{1,0} \oplus \widetilde{r}'_{1,1}$. Finally, the 2PC between $P_{1,0}$ and $P_{1,1}$ outputs $P_{0,0}$'s next message in its 2PC with $P_{0,1}$ to $P_{1,1}$, who then passes it to the first virtual party $P_{1,2}$ that participates in the 2PC emulating $P_{0,1}$. Note that *only* virtual parties $P_{1,1}$ and $P_{1,2}$ see and pass to each other the messages for the higher-level 2PC; as we will see later, this is *crucial* to local-simulatability, and topology-hiding in general.

We keep recursively splitting the computation of virtual parties in 2PC's in the recursion, until we reach level $l - 1$ of the recursion, in which two *real* parties, which are sibling leaves in the recursion tree, compute (many) 2PC's. Again, briefly, the 2PC's that each pair of sibling leaves computes is the emulation of the next message function of the virtual party at the parent in the recursion tree. This virtual party in turn is computing a 2PC with its sibling that emulates the next message function of the virtual party at *their* parent in the recursion tree. We continue up the tree like this, until we reach the original OR between the two largest virtual parties.

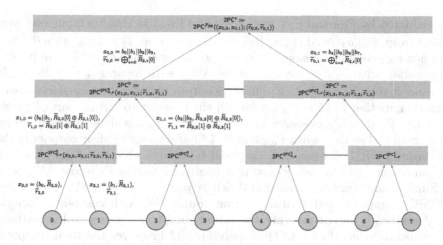

Fig. 3. Depiction of the directed path protocol $\Pi_{\text{dir-path}}$ for a path of length $\ell = 8$. Each interior node represents a 2PC which gets its inputs and randomness from its two children. This 2PC computes the next message for virtual party P_0 (resp. P_1) in the 2PC at the node's parent by combining the inputs of its two children into the input and randomness of P_0 (resp. P_1). This next message is passed from this node to its sibling in the protocol via the two *neighboring real* parties at the rightmost (resp. leftmost) and leftmost (resp. rightmost) leaves of the corresponding subtrees (indicated by horizontal lines of matching thickness).

For clarity, we depict an example computation with $\ell = 8$ in Fig. 3. We shall first focus on *real* parties P_0 and P_1. Each party has their respective input bits which we denote as b_0 and b_1. The parties also sample several random strings for (i) the emulation of virtual party $P_{0,0}$ and (ii) for the emulation of each 2PC in which virtual party $P_{1,0}$ participates (one for each of the R_{2PC} rounds of the root 2PC).

Now, for each round of each 2PC execution that virtual party $P_{1,0}$ participates in (i.e., R_{2PC}^2 in total), $P_{2,0}$ and $P_{2,1}$ execute their own 2PC to emulate $P_{1,0}$ in this round. They do so by emulating (via their 2PC execution) $P_{1,0}$'s input bits as $(b_0\|b_1)$, $P_{1,0}$'s input randomness (for emulation of the root 2PC) as $\widetilde{r}_{1,0} = \widetilde{R}_{2,0}[0] \oplus \widetilde{R}_{2,1}[0]$, and $P_{1,0}$'s random tape as $\widetilde{r}_{1,0} = \widetilde{R}_{2,0}[1] \oplus \widetilde{R}_{2,1}[1]$ (where $\widetilde{R}_{2,0}[1], \widetilde{R}_{2,1}[1]$ are freshly sampled for each execution in which $P_{1,0}$ participates). $P_{2,1}$ then receives $P_{1,0}$'s next message as output of this 2PC, and forwards it to $P_{2,2}$ (who together with $P_{2,3}$ will emulate $P_{1,1}$'s next message). Note that $P_{2,1}$ will also input to the 2PC $P_{1,1}$'s previous messages in its 2PC with $P_{1,0}$, which $P_{2,1}$ receives from $P_{2,2}$.

The 2PC's which virtual party $P_{1,0}$ executes with $P_{1,1}$ correspond to emulations of the next message function of virtual party $P_{0,0}$ in the highest level 2PC, which simply computes the OR of $P_{0,0}$'s and $P_{0,1}$'s input bits. $P_{1,0}$ and $P_{1,1}$ emulate (via these 2PC executions) $P_{0,0}$'s input bits as $(b_0\|b_1\|b_2\|b_3)$, and $P_{0,0}$'s random tape as $\widetilde{r}_{0,0} = \widetilde{r}'_{1,0} \oplus \widetilde{r}'_{1,1}$. Again, recall that, recursively, $P_{1,0}$ (resp. $P_{1,1}$)

was emulated by $P_{2,0}$ and $P_{2,1}$ (resp. $P_{2,2}$ and $P_{2,3}$) so that its input bits were $(b_0||b_1)$ (resp. $(b_2||b_3)$) and $\tilde{r}'_{1,0} = \tilde{R}_{2,0}[0] \oplus \tilde{R}_{2,1}[0]$ (resp. $\tilde{r}'_{1,1} = \tilde{R}_{2,2}[0] \oplus \tilde{R}_{2,3}[0]$). So, when $P_{1,1}$ computes its output, it will be the next message of $P_{0,0}$ in its 2PC computation with $P_{1,0}$ of the OR functionality, with input $x_{0,0} = b_0||b_1||b_2||b_3$ and random tape $\tilde{r}_{0,0} = \bigoplus_{i=0}^{3} \tilde{R}_{2,i}[0]$. This output will then be recursively passed down (via another 2PC) to $P_{2,3}$, who will then pass it to virtual party $P_{0,1}$ via real party $P_{2,4}$. $P_{0,1}$'s messages in the 2PC with $P_{0,0}$ will be similarly recursively emulated so that when $P_{0,0}$ and $P_{0,1}$ finally compute their outputs in the highest-level OR 2PC execution, they will be recursively passed down to each $P_{1,i}$, and then again to each $P_{2,i}$ so that finally, all parties $\tilde{P}_i$ receive $\bigvee_{i=0}^{7} b_i$.

Finally, note that the recursion depth is just $l = \log_2(\ell)$. Moreover, when the 2PC is implemented with a constant round 2PC with constant computational overhead, we can see that the round complexity grows multiplicatively in the recursion depth, i.e. $O(1)^l = \text{poly}(\ell)$, and moreover the total computational complexity (and hence communication complexity) is just $O(\cdots O(O(1) + \text{poly}(\lambda)) + \text{poly}(\lambda) \cdots) + \text{poly}(\lambda) = \text{poly}(\ell, \lambda)$.

Enablers for Proper Topology-Hiding Emulation and Local Simulatability. There are a few main ways in which this protocol enables proper topology-hiding emulation and local simulatability. First, 2PC messages at any depth of the recursion are only output and passed between real parties that are neighbors on the path. This is important since if this were not true, and (random-looking, and thus unique w.h.p.) messages were passed between real parties several edges away from each other, then as noted previously, these parties would know that they participate in the same execution, and thus local simulation would not be possible. This is the reason why our path protocol uses recursive 2PC's, as opposed to, e.g., 3PC's, as doing so would require real parties to pass messages to other real parties that are not their neighbors, thus revealing infromation about the topology (recall that we work in the KT_0 model, so parties should not know if they have a neighbor in common).

Second, virtual parties' random tapes are collectively emulated by each real party of which they consist. So, even if the party at the "edge" of a virtual party that sees the 2PC messages sent by the virtual party they are helping to emulate is corrupted, if at least one of the other real parties in the virtual party is uncorrupted, then this 2PC message reveals nothing about the uncorrupted parties' inputs. This is because the uncorrupted parties mix in their own fresh randomness to compute the random tape of the virtual party so that the 2PC messages are generated with randomness that looks fresh and independent to the adversary. So, by the security of the 2PC, these messages reveal nothing about the virtual party's input (and thus nothing about the uncorrupted real parties' inputs).

Finally, since we compute an OR amongst all parties, we can simulate virtual parties' views with only partial information. Simulation using generic 2PC seems challenging at a first glance, since in the 2PC in which a corrupted real party is helping to emulate a virtual party, it may receive 2PC messages from the other virtual party in the higher-level 2PC. This happens even if some of the other real parties of which the emulated virtual party consists are not corrupted. We are thus faced with using generic 2PC simulators only with partial information on the input (and output) of the corresponding virtual party. However, since we compute the OR functionality, and based on the output OR'd bit b and the fact that every real party mixes in their own independent randomness for the emulation of virtual parties, our local simulators can actually *fill in the gaps* of the uncorrupted parties. That is, if $b = 0$, then our simulator can simply fill in the uncorrupted parties' inputs as 0 and sample fresh randomness for them, which will be a perfect simulation. Even if $b = 1$, because of the 2PC security of computing ORs, our simulator can simply simulate as if *all* of the uncorrupted parties' inputs were 1. Although this will not be true for the THB protocol itself, it can be true for computing recursive ORs, and thus we leverage this along with 2PC security for our proof.

Generalizing to "Efficiently Invertible from Local Information" Functionalities. We just noted that the fact that our path protocol computes an OR is crucial to local simulatability. The important part, however, was that from a subset of parties' input bits and the output bit, one can efficiently compute all other parties' inputs (0's if the output is 0; 1's if the output is 1). In the full version [BBKM23], we further generalize this strategy to all functionalities $\mathcal{F}$ such that given a subset of parties' inputs and outputs, there exists an "inverse" algorithm that computes possible inputs of the other parties that are consistent with the original parties' outputs. We call such functionalities *efficiently invertible from local information.* Other examples of such functionalities include private set intersection, private set union, and more. However, we do note that there are some efficiently computable functionalities that nonetheless are not efficiently invertible from local information; for example, leakage resilient one-way functions. Unfortunately, we cannot extend the strategy to such functionalities.

Now recall that we use secure OR to eventually build our THB protocol, which in turn can be generically composed with any secure MPC protocol to get full-fledged THC (see Sect. 6). However, we note that if the eventual THC computes a functionality that is efficiently invertible from local information, our path protocol can just directly (and thus more efficiently) be used to compute the THC, without going through the THB + MPC composition.

3   Preliminaries

Notations. For $m < n \in \mathbb{N}$ let $[n] = \{1, \ldots, n\}$ and $[m, n] = \{m, m + 1, \ldots, n\}$. In our protocols we sometimes denote by B an upper bound on the number of participating parties. The security parameter is denoted by λ. We will use 0-indexing for many of our definitions and protocols. We also make use of dictionaries in our protocols. For a dictionary D, $D[: x]$ results in a new dictionary D' consisting of elements 0 through x of D; i.e., for $i \in [0, x]$, $D'[i] = D[i]$, but for $i > x$, $D'[i] = \bot$. Finally, we let $||_{j=i}^{n} x_j = x_i || x_{i+1} || \ldots || x_n$

Graph Notations and Properties. A graph $G = (V, E)$ is a set V of vertices and a set E of edges, each of which is an unordered pair $\{v, w\}$ of distinct vertices. A graph is *directed* if its edges are instead ordered pairs (v, w) of distinct vertices. The *(open) neighbourhood* of a vertex v in an undirected graph G, denoted $\mathcal{N}_G(v)$, is the set of vertices sharing an edge with v in G. The *closed neighbourhood* of v in G is in turn defined by $\mathcal{N}_G[v] := \mathcal{N}_G(v) \cup \{v\}$.

3.1   Topology-Hiding Computation (THC)

There are two notions of topology-hiding computation in the literature: game-based and simulation-based [MOR15]. Since we introduce a feasibility result, we use a stronger simulation-based definition.

UC Framework. The simulation-based definition is defined in the UC framework of [Can00]. We will consider computationally bounded, static, and semi-honest adversaries and environments.

Neighbourhood Models. In this work, we unify the neighbourhood models of past THC definitions in the literature (for an illustration we refer to Fig. 4). To simplify the notation, we will consider that P_v in some protocol is associated with node v in the underlying graph. Typically, THC functionalities are realized in the $\mathcal{F}_{\text{graph}}^{\mathcal{G}}$-hybrid model, where $\mathcal{F}_{\text{graph}}^{\mathcal{G}}$ is some functionality that allows parties to communicate with their neighbors in the graph. Many works have used the model of [MOR15], wherein $\mathcal{F}_{\text{graph}}^{\mathcal{G}}$ informs every party P_v of their local neighbourhood by indeed sending $\mathcal{N}_G(v)$ directly to them, and $\mathcal{F}_{\text{graph}}^{\mathcal{G}}$ thereafter facilitates communication from P_v to some other node u, only if u is indeed a neighbor of v. However, [ALM17] instead has $\mathcal{F}_{\text{graph}}^{\mathcal{G}}$ first sample a random injective function $f: E \to [n^2]$, labeling each edge with a random (unique) element from $[n^2]$. Next, $\mathcal{F}_{\text{graph}}^{\mathcal{G}}$ informs every party P_v of their local neighbourhood by instead sending them the set of edge labels $L_v := \{f((u, v)) : (u, v) \in E\}$. $\mathcal{F}_{\text{graph}}^{\mathcal{G}}$ thereafter facilitates communication from P_v along some edge with label l, only if l corresponds to some edge $(v, u) \in E$ according to f.

We refer to these two notions according to the terminology of [AGPV88], who define the **K**nowledge **T**ill **R**adius σ Model (KT$_\sigma$). These two worlds are illustrated in Fig. 4. KT$_1$ is called the 'Common Neighbours' model, and refers to the [MOR15] world. Indeed, in this world, parties are given the identities of their neighbours, so that two colluding parties that each have an edge to a common party know that this is in fact the case. KT$_0$ is called the 'Pseudonymous Neighbours' model, and refers to the [ALM17] world. In this world, parties are only given the random (unique) identities of the *edges* corresponding to their neighbourhood, as described above, but not the actual identities of the parties with which they share these edges. So, if two colluding parties each have an edge to a common party, their respective edges will have different labelings and thus will not tell them if they indeed share this common neighbour.

KT$_0$: Common Neighbours Model

KT$_1$: Pseudonymous Neighbours Model

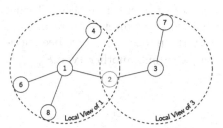

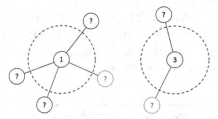

(a) In the 'Common Neighbours' model, colluding parties (①,③) know from their local views if they have common neighbours (②).

(b) In the 'Pseudonymous Neighbours' model, colluding parties (①,③) do not know from their local views if they have common neighbours (⑦).

Fig. 4. Differing views of parties in KT$_0$ and KT$_1$.

Simulation-Based THC. Now we are ready to introduce our simulation-baesd topology-hiding computation definition. The real-world protocol is defined in a model where all communication is transmitted via the functionality $\mathcal{F}_{\text{graph}}^{\mathcal{G},\text{KT}_\sigma}$ (described in Fig. 5). The functionality is parameterised by a family of graphs $\mathcal{G}$, representing all possible network topologies (aka communication graphs) that the protocol supports. It is also parameterised by the neighbourhood model KT$_\sigma$, for $\sigma \subset [0,1]$. We implicitly assume that every node in a graph is associated with a specific *party identifier*, pid.

Initially, before the protocol begins, $\mathcal{F}_{\text{graph}}^{\mathcal{G},\text{KT}_\sigma}$ receives the network communication graph G from a special graph party P$_{\text{graph}}$ and makes sure that $G \in \mathcal{G}$. Then, if $\sigma = 0$, it samples a random injective function $f\colon E \to [n^2]$, labeling each edge with an element from $[n^2]$, and gives each party P$_v$ with $v \in V$ the edge labels according to its local neighbor-set. Next, during the protocol's execution, whenever party P$_v$ wishes to send a message m along edge l, it sends (l, m) to the functionality; the functionality first checks if there is $(v, w) \in E$ such that $f(v, w) = l$, and if so delivers (l, m) to P$_w$. Otherwise, if $\sigma = 1$, it simply provides to each party P$_v$ with $v \in V$ its local neighbor-set. Next, during the protocol's execution, whenever party P$_v$ wishes to send a message m to party P$_w$, it sends (v, w, m) to the functionality; the functionality verifies that the edge (v, w) is indeed in the graph, and if so delivers (v, w, m) to P$_w$.

Note that if all the graphs in $\mathcal{G}$ have exactly n nodes, then the exact number of participants is known to all and need not be kept hidden. In this case, defining the ideal functionality and constructing protocols becomes a simpler task. However, if there exist graphs in $\mathcal{G}$ that contain a *different* number of nodes, then the model must support functionalities and protocols that only know an *upper bound* on the number of participants. In the latter case, the actual number of participating parties must be kept hidden.

Given a class of graphs $\mathcal{G}$ with an upper bound n on the number of parties, we define a protocol π with respect to $\mathcal{G}$ as a set of n PPT interactive Turing machines (ITMs) $(\mathsf{P}_1, \ldots, \mathsf{P}_n)$ (the parties), where any subset of them may be activated with (potentially empty) inputs. Only the parties that have been activated participate in the protocol, send messages to one another (via $\mathcal{F}_{\mathsf{graph}}^{\mathcal{G}, \mathsf{KT}_\sigma}$), and produce output.

Functionality $\mathcal{F}_{\mathsf{graph}}^{\mathcal{G}, \mathsf{KT}_\sigma}$

The functionality $\mathcal{F}_{\mathsf{graph}}^{\mathcal{G}, \mathsf{KT}_\sigma}$ is parametrized by a graph class $\mathcal{G}$ and neighbourhood model KT_σ; let n be the maximum number of nodes in any graph in $\mathcal{G}$. $\mathcal{F}_{\mathsf{graph}}^{\mathcal{G}, \mathsf{KT}_\sigma}$ interacts with a special graph party $\mathsf{P}_{\mathsf{graph}}$ and (a subset of the) parties $\mathsf{P}_1, \ldots, \mathsf{P}_n$ (to be defined by the graph received from $\mathsf{P}_{\mathsf{graph}}$) as follows.

Initialization Phase:

Input: $\mathcal{F}_{\mathsf{graph}}^{\mathcal{G}, \mathsf{KT}_\sigma}$ waits to receive the graph $G = (V, E)$ from $\mathsf{P}_{\mathsf{graph}}$. If $G \notin \mathcal{G}$, abort. If $\sigma = 0$, $\mathcal{F}_{\mathsf{graph}}^{\mathcal{G}, \mathsf{KT}_\sigma}$ samples a random injective function $f \colon E \to [n^2]$, labeling each edge with an element from $[n^2]$.

Output: Upon receiving an initialization message from P_v, $\mathcal{F}_{\mathsf{graph}}^{\mathcal{G}, \mathsf{KT}_\sigma}$ verifies that $v \in V$, and if so sends the following to P_v:

$$\begin{cases} \mathcal{N}_G(v) & \text{if } \sigma = 1 \text{ (``in } \mathsf{KT}_1\text{'')} \\ L_v := \{f((u,v)) \colon (u,v) \in E\} & \text{if } \sigma = 0 \text{ (``in } \mathsf{KT}_0\text{'')} \end{cases}$$

Communication Phase:

Input:

- If $\sigma = 1$: $\mathcal{F}_{\mathsf{graph}}^{\mathcal{G}, \mathsf{KT}_1}$ receives from a party P_v a destination/data pair (w, m) where $w \in \mathcal{N}_G(v)$ and m is the message P_v wants to send to P_w. (If $v, w \notin V$, or if w is not a neighboring vertex of v, $\mathcal{F}_{\mathsf{graph}}^{\mathcal{G}, \mathsf{KT}_0}$ ignores this input.)
- If $\sigma = 0$: $\mathcal{F}_{\mathsf{graph}}^{\mathcal{G}, \mathsf{KT}_0}$ receives from a party P_v a destination/data pair (l, m) where $f(v, w) = l \in L_v$ indicates to $\mathcal{F}_{\mathsf{graph}}^{\mathcal{G}, \mathsf{KT}_0}$ the neighbour w, and m is the message P_v wants to send to P_w. (If $v \notin V$ or $\nexists (v, w) \in E \colon f(v, w) = l$, $\mathcal{F}_{\mathsf{graph}}^{\mathcal{G}, \mathsf{KT}_1}$ ignores this input.)

Output:

- If $\sigma = 1$: $\mathcal{F}_{\mathsf{graph}}^{\mathcal{G}, \mathsf{KT}_1}$ gives output (v, m) to P_w indicating that P_v sent the message m to P_w.
- If $\sigma = 0$: $\mathcal{F}_{\mathsf{graph}}^{\mathcal{G}, \mathsf{KT}_0}$ gives output (l, m) to P_w, where $f(v, w) = l$, indicating that the neighbor on edge l sent the message m to P_w.

Fig. 5. The communication graph functionality (unified definition for KT_0 and KT_1).

An ideal-model computation of a functionality $\mathcal{F}$ is augmented to provide the corrupted parties with the information that is leaked about the graph; namely, every corrupted (dummy) party should learn its local neighbourhood information (in KT_0 or KT_1, respectively). Note that the functionality $\mathcal{F}$ can be completely agnostic about the actual graph that is used, and even about the family $\mathcal{G}$. To augment $\mathcal{F}$ in a generic way, we define the wrapper-functionality $\mathcal{W}_{\mathsf{graph\text{-}info}}^{\mathcal{G},\mathsf{KT}_\sigma}(\mathcal{F})$, that runs internally a copy of the functionality $\mathcal{F}$. The wrapper $\mathcal{W}_{\mathsf{graph\text{-}info}}^{\mathcal{G},\mathsf{KT}_\sigma}(\cdot)$ acts as a shell that is responsible to provide the relevant leakage to the corrupted parties; the original functionality $\mathcal{F}$ is the core that is responsible for the actual ideal computation.

More specifically, the wrapper receives the graph $G = (V, E)$ from the graph party $\mathsf{P}_{\mathsf{graph}}$, makes sure that $G \in \mathcal{G}$, and sends a special initialization message containing G to $\mathcal{F}$. (If the functionality $\mathcal{F}$ does not depend on the communication graph, it can ignore this message.) The wrapper then proceeds to process messages as follows: Upon receiving an initialization message from a party P_v responds with its local neighbourhood information (just like $\mathcal{F}_{\mathsf{graph}}^{\mathcal{G},\mathsf{KT}_\sigma}$). All other input messages from a party P_v are forwarded to $\mathcal{F}$ and every message from $\mathcal{F}$ to a party P_v is delivered to its recipient (Fig. 6).

Wrapper Functionality $\mathcal{W}_{\mathsf{graph\text{-}info}}^{\mathcal{G},\mathsf{KT}_\sigma}(\mathcal{F})$

The wrapper functionality $\mathcal{W}_{\mathsf{graph\text{-}info}}^{\mathcal{G},\mathsf{KT}_\sigma}(\mathcal{F})$ is parametrized by a graph class $\mathcal{G}$ and neighbourhood model KT_σ; let n be the maximum number of nodes in any graph in $\mathcal{G}$. $\mathcal{W}_{\mathsf{graph\text{-}info}}^{\mathcal{G},\mathsf{KT}_\sigma}(\mathcal{F})$ internally runs a copy of $\mathcal{F}$ and interacts with a special graph party $\mathsf{P}_{\mathsf{graph}}$ and (a subset of the) parties $\mathsf{P}_1, \ldots, \mathsf{P}_n$ (to be defined by the graph received from $\mathsf{P}_{\mathsf{graph}}$) as follows.

Initialization Phase:

Input: $\mathcal{W}_{\mathsf{graph\text{-}info}}^{\mathcal{G},\mathsf{KT}_\sigma}(\mathcal{F})$ waits to receive the graph $G = (V, E)$ from $\mathsf{P}_{\mathsf{graph}}$. If $G \notin \mathcal{G}$, abort. If $\sigma = 0$, $\mathcal{W}_{\mathsf{graph\text{-}info}}^{\mathcal{G},\mathsf{KT}_\sigma}(\mathcal{F})$ samples a random injective function $f \colon E \to [n^2]$, labeling each edge with an element from $[n^2]$.

Outputs: Upon receiving an initialization message from P_v, $\mathcal{W}_{\mathsf{graph\text{-}info}}^{\mathcal{G},\mathsf{KT}_\sigma}(\mathcal{F})$ verifies that $v \in V$, and if so sends the following to P_v:

$$\begin{cases} \mathcal{N}_G(v) & \text{if } \sigma = 1 \text{ (``in } \mathsf{KT}_1\text{'')} \\ L_v := \{f((u,v)) \colon (u,v) \in E\} & \text{if } \sigma = 0 \text{ (``in } \mathsf{KT}_0\text{'')} \end{cases}$$

Communication Phase:

Input: $\mathcal{W}_{\mathsf{graph\text{-}info}}^{\mathcal{G},\mathsf{KT}_\sigma}(\mathcal{F})$ forwards every message it receives to $\mathcal{F}$.

Output: Whenever $\mathcal{F}$ sends a message, $\mathcal{W}_{\mathsf{graph\text{-}info}}^{\mathcal{G},\mathsf{KT}_\sigma}(\mathcal{F})$ forwards the message to its intended recipient.

Fig. 6. The graph-information wrapper functionality (unified definition for KT_0 and KT_1).

Note that formally, the set of all possible parties V^* is fixed in advance. To represent a graph $G' = (V', E')$ where $V' \subseteq V^*$ is a subset of the parties, we use the graph $G = (V^*, E')$, where all vertices $v \in V^* \setminus V'$ have degree 0.

Definition 1 (Topology-hiding computation). *We say that a protocol π securely realizes a functionality $\mathcal{F}$ in a* **topology-hiding manner** *with respect to $\mathcal{G}$ tolerating a semi-honest adversary corrupting t parties if π securely realizes $\mathcal{W}_{\text{graph-info}}^{\mathcal{G}, KT_0}(\mathcal{F})$ in the $\mathcal{F}_{\text{graph}}^{\mathcal{G}, KT_0}$-hybrid model tolerating a semi-honest adversary corrupting t parties.*

Broadcast. In this work we will focus on topology-hiding computation of the *broadcast* functionality (see Fig. 7), where a designated and publicly known party, named *the broadcaster*, starts with an input value m. Our broadcast functionality guarantees that every party that is connected to the broadcaster in the communication graph receives the message m as output. In this paper, we assume the communication graphs are always connected. However, the broadcaster may not be participating, in which case it is represented as a degree-0 node in the communication graph (and all the participating nodes are in a separate connected component.)

Parties that are not connected to the broadcaster receive a message that is supplied by the adversary (we can consider stronger versions of broadcast, but this simplifies the proofs).

We denote the broadcast functionality where the broadcaster is P_i by $\mathcal{F}_{\text{bc}}(P_i)$.

Functionality $\mathcal{F}_{\text{bc}}(P_i)$

The broadcast functionality $\mathcal{F}_{\text{bc}}(P_i)$ is parametrized by the broadcaster P_i and proceeds as follows.

Initialization: The functionality receives the communication graph G from the wrapper $\mathcal{W}_{\text{graph-info}}$.

Input: Record the input message $m \in \{0, 1\}$ sent by the broadcaster P_i.

Output: Send the output m to every party that is in the same connected component as P_i in G. For every other party in G, the output delivered to that party is supplied by the adversary.

Fig. 7. The broadcast functionality

Definition 2 (t-THB). *Let $\mathcal{G}$ be a family of graphs and let t be an integer. A protocol π is a t-THB protocol with respect to $\mathcal{G}$ if $\pi(P_v)$ securely realizes $\mathcal{F}_{\text{bc}}(P_v)$ in a topology-hiding manner with respect to $\mathcal{G}$, for every P_v, tolerating a semi-honest adversary corrupting t parties.*

3.2 Constant-Overhead Two-Party Computation for Semi-Honest Adversaries

Definition 3 (Stateless Two-Party Computation Syntax). *A R_{2PC}-round Stateless Two-Party Computation (2PC) protocol* $2PC^{\mathcal{F}}(x_0, x_1; r_0, r_1) :=$ $(2PC_{0,i}^{\mathcal{F}}, 2PC_{1,i}^{\mathcal{F}})_{i \in [0, R_{2PC}-1]}$ *for given functionality $\mathcal{F}$ is described by two parties,* P_0 *and* P_1, *with respective inputs* x_0, x_1 *and respective randomness* r_0, r_1 *that use PPT algorithms* $2PC_{0,i}^{\mathcal{F}}(x_0, \{m_{1,j}\}_{j<i}; r_0)$ *(resp.* $2PC_{1,i}^{\mathcal{F}}(x_1, \{m_{0,j}\}_{j \leq i}; r_1)$) *to compute* P_0*'s (resp.* P_1*'s) i-th round message of the protocol,* $m_{0,i}$ *(resp.* $m_{1,i}$), *taking as input* P_0*'s 2PC input* x_0 *and the j-th round messages of* P_1 *for* $j < i$, *and using* P_0*'s 2PC randomness* r_0 *(resp.* P_1*'s 2PC input* x_1 *and the j-th round messages of* P_0 *for* $j \leq i$, *and using* P_1*'s 2PC randomness* r_1). *Algorithm* $2PC_{0,R_{2PC}-1}^{\mathcal{F}}(x_0, \{m_{1,j}\}_{j<R_{2PC}-1}; r_0)$ *(resp.* $2PC_{1,R_{2PC}-1}^{\mathcal{F}}(x_1, \{m_{0,j}\}_{j \leq R_{2PC}-1}; r_1)$) *additionally gives output* y_0 *(resp. only gives output* y_1).

We will additionally use the notation $2PC_{i,<\rho}^{\mathcal{F}}(x_0, x_1; r_0, r_1)$ *to represent the first ρ messages that party i receives from party $1-i$ on inputs x_0, x_1 and randomness r_0, r_1, respectively.*

We defer the standard real/ideal world security definition of 2PC with respect to a semi-honest adversary to the real version [BBKM23].

Constant-Overhead Constant-Round 2PC. For this work, we need to use a 2PC with constant overhead and constant round complexity. More precisely, we require that 2PC satisfies the following properties: First, for any given functionality $\mathcal{F}$ and the corresponding circuit $C_{\mathcal{F}}$ that computes it, 2PC has computational (and thus also communication) overhead $O(|C_{\mathcal{F}}|) + \text{poly}(\lambda)$, where $|C_{\mathcal{F}}|$ is the size of the circuit, i.e., the number of gates it has. Second, we require the number of rounds R_{2PC} to be constant.

3.3 Efficiently Invertible from Local Information Functionalities

In the full version [BBKM23], we define special *efficiently invertible from local information* functionalities for which we can prove local simulatability of our path protocol (the OR functionality being one example).

4 Locally Simulatable MPC

In this section we introduce the notion of locally simulatable MPC on disconnected graphs.

Towards the definition of locally simulatable MPC, we first recall the standard definition of a functionality to model a function $f: \mathcal{X}^0 \times \cdots \times \mathcal{X}^{\ell-1} \rightarrow \mathcal{Y}^0 \times \cdots \times \mathcal{Y}^{\ell-1}$ in Fig. 8.

We define local simulatability relative to a communication network $G = (V, E)$, where $V = \{0, \ldots, \ell-1\}$, and where two parties P_i and P_j can communicate if and only if they are connected by an edge $(i, j) \in E$. In the following we always assume the graph to be connected.

Functionality $\mathcal{F}_f$

The functionality $\mathcal{F}_f$ is parameterised by the function f to be computed.

Input: The functionality awaits input $x_i \in \mathcal{X}_i$ from party P_i (for $i \in \{0, \ldots, \ell - 1\}$).

Computation: The functionality computes $(y_0, \ldots, y_{\ell-1}) := f(x_0, \ldots, x_{\ell-1})$.

Output: The functionality outputs y_i to party P_i (for $i \in \{0, \ldots, \ell - 1\}$).

Fig. 8. Functionality $\mathcal{F}_f$ for computing $f \colon \mathcal{X}^0 \times \cdots \times \mathcal{X}^{\ell-1} \to \mathcal{Y}^0 \times \cdots \times \mathcal{Y}^{\ell-1}$.

We model the notion of local simulatability, by requiring a simulator to be dividable in simulators $S_1, \ldots, S_\mu$ (one for each connected component of the adversary), where simulator S_i has to simulate the view of the i-th component solely based on the inputs and outputs of the parties in this component.

Real Execution. Let Π be a protocol executed by parties $P_0, \ldots, P_{\ell-1}$ on G, i.e., a protocol where each party can only send and receive messages from their neighbors in G. Then, the view $\text{View}_i^\Pi(x_0, \ldots, x_{\ell-1})$ of party P_i consists of its input x_i, its internal randomness r_i and all messages received by party P_j with $(i, j) \in E$. Let $\mathcal{A}$ be an adversary corrupting a subset $I \subset \{0, \ldots, \ell - 1\}$ of the players. Then, the view of $\mathcal{A}$ in the real execution of Π is of the form

$$\text{REAL}_{\mathcal{A}, I}^\Pi(x_0, \ldots, x_{\ell-1}) = \left(\Pi(x_0, \ldots, x_{\ell-1}), \left\{ \text{View}_i^\Pi(x_0, \ldots, x_{\ell-1}) \right\}_{i \in I} \right),$$

where $\Pi(x_0, \ldots, x_{\ell-1})$ denotes the outputs of parties $P_0, \ldots, P_{\ell-1}$ after the execution of Π on input $(x_0, \ldots, x_{\ell-1})$ with randomness $(r_0, \ldots, r_{\ell-1})$.

Ideal Execution. Again, let $\mathcal{A}$ be an adversary corrupting a subset $I \subset V$ of the nodes and let $I_1, \ldots, I_\mu$ be a partitioning of I into *pairwise disconnected components*, i.e. such that

- $I = \bigcup_{j=1}^\mu I_j$
- I_i, I_j are *disconnected* for any $i \neq j$, i.e., for each $u \in I_i$ and $v \in I_j$ it holds $(u, v) \notin E$.

Let $\text{Sim} = (\text{Sim}_1, \ldots, \text{Sim}_\mu)$ be a tuple of algorithms[10], such that for each $j \in \{1, \ldots, \mu\}$ the following holds:

- Sim_j is a PPT algorithm,
- Sim_j obtains an input/ output pair (x_i, y_i) for all $i \in I_j$,
- Sim_j outputs a simulated view of parties $\{P_i\}_{i \in I_j}$.

---

[10] Note that the distinction into μ different simulators instead of μ copies of the same simulator is solely for the sake of clarity.

Then, we define the simulated view of Sim in the ideal execution of $\mathcal{F}_f$ as

$$\text{IDEAL}^f_{\text{Sim},I}(x_0,\ldots,x_{\ell-1}) = \left(f(x_0,\ldots,x_{\ell-1}), \{\text{Sim}_j((x_i,y_i)_{i\in I_j})\}_{j\in\mu} \right).$$

Definition 4 (Local Simulation). *Let Π be a protocol on G. We say that Π emulates $\mathcal{F}_f$ relative to G with local simulatability in the static, semi-honest model against t corruptions if for every PPT adversary $\mathcal{A}$ corrupting a set $I \subset \{0,\ldots,\ell-1\}$ with $|I| \leq t$ and for every partitioning of I into pairwise disconnected components $I_1,\ldots,I_\mu$, there exists a PPT simulator $Sim = (Sim_1,\ldots,Sim_\mu)$, such that for all $x_0,\ldots,x_{\ell-1} \in \{0,1\}^*$ it holds*

$$\left\{ \text{REAL}^\Pi_{\mathcal{A},I}(x_0,\ldots,x_{\ell-1}) \right\} \approx_c \left\{ \text{IDEAL}^f_{Sim,I}(x_0,\ldots,x_{\ell-1}) \right\}$$

4.1 Locally Simulatable Protocols Are Execution-Oblivious

In this section we first define *execution obliviousness*. Then, in the full version of the paper [BBKM23], we show that the notion of locally simulatability indeed guarantees execution-obliviousness (unless the execution can be derived from the output), as we will require to construct THC.

In the following we restrict to protocols implementing deterministic functionalities with perfect correctness, i.e. for which $\Pi(x_0,\ldots,x_{\ell-1})$ is well-defined without specifying the random coins. (Note that the requirements on inputs and randomness in the following definition are necessary for preventing a trivial distinguisher.)

Definition 5 (Execution obliviousness.). *Let $G = (V,E)$ be a graph with $V = \{0,\ldots,\ell-1\}$ and let Π be an ℓ-party protocol on G. We say Π is execution oblivious on G tolerating t corruptions, if for all sets $I \subseteq \{0,\ldots,\ell-1\}$ with $|I| \leq t$ and for any partitioning of I into pairwise disconnected components $I_1,\ldots,I_\mu$ the following holds:*

For all inputs $(x_0,\ldots,x_{\ell-1}),(x_0^{(1)},\ldots,x_{\ell-1}^{(1)}),\ldots,(x_0^{(\mu)},\ldots,x_{\ell-1}^{(\mu)}) \in \mathcal{X}_0\times\cdots\times\mathcal{X}_{\ell-1}$ with

- $x_i^{(j)} = x_i$ *for all* $i \in I_j, j \in [\mu]$, *and*
- $\Pi(x_0,\ldots,x_{\ell-1}) = \Pi(x_0^{(1)},\ldots,x_{\ell-1}^{(1)}) = \cdots = \Pi(x_0^{(\mu)},\ldots,x_{\ell-1}^{(\mu)})$,

it holds:

$$\left(\Pi(x_0,\ldots,x_{\ell-1}), \{\text{View}_i^\Pi(x_0,\ldots,x_{\ell-1};r_1,\ldots,r_{\ell-1})\}_{i\in I} \right)$$

$$\approx_c \left(\Pi(x_0,\ldots,x_{\ell-1}), \bigcup_{j=1}^\mu \{\text{View}_i^\Pi(x_0^{(j)},\ldots,x_{\ell-1}^{(j)};r_0^{(j)},\ldots,r_{\ell-1}^{(j)})\}_{i\in I_j} \right),$$

where the randomness is taken over the random coins $r_1,\ldots,r_{\ell-1},\{r_1^{(j)},\ldots,r_{\ell-1}^{(j)}\}_{j\in[\mu]}$.

Lemma 1 (Locally Simulatable Protocols are Execution Oblivious).
Let $G = (V, E)$ be a graph with $V = \{0, \ldots, \ell - 1\}$, let $\mathcal{F}_f$ be a deterministic ℓ-party functionality and let Π be an ℓ-party protocol on G. If Π emulates $\mathcal{F}_f$ relative to G with local simulatability in the static, semi-honest model against t corruptions, then Π is execution oblivious on G tolerating t corruptions.

We defer the proof of this lemma to the full version [BBKM23].

5   Locally Simulatable Protocol for Directed Paths

In this section, we formally present the protocol for computing on a directed path some functionality $\mathcal{F}$ that is *efficiently invertible from local information*. An example of such a functionality is $\mathcal{F}_{\mathsf{OR}}$, which we will use to implement THB in the next section. We refer the reader back to Sect. 2.2 for a detailed overview of the protocol. Due to space limitations, we defer the proof of local simulatability to the full version of this paper [BBKM23].

5.1   The Path Protocol

The directed path protocol $\Pi_{\mathsf{dir\text{-}path}}$ is formally presented in Fig. 9. As described in Sect. 2.2, the protocol works over a directed path $\mathsf{Path}_\ell = \textcircled{0} \rightarrow \textcircled{1} \cdots \rightarrow \textcircled{ℓ-1}$ of length $\ell = 2^l$, for some $l > 0$. Each party knows its position j on the path and we refer to each such party as $\widetilde{\mathsf{P}}_j$. The protocol recursively computes the given functionality $\mathcal{F}$. Recall that $\mathcal{F}$ must be *efficiently invertible from local information*, such as $\mathcal{F}_{\mathsf{OR}}$, which on input bits b_j from each party $\widetilde{\mathsf{P}}_j$, outputs $\bigvee_{j=0}^{\ell-1} b_j$ to every party. When computation of $\mathcal{F}_{\mathsf{OR}}$ used in our higher-level THB protocol of the next section, the input of party $\widetilde{\mathsf{P}}_{j^*}$ corresponding to the broadcaster will be $b_{j^*} = b$, the broadcast bit, and for all $j \neq j^*$, the input of party $\widetilde{\mathsf{P}}_j$ will be $b_j = 0$.

$\Pi_{\mathsf{dir\text{-}path}}$ proceeds by recursively emulating a (constant-round, constant-overhead) 2PC that computes $((y_0|| \ldots ||y_{\ell/2-1}), (y_{\ell/2}|| \ldots ||y_{\ell-1})) = \mathcal{F}'((x_0|| \ldots ||x_{\ell/2-1}), (x_{\ell/2}|| \ldots ||x_{\ell-1})) = \mathcal{F}(x_0, \ldots, x_{\ell-1})$ for two virtual parties, and then recursively sending the outputs y_j to the Parties P_j at the bottom of the recursion tree. Party $\mathsf{P}_{0,0}$ (and similarly for party $\mathsf{P}_{0,1}$) of the highest-level 2PC is recursively emulated by parties $\widetilde{\mathsf{P}}_0, \ldots \widetilde{\mathsf{P}}_{\ell/2-1}$ on the path by first computing each message that $\mathsf{P}_{0,0}$ sends in this 2PC via another lower-level 2PC between virtual parties $\mathsf{P}_{1,0}$ and $\mathsf{P}_{1,1}$. Parties $\mathsf{P}_{1,0}$ and $\mathsf{P}_{1,1}$ combine their inputs and random strings via this 2PC to emulate $\mathsf{P}_{0,0}$'s input and random tape. $\mathsf{P}_{1,1}$ then receives $\mathsf{P}_{0,0}$'s next message and sends it to $\mathsf{P}_{1,2}$ (the first party emulating $\mathsf{P}_{0,1}$). Continuing in the recursion, both $\mathsf{P}_{1,0}$ and $\mathsf{P}_{1,1}$ are then emulated by another 2PC in the same fashion, and so on, until we reach two actual parties on the path.

For each call (either the invocation or recursive calls) to $\Pi_{\mathsf{dir\text{-}path}}$ there are some parameters known to all participants: the current topology being considered (each recursive call works over a connected subgraph of the path); the R_{2PC}

round constant-overhead semi-honest stateless protocol 2PC that is being used for the execution; the recursion depth d; the message virtual party $\sigma \in \{0, 1, \bot\}$ who outputs a message for the 2PC that is being emulated by this instance (if $\sigma = \bot$, this means neither party does); output flag $o \in \{0, 1\}$, which indicates whether or not the parties produce an output in this execution; and the 2PC functionality $\mathcal{F}$ that the two virtual parties are computing. For the original invocation call, the path considered is the whole path $\texttt{Path}_\ell = \text{⓪} \to \text{①} \cdots \to \text{ⓛ-1}$, the recursion depth is $d = 0$, message virtual party is $\sigma = \bot$, output flag is $o = 1$, and the 2PC functionality that will be recursively computed is $\mathcal{F}'$; i.e., on input x_0 from $\mathsf{P}_{0,0}$ (recursively $||_{j=0}^{\ell/2-1} x_j$) and x_1 from $\mathsf{P}_{0,1}$ (recursively $||_{j=\ell/2}^{\ell-1} x_j$), output $\mathcal{F}'(x_0, x_1)$ to $\mathsf{P}_{0,0}$ and $\mathsf{P}_{0,1}$.

For each call, each party also receives some local input: their position j on the corresponding subgraph of the path; their input x_j; a dictionary of random strings $\tilde{R}_j$ that they will use for the emulation of high-level 2PC virtual parties; a set of 2PC messages M_j that they receive from some higher-level 2PC in which they are assisting the emulation of one of the virtual parties; and their neighbors on the path, $\tilde{\mathsf{P}}_{j-1}$ and $\tilde{\mathsf{P}}_{j+1}$. For the original invocation call, each party's position is of course j, their input x_j, random string dictionary $\tilde{R}_j[\cdot] = \bot$, empty message set $M_j = \emptyset$, and neighbors $\tilde{\mathsf{P}}_{j-1}$ and $\tilde{\mathsf{P}}_{j+1}$.

Efficiency. Recall that we assume the round complexity of the 2PC protocol is some constant R_{2PC} and its overhead is $c \cdot |\mathcal{C}_\mathcal{F}| + \mathrm{poly}(\lambda)$ for some constant c, where $\mathcal{C}_\mathcal{F}$ is the circuit that computes given functionality $\mathcal{F}$. Thus, the round complexity of $\Pi_{\mathsf{dir\text{-}path}}$ is $R[\ell] = 2R_{\mathsf{2PC}} \cdot R[\ell/2] + 2 = \Theta\left(\ell \cdot R_{\mathsf{2PC}}^{\log \ell}\right)$, which is $O(\ell^2)$. Furthermore, each real party on the path executes $R_{\mathsf{2PC}}^{\log \ell - 1}$ 2PC's. The overhead of the highest-level 2PC is $c \cdot |\mathcal{C}_{\mathcal{F}'}| + \mathrm{poly}(\lambda)$, the overhead of the 2PC's in the next recursion level are then $c^2 \cdot |\mathcal{C}_{\mathcal{F}'}| + c \cdot \mathrm{poly}(\lambda) + \mathrm{poly}(\lambda)$, and so on so that the overhead of the 2PC's executed by the real parties is $O(\ell \cdot (|\mathcal{C}_{\mathcal{F}'}| + \mathrm{poly}(\lambda)))$. Therefore, the total overhead of $\Pi_{\mathsf{dir\text{-}path}}$ is $O(R_{\mathsf{2PC}}^{\log \ell - 1} \cdot \ell \cdot (|\mathcal{C}_{\mathcal{F}'}| + \mathrm{poly}(\lambda))) = O(\ell^2 \cdot (|\mathcal{C}_{\mathcal{F}'}| + \mathrm{poly}(\lambda)))$.

Protocol $\Pi_{\text{dir-path}}$

Parameters: A topology $\texttt{Path}_\ell = \textcircled{0} \to \textcircled{1} \cdots \to \textcircled{\ell\text{-}1}$ of length $\ell = 2^l$, an R_{2PC}-round constant-overhead semi-honest stateless protocol $\text{2PC} = (\text{2PC}_{0,\rho}, \text{2PC}_{1,\rho})_{\rho \in [0, R_{\text{2PC}}-1]}$, recursion depth d, a message virtual party σ, output flag o, and 2PC functionality to be (recursively) computed $\mathcal{F}$. *Note:* we will use $\widetilde{\mathsf{P}}_j$ to denote the party at position j on the path.

The Protocol:

- **Initialisation:** Each party $\widetilde{\mathsf{P}}_j$ receives $(j, x_j, \widetilde{R}_j, M_j, \widetilde{\mathsf{P}}_{j-1}, \widetilde{\mathsf{P}}_{j+1})$ as input, either from the original invocation, or from a recursive call. Each party $\widetilde{\mathsf{P}}_j$ samples $\widetilde{r}_j \xleftarrow{\$} \{0,1\}^\lambda$ and sets $\widetilde{R}_j[d] \leftarrow \widetilde{r}_j$.
- **Base Case ($\ell = 2$):** Parties $\widetilde{\mathsf{P}}_0$ and $\widetilde{\mathsf{P}}_1$ directly compute the R_{2PC} round protocol $\text{2PC}^{\mathcal{F}}((x_0, \widetilde{R}_0[: d-2], \widetilde{R}_0[d-1], M_0), (x_1, \widetilde{R}_1[: d-2], \widetilde{R}_1[d-1], M_1); \widetilde{r}_0, \widetilde{r}_1)$. If $\sigma \neq \perp$, then $\widetilde{\mathsf{P}}_\sigma$ returns the output message to its invoker. Furthermore, if $o = 1$, then both parties locally return their outputs y_0 and y_1, respectively.
- For $\rho = 0, \ldots, R_{\text{2PC}} - 2$:
  - For $k \in [0,1]$, rounds $(2\rho + k) \cdot (R[\frac{\ell}{2}] + 1)$ to $(2\rho + k + 1) \cdot (R[\frac{\ell}{2}] + 1) - 1$:
    Compute virtual Party P_k's next 2PC message $m_{k,\rho}$.
    1. Parties $\widetilde{\mathsf{P}}_{k \cdot \ell/2}, \ldots, \widetilde{\mathsf{P}}_{k \cdot \ell/2 + \ell/2 - 1}$ recursively call $\Pi_{\text{dir-path}}$ with:
       * *Parameters:* $\boxed{\mathsf{k} \cdot \ell/2} \to \boxed{\mathsf{k} \cdot \ell/2 + 1} \cdots \to \boxed{\mathsf{k} \cdot \ell/2 + \ell/2 - 1}$ of length $\ell/2 = 2^{l-1}$, protocol 2PC, recursion depth $d + 1$, message virtual party $\sigma' = 1 - k$, output flag $o = 0$, 2PC functionality $\mathcal{F}_k :=$
         · $\mathsf{P}_{k,0}$'s Input: $x_{k,0}, \widetilde{R}_{k,0}, \widetilde{r}_{k,0}, M_{k,0}$

           (recursively:
           $$\|_{j=k\cdot\ell/2}^{k\cdot\ell/2+\ell/4-1} x_j, \left\{ \bigoplus_{j=k\cdot\ell/2}^{k\cdot\ell/2+\ell/4-1} \widetilde{R}_j[d'] \right\}_{d' \in [0, d-1]}, \bigoplus_{j=k\cdot\ell/2}^{k\cdot\ell/2+\ell/4-1} \widetilde{r}_j, M'_{k\cdot\ell/2};$$
           where for $k = 1$, $M'_{k\cdot\ell/2} = \{m_{0,q}\}_{q < \rho}$, i.e., messages sent so far by P_0;
           $$\text{for } k = 0, M'_{k\cdot\ell/2} = M_{k\cdot\ell/2}\Big)$$

         · $\mathsf{P}_{k,1}$'s Input: $b_{k,1}, \widetilde{R}_{k,1}, \widetilde{r}_{k,1}, M_{k,1}$

           (recursively:
           $$\|_{j=k\cdot\ell/2+\ell/4}^{k\cdot\ell/2+\ell/2-1} x_j, \left\{ \bigoplus_{j=k\cdot\ell/2+\ell/4}^{k\cdot\ell/2+\ell/2-1} \widetilde{R}_j[d'] \right\}_{d' \in [0, d-1]}, \bigoplus_{j=k\cdot\ell/2+\ell/4}^{k\cdot\ell/2+\ell/2-1} \widetilde{r}_j, M'_{k\cdot\ell/2+\ell/2-1};$$
           where for $k = 0$, $M'_{k\cdot\ell/2+\ell/2-1} = \{m_{1,q}\}_{q < \rho}$, i.e., messages sent so far by P_1;
           $$\text{for } k = 1, M'_{k\cdot\ell/2+\ell/2-1} = M_{k\cdot\ell/2+\ell/2-1}\Big)$$

Fig. 9. Protocol $\Pi_{\text{dir-path}}$ which on input x_j from each party $\widetilde{\mathsf{P}}_j$ on a directed path, computes $\mathcal{F}(x_0, \ldots, x_{\ell-1}) = (y_0, \ldots, y_{\ell-1})$ and outputs to party $\widetilde{\mathsf{P}}_j$ their output y_j. Note: each party knows their position on the path.

· $\mathsf{P}_{k,k}$'s output: $\perp$
· $\mathsf{P}_{k,1-k}$'s output: $2\mathsf{PC}^{\mathcal{F}}_{k,\rho}((x_{k,0}||x_{k,1},\{\widetilde{R}_{k,0}[d']\oplus \widetilde{R}_{k,1}[d']\}_{d'\in[0,d-2]},$

$$\widetilde{R}_{k,0}[d-1]\oplus\widetilde{R}_{k,1}[d-1],M_{k,0}),M_{k,1};\widetilde{r}_{k,0}\oplus\widetilde{r}_{k,1})$$

* *Inputs:* $\widetilde{\mathsf{P}}_j$ holds $(j \bmod \ell/2, b_j, \widetilde{R}_j, M'_j, \widetilde{\mathsf{P}}_{j-1}, \widetilde{\mathsf{P}}_{j+1})$, where for $\widetilde{\mathsf{P}}_{\ell/2-1+k}$, M'_j is as above, otherwise, $M'_j = M_j$.

2. $\widetilde{\mathsf{P}}_{\ell/2-1+k}$ waits to receive $m_{k,\rho}$ as output of the recursive call to $\Pi_{\mathsf{dir\text{-}path}}$.

Send virtual Party P_k's message $m_{k,\rho}$ to virtual Party P_{1-k}.

1. $\widetilde{\mathsf{P}}_{\ell/2-1+k}$ sends $m_{k,\rho}$ to $\widetilde{\mathsf{P}}_{\ell/2-k}$.

− For $\rho = R_{\mathsf{2PC}} − 1$ (the last 2PC round):

• Rounds $(2R_{\mathsf{2PC}}-2)\cdot(R[\frac{\ell}{2}]+1)$ to $(2R_{\mathsf{2PC}}-2)\cdot(R[\frac{\ell}{2}]+1)+R[\frac{\ell}{2}]-1$:
  Compute virtual Party P_0's last 2PC message $m_{0,R_{\mathsf{2PC}}-1}$ and output y_0.
  1. As above, except if $\sigma = 0$, then instead of using message virtual party $\sigma' = 1$ for the recursive call to $\Pi_{\mathsf{dir\text{-}path}}$, we use $\sigma' = \sigma$. Furthermore, if $o = 1$, then instead of using output flag $o' = 0$, we use $o' = 1$. Then, if $\sigma = 0$, $\widetilde{\mathsf{P}}_0$ waits to receive the output y_0 from the recursive call to $\Pi_{\mathsf{dir\ path}}$ then outputs it to its invoker themself, and sets $m_{0,R_{\mathsf{2PC}}-1} = \perp$. Otherwise, $\widetilde{\mathsf{P}}_{\ell/2-1}$ waits to receive $m_{0,R_{\mathsf{2PC}}-1}$ from the recursive call to $\Pi_{\mathsf{dir\text{-}path}}$.

• Round $(2R_{\mathsf{2PC}} − 1)\cdot(R[\frac{\ell}{2}] + 1) − 1$:
  Send virtual Party P_0's last 2PC message $m_{0,R_{\mathsf{2PC}}-1}$ to Party P_1.
  1. As above.

• Rounds $(2R_{\mathsf{2PC}}-1)\cdot(R[\frac{\ell}{2}]+1)$ to $(2R_{\mathsf{2PC}}-1)\cdot(R[\frac{\ell}{2}]+1)+R[\frac{\ell}{2}]-1$:
  Compute virtual Party P_1's 2PC output.
  1. As above, except if $\sigma = 0$, then return $\perp$. Otherwise, if $\sigma = 1$ or $\sigma = \perp$, then instead of using message virtual party $\sigma' = 0$ for the recursive call to $\Pi_{\mathsf{dir\text{-}path}}$, we use $\sigma' = \sigma$. Furthermore, if $o = 1$, then instead of using output flag $o' = 0$, we use $o' = 1$. Then, $\widetilde{\mathsf{P}}_{\ell-1}$ waits to receive the output y_1 of the recursive call to $\Pi_{\mathsf{dir\text{-}path}}$ (if any) and outputs it to its invoker themself.

Fig. 9. (*continued*)

6   Extension to All Graphs

We refer to the full version of this paper [BBKM23] for how to use our protocol with local simulatability on paths to achieve topology-hiding computation on all graphs, building on the technqiues of [ALM17]. We state the relevant Theorem and Corollaries below.

Theorem 3 (Topology-hiding OR on all graphs). *Let $\kappa \in \mathbb{N}$ the statistical security parameter. Let B be an upper bound on the number of parties, and let $\ell := 2^{\lfloor \log(8\kappa \cdot B^3) \rfloor}$. If $\Pi_{dir\text{-}path} = (\text{Init}, \text{next}^{dir\text{-}path}, \text{RetrieveOutput})$ is an $R_{dir\text{-}path}$-round locally simulatable protocol for securely computing $(x_0, \ldots, x_{\ell-1}) \mapsto \bigvee_{i=0}^{\ell-1} x_i$ on the directed path $\textcircled{0} \to \textcircled{2} \cdots \to \boxed{\ell-1}$ of length ℓ with security against $\ell - 1$ corruptions, then there exists a protocol that securely realises $\mathcal{F}_{\text{OR}}$ in a topology-hiding manner against a static semi-honest adversary corrupting up to all but one party.*

As an immediate corollary of the proof of Theorem 3 (in the full version [BBKM23]) we obtain a black-box compiler for locally simulatable protocol for $\mathcal{F}_{\text{OR}}$ from directed paths to any topology. This is simply due to the observation that the simulator described above is local. Note though that for the task of obtaining locally-simulatable OT, one can replace the correlated random walks by a fixed covering walk[11], since for that purpose the topology does not need to be hidden.

Corollary 1 (Locally simulatable OR on any graph). *Let G be a graph. Assuming the existence of a secure 2-party computation protocol with constant rounds and constant overhead, there exists a locally simulatable protocol for securely computing the $\mathcal{F}_{\text{OR}}$ functionality in the presence of a semi-honest adversary corrupting any number of parties.*

Going from THB to general THC can be achieved via standard techniques, which we briefly recall in the following. On a high level, given topology hiding broadcast the parties can first decide on an enumeration $1, \ldots, |V|$ of the parties (this can be achieved, e.g., by each party broadcasting a string in a sufficiently large interval and sorting the parties based on the lexicographic order of the strings). Given this enumeration, the parties can set up point to point channels using any key exchange protocol (which, in particular, is implied by oblivious transfer). Finally, given these topology-hiding point-to-point channels, the parties can execute any MPC protocol to achieve general topology-hiding secure computation. We therefore obtain the following corollary.

Corollary 2 (THC on all graphs). *Assuming the existence of a secure 2-party computation protocol with constant rounds and constant overhead, there exists a protocol for securely computing any efficiently computable functionality*

---

[11] A *walk* in a graph is an alternating sequence of adjacent vertices and edges; both vertices and edges may be repeated. A *covering* walk contains each vertex at least once.

against a semi-honest adversary corrupting all-but-one parties, where only the total number of parties in the graph is leaked (assuming a known apriori bound on the number of parties).

Acknowledgments. We thank Elette Boyle, Ran Cohen, and Tal Moran for helpful discussions. Marshall Ball is supported in part by the Simons Foundation. Lisa Kohl is funded by NWO Gravitation project QSC. Pierre Meyer was supported by ERC Project HSS (852952) and by AFOSR Award FA9550-21-1-0046. We thank the anonymous reviewers of TCC for helpful feedback regarding the presentation of our results.

References

[AGPV88] Awerbuch, B., Goldreich, O., Peleg, D., Vainish, R.: A tradeoff between information and communication in broadcast protocols. In: Reif, J.H. (ed.) AWOC 1988. LNCS, vol. 319, pp. 369–379. Springer, New York (1988). https://doi.org/10.1007/BFb0040404

[ALM17] Akavia, A., LaVigne, R., Moran, T.: Topology-hiding computation on all graphs. In: Katz, J., Shacham, H. (eds.) CRYPTO 2017. LNCS, vol. 10401, pp. 447–467. Springer, Cham (2017). https://doi.org/10.1007/978-3-319-63688-7_15

[ALM20] Akavia, A., LaVigne, R., Moran, T.: Topology-hiding computation on all graphs. J. Cryptol. **33**(1), 176–227 (2020)

[AM17] Akavia, A., Moran, T.: Topology-hiding computation beyond logarithmic diameter. In: Coron, J.-S., Nielsen, J.B. (eds.) EUROCRYPT 2017. LNCS, vol. 10212, pp. 609–637. Springer, Cham (2017). https://doi.org/10.1007/978-3-319-56617-7_21

[BBC+19] Ball, M., Boyle, E., Cohen, R., Malkin, T., Moran, T.: Is information-theoretic topology-hiding computation possible? In: Hofheinz, D., Rosen, A. (eds.) TCC 2019. LNCS, vol. 11891, pp. 502–530. Springer, Cham (2019). https://doi.org/10.1007/978-3-030-36030-6_20

[BBC+20] Ball, M., et al.: Topology-hiding communication from minimal assumptions. In: Pass, R., Pietrzak, K. (eds.) TCC 2020. LNCS, vol. 12551, pp. 473–501. Springer, Cham (2020). https://doi.org/10.1007/978-3-030-64378-2_17

[BBKM23] Ball, M., Bienstock, A., Kohl, L., Meyer, P.: Towards topology-hiding computation from oblivious transfer. Cryptology ePrint Archive, Paper 2023/849 (2023). https://eprint.iacr.org/2023/849

[BBMM18] Ball, M., Boyle, E., Malkin, T., Moran, T.: Exploring the boundaries of topology-hiding computation. In: Nielsen, J.B., Rijmen, V. (eds.) EUROCRYPT 2018. LNCS, vol. 10822, pp. 294–325. Springer, Cham (2018). https://doi.org/10.1007/978-3-319-78372-7_10

[BGW88] Ben-Or, M., Goldwasser, S., Wigderson, A.: Completeness theorems for non-cryptographic fault-tolerant distributed computation (extended abstract). In: 20th Annual ACM Symposium on Theory of Computing, pp. 1–10, Chicago, IL, USA, ACM Press, 2–4 May 1988

[BM90] Bellare, M., Micali, S.: Non-interactive oblivious transfer and applications. In: Brassard, G. (ed.) CRYPTO 1989. LNCS, vol. 435, pp. 547–557. Springer, New York (1990). https://doi.org/10.1007/0-387-34805-0_48

[Can00] Canetti, R.: Security and composition of multiparty cryptographic protocols. J. Cryptol. **13**(1), 143–202 (2000)

[CCD88] Chaum, D., Crépeau, C., Damgård, I.: Multiparty unconditionally secure protocols (extended abstract). In: 20th Annual ACM Symposium on Theory of Computing, pp. 11–19, Chicago, IL, USA, ACM Press, 2–4 May 1988

[DDN14] David, B., Dowsley, R., Nascimento, A.C.A.: Universally composable oblivious transfer based on a variant of LPN. In: Gritzalis, D., Kiayias, A., Askoxylakis, I. (eds.) CANS 2014. LNCS, vol. 8813, pp. 143–158. Springer, Cham (2014). https://doi.org/10.1007/978-3-319-12280-9_10

[DGH+20] Döttling, N., Garg, S., Hajiabadi, M., Masny, D., Wichs, D.: Two-round oblivious transfer from CDH or LPN. In: Canteaut, A., Ishai, Y. (eds.) EUROCRYPT 2020. LNCS, vol. 12106, pp. 768–797. Springer, Cham (2020). https://doi.org/10.1007/978-3-030-45724-2_26

[GMW87] Goldreich, O., Micali, S., Wigderson, A.: How to play any mental game or a completeness theorem for protocols with honest majority. In: Aho, A. (ed.), 19th Annual ACM Symposium on Theory of Computing, pp. 218–229, New York City, NY, USA, ACM Press, 25–27 May 1987

[Gol00] Goldreich, O.: Candidate one-way functions based on expander graphs. Cryptology ePrint Archive, Report 2000/063 (2000). https://eprint.iacr.org/2000/063

[HMTZ16] Hirt, M., Maurer, U., Tschudi, D., Zikas, V.: Network-hiding communication and applications to multi-party protocols. In: Robshaw, M., Katz, J. (eds.) CRYPTO 2016. LNCS, vol. 9815, pp. 335–365. Springer, Heidelberg (2016). https://doi.org/10.1007/978-3-662-53008-5_12

[IKOS08] Ishai, Y., Kushilevitz, E., Ostrovsky, R., Sahai, A.: Cryptography with constant computational overhead. In: Richard, E.L., Cynthia, D. (eds.), 40th Annual ACM Symposium on Theory of Computing, pp. 433–442, Victoria, BC, Canada, ACM Press, 17–20 May 2008

[Li22] Li, S.: Towards practical topology-hiding computation. In: Agrawal, S., Lin, D. (eds.) Advances in Cryptology - ASIACRYPT 2022. ASIACRYPT 2022. LNCS, vol. 13791, pp. 588–617. Springer, Cham (2022). https://doi.org/10.1007/978-3-031-22963-3_20

[LZM+18] LaVigne, R., Liu-Zhang, C.-D., Maurer, U., Moran, T., Mularczyk, M., Tschudi, D.: Topology-hiding computation beyond semi-honest adversaries. In: Beimel, A., Dziembowski, S. (eds.) TCC 2018. LNCS, vol. 11240, pp. 3–35. Springer, Cham (2018). https://doi.org/10.1007/978-3-030-03810-6_1

[MOR15] Moran, T., Orlov, I., Richelson, S.: Topology-hiding computation. In: Dodis, Y., Nielsen, J.B. (eds.) TCC 2015. LNCS, vol. 9014, pp. 159–181. Springer, Heidelberg (2015). https://doi.org/10.1007/978-3-662-46494-6_8

[MST03] Mossel, E., Shpilka, A., Trevisan, L.: On e-biased generators in NC0. In 44th Annual Symposium on Foundations of Computer Science, pp. 136–145, Cambridge, MA, USA, IEEE, Computer Society Press, 11–14 October 2003

[OW14] ODonnell, R., Witmer, D.: Goldreich's prg: evidence for near-optimal polynomial stretch. In: 2014 IEEE 29th Conference on Computational Complexity (CCC), pp. 1–12. IEEE (2014)

[RB89] Rabin, T., Ben-Or, M.: Verifiable secret sharing and multiparty protocols with honest majority (extended abstract). In: 21st Annual ACM Symposium on Theory of Computing, pp. 73–85, Seattle, WA, USA, ACM Press, 15–17 May 1989

[Yao82] Yao, A.C.: Protocols for secure computations (extended abstract). In: 23rd Annual Symposium on Foundations of Computer Science, pp. 160–164, Chicago, Illinois, IEEE Computer Society Press, 3–5 November 1982

[YZ16] Yu, Yu., Zhang, J.: Cryptography with auxiliary input and trapdoor from constant-noise LPN. In: Robshaw, M., Katz, J. (eds.) CRYPTO 2016. LNCS, vol. 9814, pp. 214–243. Springer, Heidelberg (2016). https://doi.org/10.1007/978-3-662-53018-4_9

On the Impossibility of Surviving (Iterated) Deletion of Weakly Dominated Strategies in Rational MPC

Johannes Blömer[1], Jan Bobolz[2], and Henrik Bröcher[1(✉)]

[1] Paderborn University, Paderborn, Germany
{bloemer,bhenrik}@uni-paderborn.de
[2] University of Edinburgh, Edinburgh, UK
jan.bobolz@ed.ac.uk

Abstract. Rational multiparty computation (rational MPC) provides a framework for analyzing MPC protocols through the lens of game theory. One way to judge whether an MPC protocol is *rational* is through weak domination: Rational players would not adhere to an MPC protocol if deviating never decreases their utility, but sometimes increases it.

Secret reconstruction protocols are of particular importance in this setting because they represent the last phase of most (rational) MPC protocols. We show that most secret reconstruction protocols from the literature are not, in fact, stable with respect to weak domination. Furthermore, we formally prove that (under certain assumptions) it is impossible to design a secret reconstruction protocol which is a Nash equilibrium but not weakly dominated if (1) shares are authenticated or (2) half of all players may form a coalition.

Keywords: Game Theory · Rational Secret Sharing · Multiparty Computation · Rational Cryptography · Iterated Deletion of Weakly Dominated Strategies

1 Introduction

A multiparty computation (MPC) protocol is one that allows n parties, each with their own secret input x_i, to jointly compute the value of a function $f(x_1, \ldots, x_n)$. Applications range from jointly evaluating statistics on confidential data in a privacy-preserving way, to replacing trusted parties which setup cryptographic systems, to substituting trusted hardware by software. Security typically ensures the correctness of results while guaranteeing to leak no more information about

This work was partially supported by the German Research Foundation (DFG) within the Collaborative Research Centre "On-The-Fly Computing" under the project number 160364472 – SFB 901/3.
J. Bobolz—Work done while at Paderborn University.

the inputs than the computation's result itself leaks. Traditionally, these properties must hold with respect to adversaries that are allowed to corrupt certain parties while non-corrupted parties honestly follow the protocol prescriptions.

In this paper, we are interested in *rational MPC* [14], i.e. rather than partitioning the MPC protocol participants into a set of strictly honest and a set of arbitrarily malicious parties, we instead analyze the parties' behavior from a game-theoretic point of view. This means that we assume that *every* participant is *rational* (rather than honest or malicious) and tries to maximize some utility function. Rational MPC addresses the following issues with the standard MPC definition: On one hand, the standard definition is too strong because it covers arbitrarily irrational destructive behavior. On the other hand, the standard definition is too weak because it assumes that at least one party honestly executes the protocol even if it is potentially irrational to do so. Rational MPC offers an alternative that takes game-theoretic incentives into account when evaluating MPC protocols. It is the better formalization for scenarios where one can reasonably assume participants to act rationally (e.g., in economics).

Using game theory terminology, the n MPC parties are *players*. Each player i chooses a *strategy* M_i, which is an interactive Turing machine describing how they want to behave in the protocol. Then the Turing machines run their programs, interacting with each other. At the end, the utility of each player is determined, roughly speaking, by their machine's output. An MPC protocol $(M_1, \ldots, M_n)$ is a tuple of suggested strategies for the n players, also called a *mechanism*. The goal is to design mechanisms which are stable in the sense that rational, utility-maximizing participants follow their prescriptions. A common notion of stability is the Nash equilibrium (NE), where no player i can (significantly) improve her expected utility by deviating from her prescribed strategy M_i. In some situations, especially when there is uncertainty about the other players' strategies or utilities, a NE is considered too weak and additional properties are required. For example, think of switching to a strategy which additionally to the original behaviour protects against some denial of service attack by the other players. If it is possible to protect against such an attack without additional cost, why should a player not switch? Additionally, uncertainty may generally arise in *network settings*, where the other players' strategies might be affected by external factors like connection failures or lost messages. Based on these considerations, the requirement that a NE survives the iterated deletion of weakly dominated strategies (IDoWDS) has been used in rational secret reconstruction repetitively [1,12,14,20]. A strategy M_i is weakly dominated if there exists a strategy M_i^* that does (significantly) better against *some* strategy profile of the other players, and does *not* perform (significantly) worse against *any* strategy profile. Surviving IDoWDS means that in a process where, repeatedly, all weakly dominated strategies are deleted, the original strategy M_i remains. This process is reasoned by the assumption that a rational player would always switch to a dominating strategy M_i^* since this may only increase her gain. Like [1,12,14,20], we call a protocol a *practical mechanism* or *rationally secure*, if its strategies (1) form a NE and (2) survive IDoWDS.

Typically, rational MPC protocols work in two stages: first, the parties run a standard MPC protocol with malicious security for the functionality f. As the result of that protocol, the parties receive secret shares s_i of the computation result $s = f(x_1, \ldots, x_n)$. In the second stage, the parties run a *rational* MPC secret reconstruction phase, to which each party contributes their share s_i, and the protocol yields the final result s for everyone. This structure is reminiscent of standard MPC protocols (e.g., GMW [11]), which also yield a secret-sharing of the result s and then have the parties reconstruct it. In contrast to the standard setting, where secret reconstruction amounts to simply having all the (honest) parties broadcast their shares to everyone, secret reconstruction in the rational setting is much more complicated. This is because, in some scenarios, it is irrational for a party i to simply broadcast their share s_i [14]. Broadcasting the share does not help player i to reconstruct the secret, but it may help others. So for players that prefer to learn the result and prefer others not to learn the result, the simple "everyone broadcast their shares" protocol breaks down.

As a consequence, secret reconstruction protocols play a crucial role in rational MPC. The secret reconstruction scenario can be described as follows: A dealer samples a secret s and secret shares $(s_i)_{i=1}^n$ of s, as well as digital signatures σ_i on (i, s_i) (for ease of exposition, we assume authentication via digital signatures). When using secret reconstruction as part of a larger rational MPC protocol, we can imagine that $(s_i, \sigma_i)_{i=1}^n$ are the result of some MPC computation. The player machine M_i gets as input its signed share (s_i, σ_i) (and the corresponding public key). The machines $M_1, \ldots, M_n$ then interact with each other. Finally, each M_i outputs what it thinks the reconstructed secret is. The rational utilities that player i tries to maximize are *natural*, i.e. the player prefers outputting the correct secret over outputting a wrong secret (prefers correctness) and the player prefers other players *not* to learn the secret (prefers exclusivity).

Several works have tackled the problem of rational secret reconstruction. To sidestep the issue that rational participants may be hesistant broadcasting their share for fear of unnecessarily helping others, most existing secret reconstruction protocols [1,12,14,20] take a randomized number of rounds and use dummy rounds to punish participants who refuse to broadcast. Ultimately, parties in those protocols still broadcast shares, but there is randomness and uncertainty involved about when (non-dummy) shares are broadcast.

Another challenge for rational secret reconstruction is the authentication of the result s: If a party i can broadcast a fake share so that all other parties receive a wrong reconstruction result $s' \neq s$ (while i can reconstruct the real result), then doing so is rational. For this reason, inherently, there needs to be some way for parties to check whether the correct share was broadcast or at least whether the reconstruction result is valid.

1.1   Our Contribution

We show that almost all known secret reconstruction protocols do not survive iterated deletion of weakly dominated strategies (where weak domination is adapted to the computational setting in a natural way, see Definition 9). We observe that any "natural" strategy M_i is weakly dominated by a machine M_i^* that works as follows: M_i^* behaves exactly like M_i except that it adds an additional check to messages it receives in the first round. If *all* other players $j \neq i$ happen to send messages of the format $(\mathsf{LEAK}, s_j, \sigma_j)$ such that σ_j is a valid signature on (j, s_j), then M_i^* uses the received shares $(s_1, \ldots, s_n)$ to reconstruct the secret s. In this case, M_i^* continues to behave like M_i, but outputs the s from the leaked shares in the end. In all other cases, M_i^* outputs what M_i outputs.

In other words, M_i^* hopes that all other players decide to deviate from the protocol and instead simply send this special format message containing their input in plain. And indeed, if the other players play this (artificial) strategy, then M_i^* outputs the correct secret with probability 1. This is significantly better than a typical protocol M_i, which we (for now) assume just aborts because of an unexpected first-round message format $(\mathsf{LEAK}, \ldots)$. Furthermore, M_i^* never does worse than M_i, because the only way M_i^* deviates is by outputting a secret s that is guaranteed to be the *correct* secret (assuming unforgeable signatures), which is the preferred outcome of a rational player. So M_i^* is never worse than M_i, but does significantly better against strategies that leak their input, which means that M_i^* weakly dominates M_i. This makes intuitive sense: the additional signature check can only *help* player i, so it is irrational not to include it.

Hence, any "natural" strategy M_i, which does not include such a first-message check itself, is weakly dominated by the modified strategy M_i^*. It follows that M_i does not survive iterated deletion of weakly dominated strategies (IDoWDS) (or, more specifically, M_i does not even survive the first "iteration" of IDoWDS because it is weakly dominated w.r.t. the original strategy set). We apply this observation to existing protocols in Sect. 4, demonstrating that *almost all* known secret reconstruction protocols from the literature do *not* survive IDoWDS.

In addition to falsifying claims from the literature, the goal of this paper is to characterize the extent of this IDoWDS issue. Can existing protocols be fixed? What classes of protocols are susceptible to the issue? It may be tempting to try to fix the issue by including the first-message check of M_i^* in the original protocol. If M_i already checks the first message, then M_i^* has no advantage over M_i and does not weakly dominate it. However, there is an essentially endless supply of other ways to encode the input-leaking message. Say a strategy M_i *does* check if the first messages contain messages of the format $(\mathsf{LEAK}, s_j, \sigma_j)$. Then this strategy is still weakly dominated by a strategy M_i^{**}, which works like M_i, but additionally checks whether the first messages have the format $(\mathsf{LEAK}, \overline{s_j}, \overline{\sigma_j})$, where $\overline{x}$ denotes some other encoding, e.g., base64 or the bitwise negation of the canonical representation. Similarly to above, M_i^{**} weakly dominates M_i, as it cannot do worse than M_i, but does better against the strategies that leak their input by sending $(\mathsf{LEAK}, \overline{s_j}, \overline{\sigma_j})$. Intuitively, no matter how many different ways of interpreting the first message a strategy implements, it is likely that one can come up with a new (contrived) representation not covered by it. Hence, it seems exceedingly unlikely that any reasonable strategy exists that survives IDoWDS. We formalize this idea in Sect. 5, proving that if we allow strategies to be non-uniform Turing machines and the dealer "sufficiently" authenticates the secret shares, then there exists *no* strategy that is not weakly dominated.

What could be possible ways around this issue? For this, we examine what makes the machine M_i^* work. Because the shares are signed in the examples above, M_i^* can be sure that when it receives authenticated first-round shares, M_i^* (almost) never outputs the wrong secret, no matter what the remaining $n-1$ parties do. This enables the argument that M_i^* weakly dominates M_i: If it were possible for $n-1$ parties to convince M_i^* to output a wrong secret, then M_i^* does not necessarily weakly dominate M_i anymore. So counter-intuitively, in order for the secret-sharing scenario to possess a rational mechanism (circumventing weak domination by M_i^*), the shares must not be authenticated *too well*. However, in order for a mechanism to be a Nash equilibrium, authentication must also not be *too weak*: If it were possible for a party to convince all others of a wrong secret (while receiving the correct secret himself), then doing so is rational.

There is indeed a (small) middle ground between *perfect* authentication and *no* authentication, which sidesteps our initial weak domination result. Indeed, the third protocol of Abraham, Dolev, Gonen, and Halpern [1] avoids the initial weak domination counterexample as follows: Instead of authenticating the secret-sharing with signatures or MACs (as in the first two instantiations in [1]), their third instantiation uses Reed-Solomon codes (i.e. Shamir shares with redundancy). This instantiation hits the sweet spot between too much and too little authentication: Reed-Solomon codes are strongly authenticating against up to $n/3$ parties (even providing error correction), but for $n-1$ parties, it is trivial to manipulate shares to make the last party believe in a wrong secret. This allows their protocol to be a Nash equilibrium while avoiding our initial counterexample, which requires stronger authentication.

However, the third protocol of Abraham et al. [1] is *also* weakly dominated in certain (reasonable) settings, even if it requires a different counterexample. Roughly speaking, the weakly dominating strategy for this protocol only deviates from the original protocol when the original protocol would output a reconstructed secret $s_{unlikely}$ that is only correct with negligible probability (say, for simplicity, an error symbol). Because this is almost certainly not the correct secret, deviating in this case is *never worse* than the original strategy, which has minimal utility outputting the (likely) wrong secret. The deviation is *sometimes better* against strategies that would make the original protocol consistently output a wrong secret $s_{unlikely}$. This is possible in the Reed-Solomon scenario because $n-1$ parties can easily change the shared secret in a way that is undetectable to the last party. In this case, the deviation would correct the wrong $s_{unlikely}$ to the *correct* secret instead, achieving significantly higher utility. We explain this counterexample in our full version [5, Sect. 7] in detail.

Still, while our initial counterexample rules out most (authenticated) secret sharing settings, and our second counterexample rules out using Reed-Solomon for *some* secret distributions, it may well be that there are other secret distributions for which Reed-Solomon secret sharing presents a way out of the weak domination issues. To approach this remaining possibility, we offer additional secret-distribution-agnostic insights when considering *coalitions* (as is standard in the rational MPC literature [1, 18]). In Sect. 6, we show that if we consider coalitions of at least $n/2$ rational players, then no reasonable secret reconstruction protocol exists (at least not for typical secret-sharing schemes) that is rational to play for the coalition. Essentially, we show that in that setting, either authentication is *good enough* for the weak domination counterexample to work, or authentication is *weak enough* to enable the coalition to play a strategy that is better for them than the prescribed strategy (meaning that there is no Nash equilibrium). In particular, this effectively rules out the existence of rational secret reconstruction for the important $n = 2$ setting. Overall, our results in Sect. 5, Sect. 6, and [5, Sect. 7] comprehensively characterize the extent of the IDoWDS issue for rational MPC protocols.

1.2   Consequences

Our results call into question a wide range of rational MPC protocols, for secret reconstruction in particular. The most immediate insight is that the popular strategy of authenticating shares with digital signatures, with one-time information-theoretically secure MACs (Construction 6), or with zero-knowledge proofs seem to be widely incompatible with weak domination requirements. In all those cases, this strong authentication makes adding a first-round check to the strategy weakly dominate any reasonable protocol's strategies. In particular, all secret reconstruction protocols from [1, 12, 14, 20] exhibit this weak domination flaw. We discuss concrete examples in Sect. 4, unifying several of the protocols in a common framework. See [5, Sect. 7] for the counterexample for the Reed-Solomon based secret reconstruction protocol from [1].

Our impossibility result for rationally secure secret reconstruction carries over to general rational MPC, which was approached so far by "take any actively secure general-purpose MPC protocol which computes a sufficiently authenticated secret sharing and replace the final reconstruction phase by a rationally secure one" [1, 12, 14, 20]. Since by our result such reconstruction mechanisms in many settings do not exist, such compositions which survive IDoWDS do not exist, either. Our results from Sect. 6 rule out this approach for coalitions of $n/2$ and more players, which especially covers two party computations. Therefore, these approaches have to be rethought with respect to weak domination.

In conclusion, our results (summarized in Table 1) show that in many important settings, the approaches and techniques known from the literature are incompatible with respect to the cryptographic version of IDoWDS.

1.3   The Way Forward for Rational MPC

Given the extent of the IDoWDS issue regarding our current understanding of how to design rational MPC protocols, the question arises how future rational MPC research should deal with our results. As motivated in Sect. 1.1, in network settings and, especially, cryptographic settings, the notion of IDoWDS is

Table 1. Overview of our results for coalitions of t parties and k-out-of-n secret sharing schemes having the corresponding property from column one. Each result applies to *any* mechanism in the given setting. We assume $t < k$ as otherwise coalitions are able to reconstruct secrets, which inherently leads to unstable mechanisms. Note, $t = 1$ represents the non-coalition case.

	majority coalition $t \geq n/2$	$t < n/2$
local $(n-t)$-verifiable (e.g. shares authenticated using signatures, MACs, …)	weakly dominated (for non-uniform strategies: Theorems 2 and 3)	
Reed-Solomon codes based (e.g. redundant Shamir shares)	weakly dominated for certain secret distributions (c.f. [5, Theorem 5])	
verifiable-or-fully-broken (e.g. additive sharing, Shamir's sharing for $k > n/2$)	weakly dominated or no Nash equilibrium (Theorem 4)	no result

philosophically reasonable and its ideas should be represented somehow. Given that, we see two approaches for handling the IDoWDS property in the future.

The first way is to concentrate future research on settings and protocols for rational secret reconstruction or, more generally, MPC protocols, which are not ruled out by our results. In Sect. 6.3 we show that settings with coalitions of $n/2$ and more players cannot be proven rationally secure in almost any reasonable setting. As we only rule out Reed-Solomon based reconstruction protocols *for certain secret distributions*, it is still open whether there are such protocols not prone to weak domination for *some* secret distributions. Those, however, would need to exploit properties of the secret distribution to avoid our counterexample.

The second way is to tweak the definitions of what we consider rationally secure. As our adaptation of IDoWDS to the computational setting is quite natural (as discussed in the full version [5]), it seems that one needs to find a replacement for IDoWDS on the game-theoretic side, which reflects rational behavior and in particular the idea of "weak dominance rationality", but whose computational translation is less strict and does not rule out the same wide range of protocols ruled out by the current definition. For example, Hillas and Samet [15] propose to iteratively delete so called weak *flaws* instead of weakly dominated strategies and claim this reflects "weak dominance rationality" better than IDoWDS. This is a potential candidate for a replacement. Other replacements, already suggested in the literature, are discussed below. Either option leads to many open questions and paves the way for new interesting research and results.

1.4   Organization

In Sect. 2, we discuss related work. In Sect. 3, we introduce the models of communication and non-uniform computation as well as other relevant standard primitives from cryptography and game theory. Then, in Sect. 3.4 we define the rational secret reconstruction game central to this work. In Sect. 4, we show that most previously published mechanisms are weakly dominated. We generalize this result to arbitrary mechanisms in the non-uniform setting in Sect. 5. In Sect. 6, we extend the previous results to coalitions.

2   Discussion of Related Work

For the last 20 years a lot of research has been done on the interplay between game theory and cryptography (see for example the surveys [9,17], and [21] for a more practically oriented perspective). This covers, at least, two different aspects: on the one hand, cryptographic approaches to game-theoretic problems, e.g. replacing mediators in certain games (see e.g. [8,16] and many subsequent papers); on the other hand, using game-theoretic concepts in the design of cryptographic primitives, e.g. replacing malicious adversaries by rational adversaries, or mixtures of malicious and rational adversaries (see [20]). The second line of research was initiated by Halpern and Teague [14]. They initiated the study of rational multiparty computation and, in particular, rational secret reconstruction. Instead of designing protocols resistant to malicious adversarial behavior, they studied secret reconstruction and multiparty computation under the assumption that agents act rationally. Recently, this approach led to game-theoretic notions of fairness in multiparty coin toss and leader election [3,6,7,13,27].

Most relevant to our work is the work of Halpern and Teague and the research that followed it [1,2,10,12,18,19]. In this approach, secret reconstruction, and more generally a multiparty computation of some functionality, is modeled as a game, with the goal of designing protocols that satisfy various game-theoretic properties within this game, e.g. constitute a Nash equilibrium. However, there has never been any consensus about the right definition for a good rational strategy in multiparty computation, especially around weak domination and iterated deletion of weakly dominated strategies.

In this section, we explore the history of weak domination in the literature, argue why we should not just abandon weak-domination-like properties, and then discuss more recent definitions in that context.

2.1   History of (Iterated) Deletion of Weakly Dominated Strategies

The notion of iterated deletion of weakly dominated strategies has been introduced in the computational context by Halpern and Teague [14]. They argue that every protocol with a fixed last round, in which the parties send their shares, is weakly dominated: it is better for player i to deviate and not send her share, because revealing her share can only help *others* learn the secret and does not help *her* at all. This argument is wrong: as observed by [18], this deviation can be detected and punished by the other players, e.g., by checking whether player i indeed sends her share, and *only then* revealing their own shares. Because refusing to send the share leads to not learning the secret when played against those punishment strategies, it does not weakly dominate the original strategy of simply sending the last message.

Nevertheless, their argument against last rounds inspired several secret reconstruction protocols [1,12,14,20] that introduce uncertainty about which round is the last. The underlying idea of those protocols is that not sending some round's message is risky: if it turns out that this was *not* the last round, the other parties will abort the protocol, making it impossible to learn the secret. On the positive side, the protocols of [1,12,14,20] enable reconstruction of n-out-of-n secret sharing in a Nash sense, which does indeed require hiding the last round. In particular, [1,12,20] enable two-party secret reconstruction. Note that for k-out-of-n ($k < n$) secret sharing, the simple "everyone broadcast their shares in round 1" strategy is a Nash equilibrium.

On the negative side, in this paper, we show that all those protocols are still weakly dominated, contrary to stated goals and claims. The issue with the proof sketches by [1,12,14,20] is that they (implicitly) only consider deviations that send or do not send the expected messages in some round. However, there is another form of deviation, which we will call *undetectable* deviation, which forms the basis of our counterexample: This kind of deviation keeps following the protocol (sending the expected messages) outwardly, but secretly adds an additional check to improve utility in some contrived scenarios. Undetectable deviations (which are invisible to the other parties) were seemingly overlooked in those proofs without any formal justification.

Later, Kol and Naor showed that, in a very restricted strategy space, *no* strategy is weakly dominated [18, Theorem A.3]. Their strategy space essentially only considers the choice of either sending a share in some round or keeping silent in that round. Additionally invoking purely game-theoretic criticism of weak domination [24,26], they conclude that weak domination is not a useful notion, as it does not seem to rule out several "bad" strategies.

2.2   In Defense of Weak Domination

We disagree with Kol and Naor's assessment of weak domination, given that our results show that, if we do not severely restrict our strategy space, *all* strategies are weakly dominated. As a consequence, weak domination seems to deserve criticism for being *too harsh*, rather than *too forgiving*.

To (somewhat informally) reflect on the role that weak domination serves in modeling rational behavior, consider the strategy $M_i^{backdoor}$ (Fig. 1), which allows the other players to unanimously vote to have party i self destruct. We can view this vote as a backdoor that triggers irrational behavior if all other parties collaborate. If the vote does not pass (which is the default behavior if everyone plays $M_i^{backdoor}$), $M_i^{backdoor}$ behaves reasonably. Clearly, $M_i^{backdoor}$ is not a reasonable strategy to play for a rational player. Any rational player would (at least) remove the irrational behavior (line 3), as it does not serve any positive purpose for them and may only serve to sabotage them. Hence we would expect our definitions to reflect this and identify $M_i^{backdoor}$ as a bad strategy.

Strategy $M_i^{backdoor}$
1 : Send nothing in the first round.
2 : **if** we received (shutdown, i) from all other players in first round **then**
3 :   Self-destruct (e.g., halt and output an error).
4 : **else**
5 :   Run reasonable protocol M_i.

Fig. 1. Strategy $M_i^{backdoor}$, augmenting some reasonable strategy M_i with a self-destruct if the other players unanimously vote for it. Serves as an illustration of the need for the weak domination property.

Consider the mechanism $(M_1^{backdoor}, \ldots, M_n^{backdoor})$ for $n > 2$. If everyone keeps to the prescribed strategies $M_i^{backdoor}$, then nobody sends any messages in the first round and the backdoor is not triggered. If a single party deviates, they can also not trigger the backdoor, as this requires cooperation of other players. Hence $(M_1^{backdoor}, \ldots, M_n^{backdoor})$ is a Nash equilibrium (assuming the non-backdoored $(M_1, \ldots, M_n)$ are reasonable).

The notion of a Nash equilibrium does not detect the issue with $M_i^{backdoor}$, because it only considers scenarios where almost everyone executes the prescribed protocol. This is where weak domination comes in: for weak domination, we need to consider *all possible* behavior of the other parties. It is then easy to see that $M_i^{backdoor}$ is weakly dominated by a strategy ignoring the vote outcome: this is (1) clearly better against strategies where all other players collaborate to trigger the backdoor in $M_i^{backdoor}$, and (2) it is never worse than $M_i^{backdoor}$ (assuming self-destruction has minimal utility and M_i is reasonable).

Overall, we conclude that the field should have *some* notion that detects "backdoored" strategies such as $M_i^{backdoor}$. For this, Nash equilibria are not sufficient, and weak domination, while very suitable for this very task in spirit, in actuality is too eager and removes too many strategies, as we show in this paper.

2.3   Alternative Notions

The notion of weak domination has been widely abandoned in the more recent rational MPC literature, which the literature generally justifies with Kol-Naor's observation that weak domination is too forgiving and hence not meaningful (even though this is only true in a very restricted strategy space).

As a replacement, Kol and Naor themselves suggest *strict* Nash equilibria [10,18], which essentially requires that unilateral (detectable) deviation *significantly decreases* utility (as opposed to simply *not increasing* utility as in the standard notion). While strict Nash equilibria capture some intuitions of irrational behavior, by its nature it also only considers unilateral deviations and fails to detect some issues that were (in spirit) caught by weak domination.

For example, if we consider $M_i^{\text{backdoor}'}$ that behaves like M_i^{backdoor} but also, if the vote is not unanimous, punishes everyone that voted for triggering the backdoor (e.g., by shunning them from the rest of the protocol). This way, any unilateral deviation in the first round leads to a decrease in utility, making $(M_1^{\text{backdoor}'}, \ldots, M_n^{\text{backdoor}'})$ a strict Nash equilibrium (assuming M_i is reasonable), but the backdoor is still very much present in $M_i^{\text{backdoor}'}$.

Another notion that may replace weak domination are Nash equilibria that are *stable with respect to trembles* [10]. The idea is to model deviating behavior as another strategy: we consider strategies that usually play the prescribed strategies, but "tremble" with some probability and play some completely arbitrary strategy. The notion then says that even when playing against trembling strategies, it is still rational to follow the protocol honestly. Similarly to weak domination, this notion considers deviations of *all* players (though it has only been formally defined for $n = 2$ players [10]). However, for technical reasons (probably as they noticed problems similar to our weak domination counterexample), the notion explicitly removes undetectable deviations from consideration. In somewhat simplified terms, their definition requires that any improvement against trembles strategies can be achieved in a way that does not alter behavior against the originally prescribed (non-trembles) strategies. In other words, undetectable deviations, that do not alter the behavior against the prescribed strategies (such as our weak domination counterexamples) are exempt from this definition (i.e. even if one such undetectable deviation were a significant improvement against trembling strategies, the definition would not consider this an issue). Because of this, the stability with respect to trembles notion also fails to detect backdoors such as M_i^{backdoor}, i.e. $(M_1^{\text{backdoor}}, \ldots, M_n^{\text{backdoor}})$ is a Nash equilibrium that is stable with respect to trembles (assuming M_i are reasonable). Even though removing the backdoor improves utility significantly against strategies that sometimes tremble to trigger the backdoor, M_i^{backdoor} and the non-backdoored version behave the same against non-trembling strategies, and hence this improvement is ignored by the notion.

Overall, while the field has largely moved on from weak domination, we argue that (1) it did so for the wrong reasons (believing the notion is too forgiving rather than, as we show, too strict), and that (2) it did so without adequately replacing the notion with something that can detect bad mechanisms that would be intuitively considered irrational, such as M_i^{backdoor}. This paper and its impossibility results supply more adequate reasons why weak domination may be dismissed for now by future protocols (given that it rules out many settings), and explain why one should not attempt to prove future protocols rationally secure regarding weak domination. Our results should also inform the design of future stability notions to replace weak domination, providing some baseline potential counterexamples to check new notions against.

3   Preliminaries

For more detailed intuitions and discussions on this section's definitions, we refer to the full version [5]. We will use following notation. We define $[n] := \{1, \ldots, n\}$.

For index set $I \subseteq [n]$ let $-I := [n] \setminus I$, when n is clear from the context. Similarly, let $-i := -\{i\} = [n] \setminus \{i\}$ for a single index $i \in [n]$. For sets $S_1, \ldots, S_n$, we define $S_{\times I} := \times_{i \in I} S_i$. For a vector $(s_1, \ldots, s_n) \in S_{\times [n]}$, let s_I denote the restriction of s to the indices contained in I. For $s, s' \in S_{\times [n]}$, let (s_I, s'_{-I}) denote the tuple $s^* = (s_1^*, \ldots, s_n^*)$ with $s_i^* := s_i$ if $i \in I$ and $s_i^* := s'_i$ otherwise. If the context is clear, we omit the additional parentheses, especially when being used within functions, e. g. we write $u(1^\lambda, s_I, s'_{-I})$ instead of $u(1^\lambda, (s_I, s'_{-I}))$. A function $\mu : \mathbb{N} \to \mathbb{R}_{\geq 0}$ is *negligible* if $\forall c > 0\ \exists \lambda_0\ \forall \lambda \geq \lambda_0 : \mu(\lambda) \leq \lambda^{-c}$. A function $p : \mathbb{N} \to \mathbb{R}_{\geq 0}$ is *noticeable* if $p(\lambda) \geq 1/q(\lambda)$ for some polynomial q.

3.1 Model of Computation and Communication

Interaction is modeled using interactive Turing machines (ITMs) which are probabilistic polynomial-time (ppt) with respect to security parameter λ. Communication proceeds round-based and simultaneous, where in each round k and for each pair M_i, M_j of ITMs, M_i sends a, possibly empty, message $m_j^{(k,i)}$ to M_j.

Our results also transfer to models where messages may be delayed but eventually are delivered. For our general results, we require non-uniform ITMs.

Definition 1. *A non-uniform ppt interactive Turing machine (ITM) is a pair $(M, \bar{a})$ where $\bar{a} = (a_1, a_2, \ldots)$ is an infinite sequence of auxiliary strings with $|a_\lambda|$ being polynomially bounded in λ and M is a ppt ITM with a special tape for the non-uniform advice. For given input (security) parameter $\lambda \in \mathbb{N}$ and input x, M is run on $(1^\lambda, x, a_\lambda)$ where we require the running time to be polynomial in λ and the length $|x|$ of x per round of communication.*

3.2 Secret Sharing

In the following we define secret sharing schemes with respect to access structures. We extend the standard secret sharing definition (c. f. [4]) by additional information which is used for authentication and (local) verification of shares.

Definition 2 (Access Structure). *Let $M = \{P_1, \ldots, P_n\}$ be a set of n parties. A set $\mathbb{A}$ of subsets of M is called monotone if $A \in \mathbb{A}$ and $A \subseteq B \subseteq M$ implies $B \in \mathbb{A}$. An* access structure $\mathbb{A} \subseteq \mathcal{P}(M)$ with n parties *is a* monotone collection *of non-empty subsets of M. A set $A \subseteq M$ is called qualified if $A \in \mathbb{A}$ and non-qualified if $A \notin \mathbb{A}$.*

Definition 3 (Secret Sharing Scheme with locally verifiable reconstruction). *Let $\mathbb{A}$ be an access structure with n parties and $\mathbb{S}$ be a finite set of secrets where $|\mathbb{S}| \geq 2$. A (perfect) secret sharing scheme with domain of secrets $\mathbb{S}$ realizing access structure $\mathbb{A}$ with locally verifiable reconstruction is a tuple of ppt algorithms $\Pi = (\mathsf{Setup}_\Pi, \mathsf{Share}, \mathsf{Recon})$, where*

- $\mathsf{Setup}_\Pi(1^\lambda)$, *on input security parameter 1^λ, outputs public parameters* pp *with $|\mathsf{pp}| \geq \lambda$.*

- Share(pp, s), *on input public parameters* pp *and secret* $s \in \mathbb{S}$, *outputs for each* $i \in [n]$ *a triple* $(s^{(i)}, \tau^{(i)}, \sigma^{(i)})$ *consisting of share* $s^{(i)}$, *local verification information* $\tau^{(i)} \in \{0, 1\}^*$, *and authentication information* $\sigma^{(i)} = (\sigma_1^{(i)}, \dots, \sigma_n^{(i)}) \in \{0, 1\}^*$.
- Recon(pp, $\tau^{(i)}, (s^{(j)}, \sigma_i^{(j)})_{j \in A}$), *on input public parameters* pp, P_i's *local verification information* $\tau^{(i)}$, *and, for* $A \subseteq [n]$, *tuples* $(s^{(j)}, \sigma_i^{(j)})_{j \in A}$ *of shares and authentication information, deterministically outputs an element from* $\mathbb{S} \cup \{\perp\}$.

We require correctness: For all $\lambda \in \mathbb{N}$, pp $\leftarrow$ Setup$_\Pi(1^\lambda)$, $s \in \mathbb{S}$, *and for all* $(s^{(i)}, \tau^{(i)}, \sigma^{(i)})_{i \in [n]} \leftarrow$ Share(pp, s), $A \in \mathbb{A}, i \in A$ *it holds*

$$\Pr[\text{Recon}(\text{pp}, \tau^{(i)}, (s^{(j)}, \sigma_i^{(j)})_{j \in A}) = s] = 1.$$

If $\mathbb{A} = \{A \subseteq [n] \mid |A| \geq m\}$, *we say* Π *is an* m-*out-of-*n *secret sharing scheme.*

In a secret sharing scheme with locally verifiable reconstruction, after public parameters are set up, a dealer shares a secret among n parties. Then, qualified groups of parties may correctly reconstruct this secret by pooling their shares and authentication information. Following standard notion of privacy assures that non-qualified groups do learn nothing on this secret.

Definition 4 (Perfect privacy). *A secret sharing scheme* Π *for access structure* $\mathbb{A}$ *and secret domain* $\mathbb{S}$ *has perfect privacy if* $\forall \lambda \in \mathbb{N}$, $\forall$pp $\leftarrow$ Setup$_\Pi(1^\lambda)$, $\forall A \notin \mathbb{A}$, *and* $\forall s, s' \in \mathbb{S}$, *it holds that* Share(pp, s)$_A$ *and* Share(pp, s')$_A$ *are identically distributed.*

In addition to privacy we define the non-standard property of (non-uniform) local t-verifiability. This property ensures that it is infeasible for ppt adversaries to make an honest player output a wrong secret by manipulating up to t shares.

Experiment Forge$_{\mathcal{A}, \Pi}^{\mathcal{S}, C}(\lambda)$:

1. $s^* \leftarrow \mathcal{S}(1^\lambda)$, pp $\leftarrow$ Setup$_\Pi(1^\lambda)$.
2. $((s^{(1)}, \tau^{(1)}, \sigma^{(1)}), \dots, (s^{(n)}, \tau^{(n)}, \sigma^{(n)})) \leftarrow$ Share(pp, s^*).
3. Non-uniform adversary $(\mathcal{A}, (\omega_1, \omega_2, \dots))$ is given pp, and triples $(s^{(j)}, \tau^{(j)}, \sigma^{(j)})_{j \in C}$, and outputs $(\bar{s}^{(j)}, \bar{\sigma}^{(j)})_{j \in C}$.
4. Output is 1 iff $\exists i \in [n] \setminus C, \exists H \subseteq [n] \setminus C$ with Recon(pp, $\tau^{(i)}, (\bar{s}^{(j)}, \bar{\sigma}^{(j)})_{j \in C}, (s^{(j)}, \sigma^{(j)})_{j \in H}) \notin \{s^*, \perp\}$.

Fig. 2. Experiment for local verification of secrets for secret sharing scheme Π with respect to non-uniform adversary $(\mathcal{A}, (\omega_1, \omega_2, \dots))$, set $C \subset [n]$ of corrupted parties, and family of secret distributions $\mathcal{S}$.

Definition 5 ((Non-uniform) local t-verifiability). *Secret sharing scheme Π has local verifiability against up to t corruptions if $\forall$ non-uniform ppt $\mathcal{A}$, $\forall C \subset [n], |C| \leq t$, there is a negligible function μ such that*

$$\Pr[\mathsf{Forge}_{\mathcal{A},\Pi}^{\mathcal{S},C}(\lambda) = 1] \leq \mu(\lambda),$$

where the experiment $\mathsf{Forge}_{\mathcal{A},\Pi}^{\mathcal{S},C}(\lambda)$ is defined in Fig. 2.

Note, the stronger notions of robust secret sharing (RSS) and verifiable secret sharing (VSS) (c.f. [22]) are different from local verifiability. Construction 6 is an example for a secret sharing scheme by Abraham et al. [1] which satisfies locally $(n-1)$-verifiable reconstruction. It authenticates shares from Shamir's secret sharing scheme [25] with the idea of information checking from [23].

Construction 6 (Secret Sharing Scheme Π^{ADGH} [1]). *The m-out-of-n secret sharing scheme $\Pi^{\mathsf{ADGH}} = (\mathsf{Setup}^{\mathsf{ADGH}}, \mathsf{Share}^{\mathsf{ADGH}}, \mathsf{Recon}^{\mathsf{ADGH}})$ with domain of secrets $\mathbb{S}$ is defined as follows*

- *$\mathsf{Setup}^{\mathsf{ADGH}}(1^\lambda)$: Generates and returns the description of a field $\mathbb{F}$ with $|\mathbb{F}| > 2^\lambda$ and $\mathbb{S} \subset \mathbb{F}$ as public parameters pp.*
- *$\mathsf{Share}^{\mathsf{ADGH}}(\mathsf{pp}, s)$: Generates uniformly at random a degree-$(m-1)$ polynomial $h \in \mathbb{F}[X]$ constrained by $h(0) = s$. For each $i, j \in [n], i \neq j$, it chooses uniformly at random P_i's verification information $y_j^{(i)} \leftarrow \mathbb{F}$ and computes P_j's corresponding authentication information $b_i^{(j)}, c_i^{(j)} \in \mathbb{F}$ such that $c_i^{(j)} = b_i^{(j)} \cdot h(i) + y_j^{(i)}$. For each $i \in [n]$, it sets $s^{(i)} = (i, h(i))$, $\tau^{(i)} = (y_1^{(i)}, \dots, y_n^{(i)})$, and $\sigma^{(i)} = ((b_1^{(i)}, c_1^{(i)}), \dots, (b_n^{(i)}, c_n^{(i)}))$, and returns $(s^{(i)}, \tau^{(i)}, \sigma^{(i)})$.*
- *$\mathsf{Recon}^{\mathsf{ADGH}}(\mathsf{pp}, y^{(i)}, ((j, s^{(j)}), (b_i^{(j)}, c_i^{(j)}))_{j \in A})$: Compute set of indices of valid shares as $H = \left\{ j \in A | c_i^{(j)} = b_i^{(j)} \cdot s^{(j)} + y_j^{(i)} \right\}$. If $|H| < m$ output $\bot$. Otherwise choose m values $(j, s^{(j)})$, interpolate the corresponding degree-$(m-1)$ polynomial $h \in \mathbb{F}[X]$, and output $h(0)$.*

3.3 Game-Theoretic Notions

In the following we define the game-theoretic notions necessary to model rationality of participants in a computational setting. These originate mainly from the survey of Katz [17] but are suitably adapted to our (non-uniform) setting.

Definition 7 (Typed Computational Game). *A typed computational game $\Gamma = (\{\mathcal{D}(\lambda)\}_{\lambda \in \mathbb{N}}, (S_i)_{i \in [n]}, (u_i)_{i \in [n]})$ with n players $P_1, \dots, P_n$ consists of*

- *A set $\mathbb{T}_i$ of types for each player P_i and a corresponding ppt-sampleable family of (input) type distributions $\{\mathcal{D}(\lambda)\}_{\lambda \in \mathbb{N}}$ over $\mathbb{T}_{\times [n]}$.*
- *A set S_i of ppt ITMs with (local) output space $\mathbb{O}_i \subseteq \{0,1\}^*$ for each player P_i.*
- *A utility function u_i for each player P_i which maps security parameter λ, types $(t_1, \dots, t_n) \in \mathbb{T}_{\times [n]}$, and (local) ITM outputs $(o_1, \dots, o_n) \in \mathbb{O}_{\times [n]}$ to a utility in $\mathbb{R}$.*

For a given security parameter λ and ITMs $(M_1, \ldots, M_n)$, we overload notation and define the utility $u_i(1^\lambda, (M_1, \ldots, M_n)) = \mathbb{E}\left[u_i(1^\lambda, t_1, \ldots, t_n, o_1, \ldots, o_n)\right]$, where $(t_1, \ldots, t_n) \leftarrow \mathcal{D}(\lambda)$ and o_i is the output of ITM $M_i(1^\lambda, t_i)$ after interacting with all the other ITMs. For a coalition $C \subseteq [n]$ we define utility $u_C(1^\lambda, (M_1, \ldots, M_n)) := \sum_{i \in C} u_i(1^\lambda, (M_1, \ldots, M_n))$, where each ITM $M_i, i \in C$, is run with input $(1^\lambda, (t_i)_{i \in C})$.

In a typed computational game, first the players choose their strategies, i.e. ITMs. Afterwards, the security parameter is fixed, the types $(t_1, \ldots, t_n)$ are privately sampled by an external Dealer (in game theory often called Nature), and each t_i is (privately) written on the input tape of M_i which starts the interaction. Fixing the ITMs before sampling types is of major importance with respect to types which are based on computationally hard problems.

Utilities in typed computational games depend on the (local) outputs *and* sampled types. They are (a-priori) computed as expected value over the sampling of types, interaction of machines and their final outputs. For a coalition C of players, we define the utility u_C as sum over the parties' individual utilities when their ITMs are run on their shared inputs. This reflects the idea that in a realistic setting parties who form a coalition split up their gains.

With respect to the framework from Definition 7 the notion of t-resilient equilibria, an adaption of ϵ-Nash equilibria, serves as first concept to describe stable strategy profiles.

Definition 8 (t-Resilient Computational Equilibrium). *For a typed computational game* $\Gamma = \left(\{\mathcal{D}(\lambda)\}_{\lambda \in \mathbb{N}}, (S_i)_{i \in [n]}, (u_i)_{i \in [n]}\right)$ *we call strategy profile* $M = (M_1, \ldots, M_n) \in S_{\times [n]}$ t-resilient computational equilibrium *if for all* $C \subseteq [n], |C| = t$, *and all strategies* $M'_C \in S_{\times C}$ *there exists a negligible function* μ *such that*

$$u_C(1^\lambda, M'_C, M_{-C}) \leq u_C(1^\lambda, M) + \mu(\lambda)$$

For some scenarios the stability of t-resilient equilibria is insufficient and complementary properties are demanded. One such property relies on the *dominance* of strategies which we define for typed computational games.

Definition 9 (Dominance in Typed Computational Games). *Let typed computational game* $\Gamma = \left(\{\mathcal{D}(\lambda)\}_{\lambda \in \mathbb{N}}, (S_i)_{i \in [n]}, (u_i)_{i \in [n]}\right)$. *For player* P_i *a strategy* $M_i^* \in S_i$ *weakly dominates* $M_i' \in S_i$ *if*

1. *"Never non-negligibly worse": For all* $M_{-i} \in S_{\times -i}$ *there exists a negligible function* μ *such that*

$$u_i(1^\lambda, M_i^*, M_{-i}) \geq u_i(1^\lambda, M_i', M_{-i}) - \mu(\lambda)$$

2. *"Sometimes significantly better": There exists a noticeable function* p *and an opponent strategy profile* $M_{-i} \in S_{\times -i}$ *such that*

$$u_i(1^\lambda, M_i^*, M_{-i}) \geq u_i(1^\lambda, M_i', M_{-i}) + p(\lambda)$$

If the second condition holds for all strategies, then M_i^* strictly dominates M_i'. For each player P_i, denote the set of its strictly dominated strategies by $\mathsf{sDOM}_i(\Gamma)$ *and its weakly dominated strategies by* $\mathsf{wDOM}_i(\Gamma)$.

In contrast to Nash equilibria, there does not seem to be a consensus on how to generalize domination to a setting that includes coalitions. We refer to Sect. 6 for our definition of domination with coalitions.

Note that, essentially, weakly dominated strategies are irrelevant for the game. No rational player would consider playing them. So conceptually, weakly dominated strategies can be safely deleted from the pool of considered strategies. Deleting strategies, however, may render *other* strategies weakly dominated, with respect to the reduced strategy sets. So with the same reasoning, those "new" weakly dominated strategies should be deleted as well. This process leads to following definition of *iterated* deletion of weakly dominated strategies.

Definition 10 (Iterated Deletion of Weakly Dominated Strategies).
Let typed computational game $\Gamma^0 = (\{\mathcal{D}(\lambda)\}_{\lambda \in \mathbb{N}}, (S_i^0)_{i \in [n]}, (u_i)_{i \in [n]})$. *For all* $i \in [n]$ *and* $j \in \mathbb{N}$ *define* $S_i^j := S_i^{j-1} \setminus \mathsf{wDOM}_i(\Gamma^{j-1})$ *and* $\Gamma^j = (\{\mathcal{D}(\lambda)\}_{\lambda \in \mathbb{N}}, (S_i^j)_{i \in [n]}, (u_i)_{i \in [n]})$. *Then* $S_{\times[n]}^\infty := \bigcap_{j=1}^\infty S_{\times[n]}^j$ *is the set of strategies which survives the process of iterated deletion of weakly dominated strategies and* $\Gamma^\infty = (\{\mathcal{D}(\lambda)\}_{\lambda \in \mathbb{N}}, (S_i^\infty)_{i \in [n]}, (u_i)_{i \in [n]})$ *is its corresponding game. A strategy profile* $(M_1, \ldots, M_n) \in S_{\times[n]}^\infty$ *survives the iterated deletion of weakly dominated strategies, if* $(M_1, \ldots, M_n) \in S_{\times[n]}^\infty$.

For our upcoming results, it is important to note that any weakly dominated strategy w.r.t. the original (full) strategy set is deleted in the first iteration and can never be considered rational to play according to this notion. Indeed, our results will only focus on the first iteration of iterated deletion, i. e. we generally show that strategies are weakly dominated from the start (rather than becoming weakly dominated in later iterations).

In important publications [1,12,14], founding the field of rational secret reconstruction and rational MPC, a mechanism is only considered "practical" if it both is a Nash equilibrium and survives the iterated deletion of weakly dominated strategies. Otherwise, playing such a mechanism is arguably irrational.

3.4 Rational Secret Reconstruction

In this section, we define the secret reconstruction game in the spirit of [12] as an instantiation of a typed computational game (Definition 7). For this, we need to define the types, allowed strategies, and utility functions.

Definition 11 (Secret reconstruction game with locally verifiable reconstruction). *The secret reconstruction game with family of secret distributions* $\{\mathcal{S}(\lambda)\}_{\lambda \in \mathbb{N}}$ *over secret domain* $\mathbb{S}$, *access structure* $\mathbb{A}$, *secret-sharing scheme* $\Pi = (\mathsf{Setup}_\Pi, \mathsf{Share}, \mathsf{Recon})$ *with locally verifiable reconstruction consists of*

– *Type distribution $\mathcal{D}(\lambda)$: Sample public parameters* $\mathsf{pp} \leftarrow \mathsf{Setup}_\Pi(1^\lambda)$, *secret* $s \leftarrow \mathcal{S}(\lambda)$, *and shares* $(s^{(i)}, \tau^{(i)}, \sigma^{(i)})_{i \in [n]} \leftarrow \mathsf{Share}(\mathsf{pp}, s)$. *Set type* $t_i := (\mathsf{pp}, (s^{(i)}, \tau^{(i)}, \sigma^{(i)}))$.
– *A set S_i of ppt ITMs with (local) output space* $\mathbb{S} \cup \{\bot\}$.
– *A utility function u_i for each player P_i which maps security parameter, secret* $s \in \mathbb{S}$, *and the parties' outputs* $(s_1, \ldots, s_n) \in (\mathbb{S} \cup \{\bot\})^n$ *to a utility in* $\mathbb{R}$.

Definition 11 models a scenario where players first choose the ITMs they use for reconstructing the secret which is afterwards shared among them by an external party. The secrets are sampled according to a publicly known distribution which depends on the security parameter. This dependence is especially important if the secret's length increases with the security parameter, e. g. when it corresponds to a secret key. Then each player runs their ITM on input $(s^{(i)}, \tau^{(i)}, \sigma^{(i)})$, consisting of the player's share $s^{(i)}$, local verification information $\tau^{(i)}$, and authentication information $\sigma^{(i)}$ as in Definition 3. The ITM eventually outputs a guess for the secret or an error symbol $\bot$. After the execution, a player's utility depends on the shared secret and the output guesses.

While utility functions might encode anything, previous works [1,12,14,18] modeled players to prefer learning the (correct) secret over not learning the secret, and to prefer the others *not* to learn the (correct) secret.

Definition 12. *Let u_i be the secret reconstruction utility of player P_i from a secret reconstruction game (Definition 11). We say u_i*

– prefers correctness, *if there exists a noticeable function p such that for all $\lambda \in \mathbb{N}$, secrets $s \in \mathbb{S}$, and guesses $s^*, s' \in (\mathbb{S} \cup \{\bot\})^n$ with $s_i^* = s \neq s_i'$ we have*

$$u_i(1^\lambda, s, s^*) > u_i(1^\lambda, s, s') + p(\lambda).$$

– prefers exclusivity, *if for all $j \neq i$ there exists a noticeable function p such that for all $\lambda \in \mathbb{N}$, secrets $s \in \mathbb{S}$, and guesses $s^*, s' \in (\mathbb{S} \cup \{\bot\})^n$ with $s_j^* = s \neq s_j'$ and $s_{-j}^* = s_{-j}'$ we have*

$$u_i(1^\lambda, s, s') > u_i(1^\lambda, s, s^*) + p(\lambda).$$

If u_i prefers both correctness and exclusivity, then we call it natural.

This restriction of utilities, which arguably applies to many real-world applications, was used to show negative results [1,3,14,20] as well as to construct protocols being a computational equilibrium [1,12,14,18].

Finally, we restrict the distribution of secrets to be non-trivial to rule out scenarios where ITMs are able to correctly guess the secret without any interaction: The distribution must not be concentrated too much on a single secret.

Definition 13 (Non-trivial secret distribution). *A family of secret distributions $\{\mathcal{S}(\lambda)\}_{\lambda \in \mathbb{N}}$ over secret domain $\mathbb{S}$ is called* non-trivial *if there exists a noticeable function p such that for all secrets $s \in \mathbb{S}$*

$$\Pr[\mathcal{S}(\lambda) = s] < 1 - p(\lambda).$$

4 Weak Domination in Existing Secret Reconstruction Protocols

In this section we describe several existing strategies from [1,12] which were formerly claimed to survive the iterated deletion of weakly dominated strategies in the secret reconstruction game. Contradicting these claims we construct a counterexample which weakly dominates the original strategies if the initial secret-sharing scheme is locally verifiable. This counterexample serves as blueprint for other protocols like [14,18] and provides an intuition for our general results.

The above-mentioned protocols follow the generic pattern depicted in Fig. 3. We describe this pattern using standard terminology from multiparty computation, i.e. we use an ideal functionality that has to be replaced by an appropriate protocol. Using the functionality description allows us to abstract from many irrelevant details. In accordance with the secret reconstruction game, input t_i for ITM M_i^{ADGH} includes public parameters pp and a triple $(s^{(i)}, \tau^{(i)}, \sigma^{(i)})$ consisting of share $s^{(i)}$, local verification information $\tau^{(i)}$, and authentication information $\sigma^{(i)}$. They assume there is some fake secret $\hat{s} \in \mathbb{S}$ which is not in the support of distribution $\mathcal{S}$ of secrets and, therefore, is distinguishable from the initially shared secret s^*. The main loop always begins with a first phase where the parties query an ideal functionality $\mathcal{F}^{\beta,\hat{s}}$ (Fig. 4) using their types. Functionality $\mathcal{F}^{\beta,\hat{s}}$ first checks consistency and validity of these inputs and, if successful, returns a fresh round sharing $(\overline{s}^{(i)}, \overline{\tau}^{(i)}, \overline{\sigma}^{(i)})$ of either s^* with probability β or of $\hat{s}$ with probability $1 - \beta$. Afterwards M_i^{ADGH} sends its round share $\overline{s}^{(i)}$ and authentication information $\sigma_j^{(i)}$ to each M_j as well as simultaneously obtains a message parsed as $(\overline{s}^{(j)}, \sigma_i^{(j)})$. M_i^{ADGH} uses its round verification information $\overline{\tau}^{(i)}$ to locally reconstruct a corresponding secret. If the reconstruction fails with

---

ITM M_i^{ADGH} on input $t_i = (\mathrm{pp}, s^{(i)}, \tau^{(i)}, \sigma^{(i)})$ with access to $\mathcal{F}^{\beta,\hat{s}}$ (Fig. 4)

1 : Set flag allHonest := **true**

2 : **while** allHonest **do**

3 :   Send t_i to $\mathcal{F}^{\beta,\hat{s}}$ which privately returns $(\overline{s}^{(i)}, \overline{\tau}^{(i)}, \overline{\sigma}^{(i)})$.

4 :   For all $M_j, j \neq i$: Simultaneously send $(\overline{s}^{(i)}, \overline{\sigma}_j^{(i)})$ and obtain $(\overline{s}^{(j)}, \overline{\sigma}_i^{(j)})$.

5 :   Compute $s^* = \mathsf{Recon}(\mathrm{pp}, \overline{\tau}^{(i)}, ((\overline{s}^{(1)}, \overline{\sigma}_i^{(1)}), \ldots, (\overline{s}^{(n)}, \overline{\sigma}_i^{(n)})))$.

6 :   **if** $s^* = \perp$ **then**

7 :   allHonest := **false**

8 :   **elseif** $s^* \neq \hat{s}$ **then**

9 :   Output s^* and terminate.

10 : Continue listening, but send nothing anymore.

Fig. 3. Secret reconstruction strategy generalized from several protocols of [1,12] using an ideal functionality $\mathcal{F}^{\beta,\hat{s}}$ (Fig. 4) instead of an MPC protocol.

error symbol $\perp$, M_i^{ADGH} leaves the loop and only listens to any further communication. If the reconstructed secret s^* does not equal the fake secret $\hat{s}$, s^* is locally output as final guess. Otherwise, the loop's next round begins. Note, the protocol makes each M_i correctly output the initially shared secret s^* in an expected number of $1/\beta$ loop runs.

This protocol pattern randomizes the last round in order to overcome the problem that "send no/wrong share" weakly dominates "send share" in a fixed last round. Due to the secret-sharing's privacy, it is indistinguishable for deviating parties whether the current round's secret equals the initial secret s^* or the fake secret $\hat{s}$. When a party deviates such that she makes the reconstruction either fail with $\perp$ or a wrong secret $s \neq \hat{s}$, the remaining parties stop the interaction. If this happens in a fake round, which with probability $1 - \beta$ is the case, this stop of interaction acts as punishment as the deviating party obtains no further information on s^*.

In order to instantiate M_i^{ADGH} such that "send no/wrong share" not weakly dominates "send share", the secret-sharing scheme, its access structure, and the parameter β have to be chosen suitably. Depending on the given utilities, these ingredients have to be chosen such that the expected loss of making the protocol stop in a fake round outweighs the expected gain of exclusively learning the secret by deviating in a non-fake round. In short, the punishment deters active deviations which are observable by the remaining players. This, however, does not account for local deviations which are not observable. To see this, consider our counterexample $\overline{M_i^{\text{ADGH}}}$ (Fig. 5) which extends strategy M_i^{ADGH} by a simple check at the end of its first loop run. Concretely, $\overline{M_i^{\text{ADGH}}}$ checks whether each other machine sent a specially formatted LEAK-message containing their share and authentication information. If these values reconstruct to a valid secret under the *initial* verification information $\tau^{(i)}$, then s^* is output. $\overline{M_i^{\text{ADGH}}}$ weakly dominates the original approach M_i^{ADGH} in certain settings as specified in following theorem.

Functionality $\mathcal{F}^{\beta,\hat{s}}$ on inputs $(\mathsf{pp}_i, s^{(i)}, \tau^{(i)}, \sigma^{(i)})$ from each ITM M_i
1 :   **if** $\exists i \in [n] : \mathsf{Recon}(\mathsf{pp}, \tau^{(i)}, (s^{(j)}, \sigma_i^{(j)})_{j \in [n]}) = \perp \vee \mathsf{pp}_i \neq \mathsf{pp}_1$ **then**
2 :   **return** $\perp$
3 :   **else**
4 :   Compute $s^* = \mathsf{Recon}(\mathsf{pp}, \tau^{(1)}, (s^{(j)}, \sigma_i^{(j)})_{j \in [n]})$
5 :   Compute $(\overline{s}^{(i)}, \overline{\tau}^{(i)}, \overline{\sigma}^{(i)})_{i \in [n]} \leftarrow \begin{cases} \mathsf{Share}(\mathsf{pp}_\Pi, s^*), & \text{with probability } \beta \\ \mathsf{Share}(\mathsf{pp}_\Pi, \hat{s}), & \text{with probability } 1 - \beta \end{cases}$
6 :   **return** $(\overline{s}^{(i)}, \overline{\tau}^{(i)}, \overline{\sigma}^{(i)})$ to each party P_i

Fig. 4. Functionality $\mathcal{F}^{\beta,\hat{s}}$ which, given a consistent and valid sharing of secret s^*, returns a fresh sharing of s^* with probability β and of $\hat{s}$ with probability $1 - \beta$.

Theorem 1. *Let* $\Pi = (\mathsf{Setup}_\Pi, \mathsf{Share}, \mathsf{Recon})$ *be a secret-sharing scheme (Definition 3) with perfect privacy (Definition 4). Consider a secret reconstruction game (Definition 11) for* Π, *with non-trivial distribution of secrets (Definition 13) and reconstruction utilities preferring correctness (Definition 12). If* Π *has local* $(n-1)$-*verifiability (Definition 5), then for strategy* M_i^{ADGH} *(Fig. 3) there exists a weakly dominating strategy* $\overline{M_i^{\mathsf{ADGH}}}$.

We sketch the proof idea of Theorem 1. For more details we refer to the analogous formal proof of our generalized non-uniform result Theorem 2. In order to weakly dominate M_i^{ADGH} (Fig. 3) our constructed strategy $\overline{M_i^{\mathsf{ADGH}}}$ (Fig. 5) has to be 1) noticeably better against at least one opponent strategy but 2) never more than negligibly worse against any opponent strategy. Regarding 1), consider strategies $M'_{j\to i}$ (Fig. 6) which send $(\mathsf{LEAK}, s^{(j)}, \sigma_i^{(j)})$, i.e. a specially marked message containing the initial share and authentication information, to $\overline{M_i^{\mathsf{ADGH}}}$ and terminate. With respect to strategies $M'_{j\to i}$ ITM $\overline{M_i^{\mathsf{ADGH}}}$ correctly parses the incoming messages, reconstructs the initial secret, and outputs it. Because M_i^{ADGH} is not instructed to parse the specific LEAK-format, reconstruction fails, M_i^{ADGH} leaves its loop, and only listens without a correct output. As we assume correctness-preferring reconstruction utilities, which value correct outputs with a noticeably higher utility than wrong outputs, requirement 1) is satisfied. Regarding 2), in comparison to M_i^{ADGH} ITM $\overline{M_i^{\mathsf{ADGH}}}$ may only deviate and lead to a worse utility, if the remaining $(n-1)$-parties sent shares which make $\overline{M_i^{\mathsf{ADGH}}}$ reconstruct neither the initial secret s^* nor $\perp$ under the initial $\tau^{(i)}$. Assuming local $(n-1)$-verifiability, this happens with negligible probability against any ppt strategy $M'_{j\to i}$. Hence, compared to M_i^{ADGH}, the expected loss of $\overline{M_i^{\mathsf{ADGH}}}$ is at most negligible which satisfies requirement 2).

ITM $\overline{M_i^{\mathsf{ADGH}}}$ on input $t_i = (\mathsf{pp}, s^{(i)}, \tau^{(i)}, \sigma^{(i)})$ with access to $\mathcal{F}^{\beta,\hat{s}}$ (Fig. 4)

1 :   Run M_i^{ADGH} on the given inputs until end of first communication round.

2 :   For all $j \in [n] \setminus \{i\}$: Parse message m_j from M_j as $(\mathsf{LEAK}, s^{(j)}, \sigma_i^{(j)})$.

3 :   Compute $s^* = \mathsf{Recon}(\mathsf{pp}, \tau^{(i)}, ((s^{(1)}, \sigma_i^{(1)}), \dots, (s^{(n)}, \sigma_i^{(n)})))$.

4 :   **if** $s^* \notin \{\hat{s}, \perp\}$ **then**   // Shares valid with respect to the initial $\tau^{(i)}$ were sent.

5 :   Output s^*.

6 :   Continue to execute M_i^{ADGH}.

Fig. 5. Strategy $\overline{M_i^{\mathsf{ADGH}}}$ which weakly dominates M_i^{ADGH} (Fig. 3).

ITM $M'_{j\to i}$ on input $t_j = (\mathsf{pp}, s^{(j)}, \tau^{(j)}, \sigma^{(j)})$ with access to $\mathcal{F}^{\beta,\hat{s}}$

1 :   Send $m_j = (\mathsf{LEAK}, s^{(j)}, \sigma_i^{(j)})$ to M_i.

2 :   Output $\perp$ and terminate.

Fig. 6. Strategies $M'_{j\to i}$.

Theorem 1 applies directly to all but one concrete protocol instantiations and settings of M_i^{ADGH} from [1,12], as they use locally $(n-1)$-verifiable secret sharings. In the full version [5], we explain this in detail. Also, we describe another counterexample for the last missing instantiation [1, Proposition 3].

5   Impossibility Results for Surviving Iterated Deletion of Weakly Dominated Strategies

As explained in the introduction, the counterexample shown in Sect. 4 can be counteracted by adding the same first-round check to the honest protocol. However, informally, one can argue that there are many different checks that simply expect different encodings of the special first-round message, and not all of them can be built into a polynomial-time strategy. In this section, we show that in certain settings, local $(n-1)$-verifiability and iterated deletion of weakly dominated strategy (IDoWDS) are provably incompatible. We start with a non-uniform setting in Sect. 5.1 and then discuss other settings in Sect. 5.2.

5.1   Impossibility with Respect to Non-uniform Strategies

We consider the non-uniform setting. We show that for a secret reconstruction game local $(n-1)$-verifiability and iterated deletion of weakly dominated strategy (IDoWDS) are incompatible, i.e. in this setting every non-uniform strategy is weakly dominated by some other non-uniform strategy. This is formalized in Theorem 2 and Corollary 1. The only restrictions we need are non-trivial distributions and correctness-preferring utilities. Recall that for trivial secret distributions, i.e. distributions that are concentrated on a single secret, secret reconstruction games are mostly vacuous.

Theorem 2. Let $\Pi = (\mathsf{Setup}_\Pi, \mathsf{Share}, \mathsf{Recon})$ be a secret-sharing scheme (Definition 3) with perfect privacy (Definition 4). Consider a secret reconstruction game (Definition 11) for Π, with non-uniform strategies, non-trivial distribution of secrets (Definition 13), and reconstruction utilities preferring correctness (Definition 12). Let $(M_i, \omega'_1, \omega'_2, \dots)$ be a strategy for the secret reconstruction game, i.e. a non-uniform ppt ITM. If Π has (non-uniform) local $(n-1)$-verifiability (Definition 5), then there exists another strategy $(M_i^*, (\omega_1, \omega_2, \dots))$ which weakly dominates $(M_i, \omega'_1, \omega'_2, \dots)$ (Definition 9).

Corollary 1. *In the non-uniform setting there exists no strategy profile for the secret reconstruction game setting described in Theorem 2 which survives the iterated deletion of weakly dominated strategies (Definition 10).*

Proof (Theorem 2). In order to prove Theorem 2, given strategy $(M_i, \omega_1', \omega_2', \dots)$, where we from now on drop its auxiliary inputs $(\omega_1', \omega_2', \dots)$ which are immaterial to the argument, we define a new strategy $(M_i^*, (\omega_1, \omega_2, \dots))$ as in Fig. 7.

Non-uniform ITM $(M_i^*, (\omega_1, \omega_2, \dots))$, $\omega_\lambda = (\omega_{\lambda,1}, \dots, \omega_{\lambda,n})$, for given M_i.

Setup: Sample $(t_1, \dots, t_n) \leftarrow \mathcal{D}(\lambda)$, $t_i = (\mathsf{pp}, s^{(i)}, \tau^{(i)}, \sigma^{(i)})$, and send t_i to M_i.

1 :   Run M_i on the given inputs until end of first communication round.

2 :   For all $j \in [n] \setminus \{i\}$: On message m_j from M_j set $(s^{(j)}, \sigma_i^{(j)}) := m_j \oplus \omega_{\lambda,j}$.

3 :   **if** $s^* := \mathsf{Recon}(\mathsf{pp}, \tau^{(i)}, (s^{(j)}, \sigma_i^{(j)})_{j \in [n]}) \neq \perp$ **then**

4 :   Output s^*.

5 :   Continue to execute M_i.

Fig. 7. Improved strategy $(M_i^*, (\omega_1, \omega_2, \dots))$

$(M_i^*, (\omega_1, \omega_2, \dots))$ extends M_i by an additional check whether it obtained one-time pad encryptions of the original signed shares using the non-uniform keys $\omega_\lambda = (\omega_{\lambda,1}, \dots, \omega_{\lambda,n})$. Without loss of generality we assume that the messages m_j that M_i receives from other strategies are of the same length as the advice strings $\omega_{\lambda,j}$ (which in turn have the length of shares). If this is not the case, we only consider prefixes of m_j of the appropriate length. Since $(M_i^*, (\omega_1, \omega_2, \dots))$ in its first step simulates M_i until the end of the communication round, it also needs the $M_i's$ advice string as additional input. To simplify notation, we do not include this in the description of $(M_i^*, (\omega_1, \omega_2, \dots))$.

To prove Theorem 2, first note that $(M_i^*, (\omega_1, \omega_2, \dots))$ (Fig. 7) is ppt. Next, we show its weak dominance over M_i (Definition 9). We split the proof for computational weak dominance into two Lemmas 1 and 2: On the one hand, we show that M_i^* achieves at most negligibly less utility than M_i with respect to any opponent strategy M_{-i} (Lemma 1). On the other hand, we show the existence of an opponent strategy M_{-i} that achieves noticeably higher utility than M_i (Lemma 2). Taken together, Lemmas 1 and 2 show that both requirements of computational weak dominance are satisfied which finishes the proof.   □

Lemma 1. *Let (non-uniform) ITM M_i be a strategy for the secret reconstruction game for a secret sharing scheme $\Pi = (\mathsf{Setup}_\Pi, \mathsf{Share}, \mathsf{Recon})$ with locally $(n-1)$-verifiable reconstruction and non-uniform strategies. Then for any opponent strategy profile M_{-i} and strategy $(M_i^*, (\omega_1, \omega_2, \dots))$ (Fig. 7) there exists a negligible function μ such that for all $\lambda \in \mathbb{N}$*

$$u_i(1^\lambda, M_i, M_{-i}) \leq u_i(1^\lambda, (M_i^*, (\omega_1, \omega_2, \dots)), M_{-i}) + \mu(\lambda) \qquad (1)$$

Proof. For the sake of contradiction assume that for some $(M_i^*, (\omega_1, \omega_2, \dots))$, M_{-i}, and all negligible functions μ we have

$$u_i(1^\lambda, M_i, M_{-i}) > u_i(1^\lambda, (M_i^*, (\omega_1, \omega_2, \dots)), M_{-i}) + \mu(\lambda).$$

Note that the only deviation of ITM $(M_i^*, (\omega_1, \omega_2, \dots))$ from the original strategy M_i happens within lines 2–4 (Fig. 7). Since, by assumption, reconstruction utilities prefer correctness, compared to M_i this deviation only decreases utility if the secret output in line 4 is not correct. In order to decrease utility more than negligibly, entering line 4 and outputting the wrong secret has to happen with a non-negligible probability. However, in that case from $(M_i^*, (\omega_1, \omega_2, \dots))$ and M_{-i} we immediately get an adversary violating the local $(n-1)$-verifiability property of $\Pi = (\mathsf{Setup}_\Pi, \mathsf{Share}, \mathsf{Recon})$ (see Definition 3). $\square$

Lemma 2. *Let ITM M_i be a strategy for the secret reconstruction game for secret sharing scheme $\Pi = (\mathsf{Setup}_\Pi, \mathsf{Share}, \mathsf{Recon})$ with locally $(n-1)$-verifiable reconstruction and with non-uniform strategies (Definition 11). If the distribution of secrets is non-trivial (Definition 13) and reconstruction utilities prefer correctness, then there exist auxiliary strings $(\omega_1, \omega_2, \dots)$, an opponent strategy M_{-i}, and a noticeable function p such that for all $\lambda \in \mathbb{N}$*

$$u_i(1^\lambda, (M_i^*, (\omega_1, \omega_2, \dots)), (M_{-i}, (\omega_1, \omega_2, \dots)))$$
$$\geq u_i(1^\lambda, M_i, (M_{-i}, (\omega_1, \omega_2, \dots))) + p(\lambda),$$

where each strategy in profile M_{-i} gets the same sequence of auxiliary strings.

Proof. Consider the opponent strategies $(M'_{j \to i}, (\omega_1, \omega_2, \dots)), j \neq i$, described in Fig. 8. Together they form the profile M_{-i}.

Non-uniform ITM $(M'_{j \to i}, (\omega_1, \omega_2, \dots))$, $\omega_\lambda = (\omega_{\lambda,1}, \dots, \omega_{\lambda,n})$

Setup: Sample $(t_1, \dots, t_n) \leftarrow \mathcal{D}(\lambda)$, $t_i = (\mathsf{pp}, s^{(i)}, \tau^{(i)}, \sigma^{(i)})$, and send t_i to M_i.

1 :   Send $m_j = (s^{(j)}, \sigma_i^{(j)}) \oplus \omega_{\lambda,j}$ to M_i.
2 :   Output $\perp$ and terminate.

Fig. 8. Strategies $(M'_{j \to i}, (\omega_1, \omega_2, \dots))$

The strategies in $(M'_{j \to i}, (\omega_1, \omega_2, \dots))$ are tailored towards $(M_i^*, (\omega_1, \omega_2, \dots))$ and simply send one-time pad encryptions of their shares to M_i. Obviously, these are not useful (or rational) strategies but are still relevant for weak domination.

In the following, to ease notation, we exclude the shares verification and authentication information which are not relevant to the argument itself. Also, to increase readability, we drop the auxiliary strings from the non-uniform ITMs $(M_i^*, (\omega_1, \omega_2, \dots))$ and $(M'_{j \to i}, (\omega_1, \omega_2, \dots))$ when possible.

For the sake of contradiction assume that for all $(\omega_1, \omega_2, \dots)$ and all noticeable functions p

$$u_i(1^\lambda, M_i^*, (M'_{j \to i})_{j \neq i}) < u_i(1^\lambda, M_i, (M'_{j \to i})_{j \neq i}) + p(\lambda). \tag{2}$$

First note, the strategies $M'_{j \to i}$ have the fixed output $\perp$ irrespective of M_i. Therefore, against $M'_{j \to i}$, the only difference in M_i's utility originates from the output of M_i itself. Further, because we assume utilities which prefer correctness, any output of M_i which is not the correct secret results in noticeably less utility compared to the correct secret. By construction, M_i^* always correctly reconstructs and outputs the originally shared secret in line 4 when the remaining parties run $M'_{j \to i}$. Therefore, M_i^* achieves the optimal utility with respect to the ITMs $M'_{j \to i}$. Hence, in order to satisfy Eq. (2), strategy M_i has to output the correct secret with overwhelming probability for all choices of auxiliary strings. By an averaging argument this also holds when choosing the auxiliary strings uniformly at random. Formally, there exists a negligible function μ such that

$$\Pr[s \leftarrow \mathcal{S}(\lambda), \omega_\lambda \leftarrow \{0,1\}^{\ell(\lambda)} : M_i(\mathsf{Share}(s) \oplus \omega_\lambda) = s] = 1 - \mu(\lambda).$$

for all $\lambda \in \mathbb{N}$. We rewrite above equation as

$$\Pr[s \leftarrow \mathcal{S}(\lambda), \omega_\lambda \leftarrow \{0,1\}^{\ell(\lambda)} : M_i(\omega_\lambda) = s] = 1 - \mu(\lambda).$$

In particular, by the uniform choice of ω the input of M_i is stochastically independent of s but M_i still outputs s with overwhelming probability. This, however, contradicts the non-trivial distribution of secrets because there exists a noticeable function p such that for any machine M', especially M_i, we have

$$\Pr[s \leftarrow \mathcal{S}(\lambda), \omega_\lambda \leftarrow \{0,1\}^{\ell(\lambda)} : M'(\omega_\lambda) = s] \leq \max_{s \in \mathbb{S}} \Pr[\mathcal{S}(\lambda) = s] < 1 - p(\lambda).$$

Concretely, for the negligible function μ and noticeable function p the previous equations imply relation $p(\lambda) < \mu(\lambda)$, which for λ large enough is false. $\square$

5.2 Impossibility with Respect to Other Settings

If we examine the proof above, the main challenge for proving that every strategy is weakly dominated is coming up with a first-message encoding for which we can prove that the original strategy does not check it in any way. We mask the first-round message by XORing with some bit string that is the same for all machines $M'_{j \to i}$, but to which the original strategy has no access. In the non-uniform setting, we essentially prove that a ppt machine cannot check all XOR masks, and then encode some XOR mask that is not checked in the non-uniform advice string ω of the counterexample machines $(M_i^*, (\omega_1, \omega_2, \dots)), (M'_{j \to i}, (\omega_1, \omega_2, \dots))$.

Another alternative for getting an XOR mask that is not accessed by the original strategy M_i presents itself in the random oracle model: If the original strategy M_i is such that it never queries a random oracle (e.g., any strategy in the standard model), then in the random oracle model, M_i is weakly dominated by some random oracle model strategy M_i^*. M_i^* works as in the non-uniform example, but sources the XOR mask from the random oracle (e.g., as $H(1)||H(2)||\dots$). The first-round messages of $M'_{j \to i}$ do not convey any information about the secret at all to the original non-random-oracle strategy.

Other ways are conceivable as well. For example, assume that the dealer extends each party's type t_i by some shared random bit string ω or there is some common reference string that we know is ignored by the original machine M_i (e.g., if M_i is a subprotocol in a larger protocol).

6 Impossibility of Rational Mechanisms for Majority Coalitions

In many cases, we not only want to look at individual rational actors, but also design mechanisms that are rational to follow for *coalitions* of actors [1]. So instead of standard (computational) Nash equilibria, in the coalition setting one considers t-resilient computational equilibria (Definition 8). Even though it seems not to have been done in the literature [1], we argue that in order to properly take coalitions into account, one must also account for coalitions when considering weak domination of strategies.

In this section, we provide evidence that there *cannot* be any reasonable secret-reconstruction mechanism that for coalitions of size $t \geq n/2$ is both (1) a t-resilient computational Nash equilibrium and (2) in some sense "t-resilient against weak domination", i.e. there is no *t-coalition strategy* that is sometimes (significantly) better (against some strategy of the non-coalition members) and never (non-negligibly) worse. This seems to be true as long as the secret-sharing scheme is *verifiable-or-fully-broken* (Definition 15), which is the case for the most popular secret-sharing schemes. We formally prove impossibility for those secret-sharing schemes and *non-uniform* strategies (so that we can apply a version of Theorem 2), but the result also generalizes to the settings discussed in Sect. 5.2 and intuitively, as argued in the introduction, similar results should apply to any reasonable concrete protocol with uniform strategies.

Intuitively, a mechanism designer has the choice between two options regarding authentication of the secret-sharing: The first option is to make the secret-sharing scheme very well authenticated, so that $n - t$ parties *cannot* convince t honest parties of a wrong secret. But then any (t-coalition) strategy is weakly dominated similar to Sect. 5, as the strategy that applies a share verification check to (some encoding of) the first-round messages can be sure that if the check succeeds, it outputs the *correct* secret. The alternative option is to make the secret-sharing scheme not as well authenticated, so that a coalition of $n - t$ parties *can* convince someone of a wrong secret. But in that case, no strategy can be a $(n - t)$-resilient Nash equilibrium because it is always better for a coalition of $n - t$ parties to deviate to convince the other parties of a wrong secret. But if a strategy is not a $(n - t)$-resilient Nash equilibrium, then it also cannot be a t-resilient Nash equilibrium because $t \geq n - t$ for $t \geq n/2$. Overall, no matter whether authentication is chosen to be strong or weak, you get a problem with either weak domination or Nash equilibria.

To prove this, we first introduce a notion of weak domination for coalitions in Sect. 6.1, then go on to explain our assumption on the possible secret-sharing schemes in Sect. 6.2, and finally prove the impossibility result in Sect. 6.3.

6.1 Weak Domination for Coalitions

First, we generalize the notion of weakly dominated strategies to weakly dominated strategies with respect to coalitions. While definitions of Nash equilibria with respect to coalitions (Definition 8) are widely available, it seems a similar generalization for weak domination is much less standard. For Nash equilibria, it is argued that if coalitions form, they may have an incentive to deviate from the prescribed mechanism in order to improve their utility. We argue that similarly, for weak domination with coalitions, it is reasonable for a coalition to deviate from the mechanism because there is an alternative coalition strategy that is never (non-negligibly) worse than the mechanism, but is (noticeably) better against *some* strategies of the non-coalition parties. We generalize Definition 9 for coalitions as follows.

Definition 14 (Dominance with coalition C). *Let typed computational game* $\Gamma = (\{\mathcal{D}(\lambda)\}_{\lambda \in \mathbb{N}}, (S_i)_{i \in [n]}, (u_i)_{i \in [n]})$ *and* $C \subsetneq [n]$. *A partial strategy* $M_C^* \in S_{\times C}$ *weakly dominates* $M_C' \in S_{\times C}$ *with respect to coalition C if*

1. *"Never non-negligibly worse": For all* $M_{-C} \in S_{\times -C}$, *there exists a negligible function μ such that*

$$u_C(1^\lambda, M_C^*, M_{-C}) \geq u_C(1^\lambda, M_C', M_{-C}) - \mu(\lambda)$$

2. *"Sometimes significantly better": There exists a noticeable function p and a partial opponent strategy* $M_{-C} \in S_{\times -C}$

$$u_C(1^\lambda, M_C^*, M_{-C}) \geq u_C(1^\lambda, M_C', M_{-C}) + p(\lambda)$$

where u_C is defined as in Definition 7. We say that the coalition strategy $M_C' \in S_{\times C}$ *is weakly dominated if there is some M_C^* that weakly dominates it.*

The original non-coalition definition (Definition 9) is the special case with $|C| = 1$. We omit a definition of iterated deletion of weakly dominated strategies with respect to coalitions (it is not actually clear what that should look like, but it also is not necessary to our argument).

Theorem 2 can be generalized to coalitions as follows.

Theorem 3. *Let* $\Pi = (\mathsf{Setup}_\Pi, \mathsf{Share}, \mathsf{Recon})$ *be a secret-sharing scheme (Definition 3) with perfect privacy (Definition 4). Consider a secret reconstruction game (Definition 11) for Π, with non-uniform strategies, non-trivial distribution of secrets (Definition 13), and reconstruction utilities preferring correctness (Definition 12). Let* $C \subset [n], t = |C|$, *and let* $M_C = (M_i)_{i \in C}$ *be some partial non-uniform strategy profile. If Π has (non-uniform) local $n - t$-verifiability (Definition 5), then there exists a non-uniform partial strategy profile M_C^* that weakly dominates M_C (Definition 14).*

Proof (sketch). Given partial strategy profile $M_C = (M_i)_{i \in C}$, define partial strategy profile M_C^* as follows. Choose $i \in C$ arbitrarily. Then M_C^* consists of $(M_i^*, (\omega_1, \omega_2, \ldots))$ and strategies $M_j, j \in C \setminus \{i\}$. The rest of the proof is as the proof for Theorem 2. $\square$

6.2 An Assumption on the Secret-Sharing Scheme

For the results in this section, we require the secret-sharing scheme to have a specific property. Namely, we want that for any number k of corrupted shares, it must be either (1) *infeasible* to circumvent authentication (meaning it has local k-verifiability as in Definition 5), or (2) *very easy* to circumvent authentication in the following sense: Manipulating the k corrupted shares results in a sharing of a different secret s' *related* to the original secret s^* (even if the k parties may not be able to reconstruct s^* from their shares). Then given the related secret s', it must be easy to find s^*. For example, for an additive (xor) secret-sharing, the process (2) can be accomplished by incrementing some corrupted share by 1, which results in a secret $s' = s^* + 1$, so given s', it is easy to retrieve s^*. There must not be an in-between where authentication is broken against k parties, but it also is not possible for k parties to both change the sharing to a different secret and then reliably infer the real secret.

Definition 15 (Verifiable-or-fully-broken secret sharing schemes). *Let Π be a secret-sharing scheme (Definition 3) for n parties. We say that Π is verifiable-or-fully-broken (for secret distributions $\mathcal{S}(1^\lambda)$) if for all $k \in [1, n-1]$, Π has local k-verifiability, or there is a $C \subseteq [n], |C| = k$ and a deterministic polynomial-time algorithm $\mathcal{A}$ such that $\Pr[\mathsf{ForgeRel}_{\mathcal{A}, \Pi}^{\mathcal{S}, C}(\lambda) = 1] \geq 1 - \mu(\lambda)$ for some negligible function μ, where $\mathsf{ForgeRel}_{\mathcal{A}, \Pi}^{\mathcal{S}, C}$ is as in Fig. 9.*

Experiment $\mathsf{ForgeRel}_{\mathcal{A}, \Pi}^{\mathcal{S}, C}(\lambda)$:

1. $s^* \leftarrow \mathcal{S}(1^\lambda), \mathsf{pp} \leftarrow \mathsf{Setup}_\Pi(1^\lambda)$.
2. $((s^{(1)}, \tau^{(1)}, \sigma^{(1)}), \ldots, (s^{(n)}, \tau^{(n)}, \sigma^{(n)})) \leftarrow \mathsf{Share}(\mathsf{pp}, s^*)$.
3. Adversary $\mathcal{A}$ is given pp, $(s^{(j)}, \tau^{(j)}, \sigma^{(j)})_{j \in C}$. It outputs $(\bar{s}^{(j)}, \bar{\tau}^{(j)}, \bar{\sigma}^{(j)})_{j \in C}$ and a state st.
4. Check if $((s^{(j)}, \tau^{(j)}, \sigma^{(j)})_{j \notin C}, (\bar{s}^{(j)}, \bar{\tau}^{(j)}, \bar{\sigma}^{(j)})_{j \in C})$ is valid output of $\mathsf{Share}(\mathsf{pp}, s')$ for some $s' \notin \{s^*, \bot\}$. If not, output 0 and stop.
5. $\mathcal{A}$ is given s' and st, and outputs some s_{guess}.
6. Output 1 iff $s_{\mathsf{guess}} = s^*$.

Fig. 9. Experiment for fully breaking verification of secrets for secret-sharing scheme Π with respect to deterministic adversary $\mathcal{A}$, set $C \subset [n]$ of corrupted parties, and family of secret distributions $\mathcal{S}$.

This definition covers many standard schemes (c. f. examples in [5, Sect. 6]) which are widely used and arguably the most relevant ones. Note that Shamir's secret sharing for threshold $m \leq n/2$ does not fall under this, but that case is less interesting in our setting because a coalition of $k > n/2$ can then reconstruct the secret without any interaction (in particular, if used for sharing secrets in multiparty computation, the coalition would be able to see all of it).

6.3 Proving Impossibility

We are now ready to prove the following theorem.

Theorem 4. *Let Π be a secret-sharing scheme (Definition 3) with perfect privacy (Definition 3) that is verifiable-or-fully-broken (Definition 15) for secret distributions S. Consider the secret reconstruction game for secret sharing scheme Π with non-uniform strategies, non-trivial distribution of secrets S (Definition 13), and reconstruction utilities preferring correctness and exclusivity (Definition 12). Let $t \geq n/2$. Then there exists no mechanism with the following properties:*

- *If everyone follows the mechanism, the correct secret is reconstructed with probability 1.*
- *The mechanism is a t-resilient Nash equilibrium (Definition 8).*
- *There is no coalition $C \subseteq [n], |C| = t$ such that M_C is weakly dominated (Definition 14).*

Overall, this indicates that for most typical secret-sharing schemes, there is no pleasing mechanism that could be considered fully "rational". In contrast to Sect. 5, Theorem 4 does not *assume* that the secret sharing needs to be authenticated (but rather shows that whether or not authentication is applied, both cases run into rational issues).

For the proof, there are two cases, similar to how we argued at the beginning of this section: (1) if the secret sharing scheme Π has (non-uniform) local $n - t$-verifiability (Definition 5), then every mechanism is t-weakly dominated (because of Theorem 3). Otherwise (2) the secret sharing scheme does *not* have local $n - t$ verifiability. Then it also does not have local $t \geq n - t$ verifiability. Then Definition 15 gives us an adversary $\mathcal{A}$ that manipulates the coalition shares, altering the shared secret from s^* to some $s' \neq s^*$ (for the non-coalition parties), and can output the correct s^* for the coalition parties. We use $\mathcal{A}$ to construct a coalition strategy with better utility than the mechanism, meaning that the mechanism is not a t-resilient computational Nash equilibrium.

Proof. Theorem 4 follows from Theorem 3 for the case that Π has (non-uniform) local $n - t$-verifiability, and from Lemma 3 in the other case.   □

Lemma 3. *In the setting of Theorem 4, assume Π does not have (non-uniform) local t-verifiability. Then no mechanism $(M_1, \ldots, M_n) \in S_{\times[n]}$ is a t-resilient computational Nash equilibrium.*

Behavior of ITM M_i^* in the coalition $(i \in C)$ on input $(\mathsf{pp}, (s^{(j)}, \tau^{(i)}, \sigma^{(j)}))_{j \in C}$, where M_i is the honest strategy and $\mathcal{A}$ (Definition 15) fully breaks Π.

---

1 :   Run $((\overline{s}^{(j)}, \overline{\tau}^{(j)}, \overline{\sigma}^{(j)})_{j \in C}, \mathsf{st}) \leftarrow \mathcal{A}(\mathsf{pp}, (s^{(j)}, \tau^{(j)}, \sigma^{(j)})_{j \in C})$.

2 :   Run $M_i(\mathsf{pp}, \overline{s}^{(i)}, \overline{\tau}^{(i)}, \overline{\sigma}^{(i)})$ interactively, until M_i outputs s'.

3 :   Run $s_{\text{guess}} \leftarrow \mathcal{A}(s', \mathsf{st})$.

4 :   Output s_{guess}.

Fig. 10. Improved strategy M_i^* for coalition member $i \in C$

Proof. Let $M = (M_1, \ldots, M_n)$ be a mechanism. Let C and $\mathcal{A}$ be as in Definition 15, $C \subseteq [n], |C| = t$. Let $(M_i^*)_{i \in C}$ be as in Fig. 10.

Consider a run of strategies $((M_i^*)_{i \in C}, (M_i)_{i \notin C})$ from the point of view of the coalition strategies M_i^*. If $\mathcal{A}$ outputs manipulated shares that are possible output of $\mathsf{Share}(\mathsf{pp}, s')$ for some secret s', the result of the honestly run mechanism will be s'. This is because all the coalition members get the same output from the deterministic $\mathcal{A}$, and the honestly executed mechanism always succeeds in reconstructing the input shared secret (in this case the manipulated one).

That means that from the point of view of $\mathcal{A}$, everything is exactly as in $\mathsf{ForgeRel}_{\mathcal{A}, \Pi}^{S, C}(\lambda)$. So that with overwhelming probability, the coalition members output the right secret $s^* = s_{\text{guess}}$ and the non-coalition members output a wrong secret $s' \neq s^*$. Because parties prefer exclusivity, it follows that the coalition utility $\sum_{i \in C} u_i(1^\lambda, (M_i^*)_{i \in C}, M_{-C})$ with the strategies M_i^* is noticeably larger than the coalition utility $\sum_{i \in C} u_i(1^\lambda, M)$ for the mechanism (where everyone learns the correct secret). Hence M is not a t-resilient Nash equilibrium. □

Acknowledgements. We would like to thank the anonymous reviewers for their valuable feedback and constructive comments.

References

1. Abraham, I., Dolev, D., Gonen, R., Halpern, J.Y.: Distributed computing meets game theory: robust mechanisms for rational secret sharing and multiparty computation. In: Proceedings of the 25th Annual Symposium on Principles of Distributed Computing, PODC, pp. 53–62. ACM (2006)
2. Asharov, G., Canetti, R., Hazay, C.: Towards a game theoretic view of secure computation. In: Paterson, K.G. (ed.) EUROCRYPT 2011. LNCS, vol. 6632, pp. 426–445. Springer, Heidelberg (2011). https://doi.org/10.1007/978-3-642-20465-4_24
3. Asharov, G., Lindell, Y.: Utility dependence in correct and fair rational secret sharing. J. Cryptol. **24**(1), 157–202 (2011)
4. Beimel, A.: Secret-sharing schemes: a survey. In: Chee, Y.M., et al. (eds.) IWCC 2011. LNCS, vol. 6639, pp. 11–46. Springer, Heidelberg (2011). https://doi.org/10.1007/978-3-642-20901-7_2

5. Blömer, J., Bobolz, J., Bröcher, H.: On the impossibility of surviving (iterated) deletion of weakly dominated strategies in rational MPC. Cryptology ePrint Archive, Paper 2022/1762 (2022)
6. Chung, K.-M., Chan, T.-H.H., Wen, T., Shi, E.: Game-theoretic fairness meets multi-party protocols: the case of leader election. In: Malkin, T., Peikert, C. (eds.) CRYPTO 2021. LNCS, vol. 12826, pp. 3–32. Springer, Cham (2021). https://doi.org/10.1007/978-3-030-84245-1_1
7. Chung, K.-M., Guo, Y., Lin, W.-K., Pass, R., Shi, E.: Game theoretic notions of fairness in multi-party coin toss. In: Beimel, A., Dziembowski, S. (eds.) TCC 2018. LNCS, vol. 11239, pp. 563–596. Springer, Cham (2018). https://doi.org/10.1007/978-3-030-03807-6_21
8. Dodis, Y., Halevi, S., Rabin, T.: A cryptographic solution to a game theoretic problem. In: Bellare, M. (ed.) CRYPTO 2000. LNCS, vol. 1880, pp. 112–130. Springer, Heidelberg (2000). https://doi.org/10.1007/3-540-44598-6_7
9. Dodis, Y., Rabin, T.: Cryptography and game theory. In: Algorithmic Game Theory, pp. 181–207 (2007)
10. Fuchsbauer, G., Katz, J., Naccache, D.: Efficient rational secret sharing in standard communication networks. In: Micciancio, D. (ed.) TCC 2010. LNCS, vol. 5978, pp. 419–436. Springer, Heidelberg (2010). https://doi.org/10.1007/978-3-642-11799-2_25
11. Goldreich, O., Micali, S., Wigderson, A.: How to play any mental game or A completeness theorem for protocols with honest majority. In: Proceedings of the 19th Annual ACM Symposium on Theory of Computing, pp. 218–229. ACM (1987)
12. Gordon, S.D., Katz, J.: Rational secret sharing, revisited. In: De Prisco, R., Yung, M. (eds.) SCN 2006. LNCS, vol. 4116, pp. 229–241. Springer, Heidelberg (2006). https://doi.org/10.1007/11832072_16
13. Groce, A., Katz, J.: Fair computation with rational players. In: Pointcheval, D., Johansson, T. (eds.) EUROCRYPT 2012. LNCS, vol. 7237, pp. 81–98. Springer, Heidelberg (2012). https://doi.org/10.1007/978-3-642-29011-4_7
14. Halpern, J.Y., Teague, V.: Rational secret sharing and multiparty computation: extended abstract. In: Proceedings of the 36th Annual ACM Symposium on Theory of Computing, pp. 623–632. ACM (2004)
15. Hillas, J., Samet, D.: Dominance rationality: a unified approach. Games Econ. Behav. **119**, 189–196 (2020)
16. Hubáček, P., Nielsen, J.B., Rosen, A.: Limits on the power of cryptographic cheap talk. In: Canetti, R., Garay, J.A. (eds.) CRYPTO 2013. LNCS, vol. 8042, pp. 277–297. Springer, Heidelberg (2013). https://doi.org/10.1007/978-3-642-40041-4_16
17. Katz, J.: Bridging game theory and cryptography: recent results and future directions. In: Canetti, R. (ed.) TCC 2008. LNCS, vol. 4948, pp. 251–272. Springer, Heidelberg (2008). https://doi.org/10.1007/978-3-540-78524-8_15
18. Kol, G., Naor, M.: Cryptography and game theory: designing protocols for exchanging information. In: Canetti, R. (ed.) TCC 2008. LNCS, vol. 4948, pp. 320–339. Springer, Heidelberg (2008). https://doi.org/10.1007/978-3-540-78524-8_18
19. Kol, G., Naor, M.: Games for exchanging information. In: Proceedings of the 40th Annual ACM Symposium on Theory of Computing, pp. 423–432 (2008)
20. Lysyanskaya, A., Triandopoulos, N.: Rationality and adversarial behavior in multiparty computation. In: Dwork, C. (ed.) CRYPTO 2006. LNCS, vol. 4117, pp. 180–197. Springer, Heidelberg (2006). https://doi.org/10.1007/11818175_11
21. Manshaei, M.H., Zhu, Q., Alpcan, T., Başar, T., Hubaux, J.P.: Game theory meets network security and privacy. ACM Comput. Surv. (CSUR) **45**(3), 1–39 (2013)

22. Rabin, T.: Robust sharing of secrets when the dealer is honest or cheating. J. ACM **41**(6), 1089–1109 (1994)
23. Rabin, T., Ben-Or, M.: Verifiable secret sharing and multiparty protocols with honest majority (extended abstract). In: Proceedings of the 21st Annual ACM Symposium on Theory of Computing, pp. 73–85. ACM (1989)
24. Samuelson, L.: Dominated strategies and common knowledge. Games Econ. Behav. **4**(2), 284–313 (1992)
25. Shamir, A.: How to share a secret. Commun. ACM **22**(11), 612–613 (1979)
26. Stahl, D.O.: Lexicographic rationalizability and iterated admissibility. Econ. Lett. **47**(2), 155–159 (1995)
27. Wu, K., Asharov, G., Shi, E.: A complete characterization of game-theoretically fair, multi-party coin toss. In: Dunkelman, O., Dziembowski, S. (eds.) EURO-CRYPT 2022. LNCS, vol. 13275, pp. 120–149. Springer, Cham (2022). https://doi.org/10.1007/978-3-031-06944-4_5

Synchronizable Fair Exchange

Ranjit Kumaresan[1], Srinivasan Raghuraman[2](✉), and Adam Sealfon[3]

[1] Visa Research, Austin, USA
[2] Visa Research and MIT, Cambridge, USA
srini131293@gmail.com
[3] Google Research, San Francisco, USA

Abstract. Fitzi, Garay, Maurer, and Ostrovsky (J. Cryptology 2005) showed that in the presence of a dishonest majority, no primitive of cardinality $n-1$ is complete for realizing an arbitrary n-party functionality with *guaranteed output delivery*. In this work, we introduce a new 2-party primitive $\mathcal{F}_{\mathsf{SyX}}$ ("synchronizable fair exchange") and show that it is complete for realizing any n-party functionality with *fairness* in a setting where all parties are pairwise connected by instances of $\mathcal{F}_{\mathsf{SyX}}$.

In the $\mathcal{F}_{\mathsf{SyX}}$-hybrid model, the two parties *load* $\mathcal{F}_{\mathsf{SyX}}$ with some input, and following this, either party can *trigger* $\mathcal{F}_{\mathsf{SyX}}$ with a "witness" at a later time to receive the output from $\mathcal{F}_{\mathsf{SyX}}$. Crucially the other party also receives output from $\mathcal{F}_{\mathsf{SyX}}$ when $\mathcal{F}_{\mathsf{SyX}}$ is triggered. The trigger witnesses allow us to *synchronize* the trigger phases of multiple instances of $\mathcal{F}_{\mathsf{SyX}}$, thereby aiding in the design of fair multiparty protocols. Additionally, a pair of parties may *reuse* a single *a priori* loaded instance of $\mathcal{F}_{\mathsf{SyX}}$ in any number of multiparty protocols (involving different sets of parties). (The authors grant IACR a non-exclusive and irrevocable license to distribute the article under the https://creativecommons.org/licenses/by-nc/3.0/), (This work was done in part while all the authors were at MIT).

Keywords: secure computation · fair exchange · completeness · preprocessing

1 Introduction

Secure multiparty computation (MPC) allows a set of mutually mistrusting parties to perform a joint computation on their inputs that reveals only the outcome of the computation and nothing else. Showing feasibility [7,13,22,34,37] of this seemingly impossible to achieve notion has been one of the most striking contributions of modern cryptography. However, definitions of secure computation do vary across models, in part owing to the general impossibility results for fair coin-tossing [15]. In settings where the majority of the participating parties are dishonest (including the two party setting), a protocol for secure computation only provides *security-with-abort*, and in particular is not required to guarantee important properties such as guaranteed output delivery or even fairness[1].

---

[1] Fairness means that either all parties get the output or none do. Guaranteed output delivery means that all parties get the output.

© International Association for Cryptologic Research 2023
G. Rothblum and H. Wee (Eds.): TCC 2023, LNCS 14369, pp. 411–440, 2023.
https://doi.org/10.1007/978-3-031-48615-9_15

On the other hand, when up to $t < n/3$ parties are corrupt, then there exist protocols for n-party secure computation that guarantee output delivery [7,13]. This result can be extended to a setting where up to $t < n/2$ parties are corrupt assuming the existence of a broadcast channel [22,34].

Given the state of affairs, there has been extensive research to better understand the problem of fairness and guaranteed output delivery in secure computation in setting where $t \geq n/2$. For instance, while Cleve [15] showed that dishonest majority fair coin tossing is impossible, several works [3,4,23,25] showed the existence of non-trivial functions for which fair secure computation is possible in the dishonest majority setting.

Most relevant to our work is the work of Fitzi, Garay, Maurer, and Ostrovsky [18] who studied complete primitives for secure computation *with guaranteed output delivery*. They showed that no ideal primitive of cardinality[2] $n - 1$ is complete for n-party secure computation. More generally, for $n \geq 3$ and $k < n$, they show that no primitive of cardinality k is complete when $t \geq \lceil \frac{k-1}{k+1} \cdot n \rceil$. It follows that when $t \geq \lceil n/3 \rceil$, no primitive of cardinality 2 is complete for secure computation. Also, when $t \geq n - 2$, no primitive of cardinality $k < n$ is complete for secure computation. They also show a primitive of cardinality n that is complete for n-party secure computation when $t \geq n - 2$.

It is interesting to note that the above impossibility results are derived in [18] by showing the *impossibility of broadcast* given a primitive of cardinality k.[3] Recently, Cohen and Lindell [16] showed that the presence of a broadcast channel is inconsequential to achieving the goal of fairness, i.e., they showed that any protocol for fair computation that uses a broadcast channel can be compiled into one that does not use a broadcast channel. They also showed that assuming the existence of a broadcast channel, any protocol for fair secure computation can be compiled into one that provides guaranteed output delivery. Importantly, all these transformations only require primitives of cardinality 2.

Given the above, one wonders whether the impossibility result of [18] can be bypassed if we restrict our attention to *fair secure computation* alone. Gordon et al. [24] propose primitives that are complete for fair MPC.[4] The upside of these primitives is that unlike [18], their primitive complexity is independent of the function being computed. However, these primitives are still n-wise primitives, and thus do not answer the question of whether a primitive of cardinality $n - 1$ can be complete for n-party fair secure computation.

OUR CONTRIBUTIONS. In this work, we introduce a new 2-party primitive $\mathcal{F}_{SyX}$ ("synchronizable fair exchange," or simply "synchronizable exchange") and show

---

[2] Cardinality refers to the number of parties interacting with a single instance of the ideal primitive.

[3] Although unstated in [18], we believe that their lower bound proof extends even for reactive functionalities. That is, no $(n - 1)$-wise *reactive* functionality is sufficient to realize broadcast (and consequently, secure computation with guaranteed output delivery).

[4] In fact, some of their primitives are also complete for secure computation with guaranteed output delivery.

that it is complete for realizing any n-party functionality with *fairness* in a setting where all n parties are pairwise connected by independent instances of $\mathcal{F}_{\mathsf{SyX}}$.[5] Additionally, a pair of parties may *reuse* a single instance of $\mathcal{F}_{\mathsf{SyX}}$ in any number of multiparty protocols, possibly involving different sets of parties.

Synchronizable exchange $\mathcal{F}_{\mathsf{SyX}}$ is a two-party symmetric primitive which is reactive (like the commitment functionality $\mathcal{F}_{\mathsf{com}}$ [10]) and works in two phases. In the first phase, which we call the *load phase*, parties submit their private inputs x_1, x_2 along with public inputs $(f_1, f_2, \phi_1, \phi_2)$. Here f_1, f_2 are possibly randomized functions[6], and ϕ_1, ϕ_2 are Boolean predicates. The public input must be submitted by both parties, and the submitted values must match. Upon receiving these inputs, $\mathcal{F}_{\mathsf{SyX}}$ computes $f_1(x_1, x_2)$ and delivers the respective outputs to both parties. Next, in the *trigger phase*, which can be initiated at any later time after the load phase, party P_i can send a "witness" w_i to $\mathcal{F}_{\mathsf{SyX}}$ following which $\mathcal{F}_{\mathsf{SyX}}$ checks if $\phi_i(w_i) = 1$. If that is indeed the case, then $\mathcal{F}_{\mathsf{SyX}}$ computes $f_2(x_1, x_2, w_i)$ and delivers the respective outputs along with w_i to both parties. We stress that $\mathcal{F}_{\mathsf{SyX}}$ guarantees that both parties get the output of f_2. We state our main theorem.

Theorem 1 (informal). *Assuming the existence of enhanced trapdoor permutations, there exists a two-phase two-party functionality which is complete for fair secure multiparty computation.*

To use multiple pairwise instances of synchronizable exchange to achieve n-wise fair secure computation, the main idea is to keep different instances of $\mathcal{F}_{\mathsf{SyX}}$ "in sync" with each other throughout the protocol execution. That is, we need to ensure that all pairwise $\mathcal{F}_{\mathsf{SyX}}$ instances are, loosely speaking, *simultaneously loaded*, and if so, *simultaneously triggered*. Ensuring this in the presence of byzantine adversaries is somewhat tricky, and we outline our techniques below.

Reduction to Fair Reconstruction. First, we let parties run an (unfair) MPC protocol for a function f that accepts parties' inputs and computes the function output, then computes secret shares of the function output, and then computes commitments on these secret shares. The MPC protocol outputs to all parties the set of all commitments, and to each individual party the corresponding share of the function output. Since the MPC protocol itself does not guarantee fairness, it may be that some honest party does not receive the output. In that case, all parties terminate and abort the protocol, and no party learns the function output. If the protocol has not terminated, then all that is left to perform a fair reconstruction of the function output from the secret shares. The above

---

[5] The primitive complexity of $\mathcal{F}_{\mathsf{SyX}}$ is independent of the function that is fairly computed. As mentioned before, this was the case with the primitives proposed by [24], but not [18].

[6] While we introduce $\mathcal{F}_{\mathsf{SyX}}$ in terms of arbitrary functions f_1, f_2, our (strongest) results can be obtained by, loosely speaking, setting $f_1(x_1, x_2) = (v_1 \oplus x_1, v_2 \oplus x_2)$ for randomly chosen v_1, v_2, and $f_2(x_1, x_2, w; v_1, v_2) = \mathsf{Hash}(v_1 \oplus v_2 \| w)$ (see Sect. 5).

technique of reducing fair computation of a function to fair reconstruction of a (non-malleable) additive secret sharing scheme is a well-known technique [24].

Synchronization via Trigger Conditions. The commitments generated in the above step are used to define the trigger conditions, specifically the trigger witness must include (among other things) openings to the commitments (i.e., the secret shares). That is, each pair of parties initiate the load phase with their $\mathcal{F}_{\mathsf{SyX}}$ instance. We will need to ensure that the protocol proceeds only if all $\mathcal{F}_{\mathsf{SyX}}$ instances were loaded. To do this, we let the load phase of each $\mathcal{F}_{\mathsf{SyX}}$ instance to output a *receipt* (think of these as signatures on some special instance-specific message) that indicates that the $\mathcal{F}_{\mathsf{SyX}}$ instance has been loaded. (Note that by [16], we can assume a broadcast channel while developing our protocol, and then use their compiler to remove the broadcast channel from our protocol. Note that such a broadcast channel can be used to set up a temporary PKI among the participants.) Following this parties broadcast to all other parties the receipts they have obtained in the load phase. In an honest execution, at the end of this broadcast step, each party would possess receipts from every pairwise $\mathcal{F}_{\mathsf{SyX}}$. On the other hand, corrupt parties may not broadcast some receipts, resulting in a setting where corrupt parties possess all receipts, but honest parties do not.

To maintain that $\mathcal{F}_{\mathsf{SyX}}$ instances remain in sync, we let the trigger conditions ask for all receipts (each individual $\mathcal{F}_{\mathsf{SyX}}$ instance can verify these load receipts using, e.g., digital signature verification). This way, we ensure that any $\mathcal{F}_{\mathsf{SyX}}$ instance can be triggered only if all $\mathcal{F}_{\mathsf{SyX}}$ instances were loaded. Recall that by definition, $\mathcal{F}_{\mathsf{SyX}}$ outputs the trigger witness along with the output of f_2. This in turn ensures that if, say an $\mathcal{F}_{\mathsf{SyX}}$ instance between P_i and P_j was triggered by P_i, then P_j would obtain the load receipts which it can then use as part of trigger witnesses for other $\mathcal{F}_{\mathsf{SyX}}$ instances associated with P_j. Finally, because parties only receive additive secret shares of the output, to get the final output the adversary will need to trigger at least one $\mathcal{F}_{\mathsf{SyX}}$ instance associated with an honest party. The ideas outlined above ensures that honest party (and consequently every honest party) will be able to continue triggering other $\mathcal{F}_{\mathsf{SyX}}$ instances associated with it, and obtain the final output. An additional detail to note is that in our constructions, we let the Boolean predicates ϕ_1, ϕ_2 depend on *time*. This is required to ensure termination of our protocols (i.e., force a time limit on when the adversary must begin triggering the $\mathcal{F}_{\mathsf{SyX}}$ instances to obtain output). Therefore, in the terminology of [32], our functionality $\mathcal{F}_{\mathsf{SyX}}$ is *clock-aware*. The techniques we use to ensure termination may be reminiscent of techniques used in the design of broadcast protocols from point-to-point channels in the dishonest majority setting [17].

Complexity, Preprocessing, and Assumptions. The complexity of $\mathcal{F}_{\mathsf{SyX}}$ is the sum of the complexities of the functions f_1, f_2, and the predicates ϕ_1, ϕ_2. In our construction of n-party fair secure computation of an n-input function f whose output length is ℓ_{out}, the complexity of each $\mathcal{F}_{\mathsf{SyX}}$ instance is $\mathcal{O}(n^2 \lambda \ell_{\mathsf{out}})$ (λ denotes the security parameter) and is otherwise independent of the size of the function that is being computed. With additional assumptions, specifically with a *non-interactive non-committing encryption* [31] (alternatively, a *programmable random oracle*), the use of $\mathcal{F}_{\text{SyX}}$ can be preprocessed in a network-independent manner to support any number of executions.[7] That is, a pair of parties can preprocess an instance of $\mathcal{F}_{\text{SyX}}$ by loading it once, and then reusing it across multiple independent (possibly concurrent) executions of secure computation involving different sets of parties. Of course, to enable this type of preprocessing, we rely on a variant of $\mathcal{F}_{\text{SyX}}$ which can be *triggered multiple times* (but loaded only once). In this case, the complexity of f_1 is $\mathcal{O}(\lambda)$, while the complexity of f_2 is $\mathcal{O}(n\lambda)$ per trigger invocation, and the complexities of ϕ_1, ϕ_2 would be $\mathcal{O}(n\lambda)$ per trigger invocation for a protocol involving n parties. Thus, assuming preprocessing, the total communication complexity of $\mathcal{F}_{\text{SyX}}$ invocations is $\mathcal{O}(n^3\lambda)$ (i.e., $\mathcal{O}(n^2)$ invocations of $O(n\lambda)$ each). We emphasize that in the preprocessing setting, $\mathcal{F}_{\text{SyX}}$ need not be triggered when the protocol participants behave honestly.

Theorem 2 (informal). *Let λ be a computational security parameter. Assuming the existence of enhanced trapdoor permutations, for every $n \geq 2$, there exists a two-phase two-party primitive which is complete for fair secure n-party computation of any n-input function f whose output length is ℓ_{out} such that for each instance of the primitive it holds that*

- *in the standard model, the complexity of the first phase is $O(n^2\lambda\ell_{\text{out}})$ and the complexity of the second phase is $O(n\lambda)$, and*
- *in the programmable random oracle model, the complexity of the first phase is $O(\lambda)$ and the complexity of the second phase is $O(n\lambda)$, and the inputs/outputs to the primitive are independent of the function f.*

Relationship to Other Primitives. [18] investigate a number of interesting primitives that are complete for secure computation with guaranteed output delivery for various parameter regimes. (See [18] for a discussion of complete primitives for secure computation with abort.) For $t < n/3$, they identify *secure channels* (with cardinality 2) as a complete primitive. For $t < n/2$, they identify two complete primitives *converge cast* and *oblivious cast*. Both these have cardinality 3. For $t < n$, they identify *universal black box* (UBB) as a complete primitive of cardinality n. Note that unlike $\mathcal{F}_{\text{SyX}}$, the complexity of UBB is proportional to the complexity of f. Improving on this, [24] show *fair reconstruction of a non-malleable secret sharing scheme* as a complete primitive of cardinality n, whose *complexity* is independent of the function being computed. In addition, [24] investigate the power of primitives that guarantee fairness but are restricted in other ways. For instance, they study *fair coin flipping* and *simultaneous broadcast*, and show that neither is complete for fair computation. Note that simultaneous broadcast was shown in [27] to be complete for partial fairness [26]. None of the primitives discussed in [18,24] are *reactive*. A well-known example of a reactive

---

[7] Preprocessing for a bounded number of executions may be achieved by assuming only *receiver non-committing encryption* [11].

functionality which is complete for (unfair) UC secure MPC is the two-phase two-party UC commitment functionality $\mathcal{F}_{\mathsf{com}}$ [12].

Timed commitments [9] (and numerous related works such as [19,21]) can be used to enable a fair exchange of digital signatures, fair auctions, and more under a somewhat non-standard security notion. Other works with similar security notions that consider fairness in secure computation include [20,32,33] (see also numerous references therein). Another line of research investigates the use of physical/hardware assumptions to enforce fairness. For example, [30] relies on physical envelopes which provide some form of synchronizability. There are numerous works in the optimistic model (cf. [5,6] and several follow-up works) that minimize the use of a trusted third party to restore fairness when breached. Another line of research [1,2,8] investigates a non-standard notion of fair secure computation where participants who do not obtain output are instead compensated monetarily (via cryptocurrency).

Recent work [14,36] (following [32]) has shown that fair secure computation is possible assuming the existence of trusted execution environments (alternatively, witness encryption [14]) and a bulletin board abstraction (or blockchain) to which all parties have read/write access. In these works, the bulletin board can be interpreted as a cardinality n primitive that helps in synchronizing the trusted execution environments. While not the focus of our work, we note that ideas similar to [14,36] may help to implement $\mathcal{F}_{\mathsf{SyX}}$ using trusted execution environments (e.g., Intel SGX) and a bulletin board abstraction.

Remarks. Note that our functionality $\mathcal{F}_{\mathsf{SyX}}$ is both reactive and clock-aware. One may wonder which, if not both, of these properties are essential. It has been shown in [35] that non-reactive functionalities of cardinality smaller than n do not suffice for fair multiparty coin tossing, thus answering an important question regarding the design of our functionality $\mathcal{F}_{\mathsf{SyX}}$. Indeed, $\mathcal{F}_{\mathsf{SyX}}$ must be reactive. We leave open the requirement of clock-awareness. We conjecture that non-clock-aware functionalities of cardinality smaller than n (whether reactive or not), for e.g., two-wise coin tossing, two-wise simultaneous exchange, etc., do not suffice for fair multiparty coin tossing. However, we would also like to note that we require clock-awareness only to ensure termination of the protocol (an implicit requirement), not privacy or fairness, making the answer to the question of whether clock-awareness is needed, perhaps more nuanced than one would initially presume.

2   Preliminaries

2.1   Secure Computation

We recall most of the definitions regarding secure computation from [23] and [16]. We present them here for the sake of completeness and self-containedness.

Consider the scenario of n parties $P_1, \ldots, P_n$ with private inputs $x_1, \ldots, x_n \in \mathcal{X}^8$. We denote $\mathbf{x} = (x_1, \ldots, x_n) \in \mathcal{X}^n$.

Functionalities. A functionality f is a randomized process that maps n-tuples of inputs to n-tuples of outputs, that is, $f : \mathcal{X}^n \to \mathcal{Y}^n$. We write $f = (f^1, \ldots, f^n)$ if we wish to emphasize the n outputs of f, but stress that if $f^1, \ldots, f^n$ are randomized, then the outputs of $f^1, \ldots, f^n$ are correlated random variables.

Adversaries. We consider security against *static t-threshold adversaries*, that is, adversaries that corrupt a set of at most t parties, where $0 \le t < n^9$. We assume the adversary to be malicious. That is, the corrupted parties may deviate arbitrarily from an assigned protocol.

Model. We assume the parties are connected via a fully connected point-to-point network; we refer to this model as the point-to-point model. We sometimes assume that the parties are given access to a physical broadcast channel in addition to the point-to-point network; we refer to this model as the broadcast model. The communication lines between parties are assumed to be ideally authenticated and private (and thus an adversary cannot read or modify messages sent between two honest parties). Furthermore, the delivery of messages between honest parties is guaranteed. We sometimes assume the parties are connected via a fully pairwise connected network of oblivious transfer channels in addition to a fully connected point-to-point network; we refer to this model as the OT-network model. We sometimes assume that the parties are given access to a physical broadcast channel in addition to the complete pairwise oblivious transfer network and a fully connected point-to-point network; we refer to this model as the OT-broadcast model.

Protocol. An n-party protocol for computing a functionality f is a protocol running in polynomial time and satisfying the following functional requirement: if for every $i \in [n]$, party P_i begins with private input $x_i \in \mathcal{X}$, then the joint distribution of the outputs of the parties is statistically close to $(f^1(\overrightarrow{x}), \ldots, f^n(\overrightarrow{x}))$. We assume that the protocol is executed in a synchronous network, that is, the execution proceeds in rounds: each round consists of a *send phase* (where parties send their message for this round) followed by a *receive* phase (where they receive messages from other parties). The adversary, being malicious, is also *rushing* which means that it can see the messages the honest parties send in a round, before determining the messages that the corrupted parties send in that round.

---

[8] Here we have assumed that the domains of the inputs of all parties is $\mathcal{X}$ for simplicity of notation. This can be easily adapted to consider setting where the domains are different.

[9] Note that when $t = n$, there is nothing to prove.

Security with Fairness. The security of a protocol is analyzed by comparing what an adversary can do in a real protocol execution to what it can do in an ideal scenario that is secure by definition. This is formalized by considering an *ideal* computation involving an incorruptible *trusted party* to whom the parties send their inputs. The trusted party computes the functionality on the inputs and returns to each party its respective output. Loosely speaking, a protocol is secure if any adversary interacting in the real protocol (where no trusted party exists) can do no more harm than if it were involved in the above-described ideal computation.

Execution in the Ideal Model. The parties are $P_1, \ldots, P_n$, and there is an adversary $\mathcal{A}$ who has corrupted at most t parties, where $0 \leq t < n$. Denote by $\mathcal{I} \subseteq [n]$ the set of indices of the parties corrupted by $\mathcal{A}$. An ideal execution for the computation of f proceeds as follows:

- **Inputs:** $P_1, \ldots, P_n$ hold their private inputs $x_1, \ldots, x_n \in \mathcal{X}$; the adversary $\mathcal{A}$ receives an auxiliary input z.
- **Send inputs to trusted party:** The honest parties send their inputs to the trusted party. The corrupted parties controlled by $\mathcal{A}$ may send any values of their choice. In addition, there exists a special abort input. Denote the inputs sent to the trusted party by $x_1', \ldots, x_n'$.
- **Trusted party sends outputs:** If $x_i' \notin \mathcal{X}$ for any $i \in [n]$, the trusted party sets x_i' to some default input in $\mathcal{X}$. If there exists an $i \in [n]$ such that $x_i' = $ abort, the trusted party sends $\perp$ to all the parties. Otherwise, the trusted party chooses r uniformly at random, computes $z_i = f^i(x_1', \ldots, x_n'; r)$ for every $i \in [n]$ and sends z_i to P_i for every $i \in [n]$.
- **Outputs:** The honest parties output whatever was sent by the trusted party. The corrupted parties output nothing and $\mathcal{A}$ outputs an arbitrary (probabilistic polynomial-time computable) function of its view.

We let $\mathrm{IDEAL}_{f,\mathcal{I},\mathcal{S}(z)}^{\mathrm{fair}}(\overrightarrow{x}, \lambda)$ be the random variable consisting of the output of the adversary and the output of the honest parties following an execution in the ideal model described above.

Execution in the Real Model. We next consider the real model in which an n-party protocol π is executed by $P_1, \ldots, P_n$ (and there is no trusted party). In this case, the adversary $\mathcal{A}$ gets the inputs of the corrupted party and sends all messages on behalf of these parties, using an arbitrary polynomial-time strategy. The honest parties follow the instructions of π.

Let f be as above and let π be an n-party protocol computing f. Let $\mathcal{A}$ be a non-uniform probabilistic polynomial-time machine with auxiliary input z. We let $\mathrm{REAL}_{\pi,\mathcal{I},\mathcal{A}(z)}(x_1, \ldots, x_n, \lambda)$ be the random variable consisting of the view of the adversary and the output of the honest parties following an execution of π where P_i begins by holding x_i for every $i \in [n]$.

Security as Emulation of an Ideal Execution in the Real Model. Having defined the ideal and real models, we can now define security of a protocol. Loosely speaking, the definition asserts that a secure protocol (in the real model) emulates the ideal model (in which a trusted party exists). This is formulated as follows.

Definition 1. *Protocol π is said to securely compute f with fairness if for every non-uniform probabilistic polynomial-time adversary $\mathcal{A}$ in the real model, there exists a non-uniform probabilistic polynomial-time adversary $\mathcal{S}$ in the ideal model such that for every $\mathcal{I} \subseteq [n]$ with $|\mathcal{I}| \leq t$,*

$$\left\{ \text{IDEAL}_{f,\mathcal{I},\mathcal{S}(z)}^{\text{fair}}(\overrightarrow{x},\lambda) \right\}_{\overrightarrow{x} \in \mathcal{X}^n, z \in \{0,1\}^*} \equiv \left\{ \text{REAL}_{\pi,\mathcal{I},\mathcal{A}(z)}(\overrightarrow{x},\lambda) \right\}_{\overrightarrow{x} \in \mathcal{X}^n, z \in \{0,1\}^*}$$

We will sometimes relax security to statistical or computational definitions. A protocol is statistically secure if the random variables $\text{IDEAL}_{f,\mathcal{I},\mathcal{S}(z)}^{\text{fair}}(\overrightarrow{x},\lambda)$ and $\text{REAL}_{\pi,\mathcal{I},\mathcal{A}(z)}(\overrightarrow{x},\lambda)$ are statistically close, and computationally secure if they are computationally indistinguishable.

2.2   The Hybrid Model

Let type $\in$ {g.d., fair, id-fair, abort, id-abort}. Let $\mathcal{G}$ be a functionality and let π be an n-party protocol for computing some functionality f, where π includes real messages between the parties as well as calls to $\mathcal{G}$. Let $\mathcal{A}$ be a non-uniform probabilistic polynomial-time machine with auxiliary input z. $\mathcal{A}$ corrupts at most t parties, where $0 < t < n$. Denote by $\mathcal{I} \subseteq [n]$ the set of indices of the parties corrupted by $\mathcal{A}$. Let $\text{HYBRID}_{\pi,\mathcal{I},\mathcal{A}(z)}^{\mathcal{G},\text{type}}(\overrightarrow{x},\lambda)$ be the random variable consisting of the view of the adversary and the output of the honest parties, following an execution of π with ideal calls to a trusted party computing $\mathcal{G}$ according to the ideal model "type" where P_i begins by holding x_i for every $i \in [n]$. Security in the model "type" can be defined via natural modifications. We call this the ($\mathcal{G}$, type)-hybrid model.

2.3   Fairness Versus Guaranteed Output Delivery

We recall here some of the results from [16].

Lemma 1 [16]. *Consider n parties $P_1, \ldots, P_n$ in a model without a broadcast channel. Then, there exists a functionality $f : \mathcal{X}^n \rightarrow \mathcal{Y}^n$ such that f cannot be securely computed with guaranteed output delivery in the presence of t-threshold adversaries for $n/3 \leq t < n$.*

Lemma 2 [16]. *Consider n parties $P_1, \ldots, P_n$ in a model with a broadcast channel. Then, assuming the existence of one-way functions, for any functionality $f : \mathcal{X}^n \rightarrow \mathcal{Y}^n$, if there exists a protocol π which securely computes f with fairness, then there exists a protocol π' which securely computes f with guaranteed output delivery.*

Lemma 3 [16]. *Consider n parties $P_1, \ldots, P_n$ in a model with a broadcast channel. Then, assuming the existence of one-way functions, for any functionality $f : \mathcal{X}^n \to \mathcal{Y}^n$, if there exists a protocol π which securely computes f with fairness, then there exists a protocol π' which securely computes f with fairness and does not make use of the broadcast channel.*

3   Synchronizable Exchange

We are interested in solving the problem of securely computing functionalities with fairness, most commonly referred to as fair secure computation. We begin with the case of two parties. It is known that fair two-party secure computation is impossible in the standard model as well as in the $(\mathcal{F}_{bc}, \mathcal{F}_{OT})$-hybrid model [15]. This result generalizes to the setting of n parties that are trying to compute in the presence of a t-threshold adversary for any $n/2 \le t < n$.

Preliminaries: $x_1, x_2 \in \{0, 1\}^*$; f_1, f_2 are 2-input, 2-output functionalities. The functionality proceeds as follows:

– Upon receiving inputs (x_1, f_1) from P_1 and (x_2, f_2) from P_2, check if $f = f_1 = f_2$. If not, abort. Else, send $f^1(x_1, x_2)$ to P_1 and $f^2(x_1, x_2)$ to P_2.

Fig. 1. The ideal functionality $\mathcal{F}_{2PC}$.

One could define the ideal functionality, $\mathcal{F}_{2PC}$ as in Fig. 1. Clearly, any 2-party functionality can be securely computed with fairness in the $(\mathcal{F}_{2PC}, \text{fair})$-hybrid model. One can then ask the following question in the context of $n > 2$ parties:

Consider n parties $P_1, \ldots, P_n$ in the OT-broadcast model. Does there exist a protocol that securely computes $\mathcal{F}_{MPC}$ with fairness in the $(\mathcal{F}_{2PC}, \text{fair})$-hybrid model?

We are interested in security in the presence of a t-threshold adversary for any $n/2 \le t < n$. While we do not know the answer to this question, it seems that the answer to this question would be negative. The intuition for this is that the various invocations of the ideal functionality $\mathcal{F}_{2PC}$ cannot "synchronize" with each other and thus we would run into issues similar to the those highlighted by the impossibility result in [15], namely, some party/parties obtain information about the output of the protocol before the others and if these parties were corrupt, they may choose to abort the protocol without the honest parties receiving their outputs.

Equipped with this intuition, we propose the primitive, $\mathcal{F}_{SyX}$, which we call "synchronizable exchange". We define the ideal functionality for $\mathcal{F}_{SyX}$ in Fig. 2. We associate the type g.d. to the ideal functionality $\mathcal{F}_{SyX}$ when working in the

Preliminaries: $x_1, x_2 \in \{0,1\}^*$; f_1, f_2 are 2-output functions; ϕ_1, ϕ_2 are Boolean predicates. The functionality proceeds as follows:

- **Load phase.** Upon receiving inputs $(x_1, f = (f_1, f_2, \phi_1, \phi_2))$ from P_1 and (x_2, f') from P_2, check if $f = f'$. If not, abort. Else, compute $f_1(x_1, x_2)$. If $f_1(x_1, x_2) = \bot$, abort. Else, send $f_1(x_1, x_2)$ to both parties, and go to next phase.
- **Trigger phase.** Upon receiving input w from party P_i, check if $\phi_i(w) = 1$. If yes, then send $(w, f_2(x_1, x_2, w))$ to both P_1 and P_2.

Fig. 2. The ideal functionality $\mathcal{F}_{\mathsf{SyX}}$.

$\mathcal{F}_{\mathsf{SyX}}$-hybrid model. When interacting with this functionality, parties first submit their inputs to $\mathcal{F}_{\mathsf{SyX}}$ which then gives them a "receipt" acknowledging the end of the input submission phase. Following this, the functionality simply waits for a trigger from one of the parties. Once the trigger is received (we specify conditions for the validity of a trigger), then the functionality will deliver the outputs according to the specification. In the formal specification, we allow parties P_1, P_2 to submit two functions f_1, f_2 and two Boolean predicates (that check validity of a trigger value) ϕ_1, ϕ_2 along with their inputs x_1, x_2. $\mathcal{F}_{\mathsf{SyX}}$ then computes $f_1(x_1, x_2)$ and sends this value as a "receipt" that the input submission phase has ended. The actual output of the computation is $f_2(x_1, x_2)$ and this will be provided to the parties at the end of the trigger phase. Note that the trigger phase can be activated by either party P_i. However, P_i would need to provide a "witness" w that satisfies ϕ_i.

Note that $\mathcal{F}_{\mathsf{SyX}}$ is at least as strong as $\mathcal{F}_{\mathsf{2PC}}$. In order to realize $\mathcal{F}_{\mathsf{2PC}}$ in the $\mathcal{F}_{\mathsf{SyX}}$-hybrid model, we set $f_1 = \varepsilon$ (the empty string), $f_2 = f$, $\phi_1 = \phi_2 = 1$. The hope in defining this reactive functionality, however, is to achieve synchronization of multiple invocations of the ideal functionality $\mathcal{F}_{\mathsf{SyX}}$. In a nutshell, the synchronization of multiple invocations of the ideal functionality $\mathcal{F}_{\mathsf{SyX}}$ is enabled by the "trigger" phase of functionality. We will be using f_1 to provide a proof to parties other than P_1, P_2 that the input submission phase has ended for parties P_1, P_2. In other words, if we wish to synchronize multiple invocations of the ideal functionality $\mathcal{F}_{\mathsf{SyX}}$, we set the witness for the trigger phase of each of the invocations to be the set of all receipts obtained from the inputs phases of the invocations. The set of all receipts acts as a proof that every invocation of the ideal functionality completed its load phase successfully. We use this feature of $\mathcal{F}_{\mathsf{SyX}}$ in order to design a protocol for fair secure computation.

Multiple Triggers and Witnesses. Note that as described, the load phase of the functionality $\mathcal{F}_{\mathsf{SyX}}$ can only be executed successfully once. And, once it has been successfully executed, the functionality is in the trigger phase. However, whilst in the trigger phase, the primitive may be triggered any number of times successfully or unsuccessfully. Furthermore, triggering the primitive with different witnesses may actually produce different outputs, as modeled by having the output f_2 depend on the witness w in addition to x_1, x_2. This will be important for us in Sect. 5.

Remark. We crucially require that $\perp$ is a special symbol different from the empty string. We use $\perp$ as a means of signalling that the load phase of $\mathcal{F}_{\mathsf{SyX}}$ did not complete successfully. We will however allow parties to attempt to invoke the load phase of the functionality at a later time. However, as we proceed, we will also have our functionality be clock-aware and thus only accept invocations to the load phase until a certain point in time. After the load phase times out, the functionality is rendered completely unusable. Similarly, if the load phase has been completed successfully, a clock-oblivious version of the functionality can be triggered at any point in time as long as a valid witness is provided, no matter the number of failed attempts. The clock-aware version of the functionality, however, will only accept invocations of the trigger phase until a certain point in time. After the trigger phase times out, the functionality is rendered completely unusable.

Clock-Awareness. A technicality that arises in the protocol is that of guaranteed termination. Specifically, we will need our ideal functionality to be "clock-aware". The issue of modeling a trusted clock has been studied in the literature. In this work, we stick to the formalism outlined in [32]. We recall the main ideas here. We assume a synchronous execution model, where protocol execution proceeds in atomic time steps called *rounds*. We assume that the trusted clocks of attested execution processors and the network rounds advance at the same rate. It is easy to adapt our model and results if the trusted clocks of the processors and the network rounds do not advance at the same rate. In each round, the environment must activate each party one by one, and therefore, all parties can naturally keep track of the current round number. We will use the symbol r to denote the current round number. A party can perform any fixed polynomial (in λ) amount of computation when activated, and send messages. We consider a synchronous communication model where messages sent by an honest party will be delivered at the beginning of the next round. Whenever a party is activated in a round, it can read a buffer of incoming messages to receive messages sent to itself in the previous round. To model trusted clocks in attested execution processors, we will provide a special instruction such that ideal functionalities, in particular $\mathcal{F}_{\mathsf{SyX}}$ can query the current round number. We say that a functionality $\mathcal{F}$ is *clock-aware* if the functionality queries the local time; otherwise we say that the functionality $\mathcal{F}$ is *clock-oblivious*. For the rest of the work, we will always assume that $\mathcal{F}_{\mathsf{SyX}}$ is clock-aware. We would also like to stress that we require only relative clocks - in other words, trusted clocks of all functionalities need not be synchronized, since our protocol will only make use of the number of rounds that have elapsed since initialization. Therefore, we will assume that when a functionality reads the clock, a relative round number since the first invocation of the functionality is returned. Thus, when working in this model, we assume that every party and every invocation of the ideal functionality $\mathcal{F}_{\mathsf{SyX}}$ has access to a variable r that reflects the current round number. More generally, every function and predicate that is part of the specification of $\mathcal{F}_{SyX}$ may also take r as an input. Finally, the functionality may also time out after a pre-programmed amount of time. We describe this clock-aware functionality in Fig. 3.

Preliminaries: $x_1, x_2 \in \{0,1\}^*$; f_1, f_2 are 2-input, 2-output functions; ϕ_1, ϕ_2 are Boolean predicates; r denotes the current round number; INPUT_TIMEOUT < TRIGGER_TIMEOUT are round numbers representing time outs. The functionality proceeds as follows:

- **Load phase.** If $r >$ INPUT_TIMEOUT, abort. Otherwise, upon receiving inputs of the form $(x_1, f = (f_1, f_2, \phi_1, \phi_2))$ from P_1 and (x_2, f') from P_2, check if $f = f'$. If not, abort. Else, compute $f_1(x_1, x_2, r)$. If $f_1(x_1, x_2, r) = \bot$, abort. Else, send $f_1(x_1, x_2, r)$ to both parties, and go to next phase.
- **Trigger phase.** If $r >$ TRIGGER_TIMEOUT, abort. Otherwise, upon receiving input w from party P_i, check if $\phi_i(w, r) = 1$. If yes, send $(w, f_2(x_1, x_2, w, r))$ to both P_1 and P_2.

Fig. 3. The clock-aware ideal functionality $\mathcal{F}_{SyX}$.

Infinite Timeouts. We note here that it is possible to set either one or both of INPUT_TIMEOUT and TRIGGER_TIMEOUT to be ∞. What this means is that the functionality retains its state even if it goes offline. Its state would comprise (x_1, x_2) and which phase (input or trigger) it is currently in. We also require that if the functionality does go offline and come back online, it can still access the current value of the clock, r. The only time we use this feature of the primitive is in Sect. 5 where we are able to preprocess the functionality for an unbounded number of fair multiparty computations that would be run in the future. In this case, we would need to trigger this functionality whenever an adversary attempts to break fairness. Since we have no bound on how many computations we will run, we will set the TRIGGER_TIMEOUT to be ∞. In practice, one could also just set TRIGGER_TIMEOUT to be a very large number. We stress however that the functionality is stateful and able to read time irrespective of whether it goes offline intermittently.

4   Fair Secure Computation in the $\mathcal{F}_{SyX}$-Hybrid Model

In this section, we will describe how a set of n parties in the OT-network model that have pairwise access to the ideal functionality $\mathcal{F}_{SyX}$ can implement n-party fair secure function evaluation. To begin with, we will assume that the n-parties are in the point-to-point model and develop a protocol in the $(\mathcal{F}_{bc}, \mathcal{F}_{MPC}, \mathcal{F}_{SyX})$-hybrid model. By virtue of Lemmas 3 and 4, we can get to the $\mathcal{F}_{SyX}$-hybrid model. We first provide some intuition for our construction.

4.1   Intuition

We first start with the 3-party case as a warm-up. Let P_1, P_2, and P_3 be the three parties with inputs x_1, x_2 and x_3 respectively. For $i, j \in \{1, 2, 3\}$ with $i < j$, we have that parties P_i and P_j have access to the ideal functionality $\mathcal{F}_{\mathsf{SyX}}$. In particular, let $\mathcal{F}_{\mathsf{SyX}}^{i,j}$ represent the instantiation of the $\mathcal{F}_{\mathsf{SyX}}$ functionality used by parties P_i, P_j. We wish to perform fair secure function evaluation of some 3-input 3-output functionality F.

Reduction to Single Output Functionalities. Let $(y_1, y_2, y_3) \xleftarrow{\$} F(x_1, x_2, x_3)$ be the output of the function evaluation. We define a new four input single output functionality F' such that

$$F'(x_1, x_2, x_3, z) = F^1(x_1, x_2, x_3) \| F^2(x_1, x_2, x_3) \| F^3(x_1, x_2, x_3) \oplus z = y_1 \| y_2 \| y_3 \oplus z$$

where $z = z_1 \| z_2 \| z_3$ and $|y_i| = |z_i|$ for all $i \in [3]$. The idea is that the party P_i will obtain $z' = F'(x_1, x_2, x_3, z)$ and z_i. Viewing $z' = z_1' \| z_2' \| z_3'$ where $|z_i'| = |z_i|$[10] for all $i \in [3]$, party P_i reconstructs its output as

$$y_i = z_i \oplus z_i'$$

Now, we may assume that the input of party P_i is (x_i, z_i) (or we can generate random z_is as part of the computation) which determines z. It thus suffices to consider fair secure function evaluation of single output functionalities.

Reduction to Fair Reconstruction. We will use ideas similar to [24,29] where instead of focusing on fair secure evaluation of an arbitrary function, we only focus on fair reconstruction of an additive secret sharing scheme. The main idea is to let the three parties run a secure computation protocol that computes the output of the secure function evaluation on the parties' inputs, and then additively secret shares the output. Given this step, fair secure computation then reduces to fair reconstruction of the underlying additive secret sharing scheme.

The Underlying Additive Secret Sharing Scheme. We use an additive secret sharing of the output y. Let the shares be y_i for $i \in [3]$. That is, it holds that

$$y = \bigoplus_{i \in [3]} y_i$$

We would like party P_i to reconstruct y by obtaining all shares y_i for each $i \in [3]$. Initially, each party P_i is given y_i. Therefore, each party P_i only needs to obtain y_j and y_k for $j, k \neq i$.

Fair Reconstruction via $\mathcal{F}_{\mathsf{SyX}}$. We assume that the secure function evaluation also provides commitments to all the shares of the output. That is, P_i receives $(y_i, \overrightarrow{c})$ for each $i \in [3]$, where Com is a commitment scheme and

$$\overrightarrow{c} = \{\mathsf{Com}(y_1), \mathsf{Com}(y_2), \mathsf{Com}(y_3)\}$$

---

[10] We may assume without loss of generality that the lengths of the outputs of each party are known beforehand.

Furthermore, we assume that each party P_i picks its own verification key vk_i and signing key sk_i with respect to a signature scheme with a signing algorithm Sign and a verification algorithm Verify, for each $i \in [3]$. All parties then broadcast their verification keys to all parties. Let

$$\overrightarrow{\mathsf{vk}} = \{\mathsf{vk}_1, \mathsf{vk}_2, \mathsf{vk}_3\}$$

Each pair of parties P_i and P_j then initializes $\mathcal{F}_{\mathsf{SyX}}^{i,j}$ with inputs

$$x_i = \left(\overrightarrow{\mathsf{vk}}, \mathsf{sk}_i, y_i, \overrightarrow{c}\right)$$

and

$$x_j = \left(\overrightarrow{\mathsf{vk}}, \mathsf{sk}_j, y_j, \overrightarrow{c}\right)$$

The function f_1 checks if both parties provided the same value for $\overrightarrow{\mathsf{vk}}, \overrightarrow{c}$ and checks the y_i and y_j are valid openings to the corresponding commitments. It also checks that the signing keys provided by the parties are consistent with the corresponding verification keys (more precisely, we will ask for randomness provided to the key generation algorithm of the signature scheme). If all checks pass, then $\mathcal{F}_{\mathsf{SyX}}^{i,j}$ computes

$$\sigma_{i,j} = \mathsf{Sign}((i,j); \mathsf{sk}_i) \| \mathsf{Sign}((i,j); \mathsf{sk}_j)$$

This completes the description of f_1.

Synchronization Step. The output of f_1 for each of the $\mathcal{F}_{\mathsf{SyX}}^{i,j}$ will provide a way to synchronize all $\mathcal{F}_{\mathsf{SyX}}$ instances. By synchronization, we mean that an $\mathcal{F}_{\mathsf{SyX}}^{i,j}$ instance cannot be triggered unless every other instance has already completed its load phase successfully. We achieve synchronization by setting the predicate $\phi_k(w)$ (for $k \in \{i, j\}$) to output 1 if and only if w consists of all signatures

$$\overrightarrow{\sigma} = \{\sigma_{i,j}\}_{i < j}$$

That is, each instance $\mathcal{F}_{\mathsf{SyX}}^{i,j}$ will accept the same trigger $w = \overrightarrow{\sigma}$. We define f_2 to simply output both y_i and y_j to both parties if $\phi_k(w) = 1$.

Protocol Intuition. We briefly discuss certain malicious behaviors and how we handle them. From the description above, it is clear that parties have no information about the output until one of the $\mathcal{F}_{\mathsf{SyX}}$ instances is triggered. Furthermore, note that this implies that the corrupt parties must successfully complete the load phases of the instances of $\mathcal{F}_{\mathsf{SyX}}$ that it shares with all of the honest parties in order to obtain the witness that can be used to trigger the $\mathcal{F}_{\mathsf{SyX}}$ instances. Following the load phases of all of the $\mathcal{F}_{\mathsf{SyX}}$ instances, we ask each party to broadcast the receipt $\sigma_{i,j}$ obtained from $\mathcal{F}_{\mathsf{SyX}}^{i,j}$. Now suppose parties P_i and P_j are both dishonest, and suppose they do not broadcast $\sigma_{i,j}$. Note also that since P_i and P_j collude, they do not need the help of $\mathcal{F}_{\mathsf{SyX}}$ to compute $\sigma_{i,j}$. Since honest P_k does not know the synchronizing witness $\overrightarrow{\sigma}$, it will not be able to trigger any of the $\mathcal{F}_{\mathsf{SyX}}$ instances. However, note that for the adversary to learn the output of the computation, the corrupt party P_i (without loss of generality) will need to trigger $\mathcal{F}_{\mathsf{SyX}}^{i,k}$ to obtain P_k's share of the key. However, once P_i triggers $\mathcal{F}_{\mathsf{SyX}}^{i,k}$, it follows that P_k would obtain the synchronizing witness $\vec{\sigma}$ using which it can trigger both $\mathcal{F}_{\mathsf{SyX}}^{i,k}$ and $\mathcal{F}_{\mathsf{SyX}}^{j,k}$ and learn its output.

Termination. The protocol as described up until this point does not have guaranteed termination. In particular, the honest parties will need to wait for the corrupted parties to broadcast their receipts in order to be able to trigger the instances of $\mathcal{F}_{\mathsf{SyX}}$ and obtain the output. Time outs do not help in this case as the adversary may simply wait until the last moment to trigger instances of $\mathcal{F}_{\mathsf{SyX}}$ and obtain their outputs leaving only insufficient time for the honest parties to trigger their instances of $\mathcal{F}_{\mathsf{SyX}}$ and obtain their outputs. In order to ensure termination, we make use of the clock. The main invariant that we want to guarantee is that if an instance of $\mathcal{F}_{\mathsf{SyX}}$ involving an (honest) party is triggered, then every other instance of $\mathcal{F}_{\mathsf{SyX}}$ that the (honest) party is involved in, also needs to be triggered. One way to implement this idea is to assume that all instances of $\mathcal{F}_{\mathsf{SyX}}$ time out after

$$T = \binom{3}{2} = 3$$

rounds. Furthermore, an instance of $\mathcal{F}_{\mathsf{SyX}}$ accepts triggers in some round $\tau \in [T]$ (that is, until it times out) if and only if you provide a proof that $t - 1$ other instances of $\mathcal{F}_{\mathsf{SyX}}$ were triggered until now. As before, we will have $\mathcal{F}_{\mathsf{SyX}}$ leak the triggering witness to the parties. Thus, if $\mathcal{F}_{\mathsf{SyX}}^{i,j}$ is triggered in some round t, then P_i (and/or P_j) can trigger all the other $\mathcal{F}_{\mathsf{SyX}}^{i,k}$ (and/or $\mathcal{F}_{\mathsf{SyX}}^{j,k}$) channels that it is involved in, in round $\tau + 1$.

Suppose some honest party, say P_i, does not obtain the output of the computation while the adversary has learned the output. Since the adversary learned the output, this means that the adversary triggered $\mathcal{F}_{\mathsf{SyX}}^{i,j}$ for some j (otherwise the adversary would not have learnt y_i and would not have received the output). That means P_i would have been able to trigger all the other channels that it is involved in and generate the final output in the next round. The only issue with this argument would be when $\mathcal{F}_{\mathsf{SyX}}^{i,j}$ was triggered last, that is, in round $\tau = T$. However this is not possible since until this time, at most $T - n + 1 < T - 1$, assuming $n \geq 3$, instances of $\mathcal{F}_{\mathsf{SyX}}$ could have been be triggered. This is because $n - 1$ instances of $\mathcal{F}_{\mathsf{SyX}}$ must be left untriggered in round $\tau = T - 1$ since the honest party didn't get its output.

Reducing the Duration of Time Outs. A more clever solution will allow us to terminate within $T = n$ rounds. In order to trigger an instance of $\mathcal{F}_{\mathsf{SyX}}$ in some round $\tau \in [T]$, you must provide a proof that other instances of $\mathcal{F}_{\mathsf{SyX}}$ involving at least τ different parties have been triggered. Consider the first round τ in which P_i is an honest party and $\mathcal{F}_{\mathsf{SyX}}^{i,j}$ is triggered for some j. If $\tau = 1$, then the single invocation already gives a proof that channels involving two parties, namely, i, j, have been triggered. Otherwise, by assumption, proofs of invocations of instances of $\mathcal{F}_{\mathsf{SyX}}$ involving τ different parties were needed to trigger $\mathcal{F}_{\mathsf{SyX}}^{i,j}$. But P_i is not one of these parties as τ is the first round in which $\mathcal{F}_{\mathsf{SyX}}^{i,j}$ was triggered for any j. Consequently, P_i, on this invocation, obtains a proof that instances of $\mathcal{F}_{\mathsf{SyX}}$ involving at least $\tau + 1$ parties have been triggered, and can thus trigger all channels in round $\tau + 1$. As before, the only gap in the argument is the case $\tau = T$. One can trivially see that since $\mathcal{F}_{\mathsf{SyX}}^{i,j}$ has not been triggered for any j, it is impossible to obtain a proof that instances of $\mathcal{F}_{\mathsf{SyX}}$ involving at least T different parties have been triggered.

Simulation. We look ahead for the issues that come up while trying to prove security, that is, during the simulation. The simulator will release to the adversary, the adversary's shares of the output, which can be simulated. But, it also releases commitments to all the shares of the output. Since the simulator does not know the output *a priori*, and does not know whether the adversary is going to abort the computation, in which case, no one knows the output, it has to produce commitments that it can later *equivocate*. In this context, we use, not regular commitments, but honest-binding commitments. In this case, the simulator can produce commitments to garbage but can later open them to be *valid* shares of the output. The rest of the computations can be trivially simulated. The only other detail to be looked into is that of the clock. We need to determine if the adversary has decided to abort the computation, that is, if the adversary is going to receive the output of the computation or not. This is done by noticing if and when the adversary decides to trigger the instances of $\mathcal{F}_{\mathsf{SyX}}$ that involve honest parties. We know that if the adversary ever triggers an instance of $\mathcal{F}_{\mathsf{SyX}}$ involving an honest party, then all parties will be in a position to receive the output. Thus, the simulator can simply run the adversary to determine whether it has decided to enable parties to obtain the output, in which the simulator would ask the trusted party to continue, or not, in which case the simulator would ask the trusted party to abort.

4.2 Protocol

We now present the protocol for fair secure computation in the $(\mathcal{F}_{\mathsf{bc}}, \mathcal{F}_{\mathsf{MPC}}, \mathcal{F}_{\mathsf{SyX}})$-hybrid model.

Preliminaries. F is the n-input n-output functionality to be computed; x_i is the input of party P_i for $i \in [n]$; $\mathcal{F}_{\mathsf{SyX}}^{a,b}$ represents the instantiation of the $\mathcal{F}_{\mathsf{SyX}}$ functionality used by parties P_a, P_b with time out round numbers $\mathsf{INPUT\_TIMEOUT} = 0$ and $\mathsf{TRIGGER\_TIMEOUT} = n$ for $a < b$, where $a, b \in [n]$; $\left(\mathsf{Com}, \mathsf{Open}, \widetilde{\mathsf{Com}}, \widetilde{\mathsf{Open}}\right)$ is an honest-binding commitment scheme; $\mathcal{V} = (\mathsf{Gen}, \mathsf{Sign}, \mathsf{Verify})$ is a signature scheme; r denotes the current round number.

Protocol. The protocol Π_{FMPC} proceeds as follows:

- Define F' to the be the following n-input n-output functionality: On input $\overrightarrow{x} = (x_1, \ldots, x_n)$:
  - Let $(y_1, \ldots, y_n) = F(x_1, \ldots, x_n)$ and let

    $$y = y_1 \| \ldots \| y_n$$

    Sample random strings $\alpha_i \overset{\$}{\leftarrow} \{0,1\}^*$ such that $|\alpha_i| = |y_i|$ for each $i \in [n]$. Let

    $$\alpha = \alpha_1 \| \ldots \| \alpha_n$$

    Let $z = y \oplus \alpha$.
  - Sample a random additive n-out-of-n secret sharing $z_1, \ldots, z_n$ of z such that

    $$z = \bigoplus_{i \in [n]} z_i$$

  - Compute commitments along with their openings $(c_i^z, \omega_i^z) \overset{\$}{\leftarrow} \mathsf{Com}(z_i)$ to each of the shares z_i for each $i \in [n]$. Let

    $$\overrightarrow{c^z} = (c_1^z, \ldots, c_n^z)$$

  - Sample random proof values $\pi_1, \ldots, \pi_n \overset{\$}{\leftarrow} \{0,1\}^\lambda$. Compute commitments along with their openings $(c_i^\pi, \omega_i^\pi) \overset{\$}{\leftarrow} \mathsf{Com}(\pi_i)$ to each of the proof values π_i for each $i \in [n]$. Let

    $$\overrightarrow{c^\pi} = (c_1^\pi, \ldots, c_n^\pi)$$

  - Party P_i receives output $\left(\alpha_i, \overrightarrow{c^z}, \omega_i^z, z_i, \overrightarrow{c^\pi}, \omega_i^\pi, \pi_i \right)$ for each $i \in [n]$.
- The parties invoke the ideal functionality $\mathcal{F}_{\mathsf{MPC}}$ with inputs $((x_1, F'), \ldots, (x_n, F'))$. If the ideal functionality returns $\perp$ to party P_i, then P_i aborts for any $i \in [n]$. Otherwise, party P_i receives output $\left(\alpha_i, \overrightarrow{c^z}, \omega_i^z, z_i, \overrightarrow{c^\pi}, \omega_i^\pi, \pi_i \right)$ for each $i \in [n]$.
- Each party P_i, for each $i \in [n]$, picks a random $\beta_i \in \{0,1\}^*$ and uses this randomness to pick a signing and verification key pair $(\mathsf{sk}_i, \mathsf{vk}_i) = \mathcal{V}.\mathsf{Gen}(1^\lambda; \beta_i)$. It then invokes the ideal functionality $\mathcal{F}_{\mathsf{bc}}$ and broadcasts vk_i to all other parties. If it does not receive vk_j for all $j \neq i$, it aborts. Otherwise, it obtains

  $$\overrightarrow{\mathsf{vk}} = (\mathsf{vk}_1, \ldots, \mathsf{vk}_n)$$

- For each $a, b \in [n]$ with $a < b$, define the following functions.
  - Let $f_1^{a,b}$ be the function that takes as input (γ, γ') and parses

    $$\gamma = \left(\overrightarrow{\mathsf{vk}}, \mathsf{sk}, \beta, \overrightarrow{c^z}, \omega^z, z, \overrightarrow{c^\pi}, \omega^\pi, \pi \right)$$

    and

    $$\gamma' = \left(\overrightarrow{\mathsf{vk}}', \mathsf{sk}', \beta', \overrightarrow{c^z}', \omega^{z\prime}, z', \overrightarrow{c^\pi}', \omega^{\pi\prime}, \pi' \right)$$

    It checks that:

* $\overrightarrow{\mathsf{vk}} = \overrightarrow{\mathsf{vk}}'$, $\overrightarrow{c^z} = \overrightarrow{c^z}'$, $\overrightarrow{c^\pi} = \overrightarrow{c^\pi}'$
* $(\mathsf{sk}, \mathsf{vk}_a) = \mathcal{V}.\mathsf{Gen}(1^\lambda; \beta)$, $(\mathsf{sk}', \mathsf{vk}_b) = \mathcal{V}.\mathsf{Gen}(1^\lambda; \beta')$
* $\mathsf{Open}(c_a^z, \omega^z, z) = \mathsf{Open}(c_b^z, \omega^{z'}, z') = 1$
* $\mathsf{Open}(c_a^\pi, \omega^\pi, \pi) = \mathsf{Open}(c_b^\pi, \omega^{\pi'}, \pi') = 1$

If all of these checks pass, then $f_1^{a,b}$ outputs

$$\sigma_{a,b} = (\mathcal{V}.\mathsf{Sign}((a,b); \mathsf{sk}_a), \mathcal{V}.\mathsf{Sign}((a,b); \mathsf{sk}_b))$$

and otherwise it outputs $\perp$.

- Let $\phi_1^{a,b}$ be the function that takes as input a witness w, which is either of the form $(0, \overrightarrow{\sigma})$ or of the form $\left(1, \overrightarrow{z}, \overrightarrow{\omega^z}, \overrightarrow{\pi}, \overrightarrow{\omega^\pi}, \overrightarrow{\mathsf{ind}}\right)$.
  * If w is of the first form, then it tests if $r = 1$ and

$$\mathcal{V}.\mathsf{Verify}\left(\sigma_{a,b,1}, (a,b); \mathsf{vk}_a\right) = 1$$

and

$$\mathcal{V}.\mathsf{Verify}\left(\sigma_{a,b,2}, (a,b); \mathsf{vk}_b\right) = 1$$

for all $a, b \in [n]$ with $a < b$, outputting 1 if so and 0 if not.
  * If w is of the second form, then it checks that:
    · $|\overrightarrow{\pi}| = \left|\overrightarrow{\omega^\pi}\right| = \left|\overrightarrow{\mathsf{ind}}\right| = r$
    · $\overrightarrow{\mathsf{ind}}$ consists of distinct indices in $[n]$.
    · $\mathsf{Open}\left(c_{\mathsf{ind}_j}^z, \omega_j^z, z_j\right) = 1$ for every $j \in [r]$.
    · $\mathsf{Open}\left(c_{\mathsf{ind}_j}^\pi, \omega_j^\pi, \pi_j\right) = 1$ for every $j \in [r]$.

  If all of these checks pass, then $\phi_1^{a,b}$ outputs 1 and otherwise it outputs 0.
- Let $\phi_2^{a,b}$ be identical to $\phi_1^{a,b}$.
- Let $f_2^{a,b}$ be the function that takes as input (γ, γ') where γ, γ' are as above, and outputs $(\omega^z, z, \omega^\pi, \pi, \omega^{z'}, z', \omega^{\pi'}, \pi')$.

- Set $r = 0^{11}$. Each party P_a for each $a \in [n]$ will now run the load phase to set up each instance of $\mathcal{F}_{\mathsf{SyX}}$ that it is involved in. For each pair of parties P_a, P_b with $a \neq b$ for $a, b \in [n]$, let $a' = \min(a,b)$ and $b' = \max(a,b)$. For each such pair of parties P_a, P_b, party P_a runs the load phase of $\mathcal{F}_{\mathsf{SyX}}^{a',b'}$, providing inputs (x_a, f), where

$$x_a = \left(\overrightarrow{\mathsf{vk}}, \mathsf{sk}_a, \beta_a, \overrightarrow{c^z}, \omega_a^z, z_a, \overrightarrow{c^\pi}, \omega_a^\pi, \pi_a\right)$$

and

$$f = \left(f_1^{a',b'}, f_2^{a',b'}, \phi_1^{a',b'}, \phi_2^{a',b'}\right)$$

- If $r > n$, abort. Otherwise, while $r \leq n$,

---

[11] This does not entail actually setting $r = 0$, but rather viewing the current round as round zero and henceforth referencing rounds with respect to it, that is, viewing r as the round number relative to the round number when this statement was executed.

- If a party P_a for $a \in [n]$ receives $\sigma_{a',b'}$ from each $\mathcal{F}_{\mathsf{SyX}}^{a',b'}$ it is involved in, indicating that the load phase of all such $\mathcal{F}_{\mathsf{SyX}}$ functionalities were completed successfully, and $r = 0$, it invokes the ideal functionality $\mathcal{F}_{\mathsf{bc}}$ and broadcasts

$$\overrightarrow{\sigma_a} = \{\sigma_{a',b'}\}_{a'=a \ \vee \ b'=a}$$

  to all the parties. Otherwise, it invokes the ideal functionality $\mathcal{F}_{\mathsf{bc}}$ when $r = 1$ and broadcasts abort to all the parties and aborts.
- If a party P_a for $a \in [n]$ receives $\overrightarrow{\sigma}$ such that

$$\mathcal{V}.\mathsf{Verify}\left(\sigma_{a,b,1}, (a,b); \mathsf{vk}_a\right) = 1$$

  and

$$\mathcal{V}.\mathsf{Verify}\left(\sigma_{a,b,2}, (a,b); \mathsf{vk}_b\right) = 1$$

  for all $a, b \in [n]$ with $a < b$, and $r = 1$, then it uses the witness $w = (0, \overrightarrow{\sigma})$ to invoke the trigger phase of each instance of $\mathcal{F}_{\mathsf{SyX}}$ that it is involved in. Once all such instances of $\mathcal{F}_{\mathsf{SyX}}$ involving party P_a have been triggered, use the shares $z_1, \ldots, z_n$ to reconstruct z, parses z as $z_1 \| \ldots \| z_n$ where $|z_i| = |y_i|$ for all $i \in [n]^{12}$ and computes $y_i = z_i \oplus \alpha_i$ to obtain the output of the computation.
- If party P_a for $a \in [n]$ has not received the output of the computation and an instance of $\mathcal{F}_{\mathsf{SyX}}$ involving party P_a is first triggered in round $1 \leq r < n$, it triggers each instance of $\mathcal{F}_{\mathsf{SyX}}$ that it is involved in during round $r + 1$ using the output out it receives from the instance of $\mathcal{F}_{\mathsf{SyX}}$ as follows:
  * If $\mathsf{out}_1 = (0, \overrightarrow{\sigma})$, then $r = 1$. Let $\mathcal{F}_{\mathsf{SyX}}^{a',b'}$ be the instance of $\mathcal{F}_{\mathsf{SyX}}$ that was triggered, where $a' = a \ \vee \ b' = a$. Parse

$$\mathsf{out}_2 = \left(\omega^z, z, \omega^\pi, \pi, \omega^{z'}, z', \omega^{\pi'}, \pi'\right)$$

  It prepares the witness

$$w = \left(1, (z, z'), \left(\omega^z, \omega^{z'}\right), (\pi, \pi'), \left(\omega^\pi, \omega^{\pi'}\right), (a', b')\right)$$

  * If $\mathsf{out}_1 = \left(1, \overrightarrow{z}, \overrightarrow{\omega^z}, \overrightarrow{\pi}, \overrightarrow{\omega^\pi}, \overrightarrow{\mathsf{ind}}\right)$, it prepares the witness

$$w = \left(1, \overrightarrow{z}', \overrightarrow{\omega^z}', \overrightarrow{\pi}', \overrightarrow{\omega^\pi}', \overrightarrow{\mathsf{ind}}'\right)$$

  where
  · $|\overrightarrow{z}'| = r + 1$, $\overrightarrow{z}'|_{[r]} = \overrightarrow{z}|_{[r]}$, $z'_{r+1} = z_a$
  · $\left|\overrightarrow{\omega^z}'\right| = r + 1$, $\overrightarrow{\omega^z}'\Big|_{[r]} = \overrightarrow{\omega^z}\Big|_{[r]}$, $\omega^z_{r+1}{}' = \omega^z_a$
  · $|\overrightarrow{\pi}'| = r + 1$, $\overrightarrow{\pi}'|_{[r]} = \overrightarrow{\pi}|_{[r]}$, $\pi'_{r+1} = \pi_a$

---

[12] We may assume without loss of generality that the lengths of the outputs of each party are known beforehand.

$$\cdot \left|\overrightarrow{\omega^{\pi\,\prime}}\right| = r+1, \; \overrightarrow{\omega^{\pi\,\prime}}\Big|_{[r]} = \overrightarrow{\omega^{\pi}}\Big|_{[r]}, \; \omega^{\pi}_{r+1}{}' = \omega^{\pi}_a$$

$$\cdot \left|\overrightarrow{\mathsf{ind}'}\right| = r+1, \; \overrightarrow{\mathsf{ind}'}\Big|_{[r]} = \overrightarrow{\mathsf{ind}}\Big|_{[r]}, \; \mathsf{ind}'_{r+1} = a$$

Once all instances of $\mathcal{F}_{\mathsf{SyX}}$ involving party P_a have been triggered, it uses the shares $z_1, \ldots, z_n$ to reconstruct z, parses z as $z_1 \| \ldots \| z_n$ where $|z_i| = |y_i|$ for all $i \in [n]$ and computes $y_i = z_i \oplus \alpha_i$ to obtain the output of the computation.

- If party P_a for $a \in [n]$ has not received the output of the computation and an instance of $\mathcal{F}_{\mathsf{SyX}}$ involving party P_a is triggered and $r = n$, it receives all shares of z. It uses the shares $z_1, \ldots, z_n$ to reconstruct z, parses z as $z_1 \| \ldots \| z_n$ where $|z_i| = |y_i|$ for all $i \in [n]$ and computes $y_i = z_i \oplus \alpha_i$ to obtain the output of the computation.

Remark. It is possible to replace the $\mathcal{O}(n^2)$ signatures with n other commitments to n other independent random proof values (akin to π) that can be used to prove that all the instances of $\mathcal{F}_{\mathsf{SyX}}$ completed their load phases successfully.

4.3   Proof Sketch of Security

We sketch the proof of security of the above protocol. The correctness of the computation of the functionality F' follows by definition from the correctness of the ideal functionality $\mathcal{F}_{\mathsf{MPC}}$. Furthermore, we have that at the end of the invocation of the ideal functionality $\mathcal{F}_{\mathsf{MPC}}$, either all honest parties *unanimously abort* or all honest parties *unanimously continue*. Thus, assuming that $\mathcal{F}_{\mathsf{MPC}}$ did not abort, every party receives the output of F'. For every $i \in [n]$, let $\overrightarrow{\mathsf{vk}}_i$ denote the set of verification keys that were obtained by party P_i. Note that, by the correctness of the ideal functionality $\mathcal{F}_{\mathsf{bc}}$,

$$\overrightarrow{\mathsf{vk}} = \overrightarrow{\mathsf{vk}}_i$$

for all $i \in [n]$. If $\overrightarrow{\mathsf{vk}}$ does not contain vk_j for every $i \in [n]$, which would happen in the case that some corrupt parties do not broadcast their verification keys, all honest parties *unanimously abort*. Otherwise, all honest parties *unanimously continue*. Assuming the honest parties have not aborted, we note that if the corrupt parties do not provide valid inputs to the load phase of even one of the instances of $\mathcal{F}_{\mathsf{SyX}}$ that they are involved in along with an honest party, say P_i for some $i \in [n]$, by the correctness of the ideal functionality $\mathcal{F}_{\mathsf{SyX}}$ and the binding property for the honestly generated commitments, that particular instance of $\mathcal{F}_{\mathsf{SyX}}$ will not complete its load phase successfully. In this case P_i will force all honest parties to *unanimously abort*, since no party (not even the corrupt ones) can obtain their output. We thus consider the case where all instances of $\mathcal{F}_{\mathsf{SyX}}$ have completed their load phases successfully. At this point, if all parties broadcast all the signatures they obtained from the instances of $\mathcal{F}_{\mathsf{SyX}}$, all parties can trigger the instances of $\mathcal{F}_{\mathsf{SyX}}$ that they are involved in to receive all the shares of z, reconstruct z and finally obtain their output correctly. The issue arises when some corrupt parties do not broadcast the signatures they obtained from the instances of $\mathcal{F}_{\mathsf{SyX}}$. If a corrupt party triggers any instance of $\mathcal{F}_{\mathsf{SyX}}$ involving an honest party, say P_i for some $i \in [n]$, with a witness of the form $(0, \overrightarrow{\sigma})$ in round 1, then the honest party obtains a tuple of values $(z, \omega^z, \pi, \omega^\pi)$ from the corrupt. In addition its own such tuple of values, it obtains a valid witness to trigger all the instances of $\mathcal{F}_{\mathsf{SyX}}$ that it is involved in round 2. Since $n \geq 2$, P_i succeeds in doing this and obtaining the shares of z, z and hence finally its output correctly. Consider any honest party P_j for $j \neq i$. Since $n > 2$, P_j, as did P_i, proceeds to trigger all the instances of $\mathcal{F}_{\mathsf{SyX}}$ that it is involved in round 3. If no corrupt party triggers any instance of $\mathcal{F}_{\mathsf{SyX}}$ involving an honest party with a witness of the form $(0, \overrightarrow{\sigma})$ in round 1, if the adversary is to obtain the output, it must instruct a corrupt party to trigger an instance of $\mathcal{F}_{\mathsf{SyX}}$ that it is involved in along with an honest party, but now using a witness of the form $\left(1, \overrightarrow{z}, \overrightarrow{\omega^z}, \overrightarrow{\pi}, \overrightarrow{\omega^\pi}, \overrightarrow{\mathsf{ind}}\right)$. Let r be the first round when a corrupt party triggers an instance of $\mathcal{F}_{\mathsf{SyX}}$ that it is involved in along with an honest party, say P_i for some $i \in [n]$, using a witness of the form $\left(1, \overrightarrow{z}, \overrightarrow{\omega^z}, \overrightarrow{\pi}, \overrightarrow{\omega^\pi}, \overrightarrow{\mathsf{ind}}\right)$. Then, it must be the case that $i \notin \overrightarrow{\mathsf{ind}}$ and that P_i now obtains the tuple of values $(z, \omega^z, \pi, \omega^\pi)$ corresponding to r parties other than itself. Combining this information with its own tuple of values $(z, \omega^z, \pi, \omega^\pi)$, it obtains a valid witness to trigger all the instances of $\mathcal{F}_{\mathsf{SyX}}$ that it is involved in round $r + 1$. If $r < n$, P_i succeeds in doing this and obtaining the shares of z, z and hence finally its output correctly. Consider any honest party P_j for $j \neq i$. If $r + 1 = n$, then P_j receives all the shares of z and consequently its output correctly. If $r + 1 < n$, then P_j, as did P_i, proceeds to trigger all the instances of $\mathcal{F}_{\mathsf{SyX}}$ that it is involved in round $r + 2$. Finally, we note that $r < n$ since r is the first round when a corrupt party triggers an instance of $\mathcal{F}_{\mathsf{SyX}}$ that it is involved in along with an honest party, which means that the witness it used to trigger the instance of $\mathcal{F}_{\mathsf{SyX}}$ can have the tuple of values $(z, \omega^z, \pi, \omega^\pi)$ corresponding to at most $n - 1$ parties as at least one of the parties is honest. If this does not happen, then no party (not even the corrupt ones) obtains their output. This completes the proof of correctness.

We state the following lemma and defer its proof to the full version [28].

Lemma 4. *If* $\left(\mathsf{Com}, \mathsf{Open}, \widetilde{\mathsf{Com}}, \widetilde{\mathsf{Open}}\right)$ *is an honest-binding commitment scheme and* $\mathcal{V}$ *is a signature scheme, then the protocol* Π_{FMPC} *securely computes* $\mathcal{F}_{\mathsf{MPC}}$ *with fairness in the* $(\mathcal{F}_{\mathsf{bc}}, \mathcal{F}_{\mathsf{MPC}}, \mathcal{F}_{\mathsf{SyX}})$*-hybrid model.*

4.4 Getting to the $\mathcal{F}_{\mathsf{SyX}}$-Hybrid Model

Combining Lemmas 3 and 4, we obtain the following theorem.

Theorem 1. *Consider* n *parties* $P_1, \ldots, P_n$ *in the* **point-to-point** *model. Then, assuming the existence of one-way functions, there exists a protocol* π *which securely computes* $\mathcal{F}_{\mathsf{MPC}}$ *with fairness in the presence of* t*-threshold adversaries for any* $0 \leq t < n$ *in the* $(\mathcal{F}_{\mathsf{OT}}, \mathcal{F}_{\mathsf{SyX}})$*-hybrid model.*

As discussed in Sect. 3, $\mathcal{F}_{2PC}$, and hence $\mathcal{F}_{OT}$, can be realized in the $\mathcal{F}_{SyX}$-hybrid model. We thus have the following theorem.

Theorem 2. *Consider n parties $P_1, \ldots, P_n$ in the* point-to-point *model. Then, assuming the existence of one-way functions, there exists a protocol π which securely computes $\mathcal{F}_{MPC}$ with fairness in the presence of t-threshold adversaries for any $0 \leq t < n$ in the $\mathcal{F}_{SyX}$-hybrid model.*

It is important to note that via this transformation, we have not introduced a need for the parties to have access to multiple instances of the ideal functionality $\mathcal{F}_{SyX}$ as opposed to one. This is because, in the protocol Π_{FMPC}, the ideal functionality $\mathcal{F}_{OT}$ will only be used to emulate the ideal functionality $\mathcal{F}_{MPC}$. During this stage, we do not make any use of the ideal functionality $\mathcal{F}_{SyX}$. Once we are done with the single invocation of $\mathcal{F}_{MPC}$, we only invoke the ideal functionality $\mathcal{F}_{SyX}$. As a consequence, parties can reuse the same instance of $\mathcal{F}_{SyX}$ to first emulate $\mathcal{F}_{OT}$ and then as a complete $\mathcal{F}_{SyX}$ functionality. We note that this however does increase the number of times the functionality is invoked.

5 Preprocessing $\mathcal{F}_{SyX}$

In this section, we will describe how a pair of parties can "preprocess" an instance of the ideal functionality $\mathcal{F}_{SyX}$. We first describe what we mean by "preprocess". What we would like to enable is the following. We already know that the ideal functionality $\mathcal{F}_{SyX}$ allows the pair of parties to perform fair two-party computations. We would like to set up the $\mathcal{F}_{SyX}$ functionality such that after a *single* invocation of the load phase, the two parties can perform an arbitrary (a priori unknown) polynomial number of fair two-party computations. Furthermore, if the parties are honest, they would not need to invoke the ideal functionality, that is, the "preprocessing" of the functionality is optimistic. Combining this with the protocol for fair multiparty computation in the $\mathcal{F}_{SyX}$-hybrid model from Sect. 4, we are able to show how an arbitrary set of n parties in the point-to-point model that have pairwise access to the ideal functionality $\mathcal{F}_{SyX}$ that has been preprocessed, can perform an arbitrary (a priori unknown) polynomial number of fair multiparty computations. To begin with, we will assume that the n-parties are in the point-to-point model and develop a protocol in the $(\mathcal{F}_{bc}, \mathcal{F}_{MPC}, \mathcal{F}_{SyX})$-hybrid model. We first provide some intuition for our construction. Our full protocol and proof can be found in the full version [28].

5.1 Intuition

We first start with the 3-party case as a warm-up. Let $P_1, P_2,$ and P_3 be the three parties, subsets (or all) of which would like to perform an unbounded (a priori unknown polynomial) number of secure function evaluations. For $i, j \in \{1, 2, 3\}$ with $i < j$, we have that parties P_i and P_j have access to the ideal functionality $\mathcal{F}_{SyX}$. In particular, let $\mathcal{F}_{SyX}^{i,j}$ represent the instantiation of the $\mathcal{F}_{SyX}$ functionality used by parties P_i, P_j. We wish to perform fair secure function evaluation of some 3-input 3-output functionality F. We assume, as before, a reduction to single output functionality F'.

Instance and Party Independence. Looking ahead, as in Sect. 4, we will use the instances of the ideal functionality $\mathcal{F}_{\mathsf{SyX}}$ to perform fair reconstruction. In order to be able to preprocess the instances of the functionality for arbitrary reconstructions, what is being reconstructed must be independent of the secure function evaluation and, in particular, the inputs of the parties. Furthermore, it must also be independent of the specific parties that are performing the reconstruction. However, until now, we have been assuming that the output of the secure function evaluation on the parties' inputs is what is being reconstructed, which does not satisfy our requirements and hence would not allow preprocessing. In order to fix this, we assume that the output of the secure function evaluation on the parties' inputs is encrypted under a key and that key is what will be reconstructed fairly. Note that the key can be chosen independent of the secure function evaluation and the parties' inputs. We would also like it to be the case that even after reconstructing once, our preprocessing is valid. This would require that the preprocessing allows for the generation and fair reconstruction of multiple independent (to a computational adversary) keys, one for each secure function evaluation. Thus, what is actually done during the preprocessing phase is the following. Each pair of parties P_i and P_j then initializes $\mathcal{F}_{\mathsf{SyX}}^{i,j}$. The function f_1 samples two random values $v_{i,j}, v_{j,i} \overset{\$}{\leftarrow} \{0,1\}^\lambda$ and sends these respectively to P_i and P_j. Let

$$V_{i,j} = V_{j,i} = v_{i,j} \oplus v_{j,i}.$$

The Underlying Additive Secret Sharing Scheme. For the instance of secure function evaluation with identifier id, we sample a unique key, K_{id}, to encrypt the output y_{id} of the secure function evaluation. Let Enc denote the encryption algorithm of an encryption scheme. The parties would receive $\mathsf{ct}_{\mathsf{id}} = \mathsf{Enc}(y_{\mathsf{id}}; K_{\mathsf{id}})$ and then fairly reconstruct K_{id}. We use an independent additive secret sharing of the key K_{id} for each party. Let the shares be $k_{\mathsf{id},i,j}$ for $i,j \in [3]$. That is, it holds that

$$K_{\mathsf{id}} = \bigoplus_{j \in [3]} k_{\mathsf{id},i,j}$$

for each $i \in [3]$. We would like party P_i to reconstruct K_{id} by obtaining all shares $k_{\mathsf{id},i,j}$ for each $j \in [3]$. Initially, each party P_i is given $k_{\mathsf{id},i,i}$. Therefore, each party P_i only needs to obtain $k_{\mathsf{id},i,j}$ and $k_{\mathsf{id},i,j'}$ for $j, j' \neq i$. Looking ahead, we would use the instances of the ideal functionality $\mathcal{F}_{\mathsf{SyX}}$ to allow parties to fairly learn all their shares of K_{id}. However, since we are preprocessing the instances, the information needed to compute these shares must be independent of the instance of secure function evaluation. The value that the instance $\mathcal{F}_{\mathsf{SyX}}^{i,j}$ would release fairly to parties P_i and P_j is $V_{i,j}$. Thus, party P_i additionally receives

$$\mathsf{ct}_{\mathsf{id},i,j} = \mathsf{Enc}(k_{\mathsf{id},i,j}; h_{\mathsf{id},i,j})$$

where
$$h_{\mathsf{id},i,j} = H(V_{i,j}\|\mathsf{id})$$

where H is a hash function (random oracle). The intuition is that the instances of the ideal functionality $\mathcal{F}_{\mathsf{SyX}}$ to allow parties to fairly learn the $V_{i,j}$s, and hence the $h_{\mathsf{id},i,j}$s and finally $k_{\mathsf{id},i,j}$s, thus fairly reconstructing K_{id}. It is important to note that using $V_{i,j}$s that are independent of the instance of secure function evaluation, we can fairly reconstruct, using per-instance (computationally independent) hash values $h_{\mathsf{id},i,j}$ generated using $V_{i,j}$s, per-instance (independent) encryption keys K_{id}.

An Attempt at Fair Reconstruction via $\mathcal{F}_{\mathsf{SyX}}$. We assume that the secure function evaluation with identifier id provides the encryption $\mathsf{ct}_{\mathsf{id}}$ of the output y_{id} of the secure function evaluation. Additionally, party P_i receives $\mathsf{ct}_{\mathsf{id},i,j}$ for each $j \in [n]$ and $k_{\mathsf{id},i,i}$. From our earlier discussion, the instances of the ideal functionality $\mathcal{F}_{\mathsf{SyX}}$ allow parties to fairly learn the $V_{i,j}$s. In order to allow reuse of the preprocessing, however, the instances of the ideal functionality $\mathcal{F}_{\mathsf{SyX}}$ must only allow parties to fairly learn the $h_{\mathsf{id},i,j}$s. As a first attempt to ensure this, we require the secure function evaluation to also give party P_i a signature σ_i on id. That is, P_i receives

$$\left(\mathsf{ct}_{\mathsf{id}}, \{\mathsf{ct}_{\mathsf{id},i,j}\}_{j\in[3]}, k_{\mathsf{id},i,i}, \sigma_i\right)$$

We will have the parties fairly learn the $h_{\mathsf{id},i,j}$s using the instances of the ideal functionality $\mathcal{F}_{\mathsf{SyX}}$. We achieve this by setting the predicate $\phi_k(w)$ (for $k \in \{i,j\}$) to output 1 if and only if w consists of both signatures (σ_i, σ_j). That is, each instance $\mathcal{F}_{\mathsf{SyX}}^{i,j}$ will accept the trigger $w_{i,j} = (\mathsf{id}, \sigma_i, \sigma_j)$. We define f_2 to simply output $h_{\mathsf{id},i,j}$ to both parties if $\phi_k(w) = 1$. Parties learn signatures of other parties by broadcasting their signatures and waiting for other parties to do so. If party P_i receives signatures from every other party, it can trigger every instance of the ideal functionality $\mathcal{F}_{\mathsf{SyX}}$ it is involved in, thus learning $h_{\mathsf{id},i,j}$ for each $j \in [3]$ and finally learning K_{id}. Malicious parties may however not broadcast their signatures. Concretely, we have the following attack: Suppose P_1 is honest while P_2 and P_3 are corrupt. P_2 and P_3 already know σ_2 and σ_3 and only need σ_1 to learn the output. P_1 broadcasts σ_1 while P_2 and P_3 do not broadcast σ_2 and σ_3. Finally, P_2 triggers the ideal functionality $\mathcal{F}_{\mathsf{SyX}}^{1,2}$ using (σ_1, σ_2) and learns the output. P_1, on the other hand, only learns σ_2 and hence does not learn the output.

Fair Reconstruction via $\mathcal{F}_{\mathsf{SyX}}$. We fix the protocol sketch described above using a technique we developed for termination of the protocol described in Sect. 4. The protocol for reconstruction proceeds in $T = n$ rounds. In order to trigger an instance of $\mathcal{F}_{\mathsf{SyX}}$ in some round $\tau \in [T]$, you must provide a proof that other instances of $\mathcal{F}_{\mathsf{SyX}}$ involving at least τ different parties have been triggered. Consider the first round τ in which P_i is an honest party and $\mathcal{F}_{\mathsf{SyX}}^{i,j}$ is triggered for some j. If $\tau = 1$, then the single invocation already gives a proof that channels involving two parties, namely, i, j, have been triggered. Otherwise, by assumption, proofs of invocations of instances of $\mathcal{F}_{\mathsf{SyX}}$ involving τ different parties were needed to trigger $\mathcal{F}_{\mathsf{SyX}}^{i,j}$. But P_i is not one of these parties as τ is the first round in which $\mathcal{F}_{\mathsf{SyX}}^{i,j}$ was triggered for any j. Consequently, P_i, on this invocation, obtains a proof that instances of $\mathcal{F}_{\mathsf{SyX}}$ involving at least $\tau + 1$ parties have been triggered, and can thus trigger all channels in round $\tau + 1$. The only gap in the argument is the case $\tau = T$. One can trivially see that since $\mathcal{F}_{\mathsf{SyX}}^{i,j}$ has not been triggered for any j, it is impossible to obtain a proof that instances of $\mathcal{F}_{\mathsf{SyX}}$ involving at least T different parties have been triggered.

Optimistic Preprocessing. In the case where parties are honest, we can simply have the secure function evaluation provide the output instead of parties having to trigger their instances of the ideal functionality $\mathcal{F}_{\mathsf{SyX}}$. We are guaranteed, by virtue of the fair reconstruction techniques discussed thus far, that in the case where parties behave adversarially, the honest parties do have a way to obtain the output of the computation. In this way, in the optimistic setting, parties never have to trigger the instances of the ideal functionality $\mathcal{F}_{\mathsf{SyX}}$. Combined with the fact that the actual preprocessing phase is extremely simple, we see that this paradigm makes fair secure function evaluation just as efficient as secure function evaluation with abort in the optimistic case.

Simulation. We look ahead for the issues that come up while trying to prove security, that is, during the simulation. The simulator will release to the adversary, the encryption of the output and encryptions of the adversary's shares of the key used to encrypt the output. Since the simulator does not know the output *a priori*, and does not know whether the adversary is going to abort the computation, in which case, no one knows the output, it has to produce encryptions that it can later *equivocate*. In this context, we use, not a regular encryption scheme, but non-interactive non-committing encryption commitments. In this case, the simulator can produce encryptions to garbage but can later decrypt them to be *valid* shares of the key and the actual output. The rest of the computations can be trivially simulated. The only other detail to be looked into is that of the clock. We need to determine if the adversary has decided to abort the computation, that is, if the adversary is going to receive the output of the computation of not. This is done by noticing if and when the adversary decides to trigger the instances of $\mathcal{F}_{\mathsf{SyX}}$ that involve honest parties. We know that if the adversary ever triggers an instance of $\mathcal{F}_{\mathsf{SyX}}$ involving an honest party, then all parties will be in a position to receive the output. Thus, the simulator can simply run the adversary to determine whether it has decided to enable parties to obtain the output, in which the simulator would ask the trusted party to continue, or not, in which case the simulator would ask the trusted party to abort.

We state our main theorem below and refer the reader to the full version [28] for further details.

Theorem 3. *Consider n parties $P_1, \ldots, P_n$ in the* point-to-point *model. Then, assuming the existence of enhanced trapdoor permutations, there exists a protocol π in the programmable random oracle model which securely preprocesses for and* *computes and arbitrary (polynomial) number of instances of $\mathcal{F}_{\mathsf{MPC}}$ with fairness in the presence of t-threshold adversaries for any $0 \leq t < n$ in the $\mathcal{F}_{\mathsf{SyX}}$-hybrid model. Furthermore, for each $\mathcal{F}_{\mathsf{SyX}}$ instance, the complexity of its load phase is $O(\lambda)$ and the complexity of its trigger phase is $O(n\lambda)$.*

Disclaimer

References

1. Andrychowicz, M., Dziembowski, S., Malinowski, D., Mazurek, L.: Fair two-party computations via bitcoin deposits. In: Böhme, R., Brenner, M., Moore, T., Smith, M. (eds.) Financial Cryptography and Data Security - FC 2014 Workshops, BITCOIN and WAHC 2014, Christ Church, Barbados, 7 March 2014, Revised Selected Papers. LNCS, vol. 8438, pp. 105–121. Springer, Cham (2014). https://doi.org/10.1007/978-3-662-44774-1_8
2. Andrychowicz, M., Dziembowski, S., Malinowski, D., Mazurek, L.: Secure multiparty computations on bitcoin. Commun. ACM **59**(4), 76–84 (2016)
3. Asharov, G.: Towards characterizing complete fairness in secure two-party computation. In: Lindell, Y. (ed.) Theory of Cryptography - 11th Theory of Cryptography Conference, TCC 2014, San Diego, CA, USA, 24–26 February 2014, Proceedings. LNCS, vol. 8349, pp. 291–316. Springer, Cham (2014). https://doi.org/10.1007/978-3-642-54242-8_13
4. Asharov, G., Beimel, A., Makriyannis, N., Omri, E.: Complete characterization of fairness in secure two-party computation of boolean functions. In: Dodis, Y., Nielsen, J.B. (eds.) Theory of Cryptography - 12th Theory of Cryptography Conference, TCC 2015, Warsaw, Poland, 23–25 March 2015, Proceedings, Part I. LNCS, vol. 9014, pp. 199–228. Springer, Cham (2015). https://doi.org/10.1007/978-3-662-46494-6_10

5. Asokan, N., Schunter, M., Waidner, M.: Optimistic protocols for fair exchange. In: CCS 1997, Proceedings of the 4th ACM Conference on Computer and Communications Security, Zurich, Switzerland, 1–4 April 1997, pp. 7–17 (1997)
6. Asokan, N., Shoup, V., Waidner, M.: Optimistic fair exchange of digital signatures. IEEE J. Sel. Areas Commun. 18(4), 593–610 (2000)
7. Ben-Or, M., Goldwasser, S., Wigderson, A.: Completeness theorems for non-cryptographic fault-tolerant distributed computation (extended abstract). In: Proceedings of the 20th Annual ACM Symposium on Theory of Computing, 2–4 May 1988, Chicago, Illinois, USA, pp. 1–10 (1988)
8. Bentov, I., Kumaresan, R.: How to use bitcoin to design fair protocols. In: Garay, J.A., Gennaro, R. (eds.) Advances in Cryptology - CRYPTO 2014–34th Annual Cryptology Conference, Santa Barbara, CA, USA, 17–21 August 2014, Proceedings, Part II. LNCS, vol. 8617, pp. 421–439. Springer, Cham (2014). https://doi.org/10.1007/978-3-662-44381-1_24
9. Boneh, D., Naor, M.: Timed commitments. In: Bellare, M. (ed.) Advances in Cryptology - CRYPTO 2000, 20th Annual International Cryptology Conference, Santa Barbara, California, USA, 20–24 August 2000, Proceedings. LNCS, vol. 1880, pp. 236–254. Springer, Cham (2000). https://doi.org/10.1007/3-540-44598-6_15
10. Canetti, R., Fischlin, M.: Universally composable commitments. In: Kilian, J. (ed.) Advances in Cryptology - CRYPTO 2001, 21st Annual International Cryptology Conference, Santa Barbara, California, USA, 19–23 August 2001, Proceedings. LNCS, vol. 2139, pp. 19–40. Springer, Cham (2001). https://doi.org/10.1007/3-540-44647-8_2
11. Canetti, R., Halevi, S., Katz, J.: Adaptively-secure, non-interactive public-key encryption. In: Kilian, J. (ed.) Theory of Cryptography, Second Theory of Cryptography Conference, TCC 2005, Cambridge, MA, USA, 10–12 February 2005, Proceedings. LNCS, vol. 3378, pp. 150–168. Springer, Cham (2005). https://doi.org/10.1007/978-3-540-30576-7_9
12. Canetti, R., Lindell, Y., Ostrovsky, R., Sahai, A.: Universally composable two-party and multi-party secure computation. In: STOC, pp. 494–503 (2002)
13. Chaum, D., Crépeau, C., Damgård, I.: Multiparty unconditionally secure protocols (extended abstract). In: Proceedings of the 20th Annual ACM Symposium on Theory of Computing, 2–4 May 1988, Chicago, Illinois, USA, pp. 11–19 (1988)
14. Choudhuri, A.R., Green, M., Jain, A., Kaptchuk, G., Miers, I.: Fairness in an unfair world: fair multiparty computation from public bulletin boards. In: Proceedings of the 2017 ACM SIGSAC Conference on Computer and Communications Security, CCS 2017, Dallas, TX, USA, 30 October–3 November 2017, pp. 719–728 (2017)
15. Cleve, R.: Limits on the security of coin flips when half the processors are faulty (extended abstract). In: Proceedings of the 18th Annual ACM Symposium on Theory of Computing, 28–30 May 1986, Berkeley, California, USA, pp. 364–369 (1986)
16. Cohen, R., Lindell, Y.: Fairness versus guaranteed output delivery in secure multiparty computation. J. Cryptology 30(4), 1157–1186 (2017)
17. Dolev, D., Strong, H.R.: Authenticated algorithms for byzantine agreement. SIAM J. Comput. 12(4), 656–666 (1983)
18. Fitzi, M., Garay, J.A., Maurer, U.M., Ostrovsky, R.: Minimal complete primitives for secure multi-party computation. J. Cryptology 18(1), 37–61 (2005)
19. Garay, J.A., Jakobsson, M.: Timed release of standard digital signatures. In: Blaze, M. (ed.) Financial Cryptography, 6th International Conference, FC 2002, Southampton, Bermuda, 11–14 March 2002, Revised Papers. LNCS, vol. 2357, pp. 168–182. Springer, Cham (2002). https://doi.org/10.1007/3-540-36504-4_13

20. Garay, J.A., MacKenzie, P.D., Prabhakaran, M., Yang, K.: Resource fairness and composability of cryptographic protocols. J. Cryptology **24**(4), 615–658 (2011)
21. Garay, J.A., Pomerance, C.: Timed fair exchange of standard signatures: (extended abstract). In: Wright, R.N. (ed.) Financial Cryptography, 7th International Conference, FC 2003, Guadeloupe, French West Indies, 27–30 January 2003, Revised Papers. LNCS, vol. 2742, pp. 190–207. Springer, Cham (2003). https://doi.org/10.1007/978-3-540-45126-6_14
22. Goldreich, O., Micali, S., Wigderson, A.: How to play any mental game or a completeness theorem for protocols with honest majority. In: Proceedings of the 19th Annual ACM Symposium on Theory of Computing, 1987, New York, New York, USA, pp. 218–229 (1987)
23. Gordon, S.D., Hazay, C., Katz, J., Lindell, Y.: Complete fairness in secure two-party computation. J. ACM **58**(6), 24:1–24:37 (2011)
24. Gordon, S.D., Ishai, Y., Moran, T., Ostrovsky, R., Sahai, A.: On complete primitives for fairness. In: Micciancio, D. (ed.) Theory of Cryptography, 7th Theory of Cryptography Conference, TCC 2010, Zurich, Switzerland, 9–11 February 2010, Proceedings. LNCS, vol. 5978, pp. 91–108. Springer, Cham (2010). https://doi.org/10.1007/978-3-642-11799-2_7
25. Gordon, S.D., Katz, J.: Complete fairness in multi-party computation without an honest majority. In: Reingold, O. (ed.) Theory of Cryptography, 6th Theory of Cryptography Conference, TCC 2009, San Francisco, CA, USA, 15–17 March 2009, Proceedings. LNCS, vol. 5444, pp. 19–35. Springer, Cham (2009). https://doi.org/10.1007/978-3-642-00457-5_2
26. Gordon, S.D., Katz, J.: Partial fairness in secure two-party computation. In: Gilbert, H. (ed.) Advances in Cryptology - EUROCRYPT 2010, 29th Annual International Conference on the Theory and Applications of Cryptographic Techniques, Monaco/French Riviera, 30 May–3 June 2010, Proceedings. LNCS, vol. 6110, pp. 157–176. Springer, Cham (2010). https://doi.org/10.1007/978-3-642-13190-5_8
27. Katz, J.: On achieving the "best of both worlds" in secure multiparty computation. In: Proceedings of the 39th Annual ACM Symposium on Theory of Computing, San Diego, California, USA, 11–13 June 2007, pp. 11–20 (2007)
28. Kumaresan, R., Raghuraman, S., Sealfon, A.: Synchronizable exchange. IACR Cryptol. ePrint Arch. 976 (2020)
29. Kumaresan, R., Vaikuntanathan, V., Vasudevan, P.N.: Improvements to secure computation with penalties. In: Proceedings of the 2016 ACM SIGSAC Conference on Computer and Communications Security, Vienna, Austria, 24–28 October 2016, pp. 406–417 (2016)
30. Lepinski, M., Micali, S., Peikert, C., Shelat, A.: Completely fair SFE and coalition-safe cheap talk. In: Proceedings of the Twenty-Third Annual ACM Symposium on Principles of Distributed Computing, PODC 2004, St. John's, Newfoundland, Canada, 25–28 July 2004, pp. 1–10 (2004)
31. Nielsen, J.B.: Separating random oracle proofs from complexity theoretic proofs: the non-committing encryption case. In: Yung, M. (ed.) Advances in Cryptology - CRYPTO 2002, 22nd Annual International Cryptology Conference, Santa Barbara, California, USA, 18–22 August 2002, Proceedings. LNCS, vol. 2442, pp. 111–126. Springer, Cham (2002). https://doi.org/10.1007/3-540-45708-9_8

32. Pass, R., Shi, E., Tramèr, F.: Formal abstractions for attested execution secure processors. In: Coron, J.S., Nielsen, J. (eds.) Advances in Cryptology - EUROCRYPT 2017–36th Annual International Conference on the Theory and Applications of Cryptographic Techniques, Paris, France, 30 April–4 May 2017, Proceedings, Part I. LNCS, vol. 10210, pp. 260–289. Springer, Cham (2017). https://doi.org/10.1007/978-3-319-56620-7_10

33. Pinkas, B.: Fair secure two-party computation. In: Biham, E. (ed.) Advances in Cryptology - EUROCRYPT 2003, International Conference on the Theory and Applications of Cryptographic Techniques, Warsaw, Poland, 4–8 May 2003, Proceedings. LNCS, vol. 2656, pp. 87–105. Springer, Cham (2003). https://doi.org/10.1007/3-540-39200-9_6

34. Rabin, T., Ben-Or, M.: Verifiable secret sharing and multiparty protocols with honest majority (extended abstract). In: Proceedings of the 21st Annual ACM Symposium on Theory of Computing, 14–17 May 1989, Seattle, Washington, USA, pp. 73–85 (1989)

35. Raghuraman, S., Yang, Y.: Just how fair is an unreactive world. IACR Cryptol. ePrint Arch. **2022**, 1655 (2022)

36. Sinha, R., Gaddam, S., Kumaresan, R.: LucidiTEE: policy-based fair computing at scale. IACR Cryptol. ePrint Arch. **2019**, 178 (2019)

37. Yao, A.C.: How to generate and exchange secrets (extended abstract). In: 27th Annual Symposium on Foundations of Computer Science, Toronto, Canada, 27–29 October 1986, pp. 162–167 (1986)

DORAM Revisited: Maliciously Secure RAM-MPC with Logarithmic Overhead

Brett Falk[1], Daniel Noble[1]([envelope]), Rafail Ostrovsky[2], Matan Shtepel[1], and Jacob Zhang[2]

[1] University of Pennsylvania, Philadelphia, USA
{fbrett,dgnoble}@seas.upenn.edu, matan.shtepel@ucla.edu
[2] UCLA, Los Angeles, USA
rafail@cs.ucla.edu, jacobzhang@g.ucla.edu

Abstract. Distributed Oblivious Random Access Memory (DORAM) is a secure multiparty protocol that allows a group of participants holding a secret-shared array to read and write to secret-shared locations within the array. The efficiency of a DORAM protocol is measured by the amount of communication required per read/write query into the array. DORAM protocols are a necessary ingredient for executing Secure Multiparty Computation (MPC) in the RAM model.

Although DORAM has been widely studied, all existing DORAM protocols have focused on the setting where the DORAM servers are semi-honest. Generic techniques for upgrading a semi-honest DORAM protocol to the malicious model typically increase the asymptotic communication complexity of the DORAM scheme.

In this work, we present a 3-party DORAM protocol which requires $O((\kappa+D)\log N)$ communication per query, for a database of size N with D-bit values, where κ is the security parameter. Our hidden constants in the big-O nation are small. We show that our protocol is UC-secure in the presence of a malicious, static adversary. This matches the communication complexity of the best semi-honest DORAM protocols, and is the first malicious DORAM protocol with this complexity.

1 Introduction

In this work, we develop the first Distributed Oblivious RAM (DORAM) protocol secure against *malicious* adversaries while matching the communication and computation costs of the best-known semi-honest constructions.

Poly-logarithmic overhead Oblivious RAM (ORAM) [Ost90, Ost92, GO96] was developed to allow a client to access a database held by an untrusted server,

---

M. Shtepel–Work done while at UCLA.

Supplementary Information The online version contains supplementary material available at https://doi.org/10.1007/978-3-031-48615-9_16.

© International Association for Cryptologic Research 2023
G. Rothblum and H. Wee (Eds.): TCC 2023, LNCS 14369, pp. 441–470, 2023.
https://doi.org/10.1007/978-3-031-48615-9_16

while hiding the client's access pattern from the server itself with poly-log overhead. In this work, we focus on *Distributed* Oblivious RAM, which allows a group of servers to access a secret-shared array at a secret-shared index. The secret-shared index can be conceptualized as coming either from an external client or as the output of a previous secure computation done by the servers.

The efficiency of an ORAM protocol is usually measured by the (amortized) number of bits of communication required to process a single query. If privacy were not an issue, in order to retrieve a single D-bit entry from a table of size N, the client would need to send a $\log(N)$-bit index, and receive a D-bit value, so the communication would be $\log(N) + D$. In order to make the queries *oblivious*, it is known that a multiplicative communication overhead of $\Omega(\log(N))$ is required [GO96, LN18]. That is, the optimal communication in the traditional, passive-server ORAM setting is $\Omega((D + \log N)\log N)$.[1] Several ORAM protocols have achieved this "optimal" communication complexity (in slightly different settings). [LO13] achieved logarithmic amortized overhead in the two-server setting (Fig. 1b), OptORAMa [AKL+20] achieved amortized logarithmic overhead in the single-server setting (Fig. 1a) with constant $> 2^{228}$ hidden by the big-O notation. The constant was later reduced to 9405 in [DO20] and de-amortized in [AKLS21]. However, despite all these improvements, these works are of only theoretical interest, due to large constants. In Appendix A.4 we discuss why none of these semi-honest constructions can be naïvely compiled to a maliciously secure DORAM without asymptotic blowup. When a DORAM can store N, D-bit elements with security parameter is κ, we prove the following theorem:

Theorem 1 (Malicious DORAM, Informal). *If Pseudo-Random Functions exist with $O(\kappa + l)$ circuit size (where l is the number of input bits and κ is the computational security parameter), then there exists a (3,1)-malicious DORAM scheme (see Definition 2) with $O((\kappa + D)\log N)$ communication complexity between the servers per each query.*

The best DORAMs in the *semi-honest* model have either $O((\kappa + D)\log(N))$ [LO13, FNO22] or $O((\log^2(N) + D)\log(N))$ [WCS15] communication complexity per query. Which of these is better depends on the parameter choices. If D is large ($\Omega(\log^2(N) + \kappa)$) they are equally good. If D is small, [LO13, FNO22] are better when $\log(N) = \omega(\sqrt{\kappa})$ and [WCS15] is better otherwise. Thus, our server-to-server communication overhead of $O((\kappa + D)\log(N))$ matches the best communication complexity of the best DORAM protocols in the semi-honest model [FNO22, LO13], achieving security against malicious adversaries with *no* asymptotic increase in communication costs.

Note that a non-private solution would still require communicating $\Theta(\log(N) + D)$ bits to simply send the secret-shared query and secret-shared response. Thus, our cost of $\Theta((\kappa + D)\log(N))$ has logarithmic overhead when

---

[1] Most ORAM works assume $D = \Omega(\log N)$, so $O((D + \log N)\log N) = O(D\log N)$ which is described as a logarithmic "overhead" or a logarithmic "blowup" over $O(D)$ communication needed to make a query in the insecure setting.

the block size, $D = \Omega(\kappa)$. Our title refers to this (common) scenario. If $D = o(\kappa)$, the overhead is $\Theta(\log(N)\kappa/D)$.

As we discuss below, one of the main motivations for studying DORAM is in service of building efficient, secure multiparty computation (MPC) protocols in the RAM model of computation.

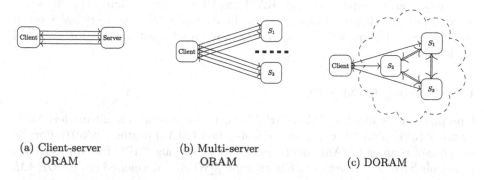

(a) Client-server
    ORAM

(b) Multi-server
    ORAM

(c) DORAM

Fig. 1. *Abstract view of different ORAM "flavors" in the client-server model. In client-server ORAM the client and the server communicate over many rounds. In multiserver ORAM the client communicates with each server individually over many rounds. In DORAM, the client communicates a secret shared query to the servers, the DORAM servers communicate among themselves for several rounds, and respond to the client. The client's work is the lowest in the DORAM setting.*

1.1 MPC in the RAM Model

Secure Multiparty Computation (MPC) protocols enable a set of mutually distrusting parties, $P_1, ..., P_n$, with private data $x_1, ..., x_n$ to compute an agreed-upon (probabilistic) polynomial-time function, f, in such a way that each player learns the output, $f(x_1, ..., x_n)$, but no additional information about the other participants' inputs [Yao82, Yao86, GMW87, CCD88].

The majority of MPC protocols work in *the circuit model of computation* [Vol99], where the functionality, f, is represented as a circuit (either a boolean circuit, or an arithmetic circuit over a finite field $\mathbb{F}$). Computing in the circuit model has been advantageous for MPC protocols because circuits are naturally *oblivious*, i.e., the sequence of operations needed to compute f is independent of the *private* inputs $x_1, ..., x_n$. This reduces the problem of securely computing an arbitrary function, f, to the problem of securely computing a small set of universal gates (e.g. AND and XOR).

Although the circuit model of computation is convenient for MPC, many common functionalities cannot be represented by *compact* circuits, which means generic circuit-based MPC protocols cannot compute them efficiently. A simple database lookup highlights the inefficiency of the circuit model. Consider the function $R(i, y_1, ..., y_N) = y_i$, which outputs the ith element in a list or the function $W(i, Y, y_1, \ldots, y_N)$ which produces no output but sets $y_i = Y$. These functionalities can run in constant time in the RAM-model of computation, but in the *circuit model*, both R and W have circuit complexity $O(N)$.

In contrast to circuit-based MPC protocols, RAM-MPC framework [OS97] provides a method of securely computing functions specified in the RAM model of computation. Efficiency is often a barrier to the deployment of MPC protocols in practice, and compilation from RAM model into circuits hurts the efficiency of programs which use random access. Thus, RAM-MPC is a critical step in making general-purpose MPC protocols that are efficient enough for practical applications.

1.2   Building RAM-MPC

One method for building RAM-MPC is to use a generic (circuit-model) MPC protocol to simulate the client for a client-server ORAM protocol [OS97]. For the purpose of running ORAM clients under MPC, various "MPC friendly" ORAM protocols have been developed. For example, [WCS15] developed *circuit ORAM*, an ORAM maintaining the stringent one-trusted-client one-untrusted-server security model of traditional ORAM while decreasing the circuit-complexity of the client. Another example of such efforts, are *multi-server ORAM* protocols where the trusted client's data is shared and accessed across multiple servers. Assuming some fraction of the servers are honest [OS97, GKK+12, GKW18, KM19] these works shift some of the communication burden to servers. These multi-server ORAMs can also be adapted to the MPC context by simulating the client using (circuit-based) MPC, allowing the MPC participants to play the role of the additional ORAM servers. Some of these protocols have been implemented [GKK+12, LO13, ZWR+16, WHC+14, Ds17].

A recent direction in the search for MPC-friendly ORAMs is *Distributed ORAM* (DORAM). In a DORAM protocol, both the index i and the database $y_1, \ldots, y_N$ are secret shared among a number of servers. The goal of the protocol is to obtain a secret-sharing of y_i at minimal communication between the servers while not exposing *any* information about i or $y_1, \ldots, y_N$. DORAM has been widely studied in the semi-honest model [LO13, GHL+14, FJKW15, ZWR+16, Ds17, JW18, BKKO20, FNO22, JZLR22, VHG22]. These works have taken several interesting approaches, emphasizing different parameters, and often presenting implementations [ZWR+16, Ds17, VHG22, JZLR22].

In this paper, we study DORAM in the malicious model. In particular, we provide the *first* DORAM protocol that provides security against *malicious* adversaries while *matching the asymptotics of the best-known semi-honest construction*. We use the generic transformation to compile our DORAM into RAM-MPC, giving RAM-MPC which is secure against *malicious* adversaries with an asymptotic cost on par with *the best existing semi-honest constructions*.

2 Notation and Definitions

We denote the 3 parties as P_0, P_1, P_2, and use $\mathbb{F}_{2^l}$ to denote the finite field of 2^l elements. For $x = x_0 \ldots x_{n-1} = x \in \mathbb{F}^n$ we let $x[i : j] = x_i \ldots x_j$. For $a \in \mathbb{Z}^+$, $[a]$ represents the set $\{1, \ldots, a\}$. For any set S, $x \in_R S$ represents choosing x uniformly at random from S.

N is the number of elements in the DORAM. Each element stored in the DORAM is a pair (X, Y), where $X \in [N]$ is the "virtual index" of the D-bit payload, Y. We assume that only indices in the range $[N]$ are queried. We use $\perp \notin [N] \cup \{0,1\}^D$ to represent a reserved null-value. κ is the computational security parameter and σ is a statistical security parameter. Since we want to achieve failures with probability negligible in N, we must have both $\kappa, \sigma = \omega(\log N)$.

The primary secret-sharing our protocol uses is $(3, 1)$ Replicated Secret Sharing (RSS) (also called a CNF sharing [CDI05]). $[\![x]\!]$ denotes a RSS of a variable x. In a $(3, 1)$ RSS sharing, each party holds two shares of an additive sharing:

Definition 1 (replicated secret sharing). Let $x, x^{(0)}, x^{(1)}, x^{(2)} \in \mathbb{F}$ s.t $x^{(0)} + x^{(1)} + x^{(2)} = x$. we say that P_0, P_1, P_2 hold a replicated secret sharing of x if P_i hold all $x^{(j)}$ s.t $j \neq i$.

We also use two-party additive sharings. $[x]^{(i,j)}$ denotes an additive sharing of x held by parties P_i and P_j, that is P_i holds $x^{(i)}$ and P_j holds $x^{(j)}$ where $x^{(i)} + x^{(j)} = x$.

We use standard Boolean operators $(\wedge, \vee, \neg)$. We also represent by $x \overset{?}{=} y$ the Boolean-output operation that outputs 1 if x equals y and 0 otherwise, and use $(b?x : y)$ to represent an if-then-else statement which evaluates to x if b, and y otherwise.

Functionality $\mathcal{F}_{\textbf{DORAM}}$

$\mathcal{F}_{\text{DORAM}}.\textbf{Init}([\![Y]\!])$: Given a secret-shared N element array, s.t for all $i \in [N]$, $Y_i \in \{0,1\}^D$, store Y internally. No output.
$\mathcal{F}_{\text{DORAM}}.\textbf{ReadAndWrite}([\![X]\!], [\![Y_{\textbf{new}}]\!])$: Given a secret-shared address $X \in [N]$ and secret-shared value $Y_{\text{new}} \in \{0,1\}^D \cup \perp$:

1. Output $[\![Y_X]\!]$ to the players.
2. If $Y_{\text{new}} \neq \perp$, update $Y_X = Y_{\text{new}}$.

Fig. 2. $\mathcal{F}_{\text{DORAM}}$: The DORAM functionality

In this work, we define security using the Universal Composability (UC) framework [Can01], which allows us to formally define DORAM.

Definition 2 (DORAM). *A protocol, Π, is said to be a UC maliciously-secure (n, t)-Distributed ORAM protocol if for all $N, D, \kappa \in \mathbb{Z}^+$, Π UC-realizes the DORAM functionality (Fig. 2).*

3 Related Work

In this section we present a brief overview of related work; Appendix A contains a more detailed discussion.

Many DORAMs start with a client-server ORAM and simulate the client inside of a secure computation. This was the approach taken by [WCS15] and [ZWR+16]. The generic MPC can be achieved from Garbled Circuits (GC), which allows for 2 parties, low round complexity, but requires $\Theta(\kappa)$ communication for each AND gate. Alternatively, it can be achieved using honest-majority secret-sharing approaches derived from the BGW protocol [BOGW88], which have $\Theta(1)$ communication per AND gate, but need 3 parties and more rounds.

Similarly it is also possible to convert a multi-server ORAM, such as [LO13] to a DORAM, again by simulating the client inside of a secure computation, and having each server run by a different party.

Other protocols build DORAM directly. This includes [Ds17, HV20, FJKW15, JW18, BKKO20, VHG22, FNO22]. This allows use of techniques that are not applicable for client server ORAMs, such as Function Secret Sharing (FSS), Secret-Shared PIR (SS-PIR) and efficient shuffles.

Table 1 presents these protocols, with their communication costs. Our communication cost is asymptotically identical to [FNO22] and a BGW-style instance of [LO13]. Depending on the relationship between κ and $\log(N)$ it may be either asymptotically better or worse than a BGW-style instance of [WCS15]. For small block sizes the communication cost is strictly better than all previous protocols. Unlike all previous protocols, it is secure against malicious adversaries.

Table 1. Complexity of DORAM protocols. N denotes the number of records, κ is a cryptographic security parameter, σ is a statistical security parameter, and D is the record size.

Protocol	Communication	Parties	Security
Circuit ORAM [WCS15] (GC)	$O\left(\kappa \log^3 N + \kappa D \log N\right)$	2	Semi-Honest
Square-root ORAM [ZWR+16] (GC)	$O\left(\kappa D \sqrt{N \log^3 N}\right)$	2	Semi-Honest
FLORAM [Ds17]	$O\left(\sqrt{\kappa D N} \log N\right)$	2	Semi-Honest
[HV20]	$O\left(\sqrt{\kappa D N} \log N\right)$	2	Semi-Honest
Circuit ORAM [WCS15] (BGW)	$O\left(\log^3 N + D \log N\right)$	3	Semi-Honest
[LO13] (BGW)	$O((\kappa + D) \log N)$	3	Semi-Honest
[FJKW15]	$O\left(\kappa \sigma \log^3 N + \sigma D \log N\right)$	3	Semi-Honest
[JW18]	$O\left(\kappa \log^3 N + D \log N\right)$	3	Semi-Honest
[BKKO20]	$O\left(D\sqrt{N}\right)$	3	Semi-Honest
DuORAM [VHG22]	$O(\kappa \cdot D \cdot \log N)$	3	Semi-Honest
[FNO22]	$O((\kappa + D) \log N)$	3	Semi-Honest
Our protocol	$O((\kappa + D) \log N)$	3	Malicious

4   Technical Overview

Our protocol is based on the Hierarchical solution [Ost90]. While this technique has primarily been applied in many client-server ORAMs [GMOT12, KLO12, LO13, PPRY18, AKLS21], we, like several other works [KM19, FNO22], apply it to DORAMs. Before understanding our protocol, it is important to understand the Hierarchical solution in general.

The Hierarchical Solution in Client-Server ORAM: A client-server ORAM must ensure that the physical access pattern on the server is (computationally) independent of the client's queries, regardless of the query sequence. Let us first consider a slightly weaker primitive: a protocol in which the access pattern on the server is (computationally) independent of the client's queries *provided each item is queried at most once*. This primitive is called an Oblivious Hash Table (OHTable) and is much easier to instantiate. Most common hash tables become oblivious when the hash functions themselves are pseudorandom. If the hash table can also be *constructed* on the server in a way that leaks no information about the contents, or their relation to any later queries, then a full OHTable protocol has been achieved.

An OHTable may seem significantly weaker that an ORAM, but in fact an ORAM of size N can be constructed using only $\Theta(\log(N))$ OHTables through a recursive construction known as the "hierarchical solution", first introduced in [Ost90]. Assume we have access to a sub-ORAM of capacity $N/2$. The protocol then stores all N elements in a single OHTable, and each time an item is accessed, the item is cached in the sub-ORAM. When an item is queried, the sub-ORAM is queried first. If the item is not in the sub-ORAM, it has not been queried in the OHTable, so it can be queried in the OHTable and this will not be a repeated query into the OHTable. On the other hand, if the item is in the sub-ORAM, we must still query the OHTable, but in this case, we query random locations in the OHTable (independent of the client's query). This ensures that if the client makes at most $N/2$ queries, no element is ever queried twice in the OHTable, and the security of the OHTable is preserved. When the sub-ORAM becomes full, its contents can be extracted, as well as the contents of the OHTable, and the OHTable can be rebuilt, with new secret keys for the PRF/hash functions. If the sub-ORAM is implemented recursively, this results in $\Theta(\log(N))$ OHTables, and a small base-case. Typically we conceptualize the OHTables as arranged vertically in a "hierarchy" of levels of geometrically increasing size, labeled from Level 0, the base-case, also called the *cache*, to the largest level of size N. The cache could be of constant size, though it is often of size $\Theta(\log(N))$ and in our work is larger (of size $\Theta(\kappa) = \omega(\log N)$). Since the cache is very small it can be implemented using a less efficient "ORAM."

OMaps: Actually, the recursive construction requires the sub-ORAMs to be slightly more versatile than an ORAM. Notice that the sub-ORAM has capacity $N/2$ but may be required to store elements from the index space $[N]$. The ORAM definition requires the size of the ORAM to be the same size as the index space.

To implement the recursive hierarchical construction, the sub-ORAMs really need to implement an *Oblivious Map (OMAP)*. An OMap is essentially just an ORAM for storing key-value pairs instead of index-value pairs. The OMap functionality is defined formally in Fig. 3. Note that most existing ORAM protocols actually instantiate the slightly stronger OMap functionality.

Functionality $\mathcal{F}_{\mathsf{OMap}}$

$\mathcal{F}_{\mathsf{OMap}}.\mathbf{Init}(\llbracket X \rrbracket, \llbracket Y \rrbracket, w, n, N)$: Store (X_i, Y_i) in a dictionary for all $1 \leq i \leq w$, where $\mathrm{len}(X) = \mathrm{len}(Y) = w$.

$\mathcal{F}_{\mathsf{OMap}}.\mathbf{Query}(\llbracket x \rrbracket, \mathbf{res})$: If x is stored in the dictionary, store the corresponding value, y, as $\llbracket res \rrbracket$.
If x is not stored in the dictionary, store $\bot$ as $\llbracket res \rrbracket$.

$\mathcal{F}_{\mathsf{OMap}}.\mathbf{Add}(\llbracket x \rrbracket, \llbracket y \rrbracket)$: Store (x, y) in the dictionary (writing over an old value if need be).

$\mathcal{F}_{\mathsf{OMap}}.\mathbf{Extract}(\mathbf{res})$: Create array Z consisting of the key-value pairs from the dictionary, i.e. $Z_i = (X_i, Y_i)$ for some (X_i, Y_i) stored in the dictionary. Pad Z to length n with $(\bot, \bot)$. Shuffle Z randomly and store it as $\llbracket res \rrbracket$.

Fig. 3. OMap Functionality

Cuckoo Hashing: ORAMs and DORAMs often use Cuckoo Hashing [PR01] to implement OHTables (e.g. [PR10, GMOT12, LO13, KM19, PPRY18, AKL+20, FNO22].) In Cuckoo Hashing, there are 2 hash tables, and each item can be stored in one location in each table. This makes oblivious queries efficient. The hash output for each table can be revealed and both locations accessed. However, cuckoo hashing has a non-negligible failure probability. To alleviate this, items which are unable to be stored can be placed in a super-constant sized "stash".

Unfortunately, the cuckoo stash introduces some problems in the ORAM setting. To handle the cuckoo stashes, a standard approach to use a weaker OHTable which rejects a fixed number of stash elements, and store this stash in the sub-ORAM [KLO12]. There are two challenges with this approach. First, if the table is small (say $\Theta(\log(N))$), the probability of a build failure is no longer negligible in N. We address by making our smallest OHTable of size $\Theta(\kappa)$, thanks to our efficient QuietCache. The second problem is more subtle. The first time a stashed item is queried, it will always be found in the sub-ORAM, and random locations will be queried in the OHTable. This effectively resamples the locations that will be queried in the OHTables, which can leak information about whether the queried items were stored in the table. We use the Alibi technique [FNO21] to solve this. When a stash item is placed in the sub-ORAM during builds, it is tagged with a bit to show that the item should still be queried in the OHTable during a query. See Supplementary Material B for more details.

The Hierarchical Solution for DORAMs: *Distributed* ORAMs can also be built using the Hierarchical solution. Distributed Oblivious Hash Tables (DOHTables) are multi-party protocols that implement a dictionary data structure, subject to the fact that no adversarially-controlled subset of parties can learn anything about the query pattern from their views of the protocol, *provided each item is queried at most once*. Like before, we can cache responses of queries to a large DOHTable in a sub-DORAM and query the sub-DORAM first. If the item is not found in the sub-DORAM, the item is queried at the DOHTable; if it is found, the parties execute a protocol that is indistinguishable from a real, unique query to the DOHTable. By recursively implementing the sub-DORAMs using this technique, a DORAM can be constructed using $\Theta(\log(N))$ DOHTables.

Overview of Our Solution: One approach to building DORAM is to take an existing ORAM and simulate the client inside of a secure computation (e.g. [WCS15]). We depart from this approach, noting that DORAM actually allows for many efficiency improvements that would not be possible in a classic client-server ORAM. While DORAM has no trusted client, it does have multiple non-colluding servers which perform local computation and can communicate between each other. In particular, we examine the (3,1)-setting, where there are 3 servers and at most one corruption. This allows us to do many things more efficiently than in the client-server ORAM setting.

1. Efficient Shuffles: In the (3,1) setting, similar to [LWZ11] we can secret-share a list between 2 parties. These parties can then shuffle the list using a permutation known to them but not the third party. If this process is repeated 3 times, with parties taking turns to be the uninvolved party, the final permutation will be unknown to all parties. This allows us to shuffle n items of size D with $\Theta(nD)$ communication and small constants.

While this protocol is simple, its significance can be appreciated when compared to the difficulty of shuffling in the classical ORAM setting. In that setting, shuffling n items requires $\Theta(n \log(n)D)$ communication with huge constants, or $\Theta(n \log^2(n)D)$ communication with small constants. A core insight of recent ORAM protocols [PPRY18, AKLS21] is that full shuffles can be avoided by re-using randomness and using oblivious tight compaction instead of shuffles. This brings the cost down to $\Theta(nD)$ but the constants are still impractical [DO20].

2. Efficient multi-select: In the (3, 1) setting, it is possible to evaluate circuits of AND-depth 1 with communication equal to that of a single AND gate. Using this, we can construct an efficient multi-select protocol. That is, given n secret-shared items of size D, we can efficient select the kth item for any secret-shared $k \in [n]$ with only $\Theta(n + D)$ communication. (See Sect. 6 for more details.) To the best of our knowledge, efficient multi-selects have not been used to build DORAMs prior to our work.

3. Separating Builders from Holders: In the classical ORAM setting, the server can see the access patterns during both builds and queries to an OHTable. This creates a problem: for efficiency the possible locations in which an item may be stored are revealed during a query. To ensure security, the build must *obliviously* move each item to its correct location. In the $(3, 1)$ setting we can instead have a single party, the *builder*, learn the locations in which items in the table may be stored. This allows the builder to *locally and non-obliviously* calculate the allocation of items to locations. After this, the table is secret-shared between the other 2 parties, called the *holders*. During a query, the holders (but not the builder) learn the locations in which the queried item may be stored and return their shares of the items in these locations. Since the adversary controls at most one party, it can either learn the physical locations of stored items (from the builder) or the potential physical locations of queried items (from a holder) but not both, preventing it from learning information about whether the queried items were stored in the table. (Our actual protocol, in fact allows the builder to construct a useful data-structure for set queries entirely by itself, and secret-share this to the holders. This is then used to build a DOHTable.)

However, in the malicious setting it is difficult to take advantage of these techniques, especially the technique of separating builders from holders. If the builder is malicious, how can we ensure that they build data structures correctly? Naturally, zero knowledge proofs allow the builder to prove any claim, but how can it do so efficiently? Furthermore, after we secret-share the data-structure between two holders, how can we guarantee that they provide the correct shares during reconstruction? (We can use a $(3,1)$ replicated secret sharing (Sect. 2) to detect modification of shares when all three parties are involved, but this will not work with only 2 parties.) Similarly, the multi-select and shuffle protocols described above are only secure against semi-honest adversaries.

Core Contributions: In this paper, we show how to take advantage of the existence of multiple non-colluding servers even when one of these parties is malicious. The primary techniques are as follows:

- **Proving in zero-knowledge a distributed statement that builder built data structures correctly:** We present a method by which it can be efficiently verified that the builder has built and secret shared their data structure correctly to the two holders without revealing any information to the holders. Our method is linear in the data-structure size and has small constants.
- **Designing QuietCache and restructuring the DORAM hierarchy:** We present a more efficient distributed, oblivious, maliciously-secure cache protocol, QuietCache (Sect. 6), which serves as a top level of our DORAM hierarchy. Querying the standard cache used in the literature when it stores n elements costs $O((n + D) \log N)$ communication. For works targeting the best-known complexity of $O((\kappa + D) \log N)$, this has restricted the size of the cache to $O(\log N)$. Since Cuckoo Hash Tables with a Stash (CHTwS) of $\Theta(\log N)$ elements have non-negligible failure probability and, generally speaking, all efficient-to-query OHTables are based on CHTwS, previous constructions had to design a different type of OHTable for small levels (e.g. [LO13, FNO22]). Unfortunately, we find that a small size maliciously secure

OHTables are difficult to construct. To resolve this, we design QuietCache, which costs $O(n \log N + D)$ communication to query. This allows us to have a large cache (of size $\Theta(\kappa) = \omega(\log N)$), thus completely avoiding the need for small OHTables.

- **Mixing Boolean and $\mathbb{F}_{2^l}$** *secret-sharings:* Our solutions to the above require a combination of large-field arithmetic (for MACs and polynomial equality checks) and bit-wise operations (for equality tests and PRFs). We therefore require efficient methods of converting between these two types of secret-sharing: by using the field $\mathbb{F}_{2^l}$ we can actually convert between these two types of sharing for free.

In addition, we design an expanded, versatile Arithmetic Black Box (Sect. 5), and prove it UC-secure against a $(3, 1)$ malicious adversary. This greatly simplifies our later protocol descriptions and proofs.

5   The Arithmetic Black Box (ABB) Model

In order to simplify our protocol descriptions and analysis we use the Arithmetic Black Box (ABB) model. In the words of its creators an "ABB can be thought of as a secure general-purpose computer" [DN03]. The ABB is a reactive functionality that allows secret data to be "stored" and allows other functionalities to compute on secret data. This will be implemented by the stored values being secret-shared between parties, but the ABB will extract away these details. Most functionalities will take as inputs (public) identifiers to secret variables already stored in the ABB and output (public) identifiers to secret variables added to the ABB. For instance $[\![z]\!] = [\![x]\!] + [\![y]\!]$ indicates that secret variables x and y are already stored in the ABB, their sum is computed securely, and the sum is stored in the ABB under the name z.

We use bit-wise RSS as the underlying secret-sharing scheme for the ABB. Boolean operations (AND, OR, NOT) are achieved using [FLNW17], and denoted using standard infix operators $(\vee, \wedge, \neg)$. For any field $\mathbb{F}_{2^l}$ $l \in \mathbb{Z}^+$ we support the addition (bitwise XOR) and multiplication using [CGH+18]. Both of these are $(3, 1)$ UC-maliciously secure protocols. Since we use RSS, we can

Table 2. Communication costs of ABB operations.

ABB operation(s)	Communication (bits)
Input(x, P_i)/Output($[\![x]\!]$, P_i)/Mult($[\![x]\!]$, $[\![y]\!]$)	$\Theta(|x|)$
RandomElement(ℓ)/Add($[\![x]\!]$, $[\![y]\!]$)/NOT($[\![x]\!]$)	0
OR($[\![x]\!]$, $[\![y]\!]$)/AND($[\![x]\!]$, $[\![y]\!]$)	$\Theta(1)$
Equal($[\![x]\!]$, $[\![y]\!]$)/IfThenElse($[\![b]\!]$, $[\![x]\!]$, $[\![y]\!]$)	$\Theta(|x|)$
CreateMAC($[\![x]\!]$)/ CheckMAC($[\![x]\!]$)/PRFEval($[\![x]\!]$, $[\![k]\!]$)	$\Theta(|x| + \kappa)$
ReplicatedTo2Sharing($[\![x]\!]$, i, j, varName^{i,j})	$\Theta(|x|)$
2SharingToReplicated($[x^{i,j}]^{(i,j)}$, varName)	$\Theta(|x|)$
ObliviousShuffle($[\![X]\!]$) $(X \in (\{0,1\}^\ell)^n)$	$\Theta(n\ell)$
SilentDotProduct($[\![X]\!]$, $[\![Y]\!]$, $[\![M]\!]$) $(X, Y \in (\{0,1\}^\ell)^n$	$\Theta(\ell + \kappa)$

actually switch between viewing an element as a string of bits and as a field element at no cost.

We extend the ABB to support various functionalities. The full ABB is presented in Fig. 4, with costs shown in Table 2. In Supplemental Material C, we show how all of these functionalities are instantiated. Of note, we add functionalities that allow conversion to a 2-sharing. In the context of the ABB, this means that the variable names are no longer public, but are known to only 2 parties. This, for instance, allows them to access an element of a secret array using an index known to them, but not the third party. This is critical in allowing the Holders to store and access data without the Builder learning the accessed locations.

6   QuietCache: Maliciously-Secure Oblivious Cache Construction

In this section, we design a novel, distributed, oblivious, "cache" protocol which we will use to instantiate the topmost level of our hierarchy.

Unlike the OHTables at all other levels of the hierarchy, the cache must allow items to be queried more than once, since there is no smaller level to which an item may be moved. Furthermore, it should allow new items to be added without requiring an expensive rebuild process. We formalize the functionality that the cache must satisfy as Functionality $\mathcal{F}_{\mathsf{OMap}}$, (Fig. 3).

In similar works, the cache is often instantiated by executing a linear-scan under MPC [FNO22] this has append complexity $O(1)$ and query complexity $O((D + \log N)c)$ where c is the number of elements in the cache.

There is a fundamental tension here regarding the size of the cache. Since every (D)ORAM query accesses the cache, performing a linear scan of the cache adds $\Omega((D + \log N)c)$ to the (D)ORAM query complexity. When $c = \Omega(\log N)$, querying the cache becomes the bottleneck for the entire (D)ORAM protocol, so most (D)ORAM protocols set $c = O(1)$. Unfortunately, there are multiple problems with a small cache. First, the "cache-the-stash" technique requires a cache of at least size $\Omega(\log(N))$. Second, small cuckoo hash tables always have a non-negligible probability of build failure [Nob21], and when the cache (L_0) is small, so are the smaller levels in the hierarchy ($L_1, L_2, \ldots$) For this reason, many hierarchical (D)ORAM protocols (e.g. [LO13]) are forced to use different types of tables for the smaller levels of the (D)ORAM hierarchy.

We resolve this tension by designing a novel, distributed, oblivious cache protocol $\Pi_{\mathsf{QuietCache}}$ that allows us to increase c to $c = \kappa = \omega(\log N)$, while still maintaining efficient access to the cache. Notably, our protocol requires $O(\max D, \kappa)$ communication to store a new item and $O(D + n \log N)$ communication to query an item. This will mean that our smallest OHTables will be of size $\Omega(\kappa) = \omega(\log(N))$, allowing them to instantiate cuckoo hash tables with a stash with at most negligible build failure negligible in N, as required.

Our protocol, $\Pi_{\mathsf{QuietCache}}$ works as follows. The protocol maintains an array of all items that have been added (either during initialization or later), with

---

Functionality $\mathcal{F}_{ABB}$

Inputs and outputs are in $\mathbb{F}_{2^l}$ for various $l \in \mathbb{Z}$. All functionalities allow the adversary to abort the protocol, seeing their outputs first if applicable.

$\mathcal{F}_{ABB1}$: Basic ABB Functionalities

Input(x, P_i): Receive x from party P and return $[\![x]\!]$.
RandomElement(l): Sample $x \in_R \mathbb{F}_{2^l}$, return $[\![x]\!]$.
OR($[\![x]\!]$, $[\![y]\!]$): For $x, y \in \mathbb{F}_2$, compute $z = x \vee y$. Return $[\![z]\!]$.
Add($[\![x]\!]$, $[\![y]\!]$): Compute $z = x + y$ and return $[\![z]\!]$.
Mult($[\![x]\!]$, $[\![y]\!]$): Compute $z = x * y$ and return $[\![z]\!]$.
Output($[\![z]\!]$, P_i): Output z to P_i.

$\mathcal{F}_{ABB2}$: Circuit-based Operations

Equal($[\![x]\!]$, $[\![y]\!]$): If $x \overset{?}{=} y$ set z to 1, otherwise to 0. Return $[\![z]\!]$.
IfThenElse($[\![b]\!]$, $[\![x]\!]$, $[\![y]\!]$): If $b \overset{?}{=} 1$, set z to x, otherwise set z to y. Return $[\![z]\!]$.
CreateMAC($[\![x]\!]$): Create a "tag," τ, on the data X, and return $[\![\tau]\!]$.
CheckMAC($[\![x]\!]$, $[\![\tau]\!]$): If τ is a valid tag on the message, x, return $[\![1]\!]$, otherwise return $[\![0]\!]$.
PRFEval($[\![x]\!]$, $[\![k]\!]$): Compute $z = \text{PRF}_k(x)$, a pseudorandom function on input x over key $k \in \mathbb{F}_{2^\kappa}$. Return $[\![z]\!]$.

$\mathcal{F}_{ABB3}$: Sharing to and from a 2-sharing

ReplicatedTo2Sharing($[\![x]\!]$, i, j, varName^{i,j}): Given a handle, varName, known to (distinct) P_i and P_j, store x as $[varName]^{(i,j)}$
2SharingToReplicated($[x^{i,j}]^{(i,j)}$, varName): Given a handle, $x^{i,j}$, known to (distinct) P_i and P_j, for a variable stored in $[x]^{(i,j)}$ and a public handle, varName, store $x^{i,j}$ in $[\![varName]\!]$

$\mathcal{F}_{ABB4}$: Specialized Functionalities

ObliviousShuffle($[\![X]\!]$): Let $X = X_0, \ldots, X_{n-1}$. Sample a random (secret) permutation $\pi \in_R S_n$ and return $[\![\pi(X)]\!] = [\![\pi(X_0)]\!], \ldots, [\![\pi(X_l)]\!]$. This naturally allows multiple arrays of the same length to be shuffled using the same secret shuffle, by combining elements at the same index from different arrays, shuffling, then separating the elements into their original arrays. We denote this by ObliviousShuffle having multiple inputs and outputs.
SilentDotProduct($[\![X]\!]$, $[\![Y]\!]$, $[\![M]\!]$): $X = X_0, \ldots, X_{n-1}$, $Y = Y_0, \ldots, Y_{n-1}$. $M_i = \alpha Y_i$ for all $0 \leq i \leq n-1$. Compute $z = \sum_{i=0}^{n-1} X_i Y_i$ and return $[\![z]\!]$.

Fig. 4. Arithmetic Black Box functionality.

Protocol $\Pi_{\text{QuietCache}}$

Hybrids: The protocol is defined in the $\mathcal{F}_{\text{ABB}}$-hybrid model.

$\Pi_{\text{QuietCache}}.\textbf{Init}([\![X]\!], [\![Y]\!], w, n, N)$:

1. Store arrays $[\![X]\!]$ and $[\![Y]\!]$.
2. Initialize counter t to w.
3. Initialize MACs for all elements. For $i \in [w]$: $[\![M_i]\!] = \mathcal{F}_{\text{ABB}}.\text{CreateMAC}([\![Y_i]\!])$

$\Pi_{\text{QuietCache}}.\textbf{Store}([\![x]\!], [\![y]\!])$:

1. Increment t.
2. Set $[\![X_t]\!] = [\![x]\!]$, $[\![Y_t]\!] = [\![y]\!]$.
3. Create MAC for new value: $[\![M_t]\!] = \mathcal{F}_{\text{ABB}}.\text{CreateMAC}([\![y]\!])$

$\Pi_{\text{QuietCache}}.\textbf{Query}([\![X]\!], \text{outName})$:

1. First create a t-bit indicator array, $[\![b]\!]$ which shows the index of the copy of $[\![x]\!]$ that was most recently stored (or the all-zero vector if $[\![x]\!]$ has never been stored).
   (a) For $i = t, \ldots, 1$
      i. $[\![isMatch_i]\!] = \mathcal{F}_{\text{ABB}}.\text{Equal}([\![X_i]\!], [\![X]\!])$
      ii. $[\![isBeforeMatch_i]\!] = [\![isBeforeMatch_{i+1}]\!] \vee [\![isMatch_{i+1}]\!]$ (Except that $[\![isBeforeMatch_t]\!] = 0$)
      iii. $[\![b_i]\!] = [\![isMatch_i]\!] \wedge (\neg [\![isBeforeMatch_i]\!])$
2. Then efficiently select the item based on this indicator array using $\mathcal{F}_{\text{ABB}}.\text{SilentDotProduct}$:
   (a) $[\![y]\!] = \mathcal{F}_{\text{ABB}}.\text{SilentDotProduct}(([\![b_i]\!]^D)_{i=1}^t, [\![Y_i]\!]_{i=1}^t, [\![M_i]\!]_{i=1}^t)$
   (b) Return $[\![y]\!]$.

$\Pi_{\text{QuietCache}}.\textbf{Extract}()$:

1. For every index, x, set all but the latest copy of (x, y) to $(\bot, \bot)$. For $i = 1, \ldots, t$:
   (a) $[\![\hat{X}]\!]_i = [\![X]\!]_i$, $[\![\hat{Y}]\!]_i = [\![Y]\!]_i$
   (b) For $i < j \leq t$:
      i. $[\![b_{ij}]\!] = \mathcal{F}_{\text{ABB}}.\text{Equal}([\![X_i]\!], [\![X_j]\!])$
      ii. $([\![\hat{X}_i]\!], [\![\hat{Y}_i]\!]) = \mathcal{F}_{\text{ABB}}.\text{IfThenElse}([\![b_{ij}]\!], ([\![\bot]\!], [\![\bot]\!]), ([\![\hat{X}_i]\!], [\![\hat{Y}_i]\!]))$
2. Shuffle items and return the result:
   (a) $[\![\hat{X}]\!], [\![\hat{Y}]\!] = \mathcal{F}_{\text{ABB}}.\text{ObliviousShuffle}([\![\hat{X}]\!], [\![\hat{Y}]\!])$
   (b) Return $[\![\hat{X}]\!], [\![\hat{Y}]\!]$.

Fig. 5. $\Pi_{\text{QuietCache}}$: Protocol for the cache (implementation of smallest $\mathcal{F}_{\text{OMap}}$).

items that were added later appearing later in the array. When a new item is added, $\Pi_{\text{QuietCache}}$ does not attempt to delete the old item, but merely places the new item at the end of the array to indicate it is newer. Authentication tags are also added to values each time an item is inserted, which will later allow for efficient queries. To query, we perform a linear scan of the indices, but not the values. We create a bit-array that is 1 in the location of the array where the index was most recently added (if any) and 0 elsewhere. Since the values are all authenticated, we can use our bit-array to very efficiently access the correct value using $\mathcal{F}_{\text{ABB}}$.SilentDotProduct (Fig. 4). In the honest-majority 3-party setting, this is very efficient and has essentially the same cost as a single multiplication. Leveraging the silent dot product is the key trick which enables $\Pi_{\text{QuietCache}}$'s efficiency. Finally, when items need to be extracted we need to delete old copies of items. We do this using a brute-force check under MPC.

We now show that $\Pi_{\text{QuietCache}}$ implements $\mathcal{F}_{\text{OMap}}$ securely.

Proposition 1. *Against a static malicious adversary controlling at most one party out of three, Protocol $\Pi_{\text{QuietCache}}$ (Fig. 5) UC-realizes functionality $\mathcal{F}_{\text{QuietCache}}$ (Fig. 5) with abort in the $\mathcal{F}_{\text{ABB}}$-hybrid model.*

The proof of Proposition 1 is in Appendix G.1. In Appendix H.1 we prove that:

Proposition 2. *The communication complexity of $\Pi_{\text{QuietCache}}$.Init, $\Pi_{\text{QuietCache}}$. Store, $\Pi_{\text{QuietCache}}$.Query, $\Pi_{\text{QuietCache}}$.Extract is $\Theta(\kappa w), O(\max D, \kappa), O(D + n \log N), O(n^2 \log N + nD)$, respectively.*

7   Maliciously-Secure Oblivious Set Construction

At a high level, our DORAM has a hierarchy of Oblivious Hash Tables (OHTables), one in each level. It was observed by [MZ14] that once it is known whether an item is in a given level, it is much easier to access it obliviously. We therefore adopt the approach of [FNO22] to first have a protocol exclusively to securely determine whether the item exists at a given level. We call such a protocol a *Distributed Oblivious Set* or OSet and we implement (a variant of) this functionality in this section. In the next section (Sect. 8) we use this as a sub-protocol to build (a variant of) an OHTable.

At a high level, Π_{OSet} obtains efficiency by separating the players into the roles of "builder" and "holders" [LO13,FNO22]. The Builder constructs a data structure locally, which is secret-shared between two Holders. The Builder can learn information about where data is stored in the data structure during a build, while the Holders can learn the locations that queried items may be located during queries. If an adversary can only corrupt a single party it therefore is unable to use this information to learn whether queried items are stored in the table.

There are two major challenges with this approach. The first is achieving *privacy*. The Builder must somehow build the data structures based on knowledge of the *locations* of items, without learning any information about the items

---

Functionality $\mathcal{F}_{\text{OSet}}$

$\mathcal{F}_{\text{OSet}}$.**Build**($[\![X]\!]$, n, N, **stash**): X is an array of n distinct items, each chosen from $[N]$, which is stored in the ABB. Set $s = \log(N)$. It is assumed that $n = \omega(s)$.

1. Let S be an arbitrary bit array of length n, with s ones and $n - s$ zeros.
2. Store S in $[\![stash]\!]$ in the ABB.

$\mathcal{F}_{\text{OSet}}$.**Query**($[\![x]\!]$, **res**):

1. If $x \in \{X_i\}_{i \in [n] \setminus S}$, then set $z = 1$, otherwise set $z = 0$. That is, set z to 1 iff x is one of the $n - s$ elements that are stored.
2. Store z in $[\![res]\!]$ in the ABB.

Protocol Π_{OSet}

Hybrids: $\mathcal{F}_{\text{ABB}}, \mathcal{F}_{\text{ZKPOfValidCHT}}$.
Π_{OSet}.**Build**($[\![X]\!]$, n, N, **stash**):

1. Set public parameters for the Cuckoo Hash Table. Table size $c = 2^{\lfloor \log_2(3n) \rfloor}$, stash size $s = \log N$, and hash functions

$$h_0(x) \stackrel{\text{def}}{=} 0 \parallel x[0 : \log(c) - 1] \tag{1}$$

$$h_1(x) \stackrel{\text{def}}{=} 1 \parallel x[\log(c) : 2\log(c) - 1] \tag{2}$$

2. Generate a secret-shared PRF key: $[\![k]\!] = \mathcal{F}_{\text{ABB}}.\text{RandomEl}(\kappa)$.
3. Evaluate the SISO-PRF on inputs: $[\![Q_i]\!] = \mathcal{F}_{\text{ABB}}.\text{PRF}([\![X_i]\!], [\![k]\!])$ for $i \in [n]$.
4. Reveal PRF evaluations to P_0: $Q = \mathcal{F}_{\text{ABB}}.\text{Reveal}([\![Q]\!], \{0\})$
5. P_0 locally builds a CHTwS of the PRF evaluations $\text{CHT} \cup \text{Stash} = \{\text{CHT}, (i_1, \ldots, i_s)\} = \text{BuildCHTwS}(\tilde{Q}, h_0, h_1)$
6. Define the vector $S \in \{0, 1\}^n$, and set $S_i = 1$ if $i \in \{i_1, \ldots, i_s\}$.
7. P_0 secret shares the CHT and the stash bit-array:
   (a) $[\![\text{CHT}]\!] = \mathcal{F}_{\text{ABB}}.\text{Input}(\text{CHT}, 0)$.
   (b) $[\![stash]\!] = \mathcal{F}_{\text{ABB}}.\text{Input}(S, 0)$.
8. Verify that there are s stash elements, and remove these:
   (a) $[\![\hat{Q}]\!], [\![\hat{S}]\!] = \mathcal{F}_{\text{ABB}}.\text{ObliviousShuffle}([\![Q]\!], [\![S]\!])$
   (b) For all $i \in [n]$, $\hat{S}_i = \mathcal{F}_{\text{ABB}}.\text{Output}([\![\hat{S}_i]\!])$
   (c) If there are exactly s values in $\hat{S}_i$ set to 1 continue, else abort.
   (d) $[\![\tilde{Q}]\!] = \{[\![\hat{Q}_i]\!]\}_{\hat{S}_i = 0}$.
9. Verify that P_0 built and shared a *valid* CHT on the non-stash elements:
   (a) $[\![b]\!] = \mathcal{F}_{\text{ZKPOfValidCHT}}.\textbf{Verify}([\![\tilde{Q}]\!], [\![\text{CHT}]\!], c, h_0, h_1, \log(N))$
   (b) $b = \mathcal{F}_{\text{ABB}}.\text{Reveal}([\![b]\!])$. Abort if not b.
10. Secret-share the CHT to P_1 and P_2:
    $[\text{CHT}]^{(1,2)} = \mathcal{F}_{\text{ABB}}.\text{ReplicatedTo2Sharing}([\![\text{CHT}]\!], \{1, 2\})$.

Π_{OSet}.**Query**($[\![x]\!]$, **res**):

1. $[\![q]\!] = \mathcal{F}_{\text{ABB}}.\text{PRFEval}([\![x]\!], [\![k]\!])$.
2. $q = \mathcal{F}_{\text{ABB}}.\text{Reveal}([\![q]\!], \{1, 2\})$
3. P_1 and P_2 access the locations in the CHT which may store q and re-share their contents without revealing the locations to P_0:

$$[\![Q_b^*]\!] = \mathcal{F}_{\text{ABB}}.\text{2SharingToReplicated}([\text{CHT}[h_b(q)]]^{(1,2)}) \text{ for } b \in \{0, 1\}$$

4. $[\![res]\!] = \mathcal{F}_{\text{ABB}}.\text{Equal}([\![q]\!], [\![Q_0^*]\!]) \vee \mathcal{F}_{\text{ABB}}.\text{Equal}([\![q]\!], [\![Q_1^*]\!])$

Fig. 6. $\mathcal{F}_{\text{OSet}}$ and Π_{OSet}: Functionality and Protocol for a Distributed Oblivious Partial Set

---

Functionality $\mathcal{F}_{\text{ZKPOfValidCHT}}$

$\mathcal{F}_{\text{ZKPOfValidCHT}}.\textbf{Verify}([\![X]\!],\ [\![CHT]\!],\ c,\ h_0,\ h_1,\ \ell,\ \textbf{varName})$:

X is an array of length n of unique elements from $\{0,1\}^\ell$, stored in the ABB.
CHT is an array of length $2c$ of elements from $\{0,1\}^\ell \bigcup \{\bot\}$, stored in the ABB.
$h_0, h_1 : 2^\ell \to \{0,\ldots,c-1\}$ are two public hash functions.
If CHT stores X and $2c - n$ copies of $\bot$ the CHT stores exactly the correct set.
If for every $CHT_i \neq \bot$, $h_0(CHT_i) = i$ or $h_1(CHT_1) = i + c$, the stored items are
in the correct positions. If either condition is false, set $z = 0$, otherwise set $z = 1$.
Store z in the ABB under handle varName.

Protocol $\Pi_{\text{ZKPOfValidCHT}}$

$\Pi_{\text{ZKPOfValidCHT}}.\text{Verify}([\![X]\!],\ [\![CHT]\!],\ c,\ h_0,\ h_1,\ S,\ \text{varName})$:

1. Check CHT holds correct set using Multi-Set Polynomial Check.
   (a) Append $2c - n$ copies of $[\![\bot]\!]$ to array $[\![X]\!]$.
   (b) Represent $[\![X]\!]$ and $[\![CHT]\!]$ as items from $GF(2^l)$, where $l = \max\{S + 1, \sigma + \log(2c)\}$. Specifically, represent $\bot$ as 0^ℓ and add the prefix $1||O^{\ell-S-1}$ to all real elements.
   (c) Pick a random evaluation point for the polynomial:
   $[\![w]\!] = \mathcal{F}_{\text{ABB}}.\text{RandomElement}(\kappa)$
   (d) Using $\mathcal{F}_{\text{ABB}}.\text{Mult}$ and $\mathcal{F}_{\text{ABB}}.\text{Add}$, securely evaluate the polynomial for the input elements (with copies of $\bot$):

   $$[\![u]\!] = \prod_{[\![a]\!] \in [\![X]\!]} ([\![a]\!] - [\![w]\!])$$

   (e) Likewise evaluate the polynomial for the contents of the CHT:

   $$[\![v]\!] = \prod_{[\![b]\!] \in [\![CHT]\!]} ([\![b]\!] - [\![w]\!])$$

   (f) Check that the evaluations are the same:
   $[\![check_1]\!] = \mathcal{F}_{\text{ABB}}.\text{Equal}([\![u]\!], [\![v]\!])$

2. Verify CHT locations are either empty ($\bot$) or are real items in a valid position.
   (a) For all $i \in \{0,\ldots,2c-1\}$
      i. $[\![empty_i]\!] = \mathcal{F}_{\text{ABB}}.\text{Equal}(CHT_i, \bot)$
      ii. $[\![eq_{0,i}]\!] = \mathcal{F}_{\text{ABB}}.\text{Equal}(i, h_0(CHT_i))$
      iii. $[\![eq_{1,i}]\!] = \mathcal{F}_{\text{ABB}}.\text{Equal}(i, h_1(CHT_i))$
      iv. Using $\mathcal{F}_{\text{ABB}}.\text{OR}$ securely evaluate

   $$[\![b_i]\!] = [\![empty_i]\!] \vee [\![eq_{0,i}]\!] \vee [\![eq_{1,i}]\!]$$

   (b) Using $\mathcal{F}_{\text{ABB}}.\text{AND}$ evaluate

   $$[\![check_2]\!] = \bigwedge_{i \in \{0,\ldots,2c-1\}} [\![b_i]\!]$$

3. Set $[\![varName]\!] = \mathcal{F}_{\text{ABB}}.\text{OR}(check_1, check_2)$

Fig. 7. $\mathcal{F}_{\text{ZKPOfValidCHT}}$ and $\Pi_{\text{ZKPOfValidCHT}}$: Functionality and Protocol for verifying in zero knowledge the correctness of a Cuckoo Hash Table.

themselves. The second is ensuring *correctness*. In the malicious setting, there must be a method to verify that the Builder constructed data structures correctly. If the Builder were to place an item in the incorrect location, the protocol would not find the item during queries.

We address the privacy challenge by storing pseudorandom "tags" (based on a PRF applied each item) rather than the items themselves. We evaluate the PRF inside of the ABB, so only the PRF output is revealed to the Builder. The security of the PRF guarantees that no information about the items themselves is leaked by their outputs. It also guarantees that collisions occur with negligible probability, so an item will be in the set only if its PRF is in the set of PRF evaluations (except with negligible probability).

We address the correctness challenge by the protocol proving, in zero-knowledge, that the data structure which the Builder constructed and shared is a valid Cuckoo Hash Table of the underlying data. First, we must prove that the set of items in the table is equal to the set of items that should be there. We prove this using a multi-set polynomial equality test. Second, we must prove that each item is in a correct location. This is done by evaluating the hash functions on each item in the table ensuring that the table location matches one of these hash functions. While we will describe our verification protocol in terms of general hash functions, in our case, since the item is itself the output of a PRF, it actually suffices for our "hash functions" to simply be bit-truncations of the items. This is very efficient: the bit-truncation itself requires no communication, after which we can evaluate a standard circuit for an equality test.

Note that we verify the first property using polynomials over large fields whereas we verify the second property using bitwise operations. We can do this efficiently due to the fact that we represent data in the field $\mathbb{F}_{2^\ell}$, which is also a valid Boolean sharing (i.e., over $\mathbb{F}_2^\ell$) (see Appendix C.1). This allows us to convert between these sharings for free. We therefore cast the data as a field for efficient polynomial evaluation, while casting it as a Boolean array for efficient bit-wise equality testing.

One final challenge in constructing our OSet is handling the stash. We will use Cuckoo Hashing with a Stash in order to ensure that the build failure probability is negligible. However, for efficiency, the stashed items will not be part of the OSet (or OHTable), but will instead be inserted into a sub-DOMap. As such, we will not implement a full Oblivious Set storing all n items, but a Distributed Oblivious Partial-Set storing $n - s$ of the n items, and rejecting the s items in the stash. However, allowing the stash to leave the protocol/functionality is risky. If information about which queries correspond to stashed items is leaked, this breaks the obliviousness of queries. For instance, the locations of stashed elements necessary collide with elements that were stored in the OSet. This means that if a Holder is corrupted and the environment knows some queries that correspond to stashed elements, it can conclude that any other query that accesses the same locations is more likely to have been a member of the set. This coin has another side to it: if the environment can *influence* the probability of a stashed item being queried compared to a stored item it can likewise cause the accesses to be dependent. (This is exploited for instance by the Alibi attack (Appendix B) where stash items are never queried, which leaks information about whether the other queried items were in the set.) Our OSet functionality will therefore have the limitation that no information about the stash leaves the ABB *outside the protocol*, and the calls to build do not depend on which items were stashed (even conditioned on ABB-revealed values) to avoid leaking information *inside the protocol*.

Our OSet also has the limitation that it is only secure if queries are never repeated. Furthermore, we will need to limit the number of queries to the OSet data structure. We will later show that the uses of our OSet by the larger protocol obey all these restrictions. These restrictions are formalized in the following conditions:

Condition 1 (No Repeats). *For all x, $Query([\![x]\!], res)$ is called at most once.*

Condition 2 (Limited Queries). *Query is called at most n times.*

Condition 3 (ABB-Stash Independence). *Let $stash_1$, $stash_2$ be two different possible values of stash. The distribution of all outputs of the ABB by the environment when $stash = stash_1$ must be computationally indistinguishable from the distribution when $stash = stash_2$.*

Condition 4 (Query-Stash Independence). *Let stash be the output of the Build. If $x = X_i$ for any $i \in [n]$, the probability that $Query(x, res)$ occurs/occurred, conditioned on any values revealed by $\mathcal{F}_{ABB}$ either before or after, is computationally indistinguishable from independent of $stash_i$.*

Our OSet functionality and protocol are presented in Fig. 6. This makes use of our functionality for verifying, in zero-knowledge, that the Builder (P_0) correctly constructed the Cuckoo Hash table (on the non-stash elements). This functionality, and the protocol that implements it, are presented in Fig. 7. We now prove that these protocols correctly implement the desired functionalities.

Proposition 3. *Protocol $\Pi_{ZKPOfValidCHT}$ statistically UC-securely implements $\mathcal{F}_{ZKPOfValidCHT}$ in the $\mathcal{F}_{ABB}$-hybrid model.*

Proof. Note that this protocol makes no assumptions about the parties or the adversary setting, as all operations are exclusively within the ABB. It inherits whichever security the ABB is implemented with. Implementing with our ABB from Fig. 4 yields a 3-party protocol with statistical UC-security with abort against a malicious adversary statically corrupting one party. Also, note that this protocol and functionality provide no guarantees that CHT was chosen uniformly at random from the set of valid CHTs for X, only that it was one such valid CHT.

By Corollary 1, since $\Pi_{ZKPOfValidCHT}$ does not reveal any values, it suffices to prove that the output stored in the ABB is correct (except with negligible probability).

Let $f(x) = \Pi_{[\![a]\!]\in[\![X]\!]}([\![a]\!]-x)-\Pi_{[\![b]\!]\in[\![CHT]\!]}([\![b]\!]-x)$. If $[\![X]\!]$ and $[\![CHT]\!]$ contain the same multiset, then $f(x)$ will be the zero polynomial. Otherwise, it will be a non-zero polynomial of degree at most $2c$. In this case, by the Schwartz-Zippel Lemma, the probability that $f(x)$ evaluates to 0 on a point chosen randomly from $GF(2^\ell)$ is at most $\frac{2c}{2^\ell}$, which is at most $2^{-\sigma}$. Note that $u = v$ if and only if $f(w) = 0$, where w was chosen randomly from $GF(2^\ell)$. Therefore $check_1 = 1$ if and only if $[\![X]\!] = [\![CHT]\!]$, except with negligible probability.

Now we examine the part of the $\Pi_{\text{ZKPOfValidCHT}}$ that verifies that items are in the correct locations. If $check_1 = 1$, every item in X is in the table (except with negligible probability). Assuming this is true, if every item is stored in a correct location, $check_2$ will evaluate to 1, otherwise it will evaluate to 0. (If $check_1 = 0$, then it does not matter what $check_2$ evaluates to as $varName$ will be set to 0.) Therefore $varName$ will be set to 1 if, and only if, all items in X are stored in CHT at a correct location.

We now prove that Π_{OSet} realizes $\mathcal{F}_{\text{OSet}}$ subject to our conditions:

Proposition 4. *Against a static malicious adversary controlling at most one party out of three and an environment satisfying Conditions 1, 2, 3 and 4 Protocol Π_{OSet} (Fig. 6) statistically (with failure probability negligible in N) realizes functionality $\mathcal{F}_{OSet}$ (Fig. 6) with abort in the $\mathcal{F}_{ABB}, \mathcal{F}_{ZKPOfValidCHT}$-hybrid model.*

The proof of Proposition 4 is in Appendix G.2. In Appendix H.2 we prove that:

Proposition 5. *$\Pi_{OSet}.Build$ has complexity $O(n(\kappa+D))$ and $\Pi_{OSet}.Query$ has complexity $O(\kappa)$.*

8 Maliciously-Secure Oblivious Hash Table Construction

In this section, we build a Distributed Oblivious Hash Table (OHTable) using the OSet protocol outlined in Sect. 7. The OHTable is a protocol for securely mapping indices to values provided each item is only queried once.

The purpose of the OSet is to check whether the item being queried is in the domain of the Hash Table. If so, the item will be accessed in the ABB based on a public tag (which is a PRF evaluation of the index). If not, a pre-inserted dummy item will be accessed based on its public tag (which is a PRF evaluation of a counter). The real items and pre-inserted dummies are shuffled prior to the tags being revealed, hiding which items are real.

The OHTable's Query function will also provide a way to do a no-op query that is indistinguishable from a real query. This will be critical in ensuring the no-repeats condition is satisfied: when the DORAM is queried multiple times for an item, it will query the item in the OHTable the first time and henceforth will ask the OHTable to perform a no-op query. Additionally, our OHTable supports an Extract functionality which returns (in the ABB) an array of the items which were not queried (padded to length n with copies of $(\bot, \bot)$).

Functionality $\mathcal{F}_{\text{OHTable}}$

Build($([\![X]\!],[\![Y]\!]$, n, N, X^{stash}, Y^{stash}):
X is an array of n distinct elements from $[N]$. Y is an array of n elements of
length D bits. Let $s = \log(N)$. An arbitrary array of s distinct items from X, and
their corresponding values from Y are stored in the ABB under handles X^{stash}
and Y^{stash} respectively.

Query($[\![x]\!]$, res):
$x \in [N] \cup \{\perp\}$. If $\exists j \in [n]; x = X_j$ and $x \notin X^{\text{stash}}$, set $z = [\![Y_j]\!]$. Else, set $z = [\![\perp]\!]$.
Store z in the ABB under handle res.

Extract(res):
For all $i \in [n]$ such that $X_i \notin X^{\text{stash}}$ and Query(X_i, res) was never called store
(X_i, Y_i) in an array Z. Pad Z to length $n - s$ with copies of $(\perp, \perp)$. Randomly
shuffle Z. Store Z in the ABB under handle res.

Protocol Π_{OHTable}

Hybrids: $\mathcal{F}_{\text{ABB}}$, $\mathcal{F}_{\text{OSet}}$.
Build($[\![X]\!]$, $[\![Y]\!]$, n N, X^{stash}, Y^{stash}):

1. Build OSet from the indices. Create arrays of the stashed indices and values:
   (a) $[\![S]\!] = \mathcal{F}_{OSet}.\text{Build}([\![X]\!], n)$
   (b) $[\![\tilde{S}]\!], [\![\tilde{X}]\!], [\![\tilde{Y}]\!] = \mathcal{F}_{\text{ABB}}.\text{ObliviousShuffle}([\![S]\!], [\![X]\!], [\![Y]\!])$
   (c) $\tilde{S} = \mathcal{F}_{\text{ABB}}.\text{Output}([\![\tilde{S}]\!])$
   (d) $[\![X^{\text{stash}}]\!], [\![Y^{\text{stash}}]\!] = ([\![\tilde{X}_i]\!], [\![\tilde{Y}_i]\!])_{\tilde{S}_i=1}$
2. Tag items with PRF evaluations of the indices under a new PRF key:
   (a) $[\![k]\!] = \mathcal{F}_{\text{ABB}}.\text{RandomElement}(\kappa)$
   (b) $[\![Q]\!] = \{\mathcal{F}_{\text{ABB}}.\text{PRFEval}([\![X_i]\!], [\![k]\!])\}_{i \in [n], \tilde{S}_i = 0}$
   (c) For $i \in [n-s]$, let $[\![Q_{n-s+i}]\!] = \mathcal{F}_{\text{ABB}}.\text{PRFEval}([\![N+i]\!], [\![k]\!])$, $[\![X_{n-s+i}]\!] = [\![\perp]\!]$ and $[\![Y_{n-s+i}]\!] = [\![\perp]\!]$
3. Build data structure allowing items to be accessed based on their tags.
   (a) $[\![\hat{Q}]\!], [\![\hat{X}]\!], [\![\hat{Y}]\!] = \mathcal{F}_{\text{ABB}}.\text{ObliviousShuffle}([\![Q]\!], [\![X]\!], [\![Y]\!])$
   (b) For $i \in [2n-2s]$, set $\hat{Q}_i = \mathcal{F}_{\text{ABB}}.\text{Output}(\hat{Q}_i)$
   (c) Store $(\hat{Q}_i, i)_{i \in [2n-2s]}$ in a local dictionary.
4. Initialize local query counter: $t = 0$

Query($[\![x]\!]$, res):

1. Locally increment counter: $t = t + 1$.
2. Query x to the OSet or, if $x = \perp$, query a counter (not in $[N]$) to the OSet.
   (a) $[\![x_{OSet}]\!] = \mathcal{F}_{\text{ABB}}.\text{IfThenElse}([\![x]\!] \stackrel{?}{=} [\![\perp]\!], [\![N+t]\!])$
   (b) $[\![in]\!] = \mathcal{F}_{OSet}.\text{Query}([\![x_{OSet}]\!])$
3. If the item was found in the OSet, access the item's value using its tag,
   otherwise access a pre-inserted dummy:
   (a) $[\![x_{used}]\!] = \mathcal{F}_{\text{ABB}}.\text{IfThenElse}([\![in]\!], [\![x]\!], [\![N+t]\!])$
   (b) $[\![q]\!] = \mathcal{F}_{\text{ABB}}.\text{PRFEval}([\![x_{used}]\!], [\![k]\!])$
   (c) $q = \mathcal{F}_{\text{ABB}}.\text{Output}([\![q]\!])$
   (d) Find i such that $q = \hat{Q}_i$.
   (e) Set $[\![res]\!] = [\![\hat{Y}_i]\!]$
4. Delete the accessed item: Delete $[\![\hat{Y}_i]\!]$ from $[\![\hat{Y}]\!]$, $[\![\hat{X}_i]\!]$ from $[\![\hat{X}]\!]$ and $[\![\hat{Q}_i]\!]$ from $[\![\hat{Q}]\!]$.

Extract(res):

1. Shuffle the remaining items of $[\![\hat{X}]\!]$ and $[\![\hat{Y}]\!]$ and return them:
   (a) $[\![\bar{X}]\!], [\![\bar{Y}]\!] = \mathcal{F}_{\text{ABB}}.\text{ObliviousShuffle}([\![\hat{X}]\!], [\![\hat{Y}]\!])$.
   (b) Store $[\![\bar{X}]\!], [\![\bar{Y}]\!]$ in $[\![res]\!]$.

Fig. 8. $\mathcal{F}_{\text{OHTable}}$ and Π_{OHTable}: Functionality and Protocol for Distributed Oblivious
Partial Hash-Table

Since the OHTable uses our OSet construction which generates a stash, our OHTable will also generate a stash. The stash elements will be not be stored in the table; they will be rejected and returned by the Build functionality. Like the OSet, our OHTable will only be secure if stashed items are queried with probability equal to items stored in the set.

Like our OSet protocol, our OHTable protocol has a limit on the number of times Query is executed. It has an additional Extract function which must be called so the OHTable can be rebuilt when this limit has been reached.

Our protocol is subject to similar conditions as that of our OSet protocol, but with some modifications. While OSet did not allow repeated queries, OHTable does not allow repeated queries of real items, but does allow repeated queries of the null-value $\perp$, which is used for the no-op queries. Like in the OSet protocol we need to limit to n queries. We also need independence from the stash, both for values revealed by the ABB by the environment and for queries to the OHTable. However in this case, the stash consists of an array of both indices and values. In addition, we have a condition that the Extract function will only be called after the queries have been depleted. We formally state our conditions below:

Condition 5 (No Repeats of Real Items). *For all $x \in [N]$, $Query(\llbracket x \rrbracket, res)$ is called at most once. ($Query(\llbracket \perp \rrbracket, res)$ may be called many times.)*

Condition 6 (Limited Queries). *Query is called $n - s$ times.*

Condition 7 (ABB-Stash Independence). *Let $(stashX_1, stashY_1)$, $(stashX_2, stashY_2)$ be two different possible values of (X^{stash}, Y^{stash}). The distribution of all outputs of the ABB by the environment when $(X^{stash}, Y^{stash}) = (X_1^{stash}, Y_1^{stash})$ must be computationally indistinguishable from the distribution when $(X^{stash}, Y^{stash}) = (X_2^{stash}, Y_2^{stash})$.*

Condition 8 (Query-Stash Independence). *Let (X^{stash}, Y^{stash}) be the output of Build. If $x = X_i$ for any $i \in [n]$, the probability that $Query(x, res)$ is called at any time, conditioned on any values revealed by the ABB either before or after, is computationally indistinguishable from independent of whether $x \in X^{stash}$.*

Condition 9 (Extract at End). *The function Extract will only be called at most once, and only after $n - s$ calls to Query.*

We present our OHTable protocol (Π_{OHTable}) and functionality ($\mathcal{F}_{\text{OHTable}}$) in Fig. 8. We now prove its security. Firstly, we need to demonstrate that if Π_{OHTable} is accessed consistently with its conditions, it will also access $\mathcal{F}_{\text{OSet}}$ in a manner that is consistent with its conditions. Formally:

Proposition 6. *Assuming an environment that follows Conditions 5, 6, 7, 8 and 9 when accessing $\Pi_{OHTable}$, Conditions 1, 2, 3 and 4 will also be satisfied in calls to $\mathcal{F}_{OSet}$.*

The proof is in Appendix G.3

Proposition 7. *Assuming an environment that follows Conditions 5, 6, 7, 8 and 9 $\Pi_{OHTable}$ is a secure implementation of $\mathcal{F}_{OHTable}$ with abort in the $\mathcal{F}_{ABB}, \mathcal{F}_{OSet}$-hybrid model in the 3-party setting against one static malicious adversary, where $\mathcal{F}_{OSet}$ is subject to Conditions 1, 2, 3 and 4.*

The proof is in Appendix G.4. Finally, in Appendix H.3 we show that:

Proposition 8. *$\Pi_{OHTable}.Build$ has complexity $O(n(\kappa + D))$ and $\Pi_{OHTable}.Query$ has complexity $O(\kappa)$ and $\Pi_{OHTable}.Extract$ has complexity $O(nD)$.*

9   Maliciously-Secure Oblivious Map Construction

As noted above, Oblivious Hash Tables (Sect. 8) have multiple limitations (formalized by Conditions 5–9). In particular, it does not allow real items to be queried multiple times and has very particular restrictions about how the stash is used by the environment. In this section, we present an Oblivious Map (OMap) construction that removes these limitations.

We will use the hierarchical solution, but with a twist. We will define our OMap recursively[2]. An OMap will consist of an Oblivious Hash Table and a smaller OMap of roughly half the capacity. This implicitly creates a hierarchy of OHTables, with the levels corresponding to levels of the recursion. Viewing the hierarchical solution in terms of recursion will make it much simpler to present our protocols and prove them secure. We will evidently need a base case: we use $\Pi_{QuietCache}$ for this as $\Pi_{QuietCache}$ already implements OMap (although it is only efficient for smaller table sizes). Our OMap will have a limitation that it can only be queried a certain number of times. Our final ORAM will be able to remove this limitation by taking advantage of the fact that its capacity is equal to the size of the index space. Our condition on the order that OMap should be accessed is formally stated below.

Condition 10 (OMap Call Pattern). *First Init($[\![X]\!], [\![Y]\!], n$) is called, where $len([\![X]\!]) = len([\![Y]\!]) = w \leq \log(N) < \frac{\kappa}{4}$.*
Then there are at most $n - w$ calls to Query($[\![x]\!]$) each followed immediately by a call to Add($[\![x]\!], [\![y]\!]$) (for the same x and some value of y other than $\bot$).
Finally, there is a call to Extract.

In more detail, an OMap of capacity n will contain two data objects: an OHTable with capacity roughly $\frac{n}{2}$ and a smaller sub-OMap of capacity roughly $\frac{n}{2}$. We first store items in the sub-OMap, until it becomes full. When this happens, we extract the contents of the sub-OMap and build an OHTable from its contents. We then initialize a new sub-OMap, in which we store new items. To avoid querying an item to the OHTable more than once, we first query the sub-OMap. If the item has already been queried, it will have been re-added (see Condition 10) and therefore placed in the sub-OMap. If it is found in the

---

[2] Recall that we need to recurse on OMaps rather than ORAMs, since the smaller levels in the hierarchy need to be able to hold indices from the full space.

Protocol Π_{OMap}

$\Pi_{\text{OMap}}.\text{Init}(\llbracket X \rrbracket, \llbracket Y \rrbracket, w, n, N)$:

1. Initialize counter for the number of stored items (including overwrites): $t = w$
2. Create a sub-OMap. Store the initial values in this sub-OMap. (Alibi bits are not needed here, as there is no OHTable yet.)
   (a) $s = \log(N)$
   (b) $\mathcal{F}_{\text{OMap}}.\text{Init}(\llbracket X \rrbracket, \llbracket Y \rrbracket, w, \frac{n}{2} + \frac{s}{2}, N)$

$\Pi_{\text{OMap}}.\text{Query}(\llbracket x \rrbracket)$:

1. If $t < \frac{n}{2} + \frac{s}{2}$: This means the OHTable has not yet been built. Only query the sub-OMap and pass on the value:
   (a) Return $\mathcal{F}_{\text{OMap}}.\text{Query}(\llbracket x \rrbracket)$
2. Else: The OHTable has been built. First query the sub-OMap. If the item is not found, search for it in the OHTable and return the result. If the item was found but has an Alibi bit of 1 it was stashed from the OHTable, so must also be searched for in the OHTable. Otherwise, perform a no-op query:
   (a) $\llbracket y \rrbracket = \mathcal{F}_{\text{OMap}}.\text{Query}(\llbracket x \rrbracket)$
   (b) $\llbracket b_{Alibi} \rrbracket = \llbracket y[-1] \rrbracket$
   (c) $\llbracket b_{found} \rrbracket = \mathcal{F}_{\text{ABB}}.\text{Equal}(\llbracket y \rrbracket, \llbracket \bot \rrbracket)$
   (d) $\llbracket x_{query} \rrbracket = \mathcal{F}_{\text{ABB}}.\text{IfThenElse}(\llbracket b_{Alibi} \rrbracket \cup (\neg \llbracket b_{found} \rrbracket), \llbracket 0 \rrbracket \| \llbracket x \rrbracket, \llbracket \bot \rrbracket)$
   (e) $\llbracket y_{table} \rrbracket = \mathcal{F}_{\text{OHTable}}.\text{Query}(\llbracket x_{query} \rrbracket)$
   (f) $\llbracket y_{map} \rrbracket = \llbracket y[1:-1] \rrbracket$ (Drop the Alibi bit for this level.)
   (g) $\llbracket y_{ret} \rrbracket = \mathcal{F}_{\text{ABB}}.\text{IfThenElse}(\llbracket b_{found} \rrbracket, \llbracket y_{map} \rrbracket, \llbracket y_{table} \rrbracket)$
   (h) Return $\llbracket y_{ret} \rrbracket$

$\Pi_{\text{OMap}}.\text{Add}(\llbracket x \rrbracket, \llbracket y \rrbracket)$:

1. If $t \geq \frac{n}{2} + \frac{s}{2}$ (the OHTable has been built, so the Alibi bit must be appended to show this is not a stashed item):
   (a) $\llbracket y \rrbracket = \llbracket y \rrbracket \| \llbracket 0 \rrbracket$
2. $\mathcal{F}_{\text{OMap}}.\text{Add}(\llbracket x \rrbracket, \llbracket y \rrbracket)$
3. $t = t + 1$
4. If $t = \frac{n}{2} + \frac{s}{2}$: The sub-OMap is full. It must be extracted and built into the OHTable. The sub-OMap may contain empty items due to overwrites, these are assigned an index from a disjoint space so they can be inputs to the build:
   (a) $(\llbracket X \rrbracket, \llbracket Y \rrbracket) = \mathcal{F}_{\text{OMap}}.\text{Extract}()$
   (b) For $i \in [\frac{n}{2} + \frac{s}{2}]$:
       i. $\llbracket \hat{X}_i \rrbracket = \mathcal{F}_{\text{ABB}}.\text{IfThenElse}(\llbracket X_i \rrbracket \overset{?}{=} \llbracket \bot \rrbracket, \llbracket 1 \rrbracket \| \llbracket i \rrbracket, \llbracket 0 \rrbracket \| \llbracket X_i \rrbracket)$
   (c) $(\llbracket stashX \rrbracket, \llbracket stashY \rrbracket) = \mathcal{F}_{\text{OHTable}}.\text{Build}(\llbracket \hat{X} \rrbracket, \llbracket Y \rrbracket, \frac{n}{2} + \frac{s}{2}, 2N)$
   (d) Set the Alibi bits to 1 for stashed items:
       i. For $i \in [s]$ $\llbracket stashY_i \rrbracket = \llbracket stashY_i \rrbracket \| \llbracket 1 \rrbracket$
   (e) If an item was empty before it was put in the table, make it empty again:
       For $i \in [s]$
       i. $\llbracket stashX_i \rrbracket = \mathcal{F}_{\text{ABB}}.\text{IfThenElse}(\llbracket stashX_i[1] \rrbracket, \llbracket \bot \rrbracket, \llbracket stashX_i[2:] \rrbracket)$
   (f) $\mathcal{F}_{\text{OMap}}.\text{Init}(\llbracket stashX \rrbracket, \llbracket stashY \rrbracket, s, \frac{n}{2} + \frac{s}{2}, N)$

$\Pi_{\text{OMap}}.\text{Extract}()$:

1. Extract contents from the OMap and the OHTable. Combine and shuffle them, then return the result (which may include empty items):
   (a) $\llbracket X^{map} \rrbracket, \llbracket Y^{map} \rrbracket = \mathcal{F}_{\text{OMap}}.\text{Extract}()$
   (b) $\llbracket X^{table} \rrbracket, \llbracket Y^{table} \rrbracket = \mathcal{F}_{\text{OHTable}}.\text{Extract}()$
   (c) If an item was empty before it was put in the table, make it empty again.
       For $i \in [\frac{n}{2} - \frac{s}{2}]$:
       i. $\llbracket X_i^{table} \rrbracket = \mathcal{F}_{\text{ABB}}.\text{IfThenElse}(\llbracket X_i^{table} \rrbracket[1], \llbracket \bot \rrbracket, \llbracket X_i^{table}[2:] \rrbracket)$
   (d) $\llbracket X \rrbracket = \llbracket X^{map} \rrbracket \| \llbracket X^{table} \rrbracket, \llbracket Y \rrbracket = \llbracket Y^{map} \rrbracket \| \llbracket Y^{table} \rrbracket$
   (e) $\llbracket \hat{X} \rrbracket, \llbracket \hat{Y} \rrbracket = \mathcal{F}_{\text{ABB}}.\text{ObliviousShuffle}(\llbracket X \rrbracket, \llbracket Y \rrbracket)$
   (f) Return $\llbracket \hat{X} \rrbracket, \llbracket \hat{Y} \rrbracket$

Fig. 9. Recursive OMap protocol

sub-OMap we therefore do a no-op query to the OHTable. Extract will be called exactly when the sub-OMap becomes full again, and the contents of both the OHTable and sub-OMap will be extracted and returned.

Things are complicated slightly by the fact that because of the "cache-the-stash" technique, our OHTable for storing n elements, actually stores only $n - s$ elements, and returns a stash of s items which is intended to be "cached." To handle this, we increase the capacity of the both the sub-OMap and the OHTable by $\frac{s}{2}$, thus both have a size of $\frac{n}{2} + \frac{s}{2}$. Note that since the OHTable caches s items, it will only hold $\frac{n}{2} - \frac{s}{2}$ real items. This means that each recursive call to the OMap causes the size to be reduced by slightly less than half; nevertheless as s is very small relative to n ($s = \Theta(\log(N)) = o(\kappa)$ and κ is the size of the base level), the total recursive depth will still be $\Theta(\log(N))$. Additionally, since stashed items need to be queried in the OHTable with probability equal to stored items, the OMap will tag stashed items with an Alibi bit (c.f. Appendix B) before placing them in the sub-OMap. This will slightly increase the size of payloads at smaller levels of the recursion, but will not affect asymptotic performance.

Our protocol Π_{OMap}, as well as the functionality $\mathcal{F}_{OMap}$ that it implements, are presented in detail in Figs. 9 and 3 respectively. We next prove the security of Π_{OMap} with respect to $\mathcal{F}_{OMap}$. Note that since Π_{OMap} reveals no values from the ABB, this security proof is not particular to our 3-party honest-majority setting. Rather, it applies in any setting given a $\mathcal{F}_{ABB}, \mathcal{F}_{OHTable}, \mathcal{F}_{OMap}$-hybrid setting, where $\mathcal{F}_{OHTable}$ is subject to at most Conditions 5, 6, 7, 8 and 9, and $\mathcal{F}_{OMap}$ is of a smaller capacity and subject to at most Condition 10.

Since Π_{OMap} does not reveal any values from the ABB, to prove its security we need only prove two things (see Corollary 1): that the outputs (to the ABB) are correct and that the conditions on the functionalities it uses are upheld. We prove these below.

Proposition 9. *Assuming an environment that follows Condition 10 and that $n \geq \kappa = \omega(\log(N))$, $\Pi_{OMap}[n, N]$ is a secure implementation of $\mathcal{F}_{OMap}[n, N]$ in the $\mathcal{F}_{ABB}, \mathcal{F}_{OHTable}, \mathcal{F}_{OMap}[\frac{n}{2} + \frac{\log(N)}{2}, N]$-hybrid setting, where $\mathcal{F}_{OHTable}$ is subject to Conditions 5, 6, 7, 8 and 9, and $\mathcal{F}_{OMap}$ occurs as a single instance of $\mathcal{F}_{OMap}[\frac{n}{2} + \frac{\log(N)}{2}, N]$ and is subject to Condition 10.*

The proof is in Appendix G.5.

Proposition 10. *If Π_{OMap} is implemented with its functionalities instantiated in the following ways:*

- *$\mathcal{F}_{OMap}$ implemented recursively with Π_{OMap} for all $n \geq \kappa$ and with $\Pi_{QuietCache}$ once $n < \kappa$.*
- *$\mathcal{F}_{OHTable}$ implemented using $\Pi_{OHTable}$, which in turn implements $\mathcal{F}_{OSet}$ using Π_{OSet}*
- *$\mathcal{F}_{ABB}$ is implemented as described in Sect. 5*

the resulting protocol will have the following costs:

- *Init* : $\Theta(\kappa w)$
- *Query:* $\Theta(\log(N)(\kappa + D))$
- *Add and Extract (combined, amortized over n accesses):* $\Theta(\log(N)(\kappa + D))$

The proof is in Appendix H.4

Acknowledgments. Supported in part by ONR under grant N00014-15-1-2750, Ripple Labs Inc., DARPA under Cooperative Agreement HR0011-20-2-0025, the Algorand Centers of Excellence programme managed by Algorand Foundation, NSF grants CNS-2001096 and CCF-2220450, US-Israel BSF grant 2015782, Amazon Faculty Award, Cisco Research Award and Sunday Group. Any views, opinions, findings, conclusions or recommendations contained herein are those of the author(s) and should not be interpreted as necessarily representing the official policies, either expressed or implied, of ONR, Ripple Labs Inc., DARPA, the Department of Defense, the Algorand Foundation, or the U.S. Government. The U.S. Government is authorized to reproduce and distribute reprints for governmental purposes not withstanding any copyright annotation therein.

References

[AKL+20] Asharov, G., Komargodski, I., Lin, W.-K., Nayak, K., Peserico, E., Shi, E.: OptORAMa: optimal oblivious RAM. In: Canteaut, A., Ishai, Y. (eds.) EUROCRYPT 2020. LNCS, vol. 12106, pp. 403–432. Springer, Cham (2020). https://doi.org/10.1007/978-3-030-45724-2_14

[AKLS21] Asharov, G., Komargodski, I., Lin, W.-K., Shi, E.: Oblivious RAM with *Worst-Case* logarithmic overhead. In: Malkin, T., Peikert, C. (eds.) CRYPTO 2021. LNCS, vol. 12828, pp. 610–640. Springer, Cham (2021). https://doi.org/10.1007/978-3-030-84259-8_21

[AKST14] Apon, D., Katz, J., Shi, E., Thiruvengadam, A.: Verifiable oblivious storage. In: Krawczyk, H. (ed.) PKC 2014. LNCS, vol. 8383, pp. 131–148. Springer, Heidelberg (2014). https://doi.org/10.1007/978-3-642-54631-0_8

[ARS+15] Albrecht, M.R., Rechberger, C., Schneider, T., Tiessen, T., Zohner, M.: Ciphers for MPC and FHE. In: Oswald, E., Fischlin, M. (eds.) EUROCRYPT 2015. LNCS, vol. 9056, pp. 430–454. Springer, Heidelberg (2015). https://doi.org/10.1007/978-3-662-46800-5_17

[BBVY21] Banik, S., Barooti, K., Vaudenay, S., Yan, H.: New attacks on LowMC instances with a single plaintext/ciphertext pair. IACR ePrint 2021/1345 (2021)

[BGI15] Boyle, E., Gilboa, N., Ishai, Y.: Function secret sharing. In: Oswald, E., Fischlin, M. (eds.) EUROCRYPT 2015. LNCS, vol. 9057, pp. 337–367. Springer, Heidelberg (2015). https://doi.org/10.1007/978-3-662-46803-6_12

[BIKO12] Beimel, A., Ishai, Y., Kushilevitz, E., Orlov, I.: Share conversion and private information retrieval. In: 2012 IEEE 27th Conference on Computational Complexity, pp. 258–268. IEEE (2012)

[BKKO20] Bunn, P., Katz, J., Kushilevitz, E., Ostrovsky, R.: Efficient 3-party distributed ORAM. In: Galdi, C., Kolesnikov, V. (eds.) SCN 2020. LNCS, vol. 12238, pp. 215–232. Springer, Cham (2020). https://doi.org/10.1007/978-3-030-57990-6_11

[BOGW88] Ben-Or, M., Goldwasser, S., Wigderson, A.: Completeness theorems for non-cryptographic fault-tolerant distributed computation. In: STOC, New York, NY, USA. ACM (1988)

[Can01] Canetti, R.: Universally composable security: a new paradigm for cryptographic protocols. In: FOCS, pp. 136–145. IEEE (2001)

[CCD88] Chaum, D., Crépeau, C., Damgård, I.: Multiparty unconditionally secure protocols. In: STOC (1988)

[CDG+17] Chase, M., et al.: Post-quantum zero-knowledge and signatures from symmetric-key primitives. IACR ePrint 2017/279 (2017)

[CDI05] Cramer, R., Damgård, I., Ishai, Y.: Share conversion, pseudorandom secret-sharing and applications to secure computation. In: Kilian, J. (ed.) TCC 2005. LNCS, vol. 3378, pp. 342–362. Springer, Heidelberg (2005). https://doi.org/10.1007/978-3-540-30576-7_19

[CFP13] Cramer, R., Fehr, S., Padró, C.: Algebraic manipulation detection codes. Sci. China Math. **56**, 1349–1358 (2013)

[CGH+18] Chida, K., et al.: Fast large-scale honest-majority MPC for malicious adversaries. In: Shacham, H., Boldyreva, A. (eds.) CRYPTO 2018. LNCS, vol. 10993, pp. 34–64. Springer, Cham (2018). https://doi.org/10.1007/978-3-319-96878-0_2

[CHL22] Casacuberta, S., Hesse, J., Lehmann, A.: SoK: oblivious pseudorandom functions. In: EuroS&P, pp. 625–646. IEEE (2022)

[DFK+06] Damgård, I., Fitzi, M., Kiltz, E., Nielsen, J.B., Toft, T.: Unconditionally secure constant-rounds multi-party computation for equality, comparison, bits and exponentiation. In: Halevi, S., Rabin, T. (eds.) TCC 2006. LNCS, vol. 3876, pp. 285–304. Springer, Heidelberg (2006). https://doi.org/10.1007/11681878_15

[DK12] Drmota, M., Kutzelnigg, R.: A precise analysis of Cuckoo hashing. ACM Trans. Algorithms (TALG) **8**(2), 1–36 (2012)

[DLMW15] Dinur, I., Liu, Y., Meier, W., Wang, Q.: Optimized interpolation attacks on LowMC. IACR ePrint 2015/418 (2015)

[DN03] Damgård, I., Nielsen, J.B.: Universally composable efficient multiparty computation from threshold homomorphic encryption. In: Boneh, D. (ed.) CRYPTO 2003. LNCS, vol. 2729, pp. 247–264. Springer, Heidelberg (2003). https://doi.org/10.1007/978-3-540-45146-4_15

[DO20] Dittmer, S., Ostrovsky, R.: Oblivious tight compaction in $O(n)$ time with smaller constant. In: Galdi, C., Kolesnikov, V. (eds.) SCN 2020. LNCS, vol. 12238, pp. 253–274. Springer, Cham (2020). https://doi.org/10.1007/978-3-030-57990-6_13

[DPSZ12] Damgård, I., Pastro, V., Smart, N., Zakarias, S.: Multiparty computation from somewhat homomorphic encryption. In: Safavi-Naini, R., Canetti, R. (eds.) CRYPTO 2012. LNCS, vol. 7417, pp. 643–662. Springer, Heidelberg (2012). https://doi.org/10.1007/978-3-642-32009-5_38

[Ds17] Doerner, J., Shelat, A.: Scaling ORAM for secure computation. In: CCS (2017)

[DvDF+16] Devadas, S., van Dijk, M., Fletcher, C.W., Ren, L., Shi, E., Wichs, D.: Onion ORAM: a constant bandwidth blowup oblivious RAM. In: Kushilevitz, E., Malkin, T. (eds.) TCC 2016. LNCS, vol. 9563, pp. 145–174. Springer, Heidelberg (2016). https://doi.org/10.1007/978-3-662-49099-0_6

[FJKW15] Faber, S., Jarecki, S., Kentros, S., Wei, B.: Three-party ORAM for secure computation. In: Iwata, T., Cheon, J.H. (eds.) ASIACRYPT 2015. LNCS, vol. 9452, pp. 360–385. Springer, Heidelberg (2015). https://doi.org/10.1007/978-3-662-48797-6_16

[FLNW17] Furukawa, J., Lindell, Y., Nof, A., Weinstein, O.: High-throughput secure three-party computation for malicious adversaries and an honest majority. In: Coron, J.-S., Nielsen, J.B. (eds.) EUROCRYPT 2017. LNCS, vol. 10211, pp. 225–255. Springer, Cham (2017). https://doi.org/10.1007/978-3-319-56614-6_8

[FNO21] Hemenway Falk, B., Noble, D., Ostrovsky, R.: Alibi: a flaw in Cuckoo-hashing based hierarchical ORAM schemes and a solution. In: Canteaut, A., Standaert, F.-X. (eds.) EUROCRYPT 2021. LNCS, vol. 12698, pp. 338–369. Springer, Cham (2021). https://doi.org/10.1007/978-3-030-77883-5_12

[FNO22] Falk, B.H., Noble, D., Ostrovsky, R.: 3-party distributed ORAM from oblivious set membership. In: Galdi, C., Jarecki, S. (eds.) Security and Cryptography for Networks. SCN 2022. LNCS, vol. 13409, pp. 437–461. Springer, Cham (2022). https://doi.org/10.1007/978-3-031-14791-3_19

[FNR+15] Fletcher, C.W., Naveed, M., Ren, L., Shi, E., Stefanov, E.: Bucket ORAM: single online roundtrip, constant bandwidth oblivious RAM. IACR ePrint 2015/1065 (2015)

[GHL+14] Gentry, C., Halevi, S., Lu, S., Ostrovsky, R., Raykova, M., Wichs, D.: Garbled RAM revisited. In: Nguyen, P.Q., Oswald, E. (eds.) EUROCRYPT 2014. LNCS, vol. 8441, pp. 405–422. Springer, Heidelberg (2014). https://doi.org/10.1007/978-3-642-55220-5_23

[GI14] Gilboa, N., Ishai, Y.: Distributed point functions and their applications. In: Nguyen, P.Q., Oswald, E. (eds.) EUROCRYPT 2014. LNCS, vol. 8441, pp. 640–658. Springer, Heidelberg (2014). https://doi.org/10.1007/978-3-642-55220-5_35

[GKK+12] Gordon, S.D., et al.: Secure two-party computation in sublinear (amortized) time. In: CCS (2012)

[GKW18] Gordon, S.D., Katz, J., Wang, X.: Simple and efficient two-server ORAM. In: Peyrin, T., Galbraith, S. (eds.) ASIACRYPT 2018. LNCS, vol. 11274, pp. 141–157. Springer, Cham (2018). https://doi.org/10.1007/978-3-030-03332-3_6

[GMOT12] Goodrich, M.T., Mitzenmacher, M., Ohrimenko, O., Tamassia, R.: Privacy-preserving group data access via stateless oblivious RAM simulation. In: SODA (2012)

[GMW87] Goldreich, O., Micali, S., Wigderson, A.: How to play any mental game. In: STOC (1987)

[GO96] Goldreich, O., Ostrovsky, R.: Software protection and simulation on oblivious RAMs. JACM 43(3), 431–473 (1996)

[Gol87] Goldreich, O.: Towards a theory of software protection and simulation by oblivious RAMs. In: STOC 1987, pp. 182–194. ACM (1987)

[HV20] Hamlin, A., Varia, M.: Two-server distributed ORAM with sublinear computation and constant rounds. IACR ePrint 2020/1547 (2020)

[IKH+23] Ichikawa, A., Komargodski, I., Hamada, K., Kikuchi, R., Ikarashi, D.: 3-party secure computation for RAMs: optimal and concretely efficient. IACR ePrint 2023/516 (2023)

[IKK+11] Ishai, Y., Katz, J., Kushilevitz, E., Lindell, Y., Petrank, E.: On achieving the "best of both worlds" in secure multiparty computation. SIAM J. Comput. **40**(1), 122–141 (2011)

[JW18] Jarecki, S., Wei, B.: 3PC ORAM with low latency, low bandwidth, and fast batch retrieval. In: Preneel, B., Vercauteren, F. (eds.) ACNS 2018. LNCS, vol. 10892, pp. 360–378. Springer, Cham (2018). https://doi.org/10.1007/978-3-319-93387-0_19

[JZLR22] Ji, K., Zhang, B., Lu, T., Ren, K.: Multi-party private function evaluation for RAM. IACR ePrint 2022/939 (2022)

[KLO12] Kushilevitz, E., Lu, S., Ostrovsky, R.: On the (in) security of hash-based oblivious RAM and a new balancing scheme. In: SODA (2012)

[KM19] Kushilevitz, E., Mour, T.: Sub-logarithmic distributed oblivious RAM with small block size. In: Lin, D., Sako, K. (eds.) PKC 2019. LNCS, vol. 11442, pp. 3–33. Springer, Cham (2019). https://doi.org/10.1007/978-3-030-17253-4_1

[KMW09] Kirsch, A., Mitzenmacher, M., Wieder, U.: More robust hashing: Cuckoo hashing with a stash. SIAM J. Comput. **39**, 1543–1561 (2009)

[KO97] Kushilevitz, E., Ostrovsky, R.: Replication is NOT needed: SINGLE database, computationally-private information retrieval. In: FOCS (1997)

[KS14] Keller, M., Scholl, P.: Efficient, oblivious data structures for MPC. In: Sarkar, P., Iwata, T. (eds.) ASIACRYPT 2014. LNCS, vol. 8874, pp. 506–525. Springer, Heidelberg (2014). https://doi.org/10.1007/978-3-662-45608-8_27

[Lau15] Laud, P.: Parallel oblivious array access for secure multiparty computation and privacy-preserving minimum spanning trees. In: PoPETs (2015)

[LIM20] Liu, F., Isobe, T., Meier, W.: Cryptanalysis of full LowMC and LowMC-M with algebraic techniques. IACR ePrint 2020/1034 (2020)

[LN17] Lindell, Y., Nof, A.: A framework for constructing fast MPC over arithmetic circuits with malicious adversaries and an honest-majority. In: CCS, pp. 259–276 (2017)

[LN18] Larsen, K.G., Nielsen, J.B.: Yes, there is an oblivious RAM lower bound! In: Shacham, H., Boldyreva, A. (eds.) CRYPTO 2018. LNCS, vol. 10992, pp. 523–542. Springer, Cham (2018). https://doi.org/10.1007/978-3-319-96881-0_18

[LO13] Lu, S., Ostrovsky, R.: Distributed oblivious RAM for secure two-party computation. In: Sahai, A. (ed.) TCC 2013. LNCS, vol. 7785, pp. 377–396. Springer, Heidelberg (2013). https://doi.org/10.1007/978-3-642-36594-2_22

[LWZ11] Laur, S., Willemson, J., Zhang, B.: Round-efficient oblivious database manipulation. In: Lai, X., Zhou, J., Li, H. (eds.) ISC 2011. LNCS, vol. 7001, pp. 262–277. Springer, Heidelberg (2011). https://doi.org/10.1007/978-3-642-24861-0_18

[Mit09] Mitzenmacher, M.: Some open questions related to Cuckoo hashing. In: Fiat, A., Sanders, P. (eds.) ESA 2009. LNCS, vol. 5757, pp. 1–10. Springer, Heidelberg (2009). https://doi.org/10.1007/978-3-642-04128-0_1

[MV23] Mathialagan, S., Vafa, N.: MacORAMa: optimal oblivious RAM with integrity. IACR ePrint 2023/083 (2023)

[MZ14] Mitchell, J.C., Zimmerman, J.: Data-oblivious data structures. In: STACS. Schloss Dagstuhl-Leibniz-Zentrum fuer Informatik (2014)

[NIS21] NIST. Post-quantum cryptography PQC: Round 3 submissions (2021). https://csrc.nist.gov/Projects/post-quantum-cryptography/post-quantum-cryptography-standardization/round-3-submissions

[Nob21] Noble, D.: Explicit, closed-form, general bounds for cuckoo hashing with a stash. IACR ePrint 2021/447 (2021)

[OS97] Ostrovsky, R., Shoup, V.: Private information storage. In: STOC, vol. 97 (1997)

[Ost90] Ostrovsky, R.: Efficient computation on oblivious RAMs. In: STOC (1990)

[Ost92] Ostrovsky, R.: Software protection and simulation on oblivious RAMs. Ph.D. thesis, Massachusetts Institute of Technology (1992)

[PPRY18] Patel, S., Persiano, G., Raykova, M., Yeo, K.: PanORAMa: oblivious RAM with logarithmic overhead. In: FOCS (2018)

[PR01] Pagh, R., Rodler, F.F.: Cuckoo hashing. In: ESA (2001)

[PR10] Pinkas, B., Reinman, T.: Oblivious RAM revisited. In: Rabin, T. (ed.) CRYPTO 2010. LNCS, vol. 6223, pp. 502–519. Springer, Heidelberg (2010). https://doi.org/10.1007/978-3-642-14623-7_27

[PSSZ15] Pinkas, B., Schneider, T., Segev, G., Zohner, M.: Phasing: private set intersection using permutation-based hashing. In: USENIX, pp. 515–530 (2015)

[RFK+14] Ren, L., et al.: Ring ORAM: closing the gap between small and large client storage oblivious RAM. IACR ePrint 2014/997 (2014)

[SVDS+13] Stefanov, E., et al.: Path ORAM: an extremely simple oblivious RAM protocol. In: CCS (2013)

[Tof07] Toft, T.: Primitives and applications for multi-party computation. Unpublished doctoral dissertation, University of Aarhus, Denmark (2007)

[VHG22] Vadapalli, A., Henry, R., Goldberg, I.: Duoram: a bandwidth-efficient distributed ORAM for 2- and 3-party computation. IACR ePrint 2022/1747 (2022)

[Vol99] Vollmer, H.: Introduction to Circuit Complexity: A Uniform Approach. Springer, Cham (1999). https://doi.org/10.1007/978-3-662-03927-4

[WCS15] Wang, X., Chan, H., Shi, E.: Circuit ORAM: on tightness of the Goldreich-Ostrovsky lower bound. In: CCS (2015)

[WHC+14] Wang, X.S., Huang, Y., Chan, T.-H.H., Shelat, A., Shi, E.: SCORAM: oblivious RAM for secure computation. In: CCS (2014)

[Yao82] Yao, A.: Protocols for secure computations (extended abstract). In: FOCS (1982)

[Yao86] Yao, A.: How to generate and exchange secrets. In: FOCS (1986)

[ZWR+16] Zahur, S., et al.: Revisiting square-root ORAM: efficient random access in multi-party computation. In: S & P (2016)

3-Party Secure Computation for RAMs: Optimal and Concretely Efficient

Atsunori Ichikawa[1]($\boxtimes$), Ilan Komargodski[2,3], Koki Hamada[1], Ryo Kikuchi[1], and Dai Ikarashi[1]

[1] NTT Social Informatics Laboratories, Tokyo, Japan
{atsunori.ichikawa,koki.hamada,ryo.kikuchi,dai.ikarashi}@ntt.com
[2] The Hebrew University of Jerusalem, Jerusalem, Israel
ilank@cs.huji.ac.il
[3] NTT Research, Sunnyvale, USA

Abstract. A distributed oblivious RAM (DORAM) is a method for accessing a secret-shared memory while hiding the accessed locations. DORAMs are the key tool for secure multiparty computation (MPC) for RAM programs that avoids expensive RAM-to-circuit transformations.

We present new and improved 3-party DORAM protocols. For a logical memory of size N and for each logical operation, our DORAM requires $O(\log N)$ local CPU computation steps. This is known to be asymptotically optimal. Our DORAM satisfies passive security in the honest majority setting. Our technique results with concretely-efficient protocols and does not use expensive cryptography (such as re-randomizable or homomorphic encryption). Specifically, our DORAM is 25X faster than the known most efficient DORAM in the same setting.

Lastly, we extend our technique to handle malicious attackers at the expense of using slightly larger blocks (i.e., $\omega((\lambda + b) \log N)$ vs. $\lambda + b$ where $b = \Omega(\log N)$ is original block size). To the best of our knowledge, this is the first concretely-efficient maliciously secure DORAM.

Technically, our construction relies on a novel concretely-efficient 3-party oblivious permutation protocol. We combine it with efficient non-oblivious hashing techniques (i.e., Cuckoo hashing) to get a distributed oblivious hash table. From this, we build a full-fledged DORAM using a distributed variant of the hierarchical approach of Goldreich and Ostrovsky (J. ACM '96). These ideas, and especially the permutation protocol, are of independent interest.

1 Introduction

Secure multiparty computation (MPC) is a method that enables mutually distrustful parties to jointly compute an arbitrary function over their private inputs. Since breakthrough feasibility results in the 80s, the quest for practically efficient MPC protocols is a central research area in cryptography. Efficiency is measured in terms of local computation and/or communication, as a function of the size of the representation of the function that needs to be computed.

© International Association for Cryptologic Research 2023
G. Rothblum and H. Wee (Eds.): TCC 2023, LNCS 14369, pp. 471–502, 2023.
https://doi.org/10.1007/978-3-031-48615-9_17

There are several common ways to represent computation, e.g., the circuit model or Random Access Memory (RAM) model. Any function can be computed in either of the models and a representation in one model can be translated to the other. However, such translations have a cost: a RAM program of size N can be turned into a circuit of size $O(N^3 \log N)$ [38]. Therefore, due to efficiency reasons, it would be highly desirable to be able to perform secure computation for RAM programs, *directly*.

This is challenging because MPC protocols need to guarantee, in particular, that the running time, memory accesses and communication patterns of the participants, do not depend on their private inputs. The circuit model guarantees these properties for free as circuits can be computed in a gate-by-gate fashion, independently of the inputs. In general, RAM programs do not have these features and therefore some extra work is needed.

There is a generic way to turn any RAM program into another that computes the same functionality but whose memory accesses do not reveal anything about the program's secret inputs. This is called an *Oblivious RAM* (ORAM), originally proposed by Goldreich and Ostrovsky [23,24,35]. The traditional setting for ORAMs is one client and one server. That is, a large memory is stored on an untrusted server and a client can make accesses to it using a small trusted memory. Ostrovsky and Shoup [36] observed that by simulating the client of an ORAM using traditional circuit-based MPC protocol, one can generically get an MPC for RAM programs. However, designing an efficient ORAM with a client that is "compatible" with circuit-based MPC is not at all obvious and has been (so far) sub-optimal in terms of the efficiency of the resulting protocol (see, e.g., [40]).

Due to the inherent inefficiency of circuit-based MPC for certain computations, there have been significant efforts in the last decade in building efficient MPCs for RAM programs, for example [6,9,16,19,33,40]. By now, due to its relation to oblivious simulation, the common terminology for this problem is **Distributed Oblivious RAM** (DORAM)—informally, this is a protocol that allows parties to collectively maintain and perform reads/writes on a memory (a formal definition appears in Sect. 3.2).

The complexity measure of DORAMs of interest to us is their *computational overhead*. That is, the maximal amount of CPU instructions[1] performed by each of the parties when serving a single logical request.[2] Some prior works measure *bandwidth* overhead which accounts only for the maximal amount of bits communicated between the parties. Computational overhead is harder to optimize since an upper bound on the computational overhead implies an upper bound on the communication overhead, i.e., computational overhead $\geq$ communication overhead. The other direction is not necessarily true; indeed, some prior works

---

[1] We model parties as RAM machines that can perform word-level addition and standard Boolean operations at unit cost.

[2] As commonly done, we sometimes settle for overhead in an amortized sense, that is, we measure the average overhead over a sequence of requests. Known schemes can be made worst-case ("de-amortized") [5,36].

(e.g., [19]) optimize communication overhead at the expense of increased computational overhead. In this work, we choose the more stringent measure. This is particularly important if we aim for concretely efficient and practically useful DORAMs.

Furthermore, we focus on the honest majority setting and more specifically on the 3-party setting, where at most one server is corrupted. We mention that there are several schemes in the 2-party setting (e.g., [15,33,40]), but due to the nature of the dishonest majority setting, existing techniques result with asymptotically and concretely less efficient schemes than in the 3-party honest majority setting.

A variant of a scheme due to Lu and Ostrovsky [33], suggested by Faber et al. [16],[3] gives a (3-party) DORAM with $O(\log N)$ computational overhead with block size $\Omega(\log N)$. While the asymptotical overhead of this construction is optimal, the concrete efficiency is quite poor. The reason is that their compiler requires the parties to securely and jointly compute a linear number of encryptions once in a while (which requires a circuit-based secure computation protocol of AES computation).

Later works attempt to present concretely efficient DORAMs. Wang et al. [40] and Faber et al. [16] proposed DORAMs with $O(\log N)$ computational overhead, but their block size is $\Omega(\log^2 N)$ which is less standard. Bunn et al. [6] constructed a DORAM with small concrete constants but poor asymptotic overhead ($\Omega(\sqrt{N})$). Most recently, Falk et al. [19] reduced the large constant factor of [16,33] and achieved a scheme with $O(\log^2 N)$ computational overhead (see Section 1.4 of full version [26] for details) and $O(\log N)$ communication overhead.

Moreover, all of the above schemes only guarantee security against a passive attacker, i.e., any single server cannot learn any non-trivial information about the others' inputs, as long as it follows the prescribed protocol. There are generic methods to boost security to the more standard setting of active security, where security holds even if a rouge server arbitrarily deviates from the protocol. However, these techniques do not preserve efficiency.

The current state of the art for 3-party DORAMs is summarized in Table 1. This brings us the main problems that we consider in this work:

> *Is there a 3-party DORAM that is asymptotically optimal in terms of computational overhead and concretely efficient? Additionally, is there an efficient actively secure DORAM?*

---

[3] The protocol of Lu and Ostrovsky [33] is in the multi-party setting where there are two non-communicating servers and a single trusted lightweight client (see full version for details). Faber et al. [16] observed that the client in [33]'s scheme can be efficiently simulated by an MPC.

Table 1. Summary of known *3-party DORAMs in the honest majority setting* together with our own schemes. Let N be the number of input elements and also treated as the statistical security parameter, $b = \Omega(\log N)$ be the size of the input element, and λ be the computational security parameter. The first column points to the paper that obtained the DORAM. The second column states the communication overhead of the proposed construction. The third column states the computational overhead of the proposed construction. The fourth column states whether the security guarantee is for passive or active attackers. The fifth column mentions the block size used in the construction. Lastly, the sixth column states whether the hidden constants are considered large or small.

Ref.	Communication	Computation	Security	Block size	Hidden const.
[36]	$O(\log^3 N)$	$O(\log^3 N)$	Passive	b	Large
[16,33]	$O(\log N)$	$O(\log N)$	Passive	$\lambda + b$	Large
[16,40]	$O(\log N)$	$O(\log N)$	Passive	$b + \Omega(\log^2 N)$	Large
[6]	$O(\sqrt{N})$	$O(\sqrt{N})$	Passive	b	Small
[19]	$O(\log N)$	$O(\log^2 N)$	Passive	$\lambda + b$	Small
[17][a]	$O(\log N)$	$O(\log N)$	Active	$\omega((\lambda + b)\log N)$	Small
Our	$O(\log N)$	$O(\log N)$	Passive	$\lambda + b$	Small
Our	$O(\log N)$	$O(\log N)$	Active	$\omega((\lambda + b)\log N)$	Small

[a] A concurrent work that is realized in a different and independent way from ours. See also Sect. 2 for the comparison.

1.1 Our Contributions

An Optimal 3-Party DORAM: We present an asymptotically optimal and concretely efficient 3-party DORAM in the honest majority setting. Specifically, our DORAM has the computational overhead of $O(\log N)$ and the hidden constant is rather small. Our DORAM requires at most $4 \log N$ oblivious pseudorandom function (OPRF) calls per access (amortized). This is about 2 times greater than that of the DORAM of Falk et al. [19],[4] but it is significantly more efficient than the known optimal DORAM of Lu and Ostrovsky [16,33] that requires at least $100 \log N$ calls per access (see full version for more details). This protocol is secure against passive (honest-but-curious) attackers.

A Distributed Oblivious Permutation: Our main technical novelty is a new (concretely efficient and asymptotically optimal) 3-party oblivious permutation protocol. Our protocol can apply any permutation to the data with communication of $4nb + 2n\lceil \log n \rceil$ bits and $12nb + 2n\lceil \log n \rceil$ local CPU computation steps where n is the number of data elements to be shuffled and b is the bit-length of each data element. We also construct a procedure to invert that permutation. This procedure requires $8nb + 2n\lceil \log n \rceil$ bits of communication and $19nb + 2n\lceil \log n \rceil$ steps of local computation.

---

[4] Here, we emphasize again that the DORAM of Falk et al. [19] requires $O(\log^2 N)$ *computational* cost in addition to the communication cost. We only have $O(\log N)$ computational cost.

A Distributed Oblivious Hash Table: Our DORAM construction is modular and, at a high level, is reminiscent of the hierarchical ORAM technique of Goldreich and Ostrovsky [24]. Recall that [24]'s hierarchical method basically reduces the problem of maintaining a memory to the problem of building a static hash table (supporting only lookups after an initial build). To this end, we implement a concretely efficient *distributed* oblivious hashing scheme. This is the first concretely efficient and asymptotically optimal distributed oblivious hash table construction. To store n data blocks of size b bits into a distributed hash table, each party needs to perform at most $O(n \cdot (\lambda + b + \lceil \log n \rceil))$ local CPU computation steps, and our lookup protocol requires $O(\lambda + b) + O(\sigma \cdot b)$ local CPU computation steps, where the first term is for a lookup in a main table and the second for a linear scan of a σ-size stash. The storage size of the hash table is $O(nb)$. We obtain our distributed oblivious hash table by first randomly permuting the data to be hashed (using the above-mentioned permutation protocol) and then simply invoking an off-the-shelf (non-oblivious) distributed hashing technique.

Active Security: We extend our passively secure schemes from above to be *actively* secure, without hurting efficiency, except that we rely on somewhat larger blocks. Specifically, we get a 3-party DORAM with $O(\log N)$ computational overhead and block size $\omega((\lambda+b) \log N)$. As far as we know, this is the first result of achieving active security for DORAM with practical efficiency guarantees. We do not know how to achieve similar concrete efficiency guarantees with logarithmic size blocks and we leave it as an exciting open problem.

1.2 Technical Overview

Before showing the fundamental idea of our schemes, we first revisit the optimal DORAM of Lu and Ostrovsky [16,33]. Their DORAM consists of a hierarchy of *permuted arrays*, i.e., oblivious hash tables, that are managed by multi-party protocols while hiding access patterns. The fundamental idea of their oblivious hashing (which comes from the 2-server setting [33]) is as follows. One of the two servers is *the permuter*, and the other is *the storage*. The storage sends all data that should be permuted to the permuter while *rerandomizing*, and the permuter constructs a hash table consisting of the data. The permuter sends the hash table to the storage while rerandomizing. Now, the storage can explore the table with a (randomized) query.

Though the storage can observe the access patterns on the table directly in the above scheme, the access patterns achieve obliviousness against the storage with non-duplicate access since it does not know the permutation for building the table. In other words, the table seems to be shuffled from the storage's point of view, and hence a single lookup looks completely random. On the other hand, since the permuter does not observe any access to the table, it never knows the access patterns even if it knows how to construct the table.

Due to the ingenuity of the server role splitting, they achieved optimal DORAM with optimal oblivious hashing. However, as Falk et al. [19] pointed out, while this DORAM is *asymptotically* optimal it is *not practically* efficient because of the large frequency of required rerandomizations. Their rerandomization can be implemented by *oblivious pseudorandom function* (OPRF) in the context of secure multiparty computation, but as mentioned in [19], the DORAM of Lu and Ostrovsky requires at least $100 \log N$ OPRFs per access. Falk et al. improved this by a factor of 50, at the expense of increased local computation overhead—i.e., $O(\log^2 N)$ local hash function evaluations per access.

An Oblivious Distributed Permutation Protocol. Our starting point is the idea of role splitting, but with a novel modification that maintains optimality and greatly improves practical efficiency. Our fundamental idea is as follows. Set the role of one of the *three* servers as the permuter; this server knows a permutation for hashing. The other two servers will be the storage that holds data in a secret-shared form. The servers obliviously compute hash values of all secret-shared data (which can be implemented by ORPFs) and reveal them to the permuter. The permuter calculates a permutation that sorts the data to make a hash table. The servers run a role-asymmetric oblivious permutation to apply the above permutation to the data obliviously. As the output of this protocol, the two storages obtain a hash table in secret-shared form. Now, the storages can explore the table with a secret-shared query.

By the description above, only one round of OPRF evaluations is required to build a hash table. Our permutation protocol is for 3-party computation, and if one party knows a permutation, it can apply the permutation to a secret-shared array in linear time while keeping the permutation secret from the other two parties (see Sect. 5.1 for more details).

From an Oblivious Distributed Permutation to a DORAM. We obtain a DORAM using only $4 \log N$ OPRF evaluations and optimal computational complexity per access. This is obtained via the following very useful observations: (1) given an oblivious permutation protocol, there is an extremely efficient way to get an oblivious distributed hash table, and (2) given the latter, we can adapt the hierarchical ORAM framework (or its optimizations) to the distributed setting. We elaborate on both bullets next. First, we observe that the shuffle-sort paradigm can be applied to hashing: if data is randomly shuffled, we can invoke an insecure oblivious hashing algorithm. This allows us to completely get rid of complicated (distributed) oblivious hashing approaches by first shuffling the input and then invoking a simple hashing procedure. Concretely, we use (plain) cuckoo hashing with a stash [30] to achieve constant lookup time (ignoring scanning a logarithmic-size stash, which we will do once per logical access).

Once we have obtained our distributed hash table, we plug it into the hierarchical ORAM setting, while extending it to the distributed setting. I.e., we implement every level in the hierarchy with an oblivious distributed hash table, as above, and where each level can hold twice more elements than its previous level. The stashes from all levels are merged into one common stash and scanning it is done once per lookup.

Maliciously Secure DORAM. In our permutation protocol roles of parties are asymmetric, and in particular, the permuter has complete control over the chosen permutation. Thus, it is non-trivial to extend our ideas to the malicious setting. Note that, it is not trivial to compile the known passively secure DORAMs [16,19,33] to active security despite the existence of actively secure MPC frameworks [10,20,27,29]. The oblivious hashing of [16,33] highly depends on oblivious permutation, thus to compile it to active security, one would need an actively secure variant of their permutation protocol (a task that we achieve as one of our main technical contributions). Alternatively, extending [19]'s DORAM to a malicious setting would require some form of an active hash table based on Bloom filters; this is closer to the strategy employed in the concurrent work of [17] (see Sect. 2).

To this end, we augment our permutation evaluation protocol to check that *all elements in a hash table are actually in their correct cell.* The key insight is that the correctness of a hash table can be evaluated by hash values of elements calculated by OPRF whose correctness (in turn) can be guaranteed using a known actively secure MPC framework. That is, comparing the virtual address (obtained obliviously by OPRF) and the real address (known by all parties) of each element in a hash table, the correctness of the table can be achieved regardless of whether the permuter is the adversary or not. We observe that any attack of the permuter can be translated into some form of an *additive attack* [21,22]. Thus, to achieve malicious security, we incorporate the permutation evaluation into an efficient evaluation process of security-with-abort MPC (e.g., [10,27,29]) and only need to deal with "additive attacks". This makes our hash table validation have almost no effect on overall efficiency except the required increase in block size.

Organization. We describe our passively secure oblivious permutation and oblivious hashing protocols in Sect. 5. We combine them to get our passively secure DORAM in Sect. 6. The actively secure extension is described in Sect. 7. Due to lack of space, we defer various non-essential or standard parts to the full version [26].

2   Comparison with [17]

A concurrent and independent work of Falk, Noble, Ostrovsky, Shtepel, and Zhang [17] achieves very similar results to us (both passive and active DORAMs) albeit with somewhat different techniques. As opposed to us, they rely and extend [19]. In particular, they obtain the optimal $O(\log N)$ overhead by a new $\omega(\log N)$-size cache that can be accessed efficiently, thereby avoiding the usage of a hierarchy of Bloom filters for small inputs.

We note that the usage of asymptotically larger than logarithmic size blocks in the actively secure DORAM is common to both works. For us, it stems from the usage of MACs that have negligible probability (in N) of being forged. For them, it stems from the usage of an actively secure MPC by Furukawa et al. [20] which requires $\omega(\log N)$ bits of communication per AND gate computation, assuming $\mathsf{negl}(N)$ statistical security is required. (The authors of [20] mention an optimization to perform multiplication in constant time but guaranteeing security only 2^{-40}.) Overall, treating N (the input size) as the statistical security parameter, the complexity of [17]'s DORAM is $O((\lambda + b)\log N) \cdot \omega(\log N)$. Alternatively, $O(\log N)$ overhead in accesses with block size $\omega((\lambda + b)\log N)$, which is identical to our complexity.

3   Preliminaries

3.1   Secret Sharing Schemes

A (threshold) secret sharing scheme (SSS) is a technique for "splitting" a secret between a collection of m parties such that a set of parties of some predefined cardinality, say $t + 1$ for $1 \le t \le m - 1$, can reconstruct the secret while smaller sets cannot. A "piece" that is held by a party is called a *share*. We refer to such a scheme as (t, m)-SSS. Shamir's scheme [39] or the so-called replicated secret sharing scheme [28] are well-known implementations of such schemes.

To share and reconstruct a secret, we introduce three functionalities as follows. We use the notations $[\![\cdot]\!]_i$ to represent the share of party $i \in [m]$.

- $\mathcal{F}_{\mathrm{SHARE}}$ receives a secret s and distributes the shares among the parties; share $[\![s]\!]_i$ is sent to party i.
- $\mathcal{F}_{\mathrm{REVEAL}}$ receives shares $[\![s]\!]_i$ from at least $t + 1$ parties, recovers the secret s, and sends it to all parties.
- $\mathcal{F}_{\mathrm{REVEAL}}^{\mathcal{P}}$ behaves the same as $\mathcal{F}_{\mathrm{REVEAL}}$ except that it sends the recovered secret s only to parties $\in \mathcal{P}$.

Also, we use the notations $\langle \cdot \rangle_{i \in \{0,1\}}$ to represent the shares in a $(1,2)$-*additive* SSS, i.e., $a = \langle a \rangle_0 + \langle a \rangle_1$ for any secret a. Under Shamir's SSS [39] or the replicated SSS [28], any two parties $P_i, P_{i+1 \bmod 3}$ can convert their shares $[\![s]\!]_i, [\![s]\!]_{i+1 \bmod 3}$ to $\langle s \rangle_0, \langle s \rangle_1$ by performing local computation.

We extend the notation to sharing arrays. For an array $\mathbf{A}$ of length X, we denote its x-th element by $\mathbf{A}[x]$. When secret sharing such an array, we denote its sharing by $[\![\mathbf{A}]\!] := ([\![a_0]\!], \ldots, [\![a_{X-1}]\!])$ and $\langle \mathbf{A} \rangle = (\langle a_0 \rangle, \ldots, \langle a_{X-1} \rangle)$, where $a_x = \mathbf{A}[x]$.

For concreteness and clarity of this work, we assume that all shares $[\![s]\!]$ are of the $(1,3)$-replicated SSS on the extension field $\mathbb{Z}_{2^\ell}$ as [2,12], i.e., for any $s = \sum_{i=0}^{\ell-1} s_i 2^i$; $s_i \in \mathbb{Z}_2$, its share is of the form $[\![s]\!] = \sum_{i=0}^{\ell-1} [\![s_i]\!] 2^i$. In this setup, all shares have the following properties.

Linear Homomorphism: The replicated SSS [28], by definition, supports share-to-share addition by performing only local operations on each party's shares. That is, for any $a, b, c \in \mathbb{Z}_{2^\ell}$, without any interaction, the parties can compute

$$[\![a]\!] + [\![b]\!] = [\![a + b]\!] \text{ and } c \times [\![a]\!] = [\![ca]\!].$$

We extend the above notation and operations to arrays of secrets. For any arrays $[\![\mathbf{A}]\!] = ([\![a_0]\!], \ldots, [\![a_{X-1}]\!])$ and $[\![\mathbf{B}]\!] = ([\![b_0]\!], \ldots, [\![b_{X-1}]\!])$ where $a_i, b_i \in \mathbb{Z}_{2^\ell}$, we denote entry-wise addition as $[\![\mathbf{A}]\!] + [\![\mathbf{B}]\!] := ([\![a_0]\!] + [\![b_0]\!], \ldots, [\![a_{X-1}]\!] + [\![b_{X-1}]\!])$ and entry-wise multiplication by a scalar as $c \times [\![\mathbf{A}]\!] := (c \times [\![a_0]\!], \ldots, c \times [\![a_{X-1}]\!])$.

Bit-Decomposition: Since all shares are of the form $[\![s]\!] = \sum_{i=0}^{\ell-1} [\![s_i]\!] 2^i$ where each $[\![s_i]\!]$ is a share of the replicated SSS on $\mathbb{Z}_2$, parties can perform the bit-decomposition operation $[\![s]\!] \to ([\![s_{\ell-1}]\!], \ldots, [\![s_0]\!])$ by their local conversion.

3.2   Distributed Oblivious RAM

A RAM consists of a memory of N cells and each cell is of size w bits and it allows for "clients" to perform read and write operations of the form $(\mathsf{op}, \mathsf{addr}, \mathsf{d})$, where $\mathsf{op} \in \{\mathsf{read}, \mathsf{write}\}$, $\mathsf{addr} \in [N]$ and $\mathsf{d} \in \{0,1\}^w \cup \{\bot\}$. If $\mathsf{op} = \mathsf{read}$, then $\mathsf{d} = \bot$ and the returned value is the content of the block located in logical address addr in the memory. If $\mathsf{op} = \mathsf{write}$, then the memory data in logical address addr is updated to d. We can think of this as an ideal (reactive) functionality $\mathcal{F}_{\mathrm{RAM}}$ that supports the following operation:

$\mathcal{F}_{\mathrm{RAM}}$:

- $v \leftarrow \textsc{Access}(\mathsf{op}, \mathsf{addr}, \mathsf{d})$: The input is an operation $\mathsf{op} \in \{\mathsf{read}, \mathsf{write}\}$, a key $\mathsf{addr} \in [N]$, and a value $\mathsf{d} \in \{0,1\}^w \cup \{\bot\}$. An internal size N array $\mathbf{X}$, initialized to all 0s, is maintained. The procedure does:
  1. If $\mathsf{op} = \mathsf{read}$, then set $\mathsf{d}^* = \mathbf{X}[\mathsf{addr}]$.
  2. If $\mathsf{op} = \mathsf{write}$, then set $\mathbf{X}[\mathsf{addr}] = \mathsf{d}$ and $\mathsf{d}^* = \mathsf{d}$.
  3. Output d^*.

Distributed Oblivious Simulation. Our goal is to simulate a RAM correctly while guaranteeing the standard security notion of secure multi-party computation. Towards this goal, we have m servers that can communicate between themselves over a fully connected network in synchronous rounds of communication. Each server can further perform arbitrary local computation between rounds. We model each server machine as a RAM. The view of each machine includes the contents of its own memory and the contents of the incoming messages, where the latter include addresses of memory cells to access. Such a secure system is called *Distributed Oblivious RAM* (DORAM). The security guarantee stipulates that the view of a colluding subset of dishonest servers cannot learn anything about the computation being performed, except what is absolutely necessary (e.g., the length of the computation). We shall consider a passive (semi-honest) or active (malicious) adversary who controls up to $t < m$ servers.

We shall define distributed oblivious simulation with respect to an arbitrary (possibly reactive or stateful) functionality. The definition for the RAM functionality will be implied as a special case. For concreteness, it is convenient (though not necessary) to imagine that the input and RAM state are secret-shared between the servers, that is, each party holds one out of m shares of the

RAM, and operations from a client are also written to each server in a secret shared fashion. We follow the real-ideal paradigm by defining two "worlds" and requiring that they are indistinguishable (following, e.g., Canetti [7]).

Definition 3.1 (View). *The view of party i consists of its auxiliary input and randomness followed by the honest input and all the messages sent and received by the party during the computation. Since we model parties as RAMs, the incoming and outgoing messages contain physical memory locations.*

In what follows, we suppress mentioning the auxiliary information to simplify notation and presentation. All of the definitions and results readily extend to the setting where auxiliary input is present.

Non-reactive Functionalities. Let $\mathcal{F}$ be a non-reactive functionality. Let Π be a distributed protocol implementing $\mathcal{F}$, $C \subseteq [m]$ be the set of $\leq t$ corrupted servers, and Sim be a PPT simulator. Denote $\bar{C} = [m] \setminus C$. We introduce the following experiments to define active (malicious) security and remark the necessary changes for passive (semi-honest) security.

- $\mathsf{Real}^{\mathsf{nr}}_{\Pi,C,\mathcal{A}}(\lambda, \{x_i\}_{i \in [m]})$: Run the protocol with security parameter λ, where honest parties (ones not in C) run the protocol Π honestly with their private input $x_i^* = x_i$, whereas corrupt parties (ones in C) get the corresponding x_i's but can deviate from the prescribed protocol arbitrarily, according to $\mathcal{A}$'s strategy. Let V_i be the view of server $i \in C$ throughout the execution and let y_i be the output of some honest party $i \in \bar{C}$. Output $(\{V_i\}_{i \in C}, \{y_i\}_{i \in \bar{C}})$.
  In the passive (semi-honest) setting, the experiment is the same except that corrupt parties use $x_i^* = x_i$ and they follow the specification of the protocol (i.e., $\mathcal{A}$ is passive).
- $\mathsf{Ideal}^{\mathsf{nr}}_{\mathcal{F},\mathsf{Sim},C,\mathcal{A}}(\lambda, \{x_i\}_{i \in [m]})$: First, the adversary sees the inputs of corrupted parties $\{x_i\}_{i \in C}$ and outputs $\{x_i^*\}_{i \in C}$ that may depend on them. Denote $x_i^* = x_i$ for each $i \in \bar{C}$. Then, we invoke the functionality $y_1, \ldots, y_m \leftarrow \mathcal{F}(x_1^*, \ldots, x_m^*)$. Finally, the simulator is executed and the following pair is outputted $(\mathsf{Sim}^{\mathcal{A}}(\lambda, C, \{x_i^*\}_{i \in C}), \{y_i\}_{i \in \bar{C}})$.
  In the passive (semi-honest) setting, the experiment is the same except that the adversary is passive and uses $x_i^* = x_i$.

A distributed protocol obliviously simulates a functionality $\mathcal{F}$ against active (resp. passive) adversaries if the corrupted servers in the real world have views that are indistinguishable from their views in the ideal world.

Definition 3.2 (Distributed oblivious simulation of non-reactive functionalities). *An m-server protocol Π (t, m)-obliviously simulates $\mathcal{F}$ if for any attacker there exists a PPT simulator Sim such that, for every subset of t passive/active corrupt parties C, any non-uniform PPT adversary $\mathcal{A}$, and all inputs $x_0, \ldots, x_{m-1}$, the distributions $\mathsf{Real}^{\mathsf{nr}}_{\Pi,C,\mathcal{A}}(\lambda, \{x_i\}_{i \in [m]})$ and $\mathsf{Ideal}^{\mathsf{nr}}_{\mathcal{F},\mathsf{Sim},C,\mathcal{A}}(\lambda, \{x_i\}_{i \in [m]})$ are computationally indistinguishable.*

Reactive Functionalities. A reactive functionality is one that can be repeatedly invoked and it may keep an internal secret state between invocations (a

RAM is, in particular, a reactive functionality). The adversary $\mathcal{A}$ chooses the next operation $(\mathsf{op}, \{x_i\}_{i \in [m]})$ adaptively in each stage. In the real execution, the corrupt parties may deviate arbitrarily from the prescribed protocol and the goal is to ensure that they do not learn anything beyond what is absolutely necessary. That is, we execute the protocol in the presence of the malicious adversary. In the ideal execution, the adversary obtains inputs $\{x_i\}_{i \in C}$ and may choose new inputs $\{x_i^*\}_{i \in C}$. The new inputs are fed (together with the inputs of the honest parties) into the functionality $\mathcal{F}$ which outputs an output $\{y_i\}_{i \in \bar{C}}$. At this point, using the output of malicious parties, a simulator must simulate the view of the malicious parties, including their internal state and the obtained messages (and access pattern) from other servers. The adversary can then choose the next command, as well as the next input, in an adaptive manner, based on everything it has seen so far.

Definition 3.3 (Distributed oblivious simulation of a reactive functionality). *We say that a stateful protocol Π is a (t, m)-distributed oblivious implementation of the reactive functionality $\mathcal{F}$ if there exists a stateful PPT simulator Sim, such that for any non-uniform PPT (stateful) adversary $\mathcal{A}$, the view of the adversary $\mathcal{A}$ in the following two experiments $\mathsf{Real}_{\Pi,C,\mathcal{A}}(\lambda, \{x_i\}_{i \in [m]})$ and $\mathsf{Ideal}_{\mathcal{F},\mathsf{Sim},C,\mathcal{A}}(\lambda, \{x_i\}_{i \in [m]})$ is computationally indistinguishable:*

$\mathsf{Real}_{\Pi,C,\mathcal{A}}(\lambda, \{x_i\}_{i \in [m]})$:	$\mathsf{Ideal}_{\mathcal{F},\mathsf{Sim},C,\mathcal{A}}(\lambda, \{x_i\}_{i \in [m]})$:
Let $(\mathsf{op}, \{x_i\}_{i \in [m]}) \leftarrow \mathcal{A}(1^\lambda)$.	Let $(\mathsf{op}, \{x_i\}_{i \in [m]}) \leftarrow \mathcal{A}(1^\lambda)$.
Loop while $\mathsf{op} \neq \perp$:	Loop while $\mathsf{op} \neq \perp$:
$\quad$ Let $x_i' = (\mathsf{op}, x_i)$ for each $i \in [m]$.	$\quad$ Let $x_i' = (\mathsf{op}, x_i)$ for each $i \in [m]$.
$\quad \{V_i\}_{i \in C}, \{y_i\}_{i \in \bar{C}} \quad \leftarrow$ $\quad \mathsf{Real}^{\mathsf{nr}}_{\Pi,C,\mathcal{A}}(\lambda, \{x_i'\}_{i \in [m]})$.	$\quad \{V_i\}_{i \in C}, \{y_i\}_{i \in \bar{C}} \quad \leftarrow$ $\quad \mathsf{Ideal}^{\mathsf{nr}}_{\mathcal{F},\mathsf{Sim},C,\mathcal{A}}(\lambda, \{x_i'\}_{i \in [m]})$.
$\quad (\mathsf{op}, \{x_i\}_{i \in [m]}) \quad \leftarrow$ $\quad \mathcal{A}(1^\lambda, \{V_i\}_{i \in C}, \{y_i\}_{i \in \bar{C}})$.	$\quad (\mathsf{op}, \{x_i\}_{i \in [m]}) \quad \leftarrow$ $\quad \mathcal{A}(1^\lambda, \{V_i\}_{i \in C}, \{y_i\}_{i \in \bar{C}})$.

4   Secure Computation Building Blocks

Our schemes rely on various existing building blocks from the secure computation literature. To encapsulate these building blocks, we assume the existence of an Arithmetic Black Box (ABB) functionality, $\mathcal{F}_{\mathsf{ABB}}$, which is a (reactive) multiparty functionality. $\mathcal{F}_{\mathsf{ABB}}$ should consist of functions MULT, RND, RESHARE, EQ, IFELSE, BITEXT, TRUNC, and PRF, each listed below.

To simplify the notation, we denote *"calling a function p of $\mathcal{F}_{\mathsf{ABB}}$"* as *"calling $\mathcal{F}_p$"*, e.g., *"parties call $\mathcal{F}_{\mathsf{MULT}}$"* represents that the parties invoke $\mathcal{F}_{\mathsf{ABB}}$ to call its function MULT with their inputs.

Assuming that all secrets are in $\mathbb{Z}_{2^b}$, all implementations we introduce below consume $O(b)$-bit communication and $O(b)$ local CPU computation steps except OPRFs that consume $O(\lambda + b)$-bits and steps.

Multiplication: Let $\mathcal{F}_{\text{MULT}}$ be a secure multiplication functionality that receives $[\![a]\!]$ and $[\![b]\!]$ and returns $[\![ab]\!]$. For the $(1,3)$-replicated SSS on the extension field $\mathbb{Z}_{2^\ell}$, we can use the implementation of Araki et al. [2] or Chida et al. [12]. For ease of notation, we occasionally denote $\mathcal{F}_{\text{MULT}}$ as $[\![a]\!] \times [\![b]\!]$.

Generating Random Shares: Let $\mathcal{F}_{\text{RND}}$ be a functionality that requires no inputs but returns a share $[\![r]\!]$ of a secret random value r. In the $(1,3)$-replicated SSS, since the form of shares is $[\![a]\!]_{i \bmod 3} = (a_i, a_{i+1})$; $a = a_0 + a_1 + a_2$, $\mathcal{F}_{\text{RND}}$ is simply implemented in information-theoretical security as that: Each party P_i locally generate a random r_i, send it to P_{i-1} and set $[\![r]\!]_i$ as (r_i, r_{i+1}). It is also known that, trading off the information-theoretical security, a pseudorandom r can be shared without any communication except a pre-computation. This is called Pseudorandom Secret Sharing (PRSS) [13].

Resharing: Let $\mathcal{F}_{\text{RESHARE}}$ be a functionality that receives $\langle a \rangle_0$ and $\langle a \rangle_1$, and returns $[\![a]\!]$. It can be simply implemented as that the parties P_{i_0} and P_{i_1}, who have $\langle a \rangle_0$ and $\langle a \rangle_1$ respectively, secret-shares their shares as $[\![\langle a \rangle_i]\!]$ for all parties and then they observe $[\![a]\!] = [\![\langle a \rangle_0 + \langle a \rangle_1]\!]$. Under the use of PRSS, the slightly efficient implementation is known [11].

Equality Test: Let $\mathcal{F}_{\text{EQ}}$ be a functionality that receives $[\![a]\!]$ and $[\![b]\!]$ then return $[\![c]\!]$ where $c \in \{0,1\}$ is equal to $(a =_? b)$. Though there are numerous implementations of these functionalities, for concreteness, we expect to use the one of Catrina and de Hoogh [8].

Selection: Let $\mathcal{F}_{\text{IFELSE}}$ be a functionality that receives $[\![c]\!]$, $[\![t]\!]$ and $[\![f]\!]$ such that $c \in \{0,1\}$, and returns $[\![t]\!]$ if $c = 1$, or $[\![f]\!]$ otherwise. Observe that $\mathcal{F}_{\text{IFELSE}}$ is equal to $f + c(t - f)$.

Bit Operations: Let $\mathcal{F}_{\text{BITEXT}}, \mathcal{F}_{\text{TRUNC}}$, and $\mathcal{F}_{\text{R\_SHIFT}}$ each be a functionality that receives shares $[\![a]\!]$, whose bit-representation is $a = a_\ell \ldots a_1$, and an integer $i; 1 \leq i \leq \ell$, then returns the following output:

- $\mathcal{F}_{\text{BITEXT}}([\![a]\!], i) \to [\![a_i]\!]$ s.t. $a_i (\in \{0,1\})$ is the i-th least significant bit of a.
- $\mathcal{F}_{\text{TRUNC}}([\![a]\!], i) \to [\![a']\!]$ s.t. $a' = a_\ell \ldots a_{i+1} \parallel 0^i$.
- $\mathcal{F}_{\text{R\_SHIFT}}([\![a]\!], i) \to [\![a']\!]$ s.t. $a' = 0^i \parallel a_\ell \ldots a_{i+1}$.

Using the local bit-decomposition described in Sect. 3.1, $\mathcal{F}_{\text{BITEXT}}$ can be implemented straightforwardly as follows: For $[\![a]\!] = \sum_{i=0}^{\ell-1} [\![a_i]\!] 2^i$, parties extract the target bit $[\![a_i]\!]$, generate $[\![\vec{0}]\!] = \sum_{i=0}^{\ell-1} [\![0]\!] 2^i$, and compute $[\![\vec{0}]\!] + ([\![a_i]\!] 2^0)$. $\mathcal{F}_{\text{TRUNC}}$ and $\mathcal{F}_{\text{R\_SHIFT}}$ can be realized in a similar manner.

Oblivious PRF (OPRF): Let $\mathcal{F}_{\text{PRF}}$ be a functionality that receives shares $[\![\mathsf{sk}]\!]$ and $[\![x]\!]$ from all parties and sends them $[\![y]\!]$ where y is given by a PRF $\mathsf{F}_{\mathsf{sk}}(x)$. A combination of known oblivious block ciphers [1,12,14,31] and $\mathcal{F}_{\text{R\_SHIFT}}$ implements $\mathcal{F}_{\text{PRF}}$.

5 Efficient Passively Secure Distributed Oblivious Hashing

A (static) hash table is a data structure supporting three operations BUILD, LOOKUP, and EXTRACT, that realizes the following reactive functionality. The BUILD procedure creates an in-memory data structure from an input array $\mathbf{I}$ containing real and dummy elements where each element is a (key, value) pair. Dummy elements have their key be $\perp$. It is assumed that all real elements in $\mathbf{I}$ have distinct keys. The LOOKUP procedure allows a requestor to look up the value of a key. A $\perp$ symbol is returned if the key is not found or if $\perp$ is the requested key. We say a (key, value) pair is visited if the key was searched for and found before. Finally, EXTRACT is the destructor and it returns a list containing unvisited elements padded with dummies to the same length as the input array $\mathbf{I}$.

The description of this functionality, denoted $\mathcal{F}_{HT}$, is described next:

$\mathcal{F}_{HT}$:

- BUILD($\mathbf{I}$): The input is an array $\mathbf{I} = (a_1, \dots, a_n)$ containing n elements, where each a_i is either dummy or a (key, value) pair denoted $a_i = (k_i, v_i)$. It is assumed that keys and values fit into $O(1)$ memory words and that all real keys are distinct. The procedure does:
  1. Initialize the state $\mathsf{H} = (\mathbf{I}, \mathbf{P})$ where $\mathbf{P} = \emptyset$.
- LOOKUP(k): The input is a key k (that might be $\perp$, i.e., dummy). The procedure does:
  1. If $k \in \mathbf{P}$ (i.e., k is a recurring lookup), then halt and return $\perp$.
  2. If $k = \perp$ or $k \notin \mathbf{I}$, set $v^* = \perp$.
  3. Otherwise, set $v^* = v$, where v is the value corresponding to $k(\in \mathbf{I})$.
  4. Update $\mathbf{P} = \mathbf{P} \cup \{k\}$.
  5. Output v^*.
- EXTRACT(): The procedure does:
  1. Define $\mathbf{I}' = \{a_1', \dots, a_n'\}$ such that: For $i \in [n]$, set $a_i' = a_i$ if $a_i = (k, v)$ and $k \notin \mathbf{P}$. Otherwise, set $a_i' = \perp$.
  2. Output $\mathbf{I}'$.

In this section, we propose a simple $(1, 3)$-distributed oblivious implementation of $\mathcal{F}_{HT}$ that is inspired by Lu et al. [33]. Since Lu's DORAM requires too many (at least $100 \log N$) OPRF calls for distributed blocks, the practical computation cost becomes expensive even if the asymptotic overhead is down to $O(\log N)$. To reduce the practical computation complexity without increasing the asymptotic overhead, we construct a concretely efficient distributed oblivious hashing from a simple new permutation protocol for 3-party computation.

We present two different oblivious distributed hash table constructions. One hash table will be very efficient but will only work (i.e., be secure) if $n \in \Omega(\log^2 N)$. The other construction is much simpler and will work for smaller tables, which is a standard technique from prior works (e.g. [25]). At a very high level, both hash table constructions work as follows (assuming a permutation protocol):

1. Starting with $(1,3)$-shares of input blocks, the parties securely compute (pseudorandom) addresses for the blocks to be placed.
2. The parties divide their roles into one *permuter* and two *storages*, and then only the permuter reveals the addresses of the blocks.
3. The permuter computes a permutation for the blocks, which is a *sorting permutation* depending on the addresses.
4. The parties obliviously apply the permutation (that is secret for the storages) and the storages receive the $(1,2)$-shares of the permuted blocks.
5. Now, the permuted blocks can take the form of some hash table (if the permutation is valid), and only the storages can access the table.
   (a) If the input array is long enough (say $\Omega(\log^2 N)$) we can directly apply a distributed version of Cuckoo hashing. This results with linear time build and constant time lookup.
   (b) Otherwise, if the input array is too short (say $O(\log^2 N)$), we use a much simpler and standard hash table construction (also used by [25,33] in a similar context). Set $\ell = 3\log N/\log\log N$. We split the input into N/ℓ bins each of size ℓ by sending element with key k to bin $\mathsf{PRF}(k)$. Overflowing elements are routed to a σ-size stash (we will use $\sigma = \log N$). Lookup then costs $O(\ell+\sigma)$. Looking forward, we will use this hash table construction for arrays of size $\log N, 2\log N, 4\log N, \ldots, \log^2 N$ and combine all of their stashes. Since there are $O(\log\log N)$ such tables and the lookup cost in each one is $O(\log N/\log\log N)$, the total cost will be $O(\log N + \sigma)$, as we want.

5.1   Distributed Oblivious Permutation

As a building block for our distributed oblivious hash table, we first construct an efficient 3-party secure permutation protocol. The precise functionality that we implement is described below. This section is devoted to the implementation of these functionalities via a 3-party protocol where at most one may be corrupted.

$\mathcal{F}_{\mathrm{PERM}}$:

1. Receive a permutation π from the *permuter* P, and receive $(1,3)$-shares of an array $[\![\mathbf{I}]\!]$ from all parties.
2. Obtain $\mathbf{I}$, compute $\pi \cdot \mathbf{I}$, and choose a random string $\mathbf{R}$ of the same size as $\mathbf{I}$.
3. Send $\langle \mathbf{I}'\rangle_0 = \mathbf{R}$ to the first *storage* S_0 and $\langle \mathbf{I}'\rangle_1 = \pi \cdot \mathbf{I} - \mathbf{R}$ to the second S_1.

$\mathcal{F}_{\mathrm{UNPERM}}$:

1. Receive a permutation π from the *permuter* P and 2-out-of-2 shares of an array $\langle \mathbf{I}\rangle_0, \langle \mathbf{I}\rangle_1$ from the *storages* S_0, S_1.
2. Reconstruct $\mathbf{I}$ and compute $\pi^{-1} \cdot \mathbf{I}$.
3. Return $[\![\mathbf{I}']\!] \leftarrow \mathcal{F}_{\mathrm{SHARE}}(\pi^{-1} \cdot \mathbf{I})$ for all parties.

Lemma 5.1 (Realization of $\mathcal{F}_{\mathbf{Perm}}$). *There is a (1,3)-distributed oblivious implementation, described as Algorithm 1, of $\mathcal{F}_{\mathrm{PERM}}$ in the presence of a passive adversary that controls one party. The protocol consumes $4nb + 2n\lceil \log n \rceil$ bits of communication and $12nb + 2n\lceil \log n \rceil$ local CPU computation steps where n is the number of blocks in the input array and b is the bit-length of each block. It also consumes 2 communication rounds.*

Lemma 5.2 (Realization of $\mathcal{F}_{\mathbf{Unperm}}$). *There is a distributed 3-party protocol, described as Algorithm 2, that securely realizes $\mathcal{F}_{\mathrm{UNPERM}}$ in the presence of a passive adversary that controls one party and in the $\mathcal{F}_{\mathrm{RESHARE}}$-hybrid model. By composition and using the implementation of $\mathcal{F}_{\mathrm{RESHARE}}$ described in Sect. 4, the protocol consumes $8nb + 2n\lceil \log n \rceil$ bits of communication cost and $19nb + 2n\lceil \log n \rceil$ local CPU computation steps where n is the number of blocks in the input array and b is the bit-length of each block. It also consumes 3 communication rounds.*

Proof of Lemma 5.1. The output of S_0 is $\mathbf{V}$ and the output of S_1 is

$$\widetilde{\mathbf{I}}_0 + \pi_1 \cdot \widetilde{\mathbf{I}}_1 = \pi \cdot \langle \mathbf{I} \rangle_0 - \pi_1 \cdot \mathbf{U} - \mathbf{V} + \pi_1 \circ \pi_0 \cdot \langle \mathbf{I} \rangle_1 + \pi_1 \cdot \mathbf{U}$$
$$= \pi \cdot \mathbf{I} - \mathbf{V}.$$

Together, they form a $(1,2)$-share of $\pi \cdot \mathbf{I}$, as needed for correctness. The claimed efficiency follows by direct inspection. The strings $\mathbf{U}$ and $\mathbf{V}$ are each nb bits long, similarly to $\widetilde{\mathbf{I}}_0$ and $\widetilde{\mathbf{I}}_0$. The bit-length of π_0 and π_1 is $n\lceil \log n \rceil$, each.

Algorithm 1. $(\cdot, \langle \mathbf{I}' \rangle_0, \langle \mathbf{I}' \rangle_1) \leftarrow \Pi_{\mathrm{PERM}}((\pi, [\![\mathbf{I}]\!]_0), [\![\mathbf{I}]\!]_1, [\![\mathbf{I}]\!]_2)$

Notation: P is the "permuter" and S_0, S_1 are two "storages."
Require: P has a permutation π and each party has shares of an array $[\![\mathbf{I}]\!]$.
Ensure: $\mathbf{I}' = \pi \cdot \mathbf{I}$.
1: P and S_0 convert their $(1,3)$-shares $[\![\mathbf{I}]\!]_0, [\![\mathbf{I}]\!]_1$ to $(1,2)$-shares $\langle \mathbf{I} \rangle_0, \langle \mathbf{I} \rangle_1$, respectively.
2: P chooses random strings $\mathbf{U}, \mathbf{V}$ of the same size as $\langle \mathbf{I} \rangle_0$, and random permutations π_0, π_1 s.t. $\pi_1 \circ \pi_0 = \pi$.
3: P sends $\pi_0, \mathbf{U}, \mathbf{V}$ to S_0 and $\pi_1, \widetilde{\mathbf{I}}_0 := \pi \cdot \langle \mathbf{I} \rangle_0 - \pi_1 \cdot \mathbf{U} - \mathbf{V}$ to S_1.
4: S_0 sends $\widetilde{\mathbf{I}}_1 := \pi_0 \cdot \langle \mathbf{I} \rangle_1 + \mathbf{U}$ to S_1.
5: S_0 outputs $\langle \mathbf{I}' \rangle_0 := \mathbf{V}$, and S_1 outputs $\langle \mathbf{I}' \rangle_1 := \widetilde{\mathbf{I}}_0 + \pi_1 \cdot \widetilde{\mathbf{I}}_1$.

Algorithm 2. $[\![\mathbf{I}']\!]_0, [\![\mathbf{I}']\!]_1, [\![\mathbf{I}']\!]_2 \leftarrow \Pi_{\text{UNPERM}}(\pi, \langle\mathbf{I}\rangle_0, \langle\mathbf{I}\rangle_1)$

Notation: P is the "permuter" and S_0, S_1 are two "storages."
Require: P has a permutation π and S_0, S_1 have a shares $\langle\mathbf{I}\rangle_0, \langle\mathbf{I}\rangle_1$, respectively.
Ensure: $\mathbf{I}' = \pi^{-1} \cdot \mathbf{I}$.

1: S_1 chooses a random strings $\mathbf{U}, \mathbf{V}$ of the same size as $\langle\mathbf{I}\rangle_0$.
2: P chooses random permutations π_0, π_1 s.t. $\pi_1 \circ \pi_0 = \pi$.
3: S_1 sends $\mathbf{U}$ to P and $\mathbf{V}$ to S_0. P sends π_0 to S_0 and π_1 to S_1.
4: S_0 sends $\widetilde{\mathbf{I}}_0 := \langle\mathbf{I}\rangle_0 + \mathbf{V}$ to P. S_1 sends $\widetilde{\mathbf{I}}_1 := \pi_1^{-1} \cdot (\langle\mathbf{I}\rangle_1 - \mathbf{V}) - \mathbf{U}$ to S_0.
5: P computes $\langle\mathbf{I}'\rangle_0 := \pi^{-1} \cdot \widetilde{\mathbf{I}}_0 + \pi_0^{-1} \cdot \mathbf{U}$, and S_0 computes $\langle\mathbf{I}'\rangle_1 := \pi_0^{-1} \cdot \widetilde{\mathbf{I}}_1$.
6: Parties call $\mathcal{F}_{\text{RESHARE}}$ to convert $\langle\mathbf{I}'\rangle_0, \langle\mathbf{I}'\rangle_1$ to $[\![\mathbf{I}']\!]_0, [\![\mathbf{I}']\!]_1, [\![\mathbf{I}']\!]_2$.

For security, observe that the permuter P never receives any message and does not have any output, and therefore it is trivial to simulate its view. Similarly, the first storage server S_0 only gets one message $\mathbf{U}, \mathbf{V}, \pi_0$ (from P), all of which are uniformly random and independent of the inputs of all parties. The output of S_0 contains $\mathbf{V}$ and so overall it is immediate to simulate its view. The only case remaining is when S_1 is corrupted. Its view in the protocol consists of $\pi_1, \widetilde{\mathbf{I}}_0, \widetilde{\mathbf{I}}_1$ which can be simulated by 3 uniformly random strings of appropriate length. Indeed, $\widetilde{\mathbf{I}}_0$ is masked by $\mathbf{V}$ and then $\widetilde{\mathbf{I}}_1$ is masked by $\mathbf{U}$, all of which are not known to S_1. $\qquad\square$

Proof of Lemma 5.2. Since we are in the $\mathcal{F}_{\text{RESHARE}}$-hybrid model, for correctness we need to show that $\langle\mathbf{I}'\rangle_0 + \langle\mathbf{I}'\rangle_1 = \pi^{-1} \cdot \mathbf{I}$. Indeed,

$$\langle\mathbf{I}'\rangle_0 + \langle\mathbf{I}'\rangle_1 = \pi^{-1} \cdot (\langle\mathbf{I}\rangle_0 + \mathbf{V}) + \pi_0^{-1} \cdot \mathbf{U} + \pi_0^{-1} \cdot (\pi_1^{-1} \cdot (\langle\mathbf{I}\rangle_1 - \mathbf{V}) - \mathbf{U})$$
$$= \pi^{-1} \cdot \mathbf{I}.$$

The claimed efficiency follows by direct inspection. The strings $\mathbf{U}$ and $\mathbf{V}$ are each nb bits long, similarly to $\widetilde{\mathbf{I}}_0$ and $\widetilde{\mathbf{I}}_0$. The bit-length of π_0 and π_1 is $n\lceil\log n\rceil$, each.

For security, if S_1 is corrupted, we can easily simulate its view as it does not receive any message except π_1 which is uniformly random and independent of the other inputs. If P is corrupted, then it again immediately simulates its view since it only receives $\mathbf{U}$ and $\widetilde{\mathbf{I}}_0 := \langle\mathbf{I}\rangle_0 + \mathbf{V}$ throughout the execution, both of which are uniformly distributed (in P's view). Lastly, assume that S_0 is corrupted. Its view consists of $\mathbf{V}, \pi_0$ and $\widetilde{\mathbf{I}}_1 := \pi_1^{-1} \cdot (\langle\mathbf{I}\rangle_1 - \mathbf{V}) - \mathbf{U}$. Since it does not know $\mathbf{U}$, the term $\widetilde{\mathbf{I}}_1$ looks completely uniform and therefore the whole view can be simulated by 3 uniformly random strings of the appropriate length. $\qquad\square$

5.2 Distributed Oblivious Hashing for Short Inputs

Equipped with the above permutation protocols, we present a distributed oblivious hash table for short input. Specifically, the hash table that we give out here works best when n, the input array size, is $O(\log^2 N)$. Similar hash was employed in [25,33] in a similar context.

Consider a balls-into-bins hash table T of size τ with bin size β and a stash S of size σ. Below, we construct a distributed hash table $\langle T \rangle$ and stash $[\![S]\!]$ from n elements (Algorithm 3), support lookup in the main table (Algorithm 4) and in the stash (Algorithm 5), and finally deconstruct the structure (Algorithm 6). We rely on our role-splitting permutation protocols and an OPRFs.

Algorithm 3. $\pi, \langle T \rangle_{0,1}, [\![S]\!], [\![s]\!], \mathsf{ctr}, \mathbf{P} \leftarrow \Pi_{\mathrm{BUILD}}([\![D]\!]_0, [\![D]\!]_1, [\![D]\!]_2)$

Notation: Let P be the permuter and S_0, S_1 be the storages. Let $\tau := |T|$ and $\sigma := |S|$ be the size of expected hash table and stash (T, S) storing n items, and let $n' = \tau + \sigma$.

Require: Parties have $(1,3)$-shares of a dataset $[\![D]\!]_{i \in \{0,1,2\}} = ([\![d_0]\!]_i, \ldots, [\![d_{n-1}]\!]_i)$.

Ensure: S_0 and S_1 obtain $(1,2)$-shares of a balls-into-bins hash table, $\langle T \rangle_0$ and $\langle T \rangle_1$, respectively. P obtains a permutation π, and all parties hold $(1,3)$-shares of a stash $[\![S]\!]$ and a PRF key $[\![s]\!]$. Parties also hold a query counter ctr, and S_0, S_1 hold a set $\mathbf{P}$, as their states.

(Computing pseudorandom addresses for the input data.)

1: Parties call $\mathcal{F}_{\mathrm{RND}}$ to generate a random PRF key $[\![s]\!]$.
2: **for all** $i \in [n]$ **do**
3:     Parties call $\mathcal{F}_{\mathrm{EQ}}$ to obtain $[\![\mathsf{isDummy}_i]\!] := [\![k_i =_? \bot]\!]$.
4:     Parties call $\mathcal{F}_{\mathrm{IFELSE}}$ to simulate:
        If $\mathsf{isDummy}_i = 1$, *then* $[\![\widetilde{k_i}]\!] := [\![\bot + i]\!]$; *otherwise* $[\![\widetilde{k_i}]\!] := [\![k_i]\!]$.
5:     Parties call $\mathcal{F}_{\mathrm{PRF}}$ to obtain virtual addresses $[\![\mathsf{addr}_i]\!]$ from $([\![s]\!], [\![\widetilde{k_i}]\!])$.

(Building a balls-into-bins hash table via permutation.)

6: Parties call $\mathcal{F}_{\mathrm{SHARE}}$ to generate an array $[\![E]\!]$ consisting of $n' - n$ dummy blocks.
7: Let $[\![\widetilde{D}]\!] := [\![D]\!] \,\|\, [\![E]\!]$ be a concatenated dataset.
8: Parties call $\mathcal{F}_{\mathrm{REVEAL}}^{\{P\}}$ to reveal to P all $\mathsf{addr}_{i,0}, \mathsf{addr}_{i,1}$ for $i \in [n]$.
9: P computes a permutation $\pi \colon [n'] \to [n']$ that indicates the bin-placements of elements. That is, π says where to place $\widetilde{D}$'s elements into T (or S) as indicated by addr_i.
10: Parties call $\mathcal{F}_{\mathrm{PERM}}$ with π and $[\![\widetilde{D}]\!]$ to make S_0 and S_1 obtain $\langle \widetilde{D'} \rangle_0$ and $\langle \widetilde{D'} \rangle_1$ respectively, where $\widetilde{D'} = \pi \cdot \widetilde{D}$.
11: Each S_i for $i \in \{0,1\}$ organizes the array $\langle \widetilde{D'} \rangle_i$ into a hash table $\langle T \rangle_i$ and stash $\langle S \rangle_i$, by separating $\langle \widetilde{D'} \rangle_i$ into the first τ and the last σ elements.
12: Parties call $\mathcal{F}_{\mathrm{RESHARE}}$ to convert $\langle S \rangle_{0,1}$ to $[\![S]\!]$.
13: Parties set their state $\mathsf{ctr} = 0$, and S_0, S_1 allocate an empty set $\mathbf{P} = \emptyset$.
14: **Return** $\pi, \langle T \rangle_{0,1}, [\![S]\!], [\![s]\!], \mathsf{ctr}, \mathbf{P}$

Algorithm 4. $[\![d]\!], [\![\text{found}]\!] \leftarrow \Pi_{\text{LOOKUP}}([\![k]\!], \langle T \rangle_{0,1}, [\![s]\!], \text{ctr}, \mathbf{P})$

Notation: Let P be the permuter and let S_0, S_1 be the storages. Let β and γ be the bin size and number of bins, respectively, i.e., $|T| = \tau = \beta\gamma$.

Require: $[\![k]\!]$ is a $(1,3)$-share of an input key to be searched for. S_i have the distributed hash table $\langle T \rangle_i$ and a set $\mathbf{P}$. Parties have $(1,3)$-shares of a PRF key $[\![s]\!]$ and a query counter ctr.

Ensure: $\text{d} = (k, v), \text{found} = 1$ if T contains (k, v). Otherwise, $\text{d} = (0, 0), \text{found} = 0$.

(Computing pseudorandom addresses to be fetched.)

1: Parties call $\mathcal{F}_{\text{EQ}}$ to obtain $[\![\text{isDummy}]\!] := [\![k =_? \bot]\!]$.

2: Parties call $\mathcal{F}_{\text{IFELSE}}$ to simulate:
   $\quad$ *If* isDummy $= 1$, *then set* $[\![\widetilde{k}]\!] := [\![\bot + \text{ctr}]\!]$; *otherwise* $[\![\widetilde{k}]\!] := [\![k]\!]$.

3: Parties call $\mathcal{F}_{\text{PRF}}$ to obtain $[\![\text{addr}]\!]$ from $([\![s]\!], [\![\widetilde{k}]\!])$.

4: Parties call $\mathcal{F}_{\text{REVEAL}}^{\{S_0, S_1\}}$ to recover addr to both S_0 and S_1. If addr $\in \mathbf{P}$, S_0 and S_1 halt. Otherwise, they update $\mathbf{P} \leftarrow \mathbf{P} \cup \{\text{addr}\}$.

(Searching for the table T.)

5: **for all** $i \in [\beta]$ **do**

6: $\quad$ Parties call $\mathcal{F}_{\text{RESHARE}}$ to convert $\langle T[\gamma \cdot \text{addr} + i] \rangle$ to $([\![k_i]\!], [\![v_i]\!])$,
   $\quad$ i.e., fetch the i-th element of the addr-th bin.

7: $\quad$ Parties call $\mathcal{F}_{\text{EQ}}$ to obtain $[\![\text{isQueried}_i]\!] = [\![k_i =_? k]\!]$.

8: $\quad$ Parties call $\mathcal{F}_{\text{IFELSE}}$ and $\mathcal{F}_{\text{MULT}}$ to simulate:
   $\quad$ *If* isDummy $= 0$ *and* isQueried$_i = 1$,
   $\quad\quad$ *then* found $= 1$, $[\![d]\!] = ([\![k_i]\!], [\![v_i]\!])$, *and* $\langle T[\gamma \cdot \text{addr} + i] \rangle = \langle d^{\text{dummy}} \rangle$.

9: Parties increment ctr.

10: **Return** $[\![d]\!], [\![\text{found}]\!]$

Lemma 5.3. *Assume that the input array consists of $n \leq \log^2 N$ blocks and each block is b bits. Also assume that the table size $\tau = n$, the bin size $\beta = \lceil 3 \log N / \log \log N \rceil$, and the stash size $\sigma = \lceil \log N \rceil$. There exists a distributed 3-party protocol, described as Algorithms 3, 4, 5, and 6, that securely realizes $\mathcal{F}_{\text{HT}}$ in the $(\mathcal{F}_{\text{SHARE}}, \mathcal{F}_{\text{REVEAL}}^P, \mathcal{F}_{\text{ABB}}, \mathcal{F}_{\text{PERM}}, \mathcal{F}_{\text{UNPERM}})$-hybrid model and in the presence of a passive adversary that controls one party.*

- *The BUILD procedure consumes $O(n(\lambda + b + \log n))$ local computation steps.*
- *The LOOKUP procedure consumes $O((\lambda + b)\frac{\log N}{\log \log N})$ local computation steps.*
- *The STASHSEARCH procedure consumes $O(b \log \lambda)$ local computation steps.*
- *The EXTRACT procedure consumes $O(nb)$ local computation steps.*

Furthermore, all of the above procedures consume $O(1)$ communication rounds.

Proof Sketch. We sketch complexity and why the construction is secure for completeness because this hash table has been used many times in the ORAM literature. For instance, in our range of parameters, it was directly used in [33, Section 3.5 of the full version]. Recall that our input is already randomly shuffled and so which element goes to which bin is completely hidden from the adversary. Also the bins are padded to their maximum capacity. (Notice that the permuter

Algorithm 5. $[\![d]\!], [\![\text{found}]\!] \leftarrow \Pi_{\text{StashSearch}}([\![k]\!], [\![S]\!])$

Require: $[\![k]\!]$ is a $(1,3)$-share of an input key to be searched for, and $[\![S]\!]$ is an array consisting of σ shares of key-value pairs.

Ensure: $d = (k, v), \text{found} = 1$ if S contains (k, v). Otherwise, $d = (0, 0), \text{found} = 0$.

1: **for all** $([\![k_u]\!], [\![v_u]\!])_{u \in [\sigma]}$ in $[\![S]\!]$ **do**
2:     Parties call $\mathcal{F}_{\text{EQ}}$ to obtain $[\![\text{isQueried}_u]\!] = [\![k_u =_? k]\!]$.
3:     Parties call $\mathcal{F}_{\text{IFELSE}}$ and $\mathcal{F}_{\text{MULT}}$ to simulate:
        If $\text{isQueried}_u = 1$, then $\text{found} = 1$, $[\![d]\!] = ([\![k_u]\!], [\![v_u]\!])$, and $[\![S[u]]\!] = [\![d^{\text{dummy}}]\!]$.
4: **Return** $[\![d]\!], [\![\text{found}]\!]$

Algorithm 6. $[\![D]\!]_0, [\![D]\!]_1, [\![D]\!]_2 \leftarrow \Pi_{\text{EXTRACT}}(\pi, \langle T \rangle_{0,1}, [\![S]\!])$

Notation: Let P be the permuter and let S_0, S_1 be the storages.

Require: S_0 and S_1 have the distributed hash table $\langle T \rangle_{0,1}$, respectively. P has the permutation π and all parties have the distributed stash $[\![S]\!]$.

Ensure: A dataset D contains all real elements in T and S.

1: Each S_i converts $[\![S]\!]$ to $\langle S \rangle_i$ and reorganizes an array $\langle \widetilde{D} \rangle_i$ as $\widetilde{D} = T \| S$.
2: Parties call $\mathcal{F}_{\text{UNPERM}}$ with $(\pi, \langle \widetilde{D} \rangle_0, \langle \widetilde{D} \rangle_1)$ to obtain $[\![\widetilde{D'}]\!]_{j \in \{0,1,2\}}$ where $\widetilde{D'} = \pi^{-1} \cdot \widetilde{D}$.
3: Let $[\![D]\!]_j$ be the first n elements of $[\![\widetilde{D'}]\!]_i$.
4: **Return** $[\![D]\!]_0, [\![D]\!]_1, [\![D]\!]_2$

---

knows the PRF key and so can pad appropriately but never sees lookup queries.) Also, by the analysis of [33, Section 3.5 of the full version], except with negligible probability in N, a σ-size stash suffices to store all overflowing elements and so the construction is successful. □

5.3 Distributed Oblivious Hashing for Long Inputs

The idea is simple to describe at a high level: given a set of elements we first obliviously permute them and then we index the permuted set using a non-oblivious efficient hashing scheme. For the latter, we use *Cuckoo hashing* [37], a hashing paradigm that resolves collisions in a table by using two hash functions and two tables, cleverly assigning each element to one of the two tables, and enabling lookup using only two queries. The standard version of Cuckoo hashing suffers from inverse polynomial probability of build failure which does not suffice for our application (since we aim for negligible error). To this end, we use a variant of Cuckoo hashing where items that cannot be stored in one of the two tables are stored in a (typically small) "stash". According to Noble [34], for any number of elements $n = \omega(\log N)$, there exists Cuckoo hashing that has the table of size $\tau = (1 + \epsilon)n$ and the stash of size $\sigma = \Theta(\log N)$ with negligible failure probability. Henceforth, we specify $\tau = 2n$ and $\sigma = \lceil \log N \rceil$ for concrete efficiency analysis.

To ease presentation of our implementations, we use the following notations to represent shares of real/dummy blocks.

Algorithm 7. $\pi, \langle T \rangle_{0,1}, [\![S]\!], [\![s_0]\!], [\![s_1]\!], \mathsf{ctr}, \mathbf{P} \leftarrow \Pi_{\text{BUILD}}([\![D]\!]_0, [\![D]\!]_1, [\![D]\!]_2)$

Notation: Let P be the permuter and S_0, S_1 be the storages. Let $\tau := |T|$ and $\sigma := |S|$ be the size of expected hash table and stash (T, S) storing n items, and let $n' = \tau + \sigma$.

Require: Parties have $(1,3)$-shares of a dataset $[\![D]\!]_{i \in \{0,1,2\}} = ([\![d_0]\!]_i, \ldots, [\![d_{n-1}]\!]_i)$.

Ensure: S_0 and S_1 obtain $(1,2)$-shares of Cuckoo hash table, $\langle T \rangle_{0,1}$, respectively. P obtains a permutation π, and all parties hold $(1,3)$-shares of a stash $[\![S]\!]$ and PRF keys $[\![s_0]\!]$ and $[\![s_1]\!]$. Parties also hold a query counter ctr, and S_0, S_1 hold a set $\mathbf{P}$, as their states.

(Computing pseudorandom addresses for the input data.)
1: Parties call $\mathcal{F}_{\text{RND}}$ to generate random PRF keys $[\![s_0]\!]$ and $[\![s_1]\!]$.
2: **for all** $i \in [n]$ **do**
3:      Parties call $\mathcal{F}_{\text{EQ}}$ to obtain $[\![\mathsf{isDummy}_i]\!] := [\![k_i =_? \bot]\!]$.
4:      Parties call $\mathcal{F}_{\text{IFELSE}}$ to simulate:
         If $\mathsf{isDummy}_i = 1$, *then* $[\![\widetilde{k}_i]\!] := [\![\bot + i]\!]$; *otherwise* $[\![\widetilde{k}_i]\!] := [\![k_i]\!]$.
5:      Parties call $\mathcal{F}_{\text{PRF}}$ to obtain virtual addresses $[\![\mathsf{addr}_{i,0}]\!]$ and $[\![\mathsf{addr}_{i,1}]\!]$ from $([\![s_0]\!], [\![\widetilde{k}_i]\!])$ and $([\![s_1]\!], [\![\widetilde{k}_i]\!])$, respectively.

(Building a Cuckoo hash table via permutation.)
6: Parties call $\mathcal{F}_{\text{SHARE}}$ to generate an array $[\![E]\!]$ consisting of $n' - n$ dummy blocks.
7: Let $[\![\widetilde{D}]\!] := [\![D]\!] \,\|\, [\![E]\!]$ be a concatenated dataset.
8: Parties call $\mathcal{F}_{\text{REVEAL}}^{\{P\}}$ to reveal to P all $\mathsf{addr}_{i,0}, \mathsf{addr}_{i,1}$ for $i \in [n]$.
9: P computes a permutation $\pi \colon [n'] \to [n']$ that indicates the bin-placements of Cuckoo hashing. That is, π says where to place $\widetilde{D}$'s elements as indicated by either $\mathsf{addr}_{i,0}$ or $\mathsf{addr}_{i,1}$.
10: Parties call $\mathcal{F}_{\text{PERM}}$ with π and $[\![\widetilde{D}]\!]$ to make S_0 and S_1 obtain $\langle \widetilde{D'} \rangle_0$ and $\langle \widetilde{D'} \rangle_1$ respectively, where $\widetilde{D'} = \pi \cdot \widetilde{D}$.
11: Each S_i for $i \in \{0,1\}$ organizes the array $\langle \widetilde{D'} \rangle_i$ into a hash table $\langle T \rangle_i$ and stash $\langle S \rangle_i$, by separating $\langle \widetilde{D'} \rangle_i$ into the first τ and the last σ elements.
12: Parties call $\mathcal{F}_{\text{RESHARE}}$ to convert $\langle S \rangle_{0,1}$ to $[\![S]\!]$.
13: Parties set their state $\mathsf{ctr} = 0$, and S_0, S_1 allocate an empty set $\mathbf{P} = \emptyset$.
14: **Return** $\pi, \langle T \rangle_{0,1}, [\![S]\!], [\![s_0]\!], [\![s_1]\!], \mathsf{ctr}, \mathbf{P}$

- Let $[\![d]\!] = ([\![k]\!], [\![v]\!])$ be a share of a data block that contains shares of a key k and value v.
- Let $[\![d^{\mathsf{dummy}}]\!] = ([\![\bot]\!], [\![\bot]\!])$ be a share of a dummy block. We assume that $\bot$ is a number greater than any real k.
- Let $[\![D]\!] = ([\![d_0]\!], \ldots, [\![d_{n-1}]\!])$ be a share of a dataset of size n.

Algorithm 7 constructs 2-out-of-2 shares of a Cuckoo hash table, $(\langle T \rangle, \langle S \rangle)$, from 2-out-of-3 shares of a dataset $[\![D]\!]$. In this protocol, the party assigned the role of *permuter* obtains all addresses the data should be placed and then computes a permutation π that moves the data to (one of) the corresponding addresses. Now, parties can efficiently convert D into the table (T, S) via $\mathcal{F}_{\text{PERM}}$.

Algorithm 8 fetches a queried item from the Cuckoo hash table. The main part of this protocol is that the parties assigned the role of *storage* obtain two addresses of the queried item, access T of the location indicated by them, and select one out of the two items of T. When the parties receive a dummy query, random locations of T are fetched.

Algorithm 8. $\llbracket d \rrbracket, \llbracket \text{found} \rrbracket \leftarrow \Pi_{\text{LOOKUP}}(\llbracket k \rrbracket, \langle \mathsf{T} \rangle_{0,1}, \llbracket s_0 \rrbracket, \llbracket s_1 \rrbracket, \text{ctr}, \mathbf{P})$

Notation: Let P be the permuter and let S_0, S_1 be the storages.

Require: $\llbracket k \rrbracket$ is a $(1,3)$-share of an input key to be searched for. S_0, S_1 have the distributed hash table $\langle \mathsf{T} \rangle_{0,1}$ and a set $\mathbf{P}$. Parties have $(1,3)$-shares of PRF keys $\llbracket s_0 \rrbracket, \llbracket s_1 \rrbracket$ and a query counter ctr.

Ensure: $\mathsf{d} = (k, v), \text{found} = 1$ if T contains (k, v). Otherwise, $\mathsf{d} = (0, 0), \text{found} = 0$.

(Computing pseudorandom addresses to be fetched.)
1: Parties call $\mathcal{F}_{\text{EQ}}$ to obtain $\llbracket \text{isDummy} \rrbracket := \llbracket k =_? \perp \rrbracket$.
2: Parties call $\mathcal{F}_{\text{IFELSE}}$ to simulate:
   If isDummy $= 1$, then set $\llbracket \widetilde{k} \rrbracket := \llbracket \perp + \text{ctr} \rrbracket$; otherwise $\llbracket \widetilde{k} \rrbracket := \llbracket k \rrbracket$.
3: Parties call $\mathcal{F}_{\text{PRF}}$ to obtain $\llbracket \text{addr}_0 \rrbracket$ and $\llbracket \text{addr}_1 \rrbracket$ from $(\llbracket s_0 \rrbracket, \llbracket \widetilde{k} \rrbracket)$ and $(\llbracket s_1 \rrbracket, \llbracket \widetilde{k} \rrbracket)$, respectively.
4: Parties call $\mathcal{F}_{\text{REVEAL}}^{\{S_0, S_1\}}$ to recover $\text{addr}_0, \text{addr}_1$ to both S_0 and S_1. If $(\text{addr}_0, \text{addr}_1) \in \mathbf{P}$, S_0 and S_1 halt. Otherwise, they update $\mathbf{P} \leftarrow \mathbf{P} \cup \{(\text{addr}_0, \text{addr}_1)\}$.

(Searching for the table T.)
5: for all $i = 0, 1$ do
6:     Parties call $\mathcal{F}_{\text{RESHARE}}$ to convert $\langle \mathsf{T}[\text{addr}_i] \rangle$ to $(\llbracket k_i \rrbracket, \llbracket v_i \rrbracket)$.
7:     Parties call $\mathcal{F}_{\text{EQ}}$ to obtain $\llbracket \text{isQueried}_i \rrbracket = \llbracket k_i =_? k \rrbracket$.
8:     Parties call $\mathcal{F}_{\text{IFELSE}}$ and $\mathcal{F}_{\text{MULT}}$ to simulate:
       If isDummy $= 0$ and isQueried$_i = 1$,
         then found $= 1$, $\llbracket d \rrbracket = (\llbracket k_i \rrbracket, \llbracket v_i \rrbracket)$, and $\langle \mathsf{T}[\text{addr}_i] \rangle = \langle \mathsf{d}^{\text{dummy}} \rangle$.
9: Parties increment ctr.
10: **Return** $\llbracket d \rrbracket, \llbracket \text{found} \rrbracket$

Algorithm 9 is a deconstruction procedure that applies the inverted permutation π^{-1} to the hash table. This π^{-1} sorts all real blocks in the hash table into the order in which they were input to Π_{BUILD}. The stash lookup procedure is the same as Algorithms 5 and so we reuse the code and avoid repetition.

Lemma 5.4. *Assume that the input array consists of $n > \log^2 N$ blocks and each block is b bits. There exists a distributed 3-party protocol, described as Algorithms 5, 7, 8 and 9, that securely realizes $\mathcal{F}_{\text{HT}}$ in the $(\mathcal{F}_{\text{SHARE}}, \mathcal{F}_{\text{REVEAL}}^P, \mathcal{F}_{\text{ABB}}, \mathcal{F}_{\text{PERM}}, \mathcal{F}_{\text{UNPERM}})$-hybrid model and in the presence of a passive adversary that controls one party.*

– The BUILD procedure consumes $O(n(\lambda + b + \log n))$ local computation steps.

Algorithm 9. $\llbracket \mathsf{D} \rrbracket_0, \llbracket \mathsf{D} \rrbracket_1, \llbracket \mathsf{D} \rrbracket_2 \leftarrow \Pi_{\text{EXTRACT}}(\pi, \langle \mathsf{T} \rangle_{0,1}, \llbracket \mathsf{S} \rrbracket)$

Notation: Let P be the permuter and let S_0, S_1 be the storages.

Require: S_0 and S_1 have the distributed hash table $\langle \mathsf{T} \rangle_{0,1}$, respectively. P has the permutation π and all parties have the distributed stash $\llbracket \mathsf{S} \rrbracket$.

Ensure: A dataset D contains all real elements in T and S.
1: Each S_i converts $\llbracket \mathsf{S} \rrbracket$ to $\langle \mathsf{S} \rangle_i$ and reorganizes an array $\langle \widetilde{\mathsf{D}} \rangle_i$ as $\widetilde{\mathsf{D}} = \mathsf{T} \| \mathsf{S}$.
2: Parties call $\mathcal{F}_{\text{UNPERM}}$ with $(\pi, \langle \widetilde{\mathsf{D}} \rangle_0, \langle \widetilde{\mathsf{D}} \rangle_1)$ to obtain $\llbracket \widetilde{\mathsf{D}'} \rrbracket_{j \in \{0,1,2\}}$ where $\widetilde{\mathsf{D}'} = \pi^{-1} \cdot \widetilde{\mathsf{D}}$.
3: Let $\llbracket \mathsf{D} \rrbracket_j$ be the first n elements of $\llbracket \widetilde{\mathsf{D}'} \rrbracket_i$.
4: **Return** $\llbracket \mathsf{D} \rrbracket_0, \llbracket \mathsf{D} \rrbracket_1, \llbracket \mathsf{D} \rrbracket_2$

- *The* LOOKUP *procedure consumes* $O(\lambda + b)$ *local computation steps.*
- *The* STASHSEARCH *procedure consumes* $O(b \log N)$ *local computation steps.*
- *The* EXTRACT *procedure consumes* $O(nb)$ *local computation steps.*

Furthermore, all those procedures consumes $O(1)$ *communication rounds.*

Proof. The proof of security and correctness is given in the full version. We focus on the efficiency analysis below.

Algorithm 7 consists of $O(n)$ calls of $\mathcal{F}_{\text{EQ}}, \mathcal{F}_{\text{IFELSE}}, \mathcal{F}_{\text{PRF}}, \mathcal{F}_{\text{SHARE}}$, and $\mathcal{F}_{\text{REVEAL}}$, and an invocation of $\mathcal{F}_{\text{PERM}}$. In Algorithm 8, the parties need to call $\mathcal{F}_{\text{MULT}}$, $\mathcal{F}_{\text{RESHARE}}, \mathcal{F}_{\text{EQ}}, \mathcal{F}_{\text{IFELSE}}, \mathcal{F}_{\text{REVEAL}}$, and $\mathcal{F}_{\text{PRF}}$ $O(1)$ times for the table lookup. Algorithm 9 requires $\mathcal{F}_{\text{UNPERM}}$ at once. In addition, all iterative operations in Algorithm 7, 8, and 9 can be performed in parallel. Lastly, the cost of STASHSEARCH was analyzed in Lemma 5.3.   □

6   Optimal DORAM Against Passive Adversary

In this section, we give our optimal 3-party DORAM that is secure against a passive adversary who colludes with one of the three servers.

Our DORAM is on the known hierarchical paradigm, i.e. the data structure is built via a hierarchy of $L := \lceil \log N - \log \log N \rceil$ distributed hash tables and one top-level array. All levels $i = 1, \ldots, L$ in the hierarchy are implemented using our distributed oblivious hash table $\mathcal{F}_{\text{HT}}$ from Sects. 5.2 and 5.3. The size of the stash in our distributed oblivious hash table is set to $\sigma = \lceil \log N \rceil$. The top-level array, $[\![S]\!]$, can store up to $c = 2\sigma$ data blocks. The capacity of level $i \in [L]$ is $c2^{i-1}$. Each data block may be associated with metadata that is used to keep track of the location of an element. Specifically, an "augmented data block" $[\![\tilde{d}_i]\!] := ([\![d_i]\!], [\![lv_i]\!])$ consists of the main data block $[\![d_i]\!] = ([\![k_i]\!], [\![v_i]\!])$ and additional information $[\![lv_i]\!]$; $lv_i \in \{0,1\}^{L-1}$ that indicates the levels to which $[\![\tilde{d}_i]\!]$ is associated.[5]

The smaller tables of level $i = 1$ to $2 \log \log N$, i.e., tables that hold up to $\log^2 N$ elements, are implemented with our hash table for short inputs (Sect. 5.2). For them, each instance consists of a single table, split into bins and a stash. Recall that we merge all stashes of all levels together into one logarithmic-size stash. Lookup goes into one of the bins and scans it. For the tables holding longer arrays, from $i = 2 \log \log N + 1$ to L, the hash table is implemented with our hash table for long inputs (Sect. 5.3). Each such hash table consists of two parts: the main table and a stash. Again, the stashes from all levels are combined into the top-level array, as commonly done (e.g., in [33]).

Theorem 6.1. *There is a 3-party protocol, described as Algorithm 10 and 11, that securely realizes* $\mathcal{F}_{\text{RAM}}$ *in the* $(\mathcal{F}_{\text{ABB}}, \mathcal{F}_{\text{HT}})$-*hybrid model and in the presence*

---

[5] The metadata associated with each data blocks is used to avoid the stash-resampling attack of [18], same as was done in [3,4,18].

[5] Note that if $p \le \log \log N$, the obtained PRF key is single, $[\![s_p]\!]$.

Algorithm 10. $[\![d]\!] \leftarrow \Pi_{\text{Access}}([\![\text{op}]\!], [\![k]\!], [\![v']\!])$

Require: The input contains shares of an operation $[\![\text{op}]\!]$; op $\in \{\text{read}, \text{write}\}$, key $[\![k]\!]$, and value $[\![v']\!]$.

Ensure: $d = (k, v)$ if the ORAM holds (k, v), or $d = (k, v')$ if op = write. Otherwise, $d = (\bot, \bot)$.

(Searching for the top-level array.)

1: Parties run $\Pi_{\text{StashSearch}}([\![k]\!], [\![S]\!])$ for the top-level array $[\![S]\!]$ to obtain $[\![\tilde{d}]\!], [\![\text{found}]\!]$.

(Searching for hash tables in the hierarchy.)

2: **for** $\ell = 1$ to L **do**

3:     Parties call $\mathcal{F}_{\text{Bitext}}$ to obtain $[\![\text{lv}_\ell]\!]$ where lv_ℓ is the ℓ-th bit of lv of $\tilde{d}$.

4:     Parties call $\mathcal{F}_{\text{IfElse}}$ and $\mathcal{F}_{\text{Mult}}$ to simulate:

    If found = 1 *and* $\text{lv}_\ell = 0$ *then* $[\![\tilde{k}]\!] := [\![\bot]\!]$, *otherwise* $[\![\tilde{k}]\!] := [\![k]\!]$.

5:     Parties call $\text{HT}_i.\text{Lookup}([\![\tilde{k}]\!])$ (only in the main tables, ignoring the stash) to obtain $[\![\tilde{d}_i]\!], [\![\text{found}_i]\!]$ with its state

    $(\langle T_i \rangle_0, \langle T_i \rangle_1, [\![s_i]\!], \text{ctr}_i, \mathbf{P}_i)$ when $1 \le i \le \log \log N$, or

    $(\langle T_i \rangle_0, \langle T_i \rangle_1, [\![s_{i,0}]\!], [\![s_{i,1}]\!], \text{ctr}_i, \mathbf{P}_i)$ when $\log \log N < i$.

6:     Set $[\![\tilde{d}]\!] = [\![\tilde{d}]\!] + [\![\tilde{d}_i]\!]$ and $[\![\text{found}]\!] = [\![\text{found}]\!] + [\![\text{found}_i]\!]$.

(Rewriting (if needed) and re-storing the retrieved data.)

7: Parties call $\mathcal{F}_{\text{IfElse}}$ to simulate: *If* found = 0 *then set* $[\![d]\!] = [\![d^{\text{dummy}}]\!]$.

8: Parties call $\mathcal{F}_{\text{IfElse}}$ to simulate: *If* op = write *then set* $[\![d]\!] = ([\![k]\!], [\![v']\!])$.

9: Parties set $[\![\tilde{d}]\!] = ([\![d]\!], [\![0]\!])$ and concatenate it into the end of the top-level array.

10: If the size of the top-level array is c, parties run $\Pi_{\text{Reshuffle}}()$ to refresh the hierarchy.

11: **Return** $[\![d]\!]$

---

of a passive adversary that controls one party. The construction costs $O(\log N)$ amortized computational overhead and $O(\log N)$ communication rounds with $\lambda + b$ block size, where $b = \Omega(\log N)$.

Proof. The proof of security is given in the full version. Correctness is clear from the algorithms since we are in the $\mathcal{F}_{\text{HT}}$-hybrid model,. Indeed, a lookup is performed through the whole hierarchy and when an element is found, it is re-inserted into the hierarchy. Hence, we focus on efficiency analysis next.

Algorithm 10 requires one call of $\Pi_{\text{StashSearch}}$ with input size c, $O(L)$ calls of $\mathcal{F}_{\text{Bitext}}, \mathcal{F}_{\text{IfElse}}$, and $\mathcal{F}_{\text{Mult}}$, $O(\log \log N)$ calls to of $H.\text{Lookup}$ of the balls-and-bins-based scheme, calls $O(L)$ calls of $H.\text{Lookup}$ (without stash) for the Cuckoo-hash based scheme, and an invocation of $\Pi_{\text{Reshuffle}}$, for $c = L = O(\log N)$. For any block size $b = \Omega(\log N)$ bits, this procedure requires $O((\lambda + b) \log N) + \mathcal{C}$ computational steps where $\mathcal{C}$ is the amortized cost of $\Pi_{\text{Reshuffle}}$. Algorithm 11 costs $H_i.\text{Extract}$ for all $i = 1, \ldots, p$, $H_p.\text{Build}$ at once, and $O(c2^{p-1})$ calls of $\mathcal{F}_{\text{Trunc}}$, per $c2^{p-1}$ access. Hence, its amortized cost can be estimated as $\mathcal{C}_{\text{Reshuffle}} = \sum_{p=1}^{L} \frac{O(c2^p(\lambda+b))}{c2^{p-1}}$. $\qquad \square$

Concrete Efficiency. As we mentioned in Sect. 1.1, the overhead claimed above depends on a small hidden constant. Specifically, our Π_{Access} consists of at most $4 \log N$ (amortized) calls of $\mathcal{F}_{\text{PRF}}$ per access, which is 25 times smaller than the known optimal DORAM [33]. For a more detailed analysis, see full version [26].

Algorithm 11. $\Pi_{\text{RESHUFFLE}}()$

Require: p is the level s.t. all $\mathsf{HT}_{i<p}$ in the hierarchy is full and HT_p is not.
Ensure: All $\mathsf{HT}_{i<p}$ in the hierarchy become empty, and HT_p becomes full.
(Extracting all the data that needs to be reshuffled.)
1: Allocate an array $[\![\mathbf{A}]\!]$ of sufficient capacity and insert all elements of $[\![\mathsf{S}]\!]$ to $[\![\mathbf{A}]\!]$.
2: For all $i = 1, \ldots, p-1$, parties call $\mathsf{HT}_i.\text{EXTRACT}()$ with its state $(\pi_i, \langle \mathsf{T}_i \rangle_0, \langle \mathsf{T}_i \rangle_1)$
   to extract all real elements as $[\![\mathsf{D}_i]\!]$ and combine them to $[\![\mathbf{A}]\!]$ as $\mathbf{A} = \mathbf{A} \parallel \mathsf{D}_i$.
3: For all elements $[\![\widetilde{\mathsf{d}}_j]\!] = ([\![\mathsf{d}_j]\!], [\![\mathsf{lv}_j]\!])$ of $[\![\mathbf{A}]\!]$, parties call $\mathcal{F}_{\text{TRUNC}}$ to set the p first
   indices of lv_j to 0.
(Building a new hash table.)
4: Parties call $\mathsf{HT}_p.\text{BUILD}([\![\mathbf{A}]\!])$ to construct a distributed hash table
   $(\pi_p, \langle \mathsf{T}_p \rangle_{0,1}, [\![\mathsf{S}_p]\!], [\![s_{p,0}]\!], [\![s_{p,1}]\!], \mathsf{ctr}, \mathbf{P})$. [9]
5: Parties set $[\![\mathsf{S}]\!]$ as a new top-level array, and for all $[\![\widetilde{\mathsf{d}}_u]\!] = ([\![\mathsf{d}_u]\!], [\![\mathsf{lv}_u]\!])$ of $[\![\mathsf{S}]\!]$, call
   $\mathcal{F}_{\text{EQ}}$ and $\mathcal{F}_{\text{IFELSE}}$ to simulate:
   $\qquad$ *If $k_i \neq \perp$, set $[\![\mathsf{lv}_u]\!] = [\![\mathsf{lv}_u]\!] + [\![1]\!]2^{p-1}$.*

---

7 Actively Secure Extension

We extend our oblivious hashing and DORAM to be secure against an adversary that can deviate from the prescribed protocols. Though it is *almost* feasible by a generic framework of actively secure MPC, we require a new permutation (Sect. 7.1) and *verifying permutations* protocol (Sect. 7.2) in addition.

By known frameworks of actively secure MPC with abort [10,27,29], we assume that our protocols are in the flow of the following three phases:

- **Randomization phase.** For any share $[\![a]\!]$, parties compute $[\![ra]\!]$ with random secret r and store $([\![a]\!], [\![ra]\!])$ as the share of a *with a MAC*. This r serves as a blinding factor and is unknown to any party.
- **Computation phase.** Parties compute a target function F on input $([\![a]\!], [\![ra]\!])$ while recording checksums. For example, let $F = f_0 \circ f_1$ and assume Π_{f_0}, Π_{f_1} that are protocols used to compute $([\![f_{\{0,1\}}(a)]\!], [\![rf_{\{0,1\}}(a)]\!])$ from $([\![a]\!], [\![ra]\!])$ and are further secure up to additive attacks [21,22]. Now, the parties allocate a set of checksums $\mathcal{S} = \emptyset$ and perform Π_{f_2} and Π_{f_1} in sequence to obtain $[\![F(a)]\!]$ while storing all inputs and outputs of the protocols, i.e., $([\![a]\!], [\![ra]\!])$, $([\![f_2(a)]\!], [\![rf_2(a)]\!])$ and $([\![F(a)]\!], [\![rF(a)]\!])$, into $\mathcal{S}$.
- **Proof phase.** To detect cheating, parties evaluate the shares and their MACs recorded as checksums. Following the above example, the parties generate new random shares $[\![\rho_0]\!], [\![\rho_1]\!]$ and $[\![\rho_2]\!]$, and compute inner products

$$[\![\phi]\!] = ([\![\rho_0]\!] \times [\![a]\!] + [\![\rho_1]\!] \times [\![f_2(a)]\!] + [\![\rho_2]\!] \times [\![F(a)]\!]) \text{ and}$$
$$[\![r\phi]\!] = ([\![\rho_0]\!] \times [\![ra]\!] + [\![\rho_1]\!] \times [\![rf_2(a)]\!] + [\![\rho_2]\!] \times [\![rF(a)]\!]).$$

The parties recover $[\![\eta]\!] = [\![r]\!] \times [\![\phi]\!] - [\![r\phi]\!]$, and if $\eta \neq 0$ then they abort.

For our DORAM, we should be more concerned about the form of shares than in the passive security model. Since part of building blocks in Sect. 4, e.g.,

$\mathcal{F}_{\mathrm{PRF}}$, requires bit-wise operations, we should assign MACs to bits $a_{b-1}, \ldots, a_0 \in \mathbb{Z}_2$, instead of the whole $a \in \mathbb{Z}_{2^b}$. According to Kikuchi et al. [29], we can provide a MAC for a bit $u \in \{0, 1\}$ as $[\![ru]\!] := ([\![r_{\kappa-1}u]\!], \ldots, [\![r_0 u]\!])$ where each r_j is in $\mathbb{Z}_2$. To detect cheating with overwhelming probability $1 - \mathrm{negl}(N)$, this κ should be $\omega(\log N)$. Hence, by encoding $([\![a]\!], [\![ra]\!])$ as $(([\![a_{b-1}]\!], \ldots, [\![a_0]\!]), ([\![ra_{b-1}]\!], \ldots, [\![ra_{b-1}]\!]))$, the $\mathcal{F}_{\mathrm{ABB}}$ functionality described in Sect. 4 is also available in active security model.

To simplify the notation, we denote $([\![a]\!], [\![ra]\!])$ as $[\![a]\!]^m$ in the following.

7.1 Secure Oblivious Permutation up to Additive Attacks

We start with constructing a secure permutation protocol up to additive attacks. In contrast to Sect. 5.1, we assume that a permutation π provided by one party has been already separated into π_0 and π_1 s.t. $\pi = \pi_1 \circ \pi_0$ and shared between parties. We discuss verification for the permutation π in Sect. 7.2, and here we focus on cheating on an array that should be permuted.

Our permutation protocol described in Algorithm 1 relies on (semi-)honest parties and is difficult to convert to be secure up to additive attacks. Instead, we construct a permutation protocol using a reshare-based shuffling as in Ikarashi et al. [27]. Let $\mathcal{F}_{\mathrm{SHUFFLE}}$ be functionality for secure shuffling up to an additive attack s.t. it receives shares of an array $[\![\mathbf{I}]\!]$ and a permutation π from honest parties and an array Δ of the same size as $\mathbf{I}$ from an adversary, then it returns $[\![\pi \cdot \mathbf{I} + \Delta]\!]$. Now, the following protocol, originally proposed by Laur et al. [32], is the implementation of $\mathcal{F}_{\mathrm{SHUFFLE}}$ that costs n calls of $\mathcal{F}_{\mathrm{RESHARE}}$.

$[\![\mathbf{I}']\!]_0, [\![\mathbf{I}']\!]_1, [\![\mathbf{I}']\!]_2 \leftarrow \Pi_{\mathrm{SHUFFLE}}((\pi, [\![\mathbf{I}]\!]_0), (\pi, [\![\mathbf{I}]\!]_1), [\![\mathbf{I}]\!]_2)$:

1. P_0 and P_1 convert their $[\![\mathbf{I}]\!]_{i \in \{0,1\}}$ to $\langle \mathbf{I} \rangle_i$ and compute $\langle \mathbf{I}' \rangle_i = \pi \cdot \langle \mathbf{I} \rangle_i$ each.
2. Parties call $\mathcal{F}_{\mathrm{RESHARE}}$ to obtain $[\![\mathbf{I}']\!]_{\{0,1,2\}}$ from $\langle \mathbf{I}' \rangle_{\{0,1\}}$.
3. Output $[\![\mathbf{I}']\!]_{\{0,1,2\}}$.

Algorithm 12. $[\![\mathbf{I}']\!]_0^m, [\![\mathbf{I}']\!]_1^m, [\![\mathbf{I}']\!]_2^m \leftarrow \Pi_{\mathrm{PERM}}^{\mathrm{active}}((\pi_0, \pi_1), [\![\mathbf{I}]\!]_0^m, [\![\mathbf{I}]\!]_1^m, [\![\mathbf{I}]\!]_2^m)$

Notation: Let P be the permuter and let S_0, S_1 be the storages. Let S be a set of checksums.

Require: P has both π_0, π_1 and $[\![\mathbf{I}]\!]_0^m$. Each $S_{i=0,1}$ has π_i and $[\![\mathbf{I}]\!]_{i+1}^m$.

Ensure: $\mathbf{I}' = \pi \cdot \mathbf{I}$ and $r\mathbf{I}' = \pi \cdot (r\mathbf{I})$ where $\pi = \pi_1 \circ \pi_0$.

1: Parties record their input shares into S as $S = S \cup \{[\![\mathbf{I}]\!]^m\}$, and let $[\![\mathbf{I}_0']\!]^m = [\![\mathbf{I}]\!]^m$.
2: **for** $i = 0, 1$ **do**
3:     Parties call $\mathcal{F}_{\mathrm{SHUFFLE}}$ with inputs π_i and $[\![\mathbf{I}_i']\!]^m$ to obtain
        $[\![\mathbf{I}_{i+1}']\!]^m = [\![\pi_i \cdot \mathbf{I}_i']\!]^m$.
4:     Parties record their shares into S as $S \leftarrow S \cup \{[\![\mathbf{I}_{i+1}']\!]^m\}$.
5: Parties store $[\![\mathbf{I}_2']\!]_0^m, [\![\mathbf{I}_2']\!]_1^m, [\![\mathbf{I}_2']\!]_2^m$ as $[\![\mathbf{I}']\!]_0^m, [\![\mathbf{I}']\!]_1^m, [\![\mathbf{I}']\!]_2^m$, respectively.
6: **Return** $[\![\mathbf{I}']\!]_{\{0,1,2\}}^m$

In Algorithm 12, we describe an actively secure permutation protocol for our distributed oblivious hashing in the $\mathcal{F}_{\mathrm{SHUFFLE}}$-hybrid model. An actively secure unpermutation protocol, $\Pi_{\mathrm{UNPERM}}^{\mathrm{active}}$, is achieved from $\Pi_{\mathrm{PERM}}^{\mathrm{active}}$ straightforwardly, i.e., parties first compute $[\![\mathbf{I}']\!]^m = [\![\pi_1^{-1} \cdot \mathbf{I}]\!]^m$, then obtain $[\![\mathbf{I}'']\!]^m = [\![\pi_0^{-1} \cdot \mathbf{I}']\!]^m$.

7.2 Actively Secure Distributed Hashing

Even though an actively secure oblivious hashing can be obtained *almost* completely straightforwardly by replacing all functionalities used in our distributed oblivious hashing (Sect. 5.2 and 5.3) by actively secure ones, it is still *not secure against a corrupted permuter* that can input an invalid permutation. We thus focus on solving this problem. We can say the permutation π is *valid* if all keys are always found in their place, *whatever π actually is*. This means that the pseudorandom addresses can work as *witnesses* for the correctness of the hash table, i.e., we can verify π by checking whether

(*one of two pseudorandom addresses computed from a non-dummy key*)

$-$ (*the actual address where the element resides*)

is equal to 0 for all real keys (in Cuckoo hashing). This verification can be done in the BUILD procedure as follows: For all real blocks $[\![d_i]\!]$ located in $\mathsf{T}[\mathsf{addr}_i^r]$ and assigned to the pseudorandom addresses ($[\![\mathsf{addr}_{i,0}^p]\!]$, $[\![\mathsf{addr}_{i,1}^p]\!]$), parties check the following equation with uniformly random ρ_i.

$$0 =_? \sum_i [\![\rho_i]\!] \times ([\![\mathsf{addr}_{i,0}^p]\!] - \mathsf{addr}_i^r) \times ([\![\mathsf{addr}_{i,1}^p]\!] - \mathsf{addr}_i^r). \tag{7.1}$$

In addition, for efficiency, we combine the above verification with the MAC verification. Remember that, in the Proof phase for MACs, fresh random shares $[\![\rho_i]\!]$ are given for each checksum ($[\![a]\!]$, $[\![ra]\!]$). Noticing the similarity in the use of the random ρ_i, for any r, we can transform Eq. (7.1) as below:

$$[\![r]\!] \times \sum_i [\![\rho_i]\!] \times ([\![\mathsf{addr}_{i,0}^p]\!] \times [\![\mathsf{addr}_{i,1}^p]\!] + (\mathsf{addr}_i^r)^2) =_?$$

$$\sum_i [\![\rho_i]\!] \times ([\![r \times \mathsf{addr}_{i,0}^p]\!] + [\![r \times \mathsf{addr}_{i,1}^p]\!]) \times \mathsf{addr}_i^r. \tag{7.2}$$

Now, to make parties evaluate the above equation in the Proof phase, we propose the following new protocol that checks the consistency between the virtual address and the actual address of each non-dummy block.

$\Pi_{\mathrm{VERPERM2}}([\![\mathsf{addr}_{i,0}^p]\!]^m, [\![\mathsf{addr}_{i,1}^p]\!]^m, \mathsf{addr}_i^r)$:

1. At first, parties call the actively secure $\mathcal{F}_{\mathrm{MULT}}$ to obtain

$$[\![\mathsf{addr}_i']\!]^m = ([\![\mathsf{addr}_i']\!], [\![r \times \mathsf{addr}_i']\!]) = [\![\mathsf{addr}_{i,0}^p]\!]^m \times [\![\mathsf{addr}_{i,1}^p]\!]^m.$$

$[\![\mathsf{addr}_{i,0}^p]\!]^m$, $[\![\mathsf{addr}_{i,1}^p]\!]^m$ and $[\![\mathsf{addr}_i']\!]^m$ are recorded in $\mathcal{S}$ as checksums.

2. Parties locally compute below and record $[\![\mathsf{ver}_i^{(1)}]\!]^m$ and $[\![\mathsf{ver}_i^{(2)}]\!]^m$ to $\mathcal{S}$.

$$[\![\mathsf{ver}_i^{(1)}]\!]^m := ([\![\mathsf{addr}_i']\!] + (\mathsf{addr}_i^r)^2, ([\![r \times \mathsf{addr}_{i,0}^P]\!] + [\![r \times \mathsf{addr}_{i,1}^P]\!]) \times \mathsf{addr}_i^r), \text{ and}$$

$$[\![\mathsf{ver}_i^{(2)}]\!]^m := (([\![\mathsf{addr}_{i,0}^P]\!] + [\![\mathsf{addr}_{i,1}^P]\!]) \times \mathsf{addr}_i^r, [\![r \times \mathsf{addr}_i']\!] + [\![r]\!] \times (\mathsf{addr}_i^r)^2).$$

Since whether the permuter has provided a valid permutation is equivalent to whether $\mathsf{addr}_i^{(1)} = \mathsf{addr}_i^{(2)}$, the verification for *checksums* $[\![\mathsf{ver}_i^{(1)}]\!]^m$ and $[\![\mathsf{ver}_i^{(2)}]\!]^m$ includes Eq. (7.2) and its transformation. Furthermore, since the input and output of $\mathcal{F}_{\mathrm{MULT}}$, $[\![\mathsf{addr}_{i,0}^P]\!]^m, [\![\mathsf{addr}_{i,1}^P]\!]^m$ and $[\![\mathsf{addr}_i']\!]^m$, are recorded as checksums, we can attribute the attack providing an invalid permutation to an additive attack that modifies addr_i^r to $\mathsf{addr}_i^r + \delta$ for some δ.

In addition, we can also achieve a simpler permutation verification protocol for our balls-into-bins hashing as follows:

$\varPi_{\mathrm{VERPERM1}}([\![\mathsf{addr}_i^P]\!]^m, \mathsf{addr}_i^r)$:

1. Parties locally compute below and record $[\![\mathsf{ver}_i]\!]^m$ to $\mathcal{S}$.

$$[\![\mathsf{ver}_i]\!]^m := ([\![\mathsf{addr}_i^P]\!] - \mathsf{addr}_i^r, [\![r \times \mathsf{addr}_i^P]\!] - [\![r]\!] \times \mathsf{addr}_i^r).$$

Algorithm 13. $\pi_0, \pi_1, \langle \mathsf{T} \rangle_{0,1}^m, [\![S]\!]^m, [\![s]\!]^m, \mathsf{ctr}, \mathbf{P} \leftarrow \varPi_{\mathrm{BUILD}}^{\mathrm{active}}([\![\mathsf{D}]\!]^m)$

(Constructing a balls-into-bins hash table.)

1. Parties do the same as Algorithm 3 with actively secure components to obtain $\pi_0, \pi_1, \langle \mathsf{T} \rangle_{0,1}^m, [\![S]\!]^m, [\![s]\!]^m, \mathsf{ctr}, \mathbf{P}$. Note that, in the actively secure variant, once the original construction permutation π is split into π_0, π_1; $\pi = \pi_1 \circ \pi_0$, each π_i should be held by the storage S_i until EXTRACT for the consistency of the permutation.

(Verifying π.)

2. For the virtual addresses $[\![A]\!]^m = ([\![\mathsf{addr}_0]\!]^m \dots, [\![\mathsf{addr}_{n-1}]\!]^m)$, which are obtained in Line 5 of Algorithm 3, parties set $[\![\tilde{A}]\!]^m = [\![A \parallel E]\!]^m$ of size n' in the same way as Line 6 and 7 of Algorithm 3. Then, parties run $[\![\tilde{A}']\!]^m \leftarrow \varPi_{\mathrm{PERM}}^{\mathrm{active}}(\pi_0, \pi_1, [\![\tilde{A}]\!]^m)$.

3. **for all** $i \in [\tau]$ **do**

4.   Let $(\langle k_i \rangle^m, \langle v_i \rangle^m)$ be the i-th element of $\langle \mathsf{T} \rangle^m$.

5.   Let $[\![\widetilde{\mathsf{addr}_i'}]\!]^m$ be the i-th element of $[\![\tilde{A}']\!]^m$.

6.   Let $\mathsf{addr}_i^r := \lfloor i/\beta \rfloor$ where β is bin size of T.

7.   Parties call $\mathcal{F}_{\mathrm{RESHARE}}, \mathcal{F}_{\mathrm{EQ}}$ and $\mathcal{F}_{\mathrm{IFELSE}}$ to simulate:
      If $k_i = \perp$ then $[\![\mathsf{addr}_i^P]\!]^m = [\![\mathsf{addr}_i^r]\!]^m$, *otherwise* $[\![\mathsf{addr}_i^P]\!]^m = [\![\widetilde{\mathsf{addr}_i'}]\!]^m$.

8.   Parties perform $\varPi_{\mathrm{VERPERM1}}([\![\mathsf{addr}_i^P]\!]^m, \mathsf{addr}_i^r)$.

9. **Return** $\pi_0, \pi_1, \langle \mathsf{T} \rangle_{0,1}^m, [\![S]\!]^m, [\![s]\!]^m, \mathsf{ctr}, \mathbf{P}$

Now, we can obtain our actively secure BUILD procedure as Algorithm 13 and 14. Note that new LOOKUP, STASHSEARCH, and EXTRACT procedures can be achieved by natural conversion from the passive MPC to active, thus we skip detailing their pseudocode here.

Lemma 7.1. *There exists a 3-party distributed balls-into-bins hashing of which the* BUILD *procedure is described in Algorithm 13 and the other procedures are achieved from the actively secure conversion of Algorithm 4, 5, and 6 that securely realizes* $\mathcal{F}_{\mathsf{HT}}$ *in the* $(\mathcal{F}_{\mathsf{SHARE}}, \mathcal{F}_{\mathsf{REVEAL}}^{P}, \mathcal{F}_{\mathsf{ABB}})$-*hybrid model in the presence of an active adversary that controls one party.*

Assume that the input size n and $b' = b \cdot \omega(\log N), \lambda' = \lambda \cdot \omega(\log N)$.

- *The* BUILD *procedure consumes $O(n(b' + \lambda' + \log n))$ local computation steps.*
- *The* LOOKUP *procedure consumes $O((b'+\lambda')\frac{\log N}{\log \log N})$ local computation steps.*
- *The* STASHSEARCH *procedure consumes $O(b' \log N)$ local computation steps.*
- *The* EXTRACT *procedure consumes $O(nb')$ local computation steps.*

Algorithm 14. $\pi_0, \pi_1, \langle \mathsf{T} \rangle_{0,1}^m, [\![\mathsf{S}]\!]^m, [\![s_0]\!]^m, [\![s_1]\!]^m, \mathsf{ctr}, \mathbf{P} \leftarrow \Pi_{\mathrm{BUILD}}^{\mathrm{active}}([\![\mathsf{D}]\!]^m)$

(Constructing a cuckoo hash table.)

1: Parties do the same as Algorithm 7 with actively secure components to obtain $\pi_0, \pi_1, \langle \mathsf{T} \rangle_{0,1}^m, [\![\mathsf{S}]\!]^m, [\![s_0]\!]^m, [\![s_1]\!]^m, \mathsf{ctr}, \mathbf{P}$.

(Verifying π.)

2: For the virtual addresses $[\![\mathsf{A}]\!]^m = \left(([\![\mathsf{addr}_{i,0}]\!]^m, [\![\mathsf{addr}_{i,1}]\!]^m) \right)_{i \in [n]}$, which are obtained in Line 5 of Algorithm 7, parties set $[\![\widetilde{\mathsf{A}}]\!]^m = [\![\mathsf{A} \parallel \mathsf{E}]\!]^m$ of size n' in the same way as Line 6 and 7 of Algorithm 7. Then, parties run $[\![\widetilde{\mathsf{A}}']\!]^m \leftarrow \Pi_{\mathrm{PERM}}^{\mathrm{active}}(\pi_0, \pi_1, [\![\widetilde{\mathsf{A}}]\!]^m)$.

3: **for all** $i \in [\tau]$ **do**

4:    Let $(\langle k_i \rangle^m, \langle v_i \rangle^m)$ be the i-th element of $\langle \mathsf{T} \rangle^m$.

5:    Let $([\![\widetilde{\mathsf{addr}}'_{i,0}]\!]^m, [\![\widetilde{\mathsf{addr}}'_{i,1}]\!]^m)$ be the i-th element of $[\![\widetilde{\mathsf{A}}']\!]^m$.

6:    Let $\mathsf{addr}_i^r := i$.

7:    Parties call $\mathcal{F}_{\mathrm{RESHARE}}, \mathcal{F}_{\mathrm{EQ}}$ and $\mathcal{F}_{\mathrm{IFELSE}}$ to simulate:
     If $k_i = \bot$ then $([\![\mathsf{addr}_{i,0}^p]\!]^m, [\![\mathsf{addr}_{i,1}^p]\!]^m) = ([\![\mathsf{addr}_i^r]\!]^m, [\![\mathsf{addr}_i^r]\!]^m)$,
     otherwise $([\![\mathsf{addr}_{i,0}^p]\!]^m, [\![\mathsf{addr}_{i,1}^p]\!]^m) = ([\![\widetilde{\mathsf{addr}}'_{i,0}]\!]^m, [\![\widetilde{\mathsf{addr}}'_{i,1}]\!]^m)$.

8:    Parties perform $\Pi_{\mathrm{VERPERM2}}([\![\mathsf{addr}_{i,0}^p]\!]^m, [\![\mathsf{addr}_{i,1}^p]\!]^m, \mathsf{addr}_i^r)$.

9: **Return** $\pi_0, \pi_1, \langle \mathsf{T} \rangle_{0,1}^m, [\![\mathsf{S}]\!]^m, [\![s_0]\!]^m, [\![s_1]\!]^m, \mathsf{ctr}, \mathbf{P}$

Lemma 7.2. *There exists a 3-party distributed Cuckoo hashing of which the* BUILD *procedure is described in Algorithm 14 and the other procedures are achieved from the actively secure conversion of Algorithm 5, 8, and 9 that securely realizes* $\mathcal{F}_{\mathsf{HT}}$ *in the* $(\mathcal{F}_{\mathsf{SHARE}}, \mathcal{F}_{\mathsf{REVEAL}}^{P}, \mathcal{F}_{\mathsf{ABB}})$-*hybrid model in the presence of an active adversary that controls one party.*

Assume that the input size n and $b' = b \cdot \omega(\log N), \lambda' = \lambda \cdot \omega(\log N)$.

- *The* BUILD *procedure consumes $O(n(b' + \lambda' + \log n))$ local computation steps.*
- *The* LOOKUP *procedure consumes $O(b' + \lambda')$ local computation steps.*
- *The* STASHSEARCH *procedure consumes $O(b' \log N)$ local computation steps.*
- *The* EXTRACT *procedure consumes $O(nb')$ local computation steps.*

Proof of Lemma 7.1 *and* 7.2. Since each output of Algorithm 13 and 14 is obtained from a general actively secure conversion of Algorithm 3 and 7 respectively, the correctness of them are also given by Lemma 5.3 and 5.4.

In addition, the security of the algorithms is also guaranteed from a known actively secure MPC and our additional evaluations $\Pi_{\text{VerPerm1}}, \Pi_{\text{VerPerm2}}$. Though known actively secure MPC frameworks cannot prevent a malicious permuter from tampering with a permutation, Π_{VerPerm1} and Π_{VerPerm2} can detect blocks that are located in invalid places of a hash table since the *checksums* provided in $\Pi_{\text{VerPerm1}}, \Pi_{\text{VerPerm2}}$ cannot be a valid pair of MAC with overwhelming probability when the adversary that does not know the MAC key r tampers with the real addresses of the blocks (remember that the virtual addresses, addr_i^P, are derived from actively secure OPRFs, and the real addresses, addr_i^r, are the result of the permutation).

For the efficiency analysis, we show the following claim.

Claim. Π_{VerPerm1} and Π_{VerPerm2} each consumes $O(b')$ local computation steps.

This claim is clear from their algorithms, and hence it shows that the additional $O(n)$ calls of Π_{VerPerm1} or Π_{VerPerm2} do not affect to the asymptotic cost of Algorithm 13 or 14, each. □

7.3 Actively Secure Distributed ORAM

Given our actively secure distributed oblivious hashing, we achieve an actively secure DORAM.

Theorem 7.3. *There exists a 3-party protocol that securely realizes $\mathcal{F}_{\text{RAM}}$ in the presence of an active adversary that controls one party. In addition, this implementation consumes $O(\log N)$ amortized overhead and $O(\log N)$ communication rounds with $\omega((\lambda + b) \log N)$ block size where $b = \Omega(\log N)$.*

Proof. By straightforward composition, we can replace all functionalities related to $\mathcal{F}_{\text{ABB}}$ and $\mathcal{F}_{\text{HT}}$ in Algorithms 10 and 11 with their concrete implementations and thereby get a concrete actively secure DORAM. For security, we refer to the full version [26]. Moreover, since the efficiency of each $\mathcal{F}_{\text{ABB}}$ and $\mathcal{F}_{\text{HT}}$ is asymptotically the same as in passive security except for the increased block size, the actively secure DORAM achieves $O(\log N)$ overhead using a slightly larger block size $\omega((\lambda + b) \log N)$. □

8 Conclusion

We proposed an optimal DORAM of $O(\log N)$ overhead with small hidden constant, that relies on only $4 \log N$ OPRF calls. The key building block is a novel 3-party permutation protocol, in which parties split their roles into one permuter that knows the whole permutation and two storages that hold a permuted table. Since these roles do not overlap, the permuter never observes access patterns to the permuted table even though it knows the structure of the table.

In addition, we extended the above (passively secure) DORAM to an actively secure one. Since our passively secure construction depends on the permutation protocol in which one party has full control of a permutation, we additionally construct a novel protocol to verify the permutation provided by the (possibly dishonest) party. Then, we achieved an actively secure DORAM of $O(\log N)$ overhead with slightly larger $\omega((\lambda + b) \log N)$-bit block size.

Acknowledgements. We thank Brett Hemenway Falk, Daniel Noble, Rafail Ostrovsky, Matan Shtepel, and Jacob Zhang for observing a gap in a previous version of this work. Ilan Komargodski is the incumbent of the Harry & Abe Sherman Senior Lectureship at the School of Computer Science and Engineering at the Hebrew University. Research supported in part by an Alon Young Faculty Fellowship, by a grant from the Israel Science Foundation (ISF Grant No. 1774/20), and by a grant from the US-Israel Binational Science Foundation and the US National Science Foundation (BSF-NSF Grant No. 2020643).

References

1. Albrecht, M.R., Rechberger, C., Schneider, T., Tiessen, T., Zohner, M.: Ciphers for MPC and FHE. In: Oswald, E., Fischlin, M. (eds.) EUROCRYPT 2015. LNCS, vol. 9056, pp. 430–454. Springer, Heidelberg (2015). https://doi.org/10.1007/978-3-662-46800-5_17
2. Araki, T., Furukawa, J., Lindell, Y., Nof, A., Ohara, K.: High-throughput semi-honest secure three-party computation with an honest majority. In: CCS, pp. 805–817 (2016)
3. Asharov, G., Komargodski, I., Lin, W., Nayak, K., Peserico, E., Shi, E.: Optorama: optimal oblivious RAM. J. ACM **70**(1), 4:1–4:70 (2023)
4. Asharov, G., Komargodski, I., Lin, W., Peserico, E., Shi, E.: Optimal oblivious parallel RAM. In: ACM-SIAM Symposium on Discrete Algorithms, SODA, pp. 2459–2521 (2022)
5. Asharov, G., Komargodski, I., Lin, W.-K., Shi, E.: Oblivious RAM with *worst-case* logarithmic overhead. In: Malkin, T., Peikert, C. (eds.) CRYPTO 2021. LNCS, vol. 12828, pp. 610–640. Springer, Cham (2021). https://doi.org/10.1007/978-3-030-84259-8_21
6. Bunn, P., Katz, J., Kushilevitz, E., Ostrovsky, R.: Efficient 3-party distributed ORAM. Cryptology ePrint Archive (2018)
7. Canetti, R.: Security and composition of multiparty cryptographic protocols. J. Cryptology **13**(1), 143–202 (2000)
8. Catrina, O., de Hoogh, S.: Improved primitives for secure multiparty integer computation. In: Garay, J.A., De Prisco, R. (eds.) SCN, pp. 182–199 (2010)
9. Chan, T.H., Shi, E.: Circuit OPRAM: unifying statistically and computationally secure ORAMs and OPRAMs. In: TCC, pp. 72–107 (2017)
10. Chida, K., et al.: Fast large-scale honest-majority MPC for malicious adversaries. In: Shacham, H., Boldyreva, A. (eds.) CRYPTO 2018. LNCS, vol. 10993, pp. 34–64. Springer, Cham (2018). https://doi.org/10.1007/978-3-319-96878-0_2
11. Chida, K., Hamada, K., Ikarashi, D., Kikuchi, R., Kiribuchi, N., Pinkas, B.: An efficient secure three-party sorting protocol with an honest majority. Cryptology ePrint Archive (2019)

12. Chida, K., Hamada, K., Ikarashi, D., Kikuchi, R., Pinkas, B.: High-throughput secure AES computation. In: WAHC, pp. 13–24 (2018)
13. Cramer, R., Damgård, I., Ishai, Y.: Share conversion, pseudorandom secret-sharing and applications to secure computation. In: TCC, pp. 342–362 (2005)
14. Damgård, I., Keller, M.: Secure multiparty AES. In: FC, pp. 367–374 (2010)
15. Doerner, J., Shelat, A.: Scaling ORAM for secure computation. In: CCS, pp. 523–535 (2017)
16. Faber, S., Jarecki, S., Kentros, S., Wei, B.: Three-party ORAM for secure computation. In: Iwata, T., Cheon, J.H. (eds.) ASIACRYPT 2015. LNCS, vol. 9452, pp. 360–385. Springer, Heidelberg (2015). https://doi.org/10.1007/978-3-662-48797-6_16
17. Falk, B., Noble, D., Ostrovsky, R., Shtepel, M., Zhang, J.: DORAM revisited: maliciously secure RAM-MPC with logarithmic overhead. IACR Cryptology ePrint Archive, p. 578 (2023)
18. Hemenway Falk, B., Noble, D., Ostrovsky, R.: Alibi: a flaw in cuckoo-hashing based hierarchical ORAM schemes and a solution. In: Canteaut, A., Standaert, F.-X. (eds.) EUROCRYPT 2021. LNCS, vol. 12698, pp. 338–369. Springer, Cham (2021). https://doi.org/10.1007/978-3-030-77883-5_12
19. Falk, B.H., Noble, D., Ostrovsky, R.: 3-party distributed ORAM from oblivious set membership. In: SCN, pp. 437–461 (2022)
20. Furukawa, J., Lindell, Y., Nof, A., Weinstein, O.: High-throughput secure three-party computation for malicious adversaries and an honest majority. In: Coron, J.-S., Nielsen, J.B. (eds.) EUROCRYPT 2017. LNCS, vol. 10211, pp. 225–255. Springer, Cham (2017). https://doi.org/10.1007/978-3-319-56614-6_8
21. Genkin, D., Ishai, Y., Polychroniadou, A.: Efficient multi-party computation: from passive to active security via secure SIMD circuits. In: Gennaro, R., Robshaw, M. (eds.) CRYPTO 2015. LNCS, vol. 9216, pp. 721–741. Springer, Heidelberg (2015). https://doi.org/10.1007/978-3-662-48000-7_35
22. Genkin, D., Ishai, Y., Prabhakaran, M.M., Sahai, A., Tromer, E.: Circuits resilient to additive attacks with applications to secure computation. In: STOC, pp. 495–504 (2014)
23. Goldreich, O.: Towards a theory of software protection and simulation by oblivious rams. In: STOC, pp. 182–194 (1987)
24. Goldreich, O., Ostrovsky, R.: Software protection and simulation on oblivious rams. J. ACM **43**(3), 431–473 (1996)
25. Goodrich, M.T., Mitzenmacher, M.: Privacy-preserving access of outsourced data via oblivious ram simulation. In: ICALP, pp. 576–587 (2011)
26. Ichikawa, A., Komargodski, I., Hamada, K., Kikuchi, R., Ikarashi, D.: 3-party secure computation for rams: optimal and concretely efficient. IACR Cryptology ePrint Archive, p. 516 (2023)
27. Ikarashi, D., Kikuchi, R., Hamada, K., Chida, K.: Actively private and correct MPC scheme in $t < n/2$ from passively secure schemes with small overhead. Cryptology ePrint Archive (2014)
28. Ito, M., Saito, A., Nishizeki, T.: Secret sharing scheme realizing general access structure. In: GLOBECOM, pp. 99–102 (1987)
29. Kikuchi, R., et al.: Field extension in secret-shared form and its applications to efficient secure computation. In: ACISP, pp. 343–361 (2019)
30. Kirsch, A., Mitzenmacher, M., Wieder, U.: More robust hashing: cuckoo hashing with a stash. J. Computing **39**(4), 1543–1561 (2009)
31. Laur, S., Talviste, R., Willemson, J.: From oblivious AES to efficient and secure database join in the multiparty setting. In: ACNS, pp. 84–101 (2013)

32. Laur, S., Willemson, J., Zhang, B.: Round-efficient oblivious database manipulation. In: ISC, pp. 262–277 (2011)
33. Lu, S., Ostrovsky, R.: Distributed oblivious ram for secure two-party computation. In: TCC, pp. 377–396 (2013). https://eprint.iacr.org/2011/384
34. Noble, D.: Explicit, closed-form, general bounds for cuckoo hashing with a stash. Cryptology ePrint Archive (2021)
35. Ostrovsky, R.: Efficient computation on oblivious rams. In: STOC, pp. 514–523 (1990)
36. Ostrovsky, R., Shoup, V.: Private information storage (extended abstract). In: STOC, pp. 294–303 (1997)
37. Pagh, R., Rodler, F.F.: Cuckoo hashing. J. Algorithms **51**(2), 122–144 (2004)
38. Pippenger, N., Fischer, M.J.: Relations among complexity measures. J. ACM **26**(2), 361–381 (1979)
39. Shamir, A.: How to share a secret. Commun. ACM **22**(11), 612–613 (1979)
40. Wang, X., Chan, T.H., Shi, E.: Circuit ORAM: on tightness of the goldreich-ostrovsky lower bound. In: CCS, pp. 850–861 (2015)

Author Index

© International Association for Cryptologic Research 2023
G. Rothblum and H. Wee (Eds.): TCC 2023, LNCS 14369, pp. 503–504, 2023.
https://doi.org/10.1007/978-3-031-48615-9